A LION HANDBOOK
THE WORLD'S RELIGIONS

Consulting Editors

R. Pierce Beaver   Emeritus Professor of Mission
University of Chicago, USA

Dr Jan Bergman   Professor of the History of Religions
Uppsala University, Sweden

Dr Myrtle S. Langley   Head of Practical Theology and Missiology
Trinity College, Bristol, England

Dr theol. Wulf Metz   Professor at the Fachhochschule
Munich, Germany

Dr Arild Romarheim   Lecturer in World Religions
The Free Faculty of Theology
Oslo, Norway

Professor Andrew Walls   Head of the Department of Religious Studies
University of Aberdeen, Scotland

Dr Robert Withycombe   Librarian, St Mark's Library and Theological Institute
Canberra, Australia

Canon R.W.F. Wootton   Formerly Leicester Diocesan Chaplain for Community Relations
Leicester, England

Copyright © 1982 Lion Publishing

Published by
Lion Publishing
Icknield Way, Tring, Herts, England
ISBN 0 85648 187 4
Albatross Books
PO Box 320, Sutherland, NSW 2232, Australia
ISBN 0 86760 354 2

First edition 1982
Reprinted 1982
Reprinted 1983
Reprinted 1984

Printed and bound in Hong Kong
by Mandarin Offset International (HK) Ltd.

A LION HANDBOOK
The World's
Religions

Contents

Preface

As far back as we can go, even before the earliest written records, there is evidence that religion was a key aspect of life. The mystery of birth and death, the challenge of life itself, has always moved mankind to reach out to something – someone – beyond, in search of meaning. 'No one', it has been said, 'can understand mankind without understanding the faiths of humanity.'

This book is intended to present the reader with a comprehensive, clear and stimulating introduction and guide to the world's religions, from man's earliest forms of worship to the present day.

After setting the scene and discussing the origins of religion the Handbook describes the ancient religions – Egypt, Greece, Rome, the Norse gods . . . Primal religions today are illustrated with a series of case-studies from many parts of the world. On the major Eastern and world religions, articles give information on the history, scriptures, worship, beliefs and practices of the various faiths.

More than fifty specialist authors from many different countries have contributed to the Handbook. They write from a Christian concern to describe each faith 'as it is', presenting different viewpoints clearly and objectively so that they speak for themselves. As reporters, they have no wish to erect images of a religion which they then knock down; nor do they try to cover up facts which an insider may not want brought out into the light of day.

In the section on Christianity, there has been a real attempt to be equally dispassionate! If conviction shows through, however, it is because there can never be total objectivity when it comes to deeply-held matters of belief. Different religious faiths cannot be put on the supermarket shelves and one labelled 'best buy'. So the section title puts a question: is Christianity in fact a 'religion' at all, or does it claim more, to be the fulfilment of religion?

The evidence is presented. The response – whether the faiths of mankind are being studied simply from academic interest or as part of a deep personal search – must be left to the reader.

Contributors

John Allan, former Head of Religious Education, Hreod Burna School, Swindon, Wilts, England; Director of Training, British Youth for Christ. *A Fusion of Religion: Syncretism.*

Professor Sir Norman Anderson, formerly Professor of Oriental Studies and Director of the Institute of Advanced Legal Studies, London University. *The Law of Islam*; *The Future of Islam.*

Dr George Bankes, Assistant Keeper of Ethnology, The Manchester Museum, Manchester, England. *Land of the Aztecs and Incas: America before Columbus.*

Dr Robert Banks, Visiting Fellow, Department of History, Faculty of Arts, Australian National University, Canberra. *The Covenant*; *Torah and Mishnah*; *The God Who Speaks*; *Competing Ideologies Today: Communism.*

Dr Axel-Ivar Berglund, Lecturer in Missiology and Cultural Anthropology, Uppsala University, Sweden. *Primal Religions, Case-study 10: The Zulus.*

Dr John Berthrong, Lecturer at the Centre for Religious Studies, Toronto University, Canada. *Sages and Immortals: Chinese Religions.*

Dr Barbara M. Boal, Lecturer in Primal Religions, Selly Oak Colleges, Birmingham, England. *Primal Religions, Case-study 1: Asia*; *Cao-Dai and Hoa-Hao.*

Newell S. Booth, Jr., Professor of Religions, Miami University, Oxford, Ohio, USA. *African Religions*; *The Luba Epic.*

The Rev. Robert Brow, Rector of St James' Church, Kingston, Ontario, Canada. *Origins of Religion.*

The Rev. Colin Buchanan, Principal, St John's Theological College, Bramcote, Nottingham, England. *Christian Worship.*

Chua Wee Hian, General Secretary, International Fellowship of Evangelical Students. *The Worship of Ancestors*; *Community of a Common Life.*

Harvie M. Conn, Associate Professor of Missions and Apologetics, Westminster Theological Seminary, Philadelphia PA, USA. *Primal Religions, Case-study 2: Korea.*

Dr Geoffrey Cowling, Senior Lecturer in History, Macquarie University, North Ryde, New South Wales, Australia. *Story of a Nation* (Judaism); *Developments in Judaism*; *Moses*; *Ezra*; *Theodore Herzl.*

The Rev. Dr Clyde Curry Smith, Professor of Ancient History and Religion, University of Wisconsin, River Falls, USA. *The Ancient Religions of Greece and Rome.*

The Rev. Douglas Davies, Lecturer, Department of Theology, Nottingham University, England. *The Study of Religion*; *Myths and Symbols*; *Religion of the Gurus: The Sikh Faith.*

Richard H. Drummond, Professor of Ecumenical Mission and History of Religions, University of Dubuque, Theological Seminary, Dubuque, Iowa, USA. *Gautama The Buddha in His Setting*; *The Buddha's Teaching.*

The Rev. William H. Edwards, Pitjanjatjara Area Chaplain, Uniting Church in Australia. *The Aborigines.*

The Rev. Dr R.T. France, Senior Lecturer in New Testament Studies, London Bible College. *Jesus*; *The Bible.*

Dr Raymond Hammer, Director, Bible Reading Fellowship. *The Eternal Teaching: Hinduism*; *Roots: The Development of Hindu Religion*; *Approaches to Truth: The Great Interpreters*; *Concepts of Hinduism*; *Hindu Worship and the Festivals*; *Men and Movements*; *Escape from Life?*; *Karma and Dharma: Hindu Ethics*; *Hinduism Outside India.*

The Rev. C.D. Harley, Lecturer in Old Testament and Jewish Studies, All Nations Christian College, Ware, Herts, England. *Chosen People: Judaism*; *Life in a Jewish Family.*

Antony J. Harrop, United Bible Societies Distribution Adviser in South Asia. *A Day in the Life of a Muslim Family.*

Dr John R. Hinnells, Lecturer in Comparative Religion, Manchester University, England. *The Cosmic Battle: Zoroastrianism*; *Mithraism: Cult of the Bull*; *Courage and Faith: The Parsis.*

Leslie Hoggarth, Lector in the Centre for Latin American Linguistic Studies, St Andrews University, Scotland. *Primal Religions, Case-study 12: The Andes.*

Dr Åke Hultkrantz, Professor in the History of Religions, Stockholm University, Sweden. *Religion Before History*; *Nomads of the Steppes.*

The Rev. James Irwin, Dean of Maori and Polynesian Studies, Theological Hall, Knox College,

Presbyterian Church of New Zealand. *Primal Religions, Case-study 7: The Maoris.*

Dr David Kerr, Director of the Centre for the Study of Islam and Christian Muslim Relations, Selly Oak Colleges, Birmingham, England. *The Worship of Islam; The Unity and Variety in Islam.*

The Rev. Christopher Lamb, BCMS/CMS Other Faiths Theological Project, Birmingham, England. *The Claim to be Unique.*

Dr Myrtle S. Langley, Head of Practical Theology and Missiology, Trinity College, Bristol, England. *Respect for All Life: Jainism.*

Robert D. Linder, Professor of History, Kansas State University, Manhattan, Kansas, USA. *The Future of Christianity.*

Dr Carl Loeliger, Senior Lecturer in Religious Studies, History Department, University of Papua New Guinea. *Primal Religions, Case-study 4: Melanesia; New Myths: The Cargo Cults.*

I. Howard Marshall, Professor of New Testament Exegesis, Aberdeen University, Scotland. *Christian Beliefs.*

Dr Theol. Wulf Metz, Professor at the Fachhochschule, Munich, Germany. *The Enlightened One: Buddhism; The Buddhist Lands; One Goal, Many Paths; Buddha – Just a Good Hindu?; From Memory to Writing; The Appeal of Buddhism in the West.*

A.R. Millard, Rankin Senior Lecturer in Hebrew and Ancient Semitic Languages, Liverpool University, England. *Cradle of Civilization: The Ancient Near East.*

Wm. Montgomery Watt, formerly Professor of Arabic,

Edinburgh University, Scotland. *The Way of the Prophet* (Islam).

J.W.E. Newbery, Professor Emeritus (Native Studies), University of Sudbury, Canada. *Primal Religions, Case-study 11: North American Indians.*

Dr Michael Pye, Lecturer in the History of Religions, Leeds University, England. *A Tapestry of Traditions: Japanese Religions.*

The Rev. A.D. Rogers, Principal Lecturer in Theology and Religion, Dorset Institute of Higher Education, England. *Primal Religions, Case-study 8: Madagascar.*

John Ruffle, Keeper of Archaeology, Ethnography and Birmingham History, Birmingham City Museums and Art Gallery, England. *Ancient Egypt: Land of the Priest-King; Egyptian Temples: Houses of Power.*

Joan E. Rule, Senior Lecturer in English, Dauli Teachers' College, Papua New Guinea. *Primal Religions, Case-study 5: The Foe of Papua New Guinea.*

The Rev. Michael Sadgrove, Vice-Principal, Salisbury and Wells Theological College, England. *The Christian Life; Branches of the Church.*

The Rev. Dr Werner Schilling, Lecturer in Foreign Religions and Missiology, Free Theological Academies, West Germany. *Unity and Peace: The Baha'i Faith; Persecution of the Baha'is.*

Lothar Schmalfuss, Director of Studies, the University, Neubiberg, Germany. *Muhammad; Science, Art and Culture in Islam.*

Eric J. Sharpe, Professor of Religious Studies, University of Sydney, Australia. *Six Major Figures in Religious Studies.*

The Rev. Dr Anthony C. Thiselton, Senior Lecturer in Biblical Studies, Sheffield University, England. *Competing Ideologies Today: Existentialism.*

Angela Tilby, Producer, Religious Programmes, BBC Television, England. *Part Seven: Rapid Fact-finder* (joint author with Dr John-David Yule).

Dr A.R. Tippett, Research Fellow, St Mark's Library, Canberra, Australia. *Primal Religions, Case-study 3: Oceania.*

Dr Harold W. Turner, Director, Project for the Study of New Religious Movements in Primal Societies, Aberdeen University, Scotland. *Holy Places, Sacred Calendars; World of the Spirits; Christianity and the Primal Religions.*

Professor Andrew Walls, Head of the Department of Religious Studies, Aberdeen University, Scotland. *The Old Gods: Religions of Northern Europe.*

J. Christy Wilson, Jr, Professor of World Evangelization, Gordon-Conwell Theological Seminary, South Hamilton, Massachusetts, USA. *The Qur'an.*

Marvin R. Wilson, Ockenga Professor of Biblical Studies and Chairman of the Department of Biblical Studies, Gordon College, Wenham, Massachusetts, USA. *Branches of Judaism; The Influence of Judaism.*

Dr Edwin M. Yamauchi, Professor and Director of Graduate Studies, History Department, Miami University, Oxford, USA. *Secret Knowledge: The Gnostics; The Mandaeans: Gnostic Survivors; Faith of Light and Darkness: the Manichaeans.*

The Rev. Dr John-David Yule, Assistant Curate of St Andrew's Church, Cherry Hinton, Cambs, England. *Part Seven: Rapid Fact-finder* (joint author with Angela Tilby).

Part One
The Development of Religion

The Study of Religion

Douglas Davies

Every adult male Muslim is required to make the pilgrimage to Mecca once in his lifetime. These pilgrims are setting out from Aswan.

What is religion? There have been many definitions. Some have simply described it as 'belief in spiritual beings'. Others have attempted more comprehensive definitions in terms of beliefs or a description of practices.

Some of the different approaches to religion are as follows:

● **Anthropologists** describe religious beliefs and practices as they find them in living communities. Religion helps to unite people in a shared experience and explanation of life. It provides a pattern of human behaviour, often in response to the hazards of life.

● **Sociologists** stress the social dimension of religious ideas. Religion provides an agreed way of looking at the world. It gives the individual a sense of purpose and meaning.

● **Historians** describe religion in terms of events resulting from beliefs; **theologians** are concerned with the beliefs themselves, the question of whether they are true or false, and with people's response to them.

The different approaches are valid in different ways and within their own limitations. The basic difference is that of standpoint: there is the way of the believer and the way of the scholar.

The believer

Theology is the term usually given to the study of one's own religion. It is concerned with the meaning of the doctrines which have developed over the years, with the way doctrine is derived from *scriptures*, and the interpretation of the scriptures. This often leads to the formation of different schools of tradition and to sectarian divisions within major religions.

It also leads to the application of this knowledge to ordinary behaviour —*ethics*—and to special acts of worship—*liturgy*.

These are the names used of Christian theology, but similar strands can be found in other world religions.

Theology, then, is the study of a religion from the inside. It assumes that the faith is true. Then it seeks to explore it more fully, and often attempts to relate that faith to changing world situations. Theology is always grounded in a religious tradition.

The scholar

The 'scholarly approach' to religion means a neutral, non-committed form of study. It looks at the form of a religion: it does not ask whether it is true.

The phrase 'scholarly approach' is deceptive if it means that religious people cannot adopt an intellectual approach to religious things. Very often they can and do. But the scholarly, objective or scientific perspective is one which emphasizes the outward and visible aspects of a religion, even when this means describing the nature of people's religious experiences, rather than pinpointing the great issues of truth and awareness of God as felt by the believer himself. It is possible for the religious person to speak in one context as a believer about the intimate things of his religion, and in another as a scholar about the way his fellow-believers see things.

What, then, are the different methods scholars have adopted in studying the whole subject of religion? And what are the key ideas that will help us understand the 'scholarly approach'?

Reductionism

The different approaches are not, of course, mutually exclusive. In fact each method of study can add to our total picture.

This is in contrast to the 'reductionism' of some approaches which try to explain everything in terms of one theory. Religion is 'nothing but' economic, sexual or evolutionary drives.

For instance, Marx explained religion in economic terms. Freud explained it in sexual terms. Some nineteenth-century anthropologists explained it simply in terms of evolution.

The anthropologists

Anthropology is the study of human behaviour: religion as a pattern of behaviour can be observed like any other human activity.

As a discipline it has added enormously to what we know of peoples throughout the world, particularly the more primitive tribes. Anthropologists from the last century on have been particularly keen to study such tribes because they were interested to relate the new science to the theory of evolution.

Evolution

The work of Charles Darwin provided scholars with the kind of theoretical explanation of religion which had not been present in the eighteenth-century arguments of philos-

'**No-one can understand mankind without understanding the faiths of humanity. Sometimes naive, sometimes penetratingly noble, sometimes crude, sometimes subtle, sometimes cruel, sometimes suffused by an overpowering gentleness and love, sometimes world-affirming, sometimes negating the world, sometimes inward-looking, sometimes universalistic and missionary minded, sometimes shallow and often profound— religion has permeated human life since early and obscure times.'**

Ninian Smart, *Religious Experience*

ophers such as G.W.F. Hegel and J.G. Herder.

Instead of abstract ideas of progress and development, scholars such as E.B. Tylor, J.G. Frazer and W. Robertson Smith, whose works spanned the period between 1870 and 1920, sought to identify specific periods through which man had passed, by characterizing the beliefs held during these successive eras. They named these stages of religious life according to their own, largely speculative, theory of the dominant concern present in each one.

Often religion was said to cease to be significant once science replaced it as a stage in human thought. This was a characteristic argument of Sir J.G. Frazer, whose book *The Golden Bough* is still in print even though it is more a work of speculation than of fact.

Functionalism

The twentieth century saw a marked difference of approach to the study of religion, and in particular the question of the development of religion changed its form. Instead of asking the evolutionary question of how religion first originated, anthropologists chose to ask what function was served by religion in each particular society where it occurred. The anthropologist E.E. Evans-Pritchard expressed this neatly, saying that 'religion is what religion does'. Bronislaw Malinowski (1884–1942) abandoned the historical dimension, preferring to study intensively the role played by religion in the Trobriand Island community where, as an Austrian citizen, he was interned during World War I.

Malinowski believed that there were scientific laws of culture and that they could also be applied to religion. The individual biological needs of food, shelter, sex and security could also be viewed as social needs which people provide for corporately through economic, political, kinship and religious institutions. Magic was useful because it brought one man into a leadership position during times of crisis in society. It made some sort of positive action possible and thereby pre-vented chaotic behaviour. Religion along with magic provided the basic integrating force in society, for it was the response to the human desire for survival. Magic, performed in the face of natural calamity, provided a psychological support for people's fear. Much of this theory resulted from Malinowski's observation of primitive society, but as his private diaries show—published long after his death—his own fears of loneliness, the dark, and of death probably guided the way he constructed his theory of religion.

Structuralism

After the 1950s, anthropologists turned their attention more to the role of religion as an expression of the structure of the ideas, values and beliefs of a society. They drew a picture of the relationships which existed between doctrines. They asked how people argued, how they organized their beliefs, and what was the inner logical pattern of a religion.

For example, village Buddhists escape painful experiences by means of exorcists: how do they square this with the Buddhist ideal which denies the validity of such exorcism? Or how do Christian groups relate their beliefs about everyday life to the concept of the Trinity? This structuralist approach draws attention to the organization of human thought, and to the way man brings an ordered pattern to his complex world. For instance, the French anthropologist Claude Levi-Strauss has studied the question of how this works out in the case of myths.

The psychologists

Whereas in the nineteenth century scholars were happy to combine anthropological ideas with those concerning the human mind, in the twentieth century the mind has been singled out for special attention by the psychologists. Sigmund Freud drew heavily from evolutionary anthropology, especially from William Robertson Smith's famous *Lectures on the Religion of the Semites* (1889), but his wish was to show how the underlying power of the human

Hindus bathe in the sacred rivers such as the Ganges, to wash away pollution, both physical and spiritual.

mind, grounded in a kind of sexual energy called the libido, ascribed to a god-figure attitude which originated in the child's relationship with his human father.

Projection

This introduces a major concept in religious studies: that of 'projection', a term which embraces not only the psychological approach of Freud but also the earlier philosophical argument of Feuerbach (1804–72), who claimed that statements about God were really to be understood as statements about man. Man had tended to construct ideas of God and then to look at them as though they had a reality of their own. For a proper understanding of theology one should reverse this process and interpret religious doctrine in human terms. Feuerbach influenced Marx and Engels, and thereby the rise of communist society and its view of religion as an outmoded way of interpreting life.

Freud also decided that religious positions were no longer useful to man, as his book *The Future of an Illusion* (1927) clearly showed: here projection is seen as illusion, the human mind leading man away from truth and reality, and therefore to be deplored.

The psychologist William James adopted a rather more positive attitude to the role of religion. In *The Varieties of Religious Experience* (1902), he gave a full description of religious experiences possessed by various people, comparing and contrasting what he called 'the religion of healthy-mindedness' with that of 'the sick soul'.

For James, religion was of value in helping man to live a positive and courageous life. It was seen as ultimately about the fact that there is something wrong with us, and with ways of saving us from that wrongness. In other words, religion helps man to accept himself and his life-condition rather than falling prey to the infirmities of his life. All this is of positive advantage to man, so that James did not see religion as an illusion with no real future as Freud thought it to be.

The sociologists

The discipline of sociology also developed rapidly in the early twentieth century. Here too the idea of projection was of great significance, particularly for Emile Durkheim (1858–1917). His famous study of *The Elementary Forms of the Religious Life* owed much to the same lectures by Robertson Smith which had also influenced Freud. It presupposed an evolutionary approach to religion, but did not accept the view that religious ideas were simply misleading products of the human mind. Here Durkheim as a sociologist parted company both with the psychology of Freud and the speculative anthropology of Frazer. Durkheim was convinced that there was something real in religion, and that man was not deceiving himself. In identifying the reality underlying religious behaviour he also parted company with theological explanations, for the reality influencing religion, he came to believe, is society itself.

Durkheim was as preoccupied with the idea of society as Freud was with the unconscious mind: he believed that there was a different sort of reality at work in social groups from that in individual lives. Society could be studied much as botanists studied plants. Religion was the human activity which spoke about social reality while using words about gods.

In one sense Durkheim was adopting a similar outlook to Feuerbach— that man merely seems to believe in and to speak about God, while really talking about his own social group without realizing it. But for Durkheim, who did not believe in a God who exists in his own right and independently of man, society is such an important thing that it can completely fill the place of God. Society is there before I am born and exists after my death. It gives me ideas and language to think and speak with. It protects me and makes me feel worthy of life. So, despite the fact that man projects all these ideas onto a god-figure, the ideas themselves are true, and what is more, they are necessary if society is to be held together as a moral community.

Six Major Figures in Religious Studies

Eric Sharpe

FRIEDRICH MAX MÜLLER (1823–1900)

Often called 'the father of comparative religion', Friedrich Max Müller was the son of a German Romantic poet. He studied in Leipzig and in Paris, where he began his first major work, a monumental edition of the Sanskrit text of the *Rig Veda*, published in four volumes between 1849 and 1862. He settled in England in 1846, and spent most of the remainder of his life in Oxford, becoming Professor of Comparative Philology in 1868. A prolific writer, his later books included *Comparative Mythology* (1856), *Introduction to the Science of Religion* (1873), *India, What can it teach us?* (1883), and many other works, including three series of Gifford Lectures and two volumes of personal reminiscences. He was also responsible for editing the fifty-volume series of *Sacred Books of the East*—still an invaluable source for the study of religion.

Max Müller brought the religions of the world for the first time to the notice of the English-speaking public, interpreted to the West the ancient and modern religions of India, in a vital, if sometimes idiosyncratic, way. His theories that religion arose through the personification of natural phenomena have, on the other hand, been wholly superseded.

EDWARD BURNETT TYLOR (1832–1917)

In its early years, the study of comparative religion was much concerned with the origin and evolution of religion as a universal human phenomenon. E.B. Tylor, who in 1896 became Britain's first professor of anthropology, in the 1860s coined the term 'animism' to describe what he believed to be the earliest stage in this evolutionary process, a simple 'belief in spiritual beings'. Tylor studied in Mexico; this visit resulted in his first book, *Anahuac* (1861). He subsequently published *Researches into the Early History of Mankind* (1865), and his most important work, *Primitive Culture* (1871), in which the 'animism' theory is clearly stated. Briefly, it is that early man's experiences of dream and trance led him first to a belief in a separate 'soul' (*anima*) in himself, and later to postulate the existence of surviving souls (ghosts), and of many such 'souls' in animals, plants, the atmosphere, etc. Out of this belief in souls or spirits, there eventually developed belief in gods.

As an evolutionary theory, this is of very little value, but it does represent accurately the way in which primal (and other) peoples look on the unseen world. Tylor's example, as well as providing for the first time a way of understanding religion at a basic level, served to point anthropology along a path which it still to some extent follows.

WILLIAM JAMES (1842–1910)

William James, the brother of the celebrated American novelist Henry James, was chiefly responsible, in the years around the turn of the century, for popularizing the new subject of the psychology of religion. His book *The Varieties of Religious Experience* (1902) is a classic, and still widely read today. Trained in medicine, he taught both physiology and psychology at Harvard as early as the 1870s, and in 1890 published a celebrated textbook, *The Principles of Psychology*. Most of his other books, including *The Will to Believe* (1896), *Pragmatism* (1907) and *Human Immortality* (1908), were originally courses of lectures.

In his *Varieties* he drew many valuable distinctions between types of religious experience, the best-known being that between the optimistic 'religion of healthy-mindedness' (typified by Christian Science) and the pessimistic 'religion of the sick soul' (traditional Calvinism). He also had much to say on mysticism, and discussed 'altered states of consciousness' many years before the subject became fashionable. He came from a Swedenborgian background, and his own religion was an indistinct theism, far removed from orthodox Christianity. Although he is still worth reading, his approach was too individualistic, and he had little to say about the corporate aspects of religion. His methods, too, were seriously called in question by the depth-psychologists (Freud, Jung and their followers), and are hardly applicable today.

WILLIAM ROBERTSON SMITH (1846–94)

Robertson Smith, best known for his magisterial book *Lectures on the Religion of the Semites* (1889), was a minister of the Free Church of Scotland. In 1870 he became Professor of Old Testament Studies at the Free Church College in Aberdeen. In the early 1880s he was dismissed from his chair for 'unscriptural' teaching, and in 1883 was elected Professor of Arabic at Cambridge. A liberal evangelical, he was responsible for bringing together traditional philological study of the Bible and the new insights of anthropology.

He first visited North Africa in 1879, and was impressed by the existence of 'totemism' among the Sinai Bedouin: this resulted in his first major work, *Kinship and Marriage in Early Arabia* (1885). In his later *Lectures*, he concentrated on the concept of sacrifice, which he saw less as a legal transaction than as a practical means of establishing communion with deity. He also recognized that in religion, custom and ritual are often more significant than systems of belief, and that it is vitally important that the student be an accurate and sympathetic observer of the practical side of religion. His influence was widespread: he inspired J.G. Frazer to study totemism, and was a forerunner of the sociological study of religion – for which reason he, almost alone among his contemporaries, is still respected among sociologists and anthropologists. Despite his brush with ecclesiastical authority, he remained warmly evangelical in his personal beliefs.

NATHAN SÖDERBLOM (1866–1931)

The link between comparative religion and Christian theology was firmly established in the early part of the twentieth century by a group of scholars of whom Nathan Söderblom was perhaps the most outstanding. Born the son of a Lutheran country minister in Sweden, from 1894 to 1901 he was Swedish legation pastor in Paris; in 1901 he became Professor of Comparative Religion in Uppsala, and remained in this post until his elevation to the archbishopric of Uppsala in 1914, a post he occupied until his death in 1931. His scholarly work spanned many fields, among them Iranian studies, Luther studies, mysticism, Catholic modernism and general comparative religion.

Though few of his many books were translated into English, his Gifford Lectures *The Living God* (published posthumously in 1931) were widely read in their day. He endeavoured to locate historical Protestantism within Christianity, and Christianity within the religions of the world. He drew valuable distinctions between 'mystical' and 'revealed' forms of religion, and later between two forms of mysticism, 'mysticism of personality' (Paul, Luther) and 'mysticism of the infinite' (Indian religion). As well as this academic work, Söderblom made an invaluable contribution to twentieth-century Christianity as one of the fathers of the ecumenical movement.

RUDOLF OTTO (1869–1937)

Educated at Erlangen and Göttingen, most of Otto's career was spent in teaching posts at Göttingen, Breslau and Marburg. After early work in Luther studies, he turned his attention to the philosophy and psychology of religion, and after 1911 to the study of Indian religions. His best-known and most important work, *The Idea of the Holy*, first appeared in German in 1917, and in English in 1923. In it, he attempted to show that religion begins with 'the sense of the numinous', that is, of a mysteriously 'other' deity both fearsome and fascinating (*numen* = deity). This book became a religious classic.

His later Indian studies included *Mysticism East and West* (1932) and *India's Religion of Grace* (1930), and a critical edition of the *Bhagavad Gita* (*The Original Gita*, 1939). In 1921, convinced of the importance of living, inter-religious dialogue, he inaugurated the Inter-Religious League, which was not a success. In his last years his internationalism caused him to fall foul of the Nazi government in Germany, and he died in 1937.

Otto's most lasting contribution to the study of religion lay in his insistence on the importance of immediate, non-rational experience to any estimate of the nature of religion. Although *The Idea of the Holy* was not always well understood, it spoke directly to the mind of the twentieth century, and helped lay the foundations for much later work in the area of personal religious experience and of mysticism.

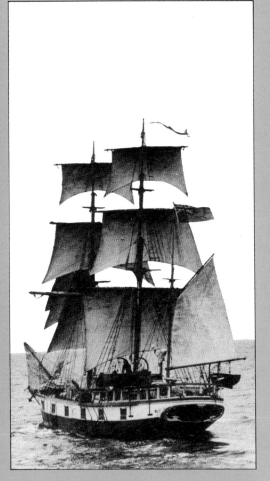

The nineteenth-century interest in anthropology was aroused by expeditions such as Charles Darwin's world voyage on board HMS Beagle.

The positive function of religion was something taken up by the sociologist Max Weber (1864–1920) who sought to show how religious ideas influenced the active social life of a group. His famous study of *The Protestant Ethic and the Spirit of Capitalism* sought to show how the Calvinist idea of predestination led believers to adopt an earnest and rational life in which they endeavoured to fulfil their calling as good stewards of God's grace. This led to the situation in which commerce and industry could develop rapidly, with maximum investment of capital and minimum loss of energy by those responsible for production of goods. Religious ideas thus motivate man's action in the world, rather than—as Marx claimed—providing an anaesthetic for worldly life.

Religion as phenomenon

'Phenomenology' differs from the previous approaches by concerning itself neither with the historical origin of religion nor with the function of a religion in contemporary situations. It sets out to classify the phenomena that are associated with religious traditions: objects, rituals, doctrines, or feelings. Each phenomenologist identifies what he thinks is the essence of these phenomena, and sets about describing their influence upon man.

Gerardus van der Leeuw (1890–1950) was among the most distinguished of phenomenologists of religion. For him, power is the source and underlying essence of all religion; it is manifested in many ways, from the idea of man in Melanesian religion to the awe and wonder experienced in the world religions. His phenomenology is a description of the many ways in which 'man conducts himself in his relation to power'. Salvation comes about when the source of power is possessed or attained.

A person's religious experience cannot, of course, be observed by someone else. The phenomenologist can only see the consequences of people's experience. So phenomenology cannot deal with questions of truth. It can only describe what can be seen by an outside observer.

The historical approach

Mircea Eliade was born in Bucharest in 1907, and has worked and taught in many parts of the world. He is the best-known and most influential representative of the study of the history of religions. It is difficult to distinguish clearly between historians and phenomenologists of religion because their perspectives are similar. So while Eliade seeks to discover how religions have developed through their historical phases, his major concern is with the idea of the 'holy'.

A Buddhist believer kneels before images of the Buddha in a shrine in Kampuchea.

The enormous Hindu Wat at Angkor, Kampuchea, is almost a mile square. Surrounded by a vast cloister and moat, the central shrine represents the hub of the universe.

What are the various ways in which mankind becomes aware of the holy? His task leads him to discuss 'hierophanies'—the ways in which the sacred is manifested—including sacred places and persons.

For instance, Jesus Christ was said to be the supreme hierophany because in him the sacred, which normally belongs to a realm totally different from our own, is manifested in something belonging entirely to our world, his human nature. Eliade believes that the Western world has allowed its ability to perceive the sacred to wither, and that the task of the history of religions is to help it to regain this sense of the holy within its materialistic life.

Eliade resembles Rudolf Otto (1869–1937) whose famous book *The Idea of the Holy* asserted that the central reality of true religion lies in a sense of the magnetic and awe-inspiring nature of the source of religious experience. Some critics argue that this approach, which does not question the existence of a divinity but rather seems to presuppose the existence of a supernatural realm, has sought to foster religion rather than to be a dispassionate study. Historians and phenomenologists may reply that they seek only to avoid reductionism and to treat the evidence with the seriousness it deserves and in a method appropriate to it.

Comparative linguistics

In 1888, the same year that Smith gave the Burnett Lectures on *The Religion of the Semites*, Friedrich Max Müller delivered the Gifford Lectures entitled *Natural Religion*. Müller told how he became entranced as a young man with the idea of translating the sacred texts of India, how his early work in the 'science of language' led him to a study of mythology and finally to 'the science of religion'. Religion is that mental state which 'enables man to apprehend the Infinite under different names', and the science of religion is the attempt to retrace the development of the names given to the gods.

Müller's study of religion is thus a study of language. For instance, the Latin *deus*, the Sanskrit *deva*, and the Greek *theos* are related and refer to the idea of brightness. He is usually remembered for his notion of the 'disease of language': the description given to something actually becomes its name, and then is imbued with a nature all of its own. It is as though man forgets that he has given a name to something, and comes to believe that it has a reality and power in itself, as in the case of the bright sun becoming a deity in its own right. Müller's work has been largely forgotten in the West, but he is still recalled in India as the man who opened up the study of Eastern texts and stimulated an entire generation of later scholars of comparative religion. He laid the solid foundation of attempting to classify and order the vast amount of material in a systematic way.

Theory of meaning

In place of the evolutionary approach to religion inherited from the nineteenth century, there is now emerging another idea which may well provide an integrating theory for the study of religion. This approach stresses man's drive to establish a meaningful world of thought and life. It avoids all simple cause-and-effect arguments, and encourages us to look at the complex inter-relationships which exist between man and his environment.

We might call this approach the 'theory of meaning'. It is much more concerned with what religion does for people now, than with how religion might have originated in the past. It sees each man as one partner involved in an extensive series of communications with others, receiving feedback from them and changing his own outlook in the process. This model of meaning further emphasizes the dynamic nature of religion and of religious experience.

Holy Places, Sacred Calendars

Harold Turner

The places where the gods are revealed or act, and the times when they do so, are central to religious experience.

The place of a vision, healing, miracle or sign tends to be set aside as a special holy space where the gods may be expected to act again. This may begin as a mere cleared circle in the grass, where people come with prayers and offerings. Symbolic objects representing the divinity, altars for the offerings and sacrifices, and buildings to protect both images and altars and to serve as a 'house for the god' may then be added. As the shrine is elaborated it may become a vast temple space with massive structures.

Such sacred places have a symbolic significance. They may be regarded as the 'centre of the world' or 'navel of the earth', as the meeting-place between the gods and men, and the earthly replica of the heavenly realms. The inner cell where the image rests is the 'most holy place', often followed by a series of courts, with degrees of lesser holiness, to the entrances.

Ascent from the earthly to the heavenly realm is symbolized by vertical features—massive stairways, sacred pillars or trees, and sanctuaries on holy mountains. Similar ideas may attach to sacred caves, groves, healing wells, mysterious rock formations, or the tombs of saints or martyrs. Since divine power is more accessible at sanctuaries, these become places of pilgrimage.

The synagogues, churches and mosques of Judaism, Christianity and Islam, however, should be seen as meeting-places for the worshippers, not as sacred dwelling-places for God. They may have a historical or devotional value. But they do not possess a special holiness' because God is more active there than anywhere else.

Distance in time separates people from the divine creative acts of the past. In many religions this is overcome by regular recital of sacred myths, retelling what the gods did in creating the world, giving the land, and showing how to make fire, to hunt, farm, build and live together. The recital brings these foundation events to life again. Similarly periodic rituals re-enact and so renew the actions of the gods.

Together myths and rites make up great religious ceremonies which are timed by the rhythms of the seasons or of the heavenly bodies. The most basic is the new year renewal rite when both human and earthly vitalities, which have been used up, corrupted or attacked by evil forces, are purified and given fresh life from the spirit world.

Calendars first developed as schedules telling when to be ready for the next renewal of divine blessing or power. Calendars, however, could not tell the right time to secure divine blessing on activities such as building a new village, making war, trading, travel, marrying or anything else of special importance.

For these, diviners sought to read the signs of divine approval in the position of the stars (astrology), the flight of birds, by casting lots, consulting oracles, and in many other ways. Divination is therefore important where people feel totally dependent on gods who do not otherwise disclose their will.

Religions with scriptures, such as Judaism, Christianity and Islam, have other means of revelation, and at their best have opposed divination. On the other hand, they have their calendars of times for renewal, whether in daily devotions, weekly worship or annual renewals of experience of the divine blessing.

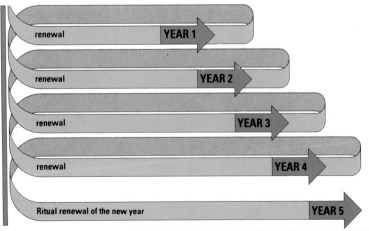

The Cycle of the Years

One year does not move directly into the next. Each year dies and is buried, returning to the time of origins, before history, to be renewed and brought back to life as the new year.

THE TIME OF ORIGINS

renewal   YEAR 1

renewal   YEAR 2

renewal   YEAR 3

renewal   YEAR 4

Ritual renewal of the new year   YEAR 5

Australian aborigines believe that before the time of man, spirits moved over the earth. Landmarks such as rock outcrops are marks of the spirits. This rock represents a mythical water-serpent who opened up water-holes.

The Golden Pavilion at Kyoto in Japan was built as a garden house. After its owner's death its great beauty led to its use as a Zen temple.

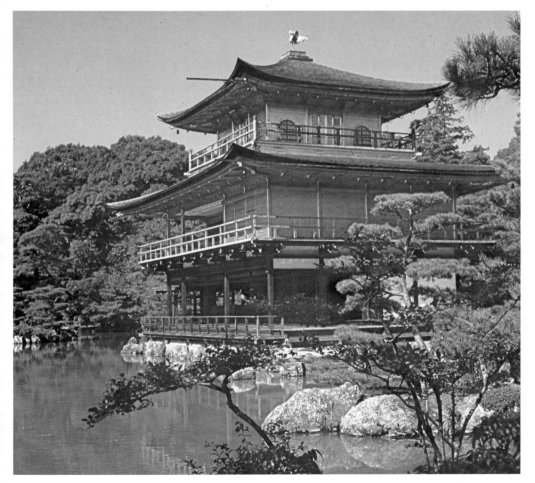

Religion Before History

Åke Hultkrantz

Evidence from archaeology

Most religions are known to us through written sources. 'Prehistoric' means that we are dealing with the time before recorded history; that is, before there were written records about myths, rituals and beliefs. Writing was developed in the ancient civilizations of the Near East, China and Middle America. The literate era started about 3000 BC in the Old World, and shortly after the birth of Christ in the New World. For the sake of convenience we may designate all religions before 3000 BC as prehistoric.

Non-religious man?

The question of the origins of religion will not concern us here. Earlier evolutionists thought that there had been an original non-religious phase in human history. Their information has, however, proved to be false. All we can say is that some groups, for example the Maasai in Kenya, appear to lack a belief in life after death.

Some students of religion consider that man's religious consciousness was born during the time when man first appeared. Others find traces of 'religious' behaviour even in the animal kingdom. Despite some startling progress in animal-behaviour studies (ethology) and the study of ancient man (palaeoanthropology), nothing certain can be said about these alternatives. All that we know is that some early human cultures seem to have contained traces of religious orientation.

Archaeological finds

The main difficulty in any approach to prehistoric religion lies, of course, in the absence of written sources from this extensive period in the history of mankind. The prehistorian is referred to silent survivals of the past: bone materials, stone arrangements, rough stone figures, rock drawings and similar materials. Such objects are difficult to decipher. For example, it is difficult to tell whether a Danish bog find from the Iron Age—be it a well-preserved human body or a golden dish—was used as a gift of offering or not, since there are no documents from that time to illuminate what really happened. (Some modern archaeologists even question whether Denmark, or even Scandinavia, had a religion during the Bronze Age!) We shall never know for certain what the people of those days thought.

However, there are means to come closer to an understanding of at least some general ideas of those distant times. Let us first see how the prehistoric source materials can be classified. The difficulty of such a classification is obvious: we cannot know if a particular type of artifact—an axe, say, or a wagon—ever had a ritual purpose. Nevertheless, a survey of materials which seem to qualify as connected with religion calls for a division along the following lines:
● burial places and burial finds;
● deposition of offerings;
● representations of deities, spirits and cultic figures (carved idols, reliefs, rock paintings, rock drawings, etc.);
● remains of constructions with religious associations, such as altars, temples, or foundations of world pillars.

Archaeologists usually point out that this material can be interpreted only by analogy. The prehistoric material must be placed in a context which may suggest its original meaning. Of course, all such conclusions are hypothetical. The history of prehistoric research has seen a succession of interpretations. The methods of archaeological reconstruction have become more refined, comparisons with the world of the science of the peoples of mankind (ethnology) more restricted in scope, and ecological perspectives more decisive. Nevertheless, much of our reconstruction of prehistoric religion remains guesswork. Almost every interpretation of beliefs can be and has been contested.

Prehistoric versus historic

The prehistoric era of religion stretches from the beginning of mankind—probably about two or three million years ago—until approximately 3000 BC. During all this time religious knowledge was transmitted through the spoken word (beliefs and myths) and through imitative behaviour (rituals). This somewhat restricted how much knowledge could be accumulated—although it is amazing how much tribal keepers of oral traditions are able to memorize.

In many prehistoric societies the fight for subsistence may likewise have precluded the growth of sophisticated religious thought (although there are examples of primal societies with a good deal of leisure time at their disposal). We therefore find some basic differences between representatives of preliterate and literate religions; for instance, the former value repetition in myth and ritual, the latter develop dogma and may go in for intricate speculations.

The perspective of society

The main differences between prehistoric and historic religions are, however, that the former are organized around the perspectives of the hunter, food-gatherer, fisherman or early farmer, whereas historic religions on the other hand, represent the world-view of the developed civilizations, beginning with Egypt, Mesopotamia and China. In other words, prehistoric religions were at home in small-scale, tribal societies where family or kin-groups meant more than other forms of social organization, and where the influence of

natural forces had a tremendous impact on daily life and religion. Such primitive societies still linger on today, and it is possible to link the types of these societies with prehistoric periods.

The first period is the Palaeolithic, or Old Stone Age, during which people were hunters, food-gatherers and fishermen. Latter-day hunting societies have been organized along similar lines, and the patterns of their religions are probably reminiscent of those of Palaeolithic times.

Farmers and herdsmen

The Palaeolithic was followed by the Neolithic, or New Stone Age, about 10,000 BC. This was the time when many hunters turned into primitive farmers. In the following millennia pastoral nomadism developed out of this agriculture in places where the cultivated lands met the grasslands and deserts. The world of the farmers and herdsmen is still with us. There is every reason to expect that their religious practices resemble those of their prehistoric predecessors.

These analogies between past and present are very rough and ready. Ecological, technological, social and historical differences may cast doubts upon their validity. But they do give us certain clues on which to base our interpretation.

Lower Palaeolithic religion

It is extremely difficult to tell from the finds at our disposal what religion was like during the long period called the Early or Lower Palaeolithic (before 30,000 BC). This was the time of the pre-human members of the family of man, the early hominids such as *Australopithecus africanus*, *Homo habilis* (2,500,000 BC), *Homo erectus* (1,600,000 BC) and *Homo neanderthalensis* (100,000–30,000 BC). Originating

in Africa, perhaps—only Africa has the earliest skeletons and a continuous succession of species—the hominids spread to Europe (where they appeared before 1,000,000 BC) and to Asia; Peking man and Sangiran man in Indonesia were both representatives of *Homo erectus*.

The beginnings of culture

We have some information about the modest cultural achievements of early man. For instance, we know that two-and-a-half million years ago groups of hominids in East Africa used choppers, scrapers and other stone utensils that they had shaped themselves. They practised division of labour between the sexes, and food-sharing.

However, their religious ideas, if any, are unknown to us. This is what we might expect, for the cultural capacity of early man was crude and he did not express clear religious ideas that can be recognized as such by today's archaeologists. We have neither burials, drawings, nor stone monuments to guide our search. However, the tool-making of these early individuals suggests that they had creative intelligence and therefore, very possibly, a form of religion.

Peking man

Many prehistorians have assumed that Peking man, who lived about half a million years ago, had some concept of religion or magic. In his cave near Chou Kou Tien he assembled human skulls which were broken at the *foramen magnum*. This gives easy access to the brain, and it would seem that Peking man extracted and ate the brain. If this was the case (we can never be sure, of course), the motive was religious or magical rather than for food, for Peking man had many animals to hunt. Such cannibalism, when practised in present-day primal societies, usually implies the incorporation of the dead man's vigour and power.

This is a most hypothetical interpretation, and, unfortunately, practically all finds from the Lower Palaeolithic that lend themselves to a religious interpretation are subject to the same difficulty.

Take, for instance, the discoveries of circles of mammoth skulls in Russia and the Ukraine. We are familiar with similar skull arrangements from North America in historical times, the circles of buffalo skulls on the plains which were important in worship. However, the Palaeolithic mammoth skulls *may* have served as weights on the tent-cloths instead of stones. In several instances there are bone circles surrounding fire-places, and in these cases a religious purpose is probably out of the question.

Neanderthal man

Almost all the early remains that may have religious significance are associated with Neanderthal man and the last 50,000 years of the Lower Palaeolithic—the so-called Mousterian period.

Neanderthal man buried his dead with proper ceremonies, and he seems to have believed in some kind of life after death. In the cave of Shanidar, northern Iraq, a dead person was buried under a heap of stones, resting on a bed of many flowers. At Techik Tach in Turkestan, a child was buried surrounded by five pairs of horns of the mountain goat, apparently placed in a circle. A cave at Monte Circeo in Italy contains a human skull within a small circle of stones; here is one of the so-called 'skull burials' that continue throughout the Palaeolithic period.

Grave gifts are common in many instances (for example, at La Chapelle-aux-Saints in France). Towards the end of the Mousterian period the dead were buried in a contracted position ('flexed burials') and painted with red ochre. Both these measures may reflect a belief in a future life: a return to the womb

This limestone fertility figure, discovered in Karpathos, dates from around 3,500 BC.

of Mother Earth, a continued existence in another world through the red 'blood'. Studies of certain modern peoples support these interpretations, but others are of course possible.

From this time also we have evidence of sacred objects: round fossils and pieces of iron pyrites. One round fossil from Tata, Hungary, is engraved with two lines, forming a cross; this could be the first clear evidence of the idea of a quartered universe, a concept widely represented in both Old and New World cosmology.

Bear worship

Even in recent times some Arctic peoples have worshipped bears. It is quite possible that similar religious beliefs were represented in Central Europe (France, Switzerland and Italy) in Mousterian times. Thus, in the Drachenloch Cave in Switzerland, bear skulls have been found enclosed in a stone coffin covered by stone slabs. This looks like a regular bear burial. Some reputable scholars today (Koby, Leroi-Gourhan, Kurtén) insist, however, that the bears in question—

they are cave-bears—had died a natural death in their winter lairs. The apparent burial chests would then be due to natural rockfall from the ceiling of the cave. This is a plausible explanation, but the 'cultic' interpretation seems no less plausible. Finds from Dordogne (in France) and Weimar (in Germany) suggest deliberate burial of bears—brown bears in these cases.

The main idea behind bear ceremonialism is that the dead animal will return to life, or persuade its relatives to make themselves available to the hunter, provided it has received a correct burial. The pattern of burial has been taken from human burials.

Modern man

Neanderthal man belonged to Europe, the Middle East, North Africa and northern Asia. He was slowly replaced by another species, *Homo sapiens*, our own direct ancestors, who had already spread over the continents before the end of the Lower Palaeolithic: Siberian mongoloid peoples entered the New World as early as 60,000 years ago, or perhaps even earlier, and Australia received its population from Indonesia more than 30,000 years ago. This is of some importance for our reconstruction of religious history. It means that the main structures of American and Australian hunting religions go back to the Lower Palaeolithic. And it may even imply that the totemism and high-god beliefs both appearing in these religions are just as old.

Upper Palaeolithic religion

At the beginning of the Upper Palaeolithic period about 30,000 years ago, Neanderthal man had left the scene in Europe and modern man, *Homo sapiens*, took over. The main periods were the Aurignacian (from 30,000 BC), the Solutrean (from 20,000 BC) and the Magdalenian (15,000–10,000 BC). It is now that the religious patterns, which we could glimpse in earlier periods, take a more discernible form. The world-view is still that of hunting peoples, but it varies in different parts of Eurasia. The religious developments in Africa, southern Asia, Australia and America are as yet hidden from us.

The burial customs give evidence of a clear belief in life after death. For example, in some caves near Menton in south-east France some 'flexed' skeletons were found, stained with iron oxide, adorned with rows of pierced shells and bracelets, and equipped with quartzite tools and flint knives. Skeletons from Italy to Russia testify that the dead were buried with their most precious property. No doubt, they were thought to take it with them to another world.

The mother-goddess

It is from this time that the famous sculptured 'Venus'-figurines in ivory, bone and stone appear (Gravettian period, 25,000 BC). They are distributed from France to eastern Siberia, and the best-known of them all is the Venus from Willendorf in Austria. They all have characteristic, distorted features: the parts of the body which serve sexual and child-bearing functions—the breasts, the hips, the buttocks, the private parts—are excessively enlarged, whereas little attention is paid to the face, the arms and the legs.

It has been suggested that these fat-rumped (steatopygous) figures are just representatives of mortal women, portrayed in the fashion of the time. This is scarcely probable, however. The emphasis on the sexual parts shows very clearly that these Venuses were supposed to represent deities of fertility, growth and fruitfulness. Here we have for the first time real representations of a deity, the mother-goddess, conceived as one or many.

There is a seemingly puzzling question here. How could the mother-goddess, forerunner of Ishtar, Cybele and Artemis, be such a prominent divinity in a hunting culture? The answer is simple. In recently-studied northern Eurasian cultures, the

Magnificent cave-paintings have been discovered in several sites in southern France, dating from before 10,000 BC. Was this simply the self-expression of man the hunter-gatherer? Or were these caves used (as has been suggested) for 'religious' purposes.

women had similar birth goddesses protecting them during pregnancy and childbirth. Many Siberian tribes believed in a mother of the wild animals, a mistress who protects the wild creatures she has given life to. We also know that women played a very important role during the Stone Age as mothers, housekeepers and gatherers of roots and berries.

Do these figurines prove that the concept of a male god was introduced later than the concept of a goddess? Such a conclusion seems unwarranted. Before the emergence of the Middle Eastern city-states, the Supreme Being was never represented in art as far as we can tell. As a diffuse sky-god he was not easy to picture.

We know that bull-roarers have been used to imitate the voice of the Supreme Being, or the voices of dead ancestors, in some modern primal hunting religions (in Australia, South Africa, Brazil and California). Some perforated, ornate stone slabs that have been found in Upper Palaeolithic caves may have been bull-roarers symbolizing the presence of the Supreme God, or other supernatural beings. However, this is far from certain.

Cave paintings

The most telling artistic creations from the Upper Palaeolithic are the engravings and paintings on cave walls. They first appear in the Aurignacian period, but receive their full development in the Magdalenian. Their focus is in southern France and northernmost Spain. The most famous and most numerous rock-paintings stem from 15,000 to 11,000 BC; this is the time of the caves of Dordogne (Lascaux), Ariège (Niaux, Les Trois-Frères, Montespan) and northern Spain (Altamira).

Four-fifths of the figures are animals, and of these most are horses and bisons, the hoofed fauna of the frost-bitten plains. Reindeer occur only at a late stage, at the same time as the glaciers made their last push forward. The composition of the beautiful, realistic animal scenes has been interpreted in various ways. In spite of some recent speculations in another direction, it seems quite reasonable to believe that the animals refer to hunting ritual and hunting magic. Hunting was the major occupation of Palaeolithic man, and ceremonies to secure a successful hunt were most certainly part of the hunting craft, just as they have been among traditional hunters up to the present day.

Only 4 per cent of the pictured animals show arrows (or wounds resulting from arrows). Does this mean that they cannot be associated with hunting magic? Not necessarily. Among primal peoples hunting ceremonies are often very complicated, and real magic—indicating the anticipation of success in the hunt—is only part of a wider pattern. The mere representation of an animal form may lead to the kill—so it was believed.

Why did this animal ceremonialism take place in caves, often in the depths of scarcely accessible inner chambers? We do not know, but it may, perhaps, have something to do with the fact that in widespread tales, recorded even in this century, the animals are supposed originally to have come from underground, or to have once been secluded in caves.

Some wall scenes depict human beings in animal disguise. They may represent ritual performers, perhaps magicians or ritual dancers, or maybe mythical beings. Well-known is the 'sorcerer' of the cave Les Trois-Frères: a picture of a human being with reindeer antlers, long beard, bear's paws and a horse's tail. He has been interpreted as a shaman or a god of the cave, but his position in the picture over a great number of animals makes it more likely that he was a lord of the animals, a master of the game.

All these interpretations are of course tentative. There is a host of pictures which do not easily lend themselves to interpretation, such as pictographs of headless animals (there is even a sculpture of a bear without a head), of women dancing around a phallic man, and so on. However, such representations strengthen the general impression that Upper Palaeolithic European religion was concerned with the animals and sexual fertility — natural targets in a religion chiefly concerned with hunting. We can say the same about animal ceremonialism in Siberia in the same era: reindeer skeletons were carefully buried in anatomical order. Such hunting rites have survived in this area into the twentieth century. As in the bear rites, the aim has been to restore the animal to a new life, in this world or hereafter.

From the end of the Palaeolithic, or the Mesolithic, we have evidence of what appear to have been sacrifices to the supernatural rulers of the reindeer in northern Germany. Reindeer were submerged in a lake close to present-day Hamburg, and weighted down with stones. It is less likely that these reindeer were caches for the hunters, as has been suggested.

Neolithic religion

The Neolithic is, strictly speaking, the period when objects of stone were no longer chipped but ground and polished. More important, this is the age, from about 10,000 BC, when man went over to producing rather than hunting or gathering his own food. The population of the world was probably then around 10 million people. The climate had changed—the melting of the ice was in full flux—and the warmer weather made new inventions in subsistence possible.

Farming and village life

Agriculture was born, possibly as a consequence of the gathering of seeds by the women. This new way of life made it possible for a rapidly-growing population to settle in one place—to live in villages, and to practise pottery-making and weaving. Village life had a tremendous impact on religion, and so had the new food sources, the products of agriculture (or horticulture, as primitive agriculture is sometimes called).

The Neolithic period provides us with archaeological materials from the whole world. There are at least three independent centres where farming began. One is the Middle East, more specifically the mountain slopes of the Fertile Crescent. Wheat and corn were cultivated here, and dogs and goats were domesticated. The taming of animals slowly developed into pastoral nomadism on the outskirts of the area. In the north where the grasslands were wide and open, horse riding was introduced in about 900 BC.

Another centre of agriculture was south-east Asia, homeland of the cultivation of root-crops such as yams. Close by, in Assam, rice was introduced as a staple food that quickly spread to China and the surrounding areas.

A third centre was Central America, where the cultivation of maize began around 5000 BC.

The religions of the Neolithic peoples were closely adapted to these three agricultural civilizations and spread with them. When pastoral nomadism appeared on the scene a new profile of religion was formed that changed the course of world religions.

Death and burial

If we now concentrate on the west Asian–Mediterranean Neolithic religions, it is easy to see how the archaeological finds fit in with this picture. People lived in villages and similar settlements; outside these, true cemeteries have been found (although in some cases the bodies were buried under the floors of the houses). Graves were provided with gifts and offerings, such as beads, shells, utensils like ivory combs, and female figurines—perhaps symbolizing servants for the next life, or protective goddesses.

The closer we come to the time of the developed civilizations, the more differentiated are the burials according to rank or class. Social distinctions (stratification) developed as the political organization based on kinship was succeeded by one based on territory, and a surplus of products made it possible for some men to become relatively rich and important. This development was reflected in the burial customs. 'Inhumation' was now common: man was interred in the ground like the grain, to arise again in another world. Coffins became more commonly used as time went by. Towards the end of the Neolithic, cremation was practised here and there, perhaps associated with a more spiritual view of the afterlife.

In some early Neolithic burials the heads of the dead were removed and placed in a circle, facing the centre. This seems to be the last survival of an old Palaeolithic tradition. The beliefs behind this arrangement are hidden from us. Perhaps the circle as a symbol of the universe had something to do with it.

Male and female

Many female sculptures, fat-rumped and violin-shaped figures in bone, clay and terracotta, testify to the prominence of fertility cults. Figurines from Romania (5000 BC) show a mother with her child, later a favourite motif in the Egyptian and Christian religions. In some places there are also phallic statuettes, most certainly representing the male companion of the fertility goddess. The female statuettes are, however, in the majority, no doubt reflecting the elevated position of the woman, and so also the goddess, in a matrilinear agrarian society. The functions of the mother-goddess were now adapted to farming needs: she appeared as goddess of earth and vegetation.

Other fertility divinities were also portrayed, sometimes through animal masks, sometimes in sculpture. Serpentines around the goddess hint that she was a snake-goddess; in later Cretan culture the goddess raises her hands holding snakes. The snake was a fertility symbol in historical times in Europe, the Middle East, India and China (as the dragon).

Another divinity is probably represented in the bull effigies with human masks in the Balkan area. The cult of the bull, symbol of fertility, seems to have been distributed over the Mediterranean and Middle Eastern world. In historical times, it became associated with gods like Baal and Dionysus, with the supernatural master of the bull figures in Zoroastrian religion, and Mithra is represented as killing the bull to rejuvenate the world. The bull-fights in south-western Europe are probably reminiscences of ancient rituals in the worship of the bull-cult.

Priests and temples

This was the time when a form of priesthood evolved and temples of wood, stone and clay became common. The casual sacrificial places of the earlier nomadic hunting culture were succeeded by large buildings for divine service. Here were kept altars, vessels, inscribed objects, vases with paintings of ritual scenes, sculptures in clay and, later on, copper and gold. All these were used in the rituals.

In the Ukraine and surrounding areas archaeologists have found remains of temples, and clay models of temples. For instance, in the southern Bug Valley, now in Soviet Moldavia, Russian prehistorians have discovered a temple at Sabatinovka dating from about 5000 BC. Built of wattle-and-daub, it occupied about seventy square metres. Its big rectangular room, with a floor plastered with clay, contained at the back a clay altar, upon which sixteen female figurines were found. They had large buttocks and were seated on horn-backed stools. Beside the altar was a chair of clay, perhaps intended for the high priest.

European and west Asian Neolithic developments are paralleled in east Asia, and are definitely connected with the Chinese Neolithic period. But the developments in south-east Asia are more difficult to follow. In America the fertility religion of the horticulturists was simply a transfer of the hunter's conceptual world to the planter's; agrarian rituals did not vary basically from hunting rituals in post-Columbian eastern North America. However, some mythological motifs connected with the 'maize mother' point to communications with Indonesia. In large areas of agricultural America the Neolithic period continued until the arrival of Columbus, and even beyond this date.

Megalithic monuments

Towards the end of the Neolithic era structures composed of large stones, or megaliths, were erected in Europe. Perhaps most of them were burial structures: the striking tombs (dolmens) consisting of a large, flat stone supported on uprights, and the passage graves, found on the islands and shores of the Mediterranean and Western Europe.

However, beside the megalithic tombs there are also huge stones in alignment, or menhirs, as at Carnac in Brittany. Their purpose is hidden from us; perhaps they marked ritual procession routes. Some large constructions, such as the Hal Tarxien stone buildings in Malta, were evidently temples. Chalk sculptures found in them show realistic human features and some kind of gowns, and may represent gods and goddesses and their priests.

Other megalithic structures give the impression of having had astronomical functions. Perhaps they helped to determine the calendar and the agricultural seasons, always important to the farmer. Stonehenge, on Salisbury Plain in England, for instance, has a circle of sarsen stones; certain stones line up with the sunrise at midsummer. Whatever calendar purpose Stonehenge had, it was also a place of worship. Fertility-gods and goddesses were probably worshipped here, as has been suggested by archaeologists.

Megalithic monuments have been found from Britain in the west to Assam in the east, and reached south-east Asia, Polynesia and—according to some scholars—even the New World. Certainly, the Egyptian pyramids and the Maya pyramids in Yucatan do resemble each other, and in both cases they served as burial chambers. All over Eurasia and America, astronomers and prehistorians have identified stone constructions as observatories and megalithic calendars. If this is true, it is almost certain that astronomy was pursued within the frame of religious and ceremonial interests.

The great civilizations

The megalithic monuments are, like the Bronze-Age finds that date from approximately the same time, stepping stones to the era of the great civilizations, or 'high cultures'. The latter started on the river plains in Egypt, Mesopotamia and other Near Eastern areas around 3000 BC. They introduce the age of history, that is, of writing. Living in towns, central political power, large economic surpluses and strict class differentiation are the characteristics of these new kingdoms. In the religious sphere they are distinguished by sacred kings, a priestly hierarchy, developed ritual, hecatombs of blood-sacrifices and imposing temple buildings. Their religious world is populated by great gods and goddesses (usually arranged in hierarchical order under a supreme god); their realm of the dead is stratified.

We have come a long way from the simple stone arrangements of the Palaeolithic peoples. Despite the 'Neolithic revolution', it is a continuous road that leads from the simple beliefs of Palaeolithic hunting groups to the polytheism of the great ancient kingdoms.

The Megalithic monument of Stonehenge dates from the early Bronze Age. It is thought to have been used for astrological and religious purposes.

Origins of Religion

Robert Brow

What was the first religion of man? Answers to this question differ widely and depend very much on what view is taken of man's origin. Those who go to the early chapters of the Bible as their source point out that religion was not invented, evolved or discovered by man: from the day of his creation man knew the one Creator-God who had made him, and from the time of his fall man worshipped this God through sacrifice. Monotheism and the practice of animal sacrifice—these, they say, are clearly shown by the Bible to be the twin characteristics of original religion. God was God, and sinful man could not approach him in his own righteousness.

In support of this view it is often pointed out that the most ancient literature of the Greeks, the Egyptians, the Chinese, the Hindus, and the traditions of many races agree that the first men brought animals to represent and substitute for them in their worship of God. As we shall see, there came a time when Buddha in India, Confucius in China, and the Greek philosophers reacted against the animal sacrifices of a corrupt priesthood, and the main non-Christian world religions were built on other premises. At this stage, however, we are not concerned with the merits or demerits of animal sacrifice. What we are discussing is basically a matter of history, and obviously the evidence provided by the ancient documents of the Bible about man's original religion must be taken seriously.

Evolution of religion

There is, however, another answer to the question which denies all this. It starts with the view that man evolved from a pre-simian ancestor. Since animals have no religion, there must have been, it is said, a long ascent through apish chatter and fear of the dark unknown to what Bouquet calls 'animatism', a 'belief in a vague, potent, terrifying inscrutable force'.

Animatism developed into 'animism', the spirit-fearing religion of most isolated tribal people. Then came the polytheism immortalized in the Greek mythologies. Israel's glory, so this summary of the development of religion suggests, was that she was able to narrow down the many gods of the surrounding nations to one tribal god. And eventually the one Creator-God of the Hebrew prophets, together with the philosophical monotheism of Plato, paved the way for higher religion.

This answer has held the field among many scholars since Darwin. Evolution was regarded as proved, and it was attractive to infer the evolution of religion from it. The only problem was how to fit the Bible into this scheme. This was neatly solved, however, by Wellhausen's documentary hypothesis which rearranged the Old Testament scriptures in line with the evolution of religion theory.

Wellhausen's reconstruction has now, however, been discredited. And we also have examples of monotheism and elaborate priestly religion from long before the time of Abraham. The theory of the upward evolution of religion is therefore being restated to push the emergence of monotheism back into the shadows of prehistory. Led by Wilhelm Schmidt of Vienna, anthropologists have shown that the religion of the hundreds of isolated tribes in the world today is not primitive in the sense of being original. The tribes have a memory of a 'high god', a benign creator-father-god, who is no longer worshipped because he is not feared. Instead of offering sacrifice to him, they concern themselves with the pressing problems of how to appease the vicious spirits of the jungle. The threats of the medicine man are more strident than the still, small voice of the father-god.

We see, then, that the evolution of religion from animatism can no longer be assumed as axiomatic and that some anthropologists now suggest that monotheism may be more naturally primitive as a world-view than animism. Their research suggests that tribes are not animistic because they have continued unchanged since the dawn of history. Rather, the evidence indicates degeneration from a true knowledge of God. Isolation from prophets and religious books has ensnared them into sacrificial bribery to placate the spirits instead of joyous sacrificial meals in the presence of the Creator.

So the evidence of history brings us back to reconsider the biblical answer. This, as we have seen, states that the first man was created in the image of God; he was a monotheist; and he practised animal sacrifice. But how, you may ask, can this be squared with evolution, the apish chatter, the cave-men, and the images of hundreds of textbooks?

Evidence

Let us first remove some misconceptions and clear the ground a little to enable us to look again at man's early religious history. Even if it were conclusively proved that God created man by some process of mutations and selection, it would not follow that the process was a chance one. The Christian insists that, whatever methods were used—and the scientists should be encouraged to find out what they were—God planned the creation of man and he carried it out in accordance with his own purposes.

Science's function is to describe processes, but it cannot pronounce on the purpose of things. Physicists and biologists have a right to say that in looking at matter and life scientifically, no evident purpose is discovered. They overstep their limits if they go on to require faith in pure chance as opposed to faith in a creator. In any decision which may have to be made between faith in God or in 'blind chance', the science of evolution is strictly neutral, and cannot be anything else.

As scientists recognize their limitations, it is also important for Christians not to go beyond what is written in the first book of the Bible. Genesis man is not defined in terms of bone structure, or brain-size, tool-using, agriculture, social organization, or even artistic ability. Adam is the first creature who can talk back to his Creator, worship him, and choose among alternative ideologies. Any previous hominids, cave dwellers, Neanderthals, etc., who might have walked upright for thousands or millions of years, were by this definition animals who did not have what was required to make them in the image of God.

Sacrifice

According to the Bible, the first true man is a monotheist, and when he falls into sin, he seeks restoration through animal sacrifice. The theory of the evolution of religion suggests that man is an animal taking a long time to become divine. The Bible describes a human couple made in the image of God, who degenerated into what we are now. The question at issue is the real nature of man, not the names of Adam and Eve.

There is one more piece of ground to clear before we begin our dig down through the mound of religious history. Even though we may accept that early man was a monotheist and practised animal sacrifice, we should not expect prehistory to give us any proof of this type of religion. Whether animals were sacrificed to God or not cannot be known from their bones. God required altars to be of earth or uncut stones, whereas elaborate altars indicate a developed priestly system. Since earth crumbles and stones are used in building, most of the early altars will be unrecognizable even if they are found.

Nor does the true monotheist use idols or images. Idolatry always indicates that monotheism has degenerated into polytheistic confusion. The fact that the dead were buried in various ways does not affect the evidence either way. We should not therefore expect any evidence of religion till it is well past the original stage. By the time a professional priesthood develops, and temples, idols and elaborate altars leave their archaeological evidence, literature has begun and we are on surer ground.

Ancient literature

As we consider some of the evidence which illustrates the biblical view of the origin of religion, it would be foolish to claim the case is proved. Since we have no way of examining the religion of the first true man, and actually true religion is never examinable, the matter is unlikely ever to be proved either way. All we can do is to show that an original monotheism gives an explanation of many historical facts which are very intractable on the evolution of religion hypothesis.

If we could look down on the ancient world in about 1500 BC, we would see ordinary men and women still offering animal sacrifice as their normal way of approaching God or the gods. The earliest literature of India, the Sanskrit *Vedas*, picture the nomadic Aryan tribes who fought their way eastwards across the Indus and Ganges plains. The head of the tribe offered animal sacrifice with the same simplicity as Abraham.

When they settled in India, the Aryans developed a regular priesthood, and the *Vedas* are the hymns which the priests chanted as the sacrificial smoke ascended to God. The hymns address God under various names such as 'the sun', 'the heavenly one' and 'the storm', but the interesting thing is that, whatever name they gave to God, they worshipped him as the supreme ruler of the universe. This practice is called henotheism. God has several names, just as Christians today have several names for God, but the names do not indicate different gods. They are different facets of one God.

Henotheism changes into polytheism when the names of God are so personified that various gods are separated, and they begin to disagree and fight among themselves. The later Vedic literature has certainly become polytheistic by, say, 1000 BC, but the earliest Aryans must have been monotheists.

Gods and myths

The original Creator-God of the Aryans was known among all the Indo-European nations. His first name was Dyaus Pitar ('divine father') which is the same as the Greek Zeus Pater, the Latin Jupiter or Deus, the early German Tiu or Ziu, and Norse Tyr. Another name was 'the heavenly one' (Sanskrit *varuna*, Greek *ouranos*), or 'the friend' (Sanskrit *mitra*, Persian *mithra*). By metaphor and simile other names were added. God is called 'the sun', 'the powerful one', 'the guardian of order'. The sacred fire (Sanskrit *agni*, Latin *ignis*, Greek *hagnos*), common to all early sacrificial worship, had a peculiar fascination and was soon endowed with divine qualities.

Gradually story-tellers embellished their tales with love and jealousy and war and drunkenness, and so the mythologies appeared. The earth became God's bride, attracted worship to herself as 'the queen of heaven', and added sex to worship in her fertility cults. Where there are no written scriptures, and no prophets to apply God's truth, degeneration into polytheism is the rule of religion. Even the great monotheistic religions, Judaism, Islam and the Christian church, all give evidence that a pure monotheism can quickly be corrupted. The emergence of mythological polytheism among the Greeks and Aryans is proof of the inventiveness of the bards, but no evidence against a primitive monotheism.

The early Semites of Babylonia, Assyria, Syria and Phoenicia also practised animal sacrifice in their approach to God. Instead of adding mythological families and friends and enemies to the Creator, the Semites tended to nationalize him into a tribal deity. He was the one who helped the nation in war. The Babylonian Bel vied with the Syrian Rimmon, while the prophets of Israel had to keep pointing out that there could be only one Creator-God, not Ammon's Molech, and Moab's Chemosh, and Israel's Yahweh as one among many.

Israel was always monotheistic, though she was often tempted to think of the Lord as a lord among many local lords (Canaanite Baal meant 'lord' or 'husband'). Much has been written about the names of God, but whether he was called Elohim ('the mighty one') or Yahweh ('he was, he is, he will be') or Adhonay ('the Lord'), he was One. A thousand years later Muhammad proclaimed the same truth about Allah, though in Islam also 'the One' has many names. It is interesting that Islam, true to its Semitic origin, considered Allah as the conquering Arab tribal god.

Cities and science

The Semites were not the first rulers of the Middle East. An interesting people called the Sumerians had a city-state civilization which flourished before 2500 BC. They were related to the Indus Valley people of north India, whose great cities flourished till they were ousted by the invading Aryans about 1500 BC. Little is known about the religion of the Indus Valley people as their script has not yet been deciphered but, like the Sumerians, they were already polytheists. Sumerian gods lied and fought and lusted against each other resulting in a gradual decadence and collapse of their civili-

zation. They were an easy prey to Semites in the west, and invading Aryans in India, just as a later Hindu polytheism was conquered by Islam in the eleventh century AD.

We cannot prove the Sumerians were originally monotheists before their decadence into crude polytheism, but it could be argued that their science and civilization was the product of a time when they knew An, the one Creator-God of heaven. It is a fact of history that polytheism has always weakened a nation, whereas monotheism invigorates and unifies.

Case-histories

If this interpretation of history is

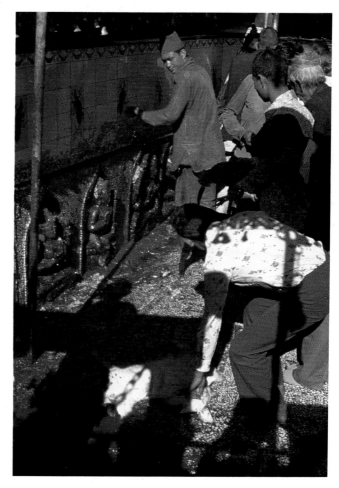

The sacrifice of animals to the gods still plays an important part in Hinduism.

correct, then it is obvious that some of the Semites and Indo-Europeans must have retained a monotheistic faith when other nations had already long degenerated into polytheism. The Egyptian priesthood, for example, continued the practice of animal sacrifice, but polytheism predominated until Akhenaten reinstated a kind of monotheism for a few years. The Minoan civilization of Crete also had animal sacrifice at the centre of its religion, but a degenerate view of the gods is evident before its overthrow.

The earliest religious history of China is very hard to study. The Chinese script, not being phonetic, gives us no linguistic clues to the names of God. In the sixth century BC the joint attack of Taoism and Confucianism virtually obliterated the ancient Chinese priestly and sacrificial worship. We can dimly trace, however, the supreme sky-god who was worshipped as Shang-ti or Hao-Tien. He was approached through the Kiao, Hsian and Hsien sacrifices. These were offered in the open air and, like the biblical sacrifices, included killing an animal, sprinkling its blood, and burning the carcass on an altar. In spite of successive waves of Taoism, Confucianism, Buddhism and early Christianity, Chinese sacrificial worship continued in temples here and there until the communists took over.

So the case for an original monotheism and worship through animal sacrifice, with subsequent degeneration into polytheism, is by no means proved. But it is certainly much easier to fit it into the recurring cycles of history than a gradual upward evolution of religion. Where documented case-histories are available, as among the early Aryans and Hebrews, the evidence for degeneration is strong.

The whole of biblical history, and the subsequent history of the Christian church, illustrates that God reveals himself as Creator, provides a way of forgiveness and fellowship through sacrifice, and all sacrifices have their meaning and fulfilment in the death of Jesus Christ. The Bible and church history also furnish many tragic illustrations of man's inveterate desire to add deities which are less demanding, and turn sacrifice or the communion service into a bribe to force God's hand.

Priests and priestcraft

Why was the emergence of priestcraft as an institution common to ancient India, China, Egypt, classical Greece and Rome, many other civilizations, and even the medieval Christian church?

First we must try to picture worship based on animal sacrifice in its simplest form. To modern man the very idea of animal sacrifice conjures up revolting images of dark, superstitious rites and gory victims. It is important to realize that before the rise of Jainism and Buddhism in the sixth century BC men were meat-eaters, as they still are in most parts of the world. If animals are to be eaten, they have to be killed, and most races have agreed that the blood should be drained out from the carcass. This happens in our Western civilization in thousands of slaughterhouses. We turn away our eyes, but for early man each 'sacrifice' had a spiritual significance. When we read of thousands of animals being sacrificed by Solomon, we could simply paraphrase 'he gave a big feast for all the people'. In both Greek and Hebrew the same word is used for sacrifice and killing animals.

The important thing about animal sacrifice in the Bible is that God used the joyous occasions of eating meat as visual aids to teach spiritual truths. There is nothing more primitive or obnoxious about attaching spiritual truths to animal sacrifice than to bread and wine. The animal sacrifices looked forward to Christ's death and resurrection just as the Christian communion services look back. That a wide variety of spiritual meanings was attached to animal sacrifice is evident from the Old Testament books of Exodus, Leviticus and Numbers. These various rites can be seen as different facets of the death of Christ and the same facets of his death are now expressed in the communion service or eucharist.

Myths and Symbols

Douglas Davies

If we had just heard a moving piece of music, we would find it strange if someone asked us whether the music were true or false. Music, we might reply, is neither true nor false. To ask such a question is inappropriate. Most people know that music can, as it were, speak to them even though no words are used. In fact, some of the great symphonies can affect us almost more deeply than any number of words, while choral works such as Handel's *Messiah* can produce an effect greater than the text alone could ever do.

As with music so with people. The question of what someone 'means' to you cannot fully be answered by saying that he is your husband or she is your wife, because there are always unspoken levels of intuition, feeling and emotion built into relationships. The question of 'meaning' must always be seen to concern these dimensions as well as the more obviously factual ones.

Myths

Myths take many forms depending on the culture in which they are found. But their function is always that of pinpointing vital issues and values in the life of the society concerned. They often dramatize those profound issues of life and death, of how man came into being and of what his life is really about, of how he should conduct himself as a citizen or husband,

as a creature of God or as a farmer, and so on.

Myths are not scientific or sociological theories about these issues. They are the outcome of the way a nation or group has pondered the great questions. Their function is not merely to provide a theory of life which can be taken or left at will; they serve to compel a response from man. We might speak of myths as bridges between the intellect and emotion, between the mind and heart—and in this, myths are like music. They both express an idea and trigger off our response to it.

Sometimes myths can form an extensive series, interlinking with each other and encompassing many aspects of life, as has been shown for the Dogon people of the River Niger in West Africa. On the other hand, they may serve merely as partial accounts of problems such as the hatred between men and snakes, or the reason for the particular shape of a mountain.

One problem in our understanding of myths lies in the fact that Western religions—Judaism, Christianity and Islam—are very concerned with history. They have founders and see their history as God's own doing. This strong emphasis upon actual events differs from the Eastern approach to religion, which emphasizes the consciousness of the individual. Hinduism and Buddhism possess a different approach to

history, and hence also to science.

In the West, the search for facts in science is like the search for facts in history, but both these endeavours differ from the search for religious experience in the present. In the West, history and science have come to function as a framework within which religious experiences are found and interpreted, and one consequence of this is that myths have been stripped of their power to evoke human responses to religious ideas.

The eminent historian of religion, Mircea Eliade, has sought to restore this missing sense of the sacred to Western man by helping him to understand the true nature of myths. The secularized Westerner has lost the sense of the sacred, and is trying to compensate, as Eliade sees it, by means of science fiction, supernatural literature and films. One may, of course, keep a firm sense of history and science without seeking to destroy the mythical appreciation of ideas and beliefs.

Symbols

Religious symbols help believers to understand their faith in quite profound ways. Like myths, they serve to unite the intellect and the emotions for the task of discipleship. Symbols also integrate the social and personal dimensions of religion, enabling an individual to share certain commonly-held beliefs expressed by symbols, while also giving him freedom to read his own private meaning into them.

We live the whole of our life in a world of symbols. The daily smiles and grimaces,

handshakes and greetings, as well as the more readily acknowledged status symbols of large cars or houses—all these communicate messages about ourselves to others.

To clarify the meaning of symbols, it will help if we distinguish between the terms 'symbol' and 'sign'. There is a certain arbitrariness about signs, so that the word 'table', which signifies an object of furniture with a flat top supported on legs, could be swapped for another sound without any difficulty. So the Germans call it *Tisch* and the Welsh *bwrdd*.

A symbol, by contrast, is more intimately involved in that to which it refers. It participates in what it symbolizes, and cannot easily be swapped for another symbol. Nor can it be explained in words and still carry the same power. For example, a kiss is a symbol of affection and love; it not only signifies these feelings in some abstract way: it actually demonstrates them. In this sense a symbol can be a thought in action.

Religious symbols share these general characteristics, but are often even more intensely powerful, because they enshrine and express the highest values and relationships of life. The cross of Christ, the sacred books of Muslim and Sikh, the sacred cow of Hindus, or the silent, seated Buddha—all these command the allegiance of millions of religious men and women. If such symbols are attacked or desecrated, an intense reaction is felt by the faithful, which shows us how deeply symbols are embedded in the emotional life of believers.

The power of symbols lies in this ability to unite fellow-believers into a community. It provides a focal point of faith and action, while also making possible a degree of personal understanding which those outside may not share.

In many primitive societies the shared aspect of symbols is important as a unifying principle of life. Blood, for example, may be symbolic of life, strength, fatherhood, or of the family and kinship group itself. In Christianity it expresses life poured out in death, the self-sacrificial love of Christ who died for human sin. It may even be true that the colour red can so easily serve as a symbol of danger because of its deeper biological association with life and death.

Symbols serve as triggers of commitment in religions. They enshrine the teachings and express them in a tangible way. So the sacraments of baptism and the Lord's Supper in Christianity bring the believer into a practical relationship with the otherwise abstract ideas of repentance and forgiveness. Man can hardly live without symbols because he always needs something to motivate his life; it is as though abstract ideas need to be set within a symbol before men can be impelled to act upon them. When any attempt is made to turn symbols into bare statements of truth, this vital trigger of the emotions can easily be lost.

In Bali the myths and legends of Hinduism are re-enacted each year in dramatic dances. Here Hanuman the monkey-god had come to help the prince Rama rescue his wife from the demon-king Ravana. Behind is the Barong, a friendly dragon.

Even before Moses we find four aspects of sacrifice which were common knowledge to the Hebrew patriarchs, the Aryans of India, the ancient Greeks, and probably many other races.

● The most common was the sacrificial *fellowship meal*, whenever men sat down to eat joyfully before God.

● An extension of this was the idea of a *covenant*, based on eating together, witnessed by the blood of the animal. The covenant might be between two men or tribes, or between men and God.

● Then there were occasional whole burnt offerings, usually presented by a king or patriarch to indicate *worship, consecration, or thanksgiving to God*.

● And when there was known sin, or a flagrant breaking of the moral order, a *sin offering* or expiatory sacrifice was required.

The earliest sacrificial worship was conducted by the head of the family or tribe. In settled conditions the development of a regular priesthood was inevitable, especially with the growth of cities and the increasing pomp of a royal court. There were dangers, but nothing inherently wrong, in having a full-time or even a hereditary priesthood. Moses appointed his own brother Aaron as the head of a hereditary, exclusive line of priests. His own tribe, the Levites, became full-time attendants on the service of God, and were supported by the tithes of the other tribes.

Similarly in the settled conditions of city life, the building of permanent facilities for sacrificial worship was acceptable to God. A temple with altars for large numbers of people, together with the attendant buildings, was required in the reign of Solomon. It is interesting, however, that the argument of the New Testament letter to the Hebrews goes back to the mobile tabernacle rather than the elaborate temple. There were certainly great dangers in the use of temple and elaborate altars, as there were in the development of a full-time priesthood, and the prophets constantly had to fight priestly rapacity and the misconceptions of the people. Where there were no prophets, priesthood and temple worship always degenerated into the ugliness of priestcraft.

Ritual

The clearest documented account of this degeneration appears in the history of the Brahmin priesthood of India. The earliest group of Vedic hymns called the *Rig Veda* were first collected in an oral form, say about 1500 BC, as the Aryan tribes were invading north-western India. The collection may have been the work of the first regular priests. At this time sacrifice could still be offered by any Aryan, and priesthood was by inclination, probably on a part-time basis. Under settled conditions the power of the priests tended to increase. They suggested that unless the right sacrifices were offered the gods would be displeased, and therefore only highly trained priests could learn the prayers and rituals which were necessary.

Some specialization began, and a school of singing priests (Udgatri) arose who chanted the special hymns for each sacrificial occasion. Their collection of 1,225 hymns (the *Sama Veda*) were all from the *Rig Veda*, except for seventy-five new ones. Then a third book called the *Yajur Veda* was produced by a class of priests who did the actual offering of sacrifice. Their collection was mainly the ritual formulae muttered in a low voice during the various stages of the sacrifice.

Thus by about 900 BC there were at least three groups of priests with their own special duties and training schools. The priests had leisure to study and teach, and knowledge brought power. It was only natural that the priestly schools should produce notes and commentaries on their books (the same kind of thing happens today). The material is called *Brahmanas*, which includes explanation of the hymns, the rituals of sacrifice and the duties of the priests. The study of this material produced an elaborate scholasticism.

By the time of the *Brahmanas* (about 800–700 BC), the Brahmins had become a hereditary priesthood in charge of all sacrificial duties, for which they were paid fees by the people. The Brahmins were now suggesting that by the right sacrifices, which they alone could offer, they could procure the favours of the gods, various temporal blessings, and a good place in heaven. Gods, men, governments, all were under priestly control.

Priestcraft and magic

About the same time as the *Brahmanas*, a fourth *Veda* was compiled called the *Atharva Veda*. Because of its lateness and the low ethical quality of its contents, this *Veda* is still not recognized in some parts of south India. The *Atharva Veda* has 6,000 stanzas, of which 1,200 are taken from the *Rig Veda*. Most of the remaining stanzas consist of charms and incantations for magical purposes. This shows how easily priestcraft degenerates into magic. Once sacrifice becomes a meritorious act which forces God to give blessings, it can be used to obtain benefits for oneself and harm for one's enemies. Obviously we are now only one stage removed from the medicine man. He still uses sacrifice, but it is directed to spirits instead of to God, and all ethical or worship content has disappeared.

The progress of modern cultural anthropology indicates that virtually all primal tribes still use animal sacrifice, and there is growing evidence to show that their sacrificial practices are a degeneration from one of the ancient priesthoods, just as those are a degeneration from the original religion of man.

As we shall see, there were great movements of revolt against priestcraft in the sixth and fifth centuries BC. The resulting great world religions and the rise of Christianity largely obliterated animal sacrifice as a significant stream in the history of religion. Before leaving the subject, however, we must note how prevalent priestcraft was in all civilizations, and how it even threatened to throttle the Christian church.

The essence of priestcraft is the rise of a group of people who claim to control access to God, and who suggest that the offering of sacrifice is a meritorious act which forces God to grant favours. Priestcraft always takes away the joy of worship. It stifles individual piety, truth and justice, and divorces morality from religion. Its tragedy is that it forces honest and true men to fight against God, since God appears to be the ally of the priests. This explains the strange alliance of poets, philosophers, Marxists, continental freemasons, humanists, pietists, university students, and the middle-class conscience against that 'opium'.

Government and religion

Many learned treatises have described early religion before 3000 BC, but without written records such dogmatism is guesswork based on less than one per cent of the evidence. If all our modern books were destroyed, what would an archaeologist be able to make of our religion from our ruins and graves? A creator-god worshipped through animal sacrifice leaves no archaeological evidence. We must therefore confine ourselves to civilizations which have left written documents.

The most ancient religion accessible in a deciphered script is that of Sumer. Hundreds of documents list sacrifices to the gods at the temples of Ur, Nippur and other cities. By about 2500 BC we know that the city temples had acquired vast lands, and there was a fierce rivalry between the priests and the government. Already Enlil, the god of creation, had been joined by numerous other gods who lied, lusted and fought against each other. A corrupt priestcraft serving degenerate gods heralded the overthrow of this city-state civilization by Semites from Babylonia.

The Babylonians also had an elaborate priesthood with vast temples and hordes of temple servants. The main difference was that the priests were mostly of the royal family, and the supreme head was a priest-king. This may reflect the original nomadic practice of having the head of the tribe act as priest. For the Babylonians the supreme god was An (who corresponded to the Semitic El, Hebrew Elohim and Arabic Allah), but many extra divinities were absorbed from the conquered Sumerians.

Where the priesthood is a department of state and the high priest is also king, the running battle between government and religion is avoided. It is also possible that the vicious effects of priestcraft are tempered by the need to maintain an ordered government. On the other hand, when religion has become a department of government, a seeker after the city of God, like Abraham, has no alternative but to leave. The Bible pictures Abraham as a man who abandoned the city-state religion of Ur to follow and serve God. Wherever he stopped, he built an altar of uncut stones and worshipped with the primitive simplicity of animal sacrifice.

Priesthood

In Egypt we find the priesthood of the sun-god Re overshadowing the king from about 2400 BC. This was followed by a revolt of the barons who divided Egypt into a collection of warring states, and brought the priests under control. After the expulsion of the Hyksos in about 1570 BC, Egypt attained her greatest political power. The secret was that, instead of one powerful priesthood, there were several (the priesthoods of Amun, Ptah, and Re) which the pharaohs played off against each other. That the priesthood had degenerated to magic not far removed from the medicine man is evidenced both from Egyptian records and from the account of the Exodus in the Bible.

The early religion of Crete may be clarified when the linear A script is deciphered. We know from Greek sources, however, that it was centred on the sacrifice of a bull and was attended by a priesthood. The earliest Greek epics describe animal sacrifice on numerous occasions, very similar to the worship of Abraham in Palestine and the Aryans in India. The Greek priesthood was weakened by being attached to a particular deity at a particular shrine and none other. The priesthood was not necessarily hereditary, and no intellectual qualifications nor elaborate teaching were required. The priesthood was often laughed at, but its scattered weakness meant that the Greek thinkers never engaged the ancient religion in open battle. The supreme place of Zeus indicates that before the inventive period of Greek mythology, the creator was worshipped through animal sacrifice as among the other Indo-European nations.

The only other ancient priesthoods of which we have written evidence before 500 BC are the Persians and the Chinese. Zoroaster of Persia and Confucius of China were contemporaries, and they both proclaimed ethical religions in opposition to the degenerate priesthood and polytheism which existed before them. We know as little about the Magi priesthood of Persia as about the Wu priesthood of China. Both practised animal sacrifice, presumably without any ethical content, and both failed to satisfy the questions of thinking men. As we shall see, Zoroaster and Confucius were part of a great movement of freedom for the human mind from priestcraft in the sixth century BC. Its importance for world history may be compared with that of the Renaissance and Reformation in Europe 2,000 years later.

Passing over the many other priesthoods, such as the Roman Flamens, who sacrificed white lambs on the ides of the month, the Aztecs, who offered human victims, and the Nordics and Germans, whose altars were overthrown by the early Christian missionaries, we must briefly mention the phenomenon of the emergence of the vast system of medieval priestcraft within Christendom. The New Testament letter to the Hebrews makes it clear that all the Old Testament sacrifices were fulfilled in Jesus Christ. From the death of Christ onwards there could be no more animal sacrifices looking forward to the cross; the bread and wine of the communion service were to look back.

But just as the true meaning of animal sacrifice always tended to be transformed into a meritorious act which had merit in itself and forced God to be gracious, so with the com-

Religions of the World

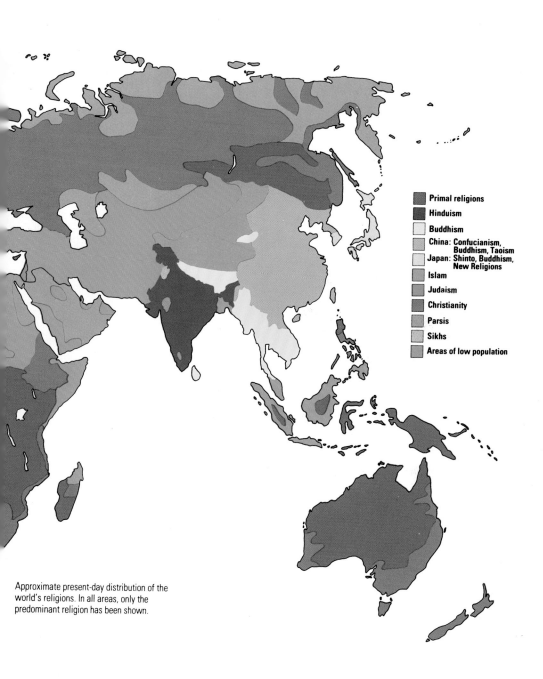

Primal religions

Hinduism

Buddhism

China: Confucianism, Buddhism, Taoism

Japan: Shinto, Buddhism, New Religions

Islam

Judaism

Christianity

Parsis

Sikhs

Areas of low population

Approximate present-day distribution of the world's religions. In all areas, only the predominant religion has been shown.

munion service. Then, gradually, it was suggested that without a properly ordained priest a communion service was not valid. Meanwhile the services became more elaborate and required special training. By the end of the Middle Ages all the characteristics of priestcraft were evident.

The sixth-century revolt

In the sixth century BC there was a tidal wave of revolt against the priestcraft of the ancient world. This wave shattered the power of the old religions, though their cults continued to exist as backwaters for centuries. Seven world religions appeared within fifty years of each other and all continue to this day: Zoroastrianism, Judaism, Buddhism, Jainism, Confucianism, Vedanta Monism, Taoism.

The wave seems to have had its origin in Persia. Zoroaster's actual teaching remains obscure. Scholars are still discussing whether he was a dualist or a monotheist. Some have given him a very early date, but the most likely seems to be some time in the first half of the sixth century. He must certainly have influenced Cyrus, who overthrew the Babylonian Empire in 539 BC, and sent the first group of Jews back to Palestine to rebuild their temple. By the time the temple was completed in 516 BC, four religious giants in India and China, Buddha, Mahavira (founder of Jainism), Confucius and Lao-Tse, had dared to question the authority of the Brahmin and Chinese priests. Socrates (470–399 BC) came at least a hundred years after Zoroaster, but he was preceded by Pythagoras (flourished about 530 BC), who first brought the new ideas of the sixth-century religious revolt into Greece.

The first causes of this great movement are probably as complex as the Renaissance and Reformation in Europe 2,000 years later. One obvious possible source is the preaching of Isaiah (about 740 BC onwards) and the other eighth-century prophets of Israel, with the refrain from Jeremiah and Ezekiel a century or so later. Certainly we can find most of the ethical emphases of Zoroaster, Buddha (about 563–483 BC), Mahavira (599–527 BC) and Confucius (551–479 BC) in the great prophets.

It is hard to believe that the prophets were heard by no one else but Israel and Judah. Isaiah's language was intelligible without translation in cities all over the Fertile Crescent. The transmission of religious ideas, especially when they were so revolutionary, would be exceedingly rapid. By the time it takes us to write and publish a book, the ancient world would have gossipped the ideas far more extensively. The number of major cities from Athens to China were comparatively few, and all were cosmopolitan with several languages spoken by the various national groups who lived there. Religious teachers and their disciples travelled constantly and, most important of all, people had the time and interest to listen to them.

The revolt in India

Whatever the cause of the tidal wave, the actual force of its impact can be seen most clearly in India. The sequence of the *Vedas*, and *Brahmanas*, the *Upanishads*, and the writings of the early Buddhists and Jains give us a picture of what happened with a clarity which is unequalled except in the Bible. From a study of the sixth-century revolt in India, we can postulate with some degree of certainty what must have happened in other parts of the ancient world.

As we have seen, Indian life was dominated by the Brahmin priests. From the primitive simplicity of animal sacrifice 1,000 years before, they had developed an elaborate system of ritual. Specialization into various schools with their own literature, the leisure to study, and access to weighty books, all enabled them to increase their hold on the common people. They, and they only, could offer sacrifice, and their sacrifices and magical prayers were so powerful that men and even gods had to submit to them. Economically their rapacious demands had become intolerable. For every occasion of birth, puberty, marriage, war, death, or transgression of the ritual laws, the

Brahmins demanded *dakshina* (money gifts).

All these might have been tolerated, but when they insisted on interfering in politics, the pressure of discontent among the second caste of warriors, nobles and kings increased till a revolt was inevitable. The actual spark may or may not have come from Israel via Persia, but it is significant that the revolt was simultaneous in both India and China. It took several different forms.

Atheism

Some of the warrior caste became atheists (*charvakas*). They said that since God did not exist, the whole system of priests, sacrifices and the mumbo-jumbo Vedic prayers was all nonsense. The first recorded example of true atheism is in Jerusalem, 'The fool says in his heart, "There is no God"' (Psalm 14:1). It is interesting that the second should be a vigorous group of atheists in India five centuries before Christ.

Of course, in the ancient world it was impossible just to declare atheism. The atheist had to state his way to salvation. Since there is no God, what must man do? The answer that the *charvakas* gave was that the only good that man knows is happiness, so the highest good was to do what made one truly happy. In this modern opinion they preceded the Epicureans of Greece by two centuries and our atheists by twenty-four.

Buddhism

Buddha, who lived around 563–483 BC, was a prince of this second or warrior caste. The first written accounts of his life are at least two hundred years after his death, and scholars agree that the two main forms of Buddhism existing today have moved far from their founder's teachings. Certain facts, however, do seem established. The tradition is that he was shocked into seeking the meaning of life by the sight of a leper, an old man and a corpse. He practised austerities for many years till he attained the illumination he was seeking. He certainly knew about the

Hindu priests still carry out the age-old rituals of the Vedic scriptures. Chanting hymns in Sanskrit, these priests are performing a fire ritual to ensure a good harvest.

religion offered by the Brahmin priests, and rejected this decisively. He seems to have been an atheist, or at least to have abandoned the usual worship of the gods. He had no time for animal sacrifice, Brahmin priests, or even the caste system.

Buddha's doctrine was simple and down to earth. The cause of all unhappiness is desire. The lust for power, success, money, sex, comfort and other bodily pleasures causes all the ills of life. Salvation (*nirvana*) is therefore the losing of all desire. It is not necessary to become a hermit or stop doing the necessities of life, but it is essential to have no passion in doing them. The practising Buddhist tends as a result to develop a quiet, serene type of personality, but the desire for the good of others and the passion for social justice is eradicated along with the desires for self. Jesus expected us to love our neighbours as ourselves. Buddha denied love for self so that practical love for others was also lost. The main sects of Buddhism vary enormously in their basic practices and philosophy, and they will be looked at in their own section. Here we have only noted that Buddha fits exactly into his time and the movement of revolt against priest craft that swept the ancient world.

Ethicism

A contemporary of Buddha, also a prince of the warrior caste, was Vardhamana Mahavira (599–527 BC). His reaction against the amorality of priestcraft was to stress the need for good deeds. Priests and sacrifices and even God were unnecessary, since this world had an inbuilt, ruthless moral order which automatically rewarded goodness and punished evil. Salvation was therefore attained by destroying the evil of one's heart through doing good. The details of his philosophical system, called Jainism, were only recorded nearly 1,000 years later, and are held by a small fraction of the people of India.

An interesting fact is that Mahavira's ethical system for the first time required vegetarianism to the extent that no animal life was to be harmed. Jainism gave to India the word *ahimsa* (no-harming), which was taken up and used with a very different meaning by Gandhi. Originally it was connected with the sacredness of all animal and insect life, which is very hard to practise in the modern world, though it was professed by Albert Schweitzer in Africa.

If we omit the inclusion of respect for animal life as part of his system of ethics, it is obvious that Mahavira's 'way' was similar to that of his predecessor Zoroaster in Persia, and his contemporary Confucius (551–479 BC) in China. All three were first and foremost preachers of ethics. The desire to do what is right and good, quite apart from any doctrines about God, is a recurring theme in the history of philosophy. Aristotle (384–322 BC) and the Stoics of Greece, the high-principled Chinese, Roman and English 'gentleman', the modern humanist, and many liberal Jews, adhere to this religious genus. I have called ethicism a type of religion because it has a 'way' enforced by a real conscience, and an experience of feeling right or righteous. Whether or not God exists, the devotee has an assurance that all is and will be well. There are many examples of this kind of thinking in nineteenth- and twentieth-century modernism in the West.

Monism

We have looked briefly at three types of revolt against an intolerable priestcraft. They all agreed in their rejection of animal sacrifice, the priests who controlled it and even the God to whom the sacrifices were directed. Because of this direct attack on Brahmanism and the caste system, the three forms of revolt were excommunicated from Hinduism for over 2,000 years. Now that the Brahmins have found other ways of establishing their position through education and the key positions in India, Buddhism, Jainism and even atheism have been readmitted as accepted paths within Hinduism. Protestantism has also come perilously close to including ethicism and even atheism as acceptable 'ways' within the Christian fold.

We must now look at a fourth kind

of revolt, which is philosophically far more important, and may in this century become the main threat to Christian theism. Monism is a type of thinking which first appeared in the Hindu *Upanishads* (teachings for a disciple). Over 200 of these writings exist. The main group belongs to our period in the sixth century BC, although some are much later additions.

The writers of the *Upanishads* did not seek to banish the gods and priests and sacrifices, but offered a parallel and deeper way of union with the absolute. The sacrifices are spiritualized, and God is given a new meaning. He is no longer a theistic Creator, but the absolute, the deepest self, ultimate reality, or what modern writers call 'the ground of all being'. Priests and sacrifices were suitable for the uninitiated, but the true monist had a direct access to the absolute which bypassed the need for ritual. The discipline developed to attain this union with the absolute was called yoga. It is still widely practised in India, and is now being vigorously propagated in the West.

The extensive literature of Hinduism describes the various types of monism in the greatest detail. Our task here is to note that this type of religion has appeared again and again in the history of the world. The four main monistic positions can be set out as follows, though there are refinements and sub-divisions for each of these:

Pantheism
● Absolute pantheism: Everything there is is God.
● Modified pantheism: God is the reality or principle behind nature.

Vedanta
● Modified monism: God is to nature as soul is to body.
● Absolute monism: Only God is reality. All else is imagination.

The Chinese teacher Lao-Tse (born about 550 or 600 BC) was a contemporary of Confucius, and obviously belongs to the same wave of revolt against priestcraft. He insisted on freedom from elaborate ritual and regulations. He rejected the man-made restraints typical of ethicism, so that Confucius found him incomprehensible. Positively he recommended conformity to the way (Tao) of the universe. Of the four kinds of monism, Taoism would appear to have been closer to pantheism or modified pantheism than to the typical Vedanta type of Hindu monism. Instead of a stress on meditation, it was more a seeking to be natural, or at one with the course of nature. But in any case, Taoism was certainly monistic as opposed to the ancient theism and polytheism of China.

Monism and Christianity
Monism has since had a long history, not least in Christianity. After the powerful attack from the direction of Gnosticism in the second century, the Christian church had to face a monistic counter-attack from the Neo-Platonists in the third century. Plotinus (about 205–269) made a journey to the East and returned with an arsenal of monistic ideas against

Confucius, the Buddha and Lao-tzu were all teachers who reacted against the 'priestcraft' of their time. This scene shows an imaginary meeting between them.

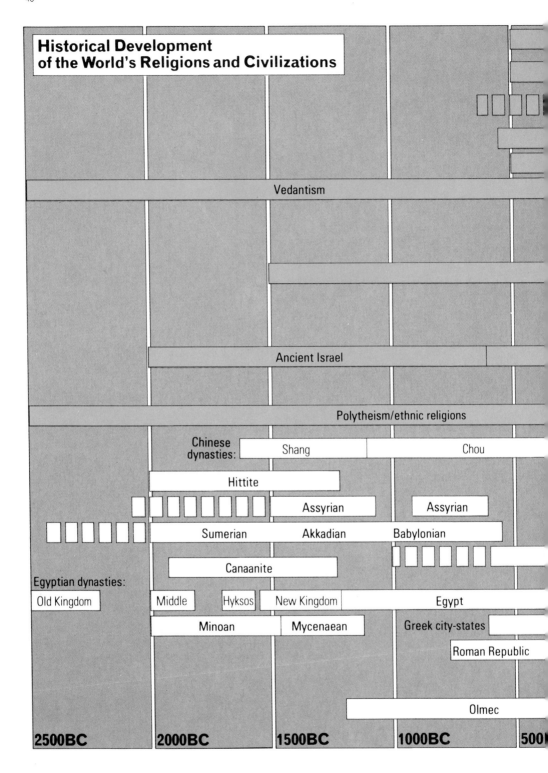

46

**Historical Development
of the World's Religions and Civilizations**

Vedantism

Ancient Israel

Polytheism/ethnic religions

Chinese dynasties:	Shang	Chou

Hittite

Assyrian | Assyrian

Sumerian | Akkadian | Babylonian

Canaanite

Egyptian dynasties:

| Old Kingdom | Middle | Hyksos | New Kingdom | Egypt |

Minoan | Mycenaean | Greek city-states

Roman Republic

Olmec

2500BC   **2000BC**   **1500BC**   **1000BC**   **500**

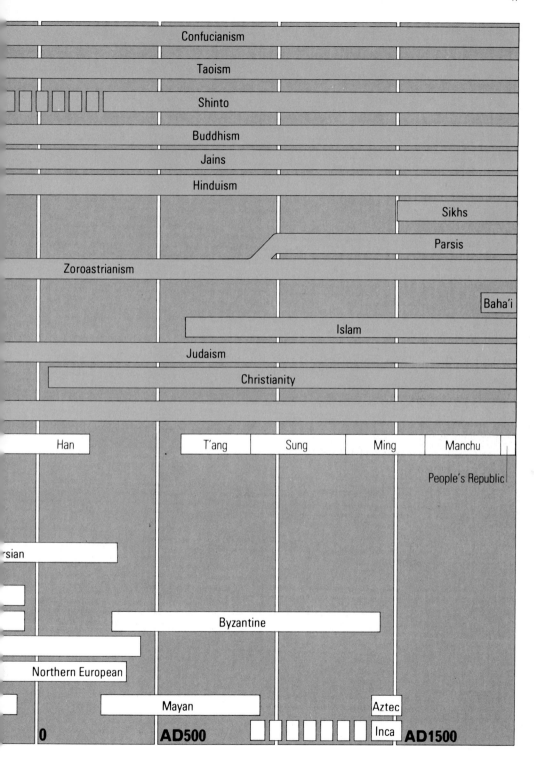

Confucianism

Taoism

Shinto

Buddhism

Jains

Hinduism

Sikhs

Parsis

Zoroastrianism

Baha'i

Islam

Judaism

Christianity

Han

T'ang

Sung

Ming

Manchu

People's Republic

sian

Byzantine

Northern European

Mayan

Aztec

Inca

0

AD500

AD1500

the rapidly-growing Christian church in the Roman Empire. To claim the Greek philosophical heritage he included some ideas from Plato, but his system of contemplation was identical with the yoga of Hindu monism.

Plotinus failed to rally the Roman Empire against Jesus Christ, but he was rediscovered and introduced through the back door many centuries later. An Italian philosopher, Giordano Bruno (1548–1600), represented the first Western monistic reaction to medieval priestcraft, and his pantheism influenced the Jew Spinoza (1632–77). Meanwhile many of the mystics had been influenced by Neo-Platonism through a forgery attributed to Dionysius the Areopagite. Most of the readers of *Pseudo-Dionysius* thought that they were still Christians, but their piety had become strangely Hindu, and one of them, Eckhart (about 1260–1327), was nearly condemned for heresy.

Philosophical monism entered the German church through Johann Fichte (1762–1814), who is described as an ethical monist. He was dismissed from the University of Jena for atheism in 1799, but was later appointed to the University of Berlin. Through G.W.F. Hegel (1770–1831) one wing of the idealists became the true materialists like Feuerbach (1804–72) and Karl Marx

(1818–83). Friedrich Schelling (1775–1854) led a group who had a less materialistic view of reality which was closer to the Hindu Vedanta type of monism. Another wing was championed by Schleiermacher (1768–1834), who tried to show that true Christianity is in fact a kind of monism.

The renewed invasion of Eastern religious ideas in our own day by Hindu gurus, Zen masters and Tibetan rituals, is evidence that the struggle of alternative religions and ideologies is as strong as ever.

The chart (below) shows the main religious systems preached in the sixth century BC and the later developments classified under them. Priestcraft was a degeneration from the original religion of man. Atheism, Buddhism, ethicism and monism are the four possible reactions of a thinking man against it, and all are at least twenty-five centuries old.

Obviously all five of these options are very much with us today. Christianity contradicts the major premiss of each of them and offers salvation from outside ourselves altogether, so it is not dependent on our own stumbling attempts at happiness or spiritual fulfilment. But that must be the subject of a later section.

Religious systems sixth century BC and their later developments

Ritualism	Atheism	Buddhism	Ethicism	Monism
Salvation by right ritual	*Salvation by doing what makes you happy*	*Salvation by losing all desire*	*Salvation by right actions*	*Salvation by union with the Absolute*
Brahmanism	Charvakas	Buddhism	Zoroastrianism	Taoism
Priestcraft	Epicureans	Monasticism	Jainism	Neo-Platonists
	Atheists		Confucianism	Spinoza
	Existentialists		Aristotle	Sufis
			Stoics	Idealism
			Humanists	Unity
			Liberal Judaism	

Part Two
Ancient Religions

Land of the Aztecs and Incas: America before Columbus

George Bankes

'Pre-Columbian' America is a term generally applied to Middle and South America before its conquest by the Spaniards in the sixteenth century AD. The native inhabitants of this area were all American Indians.

In much of Middle America, now mainly the modern states of Mexico and Guatemala, and the central Andes, largely modern Peru and highland Bolivia, high cultures with polytheistic religions developed. In both areas, however, there were two levels of religion. The common people had their local shrines at which offerings were made. But there were also the organized state religions with temples and systematic theologies.

What we know about these religions comes from archaeology, contemporary native documents such as the Aztec and Maya codices, and Spanish accounts. The origins of formalized religions in both Mexico and Peru can be traced back to temple structures with associated cults as early as 1200 BC.

Middle America

Sacred jaguar: the Olmecs

Between about 1200 and 100 BC a people, called the Olmecs by archaeologists, lived on the Gulf Coast of Mexico. They built ceremonial centres such as La Venta which were carefully planned temple communities. At La Venta a group of buildings was arranged symmetrically along one axis. At the south end was a clay pyramid, shaped like a fluted cone.

Olmec religion seems to have centred around the jaguar in various guises. At La Venta three identical mosaic pavements, made from blocks of green serpentine, were discovered.

America before Columbus

Chichen Itza

THE AZTECS
AD 1519

Tenochtitlan

Teotihuacan

THE MAYA
AD 300 - 900

THE MOCHE
6th century AD

Pachacamac

Cuzco

Tiahuanaco

THE INCAS
AD 1525

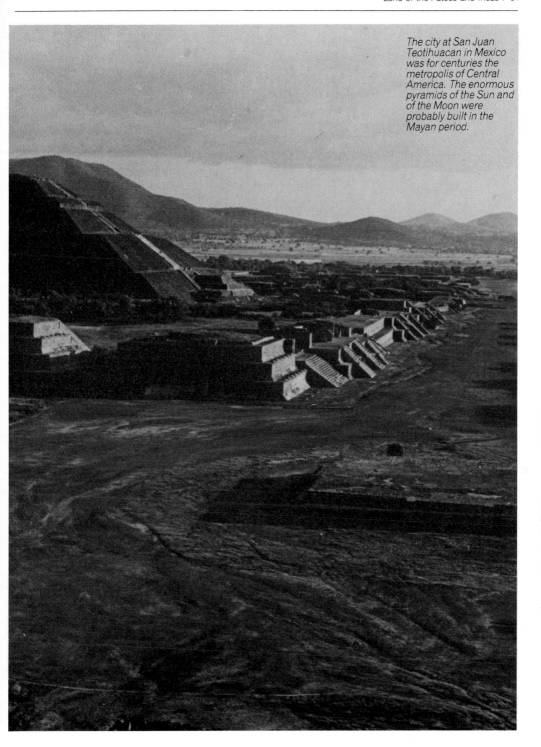

The city at San Juan Teotihuacan in Mexico was for centuries the metropolis of Central America. The enormous pyramids of the Sun and of the Moon were probably built in the Mayan period.

Each was laid out in the form of a stylized jaguar face, and as soon as it was finished it was covered up. These could have been some kind of offering to the beast.

On the lid of a stone coffin, or sarcophagus, at La Venta a jaguar mask is depicted with feathers for eyebrows and a forked tongue of the type only found in snakes. This seems to show him as part bird and part snake, suggesting that he may be the ancestor of the Mexican god Quetzalcoatl, usually shown as a plumed serpent. It also suggests that in Olmec times different animals were combined to form one god, which is an idea basic to Middle American deities.

The Olmec jaguar could also assume human characteristics. A carving from the site of Potrero Nuevo shows his union with a woman. This act was believed to have produced a race of creatures half human and half jaguar. The human element is generally childish, with a paunch and stubby limbs. Onto this are grafted the jaguar characteristics: fangs, sometimes claws, and a snarling mouth turned down at the corners. The heads are often cleft at the top. These hybrid creatures were probably deities, possibly of fertility.

The Maya

Successors to the Olmecs were the Maya, a Middle American people who lived in the semi-tropical rain forest of the Guatemalan department of El Peten and the adjacent parts of Mexico and Belize. The Maya developed an elaborate state religion based on ceremonial centres or cities containing temples. Alongside this existed a native folk religion. The earliest temples were being built about 200 BC at Tikal and Uaxactun. However, it was during the 'Classic Period', between AD 300 and 900, that Maya culture and religion fully developed. After AD 900 the state religion largely collapsed, though the folk one has partially survived.

Maya religion was—and still is—a contract between man and his gods. The gods helped man in his work and provided him with his food. In return they expected payment which usually had to be in advance. Prayer was directed towards material ends such as obtaining rain to make the crops grow.

Before an important ceremony there seems to have been little difference, except in scale, between the preparations in the village and those at the ceremonial centre or city. Before all ceremonies there had to be sexual continence, fasting and usually confession. Continence involved sleeping apart from wives for a specified period. If this was not carried out, both the ceremony and the guilty person might be endangered. In antiquity the body was painted black, the colour of unmarried men, during fasting.

Sacrifices in many forms played an important part in Maya religion. They could consist of one's own blood or that of human or animal victims. Also produce such as maize might be offered. Human sacrifice involved extracting the heart while the living victim was held down by the arms and legs. The rain-gods preferred small offerings, such as miniature corn grindstones, and in the case of human sacrifice the preferred victims were children.

In Maya theology there was no general assembly of gods. Maya deities usually only wanted recognition in the form of frequent offerings. Few of them were human in form, and most showed a blending of human and animal features. For example, the all-important Chacs or rain gods are shown in the Maya codices as long-nosed gods with snake features. In addition, gods like the Chacs were conceived of in fours, each one being associated with a compass direction and a colour. For example, there was one Chac for the east with the colour red.

These gods of the Maya had a dual character: both benevolent and malevolent. Also there was a sexual duality. The Chacs are generally masculine, but one is sometimes shown as female. The Maya indiscriminately marshalled their gods in large categories, and a god could belong to two diametrically-opposed groups. The sun-god was mainly a sky-god, as one would expect. However, at night he passed through the underworld on his way eastward from the point of sunset to that of sunrise. During this passage he became one of the nine lords of the night and the underworld.

The great city of Teotihuacan

Teotihuacan was a large city that flourished in the Valley of Mexico at much the same time as the Maya zenith, between AD 300 and 700. To judge from the number and size of the temples at Teotihuacan it appears to have been a theocracy. The city seems to have fallen to outside invaders about AD 700.

On Teotihuacan's temple walls, religious symbolism features strongly. The rain-god, called Tlaloc or 'he who makes things grow', is frequently depicted, suggesting that he was held in great esteem. One fresco shows him with a spectacle-like mask over his face and fangs protruding from his mouth. The other deity who features prominently at Teotihuacan is Quetzalcoatl. He can be seen on a temple façade bearing his name, where he is surrounded by sea shells and snail shells. He may have represented the waters of the earth.

The Toltecs

The Toltecs were a coalition of nations in north-central Mexico. They established their capital at Tula, about fifty miles/eighty kilometres

The mythological figure Quetzalcoatl appears in many pre-Columbian religions. He is often represented as a plumed serpent, as in this carving from the Toltec city of Chichen Itza.

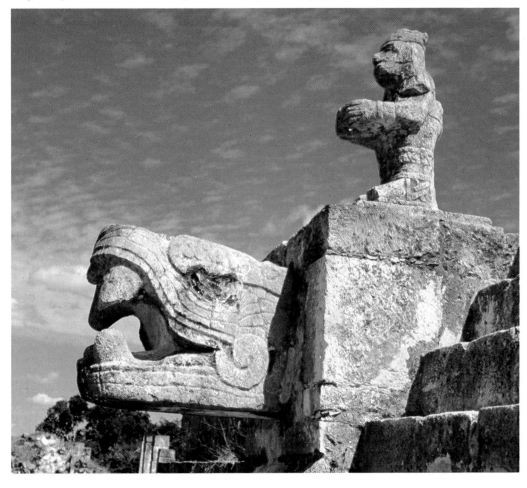

north of Mexico City, about AD 980.

The fifth ruler of the Toltecs, the semi-legendary Ce Acatl, was a priest-king who took the name of the god Quetzalcoatl. Soon after his accession he was expelled by devotees of the god Tezcatlipoca and migrated with his followers to Yucatan where he founded Chichen Itza. The two principal Toltec pyramids, the Castillo at Chichen Itza and the Temple of the Morning Star at Tula, illustrate how religious life had changed since the collapse of the theocracy at Teotihuacan. At the foot of the stairway of each pyramid was a large colonnaded hall. Here warriors could gather together at religious festivals to use their own altar platforms and sacrificial stones. Theocracy had been largely superseded by militarism.

Among the Toltecs Quetzalcoatl became a sky symbol instead of one of water. Another Toltec deity was a combination of the eagle and jaguar, representing the earthly warrior caste. The latter had the duty of feeding the sun and morning star with the hearts and blood of sacrificial victims.

Aztec religion traced several important elements back to Toltec times. Both Toltec and Aztec religion displayed a close connection between kingship and warriorhood on the one hand and fire, the sun and the morning star on the other. Also the Toltec method of human sacrifice was continued by the Aztecs. The victim was held down on a low stone block, his chest opened with a knife and the heart torn out.

Religion of the Sun: the Aztecs

The Aztecs migrated into the Valley of Mexico in the late twelfth century and founded their capital city of Tenochtitlan about AD 1370. However, they did not start their political expansion until after AD 1430.

The Aztecs believed that two primordial beings originated everything, including the gods. They were Ometecuhtli, 'Lord of the Duality', and Omeciuatl, 'Lady of the Duality'. They lived at the summit of the world in the thirteenth heaven. These two produced all the gods and also all mankind. However, by the time of the Spanish Conquest, the two primordial beings had largely been pushed into the background by a crowd of younger and more active gods.

The Aztecs believed that the gods in their turn created the earth. The most important act in this creation was the birth of the sun. The sun is supposed to have been born at Teotihuacan through the self-sacrifice of a little leprous god. The remaining gods followed his example of sacrifice to provide the blood needed to set the sun moving across the sky.

In order to keep the sun moving on its course it had to be fed every day with human blood. The Aztecs regarded sacrifice as a sacred duty towards the sun. Without this the life of the world would stop. Therefore constant human sacrifices—mainly of war captives—had to be provided. It is thought that more than 20,000 were slain each year.

There was a strong solar element in Aztec religion. Huitzilopochtli, the tribal god of the Aztecs, personified the sun at its height. He was the god of the warriors. In contrast there was the rain-god Tlaloc, who was the supreme god of the peasants. Tlaloc was rated equal with Huitzilopochtli, and their high priests were equal in status. This clearly shows how Aztec religion combined both ancient and modern elements in the form of the old rain-god and the later tribal one.

Aztec warriors who were sacrificed or died in battle were believed to join the sun in the sky for four years. Afterwards they were reincarnated as humming-birds. When the peasants died they went to Tlalocan—a lush tropical paradise. Those who did not get to either of these places went to Mictlan, a cold, twilit underworld.

Central Andes

Chavin

Between 1200 and 400 BC a cult connected with the worship of a feline animal spread over northern, central and part of southern Peru. It appears to have emanated from a stone-built temple at Chavin de

Huantar in the north Peruvian highlands.

The temple at Chavin is riddled with interior galleries. Some of these contained offerings of fine pottery, guinea-pigs and llamas as well as sea shells. In the oldest part of the temple is a gallery containing a tall sculptured standing stone. Carved on this is a stylized feline—probably a jaguar—in human form. Snakes represent the eyebrows and hair. The upturned lips of this creature have earned it the name 'The Smiling God'.

Another version of the Chavin feline is the 'Staff God'. This is a standing feline figure with a large rectangular head and outstretched arms, holding a sort of staff in each hand. The fingers and toes have claws, while snakes represent the hair. This could have been a nature-god who was thought to live up in the sky with the eagles and hawks also carved on pillars at Chavin.

The Moche

The Moche people revived the Chavin feline cult on the coast of north Peru during the first millennium AD. They made many pots showing fanged humans, often with snake belts. Frequently they are depicted fighting a monster, part human and part animal, which they generally defeat. Human prisoners were sacrificed to these fanged beings. There seem to have been a number of other animal deities, such as one which was part owl and part human. The moon also was probably an important deity.

Tiahuanaco

The ruins of the city of Tiahuanaco are on the eastern side of Lake Titicaca, just in present-day Bolivia. Most of the buildings there are ceremonial and were erected during the period AD 200–500, when the city's influence was widespread.

The principal deity of Tiahuanaco appears to have been a standing figure carved on a monolithic gateway. In each hand he holds a vertical staff with eagle-headed appendages. His radiating head-dress includes six puma heads. From his belt hang a row of trophy heads suggesting human sacrifice. This figure could represent Viracocha, the creator god of Inca mythology.

The Chimu

The Chimu established a kingdom on the coast of north Peru between AD 1200 and their conquest by the Incas in the 1460s. Their greatest divinity was the moon. She was believed to be more powerful than the sun since she appeared by both day and night. The sun was believed to be an inferior supernatural being. Several constellations were highly regarded; Fur or the Pleiades was the patron of agriculture. The sea (Ni) was also very important. White maize flour and red ochre were offered to Ni with prayers for fish and protection against drowning. The feline cult of earlier times appears to have largely died out by this period.

The Incas—an empire built on sacrifice

The Incas first established themselves in the Cuzco area about AD 1200. However, their conquest of highland and coastal Peru was not completed until about AD 1470, by which time their empire covered some 400,000 square miles/a million square kilometres.

In the Inca Empire there were numerous local shrines which were allowed to exist alongside the state religion. Some of these were of great antiquity and a few, like the oracle at Pachacamac, were noted for their pronouncements. There were numerous Inca shrines round Cuzco which ranged from natural features such as hills to temple buildings.

The Inca state religion was largely concerned with organization, particularly that of the food supply, and ritual, rather than with mysticism and spirituality. Divination was essential before taking any action. Nearly every religious rite was accompanied by sacrifices. These were usually of maize beer, food or llamas, but were occasionally of virgins or children.

The Inca emperor Pachacuti instituted the worship of a creator-god called Viracocha (or Huiracocha).

Viracocha created the sun, moon, other supernatural beings and all mankind. He was the theoretical source of all divine power, and had supernatural beings like the sun to help administer his creation.

The cult of the sun was very important to the Incas. He was thought of as a male god, Inti, who protected and matured the crops. Sun temples were established along with fields to support the religious officials. These temples also housed the images of all the other sky-gods like the thunder-god who was the servant and messenger of the sun.

In contrast to many Middle American peoples, the Incas and their predecessors had a widespread ancestor cult. Elaborate offerings including food and drink were placed with the dead. The mummies of Inca emperors were preserved in their palaces and brought out at festivals.

After death the Incas believed that virtuous people went to live in the 'upper world' (*Janaq Pacha*) which was rather like earth. Sinners went to the 'lower world' (*Uku Pacha*) where they were cold and only had stones to eat.

The Spanish conquest

At the height of its political power and cultural achievements, the Inca Empire was destroyed by the Spanish invasion of 1532. Their ruler was deposed and killed, and within fifty years the last vestige of Inca resistance had ceased. Roman Catholic Christianity, imposed by force, displaced the old religion officially. However, it lingered on among the people, and some of its features are still recognizable in present-day Indian beliefs.

Human sacrifice was central to the religion of the Aztecs and, to a lesser extent, of the Incas. This altar is in the ancient Inca city of Macchu Picchu.

Cradle of Civilization: the Ancient Near East

Alan Millard

The wheel and writing originated in the Near East; so too did many other inventions basic to Greek, Roman and modern Western civilization. It is also, of course, the region in which Judaism and Christianity began. In modern terms it embraces western Iran, Iraq, Turkey, Syria, Lebanon, Jordan, Israel and northern Arabia.

In parts of this region the basic cereals—barley, emmer and wheat—grew wild. The animals that could be domesticated most easily roamed there, and the climate followed a regular pattern. Raw materials of every sort were ready to hand: reeds in the rivers, timber in the hills, stones that could be chipped into tools, copper for smelting and casting.

After the last Ice Age, about 10,000 BC man began to settle in the Near East, developing agriculture and metallurgy. Varying natural resources caused development in different ways. Some areas grew richer than others, some were more self-sufficient than others. The whole area depended upon the weather for its prosperity. If there was too little rain in the winter, the soil would become too dry for the crops to grow, there would be little pasture for the animals, and man would starve. Too much rain could bring disastrous floods; too much sunshine could dry up the water supplies and burn the plants. It is not surprising that man's earliest religious beliefs, so far as we

can trace them in this region, were concerned with survival, with the powers of the weather, the growth of crops, and the breeding of man and animals.

Over the period from 3000 BC to 500 BC, many different cultures rose and fell in the Near East. Some are well-known to us because their ruined temples and palaces have been explored, their writings deciphered and read. Others are little known because their major cities have not been found or uncovered, or none of their records survive. Thousands of written texts are available to us from the culture of the Babylonians, many informing us about their religion. On the other hand, for the Philistines we have no more than the incidental information given in the Old Testament, and the ruins of a single small temple. The Babylonian culture was the most ancient and the most influential, affecting the whole of the Near East in some way at some time.

The first empires: ancient Mesopotamia

Mesopotamia is the Greek name (meaning 'between the rivers') for the land of the Tigris and Euphrates rivers, the area now ruled by Iraq and Syria. To the north the mountains of Turkey and to the east the Zagros range loom over the plains. On the west the steppe country reaches out to the Arabian Desert, while the two great rivers drain through marshes and lagoons to the Persian Gulf in the south.

Mesopotamia was a region, therefore, that had no easily defensible frontiers. It was open to invasion and infiltration from each direction. Throughout historical times we learn of fierce hill-folk making raids from the east, and of hungry desert herdsmen overrunning the fertile lands from the west and south. This process began as soon as man realized the possibilities of cultivating the rich soil and harvesting the fish of the rivers. The northern part of Mesopotamia receives enough rain each year for farmers to grow grain and find pasture for their flocks. Men have lived in the hills and near the rivers since the Neolithic age, about 12,000 years ago.

The south, ancient Babylonia, depends upon artificial irrigation by drawing the water from the rivers and carefully controlling it, in order to grow any crops. It appears that this skill was put into practice there about 5000 BC. From then onwards we can trace a steady development of settled life until we find great cities

flourishing by the rivers and canals at the end of the fourth millennium BC. From these cities traders and colonists spread up the Euphrates into Syria, eastwards into Persia, and south down the Persian Gulf, carrying with them the inventions and ideas of their culture.

Amongst these was one of man's greatest inventions, writing. Without wide-ranging written documents, relatively little can be learned about the life and religion of a long-dead society. The objects surviving from an ancient religion can be misunderstood very easily without the precise information that written texts can give. It was apparently the need to organize and administer the large settlements and their vital irrigation systems that stimulated the development of writing in Babylonia, and, at the same time—possibly by imitation—in Egypt.

The Sumerians

The Babylonian cuneiform writing on clay tablets was produced for the dominant people of the south, the Sumerians. Their religious beliefs are the earliest we can learn about in

The Civilizations of the Ancient Near East

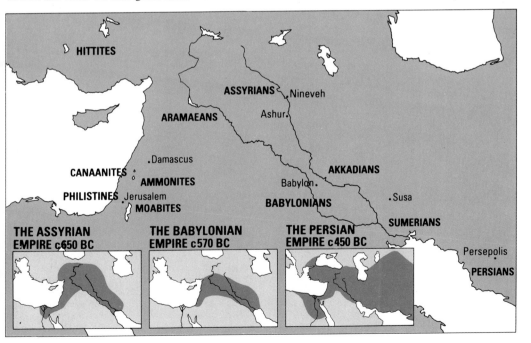

This clay tablet from Ugarit, written in cuneiform script, is a listing of fields with the owners' names.

This clay tablet from Ugarit, written in cuneiform script, is a listing of fields with the owners' names.

Mesopotamia, but it is impossible to be sure that any feature is purely Sumerian because the land was always inhabited by a mixture of races. Indeed, apart from their language, there is very little that can be called distinctively Sumerian.

In Uruk, the city of about 3000 BC best known from excavations by archaeologists and from the earliest texts, there were two main temples. One was for Anu, the supreme god, the king of heaven; the other was for Inanna, the great mother, goddess of fertility, love and war. Inanna was, undoubtedly, the principle of life men had worshipped from time immemorial, the goddess found depicted on paintings, carved in stone and modelled in clay in almost every prehistoric dwelling-place.

At Uruk the temples employed large numbers of people, and owned large estates. Beside the farmers and herdsmen who tilled their land, there were craftsmen making fine objects for use in the temple services, weavers making clothes for the sacred statues and for the priests, and scribes keeping check on all the temple affairs. The priests had an important place in city life, the high priest sometimes being the king of the city. This seems to have been the normal structure of temple life in the Babylonian cities for many centuries.

Records of temple business from about 2300 BC show at least 1,200 people in the employ of a temple in one city, a temple that was dedicated to an unimportant goddess.

Each major city in the south was the centre for worship of a particular deity. During the third millennium BC, beside Anu and Inanna at Uruk, there were Enlil, lord of the atmosphere, who was worshipped at Nippur, and was, next to Anu, the chief of the gods; Enki, ruler of the fresh waters that come from beneath the earth, who had his shrine at Eridu; the sun-god, Utu, whose home was at Larsa; and the moon-god, Nanna, who lived at Ur. In some places the chief deity was simply called 'Lord of the City X'.

Ancient theologians organized the relationships between the gods and goddesses. Each principal god had a family and servants, and they were honoured with temples and chapels also. Enlil's son, Ninurta, was lord of Lagash, for example. The less important deities had shrines inside the larger temples, but they were also revered in small shrines set amongst the houses of the citizens.

The temples dominated the cities. When a temple grew old, or was thought to be too small, a new one was built, often on top of the ruins of the previous one. Over the years, the temples came to be set up above the houses round about on the platforms that covered the earlier buildings. Stone is scarce in Babylonia, so the temples were built of mud-bricks, giving them a very solid appearance. The most important part was the holy room where the statue of the god stood. Each day the statue had to be washed, dressed and fed. The clothes and food were supplied by the worshippers as offerings, or drawn from the wealth of the temple. Store-rooms around the temple courtyard held reserves of all sorts, and items that could be exchanged for goods the temple needed. There were also houses for the priests. The holy room always seems to have been enclosed. The statue was not visible to everyone entering the temple, only to those permitted to enter the innermost part.

Myths of the gods

From 3000 to 2000 BC Sumerian culture continued to flourish. Poets of those centuries told stories about the gods, probably setting them to music. Some of these myths survive, a few in copies made about 2500 BC, many in copies of around 1700 BC.

The gods of the Sumerians were the powers of nature as revealed in the world. So the sun-god was the sun and the power within it. Just as human activities are limited, so were the gods each restricted to their own sphere. The myths show the gods acting in their own positions. They fight to hold their places against evil powers that want to break down their ordered way of life, they quarrel over their areas of influence, they engage in trickery and show every kind of human emotion and vice.

Like most people, the Sumerians asked why the world existed, why man was made. Several myths give answers. In one, Enlil separated the heaven from the earth. On the earth he made a hoe to break the soil. Out of the hole made by his hoe sprang man, like a plant. Another myth tells how Enki and the mother-goddess created man. The gods were tired of the work they had to do, tilling the ground and digging canals to grow the crops for their food. Enki had the idea of making a clay figure which the mother-goddess would bring to birth. This was done, resulting in man. Ever since, man has had to work the ground in order to grow food for the gods and for himself.

The myth goes on to tell how the god and goddess drank too much beer in their celebration afterwards. They quarrelled, and the goddess boasted she could spoil their creation. Enki challenged her, boasting that he could find a place for any creature she made. The goddess produced all sorts of cripples and freaks, but Enki found each a place in society. So the story not only explained why man was made, but also offered a reason for the existence of the deformed.

Another topic the poets took up was the story of Dumuzi, later known as Tammuz. He was a shepherd who wooed and married the goddess Inanna. Afterwards, Dumuzi was carried off to the world of the dead. There is more than one version of the story. In the clearest, Dumuzi was the substitute provided by his wife who had dared to enter the realm of the dead in order to obtain her release. In other versions Dumuzi was captured by police from the underworld. There follows in all the stories great lamenting for the dead god, and attempts to restore him to life. The idea that he did rise from the dead is hard to find in the Sumerian texts. It is very likely that the story arose from the cycle of nature when the fresh growth of spring dies in the summer heat. Certainly the story was significant for the Sumerians. In many cities it was retold each year as the king performed a symbolic marriage with a priestess in a rite aimed at securing prosperity for the year.

The Akkadian Empire

During the third millennium BC Semitic peoples settled in Babylonia in increasing numbers. They mixed with the Sumerians, adopting their culture and their writing. From 2300 BC they came to dominate Mesopotamia when Sargon of Akkad set up the first Semitic empire, ruling all the lands from the Persian Gulf through Syria to the Mediterranean.

This was a time of high artistic achievement, and probably the time when the Sumerian stories began to be put into the Semitic language we call Akkadian. Semitic compositions, too, were recorded in writing. These Semites identified some of their gods with the Sumerian ones. Thus Anu was equated with El, the chief god; Inanna with Ishtar; Enki was known as Ea, a name that seems to mean 'living'; and the sun and moon became Shamash and Sin. It can be argued that El was at first the name of a single, unique god, and that an original monotheism developed into polytheism, but this is very doubtful.

Sargon's dynasty fell to mountain raiders, then a new line of kings arose, at Ur. There they built a magnificent temple-tower (*ziggurat*) for the moon-god, which still rises over the ruins. More invaders ended Ur's rule, and made the Semitic

Akkadian or Babylonian language the normal one, ending the use of Sumerian outside of the schools.

It was in the schools that many of the Sumerian myths were copied out as writing exercises alongside a growing number of tales in Akkadian. Some of these were new compositions, some were new forms of the ancient Sumerian stories.

The Gilgamesh epic

The most famous are those that tell of the great King Gilgamesh. He had ruled Uruk, there is now evidence to suggest, about 2700 BC. Somehow he had captured the story-tellers' imaginations, and become a legendary figure. In Sumerian there are several separate stories about him; in Akkadian there is one long epic. Its basic theme is the problem of man's mortality. Gilgamesh did many great deeds, but he was forced to recognize that he would die one day. He set out on a quest to gain immortality. After many adventures, he came to the place where there lived an old man, the Babylonian equivalent of the biblical Noah. This man, Ut-napishtim, was the only mortal who had won immortality. But Gilgamesh was disappointed, for the man was incredibly old and lay on his back doing nothing. Perhaps immortality was not so good after all!

He told Gilgamesh how he had reached his state. The gods had created mankind, but man disturbed

them by his noise. Unable to quell the noise, the gods decided to destroy mankind by a great flood. Enki, who had made man in the first place, warned his particular devotee and told him to build a large boat in which he might escape. When the flood came, Ut-napishtim, his family and a variety of animals were safe. After the flood, the ship grounded on a mountain in the north-east of Mesopotamia, and the gods rewarded Ut-napishtim with immortality. But Gilgamesh could not have that experience.

Ut-napishtim told him how to get a plant that might make him young again. Gilgamesh found it, and was taking it home to Uruk to test on an old man, when he put it on the ground while he had a swim. A snake ate it, and went away sloughing its skin. The power of the plant was proved, but there was no other, and Gilgamesh could only go home with the thought that his noble deeds would live long after his death.

This story summarizes the basic outlook of the Babylonians. For them, life on earth was the main concern, life after death was a vague and shadowy concept. They thought of the world of the dead as a place of dust and gloom. Yet it was necessary for the dead to be properly buried; for if not, they would return to haunt their relatives. Offerings were made for the dead, too, partly to keep their memories alive.

Omens: the fingers of the gods

The present life of man was entirely under the control of the gods. To have success or a happy life, it was essential to keep the gods in a good humour. There were special days of festival when the worshippers would attend ceremonies at the temple, or carry the statues through the streets. There were sacrifices that could be made to show devotion or ask for help. An ordinary man could not simply walk into the presence of a great god. He had to be introduced by a servant. This is the scene engraved on the cylinder seals current during the Third Dynasty of Ur and following centuries. The owner of the seal would identify himself with the

This is a modern reconstruction of the Ninmah Shrine, one of the magnificent temples of ancient Babylon.

figure on it, and pray for the god's blessing. But the gods were unpredictable. The Babylonian could hope, but he could have no assurance of divine favour. This led to the development of another aspect of Babylonian religion which is not yet extinct, the taking of omens.

The Babylonians, and the Sumerians before them, believed they could find out about the future from all sorts of strange happenings. In the birth of monstrosities, in the movements of animals, in the shapes of cracks in the wall, or of oil poured into a cup of water, they saw the fingers of the gods pointing to the future. If a man wanted to marry, or a king to go to war, the omens would be consulted. One common way was to examine the liver of a sacrificed animal. If the form was exactly as it had been once before then the events that followed on that occasion, if good, would suggest it was a good omen; or if bad, that the proposed action should not be taken.

A special class of priests was trained to take and interpret the omens, and they built up an enormous encyclopedia about them. In watching the stars they learned a lot about them, and became able to predict eclipses and to correct the calendar. They also originated fortune-telling by astrology.

The Assyrian Empire

In northern Mesopotamia the state of Assyria grew strong about 1400 BC, and, after an interval, became the dominant power in the Near East from 900 to 612 BC. The Assyrian kings tried to copy the Babylonians, whose culture was much older. They worshipped the same gods, but the chief, identified with Enlil, was Ashur, the god after whom the land was named. When the Assyrians went to war, it was at Ashur's command they marched, it was to defend or extend his frontiers they fought, and it was for his glory they conquered other states. Of course, it was the king on whom all the glory actually fell, and the disgrace in defeat.

When the Assyrians conquered other lands, they did not interfere in the local religion, and, if the people

The Babylonians made models of demons from clay. They were hung in doorways or buried under doorsteps to ward off evil.

were submissive, they allowed them to continue their own customs. If they revolted, then their gods might be taken away captive, to be set in the Assyrian temples. Usually they were respected, and were sometimes returned when a once-rebellious land was made to submit.

The Babylonians

The Assyrians fell to the Babylonians or Chaldeans, of whom Nebuchadnezzar is the most famous ruler. He rebuilt Babylon and the great temple of Marduk, the patron god of the city. Marduk had risen to prominence under Hammurabi of Babylon in about 1750 BC, and was popular when Babylon's power was greatest. It was in his honour that the Babylonian creation story was written.

This describes the beginning of the world, when all was sea. The gods born by the sea disturbed her, and she planned to destroy them. They chose a champion to fight her lieutenant, but he failed. Another was chosen and failed. Then Marduk, a god of no importance, offered a plan, and succeeded. His prize was the kingship of the gods. His gift to the gods was the creation of man, with the aid of his father Enki-Ea, to do the work they so disliked. The poem ends with a long list of Marduk's powers. By the time of Nebuchadnezzar there were some theologians who tried to explain all the gods as

The Babylonian answer to the quest for immortality was given by a divine 'barmaid' to the hero Gilgamesh:

Gilgamesh said: 'O barmaid, let me not see the death I constantly fear.'

The barmaid said to him, to Gilgamesh: 'Gilgamesh, where are you wandering to? You will not find the life you seek. When the gods made mankind, They set death aside for men, But they kept life in their own hands. So, Gilgamesh, do you fill your belly, Be happy day and night, Take pleasure every day, Day and night dance and play. Wear clean clothes, Wash your head, bathe in water, Attend to the child who holds your hand, Let your wife be happy with you. This is what man's lot is.'

aspects of one god, Marduk or another, in an attempt to reduce the diversity of the gods to some sort of order, perhaps from a feeling that there could not be so great a variety of powers ruling the world.

The Persians who conquered Babylon kept the local religion alive, and in a few centres it flickered on until the first century AD. Some of the gods and goddesses continued to be worshipped by local people until the coming of Islam to Iraq.

Canaan: gods of nature

Canaan was the name for Palestine from about 1800 to 1200 BC. The people living there were a mixture of races, basically Semitic, with close relatives in Syria to the north. After Israel took control of the land, by about 1100 BC, some of the Canaanites maintained separate states in the north, in the area the·Greeks called Phoenicia (modern Lebanon). Their culture and religion continued to flourish there, and influenced the people who occupied neighbouring lands.

Temples, religious objects and inscriptions that have been unearthed tell us something about the religion of the Canaanites and Phoenicians. Other information is given by Hebrew, Greek and Latin books. Ancient Israel was warned to avoid all contact with Canaanite religion, in fact, to wipe all traces of it from the land in which they were to settle (Exodus 23).

Canaanite temples

Excavations have uncovered remains of many small temples in the towns of Canaan. They were single rooms with a niche opposite the doorway where a statue of the deity might stand. Other rooms in front of, or beside the shrine could be for the priests or for storage. In a few cases, the thickness of the walls suggests there was an upper storey, and models in pottery show that some temples had towers. Presumably these were for special rites, perhaps for the worship of the sun or the stars.

Where the temple had a courtyard,

This pillared Canaanite temple is in Byblos in Lebanon. The stone trough in the foreground would have been used for sacrifices, sometimes of humans.

it is likely that the worshippers stood there while the priests alone entered the sanctuary. A large altar may have stood in the courtyard, with a smaller one inside the building. Animal bones suggest the animals commonly sacrificed were lambs and kids, and at one place piglets had been slaughtered. Liquid offerings of wine and oil were made, and incense was burned.

In some temples stone pillars stood as memorials to the dead. Other pillars were symbols of the gods. They were objects of worship which were covered with fine cloth, and carried in procession for the faithful to see. Their ancient name, *bethel*, 'house of god', suggests that the god was supposed to live in them.

Statues of gods and goddesses were carved in stone or wood, or moulded in metal. They were overlaid with gold, dressed in expensive clothes, and decorated with valuable jewellery given by the devotees. They have not survived, but there are many small bronze figures that are still to be seen, and they are probably copies of the larger images that stood in the temples. These small ones were made for the worshipper to offer at the temple, or to use in private devotions at home. When new, most of them were probably plated with gold or silver. The most common figures are cheap pottery representations of a naked female, thought to be the mother-goddess, giver of fertility. They were used as charms.

War, love and power

To the north of ancient Canaan, but sharing much of the same culture, lay the merchant city of Ugarit. Excavations there since 1929 have yielded a lot of information about the local religion. In particular, clay tablets, written about 1300 BC, have added an important dimension to our understanding of Canaanite thought, a dimension that could not be obtained from the material remains alone.

These texts from Ugarit contain stories about the gods, and instructions about their worship. We learn that the Canaanite gods were like many others of the Ancient Near East. They were the powers of the

Babylonian worshippers hoped to relieve their troubles by prayers in which they confessed their faults and praised their gods, although they usually speak in very general terms, often saying that man cannot really understand what he should do.

Part of a prayer to Marduk:

'**Warrior Marduk,
whose anger is like a flood,
Whose forgiveness is like a loving father's,
I am sleepless through speaking but not being heard,
I am depressed from calling but receiving no answer.
This has made my heart grow weak,
And made me bent like an old man.
Great lord, Marduk,
forgiving god,
Who among all kinds of men,
Can understand his nature?
Who has not been at fault, who is there who has not sinned?
Who can know the way of a god?
O that I were careful not to sin,
O that I would seek the places of life always!
Mankind is set by the gods on a hapless course,
To endure what the gods inflict upon him.
If I, your servant, have sinned,
If I have passed the divine bounds,
What I did in my youth, forget it, whatever it was,
And absolve my fault,
Remove my wrong,
Lighten my troubles,
relieve my distress ...
Warrior Marduk, let me live to sing your praise!'**

natural world. At their head was El, whose name means simply 'god'. He was the father of gods and of men. His wife was Asherah, the mother-goddess. El appears in some of the myths as an old man, too old to act effectively, bullied by his wife and his children. In one story he is shown in a drunken stupor; in another he marries two girls who bear him two sons, Dawn and Dusk.

El had a daughter, Anat. She personified war. One poem tells how she slaughtered the people of a city, tied their heads to her waist, and waded up to her thighs in their blood, laughing with joy. Anat was also the goddess of love, and is described in some stories as the lover of her brother Baal. He was the best-known of the Canaanite gods. His name means 'master' or 'lord', and he was actually the god of the weather, Hadad, 'the thunderer'. The texts of Ugarit tell how Baal fought and conquered Yam, the sea, with Anat's help. She also helped him in his fight against Mot, god of death. Although Anat ground Mot like corn, he recovered to live in unresolved tension with the other gods. Some interpret this long myth as an explanation of the cycle of nature through the seasons, others as an account of recurrent famine, and yet others as a parable about death.

Baal's control of the seasonal rain made him popular. There is a vivid account of the effect his presumed absence had in 1 Kings 18 in the Bible. There the priests of Baal implore him to end the drought that had hit the land. Crying to him to send rain, his frenzied servants gashed themselves with swords and spears in a display of devotion.

Other gods

Other gods and goddesses whom the Canaanites worshipped include Shapash, the sun-goddess, Yarikh, the moon-god, and his wife Nikkal. There was Reshef, the god who shot his arrows of plague and illness into men; Eshmun, the healer; Kothar-and-Khasis, the divine craftsman. Each city had its chief deity who was often called 'master' (*baal*) or 'mistress' (*baalat*) of the place. At Tyre

the city-god was Melqart, meaning 'king of the city'. There were many minor gods and goddesses, the spirits of hills, springs and rivers, who are now forgotten.

One of them is known because his cult existed in Roman times. He was Adonis, whose name also means 'lord'. A legend tells how the goddess Astarte fell in love with the young hunter Adonis, but her husband was jealous and, disguised as a wild boar, killed the hunter. Each year at a certain time, a river that runs from the Lebanon into the sea at Byblos turns red with the blood of Adonis, and all the women mourn for him. No doubt this is one of many local cults that were practised by the Canaanites. The Canaanite religion was not exclusive; foreign gods were taken into the pantheon, identified with Canaanite gods, or worshipped beside them.

Beliefs of the common man

It is difficult to discover what the ordinary man believed, or how he worshipped. In offering sacrifices, the person could share in the meat at a cultic banquet with the priest and the god, the sacrifice being a sign of devotion, the payment of a vow, or an offering for pardon. Beside the chief gods there were many spirits and demons who had to be placated or warded off. Dead relatives, too, required regular commemoration to prevent their ghosts from haunting the living.

The priests in major temples had many colleagues serving small shrines on hill-tops, the 'high places', mentioned in the Bible, and in every town and village. These men, and others, cast spells and forecast the future, telling the anxious inquirer if it was a lucky day for a business venture, a war or a wedding. Divination was a skill Canaanites learned with the help of Babylonian manuals, and applied in every possible way.

According to Hebrew and Greek writings, popular worship included ritual prostitution and other excesses. Child sacrifice was believed by the Romans to be a custom of the Phoenicians, and the people of Israel were instructed not to 'pass their children through fire to Molech', another form, apparently, of infant sacrifice (see, for example, Leviticus 18:21). Remains of such offerings have come to light in the ruins of Carthage in North Africa. At a small shrine near Amman in Jordan, burnt human bones were buried in the floor in considerable quantity. The majority of the bones belonged to children. The archaeologists cannot determine whether these were the remains of children sacrificed to a deity, or of children who had died naturally and who had been cremated. Such uncertainty often attends archaeological discoveries.

A happier side of Canaanite religion can be seen in the titles 'merciful' and 'gracious' applied to El. The main impression, however, is of gods and goddesses who were imagined as wilful and capricious, just like their human followers. Whatever a Canaanite might do, he could not be sure of divine approval or blessing, for he could not know his gods.

The gods of the nations

At the same time as the Israelites took control of Canaan, other peoples were settling in adjacent lands. Along the coast, in the south-west of Palestine, were the Philistines; eastwards, across the Jordan, were Edomites, Moabites and Ammonites, while the Aramaeans occupied Syria to the north.

The religions of all but the Aramaeans are little known, for these people have left us very few inscriptions, and their cities have not been extensively explored. The Bible speaks of Chemosh as the national god of Moab, and a little more can be discovered about him from the famous Moabite Stone. This inscription, engraved about 830 BC, describes Chemosh in much the same way as the God of Israel is depicted; he is angry with his land, so hands it over to an enemy, then he gives relief, and the enemy is defeated. Booty and captives were dedicated to him by the victorious king of Moab, Mesha, who set up the stone in a temple of Chemosh at Dibon. When under attack, another king of Moab

sacrificed his son in a bid to arouse Chemosh's aid (2 Kings 3:27). It was to Moab that the seer Balaam was brought to curse Israel (Numbers 22).

Clay figures of humans and animals, and especially of the 'mother-goddess' type, are found in Moab, Edom and Ammon, just as in Canaan and Israel. From the little known of Moabite religion, similarities with Canaanite beliefs are evident, although the position of Chemosh as a national god is more like the position of Israel's deity. It is reasonable to assume that Edomite and Ammonite religions, of which even less is known, were very like the Moabite one. Edom's national god was Qaus, and his name formed part of personal names borne by Edomites (such as Qaus-gabbar, 'Qaus is mighty').

In Ammon (the name is preserved in modern Amman) the people worshipped Milcom. He may be identified with the Molech to whom Canaanites offered children. As for the Philistines, the Old Testament suggests that they adopted Canaanite gods (Dagon, Judges 16:21ff; Baal-zebub, 2 Kings 1:2), and a small temple uncovered at Tel Aviv is similar in design and furnishings to Canaanite shrines, except that it contained Philistine pottery.

The Aramaeans

The Aramaeans of Syria also absorbed the religion of the people of the land. Hadad was revered as the chief god of Damascus, with the added title Ramman or Rimmon, 'Thunderer'. He was also called 'Lord of heaven' (Baal-shamen). Beside him was his consort Athtar. El continued to have worshippers, who gave him the title 'Creator of heaven and earth'. The 'Queen of heaven' was a name for the mother-goddess.

In course of time, these Semitic deities were identified with Greek and then with Roman gods, and some took over the attributes of others. Under the Roman Empire, magnificent temples were built for the gods at the main centres, and some still stand, most notably at Baalbek in Lebanon. There Baal-shamen was equated with Zeus and

The fertility-god Baal was worshipped in Canaan.

groups, the highest being the priests of Bel. They presided at the sacred meals following sacrifices. This was an ancient practice, followed by the Canaanites, when the priests, the offerers and the gods were all thought to eat and drink together. Wealthy citizens gave funds for the banquets to be held regularly, expecting to gain merit thereby. Admission was by small clay tokens bearing suitable pictures and inscriptions. As elsewhere in the Ancient Near East, the people of Palmyra buried their dead with care, recording their names so that their memory might not be lost.

Sun and storm: the Hittites

From about 2000 BC until 1200 BC most ofthe area of modern Turkey was controlled by an Indo-European people.They are called the Hittites, although the name really belonged to another, non-Indo-European, group. A third people, the Hurrians, possibly related tothe modern Armenians, mixed with the Hittites and influenced their religion and culture from 1450 BC. After the end of Hittite power, the language and religious beliefs continued for a long time in parts of Turkey, being known to writers of the Roman period.

The country is mountainous, each town being distinct. As a result, each town had its own god or goddess, usually the deified elements, the sun, storm, and so forth, whom the citizens worshipped in the main temple of the place. A Hittite myth makes clear how the gods depended upon their human servants: when a disaster befell the land, the gods were starving because the sacrifices were interrupted. All sorts of other powers claimed attention: the spirits of earth, of grain, of fire, of seeing, of hearing. Magic spells were recited to win their aid or ward off their evil.

At the capital city, Hattusha, modern Bogazköy, the king led the cult of the storm-god and the sun-goddess, the national deities. The king was both high priest and deputy of the storm-god, and high priest of all the other gods. He was expected to attend the major annual festival of

Jupiter, as the sun-god, while the goddess Atargatis, a fusion of Athtar and Anat, became Venus.

At Palmyra, the caravan city between Damascus and the Euphrates, a powerful state existed during the first century BC and the first three centuries AD. Baal-shamen was important there, in addition to a triad of local deities, Bol, or Bel, Yarihbol, and Aglibol, the last two being the sun and the moon. Appropriately for a trading city, Gad, 'good luck', was prominent, too. The great temple of Bel still stands, its size and extensive outbuildings showing the wealth of the city and the number of staff employed in the cult.

The priests were organized in

each god in that god's city. Elaborate rituals were performed to ensure that he was cultically pure for such occasions. If the king did not attend, or committed some other error, a catastrophe could overtake the land. This is seen in a series of prayers offered by a king for relief from a plague that affected the land. The king discovered that certain actions of the past were wrong, and tried to put them right. His confession reads in part:

'Weather god of Hatti, my Lord, and you gods, my lords: It is the case that (men) are sinful. My father too has sinned by transgressing against the word of the weather god of Hatti, my lord. But I have sinned in nothing. Now it is (true) that the father's sin falls on the son. So the sin of my father has also fallen upon me.

See, now I have confessed it to the weather god of Hatti, my lord, and to the gods, my lords: it is so, we have done it. Now because I have confessed my father's sin, may the mind of the weather god, my lord, and the gods, my lords, again be pacified! Again be graciously inclined towards me, and drive the plague away from the Hatti land once again. And may the few who are left to offer thick bread and wine no longer continue to die.'

The causes of divine anger might be petty, as when the god's robe was worn out, or significant, the breaking of an oath. They could be discovered only by asking the god to give a sign through an omen of some sort. Only in such ways could man learn the mind of the gods, and hope to gain their goodwill.

Ancient Egypt:
Land of the Priest-King

John Ruffle

The magnificent pyramids at Giza, outside Cairo, have stood for four-and-a-half thousand years.

Ancient Egypt is the name given to the civilization in the lower reaches of the Nile Valley, from about 3100 BC to 30 BC, when the Romans occupied Egypt. It covers periods of strength such as the Old Kingdom (about 2700–2200 BC), when a line of powerful rulers left their pyramids as monuments, the Middle Kingdom (about 2000–1800 BC), another time of strong central government with influence amongst Egypt's neighbours, and the New Kingdom (about 1550–1225 BC), when Egypt was one of the dominant countries of the Near East. It also covers periods of weakness when Egypt was torn by internal strife and occupied by foreign powers.

Obviously such changes in political strength and economic fortunes over 3,000 years meant that philosophical and religious attitudes also changed, but there are enough consistent features for us to be able to talk about Egyptian religion as a whole.

Naked figures

Writing was not practised in Egypt until about 3100 BC, when a single central government was established. What we know about Egyptian religion before then, therefore, has to be deduced from objects found by archaeologists. These take us back another 2,000 to 3,000 years and mainly consist of amulets, usually connected with hunting or fertility. Animal tusks worn as pendants were probably intended to protect the hunter and make him successful; earthenware figures of naked women were meant to ensure plenty of healthy children.

Some pictures painted on pots, or scratched onto rocks, seem to suggest religious rituals, but without a written explanation it is impossible to understand them fully. Sometimes they seem to refer to ceremonies or figures that we recognize from later periods, and it is fairly safe to assume that the basic beliefs and practices did not greatly change in the historical period.

Animal-headed gods

The gods of ancient Egypt—as they are represented in the temples and tombs—present a bewildering complexity of strange forms, half animals, half men. In fact we know very little about Egyptian religious beliefs, since there are no studies of Egyptian theology made by the ancient Egyptians themselves.

Many of the Egyptian gods represented strong forces in the natural world. Egypt's prosperity depended on the daily reappearance of the sun and the annual flooding of the river, and these natural forces (with others) were thought of as gods needing to be cajoled and encouraged by sacrifice

and worship. The Egyptians often portrayed them as animals. For example, they chose the hawk, which flies high in the sky, as a representation of the sun; and the cobra, which was often found basking on the hot threshing floors, as a symbol of the harvest goddess.

At an early stage other characteristics were associated with some of the gods. The ibis-headed god, Thoth, was thought of as the god of scribes and writing; Khnum, the ram-headed deity, was considered the creator of men on his potter's wheel, and so on. How these special attributes came to be given to particular deities is not clear, but they seem to be established in these roles at an early date.

The gods were often associated with particular cities. This probably dates back into the prehistoric period when Egypt was a series of individual communities. As these came together into larger political units, so their local deities gradually became important in the nation as a whole. For example, the god Amun from the city of Thebes was a kind of national god, protecting and leading the whole nation for a time during the New Kingdom while Thebes was the home city of the ruling family.

This was not exclusive, however. The town-folk of other communities would continue to worship their own local god or they would feel free to pray to any other god who might offer special favours. So a scribe who hailed from Denderah might accompany the king to the temple of Amun at Thebes after some notable victory, but would pay his respects to Hathor whilst at Denderah. He would also pray to Thoth, the god with a special interest in writing, for help in his career.

There are also references to 'God' or 'The God', who seems to have been an unnamed universal divine power who controlled the universe and upheld good against evil.

The 'reform' of Akhenaten

For a short while, from about 1375 to 1350 BC, there was an attempt to impose a form of monotheism. The Pharaoh Amenophis IV, who is vari-

The solid-gold death-mask of the young King Tutankhamun.

The Egyptian king acted as an intermediary between gods and people. This relief shows the hawk-god, Horus, speaking with King Ptolemy.

Wealthy Egyptian women dressed luxuriously in fine linen. They wore elaborate jewellery and used an array of cosmetics.

ously described as a visionary or a lunatic, gradually built up the worship of the Aten, or the sun's disk, until he was the only god whose worship was tolerated. The other gods were proscribed, their temples closed, their priesthoods disbanded and their names erased from all monuments where they could be found. The worship of Amun, in particular, was strongly attacked. The Aten was regarded as the source of all life. This gift of life was passed to the king, who changed his name to Akhenaten (which means 'the one who is beneficial to the Aten'), and to his family and thence to the people.

This 'reform' probably had some political cause, such as an attempt to stabilize and unite the nation, but was also influenced by Akhenaten's bizarre personality. It was apparently not popular; the priests would certainly have been against it since it deprived them of their living, and it survived only briefly after Akhenaten's death. The power of the priests of Amun could not so easily be destroyed. This period was exceptional, since normally the gods seemed happy to exist side by side even when ideas claimed on their behalf appear contradictory.

Other gods

As well as the 'mainstream' gods, other deities were adopted by the Egyptians. Some private individuals who had distinguished themselves in

some way were deified. Imhotep, for instance, a vizier of King Djoser (about 2680 BC) who also wrote a medical treatise and a wisdom book and was credited with the building of the first pyramid—he appears to have been an early Leonardo da Vinci—was worshipped as a minor deity who had special power to heal the sick. His cult was especially popular during the period of Greek influence in Egypt in the first three centuries BC.

The king or pharaoh was also thought of as a god; he was referred to as 'The Good God', but it was a restricted idea of divinity because he was, plainly, mortal. Very few rulers actually had a statue placed in the temple shrine as an object of worship. The fact that the king could be both god and priest is an indication of some of the contradictions of Egyptian religion.

Sacred animals

Animals too form an interesting aspect of Egyptian religion. The actual practice varied according to the place and the time. In some cases all the animals of one species were regarded as sacred, and they were mummified and buried in huge numbers: baboons, crocodiles, ibises, and even cats and dogs, received this treatment on occasions. In other cases one individual animal was singled out as the incarnation of a god. There were several places where a particular bull was selected, perhaps because it had some distinctive markings, and was then taken into the temple, pampered throughout its life and mummified and ceremonially interred at death.

Well-travelled gods! festivals and services

The festivals and daily services in the temples show that the Egyptians thought of their gods as having the same needs and instincts as themselves. The day began with a ritual in which the god was wakened by a choir. The night attire was then removed from the image of the god, which was washed, dressed and offered food and drink. After this the god might be called upon to receive

visitors, deliver oracles or undertake some other duties. We may assume that his behaviour and his decisions would reflect the views and wishes of the priests who could claim to interpret them on his behalf. He would receive other offerings of food during the day, and eventually be put to bed for the night in his shrine.

The daily routine was broken by festivals. Some were short, involving only a special offering or a procession inside the temple. Others involved long journeys by river to the temple of another god. Amun, for example, went by boat from his great national temple at Karnak to the smaller shrine at Luxor which was regarded as his private home, where he stayed for several days with his consort Mut and then returned along the processional way. Hathor travelled nearly 100 miles by boat from Denderah on her annual visit to the temple of Horus at Edfu.

The festivals which involved processions along the river or in the town were treated as holidays by the people, who lined the route to cheer and wave at the god's shrine. Some travelled on long pilgrimages to attend. One writer records 700,000 pilgrims gathering for a festival. Some festivals we know only by name; it is intriguing to try to imagine what happened on The Day of Smelling Onions!

The actual images of the gods that were the centre of this worship have not survived. They may have been of stone or fine metal, probably richly ornamented. At festivals they were carried (hidden from public gaze) in ornate wooden shrines in a large model boat which was borne on the shoulders of several bearers. For the river journeys they travelled in special boats built of wood but shaped to resemble the early reed boats, a reminder that these festivals had their origin in very early times.

The priest who performed all the religious ceremonies was in theory the king. All the temple reliefs show him making the offerings, but in fact of course they would be made by his deputies. The priesthood was at first a duty taken on by the local dignitaries working according to a roster, but gradually a professional priesthood was set up. At certain periods when the king was weak, the high priest of Amun or another major god was the real ruler of Egypt.

In addition to the high priest there was a whole range of other clergy with carefully graded ranks and titles. Women also served as priestesses, and of course there were numerous other people in the temple service, ranging from choristers and librarians to cooks and gardeners.

Born from water

There is no ancient Egyptian sacred book, equivalent to the Bible or Qur'an, which was accepted as a revelation of divine truth. The Egyptians had their myths like those of the ancient Greeks. The Egyptian myths told the story of the relationships between the gods, but very few have survived intact. All we have are short scattered references which can sometimes be pieced together to tell the whole story, though we cannot be sure that we have it correct.

Various creation myths abounded, for example. The Egyptians generally imagined the universe as originally filled with water, from which a hill arose on which life began. This was no doubt derived from what they observed each year as the Nile flood subsided. Thereafter the stories become extremely complex. Different gods were thought to have somehow emerged from the hill or the water, and in various ways to have created other gods. Many of the great temples were claimed to be built on this primeval hill.

An interesting claim was advanced by the priests of Memphis on behalf of their god Ptah. They declared that he was the great god who somehow was also the great watery universe from which the other gods were born, their acts of creation being simply the carrying out of his will.

As well as the myths there are prayers and hymns to the gods, which read very much like the Old Testament psalms. Books of wisdom are also known, which, rather like the biblical book of Proverbs, range from practical and moral advice to

Egyptian Temples: Houses of Power

John Ruffle

The outward appearance of an Egyptian temple was not particularly elegant. To us, whose ideas are perhaps coloured by Gothic cathedrals or even Greek temples, they appear more like power stations than temples. This in fact reflects their purpose. They were less concerned with telling people outside about the majesty and power of the god to whom they were dedicated, and more concerned with the ritual that went on inside. This ritual was intended to ensure that the gods would continue their favour towards Egypt, and it was therefore the prime consideration in the design of the building.

The plan of the temple

The two main types of temple were the cult temple, dedicated to a particular god, usually the principal god of the city or area, and the funerary temple, dedicated to the memory of a dead king who was treated as a god. To all intents and purposes the plans of these two types were the same.

The temple was thought of as the house of the god and its plan was similar to the plans of the houses of nobles and officials. These usually consisted of a number of reception rooms leading to the private family rooms and ultimately to the owner's bedroom. In the temples the same types of room were used, with large courts and halls corresponding to the reception room, and the shrine corresponding to the main bedroom. The main difference was that the rooms of the temple were laid out in a straight line so that processions could pass from the main gate to the sanctuary without awkward bends.

Some temples were in use for several hundreds of years and were extended and altered, demolished and rebuilt during that time, but the same general arrangement was followed throughout. Even those cut in the rock cliffs of Nubia, like the temples of Ramesses II at Abu Simbel, kept to the same basic plan. A few exceptions occurred, as when for example two deities of equal rank occupied the same temple at Kom Ombo; a double aisle and twin shrines were provided.

The temples represented Egypt in miniature. The great monumental entrance was similar in shape to the hieroglyph which stood for the horizon or limits of the country. On the outside walls of this gate we see the king destroying his foreign enemies. Inside, the halls were decorated as huge thickets, the floors painted to represent water, and the ceilings painted with stars. Egyptian architects did not use vaulting, so the flat stone blocks that formed the ceilings had to be supported by closely arranged pillars which were based on plant shapes, usually with papyrus or lotus capitals.

Ritual protection of the temple

As far as possible the temple was cut off from the outside world to protect its ritual purity. At the foundation ceremony, a pit was filled with clean sand containing magic amulets which warded off any evil influence that might attack from below. The corners of the building were further protected by foundation deposits, consisting of animal sacrifices, groups of model tools and other items. A high wall protected the temple estate, and the building itself was erected within another wall and an ambulatory or corridor which formed a further protective layer around it.

Elaborate precautions were even taken to remove rain-water from the roof, with a complex series of channels and huge gargoyles. The shrine itself was often constructed as a separate building within the main temple, complete with its own roof. So it was again separated from contact with the world outside.

Within the main building various rooms were set aside for special purposes. There would be a library for the papyrus rolls with the ritual texts, a vestry for the special clothing and store-rooms for the chalices, censors and other vessels used in the rituals. Often, in addition to the main god who occupied the central shrine, there were other gods, perhaps members of his family who shared the temple. Their images were kept in smaller shrines built around the central shrine in the sanctuary area.

Deepening mystery

The walls of the temple were decorated with relief carvings of scenes from the temple rituals. The words that were recited at the ritual were also inscribed on the walls. From the position of these carvings within the temple it is sometimes possible to tell the uses of the different rooms. These carvings were not just a large-scale service-book; the ceremony that was performed when the completed building was formally presented to the god included an *Opening of the Mouth* ritual by which all these carvings were given life and everlasting effectiveness. So the mere portrayal of the ritual supposedly guaranteed that it would continue for ever, even if the priests ceased to perform it.

As the worshippers moved from the temple entrance to the sanctuary the air of mystery gradually deepened. The size of the rooms was reduced in stages, the roof level came lower and the floor was stepped up. Daylight was also gradually excluded. From the open court one passed to courts lit by a clerestory or openings in the first wall which was sometimes only constructed half-way to the roof; the innermost rooms were completely cut off from daylight. Even today some temples are visited by the light of oil lamps, and it is easy to imagine how the flickering, leaping light of torches playing on the richly-painted figures and hieroglyphs on the walls must have combined with the singing and incense to create a feeling of awe and wonder in the worshippers.

The roof of the temple was also important. Some ceremonies, involving, for instance, the union of the divine image with the sun, were performed there. Special stairs with shallow steps were used so that the image of the god could be carried up to the roof in a small portable shrine. Small roof-top chapels were built for these ceremonies.

Shrines

Outside the main building of the temple, but within the enclosure wall, were many other buildings. These may still be seen in some temples such as Karnak and Denderah. There are small shrines and chapels, often including one where a divine marriage and birth ritual was enacted. There was also housing for the priests, slaughter-yards and bakehouses where offerings were prepared, a well that provided holy water, and a sacred lake on which other rituals would be performed, rather like medieval mystery plays.

The bulky stone construction of the temples has meant that, along with the pyramids and rock-cut tombs, they have survived the passage of the years. Long after their original use was superseded, many provided refuge for later inhabitants such as Christian monks, and even whole village communities.

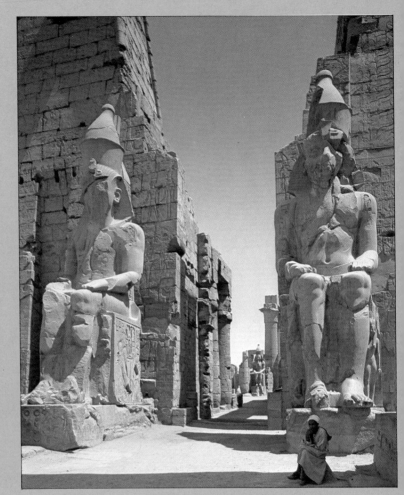

The temple at Luxor.

1	2	3
4		5
6		7

1. The ankh amulet was the symbol of life triumphant over death. 2. The entrance to the temple at Dendera. 3. The hawk-headed god Horus in a tomb-painting. 4. Outside the temple complex at Luxor. 5. The terrace temple of Queen Hatchepsut near Thebes. 6. Inside the temple at Luxor. 7. A processional avenue at Karnak, flanked by ram-headed sphinxes.

The Egyptians believed in judgement after death, when a person's soul was weighed in a balance by the gods.

the Egyptians thought such a life would be. Generally it was thought to be similar to this world but better, with successful hunting and harvests, rich banquets and pretty girls.

The idea went through various stages of development. At first it was thought that the king would spend his afterlife alongside the sun-god Re on his daily journey across the heavens. Soon, however, his future became linked with the god Osiris, and each king in turn as he died became identified with him. Gradually this privilege was extended, first to the nobles and later to all classes, so that each man on his death somehow became identified with Osiris.

The story of Osiris himself was not recorded in full until the Greek writer Plutarch (about AD 100) recounted how the good king Osiris was murdered by his jealous brother Seth. With the help of his wife Isis and other gods, Osiris eventually became the ruler of the afterworld and a symbol of continued life after death. There are several references to the story in Egyptian literature which make it clear that there were differing versions of this account.

The journey to the afterworld was fraught with difficulty. All sorts of obstacles lay in the way, and demons were ready at every turn to seize the traveller. A successful journey was assured by possession of a papyrus roll containing a series of incantations which could be recited to allow the dead man to pass when an obstacle or demon was encountered. These books are usually called *The Book of the Dead*, although there are several different titles. Copies were placed in the tomb with the dead man for his use, or at different periods they were inscribed inside the coffin or on the tomb walls.

It was, of course, plain to the Egyptians that the physical body remained in this world and that it was the dead man's spirit that passed on. They thought that this spirit needed the body as a kind of base, and for this reason they made elaborate attempts to preserve the body by mummification. It was particularly serious if a body was lost at sea or destroyed

general theological reflections on the nature of life.

There are also many magical spells, which may be counted as religious since they invoke the gods and try to persuade them to give help and protection from all sorts of evils.

Living and dying well

Several of the wisdom books encourage their readers to live according to a moral and ethical code of personal piety. They urge this partly because it is the way to earn respect from one's fellows, partly beause it is pleasing to 'the god'.

Living a good life was thought to be a way of ensuring a safe passage to the afterworld. There are many representations of a judgement scene in which the dead man's heart is weighed in a balance against a feather which represents Truth. The result was recorded by Thoth, the scribe of the gods, in the presence of Osiris, and those who failed were destroyed for ever. This judgement was not, however, a great incentive to piety, since the result could be influenced by correctly reciting an incantation in which the man denied that he had ever committed a whole range of sins.

Journey to the next world

The Egyptians seem always to have had a belief in an afterlife. The very earliest tombs contain items of food and equipment, and later on the decoration of the tombs tells us how by fire, although in extreme cases a statue or portrait of the departed might serve as a substitute.

The funeral service included a ceremony called *The Opening of the Mouth* in which the mouth and other openings of the body were magically treated to ensure that the dead man might continue to use his body to feed, see, hear and so on. The same ceremony performed over statues and paintings endowed them with a form of life in the afterworld.

The Gods of Ancient Egypt

AMUN
King of the gods, patron deity of the pharaohs. Later identified with the sun-god Amun-Re.

ANUBIS
God of the dead, guardian of tombs and cemeteries.

ATEN
The sun. For a short time became the chief and only god.

HATHOR
Sky-goddess. Later became the cow-goddess, goddess of love and dance, lady of the underworld and mistress of the stars.

HORUS
God of Lower Egypt. The sky-god.

ISIS
Queen of the gods, the great mother-goddess. Corn-goddess and fertility-goddess.

KHNUM
Old Egyptian god of the Upper Nile. Creator of gods, men and waters.

THOTH
Moon-god. Later the god of learning and wisdom, the inventor of writing.

OSIRIS
Fertility and vegetation-god. Later became supreme god of Egypt with Re and king of the dead.

SEBEK
Water-god. Sometimes the personification of evil and death.

PTAH
God of the dead. Creator and fertility-god.

SETH
God of storms. Violent and dangerous, he was the murderer of Osiris.

RE
Sun-god, the great state-god of ancient Egypt. King of the gods, father of mankind and protector of kings.

The Cosmic Battle: Zoroastrianism

John Hinnells

The story of Zoroastrianism begins in the third millennium BC with the Indo-Europeans. Somewhere to the east of Europe about 3000 BC a group of tribes began to split up. Some travelled south and settled in Greece and Rome, others went north and settled in Scandinavia, and others went east to Persia (now Iran) and India. It is because of this common descent that the ancient languages of these countries have a similar pattern.

The important group for Zoroastrian studies is the third one which settled in India and Persia. These people are called the 'Indo-Iranians' by scholars. They referred to themselves as the 'Aryas' (Aryans), 'the noble ones'. They travelled eastwards in two main waves. The first, in approximately 2000 BC, passed through northern Persia leaving only a few settlers there, with the main body carrying on into north-west India where they gradually overthrew the Indus Valley civilization. The second wave of Indo-Iranians settled in Persia about 1500 BC.

Natural powers

The religion of the Indo-Iranians provides the background to Zoroastrianism just as ancient Israelite religion does to Christianity. The Indo-Iranians were nomads, travelling from pasture to pasture on foot with their herds, not staying long enough to build temples, travelling light so that they did not have statues of the gods.

Theirs was a religion of the mountain-top, with the dome of the sky for their temple, using the ordinary household fire as the focus for their ritual offerings. Their imagery was drawn from wind and storm, from sun and rain. Their gods were not thought of in human form, but as the forces which surround man—the gods of True Speech and Hospitality, of Contract and Victory. Their demons were similarly abstract: Wrath and Greed, the Lie and Procrastination. The world was full of spirits that man must treat with caution, and make the due offerings so that they might not be angry. The peasants had no real hope of life after death: the sunlit paradise was only for men of power and wealth, priests and princes.

The prophet Zoroaster

Zoroaster is the name by which the West knows the prophet of ancient Persia, more correctly called Zarathushtra. It was usual to date him about 600 BC, but the evidence of language is persuading more scholars nowadays to date him about 1500 BC, which means that he lived when Persia was emerging from the Stone Age. This would make him the first of the great prophets of the world's religions.

Zoroaster's life

Zoroaster was a descendant of the first wave of Indo-Iranians. His people had become settled agriculturalists who were threatened by the second wave of Indo-Iranian settlers. We know little of the prophet's life. He was a priest (interestingly, the only one of the great prophets who was); he was married and had several children.

At the age of thirty he had the first of a series of visions which inspired him to preach a new message. His teaching was at first rejected, and he suffered persecution, being forced to leave his home. It took ten years before he made his first convert, his cousin. Then his message found favour with a local king, Vishtasp, and Zoroaster's religion became the official teaching of a small kingdom somewhere in north-east Persia, in what is now part of the southern USSR (the precise location is not known). Zoroaster's religion in time spread throughout Persia and became the official religion of what was, for 1,000 years, one of the major world empires.

Zoroaster's teaching

Zoroastrians believe that their prophet is the one chosen by God to receive his unique revelation. This is contained in seventeen hymns, the *Gathas*. Obviously the prophet gave more teaching than this, but all that has survived is a fragment cast into verse-form to help memorize the words in an age and region where writing was unknown. These hymns are now the central part of a major act of worship (*yasna*).

The great choice

Perhaps *the* characteristic feature of Zoroaster's teaching is his emphasis on personal religion, inspired presumably by his conviction that God had called him and appeared to him personally. All men (and women, both sexes have the same duties in Zoroastrianism) have a personal responsibility to choose between good and evil. On the basis of their exercise of their free-will, men will be judged in the hereafter. Those whose good thoughts, words and deeds out-weigh the evil will go to heaven, regardless of their social status; those whose evil thoughts, words and deeds outweigh the good will go to hell, again regardless of their social status. This moral democracy offended the established priests and princes who had considered paradise their sole preserve.

A similar prophetic emphasis can be seen in the badge Zoroaster took for the religion. For the Indo-Iranians a sacred cord was the symbol of priesthood, as it still is with the Brahmins in India. Zoroaster made this and a sacred shirt (made of white cotton rather like a vest) the symbolic armour which all believers should wear at all times after initiation, to remind them of the battle they must fight against evil.

Good and evil

God, Zoroaster taught, was the wholly Good Creator of all things, of sun, moon and stars, of the spiritual and material worlds, of man and beast. The Wise Lord (Ahura Mazda) is the bountiful sovereign, the friend not only of Zoroaster but of all men.

He is in no way responsible for evil in the world; this comes from the Destructive Spirit (Angra Mainyu) whose nature is violent and destructive. It was he who created the demons, who rules in hell and who has opposed God from the beginning. In Zoroastrianism the 'Devil' is

Modern Zoroastrian tradition identifies this as the symbol of man's spiritual self.

not a fallen angel, for that would make the Good Creator ultimately responsible for evil—an inconceivable idea for Zoroastrians. The world is the battleground in which the forces of good and evil do battle. The world and man were created by God to aid him in this battle.

He also created a number of heavenly beings. Foremost among them were the Bounteous Immortals (Amesha Spentas), the sons and daughters of God, as they became known. In some ways they resemble the Christian idea of archangels (which belief some scholars think was influenced by Zoroastrianism). But like the gods of the Indo-Iranians there is an important abstract dimension to their nature, as their names show. They are: Good Mind (Vohu Manah); Righteousness (Asha); Devotion (Armaiti); Dominion (Kshathra); Wholeness and Immortality (Haurvatat and Ameretat). These are not only heavenly beings, they are also ideals to which the righteous should aspire. So by sharing in the good mind, by a life of devotion and righteousness, man shares in God's dominion and attains wholeness and immortality.

Each of the Bounteous Immortals is thought to protect, and be represented by, one of the six creations which together constitute the Good Creation of God: cattle, fire, earth, metal, water and plants. At important acts of worship, a representative of each creation and therefore of the Bounteous Immortal, is present so that the earthly and heavenly worlds are both symbolically present. The seventh creation is man himself, the representative of God, and present at the rite in the person of the priest.

Zoroaster taught that the world was essentially good, but spoiled at present by the attacks of evil. He looked forward to the day when the battle with evil would reach its climax, when good would triumph and the world would be restored to the perfect state its Creator gave it. At the last the dead will be raised and judged, the wicked will go to hell, and the righteous dwell with God in perfection for eternity.

Persepolis was the chief royal palace of the Achaemenid kings.

The spread of Zoroastrianism

The first 1,000 years after the death of the prophet are shrouded in mystery. There simply are not the sources to reconstruct Zoroastrianism's early history. It appears to have spread across the Persian plateau largely through the movements of tribes and through tribal battles. The Medes came to power in western Persia in the seventh century BC, and the Persians in the sixth century. By that time Zoroastrianism was evidently a power in the land.

The Persian Empire

Persia really emerges into the light of history in 559 BC when Cyrus ascended the throne of a small Persian kingdom called Anshan in the southwest of the country. In 550 he seized the throne of the Medes, then captured the fabulously wealthy king of Lydia in distant Anatolia (modern Turkey). Then in 539 the mighty Babylonian Empire capitulated before him. So in twenty years he rose from being the ruler of a petty kingdom to emperor over what was then the world's largest empire.

In capturing Babylon, Cyrus liberated the Jews from their exile, an act which the biblical book of Isaiah ascribes to the powerful guidance of God, who specially chose Cyrus to accomplish his purposes. No other foreign king is spoken of in such glowing terms in the Bible. Cyrus established for himself a considerable and widespread reputation for tolerance and justice. The dynasty which ruled Persia after him—the Achaemenids (named after a legendary ancestor)—continued to uphold these ideals. It also spread Zoroastrianism throughout the realm.

The people largely responsible for its propagation were the Magi, the priestly tribe of the Medes who continued in office throughout all periods of the Zoroastrian history of Persia. The Magi acted as royal chaplains, and travelled with all important delegations, whether on military or diplomatic missions. They also lived in the many Persian settlements in various parts of the empire. So when Matthew's Gospel refers to wise men (Magi) visiting the infant Jesus, his readers would know well the significance of that. The later Christian legend that they were kings is wrong.

Alexander 'the vandal'

The Achaemenid Empire was brought to an end by Alexander in 331 BC. In Persian history he is not known as 'Alexander the Great' but rather 'Alexander the vandal', because he killed priests and burned down the royal palace of Persepolis. He said he wanted to unite the cultures of Persia and Greece, but he and his successors, the Seleucids, are remembered as the foreign interlopers who intruded into Persian life.

The Parthian Empire

A native Persian dynasty gradually expelled Seleucid power from the land in the middle of the second century BC. They are known as the Parthians, because of the region in Persia from which they came. They did not bring an advanced technology with them from this remote region, so in the early part of their rule they took over certain Hellenistic features such as coin-types and some architectural styles. But their own feudal Persian culture is better reflected in the surviving minstrel tales and epic legends. It was during the Parthian period that the first moves were made to collect together the ancient traditions which made up the Zoroastrian holy book, the *Avesta*.

The Parthians have not received the attention they deserve, mainly because the archaeological and written sources are so few. Yet they ruled Persia for about 400 years, with an empire as large as that of their more famous Achaemenid forebears, stretching at times from north India to what is now Turkey. They were the largest power to confront the might of Rome. They had good relations with Israel; invading the land in 40 BC, they deposed the hated Herod and put a Jew in his place. The Romans returned two years later and restored Herod.

It is interesting to speculate how different history would have been if

Israel, at the time of Jesus, had been under the sway of the tolerant Parthians instead of the widely-hated Romans. What is not generally realized is that at the time of Jesus, the Parthians had made Zoroastrianism the most powerful religion of the then-known world.

'Church and state'

In AD 224 the ruler of a province in the south-west of Persia rebelled against the Parthians. The new dynasty was named after a legendary ancestor, Sasan. The Sasanians ruled Persia until the Muslim invasion in the seventh century. They left behind a wealth of material splendour and a number of writings, creating the impression that this was the most glorious epoch in the history of Zoroastrian Persia.

The high priest was a major power behind the throne, determining much of imperial policy. After Constantine and his successors made Christianity the official religion of the Roman Empire, providing a religious basis for its unity, a comparable unity was necessary in the major Eastern empire. Zoroastrianism had always stressed the unity of church and state, and this was developed to the full in Sasanian times.

The Islamic conquest

The Arab armies of the new Muslim religion entered Persia in AD 633, only one year after the death of Muhammad. At first they came for booty, but later battles were aimed at permanent conquest. The intention was primarily to enforce submission to the rule of Islam. In theory religions which the Muslim authorities recognized as 'people of a book', that is, those who had received a revelation from God (mainly Jews and Christians), were allowed to continue their religion, subject only to the imposition of an extra tax.

But the position of Zoroastrianism as a religion of a book was less clear, and as the new world empire took hold, the position of Zoroastrians in their own land became increasingly threatened. Education, promotion, equality before the law, all were

denied to the followers of Zoroaster. Gradually they were forced to retreat into the obscurity of desert villages. So the religion of the land became associated with poverty and backwardness.

Persecution

Zoroastrians, as the oppressed poor, were often the subjects of vicious attacks from Muslim 'bully boys'. Even in the twentieth century under the protective Pahlavi dynasty, 'infidel-baiting' was common in the remote villages far from official gaze. Because dogs are holy animals to Zoroastrians, one favoured approach was to hack a dog to pieces and throw the remains into the yard of a devout Zoroastrian house. Any Zoroastrian venturing alone into a Muslim quarter could expect verbal and often physical abuse.

Persecution, oppression, poverty, injustice, isolation—these have been the conditions which Zoroastrians have faced in their own land for over 1,300 years of Muslim rule. It is an enormous tribute to their courage, determination and faith that there are any followers of Zoroaster left in present-day Iran. There are a few in the cities, but the majority continue to shelter in the villages of the Yazdi plain. Altogether there are about 17,000 still following the religion of ancient Persia.

The Parsis

The main base of the religion today, in numerical terms, is in India, among the Parsis. In the tenth century AD a small band of the faithful set out to seek a new land of religious freedom, preferring to leave Persia rather than give up the religion of their forefathers. In India they have lived in peace and security, in time even achieving a position of wealth and power which they used to campaign for and support their co-religionists back in the homeland.

Zoroastrian beliefs

The tenth century was not only the time when the 'Pilgrim Fathers' of Zoroastrianism set out for India, it was also a time of literary activity among the Zoroastrians of Persia. A number of texts were produced to encourage, inspire and instruct the faithful in the contemporary language known as Pahlavi or Middle Persian. The holy book, the *Avesta*, was in a language which only a few learned priests understood. Translations, summaries and explanations were produced, as well as defences of the faith against Muslim, Christian and Hindu teachings. Although they were written in the ninth and tenth centuries, they can be taken as the definitive statements of traditional Zoroastrian thought. These Middle Persian texts codify, elaborate and systematize the teaching of Zoroaster himself, from which they stem.

Creation

The Middle Persian forms of the names of God and the 'Devil', ancient Ahura Mazda and Angra Mainyu, are Ohrmazd and Ahriman. Ohrmazd, it is taught, dwells on high in perfect goodness and light whereas Ahriman dwells from eternity in darkness below in the abyss. Battle between these two primal spirits was inevitable, so Ohrmazd created the heavenly and material worlds to aid him in the battle. First he created the heavenly beings, then the world in purely spiritual form, that is, invisible and intangible. In Zoroastrian belief the material world is not evil or corrupt, rather it is the visible, tangible manifestation of the spiritual creation. It is the creation of God, therefore it is good.

The essential characteristics of evil are violence, chaos and the will to destroy. When Ahriman saw the Good Creation of God, he tried to destroy it, afflicting it with misery, suffering, disease and death. None of these evils, therefore, came from God, nor were they part of his plan for creation. They are unnatural afflictions wrought by a wholly independent 'Devil' who seeks to ruin the perfection of the divine creation.

In the myth of creation it is said that Ahriman defiled all parts of creation: the ordered creation was afflicted with chaos; the round, flat earth was shaken so that valleys were opened up, and mountains raised; the sun was dislodged from its ideal noonday position; fire was afflicted with smoke; the archetypal man and bull were afflicted with suffering and death. Ahriman was apparently triumphant. Then a miracle occurred: the dying bull and man emitted sperm; from the bull's seed grew cattle, from man's came a plant whose leaves grew, separated and formed the first human couple. In Zoroastrian thought man is literally at one with his environment.

The cosmic battle

Then Ahriman sought to escape from the world, but found he was trapped within it. Thus the cosmic battle between good and evil is now fought out in the arena of world history. For the first 3,000 years after Ahriman's attack, the two forces were reasonably evenly balanced in what is known as 'the period of mixture' (that is, of good and evil). Then the prophet Zoroaster was born. With the revelation of the Good Religion the defeat of Ahriman was assured. From this time on, the defeat of evil began.

But in Zoroastrian thought it does not come suddenly and unexpectedly like a thief in the night, it is a further 3,000-year conflict as Ahriman makes a desperate bid to destroy all that is good. This final fling is in vain. At 1,000-year intervals three saviours are born: each born of a virgin who had been impregnated with the prophet's seed preserved in a lake where the maidens bathed. They are, therefore, of the line of the prophet, though born of a virgin. A part of the evil creation is destroyed by each of them, until the third saviour raises the dead and introduces the last judgement. From this, men will return to heaven and hell for a limited period before they re-emerge to pass through a stream of molten metal—the final ordeal before all men dwell in total perfection with Ohrmazd.

During these cataclysmic events the heavenly forces will have been engaged in the final battle with the demonic powers, finally overcoming them. The molten metal which had already restored the earth to its original state by reducing mountains and filling up the valleys, and which finally tested men, now fills up hell. So Ahriman is rendered powerless for eternity. For the first time Ohrmazd becomes all-powerful. Evil is wiped out. So, in the myth, the earth ascends to the moon, the heaven descends to the moon—neither is done away with. Zoroastrians do not speak of 'the end of the world', for that would be the end of what God made. Instead they look forward to the 'renovation of creation', the time when heaven and earth join together to make what is literally the best of both worlds.

Man's nature and destiny

In Zoroastrian thought man faces two judgements. One comes after death when his thoughts, words and deeds are weighed in the balances. If good outweighs evil, then man's own conscience guides him across the Bridge of the Separator (Chinvat Bridge) to heaven. If evil predominates then his conscience leads him trembling to the bridge from which he falls into the abyss of hell. The second judgement is after the resurrection.

Whereas Christianity has no explanation for the belief in two judgements, Zoroastrianism has. Man has two sides to his being, the physical and the spiritual. Both are the creations of God. Man must be judged, rewarded or punished in both aspects

of his being. The first judgement after death is evidently one in the spirit because the body can be seen to remain on earth. But hell is not eternal in Zoroastrian belief. The purpose of punishment, they believe, must be corrective. However 'eternal' is defined—whether as everlasting or absolute—eternal hell cannot involve corrective punishment. In hell, Zoroastrians believe, the punishment is made to fit the crime, so a cruel ruler who tortures or starves his people is himself tortured and starved in hell. But at the resurrection all men return from heaven or hell to face their second judgement, this time in the body; and again they return to heaven or hell as appropriate so that they may be physically rewarded or corrected.

The purpose is that the whole man, body and soul, should be so corrected that he may dwell, in the perfection of his united being, with God. Man is a divine creation, intended to be a fellow-worker with God; his final destiny must be with God. During his earthly life he has complete free-will to act as he chooses, to support the forces of good or evil. He can live contrary to his nature, but he cannot, in eternal terms, change that nature. Through judgement, heaven and hell, he is corrected and rewarded, for his part in the great battle between good and evil.

This rock relief is at Naqsh-i Rustam, the 'valley of the kings' near the palace of Persepolis. The Sasanian monarch Shapur I (c. AD 242–273) rides in triumph and majesty before the kneeling figure of his defeated Roman enemy. Like their Achaemenid and Parthian forbears, the Sasanian monarchs ruled over an empire stretching from India to the shores of the Mediterranean. For over 1,000 years, Zoroastrian Iran was the major power in the known world.

Body and soul

Man's foremost duty is to make his body the dwelling-place of the Bounteous Immortals; as we have seen, his life is to be determined by the Good Mind of Righteousness and Devotion directed towards divine Dominion, Wholeness and Immortality—and to reject the demons such as Violence, Greed and the Lie. He should seek to reflect the bounteous, creative spirit of God and reject the negative path.

In doing this he must keep the spiritual and material sides of his nature in balance. So man has a religious duty to expand God's material creation as well as to support his spiritual creation. He should get married and have children; he should seek to expand his herds and the natural environment through agriculture. To remain celibate is sinfully to refrain from this duty. On the other hand, man should not abuse the divine gift of marriage through lechery. In Zoroastrian belief a monk is as great a sinner as a lecher—both deny what God wills. Similarly man should not fast so that the spirit is exalted over the body, nor should he be gluttonous and exalt the body over the soul. The health of body and soul are interdependent and should be cared for equally.

The world is God's Good Creation, and it is man's religious duty to care for and enjoy that creation, for Zoroastrians believe that 'misery drives away the divine'. There is no belief here that man is a spiritual self imprisoned in an alien material universe, as there is in some religions. Indeed, it is practically the reverse—the 'Devil' is a spiritual being trapped in what is to him an alien good universe. The spirit of happiness permeates not only Zoroastrian ethics, but also their rituals, which are described in the section on the Parsis.

The sacred fire, symbol of Ahura Mazda, is nowadays housed in fire temples. Originally, Zoroastrian worship was conducted in the open air, but a temple cult was introduced in Achaemenid times and received lavish royal patronage.

If evil is associated with death and decay in the material world, then man has a duty to avoid contact with any matter that aids these evils. Dirt, rotting and dead matter are places where death, and therefore evil, is present. The housewife cleaning the home, rites associated with birth, marriage and death, standards of personal hygiene—all are concerned with the great cosmic battle between good and evil. In this way man, the fellow-worker with Ohrmazd, seeks to wipe out evil and restore the world to its God-created perfection.

Personal responsibility

Zoroastrianism is a religion which is concerned with the *Good* God, the *Good* Creation and the *goodness* of man. The term its followers often use of it is 'The Good Religion'. It has no doctrine of original sin, nor of one man dying to save all. Every man is responsible for his own part in the cosmic battle, and for his own destiny. It is a religion of stalwart determination—which is perhaps what has enabled it to survive for so long, despite a millennium of oppression.

Mithraism: Cult of the Bull

John Hinnells

Mithra is perhaps unique in history in that he is one god who has been worshipped in four different religions. He appears in Hinduism and Zoroastrianism because both derive from the Indo-Iranian religion of which Mithra was a part, and in Manichaeism because of the form that religion took in Persia.

The Romans

A basic question scholars cannot answer with certainty is what is the relationship of those forms of Mithra worship with the Roman cult of Mithras. It used to be assumed that the Romans took over the Persian form, but increasingly scholars argue that the Roman cult was a new Western religion with a veneer of Persian and oriental learning to make it appeal to the many people in the empire who were fascinated by Eastern cults.

The earliest reference to the Roman Mithras is by the poet Statius who died in AD 96. The earliest-known temples were built in the mid-second century, and building continued until the fifth century. Temples are found as far apart as Wales in the west, Hadrian's Wall in northern England, Dura on the Euphrates, and Alexandria in Egypt. The areas of greatest concentration are the city of Rome and its port of Ostia, and the frontier regions of the empire, especially along the Danube and Rhine rivers.

The army appears to have provided the greatest number of recruits, but traders and officials were also members of the cult. Both military and civilian initiates were of a respected social class, inscriptions suggesting a fairly high proportion of centurions and officers. The portrait of a Mithraist in one temple shows a clean-shaven, very respectable young man. The male is significant—women were excluded from the cult.

Statues and temples

There are enormous problems in reconstructing what the Mithraists believed and did. No text written by a Mithraist has survived, only the comments of outside observers, mainly Christians, who (with the possible exception of the Neo-Platonist Porphyry) were generally biased and ignorant. There is no Mithraic 'Prayer Book' that we know of. So the main source of information is the products of archaeology, silent stones and stereotyped inscriptions dedicating a statue or temple. Religious iconography is notoriously difficult to interpret, and this is especially true in the case of Mithraism.

Mithraic temples were generally small and built to resemble a cave, in imitation of what they thought was the 'world cave' which Mithras had created, with the vault of the sky spanning the earth. On each side of a central aisle were benches on which the initiates reclined. At the end opposite the entrance was a main cult relief, usually carved in stone in the round, though in Italy some painted scenes are found. Often, in the central aisle and near the main relief, were set small altars on which incense was burned.

The bull-slaying scene

The theme of the main cult relief was virtually always Mithras slaying a bull. This act was represented with remarkable consistency of detail. The god generally puts his left knee on the bull's back, keeping his right foot on the creature's hoof, pulls back its head with his left hand and stabs it with his right. A dog leaps towards the blood from the wound, as does a snake, while a scorpion grasps the bull's genitals. At either side of the main scene are two torchbearers, one with a raised torch, the other a lowered torch. How to interpret this scene without any explanatory texts is a real problem. It used to be thought a variation of the Zoroastrian creation myth; only here it is not the 'Devil', but Mithras, who takes the first life, from which all creation proceeds. But this has been shown to be unlikely—if not impossible.

The view most scholars favour nowadays is that the scene has to be understood in astrological terms, because so many of the symbols can be interpreted astrologically—snake (hydra), dog (canis), bull (taurus), scorpion (scorpio), to list only a few. Precisely what is being depicted astrologically we still do not know—perhaps the date at which the cult started, or when it was thought creation had taken place.

Ascent of the soul

Each community of believers was divided into seven grades of initiation. In ascending order these were: Raven, Bride, Soldier, Lion, Persian, Runner of the sun, and Father. Progression through the grades was thought to reflect the spiritual ascent of the soul through the planetary spheres which bind it to the material world. The Father was a man of piety and wisdom, rather ascetic and in charge of the discipline in each group. It is reasonable to suppose that with progression through the grades, the initiate was taught deeper levels of spiritual learning, so that the cult relief may have had more than one interpretation.

Each grade clearly had a different cultic function. The main ritual which we know of is a feast enjoyed by the members in imitation of a meal shared by Mithras and Sol (the sun) over the body of the slain bull. One ritual which Mithraists did not practise, but which many popular books say they did, was the 'taurobolium'. This was a known rite in Roman religion where an initiate entered a pit over which a bull's throat was cut, and the initiate washed himself in and drank the blood. Mithraic temples were far too small to get a bull in, and presumably they did not want to. Clearly the act of slaying the bull was one which only the god could perform, even though the initiates could imitate the ritual meal which

Statues from temples to Mithras show the god slaying a bull.

followed. One inscription refers to Mithras saving his followers by the shedding of eternal blood, so it was he alone who could save them. They shared in this salvation through the meal (of bread and wine, apparently) and through a lifetime's personal discipline as each person progressed up the spiritual ladder of the seven grades.

Destroyed

Mithraism died out largely because of the success of Christianity. Christians had a special hatred of Mithras— Tertullian described Mithraism as a devilish imitation of what he believed was the true religion. Whenever Christians could break into a Mithraic temple they destroyed it and the reliefs with axes. But at least one Mithraic practice survived—25 December is celebrated in various cultures as the birth-day of a new sun. Mithraists used the date to celebrate the birth of Mithras, and Christians took it over for the celebration of Jesus' birth.

The Ancient Religions of Greece and Rome

Clyde Curry Smith

The ancient history of Greece covers some 6,000 years or more of development from the first permanent settlement based upon grain agriculture until Greece was absorbed by Rome. Within this immense period, only the last 2,000 years at most are definitely Greek by language.

The ancient history of Rome, by contrast, begins in the eighth century BC and extends into the fifth century AD, and the Latin language is present over that whole span.

For our beginning we must look at the environment of that great inland sea—the Mediterranean basin. This large, deep trench is bordered by mountainous folds. An earthquake and volcanic belt along its whole length is the fundamental feature with which man here has always had to contend. And that vital force was seen as centred in the sea. So we meet the sea-god Poseidon: the one who both 'embraces the earth' and 'shakes' it, as Homer would say.

Five larger islands define the sub-basins of the Mediterranean: Sicily (which divides the whole), Sardinia and Corsica, Crete (which separates off the Aegean) and Cyprus.

The rugged Mediterranean coastlands offered little good land for the development of civilization. It was the sea itself which became a major force in Mediterranean development. The seaways meant transport and profit in trade (and booty in piracy), relying only on the stars and fair winds—those unpredictable elements which provided the context for man's religious response.

Hence, the wanderers—the Greek word for 'planet' means 'wanderer'—in the sky were understood by the wanderers upon the sea to be those greater forces which guided them. Thus in Greek (and Latin) we meet: Zeus (Jupiter), Aphrodite (Venus), Ares (Mars), Hermes (Mercury), and Khronos (Saturn). They, along with the sun and moon, defined times and seasons, regulating human life and its economic base.

The Aegean basin

When the south-eastern mountain ranges, which originally connected the Balkan and Anatolian peninsulas, were shattered, the Aegean was formed, its main island chains being the tops of the earlier mountains.

For the Aegean region as a whole there has been no essential climatic change since prehistoric times. Only about one-tenth of the land area was level enough to be cultivable. Vegetation depends on elevation, latitude and coastal influence, but it is also under human control. One of the major effects the human agriculturalists had on the landscape was the progressive removal of woodland. In its place came the cereal grains, wheat and barley, personified by Demeter (Ceres), the Lady who nourished all.

Prehistoric religion in Greece

Because of its mountainous condition, the Greek mainland shows fewer and less spectacular examples of human presence during the long Palaeolithic period than the steppes of Eurasia. Yet its forests and scrublands were home to hunters' game, and it was open to entrance by land passage through Macedonia into the Thessalian plains or through Epeiros into the Ionian islands.

The known burial practices of Neanderthal man throughout Eurasian sites are not yet documented specifically in the Aegean basin. Their response to the mystery of birth is also not known, unless it lay in the so-called 'Venuses' (exaggerated female figurines). Otherwise we can at best describe their technological skills and assembled tool-kits, their domestic construction and hunting prowess, from skeletal debris and collections of tools of some 70,000 years ago, found since 1960 at Petralona in Macedonia and at Pantanassa in Epeiros.

The oldest farming village known is Nea Nikomedia in Macedonia, dating from before the end of the seventh millennium BC.

When barley and wheat entered the larger European and Mediterranean worlds, they were accompanied by those who understood their cultivation. These people's way of thinking included observing the seasonal cycle, and its ritual correlation with preparing, planting, weeding and harvesting, or breeding, pasturing, tending and milking. In this we see the base for *all* later development of religious ideas.

The impact of the Neolithic agricultural transformation can best be measured by the shift in population density from, at most, one person to every ten square miles under hunting and gathering conditions, to ten to one hundred persons per square mile under farming conditions. The Aegean basin never had enough space; population growth was always a critical factor, leading to social instability which produced migrations and the practice of killing unwanted children by exposure.

The Parthenon in Athens was sacred to the city's patron goddess, Athena Parthenos.

This rich Mycenaean funeral mask is known as the mask of Agamemnon. According to Homer, Agamemnon was the leader of the Greeks in the siege of Troy.

forces and dimensions of life which were to dominate the new age.

The early Bronze Age

Metal technology yielded specialized craftsmen, a new group set apart from the routine of village-farming life with its industries of pottery and weaving. The technology itself required a religious rhythm for the reduction of the metal from the ore, just as much as the secret lore related to the firing, alloying, casting or hammering processes.

For the earliest phase of the Bronze Age on the Greek mainland, objects of religious significance are minimal. There is much better evidence from the group of islands called the Cyclades. Best-known of all Cycladic objects are the marble figurines. The two most common are the elongated female (frequently highlighted with red and gold paint, standing erect, with just the nose represented on the head, arms crossed below the breasts, occasionally pregnant) and the abbreviated 'fiddle-shaped' version, which emphasizes only the necklace and the sexually-explicit features. We also know of a few nude males in a posture similar to that of the females, a few seated figures playing the lyre or pipes, and some animal-shaped terracottas. Although the figurines are usually less than twelve inches (thirty centimetres) tall, several life-sized examples exist. These were broken at the neck and knee to fit into the grave, and may well have stood elsewhere before burial. These Cycladic graves may themselves imitate a house or house-shrine.

The Middle Bronze Age, which roughly coincides with the first half of the second millennium (2000–1550 BC), seems to be an era of human reshuffling. Indo-European language groups appear not only in Anatolia (the Hittites) and the Aegean (the Greeks) but also in a great segment of the Eurasian continent, from India in the south-east to the Hebrides in the north-west.

The Middle Helladic period of the mainland was marked by the arrival of the first of several waves of

Minoan-Mycenaean civilizations

The new technology which completed the thrust towards civilization was development in metal-working. Gold and silver had previously been used as rare ornaments. But now (3000–2000 BC) the discovery of how to reduce metals and produce alloys—especially of copper with tin—made it possible to make tools much stronger than the old stone ones, so that tougher lands could now be cleared and ploughed.

The crafts of smiths became economically competitive. They also introduced a rich source of analogy and myth in speaking about the creative process. The stone-workers' skill was turned towards architecture and sculpture, the potters' craft diverted towards aesthetic expression. In their place the moulding and hammering—often noisy and dirty—and extraction by fire of strong and glistening metals from apparently fragile and earth-like ores, became the significant imagery for the vital

'Greeks', who were the ancestors of the Late Bronze Age Mycenaeans. The sites that archaeologists have investigated reveal the poverty both of towns (again without walls) and of shallow graves (without goods).

For the remainder of the Middle Bronze Age on the mainland there was no significant architecture. It was therefore very surprising when the Shaft Grave circles were discovered on the high citadel (*acropolis*) of Mycenae. Their gold treasures indicate the presence of aristocratic sea-going warriors who had amassed considerable wealth in portable loot.

Over these same centuries, from Crete, there is evidence of royal palace complexes. The palace rulers are said to be 'theocratic', because excavations have revealed no separate structures which can be called 'religious'.

The Minoans seem to have worshipped bulls and sacrificed them. There were 'bull-leapers', who performed dangerous acrobatics over a bull for religious purposes. This is often portrayed in wall-paintings, seals and the minor arts, bronze and terracotta. These ceremonial games took place in the large central courts of the palaces.

The palaces also contained 'pillar crypts', decorated with the double-headed axe, the chief Minoan religious symbol, possibly from its use in animal sacrifices. (The word 'labyrinth' comes from *labrys*, the Lydian for double-axe.) The double-axe was a woodsman's tool rather than a weapon. Actual examples have been found, with other carpentry tools.

Storage magazines were sometimes connected with the pillar crypts. In the floor of one at Knossos were 'temple repositories' containing faience figurines handling snakes. Snakes were used as house-guardians and so became the sacred animal of the household-goddess.

Minoan seals portraying cult-scenes are another important source for our knowledge of Minoan religion.

Citadels of the Mycenaeans

The Minoan epoch came to an end disastrously, probably when the vol-

The double axe was a religious symbol for the Minoans. It may have been used in animal sacrifice.

canic island of Thera erupted with extreme violence in about 1450 BC. This was documented fully at Kato Zakro. Of the palaces, neither Phaistos nor Mallia were to recover. Knossos alone, though in less grand fashion, was to be rebuilt, apparently by others. The old Minoan people had to desert their ash-covered valleys. The few who survived did so on isolated hills in the mountainous and western districts of the island.

The Late Bronze Age or Late Helladic era belongs to the Mycenaeans, both on the mainland and the islands, including Crete. The Middle Bronze mainland had been dominated by Minoan cultural influence, but as the Late Bronze Age began we find the *tholos* tomb builders. There are no surviving indications of the dwellings of these aristocratic warrior-rulers, though they may well have been built on the sites on which the Mycenaean palaces were to appear. The *tholos* tombs were underground beehive-shaped vaults, entered by way of a long, gently-sloping tunnel, and topped by an earth mound.

The principal grave goods were those of the warrior entombed. Minor objects show fishes, animals and birds, heroic figures doing battle with fellows or heraldic creatures, and female figures, in Minoan style, bare-breasted, tending domestic animals or plants. The gold cups from the Vapheio grave have scenes of netting and mating of great bulls.

'There is a land called Crete in the midst of the wine-dark sea, a fair country and fertile, seagirt, and there are many peoples, innumerable; there are ninety cities ... and there is Knossos, the great city, the place where Minos was king for nine-year periods, and conversed with great Zeus.'

Odyssey 19.172–174, 178–179

The Mycenaean palace complexes are neither towns nor houses, but fortified centres for developing valley communities. What most distinguishes these complexes from their Minoan predecessors is their location on high citadels, and their massive fortification walls. Five major sites on the mainland are known: Thebes, under the modern city; Athens, levelled for the fifth-century *acropolis*; Tiryns and Pylos, both well-preserved; and Mycenae, the best example, though part of the palace itself has collapsed down the slope. From Mycenae the civilization takes the name 'Mycenaean'.

The new ingredient in the Late Bronze Age is the earliest written texts, in a script called 'Linear B'. This was deciphered in 1952 and shown to be an archaic form of Greek.

The Linear B texts give a wholly new dimension to investigation. To date, tablets have been found only at Knossos, Pylos, Mycenae and Thebes. They include inventory lists of people and their occupations, livestock and agricultural produce, land ownership with some usage, textiles, vessels, furniture, metals and military equipment, and a grouping defined as 'proportional tribute and ritual offerings'.

It seems that commodities could serve as either tribute or offering, and that these were assessed seasonally according to fixed schedules, that receipts varied from assessments, and, most important of all, that there were functionaries of all sorts, as well as deities known by name or title. Poseidon is of considerable importance, as is 'the Lady' of different places. Zeus, Hera, Ares, Hermes, Athena, Artemis, Dionysus, and a few other classical deities are named. Among the great variety of functionaries which made up this administrative complex a 'priestess' or 'priest' is very occasionally mentioned.

The epics of Homer

There is a gap at the end of the Bronze Age, with the destruction of the Mycenaean world. The palace bureaucracies disappeared. Migrants and invaders worked the land on both sides of the Aegean basin. Some peoples simply survived the transition, to pass on in their own time. It is impossible to document which tribes were descended from old or new or intermixed inhabitants, though that must have been one of the functions of the great interest in genealogy.

Pottery remains from this period are very few. We have nothing which documents the religious response to reality—nothing, that is, except the 'epic interlude': the unsurpassed poetry of Homer, regarded by many later Greeks almost as sacred scripture.

The epic language is peculiar in that it was apparently not a spoken dialect, nor equivalent to any of the historic dialects found in inscriptions or subsequent literature. It was, however, designed to be recited.

The nearly 28,000 lines of Homer which form the *Odyssey* and the slightly longer *Iliad*, constitute the surviving bulk of this epic form with its strict metre.

The Homeric gods

The gods are portrayed in essentially human terms, but they do not grow old, and they are immortal. The gods have power (*daimon*) to change their appearance, size and attributes beyond the bounds of the human form they may take.

Their awesome status causes man to feel dread, fear, shame, or reverence. In response man feels impelled to pray, to entreat, to praise, take an oath, make sacrifice of a victim, or pour out a libation of wine. Many of these activities can be tied quite naturally to daily domestic routine. The communication between god and man may be direct or via an intermediary (including the god in disguise as human friend), or by a dream. The gods may be consulted through an agent accomplished in the art of divining, most commonly through birds or the interpretation of dreams. Lightning, thunder or falling stars may also serve as omens. And places where there was an oracle, such as Dodona with its great oak-tree at which people listened for the voice of Zeus, played a lesser role.

Life in Homer takes on some specific burden which humans must bear, sometimes even the delusion with which the gods affect them. The human characters tend to explain the course of events as the destiny imposed by the gods—even if, as Helen says to Hector, 'so that hereafter we shall be made into things of song for the men of the future'. With gifts and prayers these gods may be implored to change the situation. The god might sometimes do so, or might merely turn his head away in rejection. For these gods—even Zeus himself—are equally bound by fate. Whatever else may be granted, humans are not permitted to escape death, which is their final destiny. Within that framework all phenomena, religious as well as otherwise, are set. Although the gods manipulate human actions, they neither make nor change human nature.

The heroes

Heroes seek honour, glory and renown, believing that to obtain these is of much greater worth than life itself.

The burial of the dead is of great importance. They require that last honour, even though their souls go forth immediately to the underworld (Hades), lest they become the god's curse upon the living. In Homer, the funeral would seem to include cremation (if that of a warrior, dressed in his full armour) and some kind of interment of the burned remains accompanied by lamentations. A mound was heaped over the grave, with a stone indicating the dead man's profession.

Anger of the gods

The other side of heroic life is an overbearing, presumptuous pride, violence and transgression. Although it cannot be shown that in any final sense, other than death, recompense is required for sin, there nevertheless are hints at some larger levels of justice and decency which the gods love in preference to cruelty, or to excessive glorification over slain men. Since fate determines all, the anger of the gods, like the anger of men towards one another, must work out its destined course. Yet their full destructive anger may be averted by means of prayer, libation (a poured-out drink offering), and sacrifice. The gods may be offended by perverse judgements, refusal or neglect of funeral rites, brutal conduct in a host's home, and murder of a guest. Ultimately, the values of the society are vindicated by the gods.

The writings of Hesiod

Hesiod's *Theogony* does not provide us with much insight into religious belief. Much of *Works and Days* provides specific seasonal information concerning work, especially agricultural, which needs to be done. Similarly, much concerns the ritual for domestic necessities, or the omen-like significance of days in the month. Pithy words of wisdom and matters of general behaviour constitute the basic ingredients of the rest, with several famous parables as illustration. The poem concludes: 'But that man is fortunate and blessed who, knowing all these matters, simply works, blameless towards immortals, watching all bird-signs, and avoiding wrong-doing.' The path of religious duty is not neglecting what ought to be done, and avoiding what ought not to be done.

Temple and city-state

The Mycenaean age ended in destructive violence brought about by human efforts around 1100 BC and, with it, not only palace and palace art but also the Linear B script pass into obscurity. The archaic phase of classical Greece opens on a new world with the coming of alphabetic writing. The fundamental factor is a devastating decline in total population. Whereas some 320 inhabited sites are known from the thirteenth century BC, many of them large centres, only forty are known from the eleventh century, and all of these are small.

What remained intact through that major alteration, was a legacy of technology in the mundane matters of mixed farming, building, carpentry, boat-building, spinning, weaving, pottery and metallurgy. The simultaneous shift from bronze to iron carried with it the 'hateful strife of evil war', rather than healthy competition among hard-working neighbours.

Greece was divided among the Hellenes into at least twelve separate regions, and the Greek language into five major linguistic blocks. It is not surprising that Greece consisted ultimately of no fewer than 158 independent city-states. Most were quite small (some fifty to a hundred square miles on average), and were incapable of sustaining a total population above 10,000. By colonial expansion even more city-states were founded throughout the greater Mediterranean basin.

Their history is one of warring states achieving from time to time a truce which enabled them to translate their hostility into competitive athletics at the four great Panhellenic festivals. According to tradition, the Olympic games began in 776 BC. The Pythian, Isthmian and Nemean games began not more than two centuries later. On the Anatolian side of the Aegean, the Panionian festival dedicated to Poseidon was celebrated by another cluster of twelve Greek city-states, just as Attic Greeks combined annually for the Panathenaia dedicated to the goddess Athena, patroness of Athens, on her birthday.

Festivals required proper facilities. In the earlier era separate 'houses for cult images' did not exist. When separate temples were invented after the catastrophic transition, three sources were drawn on: the oval country hut, the throne and hearth chamber abstracted from the Mycenaean palace, and the elongated house of rulers of the period 900–700 BC. The first type has as its example the earliest known temple, dedicated to Hera Akraia at Perachora, built by the beginning of the eighth century BC.

By the sixth century BC, to use Lewis Mumford's words, 'a new god had captured the Acropolis, and had, by an imperceptible passage, merged with the original deity'. What he had in mind was the city (*polis*) itself. Just as ordinary men insinuated themselves by warfare into the political life, so the city assembly (*ekklesia*) insinuated itself into what religious structure was still considered relevant. This humanizing transition is evidenced by the development in sculpture of the perfected human form, as well as by contemporary inscriptions and decrees.

Yet several major groups remained outside the pale of citizenship-participation: the children, the large cluster of slaves descended from suppressed indigenous inhabitants or taken captive in war, and also the resident aliens.

This means that not more than one fifth of the total population in fact functioned politically, and hence religiously. Those who were excluded from the official cult of the city sought an alternative expression of their religious nature.

Official city religion is clearly manifest in the very layout and architecture of the city. The lofty citadel (*acropolis*) which had been the Mycenaean fortress and palatial residence was now abandoned—left for the gods alone. The new city lies within the plains whose agriculture supports its economy. The centre of life is the market-place (*agora*), whose purpose reveals that economics is central to this renewed urban life, and whose architecture reflects the necessity for public access. Although public inscriptions bear witness of dedication and piety to the official religion, no gods dwell there. At some distance from the city centre, or perhaps on the old *acropolis*, decorative and elaborate temples were created and maintained, with more than a hint that a major function was as treasury for the wealth of the city.

The growth of temples typifies this new era of the growth of the city-state and of law and order. The decorative arts were used to portray mythical events that expressed this sense of order. Victory over the great uncivilized forces was personified in the victory of lapiths against centaurs, or of their legendary ancestors against amazons. The final form of Greek mythology is the end product of the creative formation of the Greek city-states. Their nature is also reflected in the temple architecture with its basic patterns or 'orders'.

At the individual level of society, from the Geometric period onwards come marker-stones (*stela*), especially those set up at graves. Thus names and titles, genealogies and deeds enter into history. Objects of all kinds were dedicated to the gods, but the funeral *stele* is fully human.

Temple styles

The history of temple styles is summarized in three successive 'orders': Doric, Ionic and Corinthian. The columns of these orders are increasingly elaborate and more highly embellished. As Gisela Richter has stated: 'A central hall was provided with a columned porch, practically always in front and often also at the back; pilasters terminated the side walls of the central hall. Rows of columns were placed in front, at the back, and sometimes all around to form a colonnade; occasionally columns were added also in the interior to support the roof.' The pitched roof created triangular space at each end, the pediment, which came to be decorated often with a central mythological theme for the particular temple.

Even the largest temples are quite small: few exceed thirty metres (one hundred feet) in over-all width, nor much more than twice that in length. The inner hall, being open only in one direction, could not have allowed easy access to many people at once. Clearly the major purpose was to provide a space for the great statue of the god who was worshipped.

Painting and sculpture

Vase-painting styles developed from the earlier black-figure to red-figure techniques. Athenian examples dominate both varieties. Some shapes in the black-figure style were exclusively intended for ritual use: as grave-offerings, or for other uses at funerals, or for use in marriage ceremonies.

Although the illustration focussed

Greek architecture flourished in the sixth century BC. This temple at Hatra is exceptionally well preserved.

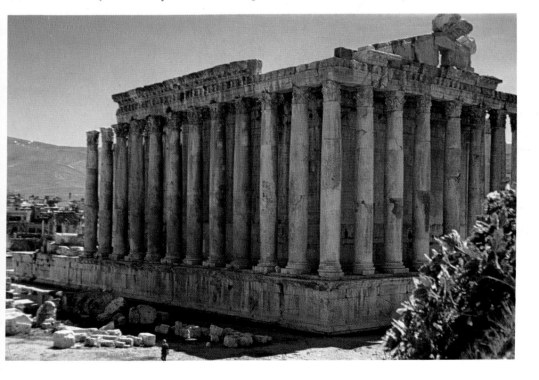

'I am Demeter the honoured, the greatest benefit and joy to undying gods and to mortals. But come now, let all the people build me a great temple and beneath it an altar under the steep walls of the city, above Kallikhoron, on the rising hill. I myself shall introduce rites so that later You may propitiate my mind by their right performance.'

Homeric *Hymn to Demeter* 268–274

on a god or myth, that is no guarantee of explicit religiousness. The world of vase-painting is basically secular, reflecting the structure of the city-state. Yet, as well as maenads—the ecstatic female followers of Dionysus—with their attendant satyrs, with the onset of the red-figure phase, women of all sorts, increasingly in domestic scenes, are more often portrayed.

Temples are rare in these paintings; but altars with sacrifice are often shown. The deities invoked are rarely to be seen, and the attendants cannot be distinguished from those in domestic life. Since there was no explicit ceremony, marriage processionals indicate that event. Funerals show chiefly the laying out of the body, the women mourning—only the men approaching in ritual gesture. The strange phenomenon of the *herm*—that human-headed, otherwise unhewn pillar, in the form of an erect penis, which stood everywhere throughout the city, outside the doors of ordinary houses—is illustrated in scenes beginning with its carving to the perfunctory act of worship made by passers-by. Similarly, the phallus-bearing celebrants in some revelry, often dedicated to Dionysus, are commonplace. Erotic scenes, both hetero- and homosexual, were considered appropriate subjects even on votive and funeral plaques.

The Greek world-view

Although the fifth century BC has often been interpreted as a crucial age for human civilization, its achievements were built on the whole period from the time of Homer. The boundary is not only the turn of a century, but the life and death of one man, Socrates (469–399 BC).

Before Socrates it was thought that all things were made out of one or more of the four basic ingredients: air, earth, fire and water. The one fully preserved example of pre-Socratic cultural inquiry is Herodotus (about 490–430), who divided the known world into five intellectual components. The Greek was set over against the Egyptian, Libyan, Scythian and Persian, collectively con-

sidered as 'barbarian'—that is, incapable of Greek language and hence of civilized Greek thought. Pre-Socratic understanding turned on the assumed relationship between nature and custom, but this broke down in the crisis which accompanied the destructive half-century of war among the Greek city-states.

The literary response to the Peloponnesian war is provided by two groups of Athenian writings. The first consists of plays, cast in metrical poetry. These portray the actions of the gods in relation to men, especially in the growing horror of a world at war. Beginning with the self-esteem which all Greeks shared from their common resistance to the Persian invasions, all the cherished assumptions of Greek society were questioned by Aeschylus (525–456), Sophocles (497–405) and Euripides (485–406), as Athens, whose democracy had become imperialistic in regard to its allies, struggled with Sparta, whose militaristic regime championed the freedom of the other city-states.

The second (prose) grouping came to be called 'Sophist'. They taught rhetoric, 'the art of persuasion'. The major surviving fifth-century author in whose work these ingredients are found is Thucydides (about 455–400).

Both analyses, poetic and prose, arrive at the role of the irrational in human affairs, and particularly in power politics. For in both Thucydides and Euripides, we are introduced to the pathology of human nature under stress. Human affairs cannot ultimately be blamed on the gods, though perhaps some fortune or necessity controls the mysterious past which has produced the present disastrous situations at both the urban and the individual levels. When human nature is aroused to do something—anything—it is not possible to turn it aside, either by law or fear of punishment. Consequences cannot be anticipated. This somewhat sceptical approach was accompanied by a sense that the Olympian gods were remote—and scarcely model examples of ethical behaviour.

The Hellenistic world-state

The ridicule of the gods in the plays of Aristophanes (about 450–385) received no apparent criticism at the time, although dedications to the gods continued to be made in the state's official inscriptions. But after the defeat of Athens in the war, the trumped-up charges against Socrates were said to be: not acknowledging the gods worshipped by the state, and introducing new divinities or an educational atheism which served to corrupt the young men from their attitudes as good citizens.

It is less than clear what, in their own times, either Plato (about 429–347) or Aristotle (384–322) contributed to religious thought. Aristotle's treatise format has a greater precision than Plato's dialogues. His discussion of fundamental substance as the basic constituent of reality served the growing sense of the nature of God, so that *Metaphysics* contains reference to the 'unmoved-mover'—God—as First Cause.

By the fifth century there was an unprecedented enlargement of religious vocabulary. From Herodotus comes a word for 'religious observance', almost 'religion' itself, and a verb 'to observe religiously' or to *do* religion. In contrast, by the time of Theophrastos (371–287), a word was in common use whose meaning, 'fear of' or 'reverence for' divinity, already had such negative overtones that it could designate the 'superstitious' man. Interestingly, the era produced no words for 'believing in' gods.

Rulers who became gods

Hellenization was taking place even before the advent of Alexander the Great (356–323), though it was his conquest of the vast Persian Empire in the east which brought the process to fruition. Alexander founded some seventy cities on the Greek pattern, mostly named after himself, 'Alexandria'. With easy transport and communication within the empire, Greek being the common language, Hellenization opened up the Mediterranean world to Eastern influences, including religious beliefs. This era was one of conspicuous luxury among the rich and powerful, while inflated prices and lower wages were the lot of the poor.

At the very top of the society were the Hellenized rulers, who declared themselves to be divine. Alexander, whose heroic deeds could not be doubted, was believed to have been received among the gods on his death, like Heracles before him. This soon degenerated into automatic deification for the king.

Even the Athenians, in response to their 'liberation' in 307 BC by the Macedonian king, Demetrios Poliorketes (336–283; 'sacker of cities'), hailed him Saviour and Benefactor, incorporating him and his father into the city-cult, with an annually-elected priesthood whose name was placed at the head of their decrees and contracts.

In a hymn by Duris of Samos (about 340–260), this 'liberating' Demetrios could be integrated with Demeter and her local solemn processional 'mysteries', identified with the offspring of Poseidon (the mightiest of the gods) and Aphrodite, and even prayed to under the assurance that while: 'the other gods are either far away or have no ears, or are not, or pay not the slightest heed to us; you we see face to face, not in wood and not in stone, but verily and in truth'!

Mysteries and healing cults

The specific technical term 'the mysteries' first occurs in Herodotus and the tragedians, though their usage had clearly grown out of urban ceremonial and temple festivals. It is amazing that 'the mysteries' were successfully kept such a close-lipped secret by all who referred to them, whether initiates or not. By Hellenistic times, however, the process of initiation was open to all Greek-speaking people not ritually impure who could afford the initiation fee.

Ultimately, *the* mysteries, meaning those primarily of Eleusis near Athens (commonly called 'Greater') must be said to lie in the initiate to whom something real is revealed, rather than in the ritual act or paraphernalia. The total complex included: 'things said', 'things shown' and 'things performed'.

Initiation promised happiness, perhaps simply in a glorious vision of the god. Although at first no particular good life was implied beyond death, the mystery religions were highly syncretistic and tended to absorb Eastern myths which hinted that this happiness continued into an afterlife, perhaps by a unification with the gods or by a deification of the human. But no kind of group association followed, and no moral demands were required for this bliss—except purity at the cult and silence ever after on 'the mysteries'.

The mythological and ritual complex at Eleusis, involving the goddess Demeter and her daughter, was tied to cereal grain. The processional and festival celebration, which was the context for initiation, took place in September–October—the ploughing season. Unlike other Greek temples, the one at Eleusis was meant for a large gathering and could hold up to 10,000 people.

Another cult, involving Dionysus, was tied to wine-making. Celebration of the country Dionysia began with the picking of the grapes and the initial pressing. The following month, festivities shifted to the sanctuary within the city. During the classical period, comedies ('revelling songs') could be performed there and then. By late winter, the wine in vats had clarified and the sediments had

Delphi was the site of the most important Greek oracle. The oracles were generally consulted on personal matters.

settled. In early spring came the ceremony at which the new wine was first tasted, offered to the god, then consumed by officiants from a sanctuary in the marshes.

The city Dionysia was celebrated in March–April. It shows a toning-down under urban control of the excesses of the rural activities, though phallic processions out from the walls to a shrine used only once a year, then back into Athens, remained an ingredient. This was the season for the complex cycles of plays—three tragedies and a satyr-play, as well as another series of comedies.

The word of the god

Herodotus tells us that the most ancient oracular site in all Greece, and the only one in his time, was that at Dodona with its great oak-tree. Preserved inscriptions of questions asked of the oracle at Dodona reveal concern for health, including successful pregnancies. There were also oracles in Amphiaraus and Trophonius. In each case some kind of earth-fault or warm spring provide the context for belief in a divine presence and a cultic sacrifice. After this the inquirer, sleeping at the spot, received by dream an appropriate response to his inquiry. Individuals brought their own private concerns; officials consulted about matters of state.

A vase-painting of the famous oracle at Delphi shows the priestess (called the Pythia) without mystery, as a woman seated on a tripod. The 615 responses known from Delphi are made up of contemporary enquiries and those which are set in Homeric times but recalled by later writers. The contemporary enquiries relate mainly to matters of worship, law, custom or sacrifice. The latter relate to personal affairs whose fulfilment is usually neither explicitly religious nor political. The oracles were chiefly designed to give simple commands on religious matters. Their use by states in matters of political importance was rare. Individuals were chiefly concerned for healing or good fortune.

Divine healing: Asclepios

The temple-cult of Asclepios, the god of healing, was set up principally in times of great need, expecially by city-states threatened by disease. It thrived because rich people who were healed rewarded the cult with wealth, though payment was not required from the poor. It became the most widespread of all the newer cults, with important centres at Pergamon and Corinth as well as Epidauros and Kos.

Apart from the environment of cleanliness and pure air, a combination of exercise, cold baths, rest, herbal prescriptions and diet were employed, along with dreams induced by suggestion. The god was believed to visit the supplicant as he slept.

The rites at Samothrace were open to men and women, children, slave and free. There were both public and private aspects. Initiation took candidates through several levels. The first stage was performed in the *anaktoron*, divided into a main hall, which even the uninitiated could enter, plus an inner sanctum. The higher stage was performed in a separate building, the *hieron*. This was an assembly hall, with benches along the side wall for spectators. An inscription at the entrance in Greek and Latin proclaimed 'the uninitiated may not enter here'. Initiates undressed and, as shown in a relief of Demeter pouring water over a naked man, underwent a ritual bathing, before receiving a purple garment. The initiate proceeded to the central area of the hall, and pledged ultimate secrecy before a sacred hearth on which small animals were offered.

At a much later (Roman) stage, in the second century AD, the structure underwent remodelling to accompany a dramatic change in the ceremonies. The apse was restructured so that one could descend into a crypt beneath. The space above was separated from that below by a grating. Over this a bull or goat was slaughtered, so that the one beneath—initiate or priest—was drenched in its blood.

The great Roman goddess Juno was associated with women, the moon and hunting. She was often identified with the Greek goddess Hera.

Mars was the Roman god of war, first in importance after Jupiter.

The Gods of Ancient Greece and Rome

The ancient Greeks had a very precise understanding of their gods, including their family histories and their characters. The gods lived on Mt Olympus, ruled by Zeus. The gods of ancient Rome, by contrast, were not clearly defined. But when the Romans conquered Greece, they took over the Greek gods, giving them new names and identifying them with their own gods.

Greek name
Roman name

ARES
   MARS

The violent and quarrelsome god of war.

APHRODITE
   VENUS

The goddess of love, beauty and fertility.

APOLLO

The god of flocks and herds, archery, music, prophecy and medicine. As Phoebus, 'the bright one', he was also the sun-god.

ARTEMIS
   DIANA

The goddess of hunting, fertility and childbirth.

ASCLEPIOS
   AESCULAPIUS

The god of healing. His staff coiled with snakes is still the symbol of medicine.

ATHENA
   MINERVA

The goddess of war and handicrafts.

Neptune, the Roman god of the sea, was identified with the Greek god Poseidon.

Mercury, the equivalent of the Greek Hermes, was god of trade and merchandise and also messenger of the other gods.

Greek name
Roman name

DEMETER
CERES

The goddess of corn and crops.

DIONYSUS
BACCHUS

Associated with the underworld, and with crops, fruit and wine. Worship of Dionysus involved ecstatic dances and orgies.

HEPHAESTUS
VULCAN

The god of fire, especially volcanoes and the blacksmith's forge. Also patron of crafts.

HERA
JUNO

Wife of Zeus. The patroness of marriage, childbirth and women.

HERMES
MERCURY

The messenger of the gods. Also god of merchants and traders.

HESTIA
VESTA

The goddess of the hearth, the home and the family. Also the goddess of the city of Rome.

POSEIDON
NEPTUNE

First called the 'earthshaker', the causer of earthquakes, but later identified as god of the sea.

ZEUS
JUPITER

The father of gods and men, though not the creator-god. Also god of the sky and weather.

Syncretism in Egypt

Two cults from Egypt provide an interesting illustration of further syncretism with the Ancient Near East. The cult of Serapis was created in Egypt under the Ptolemies as an intentional fusion of the Greek mysteries with the native Egyptian cult of Osiris, a funerary deity. The name itself was a compound of Osiris and Apis, the sacred bull. Serapis became a manifestation of the one god. Attached to his cult-centres were functionaries who proclaimed the power and mighty deeds of the god.

The second cult is that of Isis, originally the personification of the pharaoh's throne. In the ancient myth she became important as the king's divine mother in whose lap he sat, a 'madonna-and-child' image. She also became associated with the royal succession myth of Osiris and Horus, in which she was a deliverer.

Under the impact of Hellenistic syncretism these two cults of Isis and Serapis may be brought together. These deities had the power of deliverance from war, prison, pain, wandering, shipwreck, even death; and were believed to guide mankind, for they saw the manifold deeds of both the wicked and the just. They were expected to grant to the righteous, where such righteousness is individual virtue, appropriate sacrifice, and a share of blessings received.

The Western enigma

As the Greek world entered the Iron Age, the loosely-knit Etruscan confederation of twelve fortified cities in north-west Italy shared a Late Bronze culture. The Etruscans imitated both Greek vases and Near Eastern bronzes, and blended their themes. Greek and Eastern gods and myths were also absorbed and blended.

The Etruscans, like the Greeks, adapted the Semitic alphabet for inscriptions, notably on tombs. The later Roman tradition, with access to Etruscan religious writings now lost, credited the Etruscans with being 'a people who above all others were distinguished by their devotion to religious practices'.

The Roman Republican expansion

Rome—the beginnings

Historically, the event which marked the beginning of actual Roman achievement was the sacking of the city of Rome in 387 BC by those same marauding Gauls who helped eliminate the Etruscans. Until then the central Mediterranean had suffered rivalry among the Greeks of Magna Graecia in southern Italy, the Phoenicians centred on Carthage, and the Etruscans. The conflict focussed on Sicily. It was the disruption of this balance of power which permitted Rome to move swiftly, deploying the sword, founding colonies and building roads, to bring all Italy south of the Po under their rule within a century.

The extension of Roman citizenship to the conquered peoples redefined the relation between old adversaries. A new world power was created, charged with the religious spirit of *Roma*. To the original twelve Etruscan and thirty Latin cities, this expansion added a further 350 towns south of the Apennines and another eighty in the Po Valley, all under the dominion of Rome.

The historical character of Rome, which took shape in the centuries between the two sackings of the city—by Gauls in 387 BC and by Goths in AD 410—is best described on two levels: the social institutions on which the structure of urban life rests, and the buildings, known to archaeology, in which the structure was contained. At the first level the focus of attention is on the army, the law, the populace and the religion. The architectural needs of each caused the city's buildings to be erected. Nothing was planned, it simply grew.

Religion of hearth and field and city

Just as the myth of Rome as *the* city of cities was to dominate the political aspect of Roman self-understanding, so the myth of their own religiousness was to dominate their personal and cultic insights. Cicero (106–43) put it clearly: 'If we compare ourselves with other peoples, in various things we appear equal or even inferior, except that of religion, meaning the worship of the gods, in which we are by far superior.' 'Religion' (*religio*) is a Latin concept; there was no exact equivalent in Greek.

Latin authors could speak of a person as having a 'religious nature free of superstition'; or affirm that 'it is proper to be religious but not to be superstitious', contrasting the positive and negative elements of belief. On the other hand, the late Republic came to be sceptical of older religious forms still practised. Authors, with the bondage of religious duties in mind, could affirm that religion is that from which the soul (Lucretius), or oneself and one's household (Livius), ought to be freed.

The documented evidence provides little knowledge of early Roman domestic religion. The structure of the laws, especially those relating to women and marriage, children and inheritance, bears out the links of household and hearth, with paternal domination expressed in religious custom and ritual. The 'Twelve Tables', the oldest law code, are strictly civil.

To the Romans, gods were functions. Irrespective of what myths might have been attached to a particular deity, the Roman concern was to assign the precise office, so that the office rather than the older personification received appropriate worship. Agricultural deities could simply define the basic processes: Vervactor (first ploughing, or digging up stubble), Redarator (second ploughing), Imporcitor (cross-ploughing), Insitor (seeding), Obarator (covering of seeds), Occator (harrowing), Sarritor (hoeing), Subruncinator (weeding), Messor (harvesting), Convector (transporting), Conditor (storing), Promitor (utilizing). In a similar vein the ancient 'Calendar of Numa' details the days of each month on which business or assemblies might (or might not) be conducted, as well as the great variety of festivals.

The houses at Pompei, buried following the erruption of Vesuvius in AD 79 show vividly the domestic, social and religious life of a Roman city.

The communal religion was related to the basic agricultural economy, and so was dependent upon the Etruscans and others, for Rome developed too late to foster more than the mythology of her own creation. This religion was primarily that of the state, with the city personified as the chief deity. The Romans were aware of the need to accept some foreign gods, especially Greek, into their state-cult, and they modified these deities to fit their functional need. Livius (59 BC–AD 17) claims that the first celebration in Rome of a public offering of a sacred meal to images of Greek deities placed on couches (*lectisternium*) took place in 399 BC. To justify the adoption of foreign gods, the Romans claimed to confuse foreign deities with their own.

Three of the oldest deities—Jupiter, Juno and Minerva—were worshipped in an impressively large temple on the Capitoline hill. They are thus known as the 'Capitoline Triad'. The temple was dedicated to Jupiter the Best and Greatest (*Jupiter Optimus Maximus*): his was the central hall of worship, flanked by those of Juno and Minerva to the right and left.

Other deities followed in the remaining centuries BC in response to various communal needs or crises, such as the cult of Aesculapius (Greek Asclepios) to overcome pestilence in 293–291, or that of the Cybele to counteract Hannibal's military threat in 204. At the turn of the era, Augustus (63 BC–AD 14) could still be described as one who 'treated with great respect such foreign rites as were ancient and well-established, but held the rest in contempt'. That distinction of old versus new in matters of religion was characteristic. Conservatism was maintained by the high priest, *pontifex maximus*; open-mindedness was fostered by the *viri sacris faciundis*, religious officials who were responsible for the introduction of a new idea precisely when it was most appropriate.

Foreign elements could be brought into Rome; and equally, those already present might be suppressed or driven out. Hence the official Senate decree of 7 October, 186 BC, which severely limited the celebrations of the Bacchanalia and the number of its followers. This applied not only to Rome but also to its allies, and arose from the supposed threat of societies which meet in secret or conduct secret rites.

Among legitimate groupings within Rome were various associations of pontiffs, augurs and auspices; flamens or special priests for individual gods; and the vestal virgins.

If we explore the relation of domestic with communal religion in Rome, the observation made as early as 1911 by W.W. Fowler remains most pertinent: 'In no other ancient State that we know of did the citizen so entirely resign the regulation of all his dealings with the State's gods to the constituted authorities set over him. His obligatory part in the religious ritual of the State was simply *nil*, and all his religious duty on days of religious importance was to abstain from civil business and to make no disturbance.'

Beliefs and philosophy

Marcus Tullius Cicero wrote *On the Nature of the Gods* in 45 BC in the form of a dialogue among several of the intellectual positions of his day: Sceptic, Epicurean and Stoic. Two important traditions are absent: the Peripatetic (if the Stoics were really different from Aristotle as he was by then understood) and the Cynic position which was merely described.

The importance of the various positions lies simply in the fact that religion until then had no explicit intellectual content. It hinged exclusively on ritual: right doing, not right thinking, and certainly not yet right believing. For until the first century

'... there are many things in philosophy which have not yet been satisfactorily explained, particularly that most obscure and most difficult question concerning the nature of the gods, which is so extremely important both for a knowledge of the human soul and also for the regulation of religion.'

Cicero, *The Nature of the Gods* 1.1

The Romans used charms to ward off evil. These bronze hands are covered with magic symbols.

The later Roman emperors were considered to be divine. This cameo shows the Emperor Augustus being crowned as he sits beside the goddess Roma.

BC the vocabulary of belief was hardly coined. The value of this practical religion can be quite bluntly stated: 'Men describe Jupiter as best and greatest not because he makes us just or temperate or wise, but because he makes us healthy, rich and prosperous.'

For the relatively few who were caught up in the discussion or could read, or for the larger audience to whom the philosophical views were preached by itinerants, there began that transformation by which religion came to mean an intellectual consideration of god, gods and the world. The several philosophies ask essentially three questions: 'What is the nature of the world?' 'How do I know the world?' 'How am I to live in the world?' Although theologically they produced different systems in response, they began with similar assumptions in answer to these questions:

● Matter is the sole reality.

● Senses are the sole source of knowledge.

● Being untroubled and undisturbed

is the nature of happiness or pleasure.

The Epicurean position was that gods exist but they have no concern for the world. The Stoic position was that the world is ruled by a divine rationality (*logos*), manifest as fate and providence, and closely related to human reason. Scepticism was a by-product of the Platonic Academy, sharing in the common assumptions. Its appeal was to the one who 'suspends judgement about things that are either good or bad by nature, or that are to be practised or not practised, and in so doing he resists the dogmatic tendency and follows without strong convictions either way the observances of everyday life', achieving thereby the desired untroubled state. Cynics are 'dog-like' (*kunikos*) because they substitute for a system a way of life blatantly rejecting all imposed values. They identified the ideal life with that of nature. Taking nothing but the beggar's knapsack and staff, delighting in flouting all standards of decency, they wandered about with a minimum of food or shelter, though often functioning as missionaries by preaching on the street corners.

Empire— the Roman world

When Vergil (70–19 BC) wrote the *Aeneid* to honour the emperor Augustus by linking him with Rome's past, Augustus not only restored the hut of Romulus, but—with due conservative propriety and patience—absorbed into himself the whole religious tradition of the city by assuming the office of high priest. A temple of Roma and Augustus at Ostia expresses the result. Throughout the time of the empire, even the older gods of the state cult, with the exception of the major deities—Jupiter, Juno and Minerva—gave way to the increasingly dominant cult of the imperial house.

Deification Roman style

Republican Rome, even with its dictators, had avoided constitutionally the absolute rule of Hellenistic kings. A precedent was set by the Roman Senate on the assassination of Julius Caesar in 44 BC, when he was enrolled among the gods. The deification of his successor, Augustus, had been demanded in parts of the empire, especially the east, while Augustus was still alive, and divine honours were accorded him in some places. Though the Senate's action in proclaiming Augustus divine followed the precedent, Tiberius (42 BC–AD 37), who succeeded him, stoutly resisted deification, and so much angered the Senate that he was not even acclaimed as a god upon his death. Thereafter, apart from Nero and the three unsuccessful military. contenders for his position, all the early emperors received a place among the gods: even Gaius Caligula (AD 12–41), who had assumed it for himself while living, and Domitian (AD 51–96), who did likewise, though without reaffirmation by the Senate.

From the days of Augustus oaths of allegiance to the emperor were required from the Roman businessmen making money in the provinces. These show him as already 'son of a god' and express loyalty not only to him but 'to his children and descendants'. From the coronation of Caligula, the oath includes Augustus between 'Zeus the Saviour' and 'the holy Virgin of our city' (Athena Polias). Such oaths were engraved in bronze (at the oath-takers' expense) and mounted for all to see.

The religious mix of imperial Rome

The disastrous eruption of Vesuvius began on the morning of 24 August, AD 79, and by evening had buried the two flourishing cities of Pompeii and Herculaneum and the coastal resort of Stabiae. Martial asserted that 'even for gods this was going too far'. Many other cities of the ancient Mediterranean world have been destroyed and buried, but none so completely preserved in the process.

The religious evidence from Pompeii is of two principal forms. There are buildings: both official buildings, innumerable domestic shrines and wayside altars. We also have works of art, especially frescos, and inscriptions of all sorts, including graffiti and even papyri.

Family cults flourished. Nearly every house and workshop had its private shrine (*lararium*), normally housing busts of ancestors and other traditional household gods (the *Lares* and *Penates*). The simple rites at these shrines were part of daily life and under the care of the paternal head of the household, and would have included rituals for important family events such as the coming of age of the heir. Many plaques and statues have been found, representing various minor deities—Faunus, Silvanus, Flora, Priapus and so on. They are largely concerned with fruitfulness and reproduction, plenty and gain. Wreaths of fruit, or horns of plenty (*cornucopiae*) were commonplace. So too was the phallus, either alone or gigantically displayed on a little deity, often with scales to weigh its fullness.

Official cults were more elaborate but their remains are fewer. Pompeii had ten temples, but three had been wrecked in the earlier earthquake of AD 62 and were still unrepaired at the

'It is hard to say whether the birthday of the most divine Caesar is more joyful or more advantageous; we may rightly regard it as like the beginning of all things, if not in the world of nature, yet in advantage. There is nothing that was decaying and declining to unfortunate state that he did not restore, and he gave a fresh appearance to the whole universe, which would have been content to accept its own ruin if there had not been born the universal blessing of all— Caesar Augustus. The birthday of the god was the beginning of the good news (*evangelion*) to the world on account of him.'

Roman Proconsul to Provincial Assembly of Asia, 9 BC

Secret Knowledge: the Gnostics

Edwin Yamauchi

The Gnostics were followers of a variety of religious movements in the early Christian centuries which stressed salvation through 'secret knowledge' (gnosis). We know about these movements, known as Gnosticism, through the writings of the church fathers of the second century, who viewed the various Gnostic groups as heretical perversions of Christianity.

Another source of information, though admittedly very late, is the writings from the Mandaeans. The Mandaeans, who live in present-day Iraq and Iran, are the sole surviving remnants of the ancient Gnostics.

In 1945 a priceless cache of twelve Coptic codices was found at Nag Hammadi in Upper Egypt. The collection, which was deposited about AD 400, contains fifty-three treatises, including both Christian and non-Christian Gnostic texts.

Pre-Christian Gnosticism

As a result of these discoveries, modern scholars see Gnosticism as a religious phenomenon which may have been quite independent of Christianity. There is as yet no clear agreement about when or how it originated.

In spite of the lack of clear and early evidences, some scholars, such as R. Bultmann, have assumed a pre-Christian origin of Gnosticism. Bultmann explained the Prologue to the Gospel of John as the revision of an originally Gnostic document. Such a reconstruction is extremely speculative.

The safest conclusion from the available evidence is that Gnosticism existed in rudimentary form at the end of the first century AD. It is altogether hazardous to read back the fully-developed Gnosticism of the second century AD into earlier texts.

Spirits and demons

In clearly Gnostic systems there is a sharp dualism—an opposition between a transcendent God and an ignorant 'demiurge' or creator (who is often a caricature of God in the Old Testament). The material creation is viewed as evil. Sparks of divinity, however, have been encapsulated in the bodies of certain 'spiritual' individuals destined for salvation.

These 'spiritual' persons are ignorant of their celestial origins. God sends down to them a redeemer, often a Christ who merely seems to be human, to bring them salvation in the form of gnosis. Thus awakened, the 'spiritual' escape from the prison of their bodies at death and traverse the planetary spheres of hostile demons to be reunited with God.

Since salvation is not dependent upon faith or works but upon the knowledge of one's 'spiritual' nature, some Gnostics indulged in extremely licentious behaviour. Most Gnostics, however, took a radically ascetic attitude towards sex and marriage, deeming the creation of woman the source of evil, and the procreation of children to be but the multiplication of souls in bondage to the powers of darkness.

The Mandaeans: Gnostic Survivors

Edwin Yamauchi

The 15,000 or more Mandaeans who live in southern Iraq and Iran are the sole surviving remnants of ancient Gnosticism. Their texts, which are written in an eastern Aramaic dialect known as Mandaic, are an important source of Gnostic teachings.

The oldest texts are lead amulets from about the third century AD, followed by magic bowls from about AD 600. The important religious manuscripts are not older than the sixteenth century, with most coming from the eighteenth and nineteenth centuries.

Knowledge of life

The most important work, the Ginza, relates the creation of the universe and the fate of the soul after death. The Johannesbuch reveals that the Mandaeans venerate John the Baptist. They regard Jesus, however, as a false prophet. The Haran Gawaita gives us a legendary account of their alleged migration from Palestine.

In their dualistic world-view, it is Ptahil who creates the world with the aid of the evil Ruha, 'Spirit'. Manda d-Haiye, 'Gnosis (Knowledge) of Life', reveals himself to man as an incarnation of three heavenly spirits (uthras). At death the soul of the Mandaean leaves behind his 'stinking' body and ascends to the world of light.

The Mandaeans observe elaborate rituals. The masbuta is a magically purifying rite of baptism. At death a sacramental meal (masiqta) is celebrated to assist the soul in its journey to the world of light. The Mandaeans have a highly-developed code of ethics, including a stress upon marriage and children which is quite unique among Gnostics.

Many scholars have argued for a pre-Christian origin of the Mandaeans from Palestine. The objective evidence, however, does not prove that Mandaeism existed earlier than the second century AD.

time of their burial. One had been converted to the use of a private association; two were dedicated to the imperial cult, one to the most recently enrolled member, Vespasian (AD 9–79), who died just one month before the eruption, and the other to Fortuna Augusta. Graffiti bear out the people's nonchalant attitude towards this cult: 'Augustus Caesar's mother was only a woman!' Of the remaining four temples, only that dedicated to the cult of triune Isis, her consort Serapis and their divine child Harpocrates showed the signs of prosperity coming from popular support. Wall-size frescos indicate the religious life within this sanctuary as conducted by its white-robed, shaven-headed priests.

Apart from the buildings designed for religious use, we have the houses of rich and poor, in which were displayed not only wealth and varying aesthetic taste and styles, but also frescos or mosaics of religious themes. The most important of these is the sixty-roomed 'Villa of the Mysteries': one room presents on three walls twenty-nine figures nearly life-size, subdivided into ten group scenes, acting out a complex Bacchic ritual. This was entirely a woman's rite. It is impossible to say what place this great house or its spectacular scene played within the religious life of the city—perhaps somewhere in between the few great temples and the numerous little shrines.

The preserved ruins of Ostia, the port of Rome, show a different array within this religious mix, including (by the third century AD) not less than fifteen Mithraea—shrines devoted to Mithras (see *Mithraism*).

Philosophical religion

Roman religion was thus a complex mixture from varied sources. Later in the third century AD the mix was to receive a more systematic treatment blending the religious and philosophical elements into a form of Neo-Platonism. Plotinus (205–269) was its founder, and Porphyry (232–305) his expositor. This revived Platonism was a blend of elements from the traditions of Plato himself, Pythagoras, Aristotle, and the Stoics. World-

mind, World-soul and Nature are the descending levels of reality between the Ultimate One, which is the ground of existence and the source of values, and Bare Matter. All these ingredients lie within human nature, whose purpose is to achieve unification in a kind of ecstatic union with the One. This rare union was believed to occur as a result of prolonged effort of the will and understanding. Plotinus makes little explicit reference to religious ritual or particular gods, though the writings of his followers do contain hymns to certain gods. The result is the philosophical equivalent of the 'mysteries'.

A crutch for a tottering state

Of the thirty-five Roman emperors from AD 192 to 284, only three reigned for more than ten years, and only one died a natural death. All the others died of unnatural causes at the hands of troops or counter-claimants, after a reign of less than a year in at least twelve cases. Consequently, few of these imperial figures lived long enough or died in such a way as to receive deification. Most of the emperors, even the stronger ones, preferred to rule under the aegis of some greater deity, since they had perceived that to be declared divine themselves hardly secured them a long life. The most important such god is Aurelianus' choice: *Sol Invictus*, the Unconquered Sun.

It was a mere matter of time before the one resilient religion would be imposed upon the state. This took place in the 'Edict of Milan' issued in 313, jointly by Licinius and Constantine. Christian worship, like any other, was allowed to take place freely; and the Christian church, alone among the competitive cults, was singled out for 'compensation from our benevolence'. It was its organization that gave it an edge over all alternatives, from the authorities' viewpoint, for Christianity, as Arnold Toynbee has said, 'was singular in building up for itself a world-wide administrative organization, instead of letting each local group of converts go its own way'.

'Hence it is that throughout wide empires, provinces, and towns, we see each people having its own individual rites and worshipping the local gods ... but the Romans one and all.'

Minucius Felix, *Octavius* 6.23

The end of antiquity

The remoulding of the Roman Empire as Christian in all senses took more than a century, though Theodosius I had proscribed other religions by AD 381. The old forms, however, lingered on in several ways. Initially 'pagan' (*paganus*) had meant a rural in contrast to an urban dweller, and Christianity had made little headway in the former environment before it became the state religion. By this later date, the term came to designate civilians in general, over against soldiers, and thus took on its 'religious' connotation.

Several remnants of the older religion survived for a while. The short-reigned Julian (361–363), a philosopher like Marcus Aurelius, was the last non-Christian emperor. Symmachus, as prefect of the city in 382, could address to the Western emperor Gratian a passionate plea, upon the removal of the altar of victory from the assembly hall of the Senate, not to terminate all those 'ancestral customs' which 'promote the status of the public worship which has proved an advantage to the state for so long a time'. Rome itself, however, was becoming less advantageous as the capital. Once it had proved vulnerable to Visigothic assault in 410, it was but a matter of time before the imperial government was withdrawn to a safer location.

The sacking of the city after 800 years precipitated a crisis of ideas for a state newly allied to the Christian religion. Augustine of Hippo (391–430) in his *City of God*, carefully sifted all the religiousness of the ancient city and its empire; what was worthwhile was baptized into Christ, the rest was to be put aside for ever. The city, now greatly reduced in dignity and size, became the Christian Rome. Its bishop became the sole remaining officer of rank when the imperial government of the West was transferred north to Ravenna, and then in 476 when the Western empire itself ceased to exist. Rome's change of hands is well illustrated when its bishop, Leo the Great, in office from 440 to 461, assumed the defunct urban title of *pontifex maximus* ('Supreme Pontiff'). The Christian church was the final successor to the ancient religion which was the city, and in such terms the primacy of the church at Rome came to be declared.

Faith of Light and Darkness: the Manichaeans

Edwin Yamauchi

Mani (AD 216–276), a Persian prophet born in Mesopotamia, established a dualistic religion which he claimed was the final, universal revelation.

The Prophet Mani

In 1970 the discovery of a tiny Greek parchment, the Cologne Codex, confirmed Arabic traditions that Mani was raised among the Elchasaites, a Jewish-Christian baptist group. When he was twenty-four, Mani spoke against the water baptisms of the Elchasaites and preached instead salvation by secret knowledge (*gnosis*).

Mani preached in Mesopotamia, Persia and even India. He enjoyed the patronage of Shapur I, a Sasanian (Persian) king. Shapur's son, Bahram I, however, persecuted Mani. After being bound in chains for twenty-six days, Mani died in prison.

Mani, who was a gifted painter, composed a picture-book to propagate his faith among the illiterate. He also wrote seven works, including *The Shapurakan*, dedicated to King Shapur, and *The Living Gospel*, which proclaimed Mani as the Paraclete foretold by Christ. Though we have but few of the earliest texts in Syriac and in Middle Persian, we have thousands of pages of Coptic Manichaean texts which were found in Egypt in 1930. Another later collection of Manichaean texts (eighth and ninth centuries AD) comes from Chinese Turkestan.

Light and Darkness

Mani taught that there were two independent principles, Light and Darkness. In the first epoch Light and Darkness were separate; in the second they were intermingled; and in this the final epoch they were to be separated once more.

Christ is sent to liberate the particles of light in men. Perfected Manichaeans must persevere through ascetic practices until death, when their particles of light will rise up in the Column of Glory (the Milky Way) to paradise.

The Manichaeans were sharply divided between an elite circle known as 'the chosen' (*electi*), and the mass of laymen known as 'hearers' (*auditores*). The 'hearers' lived the lives of ordinary citizens. They offered daily gifts of fruit, cucumbers and melons—which were believed to possess a great deal of light—to the elect.

The Manichaeans were zealous missionaries who carried their faith to Africa, to Europe and even to China. They posed a threat to the Christian church in the fourth century, and numbered among their 'hearers' Augustine before his conversion. They bequeathed some of their dualistic beliefs to heretical groups which flourished in Europe in the Middle Ages, such as the Paulicians, the Bogomils and the Albigenses.

The Old Gods: Religions of Northern Europe

Andrew Walls

The religion of the Northern peoples underlies all modern European life and thought. Northern Europe has been significant in Christian history for its peoples began to embrace the Christian faith in substantial numbers in a period when the faith was losing its hold in some other areas. But to much of the Northern world the faith came late and penetrated slowly. Gaul (modern France) and Spain, nearer to the early Christian Mediterranean heartlands, were long in seeing the rapid conversion movements that had marked those heartlands with their inheritance of Greek and Roman. In Britain the penetration was slower still; the adoption of Christianity by some Celtic peoples was speedily submerged under successive waves of Germanic newcomers.

Not until AD 960 was there a breakthrough in Denmark; later still in Norway, Iceland and Orkney; not until the early twelfth century in Sweden. And thoughts and ways associated with the old life remained for centuries—perhaps still remain—in uneasy tension with biblical religion. The ancient 'primal' religions of the West have been part of modern Europe's unconscious formation, and occasionally come to the surface—as when Nazi Germany artificially revived Teutonic mythology, and gave it a new meaning.

The Northern peoples

Two groups of Northern peoples who dominated the land north of the Mediterranean civilization concern us here, the Celtic and the Germanic. The original home of the Celtic peoples seems to have been in what is now Bavaria. By about 300 BC they had spread out eastward and westward in a vast arc from Ireland to Anatolia. Caesar's Gauls and, if not Paul's Galatians, then at least their neighbours, were Celtic. Successive migrations covered the British Isles. Roman power conquered many of these tribes, and assimilated them in varying degrees to Roman culture; others remained untouched.

The 2,000-year-old 'Tollund man' was discovered in a peat bog in Denmark. He had been ritually strangled, probably as a sacrifice to the goddess of fertility.

Race and language

For centuries Celtic pressure kept the Germanic peoples to Northern lands. Romans, indeed, were often somewhat hazy as to the distinction between these barbarian peoples. But as Roman power declined, that of the various Germanic peoples increased, and the Dark Ages saw their vast expansion. Our concern lies especially with the peoples of Germany (who expanded into Celtic Britain) and those of Scandinavia, famous for their enterprising voyages, their settlements in harsh conditions and their unquenchable predatory instincts. In race, language and the structure of their religion these peoples were related, though we know more details of the religion of the Scandinavian than of the German peoples.

Both the Celtic and the Germanic complexes belonged to the Indo-European language group, which also includes Greek, Latin and Sanskrit; and some scholars (such as Dumézil) have discerned a common structure in the religion between Celtic, Germanic, Roman, Greek, old Persian and Vedic religion in which godhead appears in threefold form. However this may be in principle, the actual worship of one group could strike another as strange and exotic, as we know from Roman accounts of Gauls and Germans.

Our knowledge, very fragmentary and incomplete, comes from four main sources:

Early writers

Writers such as Polybius, Caesar and Tacitus give accounts for readers in civilized Mediterranean lands of the way of life of certain 'barbarian' peoples who were or had been Rome's enemies. They often write in the manner of nineteenth-century anthropological writers, their accent on the quaintness of their subjects tinged with some wistful admiration for these 'noble savages'. Naturally they tend to translate into terms they think their readers will understand, but from comparison with the other sources they come out reasonably well.

Myths and folk tales

Stories of the 'other-world' were preserved by oral tradition and written down in the Christian period. The Scandinavian myths, preserved in Iceland (where Christianity was established in AD 1000) by a writer of genius, Snorri Sturluson (died in 1264), and reflected in other sagas and poems (notably the vivid but tantalizing *Voluspà*) give the fullest account we have of the belief-system of any ancient preliterate people; but even here we must beware of taking everything as of equal value or as reflecting the same religious setting.

Some of the best-known stories, such as the adventures of Thor, dressed as a bride trying to get his

The splendid prow of a Viking ship.

hammer back, are probably not myths at all, but stories for entertainment belonging to a period when belief in the old gods was losing its hold: no one mocks the one who has the power of life and death. The rich Celtic literature is even harder to interpret, for the stories have been divorced from the original religious context altogether, and been preserved through a long period of Christian oral transmission, so that their religious significance has to be pieced together by hints and analogies and comparison.

Christian missionaries

Sometimes Christian writers tell us, usually incidentally, something of the old religion: its survival or its ways of thought. For instance, the correspondence of the English missionary Boniface (680–755) who worked in Frisia, or of the historian Bede writing when Christianity was the dominant faith in England, are full of hints—but only hints, for the Christian writers were rarely interested in the old religion for its own sake—indeed, it revolted them. Occasionally one gets an eyewitness description: most vividly, perhaps, that of Adam of Bremen of the old Swedish religion.

Archaeological finds

This source of material is constantly increasing, and has immensely deepened our knowledge of religious practice. It is, of course, notoriously hard to interpret with assurance, but can be effectively used in combination with the literary sources.

In assessing all the sources it must be remembered that we are dealing with a period of many centuries, and seeing much of that vast period through material collected still later. The religions of primal, preliterate societies have histories just as Christianity, Islam or Buddhism have—they change and develop, and appear in various guises. It is thus perilous to generalize from one place or period to another. This said, the degree of consistency across our fragmentary sources is remarkable.

The Celts: worshippers of the horned god

The history of the Celts before their contact with the Roman Empire is particularly obscure, and their religion hard to interpret. Celtic peculiarities mentioned by classical writers correspond with details revealed by archaeology, but may have been misunderstood. For instance, Lucian of Samosata, the satirist, describes an old man in skins leading adoring disciples by chains attached to his tongue. This was interpreted for him by a Hellenized Celt as representing the Herculean strength of eloquence; how does this connect with the Gaulish coins and Irish stories which depict chains from a head or mouth with severed heads attached?

Julius Caesar's account of the Gauls he fought (*Gallic War* 6.14) is based on personal acquaintance: but when he says that the Gauls worship Mercury above all gods, while keeping appropriate worship for Apollo, Mars, Jupiter and Minerva, we may suspect that he is imposing a framework he knew on something he did not fully understand.

The inscriptions in Britain and Gaul show Romanized expressions of Celtic religion: Celts who are using some of the language or images or divine names of the Romans, or perhaps Roman soldiers keeping on the right side of the local gods. The Irish and Welsh stories come from a still later period, when the old gods had been formally abandoned. It is clear, however, that some of the strange figures in the stories are in fact the old divine beings described in human form.

Local gods

As we have seen, Caesar assumed the Gallic Celts worshipped the same gods as the Romans, though under different names. 'Of these deities', he says, 'they have almost the same idea as all other nations.' Certainly some inscriptions show the imagery associated with the Roman gods Mercury, Mars and Silvanus. But while many divine names—Cocidius, Nodons, Braciaca and others—appear in in-

A Viking helmet from the Sutton Hoo treasure in Britain shows both the rich culture and the warlike nature of the northern peoples.

scriptions, no single name appears so consistently as to suggest his universal worship. Clearly local names were used at local shrines for deities associated particularly with those places. In Romanized areas these gods might be linked with the Roman deities whose functions theirs most nearly resembled.

Cernunnos: The Horned One

The most widely distributed Celtic divine symbol is of a god with horns. There are signs of an antlered god amongst the Bronze Age predecessors of the historic Celts, and in many parts of the Celtic world and in many periods one can find symbols of the stag, or a horned naked god with phallus erect (a common fertility symbol in many cultures), or a serpent with a ram's head. The symbols range from crude scrawls to the beautiful artistry of the Gundestrup bowl. One inscription seems to identify the antlered god as 'Cernunnos', perhaps meaning 'The Horned One'.

That the Horned One is a symbol of fertility is not open to doubt; but some of the Romanized inscriptions clearly make him also a warrior-god, a Celtic Mars. Such indications raise the question of whether the Celts 'departmentalized' the universe under different divinities, or whether their devotion tended to be directed to a divinity associated with a particular place or people, but manifesting himself in various ways as fertility or war predominated in their concerns.

The Horned One sometimes has a consort; and 'Earth Mothers' clearly played a part in worship. The forceful female figures of some of the Irish stories are doubtless memories of them—mysterious, vigorous, beautiful and consuming. They are often represented (and again the stories have similar features) in groups of three.

A High God

Did the Celts have a High God? No trace of such a cult can be found among the physical remains; yet a modern observer might visit hundreds of African peoples where the High God is recognized and see no material sign of his worship.

In the Irish stories concerning the mighty figure of Dagda one can trace, in reduced, humanized form, something of a great divinity of the past, who cannot be seen as simply a fertility or a warrior symbol. Yet the name is found only in the stories. Perhaps the stories of Dagda are a pointer to a more enlarged concept of divinity than one would receive from archaeology alone; and perhaps Celtic concepts were either more comprehensive or less tidy than Roman writers imagined.

Human sacrifice

Water-sources—wells and springs, and the sources of rivers necessary to fertility of the soil and the support of life—seem to have been favourite centres of Celtic worship, and shafts and pits found at such places were presumably used in sacrifice. Some elaborate pre-Roman structures have been found at Entremont and Roquepertuse, for instance, but in general early sanctuaries would have seen simple. In the Roman period temples on the Roman pattern occur, sometimes enclosing thermal springs. Several classical writers speak of Celtic worship being conducted in sacred groves.

The feature of Celtic religion that most impressed Roman writers was its violence and prevalence of human sacrifice. Possibly they exaggerated, as observers often exaggerate exotic features; none the less, there is plenty of other evidence in their favour.

The human head had a significance we cannot fully fathom. It is central to the great early sanctuaries at Entremont and Roquepertuse, the latter full of niches for heads, and the severed head is perhaps the most widespread feature in all Celtic imagery. Just a hint of what the head cult must have meant in the old religion is given in the Welsh *Mabinogion*, where the companions of Bendigeid Vran, having removed his head, enjoy eighty gloriously happy years, known as 'the Entertaining of the Noble Head', and 'it was not more irksome to them having the head with them than if Bendigeid Vran had been with them himself'.

Ancestor-cult is suggested both by the signs of worship at grave mounds and Caesar's insistence that the Gauls claim common descent from a deity, otherwise unattested, that he refers to as Dis Pater.

Life after death

The evidence of the graves with carefully-chosen grave goods points to some emphasis on the afterlife. Caesar speaks as though the Gauls believed in transmigration of souls. Some have thought that he simply means shape-changing, as practised by the shamans of the older peoples of Central Europe; but Irish stories such as that of the rebirth of Etain may suggest that Caesar's words should be taken seriously. At any rate, he had noted something about Celtic belief in the afterlife which to a Roman seemed strange.

The Druids

All the classical writers were impressed by the Druids, the Celtic religious functionaries. When Strabo speaks of them as students of moral philosophy he is probably idealizing: their role in sacrifice, divination and liturgy ('they commit to memory immense amounts of poetry', says Caesar) is better attested.

The possible links of Celtic tradition with that of Vedic India remain tantalizingly speculative. After the Christian triumph in Celtic lands residual beliefs were diverted, some local divinities became identified as evil spirits, some others, with their healing cults, perhaps being merged into Christian saints.

The Germanic peoples: mortal gods

The Roman historian Tacitus, about AD 98, describing the *Germani* of his day, is very conscious of the gulf between them and 'civilized man' in Roman society, but betrays envy of their vigour and simplicity. Like other Romans, he is most conscious of the militancy of the Germans, their proneness to battle, the constant flowing of blood; but he admires the austere family morality of a chaste and essentially monogamous people.

Like other Roman writers, he identifies the Germanic gods with what he assumes to be their Roman equivalents, and detects a triad of Mercury (the god most venerated), Mars and Hercules at the heart of Germanic devotion. He also notes the cult of a female deity, which he believes to be imported and identifies with that of Isis. Hercules is elaborately invoked before battle, and the war god presides over the administration of justice. With some surprise, Tacitus notes that it is the priests who prescribe the punishment of offenders.

Divination practices, he observes, are similar to the Roman, but include strange practices such as those associated with horses. And women have something of 'holiness and prophecy' about them which gives them some influence in German society, though he does not elaborate on this 'prophetic' function.

German deities

The triad noted by Tacitus was presumably Wotan, Tiwaz and Thor. The Germanic peoples were essentially polytheistic, and many divine names are known. Nevertheless, over the millennium and more which separates Tacitus from the Icelandic writer Snorri Sturluson and the observer of late Swedish paganism, Adam of Bremen, three, or sometimes four, divine names tend to be mentioned as though they summed up the Germanic divine world. Two

The richly-carved 'Franks casket' shows many scenes from Norse mythology. These are the three norns, who watered and tended Yggdrasil, the tree of life.

are constant: the divinity known by the Southern peoples as Wotan or Woden (whose name is perpetuated in the calendar as Wednesday) and by the Norse peoples as Odin; and the thunder-deity Thor, who has left his name as Thursday.

In early accounts Tiwaz (of Tuesday) the legislator divinity, is crucial, but in the Norse literature his successor Tyr plays a rather marginal part. There, however, the fertility-god Frey (of Friday), with or without his female counterpart Freyja, is very prominent.

According to Sturluson, there are two groups of divinities, of differing origins, once at war but now united: the Aesir (including Odin and Thor) and the Vanir (including Frey). While some have followed Sturluson in seeing this as having a basis in historical fact, an Aesir-worshipping people vanquishing a Vanir-worshipping people but adopting something of their religion, others see the tension between the active, intervening deities (Aesir) and the maintaining, reproductive deities (Vanir) as funda-

mental to all Germanic, and perhaps all Indo-European, religion.

Aristocratic Odin

Norse religion, of which (thanks to Snorri and the other saga-tellers) we know a little more than we do of related peoples like the Saxons, varied according to social divisions and preoccupations. The active cult of Odin was for leaders and warriors, for the Viking in fact. Odin gives victory—but, fickle and capricious, he is as likely to take it away again. Through the Valkyries he collects heroes for his great hall, Valhalla, where the days are spent in battle and the nights in feasting. He has one eye (for he surrendered one for a single drink of the spring of wisdom and understanding); he hung nine days and nights from the world-tree Yggdrasil, to learn how to read the hidden runes. A whole complex of ideas—wisdom, poetry, heroic warfare, shape-changing, strangulation, death—belong to him, and the grim stories of ritual killings by noose and spear suggest something of early

The most spectacular feat performed by the god Thor was his encounter with the Midgard serpent which encircles the earth. Thor attempted to catch it from a fishing-boat.

forms of devotion to him.

For other people dependent on agriculture the fertility cult of Frey could not be neglected. Adam of Bremen tells us of this deity's mighty phallic image at Uppsala about 1070.

The hammer of 'Black Thor'

The most widespread devotion of all would seem to belong to Thor. At Uppsala his throne stood between that of Odin and that of Frey; and in the late Northern paganism 'Black Thor (from the colour of his images?) was above all the enemy of the 'White Christ'. His sign, the hammer, was used in weddings and as a protective act, rather as Christians used the sign of the cross; and, as archaeology reveals, Christians took a cross to the grave, when traditional pagans took a hammer.

Thor, like the Vedic Indra, is a thunder-god, full of chaotic energy and boundless power. And if princely leaders saw Odin as their patron, the ordinary man was more likely to seek a friend in Thor.

In many stories Thor is associated with Loki, a strange, ambivalent trickster figure. It is Loki who secures by a trick the death of Odin's son Balder, the fairest of the gods. The Balder myth is beautiful, but there is little sign that he was worshipped.

The doom of the gods

Nor is there any sign of a High God. In the chaos of divine energy, the worshipper chooses the divinity most likely to favour him. The gods themselves will pass away—for at some time there will fall the day of Ragnarök, the doom of the gods, when each will fall in mortal combat, and earth and mankind will perish with them. Then a new heaven and earth will arise, and Balder return from the dead, and the male and female creatures sheltering in the world-tree will people the new world. In the end, Yggdrasil, the self-renewing world-tree, must be greater than Odin, the great god, who hung in its branches to gain its secrets.

The Norse Gods

Aesir

The great gods who lived in Asgard

ODIN/WODEN/ WOTAN
Father of all the gods and 'father of the slain'. God of war, worshipped especially by leaders and warriors.

THOR
'The thunderer', depicted as a great giant with a hammer. The strongest of the gods. God of fertility.

BALDER
'The bright one', the most beautiful of the gods. Son of Odin and Freyja.

LOKI
A mischievous god, the father of monsters. He brought harm to the gods, especially by causing the death of Balder.

Vanir

Lesser gods, formerly at war with the Aesir, but later reconciled.

NJORD
Ruler of the wind and sea.

FREY
Ruler of the rain and sun. God of fertility. Son of Njord.

FREYJA/FRIGG
Goddess of love and fertility. Consort of Odin, sister of Frey.

HEIMDALL
'The white god', watchman of the gods.

Valkyries

Odin's war-maidens. They chose warriors who died in battle to be received into Valhalla, the favourite home of Odin.

Nomads of the Steppes

Åke Hultkrantz

Some 3,000 years ago the wide steppes of southern Russia were sparsely populated by Indo-European peoples: the Cimmerians west of the Caspian Sea, the Persians east of it. The northern Persians, or Scythians, developed into horse-riding nomads about this time or soon afterwards.

This had tremendous historical consequences. Not only did they, in the seventh century BC overrun the Cimmerian lands, so that their territory stretched from present-day Romania to Turkestan; they also opened communications between East and West, so that religious ideas and art forms ('animal style') streamed over the open steppes. Long after the disappearance of the Scythians, this road to China constituted a major link between Western (Christian) and Eastern religious ideas. The famous silk route (from the first century AD) partly followed the same way.

The Greek historian Herodotus (fifth century BC) gives some interesting information on Scythian religion. The foremost divinities were the Sky Father, Papa, married to Mother Earth, Api. Among other deities, all apparently heavenly beings, were the fire- and war-gods. There were no images of the gods, altars or temples. The gods received animal sacrifices, usually horses. They were strangled, and their meat cooked over a fire that was made on their bones. A piece of the meat was thrown into the fire.

They had a war-god who was represented by an iron sword raised on a heap of brushwood. To him were sacrificed cattle and horses in large numbers, as well as prisoners of war; their blood was poured over the god's sword. Herodotus also mentions diviners, who, however, were killed when they were unsuccessful.

When a king died his corpse was carried around on a wagon among the tribes of his domain, followed by his wives and servants in a long procession. He was finally buried in a wooden chamber together with several court servants (who were strangled), his horses and some golden bowls. An enormous earth mound was heaped over the burial place. The bereaved cleansed themselves by entering a tent filled with steam from hemp seeds that had been thrown on red-hot stones.

This is the first description we have of a religion of the horse nomads. Its essentials fit in rather well with what we know of later religions among equestrian pastoralists. The pattern of horse nomadism spread to the Mongol and Turko-Tataric tribes to the east of the Scythian area and on the plateaux of central Asia. Here the war-like religion of the plains joined the traditional hunting religions with master-of-the-animals concepts and shamanism, and formed a new type of religion.

The Mongols: a sense of wonder

A good illustration of this kind of religion is offered by the Mongols of central Asia. From tribal beginnings in north-eastern Asia they ousted the Turkish peoples of Mongolia and then built up an empire that stretched from the Amur River to the Volga and beyond—the greatest empire the world had seen (thirteenth and fourteenth centuries AD). Their primitive beginnings, nomadic way of life and stratified patriarchal society were all reflected in their religion.

Tengri

The supreme god was Tengri, a name by which both the god and the blue sky were designated. Prayers were directed to him by lone supplicants bowing down on mountain-tops, and juniper incense was burned in his honour. Like other nomadic high gods Tengri was not represented by pictures. He did not create the world. In all of central Asia the beginning of the world was referred to two creators, one a good spirit (but not Tengri), the other a devil. This story of creation was diffused from Europe to North America and was sometimes combined with the flood myth, sometimes with the myth of a primeval sea.

'Tengri' is, however, also a word for everything 'heavenly', wonderful or marvellous, and for ninety-nine tengri gods that in particular protect the herds. For instance, Ataga tengri gives luck in horse-breeding, another tengri protects the cows, still another the yaks. Manaqan tengri is the guardian of the wild game.

Landmarks like mountains, lakes and rivers were worshipped. In particular the mountains inspired great awe. Passes and mountain-tops were residences of spirits, and whoever passed by had to propitiate these spirits by throwing a stone on a pile of rocks, a so-called *obo*. The ground was sacred, and libations were poured out for Mother Earth.

Genghis Khan

Dead princes and tribal ancestors had their own shrines. Chingis Khan—better known as Genghis Khan—the mighty ruler of the Mongols (died AD 1227), was considered to be of heavenly descent. A statue representing him was raised on a wagon in the military camp, and horses were dedicated to him. Sometimes he was mentioned as Tengri himself, sometimes as a culture-hero who had initiated all cultural and religious institutions. Offerings were also given to other deceased great princes by their descendants: most often horses were impaled above their graves. The Mongols of the Golden Horde in southern Russia suspended horse skins upon poles over the graves of their great leaders.

At the entrance of their tents the Mongols placed house idols (*ongons*) to whom they offered milk. These *ongons* were made of felt.

There was a 'fire mother' to whom butter was offered regularly. At the end of the year she also received a bone from a sheep, and ritual hymns were addressed to her. Fire was supposed to have cleansing power.

Shamanism

The tribal leaders were also shamans, that is, experts who cured diseases and who divined hidden knowledge while in a trance. Shamanism, a heritage from very ancient times, was strongly integrated with ancestor-worship—the shaman's guardian spirits were his ancestors—and con-

The Scythians were among the first peoples to excel at horsemanship.

centrated on the exorcism of evil spirits. Shamans performed many of the customary sacrifices.

Of the Mongol and Turkish tribes that invaded Europe during the first Christian millennium, the Huns were known for their belief in Tengri and the Magyars (Hungarians) for their high-god beliefs and their shamanism.

Slavic religions: gods of fear

From their ancient homes in Poland and White Russia the Slavs spread over Eastern Europe during the first millennium of the Christian era. They were organized in numerous tribes which, as time passed, formed themselves into larger groups. Of these only the western Slavs, formerly living east of the Elbe, and the Russians have left traces in the history of religions. What they believed is not at all clear, however, and interpretations differ widely among scholars.

Thunder-god

Thus, we can only guess what the religion of the Russians was like before the emergence of the Russian grand duchy in the ninth century. The most well-known god seems to have been Perun, a god of thunder and lightning, and apparently a Supreme Being.

His position was probably reinforced when in about 980 Vladimir the Great—of Viking descent—created two cultic centres for him, one in Kiev, the other in Novgorod. In Kiev, Perun was represented in wood on a hill outside the princely palace together with a few other gods. His image was adorned with a head of silver and a beard of bronze. Cattle and even human beings were sacrificed to this god. When in 988 Vladimir was baptised, the idol was dragged into the River Dnieper and the sacrificial grove destroyed. It is obvious that the cult of the thunder-god had developed under the influence of the cult of Thor in Scandinavia; Kiev was effectively a Viking colony.

Other Russian gods were Svarog and Dashbog, father and son, both representing the sun and the fire. The common element in their names, *bog* (compare the Indian *bhaga*), stands for 'richness' and also 'god'. Volos is mentioned as the god by whose name one swears solemn oaths. Perhaps he was a master of meadows and herds.

Vampires and werewolves

The folk beliefs in Russia, Poland and Yugoslavia have probably preserved traits of ancient Slavic religion. Best-known are the vampires, dead people who suck the blood of the living, and the werewolves, human beings transformed into wolves. *Rusalki* are maidens who have suffered premature death. Bogs are the abodes of *bagnik* and *bolotnik*, old and dirty men. Very commonly referred to are river-maidens, *vila*, seen as beautiful and cunning.

Western Slavic temples

In the western Slavic area the old religion continued until 1168 when the temple in Arkona on the River Rügen was destroyed by King Valdemar I of Denmark. Unlike the Russians the west Slavs built temples to their gods, probably very late, and possibly influenced by Germanic peoples. The temple clergy seem to have enjoyed high prestige. In Arkona, for instance, only the priest was allowed into the temple where he made libations and, at the harvest, sacrifices of meat. He also performed divination; for instance, he took omens from the movements of the white horse dedicated to the chief god, Svantevit ('the sacred lord').

The west-Slavic gods were very war-like and all-knowing. The latter quality was expressed by their statues having several heads or faces. Thus, Svantevit's huge image had four heads, two looking ahead, two looking backwards. Triglav in Stettin (modern Szczecin) had three heads, Rugievit at Garz on the Rügen one head with seven faces (and seven swords hanging from his belt), Porsevit at the same place had five heads, and so on. The idea of multi-headed gods is truly Slavic. Even in late

Chingis Khan was the greatest ruler of the Mongols. His empire stretched from the Caucasus mountains to the Indus river, from the Caspian Sea to Peking.

Serbian folklore there is a three-headed mysterious nightly rider, Trojan (probably called after Emperor Trajan).

The temples sometimes contained precious things. Triglav's statue was made of gold (but Svantevit's image in Arkona was a wooden idol, chopped up and put into the fire by the Christian king, Valdemar). In the temple belonging to the war-god Jarovit of Wolgast a shield was preserved which was brought forth every time they prayed for victory in battle. Sacred groves were next to the temples. In Stettin Triglav had a sacred oak with a spring beneath. The god Proven who was venerated at the site of Oldenburg (north of Eutin) owned a grove of sacred oaks surrounded by a wooden fence. Here the prince executed his justice in the middle of his subjects, just as the Germanic kings did under an oak.

Baltic religions: a late survival

The old religions of the Baltic peoples—the Latvians, Lithuanians and the now extinct ancient Prussians—lived on until very recent times. Thus, the sacred groves in Latvia were not felled until the eighteenth century, and the cult of Perkons (Perkunas in Lithuania), god of thunder and fertility, and closely related to the Slavic Perun, prevailed in Latvia until 1750. As a matter of fact, Lithuania did not turn Christian until the fifteenth century. Thus it was still possible to observe these indigenous religions until the end of the last century.

Baltic religions are of interest because they are supposed to have been very close to the original Indo-European religion in Persia and India. The heavenly god, Dievs, has his counterpart in the Indian Dyaus, and Perkunas is identical with the Indian Parjanya.

A characteristic feature of Baltic religions is that there are many female divinities (whereas Slavic religions are noted for their lack of goddesses). We find a host of 'mothers', among them Mother Earth (Zemes mate) and the Fire Mother (Uguns mate). The Sun (Saule in Latvia) is represented as a beautiful maiden with golden hair who rides in a wagon drawn by horses. Laima and Mara (St Mary) are important goddesses of fate, and guardians of human beings. Laima receives sacrifices of dogs, sheep and pigs and blesses the fields and the cattle.

Besides Dievs, who is thought of as a farmer with a family, there are other sky-gods, such as Usinsh. The latter is a god associated with the spring and is a patron of horses.

Among terrestrial gods should be mentioned the earth-god, Zemes dievs, who has developed into a lord of the farmstead, and the fertility-god Jumis, who is represented by a double ear of corn. Jumis is connected with the harvest feast in the autumn, when he is identified with the last sheaf of the cornfields.

Part Three
The Primal Religions

World of the Spirits

Harold Turner

When we hear of primitive super-stitions, witchcraft and ju-ju, fetish-ism or mumbo-jumbo, we may think of tribal peoples with no real religion. In fact, many tribal peoples are much more religious than many modern Westerners. They live close to nature and sense its mysterious powers. They are at the mercy of natural disasters, storm and flood, famine, disease, fire and earthquake, which are all seen as evil forces. They meet other peoples who are hostile, or find evil people in their midst. Death is close and often comes tragically early.

Tribal peoples therefore feel them-selves defenceless, weak, surrounded

Primal religions in the world today

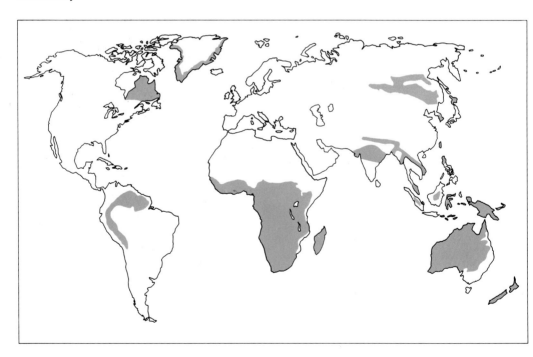

by evils, and unable to cope with life or to achieve the happiness we all long for. They readily become aware that an invisible, more-than-human power surrounds them, and develop their own religious systems to forge links with this power.

Ants before God

The religions of tribal peoples are therefore linked with real human needs, and have the hallmarks of true religion. They have a realistic view of life, a humble view of human nature, and a sense of depending on the spirit world. As the Nuer of the Sudan say, 'Man is like an ant before God.'

Many Westerners have despised tribal religions because the outward forms are different—no church buildings or Sunday services, no scriptures, hymn-books or creeds. Some have even claimed, like Charles Darwin in Patagonia, that such peoples have no religion at all. In a few cases this seems to be true; but most of the 200–300 million tribal peoples of the Americas, Africa, Asia and Oceania are very religious indeed. In

the last 100 years, through close study by missionary scholars, anthropologists and others, we have come to understand these religious systems much better.

Superstitious mumbo-jumbo?

Most of the common terms for these religions are either offensive or inaccurate. People do not like their religion to be called heathen, savage, primitive or superstitious, and words such as animistic, pre-literate, traditional or ethnic are not accurate enough. The word 'superstition' should be kept for the few customs and beliefs that linger on after a religious system has collapsed, or has been replaced by another one. Religion must be carefully distinguished from magic, where people try to use spirit powers for their own selfish ends. Magic is a kind of religion in reverse. Since there are parts of the world where 'tribalism' is a bad word, it is not easy to speak even of tribal religions.

Some people are now using the word 'primal'. This means religions

The ancient religion of Tibet is called Bön. Like many primal religions, it considers that mountains such as Kangchenjunga, are the sacred abode of the gods.

that are *prior* to those we call the 'universal' religions. These include Christianity and the great Asian religions, which appeared later in history, usually have scriptures, and often see themselves as applying universally, to all peoples. Primal religions are not religions for all peoples, and so do not become missionary, as the universal religions often do. They are the religion of one tribe or people who realize that other peoples have their own gods and systems. The word primal also means *primary* or basic. Primal religions usually have the main basic features that belong to all religions.

The spirit world

Basic to primal religions is a belief in a spiritual world of powers or beings stronger than man himself. We are not alone in the universe. Behind ordinary things and daily events there is spirit power. Sometimes this is seen as a power running through everything, but specially concentrated in anything unusual or in any

special skill of a human being. This is called *mana*.

Often this power is seen in a host of spirits dwelling in all kinds of places, or just wandering about. Some of these spirits may be friendly to people and be thanked for their help with prayers and offerings; others may play tricks on them and be a nuisance; and others again may be evil spirits or demons, who are dangerous and must be avoided or placated. So we use 'animism', from the Latin for spirit. Such beliefs emphasize that we do not control everything, and that superior spiritual forces are also at work.

Some primal religions have another group of spirit powers we can call gods. These rule over some area of the world or of human life, such as hunting, farming, fighting or metalworking. For example, among the Yoruba people of Nigeria, Ogun is the god of both metal-working and war. These major gods often have temples or shrines, with special priests and festivals, and are much more important than the spirits.

At Lomé in Central Togo, a strange selection of stones, skulls and bones are on sale as fetishes. Spirits are believed to reside in the fetishes.

'High God', 'Sky-god'

Many primal religions have a single supreme god above all other powers. Sometimes he is even thought of as a universal God for all peoples. For instance, North American Indians think of the Great Spirit, and the New Zealand Maoris of Io. This God is usually the creator of all things. Sometimes he is concerned that people live moral lives, and deals with them through the lesser gods. At other times he is believed to have been angry with mankind and to have withdrawn from the world, or else he is so high and mysterious that we cannot possibly reach him. This 'High God' or 'Sky-god' may have no temples, priests, organized worship or sacrifices, and so he is easily missed by outsiders.

The living dead

Most tribal peoples also believe that the spirits of those who have died live on. These 'living dead' have dealings with those still living in this world. The living must honour these ancestral spirits, and can rely upon them to protect or guide, and also to take their prayers to the higher spirit powers. Sometimes this system is called 'ancestor-worship'; indeed, notable ancestors have been promoted to gods. But usually, these practices show a strong sense of the continuing presence of ancestors, who are honoured rather than worshipped, and who are remembered, at least for a few generations, as human beings, not gods.

Dreams and visions

Primal religions depend on myths rather than scriptures and creeds to learn about the spirit powers. Such myths relate the great things the spirit powers did in making the world and in giving people various natural resources and skills needed to sustain life—hunting, fishing, growing crops and making fire, pottery and houses. Myths are not fairy-tales, but long and often complicated stories containing a people's theology and philosophy of life. In them we can find a deep understanding of human nature and of basic human problems.

Individuals may also meet the spirit world through ecstasy or visions, by being possessed by a spirit which for a short while controls a person's behaviour and speaks through him, perhaps in a strange spirit language, and especially through dreams. When dreams are vivid or unusual, people ask others to help interpret what the spirit powers are saying to warn, command or reward.

Bringing in the New Year

Rituals are another way of communicating between the two worlds. Sometimes they are laid down in the ancient myths; the ritual and the myth together form a complex act of worship or a great festival. In such ceremonies, the stories in the myths may be acted out afresh so that people believe that they are sharing once again the full power of the gods, and renewing life from its origins.

Some of the most important rituals concern the New Year; the old, worn out and corrupted world is discarded and replaced by a renewed creation fresh from the gods, just as in the beginning. The ritual may include such ceremonies as putting out the old village fires that have been kept alight all year, and lighting a new fire for the next year by striking flint on stone, or using some other method the gods first taught to men. Although the ceremonies may also involve much merry-making, there is a deep religious awareness of the corruption and shortcomings of humans and their world, and of the need for regular renewal from the sources of life.

Killing for the gods

Prayers and offerings to the gods feature prominently in the rituals. Some of the prayers are both beautiful and deeply spiritual, and can be used in worship by the universal religions. Others tend to be rather self-centred, asking for prosperity and practical blessings. Not all peoples sacrifice to the gods, but many primal religions have well-defined systems listing the items to be given by killing, burning, pouring out or in other ways, or food to be shared with the god in a communion meal.

**'Those who are dead are never gone:
They are there in the thickening shadow.
The dead are not under the earth:
They are in the tree that rustles,
They are in the wood that groans,
They are in the water that runs,
They are in the water that sleeps,
They are in the hut,
they are in the crowd,
The dead are not dead.**

**Those who are dead are never gone,
They are in the breast of the woman,
They are in the child who is wailing,
And in the firebrand that flames.
The dead are not under the earth:
They are in the fire that is dying,
They are in the grasses that weep,
They are in the whimpering rocks,
They are in the forest, they are in the house,
The dead are not dead.'**

From *Chants d'ombre Suivis de Hosties Noires*, ed. Leopold Senghor

Medicine men

To help with all these religious activities most primal religions have some kind of specialist, usually best called a 'medicine man'. He may perform the activities of a priest, medium, diviner, healer and herbalist, and shaman but not of a witch, sorcerer, or mere magician. Priests look after the shrines and organize the festivals; mediums become 'possessed' by the spirit power; diviners are skilled at interpreting omens or signs showing the will of the gods; healers may know useful techniques and remedies (such men first used quinine, cocaine, morphine and other drugs); shamans specialize in travel in trances to the world of the spirits to learn from its mysteries. Many of these tasks require long apprenticeships, but more importantly a special gift at birth, or a special divine call. Thus the gods keep the final control in their dealings with this world.

Although many primal religions have collapsed under modern pressures in developing areas of the world, others have persisted remarkably and have adapted to change. They should never be regarded as the childish religions of primitive peoples, or the crazy antics of savages dominated by 'witch-doctors'. They are serious efforts by adult peoples to create and preserve a spiritual system which can sustain them in both life and death.

A wooden figure for scaring away the 'devils of disease', from the Nicobar Islands, north of Sumatra.

Case-study 1: Asia

Barbara Boal

ecstatic trances to communicate with the spirits. They bring back instructions for correcting the erring community. They seek to restore harmony between man, the spirit world and everything created. This harmony is fundamental to their beliefs. Similar beliefs are held by the Ainus of northern Japan, the mountain peoples of Taiwan and, to some extent, the Hakka.

Nomadic groups

Many people think these nomadic groups are the descendants of Asia's ancient peoples and have preserved traditional ways down the ages. Today they live in small bands, usually in remote, forested hill-country, where they were probably pushed long ago by more highly organized immigrants. They include very small tribes in west-central and south India and in Chota Nagpur. The Andaman Islands are almost entirely inhabited by such peoples; they are also scattered in remote forest and swamp areas of coastal Kampuchea. Better known, perhaps, are the tiny minority groups of Semang-Negritoes and their neighbours, the Senoi, inhabiting the jungle hills of northern and central peninsular Malaysia; also the Aëtas-Negritoes of Luzon, Mindanao and Mindoro in the Philippines. Other hunter-gatherer groups can be found wandering in central Kalimantang (Borneo), the Celebes and eastern Sumatra.

Such groups may be made up of simply one elder and his family or several families. Scarcity of food dictates the smaller groups which, however much they roam, usually keep within their own boundaries. Food is always shared out equally—roots, tubers, leaves and fruits from the forest, possibly fish speared or trapped. Small game are hunted by bow-and-arrow except on the Malaysian peninsula, where Senoi blowgun and poisoned dart have also been adopted by the Semang.

Asia and Oceania

Asian tribal peoples do not separate the sacred and secular. Their religious concepts are expressed in ritualized activities involving the community.

But these concepts and actions do not result from verbal 'beliefs'. In this they differ from 'religion' as we know it in the world's major faiths.

The key to understanding Asian tribal world-views is 'relationship': with gods and spirits; with fellow human beings; with nature.

These cannot be separated: they are parts of one whole. Each group has religious practices appropriate to themselves and their environment. But everywhere they seek to restore the good order that was created 'in the beginning'. So there is a great variety of belief among these tribal groups stretching across Asia and the neighbouring islands.

The spirits

Shamans dominate religion in Siberia. They believe in a high god, beyond all good and evil. Chosen by family then later by the spirits, male and female shamans enter rigorous training. Their souls leave the body by

When humans were sacrificed, the Konds used to place emblems beneath the sacrificial stakes. This is an emblem of the leopard clan, with its victim in its mouth.

everybody; for the person's soul has wandered out of the group and must be brought back. The shaman employs the power of certain herbs and plants disliked by the spirit world, to drive away the evil and call back the wandering soul.

Taboo

In cases of more serious illness, the whole group is involved in taboos and ritual observances, perhaps in days and nights of music and spirit-possessed dance. Finally, on receiving the blood sacrifice offered by the head of the house, the spirit is driven out. If the patient dies, another set of group taboos to do with pollution begins. Deaths, like births, are full of danger and the group must isolate itself both for its own safety and that of its neighbours. If any member breaks the taboo, terrifying tropical storms will follow. These come from a supreme god. But there is little idea of a hierarchy of spirit beings. The idea that spirits of the ancestors are present is vague and unwelcome. Safety and well-being depend on the unity and harmony of the

Land and ritual

Their home area of land and its produce appear to have great religious significance. However far they wander and set up temporary dwellings, they return repeatedly to the place they regard as their own. Many, such as the Malaysian Senoi hill-people— widely known as 'slave' (*Sakai*)—have changed to slash-and-burn cultivation for part of each year. They still live in very temporary shelters during food-collecting expeditions, but cultivation demands settled base camps for part of each year. It also sets up a different religious attitude to the land and to the

Each Bontoc village has its council platform. Under each large leaning-stone is buried at least one head from a former head-hunting expedition.

spirits.

The Senoi are surrounded by taboos and work restrictions as soon as they choose which trees to fell and fire to prepare a hill-plot. There is a series of rituals seeking the spirits' help in securing a good crop, until the final harvest celebration. These are performed by the whole tiny community. For instance, the whole group is in 'quarantine' on the first day of planting. Similarly, one person's sickness involves living community.

Tribes with more complex social structures and more settled and advanced economic patterns develop a stronger pattern of rituals. These in turn demand ritual specialists for proper celebration. Nevertheless, there are still three levels of relationships. Though certain rites may be performed for the individual they still involve the wider community. The Konds are an example.

Human sacrifice

The Konds—or Kui, as they call themselves—live in the jungle-covered Eastern Ghats of Orissa, India, and number nearly a million. Traditionally they supported themselves by slash-and-burn hill-plots, and by hunting and gathering during the dry 'hungry season'. Paddy-cultivation has now steadily increased.

In 1835 the East India Company first encountered the Konds' human sacrifices to satisfy the earth's demands. Emphasizing the need for right relationships between man, the gods and the world, they felt that human sacrifice was needed for wholeness and fertility.

Earth-goddess

The creator-god, Bura, formed the earth-goddess, Tari, as his companion but found her sadly lacking in wifely attentions. She tried in vain to prevent his creating the world and man. All was paradise in the created world except for her growing jealousy. This led to a fierce conflict between the two. All the Konds except a small minority believed that the earth-goddess had won, though she let the creator keep second place. She taught man the arts of hunting, war and cultivating only in return for human sacrifice, her proper food.

Though now replaced by buffalo as victims, this ritual continues. Strips of flesh are hacked from the victim and buried in the village and in neighbouring villages to release her gift of fertility. Many villages were formerly at war. Brief, strict peace-pacts are therefore made for each annual stage of this three- or four-year ritual, ensuring co-operation for the set few days. In some areas it is still annually celebrated in each district, also at certain farming seasons or when the health of the people or its livestock is affected. This binds the people together as Konds, when otherwise the strongest unit is the lineage group.

A number of myths and dialogues show how the Konds tried to avoid the earth-goddess's demands:

'We will die rather than give you human beings!'

But breaking the relationship with her also involved breaking the relationship with the land—bringing drought and famine—and with mankind, bringing pestilence and death. Hence she always made them submit, as the means of re-creating harmony and well-being.

Kond rituals

The Konds try to use mystical powers in many other rituals to increase or restore relationship—and strength and well-being—in the district, village, kin-group or household. Rituals:

● **between the god, man and the land.** Many rituals follow the farming calendar, from ground preparation and sowing to reaping and threshing; also taboo-lifting rituals on hunting and gathering wild produce.

● **to seek the blessing and help of the ancestors.** Some of these matters involve other clans: such as marriage or the taking of a second wife, or the removal of an entire village with its ancestors, if problems and pestilences show the need.

● **to guard against loss of well-being through pollution.** Ritual impurity runs the full gamut from small household avoidances to incest, which pollutes the earth and everybody in the area.

The Konds follow a slash-and-burn agriculture. But the trees at the crown of the hill are left untouched out of reverence for the hill-god.

All births and deaths pollute, but most serious for the Konds are deaths before due time, by tiger-mauling, in childbirth, or by hanging, falling from a tree or drowning. These place the entire village in 'quarantine', traditionally for a month, but nowadays for a shorter period, while priest and people undergo daily purification rites.

● **to safeguard life.** The danger may come from high-ranking spirits: gods of the hill, of smallpox, of boundaries, of iron (war), or hunting. These are stronger than spirits of springs, trees and lesser hills. Offence against them rapidly brings disaster. Also life-destroying is an overpowering belief in evil eye, sorcery and witchcraft. These powers, neutral in themselves, become evil and deeply feared when someone uses them against his fellow. This reverses Kond beliefs about community well-being. Counter-rituals by 'witch-detectives' may return the evil to its originator, but the victim may nevertheless fall sick or die.

One community

Seers communicate with the spirits through trances or divination to find out who caused the problem and why. Seers or priests perform the rituals, sacrificing cocks, goats, pigs or buffalo. A spirit-chosen keeper of the village's shrine-stones performs many annual purification rituals. Many villages also have groves sacred to the hill-god or guardian spirit. The household head is priest for ancestor rites and some look after bronze emblems—such as animals and reptiles or other household spirits.

The ancestors, the unborn and the living are all one community. The same daily activities continue in the shade-world. Death in old age with a full funeral gives the best hope of passing peacefully to the ancestors. The dead are also rehabilitated into the bereaved home in the form of a spider, found near the funeral pyre. Sudden death in the feared forms mentioned earlier rules out being accepted by the ancestors. This results in unbearable loneliness for the dangerous spirit. For the Konds, it is as necessary to live in community after death as before it. The manner of death, not good or evil behaviour in this life, decides the future life.

Village centres

The Bontocs and Kalingas of Mountain Province in north Luzon have some similarities to the Konds, but many striking differences. In north Luzon the north–south ranges rise well over 6,000 feet/1,828 metres, often in almost vertical paddy terraces.

For the Bontocs the village is the centre of life. Large villages are sub-divided, with councils meeting on raised stone platforms circled by large, upright stones. These serve as social, ritual and political centres. Head-hunting forays ritually began and ended there, and no elder could sit in council until he had buried a head under his leaning-stone, in this way adding his victim's power and wisdom to his own. Status is all-important. It may be inherited or achieved by great community feasts of many buffalo. The number of buffalo horns nailed above the donor's door proves to both spirits and men the size of the offering.

Several features are similar to the Konds. Women do not sit in council. But they have considerable voice in making decisions. There are separate dormitories for youths and girls, with visiting between them permitted before marriage. Childlessness proves that the spirits are ill-disposed and offends the ancestors, so is reason for divorce. Both peoples revere sacred groves. Both sexes may be seers and priests. The whole farming year has rituals showing constant struggle to win fertility from wilful spirits.

Omens

Unlike the Konds, the Bontoc emphasize omens. These are central to everything. The movements of birds, insects and natural phenomena, the entrails of animals, the silence or crow of a cock held by a priest, and many such 'trials' postpone major ritual celebrations or guide an individual. The Bontoc respect family pigs in their stone-built sties; Kond pigs are scavengers, sacrificed only in pollution rituals, and are taboo to women.

Ancestors are important to both peoples. But Bontocs do not cremate their dead. They ritually seat them in chairs for long periods before putting them in caves at the foot of ravines, where they are visited every year.

Since head-hunting was so important for Bontocs and their northern neighbours, the Kalingas, inter-village feuding was a way of life. Violent incidents are now avoided by their peace-pact system, much stronger than the Konds'. In every village respected elders have been appointed to arrange settlements by traditional methods.

For both Kalingas and Bontocs, religious ceremonies are bound up with status-feasting. A powerful liquor is distilled from fermented rice or sugar-cane and shared between ancestors and the living, or offered with chicken, pig or buffalo sacrifice to particularly feared mountain spirits. A family may run into debt for years or generations, slaughtering many buffalo to ward off disease by feasting both spirits and the village.

The high regard for old village councillors is dying as authority passes into the hands of younger, educated men. With it passes the way of life that held together ancient lore, religious ritual and the elders' responsibility for the well-being of their community.

A special platform is built for the priest to perform the buffalo sacrifices.

Case-study 2: Korea

Harvie Conn

Korea's traditional religion, Sinkyo, has been called 'the religion without a name'. It is not so much a structured set of uniform beliefs as a religious way of seeing the world and a person's sacred link with it. This used to be called 'animism'. Like all religions it has five 'magnetic points'.

● **I and the cosmos.** Man is in rhythm with the world. The forces of nature controlling life and death, fertility and sterility, become personified and god-like. This world is a religious arena inhabited by spirits of heaven and the soil, water and the trees.

● **I and the norm.** The myth of Tan'gun, legendary founder of Korea, underlines that sense of cosmic norm to which the Korean must conform. Ung, the son of heaven, changed a bear into a woman. The bear-woman could find no one to marry. Ung changed his form, married her and fathered her child, Tan'gun. The myth is remembered on 'opening of heaven day' (*Kaech'onjol*), an annual national holiday. Similar tales surround the archetypal tribal leaders, and mythical ancestors of present-day clan families.

● **I and destiny.** How do we reconcile the fact that we are active beings and also victims of fate or destiny? Borrowing from

Yin and Yang represent the interdependent female and male, negative and positive forces of life.

pre-Confucian roots, Sinkyo finds its answer in a cosmic pattern where heaven, man and nature make a harmony of opposites. These opposites complement each other. They are the great forces of the Yin and the Yang, non-being and being. The Yin is negative, passive, weak and destructive. The Yang is positive, active, strong and constructive. As they act and interact, harmony is achieved and recreated again and again. Our individuality comes from these opposites. The Yin is the female, mother, soft, dark, wet. The Yang is male, father, strong, hard, bright.

Out of these opposites comes the system called 'geomancy'. Where shall we live?, becomes a religious question of choosing a good house-site or grave-site in harmony with these opposites. The house or burial place, for instance, must be arranged in conformity to the cosmic workings of yin-yang and the harmony of the five elements: wood, metal, fire, water, earth. The interacting flow of these forces must not be disturbed.

● **I and salvation.** Since this harmony is often broken, Sinkyo must also meet man's craving for salvation. When the rice paddies are ploughed in the spring, a farmers' band pacifies the spirits of the earth with music and ritual. When the ridge-pole of a new house is raised, wine and food are thrown at it, while a member of the household chants, 'Please, Grandfather and Grandmother of the ridge-pole, bless us with good luck and long life, and many sons!'

Life is under a curse, a shadow darkening the cosmic harmony. The way back to 'paradise lost' is by ritual sacrifice. Throwing a stone on a simple altar keeps you from getting sore feet on a journey. Spitting on the altar is a sign of purification, and wards off evil spirits. Earth spirits must be satisfied before a corpse can be laid to rest. The 'sin' is not that of a personal violating of the will of a personal 'god' but the corporate breaking of cosmic unity.

The chief role in restoring unity is often played by the Mudang. Always a woman, her most important task is curing mental and physical disease. Like the shamans of Siberia, she also conducts communal sacrifice, assures the farmers of good crops, fishermen of safe journeys and a good catch. She will produce sons for a barren woman, recall the spirits of the dead after a funeral, or lead them to the kingdom of the blessed. She will pacify the spirits of those who die violent or tragic deaths. Her role is regarded as beneficial.

Sinkyo feels deep horror at the threat of death which destroys cosmic harmony. Some 2,000 years ago, it was common for Koreans to bury the dead with their personal belongings, including gold and silver.

With the growing influence of Confucianism on Korea from the third century AD, Sinkyo saw the spirit world in a new way. The Confucian concept of filial piety as the summit of all virtues strengthened, if it did not create, Korea's early ancestor-cult. Food was offered to kinsmen at death and at memorial times in the following years. They hoped the ancestor would favour the descendants.

● **I and the Supreme Being.** Koreans read about the gods in the great picture-book we call the cosmos. Among the spirits of nature, the spirit of heaven (Hananim or Hanunim) has a special place. Not a 'high god', remote and supreme, he is said to bring sunlight and rain. Lightning, drought and other disasters are his judgement on the wicked. By his favour we live and breathe. When national disaster came, the king used to appeal to Hananim by confessing his own sins and those of his people. In some sense a 'heavenly father', Hananim was the grandfather of Tan'gun, the aboriginal hero of Korea.

Sinkyo and the new religious movements

As Korea was invaded by Confucianism, Buddhism and Christianity, Sinkyo did not shrink but was altered and strengthened. From Confucianism came the ethical codes surrounding the ancestor-cult. Taoism and neo-Confucianism strengthened the magical side of Sinkyo and its geomancy. From Buddhism came a stress on suffering and pain, now linked with healing and divining.

Sinkyo has also provided the background for Korea's new religions. Chondogyo was founded in the mid-eighteenth century in reaction to the coming of Christianity. It reinforced man's sacred links with the universe. Sun Myung Moon, the Korean founder of the Unification Church, can be seen as the great link-man between the people and the spirit world.

When the rice-paddies are ploughed in the spring, the spirits of the earth are pacified by music and special rituals.

Case-study 3: Oceania

Alan Tippett

In Oceania beliefs range widely from a hierarchy of high gods to a host of vague spirit forces, forest imps, culture heroes, ancestor-gods and totemism. Some places emphasize religious experience, others formal rituals. Rituals, in turn, may range from a simple chant to a highly elaborate cult.

In Papua New Guinea many tribes were untouched by Western civilization until very recently. One such tribe is the Melpa.

The practitioner may be a simple all-purpose village priest, a healer (shaman), a diviner, a prophet or a complex priest-hood—or a sorcerer. The sorcerer is normally an anti-social individual. A village priest or curer may use counter-sorcery to defeat him.

Magic and religion are inter-twined, but quite different, with different goals and usually different practitioners. For example, many island communities threw over their old religion with its belief in a hierarchy of high gods, priesthoods and temples, and turned to Christianity. Yet they had trouble ridding themselves of sorcery and domestic magic.

Creation

Attitudes to creation vary widely. Some societies believe the earth always existed. Others have elaborate creation myths and a supreme creator-god (or goddess). In many, however, he or she completed creation and retired, and is not worshipped like the gods of the house and garden. Beside the creator-gods we often find departmental gods, such as the god of the sea, embodied, say, in the shark, who is approached at times of sea travel or fishing.

Spirits and totems

Spirits may always have existed or be ghosts—spirits of the dead who once existed on earth as people and have not been properly despatched to the afterworld, or are disgruntled by unpleasant memories of earth. These are different from culture heroes, recent and remembered ancestor-gods for whom special rituals may be used to gain particular ends, or the living dead, who still belong to the lineage or clan.

Totemism is not found everywhere and does not always mean the same thing. By totems we usually mean land creatures, water creatures, trees or plants, or even natural phenomena which are specially linked with the gods and the individual or group. Their fortunes are interwoven by belief and symbolic ritual, and group survival depends on these sacred links. Totemism is hedged with taboos and learned by symbolic performances such as dances and chants. In some places totems are mainly linked with marriage patterns, but they may bear on war or even relationships with other people in the community.

Power and custom

There is a belief in a dynamic power for good or evil, *mana*, which depends on the intention of the person using it. This power is transmitted, controlled and encountered quite logically, and religious and magical rituals depend on it. *Mana* may be activated by ritual or by accidental touch. Good health, long life, fertility, security, success, good harvests and trade depend on the right use of *mana*. Its misuse is dangerous; taboo is used for protection.

Religion, and especially ritual, ties up with every stressful situation or point of social, economic or political anxiety. It helps maintain balance in the group.

Ritual is also used in agricultural fertility rites, passing of the seasons, first-fruits, rites of passage (including funerary rites), ceremonial welcomes and farewells, trade exchanges, ceremonies before war and after victory, and (in pre-Christian times) in head-hunting, cannibalism, widow-strangling and other local customs.

Spiritual beings may or may not have a fixed living-place, but there is always a right place and way of approach for consulting or sacrifice. Gods and spirits may embody themselves in a myth, animal or person, or enter objects to be venerated or consulted. Sacred places are usually recognizable by rock formations, groves or buildings, and are protected by taboos.

Numerous waves of migration have contributed new religious features to Oceanic religion. For instance, in Fiji we find the snake-cults, ancestral cults and totemism. Frequently the names of the earlier gods of the land have been taken over by later invaders.

The dead
Probably all the Oceanic peoples believe in life after death, but views of the afterlife vary. For some there are different levels in the afterlife. In some, worthy ancestors in living memory may be made gods and called on to help in the areas where they once excelled—in war, magic, agriculture. Sometimes an ancestor has a strong cult backed by long genealogies and origin myths. Frequently the dead go to a place of waiting, or pass through a series of trials. In some places we find a 'place of the dead' for each village or district, which seems to clash with the wider idea of a 'heaven' for the whole tribe found in the same region.

Survival
How far primal religion survives today in Oceania is a moot point.

Kukailimoku is the Hawaiian god of war. This wooden statue stands over six feet high.

The Melpa have periodic pig-feasts when scores of pigs are slaughtered to fulfil the social and religious obligations of the group.

Much of the region is now Christianized, and the great religions of Tonga, Maoriland and Fiji have disappeared. Nevertheless, pockets of animism, magic and sorcery survive even in the urban centres of Oceania, and primal religion is still practised in the mountainous interiors of the larger islands. Rites associated with fishing, subsistence farming, barter and daily home life are still practised in western Melanesia, Papua New Guinea and West Irian.

Many forms of sorcery are still used and very much feared, even by educated persons; a person who knows how to counter sorcery is assured of a good livelihood in any town. Colonial governments prohibited cannibalism, head-hunting and other forms of ceremonial cruelty, undermining their basic religious belief, but primal religion has adjusted to such changes and often co-exists with some local form of Christianity.

Case-study 4: Melanesia

Carl Loeliger

Melanesia is the area of the Pacific Ocean from the western end of New Guinea (Irian Jaya) to Fiji in the east, from the northernmost islands of Papua New Guinea to New Caledonia in the south, and includes Irian Jaya, Papua New Guinea, the Torres Strait Islands, the Solomon Islands, the New Hebrides and New Caledonia. There are no fewer than 1,200 vernacular languages among its roughly 5 million inhabitants.

More than a century of close contact with foreign cultures and Christianity has changed Melanesian primal religion, but has not everywhere reduced its vitality and pervasiveness.

World-view

Melanesians make no distinction between the 'religious' and the 'secular', between the 'natural' and the 'supernatural'. Their religion can be seen as a particular view of the universe, and a set of relationships with it, including people, gods, spirits, ghosts, magical powers, totems, the land and features of the landscape, living creatures, trees, plants and all physical objects, all of which are in some sense potential sources of power.

Relationships with people and ancestral spirits are universally the most important, for at the centre of life is 'the community of men and spirits all of whom are alive'. This community, with membership of an extended family and links with a particular piece of land give a person identity and security, a reason for living, a sense of history and an approach to the future. All the rituals of birth, initiation into adult life, marriage and death are directed towards maintaining these links.

Melanesian primal religion aims at life, fertility, prosperity, harmony, control and balance in all relationships, particularly with men and spirits, and in this world rather than the next. However, as with many other religions, not all its activities match these ideals. Narrow concern with the clan, suspicions and hostility between and within groups, and in some areas between the sexes, have helped foster seemingly harsh and inhuman attitudes and practices.

Myths and stories

Melanesian primal religion features a range of migration stories, myths and other stories, legends, songs, prayers and incantations similar to that of any major religion. Parts are known only by initiated males, or by specialists or adult women. Especially sacred knowledge is restricted to elderly initiated people. There is a variety of creation stories, but little speculation about the origins and nature of the universe. Many people believe that important parts of culture—social, economic and political life—were created for, or given to, the people by gods.

Gods and spirits

Not all Melanesian peoples have believed in a god of the whole universe, or in a powerful god or gods, or that the god or gods are interested in human activities. But some believe gods to be creators who continue to care for the world. Many believe in a variety of spirit beings including evil 'ghosts', demons and witches (not widespread), many of which can harm or kill people. Ancestral spirits are important everywhere; some societies look forward to the return of the dead, others fear it. Some societies regard the spirits of the recent dead as dangerous; others think they are friendly towards the living. They believe that elaborate rituals in honour of the dead—mourning, food offerings, dances, exchanges of pigs, food and valuables—will ensure that the dead will protect the living. Where beliefs in totems occur, the totems—animals, birds, fish, trees, plants—are sometimes seen as ancestors, sometimes simply as emblems.

Ritual and magic

Rituals vary from simple acts linked with everyday activities (hunting, gardening, fishing) to complex rituals, festivals and festival cycles lasting days, weeks, even months and years. In the major activities initiated men take the central role; women and juniors have only minor roles. The pig figures in many of these rituals and festivals. Food, drink and sexual taboos accompany most important rituals. Some peoples believe rituals force the spirits or gods to act; others believe the gods are free to act as they will.

Magic has a place in most societies. The sorcerer is an important person in many Melanesian societies; deaths are often credited to his activity, since a death is usually regarded as being caused by someone. Every Melanesian society includes people with special ritual responsibilities, temporary, permanent or hereditary.

For Melanesians, sacred places can include features of the landscape, such as caves, pools, streams and rocks, but also man-made constructions varying from simple structures to large elaborate buildings such as the Sepik ancestral spirit houses.

Conduct

In some societies ethics and religion seem to have no connection; in others the spirits and gods are clearly concerned with behaviour. Ethical conduct is the particular interest of the god Datagaliwabe among the Huli people of the Southern Highlands of Papua New Guinea.

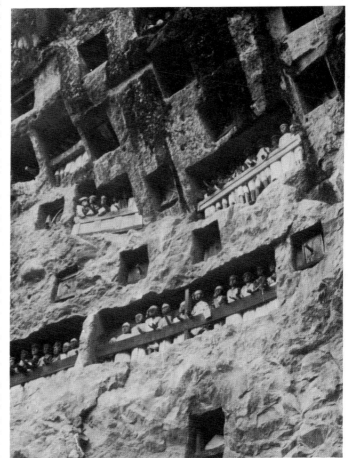

A carved image of the dead person stands guard over his rock tomb.

Toradja funeral celebrations can last for several months. At the climax dozens of sacred buffalos may be slaughtered.

The Toradja coffins are boat-shaped, like their houses.

The Toradja people from the highlands of Sulawesi were almost completely cut off from all outside civilization until the beginning of this century.

New Myths: The Cargo Cults

Carl Loeliger

New religious movements in Melanesia have become widely known since the Pacific War (1942–45) as 'cargo cults', a term often used to ridicule or condemn. This term and others have frequently led to a complete misunderstanding of these movements. Scholars justify use of the term by pointing to the term 'kago cult' in Melanesian Pidgin, and belief in the 'cargo myth (or story)' in about half the movements.

There were new religious movements in Melanesia before the modern colonial period, and there have been many in the colonial period, all with their main roots in Melanesian culture and primal religion. These movements use myths to justify changes and provide the dynamic for renewal.

A new era

Typically, somebody claims that, through a dream or vision, supernatural powers have told him that a messiah (sometimes) and the ancestors or spirits of the dead will soon return in ships, aeroplanes or trucks bringing huge supplies of manufactured goods. Their arrival will usher in a wonderful new era when Melanesians will have their identity, dignity and honour restored. Inequality, suffering and death will cease.

Sometimes the 'prophet', his associates and whole communities are seized by mass shaking fits, or fall into an ecstatic state. There may be slaughtering of pigs, harvesting or destruction of food crops and dispersal of wealth ready for the new life. Facilities to handle and store the new wealth may also be built. Graveyards get special attention, ready for the return of the ancestors. New, revived or modified rituals and customs may be announced for the faithful to follow.

The movement unites previously separated or hostile groups, although not everybody in an area always joins. Unlike primal religion, the new religious movement reaches beyond the clan and village. When the ancestors, wealth and new life fail to arrive, reasons are found, but the validity of the myth is not questioned. The movement may break out again at any time.

Characteristic features

The movements have characteristic features.
● Elements of primal religion;
● Christian elements;
● Belief in the return of the dead and sometimes in the coming of a messiah;
● Belief in the cargo myth;
● Belief that Melanesians will become whites and vice versa;
● Violence or threats against whites;
● Attempts to restore native political and economic control;
● Unifying separated groups.

No movement has all these features. The most widespread feature, belief in the cargo myth, appears in more than half; violence or threats to whites occur in less than half; belief in the coming of a messiah in only about one-sixth. But these movements possess an uncanny ability to survive and revive.

The movements have their roots in primal religion, even when biblical stories and Christian rituals are used. Colonial administration, European technology and culture, Christian missions and events such as the Pacific War have also influenced their rise. These movements may be traditional responses to difficulty. When Melanesians are unable to match outsiders' power and wealth, they turn to traditional means, myths and rituals to survive. They find it difficult to accept that an individual or group will not share power, goods, food and knowledge with others.

The shared life

Five major themes are found in the great variety of Melanesian myths:
● The division of humanity into two groups as a result of choices made by two original people;
● The two brothers who became separated, one being stupid or hostile (it is hoped they will meet and be reconciled and so will all people);
● A paradise lost due to the disobedience, stupidity or ingratitude of an individual or group;
● The turbulent end of the present world;
● The arrival of a legendary messiah with the ancestors and the ushering in of the new age.

Basic to all this is the shared life of men and spirits and the belief that all people belong to one family and are equal but, through some error or misfortune in the past, divisions and inequalities have arisen.

Feared by the government

These religious movements make converts beyond the village and clan, marking them off from primal religion. Their social, economic and political aspects have usually been obvious, and colonial and post-colonial administrations, missions and churches have feared them. Before the 1960s there were few 'secular' movements with political aims.

Whether or not they overtly express concern with 'cargo', the aim of the new religious movements is not merely wealth and prosperity but proper human relationships, liberation and the restoration of human rights, identity, dignity, respect and equality.

Case-study 5: The Foe of Papua New Guinea

Joan Rule

In the tribal religion of the Foe in the Southern Highlands of Papua New Guinea, the chief spirit is the 'Old One who is in the East' (Ama'a Hai Ta'o). Although he is the chief spirit, he is not the creator.

There are in addition three groups of spirits who live in fixed places:
● the evil things (ma'ame gai)
● the hisare
● the hibu yii.
Certain men in each village make a special relationship with one of these groups of spirits, and others pay them to make an offering on their behalf.

The evil things

The 'evil things' inhabit a clump of trees, a big rock or some unusual natural feature. For example, in about 1967, on a point of land on the south-eastern side of Lake Kutubu, in a swampy area of wild bamboo, a man named Igare from Gese village found a small area with red cordyline shrubs growing neatly. This, all agreed, must be a spirit house; so it was regarded as a place of the evil things. Men who made a relationship with the evil things, and who had the right spells for them, were in their favour and would not be harmed. But those who roused their anger would get swollen legs or a swol-

len stomach. Parents warned children against going near, for fear of disturbing them and making them angry. Children whose parents had garden-houses in the area had to be very careful not to make a noise near the dwelling-place of the evil things.

Further up the lake, some hisare spirits live. In the waters of the lake live a number of fearsome water spirits, the guruka. Men who make a relationship with the hisare spirits also make contact with these guruka. After the hisare men have danced with the hisare spirits, the guruka will come up from the water and dance around the hisare camp. They will bring cassowary's feathers or perhaps men's bones and present them to the hisare men, acting for the spirits. According to the gift, the following month a cassowary will be caught, a man will die, or some similarly appropriate event will occur.

Wandering spirits

Other spirit beings wander from place to place. The soro are spirits of the air who wander here and there at will, always on the lookout for some harm to do to humans. Children are afraid of the spirits of the air, being sure that they could carry them off or do dreadful things; but adults

make it plain that they must work in company with the spirits who live within living men (baisese). A pair or group of baisese must work with at least one spirit of the air. If a man has an enemy, his spirit will go out, find another man's spirit, find a spirit of the air and then go to do damage. For example, in about 1960 a stone was thrown into a man's sleeping area. He realized that his spirit was leaving him, pressed into service by a fellow villager's spirit. He said, 'There'll be a man harmed at Hegeso village', naming the man. Two days later the man was dead.

Spirits of the dead

Most feared of all are the spirits of the dead. These include the spirits of men slain, mostly in inter-village fighting, and the spirits of those who have died from other causes. Both can cause harm and serious illness, entering into a person's body in the form of stones and wood which will cause death.

The spirits of the slain (bauwabe) are the most potent. These spirits live 'up above' and are always painted all over with red. A man who makes offerings to a spirit of the slain finds that his spirit appears to him in a dream or vision, guaranteeing success and help. But if a man and his kinsmen are enemies of a man who is slain, his spirit appearing to them means trouble. If a man has a bad ulcer or abdominal pain, this is clearly the work of the spirit of the slain.

The spirit of a man who has died in any other way goes 'east', but wanders back and hovers around, at least for a time. It can cause sickness, but not death. An exasperated mother may say to a child, 'If you don't stop, the spirit will come with a bamboo and leaves, collect your tears and drink them, and if they're sweet cause you lots of harm.'

Medicine men

Medicine men once claimed to be

able to 'suck' out the stones and sticks implanted by the spirits. They were paid in strings of cowries, or with a pig. This cult died a natural death. The prices charged were high, and the number of cures not impressive. At the local health centres, on the other hand, drugs such as penicillin and chloroquine produced dramatic cures free of charge.

The other answer is to pay someone to drive away the spirit causing the trouble.

Bamboo and sorcery

The sorcerer is greatly feared. In a group of two or three hundred people, complete and electric silence resulted as a well-known sorcerer produced a small bamboo of sorcery material bought from sorcerers in the west to produce the death of named men. Foe sorcerers have three main methods.

The first, 'hitting the skin with a stick', is the most potent; the man will die in one or two days. Sorcery material from the bamboo, generally a fine, white, powdery substance, touches the skin of the doomed man, either by means of a stick, or by being shaken on him while he is asleep. If it can be put into his bamboo of water or his food, it works just as well.

In the second method, pieces of the man's belongings—a fragment of his cane leg-band, or of the leaves or cloth covering his buttocks—are put in the bamboo of sorcery material which is placed in the fork of a tree, where it wears slowly away. Or it may be placed in a large ant-mound on a tree trunk, or in a small running stream. As the friction or the eating takes place, the man will sicken and die over a period of four or five months.

The third method, white sorcery, is done with a set of small white stones. The sorcerer obtains a tree gum, and says his spell as he rubs it into the stones. This also causes death.

Case-study 6: The Aborigines

W. H. Edwards

The first Europeans to observe the Australian Aborigines thought they had no religion. In fact spiritual beliefs are basic to daily life and social relationships.

At the time of European settlement, there were about 300,000 Aborigines belonging to about 270 language groups. Myths passed from one area to another, and all groups shared a common view of the world, although differing in beliefs and practices. For example, although no group believed in a high god, some emphasized spirit figures such as the Wandjina, seen in the cave art of the north-west, and Baiame, referred to in many of the stories from the south-east. In other areas no spirit figure was given such prominence. In the west and centre, circumcision was the main rite of initiation, but this had not spread to the east.

The Dreamtime

Rather than looking forward to a life after death, the Aborigines look back to an era known as the Dreamtime. In this period the landscape as we know it today received its shape. Ancestral beings such as kangaroo-men, emu-men, bowerbird-women and fig-men moved over the face of the earth. They hunted, fought, married, defeated,

laughed and performed ceremonies. Their footprints and actions became the hills, waterholes, trees, caves, stars and other features of the landscape.

The central places of these stories are the totemic sites related to particular clans. These clans are regarded as descended from the ancestor beings. An old man can point to a rock said to be the fig-man and say: 'That is my grandfather'. The clan groups are responsible for looking after the sites, passing on the stories and performing the rituals. The major sites are considered sacred, and only men may visit them. Other sites can be visited by women and children. The activities of the ancestor beings in the Dreamtime set the pattern for human behaviour. Morality is a matter of conforming to these traditions.

Tracks of the ancestors

In some Aboriginal languages the same word is used for the Dreamtime and for the stories relating the events of that era. These stories reflect the peoples' nomadic existence. The countryside is criss-crossed with the supposed tracks of the ancestral beings. The stories of their journeys and deeds have passed down through the generations in the form of song-cycles, sung to complex rhythms. These myths are also related as stories.

The Aborigines had no priests and everyone was expected to perform a role in the ceremonies, but older men, skilled in recalling the stories and songs, were greatly respected. These men also guarded the special boards or stones on which were scratched patterns representing the stories. They were hidden in caves and brought out on ritual occasions, to recall and teach the stories. Symbolic markings painted on the walls of caves served the same purpose. The sites, the boards and rocks and some of the song-cycles and cave-paintings were all considered sacred, and to be seen or heard by men only.

Corroborees

The activities of the Dreamtime are re-enacted in ceremonies generally known as 'corroborees'. These usually consist of dancing, accompanied by the singing of the song-cycle. The painting of the body and preparation of the site are essential to the performance. Some corroborees are seen by everybody in the group; others are for men only. The women have their own songs and dances related to fertility cults and the roles of wife and mother.

Some of the ceremonies are related to the rites of passage For example, a male Aborigine becomes a man, not by reaching a certain age, but by undergoing initiatory rites such as circumcision. From this time the young man is introduced to the mysteries of the men's sacred life, learning their stories and songs, and being shown the sacred boards and sites. The youth undergoing this period of initiation is also referred to as sacred. The man who inflicts the wounds

At 'corroborees' Aborigines celebrate the events of the 'dreamtime' when primeval spirits formed the earth.

The Aborigines have their own unique art-forms, such as bark-painting.

on the young man must provide him with a wife from his own kin-group.

Food supply

Other ceremonies are known as increase rites. As hunters and gatherers, the Aborigines had no direct control over the supply of their food, by herding or cultivating. They tried to achieve some control by performing rites to increase the supply of a particular food, or to produce rain. This was done in various ways, by rubbing a special rock with a stone or red ochre, by cleaning a site, by letting blood from a vein onto sacred rocks or boards, or by performing special songs and dances.

Power

The series of Red Ochre rites passed from one group to another in the deserts of west and central

Australia, and relate the myths to social control and discipline. Rocks linked with these stories are thought to have special power. People fear to offend this power, but by properly observing the rites the power can be gained by men. By continually performing the rites, men reinvest the sites with power, and are in turn empowered by them.

Aboriginal identity

For the Aborigines the enduring reality is spiritual. The Aboriginal man believes that the same spirit which lives in him lives also in the related totem animals and plants, in the rocks and water-

At many sites in Australia there are Aboriginal rock paintings. This one shows the Lightning Brothers, who perpetuate the rain. The Aborigines believe these to be self-portraits. Whenever the colours begin to fade, they are ceremonially repainted.

holes, and in the stories and ceremonies. At death, the spirit is released from the body to return to a spiritual existence. Thus the Aborigine has links with all his surroundings, with all the members of his kin-group and of other groups in the neighbourhood, and with past and future generations. His beliefs help him to accept life's circumstances and to know that, despite the activities of evil spirits which bring death, sickness and natural disasters, he will be provided for and cared for.

Since Europeans entered Australia, many Aboriginal tribes have disappeared and others have lost all vestiges of the traditional life. Some groups in the north, west and centre have kept their traditional values, beliefs and ceremonies. In recent years, a return to traditional areas, a growth of Aboriginal identity, increasing economic independence and a change in government policies have led to an upsurge of traditional practices among some groups. But they tend to concentrate on certain aspects, such as man-making ceremonies, as other aspects are seen to be in conflict with other demands of present-day life.

Case-study 7: The Maoris

James Irwin

Maoris of New Zealand share some religious features with Polynesia (the triangle bounded by Hawaii, New Zealand and Easter Island). Their creation stories are very similar and they share a number of gods, although their roles and status differ.

Why the rain falls

Maori mythology tells of the first parents, Ranginui and Papatuanuku, who were locked in a deep embrace. As sons were born they were kept between the parents, and only allowed glimpses of light. The myth tells how the sons struggled to escape. After several abortive efforts, one son, Tane, placed his feet against Rangi, and his extended arms against Papa. Struggling fiercely, upside-down, and helped by his brothers, he forced his parents apart. Rangi became the sky, and Papa the earth—Sky Father and Earth Mother. The grief of their separation is seen in falling rain and rising mists.

Liberated in the world of light (*Te Aomarama*), the brothers fought for power. Tane became god of the forests, Tangaroa of the seas, Tumatauenga of war, Rongo of agriculture, and Whiro, the evil one, became ruler of the dark areas of life. Tawhirimatea stayed with his father, becoming god of winds

and hurricanes.

The brothers were immortal. They formed a female from the earth, and Tane breathed into it life-giving force (*hauora*); woman entered the world. Tane named her Hinetitama and took her as his wife. Their offspring became the human race. These beings are called gods or 'powers' (*atua*).

Out of nothingness

Ancient Maori philosophers thought much about beginnings, and expressed their beliefs in chants. One tells of the time of nothingness (*Te Kore*); then, long ago, the time of potential being (*Te Korekore*), then deep darkness (*Te Po*). Finally darkness was defeated and the world of light (*Te Aomarama*) appeared. This chant goes back long before the coming of Europeans to New Zealand. From these ideas comes the Maori view of a three-tier universe: the sky (*Te Rangi*), world of light (*Te Aomarama*) and the great dark, the realm of the dead (*Te Po*).

Io was the ultimate source of all supernatural power (*mana*). He lived in the highest of twelve heavens, and had ultimate control of all events. Io was known only to carefully chosen initiates, trained in complete isolation. They offered suitable rituals in

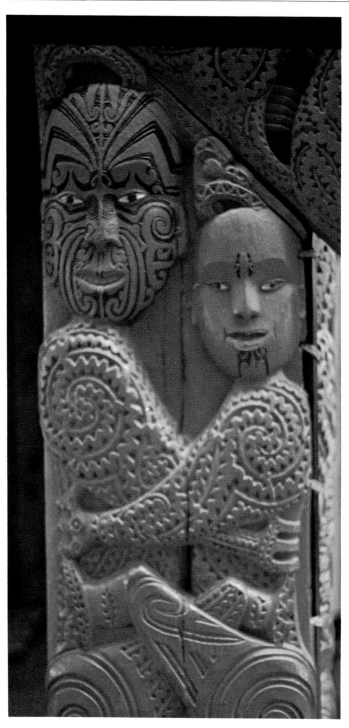

isolated places, and never spoke of Io.

Mythical monsters

As well as the gods of the 'departments of life' Maoris recognized many other powers. Some were powers of particular tribes or territory; others were family gods, known as guardians (*kaitiaki*), who warned of danger or gave encouragement. Most tribes and sub-tribes had some object called a mythical monster for example a log, or floating mass of weeds. These were to be avoided as sacred (*tapu*) objects. Many were believed to lie in deep holes in rivers or lakes, and were sometimes considered good, sometimes dangerous.

Spirits (*wairua*) could be good or evil. A departed ancestor, not given a proper funeral and so not with his ancestors, became a wandering spirit, troubling his descendants until the rites were completed. The spirits of aborted foetuses were regarded as troublesome and malicious.

God-sticks for priests

The Maoris had no temples or altars, although special secluded places were used for certain rites. Sometimes large, roughly-carved stones were placed in a clearing in a forest. These were used by a seer (*tohunga matakite*) as a place for calling his particular god. The stones were not shrines or idols. They were places where the seer would place an offering and wait until the god agreed temporarily to inhabit the stone. 'God-sticks' were used in a similar way for agricultural rituals. Minor gods, who did not do what was expected of them, were abandoned.

Eating the war victims

Sacrifice did not feature largely in Maori religion, except for food

Intricate carving on a Maori meeting-house represents the primeval parents of the Maoris. The history and customs of the Maoris are told in the paintings and carvings on the meeting-house.

offerings to pacify a god and to show respect. It was common to offer first-fruits of harvest to Rongo. The heart of the first person killed in war was offered to Tumatauenga and then, if he was a person of status, eaten by the victor to gain the spiritual power of the victim. When an important carved meeting-house was built, it was common for the body of a slave to be buried beneath the main pole.

The land used as the forecourt of a meeting-house was sacred when any gathering was held. Strict rules were observed. In death and mourning, the body was taken to the meeting-house to lie in state until the rituals were completed. This could last several days and nights, and all members of the extended family gathered. Among the Maoris, death was and is a public matter. When no rituals were taking place, the meeting-house became free from *tapu* but was still treated with respect.

If a baby sneezes...
Mauri is the life force in everyone and in certain talismans which symbolized what protected vitality, spiritual power, fertility, lands and forests. When babies sneezed at birth, it was a sign of their life force. Should someone's life force be destroyed, spiritual power would be lost and the person would soon die.
● Spiritual power is a gift from the god, and also refers to status and authority. It is powerful, and could harm individuals and communities.
● *Tapu* is the system of prohibitions warning of danger, and protecting individuals from uncontrolled spiritual power.
● *Noa* is being free from *tapu* restrictions. If *tapu* was breached, danger could only be cancelled by a purification rite (*Whakanoa*).

Maoris make up ten per cent of the population of New Zealand.

Rituals in running water
Ritual was very important to Maori people, and they emphasized the correct recital of *karakia*. Should a priest make a mistake in his incantation it was considered an ill-omen, followed by disaster.

In the rituals, water, fire and cooked food had special significance, as they could defeat evil. For special rituals, a priest would stand waist-deep in running water to protect himself from the forces he was calling up.

'Into the womb of Papa'
Maoris see the universe as sacred, so land is very important. It is to Earth Mother (Papatuanuku) that all men return at death. 'They are received into the womb of Papa.' Land is held by tribes and sub-tribes in trust for future generations and must be cared for as a man cares for his wife. Man gets from the land not only his food, but also his identity. To be without land is to be a nobody, literally worthless. To have land is to belong to the people, both alive and dead.

Waken gently!
Dreams and visions are seen as messages from the world of the spirit. A dream is usually told to a priest to have its meaning explained. It was believed that a person's spirit often left the body and travelled over wide areas during sleep. It was important to waken a sleeping person gently, to allow the spirit time to return to the body.

The last goodbye
Birth and death featured prominently in Maori religion. At birth, the father or a priest would recite a *karakia* to have supernatural power given to the child, especially the first-born. Then a feast was held. There were no rites of initiation, as the child was considered a full member of the tribe from birth.

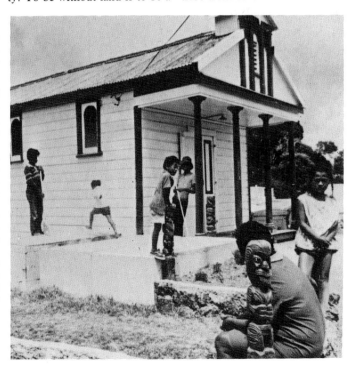

The rituals of death were elaborate and long, and still feature prominently in Maori life. It is a time to express grief, to say farewell to the dead, to make final reconciliations, and to send the dead person's spirit to the ancient homeland (*Hawaiki*), where it is installed with ancestors. Final rituals return the living relatives to ordinary life, cleansed of grief and of the *tapu* of death. The mourning is public, and whenever possible the rites are carried out at the meeting-house, for the deceased belongs to the tribe, not to the individual family.

The concept of future reward or punishment is completely absent. The departed spirits go 'above' or 'below' and seem to live a life similar to that in this world. They can interact with the living members of the sub-tribe to which they belonged in life. The realm of the dead (*Rarohenga*) is guarded by Great Hine of the Dark (*Hinenuiotepo*), through whom all must pass to reach the underworld. Originally Hinenuiotepo was Hinetitama, who fled from her husband Tane who had breathed life into her.

Glossary of Maori Words

aitua	tragedy; disaster	**rangatira**	chief of a sub-tribe; aristocracy
ao	world	**Ranginui**	Sky Father; primeval parent
ariki	high chief	**Rarohenga**	the 'below'; the underworld; realm of departed spirits
atua	supernatural powers; gods		
ahurewa	sacred place (sometimes given as *tuaahu*)	**Rongo**	god of agriculture; the moon
		rongo	peace
Hawaiki	unknown ancient homeland of the Maori	**Tane**	god of forests
		Tangaroa	god of the seas
Hinenuiotepo	guardian to the underworld	**tangi**	to weep
Hinetitama	first human being	**tangihanga**	rituals of death; funerary rites
hui	any gathering of Maori people	**taniwha**	mythical monsters; sometimes applied to important persons
Io	supreme being or high god		
iwi	people; sometimes used as a synonym for tribe	**tapu**	prohibited; sacred
		taonga	chattels; when used with plural article *nga taonga* refers to historical ornaments and weapons having *mana*
karakia	ritual incantation; invocation; prayer		
kaitiaki	guardian spirit, appears in bird or animal form		
		tipuna	ancestors
kehua	ghost	**Tawhirimatea**	a god of winds and hurricanes
mana	supernatural power; status; prestige	**tohunga**	an expert in any art or craft; especially applied to specialists of the sacred
marae	open space in front of a meeting-house		
		taura	applied to second order of specialists in the sacred
mata	face		
matakite	second sight (when used of a person means seer, or diviner)	**Tumatauenga**	god of war
		wairua	spirit (soul); spirits (supernatural powers)
mauri	life principle of anything		
ngaro	lost; hidden	**whakanoa**	to make ordinary; purificatory rites
noa	ordinary; common; free from *tapu* restrictions		
		whakairo	carved, as in *whare whakairo* (carved house)
po	night; darkness; realm of the dead		
		whare	house
Papatuanuku	Earth Mother; primeval parent (abbreviated as Papa)	**whenua**	land
		Whiro	god of evil

Case-study 8: Madagascar

Alan Rogers

Although Madagascar is close to Africa, the Malagasy people are chiefly Asiatic, and speak a Malayo-Polynesian language. Malagasy has no word for religion. 'Ancestral customs' rule every aspect of life. These customs have been slightly influenced by Arab and European cultures, but still rule the lives of more than half the population, and affect deeply the Christian and Muslim minorities. Malagasy religion has no scriptures or creeds, and has few religious stories.

Honoured by ox-skulls

In the centre of Madagascar the

twelve hills of Imerina, associated with former kings, are highly honoured. So too are the tombs of the Vazimba, half-mythical former inhabitants. Everywhere tombs of the ancestors are important. In some parts these are prominent stone buildings, in others hidden deep in the forest, and in others burial-grounds or caves marked by elaborate carved poles and the skulls of oxen killed to honour the dead. There are many upright stone pillars, usually to record an ancestor. Trees, rocks, springs, rivers and other natural features may form the centre of a cult, but the tomb of nobles are particularly important. In some tribes special cult-houses containing sacred objects set the pattern for all the houses constructed. Many villages have sacred poles at their centre, where rituals are performed.

Talismans

All sacred places have a kind of spiritual power—*hasina*. But spiritual power is present in many man-made objects. These range from charms and amulets, which protect the wearer from

In parts of Madagascar, the ancestors are honoured by being dug up periodically and danced round the family estate.

evil, to the famous talismans or fetishes (*sampy*). In former times warriors went into battle with these. They graced the accession of sovereigns, and gave advice through their human guardians. Few, if any, talismans were in human form; to call them 'idols' is misleading. They might be pieces of cloth tied to a spear, or bundles of polished wood decked with silver ornaments. The chief royal talismans were burned in 1869, but their memory is still venerated and their spiritual power continues.

Some animals convey spiritual power also, especially the crocodile, which is honoured in places by songs and occasional banquets. Cats and owls convey omens, and to some people pigs are unclean—perhaps as a result of Arab influence. No pig was allowed in the same village as a talisman. Spiritual power is a force that can be tapped in human need; but it also needs to be protected from contamination. To fail to do this is to break a taboo (*fady*)—a dangerous fault.

Dancing mania

Various sacred people act as guardians of shrines, tell the future by casting seeds on the ground, offer cures from sickness brought on by witchcraft, cast horoscopes, or guide other people through sacred rituals. Prominent men have a domestic holy man to guide all their actions. In some localities groups of people open themselves to spirit-possession (*tromba*) by smoking hemp or by other rituals. An individual may be possessed and foretell the future, using strange voices and unusual dialects. In times of national upheaval, whole bands of Malagasy have joined in a dancing mania, and broken normal taboos. Every human is valuable for his soul ('the soul makes the man' says the proverb). Above all men, all spirits and all ancestors is the fragrant

Lord Creator, Andriamanitra Zanahary—remote but good.

Bone-turning

Until the coming of European influence in the nineteenth century, an adjusted form of the Arab calendar was used. Days were marked for certain actions, or barred to others. Children born on certain days had such evil fortunes that they were killed in infancy. The New Year, at the end of the dry season, was marked by the monarch's ritual bath. The water, possessing spiritual power from the royal body, was sprinkled to bring fertility to crops, animals and people. The blood of sacrificed victims was smeared over doors, and quarrels were made up. Now there is no monarch, but the ideas and some of the customs live on. Everywhere funerals are great occasions, and the dead are regularly honoured by sacrifices and rituals. In Imerina the bones of the dead are dug up, danced round the family estate, and are thought to get pleasure from their annual outing. In return the people get protection for another year. This ceremony is called bone-turning (*famadihana*).

Rituals of family life

Important steps in life are marked by rituals. At birth, after consulting a soothsayer, the child's name is given. The after-birth is carefully disposed of. The mother purifies herself by jumping over a holy fire. All boys are circumcised at a few years old; otherwise they are not really people. Circumcision feasts are family affairs, accompanied by feasting, drinking and ribald songs. At the onset of the first menstruation girls assume the adult dress; betrothal and marriage quickly follow. Child-bearing is woman's chief function. Rituals underline this, such as climbing sacred hills, consulting a witch, or securing fragments of shroud and rotten flesh at the annual bone-turning. After fun-erals the whole family bathes and hair is shaved. Long periods of mourning follow: signs are special dress and unbraided hair.

Rum for the gods

Sacrifices are offered to the ancestors at any crisis, and holy places are honoured in the same way. The greatest sacrifice is oxen, but on lesser occasions chickens, rice, honey, rum, sugar-cane, or even sweets are enough. The prudent traveller drops small coins in rivers, hangs a scrap of cloth on each holy tree, and pours a mouthful of rum on the standing stones.

The old ordeal by poison (*tangena*) has died out, but poison is still a frequent weapon. Friends bind themselves by mingling their blood in the ceremony of *fati-dra*. In any perplexity—perhaps after breaking a taboo, or after a nightmare—people go to the local soothsayer, who prescribes a ritual to remove the threat.

'Morality' is taught by proverbs. Hundreds of these are learned, loved and used. They guide every action in life. Innovation is rash. Conforming to set patterns brings security and peace of mind. *Aza manaram-po hoatra ny kary an-efitra*—'Don't follow your own fancies: that's how cats behave in the wild.'

These model birds represent the spirits of the ancestors. They are taken to the graves to witness the annual 'bone-turning' ceremony.

Case-study 9:
African Religions

Newell Booth

By far the largest number of people in southern and central Africa speak 'Bantu' languages. The present Bantu-speaking peoples have developed through migrations and mixings of groups over the centuries, and have adapted to a number of environments, from rain forest to desert. We concentrate here on the Baluba of southern Zaire, who are in some ways typical—also mentioning other Bantu-speaking groups including the Ndembu, the Sotho-Tswana, the Zulu, the Shona and the Kikuyu.

There are other language-groups in the area such as Khoisan and Nilotic; when we use the term 'African' we include these as well as the Bantu-speaking people.

Listen to the elders

African religion is traditional; 'handed down', usually orally, from one generation to the next. A child accepts the word of the elders as final. There is no other

This article considers tribes in the southern half of Africa.

Shrines to the gods may be simple wayside altars at which offerings are made.

authority. If the elders cannot be trusted, nothing can be trusted.

It is true that what is heard from the elders is what they have received from *their* elders, and so on back. But it is also true that the tradition has been 'filtered' as it passes through several generations. The story of Nkongolo, Mbidi Kiluwe and Kalala Ilunga (see *The Luba Epic*) is told differently by various sub-groups of the Baluba, although it is the same basic story.

So we cannot say that because people today are not believing or doing exactly the same things as their ancestors 100 years ago, tradition has come to an end. If a visitor recorded a belief of 100 years ago, and a present-day African discovers that it is not now being taught by the elders, he cannot say that they have 'departed from tradition', for tradition is what the elders are handing on.

Some customs described here are no longer carried out, or have almost disappeared. This does not necessarily mean that the traditional religion is dying out, but it is undoubtedly changing.

Telling the same story

A community is made up of those who remember and share the same tradition. The Baluba are those who tell each other the story of Nkongolo, Mbidi Kiluwe and Kalala Ilunga.

In African religion community is of the highest value. The individual exists only in the community. To be cut off from the community is worse than death. But in Africa there are as many religions as there are communities.

Becoming human

African religion focusses on human beings rather than natural phenomena or supernatural beings. It aims to enhance human values in the community.

In the Bantu languages the word for 'human being' is *muntu* (or a similar word). The plural is *bantu*, from which we get the language-family name.

Birth is only the beginning of becoming *muntu*. The new-born child must first have a name, frequently an ancestral or 'spirit' name. Often it has to be decided what ancestor has 'returned' in the child, so that the child can have the right name. If a child dies before he receives this name, he was not really human at all but some sort of spirit pretending to be human.

People who are 'different' may be seen as threats to the community and therefore treated differently. Albinos, deformed people, children whose teeth came in the wrong order, and twins are all different. Most Africans consider twins to be 'special'. In some areas, one or both twins used to be destroyed for the good of the community. In other places, they were treated with special reverence; sometimes they were believed to be close to the gods. Among the Baluba, they were linked with incest and thus with the time which ended with Nkongolo.

Marking maleness

One of the most important events in the process of 'becoming human' is initiation. Among the Baluba, the male initiation ceremony is known as *mukanda*, and usually takes place at the beginning of the dry season, in May. The first stage is separation, especially from their mothers and the whole female world. This separation includes circumcision, which makes clear the maleness of the boys. Next the boys spend several months at camps away from the village, where they undergo trials and are instructed in traditional beliefs and practices. Finally, they return to the village as men prepared to take a full part in communal life. This change parallels the change in life of the whole people that took place when Kalala Ilunga replaced Nkongolo.

Similar initiations are carried out by many groups. Others have simpler ceremonies, without circumcision. The initiation of girls is usually on an individual basis, at or just before the first menstrual period. Among some groups it is quite complex, and may even be more important than male initiation.

Marriage and the community

Initiation is the gateway to full involvement in the community. The marriage of an uninitiated person would be considered an outrage. Once initiation takes place, however, marriage normally follows.

Not to marry is practically unheard of, except for seriously abnormal people. It is a community more than an individual matter; we might say that families marry, not individuals. This does not mean that the individual has no choice, but certainly his preference comes second to the good of the community. Since the purpose of marriage is to have children, any marriage which does not produce children is a failure and is usually ended.

To have children is really the most important responsibility of life. To be childless is to have failed the community, including the ancestors. A person without children cannot be an 'ancestor' and does not participate in the continuity of communal life.

The lizard and the chameleon

Life ends in death. To Africans, this is inevitable, yet in a sense unnatural. Many Africans believe that God originally intended human beings to live for ever, but due to some misunderstanding, accident or failure, death came on the scene. A common story is that God sent to mankind a message of life, but trusted it to a slow-moving animal, such as a chameleon. Later he sent a message of death, but trusted this to a swiftly-moving animal such as a lizard who, of course, arrived before the chameleon. Although God originally intended life, death cannot be escaped.

Death certainly is not welcomed. Yet there is a sense in which death makes possible the fulfilment of life. By death a person becomes an 'ancestor' living in the realm of the dead, usually believed to be underground or on the other side of our world, a land which is a mirror image of our own. Not all the dead become ancestors; only those who have children, who die in an appropriate way, and who are correctly buried. The spirits of the childless dead, of those who died of certain kinds of diseases and accidents, or far from home, and of witches, may become wandering, dissatisfied spirits who pester or harm the living in various ways.

Life continues

The kindly dead do not stay in the underworld; they continue to have dealings with their living descendants. The grave is one place where contact is made with offerings of food and drink. There may also be 'spirit houses' or shrines, frequently just outside the homes of the living, where ancestors are contacted. Snakes and other animals, especially if seen near a grave, may embody the dead. Most important, the dead may be 'reborn' into the living world.

Birth and death are complementary events. Humans move between the realms of the living and the dead. But what is 'reborn' is not the whole personality of the deceased. One who has been 'reborn' is still seen as existing in the underworld, approachable at his grave or shrine, and perhaps as appearing in an animal. A person may even be reborn in more than one descendant at a time! The dead are very much 'alive', a belief expressed in various ways.

What's in a name?

In a sense, it is the 'name' which is reborn. For Africans, the name is more than a label. It represents the basic nature of a person. So to have the name of an ancestor is to be that ancestor, inheriting something of his nature, qualities and status.

The relationship between ancestors and their descendants forms part of the 'tradition'. The ancestors 'hand down' not only myths, rituals and other information, but also their names and their being itself. All that is 'real' comes from the ancestors.

The king is dead

Most ancestors are related only to specific families. But there are also 'communal ancestors', usually linked with the founding of the present community. Among the Baluba these are called the 'superior beings' (*bavidye*). They are associated with both natural objects and heroic figures of the past. The Luba Epic suggests that originally they were nature spirits, which at a certain point entered into human beings. For example, Nkongolo is both the rainbow and an ancient chief.

The 'superior beings' continue to have a close relationship with

---

The Luba Epic

Newell Booth

A group of people with reddish skins known as the Kalanga, once lived in what is now the south-central part of Zaire. They worshipped spirits living in trees, rocks and water. But many of them were dissatisfied; they wanted the spirit powers to be more closely linked with human life. One spirit was persuaded to come from the large rock where he lived and possess a man called Mujibu, who became the first Kilumbu, one through whom the spirit could speak to the people.

The making of a tyrant

Up to this time there had been no centralized government. A young man named Nkongolo watched black ants fighting and defeating white ants. He asked his father how they did this, and his father replied, 'By organizing in bands and showing no mercy.' Nkongolo decided to follow their example. He organized a band of warriors who showed no mercy on their enemies, and soon became ruler of a large area.

Nkongolo was a tyrant, hated by his people, and suspicious of everyone except his family. He lived with his mother and sisters; possibly he was married to a sister. But Nkongolo was worried about Mujibu's prophecy that a stranger from the east would soon appear to set up a royal line in the area.

The dark stranger

One day, two of Nokongolo's sisters were collecting fish from traps along the shore of a nearby lake, when they met a hunter. He was very black, unlike the reddish local people, and obviously an aristocrat. They hurried home to tell their brother, who immediately concluded that this was the stranger from the east. He sent out warriors to capture or kill the stranger, but they could not find him.

Later Nkongolo's sisters returned and found the hunter. Nkongolo now permitted the hunter, who was called Mbidi Kiluwe, to marry his sisters. But he was still suspicious; Mbidi Kiluwe had odd habits, such as eating alone and insisting that his food be cooked on a special fire. Mujibu confirmed the view that he was the stranger from the east.

Nkongolo began to plot to get rid of Mbidi Kiluwe, who accordingly prepared to escape. His wives were now pregnant, and he gave them special arrows which only he used, saying, 'If your children are boys, and need my help, they can identify themselves with these arrows.' Then he left for his own kingdom in the east.

The dance of death

One of Mbidi Kiluwe's wives gave birth to a son, Ilunga, who grew up to be a great warrior and helped his uncle Nkongolo extend his kingdom. He was so successful that he received the title 'Conqueror' (Kalala). Nkongolo became jealous and began to plot his death. He arranged for Kalala Ilunga to lead a victory dance, secretly digging a pit in the middle of the dance area, filling it with spears with their points up, and covering it over.

When the dance began, Kalala Ilunga headed for the pit, but the drummer warned him by drumming that something was wrong. Soon Kalala Ilunga understood, threw his spear through the pit-covering, ran home to get his father's arrows, and escaped to the east. Nkongolo failed to catch him. He became fearful and hid in a cave with his sisters, who betrayed him to Kalala Ilunga on his return. Nkongolo was beheaded, and the following morning a red ant-hill had sprung up where his head had fallen.

Kalala Ilunga became king and Nkongolo, who had been resented in life as a tyrant, in death became the guardian spirit of the kingdom. 'Nkongolo' is also the Balubas word for rainbow. It is said that two large snakes, living in different lakes, sometimes rise and meet in the sky, forming the rainbow. So Nkongolo is an ancient king, a guardian spirit, and also a nature spirit. The Baluba people sometimes call themselves the 'children of Nkongolo'. But they consider Mbidi Kiluwe, the 'stranger from the east' to be the founder of the royal line which provides them with a living authority.

Spirits are responsible for many forms of evil, including sickness. To exorcise the evil, ritual dances are performed.

the kings or chiefs, who are both political rulers and religious figures. Kings and chiefs stand for the wholeness of the community, and link it with the heroic past. Sometimes it is more important for them to be in touch with the spirit world than to control the living. A ruler cannot be deformed, ill or in any way weak, because he represents the community. In some areas it was the custom to kill a ruler who was ill for more than a few days.

The house of incest

The installation of a ruler frequently involved re-enacting events of the heroic age. Among the Baluba, the new ruler was supposed to commit incest with a close female relative and then come out of the 'house of incest' to dance the victory dance of Kalala Ilunga. In this way he linked himself with the chaotic, powerful past, associated with Nkongolo, when incest occurred and brought its power into orderly society, associated with Kalala Ilunga.

Not all southern or central African groups have had centralized political systems. A village may

be the highest unit, and rule may be by consensus of elders rather than by a chief. Even where there was a chief or king, he was usually not an absolute authority but stood for the consensus of the community, which included the ancestors.

Upside-down people

We have seen that African religion involves a 'web' of past as well as present relationships. Sometimes, however, this web comes 'undone'. For instance, the dissatisfied dead are a threat to the living. There are also living persons who work against the community: witches or sorcerers. Sometimes a distinction is drawn between people who are by nature or inheritance antisocial, and even unconscious of what they are doing (witches), and those who choose to harm others (sorcerers). Both tend to do the same kind of things, destructive to the community. A witch or sorcerer is basically an 'upside-down' person. Sometimes he is actually believed to travel upside-down. He may also be 'white', whereas normal people are 'black'. He relates to animals, especially owls and hyenas, but destroys people. Normal people improve the community; a witch or sorcerer tears it down.

Death is unnatural

Individual deaths are usually blamed on a particular person. Death is seldom believed to be 'natural', except perhaps in a few cases of extreme old age. Certain kinds of death, for example from smallpox or from being struck by lightning, may be credited directly to God. Most death and disease is due to a witch or sorcerer, or to a dissatisfied spirit. It is possible that a basically kind ancestor may cause trouble, to warn the community that offerings are being neglected or standards of behaviour broken.

The basket of fortune

When disease, death or other evil occurs, the cause must be discovered through divination. There are two kinds of divination. One uses various objects to get an answer. For example, 'Ngombu', among neighbours of the Baluba such as the Ndembu, involves using a basket of objects referring to various human situations. The basket is shaken, and interpretation is based on the objects which appear at the top and how they relate to each other.

Another example would be the 'Hakata', used by the Shona people. Four pieces of wood or bone, standing for old man, young man, young woman and old woman, are marked 'up' and 'down'. The diviner throws these, and interprets on the basis of how each piece lands. Spirits are believed to be giving messages through the objects.

Secondly, spirits speak directly through persons, whom they 'possess', using their voices to speak. An example is the *kilumbu* of the Baluba, who is possessed by one of the *bavidye*. A *kilumbu* speaks especially about community matters, although he may also deal with individual problems, such as disease and childlessness.

A slightly different form is the oracle. Here a spirit dwelling in a particular spot, often a cave or a body of water, makes its will known through a medium, who is not actually 'possessed', in the sense that his or her personality is replaced by that of the spirit.

Medicine

Once the cause of a disease has been discovered, steps must be taken to produce a cure and to prevent future occurrence. Among many Bantu-speaking groups substances or actions that restore health are called *bwanga*. Africans are quite aware of the physical causes of certain problems and take practical action to deal with these. A splint would be put on a broken limb. But this is really a form of first aid, which fails to deal with the basic problems of human relationships, revealed by divination. For healing, the 'web' of tradition and community which has somehow been disturbed must be restored.

The person who uses *bwanga* to make such repairs is the 'medicine man' or 'doctor' (*nganga*), often wrongly called 'witch-doctor'. He is not a witch, who destroys relationships, but the opposite, one who repairs or protects relationships. Of course, he may use some of the same methods or powers as a witch, but he uses them positively. It is true that, using such powers, he may be tempted to use them selfishly against the community. But a *nganga* is no more a witch than a policeman is a criminal because he sometimes uses the same weapons as a criminal, and may be tempted to misuse them and become a criminal.

Many African groups have 'secret societies', with healing activities. Among the Baluba such are sometimes called *bwanga*. Members of the societies frequently perform dances which, by providing entertainment, promote harmony in the community and so keep evil away. In this way recreation, healing, politics and religion are all closely tied together in the traditional community.

The Supreme Being

Most African societies believe in a number of spirits, but also in one supreme power, responsible for creating the world. The Baluba believe in the 'superior beings' (*bavidye*); they also believe in the 'Supreme Being', *Vidye Mukulu* (*mukulu* means 'great' or 'old'). He is different from the *bavidye* who may serve him and share his being, but do not exist on the same level.

Similar beliefs appear to exist throughout southern and central Africa. Other names are used for 'God', such as Nzambe along the western coast, Leza in the south-centre, Mwari among the Shona,

In many tribes, certain people become members of a 'secret society', in order to perform special roles such as healing. These girls are about to be initiated into a secret society in Sierra Leone.

Modimo among the Sotho-Tswana, Tixo among the Zulu and neighbouring groups, Mulungu along the east coast, Ngai among both Bantu and Nilotic-speaking groups in Kenya, and Jok among several Nilotic-speaking groups. Some of these names may also mean 'spirit'; others are linked with the sky and what comes from it.

The traditional religion of most of the peoples of southern and central Africa includes belief in a Being who is in some sense the creator and ultimate power of the universe, standing behind a variety of lesser spirits. In many societies there has been little or no direct worship of this Being. He is too great, too powerful and too different from people to need or want worship of sacrifice. Or, it may be that he is too overwhelmingly present. In any case, it is unnecessary, and perhaps unwise, to call yourself to his attention. Certain groups, however, appeal to him in emergencies such as drought or epidemic, which threaten the whole community, and in a few he may receive regular worship. This seems to be more common among the Khoisan and Nilotic peoples than among the speakers of Bantu languages.

The Supreme Being holds together the 'web of relationship' between man and his environment. He is the ultimate source of the lesser spirits' power and of the power of human beings, living and dead.

Case-study 10: The Zulu

Axel-Ivar Berglund

Recent studies on African traditional beliefs have shown quite convincingly that African ideas and religious convictions are not primitive in an evolutionistic sense. Nor are they 'backward' and without sense. Quite the contrary! Thoughts and beliefs, expressed in rituals and in life-attitudes, make sense and are fully logical, if they are seen from the angle of those who live these thought-patterns.

Zulu, who live on the east coast of South Africa and belong to the Nguni family of Bantu-speaking people, are a good illustration of how an African traditional religion can adapt and accommodate itself to new ideas and symbols.

The Lord-of-the-Sky

Early literature on Zulu religious ideas, dating back some 100 years, seems to indicate that Zulu of that time hardly entertained thoughts of a god in the sky. The preoccupation was with the shades.

Due chiefly to the presence of, and challenge by, Christian missions there has developed among traditional Zulu an idea of the Lord-of-the-Sky, 'iNkosi yezulu'.

He is believed to be the eternal one; from him flows power and might. The Lord-of-the-Sky is the source of both good and evil. He is both kind and generous, but also erratic and unpredictable. In times of crisis such as drought or childlessness, Zulus turn to him; but he also sends lightning that will strike 'the one he wants to be his slave up there in heaven'. He will cause barrenness 'because the woman has irritated him, sometimes by talking too much, sometimes because the Lord-of-the-Sky is fretful'.

The chameleon is linked with the Lord-of-the-Sky. It, too, is unpredictable. It continually changes colour! It has five legs (the tail is said to be a leg because it coils around branches), and has eyes that look in different directions at the same time! 'How could such a thing as a chameleon be created? There can be no sympathy with the one that made such a creature as this.'

Although the Lord-of-the-Sky can be approached, he must be avoided lest you become insane. Only on special occasions should he be approached, and only after long preparation. Certain well-known hills in Zululand are recognized as his. On these no cattle graze and people rarely ascend them.

'Only when we plead for rain will we go up this mountain. First there must be fasting and much prayer. When everybody is ready and the set day arrives, we gather at the foot of the hill. Everybody is quiet. We climb with awe, looking down and walking humbly. Then prayer is offered by the rain-doctor. We kneel or lie down when he speaks to the Lord-of-the-Sky. When he has finished we return, without speaking. We do not talk, for the one in whose presence we are is fearful.'

The brooding shades

In the lives of the Zulu people the shades play an all-important role. But in times of crisis the shades brood over their descendants 'as a hen broods over her chickens'. The chief occasions are childbirth, puberty, marriage, death and burial. Diviners are constantly brooded over by the shades, but because they 'eat the right medicines, they do not become mad. All other people would have gone mad long ago, if they had been in the same situation'.

When a hen broods over her eggs, the chickens eventually hatch. Likewise the brooding of the shades heralds the emergence of a different person.

'It is like this. There is the bride. She is one kind of person. At marriage, when the shades brood, she becomes another person. She is now the wife. When they brood again, she changes from the childless to the mother of a child.'

A world reversed

Zulu diviners claim they see things upside-down. Shades are believed to be pale-coloured; in the world of the shades, dark stands for light and light for dark Shades are said to like gall 'because gall to them is sweet as honey'. Men work during daytime, the shades are active at night. The right hand is left, and the left is right in the world of the shades. So diviners, servants of the shades, often use the left hand when divining. Up stands for down and down for up!

These reversals and opposites make sense in the context of a flat earth viewpoint (and the global concept is, after all, relatively recent, even in Europe).

If Zululanders believe we live on top of a pancake-like world, it follows that those who live on the other side are opposite. On the top, men walk with their heads upward and feet downward; in the underworld they move upside-down.

When it is night on top it is day-time underneath! Hence people were buried at night, not to avoid the grave-site being known to thieves and evil-minded people, but so that the deceased can reach the land of the dead 'at a time when he can see in this new country'.

A diviner uses divination bones and other objects, which he throws on to a special mat in front of him.

Christianity and the Primal Religions

Harold Turner

Surprisingly, primal religion—the religion that seems farthest from Christianity and has been most despised—is in fact closer than the rest. Christianity has expanded most, not into the areas of the great culture religions of Asia, or into Islam, but among the peoples of the primal religions, starting in the Mediterranean.

The public religions of Greece, Rome and the ancient Near East were basically primal, although linked with sophisticated cultures. The religions of North Africa and Europe were also primal, like those of Oceania and black Africa south of the Sahara, and of aboriginal North and South America, whose peoples have largely been brought inside the Christian fold. Christianity has advanced most in Asia, too, where primal religions predominated—in the Philippines, in Korea with its shamanistic religions, and among the tribal hill-people of south-east Asia, Taiwan and India, and the people of Indonesia who are not Muslim.

An easy knock-down?

Some scholars explain this response as due to primal religions' fragility, primitiveness or inadequacy as compared with the great Asian religions; Christianity can deal only with religions that are an easy knock-down! This fails to take account of the deep religiousness of many primal religions. Frequently they are remarkably good at adapting to modern conditions, for example the Mwari cult of the Shona in Zimbabwe. Others have persisted through over four centuries of Western pressure and Christian penetration, for example the Hopi and other American Indian religions.

Primal religions seem to be closer to Christianity in form and structure than the major Asian religions. Often, when Christian missionaries first arrive, people say: 'This is what we have been waiting for.' A vast range of new religious movements has arisen out of a mixing of primal religions and Christianity in all continents. There is no interaction on this scale between primal religions and the other universal religions.

We are not alone

Some of the basic emphases in primal religions are also found in Christianity. These include a closeness to nature and love of the land; a profound awareness of human weakness and of the need of a greater power for successful living. There is a deep conviction that we are not alone in the universe, but that there is a spirit world from which all blessing and help come; and that while the spirits are active in the physical world, there is another world beyond death where life is purified and transformed. Not all primal religions have all these features, but many do, and clearly have much in common with Christianity.

On the other hand, there are basic differences between primal world-views and those of the Bible:
● A number of gods;
● No revelation through history;
● Efficacy of sacrifice and ritual;
● Mixing of religion and magic;
● Gods and men belong to one cosmic system and depend on each other.

By contrast, Christians worship one God with a firm moral character, who freely created the universe out of nothing, and is not tied to it, and who has acted once for all to save all peoples.

Nevertheless, primal religion often survives in syncretist folk Christianity.

Case-study 11:
North American Indians

J. W. E. Newbery

or pole, and in ceremonies such as the sacred pipe.

● **Two realities.** Tribal people also reflect upon the two-ness of life and nature. North American natives symbolize this by a divided circle, as in the Plains shields and many forms of art and craft.

Contrary to popular belief, primal religions are today reviving in many parts of the world. The superior attitude, which spread European civilization over the globe, spurred on by Western Christianity and materialism, has been discredited in the twentieth century. Native faith-ways—scorned, forbidden, almost destroyed—reached their lowest point at the end of the nineteenth century. Their flame was extinguished.

But today the disregard for the earth, for community, for spirituality, have brought the whole human enterprise into jeopardy. Arising like the phoenix from the ashes, tribal peoples are gathering again in their ceremonial circles, remembering discarded teachings, renewing the ancient ways. As they do so, perhaps they are laying the foundations for what they themselves are calling 'the fourth world', and a hope for a new beginning on the earth.

Life is one

Wisdom, for such people, is found in the past, in the long experience of the race, in tradition. A very frequent expression in their ceremonies is, 'it is said . . .' The teaching of the ancients is meant. The teacher is the Elder. He is closest to those

things of the past that are important. For tribal people, life is one. The sacred is very real—and specially real in some times and places. But the sacred is not divided off from times and places called secular. All life is sacred. All things are 'indwelt' to some degree. The whole range of life is open to spirit.

● The tribal peoples of North America proclaim the One Great Spirit. Their thought and action is governed by the circle, which they see as basic in nature: the shape of moon and sun, the wheeling stars above them, the rotating seasons, the actions of birds and animals. 'Everything tries to be round.' This form is evident in everything they do—in myth, ceremony, art and community organization.

Essential to the circle is its *centre*. From that point it is created. This is the symbol of the Great Spirit. It is reflected in all the dances around the fire, drum

Nature presents itself in pairs: dark and light, cold and hot, male and female, good and bad and so on. These are not contradictory but complementary. They are depicted in native North American shields as mirroring each other. This two-ness is also expressed in the myths, such as that of the two sons of Mother Earth; in the totems of the west coast such as Sisutl of the Kwakiutl, the two-headed serpent which punishes and protects; in the Thunderbird, threatening and caring; or in ceremonies such as the forked pole of the Sundance.

But the *two* are always seen as aspects of the one: the circle. They are different, but they appear to us in balance, in *harmony*, the over-riding virtue. We find contentment not by conflict, but by coming to terms.

An example of this is the native Arctic dweller, the Inuit. The intruding white man complains about a harsh, cruel environment, and insists when he goes north on taking with him all manner of technologies to beat the climate. The Inuit, on the other hand, lives face to face with nature and, when untouched by the intruder, is happy. He has found harmony with his surroundings, and treats the ice and snow as friends, not enemies.

● **Three-fold action.** Give and take is, for Amerindians, the basis of all healthy relationships. It can be symbolized as a triangle on a circle.

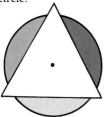

Primal people search for the support that will make their ventures succeed. This help is obtained in the *ceremonies*, whose action is three-sided. For example, a Mohawk community is threatened by drought. The corn withers in the fields. Help lies with the Thunderbeings; the rain must be sought by their aid. The thing to do is the rain dance. The community gathers in the fields. The drum and shaker sound. The dance begins. Prayer is sung. Water is sprinkled. The rains come.

The same give and take, between human need, heavenly power and particular action is found in all ceremonies for healing, guidance, power.

● **The four powers.** Native people in North America, as elsewhere, tended to see the structure of the world, and of the powers that control it, as four-sided. The symbol they used for this is a circle, with four points on the circumference.

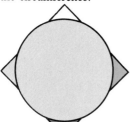

Lame Deer, a present-day Sioux, explains: 'Four is the number that is most sacred (*wakan*). Four stands for the four quarters of the earth . . . the four winds . . . seasons . . . colours . . . four things of which the universe is made (earth, air, water, fire). There are four virtues which a man should possess . . . We Sioux do everything by fours . . .'

Into this structure of fours is gathered and classified all life's variety. It is made one (the circle) through the 'great law of sacrifice', in which each part depends upon and contributes to all the others. 'One dies that another may live.' The 'wheel' is the pattern of all ceremonies, because it symbolizes the variety of life in the wholeness of life.

This concept of unity in variety and variety within unity is basic to the goal of harmony and balance in life, seen by primal people as the foundation of all health, peace and well-being in the world.

● **The seven 'Grandfathers'.** A 'mystery of sevens' lies at the root of ancient wisdom and is found among ancient cultures in all parts of the world. We find this same feeling about seven among the primal people of North America. We hear of the seven sacred rites of the Sioux, the seven prophecies (or fires) of the Ojibwa Midewiwin and the seven stopping-places in their ages-long migration westward. We hear of cycles of seven years and seven-times-seven years; we hear of the seven Grandfathers.

The seven Grandfathers are found in Ojibwa mythology. They are symbolized in the teaching staff hung in the centre of the ceremonial circle. The staff

is made up of three straight sticks bound together at their centres. These sticks have six points standing for the four directions, plus the 'above' power (sky) and the 'below' power (earth). There is a seventh, at the crossing-point. It is the 'here' place of power, the *self*, the power within. This is not to say that *I* am the centre of all, but that all the powers are available to me, are flowing through me and I can be a power with them. They come to me in visions and dreams, and in teachings and ceremonies working through me.

● **The quartered circle.** Finally, there is the simple quartered circle, the symbol of wholeness.

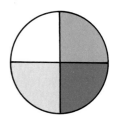

When taking part in the ceremonies, as the sweet grass is burned, the water drunk, the pipe smoked, one hears from each worshipper the words 'All my relations'. All are *related* to each and each to all. The participant is conscious that the whole universe is around him, sharing in his need and his prayer.

Case-study 12: The Andes

Leslie Hoggarth

The Andean Highlands stretch almost the whole length of the west coast of South America, from Colombia to the south of Chile. They form the longest mountain chain on any continent, with some forty-five snow peaks towering above 20,000 feet/6,080 metres.

In the mountains and valleys live many tribes, each with its own language and culture, religious beliefs and practices. The high mountainous regions are very different from the lower eastern slopes, where the rivers flow down to the Amazon forests. Physical conditions greatly affect the pattern of life and religion. But some basic concepts are common to all: beliefs about gods, spirits, the natural world, sacred places and objects possessing supernatural power and influencing every aspect of life.

Native people are concentrated in the mountain regions of Ecuador, Peru and Bolivia. Inca civilization flourished up to the time of the Spanish Conquest in 1533. It is still the homeland of some 10 million Indians. The main group are the Quechuas, but there are also about 1 million Aymara Indians, living at 12,000 feet/3,648 metres, on the 'altiplano' stretching for hundreds of miles between the main mountain ranges of southern Peru and Bolivia. The languages of the two groups differ, but there are many similarities in their life and religion.

Sacrificed to the spirits

The people of the Andes are mainly farmers, cultivating the land in the valleys and herding their sheep, llamas and alpacas as high as 14,000 feet/4,256 metres. They struggle fiercely against the harsh elements. In order to assure security and well-being, the people seek to live in harmony with their natural surroundings. Solemn rites and

The Tukano Indians live in the forests of Colombia.

An Indian shaman *from Peru.*

ceremonies are performed throughout the year to ensure good crops, animal fertility and freedom from illness and disaster. These ceremonies involve a complex ritual of prayers, offerings, drink-offerings and even animal sacrifices offered to the spirits of the region.

The mountain people see the Earth Mother, Pachamama, as the provider and sustainer of life. In the high, snow-capped peaks live the Apus. These are the 'lords' who control everything in the area. The spirits of the lower hills are known as Aukis and are not as powerful as the Apus. All the Apus and Aukis are named after the mountain or hill where they live. They are the chief gods in the Indian world. But thunder, hail, rain, wind, fire, springs, rivers and special rocks and stones are all very important. They are all alive, and possess life-power, and have to be recognized with token offerings.

The Apus, Aukis and Pachamama exercise their power in the growing of crops, making animals fertile and looking after the community. They can become hungry, angry, neglected or offended, and people must take care to give them their due and to keep up good relations with them.

Struck by lightning

August marks the beginning of the agricultural cycle. At this time Pachamama is spoken of as 'being alive'. She is ready to receive the seed; therefore the ceremonies must be performed to ensure a good harvest. Token portions of coca, food and drink are 'served' and an offering containing the foetus of a llama or some other animal, coca leaves, animal fat, and other items is burned in a special place. A prayer will be offered, such as— 'Pachamama, this is your due, that I serve you in August at the beginning of the year. You are the one who nourishes me, receive this offering. You feed me like a mother from her breast, or as a bird feeds its young. Receive this kindly, and defend me from all harm. Remove sorrow and illness far from me, and may I live well through another year.'

Similar prayers, burnt offerings, and in some places blood sacrifices, are made in animal fertility ceremonies.

In times of sickness people will consult the *paqo* (medicine man and medium) to discover the cause of the trouble. There are different types of *paqo*; some work by divination, such as reading the signs in the coca leaves— others contact the spirits direct. A genuine *paqo* is one who has been struck by lightning and survived, and is therefore considered to have been chosen as priest.

Part Four
Living Religions of the East

The Eternal Teaching: Hinduism

Raymond Hammer

The religious tradition we call 'Hinduism' is the product of 5,000 years of development. The name, however, dates only from about AD 1200, the time when the invading Muslims wished to distinguish the faith of the people of India from their own.

'Hindu' is the Persian word for 'Indian'. Indians themselves, however, prefer to speak of the eternal teaching or law (*sanatana dharma*), indicating the 'givenness' or revelatory character of the beliefs to which they are committed.

No founder, no creed

Hinduism has no founder and no prophet. It has no particular ecclesiastical or institutional structure, nor set creed. The emphasis is on the way of living rather than on a way of thought. Radhakrishnan, a former president of India, once remarked: 'Hinduism is more a culture than a creed.'

Not everyone who is born a Hindu is a practising Hindu. But it is claimed that 'they are Hindus because they were born as Hindus'. The origin of the name suggests that the common ingredient in Hinduism is the Indian origin of its adherents. (In fact, one writer somewhat cynically asserts that the only unifying features in Hinduism are the Indian character of the faith and the universal reverence for the cow!)

Mother India

The Hindu religion is closely inter-

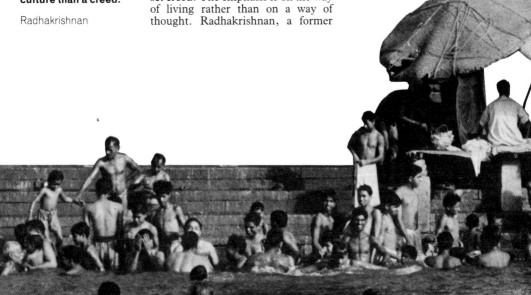

twined with tradition about the land of India, its social system and its history. The Indian subcontinent has clear geographical demarcations. Triangular in shape, it is bounded on two sides by the ocean and to the north by the impenetrable Himalayan range of mountains. The actual shape of the land recalls for Indians the figure of a mother and speaks to them of 'Mother India'.

A large part of the country is a rich, fertile plain. This is what makes the mountains, and the rivers which flow from them, so significant. In the north it is the rivers, in the south the monsoon rains, which make plentiful harvests possible throughout the year.

The whole of nature is seen as vibrant with life—trees, rocks and waterfalls provide a focus for the sacred, becoming shrines at which worshippers discover meaning in life. The mountains and forests often speak to the Indians of the powers that confront human endeavour and so become pointers to the struggle between divine and demonic powers.

Although the yogis go on pilgrimage to desolate regions in search of 'Reality', it is primarily the rivers which are seen as the source of support and spiritual life.

Sacred river

The sacred River Ganges not only provides water for the land; the water is itself the symbol of life without end. Hundreds of thousands flock to its banks daily to perform their ritual ablutions in its waters and sip from its life-giving stream. Once every twelve years as many as 10 million people share in ritual bathing at the great Kumbh Mela festival at Allahabad, where the waters of the Ganges and Jumna combine. Varanasi (on the Ganges) is the most sacred city—*the* place for a Hindu to die. Then, after cremation, the ashes can be cast upon the waters of the sacred river and life continues!

A rich variety

The population of India is far from homogeneous. Each district has its own language and customs as well as its own religious ideas and practices. The vast majority of the people are agricultural and, despite large populous cities, most live in small villages, of which there are almost 700,000. This factor contributes to the tremendous local variety within the larger regions.

The oldest continuous culture is to be found in the four southern states, where the languages are classified as 'Dravidian'. The north, as a result of the Aryan invasion which took place in the middle of the second millennium BC, possesses a group of related languages, in which Hindi is dominant. The north-eastern states are dominated by Bengal which was late in receiving Aryan influence.

About 400 million people in the Indian subcontinent may be regarded as Hindus. And wherever Indians

Varanasi (Benares) is the most holy city in India. Millions of pilgrims visit it each year, to bathe in the sacred Ganges.

Hindus cremate their dead. Scattering the ashes together with sacred marigold flowers onto the River Ganges ensures the soul's continued life.

none at all!

● He may also believe in one god *and* in several gods as manifestations of him.

● He may express the ultimate in personal or impersonal terms.

It has been suggested that Hinduism is 'a federation of cults and customs, a collage of ideas and spiritual aspirations'. So, is it possible to speak of 'Hinduism' in the singular, or are there many 'Hinduisms'?

Under one umbrella

For Hinduism, as for other religious traditions, the name is an umbrella term which does not demand a total homogeneity. (To draw a parallel: the ritual of an African independent Christian church will be far removed from a Coptic or Armenian liturgy, and yet all come under the name 'Christian'.) But if Hinduism embraces a 'family of religious beliefs', we still need to find something which can be called the 'ethos' of Indian religion.

The flow of life

One concept which is found everywhere within Hinduism today is the idea of reincarnation or transmigration. Whereas Christianity thinks in terms of the importance of decision-making within one life, and sees salvation in terms of the individual (though not neglecting the group or the whole), the Hindu thinks of the flow of life through many existences. This lies behind the notion of *samsara* which expresses this flow from birth to death and then on to rebirth, and so on. As a result the limited span of history is lengthened to billions upon billions of years.

Linked with the notion of *samsara* is the concept of *karma*. *Karma* literally means 'work' or 'action', but also indicates the *consequences* of actions within one existence which flow into the next existence and influence its character—and so the chain goes on. Hindu hope, therefore, is for release (*moksha*) from this chain or cycle.

The other great unifying feature is the attitude of Hinduism to society (see 'Roots').

have gone, they have taken with them their culture and religious ideas and practices.

One faith or many?

Hinduism embraces a wide diversity of religious belief.

● The vast majority of Hindus believe in God in some way or other, but there are some who do not.

● Some Hindus believe that a respect for all living creatures demands that they be vegetarians; others will sacrifice animals at the temple and joyfully share in a roast by the river-side.

● Some Hindus worship Shiva; others Vishnu or his incarnations (*avatars*), most notably Krishna or Rama; others again are worshippers of the goddesses.

● The inhabitants of one village do not share in the precise focus of worship which will unite the villagers in another place.

● The individual Hindu may reverence one god, a few, or many, or

Roots: The Development of Hindu Religion

Raymond Hammer

The roots of Hinduism (as we now meet it) go back thousands of years. So what do we know about the earliest forms of religion in the Indian subcontinent?

Temple-citadels

The earliest evidence we have comes from excavations that have taken place since 1922 in the Punjab and the Indus Valley. A homogeneous urban culture was established in the third millennium BC, and two cities have been excavated: Harappa, the prehistoric capital of the Punjab on the banks of the River Ravi, and Mohenjo-daro, 400 miles/645 kilometres away in Sindh, on the banks of the Indus.

It is evident that the rivers were vital for their inhabitants, irrigating the broad, fertile plains with their flood-waters. Ritual purity was most important to these early people and the ancient temples incorporated ceremonial ablutions (as they still do today). Ritual bathing was not confined simply to the baths at the sanctuary. People also bathed in the rivers which provided the livelihood for their community, and so could be thought of as 'rivers of life' and therefore sacred.

The finds at the temple-citadels suggest that there was a unity of the political and the religious. There may be parallels with the sacral kingship in ancient Babylon, where the ruler was seen as a 'son' of the divinity—in both cases a mother-goddess, the symbol of creativity and the ongoing flow of life. There are many figurines of the goddess, signifying the origin of life (a pregnant figure) or the nurture and continuance of life (figures which emphasize the breasts). All the indications are of an early matriarchal society as the background to the host of goddesses in India today. Each village seems to have its own goddess, venerated as the giver of life and fertility. They may also be seen as embodiments of the female principle, called *Shakti* in developing Hinduism.

There are figures of a male god, too, with horns and three faces (seemingly the original of the triad, *Trimurti*, later expressed by the three deities Brahma, Vishnu and Shiva). He is shown in the position of a yogi (one who practises yoga, the way of self-discipline) in a state of contemplation. He is also seen surrounded by animals, which suggests that he is the original form of the great god Shiva, who is often spoken of as 'Lord of the Beasts'. The fertility symbols, the *lingam* and *yoni* (representing the male and female sexual organs), both still present in popular forms of Hinduism, have also been found.

It would appear, therefore, that this ancient Indus Valley civilization shows traits which are still a powerful force in Indian religion.

The Aryan faith

In the middle of the second millennium BC the Aryan (literally 'noble') peoples invaded India, bringing their language and traditions and profoundly influencing, although in no way ousting, the older religions, ideas and practices. Their language developed within India into what we call Sanskrit—a parallel of Greek, Latin and other Indo-European languages. It appears that their religion, too, had close affinities with that of Homer's Greece. At any rate, the Aryan pantheon recalls the gods of *The Iliad* and *The Odyssey*—fundamentally manifestations of nature.

Whereas the older Indus Valley religion seems to have included yoga, renunciation and purification rites—all of which continue to mark the 'holy men' of India—the Aryans appear to have been much more world-affirming. They were originally nomads (coming perhaps from the Baltic regions). They appreciated the 'openness' of nature—trees, fields, sky and so on. Like Homer's Greeks, they made their sacrifices to gods who represented the forces of nature. Animal sacrifice was very much a feature of their practices. Whereas rivers provided the meeting-place for the pre-Aryan worshippers, the Aryans gathered around fire and performed their ceremonies there. They would cast grain, butter and spice into the flames.

Unfortunately there have been no archaeological finds from the early period of Aryan settlement, but we do possess a literature (written down probably about 800 BC, but reflecting an oral poetical tradition from centuries before). The Vedic texts (*Vid* expresses 'knowledge') enshrine the main evidence for the original Aryan faith.

Songs of knowledge: the Rig Veda

The *Rig Veda* ('songs of knowledge') are the oldest. Many of these religious hymns may have been composed when the Vedic peoples were still in central Asia. But most of them probably date from a time after the settlement in India. In later times they were considered to be a revelation from Brahman (the ultimate source of all being) in the form of words, received by the inspired sages (*rishis*). The sages, it was held, had been granted the ability to apprehend the knowledge which was eternal (hence the title *sanatana*—'eternal'—*dharma*) and divine. The religious tradition later distinguished between what was revealed (*shruti*) and what was remembered (*smriti*) and so possessed not direct, but only a secondary, inspiration.

The gods

The *Rig Veda* is made up of more than 1,000 hymns. They are usually addressed to a single god, and several dozen different gods feature in them. The most popular is Indra, who is portrayed as a warrior who overcomes the powers of evil and brings the world into being. The god Agni is the personification of the sacrificial fire (Latin *ignis*) and so links earth and heaven, carrying the gifts which the priests pour into the flames into the presence of the gods.

'May that Agni who is to be extolled by ancient and modern seers, conduct the gods here.'

The divine parents, Heaven and Earth, symbolize the expanses of nature. Their marriage indicates the indissoluble link between two worlds, the celestial and the terrestrial. Varuna (Greek Uranus) is the chief of the gods, because ceremonial rite (*rita*) and law (*dharma*) are administered and regulated by him. The cosmic order is within his control and he ensures that there is no transgression, cosmic or human.

The *Veda* distinguishes between the World Soul (*purusha*)

Hinduism Outside India

Raymond Hammer

From the seventh century AD Hindu culture and religion exercised a widespread influence throughout south-east Asia, taking in the modern-day countries of Burma, Thailand, Kampuchea, Laos and Vietnam as well as many of the islands of Indonesia. (For 1,000 years, even then, there had been contact with Sri Lanka, formerly Ceylon, and during the time of Ashoka who was ruler in the third century BC, Buddhist ideas had been introduced.) Generally speaking, this influence persisted for about eight centuries and is dominant on the island of Bali to the present day.

In most countries, however—and this is also true of Bali—the Hindu culture incorporates a great deal of popular, indigenous, pre-Hindu religion. The Angkor Wat structures in Kampuchea reflect interest in Brahminic religious rites, the worship of Vishnu and Shiva, as well as pronounced ideas of kingship. A stylized religious art marks most of the countries, and in Thailand and Kampuchea the sculptures bear witness to the popularity of the *Ramayana* cycle of stories.

Since Hinduism, in some form or other, is the religion of most Indians, we would expect to find Hindu wherever Indians are to be found. The dispersion takes in Europe (especially, of course, the United Kingdom), the Americas and Pacific areas as far as Fiji. Until recently, there were also a considerable number of Indians in eastern and southern Africa.

Although it has been largely through Buddhism that Indian thought (and especially religious ideas) has had its impact on the West, Indian *swamis* and gurus have had a considerable following and Hare Krishna groups are to be found in both Europe and America.

Many in the West also look to yoga. Just as Buddhism had its Eightfold Path, so royal yoga (Raja Yoga) had its eight stages—mainly physical disciplines directed to the goal of deep, concentrated meditation. This involved self-control (to which the name yoga points), observance, posture, control of breath, restraint of the senses, control of the thought-processes and contemplation.

Although many in the West regard yoga simply as a discipline which strengthens the body and provides relaxation and a quiet mind, in the context of Hinduism it is the means by which a person strives for salvation. This is achieved when the dualism of self and Brahman is overcome and all selfhood is lost in the streams of being. Movements such as Transcendental Meditation (TM) look to this goal with yoga.

and substance (*prakriti*). The former is seen as the cosmic sacrifice, which ensues in life and order. There can be no life without sacrifice, we are told, and the divisions of the World Soul are seen as the basis of the human social order. The mouth is the priestly order (the Brahmins), the arms are the rulers (Rajanya, later known as the Kshatriya), the thighs are the land-owners, merchants and bankers (*vaishya*) and the feet are the workers, artisans and serfs (*shudra*). (It is likely that the *shudras* represented the subject-peoples who came from the indigenous population and were subordinated to the conquering Aryans.)

Power for the priests

The priority of the priestly class is linked with the crucial position given to sacrifice and the magical use of incantations. The priests alone could bring the people into touch with the cosmic powers and guarantee the continuation of life. This priestly ascendancy was not accepted without question, as the ruling class seem to have held the leadership for much of the time. It was only the elaboration of rite and ceremonial which increased the power of the priests. The more complicated the forms of worship, the more essential it was to have the expert!

But the *Veda* also reflects a growing speculation which was to lead to the *Upanishads* (the *Vedanta*, the end of the *Veda*) with which the revealed word was to terminate. In the early creation myth Indra was seen as the personal agent in creation, bringing existence out of non-existence. In later speculation 'One God', described in personal terms, gives way to 'That One'—the impersonal force of creation.

There is also a questioning note:

'Who knows it for certain; who can proclaim it here; namely, out of what it was born and from what creation proceeded ... whether he made it or whether he

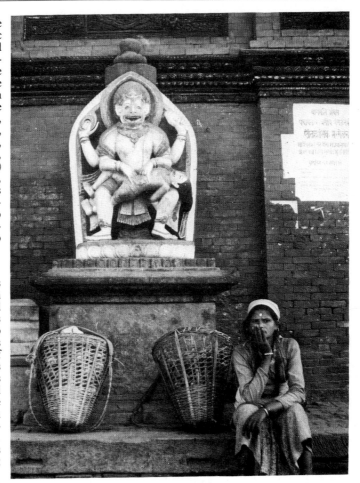

The god Shiva is the destroyer. This Nepalese carving shows him killing an evil demon.

has not? ... he alone knows, or, perhaps, even he does not know.'

In this passage we have the basis for the future philosophizing which was happier to describe the ultimate or transcendent in negative rather than in positive terms and which was to accept a basic relativism in all attempts to describe the absolute.

Classes and castes

From the four class groupings of the poem on creation, the idea grew that some hierarchic structure in society is a part of the divine intention for the natural order. The classes (*varnas*—colours) were later to proliferate into a large number of birth-groups (*jutis*), which differentiated families much more according to work done in the community.

Although some aspects of the caste system have been outlawed by the Indian government in recent times, the system continues as an integral part of Indian society. Questions of marriage and eating are all linked with the class caste groupings. The first three classes are cut off from the fourth by being 'twice-born', or 'the initiated'. They

The Ramayana *is an epic poem which tells the story of Rama, the sixth incarnation of Vishnu. He was a great hero, dedicated to ridding the earth of evil-doers.*

wear the sacred thread as an indication of superior status. In addition, birth-groups differentiate between the 'pure' and the 'impure', indicating both the importance of ritual purity and the impurity that accrues from mixing with another group.

It is likely that the *shudras* were first despised by the invading Aryans and regarded as belonging to an inferior colour (*varna*), being dark instead of light-skinned as they were. The idea of the cycle of rebirth later indicated that the *shudras* could hope for salvation only in a future life, as they were not yet among 'the initiated'.

The priests were gaining a stranglehold on society through class differentials. But this was not to go unchallenged.

Revolt in the temple!

By about 600 BC the ascendancy of the priest in society was commonly accepted in northern India. The priestly ritual of sacrifice and its appropriate *mantra* (verbal utterance) as set out in the manuals of the priestly class dominated the sacrificial system. It was at this point that the movements of Jainism and Buddhism (see relevant articles) emerged within Hinduism. At the same time the *Upanishads* provided a redirection of the Vedantic tradition, being accepted as 'revelation'. These formed an indispensable ingredient in the new synthesis which was to emerge and be called 'Hinduism'.

The Jains

Both Mahavira (?599–527 BC), the figure behind Jainism, and the Buddha (about 563–483 BC), the founder of Buddhism, belonged to small republican city-states that had emerged amongst the Aryan tribal units. They came from 'noble' families of the ruling class which had once held the leadership in society.

The Jains believe that Mahavira was the twenty-fourth 'Ford-maker' in the current era of cosmic decline. (The cyclical view of history was unquestioningly accepted.) He, like the Buddha after him, had wandered in search of 'release' or 'salvation' from the age of thirty. He found it when he was forty-two, when he became a completed soul (*kevalin*) and conqueror (*jina*). (The name 'Jain' is derived from *jina*.) He died at Pava (near Patna in Bihar) after teaching for thirty years.

Mahavira was much more of a rationalist than the Brahmanists. He rejected revelation and based his religious scheme on logic and experience. He accepted the somewhat pessimistic view of the human situation and was concerned for release. As he saw the situation, the human soul was enmeshed in matter and needed to regain its pristine purity and thereby achieve immortality. It can only gain liberation as it loses its accumulation of actions and their consequences. Each soul is seen as an entity in its own right. Jainism in this way affirms a plurality of beings as against one

Men and Movements
Raymond Hammer

Over the past 200 years Western culture and the fundamental beliefs of Christianity have had a profound impact upon Hinduism. For quite a time it was customary for the more educated Indian to identify himself with the religion of the foreign occupier of his country. Hindu belief and practice continued unchanged in the villages, but in the cities the more affluent tended to undervalue Indian culture and literature and to disassociate themselves from popular religious practice.

Rammohan Roy
Rammohan Roy (1772–1833) has been called 'the father of modern India' because of his attempt to reform Hinduism, whilst reaffirming Hindu values. He claimed that all that was of value in Christian ethics was already present in his own Hindu heritage. He came from a Brahmin family and showed himself a remarkable student from his early years. He not only studied Hindu and Buddhist texts in Sanskrit, but mastered Persian, Arabic, Greek and mathematics. He organized the Brahmo Samaj (a society for the worshippers of God) and, as the ideals of the society, selected those passages in the classical Hindu scriptures which came closest to an ethical monotheism.

Although he was not unsympathetic to Christianity and was deeply moved by the person of Jesus, he rejected what he termed the 'doctrinal shell', welcoming only what he felt to be its 'humanitarian message'. As a result of his influence, the study of the *Vedas* and *Upanishads* was popularized and he laid the basis for the Hinduism of the Indian intelligentsia.

Sri Ramakrishna
Another significant figure in Hindu renascence was Sri Ramakrishna (1836–86) who came from a Brahmin family in Bengal. From an early age he experienced religious ecstasy and was particularly involved in the Kali cult. In his mystical trances he sought for communion with the 'Divine Mother' and, from the age of twenty, he was the chief priest of the Kali temple in his neighbourhood. Later, however, he came under the influence of Vedantic philosophy and so came to approach salvation by combining the paths of devotion and knowledge. He held that there was a universal truth present in all religions and saw God present in a variety of manifestations—as the Divine Mother, as Sita, as Rama, as Krishna, as Muhammad and as Jesus Christ. He was accordingly ready to accommodate himself to the dress, food or prayer patterns of other religions when he associated with their adherents. He had great influence among the Westernized middle class in Calcutta, and his deep piety and patent sincerity led them, in

turn, to value their Hindu origins.

'I am a child of God,' he asserted; 'the son of the King of Kings; who can bind me? . . . I am not bound, I am free.'

The Ramakrishna Mission was organized in 1897, after his death, to carry on both his missionary and his social and educational work. It was reorganized in 1909, when its educational, charitable and missionary activity was separated from the monastic side (identified with the *ashrams*—open monasteries or retreat houses). The mission stresses the universal character of Hinduism (thus facilitating missionary work amongst Westerners) and adapts to the needs of a society in transition.

Vivekananda
The growing influence of the Ramakrishna movement and its international appeal were largely due to Vivekananda (1863–1902). Named Narenda Nath Datta, he had planned to study law in England, but was 'converted' by Ramakrishna. After twelve years of ascetic discipline he became famous as a religious teacher (*swami*), the apostle who carried Ramakrishna's teaching to the world. He was responsible for the stress on social work and religious education, and his fiery speeches aroused a new idealism among the young elite of India, so that they devoted themselves to uplifting the millions of poor and starving in India.

At the World Congress of Faiths in Chicago in 1893, he 'sold' to the world the greatness of the Hindu tradition. Not only

were Indians given a pride in their own culture but, for the first time, Westerners who were disillusioned with Western society and had rejected the Christianity of the West turned to India for religious values and a new spirituality. (Madame Blavatsky's Theosophical Society was one group influenced by Vivekananda.)

His fundamental message was that each person was potentially divine and so should work to unleash the unlimited power within and also enable others to do the same. The mingling of theistic and monistic language which marks much Hindu thought is present in his teaching, although 'panentheism' (i.e. everything is within God) might better describe his standpoint.

'He is in everything; he is everything. Every man and woman is the palpable, blissful, living God. Who says God is unknown? Who says he is to be searched after? We have found God eternally. We have been living in him eternally.'

Vivekananda was ready to accept caste, regarding it as part of the natural order, but he rejected the notion of privilege derived from caste differentiation. Instead, he advocated equal chances for all.

Rabindranath Tagore
A contemporary of Vivekananda was Rabindranath Tagore (1861–1941) who gained the Nobel Prize for Literature in 1913 and whose poems were quoted by the elite of British Edwardian society in their drawing-room parties. He reflected the continuing influence of the Brahmo Samaj, giving it artistic expression. Nehru once

said that 'Tagore was primarily the man of thought', as contrasted with Mohandas Karamchand Gandhi (1869–1948) whom he spoke of as the man 'of concentrated and ceaseless activity'.

Gandhi

Gandhi had been influenced by Vivekananda and once observed: 'My life is my message.' For him truth was God, and non-violence (*ahimsa*) was the way to achieve the realization of God. His life was devoted to winning independence for India and raising the country's status. His Hinduism was all-embracing. Although he respected the Vedantic tradition and had a particular affection for the *Bhagavad Gita*, he claimed that his version of Hinduism included 'all that I know to be best in Islam, Christianity, Buddhism and Zoroastrianism'.

On the other hand, his teaching cannot be understood apart from the three basic Hindu concepts of *dharma* (duty), the *karmayoga* (the discipline of action) and *moksha* (spiritual deliverance). He interpreted the *Bhagavad Gita* as selfless action (*anashakti*), seeing Arjuna as the one who has to be calm and yet generous in the midst of suffering. Non-violence is not to be thought of in terms of passivity—it is the way of action. (There is some parallel here with the fact that Christians see in the suffering of Christ God's supreme action—the liberation of mankind from sin and death. It is not without significance that the cross of Christ had a fascination for Gandhi and that his favourite hymn was 'When I survey

the wondrous cross'.

Gandhi rejected the caste system. He regarded it as an accretion to Hinduism. He was particularly concerned for the untouchables or outcaste groups, demanding that, far from being rejected by society, they should be seen as the privileged children of God (*Harijans*). In his retreat-house (*ashram*) he demanded of his followers the same vows which he had taken upon himself: the pursuit of truth, non-violence seen as love in action, abstinence from sexual activity (his own stance from 1906) and poverty.

Aurobindo Ghose

Another influential figure in recent times was Aurobindo Ghose (1870–1950). He also displayed Western influence in his thought, emphasizing cross-cultural fertilization between East and West. The son of an English-educated Bengali doctor, he studied at Cambridge, but then turned to Indian culture and politics. Like Gandhi he was influenced by Ramakrishna and Vivekananda and interpreted the Vedantic tradition through their eyes. When in prison for his political activities, he claimed to hear the voice of Vivekananda, guiding him in the practice of yoga. Although he saw all men as incarnations of God, evolving in their consciousness, he saw India's national revival as the first step in spreading 'the universal truth of Hinduism' throughout the world.

'That which we call the Hindu religion is really the eternal religion, because it is the universal religion which embraces all others.'

It is not without reason,

therefore, that some have caricatured the Hindu approach as being: 'All religions are equal, but Hinduism is a bit more equal than the rest!'

CHARISMATIC LEADERS

In addition to these reformers, a large number of charismatic leaders have been responsible for the emergence of a number of popular sects. These have been influential both within India and in Hinduism outside India. Most come within the *bhakti* tradition, although in some cases there is an attempt to fuse *bhakti* with the Vedantic understanding of Hinduism.

Swami Narayan

One example is a Gujurati called Ghanshyama (1781–1830). As leader of the Satsang sect, he was known as Swami Sahajananda and Narayana. The last name stressed his claim to be divine. A vigorous preacher and masterly organizer, he won a large following. He had a hypnotic influence on his followers, whom he prepared to face persecution and suffering. He was the 'Guru Nanak' of the Gujuratis: as the Punjabis had become Sikhs, so large numbers of the Gujuratis joined the Swami Narayan sect. They saw in the Swami authority in teaching and the focal point of their devotion. The Swami Narayan sect exercised a strong influence upon Indians in East Africa and from there it entered Britain.

Sai Baba

Another movement, largely among the Gujuratis, is that

associated with Sai Baba (died 1918). It is *bhakti* in character, but strangely enough, Sai Baba is held to have been an *avatar* of Shiva. His successor, Sathya Sai Baba (born 1926), is held to be an *avatar* of Shiva and Shakti. He has attracted a huge following. As immigrants have brought the movement to the West, there has been stress on the fact that there is only one human race and so, fundamentally, only one caste. It is sometimes affirmed that the Sai Baba movement is no new religion, nor a particular form of Hinduism, but a spiritual path that any religionist may follow, because it is held to bring fulfilment to all.

'My life is my message.'

Gandhi

ultimate reality (monism) which was the most significant affirmation of the *Upanishads*.

Though the existence of superhuman beings is not explicitly denied, the approach of Jainism is fundamentally atheistic, rejecting both the concept of creation and all thought of the operation of providence in the world. The path to knowledge is the important thing, and the Jain analysis of right conduct. (See the article on Jainism.) First of the five virtues was non-violence (*ahimsa*), or what Albert Schweitzer called 'reverence for life'. This was adopted by Buddhism and, in modern times, has been the fundamental element in Hinduism, as Mahatma Gandhi interpreted it. The other virtues in Jainism are speaking the truth, honesty, chastity and a non-attachment to worldly things.

The Buddha

If we can sift history from legend, the Buddha, Siddharta (his personal name) Gautama (his family name) rejected the sacrificial cults and the caste system, and taught a new way to release and salvation, which he described in terms of a 'quenching' (*nirvana*). What needed quenching was the desire which kept a person prisoner to the cycle of rebirth by reason of his actions. If desire was the reason for the anguish and suffering which marked the human lot, it was clear that the desire had to be set aside before release was attained and *nirvana* reached.

Like a doctor, he not only analysed the symptoms of the human malaise, but also prescribed a cure. Here he pointed to a 'middle way' which came out of his own experience. For he had found that neither a sensual life in the world nor the extreme asceticism of the hermits had satisfied him. His teaching set forth the Noble Eightfold Path to *nirvana* (see further the articles on Buddhism).

The Buddha's message was perpetuated through the community of his disciples and Buddhism spread rapidly—to the south of India and from there to Sri Lanka and Burma. Schools of Buddhism grew up and from the first century BC Mahayana ('the great vehicle') emerged.

Mahayana Buddhism made some accommodation to Hindu thought and there was interaction with it. The Buddha was thought of as the incarnation of the ultimate Buddha for this age (i.e. an historical manifestation) and the *dharma* came to be virtually identified with Brahman in the sense of an absolute and eternal law within the universe. Nagarjuna, the great Buddhist thinker, introduced the notion of accommodated teaching, which allowed for a multiplicity of religious approaches, because none, as such, was grasping at the reality. The 'Buddha nature' was within all and needed to be expressed, but the truth was to be apprehended intuitively and not through sense-experience.

The Upanishads

Although Jain and Buddhist ideas had a great influence on the development of Hinduism, later Hindu teachers regarded them as unorthodox. By contrast, there was another form of semi-secret teaching which was circulated by teachers who were within the Vedic heritage, but reshaped the Hinduism of the future. This teaching came to be known as the *Upanishads* (*upa* = near, *ni* = down, *shad* = sit), because those who received it sat down beside their teachers!

These teachers were not involved in pleading with the gods or ritual sacrifice. They were more concerned to discover the ground of the universe, the Reality (Brahman) which was prior to all other existence. At the same time they were concerned to explore the nature of human consciousness. They came to the

'Arjuna, of this be sure: None who pays me worship of loyalty and love is ever lost. For whosoever makes me his haven, base-born though he may be, Yes, women too, and artisans, even serfs— Theirs it is to tread the highest Way . . .'

Bhagavad Gita IX.31,32

'If men thought of God as much as they think of the world, who would not attain liberation (*nirvana*)?'

Maitri Upanishad 6.24

'At the heart of this phenomenal world, within all its changing forms, dwells the unchanging Lord. So, go beyond the changing, and, enjoying the inner, cease to take for yourself what to others are riches.'

The first verse of the *Isha Upanishad*

'The Self is all-knowing, it is all-understanding, and to it belongs all glory. It is pure consciousness, dwelling in the heart of all, in the divine citadel of Brahma. There is no space it does not fill.'

From the *Mindaha Upanishad*

'Thou art the Eternal among eternals, the consciousness within all minds, the Unity in diversity, the end of all desiring. Understanding and experience of Thee dissolve all limitations.'

From the *Shivatashvatara Upanishad*

The large Hindu temples are breathtaking buildings. This gate-tower or gopuram *leads into the temple of Minakshi at Madura. Minakshi is a consort of the god Shiva.*

conclusion that what was basic to the individual self (*atman*) was none other than the Reality which undergirded the cosmos.

Like the Jains and the Buddhists they were concerned to overcome the fundamental sense of anxiety and frustration which marks human existence. They also recognized the sense of flux and impermanence in life. But they looked for the essence of permanence not only outside man, but also within. Their way to salvation was that of knowledge or spiritual insight.

Like the manuals of the priests, each *Upanishad* is attached to one of the four Vedic hymn-collections. They are speculative treatises which draw upon parable to communicate their view of reality. Every book on Hindu religion quotes the story of Svetaketu in the *Chandoya Upanishad*. He is asked to split off the fruit from the banyan tree and then continue to subdivide it until he can see nothing at all. His father reminds him that nothing comes from nothing and that even within the infinitesi-

mally small there is still present the power which pervades the whole universe and is the basis of all existence.

'Have faith!' he is told. 'That is the spirit-breath (Brahman) which lies at the root of all existence, and that is what you are too, Svetaketu!' 'That is what you are' expresses the unity of the human self (or soul) with the ultimate Reality. He is told, too, to see the impossibility of extracting salt from water in a saline solution. It penetrates the whole. In the same way, he is assured that the reality within the human self (*atman*) is Reality itself (Brahman).

Radhakrishnan has stressed the subjective and the objective sides in the *Upanishads*. Svetasvatara (one of the speakers), he says, 'saw the truth owing to *his power of contemplation* and the *grace of God*.' It follows, therefore, that the truths are to be verified not only by logical reason but also by personal experience.

Although the *Upanishads* are speaking of the ultimate there is a great deal of personalized language which could later be brought into devotion (*bhakti*). We are told that 'Brahman dwells within all and outside all—unborn, pure, greater than the greatest, without breath, without mind' and yet Brahman is 'ever present in the hearts of all—the refuge of all and their supreme goal'. 'In Brahman exists all that moves and breathes.' Brahman is seen as 'the adorable one'. To 'know' Brahman is to find one's being within Brahman.

Age of the epics

The period from 300 BC to AD 300 was crucial for the emergence of what we may call classical Hinduism. Although Buddhism and Jainism reached their widest growth within India during this time, it was also the period when Vedantic 'orthodoxy' was developing. *Sutras* were written. These were for the most part collections of aphorisms which sought to highlight the teaching of the *Vedas* and *Upanishads*.

But, even more significantly for the future of popular religion, this was the time when *bhakti* (devotion to one of the gods) entered religion, so that what was already part and parcel of religion at the grass roots received approval. There was also a wider synthesis of Aryan and non-Aryan elements in the tradition. The divinities of the *Vedas* were either replaced by the older gods or identified with them. For example, Rudra, the powerful one in the Vedic hymns, was identified with Shiva, the 'dancing god' whose figurines are among the finds in the Indus Valley excavations.

Legend and story

This was also the time for writing up stories of the past. What had originated and been circulating as local legends came to be regarded as the best statement of the Indian view of the world. Although there may be some historical allusions to events long past, the epics point rather to the perennial struggle between good and evil, cosmos and chaos in human affairs. They provide the assurance that order will prevail and that there is a way through the morass of doubt and puzzlement.

The basic thesis of both the *Ramayana* (which has 24,000 couplets) and the *Mahabharata* (90,000 couplets) is that history is divided into cycles. At the beginning, righteousness and order (*dharma*) marks the world. But then, through four ages, standards deteriorate until the gods decide to destroy the world and fashion it afresh. The poems indicate the need to discover meaning and purpose, even during the period of disorder.

The loving husband and faithful wife: Ramayana

The *Ramayana* is placed within the second age, when order,

though under attack, is still largely intact. It is the story of intrigue in which Rama is ousted from the throne and his faithful wife Sita abducted and taken off to Sri Lanka. The monkey-god, Hanuman, the symbol of loyal service and ingenuity, assists in the rescue of Sita by establishing a monkey-bridge from the mainland of India to Sri Lanka. Rama is the personification of righteousness and is looked upon as one of the ten incarnations (*avatars*) of Vishnu. The notion grew up that the gods send one *avatar* for each age. (This same notion of a series of ages or aeons and the appearance of a saviour-figure in each age is also present in Buddhist thought.)

In popular Hinduism the Rama story is not only heard from earliest childhood, but becomes the basis for everyday life. Rama will be invoked at the start of any undertaking and thanked on its successful completion. His exploits become an example to follow and an encouragement to upright behaviour. His name will be used to console the aged and chanted by the assembled mourners, as the bodies of the dead are taken away for cremation.

Sita, too, becomes the model of the faithful wife who is so identified with her husband that, at one time, she would even ascend his funeral pyre and be cremated with him. Sita is praised for the virtues of piety, loyalty and unassuming courtesy.

'Song of the Lord': Bhagavad Gita

The *Mahabharata* story is set towards the end of the third age. And the civil war of which it tells ushers in the fourth age, the era of final disintegration and un-

It has been said that the one unifying theme in the diversity of Hinduism is the honour paid to cows. Why they are considered sacred is not known. But they are permitted to go anywhere and eat anything.

righteousness. Two sets of cousins claim to be the rightful rulers. The five Pandora brothers prevail in the end, but only after a bitter and lengthy conflict.

The reaction of the five brothers is crucial to the story. The eldest, Yudhishthira, finds war distasteful and wishes to opt out of the conflict. He looks in the direction of ascetic meditation. Attention finally rests on the third brother, Arjuna, who shares his brother's distaste for war, but shows great ability as a general.

The high point of the lengthy epic is the section entitled *Bhagavad Gita* ('Song of the Lord'), where Arjuna is hesitating about entering the battle against his kith and kin. He is engaged in dialogue with his charioteer, who is none other than Krishna, the eighth incarnation of Vishnu.

The *Bhagavad Gita* has some-

This modern carving shows the age-old Hindu theme of the 'wheel of life'. The doctrine of samsara teaches that after death the soul moves to a new body.

times been called 'the bible of Hinduism' because of its popular appeal. There have been more commentaries written on it than on any other Indian writing. The story tells how Arjuna is finally persuaded by Krishna to issue the order for battle against the Kuru family. Krishna argues that death does not destroy the soul and that a man must fulfil his duty in accordance with his class. To perform one's duty does not involve guilt, if it is done in a spirit of detachment. Krishna points out that knowledge, work and devotion are all paths to salvation. Through devotion to himself (in whom the impersonal Brahman becomes a personal, loving god), Arjuna can be freed

from his doubts and attachments. The *Gita* stresses that salvation is available to all: class distinctions are not a barrier but a way of securing salvation.

The Krishna cycle

There is a further cycle of stories about Krishna, which are widely circulated. The most important is the *Bhagavata Purana*. The stories begin with him as a prince of the tribe of the Yadavas, and there are miraculous stories of his birth and infancy. In devotional art-forms he is often portrayed as a plump baby full of vitality.

During his youth he fled from his wicked cousin Kamsa and dwelt among the cowherds of Vrindaban. The stories tell of his skill as a flute-player and the pranks he played upon the wives and daughters of the cowherds, outdoing Don Juan in his ways of seduction. The suggestion is that he is father, friend and elder brother to his worshippers—but also lover and husband. The sexual imagery of union with Krishna is symbolic of the intimacy of the worshipper with God, which is a feature of the *bhakti* emphasis in Hinduism. The Krishna stories are not intended to be taken literally as something to emulate!

The sacred cow

The fact that Krishna is commonly portrayed as the cowherd is also significant, for it brings Krishna-worship into the context of the ancient cult of the mother-goddess. The cow is the living symbol of Mother Earth and of the bounty she bestows upon mankind. Feeding the cow is in itself an act of worship. Even the cow's urine is seen as sacred, being used, for example, in purification rites by those who have broken caste taboo. (Although some Hindus eat meat, the majority are vegetarian, for reverence for the cow is also a symbol of reverence for all animals.)

Approaches to Truth: The Great Interpreters

Raymond Hammer

The Vedic tradition ended with the *Upanishads* and the emergence of the notion of the identity of the individual self (*atman*) with the absolute (Brahman). The next step was to see the identity of every individual with every other individual and so to postulate that there is only one reality. This understanding of existence is called monism. It is the basis of Vedantic philosophy and it became the main philosophical tradition within Hinduism, though with a great variety of interpretation.

This variety was partly due to the attempt to systematize Hindu thought—done first during the period of the epics, when Hinduism in its classical form was emerging. A number of *sutras* (collections of aphorisms) emerged, but they were often too brief to be intelligible and so a commentary was needed. The production of commentaries led on the one hand to a tradition of interpretation, and on the other to several variants in interpretation. The *Brahma Sutra* (belonging to the sixth century AD) sought to sum up the teaching and so came to be known as the *Vedanta Sutra*.

Parallel with *Vedanta* was a school which gave pride of place to scripture. It stressed those portions of the *Veda* which spoke of appeasing the gods and accumulating merit to acquire heavenly joy. There was also reasoning (*shankhya*) which stressed the two entities of spirit and matter. Matter is without feeling, but spirit acts upon it and brings about evolution within matter. It is also seen as responsible for human experience and misery. The yogic philosophy followed *shankhya*, but had a place for Ishvara as the supreme, omniscient, ever-existing teacher.

Much of the philosophical development had parallels with the earlier schools of Buddhist thought, but there was one fundamental difference. Buddhism rejected the notion of a continuing self and saw everything as subject to flux. But all Hindu thought presupposes the permanence of the self (the *atman*).

The three great interpreters of *Vedanta* were Shankara (about AD 788–820), Ramanuja (died AD 1137) and Madhva (about AD 1197–1276).

Shankara

Shankara wrote commentaries on the *Brahma Sutra* and the *Bhagavad Gita*, and also produced spiritual treatises and hymns (for he was a worshipper of Shiva). He was responsible for a revival of Hindu thought, over and against Buddhism, although he owes a debt to the Buddhist concept that nothing has substance, all being void. The mystic appreciates this and so is set free from a world which is mere illusion. Nothing can be said about reality; what is needed is mystical insight. He therefore postulated two levels of truth. At the lower level of appreciation of the truth, everything is provisional and transitory. But much of life is lived at this level.

For Shankara the world is seen as illusion (*maya*). Even the idea of each of us as a separate self is also regarded as illusory. The truth, however, is that there is only one being—the 'Brahman *atman* reality', which involves not simply my *atman*, but that of others as well. He sought to establish a link with the *Vedas*, where God is seen as the wielder of *maya*. But this, in turn, raises the question of whether God is himself an illusion and the creator of an illusory world. It is here that Shankara accepts being itself as his ultimate. The world may seem to be vividly real but, from the standpoint of the higher level of truth, it is then seen to be illusory.

Ramanuja

Ramanuja came from a background with a strong tendency

towards *bhakti*.

The *bhakti* movement had been seen as a threat to Brahmin orthodoxy, based on the *Veda*, but Ramanuja sought to create a bridge between the two, to bring *bhakti* within the classical Hindu tradition. He began by accepting the authority of the *Vedas* and the inspiration of the *Bhagavad Gita* and wrote commentaries on both the *Brahma Sutra* and the *Gita*. He saw the cosmos as God's body, but, just as the self transcends the body, so God transcends the material mani-

festation. The world functions in dependence on the purposes of God. So *karma*, too, has to be understood as the expression of God's will.

Ramanuja interpreted the 'thou art that' in the *Upanishads* as meaning not that the individual self is identical with God, but that God is the reality within the self. So he rejects Shankara's threat to the religion of worship and devotion and his assumption that salvation comes from within. Salvation, deliverance, for Ramanuja is a gift from above.

Madhva

Madhva was influenced by the Jain belief in the difference between souls and non-living matter. He therefore stresses particularity and plurality. He postulates the existence within God of attributes that no other being could possess. In the same way, each individual is different from every other, and no sequences of *karma* can ever be the same. This means that each soul must have something within itself which somehow or other determines its destiny.

The Hindu Gods

The gods of the Vedic period

AGNI
The life-force of nature. The god of fire and sacrifice.

INDRA
The sky-god and god of war.

VARUNA
The upholder of the cosmic order, with power to punish and reward.

The later gods

BRAHMA—THE CREATOR
The lord of all creatures. He is above and beyond worship, and there are hardly any temples dedicated to him.

VISHNU—THE PRESERVER
The controller of human fate. He draws near to mankind in ten incarnations (*avatars*). He is generally kindly.

SHIVA—THE DESTROYER
The source of both good and evil. The destroyer of life and also the one who re-creates new life.

SARASVATI
Consort of Brahma. The goddess of knowledge, learning and truth.

LAKSHMI
Wife of Vishnu. The goddess of fortune and beauty.

KALI/DURGA
Consort of Shiva. The 'great mother'. She is the symbol of judgement and death.

The ten avatars of Vishnu

1. MATSYA
The fish. He appeared at the time of the great flood, to warn mankind.

2. KURMA
The tortoise. He rescued treasures from the flood.

3. VARAHA
The boar. He raised the earth from the flood.

4. NARA-SIMHA
The man-lion. He defeated evil demons.

5. VAMANA
The dwarf. He defeated evil demons.

6. PARUSHA-RAMA
'Rama with an axe'. He destroyed the members of the Kshatriya warrior-caste who threatened to dominate the world.

7. RAMA-CHANDRA
The hero of the *Ramayana* epic. He was a noble hero who combatted the evil in the world. He is the epitome of virtue.

8. KRISHNA
As well as being an *avatar* of Vishnu, Krishna is a god in his own right, the most popular of all the gods. He is also the hero of many myths, depicted as a lover, a warrior and a king.

9. BUDDHA
'The enlightened one'. The ninth *avatar* is Gautama the Buddha, founder of Buddhism.

10. KALKI
The tenth *avatar* is yet to come.

Concepts of Hinduism

Raymond Hammer

In the *Veda* the ultimate or absolute is Brahman, defying all atempt at definition.

The Absolute

Brahman is neutral and impersonal—the origin, the cause and the basis of all existence. In it are to be found:

- pure being (*sat*);
- pure intelligence (*cit*);
- pure delight (*ananda*).

Brahman is the unknowable one. But the only way he can be considered is in terms of a personal deity. So it was natural for the Indians to see the several attributes or functions of divinity manifested in a multiplicity of forms. In the Vedic hymns god is not fully seen in human terms. The gods are the manifestations of nature or cosmic forces. The divine names may be countless, but they are all understood as expressions of Brahman. For, although it may have limitless forms, it is still regarded as one in essence.

So Hinduism is not troubled by the fact that each village may have its own divinity or divinities. The multiplicity is not seen as polytheism, since Brahman is One. The gods are simply ways of approaching the ultimate.

The phallic lingam pillar is the symbol of the creative god Shiva.

The Vedic gods

Indra is the god most frequently invoked in the *Veda* and many stories are told of his deeds of prowess. With his thunderbolt he was able to suppress the dragon that sought to stem the flow of the waters. He appears as conqueror of the sun, releasing from the sun's grasp the imprisoned dawns. He is depicted astride an elephant, bejewelled and with a kingly turban or tiara, thunderbolt in hand. Like the other divinities, he has his female partner, **Indrani** or **Saci**.

Agni is the god of fire and sacrifice—the one who unites earth, heaven and the atmosphere in between. He is seen as the life-force within nature. The *Rig Veda* hails him as the one who 'restores life to all beings'. 'The all is reborn through you!'

Chief of the Vedic gods is **Varuna** who is the preserver of the cosmic order. He is described as clothed in a golden mantle and is often associated with **Mitra** (the Mithra of Persian religion—the deity in Mithraism).

There are, of course, a number of other gods and goddesses—symbolizing the sun, the moon and the stars—as well as **Dyaus-pitr**, the 'heaven father' (Jupiter in Roman religion and Zeus in Greek religion), **Vayu**, the wind, and **Prajapati**, the father of the gods (*devas*) and the demons (*asuras*) and lord of all creatures.

The Vedic pantheon, however, gave place to another hierarchy of divinities, which reflect the non-Aryan elements in the religion. At the head of the other array of divine forms stands a divine triad (*Trimurti*) who share the activities of **Ishvara**, the one supreme god who symbolizes Brahman:

● The power to create belongs to **Brahma**.

● Preservation is in the power of **Vishnu**.

● **Shiva** is the great destroyer.

Their three-fold activity corresponds to the rhythm of the world. This is seen first as emerging from Brahman; next as reaching its full embodiment; then as being reabsorbed either into Brahman or into the period which precedes the next age. Creation, like history, is understood in cyclical terms. There is no true beginning or end. The beginning is an end and the end a new beginning.

Brahma

Despite his function as creator, Brahma remains fairly abstract. His function is to bring multiplicity into being in place of a primal unity. His female counterpart is **Sarasvati**, the energy that comes from him. She is identified with the Word on the one hand, the goddess of the sacred rivers; on the other, the symbol of knowledge and of 'the waters of truth'.

Brahma is often portrayed with four faces, embracing the four points of the compass, and with four arms, in which he holds the four *Vedas*. At times he is depicted as riding on a swan; at other times he sits upon a lotus—a symbol of the fact that he comes from himself and is not begotten.

Vishnu

Vishnu, as the great preserver, is thought to be in charge of human

This image of Shiva, the destroyer, is uncovered once a year, when a ritual sacrifice of bullocks is made to him.

fate. He is usually portrayed in symbolic form. He may be reclining or asleep on the ocean, which stands for chaos—the thousand-headed serpent. He may preside over the heavenly court. Or, as a symbol of the sun, he may appear mounted upon the heavenly eagle (Garuda), traversing the heights of heaven. The cult of Vishnu is very popular. He is the symbol of divine love—sometimes in company with **Lakshmi**, his female counterpart—

the symbol of beauty and good fortune; but more often drawing near in grace to mankind through his ten 'descents' or incarnations. Many of these incarnations are thought to be partial. The significance of **Krishna** (by far the most popular of the manifestations of Vishnu) is that in him the being of Vishnu is held to be totally present. There is a similar approach to Rama on the part of his worshippers. They would see in him, too, all the fullness of the being of Vishnu.

Shiva

The third of the *Trimurti* is Shiva. He is the deity in whom all opposites meet and become resolved in a fundamental unity. Although the phallus (*lingam*) is his symbol and he is naturally identified with the masculine role in fertility and procreation, he is often portrayed as perpetually chaste. (In most of the temples dedicated to Shiva there is the statue of a bull, the symbol of virility.)

He is the destroyer of life and yet also its recreator; the terrible one, and yet the epitome of mildness. In him there is both ceaseless activity and eternal rest. In him there is sexual differentiation and yet he is also the symbol of unity which transcends all division. He is the source of both good and evil.

In artistic representations from the twelfth century AD onwards he is often portrayed as the king of the dancers—the embodiment of cosmic energy. The sculptures show both the unfolding of the universe and its ultimate destruction. The dance speaks of rhythm at the heart of all existence—whether in the cosmos or in the individual consciousness, the will or the emotions, where knowledge and illusion (*maya*) are in conflict. He is also shown with many hands, one pair to express the balance between life and death, another indicating the clash between good and evil, and so on.

Both Vishnu and Shiva are the focus of cults in which the worshipper seeks for unity with the god. In the Shaivite form (which looks to Shiva) it is identity with the source of movement (life itself) which is the goal. But the sense of creatureliness is not lost. The strength of Shiva worship in south India from the twelfth century AD and also in Bihar and Bengal (areas where the Aryan influence was late) reflects the rejection of the Brahminic Aryan forms of worship—animal sacrifice, prayers for the dead and other rites.

In one popular story Shiva is the one who averted a catastrophe, when the waters of the River Ganges flowed down upon the earth. Knotting his hair, he received the waters upon his head, so that they flowed harmlessly away. But he is also the master of the yogis (the disciplined ascetics) and, in this capacity, he is portrayed as half-naked, smeared with ashes, with skulls around his waist and a necklace of intertwining serpents.

Kali

Shiva, like the other gods, has his female partner to whom his powers are delegated, but the different names probably reflect the varying qualities of the 'Great Mother', who is present in Indian thought from the earliest times. Most significant is Durga or Kali who, in her strength and dominance, reflects the matriarchal approach of the older, pre-Aryan culture. This is probably the background to Shaktism, where the divine being is thought of in female terms and the female is the dynamic and the male the more passive manifestation. There is a contrast between the inner self-sufficiency of Shiva and the creative-destructive power of Durga-Kali.

Kali is portrayed in paradoxical terms. On the one side, there is the ferocious aspect, expressing judgement and death—with the figure of Kali wearing a garland of skulls and a skirt of severed hands. On the other side, her serenity is indicated by her portrayal as the night of rest and peace between the cycles of world-creation. Even in her most fearful aspect, Kali is understood as granting peace to her followers by overcoming their fears. She can therefore be the object of an intense and passionate devotion.

Although Shiva is sometimes considered to be the supreme deity—far removed from time and creation—it is Kali who touches him and brings him into the world of time and touch as the creator and animator of all.

The act of destruction can be interpreted as the abolishing of ignorance, in order that the soul may come to knowledge, or the removal of all dross and impurity, so that the heart becomes pure and god-like.

These portrayals are never meant to be representational. Hindu art, unlike Greek art where the divinities are portrayed simply as humans, indicates that the divinities are far more than humans. Power is expressed by a multiplicity of arms, and divine wisdom (as in the case of Shiva) by a third eye in the middle of the forehead. Even animal characteristics are pointers to special qualities possessed by the god. Ganesha is always portrayed with an elephant's head and a single tusk. The portrayal speaks of the strength of the one who protects through life. The monkey form of Hanuman is the pointer to dexterity and intelligence.

Bhakti and the concept of grace

Bhakti, the devotion to a particular god, which became such a strong element in popular religion, was perhaps a reaction to the severity and rigour of yoga. The yogis had sought to suppress desire, love and feeling in general. How, then, were the worshippers' emotional needs to be met? By bringing together *bhakti*, knowledge (*jnana*) and *karma*, the *Bhagavad Gita* suggests that it is not simply the expression of the emotional; it is always associated with the intellectual and practical side of human living. Nevertheless, at the popular level, the intellectual or rational element is often lacking, and it is the ecstasy and rapture of a loving relationship which come to the fore.

Between the seventh and tenth centuries AD a number of Tamil writers (Tamil is one of the four Dravidian languages in south India) expressed their religious

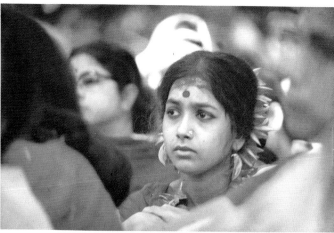

feelings and experience with tremendous warmth and fervency. And in the *Bhagavata Purana* (which was written about AD 900), the source of many of the Krishna stories, there is even more passion. One writer has said that, in this work: 'Bhakti is a surging emotion, which chokes the speech, makes the tears flow and the hair thrill with pleasurable excitement and often leads to hysterical laughing and weeping by turns, to sudden fainting fits and to long trances of unconsciousness.'

In the eleventh century Ramanuja brought *bhakti* within the classical, developed Hindu tradition. For him it was more a type of intellectual meditation, accompanied by love, but lacking the rapture and ecstasy which continue to be present at the popular level. He pointed to the significant link with the *avatara* doctrine in the Vaishnavite form of *bhakti*, when he asserted that God becomes incarnate simply out of compassion, 'to give light to the whole world with his indefectible and perfect glory and to fill out all things with his loveliness'. The Vaishnavite usually dresses in orange or white with a rosary in his hand. He paints red or white vertical lines on his forehead or red, black or white spots between his eyebrows.

In the fifteenth century AD the Chaitanya sect of the Krishna *bhakti* movement was established in Bengal. This sect lies behind the Hare Krishna movement, seen in the West, where music and dance mark the worship of Krishna and ecstatic trance is a means of achieving unity with the

A Hindu holy man meditating.

Hindus living in Jinja in Uganda hold an annual nine-day festival in honour of Kali. A sacred fire is kept burning by feeding it with ghee, a concentrate of butter.

The red mark on an Indian woman's forehead usually signifies that she is a Hindu, but practices vary from area to area.

deity. In the West, because of the stress on history in the Christian tradition, adherents of the movement tend to accept the myths attached to Krishna as historically true and they give unquestioning adherence to every utterance of Chaitanya.

If it is a person's duty to commit himself in loving devotion to God, it follows that the attainment of *moksha* (release) is made possible by God. Does this mean that it is 'grace alone', or is human effort also involved? Something like the debate about grace which emerged in Christian theology is present in the Hindu debate.

Two theories of the operation of grace were put forward: the 'kitten' and the 'monkey' approach. A she-cat seizes the kitten and carries it where she wills. This involves a total passivity on the part of the kitten and there were those who stated that God's grace operates in the same way. All is effected by God, and man does nothing to achieve *moksha*. By contrast, the baby monkey clings to its mother. The mother monkey is responsible for the baby monkey's continuance of life and movement, yet there is not total passivity. Most Hindu teachers within the *bhakti* tradition took this standpoint. We cling to God, and God effects our salvation.

The path to salvation

For the Hindu, the great goal is *moksha*. The word speaks of 're-lease'—deliverance, emancipation and liberty. On the negative side, it points to 'being loosed from' or 'rid of' something felt to be undesirable—i.e. the cycle of rebirth and attachment to the material world. On the positive side, it indicates an expanded outlook, a sense of calm and security, the notion of attainment (reaching a goal) or the power to be and to do. More often than not, this goal of salvation is described in negative terms—the

negating of evil, grief and decay.

The way of knowledge
The idea of *moksha* was not always present in Indian religion. It is likely that, as the cycle of rebirth (*samsara*) became the fundamental presupposition (about the seventh century BC), indicating an unending round of existences which were influenced by the deeds each individual performed (*karma*), the desire for release emerged.

The desire for freedom was not political, but spiritual, and the Upanishadic tradition stressed release from the bonds of ignorance. It was ignorance which tied

a person to the round of birth-death-rebirth which was expressed by *samsara*. Release would be attained as knowledge replaced ignorance—when reality was properly understood and the transient or illusory rejected.

This was, basically, the way of knowledge (*jnana-marga*) towards *moksha*. It would involve yoga and the ascetic practices associated with it. It was thought

The term 'sadhu' applies to any Indian 'holy man'. Some are ascetic hermits, others are popular wonder-workers. Devotees of Vishnu mark their foreheads with three vertical lines of ash. Devotees of Shiva have three horizontal lines.

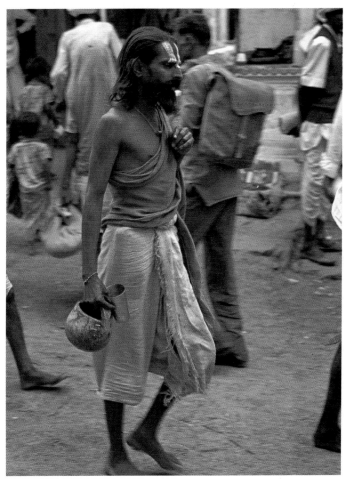

Karma and Dharma:
Hindu Ethics

Raymond Hammer

In classical Hinduism actions (*karma*) and duty (*dharma*) were the dominant concepts. *Karma*, as the accumulation of good and bad acts, would influence a person's destiny, but there was no one way to acquire good *karma*. Early in the *Veda* there had been the notion of an overriding moral law (*rita*) of which Mitra and Varuna were the guardians. Man had to recognize a divine imperative, and prayer and sacrifice were necessary to maintain a right relationship between the divine and the human. Sin, however, could be either moral or ritual.

All relative

The moral law expressed the basis of the social order, controlled by the manuals of the priests and enforced by the rulers. But responsible action was increasingly within the framework of one's class. That is why *dharma* came to be not an absolute duty, but one related to a person's status and so to the class/caste complex. The *Bhagavad Gita* considers it wrong to try to fulfil someone else's *dharma*. It is better to do your own *dharma* badly than that of another well! The action as such does not modify *karma*. It is action appropriate to the person and to the time of life. The epics stress a child's duty to parents, the love and attachment that parents must show to children, the mutual respect to be displayed in marriage, and the love and harmony belonging to other relationships.

For those living in the world, ethical pursuits— the pursuit of wealth (i.e. engagement in a livelihood), the enjoyment of pleasure or ritual piety— were all relative. The only absolute ethic was related to the release of the individual from the cycle of rebirth. This was what the ascetic concentrated on. For him the duty of 'seeking for salvation' was paramount. He had to maintain a basic morality, refraining from killing, stealing, sexual impurity, lying or the consumption of intoxicants. Unless he observed these prohibitions he could not attain the basic purity required to take him further on the path to *moksha*.

Source book

The *Laws of Manu*, a metrical work of 2,685 verses dealing with religion, law, custom and politics, is the most often quoted 'source book' of Hindu ethics. Its date is uncertain, but it belongs perhaps to the first century BC or first century AD and its author is well versed in the Vedic literature. It is concerned primarily with duty, whether the general *dharma* incumbent upon all or the particular *dharma* arising from caste or relationship. The *Laws* are concerned to bolster up conventional thought at a time when it was being threatened. They accept the class structure in terms of a common endeavour for a common good. Each has

to perform the function for which his nature best suits him. Right and wrong are determined in four ways: through the authoritative scriptures, through the other inspired writings, through good conduct and through conscience.

The four orders

Four separate orders are considered—the student, the householder, the hermit and the ascetic— and, each has an appropriate duty to perform. For example, the student has to study the *Vedas*. There is an initiation ceremony for the three upper classes, appropriate to each grouping, and rules of personal purification, of sacrifices and the morning and evening devotions to be followed are duly taught by a teacher (the guru or *rishi*). The student, we are told, gains the nether world by honouring his mother, the middle sphere by honouring his father, but the world of Brahman (the absolute) if he obeys his teacher!

It is important not to seek to discharge the *dharma* of another grouping, because this involves forfeiting membership in one's own. Ethics and ritual acts are, of course, intermingled and it is the priest's *dharma* to go through no fewer than twelve sacramental rites from his foetal period to marriage.

In modern times, there is more stress on progress than on cycles of time. Universal values such as truthfulness, kindness and love are stressed and the need to alleviate suffering. Present-day Hindus will speak, too, of the common good as a goal to be attained.

that the control of breath would allow the self to escape from the body by closing the artery from the heart to the forehead—the path by which the self was understood to move to its home in the heart. The special knowledge is attained through meditation, accompanied by yogic discipline and the repetition of the mysterious *mantra* 'Om', which represented the ultimate in all its fullness (some would say 'the triad of gods seen in their fundamental unity as Brahman, the absolute'). The repetition of the phrase would both assert and effect the unity of the worshipper with the ultimate—and this would be *moksha*. But the unity need not be identity. It is sometimes seen as the condition of a gnat in a fig or a fish in water— neither total identity nor complete disassociation.

The later songs in the *Rig Veda* saw man groping in darkness, but becoming conscious of the unfathomable mystery at the very centre of being. Nevertheless, bit by bit, he becomes assured of reality and light in the world around him, and so reaches out for *moksha*.
'From the unreal lead me to the real!
From darkness lead me to light!
From death lead me to immortality!'
But this release will also be from life as it is now experienced. The way, therefore, will be by the suppression of a craving. As the Buddha put it, the craving is itself what links a person to the cycle of rebirth. Even the rapturous assurance of release must be purified of the element of desire which may cause us to accept a fantasy for the reality.

The *Bhagavad Gita* sees *moksha* as involving liberation from evil, from the body, from lusts and anger, from decay and death, from *karma* and from *maya*. In other words, *moksha* speaks of release from bondage, however conceived. The rapture is to be experienced at the level of

Members of the International Society for Krishna Consciousness have been a familiar sight on the streets of Western cities for the past decade.

emotion, for *moksha* involves a sense of security and assurance.

The way of action

But there is also the way of action (*karma-marga*). This path to release recognizes that we live our lives in the world, where there is work to be done and there are obligations to be met. Our status in society involves duty. We are not to opt out of the ethical demands of which we are conscious. The *Bhagavad Gita* indicates that it is 'not by refraining from action' that 'man attains freedom from action'. It is not by mere renunciation that he 'attains supreme perfection'. 'Action,' we are told, 'is greater than inaction' and so there is the command to 'perform your task in life'.

The way of devotion

Faith comes in with the way of devotion or love (*bhakti-marga*). It is in commitment to God that we accept the leap from the tem-

Indra is the god of war.

Krishna was a playful and often mischievous incarnation of Vishnu.

Ganesh, the elephant-god, is very popular as god of wisdom and good fortune.

poral to the eternal, the realm of limitation to the boundlessness of what is ultimate and absolute. This path accepts the truth that the absolute confronts us in personal form—so there can be human response to divine grace. In place of an impersonal Brahman, God is seen as approachable, evoking within humanity a spirit of adoring faith.

The *Bhagavad Gita* speaks of Arjuna seeing in Krishna countless visions of wonder, as Krishna asserts that 'only by *bhakti* can men see me and know me and come to me'. For the followers of this way—and this is the path to

which most Indians instinctively lean—salvation is not the result of human striving, but is seen as a gift from God. Obviously, very few frame for themselves an articulated theology or religious philosophy. It is a faith expressed in life and not as dogma.

But *bhakti* also demands acts of worship. Apart from ritual acts and ceremonies, there are the hymns of praise to be sung and the statues to be venerated and adored. It is not 'idol-worship' as such. The idol becomes the focus through which God (who cannot be represented in any image) is worshipped.

Hindu Worship and the Festivals

Raymond Hammer

In Aryan times, worship took place in the open air, often concentrated on the sacred fire. Temple worship, as such, probably comes from the early Indus Valley practices. Early temples were made of wood and so have not survived. Later ones were patterned on the royal court. As the gods were thought to dwell in the mountains, many temples were built in the style of a mountain home. There was a tower and walls, with the symbol of the divinity in the centre, surrounded by the many symbols of the spirit world.

In the temple

The needs of the gods would be met by the worshippers who had to prepare themselves through purification rites to draw near to their god. For example, in Vaishnavite morning worship there were sixteen operations, including washing the feet, rinsing the mouth, bathing, dressing, perfuming and feeding. During these there was hymn-singing, bells were rung, incense burnt and ritual music was played. Then the worshippers would come to perform their *puja*, first paying respect to the god and

In the River Ganges at Varanasi this woman is offering up the sacred water to the rising sun.

The Festivals of Hinduism

DIVALI/NEW YEAR
A festival of lights, when presents are given. Lakshmi, the goddess of good fortune, visits every house which is lit by a lamp.

HOLI
A joyful spring festival dedicated to Krishna. Originally a fertility ceremony. It is celebrated with street dancing, processions and bonfires.

DASARA
Ten days of celebration in honour of Kali. There are processions, dances and presents are given.

Local festivals
There are many festivals specific to certain areas or towns. Some of these are held in honour of the great gods such as Shiva and Sarasvati. Others are the annual festivals of local gods.

There are many festivals are held in honour of the

Religious pilgrimages often take place at specific times of the year, accompanied by festivities.

January   March   May   July   September   November

February   April   June   August   October   December

At many Hindu festivals, worshippers go into ecstatic trances and then inflict wounds on themselves with no signs of any permanent damage.

making their requests, and then sharing in the divine banquet—water and *prasada* (the technical name for food first offered to the deity and then shared out among the worshippers). Usually the chief statue in the temple would receive food and refreshment during the day and be put to bed at night!

The statue is the symbol of the divine presence and the house in which it dwells. Ramakrishna expressed this by saying: 'We shall believe in the Divine Presence infilling the Images of the Deity.' For the more sophisticated worshipper, each part of the temple has a spiritual or symbolic meaning. The central shrine is the heart of the worshipper; the tower indicates the flight of the spirit to heaven. Each and every god stands for a particular function or attribute of the supreme.

A priest might add to the worship by reading the *Vedas* to the assembled worshippers, just as he might read to a group standing in shallow water in the Ganges at Varanasi after their ritual bathing. But any 'twice-born' Hindu (from the first three classes) may perform the reading of the prayers and *mantras*. The worshipper in the temple makes a gift of flowers or money and goes round the shrine, always keeping it to his right shoulder. Worship in the temple is never fully congregational. It is largely individual. That is why rites in the home are as significant as those in the temple.

At home

Duties in the home vary according to class, those of the Brahmin priestly caste being most arduous. Many set a room aside for *puja*—with a shrine, containing an image of the favourite deity or (in poorer homes) pictures of deities. Some have a *mandala*, a symbolic representation (usually a picture) of the universe. Fire and water are used for purification, and there are food-offerings, incense, flowers and coloured powders (for ornamentation).

'Twice-born' Hindus perform their rites three times a day. They wear the sacred thread (over the left shoulder and hanging to the right hip)—cotton for the Brahmin (priest), hemp for the Kshatriya (ruler) and wool for the *vaishya* (landowners/merchants). In addition, each has a caste mark on his forehead, and sometimes on his arms and other parts of the body.

In the early morning, worship starts with the uttering of the *mantra* 'Om', a humming to the sounds of the letters A,U,M. Then the worshipper repeats the name of his god, calls to mind the sages (*rishis*) and identifies himself with Brahman. He binds up the tuft of hair on his head and repeats the *Gayatri mantra* from the *Rig Veda*:

'We meditate on the adorable glory of the radiant sun; may he inspire our intelligence.'

He worships bare to the waist and barefoot, sitting cross-legged on the ground, with eyes looking at the tip of his nose and his face towards the rising of the sun. He then sips water, repeats the name of the god and sprinkles water around the seat. He touches six parts of the body—an indication of God within, repeats his prayers, meditates and repeats the words of the *Gayatri*. Water is offered to the images, verses from the *Veda* repeated and worship ends with a final water-offering and obeisance. Evening devotions are similar, but shorter. Midday worship may include consulting a teacher (guru). As they perform *puja*, priests, householders and ascetics (*sadhus*) incorporate special postures, gestures and utterances.

Festivals

Festivals are largely linked with the seasonal changes. But they also incorporate the myths of the *Ramayana* and of Krishna's activities.

Holi is the most popular festival of all. It is a spring festival associated with Krishna, and caste and taboo are set aside. In this festival there is a strong emphasis on pleasure.

Divali is the autumn festival (a festival of lights) linked with Kali (Shiva's female counterpart) and Lakshmi (Vishnu's counterpart). Pilgrimages are linked with the story-cycles. And centres such as Vrindaban (a focus for the Krishna cult), Varanasi and Allahabad welcome hundreds of thousands of pilgrims.

Escape from Life?

Raymond Hammer

How far is Hinduism concerned with everyday life and how far is 'escape' from life fundamental to the tradition? Life is broken into a number of orders.

● First there is the life of the student.
● Then there is the life of the householder.
● Then there is life far removed from the ordinary demands of family, community or society.

Hinduism is associated not simply with the bustling festival, but also with the wandering *sadhu* (holy man) or the almost-naked ascetic who, in yogic posture, seems entirely unconscious of physical constraints. For most of his married life Mahatma Gandhi had no sexual relationship with his wife. There are many illustrations of apparent world-denial, even though Gandhi, for instance, was at the same time fighting for political freedom and to improve the status of the outcaste groupings, demanding that they should be treated with consideration and granted their dignity.

If the world of everyday existence is illusion and if the fruit of past deeds in a previous existence determines the character of the present one, does this mean a denial of freedom? Does it remove any incentive to make life better in the present?

Unrest in the soul

There is a sense in which Indian thinking springs from an unrest in the soul rather than from intellectual curiosity, and this is what leads to a negation of the world. Philosophy, in a Hindu context, can never be an academic game, isolated from life and speculative in character. Knowledge must, therefore, be transformed into 'vision', an understanding of reality.

Whereas Western thought (in its non-religious form) sees man as 'the measure of all things' and so veers in an individualistic direction, the Hindu regards mankind as part of a cosmic whole and this involves respect for life in all its manifestations. Life 'apart' (an individualist approach) is seen as the disintegration of life. Hence the demand for a strict discipline (yoga) and meditation, so that the individual may re-integrate into the whole.

The rejection of individualism can lead to the rejection of activism. And there is often an element of passivity in Indian life, although the element of freedom would still be claimed and a charge of fatalism rejected. As a result, scientific knowledge and material progress have not traditionally been the goals of Indian endeavour.

Paradox

None the less, there is a certain paradox. Asceticism goes along with the acquiring of wealth and property (*artha*) which belongs to the duty of the householder, and the experience of pleasure (*kama*). Strict religious discipline is coupled with an extreme sensuousness and the wild abandon of cults which cast aside all inhibitions and restraints. Sculptures of the gods often show these elements.

It is likely that the two poles of 'attachment' (or affirmation) and 'aloofness' (or denial) ultimately express a unity. The extremes meet in the notion of the divinity and his female counterpart. Passivity must be wedded to creativity; weakness to strength; the negative to the positive. Only in this way can 'order' embrace 'freedom'. But it is ultimately release from the prison of meaninglessness that is sought. One Indian writer has put it that the Hindu's entire way of life and thought is determined by the 'yearnings of the soul rather than by the quest of the mind or the needs of the body'.

This tree-goddess is a typical example of Hindu carving.

Religion of the Gurus: The Sikh Faith

Douglas Davies

The Sikh religion originated in the area of Pakistan and north-west India called the Punjab, meaning 'land of the five rivers', at the end of the fifteenth century. At this time both Hinduism and Islam were present in the area, and a number of people were asking themselves whether a formal and ritual way of life would bring them near to God. The Sikh religion offered an alternative way of life.

The movement started as a small group of disciples gathered around the Guru Nanak (1469–1539) to seek the presence of God. Over the years it grew under the leadership of Nanak's nine successors. Beginning as a close fellowship of devotees whose goal was a sense of union with God, the Sikhs increased in number. They also developed a strong military power, until they became a distinct community.

Because the growth of Punjabi identity was closely related to the rise of the Sikh idea of life, the Sikh religion can be called an ethnic religion. As in Judaism and much of Hinduism, membership of the community and of the religion go hand in hand. This is what makes their faith so important to Sikhs who live outside the Punjab, for it provides them with a strong sense of identity.

God the true Guru

At the heart of Sikh religion lies the idea of the guru.

● God is the true Guru: his divine and creative word (*shabad*) came to mankind in a distinctive way through ten historical figures, each of whom was called a guru.

● The Sikh community, continuing the faith of the tenth guru, is itself called the guru.

● And the sacred scriptures are said to be a guru (the *Guru Granth Sahib*).

God is one, the ultimate and eternal Guru (*Satguru*), who provides enlightenment and understanding for the disciple who sets his heart on finding and serving him. In his transcendent state he is beyond description. But if he were no more than that, man would be unable to find and to understand him. Man would find it impossible to relate to a God without any attributes, so God manifests himself in and through certain phenomena which are known to man. Man's religious life is directed towards this more immediate and available form of God. But when Sikhs say that God, as they can experience him, possesses these characteristics, they do not mean to say that he has ever appeared or been born on the earth like the *avatars* or divine manifestations of the Hindu tradition. Rather, he has created the world, which enables man to understand something of his power and will. More than this, his grace enables sincere devotees to experience him through worship and meditation.

In its origin the Sikh religion possesses a strong mystical and devotional basis. For the early disciples who gathered around Nanak, the goal of life was to devote themselves to dwelling upon the name of God; to sing and lodge within their hearts the hymns composed by their leader. Nanak enabled his followers to gain access to the true Guru by providing a fellowship of believers who could devote themselves to the hymns. The hymns were the means by which their hearts could reach out towards God, and also by which God could move within their hearts.

Because Nanak provided such a

Sikhs meditate on the divine Name.

vital focal point for early devotees, he came to be called a guru—in the Hindu tradition of holy men who are guides to those who seek the truth, whose very presence seems to instruct the beginner, and whose direction is necessary for spiritual progress. Nanak is never considered to be a special manifestation of God, the ultimate and true Guru.

The ten gurus

One distinctive feature of Sikhism as a guru religion is that Nanak and his nine successors are seen as making up a definite historical phase of individual or living gurus. They are said to share the same truth, to have possessed the same distinctive insight into God, and even to have held a basic common identity. The Sikhs say that the ten gurus are like candles which have been lit from each other.

The orthodox Sikh gurus	
Nanak	1469–1539
Angad	1504–1552
Amar Das	1479–1574
Ram Das	1534–1581
Arjan	1563–1606
Har Govind	1595–1644
Har Rai	1630–1661
Har Krishan	1656–1664
Tegh Bahadur	1621–1675
Gobind Singh	1666–1708

Most of them served as the guru and leader of Sikhs only in later life. Each

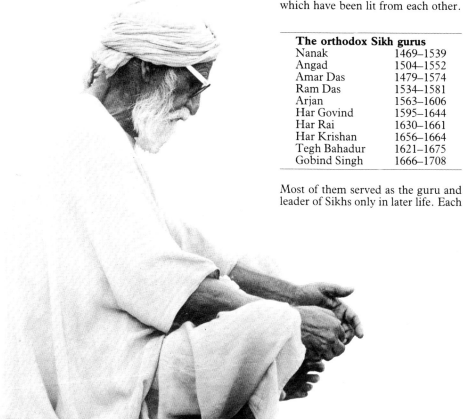

was chosen for the task by his predecessor on the basis of his spiritual insight and worthiness.

During the period of the first five gurus, most of the Sikh doctrines were developed. The community emerged as a devotional group of religious seekers. This group had much in common with the north Indian tradition of the mystics, who sought a union with God through devotion and love. Many people see the Sikh religion as possessing two basic features, one being this mystical aspect, the other more aggressive, military and world-affirming. This first major period of Sikh history—from about AD 1500 when Nanak's active ministry began until roughly 1600 when the Muslim Empire passed from Akbar, the friend of the Sikhs, to his evil successor Jehangir—was not devoid of worldly and political interest. Each of the early gurus contributed something which would become important later, when open conflict broke out between Muslims and Sikhs.

● Nanak taught that 'there is no Hindu, there is no Muslim'. This came to serve as the basis for a separate Sikh identity. What was chiefly a religious idea for Nanak later became the justification for a distinctive political and military community.

● Angad had a liking for physical fitness. He organized games among his followers. These activities were not aimed at military training, but when such training became necessary, they were seen to have prepared the way for it.

● Amar Das established the *langar* or communal eating facilities served by a common kitchen. This was paid for by Sikhs associated with a particular temple. The aim was to encourage Sikhs of all castes to eat together without the caste prejudice which characterizes much of the ordinary Indian way of life. It strengthened brotherhood and helped the underprivileged. Non-Sikhs, too, were welcome.

This great ideal of the Sikh gurus was a reaction against the Hindu caste system and involved their rejection of orthodox priesthoods such as the Brahmins. During the later period of Sikh history, when they were facing fierce aggression from the Muslims, it was relatively easy for caste divisions to be submerged in the defence of the Sikh community. Contemporary Sikhism, however, still possesses internal divisions of caste. Although the Sikh ideal speaks of the casteless brotherhood of fellow-seekers after God, in practice this ideal has not been completely achieved.

● Arjan, the fifth guru, serves as a turning-point in Sikh history. After him, there was a marked increase in political strife between Sikhs and Muslims. He built the renowned Hari Mandir, the Golden Temple at Amritsar, which became the centre of Sikh religious and national life. It was the focal point of Sikh identity and expressed many of the basic Sikh hopes and beliefs.

The war with Islam

In 1606 Guru Arjan was killed while in Muslim custody. Opinion is divided as to the justice of what happened, but the Sikhs see the death as a martyrdom. Under Arjan's leadership the Sikhs had begun to stand against Muslim aggression. This made the guru a rallying point for others in the Punjab, and soon many members of the Jat farming caste had aligned themselves with him. A switch of emphasis from a peaceful spreading of the faith to an assertion of the right to defend that faith took place among the Sikhs, now grown greater in numbers and strength. Islamic pressure forced Arjan's successor, Har Govind, into retreat, and after his death in 1644 Guru Har Rai took up the leadership and lived in the mountainous area of east Punjab. His son and successor in office, Har Krishan, could not escape the attention of Emperor Aurangzeb quite so easily, and died under house arrest at Delhi.

Tegh Bahadur had been named as the next guru but, like Har Rai, he was more of a devotional man than a soldier. It was only after Aurangzeb began to destroy temples and oppress Sikh groups in the Punjab that he was summoned from Bengal, where

1	2
3	4
5	6

1. The home of the Sikh faith is the agricultural Punjab area of north India. 2. Some Sikhs still wear the full military-style uniform. 3, 4. The Golden Temple at Amritsar.
5. Sikhs have pictures of the Gurus, especially Nanak, in their homes.
6. Inside a Sikh temple in New Zealand.

The Sikh Faith / 201

he had been living with his family, to rally the Sikhs against the enemy. As a result he was taken to Delhi, where he died as a martyr. His son Gobind Singh, then only nine years old, took up the leadership. As it turned out, over the next thirty or so years he became a renowned warrior.

Gobind Singh led the Sikhs against the Islamic powers with considerable success. He welded together an active community with a profound sense of its calling to preserve its religious tradition intact. After a first victory at Bhangani in 1686, a twenty-year period of conflict ended in defeat. Defeat in the immediate battle, though, began a period of success for Sikh religion, because Guru Gobind Singh brought about a radical difference in the way the community viewed itself.

The people and the book

According to the orthodox Sikh interpretation of what took place at the very end of the seventeenth century, the living guru transferred his authority in 1699 to the community itself on the one hand, and (in 1708) to the collection of the sacred scriptures on the other. A change in the idea of guruship was taking place. At the centre of the religion, instead of a living individual directing men in their spiritual quest and guiding them in worldly affairs, there is a community (the *Guru Panth*) and a book (the *Guru Granth*).

The tradition tells how the *Panth* (the path or way followed by the seekers; a term used to describe the community itself) was formed by Gobind Singh. He challenged his followers, who had gathered together at his request, to come forward as human sacrifices. This was a test of their faithfulness. After some thought, five men volunteered their lives to the guru. He did not, in fact, kill them but dressed them in a new form of uniform and presented them to the gathered assembly as his five beloved ones. These represented the new community of the pure ones, the *Khalsa*. (This is another name for the *Guru Panth*. It indicates the moral dedication of those who wish to follow the teaching of the historical

gurus.) This new community was to be powerful and strong in the defence of the faith and in establishing a strictly moral society. The names of *Singh* (Lion) and *Kaur* (Princess), given to the male and female members of the new community, were to express the change of status which the Sikhs were to undergo in the world, replacing names which indicated caste, and giving women a more equal standing with men.

When boys and girls are about fourteen, they may be initiated into full membership of the *Khalsa*. This ritual is often called baptism. But that is only a loose description of what actually happens. This act of 'taking *amrit*' involves present-day Sikhs in what they believe took place on that first initiation day.

Five respected members of the community represent the beloved ones of Guru Gobind Singh. After singing certain prayers and preparing a solution of sugar in water, they initiate the candidates by sprinkling the solution on their heads and eyes. They are also instructed in the basic rules of *Khalsa* membership, of loyalty and moral conduct. Their hair must be left uncut. They must avoid adultery and tobacco. And they must reject meat killed in the Muslim way.

The holy scriptures

At the heart of this ritual, as of all Sikh rites, is the holy book. The ceremony begins with a reading from it, and many of the prayers and songs are related to it. The *Guru Granth* contains the spiritual poetry of the historical gurus. It is largely the product of Guru Arjan's labour, though Guru Gobind Singh produced the final edition in which he included the work of the gurus after Arjan. This compilation is called the *Adi Granth*, or the original and first book of scriptures. Guru Gobind Singh's own hymns and poetry were not included. But the collection made by a disciple after his death is called the *Dasam Granth*—the collection of the tenth guru.

When Guru Gobind Singh invested the book with his own authority in 1708, he changed the whole structure of the Sikh religion, provid-

'There exists but one God, who is called the True, the Creator, free from fear and hate, immortal, not begotten, self-existent, great and compassionate. The True was at the beginning, the True was at the distant part. The True is at the present, O Nanak, the True will be also in the future.'

The beginning of Guru Nanak's hymn, from the *Adi Granth*. It is recited by Sikhs each morning as an expression of faith.

ing a solid, permanent focus of attention for Sikh congregations. Indian religion had always emphasized in practical ways the human need for a spiritual focus and a visible basis for worship. Temples, centres of pilgrimage, holy rivers and holy men had long been the foundation of Indian spirituality.

Although Guru Nanak himself argued that all such outward forms of religion were useless unless the heart was right with God through loving meditation, the vast majority of later Sikhs needed outward objects as a stimulus to devotion. So when Guru Gobind Singh established the book as a source of divine truth and as a vehicle of spiritual insight, it soon acquired great status. It is now always the central feature of every Sikh ritual and endeavour. Sikhs bow down before it, as Hindus before their images. When babies are brought to the temple, a random reading from the *Granth* will be used as a basis for choosing their names. Marriage centres on the book. The bride follows her groom around it four times, while songs of duty and obligation are sung. Death involves special readings from the book for seven- or ten-day periods. And continuous reading over two days accompanies certain festivals.

The Sikh temple or *gurdwara* (the guru's door) is, essentially, a place where the book is located and where

The Golden Temple

The Golden Temple can serve as a symbol of the Sikh religion, and a visual aid to our understanding of its spiritual meaning, and of how the past has influenced the present. For Sikhs this temple is the court of the Lord (*Darbar Sahib*). In its precincts are to be found peace and the possibility of access to God. The Hindi and Punjabi hymns of the early gurus, together with those of other non-Sikh mystics, were collected together in the *Gurmukhi* (mouth of the guru) script and first installed here by Arjan in 1604. Later editions of this volume, which include the devotional poetry of the later gurus, constitute the focal point of devotion and meditation. The hymns are sung from morning to night at the temple, and a constant stream of visitors and pilgrims comes to listen to the words which confer a blessing on their believing hearers.

The whole temple site consists of an outer paved area with shaded cloisters surrounding the large pool or tank from which Amritsar ('pool of nectar') takes its name. At the centre of the pool lies the beautiful Golden Temple itself, in which the sacred book is placed early in the morning. This temple has served as the basis for many interpretations of the religious life. It is, for example, like a lotus plant growing from the murky water of life, yet producing a beautiful flower of devotion and good works, teaching man to reach above the evil of the world which would choke his higher desires. The outer courtyard possesses four entrances, unlike the single doorways of Muslim and Hindu shrines, This expresses the universality of Sikh truth, which is open to all.

Another gold-topped building stands in the outer area, facing the long walkway to the inner holy place. This is the Akal Takht, a political and community centre where important pronouncements are made concerning the life of Sikhs. Built by the sixth guru, it indicates the rise of political and social awareness among Sikhs, as they sought to establish a code of conduct for themselves and a way of organizing their relations with other groups. Here in the temple area religion and politics are clearly distinguished. There are, in fact, four other major Takhts (or thrones) and many other important temples, but Amritsar provides a clear demonstration of the great unity of social and religious life which has emerged in Sikh culture.

The Golden Temple at Amritsar was built by Arjan, the fifth Guru of Sikhism, at the end of the sixteenth century.

the congregation of Sikhs may gather around it. Book plus congregation equals guru. The *Guru Granth* and the *Guru Panth* add up to the presence of the guru in the world today. An obvious consequence of this development has been the greatly increased responsibility for the faith which falls on the shoulders of each member. There are no priests; anyone can conduct the worship, though some are specially trained to read and expound the *Granth*. This has made the Sikhs particularly aware of themselves as a special group, for they are a much more congregational religion than any other in India (apart from Islam), and one in which religious and community identity correspond closely.

Despite this strong communal aspect, Sikh religious teaching is itself intensely personal. We can see this by looking at the doctrines expressed in the *Guru Granth*. One word of caution is needed here: Sikh thoughts about God and men should not be forced into overly rigid doctrinal systems. Sikh doctrines have emerged more as an attempt to express human experience of God in the course of religious living and searching, than as an exercise in academic theology.

What the Sikhs believe

As man begins to become aware of God, he is prompted to see his own life in a different way. The individual seeker realizes that he is tangled up in his own self-seeking pride, ignorance and selfishness, with a consuming passion for the world and its pleasures. It is as though people are blinded to the true nature of life by the hypnotic allure of material goods. The whole world seems to be a sea in which they are drowning with little hope of escape. Even some religious people appear to follow their rituals and creeds in a similar spirit of ignorance.

The love of God

The only hope for sinful men lies in

At Sikh gurdwaras *volunteers prepare meals for the 'free kitchen' where visitors are fed.*

the fact that the true Guru, God himself, is merciful. He will grant to the true seeker a sense of his presence which lifts and transports man from this life of evil and bondage. He should join a company of other seekers and there sing the hymns of those who have already found knowledge of God. As he dwells upon the name of God, by repeating sacred verses with sincerity and love, so the divine Lord will embrace him and give him a deep inner awareness of his nature. Then the disciple will feel at one with his master.

The language of love, often a bride's longing for her husband, is typical of the Sikh pattern of devotion and spirituality—a mysticism of love. Although God is essentially beyond description, he appears as one who is merciful, eternal, all-powerful. His will determines all that takes place, whether good or evil. He is present everywhere, in the worm as in the elephant.

True spiritual pilgrimage, which takes place in the heart and will—not by travelling to sacred sites—is a shift of emphasis from the self to God. The Sikh expressions are *manmukh* and *gurmukh*, where *man* (pronounced *mun* as in sun) indicates the entire personality of an individual, both heart and mind, and *gur* represents God. The way of salvation is therefore by regarding God, and not the self, as the centre.

Pride and selfishness

The world and its people are under a delusion—the power of *maya*—which prevents clear thought and understanding. Ultimately God is also responsible for that. But Sikhs do not focus on this as a theological problem of evil. People respond to the world in its negative aspect because they are under the power of *haumain*, the self-centred pride of men and women. Only as the power of *haumain* is destroyed by praising the name of the Lord are people set free to serve him. But without the help of the true Guru egotism is not destroyed, nor its disease removed. Salvation is a love-union with God, and that results from a devotional relationship of worship between the

disciple and God. Until that union (*sahaj*) takes place, individuals must live many times by being reincarnated. This process of transmigration of the soul ends only when a person finds the true Guru. Only a few seek him truly, and of these only a few find him.

Love and a longing to serve well up in the hearts of those who find the true Guru. Service is important in the Sikh religion. It is applied to many tasks, both menial and exalted, performed by members of the *Khalsa*. Sweeping out the *gurdwara*, cooking the food to be eaten there, representing the Sikh community to the non-Sikh world—all such acts count as service.

The style and content of the *Guru Granth* is poetical and highly metaphorical. It resembles the biblical Psalms. It is not a systematic explanation of beliefs. Its power lies in catching the mind and stimulating the heart to love God.

'**The man who is lost in selfishness is drowned without water, his mind is like a frog and his vice like mud. Yet the Lord is the ocean and the disciple a little fish; once this is realized then a union becomes possible, and that is like metal being welded to metal, like water mixing with water. This union is achieved by the word of the true Guru. Man's heart is penetrated by the Guru's word, it is imperishable and has the power to create and to destroy. Once it comes it is as though a lotus flower blossoms in the heart; it serves as a ship whereby we may cross the evil ocean of existence. The one who is asleep is awakened, and he who was aflame with fever is cooled. Once this experience comes no one will assert that he has deserved it. It is as though the disciple has no purity of his own, but the Lord seizes his arm and washes him. Then the body ceases to be a puppet of *maya* and is free to serve the true Guru.'**

Sikhs have many ways of interpreting their scriptures, but the goal of all explanation is to aid man in his search for union with God. In many respects it is a very practical religion which prefers saints to scholars, or at least wishes scholars to be saints. This has led to some interesting reactions when Sikhs have sought to make their beliefs intelligible as a world religion in the twentieth century. For the wishes of scholars are not always those of pious men, nor of the ordinary members of a religious movement.

Identity and community

The twentieth century has witnessed a rapid spread of Sikhs outside the Punjab. In the early part of the century and shortly after the Second World War, many single men and married men without their wives made their way to America, Britain, Canada and parts of South and East Africa. Many of these Sikhs abandoned the wearing of the turban, long hair and beards in an attempt to be accepted by the communities into which they moved to look for employment. Very few Sikh temples existed then but, since weekly attendance at a *gurdwara* was not an established custom in the Punjab, the fact that few attended worship did not mean any abandonment of the Sikh religion.

Sikhs in the West

The late 1960s saw a significant change in Sikh groups in the West, for this was the period when wives and families came to join their husbands and sons. It was a time when Sikh homes ceased to be mere dormitories where the men slept between shift-work, and so Sikhs became far more socially visible. There were now many women, and large numbers of Sikh children attending school. Many buildings were converted into Sikh temples in the larger industrial towns, and these served as social centres as well as places of worship. They helped the newly-arrived Punjabi women to adjust to the new world in which they found themselves.

In 1969 the Sikh Missionary Society was founded in Britain and the Sikh Research Centre in Canada, with similar movements in America.

A Sikh wedding in the Punjab. Marriage is both a social and a spiritual union.

Sikhs were becoming more aware of their community identity. They sought to produce literature which taught Sikh children about the history of the Sikh religion, as well as encouraging the teaching of the Punjabi language. The aim was to bind the Sikhs together and to enable them to gain recognition as a distinctive community. This growth in self-awareness expressed the idea that being a member of a Punjabi community could not be separated from the idea of being a Sikh.

Traditional practices

Some Sikhs now began to let their beards and hair grow again, and wore their turbans. *Khalsa* Sikhs are supposed to be distinguished by the five symbols, often referred to as the five *k*s because their Punjabi names begin with that letter. These are:

● *kesh*, or uncut hair;
● *kangha*, or comb used to keep the hair clean;
● *kara*, or metal bangle;
● *kaccha*, or special knee-length underwear;
● *kirpan*, or dagger.

Sometimes the children of Sikhs with cut hair have returned to the more traditional pattern, showing the changed relationship between the early immigrant generations and those born in their adopted country and more sure of their social standing.

Though there have been many changes in these settlements of Sikhs, some of the traditional Punjabi practices have continued, especially that of arranged marriages. In these, the families of young men and women decide on marriage partners on their behalf; they may or may not be given the chance to add their own opinion. Some youngsters prefer this decision to be taken for them, but others would rather have a love-match of their own choice. Caste is one of the most important factors in arranging marriages, despite the teachings of the historical gurus. In some towns one major caste-group meets in one *gurdwara* while other groups meet in theirs. The Jat groups are often distinguished from the Ramgarhias and Bhatras, divisions which can be traced back to occupational differences in the Punjab.

The Sikh religion is not a missionary religion in the sense that it tries to win members from outside. It is an ethnic religion which seeks to maintain the community intact. Some splinter groups in America have converted Americans to the faith, just as in the Punjab there are a few movements which believe that there is still a need for living gurus today, and which do in fact possess them. But, generally speaking, the Sikh religion is focussed on the community, and on that ethical life which brings honour to the *Khalsa*. For that is the fellowship of true believers in which alone access to God may be found. The Sikh religion does not deny the existence of truth in other faiths, but its main concern is that its members strive to be devoted to God.

Respect For All Life: Jainism

Myrtle Langley

For a religion of only 3 million people, almost all of whom live in India, Jainism has wielded an influence out of all proportion to its size and distribution. This influence has been felt most keenly in the modern world through Mahatma Gandhi. Although not himself a Jain, he grew up among Jains and embraced their most distinctive doctrine—non-violence to living things, *ahimsa*. But the influence of Jainism has also been felt in the Jain contribution to India's banking and commercial life.

As Buddhists are followers of the Buddha (the enlightened one), so Jains are followers of the *Jina* (the conqueror), a title applied to Vardhamana, last of the great Jain teachers. It is applied also to those men and women who, having conquered their passions and emotions, have achieved liberation and attained perfection. And so the very name Jainism indicates the predominantly ethical character of this religion.

The birth of Jainism

The period from the seventh to the fifth centuries BC was a turning-point in the intellectual and spiritual development of the whole world: it produced, among others, the early Greek philosophers, the great Hebrew prophets, Confucius in China and probably Zoroaster in Persia.

For north India, the sixth century BC was a time of particular social, political and intellectual ferment. The older and more familiar tribal structure of society was disintegrating. In its place were appearing a few great regional kingdoms and a number of smaller tribal groupings known, for want of a better word, as republics. These kept some of the characteristics of tribal structure but had little political power, being dependent on the largest of the kingdoms. In this transition period, when the old social order was passing away and a new one had not yet taken shape, many people felt themselves adrift, socially and morally. Religious confusion also arose as divergent streams of religious thought and practice came into contact and conflict. It was probably from this conflict that the so-called heterodox teachers associated with Buddhism, Jainism and the Ajivikas sect emerged. They, in turn, probably owed their origin to the Shramanas, the ancient religious teachers distinguished from the Brahmins by their doctrine of salvation through atheism and asceticism. They were considered heterodox because they refused to accept the authority of the *Vedas*, the authoritative Hindu texts, and rejected the institutions of caste and sacrifice.

Mahavira
the Path-Maker

Vardhamana, known to his followers as Mahavira (the Great Hero), was an elder contemporary of the Buddha. Although the legends surrounding his life are less attractive than those surrounding the Buddha's, being even more formalized and unreliable, he was undoubtedly a historical person. Under the name of Nigantha Nataputta, he is often mentioned in the Buddhist scriptures as one of the Buddha's chief opponents.

The second son of Siddhartha, a Kshatriya chieftain, Mahavira was born around 540 BC at Kundagrama, near modern Patna in Bihar, and died in 468 BC (according to scholarly opinion; tradition says 599–527 BC). On both sides of the family he belonged to the ruling warrior classes which were a powerful force at the time. Educated as a prince, according to one tradition Mahavira remained a bachelor for life; according to another he married a princess who bore him a daughter. Either way, at the age of twenty-eight, on the death of his parents, he renounced his family life to become a beggar and ascetic, seeking liberation from the dreary round of birth, death and rebirth.

At first he followed the ascetic practices of a group founded some 250 years earlier by a certain Parsva. Parsva is known as the twenty-third and Mahavira as the twenty-fourth of the *Tirthankaras*, the 'Ford-makers', 'Path-makers' or great teachers of

Jainism, who guide their followers across the river of transmigration. For over twelve years Mahavira wandered from place to place, living a life of the greatest austerity and engaging in disputation. At first he wore only a single loincloth, but after thirteen months he discarded even that encumbrance and for the rest of his life went about naked.

The enlightenment

In the thirteenth year, when aged about forty, and at the end of a long fast, he achieved liberation and full enlightenment. In the language of his followers he had become a conqueror (*jina*). He had attained a state of full, clear and unimpeded knowledge and intuition known as *kevala*, becoming a perfected soul (*kevalin*). And by attaining this omniscience, Mahavira had released himself from the forces (*karma*) which had bound him to the wheel of rebirth.

Mahavira was then acclaimed a leader of an Order (a *Tirthankara*), and for the remaining thirty years of his life he propagated his beliefs and organized his community of followers. He called himself the successor of a series of legendary *Tirthankaras* who had proclaimed Jain beliefs through countless ages. And although his claims may not be wholly true, there is little doubt that the tradition from which Jainism derives goes back beyond Mahavira, Parsva and even Nemi (alleged cousin of Krishna of the Mahabharata war) to the farthest recesses of Indian prehistory. He died, of voluntary self-starvation, at Pava, a village not far from his birthplace, and a great centre of Jain pilgrimage to this day. Thus he entered *nirvana*, his 'final rest'.

The rise of Jainism

Mahavira drew his followers mainly from the Kshatriya aristocracy and organized them into a regular community with lay and monastic members of both sexes. There is good reason to believe that before they joined him some of these followers believed that all possessions, including clothing, should be abandoned,

A Jain home shrine.

Jain temples contain images of the twenty-four Tirthankaras, *but rarely of any gods.*

The general plan of a Jain temple is of a portal and colonnades, a closed hall or open courtyard, and an inner shrine for the images. The principal image, of the *Tirthankara* to whom the temple is dedicated, is flanked by two attendants and by smaller images of the twenty-four *Tirthankaras*. In Digambara temples, the image sits naked with eyes downcast. In Svetambara temples it sits clothed with a loincloth, has protruding eyeballs and is often adorned with jewels and flowers.

Every Jain temple also has a 'saint-wheel' (*siddha cakra*). Its basic form is that of a stylized flat lotus with four petals attached to a circle in the centre. Placed in the petals and in the circle are representations of the Five Great Beings in meditative posture (seated with crossed legs). Often the principles of right knowledge, right faith and right conduct are incorporated too. The diagram is invoked for the destruction of sin and for the common good to prevail.

in the pursuit of passionless detachment, while others stopped short of making nudity a requirement. It was this difference, and later disagreement about the contents of the canon of the scriptures, which were to distinguish the two major sects of Jainism. No fundamental doctrinal differences emerged, even in later centuries.

The two sects

For two centuries, Mahavira's followers remained a small community. Then there was a big increase in Jain numbers as the founder of the great Mauryan dynasty, the Magadhan Emperor Chandragupta (about 321–297 BC), abdicated his throne and joined the order. History here confirms tradition, at least to some extent. However, towards the end of Chandragupta's reign, a serious famine led to the exodus of a large number of Jain monks from the Ganga Valley in north India south to the Deccan. There, in the state of Mysore, they established great centres of the faith.

Then, so tradition has it, when Bhadrabahu, the leader of the emigrants and eleventh elder of the community, returned to Bihar after an absence of twelve years he found that in the confusion and hardship of famine the northern monks, under Sthulabhadra, had abandoned the ancient ways laid down by Mahavira and had taken to wearing white robes.

Thus arose the two sects of Jainism, the Digambaras (the 'sky-clad' or 'space-clad') and the Svetambaras (the 'white-clad'). The schism became fixed in the first century AD and persists to this day.

The scriptures

Similarly, according to tradition, a sacred literature had been passed down orally through the generations, from Mahavira. But Bhadrabahu was the last person to know it perfectly. On his death at the beginning of the third century BC, the canon was reconstructed as far as possible in

The pessimism of Jainism is nowhere better illustrated than in the famous parable of the man in the well, said to have been told by a Jain monk to a prince in order to persuade him of the evils of the world.

'There was once a man who, oppressed by his poverty, left home and set out for another country. But after a few days he lost his way and found himself wandering in a dense forest. There, he met a mad elephant which charged him with upraised trunk. Immediately he turned to flee there appeared before him a terrible demoness with a sharp sword in her hand. In fear and trembling he looked about him in all directions for a way of escape until he saw a great tree and ran towards it. But he could not climb its smooth bole, and afraid of death, flung himself into an old well nearby. As he fell he managed to catch hold of a clump of reeds growing from the wall, and clung to them desperately. For below him he could see a mass of writhing snakes, enraged at the sound of his falling, and at the very bottom, identifiable from the hiss of its breath, a mighty black python with its mouth wide open to receive him. And even as he realized that his life could last only as long as the reeds held fast, he looked up and saw two mice, one black and one white, gnawing at the roots. Meanwhile, the elephant, enraged at not catching its victim, charged the tree and dislodged a honeycomb. It fell upon the man clinging so precariously. But even as the bees angrily stung his body, by chance a drop of honey fell on his brow, rolled down his face and reached his lips, to bring a moment's sweetness. And he longed for yet more drops and so forgot the perils of his existence.

'Now hear its interpretation. The man is the soul, his wandering in the forest is existence. The wild elephant is death, the demoness old age. The tree is salvation, where there is no fear of death, but which no sensual man can attain. The well is human life, the snakes are passions, and the python hell. The clump of reeds is man's allotted span, the black and white mice the dark and light halves of the month. The bees are diseases and troubles, while the drops of honey are but trivial pleasures. How can a wise man want them, in the midst of such peril and hardship?'

twelve sections (*Angas*) which replaced the fourteen former texts (*Purvas*). Although accepted by the Svetambaras, this canon was rejected by the Digambaras, who held that the old one was hopelessly lost. Eighty-four works are recognized as belonging to the Svetambara canon, finally fixed in the fifth century AD. Among them are forty-one Sutras, a number of unclassified works, twelve commentaries and one great commentary. All were written in the Ardha–Magadhi language.

Rise and fall

In subsequent centuries Jainism spread from east to west across India. From time to time it enjoyed the patronage of kings and princes, under whose auspices it produced some of the most magnificent temple architecture in the world. But with the rise of Hindu devotional theism (*bhakti*), particularly to Shiva and Vishnu, in the Middle Ages, it went into relative decline. It became concentrated in two regions, where it remains to this day: Gujarat and Rajasthan where the Svetambaras prevail, and the Deccan, or modern Mysore, where the Digambaras have their headquarters. But, unlike Buddhism, Jainism continued in the land of its birth. This was probably due largely to its emphasis on the lay as well as on the monastic calling. In times of persecution it had the resources of an influential and wealthy lay following to fall back on.

One final aspect of Jain history remains to be mentioned: the rise of the 'dwellers in halls' (*Sthanakavasi*) branch of the Svetambaras in AD 1653. Parallel with the Protestant Reformation in Europe, and probably owing to Muslim influence, reformers arose to condemn all forms of idolatry and temple worship as inconsistent with the teachings of Mahavira. Fundamental doctrines, however, remained unaffected by this further schism.

Jain beliefs

Mahavira and other unorthodox teachers of his age were primarily interested in seeking liberation from the wheel of rebirth.

The universe

Jain philosophy differs in important respects from the systems of Buddhism and Hinduism. Jainism upholds the existence of an infinite number of animate and inanimate substances— *jivas* or souls, and *ajivas* or non-souls, representing the mind/matter dichotomy—each of which possesses an infinite number of individual characteristics of its own. Moreover, all substances exist independently of our perceptions or awareness of them. Thus Jain philosophy is realist.

But because the number of souls inhabiting the universe is infinite, most of them will be compelled to transmigrate eternally in *samsara*, the world of birth, death and rebirth. And this world is itself subject to a process of growth and decline. It is part of a universe which, without beginning and without end, passes through an infinite number of cosmic cycles, each divided into phases of

Carving from the marble temple on Mt Abu.

ascent and descent during which civilization rises and falls. At present we are in the fifth period of a phase of descent.

The apparent fatalism and determinism of the system is opposed by Jain philosophers by means of the distinctive theory of 'many-sidedness' (*anekantavada*). This relates the truth of any proposition to the point of view from which it is made. The rise and fall of civilizations is rigidly determined from the universal point of view, but from the individual viewpoint a man is free to work out his own salvation. Only the liberated soul knows the full and absolute truth. A popular illustration of this is the parable of the six blind men and the elephant. Each, having grasped a part of the great beast, was asked what it was like. One said a wall, another a rope, another a snake, another a fan, and so on. Only the soul in *nirvana* has complete and perfect knowledge.

The soul

The soul's essential character is consciousness and knowing. In its original state, the soul knows everything: nothing is hidden from it, it commands the knowledge of existence in all its various aspects, and at all times, past, present and future. In its present state in this world, ensconced in a material body, the soul's knowledge is made imperfect and incomplete by the limitations matter places on it.

The soul is graded into five levels according to which form it takes in its earthly existence.

● At the lowest level are the souls possessing only one sense—touch; these include the elements themselves, earth, water, air and fire, and the vast vegetable kingdom.
● At the second level are the souls possessing two senses: touch and taste—including worms and shell creatures.
● At the third level are the souls possessing three senses: those of touch, taste and smell—including ants, bugs and moths.
● At the fourth level are the souls possessing four senses: touch, taste, smell and sight; these include, for example, wasps, locusts and butterflies.
● At the fifth and highest level are the souls possessing all five senses—touch, taste, smell, sight and hearing. These include four types of creatures: infernal beings, the higher animals, humans, and heavenly beings.

The soul's journey from one level of consciousness to another, and from one grade to another, up or down the scale, depends on the inexorable law of *karma*.

Karma and rebirth

Like all Indian religions, Jainism upholds the universal law of *karma*. According to this law, every action—thought, word or deed—produces an effect, which in turn serves as the cause of another action, and so on. This chain of cause and effect is known as 'karmic bondage' or simply *karma*. And because Jainism, as we have seen, subscribes also to the doctrine of transmigration and rebirth, it follows that the state of the soul at any given time is due to the *karma* accumulated over countless ages.

However, the Jain doctrine of *karma* is distinctive. Whereas Hindus view *karma* purely as a law of nature, Jains believe *karma* to consist of fine and subtle particles of matter which adhere to the soul, as clay to a pot. Yet, by effort, discipline and knowledge, man can control *karma*. Selfish, careless and cruel actions lead to the accumulation of heavy *karma* which weighs the soul down. But the *karma* accruing from good deeds is dissipated almost immediately and has no serious effects. Moreover, suffering willingly undertaken has the effect of dispersing the *karma* already accumulated, so helping to lighten the soul.

To achieve salvation (*moksha*), man must therefore free his soul from matter. Thus freed, its natural lightness will float it to the top of the universe to dwell there for ever in all-knowing bliss. The souls of heroes like Mahavira virtually achieve salvation in this life. It is only residual *karma* which binds them to the earth, but when that is exhausted through fasting and penance, they rise immediately above the highest heavens of the gods to the eternal rest of *nirvana*.

Jainism is not fatalistic, but it *is* atheistic. There is no world-soul, no supreme being, no creator and sustainer of the universe, no one beyond himself (except the *Tirthankaras* as guides and examples) to aid man in his endeavours.

Similarly, for all the subtlety and sophistication with which its doctrine of *karma* and rebirth has been elaborated, Jainism is in practice profoundly pessimistic. The world is a place of utter misery and sorrow, in no way compensated for by life's few moments of happiness.

The way of salvation

Because of the infinite number of souls in the universe and the length of the cycle of rebirth, it happens only rarely that a soul obtains human birth. Therefore, man should use every opportunity to pursue the way of salvation by acquiring the Three Jewels:

● Right knowledge;
● Right faith;
● Right conduct.

Right knowledge comes through knowing the Jain creed, right faith through believing in it and right conduct through following it. The first two are worthless without the last, and so Jain monks and nuns, laymen and laywomen take vows of right conduct, the most important and all-embracing of which is non-violence.

Non-violence

To injure living beings, even unwittingly, is to engender the most harmful of karmic effects. To injure with deliberate intent has the gravest of consequences. And since the whole universe throbs with life, this means in practice that a Jain's diet and livelihood are severely restricted. Even the Jain layman must be a strict vegetarian. He may not be a farmer, for when ploughing the soil he might injure animals and plants, not to speak of the earth itself. He may not ply certain crafts, for the metal on the blacksmith's anvil and the wood on

the carpenter's bench suffer excruciating pain as they are worked. Instead, he will follow the safe professions of trading and money-lending and most likely become a wealthy merchant or prosperous banker.

The everyday life of a Jain

Jains go through special ceremonies at birth, marriage and death as do members of most religions. But there is a difference. The rites through which the Jain passes are Hindu rather than Jain. And it is often Hindu priests or officials who perform them.

The life of a layman

Full salvation is not possible for the layman unless, as the end approaches, he takes the vow of old age, containing the promise to die by voluntary self-starvation. And, according to the Digambaras, it is never possible for a woman unless she is first of all reborn as a man.

Jainism recognizes four sources of *karma*:

● Attachment to things of this life, such as food, clothing, lodging, women and jewels;
● Giving rein to anger, pride, deceit and greed;
● Uniting the body, mind and speech to worldly things;
● False belief.

Karma can be controlled by renouncing all activity. Jainism also recognizes eight kinds of *karma*, three tenses of *karma* and fourteen steps to liberation from *karma*. Between steps one and four a person acquires knowledge and faith, but only on the fifth step does he realize the importance of conduct and thus become able to take the twelve vows which mark the layman's religious life.

First in the series of twelve vows are the five 'limited vows':

● Non-violence to souls with more than one sense.
● Truthfulness.
● Non-stealing.
● Chastity.
● Non-attachment or the limitation of possessions and worldly goods.

Next in the series are the three

The Parsvanath temple in Calcutta reflects the wealth of the Jain community.

'assistant vows' which help a person to keep the first five:

● Restriction of travel (so curtailing sin by restricting the area in which it can be committed).

● Restriction on the use of certain things, so discouraging lying, covetousness, stealing and so on.

● Discouragement of carelessness in speaking ill of others, taking life, keeping weapons and having an evil influence.

The remaining four vows in the series are intended to encourage the laity in the performance of their religious duties:

● To spend at least forty-eight minutes every day in unbroken meditation (*samayika*), thinking evil of no one, being at peace with the world and contemplating the heights which may be reached by the soul, and if possible to repeat this exercise three times, morning, afternoon and evening.

● To set aside at least one particular day to be more serious about the vows of travel restriction and meditation.

● To live as a monk for a temporary period of twenty-four hours, touching no food, drink, ornaments, scents or weapons and remaining celibate while using only three cloths by day and two by night—thus forging a link between the lay and monastic communities (called *posadha*).

● To support the ascetic community by giving its members any of the fourteen articles which they may accept without blame, such as food, water, clothing, pots, blankets, towels, beds, tables and other furniture.

Jains believe that to keep the twelve vows brings great physical and moral advantage. The body becomes fit and healthy and the soul is freed from love and enmity.

The layman wanting to reach a higher stage in the upward path towards liberation must undertake to keep a further eleven promises:

● To worship the true *deva* (i.e. a *Tirthankara*), reverence a true guru (teacher), and believe in the true doctrine (*dharma*, i.e. Jainism), while avoiding the seven bad deeds of gambling, eating meat, wine-bibbing, adultery, hunting, thieving and debauchery.

● To keep the twelve vows, facing death by voluntary self-starvation in complete peace.

● To engage in meditation at least three times a day.

● To live the life of a monk temporarily at least six times a month.

● To avoid uncooked vegetables.

● To refrain from eating between sunset and sunrise and from drinking water before daylight, in case an insect is accidentally eaten.

● To keep away from his own wife and never to scent his body so as to seduce her.

● Never to begin anything that might entangle him in worldly pursuits which might lead to destruction of life.

● To be a novice for his remaining days.

● To eat only left-overs.

● To wear the dress of an ascetic, live apart in a religious building or in the forest, and live according to the rules laid down in the scriptures for ascetics.

By the time he has taken the last of these eleven promises, the layman is virtually an ascetic.

As the layman endeavours to reach this exalted state, he will strive to develop the twenty-one qualities which distinguish the Jain 'gentleman'. He will always be 'serious in demeanour; clean as regards both his clothes and his person; good-tempered; striving after popularity; merciful; afraid of sinning; straightforward; wise; modest; kind; moderate; gentle; careful in speech; sociable; cautious; studious; reverent both to old age and old customs; humble; grateful; benevolent; and, finally, attentive to business'.

The life of an ascetic

The life of an ascetic begins with initiation. First he gives away his clothing and jewels to relatives, and dons the dress of an ascetic (*sadhu*), three upper garments and two lower ones which vary in colour according to sect. Next, he has his hair removed. From now on he is a homeless wanderer and must remain possessionless except for his robes, a few pieces of cloth with which to strain insects from his daily drink of water, a cloth mask with which to cover his mouth for fear of hurting the air, a few wooden jugs or gourds, and a brush or whisk with which to sweep insects from the path before him.

The five great vows taken by the Jain ascetic are stricter versions of the first five taken by the layman:

● Non-violence—not to kill any living thing, whether five-, four-, three-, two-sensed or immovable (one-sensed), even through carelessness.
● Truthfulness—to speak only of what is pleasant, wholesome and true.
● Non-stealing—not to take what is not given.
● Chastity—to have no dealings with gods, human beings or animals of the opposite sex.
● To renounce love for any thing or person, which means ending all likes and dislikes with regard to sounds, colours or smells as well as people—in other words, to be indifferent through anything mediated through the senses.

As there exists an ideal for the Jain layman, so too there exists the picture of a perfect monk. It has been said that the true ascetic should possess twenty-seven qualities, for he must keep the five vows, never eat at night, protect all living things, control his five senses, renounce greed, practise forgiveness, possess high

ideals, and inspect everything he uses to make sure that no insect life is injured. He must also be self-denying and carefully keep the three rules for controlling mind, speech and body, he must endure hardships in the twenty-two ways, and bear suffering till death.

Ways of worship

Jainism's rejection of God does not entail rejection of prayer and worship, more precisely termed contemplation. But of all beings, including the gods and the saints, only liberated souls or *Tirthankaras* made perfect are worshipped. Even they are not appealed to for help or mercy; they serve more as an inspiration to those still struggling for freedom and perfection.

That is the theory. The practice is very different. Many of the Jain laity pray to Hindu gods for help, many Jain temples house images of Hindu deities, and many Jain festivals incorporate Hindu customs.

Temples and domestic shrines

One of the glories of Jainism is its heritage of magnificent temple architecture. Two of its outstanding developments are the temple-cities, some of which have hundreds of shrines from many different periods, and the fretted ceilings and ornamented pillars with their delicately carved figures and flowers in marble, perhaps the finest of their kind in the world. The numerous modern temples in the towns and cities are smaller and undistinguished.

Jain homes incorporate domestic shrines. According to scriptural instruction they are supposed to be made of wood, and some with elaborately carved doors and door-frames have survived.

Prayer

Jain temples are filled with images of the *Tirthankaras*: 'Contemplating the form of the passionless Lord in a Jaina temple, the mind becomes filled automatically with a sentiment of renunciation... The mind is purified by the contemplation and worship of the *Tirthankaras*.'

The great statues of south India best convey the Jain ideal. This is a description of the sixty-foot-high stone replica of the hero Gomatesvara at Sravana Belgola:

'**[He rises] huge, stony and naked. So rigid is his stance, so austere his stillness, that creepers are growing up his legs. On his lips is an expression of total impassivity. His nudity of course symbolizes possessionlessness. It is a sign of indifference to the good things of this world. It is not even a matter of laying up treasures in heaven. The Jain saint should be indifferent even to those. Any sort of treasure binds us to this world, and even the heavenly world should be transcended. Karma which weighs us down, like weights which depress balloons, must be got rid of, destroyed. This is a supremely hard task. The saint is the culmination of a struggle which has continued over many, many lives. He gazes, unseeing, over the dry south Indian landscape, a spiritual Gulliver among dark-skinned Lilliputians. Every twelve years, the Jain faithful have a great festival in which innumerable pots of milk and curds and sandal paste are poured over the head of the stone hero. The faith celebrates those who have through heroism and insight gained liberation and thus shown the path to others.'**

Ninian Smart

Every day devout Jains rise before dawn and, with rosary of 108 beads in hand, invoke the Five Great Beings, bowing, with folded hands to east, north, west and south.

As a Jain worshipper approaches the temple, he leaves his shoes and socks outside. At the porch he puts a saffron mark on his brow and repeats the *Nissahi* (which enables him to put aside all sin and care). Inside, he comes to the shrine and bids for the right to wash the principal *Tirthankara* image. Removing the jewels and old flowers, he washes it with water, milk and five nectars. When it has dried, he then rubs it over and marks it with liquid saffron in fourteen places, from head to toe. Meanwhile, verses are sung in its praise, incense and lamps waved at the threshold and an offering of rice placed on a table before the door. Finally, the worshipper performs spiritual worship, prostrating himself three times before the image, recalling the virtues of the *Tirthankara*, singing his praises, walking backwards to the door as he repeats the *Avassahi* (which allows him to engage in worldly pursuits again), and with hands together bowing out.

Festivals

The most important festival of Jainism is held at Pajjusana, the solemn season which closes the Jain year. For eight days or longer, during the wet monsoon period, usually in August, devout Jains fast and attend special services. All householders are urged to live a monk's life for at least twenty-four hours, living in a monastery, meditating and fasting. On the closing day of the festival, every Jain abstains from food and water. At the close of the temple gathering, he performs an act of penitence in which he asks forgiveness of his neighbours for any inadvertent offence and determines to carry no grudge or quarrel over into the next year.

The second most important festival is Divali, the great Hindu festival in honour of Lakshmi, goddess of wealth, which Jains have adapted in honour of Mahavira's liberation.

Jains also observe fasts at full moon, and great excitement is found in going on pilgrimages to Jain holy places.

Jainism is a religion of austerities. Its goal—passionless detachment—is reached only through the most severe and disciplined of life-styles, culminating ideally in death by voluntary self-starvation. And the aim is to achieve it solely by self-effort, without the help of God or gods.

Yet self-imposed austerities often benefit others. And Jains have long been active in promoting public welfare. They are known especially for their endowment of schools, also of hospitals—for both people and animals.

Courage and Faith:
The Parsis

John Hinnells

The word 'Parsi' denotes the 'Persians' or people who left Persia (Iran) at the end of the ninth century AD to seek a new land of religious freedom. They were believers in the ancient Zoroastrian religion, and left Persia rather than forsake their religion, in the face of fierce Islamic persecution. The story of their voyage to India is recounted in the Tale of Sanjan, the *Qissa-i Sanjan*, written in 1600.

Acting on the advice of an astrologer-priest, a group of Zoroastrians left their home in northern Persia, journeyed across the country and set sail to Div, on the coast of present-day Pakistan. There they settled for nearly twenty years, before they moved on again at the advice of an astrologer-priest. When they were at sea, a storm blew up threatening their lives. They prayed to God to rescue them and vowed that if he answered their prayers they would build a great Fire Temple as an act of thanksgiving.

Their prayers were answered and they landed at Sanjan on the northwest coast of India in AD 936. They approached the local prince for permission to settle. This he gave on certain conditions—that they speak in the local language (Gujarati); that they should observe local wedding customs; and that the men should not carry arms. To assure him of their peaceful intentions, the Parsis presented sixteen statements (*shlokas*) regarding their faith and practice. In these they stressed those features of their faith which resembled Hinduism and the social customs which would offend no one. The ruler also gave the Parsis land on which they could build their temple.

The story shows that Parsis believe their journey to India to be part of the divine plan—written in the stars. They landed where they did as an answer to prayer; they have been required to make only minimal adaptations to their way of life in India, and there is a degree of harmony between their religion and that of their Hindu hosts. These beliefs are true of Parsis both then, in the seventeenth century, and now.

Under Hindu rule the Parsis lived a quiet, secure and settled life. In AD 1297 Muslim armies invaded Gujarat, an invasion they followed up in 1465 to secure their hold on the region. Parsis feared there would be a return to the persecution they had suffered in Persia, so they fought alongside the Hindus, but to no avail. Although there have been instances of Muslim oppression on the Parsis (and others), conditions were never as bad as those in Persia.

British rule

The arrival of European and particularly British traders in the seventeenth century was the event which most drastically affected Parsi fortunes. The British developed the islands of Bombay as a new commer-

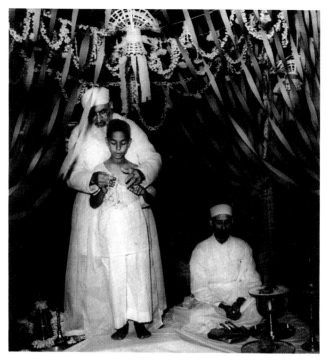

A Parsi boy is given a sacred shirt and a sacred thread at the naujote *ceremony. Following this initiation rite, Parsi children – both boys and girls – are eligible to take part fully in the religious life of the community.*

cation than any other community in proportion to their numbers.

As a result, they occupied a correspondingly high proportion of official posts. They were very influential in the early phases of the Indian National Congress, the party which led the campaign for independence and which has ruled India practically ever since. In west Indian politics they were an extremely powerful voice. Further, the only three Indians ever to be elected to the House of Commons at Westminster were all Parsis. The fact that they were elected by the English voters to represent London constituencies, not India, shows how educated and Westernized these Parsis had become. What was true of these three individuals was true of many in Bombay also. Parsis ran and owned much of India's commerce, such as banks, the textile industry and the trade with the East.

Modern trends

In the twentieth century, Parsi wealth and influence has declined as other communities have taken their share of the wealth. But still the Parsis remain a highly respected, largely middle-class, well-educated community. The numbers have begun to decline since the Second World War, largely owing to a falling birth rate. Something like 70 per cent of India's Parsi population (now about 92,000) live in the one city, Bombay, so they are hit especially hard by its typical inner-city problems.

Such tremendous social changes have inevitably influenced Parsi religion. Naturally their Western education has resulted in a Western religious influence. A number of Parsis have studied abroad, some have studied their own religion at Western universities. Most have studied under Protestant scholars and this has affected their reform movements. They have called for the use of the vernacular instead of the sacred language of Avestan in prayers, and a higher Western education for trainee Parsi priests. Some even denied that revelation was a valid religious concept, because of the educational principle that a truth per-

cial base. To do this they needed to attract immigrants to these almost uninhabited islands and so offered attractive conditions. In particular they offered freedom of religion and justice for all, which appealed particularly to minority groups such as the Parsis. As early settlers in Bombay, the Parsis played a leading part in developing it as the leading port of western India and as India's commercial capital. What is more, they obtained a substantial proportion of the wealth that flowed to the island in the nineteenth century. By 1850 it was estimated that Parsis owned half the island.

After 1857, when the government of India passed from the East India Company to the crown and parliament in London, Indians needed new resources to influence official policy. Local influence and wealth were insufficient; a Western education was essential in order to argue with the British in London. Parsis rose to positions of considerable power in these changed conditions, because more Parsis received a Western edu-ceived and learned for oneself is better understood than a truth imposed from above. Other, more secular, Parsis called for the complete Europeanization of the community.

Theosophy and the Parsis

Such extremes naturally provoked a backlash among the orthodox. The form which this took was an unexpected one, for it involved Theosophy, a religious movement started in the West which called on Indian religions not to be misled by 'the materialist West' into abandoning their ancient practices. This message inspired many Parsis who, without necessarily becoming members of the Theosophical Society, accepted a number of Theosophical teachings.

Then, early in the twentieth century, a specifically Parsi form of Theosophy was begun by Behramshah Shroff (1857–1927). He claimed that he had been taken to an unknown hideout in the Persian mountains by a wandering group of secret Zoroastrians. There, hidden in caves, he claimed, were ancient treasures and teachings from Zoroastrian Persia. The religion revealed to Shroff contains many Theosophical teachings. For thirty years after his return Shroff remained silent, but spent the last twenty years of his life preaching. There is no way of estimating the followers of his teaching (called the path of knowledge, *Ilm-i Kshnoom*), because they have not formed a clear, distinct sect. They are probably relatively few, though they are very vocal among the Parsis.

The great majority of Parsis follow neither the Westernized nor the Theosophical approach. They practise quietly, and unquestioningly, the faith of their forefathers. They know little of the official or historic theologies of their religion. What they do know are its basic ideals and values. Above all, they live out their faith in their daily lives.

Joining God's army

The rite of initiation (*naujote*) is traditionally carried out at the age of puberty, though nowadays there is a tendency for it to take place at about nine years of age. It is never performed on infants because the whole idea of the rite is that the initiate of his or her own free-will chooses to be made a member of God's army. Until a child is old enough to know the difference between right and wrong, Zoroastrians do not believe it can sin.

Naujote is not a sacrament conferring saving grace, but rather an initiation into the responsibilities of the religion. The actual rite involves the first public donning of the badges of the religion, the sacred shirt and cord. The shirt is white, a symbol of the purity of the religion, and made of cotton. It is worn at all times next to the skin. The cord is made of lamb's wool; it is untied and retied at least five times each day to the accompaniment of traditional prayers. As the worshipper rejects the devil he flicks the ends contemptuously; as he mentions God he bows his head in reverence; as he ties the knots he makes a vow to be good in thought, word and deed. These simple acts and prayers can be performed anywhere and must be said five times a day.

Death ceremonies

Death ceremonies in most religions are the ones that change least with the passage of time. Because death, to Zoroastrians, is the temporary victory of evil, it is a place where demons are present. The purpose of the funeral rites is to limit the spread of that evil. The corpse is removed as soon as possible to a place apart. It is washed and dressed in clean but old clothes—old because wastefulness is considered a sin. The funeral should take place the same day as death if possible.

After prayers, and when the mourners have taken their last look at the deceased, the bearers then carry the corpse into a *dakhma* or, as the British called them, a 'Tower of Silence'. These are round structures with high walls to prevent people seeing or getting in. There are a few steps for the corpse-bearers to enter. The tower is open to the sky and there the corpse is stripped, so that the vultures and crows may devour the flesh. It is reckoned that it takes a vulture thirty minutes to devour a

Parsis honour fire as the symbol of Ahura Mazda. The fire is kept in a fire temple, attended by a priest.

Parsis dispose of their dead in secluded buildings known as Towers of Silence.

corpse, during which time the relatives pray in a nearby building. When they return home they wash and observe certain ceremonies for three days while the soul awaits its judgement. On the third day it is usual for those who can to announce the gift of money to a charitable cause in memory of the deceased, a better memorial in Parsi belief than erecting a gravestone. The sun-bleached bones are later cast into a pit.

The initial Western reaction to this rite of exposure is one of horror, a reaction stirred up from time to time by inaccurate newspaper reports. This is a mistaken impression. In theory these places should be on a hill-top apart from all life, so that the

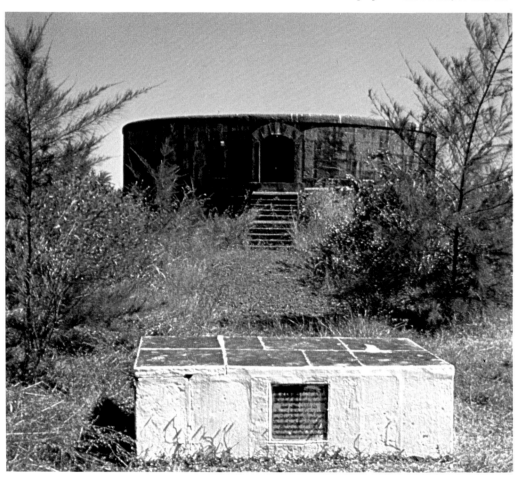

corruption of death will not affect the living. But those in cities such as Bombay and Surat have an air of natural peace and calm about them. Parsis expose bodies in this way because they believe the earth and the waters are the sacred creation of God. They must not, therefore, be polluted with death, the work of evil. Fire, too, is a sacred creation so that cremation is equally wrong. God, they believe, created the vulture for the very purpose of devouring corpses. Parsis argue that it is a far more natural form of disposal than any other, and find Christian graveyards horribly morbid!

Fire temples

Fire has been the focus of Zoroastrian rites and devotions from earliest times. The nomads used the household fire as the centre of their rites, having the sky as their dome, not a man-made temple. Temples were first introduced into Zoroastrianism by the Achaemenid monarch Artaxerxes II (404–359 BC), probably in imitation of Babylonian practice. He also introduced the cult of statues, but this was too radical a break with tradition for it to succeed. Instead of man-made statues, Zoroastrians placed the divinely created 'icon' of fire at the centre of their holy buildings. Temple worship was, then, a late entry into the religion. One can be a good Zoroastrian and never go to a temple, though in practice many do so because they find spiritual help there.

There is no set time or day for temple worship, nor any fixed ritual to perform. For the layman it involves essentially a personal pilgrimage. Before entering the temple he washes and then offers prayers, so that he is clean physically and spiritually. The prayer room itself is very simple. Against one wall there is the sanctuary, marked off by ceiling-high walls, with a door for the priest to enter and windows for the faithful to see through. The sacred fire is kept burning in a large vessel, sometimes as much as 6 feet/2 metres high. The

ordinary layman approaches the door of the sanctuary, touches the ground with his forehead, leaves an offering of wood for the fire, and takes a pinch of ash from a ladle left by the priest. He then stands to offer his prayers in private. There is no congregational worship; prayer is offered by each person directly to God.

Fire temples have an enormously powerful sense of the holy. The prayer room is bare of all decoration, so that attention is focussed exclusively on the fire, the living image of God, 'the pure flame of the fire symbolizing him who is himself eternal light', as a Parsi has said. No artificial lights must shine, lest they dim the glory of God's own creation. The priests are expected to undertake many important 'higher' ceremonies on behalf of the layman, but for the ordinary Zoroastrian his duty is primarily the life of good thoughts, words and deeds; the daily prayers and the inspiration of a personal pilgrimage to the temple.

Beauty and simplicity

It is the simplicity of the requirements and the beauty of its ideals, as well as the courage of its followers, which have kept alive the oldest of the world's prophetic religions for some 3,500 years. These have sustained it not only in the face of Muslim persecution, but also in other lands. For the Parsis have dispersed to different parts of the globe, wherever trade took them. There are now Parsi communities in Pakistan (Karachi), East Africa (though the political policies there have forced Parsis, along with other Indians, to leave), Britain (mainly in London), Canada (Toronto, Montreal and British Columbia) and the USA (mainly in New York, Washington and California). The faithful few (approximately 17,000) in present-day Iran, who have survived over 1,000 years of persecution, are now a tolerated religious group. So although the number of followers remains small—perhaps 200,000—Zoroastrianism is still a living religion.

The Enlightened One: Buddhism

Wulf Metz

There is today, in contrast to the last century, hardly any doubt that the 'historical' Buddha, founder of Buddhism, actually lived. His life is greatly interwoven with legend, and rather than a detailed biography, tradition offers an idealized portrait of what all good Buddhists should strive to become. Nevertheless, certain facts about his life can be established fairly clearly.

Siddharta Gautama, later known as Buddha, was born in about 560 BC in a village called Lumbini, near the modern border between India and Nepal. His father, Shuddhodanna, reigned as the rajah of a small principality in the area. As is common with the founder of a religion, all sorts of legends have grown up around the child's birth. In accordance with the idea of rebirth, these even include details of his previous existences! The story is told, for instance, that during his last but one incarnation, the Buddha looked down from the 'Tushita heaven', the 'seat of contented gods', to find the right time, place and parents for his reincarnation. He chose the period of history when human life could last up to 100 years—neither too long nor too short for his teaching to be grasped. As a place he chose northern India, regarded as the central land. And for his mother he took the virtuous Maya, wife of Shuddhodanna, who had shown her purity and excellence during previous existences in 100,000 ages of the world.

One night Maya, who had made a vow of chastity, dreamed that a white elephant entered her womb. Ten months later in the grove of Lumbini, on the day of the full moon in May, she bore her child. The earth trembled and supernatural beings were present at the birth; and Maya died seven days later, for she who has borne a Buddha may never serve any other purpose afterwards.

The name chosen for the boy by his parents, Siddharta, meant 'he who has reached his goal'. Later, as was the custom in noble Indian families, he chose a second name, Gautama, after a famous Hindu teacher from whom he was descended. Buddha, the name by which he came to be known, is actually a title of honour meaning 'the awakened one' or 'the enlightened one'. This title became attached to his name in much the same way that the title 'Christ' became attached to the name of Jesus.

The young prince was brought up by his mother's sister Mahapatjapati, in the greatest luxury and splendour. It had once been prophesied to his father that the boy would become either a great ruler or a homeless wanderer; in order to protect him from the second and ensure the first, Shuddhodanna sheltered his son from all outside influences. He was educated in the arts and sciences and encouraged to do physical exercises;

as he later admitted, according to the Buddhist scriptures:

'I was spoiled, very spoiled. I anointed myself only with Benares sandalwood and dressed only in Benares cloth. Day and night a white sunshade was held over me. I had a palace for the winter, one for the summer and one for the rainy season. In the four months of the rainy season I did not leave the palace at all, and was surrounded by female musicians.'

The prince married a girl called Gopa or Yashodara. He also had a harem of beautiful dancers. Yet he called his only son Rahula which means 'chain', for in the midst of all this luxury he felt as if he were in chains. Life gave him no satisfaction, and so he decided to leave and become homeless.

The great awakening

Before he left his home for good, Siddharta made three journeys on which he was faced with life's realities in a way which he had never known before. He saw the suffering of the world in three forms: a frail old man, an invalid racked with pain, and a funeral procession with weeping mourners. When he asked in amazement what all this meant, the answer was given that this was merely the common fate of all mankind. Deeply troubled, he returned to his palace.

Gautama The Buddha in His Setting

Richard Drummond

Siddharta Gautama, who came to be called the Buddha ('enlightened one') and was the founder of the Buddhist religion, was born about 560 BC, and died at the age of eighty. He lived in north-eastern India, at a time when that area was one of the world's great centres of intellectual and spiritual activity.

Gautama's birth occurred at the end of a long period of development of the Hindu religious tradition. A thousand years before, the Aryan tribes had first entered India from the north-west, and their military and political power, religious practices and other customs had increasingly come to dominate the entire subcontinent. The religious literature of the Vedas had long been composed, and most of the Upanishads were in existence by this time. Within this long tradition Buddhism came as a kind of reform movement, which was only partly accepted, and was eventually more or less expelled. Since the end of the first millennium AD, Buddhism has seen its greatest flowering outside its native land.

Gautama was born the son of the rajah of Kapilavastu, and brought up as a prince. He married at an early age, and had a son. At the age of twenty-nine, however, he was driven by an inner compulsion to leave this outwardly splendid existence for the homeless life of a holy man. His decision was evidently the result of a long-felt aspiration to higher things. It was also in keeping with the more inward religious orientation of the Upanishads, and the emergence within India of the homeless life as a proper method for earnest seekers after spiritual truth and reality.

Gautama took instruction from religious teachers, but apparently most of the first six or seven years after he left home were spent in religious exercises on his own. These exercises became increasingly severe and ascetic; for example, he fasted to the extent that the hair fell off his limbs. The key turning-point prior to his enlightenment was his realization of the spiritual and moral futility of extreme asceticism, and his adoption of the quieter methods of meditation and faith. This was the specific context of his enlightenment, the religious experience which was decisive for his entire later life.

The Buddha began to teach shortly after his experience of the enlightenment and soon won disciples who followed him into the homeless life and missionary service. His teaching, as that of his disciples, was also aimed at ordinary men and women who did not expect to enter the monastic life. The way of life of the inner group may be characterized as meditative, mendicant and missionary. They were in effect a missionary order, and the sense of universal mission which the Buddha evidently held had no parallel in the previous religious history of India. Travelling with his disciples throughout the Ganges river basin, he devoted the rest of his life to proclaiming the liberating truth of dharma and nirvana.

Siddharta Gautama spent many years of extreme asceticism, almost starving himself to death. But it was not until he renounced this way that he achieved enlightenment.

He continued on his travels until he settled at Uruvela in northern India, where he lived in extreme self-denial and discipline with five followers for six years. All this achieved was to ruin his physical health; he realized that this was not the way to set people free from the cycle of death and rebirth. External treatments were no use; what was needed was an insight into the essence of reality, and a radical change of the basic attitude of greed for life.

Despairing of finding a way out, he suddenly remembered how he had succeeded in his first meditation, at home under an apple-tree. Abandoning his strict life-style (to the horror of his friends who left him in disgust), he resolved to direct all his energies to achieving holiness by meditation.

Immersed in contemplation under a fig-tree, which came to be called 'the tree of enlightenment' or *bodhi*-tree (often shortened to *bo*-tree) he finally reached the highest knowledge, and became the Buddha. His enlightenment had three stages. In his first night of meditation he saw his previous lives pass before him. In the second night he saw with a supernatural insight the cycle of birth, death and rebirth and recognized the law that governs it. In the third night the four holy truths were revealed to him: the knowledge of suffering, the source of suffering, the removal of suffering and the way to the removal of suffering.

The reluctant teacher

Now that he was the Buddha, the 'enlightened one', Siddharta Gautama was in a state of complete redemption and could have entered *nirvana*, the Buddhist heaven, at once. Legend has it that the demon Mara, who had earlier tried to deflect him from his search for truth, now tempted him to do just that. There was no point, the demon said, in teaching the common folk what he had discovered; they were not mature enough for it, and would rather hang on to the enticements and vanities of the world.

Buddha himself had doubts about whether mankind was ready for his

On his fourth journey he met a monk, contented and joyful, travelling around with a begging bowl. This journey was decisive; it showed him that all life's pleasures and attractions are vain and worthless. What he now longed for was true knowledge.

So Siddharta left his home and family, stealing away in the night while his wife and child were asleep. He began to search for knowledge in the traditional Hindu way, striving through constant yoga exercises to unite his self (*atman*) with the origin and meaning of the world (*brahman*). But this method, under the guidance of two Brahminic teachers or gurus, did not satisfy him, or appear to lead to true knowledge.

teaching. But the god Brahma Sahampati appeared and asked him to pass it on, if only for the sake of a few people. So he decided to set the 'wheel of teaching' in motion, and preached his first famous sermon at Benares. His five former companions were present and became his first disciples.

Buddha had soon gathered around him a group of followers, convinced as much by the serene calm and unshakeable authority of his manner as by the content of his teaching. Discarding the Hindu caste system, he included in his *sangha* or community of monks both Brahmins, the highest caste, and merchants. Among them were members of his own family, including his son Rahula and his cousin Ananda. The order grew quickly; when there were sixty of them, Gautama sent them out to spread the new teaching.

Only women were excluded at first from the order; Gautama felt they were dangerous because they kept the cycle of rebirth in motion, and thus embodied the greed for life. Eventually his stepmother and cousin persuaded him to admit them; but he remained sceptical about this. He maintained that if women had not been admitted, his teachings would have lasted 1,000 years, but that now they would only last 500. History shows us that this pessimistic prophecy was not fulfilled.

A reclining Buddha at the Shwe Dagon pagoda in Rangoon.

A worshipper at the feet of Aukana Buddha in Sri Lanka. Images of the Buddha are often very large: it was believed that the Buddha's 'glorious body' was eighteen feet/ six metres high.

After his enlightenment, Gautama travelled about India for about forty-four years, living as a beggar-monk and teaching. In the rainy season from mid-June to mid-October he and his companions would stay in parks in the towns, where halls (*viharas*) had been built in the Buddha's honour. At the age of eighty, he was taken ill during a meal and died in the town of Kushinagara. Colourful legends describe his ecstatic entry into *nirvana*, and report that a terrible earthquake shook the land when his body was burned. The Buddhist scriptures record his parting speeches to his favourite disciple Ananda:

'Do not cry, Ananda. Have I not been telling you for a long time that it is in the nature of all things, however close or dear they may be to us, that we must part with them and leave them? ... The wise man sees that all created things, formed from care and suffering, disappear again, but the truth will endure. Why should I keep this fleshly body when the noble truth will last? ... You have acted well, Ananda. Make every effort, and soon you too will be free of the great evils, of sensuality, selfishness, illusions, uncertainty.'

What Buddha taught

Buddhist thinking does not centre around the veneration of one person, human or divine. Buddha is not a god, nor a god-sent mediator; he cannot act as a saviour or redeemer for others.

Far more important than the person of Buddha is the idea of teaching (*dharma*). According to the Buddhist understanding this is something timeless, not linked to history or subject to change. In line with Indian tradition, the teaching revealed by Buddha was passed on first of all by word of mouth, having been carefully memorized; only much later was it written down.

Knowledge and awakening

After his awakening it was believed that Gautama had passed from an unredeemed state to a state of re-

Buddha—Just a Good Hindu?

Wulf Metz

It is widely recognized that Siddharta Gautama, who was to become the Buddha, came out of the religious world of Hinduism. According to at least one scholar, an understanding of this background is vital to understanding his thought. Buddha, by this interpretation, was a reformer with a similar relationship to Hinduism as that which Luther had to Roman Catholicism. Just as Luther struggled with the problem of how sins can be forgiven, Gautama struggled with the question of how to be freed from the misery of endless rebirths.

It is not enough, however, to say that Buddha merely wanted to re-establish Hinduism in its original form. He was genuinely a founder of a new religion. His teaching does indeed share some central ideas with the traditional Indian religion—above all the doctrine of reincarnation and the law of *karma*. Hinduism and Buddhism can fairly be grouped together as the religions of the eternal world law. Where they differ significantly is in the idea of an individual soul (*atman*) which must be united with the source of the world (*brahman*). This Buddha absolutely rejects.

There is a belief in India that Buddha is the ninth incarnation or *avatar* of the Hindu god Vishnu. In spite of this, it must be recognized that he made a decisive break from Hinduism, most of all in not taking over the Hindu holy writings. He also abandoned the caste system and denied the existence of God in the sense of a higher being.

Of course, as Buddhism developed, many elements entered which were diametrically opposed to the original intentions of Gautama. In many of these the Hindu heritage can again be detected.

The Buddhist Lands

Wulf Metz

Theravada Buddhism

Mahayana Buddhism, including varieties

Mongolia
Korea
Japan
China
Tibet
Taiwan
Burma
Nepal
Thailand
Vietnam
Sikkim
Bhutan
Kampuchea
Sri Lanka
Laos

Strangely, Buddhism was unable to hold its own in India, the country of its birth. From the seventh century AD it declined visibly there, under pressure from Hindu piety which better suited the religious needs of the common people. Since the eleventh century it has had hardly any part to play in the Indian subcontinent. In recent years, however, vast numbers of outcastes or 'scheduled classes' have been led into Buddhism by Dr Ambedkahr. These are now estimated at about 5 million.

In other regions where it found a foothold at first, Buddhism was later driven out by Islam. Excavations and ancient monuments witness to a blossoming of Buddhism in central Asia, especially East Turkestan, which came to an abrupt end in the ninth century. In the Indonesian islands Buddhism increased in importance from the

eighth century onwards, but around the sixteenth century the area became completely Islamic.

Theravada Buddhism, the most ancient form of the religion, holds sway to this day—partly even as a 'state religion'—in Sri Lanka (formerly Ceylon) and in the countries beyond India: Burma, Thailand, Kampuchea and Laos. In other regions of the Far East, Buddhism appears in the form of the more widespread and less strict Mahayana school, or in other variations. This is the case in China,

Tibet, Korea, Japan, Vietnam, Mongolia, Ladakh, Nepal, Bhutan and Sikkim.

It is extraordinarily difficult to estimate the total number of Buddhists in the world. Religious conditions in China, Tibet and Mongolia in particular, but also in Japan, are unclear. One reason for this is that from time immemorial Buddhism has entered into the most varied alliances with other religions. It is not always easy to identify where Buddhism stops and Taoism or Shintoism

begins! The common view is that there are about 200 million Buddhists in countries excluding China (the minorities outside the Far East hardly affect these figures at all). Some people guess the 'unknown quantity' within China to be twice as high as this. So the total world membership of the Buddhist religion may be as high as 600 million people.

demption. Enlightenment and salvation are thus closely linked in a way which is typical of Buddhism. This link makes it clear that the 'knowledge' Gautama received is something very different from the intellectual understanding which Westerners generally mean when they use the word knowledge. In Buddhist terms it is essentially a special religious knowledge, a knowledge which goes far beyond the limits of reason and the intellect.

But where did Buddha's knowledge come from? The story of his experiences shows quite clearly that it did not come from any outside influence such as study, or holy writings, or a revelation from a god. The

guidance of others can certainly direct a person towards the goal of enlightenment, but no one can relieve him of the effort required to achieve it.

At the same time we cannot definitely say that Gautama brought about his own salvation. Therefore some researchers talk of an unknown quantity which defies explanation. It can neither be introduced at will nor attributed to any divine being.

Because of this, Buddhism has sometimes been described as an 'atheistic religion'. Miracles have little importance, and Buddha himself is merely a human being who has awoken from the darkness of error to live in freedom from selfishness,

1. Inside the Marble Temple in Bangkok.
2. Buddhist boys often spend several months in a monastery as part of their education. 3. The Shwe Dagon pagoda in Rangoon is said to contain the hairs of Gautama and the clothes of previous Buddhas.
4. Monks cleaning a statue of the Buddha in Vientiane, Laos.

'I have run through the course of many births looking for the maker of this dwelling and finding him not; painful is birth again and again. Now you are seen, O builder of the house, you will not build the house again. All your rafters are broken, your ridge-pole is destroyed, the mind, set on the attainment of *nirvana*, has attained the extinction of desires.'

Gautama, on receiving the light of illumination; *Dhammapuda* 153–4

Technically, a Buddha is anyone who has reached enlightenment. At Wat Po in Bangkok there are 394 gilded images of Buddhas.

greed and ignorance. He therefore stands far above the rest of humanity, at a spiritual level which even gives him magical powers.

While the Buddha himself is unique in history, other human beings are also called to Buddhahood, though according to the oldest teaching only a few will reach this goal. By looking to the Buddha they are to strive for true knowledge and become Buddhas themselves.

The fatal law

During the second night of Buddha's awakening, he understood the law governing the endless cycle of birth, death and rebirth. The term *dharma*, used earlier to describe the teaching of Buddhism, is also used of this law.

According to Buddha, every part of the universe—not only human beings—is subject to change and decay. Everything that is created must perish. Moreover, neither people nor the world are units complete in themselves and separated from other units. They are composed of many individual elements which are in a constant state of flux, always dissolving and combining with one another in new ways.

These components do not rearrange themselves at random. They are regulated by strict laws. In the case of human beings, the crucial factor is the law of *karma*, originally a Hindu idea. *Karma*, meaning roughly 'action' or 'works', is the quality which shows itself in the thoughts, words and deeds of an individual. It determines the nature of the individual's rebirth: good works automatically bring about a good rebirth, bad works a bad one. So each rebirth is conditioned by the *karma* of the previous life. This is the moral order of the world, from which no one can escape.

Dharma—in the sense of law—means not only this moral law but also the physical laws ruling the universe; indeed it also denotes the individual parts which make it up. Examples of these *dharmas* are the four elements of earth, water, fire and air; the colours and sounds; organic life; the senses, emotions, impulses of the will, the power of reasoning, consciousness, ignorance; fame, beauty, riches, true and false

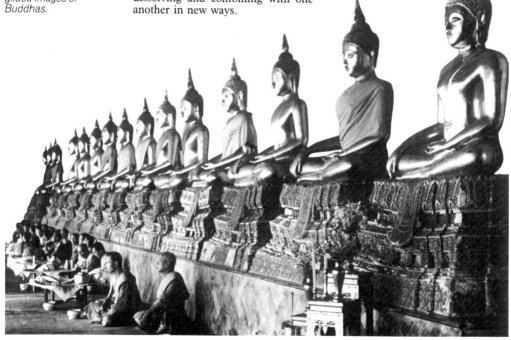

The Buddha's Teaching

Richard Drummond

Karma

The law of *karma*, or cause and effect, operates in both moral and physical dimensions of human life. Man is in bondage to this cycle of the results of good and evil actions.

Reincarnation

Through reincarnation or rebirth all human beings reap good or evil consequences of their actions. The quality of their deeds of body, their speech and thought in previous lives determines the circumstances of their rebirth.

Liberation from karma

By a proper understanding of the human situation—imprisonment in the process of *karma*—and by obedience to the right conditions, it is possible to transcend the human situation. This means, not abolishing *karma*, but liberation from its inner grip and a reorientation of life. A new process is begun by which so-called 'good *karma*' may be created and its good effects experienced in oneself and others.

The Four Noble Truths

The Buddha's experience has been summed up in the Four Noble Truths.
● The first is that the universal human experience of suffering, mental and emotional as well as physical, is the effect of past *karma*.
● The second is the perception that the cause of such suffering is craving or grasping for the wrong things, or for the right things in the wrong way. The basic human problem is a misplaced sense of values, assigning to things or persons in the world a value that they cannot sustain. Nothing in the material world is worthy of ultimate reverence, or can be depended upon in any ultimate sense.
● The third is that it is possible for suffering to cease. Gautama proclaimed that the universal human dilemma can be solved.
● The fourth is also the Noble Eightfold Path, the way to the solution.

The Noble Eightfold Path

● Right knowledge
● Right attitude
● Right speech
● Right action
● Right living (or occupation)
● Right effort
● Right mindfulness
● Right composure
The eight items of the path may be classified under three headings:
● the first two under the heading of wisdom or understanding;
● the next three under ethical conduct;
● the last three under mental discipline.

Nirvana

The goal of life is *nirvana*. This is not annihilation of the self (a Buddhist heresy). On the contrary, *nirvana* is a transformed mode of human consciousness, also an independent reality with a dynamism of its own. It is radically other than the material world: the eternal realm, the utterly dependable, the true refuge.

Dharma

Dharma is the way to the goal of *nirvana*, the 'quasi-personal' dynamism that gives inner power and quality to life.

The Buddha spoke of *dharma* as lovely and taught that the essence of the religious life 'consists in friendship, in association, in intimacy with what is lovely'. Friendship with the lovely is the prior condition for both the beginning and the sustained practice of the Noble Eightfold Path.

teachings; sexuality, sleep, hunger, illness; growing, ageing and dying.

It is impossible to classify these *dharmas* in any systematic way. The main point is that the physical world and everything in it results from the working together of these separate components. So while it seems that the human being is an independent unit, this is only an illusion. The person is actually a flowing stream of *dharmas*, which continually changes and which after death rearranges itself to form a new individual.

Thus the teaching of Buddha does not recognize the Hindu idea of the self (*atman*) which remains constant through the cycle of rebirths. It is fair to ask whether the one who has died and the one who has been reborn on the basis of his *karma* are not in fact two different beings. In one sense this is true, for there is no immortal 'soul' to link the two. Yet at the same time, the new incarnation is inseparably bound to a particular preceding life by the *karma* it inherits, and which it will now express.

All is suffering

In his third night of meditation under the *bo*-tree, Gautama discovered the Four Noble Truths. These are the core of Buddhist philosophy.
● The first truth is the knowledge of suffering. This states that all individual existence is miserable and painful. In the Buddha's own words as

The Buddhism of South Korea has been influenced by Chinese and Japanese developments.

Buddhist boys often spend a few months in a monastery as part of their education.

reported in early writings: 'Birth is suffering, ageing is suffering, illness is suffering, worry, misery, pain, distress and despair are suffering; not attaining what one desires is suffering.'

● The second truth concerns the origin of suffering. Suffering and indeed all existence (since they are the same) has its source in desire and ignorance: 'But what, O monks, is the noble truth of the origin of suffering? It is that desire (*tanha*) which results in rebirth, that desire bound up with longing and greed, which indulges itself now here, now there; the desire of the senses, the desire to be, the desire to destroy oneself.'

● The third truth deals with the destruction of suffering. Suffering must be totally extinguished; there is to be no remainder. The central aim of Buddhism is to give eternal release from suffering. This means being freed from the endless cycle of rebirth (*samsara*) and entering the blessed state of *nirvana*.

● The fourth truth indicates the way to this removal of suffering. This is

by means of the Noble Eightfold Path, which formed Gautama's basic teaching on Buddhist life-style.

Eight signposts to freedom

The Eightfold Path is as follows:

● *Right knowledge* or understanding. This of course means a recognition of the Four Noble Truths.

● *Right attitude* or thought indicates a mental attitude of goodwill, peaceableness, keeping far from oneself all sensual desire, hate and malice.

● *Right speech* Lying, useless chatter and gossip are outlawed; instead speech must be wise, truthful and directed towards reconciliation.

● *Right action* embraces all moral behaviour. Murder, stealing and adultery are especially prohibited.

● *Right occupation* means that one's way of earning a living must not be harmful to others.

● *Right effort* Evil impulses must be prevented and good ones fostered, so that the individual can develop noble thoughts, words and deeds.

● *Right mindfulness* or awareness means careful consideration, not giving in to the dictates of desire in thought, speech, action and emotion.

● *Right composure* is achieved by intense concentration, which frees the holy man from all that holds him back in his quest.

Essentially the Eightfold Path is concerned with three things: with morality (right speech, right action, right occupation); with spiritual discipline (right effort, right mindfulness, right composure); and with insight (right knowledge, right attitude). It is worth noting how far this is from any strictness or severity. It is a middle way, avoiding both the extreme of self-mortification or asceticism, and the extreme of sensuality, of giving oneself up to every impulse. This middle way cannot be called a compromise; it offers a demanding life-style that is both practical and balanced.

Nirvana: where desire ends

We have seen that according to the idea of *dharma*, the unity of the human personality is an illusion. The reality is a constantly changing arrangement of the different elements

which make up the world. Belief in the self is rejected; 'I' and 'my' are concepts bearing no relation to truth.

The man who perceives this truth will therefore no longer cling to an imaginary 'I'. Indeed, it is precisely this false attitude to life which is the main cause of suffering. The Western mind finds it hard to grasp this doctrine of the non-self (*an-atman*); nevertheless it has been described as the most important contribution of Buddhism to the field of religious thinking.

Inextricably bound up with the idea of *an-atman* is that of *nirvana*. The word is derived from a verb meaning 'to waft away', and it indicates the goal of all religious effort in Buddhism. *Nirvana* is commonly described as 'nothingness', but this is totally inappropriate. The *Tripitaka*, an early Buddhist scripture, describes it thus:

'Nirvana is the area where there is no earth, water, fire and air; it is not the region of infinite space, nor that of infinite consciousness; it is not the region of nothing at all, nor the border between distinguishing and not distinguishing; not this world nor the other world; where there is neither sun nor moon. I will not call it coming and going, nor standing still, nor fading away nor beginning. It is without foundation, without continuation and without stopping. It is the end of suffering.'

From Memory to Writing

Wulf Metz

After the death of Gautama it became necessary to establish his teaching clearly and gather it in a coherent form. So a few months later a council was held in Rajagha, and its conclusions were reviewed 100 years later at the second Buddhist council in Vesali. The crucial meeting however was the third synod, which met in Pataliputta in 253 BC, nearly 200 years after Gautama's death, under the patronage of Emperor Asoka. A thousand monks were occupied for nine months in checking, completing and finally classifying the traditions that had been passed down. At this stage the material was still in spoken form; it was not until the first century BC, on the island of Ceylon, that the first Buddhist scriptures were written down.

This basic collection of writings, or canon, is called the Pali canon, after the language in which it is written. It forms the main body of teaching for the conservative Theravada Buddhists; other groups have additional writings. More commonly, the Pali canon is called the *Tripitaka* or 'triple basket' because it is in three parts which were originally written on palm leaves and preserved in baskets.

The first part is called *Vinaya-Pitaka*, the 'basket of order'. As well as material about the life of Buddha and the origin of the monastic community, it contains the rules of discipline for monks.

The second part is known as the *Sutta-Pitaka*. *Sutta* is the Pali form of the Sanskrit *sutra* meaning 'guide-line' or 'instruction book'. It deals with the teaching of the Buddha and the monks, and also contains 547 legends and stories from previous existences of the Buddha.

The last part is the *Abhidhamma-Pitaka*, the 'basket of higher teaching'. Its seven books, probably originating from the third to the first century BC, are written in a dry, academic style, intended for specialists and not for the common people.

In addition to the Pali canon, there are many other important Buddhist writings in Pali, Sanskrit, Chinese and other Asian languages. Of these the most prominent are the *Questions of King Milinda*, written in the first century AD; the dogmatic work *The Way to Purity*, written by Buddhaghosa in the fifth century; and 'Summary of the meaning of higher teaching' (*Abhidhammattha-sangaha*), which dates back to Anuruddha in the eleventh century.

Mahayana Buddhists also recognize many more texts as authoritative than do the more traditionalist Theravada Buddhists. Among these are the 'Description of the Paradise of Sukhavati' (*Sukhavativyuha*); the 'Lotus of the Good Law' (*Sadharmapundarika*), particularly used by the Tendai sect of Japan; the 'Revelation of the teaching in Lanka' (*Lankavatara*); and above all the 'Guide to Perfect Wisdom' (*Prajnaparamita-Sutra*), a comprehensive explanation of the state of being a Buddha.

Some of these writings are geared to practical piety; others are more philosophically oriented. Whole schools of thought gathered around the various manuals or *sutras*, and then wrote their own teaching books (*shastras*), to give a thorough grounding in Buddhism and a further interpretation of it.

As you will notice, it can only be defined by negatives!

Interestingly, *nirvana* is understood as a *dharma*. It is the only one out of the 170 known to Buddhism that is unchanging and independent (all the others depend on each other) because it is not created by the power of impulse or desire.

Nirvana can be experienced before death by means of meditation. This is however not a full experience of *nirvana*, since there are still some *dharmas* at work.

Two versions of truth

The Four Noble Truths and the Eightfold Path are the heart of Buddhist teaching. Immediately after Gautama's death, however, there were arguments in the community of monks about the correct interpretation of other aspects of his teaching. Soon two groups, opposed to each other, stood out above all others. These were the strict and conservative Theravadins, and the more liberal Mahasanghikas, the 'members of the great community'.

Theravada means 'teaching of the ancients', and the Theravadins pride themselves on keeping to Gautama's original teaching as found in the earliest Buddhist writings. The group has acquired the nickname Hinayana, meaning 'small vehicle', which they dislike and find irreverent. It derives from a scripture of their rival group in which the world is likened to a burning house. To escape it, the inhabitants call for a cart to which an animal is harnessed. But there is only room in the cart for the few true believers, not for the rest of humanity.

Theravada Buddhism emphasizes the individual's efforts towards salvation and recognizes no divine help in this. It rejects all rituals and images, even frowning on statues of the Buddha; it is, of course, pointless to pray to Buddha since he has been swallowed up in *nirvana*.

This severe and spiritualized teaching is indeed in line with the teaching of Buddha himself and his early followers, for according to them it is almost impossible to become a Buddha, and even to be a holy man

(*arhat*) requires relentless effort. It goes without saying however that such strictness cannot easily satisfy the needs of the masses. Even in the countries where it does hold sway, it has been adapted for the man in the street by the inclusion of spirit and demon worship and the presence in the temples of statues of gods and other spiritual beings.

The Mahasanghikas chose for their school of thought the name Mahayana, meaning 'great vehicle'. According to them, salvation is not intended for a few people of particular moral excellence but for all mankind. Above all, Mahayana Buddhism is a humane and magnanimous religion which makes many con-

A Buddhist priest in Vietnam.

A Buddhist monk in Sri Lanka.

Bodhisattva postpones his goal of becoming a Buddha in order first to save as many others as possible. By a solemn vow he promises to help everyone, even in the reincarnations which lie ahead of him. To this end he gathers others into his own being—an idea which is not difficult when you do not believe in the reality of the individual self. The apparent difference between yourself and others can be put aside in meditation.

The sacrificial love of the Bodhisattva can be so great that he completely denies himself the promised entry into *nirvana*, so that he can continue indefinitely to work for the good of others. Thus the Bodhisattva is undeniably more than a teacher; he has become a kind of saviour or redeemer. One can expect help from him not only in the search for salvation but also in everyday life. He is the helper of the needy in every situation.

Theravada does not regard Siddharta Gautama as the only Buddha; nor did he himself. Early texts mention six forerunners and one Buddha, Maitreya, still to come. The later Theravadins list as many as twenty-eight Buddhas, though of these Gautama is certainly the most important.

Mahayana doctrine in this area is quite different. Here the number of Buddhas is said to be as many as the grains of sand. It must be stressed that these are ultimately all united in the absolute being or Dharmakaya. If the Dharmakaya is seen as personal, then it can be identified with the original Buddha or Adibuddha who has been enlightened from all eternity.

The Adibuddha has sent out from himself five 'meditation Buddhas' or Dhyanibuddhas: Amitabha, 'the one of immeasurable brilliance'; Vairocana, 'the radiant one'; Akshobya, 'the unshakeable'; Rathnasambhava, 'the one born of precious stones'; and Amoghasiddhi, 'the one of unfailing strength'.

Dhyanibodhisattvas are derived from the Dhyanibuddhas, and both can become physical beings and appear on earth. Siddharta himself is understood to be a projection of the

cessions to popular piety.

As well as accepting the basic writings of the Theravada school, Mahayana uses numerous other texts, some of which are even preferred to the older ones because they develop the Buddha's teaching and modernize it. While in Theravada Buddhism only the monk (*bhikshu*) can achieve salvation—and for this reason in the Theravada countries everyone attempts to spend at least part of his life in a monastery—in the 'great vehicle' everyone can be saved.

A particular feature of Mahayana teaching is its doctrine of the Bodhisattva—one who is destined for enlightenment, or Buddhahood. According to this doctrine, the

One Goal, Many Paths

Wulf Metz

Very early in its history Buddhism divided into two main movements: Theravada Buddhism, the strict and narrow teaching of the ancients, and Mahayana Buddhism, more liberal and open to a wider range of ideas. Later in the history of the religion, as it spread further afield, many other varieties of Buddhism grew up:

Vajrayana Buddhism

Vajrayana Buddhism is the first of these. 'Vajra' originally meant the thunderbolt of the god Indra; later it came to mean a special substance which is imagined to be bright, transparent and as indestructible as a diamond. So Vajrayana is usually translated as 'the diamond vehicle'.

This strange and impenetrable Buddhist movement originated in the middle of the first century AD in India, and from there it spread to Nepal, Tibet, China and Japan. Because of its mysterious character it is very hard to define. It could be described as a version of Mahayana Buddhism that has become overlaid with occult, magical and mystical elements. In the background can be seen the very ancient Indian philosophy of Tantrism, which has influenced both Buddhism and Hinduism.

The result is a religion which in some ways resembles the early Christian heresy of Gnosticism, though this comparison should not

be pushed too far. Certainly it is very far removed from both Theravada and Mahayana Buddhism.

Vajrayana seeks to pass beyond the appearances of things into an emptiness through which the individual is identified with the absolute. To achieve this, quite specific techniques are used:

● The *mantra* is a magic saying which is recited over and over again. Its power is believed to go out to the furthest limit of the universe. It is also possible to write the *mantra* on paper and place it in a 'prayer wheel' which sends out the magic power of the phrase when it is set in motion. The best-known *mantra* is 'Om mani padme hum', used particularly in Tibet. 'Mani padme' means 'jewel in the lotus' while 'om' and 'hum' are sounds believed to have special supernatural power.

● *Mudra*, or physical gesture, is just as important as the *mantra*. Vajrayana has a wealth of special movements, especially of the hands, that express the fact that the whole being is striving to be united with the divine. Especially in Tibet, Vajrayana has also acquired a strong erotic element, known as Shaktism, after the Indian idea of Shakti who is an eternal feminine power. Through directly orgiastic worship the worshipper is joined to the universal feminine and so realizes

the ultimate unity of all things. It need hardly be said that this addition to Buddhism is despised by other stricter movements.

● The *mandala*, meaning 'meditation circle', is a round or many-sided diagram which represents particular cosmic and spiritual relationships. Contemplation of the *mandala* and concentration on the powers that emanate from it lead to an experience of the divine.

As with all religions of this nature, it is necessary in Vajrayana to be instructed by a guru and to commit oneself to constant, devoted religious practice.

Lamaism

Lamaism is the dominant Tibetan form of Buddhism, practised by Tibetan monks both in their own country and in the lands surrounding it. Originally 'lama' was a word for a high-ranking spiritual teacher, but later it came to be used of every monk.

Lamaism's beginnings date from the seventh century AD, when King Srong-btsan-sgam-po introduced Buddhism (in the form of Vajrayana) to Tibet. At first there was strong resistance from the followers of the traditional Bon religion, which involved a ritual calling on gods and demons by magician-priests. However, towards the end of the century, the Indian missionary Padmasambhava managed to create a blend of the two religions in his monastery, and soon further orders were founded.

After the eleventh century Lamaism went into a decline, largely through the neglect of the law of celibacy and the

resulting nepotism and power politics. It was renewed by the reformer Tsong-kha-pa in the fourteenth century, and the leadership succession after this derived from his two favourite pupils. One of these was supposed to be an incarnation of the Bodhisattva Avalokiteshvara, while the other was a reincarnation of the Buddha Amitabha. From these two there evolved a dual system of leadership; firstly the Dalai Lama or 'lama great as the ocean' who has worldly rule, and secondly the Panchen Lama or 'jewel of the scholars' who is the spiritual head. When a reigning lama dies, messengers are sent throughout the country to find a child who is a reincarnation of the dead lama. This system of the 'transformed body' is known as *chubilghan*.

In 1959 the fourteenth Dalai Lama escaped to India after the Chinese communists invaded his country. After this, Buddhism lost almost all of its influence in Tibet, though liberalization in China may lead to a limited revival of religious life.

Zen Buddhism

Zen Buddhism, of great importance in Japan, originated in China under the name of Ch'an, the Chinese for meditation.

Buddhism first entered China in the first century AD, but it encountered quite strong opposition, particularly from the practical philosophy of Confucianism. In the year 526 Bodhidharma, the twenty-eighth leader of an Indian meditation sect, came to China and founded the first Ch'an school. The Ch'an movement grew and became more and more a separate entity from its parent, Mahayana Buddhism. The most important landmark after this was the transplantation of Bodhidharma's views to Japan in the twelfth century.

Central to both Chinese Ch'an and Japanese Zen is the practice of meditation according to strict rules. This was particularly prized by the Samurai warriors as a path to self-discipline. A principal means of reaching enlightenment (*satori*) is by meditation sitting in the lotus position (cross-legged, with each foot on the opposite thigh).

In addition to sitting meditation (*zazen*), the riddle (*koan*) is of great importance. These questions which have no answer serve the purpose of radically altering the Zen student's way of thinking, to help him towards *satori*. The following examples are typical *koans*:

'If you meet someone in the street who has reached the truth you may neither walk past him in silence, nor speaking. How then should you meet him?'

'When you clap both your hands together a sound results. Now listen to the sound of *one* hand clapping!'

Through these *koans* thinking is pushed to the limit of the absurd. It is useless to seek rational answers to them; the tension they produce must be borne to the utmost. Both *zazen* and *koans* must be used under the direction of a Zen master, who controls and disciplines the student.

The two branches of Zen, the Rinzai and Soto schools, differ as to whether *satori* is a

sudden and spontaneous experience or whether it can develop gradually. Common to both movements, however, is a clear opposition to intellectualism and the supremacy of reason. Concern with 'teaching' is rejected. Zen is entirely intuitive.

Zen Buddhism leaves clearly observable marks on the society that practises it, especially as it often attracts prominent individuals who may even take its philosophy into the political realm. Physical expressions of the Zen spirit are visible in such exercises as the tea ceremony, judo, the 'ikebana' art of flower arranging, landscape painting, handwriting, archery and fencing. These practices are much more than mere techniques; they have a great religious significance.

Japanese sects

Japanese sects, formed by the combination of Buddhist ideas with those of the traditional Shintoism, are numerous and varied. Since the introduction of Buddhism to Japan by Shotoktaishi in 621, history records a wide range of religious expressions, drawing partly on the influence from China, and partly on the traditional Japanese culture.

● The Tendai sect goes back to a Chinese model and was founded in 805. It concentrates on encouraging everyone to take the path to becoming a Buddha.

● The Shingon sect, founded in 807, is very mystically inclined and stresses meditation (*shingon* is the Japanese translation of the Sanskrit *mantra*).

● The Amida sects are very far from traditional Buddhism. The twelfth-

century monk Genku or Honen founded the Jodo sect which believes that only through the Buddha Amida (Japanese for the Sanskrit Amitabha) can a person be redeemed and enter the 'pure land'. Salvation cannot be gained by one's own efforts, only by calling on Amida in prayer. Influenced by Genku, Shinran Shonin founded the Shin sect, which emphasized even more the uselessness of human effort towards salvation. He dismissed the difference between monks and lay people as unimportant, rejected celibacy by getting married, and made great contributions to the equality of women.

● Nichiren, a monk of the thirteenth century, founded another sect which was later named after him. His version of Buddhism stresses the importance of the historical Buddha as an embodiment of the eternal Buddha. Enlightenment consists in recognizing that man, the world and Buddha are in the final analysis all one.

● Soka Gakkai, the 'value-creating society', is a lay movement which emerged at the turn of the century after freedom of religion was introduced in Japan in 1899. Like Nichiren from which it derives, it is intolerant of other movements and lays great stress on duty and morality. A special emphasis is placed on the creation of a 'contented society'. Soka Gakkai now has about 20 million members.

Amitabha-Buddha.

While Theravada Buddhism can describe *nirvana* only by negatives, Mahayana introduces a very concrete idea of it. The best-known description is in the story of Amitabha. As a monk he took an oath that he would become a Buddha if as a result of this a paradise could be formed in which all who had prayed to him in their lifetime could live happily after death. The resulting land of Sukhavati or 'paradise of the west' is a place where all hindrances to full salvation are removed, so that the way to *nirvana* is clear. This preliminary stage to *nirvana* has increasingly become an end in itself, where the blessed live in ecstasy after their death.

Mahayana Buddhism allows much more scope for special cults and ritual than the Theravadins do. Although following a cult (for instance, the worship of a particular Buddha) is valued less highly than following the teaching, it is accepted as a route to holiness for those who are weaker in the faith.

Buddhism today

If Buddhism has undergone many changes and developments in its early history, the same is just as true of it today. In several countries of

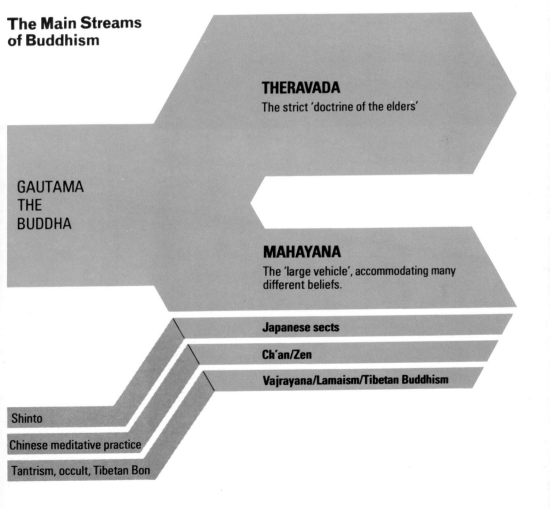

The Main Streams of Buddhism

GAUTAMA THE BUDDHA

THERAVADA
The strict 'doctrine of the elders'

MAHAYANA
The 'large vehicle', accommodating many different beliefs.

Japanese sects

Ch'an/Zen

Vajrayana/Lamaism/Tibetan Buddhism

Shinto

Chinese meditative practice

Tantrism, occult, Tibetan Bon

Tibetan Buddhists honour the maternal White Tara. She is considered to be a Bodhisattva—a perfected being who has not entered nirvana, choosing instead to help human beings on earth.

Avalokiteshvera is one of the greatest Bodhisattvas, 'the regarder of the cries of the earth'. He is the patron of Tibet.

the world. Even if Buddhist teaching originally meant something quite different by 'freedom from suffering', the idea still offered a useful way of combining the two philosophies.

In Sri Lanka, as a reaction against the capitalism of the former colonial rulers, Solomon Bandaranaike, and after his assassination his wife, revived the old ideal of a 'Buddhist welfare state' and incorporated socialism into the range of Buddhist teaching.

Of course such moves were also heavily criticized. Communism, after all, makes its own demands and is not content merely to be a support to Buddhism. The dangers of the alliance soon became visible not only in south-east Asia but also in China.

Despite the practical similarities, the two are really very different in their basic attitudes. Buddhism, unlike Marxism, has a goal which is not confined to the visible world. Political and social matters essentially play a minor part or none at all.

The Western Buddhists

The growth of Buddhism in the West owes much to the work of the Theosophical Society, founded in New York in 1875. In America the next important development was the great wave of immigration from China and Japan at the end of the nineteenth century. Temples, meditation schools and monasteries grew up; because of the origin of the immigrants, it was overwhelmingly Mahayana Buddhism which gained a foothold. Today, most of the schools and movements are united in the Buddhist Church of America, in which strong influences from American culture and Christian forms are to be seen.

In Europe, Buddhism was first widely known through the philosopher Arthur Schopenhauer, who influenced many scholars and artists including the composer Wagner. Edwin Arnold, who wrote *The Light of Asia* (1879), popularized the religion, and the Buddhist Society of England was formed at the beginning of the twentieth century.

It should not be forgotten that Buddhism is not by its nature an

south-east Asia, particularly Burma and Sri Lanka, attempts have been made to combine Buddhism with Marxism. At the end of the 1940s the then Prime Minister of Burma, U Nu, introduced and sought to propagate his 'social Buddhism'. In his opinion it was private property, above all the ownership of land and its unjust distribution, that hindered people from leading a leisured life, free from worry and completely directed towards religious goals. The seeker of *nirvana* must not be plagued with the fight for survival nor agitated by the greed for riches; both of these are obstacles in the way of meditation.

This combination was easier to make since the traditional Marxist critique of religion was not really aimed at Buddhism. The formation of a Buddhist-based anti-capitalism was influenced by experiences from the colonial days; moreover, Marxism appeared to be a suitable vehicle for a contemporary interpretation of the Buddhist religion, since after all it promised to reduce the suffering in

organized religion. Its real influence cannot therefore be measured by the number of its members. There is also what might be called an unofficial or anonymous Buddhism, which can be seen through the wealth of literature related to the subject. Eastern-inspired courses on meditation are on offer in almost every small town. Young people, weary of their own culture, reach out for 'Eastern wisdom' and create for themselves a hotch-potch of religious ideas which normally ends up having very little in common with actual Buddhism. Yet even in this climate of home-grown religiosity, elements of the Buddha's teaching and of the Buddhist way of life break through.

The Appeal of Buddhism in the West

Wulf Metz

Few of those in the Christian world attracted to Eastern spirituality actually become members of the Buddhist religion. It offers, however, an opportunity to set up one's own world-view or private religion. People often turn to books on the subject after a trip to the Far East, or perhaps a museum visit.

It is always the same few aspects of the religion that attract Westerners:

● They have the impression that Buddhism is tolerant, at least more tolerant than Christianity. There may be a body of teaching but it does not dominate or preach to people. Isn't this the ideal world-view for the modern sceptic or doubter? It offers the chance to be an atheist without having to dispense with religion.

● People also admire the justice of the Buddhist system, according to which a man reaps what he sows. The good man will receive his reward and the evil man his just deserts. Isn't that more natural than the Christian teaching of grace?

● The high quality of Buddhist ethics is held up for praise. Who would quarrel with the splendid character of the Four Noble Truths and the Noble Eightfold Path? The history of Christianity is stained with blood, which can certainly not be said of Buddhism. Which religion then is to be preferred?

● Among many other Buddhist viewpoints which are singled out for admiration, the idea of nirvana is prominent. The idea that the final goal of man is to be eliminated: isn't this a highly contemporary idea, and more natural than the Christian hope of resurrection?

Buddhism today presents a challenge the Christian must take seriously. How then might these points by answered from a Christian viewpoint?

● The breadth and tolerance of Buddhism cannot be denied. It is doubtful, however, whether this really gives a faith credibility. It must be a matter of truth, not personal preference.

● The Buddhist system may be just, but it is without mercy or grace. Buddhism is a religion of self-redemption. According to Christian teaching, however, man is not in a position to save himself. We can look to God alone for our salvation. So Christians speak not only of God's justice, but above all of his grace and mercy.

● Of course the Christian will want to show respect for Buddhist morality. But the fact that Christian works of love are imperfect and incomplete should not be blamed on the Christian religion, but on man's sin which keeps him in debt to God and his neighbour. It is true that Christian morality lives on forgiveness; but it is precisely here that its value lies. The Christian will also be ashamed of the sinfulness of Christian people. But at least Christianity is realistic about sin and evil. We can live good lives only when given new life by Jesus Christ; otherwise we are powerless to do what we ought to do, and totally unable to escape the cycle of sin and death.

● For the Christian who accepts the world as God's creation, life is not identical with suffering. Suffering is one result of humanity's estrangement from God. God however does not reject his creature: he wants to give him life in all its fullness, and this is the meaning of salvation. God does not want a human being—whom he has created in his own image—to sink into oblivion. The idea of nirvana seems pessimistic in contrast to the good news of forgiveness and new life in Jesus Christ.

Buddhism and Christianity differ completely, not only in their beliefs about man and the world, but in their view of God. On this subject Siddharta remains for ever silent.

Cao Dai and Hoa Hao

Barbara Boal

In the late nineteenth and early twentieth centuries Vietnamese nationalism was firmly, sometimes harshly, repressed by the French. The intellectuals who traditionally led nationalist movements began in the 1920s to profit financially from the situation and to enjoy privileged status like the French. Organizations therefore arose under new forms of nationalist leadership, seeking to end French domination and to establish a republic. Some of them followed communist principles, but three were under the religious leadership of monks and priests: the Cao Dai, the Hoa Hao and, less important, the Binh Xuyen. All three feared and hated things foreign. They were products of local education and aimed not only at expelling foreigners but also establishing local rule by religious leaders—something quite new to the Vietnamese pattern of rule by the privileged.

Political melting-pot

During the next decade the Communist Party of Indo-China (CPI) began to gain sympathy abroad. At this point the three religious movements began armed opposition to the French colonial troops. Their own men were well-trained local recruits. The Cao Dai held the Mekong Delta, the Hoa Hao the border of Kampuchea and the Binh Xuyen the Saigon area.

From 1941 until the end of the Second World War, Japanese military commanders directed the French colonial forces for the Vichy government in France. For a brief period in 1941 the combined French and Japanese all but defeated the local troops, but for the remainder of the war the latter again gained strength. After the final defeat of the Japanese, America, in the grip of its anti-colonial convictions, aided the communist-controlled Viet Minh, and independence was declared on 2 September 1945.

Because American and European interests in Vietnam were at variance with each other, a decade of confused political, cultural and religious action and reaction resulted. It led finally to the Geneva Accord of 1954 and the partition of North and South Vietnam. The communist Viet Minh held the North while the South was under the nationalist government of Ngo Dinh Diem. Close on 1 million refugees from North to South added to the confusion. The French, as part of their opposition to Diem, had supplied arms to the Cao Dai, Hoa Hao and Binh Xuyen, but by 1956, with American aid, Diem had smashed the military strength of the three sects. Their followers, numbering about a quarter of the total population, were resentful but remained active in a less military context.

Out of the maze of political aims, cultural diffusion and varied religious beliefs that form the background to twentieth-century Vietnam, four principal religious groups have emerged to play a significant part in more recent years. These are the Buddhists, the Roman Catholic Church, the Cao Dai and the Hoa Hao.

The Cao Dai

The Cao Dai sect arose from a séance communication received by Ngo Van Chieu, an administrator for the French in Cochin China, in 1919. In 1926 it was formally organized by a wealthy compatriot, Le Van Trung. Its name means 'Supreme Palace' or 'High Altar'.

Strikingly syncretistic, Cao Dai is also known as 'The Third Amnesty' of God. The first 'amnesty' has Moses and Jesus Christ as its principal figures; the second has Buddha and Lao Tse. Cao Dai is the third and highest because it requires no human representatives; God communicates directly through trance to certain devotees. It follows the pattern of the Roman Catholic Church, with its own pope dwelling in a village outside Tah Ninh city near Saigon, where an ornate cathedral was built in 1937 at the foot of a high mountain.

In addition to Catholicism and Buddhism, it combines Confucianism, Taoism and traditional cults of spirits and ancestors. Amongst a host of additional figures revered in its pantheon are Victor Hugo, Sun Yat Sen, Joan of Arc, Louis Pasteur and Jean Decoux, the French admiral of the Second World War who administered Vietnam for the Japanese. Its breadth thus appeals to the integrated view of peasant peoples; they have become its followers in entire village communities. The wealthy Le Van Trung had, like the Buddha, renounced the luxurious life; but for the villagers, to whom poverty is nothing new, it is the magical elements that prove attractive.

Cao Dai revived traditional Buddhist rules regarding vegetarianism, attitudes towards animals and rules for social behaviour. Female celebrants are permitted, and matrilineal descent is newly important. Its initially rapid expansion led to struggles for leadership. Despite splitting into several sects, Cao Dai has continued to grow and its numbers are thought to be over 2 million.

The Hoa Hao

This neo-Buddhist sect was started by Huynh Phu So in the village of Hoa Hao in Vietnam near the Kampuchean border. Born in 1919, he was the son of a leading Roman Catholic peasant in the local community. He received religious training as a young man in the hope of improving poor health. In 1939 he experienced a violent nervous spasm from which he emerged not only cured but with great power to preach and teach a new religion.

By claiming to be the incarnation of several past heroes, he set this religion on a supposedly ancient foundation which also indicated a political role for himself and his followers. He combined a revised form of Buddhist rituals with a teaching that no intermediary nor holy place is necessary for direct prayer to the Almighty.

There are four main precepts in his sect's teaching:

● honouring one's parents;
● love of one's country;
● respect for his interpretation of Buddhism;
● love towards one's fellow-men.

Not in temples, but in teaching-centres spread over former South Vietnam, his teachings were communicated in forms attractive to the peasant population. These sometimes had nationalistic overtones and strangely predicted the coming of Americans two decades ahead of their arrival. Viewed in the 1940s as a 'living Buddha', his reputation rapidly drew followers to the sect. The French, however, saw him as a centre of political unrest and detained him in a psychiatric hospital, then later under house arrest. This enhanced his reputation and from his home he taught continuous groups of pilgrims. A few days before a French plan to exile him to Laos could be put into action, his followers, aided by Japanese secret police, removed him to Saigon. There he was kept out of French hands.

Later it became obvious that the various nationalist movements, including Cao Dai and Hoa Hao, would each be seeking their own supremacy in the power struggle. By the late 1960s increasingly disillusioned nationalist urban intellectuals joined the Hoa peasants' religious movement, though it remained fundamentally of rural appeal.

By the time Huynh Phu So was murdered by communists in April 1947, sub-sects had arisen which were far more active and united within themselves than were the sub-sects in the Cao Dai. They utterly rejected the bribery and betrayal that discredited some Cao Dai leaders— who also suffered disunity and decline after the death of their pope in 1959. The vigorous teaching activities of Hoa Hao continued to appeal to the large rural population in the Mekong Delta and the sect has remained a powerful force in southern Vietnam.

Sages and Immortals: Chinese Religions

John Berthrong

Chinese religion is unique. This is partly due to the fact that, alone among the great religions of mankind, Chinese religion first developed in isolation, without the influence of the other great world religions. Confucianism and Taoism, two of the three faiths of China, developed their distinctive forms before there was any significant contact with the rest of the world. For this reason, Chinese religion has taken a form which often seems quite unlike any other. For example, neither Confucianism nor Taoism is like Judaism, Christianity or Islam—monotheistic religions with God at the centre. Confucianism, especially, became a religion without any great speculation on the nature and function of God. For this reason it was often not even considered to be a religion. However, it is clear that Confucianism *is* a religion and that it was the dominant tradition of pre-modern China.

The Shang

The earliest forms of Chinese religion are not clear. We know hardly anything definite about the religion of the great Shang dynasty (1751–1050? BC), the first historical dynasty. But although we know little of the detail, we are certain that religion played a very important part in the life of the Shang. In fact, the Shang lived in a world of spirits and powers who directly influenced the lives of the living—their success or failure—and who required sacrifice and appeasement.

The Shang sought to fathom the wishes of these spirits through a complicated system of divination. We still have the records of these divinations, the famous 'oracle bones'. The diviner, at the request of the king, would put the question to the spirit, and record the question and its answer on the carapace of a turtle or the shoulder-blade of an ox. The Shang were concerned to know the will of the spirits for just about everything they did.

Although the nature of Shang religion is clouded in mystery, a certain continuity remains between the

This 'oracle bone', over 3,000 years old, records questions the king asked of the spirits, and answers received by the king's diviner.

Shang and later Chinese religion. There is a persistent belief in the balance of nature, an idea which was later explicitly defined as the famous concepts of Yin and Yang: the forces of dark and light, of soft and hard, of female and male. Another important idea which continues throughout the history of Chinese religion is a constant concern for the well-being of the people. This idea of the well-being of the people later became the concept of *t'ien-ming* or the Will of Heaven.

Therefore, even if much of Shang religion is lost to us, it is clear that the Shang were distinctively Chinese and that their religion formed the basis for the development of Chinese religion, just as their political, social and material culture provided the seeds of the ongoing Chinese civilization.

Sense of concern

Prior to the rise of Confucianism, certain elements of the Shang and Chou religion took more definite shape. This is not surprising, since all great civilizations make certain choices about religion which give them their historical distinctiveness.

If there is one idea, one characteristic which informs the entire history of the development of Chinese religion, it is a 'consciousness of concern'. Even in the western Chou and eastern Chou one finds the persistent claim that high Heaven itself has concern for the well-being of the people. In fact, Heaven is said to hear and see, and as the people hear and see, and hence to have a most active concern for them.

This sense that concern is the basis of the cosmos makes Chinese religion different from such religions as Judaism, Christianity or Islam, where a sense of awe or dread of a supreme power informs religious consciousness. This is why Chinese religion has always had such a close connection with the ethical thought of the people. A sense of concern and participation pervades the Chinese understanding of mankind's relationship to the transcendent and with other people.

Philosophy or religion?

In Chinese terms, what then are Confucianism and Taoism? Are they philosophies or religions? Do they have any kind of mystical traditions which seek to aid the faithful to achieve the perfected aims of a religious life?

There is a common Chinese distinction which is helpful in answering this question—the distinction between the terms *chia* (schools of thought, philosophy) and *chiao* (teaching, religion). The former refers more to the great thinkers and their teachings, and the 'great traditions'. The latter refers to the religious and, by extension, to the unique ways in which the great traditions have been appropriated by the people at grass-roots level. A distinction between the great intellectual traditions and the cultic and devotional side of religious life has been made in all the Chinese traditions, Confucianism, Taoism and also Buddhism, after its introduction into China in the second century AD.

The Chinese traditions have never felt the need to contrast *chia* and *chiao* in a hostile fashion. In a very characteristic way, they are said to represent two different parts of one continuum. They are different yet related. In traditional China, each of the great religions operated on both levels: there were great Confucian, Taoist and Buddhist philosophers, as well as masters of the various religious arts of meditation, liturgy and ritual.

Confucianism

The Latinized name, Confucianism, is a Western invention which has come down from the seventeenth-century Jesuit missionaries. Interestingly enough, these early Western missionaries clearly saw the religious nature of Confucianism, even if they did not agree with its traditions and rituals.

The Chinese term for Confucianism, *Ju* (scholars, literati—with the special meaning of Confucian from the T'ang dynasty), points to its broader character as intellectual culture. It is usually regarded as philos-

The Worship of Ancestors

Chua Wee Hian

Ancestral worship was first introduced to China at the beginning of the Chou dynasty (1122–325 BC). It was Confucius (551–479 BC) who popularized this practice by his teaching on filial piety, decreeing that parents and elders are to be honoured and respected while they are alive. This sense of reverence continues after their deaths.

The Chinese believe that at death the soul of the deceased ancestor resides in three places. One part goes to heaven, the second remains in the grave to receive sacrifices and the third is localized in the ancestral tablet or shrine.

The soul has to be assisted as it journeys to heaven. Hence, at Chinese funerals, elaborate rituals are meticulously carried out to ensure that the soul is amply provided for on its course. With the help of a Taoist priest, members of the family chant prayers, offer sacrifices of food and burn paper money—and in some cases even paper cars, planes and servants—so that there will be no lack of provisions. Evil spirits who oppose the deceased are propitiated by appropriate sacrifices and by loud wailings.

The siting of the grave is very important. A geomancer, in Chinese *Feng shui sien sheng*, is consulted to determine the ideal location. The tomb must be maintained, and occasional offerings are made to the part of the soul that resides in it. The heirs continue to visit it, especially during the spring festival (*ts'ing meng*).

Within 100 days of the burial a memorial service is held in the home of the oldest male heir. The ancestral tablet is dedicated by a Buddhist or Taoist priest; this now normally contains a photograph of the deceased with his name, rank and status in life. Joss-sticks are burned and placed on the tablet, and on certain feast days food offerings are included. Newly-married couples in the family have to bow before this tablet. Its presence strengthens family solidarity, and it also offers protection and blessing to all in the family.

Chinese Christians have sometimes been accused of not honouring their ancestors by not becoming involved in ancestral worship rites. Their firm but gracious reply is that they will always respect and honour their elders while they are alive. Many are prepared to be the first in cleaning family tombs, and some Christians have even set up halls of remembrance for their forebears. Non-Christian relatives and friends may be invited to special memorial services where Christ is proclaimed as victor over the grave.

'While they (the parents) are alive, serve them according to the ritual (*li*): when they die bury them according to the ritual; and sacrifice to them according to the ritual.'

Confucius, *Analects* 2:5

Since the Chinese pay great reverence to ancestors, funerals are very important. At this Chinese funeral in Bangkok, the proceedings are watched over by effigies of Confucius.

Many Chinese homes, offices and factories have their own Buddhist or Taoist shrines.

A modern image of Confucius at the Tiger Balm Gardens in Singapore.

southern Sung (1126–1279 AD), explicitly states that the sage, having realized true integrity (*ch'eng*), becomes one with Heaven and Earth. Confucian moral metaphysics reaches over into the religious quest for unity with the ground of being.

None the less, Confucianism gives primary emphasis to the ethical meaning of human relationships, finding and grounding the moral in the divine transcendence. The perfect example of this is Confucius himself. He is best remembered as a great teacher. The basis of his teaching was the concept of humanity (*jen*). Just as compassion is the greatest Buddhist virtue, and love the Christian, *jen* is the ultimate goal of conduct and self-transformation for the Confucian. And whereas most of Confucius' teachings stress the ethical dimension of humanity, he made it clear that it was Heaven itself which protected him and gave him his message: 'Heaven is the author of the virtue that is in me.'

The Way of Heaven

Confucius stands as a prophet, giving an ethical teaching grounded in religious consciousness. Mencius (371–289? BC) projects the image of a teacher of mysticism. He proclaims an inner doctrine, alluding to the presence within the heart of something greater than itself.

'All things are present in me. When I reflect upon myself in all sincerity, my joy is boundless.'

What was an implicitly religious message in Confucius, becomes explicit in Mencius. For example, Confucius is said not to have discussed relationship, human nature and the Way of Heaven. Yet Mencius made his whole system of thought revolve around these two concepts. He attempted to show how the very essence of the Way of Heaven, the divine power of the cosmos, became human nature. He felt that if this human nature could be correctly cultivated and nurtured, even the common person could become a sage.

The Confucian classics (there are thirteen of them) prefer to discuss the work of spiritual cultivation in terms

ophy (*chia*), although such terms as *Ju-chiao*, *K'ung-chiao* (K'ung being Confucius' family name), or *Li-chiao* (Li referring to Confucian rituals) are also used. All of these terms refer to those elements of worship, ritual and sacrifice which are religious teachings, which is, of course, what *chiao* itself refers to.

Moral philosophy

Confucianism is best known for its moral philosophy, represented by Confucius (551–479 BC), Mencius (371–289? BC) and Hsün-tzu (fl. 298–238 BC). It is clearly grounded in religion—the inherited religion of the Lord-on-high, or Heaven. Even the great rationalist Hsün-tzu sees society founded on the penetrating insight of the sagely mind. And though Confucianism is less known for its mysticism, the *Book of Mencius* as well as other works cannot be fully understood except in the light of mysticism.

The *Chung-yung*, one of the 'Four Books' which became the basis for Confucian self-cultivation in the

of emotional harmony and psychic equilibrium—a harmony of due proportions, rather than the absence of passions. The 'Doctrine of the Mean' (*Chung-yung*), one of the 'Four Books', distinguishes between the two states of fundamental mind, the 'pre-stirred' state (before the rise of emotions), and the 'post-stirred' state (after contact with the things and events of the world). The meaning, best expressed by the concept of true integrity (*ch'eng*), lies in the harmony of emotions which have arisen, but resembles the equilibrium of the 'pre-stirred' state.

The *Chung-yung*, as we have seen before, claims that this harmony puts a person in touch with the cosmic processes of life and creativity. 'If they can assist in the transformation and nourishing process of Heaven and Earth, they can thus form a trinity with Heaven and Earth.'

Practical conduct

The third of the founding fathers of Confucianism, Hsün-tzu, is best remembered for his doctrine of ritual action (*li*). If Confucius begins Confucianism with the dramatic, almost prophetic, demand that we live a life of *jen* or perfect humanity, and Mencius expands upon the concept of *jen* to show that this is a life of heightened inter-subjectivity and intuition into the boundless joy of the enlightened sage, Hsün-tzu provides the practical side of Confucian religion.

It is his genius to demonstrate the power of correct ritual action needed to transform the human heart, which is prone to err, into the mind of a sage. In doing so, Hsün-tzu provides a model for daily life which supports the religious and ethical intuitions of Confucius and Mencius. Without a life of ritual—a liturgy of daily life ennobled by humility and graced by beautiful conduct—the supreme insights of religious geniuses such as Confucius and Mencius would be impossible to maintain.

In the course of time, the meaning of the word 'Heaven' becomes ambiguous, shifting from the early reference to a supreme deity (the *Analects* of Confucius), to a vacillation between that and moral force (Mencius), to the universe itself (Hsün-tzu).

Neo-Confucianism

Confucian mysticism, especially in its second great phase, Neo-Confucianism, leans more and more in the direction of pantheism. This is borne out by the later philosopher, Chang Tsai (1020–77). It is here that Confucian religion and mysticism show the imprint of Taoist—and Buddhist—influences. Yet Chang Tsai still shows a profoundly Confucian bent to his mystical vision of the unity of the world, by expressing this as one of a perfected family. In this vision, all the world becomes related to him as his own family. The note of inter-subjective concern sounded by Confucius and Mencius is reaffirmed.

Two ways

The first great flowering of Confucianism produced such diverse thinkers as Mencius and Hsün-tzu. Neo-Confucianism gives us Chu Hsi (1130–1200) and Wang Yang-ming (1472–1529). Both started from a desire to reform the Confucianism of their day, and then sought to give practical guidance for the perfection of the mind. Their schools, respectively, were called 'the teaching of principle' ((*li-hsüeh*) and 'the teaching of mind' (*hsin-hsüeh*). In actual fact, both were primarily concerned with the task of achieving sagehood. The great debate between them

This procession is part of a Chinese festival in Taiwan. The god of the local temple is carried through the streets.

centred on how to achieve this.

Chu Hsi believed we must go through a long and arduous process of self-cultivation and ethical activity in order to reach *jen*. He stressed the method of 'the examination of things' (*ko-wu*), as the best means to achieve this end. But this was more than a scientific interest in the material matters of the cosmos. It was to be an examination of all the various ethical and spiritual states of the mind, an attempt to know the self, in order to perfect the original nature, which he held to be good.

Chu Hsi expressed his spiritual goal in this way:

'The mind of Heaven and Earth, which gives birth to all things, is humanity (*jen*). Man, in being endowed with matter-energy receives this mind of Heaven and Earth, and thereby his life. Hence tender-heartedness and humanity are part of the very essence of his life.'

Wang Yang-ming agreed on the goal of sagehood, but rejected Chu Hsi's gradualist method. For Wang, only the 'enlightenment experience' of the absolute unity of our minds with the mind of the Tao would suffice to achieve sagehood. All other methods, including Chu Hsi's attempt at gradual self-cultivation, were a waste of time if they did not provoke this realization of the enlightenment experience. After Wang himself had had such an experience he wrote:

'My own nature is, of course, sufficient for me to attain sagehood. And I have been mistaken in searching for principle in external things and affairs.'

Life models

The great Neo-Confucians gave Confucianism a new lease of life. They provided a whole new explanation of the Confucian vision which could compete philosophically with Taoism and Buddhism. But, even more, they provided a practical set of life-models for the earnest seeker of sagehood. Although Chu Hsi consulted gradualism and Wang Yang-ming immediate experience, both sought that moment when the mind of man, precarious in its tendencies to good

and evil, would be transformed into the Mind of Heaven, the state of perfected excellence.

Taoism

The great Taoist religion is, in many ways, the opposite of Confucianism. Confucianism seeks to perfect men and women within the world, a goal of the secular as sacred. Taoism prefers to turn away from society to the contemplation of nature, seeking fulfilment in the spontaneous and 'trans-ethical'. The *Tao*, a metaphysical absolute, appears to have been a philosophical transformation of the earlier personal God. The way it teaches leads to a union with itself—a way of passive acceptance and mystical contemplation. Such is the teaching of the great Taoist thinkers, of Lao-tzu and Chuang-tzu. Little is known about their lives, if indeed they ever existed. This is perhaps fitting for men who had allegedly chosen a life of obscurity and taught a way of silence.

Taoism is not just passive contemplation. The texts of Lao-tzu and Chuang-tzu (also the name of the book, *Chuang-tzu*) served a later generation of religious-minded thinkers anxious to transcend the limited conditions of human existence. Their ambition was to 'steal the secret of Heaven and Earth', to wrench from it the mystery of life itself, in order to fulfil their desire for immortality.

The goal of the Confucian was to become a sage, a servant of society. The goal of the Taoist was to become an immortal (a *hsien*). They revived the belief in personal deities, practising a ritual of prayer and appeasement. They fostered the art of alchemy—the external alchemy, which 'internalized' the golden pill of immortality—and sought it through yoga and meditation. They also saw sexual hygiene as another means of prolonging human life.

This new Taoism has been called 'Taoist religion', to distinguish it from the classical philosophy of Lao-tzu and Chuang-tzu and its acceptance of both life and death. This Taoist religion developed its own mystical tradition, embellished with

'The Tao that can be expressed is not the eternal Tao; The name that can be defined is not the unchanging name. Non-existence is called the antecedent of heaven and earth; Existence is the mother of all things.'

The opening lines of Lao-tzu's *Tao Te Ching*

stories of marvellous drugs and wonder-working immortals, of levitations and bodily ascensions to heaven. Basing itself on the early texts—the *Lao-tzu*, *Chuang-tzu*, *Huai-nan-tzu*, and *Lieh-tzu*—the Taoist religionists created long-lasting religious institutions.

Some of these groups still exist today, and can trace their roots back to the Taoist movements at the end of the second century AD. With their esoteric and exoteric teachings, their lines of orthodox teachers, their social organizations, they more closely resemble the other great religious traditions of mankind. But their persistent Chinese style comes through: they seek unity with the *Tao* which cannot be named.

Quest for freedom

How can Taoism be distinguished from its great sister religion, Confucianism? One major goal of all the various schools and sects of Taoism was the quest for freedom. For some it was a freedom from the political and social constraints of the emerging Confucian state. For others it was the even more profound search for immortality. And for others it was the search for oneness with the *Tao* itself. This *Tao* was the sum total of all things which are and which change, for change itself was a very important part of the Taoist view of reality. As the *Chuang-tzu* tells us, the *Tao* is 'complete, all-embracing, the whole: these are different names for the same reality denoting the One'.

This One, this totality of the *Tao*, worked as a liberating concept for the Taoists. Within the ceaseless flux of the *Tao* they found the power to live life in a spontaneous fashion. Probably the most famous statement of the freedom of the Taoist immortal is that of Lao-tzu where he says, 'The ways of men are conditioned by those of Heaven, the ways of Heaven by those of the *Tao*, and the *Tao* came into being by itself.' The *Tao* is therefore the principle of the universe and is also a pattern for human behaviour, often called 'uncontrived action' (*wu-wei*).

'All things alter and change,
Never a moment ceasing,
Revolving, whirling, and rolling away,
Driven far off and returning onward,
Like the mutations of cicada,
Profound, subtle, and illimitable,
Who can finish describing it?'

'The Owl', Chia Yi (200–168 BC)

The Taoist imagination was totally unfettered by the confines of Confucian etiquette or sensibility. They provided the magic garden of the Chinese people. Some took this magic very seriously. Some found that this too was just another illusion of the changing *Tao*. For example, at the end of a report of a magical spirit journey attributed to King My of the Chou dynasty, the magician who has been his guide for the trip explains: 'Your majesty feels at home with the permanent, is suspicious of the sudden and temporary. But can one always measure how far and how fast a scene may later turn into something else?'

Or, as the next story in the *Lieh-tzu* puts it: 'The breath of all that lives, the appearance of all that has shape, is illusion.'

But unlike many of the great religions of India and the East, the Taoists never felt that the *Tao* could be called a conscious god.

'How can the Creator have a conscious mind? It spontaneously takes place but seems mysterious. The breath and matter collect together, coagulate and become shape: constant with transformation it continues on without ever ceasing.'

Life rolls on

Throughout its whole history, the diverse masters of Taoism have sought, in various ways, to become part of this 'self-so-ness' of reality. Life rolls on by itself in an unbroken wave of creative spontaneity. Neither the Confucian Heaven, nor the rule of earthly kings and emperors, nor the folly of demons or goblins can defy it.

**'Being of themselves as they are
Silently brings them about,
Gives them serenity,
gives them peace,
Escorts them as they go and
welcomes them as they come.'**

The true immortal lives to learn a life in tune with the *Tao*.

In all Taoist religion there is a poetic touch, a realization that life is a beautiful, and frightening, panorama of transformations. No religion has been more successful at invoking the sense of wonder which these transformations cause to human beings. Set within their mountain retreats and their lake pavilions, the Taoists have truly been the poets of nature. The great T'ao Ch'ien (365–427 AD) expresses this sense of wonder tinged with serene resignation and hope.

**'Just surrender to the cycle of things,
Give yourself to the waves of the Great Change,
Neither happy nor yet afraid,
And when it is time to go, then simply go,
Without any unnecessary fuss.'**

Today this sense of poetic beauty and desire to achieve oneness with the *Tao* still informs the Taoist religion. Because of the great revolutionary changes in China, it is hard to tell just how Taoism will develop there in the future. However, the Taoist Association is again functioning, and Taoism has been recognized as an important part of China's great cultural history. This means that there is probably a future for the Taoist religion very like its past. Taoism has always been at odds with the government. Yet it survives as long as Chinese culture itself exists.

Cross-fertilization

The great Chinese religions have always influenced each other's development. In early China great debates and arguments went on between the Taoists and Confucians. But the arguments helped both sides develop their own distinctive attitudes.

The picture becomes even more complicated with the introduction of

A distinctively Chinese Buddhist temple in Taiwan.

Chinese communities throughout the world have their own places of worship. This Taoist temple is in Penang.

Buddhist shrines in China take the distinctive form of pagodas.

And on the practical level, they learned a great deal about meditation, which they called 'quiet-sitting', from the Buddhists.

'The three are one'

The great heyday of cross-fertilization of religions in China came in the Ming dynasty (1369–1644). At this period many great religious thinkers, such as Lin Chao-en (1517–98), sought to effect a harmonization of the three great religions of China. Their cry was that the three religions are one.

Lin sought to combine the best features of Taoist and Buddhist meditation with a Confucian sense of shared concern for fellow creatures in a uniquely Chinese synthesis. This kind of syncretistic religious life is still present in China today. And, in fact, it would not be far wrong to say that most religious Chinese are in fact a mixture of all three great religions. The syncretists had such a great effect that no one thinks it odd to be a Buddhist, Taoist and Confucian at the same time.

Finally there is the element of Western culture in modern China's intellectual development. Along with the development and cross-fertilization of their indigenous traditions, the Chinese have been rapidly coming to terms with the West and its great missionary religion, Christianity. Christians, like the Taoists, are again active in present-day China, even if as a tiny minority. The Chinese are assimilating a new cultural perspective, just as they did in the case of Buddhism almost 1,800 years ago. Religious and secular Western influence will no doubt have just as great an impact on China— witness the tremendous transformative power of Maoist thought, based in part on Marxist concepts—as did Buddhism. The future of Chinese religion will therefore certainly be as interesting as her past, and probably just as complex. It is impossible to say what will survive from the past. But we can be absolutely certain that what will emerge will be distinctively Chinese at all levels.

Buddhism into China. Both Taoism and Confucianism borrowed a great deal from the new Indian religion. The Taoists reformed their religious structures, founded monasteries and wrote a huge canon of sacred texts in imitation of Buddhist models.

The great Neo-Confucian revival in the eleventh and twelfth centuries BC would also be unthinkable without the stimulus and challenge of Buddhist philosophy. Although the Confucians did not borrow nearly as much as the Taoists from the Buddhists, they were certainly stimulated to work out their own mature philosophic response to Buddhist thought.

A Tapestry of Traditions: Japanese Religions

Michael Pye

Religion in Japan is a rich tapestry of diverse traditions with a history of nearly 2,000 years. Many Japanese people display some kind of allegiance to more than one religion; a person will usually be expected to have a Shinto wedding and a Buddhist funeral, though Buddhist and secular weddings are also possible. With this may go a personal or family interest in a particular Buddhist denomination or practice, or membership of one of the various new religions which attract almost a third of the population.

These different forms of religion have separate organizations, buildings, festivals, sacred writings, ministers or priests and so on. However, it should always be remembered that the paths of these religions have touched at many points in Japanese history, and that they still meet in the lives of many Japanese people. For this reason it is possible to speak both of 'Japanese religions' and of 'Japanese religion'—especially as the Japanese language itself does not usually distinguish between the singular and the plural.

Land and religion

The general pattern of Japanese religion is in some ways a reflection of the country's geographical position and character. Japan has received a great deal from the Asian continent, but almost entirely from or via Korea and China. The major imported religions are therefore Buddhism, mainly in its Mahayana form, and Confucianism. The influence of Taoism, incidentally, has been largely indirect, bearing partly on divination practices and partly on the style of Zen Buddhism. It was in reaction to the powerful Buddhist and Confucian systems, with their scholarly prestige and political influence, that Japan's native Shinto faith first became clearly organized and defined. Indeed, the impact of Chinese and then of Western culture, and Japan's responses to these, provide the overall cultural perspective in which Japanese religion can be understood.

The fact that the country consists mainly of four great islands, spread over a vast distance from north to south, has also had its effect. The most famous historic Shinto shrines and Buddhist temples are found in the southern part of the main island, Honshu. Extremely ancient Shinto shrines which are still of national importance are located at Ise, where the sun-goddess Amaterasu is revered and where a new prime minister usually 'reports' on the formation of his cabinet, and at Izumo, where all the gods or *kami* of Japan are said to return once a year. Between these two sites are the former capitals, Nara and Kyoto, which themselves boast not only some well-known Shinto shrines such as the Kasuga

Worshippers at a Shinto shrine purify themselves, then approach the shrine and ring a bell or knock to attract the attention of the kami.

Shrine at Nara, but also many fine Buddhist temples and images. The thirteenth-century sectarian development of Buddhism is reflected in the temple buildings and images at Kamakura, also on the main island of Honshu, but further east near modern Tokyo.

The smaller island of Shikoku, which together with Honshu cradles the scenic Inland Sea, has never been of the slightest political importance and so lacks major religious monuments. But it does have a famous pilgrimage route which takes in no fewer than eighty-eight Buddhist temples. Today these are frequently visited by coach-parties of tourists, an example of the intimate link be-

tween holiday travel and religion in Japan today. Other pilgrimage routes are found in other parts of the country, the most famous being the thirty-three places in western Honshu where the Bodhisattva Kannon-sama is revered.

The island of Hokkaido in the north was largely undeveloped until the nineteenth century, when young Tokyoites were sent out in a pioneering spirit to cope with its less favourable climate. The main city, Sapporo, was a centre of Protestant missionary effort at that time, although its people today practise the more usual forms of Japanese religion.

Kyushu, the southernmost major

island, claims some of the oldest known historical sites in Japan, because of its proximity to Korea. Its importance as a maritime trading approach from the west meant that it became the main base for Roman Catholic missions in the sixteenth century, and also the scene of martyrdoms, especially at Nagasaki; Roman Catholic Christianity was suppressed partly because it was espoused by feudal lords in Kyushu who showed separatist tendencies. In a similar way, Kyushu was also the geographical base for the Shinto-inspired reassertion of imperial power in the mid-nineteenth century, when the central military government in Edo (now Tokyo) came to the end of its two and a half centuries of undisturbed rule.

Mountain-top shrines

The mountainous terrain of the country has also had a major effect on the forms of Japanese religious life. Many mountains have shrines at their summit, and not a few attract pilgrim groups who seek purification and heightened spiritual powers. The most famous is of course Mount Fuji itself, which is a quasi-religious symbol for the whole nation.

Buddhists had already used mountains in China as isolated retreats from the world and this practice was carried over to Japan. The most famous example was Mount Koya, one of the leading headquarters of Shingon Buddhism (see below). The mountain cult encouraged one of the most fascinating syncretistic movements in the history of religion, the Shugendo movement, which linked Buddhism and Shinto. This movement used ascetic exercises aiming at enlightenment in a quest for shamanic magical powers, performing spiritualist healing and fire-walking rites. Though it flourished in historical times, it has by no means died out today and indeed has had considerable influence on the formation of new religions.

Shinto

Shinto is the name given to a wide conglomeration of religious practices with roots in prehistoric Japan. Little is known about Japanese religion before the emergence of a unified state in the Yamato period (fourth to seventh centuries AD), but in its simplest forms it was broadly animist, believing that a supernatural living force resided in natural objects such as mountains, trees and animals.

The oldest literary works in Japan were composed on a basis of the combined myths and legends of the various clans which had been forged into political unity. The oldest of these official works is the *Kojiki* (AD 712), but this was soon replaced by the *Nihongi* (AD 720) also known as the *Nihonshoki*. These two works retain to this day an honoured position in the minds of most Japanese people and are considered especially important by the advocates of Shinto. On the other hand, they are not recited or even studied by ordinary believers.

From the Yamato period onwards, the imperial household took a central position within Shinto. Its ancestry was traced back through legendary emperors and empresses as far as Ninigi, believed to have been the grandson of the sun-goddess Amaterasu. For this reason, Ise Shrine has always had a close connection with the imperial household. From 1868 onwards, when the monarchy was restored to a central position in Japanese politics under Emperor Meiji, up until the end of the Pacific

Japanese homes often have their own small shrines.

War in 1945, the Shinto religion was focused sharply on Ise Shrine and the emperor cult. After the war, the emperor's semi-divine status was officially denied and Shinto was disestablished. Since then, religious teaching has no longer been given in state-run schools and the observance of Shinto practices has become a voluntary matter. Nevertheless the imperial family still enjoys very high esteem among the people, and leading Shinto shrines remain important symbols of Japanese nationhood.

Shinto shrines

Shinto today is based fundamentally on each individual shrine. Although most shrines large enough to have an organizing staff are affiliated to the Association of Shinto Shrines, most of the people who visit a shrine or take part in a festival are hardly aware of this. Each shrine has some individual reason for its existence, whether it be a natural phenomenon such as a mountain, a historical event of importance to the local community, or an act of personal devotion or political patronage. There is an endless variety.

For example, the ancient shrine at Kashima, near the Pacific coast of Honshu, is patronized particularly by those devoted to the martial arts, such as swordsmanship and *kendo*. At the same time it has various sub-shrines within its grounds. One of these celebrates a spring of fresh water tumbling out of the side of a hill and has its symbolic gate planted in the pool at the foot. Another is a fenced enclosure surrounding a mighty stone, of which only the rounded top is visible sticking up through the sand. This stone is supposed to hold down beneath the earth the giant catfish which is believed to be responsible for earthquakes. The god or *kami* of a shrine may be the natural object itself, it may be one of the divinities mentioned in the *Kojiki* or the *Nihongi*, or it may be a legendary or historical person. In shrines where a specific object is kept in the inner sanctuary it is usually not known what the object is, for nobody ever sees it.

Shinto shrines have certain common features which are almost always to be seen. The first of these which the visitor will notice is the large symbolic gate consisting of two uprights and two crossbars, marking the entrance to the shrine. These gates (*torii*) sometimes stand quite far off at the bottom of a busy street with shops and stalls catering for visitors; there may be two or more, or even a long line of them, leading to the shrine itself. Inside the precinct there is a large trough of clean water, usually sheltered with a roof and provided with clean wooden ladles. Here the worshipper rinses face and hands in a simple act of purification.

The main shrine buildings, of which there are several traditional architectural types, consist of a worship hall (*haiden*) and a main hall (*honden*) standing behind. The main hall is usually smaller and is not entered, being the physical location of the *kami* itself. The worship hall is entered from time to time by small groups for petitionary prayer. Individual visitors to the shrine simply stand outside before the worship hall, toss a coin into the offerings box, pull on a dangling rope with a bell or clanger at the top, clap their hands twice, bow briefly in prayer, clap their hands again and leave. The sound of the clanger and of the hand-clap are intended to alert the *kami* to the believer's presence. The front of the worship hall is often decorated with a thick rope (*shimenawa*) and folded white paper strips, which are regularly used to designate a sacred area or sacred object. Sometimes these are simply strung around a rock or a tree, indicating that these too are considered as shrines for the *kami* of the rock or the tree.

There are three main types of shrine. First, there are those of purely local significance, housing the *kami* of the locality (*ujigami*). Second, there are shrines of a particular recurrent type, such as the Inari Shrines, which are visited with a view to winning business success. These may be found in any part of the country. Third, there are shrines of great national and semi-political importance such as the Ise and Izumo Shrines mentioned earlier. Another shrine of national importance is the Meiji Shrine in Tokyo, honouring the former Emperor Meiji, which is visited by about 3 million people at New Year alone. Yet another is the Yasukuni Shrine, also in Tokyo, commemorating the souls of Japan's war dead. Since the end of the Pacific War, the status of Ise Shrine and of Yasukuni Shrine has been a matter of some controversy, because critics fear a revival of Shinto-led nationalism if relations with political leaders or with the imperial household become too close or too formal.

Other types of shrine that recur throughout the country include the Hachimangu Shrines, dedicated to the *kami* of war and martial prowess; the Toshogu Shrines, sacred to the memory of the dictator-general Ieyasu (died 1616) and reflecting the colourful pomp of his mausoleum at Nikko; and the Tenmangu Shrines where a loyal but wrongfully banished aristocrat is revered and believers pray for success in literature and study.

Shinto practices

Much of Shinto practice is an individual matter, as when a person simply visits a shrine to make his or her own request—before a journey, before an examination, before some new enterprise, or perhaps because they just happen to be passing that way. In such cases the form of wor-

The way into Shinto shrines is marked by gate-like torii. *There is sometimes just one of these; sometimes there is a whole colonnade.*

ship is as described earlier. Family occasions also involve visits to the shrine. It is common, though not universal, to take a new-born baby there so that prayers may be said for its health. Shinto priests officiate at the majority of Japanese weddings, though these usually take place in a purpose-built hall run on business lines with reception rooms and other facilities.

Shrines are visited by particularly large numbers at New Year, especially on 1 January but also on 2 and 3 January. Some people go just after midnight on 31 December, while others go at dawn. Some visitors to mountain shrines make a point of observing the rising sun and bathing their faces in its first rays. At the New Year visit there is a brisk sale of feathered wooden arrows (to drive off evil), protective charms and stiff paper strips bearing the name and seal of the shrine (*fuda*). These are taken home and kept on the *kami* shelf if there is one, or just in a high place, for the coming year. Last year's accessories are taken back to

the shrine at the New Year visit and burned on a bonfire or handed in to be burned later by shrine staff.

Another personal charm sold in great numbers at this time of year is the papier-maché *daruma* doll, originally a representation of the Zen Buddhist master Daruma (or Bodhidharma). Though Buddhist in origin, these dolls are on sale at the entrances to many shrines and are also brought back to shrines for burning. Some Buddhist temples share in the New Year practices by encouraging a first visit on a specified day in January, selling various kinds of talisman and offering prayers for safety in the home, traffic safety, prosperity in business and avoidance of bad luck.

Festivals

Perhaps the most important feature of Shinto practice is the festival (*matsuri*), since this forms the main occasion on which a particular shrine takes on meaning for all its worshippers at once. A Shinto festival usually includes a procession or a fair with stalls and side-shows, and so it easily draws large numbers of people, many returning to visit relatives at the same time. The more spectacular festivals bring in visitors and sightseers as well, thus being good for trade; for festivals which achieve national fame, special trains may be laid on and accommodation booked for months in advance. One shrine may hold several festivals in a year, but among these just one or two may be of special importance, particularly at spring or autumn.

Festivals famous throughout Japan for their huge floats hauled along in procession are the Gion Festival in Kyoto, the Takayama Festival in the Hida region and the Chichibu Festival in the mountains north-west of Tokyo. In the last of these the vehicles, representing various parts of the town of Chichibu, are illuminated by lanterns and drawn through the town at night as the *kami* from the town shrine is brought to meet the *kami* of the nearest large mountain. In many cases, the floats or the standards and banners are taken through the town by groups of young men wearing

A female priest at the Shinto shrine in Meiji.

The bronze Daibutsu statue at Kamakura is a statue of Amida Buddha, who is worshipped in Japan.

clothes representative of their part of the town. Sometimes they wear only a loincloth because of the strenuousness of the work, especially if they have to wade through water. Almost always they are fortified by plenty of rice wine (*sake*) which is particularly associated with Shinto and often offered at shrines in neatly wrapped bottles or large casks. Sometimes the processions recall a historical event such as a battle, in which case period costumes are worn.

Very often, the focal point of a procession is a portable shrine (*mikoshi*) which is taken from the main shrine to various points in the locality, symbolizing a journey made by the *kami*. Not all of those taking part in a procession enter the worship hall of the main shrine on arrival. Usually it is representatives only who go inside with the priests to present offerings such as evergreen branches of the *sakaki* tree, and to offer prayers for the safety and prosperity of the neighbourhood.

Japanese Buddhism

The history of Japanese Buddhism can be traced back to the early sixth century AD when images and *sutras* (Buddhist scriptures) were sent from Korea. The first major act of patronage took place when Prince Shotoku, regent from AD 593–622, established Buddhism as a national religion, linking it to Confucian ideals of morality and statecraft. A stream of eminent monks brought more knowledge of the new religion from Korea and China, and the early traditions at the capital of Nara were superseded in AD 805 by a much bigger Buddhist establishment on Mount Hiei, overlooking the new capital of Kyoto. This new Buddhist centre drew its inspiration from the Chinese T'ien T'ai school, which came to be known in Japan as Tendai Buddhism. This in turn was rapidly affected by the doctrines and practices of an esoteric form of Buddhism, not unlike that of Tibet. Almost immediately a rival headquarters for this type of Buddhism was set up on the then almost inaccessible Mount Koya, some distance to the south of Kyoto. This

school, Shingon Buddhism, was established by the famous monk Kukai (744–835), posthumously known as Kobo Daishi and revered as a great saint.

The Tendai and Shingon sects were rapidly supplemented by others, partly drawing on special trends in Chinese Buddhism and partly resulting from Japanese innovation. The first main development was the growth in the practice of chanting the name of Amitabha Buddha, who, according to the *sutras*, had vowed to take all living beings with him into a heavenly paradise called the 'pure land' from where they would surely attain *nirvana*. The formula chanted, called the *nembutsu*, runs in Japanese 'Namu Amida Butsu' ('Hail Amida Buddha'), though in practice the last syllable is omitted. Chanting the *nembutsu* was believed by many to have magical powers, bringing health and warding off disasters. However, according to the influential teachers Honen (1133–1212) and Shinran (1173–1262), it was symbolic of simple and sincere faith in the 'other power' (*tariki*) of the Buddha Amitabha to bring about salvation. Associated with these two teachers are the Pure Land sect (Jodoshu) and the True Pure Land sect (Jodo Shinshu) respectively.

Before long there came a new emphasis on the *Lotus Sutra* inspired by Nichiren (1222–82). The *Lotus Sutra* had already been of great importance in Tendai Buddhism, but Nichiren gave it a new centrality, and his interpretative writings provided the basis for a number of sects. Among these are counted some of the most influential lay Buddhist movements of modern times. Nichirenite sects share in common the recitation of the simple formula '*Nam(u) Myoho Renge Kyo*' ('Hail Wonderful *Dharma Lotus Sutra*').

In the meantime, the Japanese Zen masters Eisai (1141–1215) and Dogen (1200–53) had been establishing their schools of practice aimed at the direct achievement of enlightenment (*satori*). Consequently two more sects were formed, the Rinzai sect and the Soto sect, becoming the two most important Zen sects in Japan. The Rinzai sect encourages active mental training by means of well-known riddles (*koan*) such as 'What is the sound of one hand clapping?' The Soto sect prefers to concentrate on seated meditation (*zazen*) during which the practitioner is identified with the enlightenment position and with the nature of the Buddha himself.

Within each of these various types of Buddhism there are many more sub-sects, each based on some local initiative and giving emphasis to a particular practice or teaching, or simply asserting the independence of a vigorous and popular temple. A recent Japanese handbook lists no fewer than seventeen Shingon sects, nine Tendai sects, nine Nichirenite sects, sixteen Zen sects, ten True Pure Land sects and four Pure Land sects. A dictionary of Buddhist sects in Japan lists many more.

In their various ways these sects all express significant themes in the tradition of Mahayana Buddhism which spread from India across east Asia.

While some people have a clear allegiance to one or other sect, especially in the case of the *nembutsu* sects or the Nichirenite sects, there are many features of popular devotion which cut across sectarian distinctions. Two of the most widely revered saviour figures are the Bodhisattvas Jizo-sama and Kannon-sama. Jizo-sama is believed to care especially for children or for infants who have died during childbirth or pregnancy. Kannon-sama (*Avalokitesvara* in Sanskrit) offers many kinds of protection and solace and is found in many places, not least in the precincts of Soto Zen temples.

Buddhism in the home

In the home many families are reminded of Buddhism by the presence of a domestic Buddhist altar (*butsudan*). This usually contains a central Buddhist image or other symbol, tablets commemorating ancestors, a booklet with portions of Buddhist scriptures, a place for lighting incense, and various other accessories. As a morning devotion a small offer-

Zen Buddhist sand-gardens are used as an aid to meditation.

ing of food may be placed on the altar, a passage recited from a *sutra* and a stick of incense lit. Individual sects introduce many variations.

Buddhism is also particularly influential as the religion of funerals and cemeteries. Again the different sects make slightly different provisions, though cremation and a stone memorial are universal. Thin wooden posts placed by visitors at a tombstone bear texts written in heavy black ink which reflect the distinctive faith of the temple in question. Cemeteries are visited particularly at *higan*, which occurs twice a year at the spring and autumn equinoxes. The other main commemoration of the dead is in midsummer at *o-bon*, which is marked by outdoor fires and dancing.

Buddhist festivals

To some extent Japanese Buddhism borrows the characteristic Shinto concept of festival (*matsuri*). In early April, for example, some Buddhist temples celebrate a flower festival which centres on the commemoration of the Buddha's birthday on 8 April. At this time a small standing statue of the infant Buddha is placed in a framework decorated with flowers, and worshippers anoint it with liquid from a bowl beneath.

Another well-known festival, climaxing at a Buddhist temple in Tokyo, is that of the forty-seven masterless Samurai (*ronin*). These forty-seven have been applauded for centuries because they avenged the unjustly forced suicide of their master and then committed suicide themselves. This is one of the classic cases of premeditated ritual suicide (*harakiri*), carried out in connection with a feat inspired by loyalty. The theme is worked out in the well-known traditional drama *Chushingura*, regularly shown at the time of the festival in December. The festival itself consists of a procession re-enacting the arrival of the forty-seven Samurai at the temple to report the completion of their deed of vengeance. Following this, crowds of people light incense at their tombs.

Buddhism is linked to Japanese

Exuberant festivals are an important feature both of popular Shinto and Japan's New Religions.

culture at many points: through the traditional way of the Samurai, generally known as *bushido*, through the austere *no* drama with its many Buddhist themes, through the tea ceremony which is intended to communicate simplicity and naturalness, through calligraphy and painting, and so on. The most lively aspect of Japanese Buddhism however remains the popular faith directed towards the various Buddhas, Bodhisattvas and saints of the Mahayana Buddhist tradition.

The flowering of new religions

Innovation is an accepted feature of Japanese religious life. Many Shinto shrines are the result of some fresh religious experience or message from a medium, long since incorporated into the general pattern of Shinto. In some more recent cases such initiatives have led to the growth of separate religious bodies. One of the best known of these is the Religion of the Divine Wisdom (Tenrikyo), founded in the early nineteenth century by a lady named Miki Nakayama. This religion began with revelations and healings, but instead of merging into the wider pattern of Shinto it formulated its own independent sacred writings, constructed its own sacred city named Tenri, and shaped its own forms of worship including a special dance.

Another well-known example is the popularly-named Dancing Religion (Odoru Shukyo) which also has the longer formal name of Tensho Kotai Jingu Kyo, incorporating alternative names for the goddess Amaterasu and Ise Shrine. The foundress, named Sayo Kitamura, believed that a *kami* was speaking through her abdomen, and these revelations are the basis of the religion's teaching. She also initiated a form of ecstatic dance which encourages believers to experience a state of non-self (*muga*). It may be noted that this is one of the 'three marks' of Buddhist teaching. The religion known as the Teaching of the Great Source (Oomotokyo) is also a major independent religious group having a Shinto background combined with belief in a new revelation of its own.

Other new religions have moved further afield from the traditional faiths of Japan. The House of Growth (Seicho no Ie) claims to overcome disease and suffering through its new teachings propounded by Masaharu Taniguchi, a former Oomotokyo member. He has a modern headquarters in Tokyo with symbols expressing the unity of all religions and a good supply of literature for sale. The Church of World Messianity (Sekai Kyuseikyo) is also loosely derived from Oomotokyo. The leader, Mokichi Okada, preached freedom from disease and from poverty, and his following grew rapidly after the Pacific War. The movement now boasts a fine art gallery. Another body with the name of PL Kyodan sees the whole of life as art, and religion as a means of realizing this vision in the member's experience. The 'PL' in the name of this group stands for the English words 'Perfect Liberty'. There are many different explanations for the appearance of new religions, but at least it is clear that they provide a kind of barometer of the needs and aspirations of much of Japan's population.

New Buddhist movements

Japanese Buddhism also gives plenty of scope for innovation since the proliferation of sects and independent temple organizations is accepted as a normal feature of religious life. It is hardly surprising that several of Japan's new religions are in fact recently-developed forms of Buddhism. The most influential are those based in some way or other on the *Lotus Sutra*, for together they claim about a fifth of the population as adherents. Of these, the Reiyukai began as a movement caring for untended tombs and stressing the virtues of gratitude and loyalty towards ancestors. Today it boasts a huge central hall in Tokyo.

Several groups split off from the Reiyukai, however, in a series of organizational and doctrinal disputes. Of these the largest is the Rissho Kosei-kai. This movement was strongly influenced in its beginnings by the religious messages of Mrs Myoko Naganuma, whose house is still tenderly cared for today long after her death. The dominant figure, however, is the founding president, Nikkyo Niwano, who emphasized the exposition of the *Lotus Sutra* as the doctrinal basis of the movement. It is notable that this is a lay movement which is entirely independent of any previously-existing monastic sect. It also has an impressive complex of buildings in Tokyo. As far as practices are concerned, the main emphasis is on a form of group counselling in which the individual's problems are analysed in Buddhist terms, though of course the *Lotus Sutra* is recited and studied as well.

Also based on the *Lotus Sutra*, but with different doctrinal tendencies, is the lay movement commonly known as the Soka Gakkai. This is linked with a monastic sect named Nichiren Shoshu, claiming a direct tradition back to Nichiren himself, and the full name is therefore Nichiren Shoshu Soka Gakkai. The members support one of Japan's larger political parties, the Komeito (Clean Government Party) which was founded under the stimulation of Soka Gakkai leaders, although remaining legally distinct.

The future
of Japanese faiths

The new religions draw in many ways on the wider religious culture of Japan. This is formed mainly by traditional Shinto and Buddhism, but is also influenced by Confucian ideas and values, and to a lesser extent by a rather Western-looking Christianity. Historically, Confucianism has provided the main moral backing for Shinto, emphasizing family duty and loyalty and extending these concepts to school, industry and state. Though Confucianism has no organization of any note, many religious bodies in Japan stress such values as loyalty or sincerity (*makoto*), gratitude, correctness of behaviour and brightness of attitude.

Modern Christian missions have had little impact numerically or even ideologically, but they have had some unintentional influence on other Japanese religious bodies. A number of Buddhist sects now run Sunday schools, for example, and some of the new religions use books looking remarkably like Christian Bibles and prayer-books, but with different contents. Christianity itself has a total membership of less than 1 per cent of the population, probably because it is strongly identified as belonging to the Western world. The Christian churches in Japan have only the most tenuous links with the general religious culture of the country.

Secular Japan?

In spite of the startling success of several of the newer religious movements, it would be quite wrong to think that Buddhism and Shinto have lost support in recent times. In some ways, particularly in politics and education, Japan has become remarkably secularized, and there is much ignorance about the deeper teachings of the religions. At the same time, most Japanese people are involved in various kinds of religious behaviour at certain times of the year and at the appropriate points in their lives.

They also share many deeply-held, if simplistic, assumptions which draw strength from and reinforce the traditional religions. This is partly made possible by a naturalistic acceptance of the yearly routine of the calendar, which unites a wide range of religious events in a general awareness of seasonal change. It is also made possible by their pragmatic acceptance of many kinds of minor religious practices as social obligations. This general state of affairs will probably continue for a long time to come.

Unity and Peace: The Baha'i Faith

Werner Schilling

The Baha'i religion sees itself as a revelation addressed by God to the whole of mankind. It developed from the teachings of two religious visionaries in nineteenth-century Persia.

The first of these was one Mirza Ali Muhammed (1820–50), who called himself the Bab, meaning 'The Gate', and believed himself to be the latest in a long line of spiritual leaders. He attracted relatively few followers—though they were strong enough to stage armed uprisings against the government—and was executed by the Persian authorities for alleged complicity in an attempt to assassinate the Shah.

The second, who was far more influential, was Mirza Husain Ali (1817–92), a follower of the Bab who called himself Baha'u'llah, meaning 'Glory of God'. In 1863 he declared himself to be the manifestation of God foretold by the Bab, sent to redeem the world at the end of the age and to interpret God's will for a new era. He sent many proclamations of this to kings and other contemporary heads of state, an activity which brought him frequent persecution, imprisonment and exile. He lived at various times in Constantinople, Adrianople and Acre in Palestine.

His group of followers, small at first, continued · to grow after his death, until today the movement can claim to be represented in over 70,000 centres in different parts of the world. The main strength is in south-west Asia, but there are also centres in Europe, Africa, North and South America and south-east Asia. Actual statistics of followers are hardly possible to arrive at, but some very high estimates should be treated with caution.

Cycles of history

Baha'i teaching is syncretistic, derived from many religions. Running through it all is the idea that the history of mankind goes in cycles. One of these began roughly 6,000 years ago with Adam, first of its prophets. His successors were Moses, Krishna, Buddha, Zarathushtra, Christ and Muhammad. The latest and most important of these is Baha'u'llah himself—with others yet to come. The Baha'is believe that these earlier religions contained his teaching in embryonic form.

The teaching of Baha'u'llah

Baha'u'llah saw himself as the fulfilment of the promises in all religions of a coming world-renewer or messiah. He was to teach the true 'religion of God', fill the world with justice and rescue it from its lost state and from the disintegration of moral values in modern civilization. In the eyes of his followers he is a kind of divine healer, relieving the sufferings of humanity and uniting mankind. In modern times, when not only philosophers but even theologians can talk

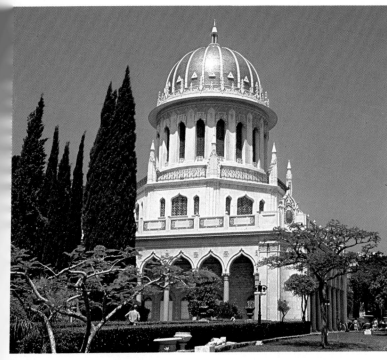

Haifa in Israel is the administrative centre of Baha'i. The Shrine of the Bab contains the body of Mirza Ali Muhammed, the forerunner of Baha'u'llah.

of God being 'dead', Baha'u'llah proclaims that the transcendent God is alive and has spoken anew to mankind. Baha'u'llah came to clear away the errors and misunderstandings of former religions and to shape a better culture in truth and righteousness; to lead mankind to unity, and to bring about the 'kingdom of God' awaited by all religions.

However, no abrupt end of this age or intervention by God is predicted. Instead, according to Baha'i teachings, there will be an inner change in man and in society. It is through this that the world will come from ruin into harmony again.

Justice is not done to the Baha'i religion if it is simply dismissed as a minor sect. It claims to be a wholly independent revealed religion. Though derived from Islam, it is not merely a sect built up from elements of another religion. On 10 May 1925 an Islamic court in the town of Baba laid down that the Baha'is had broken away from Islam; the same declaration was made by the Grand Mufti of Egypt on 11 March 1939.

Neither do the Baha'is see themselves as a religion constructed artificially from other faiths, such as Christianity or the Indian religions. The Baha'i faith claims to be one of the great universal religions of the world.

The voice of God

All the writings of Baha'u'llah are considered sacred, but they are not to be observed to the letter. He authorized his eldest son, 'Abd ul-Baha, to be the interpreter of his writings; he alone carries any weight as an interpreter. He in turn nominated an 'authorized interpreter' at his death. This was his grandson Shoghi Effendi who died in 1957. His expositions, however, and those of Baha'i writers today, no longer count as sacred literature; they interpret the 'voice of God' for the present situation.

Mankind made one

Crucial for an understanding of the Baha'i religion is its belief in a divine plan for the world which was made known to the Baha'is. Yet its ethic is not confined to the Baha'is, but open to all. World peace is striven for, as well as the settling of all social problems and the achievement of racial equality. The teaching of the Baha'is is especially concerned with the problems of the individual in the community, and Baha'is seek to work hand in hand with science. Unity is to be brought to mankind by God's universal dispensation as revealed to Baha'u'llah. This is to be brought into effect by a universal executive and legislative body, a universal language, a single currency and a uniform judicial and police system. The carrying out of Baha'u'llah's instructions is to be achieved by means of religious services through which there is spiritual preparation for these social tasks. Man is required to adopt a new attitude to his role as a partner in the family and the whole social structure.

Persecution of the Baha'is

Werner Schilling

From the start of their history the Baha'is in the Middle East have been persecuted and subjected to violent attacks as apostates from Islam, particularly in Iran. They became the object of official oppression by the government. The last Shah (Mohammed Reza Shah), in particular, made them second-class citizens by continual victimization.

The first systematic persecution was as early as 1921–22, when the Baha'i Centre in Sangsar was taken over and demolished. Baha'is were deprived of civil rights. Baha'i civil servants lost their pensions. In 1925 a law was passed by the Shah making all Baha'i marriages invalid. Children already born were declared illegitimate. Married couples were not even allowed to share a hotel bedroom. In 1932 the Baha'i schools in Tehran were closed down.

But the Baha'is refused to be defeated. In 1939 a renewed, particularly vicious press campaign was launched against them. A large number who had become officers were dismissed from the army and forced to pay back the cost of their education. After Mohammed Reza Shah had come to power in 1941, his centralized administration began an even more effective period of oppression. From 1951 onwards, the Baha'is were suspected of collaboration with the communists. The Baha'i House in Shiraz was occupied by troops, desecrated and destroyed. Even Baha'i cemeteries were violated.

The protests of Baha'is in other countries were of no avail. Discrimination against this minority was kept up constantly. During the 70s the Shah's secret police organized a systematic anti-Baha'i movement. The Baha'is were deprived of all rights and accused of being worthless citizens. Their human rights were not even considered.

Khomeini's seizure of power brought no relief to the Baha'is in Iran; indeed, a number have been put to death. The Fada'iyan-i-Islam, one of the most powerful associations in present-day Iran, was founded about twenty years ago specifically to harass the Baha'is. The same is true of the organization Tablighat-i-Islami (Society for the Propagation of Islam). No birth certificates are issued to new-born Baha'i babies because their fathers are Baha'is and the Baha'i religion is not among the recognized minority religions. In Iran, however, there are no papers other than the birth certificate by which a person can prove his identity.

Baha'u'llah's own words speak directly to such a situation.

'Nations and tribes of the world, who are always at war, turn your face towards unity and let the brightness of its light shine upon you.'

Baha'u'llah

'You are the fruit of one tree and the leaves of one branch.'

People of a Book

Chosen People: Judaism

David Harley

'The Lord ... said to
Abram ...
"I will make you into a
great nation
and I will bless you;
I will make your name
great,
and you will be a
blessing.
I will bless those who
bless you,
and whoever curses
you I will curse;
and all peoples on
earth
will be blessed
through you."'

God chooses a people:
Genesis 12:1–3

Judaism is the oldest of the world's three great monotheistic religions and is the parent both of Christianity and Islam. At the heart of Judaism is the belief that there is only one God, who is the creator and ruler of the whole world. He is transcendent and eternal. He sees everything and knows everything. He has revealed his Law (*Torah*) to the Jewish people and chosen them to be a light or example to all mankind.

The people

The choice of the Jewish people by God began when their ancestor Abraham migrated from Ur of the Chaldees to Canaan. According to the biblical narrative, God appeared to Abraham and said, 'Go from your country ... to the land that I will show you. And I will make of you a great nation, and I will bless you ... and by you shall all the families of the earth be blessed.'

Several centuries later, in the account of the exodus of the people of Israel from Egypt, God is recorded as saying to the Israelites, 'You shall be my own possession among all nations. You shall be a kingdom of priests and a holy nation.'

Both these passages imply that the Jewish people were called to a special relationship with God and a special role towards their fellow men. To be the chosen people was a great privilege but it was also a great responsibility. They were to be a 'kingdom of priests' who served the only true God and they were to be a 'holy nation' who reflected the character of that God in their personal, social and national life.

Today there are about 13 million Jews in the world: 6 million in the USA, 3 million in Israel and the rest scattered throughout the world, many in Russia and Eastern Europe. Their customs, liturgy, way of life, even their pronunciation of Hebrew may vary considerably, but they are one people, united by their common ancestors, the patriarchs Abraham, Isaac and Jacob.

The land

God promised to Abraham not only to make him and his descendants a great nation but also to give them the land of Canaan 'for an everlasting possession'. This land (later known as Palestine, or Israel) has always had a prominent place in the thinking of Jewish people. Even during periods of exile their thoughts have constantly turned towards it and the holy city of Jerusalem. Centuries of persecution by Christians led Jews to realize that the only way to avoid suffering as a religious minority was to live again in their own land. Such aspirations led to the birth of Zionism and ultimately to the founding of the State of Israel.

The Law

Judaism has no formal creed but the

A thirteen-year-old Jewish boy preparing for his Bar Mitzvah ceremony, when he will become a full member of the Jewish community. He is practising reading his portion of the scriptures.

The Ten Commandments: Exodus 20:1–17

'And God spoke all these words: "I am the Lord your God, who brought you out of Egypt, out of the land of slavery. "You shall have no other gods before me. "You shall not make for yourself an idol in the form of anything in heaven above or on the earth beneath or in the waters below. You shall not bow down to them or worship them; for I, the Lord your God, am a jealous God, punishing the children for the sin of the fathers to the third and fourth generation of those who hate me, but showing love to thousands who love me and keep my commandments. "You shall not misuse the name of the Lord your God, for the Lord will not hold anyone guiltless who misuses his name. "Remember the Sabbath day by keeping it holy. Six days you shall labour and do all your work, but the seventh day is a Sabbath to the Lord your God. On it you shall not do any work, neither you, nor your son or daughter, nor your manservant or maidservant, nor your animals, nor the alien within your gates. For in six days the Lord made the heavens and the earth, the sea, and all that is in them, but

essence of the faith is found in the *Shema*, the name given to three passages of the Bible that are read every morning and evening by the devout Jew. (*Shema* is the Hebrew word for 'hear'. The *Shema* begins, 'Hear, O Israel, the Lord our God, the Lord is one, and you shall love the Lord your God with all your heart, and with all your soul, and with all your might. And these words which I command you shall be upon your heart.' The pious Jew seeks to love God with his whole being and that love is expressed in practical obedience to the law of God in everyday life. Hence 'the Law' is of paramount importance to the Jew.

This Law is found in the first five books of the Bible (the Pentateuch or *Torah*) which record the revelation of God to Moses on Mt Sinai 3,000 years ago. It contains 613 commandments covering every area of daily life from civil law to personal hygiene and diet. These instructions, summed up most succinctly in the Ten Commandments, have proved the foundation of many of the subsequent great legal codes of the world. Although many Jews no longer rigidly adhere to all the laws of the *Torah*, orthodox Jews observe them to the finest detail. They take delight in obeying the will of God and find in these practices a meaning and significance which is not apparent to the casual observer. Some have sought to he rested on the seventh day. Therefore the Lord blessed the Sabbath day and made it holy. "Honour your father and your mother, so that you may live long in the land the Lord your God is giving you. "You shall not murder. "You shall not commit adultery. "You shall not steal. "You shall not give false testimony against your neighbour. "You shall not covet your neighbour's house. You shall not covet your neighbour's wife, or his manservant or maidservant, his ox or donkey, or anything that belongs to your neighbour.'

'Hear, O Israel: The Lord our God, the Lord is one. Love the Lord your God with all your heart and with all your soul and with all your strength. These commandments that I give you today are to be upon your hearts. Impress them on your children. Talk about them when you sit at home and when you walk along the road, when you lie down and when you get up. Tie them as symbols on your hands and bind them on your foreheads. Write them on the door-frames of your houses and on your gates.'

The 'Shema':
Deuteronomy 6:4–9

adapt the regulations of the *Torah* to life in the twentieth century. Others are selective in what they choose to observe. By and large it is left to each man's conscience as to how far he carries out the commandments of the *Torah*.

The synagogue

Most Jews belong to a synagogue, though this by no means implies that they attend every week. Synagogue (a Greek word meaning 'a place of meeting') is a translation of the Hebrew *Bet Hakeneset*. The origin of the synagogue is uncertain but it may date from the time when the Jews were exiles in Babylon, after the fall of Jerusalem in 586 BC. After the return from exile they began to set up synagogues or religious teaching houses to study the *Torah*. There were many synagogues in the temple area in Jerusalem and, after the destruction of the temple in AD 70, the synagogue assumed a role of vital importance in the preservation and development of Judaism.

The most prominent feature of a synagogue is the 'ark' or cupboard set against the eastern wall and facing towards Jerusalem. The ark contains the scrolls of the Law, written in Hebrew on parchment. These are covered in velvet, silk or brocade and carry ornaments of bells, a crown and a 'breastplate' of precious metal. Immediately in front of the ark is a lamp that is kept burning perpetually. In the centre of the synagogue is a platform or pulpit from which the service is conducted and the Law is read. The service follows the order set out in the *Siddur*, the Hebrew prayer-book. Worshippers usually cover their heads in the synagogue as a sign of reverence. In orthodox synagogues men and women sit separately.

Every Saturday during the morning service the ark is ceremonially opened and the scroll of the Law is lifted high and carried in procession around the synagogue. Several portions of the scroll are read in Hebrew using ancient Jewish modes. Members of the congregation are called up to recite the traditional blessing before and after each reading. When

the reading is complete, the scroll is again carried round the synagogue before being returned to the ark. Members of the congregation may touch the scroll with the fringes of their prayer-shawl (Hebrew *tallit*) and then kiss the fringes as an act of devotion and reverence to the word of God.

The service is led by a cantor (*chazzan*) rather than by a rabbi. The duties of a rabbi are to instruct the congregation in the faith and to make decisions concerning Jewish legal questions. He is entitled to be called 'rabbi' only after reaching a high standard of studies in Jewish Law.

The festivals

New Year

The Jewish religious year includes a number of festivals and days of fasting. The first of these is New Year's Day (*Rosh Hashanah*, 'head of the year') and it occurs in September or October. This festival speaks both of God's creation of the world and of his judgement of the world. The Hebrew prayer-book states, 'This is the day that the world was called into existence. This day He causeth all creatures to stand in judgement.' A ram's horn (*shophar*) is blown in the synagogue to remind people to return to God, and the next ten days are set aside for self-examination and repentance. It is customary to eat apple dipped in honey and to wish others 'a good and sweet year'.

Atonement

The Day of Atonement (*Yom Kippur*) is considered the holiest day in the Jewish religious year. It comes as the conclusion to the period of penitence that began on New Year's Day. The day is characterized by prayer, fasting and the public confession of sin. Traditionally this was the day when the high priest made sacrifice for the sins of the people of Israel and entered the 'holy of holies' in the temple (earlier, in the tabernacle). Today there is no temple and no sacrifice is offered, but atonement is sought through repentance. The devout worshipper fasts for twenty-four hours, spends all day in the

The Festivals of Judaism

**ROSH HASHANAH/
NEW YEAR/
TRUMPETS**
A time of reckoning with
God.

**YOM KIPPUR/THE
DAY OF ATONEMENT**
The most holy day in the
Jewish year.

**SUKKOT/
TABERNACLES**
A joyful harvest festival,
giving thanks for God's
goodness, and his care
for the Hebrews on their
forty-year journey from
Egypt to the land of Israel.

**SIMCHAT TORAH/
REJOICING IN THE
LAW**
Joyful celebration, giving
thanks for the Law—the
first five books of the
Hebrew Bible.

HANUKKAH/LIGHTS
An eight-day festival
which commemorates
the re-dedication of the
temple in Jerusalem after
Judas Maccabeus had
expelled the occupying
Syrians in 164 BC.

Months around chart: Nisan, Sivan, Av, Tishri, Kislev, Shevat, Iyar, Tamuz, Elul, Cheshvan, Teveth, Adar

PURIM
A joyful celebration which
commemorates the
events of the book of
Esther when the Jews in
Persia were saved from
massacre.

PESACH/PASSOVER
A joyful family festival
which celebrates the
deliverance of the
Hebrews from slavery in
Egypt.

FIRSTFRUITS
The week-long Passover
festival ends with a spring
harvest-festival.

**PENTECOST/
SHAVUOT**
Another harvest festival,
celebrated seven weeks
after Passover. It also
commemorates the
giving of the Law to
Moses.

THE NINTH OF AV
A day of mourning and
fasting, commemorating
the destruction of the
temple in AD 70.

synagogue and wears a white robe as
a symbol of purity and of the grave.
At the conclusion of this day he
will consider himself to have been
spiritually reborn.

Tabernacles
Five days after the Day of Atonement
comes the Feast of Tabernacles
(*Sukkot*) which lasts for a week. This
is one of the three harvest festivals in
the Jewish year (the others are Passover and Pentecost), and as such it
has served as the model for Christian
harvest celebrations. During the festival Jewish people remember how
God provided all their needs when
they wandered for forty years in the
wilderness. They build temporary

shelters or 'tabernacles' of branches
in their gardens or next to their
synagogues. They eat their meals in
them and may even sleep in them—
though this may depend on the climate, as they are left open to the sky.

Celebrating the Law
After the Feast of Tabernacles comes
the 'Rejoicing of the Law' (*Simchat
Torah*). During the course of a year
the whole of the Law, the first five
books of the Bible, is read in the
synagogue. On this festival day the
reading is completed with the last
portion of Deuteronomy and begun
again with the first verses of Genesis.
The service is characterized by great
joy and the scrolls of the Law are

carried in procession around the synagogue with singing and dancing.

Festival of Lights

At about the time that Christians celebrate Christmas, Jews celebrate *Hanukkah*, the Festival of Lights. This commemorates the victory of Judas Maccabeus over the Syrians, and the rededication of the temple in Jerusalem in 164 BC. The festival lasts eight days and many Jewish families light an eight-branched candlestick or *menorah*. (It actually has nine candles; the additional one, called 'the servant', is used to light the others.) One candle is lit on each day of the festival until on the eighth day all are alight.

Purim

In February or March comes Purim, the festival which recalls the story of Esther. Purim means 'lots' and refers to the lots cast by Haman to choose the day on which to destroy all the Jews in the Persian Empire. In the synagogue the book of Esther is read and, whenever the name of Haman occurs, the boys present make a noise with rattles or stamp their feet. In the home Purim is a time for parties, often in fancy dress, and for eating special pastries called *Hamantaschen*.

Passover

Best-known of all Jewish festivals is Passover (*Pesach*). It coincides more or less with Christian Easter and recalls the deliverance of the people of Israel from their slavery in Egypt. A special meal or *seder* (meaning 'order') is held in the home. Traditional dishes are eaten, songs are sung and the story of the deliverance from Egypt is recounted. The youngest child asks the question, 'Why is this night different from other nights?' and that is the father's cue to relate the events of the biblical book of Exodus, as they are set out in the special order of service or *Hag-*

The fertile Jordan valley runs from Galilee in the north of Israel to the Dead Sea.

gadah. (*Haggadah* means 'showing forth' or 'telling the story'.) Traditionally a place at the table is left vacant and a glass of wine is set aside for the prophet Elijah who is expected to come as the herald of the Messianic Age.

On the eve of Passover a thorough search is made in each Jewish home to ensure that no leaven (yeast) has been left anywhere. In the place of ordinary bread, flat, unleavened bread (*matzah*) is eaten. The *matzah* serves as a reminder of the 'bread of affliction' which the Jewish slaves ate in Egypt, and hence the festival is also known as the Feast of Unleavened Bread.

Pentecost

A period of seven weeks of mourning follows Passover. This is associated with the failure of the Jewish revolt against Rome in the second century AD and the loss of many Jewish scholars at about the same time through plague. The Festival of Pentecost (from the Greek word meaning 'fiftieth') or Weeks (*Shavuot*) is celebrated fifty days after the second day of Passover and commemorates the giving of the Law by God to Moses on Mt Sinai. In the synagogue service the Ten Commandments are read and some Jews sit up all night meditating on God's Law. Pentecost is also the 'Feast of the First Fruits'. The synagogue is decorated with flowers and plants, and dairy foods are eaten.

A day of mourning

On *Tishah B'Av* (the ninth day of the Jewish month Av—roughly July/August), the Jewish people remember the destruction of the temple in AD 70 by the Romans. Some also link the same date with the destruction of the first temple by Nebuchadnezzar in 586 BC. It is a day of mourning and fasting, and all ornaments are removed from the synagogue.

The Covenant

Robert Banks

At the heart of the Jewish religion lies the existence of a covenant between God and his people. The term 'covenant' signifies an agreement made between two parties and must be distinguished from related ideas such as 'testament' and 'contract'. Unlike a testament, a covenant involves a personal response on the side of the second party to make it effective. Unlike a contract, however, it is not a mutually negotiated affair but is offered unilaterally by one side to the other.

The covenants we are concerned with are between God and man. But investigation of purely civil treaties from the adjacent Hittite culture of the fourteenth and fifteenth centuries BC has provided interesting insights. These treaties between king and people always included, amongst other things, three elements:
● a historical prologue describing the deeds of the maker of the treaty;
● a list of obligations binding the lesser of the two parties;
● a list of punishments and rewards.
The Jewish covenants generally reproduce this pattern. They are grounded in certain divinely-ordered events; they contain a set of stipulations; and they are concluded with a list of 'woes and blessings'.

God's chosen people
The first covenant referred to in the Jewish scriptures is that between God and Noah (Genesis 9:8–17). The basis for this lies in God's preservation of Noah and his family during the flood. Through Noah, a promise is made to mankind and the animal world that this disaster will never be repeated. The promise has its sign, the rainbow, which is to act as a reminder, both to God and to all living creatures, of this undertaking.

The covenant with Noah provides the basis on which the later, more specialized commitment to Israel follows. To begin with there is the covenant between God and the great patriarch of Israel, Abraham. God first promises to make Abraham the ancestor of a great nation (Genesis 12) and to give him and his descendants the land of Israel (Genesis 13). The covenant itself (Genesis 15 and 17) begins with a historical introduction, stating that God is the one who brought Abraham out from Ur of the Chaldees. It then outlines obligations about living righteously and justly, which are elaborated in later books. Circumcision becomes the sign of this covenant.

Over 600 years later, this covenant is reaffirmed and extended at Mt Sinai, with all the people who have come out of Egypt (Exodus 19–20). This covenant recalls God's historical deliverance of them from Egypt and his promise that Israel will be his special possession among all nations. There is a series of obligations in the form of the Ten Commandments, and the people's acceptance of their responsibilities is also indicated.

This covenant, therefore, is again an expression of both God's grace and his demand. Even his instructions are as much a gift as an obligation, for they show Israel how they may appropriately respond to his choice of them. And since God later maintains his side of the covenant, even when certain elements within Israel fail to obey, the fact that the covenant is based on God's grace remains transparent.

These things are nowhere clearer than in the Old Testament book of Deuteronomy. Deuteronomy is the record of Moses' farewell addresses to Israel, on the eve of their entry into the promised land. Deuteronomy 5 recounts the Sinai covenant; Deuteronomy 7 refers to the covenant with the patriarchs of Israel; and Deuteronomy 29 is a renewal of the covenant with the whole people. Throughout the book, insistence on God's continued gracious maintenance of the covenant, despite Israel's failure to fulfil its conditions, is a prominent theme.

In the later historical books a still more specialized covenant is recorded—that with David and his descendants and, associated with this, with the Levitical priesthood (1 Chronicles 17:7; 28:4). Here again there are the standard elements:
● the prologue reminds David that it was God who turned him from being a shepherd into a victorious king;
● the outlining of conditions indicates that God's blessing is not automatically guaranteed (1 Chronicles 22:11);
● the promise tells of God's commitment to establish David's descendants upon the throne for ever.

A renewed covenant
So presumptuously did the people take the covenant on which their nation was based, that the great prophets (except Hosea and Jeremiah) rarely referred to the Sinai agreement. It was only after the exile had shattered Israel's presumption that the later prophets were less reticent about the covenant (Zechariah 9:11; Malachi 2:4). The later historical writings also speak of significant covenant renewals (Ezra 9; Nehemiah 9).

Most significant in a number of these writings is the promise of a new covenant to replace the broken one for which Israel had been punished (see, for example, Jeremiah 31; Ezekiel 16). The decisive difference between the two is that the new covenant will have its obligations inscribed on the wills of the people rather than existing merely as external obligations which the people must seek to observe. When this happens, Israel will receive back all that they have lost and more.

In the post-biblical writings, further changes in the understanding of the covenant take place. The idea of a new covenant either drops away altogether, or becomes simply a reiteration of the old one (Baruch 2:30).

In the apocryphal writings the word for covenant refers, much more frequently than before, just to the obligations within it. This pushes the Law into a more prominent position and the covenant into more of a contract. Meanwhile the covenant with the Fathers comes to be regarded as an irrevocable one, leading to the use of the term for the Jewish nation itself (Judith 9:13).

The apocalyptic writings preserve the same emphasis and the term for covenant is used more often than previously also for its sign, circumcision (Jubilees 15:13–14). The Law is now said to precede the covenant, moving into a position of greater prominence (Ecclesiasticus 24:6; 44:19).

The Qumran and rabbinic writings maintain this perspective. The former do take up the idea of the new covenant made with its community, but this is basically just a reaffirmation of the old covenant. The rabbinic writings occasionally suggest that God's covenant with Israel rests upon their obedience rather than his free choice.

A modern sculpture of the seven-branched candlestick which stood in the temple.

Story of a Nation

Geoffrey Cowling

A religion continually develops over ages of time. Whatever historical point we look at, religion always has links with the past. Rabbinic Judaism sees itself today as a direct development from the time of Moses, the giver of the *Torah*, over 3,000 years ago.

To understand the developing beliefs and practices, we need to know something of the social and political events which affected the Jewish communities. We also need to observe the ideas of their neighbours, to see the influences of the cultures with which they came into contact. Greek thought, Christianity, Islam, medieval philosophy, charismatic movements—all have affected the intellectual activity and popular customs of Judaism.

The Exile and after: 539–333 BC

The story of Judaism begins in the late sixth century BC (or, in Jewish terms, BCE, 'Before the Christian Era'). In the years 539–333 BC, the Persian Empire was dominant. And it was in this period that Judaism consolidated as a religion based on the Bible.

In 586 BC, Jerusalem was destroyed by Nebuchadnezzar II and the people taken captive to Babylon.

In July 539 the army of Cyrus II ('the Great') of Persia, commanded by Gubaru, in turn captured Babylon. Cyrus thus gained nominal control of the whole Babylonian Empire. Fourteen years later Egypt was captured by Cyrus' successor. Cyrus permitted the Jews to return from exile and to rebuild their temple in Jerusalem.

In both Babylon and Egypt there were communities of people who still considered themselves Judeans. These communities consisted largely of mercenary soldiers or prisoners of war and their families. The Judeans were agents of the ruling power, and privileged for that reason. In Egypt this caused much resentment, and the Judeans remained separate, following the religion (which was *not* strictly biblical) and customs they brought with them. In Babylon, biblical religion appears to have been dominant among the Judeans, though we know very little about their life there.

As soon as Cyrus made it possible, the priests returned to Jerusalem and the city was established as a temple community, led by the priests. There was a strict separation between Judean (Jew) and non-Judean in Judah which, the Bible records, was enforced by Ezra and Nehemiah. This separation was marked by circumcision, observance of the Sabbath, the Sabbatical year, recognition of the Law (*Torah*) of Moses and obligations to the temple in Jerusalem. The rigorists also required that marriage arrangements should be made only between Judeans.

The temple and the synagogue

The Judeans believed that there must be only one temple. The temple was the only place where the Jewish religious sacrifices could be carried out. And this belief, enforced by Persian authority, had far-reaching consequences. When all Judeans lived in Judah, it was possible for them all to make the pilgrimage to Jerusalem. When Judeans lived abroad this was out of the question—though the Jews of the Dispersion made great efforts to visit Jerusalem in obedience to the *Torah*. The priestly regulations in the *Torah* became a dead letter, and a new form of religion had to emerge for the ordinary Jew. This form culminated in the setting up of 'synagogues', where prayer, singing, reading, discussion and teaching (but not sacrifice) took place.

In the temple at Jerusalem the old religion continued. And here

'I was glad when they said to me,
"Let us go to the house of the Lord!"
Our feet have been standing
within your gates, O Jerusalem!
Jerusalem, built as a city
which is bound firmly together,
to which the tribes go up,
the tribes of the Lord,
as was decreed for Israel,
to give thanks to the name of the Lord.
There thrones for judgment were set,
the thrones of the house of David.
Pray for the peace of Jerusalem!
"May they prosper who love you!
Peace be within your walls,
and security within your towers!"
For my brethren and companions' sake
I will say, "Peace be within you!"
For the sake of the house of the Lord our God,
I will seek your good.'

Psalm 122

'By the rivers of Babylon we sat and wept
when we remembered Zion.
There on the poplars we hung our harps,
for there our captors asked us for songs,
our tormentors demanded songs of joy;
they said, 'Sing us one of the songs of Zion!'
How can we sing the songs of the Lord
while in a foreign land?
If I forget you, O Jerusalem,
may my right hand forget its skill.
May my tongue cling to the roof of my mouth
if I do not remember you,
if I do not consider Jerusalem
my highest joy.'

Psalm 137:1–6

the procedure was governed by written regulations, by a book. The book began to create its own ambience over and against—even in opposition to—the rituals of the priests.

Some time in this period the first scribes appear. Their home is the synagogue. Their job is to understand the *Torah* and to interpret its rules for the contemporary situation. They are also the bearers of tradition and of conduct. With hindsight, we can see how this 'guild of scholars' evolved into the rabbis of rabbinic Judaism. But at this time they were only one strand among many in Judaism.

The Hellenistic kingdoms: 333–63 BC

The victory of Alexander the Great at Issus in 333 BC began a new era, an era of much greater prosperity. Cities, founded on the Greek pattern, began to grow rapidly in size. In Egypt, Alexandria became the leading city within a few years of its foundation. The Judean community there was substantial, and Greek, instead of Aramaic, became their language. Government by democratic rule by a small nucleus of citizens (who were, or considered themselves to be, Greek) brought new political ideas to the East. The Greek language rapidly spread. People even tried to look Greek.

After the death of Alexander, his empire broke up into smaller units. The principal kingdoms were Macedonia (Greece), Egypt (ruled by the Ptolemies), and the Seleucid kingdom. (Seleucid kings did not rule Phoenicia or Judea at the beginning.) In the third century BC, the Parthian Empire rose to power. The Seleucid kingdom was gradually reduced to the Syrian region only and Babylon came under Parthian control. The Jews in Babylon became somewhat cut off from all other Jewish communities. Aramaic remained the language of Babylonia—so a barrier of speech was added to the barrier of politics.

These communities inevitably developed differently. But they were still united through having a common Bible, and also through their emphasis on Jerusalem, and the temple in particular. The priests were still undisputed leaders. The high priest was the glory of the city, powerful both politically and economically.

Tension and revolt

In 191–190 Antiochus III of Syria was defeated by the Romans, who were now turning their eyes toward the East. Prisoners of war from these battles were probably the founders of the Jewish community in Rome. Jews also settled in Antioch in Syria, and in Asia Minor (modern Turkey). The Romans

Moses

Geoffrey Cowling

Moses is central to rabbinic Judaism. In that tradition he is founder and Law-giver. He is the first and greatest of all the prophets. Through him came the instruction, the *Torah*, for all Israel, the Jewish people, and any laws are binding only if they are *halakat Moshe mi-Sinai*, 'a Mosaic rule of conduct from Sinai'. Not only is the written *Torah* the work of Moses, but the oral Law was also given to him on Sinai and passed down by word of mouth until written down in the *Mishnah*, *Tosefta* and *Baraithoth*, the

collections of the traditions and the discussions of the rabbis which aim to determine what is the *halakhah* or rule of conduct.

Nothing outside the Bible adds anything of historical value to the picture of Moses. The Bible describes him as a man born in Egypt to exiled slaves belonging to the tribe of Levi. He was educated in the Egyptian court, met with God in the desert and became leader of the 'children of Israel'. Ten miraculous plagues enabled him to lead the people out of Egypt, further miracles protected them from Egyptian pursuit and sustained them in the desert. At Mt Sinai God revealed himself again to Moses, made a covenant with the people and laid

down the pattern of their behaviour. Moses himself did not cross into Canaan, the land that God had promised to his people.

Today there is renewed debate about when Moses actually lived. Despite this uncertainty, a date round about the beginning of the Iron Age (1200 BC) is probably close.

Ezra

Geoffrey Cowling

In rabbinic Judaism, only Ezra can be compared with Moses. 'If Moses had not anticipated him, Ezra would have received the Torah' (*Tosefta Sanhedrin* 4:7). Authoritative traditions which are not traced back to Moses are traced back to Ezra.

The Bible appears to suggest that Ezra, a priest and scribe from Babylon, was an agent of the Persian government in establishing the *Torah* as the national law for Judeans in Judah and Syria. He was either a contemporary of Nehemiah's in the mid-fifth century BC, or lived a century later. His exact task and achievement are not at all clear, as he is

not credited with exercising any political authority. He is credited with extreme views on purity of genealogy, asserting that all 'foreign' wives were to be divorced. Ezra is ignored in early apocryphal books like Ecclesiasticus and 1 Maccabees.

In rabbinic tradition Ezra is seen as the founder and first leader of the legendary 'Great Synagogue'. This body (which appears to be thought of as an early Sanhedrin) was supposed to have continued until the time of Simon the Just.

Ezra was important to other groups in Judaism apart from the rabbinic circles. In 2 Esdras, an

apocryphal book probably written about AD 100 whose text is found only in Latin, Ezra finds the *Torah* burnt. Under divine inspiration he dictates ninety-four books—twenty-four of the Old Testament and seventy 'secret' books—no doubt including 2 Esdras.

'Ezra was a scholar with a thorough knowledge of the Law which the Lord, the God of Israel, had given to Moses. Because Ezra had the blessing of the Lord his God, the emperor gave him everything he asked for. In the seventh year of the reign of Artaxerxes, Ezra set out from Babylonia for Jerusalem with a group of Israelites which included priests, Levites, temple musicians, temple guards, and workmen. They left

Babylonia on the first day of the first month, and with God's help they arrived in Jerusalem on the first day of the fifth month. Ezra had devoted his life to studying the Law of the Lord, to practising it, and to teaching all its laws and regulations to the people of Israel.'

Ezra 7:6–10

imposed tribute on Antiochus. This meant increased taxes. It seems that tension between rich and poor in Jerusalem and Judah became extreme at this time. This factor, added to political and cultural differences (those for and against the Greek way of life) made for an explosive situation.

The explosion came in the reign of Antiochus IV. When the Jews resisted his nominee for the high priesthood, he sent troops to sack Jerusalem. He established pagan practices in the temple and attacked the Jewish religion. Some Jews gave in. But those who loved the Law, especially the Hasidim ('The Pious') endured great suffering. Eventually there was full-scale revolt, led by the family of the Hasmoneans.

In 165 BC Judas Maccabeus won peace with the Syrians, marched into Jerusalem, and the desecrated temple was solemnly cleansed. (The victory is still celebrated today in the Festival of Lights or *Hanukkah*.)

The Maccabee family began a line of rulers—the Hasmonean dynasty. Ironically the Hasmoneans became typical Hellenistic despots. But they won a real measure of freedom for the Jewish realm before the Romans, under Pompey, annexed Judea in 63 BC.

Under the Roman Empire: 63 BC–AD 200

Judea was now a vassal of Rome. The current Hasmonean king was confirmed as the nation's leader and high priest, but the Romans would not recognize him as king. Successive Roman governors kept a firm hold on Judea.

In 40 BC, following a Parthian invasion of Syria and Judea, the Roman Senate gave Herod the title 'king of the Jews'. Although Herod's personal life was disastrous, the country prospered under his rule. Herod is remembered as a builder—of cities (Sebaste, Caesarea), of fortresses (Masada, Herodium), of palaces, theatres and amphitheatres, of the temple in Jerusalem and pagan temples abroad. Those who opposed Rome and the Greek way of life hated him.

During the Roman period the Jewish hope of a Messiah (a king of David's line, for some a priest-king) came to the fore. He would rescue his people from the Romans and restore the Judean state.

There were several revolts in Judea during the time of Herod and his successors, and many 'prophets' drew large followings. The most serious threat to the

Jews came in the time of the Emperor Caligula (AD 37–41). He demanded that all his subjects worship him, and ordered a statue of himself (as Zeus) to be placed in the temple.

The temple is destroyed

Judea became more and more unsettled. Conflict between Greeks and Jews was constant in the coastal cities. Conflict between the Roman governors and the people increased. Finally in AD 66 the Jews rose in a general revolt against Rome. Initial success was followed by crushing defeat. Jerusalem was taken and the temple destroyed in AD 70.

The destruction of the temple was decisive for the future of Judaism. The temple and the high priesthood and the council (Sanhedrin) were finished. No longer could Jerusalem, as centre of pilgrimage, be the unifying force within Judaism. Jewish communities were now simply descent groups within larger communities. Although they remained distinct, they were inevitably affected by the culture of the city or nation in which they found themselves. Unless something took the place of the temple, the scattered com-

The world-wide distribution of Jews

Some cities with Jewish population of over 50,000 in 1980.

(Zionist Yearbook)

munities would grow apart.

It was a seemingly insignificant event which provided the new direction for Judaism. Jochanan ben Zakkai founded a school at Jamnia. The Romans made no objection because this act had no political implications. At this school the mode of address 'rabbi' ('master') became a formal title. The teachers in the school were 'rabbis'. Jochanan may not have been a Pharisee, but his successor, Gamaliel (?grandson of Hillel) was. The ethos of the school was essentially Pharisaical: and this gave the tone to emerging rabbinic Judaism.

This school at Jamnia came to exercise the function of a council, and even to adopt the name 'Sanhedrin'. Jochanan fixed the calendar for the Jews abroad, once the prerogative of the high priest. Jews began to look to this council for advice and judgements. The extent of the influence of the council is impossible to determine. As happens so often, the writings which came from the council were even more influential than the council itself. The rabbis of this early period are known as *Tanna* (plural *Tannaim*: 'teachers'). Their earliest surviving works are the 'sayings' in the *Pirkay Avot* and the second-century commentaries, or the laws, written in Hebrew.

Most other varieties of Judaism died out gradually. Jewish Christianity survived into the second century AD, even though the rabbis tried hard to exclude Jewish Christians from the synagogues after about AD 90. In the Greek world Christians broke entirely with Judaism, all too often becoming anti-Jewish.

Persecution continues
Jewish revolts were widespread and they were brutally put down.

In AD 70 the Romans sacked Jerusalem, taking the temple treasures to Rome.

The Judean revolt of 132 may have been sparked off by the establishment of the new Roman city of Aelia Capitolina on the ruins of Jerusalem. (The Old City of present-day Jerusalem is the linear descendant of this Roman town.) This revolt was led by Simeon ben Koseba, who claimed to be the Messiah, and he was supported by the greatest rabbinic scholar of the day, Rabbi Akiba, then an old man. The attempt was hopeless. Though considerable casualties were inflicted on the Romans, this only made the final defeat more disastrous.

The governors of Palestine (the name the Romans now gave the country) were now Romans of a much higher rank. Aelia Capitolina was completed and Jews were forbidden to enter the city. Galilee now became a centre of Jewish life and various towns successively became the seat of the council.

Judaism was not banned, but since the circumcision of converts was forbidden, conversion was made difficult, if not impossible. Many Jews in Palestine still hoped for a Parthian invasion to free them from the Romans.

Simeon II, son of Gamaliel II, became 'patriarch' of the Jews with—at least in theory—authority over the Jews of the Roman world. Simeon's son, Judah I ('the prince') appears to have exercised considerable political power. He appears to have been a considerable scholar, and in his time the *Mishnah* was codified and published.

The patriarchate declined in power after this, but rabbinic discussion continued in Palestine, Babylon and Rome.

In Babylon (from 223 BC a part of the Persian Empire), the recognized rulers of the Jews were the 'exilarchs' or princes of the captivity. They enjoyed a status perhaps higher even than that of Judah I and certainly much greater than that of their contemporaries in Galilee.

Israel and abroad: AD 200–640
Within the land of Israel the patriarch was almost always a descendant of Hillel. The patriarchate was abolished by the Romans in 429, but the council, the Sanhedrin, continued until 640.

The conversion of Constantine to Christianity in 313 was not auspicious for Jews. Although Judaism was never made illegal, it became very difficult to be a Jew. Many, perhaps most, Christian leaders, writers, monks and bishops hated the Jews.

In Egypt, the Jewish communities began to recover, though numbers were never the same as they had been in earlier centuries. Greek culture was on the wane, and with it Hellenistic Judaism. Relations between Jews and the Persian authorities became less amicable from the fifth century onward. The Jews there were thus ready to welcome the Arab conquerors. Similarly, in Palestine, the harshness of the Byzantine rule caused the Jews to look for redemption abroad. They aided the invading Persian forces in 614, but in 617 uprisings among the Jerusalem Jews were subdued by military force. The Byzantine army re-entered Jerusalem and the Jews were once more expelled from the city.

The age of the Gaons: 634–1096
The Muslim conquests were spectacular. In 634 the Byzantine army was defeated. Syria and Palestine were conquered. Persia fell in 637. Egypt followed soon after. Spain was invaded in 711, and an independent Muslim state was set up there around 750. The armies reached France, but were driven back to the Pyrenees.

Within 100 years, many Jews came under Muslim rule. The general conditions of life for most improved considerably. The Jews shared in the great intellec-

tual ferment of the Arab world. Great advances were made in mathematics, astronomy, philosophy, chemistry and philology. Some Jews in the enlightened Spanish area rose to influential positions in the courts of the rulers. The tenth and eleventh centuries in Spain were especially a 'Golden Age' of literary achievement. The type of Judaism known as 'Sephardic' developed in Spain with its own synagogue rituals and its own Spanish-Jewish dialect, Ladino.

The rite of the other Jews in Europe, especially in Germany, is known as the 'Ashkenazi', with its own language—the German-Jewish dialect, Yiddish.

In Christian France the Jews were relatively well-treated in the

The home is the most important religious centre for a Jewish family. Each Friday evening, at the start of the Sabbath, the wife prepares the Sabbath lights before the meal together.

ninth century. But from then on, hatred of the Jews and riots became common. The crusading armies marched to 'The Holy Land', looting and slaughtering the Jews in particular as they went. The capture of Jerusalem, hailed throughout the Christian world as a great triumph, merely meant death to the Jews there—burnt in the synagogues. Life in Christian Europe became harsh for Jews.

The Jews saw these deaths as martyrdom, the ultimate form of witness, or 'sanctification of the Name' (*kiddush ha Shem*). Some committed suicide rather than renounce their faith. It became clear that the authorities, even when sympathetic, were helpless before the Christian mob. The rules of conduct (*halakhah*) stated plainly that while laws could be broken when life was at stake, there were times when death must be preferred, to avoid the guilt of idolatry, incest or murder, or to 'sanctify the Name'.

The influence of Babylon

In Babylon, the authority of the exilarch continued under the Muslims. At this time the authority and importance of the heads of the Babylonian academies (the Gaons) grew immensely. It was these men who ensured that the Babylonian *Talmud* was accepted throughout the world. A gaonate was established in Palestine in the ninth century which was recognized as authoritative by Jews in Spain, Egypt and Italy. Under the Gaons collections of Talmudic laws were made, synagogue poetry was written, prayer-books were drawn up, the text of the Bible was fixed and annotated. Most influential of all the work of the Gaons were their *Responsa*: questions on matters of practice were sent to the Gaon, these were debated in the academies and an answer was sent out in the name of the Gaon.

There were variants from rabbinic Judaism. In the eighth century Anan ben David, and the Karaites of the tenth century, rejected the *Talmud* and all forms of oral law, taking their stand on the Bible only. The Karaites seemed likely to divide the Jewish world, but their movement soon became merely a sect. It still survives today (like the Samaritans), but in small numbers (perhaps 5,000 in the USSR, 7,000 in Israel and 1,000 or so in Egypt).

The Western teachers: 1096–1348

From the middle of the eleventh century scholars in the schools of the West became more significant than the Gaons. One French scholar is outstanding. Rabbi Solomon ben Isaac (known, from his initials, as Rashi) produced standard commentaries on the Bible and *Talmud*. His commentary on the Bible was used by Nicholas de Lyra, whom Luther often consulted, and his interpretations were frequently adopted in the translation of the Authorized King James Version of the Bible. Rashi's commentary and the additions of his successors are printed in the *Talmud* today.

Rabbi Moshe ben Maimon (see article on *Developments in Judaism*) in his *Mishneh Torah* presented a code containing all the *halakhah*, all the rules and laws that ever applied to Judaism. Other scholars applied themselves to this task after him: mostly Sephardim (after the expulsion from Spain).

Massacres in Europe

In this period Jewish communities continued to be founded in new areas and communities which had been decimated by massacres were re-established. Jews entered England in the eleventh century, but were expelled in 1290, not to return until after 1650. A new round of massacres began in the late thirteenth century. The Jewish com-

The God Who Speaks

Robert Banks

For the Jewish prophets, one of the most distinctive characteristics of their God, in comparison with the idols of the surrounding nations, was that he was the God who speaks. Moreover, in contrast to the pagan gods, he is the God who acts. In fact, these two belong inseparably together. It is precisely through his speaking or in fulfilment of his speaking, and as subsequently confirmed or interpreted by his teaching, that things happen.

This is already clear at the beginning of the biblical accounts. It is as a result of God's spoken command that the created order comes into being. And only as this is sustained by his words does it continue in existence. At the commencement of his historical purposes for Israel this same pattern is repeated. First, there is his spoken instruction to Abraham to leave the security of his homeland, then the promise made to him and his descendants. In the same way, the liberation of the Israelites from Egypt starts with God's confrontation with Moses at Horeb and finally takes place at his command. The preservation of the nation, in spite of its later defection from God, and the ultimate promise of a new covenant is also effected through his word.

Indeed, at every step of God's purpose for Israel, the sovereign power of God's word is present. Always it accomplishes what it says will happen. This word is frequently associated with, even at times described as, God's spirit or breath, and equated with his thoughts and purposes.

Prophets, priests and wise men

God spoke through people. And these fall into three main groups. Of first importance are the prophets, among whom Moses takes pride of place. The prophets proclaim and recall God's basic promises and commands to Israel, but their primary task is to deliver his contemporary word to the people, a word which sometimes includes predictions of what the future holds. They become so identified with their message that on occasions they address their audiences in first-person terms as if God himself were directly present.

One of the chief tasks of the priests within Israel was to teach what God had already revealed. They not only instructed people in what the covenant required of them but also recounted the history of God's promises and deeds which underlay these obligations. The application of past demands to present circumstances was also part of their work, with new legal decisions sometimes resulting. Occasionally they also received a direct word from the Lord.

The third group within Israel responsible for making known God's will comprised the wise men. Unlike the prophets and priests, they drew their instruction neither from God-given insight into his present purposes nor God-given deduction from his past manifestations. Their concern was with the understanding of God, man and the world drawn from human experience and observation. Indeed, their instructions and advice have a relatively timeless quality. They do not refer to God's historical covenant with Israel, or to the Mosaic Law. This does not mean that they are any less authoritative than their prophetic and priestly counterparts, for the covenant and the Law clearly provide the broader framework for their instruction.

Alongside prophet, priest and wise man, God also makes himself known through individual people's responses to their message, as, for example, in the Psalms.

The post-biblical writers continued to claim God's authority for their words. For example, the apocalyptic writings mention a prophetic concern for determining God's will in the present, though this is modified by their practice of casting such messages into the mouths of earlier figures and the fact that the chief emphasis is always upon future events. The apocryphal books display a less dynamic approach to God's law. The later wisdom literature, however, actually strengthens the authority of the wise man's instruction.

'In the beginning God created the heavens and the earth. Now the earth was formless and empty, darkness was over the surface of the deep, and the Spirit of God was hovering over the waters. And God said, 'Let there be light,' and there was light. God saw that the light was good, and he separated the light from the darkness. God called the light 'day' and the darkness he called 'night'. And there was evening, and there was morning— the first day.'

The opening words of the Bible: Genesis 1:1–5

munities in southern Italy were almost wiped out between 1290 and 1293 and many forced conversions were made. Jews were expelled from France in 1306 and further massacres occurred in 1348. The great achievements of Jews in medieval France came to an end. Jews were falsely accused of poisoning wells and causing the Black Death which killed off a third of the population of Europe in 1348. From Spain to Poland Jews were massacred.

At this time two ghastly lies were current: the so-called 'blood libel' and the 'libel of desecration of the host'. The blood libel, which claims that Jews are guilty of ritual murder, using the blood of Christian children during Passover is, alas, still perpetuated.

The Golden Age of Spain had come to an end in this period. In the twelfth century Christians tried to recapture Spain from the Muslims. In response, fanatical Muslim tribes, 'Almohades', from North Africa poured into Spain. These Muslims did not show the usual tolerance towards Jews and drove them northwards. Christian leaders welcomed these Jews at first, but their tolerance did not last long.

Jewish influence: 1348–1517

When massacres, the expulsions and the plague had ceased, the Jews were allowed to return to their cities. With other means of livelihood closed to them many Jews became moneylenders. Now the rulers needed their expertise; the new economy demanded their help.

In Christian Spain attacks on Jews reached a peak in 1391. Many Jews professed conversion, and were known by the insulting name of *Marranos* (swine). Jews left Spain in large numbers. In 1492 Jews were offered the choice of converting or leaving. Many converted, but thousands fled.

Wherever they went, in Europe and beyond, from Amsterdam to Safed in Galilee, the exiles had an enormous impact.

Europe in ferment: 1517–1700

In the sixteenth and seventeenth centuries, the Muslim Ottoman (Turkish) Empire was in the ascendancy. The Ottomans captured Palestine in 1515, Egypt in 1517, and expanded into Europe until they were halted in Vienna in 1683. During these centuries, the greatest number of Jews lived in countries of the Ottoman Empire, or else in Christian Poland—Lithuania.

Christian Europe was also in ferment. The Protestant Reformation on the whole favoured Jews, though Luther's personal attitude changed over the years from tolerance and defence to

For 2,500 years the focus of Judaism has been the study of the Law.

Torah and Mishnah

Robert Banks

The distinctive message of Judaism is that God reveals himself to his people. And the most common term for God's revelation and for the holy scriptures is *Torah*. *Torah* was also the most important term for the Law in the Jewish scriptures. The earliest codification of the leading interpretation of that Law took place in the *Mishnah*.

God's instruction

The primary meaning of the word *torah* is 'divine instruction' and its chief purpose was the practical guidance of God's people in their everyday life. This first came to clear expression in the instructions contained in the covenant at Sinai. These instructions have the character of a prophetic revelation of God's will rather than a legal code. They are grounded in the historic evidence of God; his choice of, and promises to, Abraham, and his freeing of Abraham's descendants and covenant with them. The instructions also have the character of a gift, as well as an obligation, for they reveal to the people how to respond to God's actions on their behalf. Yet they are also linked with the danger of judgement if disobedience occurs.

The instructions given at Sinai arose out of a definite historical situation and they were later reinterpreted (Deuteronomy 12), extended (Deuteronomy 20) and crystallized (Deuteronomy 6) in the face of new situations. They consist chiefly of a list of basic prohibitions which mark out the broad limits within which life is to be lived and a manageable number of more specific rulings which nevertheless leave large areas of life comparatively unregulated—personal and social relations, civil and political responsibilities, individual and family worship. But the Law does deal both with inner attitudes and with outward activities, for God desires to see the whole man and the whole of Israel's life conformed to his wishes.

The written Law

Writing down the Law began quite early in Israel's history, at the time of the exodus from Egypt, but a more comprehensive setting down of its contents took place later at the hands of the priests. Their writings display an increasing interest in extending the Law into new areas and emphasizing the ritual commandments, but the essentially non-legalistic and basically moral emphasis of the Law is always preserved.

The writings of the prophets continue to reveal the *Torah*. They continually appeal to Israel's historical beginnings but combine this with an insistent stress upon certain fundamental moral principles. They endorse the centrality of the Mosaic Law, but it is these underlying requirements such as 'righteousnesss' and 'justice' which really lie at the core of their message, and are indeed referred to as *torah* alongside the Mosaic Law.

The more general moral and prudential advice in the wisdom literature is also described as *torah*. There is no specific reference in these writings to the Mosaic Law, or to the covenant with Israel, but these undoubtedly form the base on which their instruction is built.

Torah is also used to describe the teaching of the priests, prophets and wise men. And this wide usage is a significant step on the way to its later application to the whole of scripture.

In the writings of the post-biblical period, *torah* is looked at differently. The apocryphal Jewish writings begin to talk about the Mosaic Law in more unhistorical terms. The apocalyptic books speak of it as an eternal affair which existed before God chose and made his covenant with Israel. In the wisdom literature of this period, the Mosaic Law is referred to more frequently, indeed 'Wisdom' is often bluntly equated with it. In all these writings, more stress is laid upon ritual regulations which are exclusive to the Jews. At the same time, Greek ethical ideals also begin to come in. In these two ways a more legalistic and/or humanistic note enters into Jewish thinking about the Law.

In the Dead Sea Scrolls the same characteristics can be seen but they still insist strongly on God's grace as the basis of the Law, on the need for inner as well as external obedience, and on broader ethical and social responsibilities. The teaching of the Pharisees is similar, though within it there is a more noticeable stress upon human achievement and on the development of a more extensive oral law equal in authority with the written *Torah*. This development enabled the Pharisees to get to grips with contemporary needs in a more relevant way than other Jewish parties such as the conservative Sadducees.

Studying the Law

It was at about this time that all parts of the Jewish scriptures came to be known collectively as *Torah*—in recognition that all of it is filled with God's instructions for his people. But the Pentateuch still holds the pre-eminent place.

And at this time, too, the first collections of the oral *Torah* were made. This codification, the *Mishnah*, took in leading opinions of the scribes and rabbis on matters of law. It was drawn from four centuries of *Torah* interpretation and was characterized chiefly by teaching arising from one of the schools of Pharisaism, that of Hillel. The editor of the *Mishnah* was Rabbi Judah the Prince. The *Mishnah* has sixty-three tractates, grouped according to six main divisions: laws dealing with agriculture, statutory feasts, the place of women, property and legal affairs, the temple and its accoutrements, and uncleanness. In Jewish eyes, the Talmud ranks second only to the scriptures in authority. Its contents show how dominant the Law was in post-biblical Judaism, and its increasing legalism.

The Talmud is made up of the *Mishnah* and a commentary on it called the *Gemara*. This *Gemara* is a combination of discussions on the *Mishnah* ranging over the next five or six centuries. The standard edition of the Talmud today runs to nineteen volumes and contains both the *Mishnah* and *Gemara*, together with later and other Rabbinic commentaries on these works.

Clearly this was a most unwieldy source of day-to-day guidance—particularly because the Talmud was more a record of discussion than a series of rulings. So Rabbi Joseph Karo in the sixteenth century compiled a book entitled the *Shulhan Aruch* (a Laid Table) which set out in four fairly straightforward sections the basic guidelines for a Jew's day-to-day life.

For the Jew today, the Talmud is the scholarly work and the *Shulhan Aruch* the popular source of a Jewish lifestyle in accordance with God's will.

Jews living in Frankfurt were attacked by a mob in the summer of 1614—just one example of centuries of persecution.

rabid anti-Jewish fulminations. Anti-Jewish riots continued to occur, but the authorities tended to protect the Jews, who were seen as useful. The massacres of 1648 and 1649 came as a severe blow to the Jews in the Ukraine and Poland. The Jewish writers claim that all those 'who could not flee were slain and were martyred with unnaturally cruel and bitter deaths'.

Looking more closely we see that these massacres were more than just a matter of ignorant peasant superstition. The Jewish leaders were seen to be on the side of the Polish overlords of the Ukraine, both economically and politically. It is the tragedy of history that Jews have often had the skills most appreciated by a ruling class. They have also often been forced into such occupations as money-lending, and therefore greatly resented by the lower classes.

In Italy severe penalties were inflicted on the Jews. In the Ottoman Empire conditions were generally better, but they were subject to the arbitrary and capricious actions of the rulers.

The hope of a Messiah

In the late seventeenth century a number of messianic movements arose. No doubt these were partly a product of the insecurity of Jewish life. The most important was centred on Shabbetai Zevi (1628–1716), and his prophet, Nathan of Gaza. They found acceptance and a following throughout the world.

Nathan behaved very much as a latter-day John the Baptist. He called for deep repentance, with severe ascetic practices and mortification of the body. Fasting, bathing in freezing water and constant prayer were called for and practised.

Shabbetai was imprisoned in Gallipoli in 1665–66, and in 1666 he yielded to threats and converted to Islam. Jews were devastated: 'The paradox of a traitorous Messiah is far greater than an executed Messiah', wrote Gershom Scholem. The Shabbeteans who continued to exist were viewed with deep suspicion and inevitably the general result was a great disillusionment with Messianism.

A pointer to the new times coming was Baruch Spinoza (1632–77). A great philosopher, he ceased to be a Jew without becoming a Christian—or a member of any other religion.

Enlightenment and persecution: 1700 to the present day

From the beginning of the seventeenth century, Jews gradually began to move outwards from Poland and the Ottoman Empire into the new cities of the West. There was a growing realization of the value of Jewish commercial activity and Jews began to be associated with the most developed social and economic systems. In the nineteenth century, for example, large numbers of Jews migrated to America.

Those who opposed all religion, or all revealed religion, still found Judaism a convenient target, but generally there was a growing tolerance. In the nineteenth century 'equal rights' were eventually obtained, though often with very great difficulty.

The possibility of emancipation was based on the separation of church and state. Judaism was regarded as a religion only. The Jew in England, say, or in Germany, was to be a loyal English or German citizen, differing only in religion.

The Jewish enlightenment

At the same time, there were important new directions in Judaism. The so-called Jewish enlightenment, the *haskalah*, was a humanist movement. The founder, Moses Mendelssohn (1729–86) was a practising Jew, though many of his followers were not. Mendelssohn advocated the separation of church and state, so that religious bodies should not be able to compel, only persuade. He emphasized the universal principles of religion within Judaism, and encouraged the use of German by translating the *Torah* into German. After his death the members of this movement, now led by Leopold Zunz (1794–1886), began to be more radical. They rejected the *Talmud* and traditional ideas—even the idea of revelation. Modern Jewish studies began.

The dark counterpoint to increasing tolerance was modern anti-semitism, based on spurious pseudo-biology and a belief in the 'soul' of a people. A sharp contrast was drawn between the 'Semite' nature (in practice only Jews) and the 'Aryan' or 'Slavonic' nature. The strong anti-semitic movements began in Germany and France in the 1880s.

The direct consequence of all this in 1939–40 was the 'elimination' of 6 million breathing human beings merely because they were Jewish. European Jewry almost ceased to exist. One third of all the Jews in the world were killed. The blow this dealt to security, sanity and faith is incalculable. The Holocaust, and the sorry role played by most governments and Christian leaders, is a central fact in all relations between Jews and non-Jews today.

Branches of Judaism

Marvin Wilson

The majority of Jews throughout the world today are descendants either of the Ashkenazim or the Sephardim. The Ashkenazim came from central Europe, notably Germany ('Ashkenaz' means Germany) and France, and later moved to Poland and Russia. Ashkenazic Jews developed Yiddish (medieval German) as their language. Around it they produced a rich culture in art, music and literature.

Sephardic Jews ('Sepharad' means Spain) created the language of Ladino (a vulgar Spanish). Before being driven from Spain in the Inquisition of 1492, the Sephardim became closely involved with the Muslim world. This enabled them to develop a unique intellectual culture. The wide difference in cultural background between the Ashkenazim and Sephardim is especially evident in Israel today where each supports its own chief rabbi.

Clearly the Jews are not a race. And Judaism is not an unchanging institution. Due to intermarriage, conversion, and dispersion among the nations, there has been a 'branching out' over the centuries. Wide cultural differences between Jews have resulted. The gap between the black Falasha Jews in Ethiopia and the Indian Jews in Mexico, for instance, is immense.

In addition to these cultural groupings, several religious branches can be distinguished within Judaism today. Modern Judaism is rooted in rabbinic (Talmudic) Judaism, and both evolved from biblical Judaism.

Orthodox Judaism— submission to the Law

Orthodox Judaism regards itself as the only true Judaism. During the first half of the nineteenth century it developed into a well-defined movement. It sought to preserve traditional (classical) Judaism against the emerging Reform movement in East Europe.

Orthodox Jews are characterized by a '*Torah*-true' approach to life. They teach that God personally and decisively revealed himself in giving the Law at Sinai. The words of *Torah* are therefore divine and hence fully authoritative. They are the changeless revelation of God's eternal will.

Every aspect of the orthodox Jew's life is to be governed by the commandments (*mitzvot*). Daily the Jew is to study *Torah* and conform his life obediently to its propositions and rituals, including the strict rules of Sabbath observance, dietary laws and prayer three times a day. In short, Orthodox Judaism is '*mitzvah*centric'.

The East European Jew at the start of the nineteenth century lived in a close-knit community known as a *shtetl*. In this stockaded culture he was shut off from the secular world. Toward the end of the century, however, a new orthodoxy slowly began

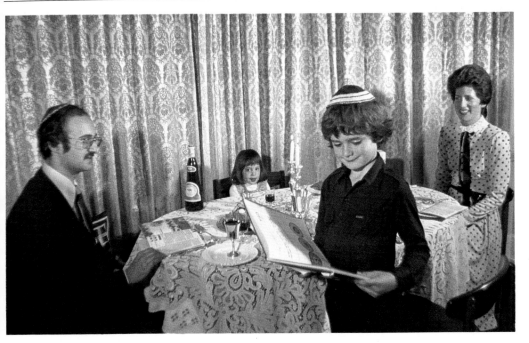

to emerge. As large numbers of Jews started to emigrate to the United States, orthodox leaders like Rabbi Samson Hirsch encouraged Jews to involve themselves in the contemporary culture of the Western world, pursue secular university education and develop philosophical minds. Today, most orthodox Jews believe that adjustment to the modern world is essential so long as it does not conflict with the teachings of *Torah*.

Orthodox Jews maintain a high regard for the rabbi as teacher and interpreter of the Law. They place a strong emphasis upon education, particularly day schools where traditional learning can be acquired. Most orthodox Jews are Zionistic and support the State of Israel. Many hope for a personal Messiah, an ideal man who will one day fully redeem Israel.

Of all the branches of Judaism, Orthodox Judaism places the greatest demands on its adherents.

Reform Judaism—response to change

Reform Judaism had its beginnings in Germany. The Enlightenment of the eighteenth century had stressed reason and progress. The Emancipation in the following century opened the Jewish people to new freedoms, to equal rights as citizens, and to new opportunities to explore secular society.

The mood of the day was geared to change and growth, scientific inquiry and critical evaluation, and Jews quickly began to adapt to this new age. To stem this tide away from Jewishness, certain changes occurred within European Judaism. Abraham Geiger (1810–74) was one of the powerful forces in this movement.

Influenced by the spirit of the age, Geiger and others taught that scientific man could no longer accept the revelation of *Torah* as factual and binding. Hence changes in ritual law and worship were encouraged. Dietary laws were abandoned. Prayers were translated from Hebrew into the vernacular. Synagogue worship changed: the organ was introduced; services were shortened; the 'family pew' replaced segregation of sexes. Some even began to worship on Sunday rather than the Sabbath.

The annual Passover meal celebrates God's deliverance of the Hebrew people from slavery in Egypt.

In the USA, dynamic leadership in the Reform movement was provided by Isaac Wise. After founding an organization of Reform congregations, in 1875 Wise established Hebrew Union College, the main seminary in the USA today for training Reform rabbis.

Reform Judaism represents the most progressive branch of modern Judaism. Liberal (Reform) Judaism is still evolving, since revelation is thought to be a continuing process. It seeks to keep current with each new generation by using reason and experience to establish the relevance or truth of a proposition. This means that the ethical teachings of the prophets are emphasized rather than the ritual Law. Reform thus provides an approach to religion which is highly individualized and non-authoritarian. A law is observed not because God said so, but because it is meaningful to modern religious experience.

Today the Reform movement remains dynamic and innovative. It has been aggressive in the area of dialogue between faiths. In the 1970s Hebrew Union College began to ordain women rabbis.

Conservative Judaism—the preservation of the people

Many European Jews were uncomfortable with the radical changes introduced by Reform Judaism. Con-

Theodore (Binyamin Ze'ev) Herzl (1860–1904)

Geoffrey Cowling

Herzl may be credited with the creation of political Zionism. He sought to secure the settlement of Jews in Palestine by political means, to win a homeland by negotiating with governments.

Herzl spent the first eighteen years of his life in Budapest. His parents then moved to Vienna, where he studied law at the university. After graduation he practised law for a short time. Then in 1884 he began writing full-time. He was a newspaper correspondent in France from October 1891 to July 1895. There he experienced the startling growth of anti-semitism which culminated in the infamous 'Dreyfus Case'. Herzl, who had once thought that assimilation—loss of peculiarly Jewish identity—was the answer to the problems of the Jews, changed his mind. He now decided they must have a state of their own. They would not be tolerated in any other country.

This conviction led him to write *Der Judenstaat* (The Jewish State). Through this he came into contact with other Zionist movements. Not all Zionists were in favour of his methods, but many gave him and his ideas their support. Particularly influential were the Hovevei Zion ('Friends of Zion', members of the Hibbat Zion movement), especially those in Eastern Europe. Herzl disagreed with their attempts to buy land in Palestine, and establish small settlements. He described this as 'infiltration'.

He tried to negotiate with the Turkish authorities to establish a Jewish state with some degree of autonomy, but part of the Turkish Empire. He also explored other possibilities—the establishment of a Jewish state in Argentina or Uganda. His support especially for the latter brought him into conflict with other members of the Zionist council, even though he declared that this was not a negation of their ultimate aim—return to Israel.

Herzl's proposal to form a united Zionist council was accepted and he chaired the first Zionist Congress in Basle in 1897. He died shortly after his efforts in April 1904 to maintain the unity of the movement.

Herzl's vision may be seen as a secularizing of Judaism's messianism. His aim was the recreation of the (biblical) state of Israel, but by political not supernatural means. There was no room for a Messiah. He kept the idea of the 'people of Israel', but without commitment to rabbinic or any other orthodox form of Judaism. The 'people' were seen as a nation without a country. Herzl was a product of the Jewish enlightenment. He accepted the nationalist movement of his time, but sought, unlike his contemporaries, to reconcile this with the continued distinctiveness of the Jews.

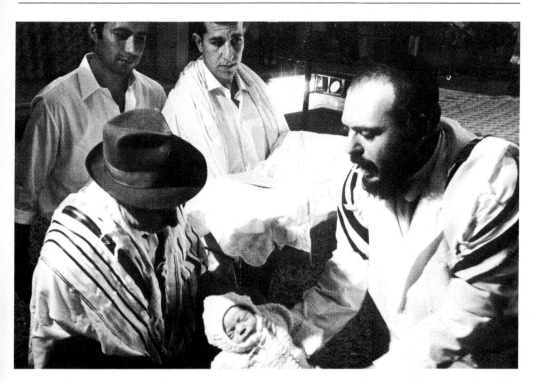

servatism arose as a new movement at the end of the nineteenth century. It sought to emphasize the positive historical elements of the Jewish tradition.

In the USA, Solomon Schechter (1850–1915) became a leading figure as president of the newly-founded Jewish Theological Seminary. He stressed the need for commitment to tradition, but with adjustment if necessary. Schechter urged that preservation of the Jewish people was the way to achieve both tradition and change. Correspondingly, Conservativism has maintained a strong emphasis on the people of Israel and modern Zionism.

Lay people have considerable influence, particularly in instituting change. Some congregations, for instance, permit the use of an organ; others reject it. Some stress keeping dietary laws; others do not.

Other branches

The Hasidim are the ultra-orthodox wing of Judaism. Living in isolation from the Gentile world, these Jews maintain a strict commitment to the Law in every phase of life. They are characterized by their distinctive style of dress (including black coats and ear locks) and their joyful form of worship (song and dance). The movement was founded in Europe by Israel Baal Shem Tov (1700–60). The Hasidim have many sects around the world, each led by its own *rebbe*. In the United States, the sects of the Lubavitch and Satmar are especially influential.

The youngest branch of Judaism is known as Reconstructionism. It was founded by Mordecai Kaplan (born 1881) who stressed Judaism as an evolving religious civilization. It gives equal importance to religion, ethics and culture.

Eight days after birth Jewish boys are circumcised by a doctor or a rabbi.

Developments in Judaism

Geoffrey Cowling

Hellenistic Judaism

When Judeans abroad adopted Greek as their mother tongue, a change in outlook inevitably followed. The Greek language was the medium by which Greek ideas, attitudes and ways of reasoning were passed on. These ideas were not necessarily terribly profound. The riches of classical Greek culture had been diluted, mixed and to a degree cheapened. But it was still a powerful, exciting and stimulating experience. People who could read Greek—especially those living in Alexandria—might have had a chance to read the great philosophers in the original.

But it seems that the Greek-speaking Jews were not drawn away from their customs as much as was feared they would be. They still regularly visited Jerusalem to celebrate the festivals in the temple, for example.

The home of Hellenistic (Greek-speaking) Judaism was the Roman Empire, and there were also branches in Palestine.

At the age of thirteen, a Jewish boy becomes 'Bar Mitzvah', 'son of the commandment', entering into full legal and religious membership of the community. This multiple Bar Mitzvah ceremony is being held at the Western 'Wailing' Wall in Jerusalem.

The most important effect of Greek thought was the conscious use of logical rules of thinking. Instead of relying on personal charisma in their teaching, the rabbis drew up rules to prescribe what methods of biblical interpretation would be accepted as valid. As well as drawing from Greek ideas, Hellenistic Jews attempted to influence Greek thought in return. But it seems that they largely failed; non-Jewish writers of the period show great ignorance of Judaism.

Philo of Alexandria sought to explain the Bible from the point of view of Greek philosophy. Philo himself was a preacher and commentator rather than a profound philosopher. He explained the great events of Israel's history as allegories of eternal truths and adopted the Stoic idea of Reason (*Logos*), which he called a 'second God', an intermediary between God and the world.

Many Jewish works, such as the *Book of Wisdom*, were written with an eye to convincing Greek readers. Their critique of Greek ideas never went very far—the greatest gulf they saw between the Jewish and the Greek world was the worship of idols—and as propaganda they were useless.

Community life

The life of the ordinary Jew in Greek-speaking areas was centred on the synagogue. Both worship and practical matters of community life were conducted there. Strangers were lodged, the poor helped, discipline enforced, public gatherings held and children taught in the synagogue. The authority was in the hands of the 'ruler of the synagogue'.

Associated with the synagogue was the 'house of study'. Here the Bible was studied and there was a library for scholars.

The synagogue was the first Jewish centre of worship which had no rite of sacrifice. Worship consisted of prayer, singing and reading of scripture. Visiting preachers might give a sermon, but the resident scholars probably did not.

The Talmuds

The *Talmud* is a vast collection of writings which contains the teaching of the rabbis. Its basis is the collection of rabbinic teachings made by Judah the Prince (the *Mishnah*). But the *Gemara*, the collection of discussions of the *Mishnah*, forms the larger part of the *Talmud*.

In fact there are two *Talmuds*, the Palestinian and the Babylonian. The former is a record of the discussion in the rabbinic schools of Galilee, especially

A Jew at a week-day morning service, wearing the prayer-shawl and phylactery–a box containing portions of the Law.

Tiberias, during the fourth century AD. The latter records the views of Babylonian schools and was not completed until the seventh or eighth century.

Both *Talmuds* have much in common—they represent parallel attacks on the same questions. Further, interchange of personnel was common, and the two *Talmuds* often quote from each other. But they differ somewhat in conclusions and interpretations.

A sea of knowledge
The bulk of the *Talmud* consists of an exhaustive discussion of the *Mishnah*. The opinions of various rabbis are quoted, with summaries of their evidence and arguments. The arguments take the biblical texts as authoritative, but

exactly *which* texts are applicable to any particular question is often open to debate. Considerable ingenuity is expended. The quality of argument may be keen and incisive on real philosophical and ethical questions. But at other times it is apparently mere cleverness.

The rabbis call on all sorts of evidence in their arguments, and it is the record of this which gives the *Talmuds* their massive encyclopedic character. Within them are found allusions to the whole store of the rabbis' knowledge—from popular sayings, folk-tales, legends, anecdotes, puns and dreams, to the scientific knowledge of the day. To the outsider this looks like the jumbled contents of a filing cabinet, a loose-leaf encyclopedia with no index. It is virtually inaccessible to all but those who have memorized it.

The traditional way of mastering the *Talmud* is by continuous reading with help of commen-

taries, arguing about it and putting forward interpretations until it becomes familiar territory. The traditional Western aids, indexes and concordances, have only recently begun to be used. Today there is still a breach between the traditional scholar with his deep acquaintance and the modern scholar with critical insight but not the knowledge.

We have to be very careful about taking any opinion in the *Talmud* as 'the teaching of Judaism'. The *Talmud* records all authoritative minority views and therefore it is necessary to discover *who* said what, how authoritative it was, whether it was accepted by the later authorities and what later commentaries said about it!

It took centuries for all the communities even to know about, let alone accept, the *Talmuds*. The Babylonian *Talmud* gained much dominance, since Judaism flourished strongly in the Muslim Empire, in which Babylonian Judaism was dominant. The Palestinian *Talmud* was most influential in Italy and in Egypt, places which had close links with Palestine.

Jewish philosophy
Oddly enough, it was thanks to the Arab Empire that Jewish philosophy blossomed in the ninth to twelfth centuries. The Arab Empire gathered the wealth of thought of past civilizations, translating into Arabic the learning of Greece, Persia and even China and India. Much of their most original work in philosophy, science, mathematics and medicine was done by Jewish scholars. And many of these were concerned with religious philosophy.

One of the greatest Jewish philosophers—Saadiah Gaon (882–942)—was concerned with the problem of 'faith and knowledge', discussing proofs of God's existence.

The most influential philosophers after Saadiah lived in Spain. Until the eleventh century the greatest influence on them was Neo-Platonism. This philosophy considers that God is separated from the world by a descending series of 'emanations'. The Jewish philosophers had an impact beyond Judaism. The work of Solomon ibn Gabirol was translated into Latin and made a profound impression on Christian thought. His influence can also be seen in the Jewish mystical tradition known as the Kabbalah. Judah Ha Levi of Toledo (1085–1140) wrote a fictional dialogue between a Jewish scholar and the king of the Khazars (a Turkish tribe converted to Judaism). He showed how philosophy could prove the existence of God, but revelation was then necessary to know more of him.

Tackling atheism

In the eleventh century there was a shift in philosophical thought: Aristotle became more important than Plato. Aristotle's science seemed to leave no room for religion, and Jewish scholars set about tackling the problem of whether his philosophy could be reconciled with biblical religion.

Ibn Daud (active around 1180) was the first, but the greatest thinker of this time was Rabbi Moshe ben Maimon (1135–1204, known as Maimonides in English). Exiled from Spain to Egypt, he brought the thought of Spain to the East. His great philosophical work was *The Guide for the Perplexed*. As the title suggests, he was concerned with the difficulties Aristotle's philosophy gave to the believer. In contrast to many Jewish scholars, Maimonides saw 'right belief' as of great importance. He met great criticism for this at the time. Maimonides drew up thirteen 'roots' of Judaism, the Thirteen Principles of the Faith:

- Belief in the existence of a creator and of providence
- Belief in his unity
- Belief in his incorporeality
- Belief in his eternity
- Belief that worship is due to him alone
- Belief in the words of the prophets
- Belief that Moses was the greatest of all the prophets
- Belief in the revelation of the *Torah* to Moses at Sinai
- Belief in the unchangeable nature of the revealed Law
- Belief that God is omniscient
- Belief in retribution in this world and in the hereafter
- Belief in the coming of the Messiah
- Belief in the resurrection of the dead.

A century later, the Christian philosopher, Thomas Aquinas, also tackled the problem of Aristotle's philosophy. He was deeply indebted to Maimonides, frequently quoting him as 'Rabbi Moyse'.

The Jewish philosophers were not concerned with the concept of 'the chosen people'. It does not appear in Maimonides' thirteen roots (except perhaps to some degree in the idea of the Messiah). They were much more concerned with universal truths. This may partly explain why, when Spanish Jews were persecuted in the fifteenth century, many of the philosophers yielded and converted, while the ordinary people (with more to lose) resisted to the death. This led to a suspicion of philosophy.

Jewish mysticism

Mysticism forms an important strand of Judaism. It is the belief in some kind of direct 'vision' of divine things, a way to experience things and events otherwise

Judaism has a mystical tradition known as Kabbalism. Amongst other things it considers that numbers and letters have an inherent creative power.

than through our ordinary senses. Mysticism may deal with the same ideas as philosophy, but it claims to rely not on argument or thought but on mystical experience.

The Kabbalah, a Jewish mystical tradition, developed in Spain. It brought together many earlier traditions, such as ideas from the *Talmud* and the 'Book of Creation' (*Sefer Yetsirot*), which emphasized the mystical meaning of the letters in the Hebrew alphabet and the philosophy of Neo-Platonism. Direct from Neo-Platonism came the idea of how God related to the world. In the Kabbalah, God was known as the 'limitless' (*En Sof*). From him came the ten aspects of God (*Sefirot*), ways in which he is manifested or made known. They are 'emanations' of God, intermediate between the *En Sof* and the world.

The most important work of Kabbalah is the *Zohar*. It was attributed to Rabbi Simeon bar Yohai (second century AD), but in reality was written in thirteenth-century Spain. The final editor/author was probably Rabbi Moses de Leon. This is a book of extreme historical importance. It is the *Talmud* of Jewish mysticism. After the Jews were expelled from Spain it became known to the West, producing the school of 'Christian Cabbalists', and still attracts those interested in the occult today.

The study of *Torah* is still central in Kabbalah, but the aim is to find hidden, secret meanings. The *Zohar* expounds the *Torah* by literal, allegorical and expository techniques and, most important, by mystical insights. Astrology is bound up in the *Zohar* as well: each day is under the influence of one of the ten *Sefirot*.

After the expulsion from Spain, Safed in Galilee became the centre of Jewish mysticism.

Here Rabbi Isaac Luria (1544–72) gave a new twist to the Kabbalah. His work, which, like the *Zohar*, made much of erotic imagery, had great influence on later movements such as Hasidism. In Luria's view, when the *En Sof* created the universe he withdrew from it. The *Sefirot* are vessels which contain the 'divine light'. But the last six *Sefirot* could not contain the light, and shattered. Some of them sank, trapping sparks of the divine light within them. This is the origin of evil; and redemption will come when these sparks are returned to their source.

Hasidism

Hasidism arose in Poland in the eighteenth century. From the start it was a popular movement. It gave hope and interest and excitement to people who were frightened, deprived and confined. The Shabbetai movement had led to disillusionment, and the 'worship through study' of rabbinism offered them no consolation. But Hasidism was a movement with emphasis on emotion and devotion. It may be paralleled with many similar movements of the time, such as the rise of Methodism in England.

The key figure in this movement was Israel Baal Shem Tov (about 1700–60). He was a dynamic, charismatic figure, widely known as a miracle worker. Baal Shem Tov means 'master of the NAME', which reflects the belief in his powers. His teaching contained much from the Kabbalah, especially the *Zohar*. Many legends are told about him, and much popular belief, indeed superstition, was caught up into the movement. But the essence was a passionate devotion to God, expressed in ecstatic prayer, singing and dancing. From the outside, Hasidic life may seem a

miserable, deprived, narrow existence, but within it is sustained by the Hasidic 'joy'—a genuine religious 'high'. In fact, from its early days asceticism was played down.

Unlike rabbis, the leaders of the Hasidic groups were more gurus than scholars. The leader, the *rebbe* or *zaddik*, is a man who is able to live the life of devotion and thus act as intermediary between his followers and God. The leader's word is absolute: his followers leave their families to be with him, they even contend to get a share of the food he has touched. Various leaders have created the different branches of Hasidism today.

Women played a much more prominent role in the beginnings of the movement than they do today. Generally, Hasidism is a man's world. Women are responsible for the survival of the community but they are definitely neglected, deprived and largely ignored.

Opposition

The Hasidic movement met strong opposition from the establishment of the Jewish communities. There was something of a class struggle, as the *rebbes* replaced the rich and learned. Excommunication was used as a weapon against them by their opponents. One of the most hostile, certainly the most influential, was the 'Gaon of Vilna', Elijah ben Solomon (1720–97). The emphases of Hasidism were anathema to his ascetically-oriented intellectualism. In his time the excommunicated were even betrayed to the hostile authorities.

It was Shneur Zalman (1745–1813), the philosopher of Hasidism, who drew the movement back to being accepted. Under his influence Hasidism, or at least his branch of it, was reconciled to Talmudic study.

The Influence of Judaism

Marvin Wilson

It is in the area of religion and ethics that Judaism has made its greatest impact upon modern civilization. What Greece brought to the world in the realm of philosophy and aesthetics, what Rome bequeathed in politics and law, Israel contributed in its understanding of the one invisible God and the revelation of his will for mankind.

Leo Tolstoy wrote concerning the Jew: 'he who has been for so long the guardian of prophecy, and who transmitted it to the rest of the world—such a nation cannot be destroyed. The Jew is everlasting as is eternity itself.'

The vocabulary of Judaism—the words of the Hebrew Bible—has itself had considerable impact on world thought. Both literature and conversation in the Western world are punctuated today by expressions such as 'lick the dust', 'apple of the eye', 'flesh of my flesh', 'put out the fleece', 'a still small voice', 'scapegoat', 'holier than thou', 'pride goes before a fall' and 'can a leopard change his spots?' All of these phrases come straight from the pages of the Bible.

Branches from the trunk

The ancient trunk of Judaism has produced two branches, Christianity and Islam, which in turn have experienced unparalleled growth over the whole earth.

Christianity has received from Judaism its basic understanding of God, his nature, his Law, his dealings with men and the standards he expects between man and man.

Many of the terms of Christianity—such words as amen, hallelujah, Satan, Sabbath, Messiah, paradise, cherub, and jubilee—have been adopted directly from the Hebrew Bible, even if they have subtly changed meaning.

The synagogue of Judaism gave birth to the Christian church as a place of assembly for the reading of scripture, prayer and worship. The sermon, the use of incense, the singing of psalms, the practice of baptism and the celebration of the Lord's Supper (Holy Eucharist), the organization of the church, the methods of biblical interpretation—each finds its root in Judaism.

The life and teaching of Jesus as recorded in the Gospels is likewise best understood in the light of his thorough Jewishness. For example, the Lord's Prayer (Matthew 6) is thoroughly Jewish, reflected in ancient Jewish prayers such as the *kaddish* and the 'Eighteen Benedictions'.

Through the influence of Muhammad its founder, Islam, the other daughter religion of Judaism, also preserves many teachings derived from the Hebrew Bible. In the Qur'an the names of Abraham, Moses and other biblical characters frequently appear. Muhammad eventually broke from Judaism when he failed to convince the Jews of his day that he was 'the Seal of the Prophets'.

Many of the laws of Islam are derived directly from, or adapted from, Judaism. Its strict monotheism, its opposition to idolatry, the practice of facing a holy city (Mecca) in daily prayer, regular fasting, the avoidance of pork and the observance of a weekly holy day all reflect the influence of Judaism upon Islam.

The wholeness of life

The distinctive theological and ethical values of Judaism have made an impact not only on the religious world, but on the political and social spheres as well.

The first distinctive value is the Jewish understanding of history. History is no aimless seasonal cycle. Rather it is unique. Events are invested with moral purpose and directed according to a divine plan. Thus the Jew is urged to remember history. Time has meaning for the future as well. History is a developing process, moving toward a glorious goal as depicted in the Hebrew prophets. So Judaism anticipates that final day of redemption when a perfected society will proclaim the God of Israel to be King of all the earth.

From the time of Moses, Judaism has also reflected a passion for maintaining justice and righteousness. Belief in the brotherhood of all peoples has resulted in displaying acts of charity, compassion and kindness. Acts of inhumanity and exploitation are a disgrace to a God of justice. Indeed, in Judaism, the obligation to 'love your neighbour as yourself' has extended not only to the poor, the widow and the orphan, but even to the animal world.

Reverence and holiness for all of life is another distinctive value of Judaism. Life is sacred, for man is created in the image of God. Man's task is to hallow every area of life— even mundane and commonplace activities can be imbued with divine meaning. The key to Jewish survival has been through following the way of holiness, a separateness from the corrupting pagan influences of the secular world. Unlike the upper classes of ancient Greece, Jews never viewed physical labour with disdain. Rather, the dedicated work of human hands could bring glory to the creator. In contrast to other religions which have sought to flee the pains of this material world for the heavenly joys of a spiritual world above, Judaism has persisted in focussing almost exclusively upon this present world of flesh and blood. Hence the laws of Judaism cover such areas of daily life as eating, sex and working the land. These commandments reflect the need to sanctify the wholeness of present human experience.

The one ideal that over the centuries Judaism has prized perhaps more than any other is that of freedom. It has been said that since the time of the escape from slavery in Egypt, the exodus, freedom has spoken with a Hebrew accent. Many of the political principles and civil liberties basic to Western democracy were originally based on the Hebrew scriptures. The historian, William Lecky, observed that 'Hebraic mortar cemented the foundations of American democracy'.

But to the Jew, freedom means far more than religious or political independence. It is a mandate for the individual to shape his own destiny and that of society. It is an affirmation that, no matter how bleak the surroundings and the future appear, progress is possible. There is an unquenchable hope that this world can be changed, and the prophetic dream of peace can be realized.

'If I am not for myself, who will be for me? If I am only for myself, what am I? If not now, when?'

Rabbi Hillel, *Mishnah*

'Why does this workman ascend the highest scaffolding and risk his life, if you do not pay him his wages as soon as they are due?'

The Talmud

'It is forbidden to destroy fruit-bearing trees but whoever breaks vessels, tears clothes, demolishes a building, stops up a fountain or wastes food, in a destructive way, offends against the law of "thou shalt not destroy".'

Maimonides

'If you wish it, it is not a dream—to live as a free people in your own land.'

Theodore Herzl

Life in a Jewish Family

David Harley

Birth and Bar-Mitzvah

According to orthodox Jewish law, a Jew is one born of a Jewish mother, although it is possible to become a Jew by conversion. On the eighth day after his birth, a Jewish boy will be circumcised. This may be either a medical operation performed by a doctor or a religious rite performed by a *mohel*, a trained and registered circumciser. When he is circumcised, the boy receives the Hebrew name which will be used at his *Bar-Mitzvah*, his wedding and on his gravestone.

During his early years his mother is responsible for his religious education. As soon as he can speak, he is taught the words of the *Shema* (see *Chosen People: Judaism*). At about the age of five he is sent to a synagogue religion class which is held after school hours on weekdays and also on Sunday mornings. One of the main activities of the religion class is to learn Hebrew and study the sacred books. For a girl it is particularly important to learn how to keep a Jewish home.

At the age of thirteen a boy becomes *Bar-Mitzvah* (son of the commandment); on the Sabbath after his birthday he reads from the scroll of the *Torah* during the synagogue service for the first time. After the service there is usually a party for family and friends. From this point on he is regarded as a responsible person. He is expected to fulfil all the duties of a Jew and may count as one of the ten adult men who are required to make a quorum for public prayer (*minyan*).

A Jewish girl automatically comes of age at twelve and is considered to be *Bat-Mitzvah* (daughter of the commandment). It is the custom of some synagogues to hold a ceremony to mark the occasion.

Prayer

A devout Jewish man prays three times a day—morning, afternoon and evening, either in his home or in the synagogue. When he prays he covers his head with an ordinary hat or a skull-cap (*yarmelka* or *kippah*). In the morning he wears a prayer-shawl (*tallit*) which has tassels or fringes at the four corners in obedience to the command found in the *Torah*. On weekdays he may also put on phylacteries (*tephillin*). These are black leather boxes containing four passages of scripture: Exodus 13:1–10 and 11–16; Deuteronomy 6:4–9 and 11:13–21. They are strapped to the forehead and left upper arm.

When he goes out, the orthodox Jew may continue to cover his head as a mark of reverence towards God in whose presence all life is lived. By the front door he passes the *mezuzah*, which is another reminder of his religious obligation to God. The *mezuzah* consists of a tiny scroll of parchment on which are written in Hebrew the opening paragraphs of the *Shema*: Deuteronomy 6:4–9 and 11:13–21. The scroll is housed in a wooden or metal container and fixed to the upper part of the right-hand doorpost of the front door. A similar *mezuzah* is fixed to the doorpost of every other living-room in the house.

Kosher food

It is the duty of a Jewish housewife to safeguard the religious purity of the home, and one of her many responsibilities is to make sure that the food eaten there is *kosher* (fit or clean according to Jewish dietary laws).

Meat and dairy products must not be served at the same meal. If meat is eaten, there can be no butter on bread or milk in coffee. To avoid any possibility of mixing meat with milk the traditional Jewish housewife uses two sets of dishes, one of which is only used for meat, the other only for milk foods. In addition she may use two sinks for washing-up and two sets of tea-towels. In Jewish hotels there are two separate kitchens.

Only certain kinds of meat may be eaten in a Jewish home. These are listed in Leviticus 11 and Deuteronomy 14. Lamb, beef and chicken are among those permitted, pork and shellfish among those that are not. The animals must be slaughtered by a trained and ordained *shochet*. He follows carefully prescribed regulations which cause the blood to drain quickly from the body and ensure the minimum of pain. After the animal is properly slaughtered, the meat must be soaked in cold water and salted to remove all the blood that remains.

Jewish people vary a great deal in the degree of their observance of these dietary laws. Some do not observe them at all. Some abstain from food that is expressly forbidden but are not so particular about the details of keeping a *kosher* kitchen. However, orthodox Jews will follow these regulations meticulously as an act of religious obedience, whereby the taking of food is sanctified and the family table becomes an altar.

Before each meal a traditional blessing is recited, and though this may vary according to the food that is being eaten, the most common words are, 'Blessed art thou O Lord our God, King of the universe, who brings forth bread from the earth.'

The Sabbath

The Sabbath is considered to be the most important of all the Jewish religious festivals. It commemorates both the creation of the world and the deliverance of the people of Israel from Egypt. It has played a significant role in the preservation of Judaism. It is a day with a special atmosphere of joy and peace, and as such is thought of as a foretaste of the age to come.

The beginning of the Sabbath, sunset on Friday evening, is marked by the lighting and blessing of the Sabbath candles by the mother. The father attends synagogue with his sons, and on his return blesses his children and praises his wife with the words of Proverbs chapter 31. The family then enjoys a Sabbath meal together, which begins with the blessing of bread and wine. The bread is a special plaited loaf called *challah*. Usually two loaves are used, in memory of the double portion of manna that fell in the wilderness on the day before the Sabbath.

No work is permitted on the Sabbath and the orthodox Jew has to be employed in an occupation which allows him to be home before sunset on every Friday throughout the year. This often means that he will be self-employed or work in a Jewish firm.

No fires may be lit on the Sabbath, though a fire which was lit before the Sabbath may be left alight. Some employ a *shabbos goy*, a non-Jew, to perform types of work not permitted to the Jew on the Sabbath. Others install time-delay switches.

No long journeys may be undertaken on the Sabbath, though those on board ship do not have to get off! An orthodox Jew will live within easy walking distance of his synagogue since he must not drive his car on the Sabbath or use public transport.

These restrictions, far from being a burden, are seen by the religious Jew as a means of releasing him from the

Orthodox Jews in Jerusalem

ardours of the daily round. It is a day when he can rest completely from his ordinary work and be spiritually renewed.

At the close of the Sabbath, the family again gathers for a brief ceremony. Blessings are recited over a cup of wine and a box of sweet spices. The spices speak of the fragrance of the Sabbath day, which, it is hoped, will be carried over into the new week.

Marriage and divorce

In Judaism marriage is considered to be a holy covenant. Before the ceremony the bridegroom signs the marriage document (*ketubbah*) in which he pledges himself to his bride. During the service the couple stand under an embroidered canopy supported by four poles, which represents their future home. The ceremony ends with the breaking of a glass under the bridegroom's foot. This symbolic act is thought by some to represent the idea that even times of great joy need to be balanced by moments of serious reflection. Others see it as a reminder of the destruction of the temple of Jerusalem, a theme which constantly reappears in Hebrew prayers.

In the event of the breakdown of a marriage, the local community tries in every way possible to reconcile husband and wife. If this is not possible, a *get* or bill of divorce may be issued by the Jewish religious court. This document, written in Aramaic and signed by two witnesses, is handed by the husband to the wife. It frees her from all her marital obligations to him. In most countries a civil divorce is required first, and then the issuing of a *get* serves as a religious ratification of the divorce.

Death and resurrection

The last words uttered by the religious Jew when he is dying—or said on his behalf if he is too weak—are the words of the *Shema* which he first learned as a child: 'Hear, O Israel, the Lord our God is one Lord . . .' At the moment of death those present make a small tear in their clothes as a mark of grief. The funeral service, which is characterized by simplicity even among wealthy families, is arranged as soon as possible and preferably within twenty-four hours of death. No prayers for the dead are offered but *kaddish*, a prayer of praise to God, is recited in their memory. It is the particular responsibility of a son to say *kaddish* on behalf of a deceased parent.

After the funeral the close relatives return home for a week of private mourning. This period is known as *shivah* or the seven days, during which those who have been bereaved sit on low stools or even on the floor. On the anniversary of the parent's death, the children light a memorial candle and recite the *kaddish* at the end of the synagogue service.

The doctrine of the resurrection is not found in the *Torah* and it is considered by some as a foreign import from Christianity. However, the idea of life after death can be traced back within Judaism at least 2,000 years, and it is expressed in the Thirteen Principles of the Faith (see *Developments in Judaism—Maimonides*) in the words, 'I believe with perfect faith that there will be a resurrection of the dead at a time when it shall please the Creator'. Yet it remains true that Judaism is concerned primarily with this life rather than the next and with obeying the Law of God in the present rather than speculating about the future.

The Way of the Prophet

Montgomery Watt

Islam began in Mecca about AD 610. The dominant religion of Arabia at this time was a form of the old Semitic religion, with shrines of various gods and goddesses in many places. There also appears to have been a widespread belief in a high god or supreme god; Allah. The other gods were sometimes regarded as angels, and could be asked to intercede with the supreme god on behalf of the worshippers.

Most of the Arabs were members of nomadic tribes and believed more in human excellence than in any divine power. They believed that what happened to them was determined by Fate or Time, which they thought of not as a being to be worshipped, but simply as 'the course of events'. Some tribes or parts of tribes had become Christian and there were Jewish communities in Medina and elsewhere in western Arabia. Thus, certain Jewish and Christian ideas were familiar to many Arabs.

Messages from God

Islam began not among nomads but among city-dwellers engaged in far-flung commercial enterprises. Towards the end of the sixth century the merchants of Mecca gained monopoly of trade between the Indian Ocean and the Mediterranean, which passed up the west coast of Arabia by camel caravan. Mecca had a sanctuary, the Ka'ba, which was an ancient pilgrimage centre, and the surrounding district was sacred. All this facilitated the growth of trade, but the wealth which poured into Mecca led to social tensions, especially among the younger men.

Muhammad (see special article) was born in Mecca around the year 570. It was in about AD 610 that he came to believe that he was receiving messages from God which he was to convey to his fellow Meccans. These messages or revelations were later collected and form the Qur'an. They asserted that God was *One* (Allah) and that he was both merciful and all-powerful, controlling the course of events. On the Last Day he would judge men according to their acts and assign them to heaven or hell. Part of the conduct which he expected of men was a generous use of wealth. In the revelations, Muhammad himself was spoken of sometimes as merely a warner telling of God's punishment for sinners, sometimes as a prophet or messenger of God. Muhammad sincerely believed that these revelations were not his own composition, but were the actual speech of God conveyed to him by an angel. This is still the belief of Muslims.

Muhammad gained a number of followers, who met frequently with him and joined him in worship of God. But his messages were not all well received. The Meccan merchants were roused to vigorous opposition by the criticisms of their

'He is Allah, besides whom there is no other god. He is the Sovereign Lord, the Holy One, the Giver of Peace, the Keeper of Faith; the Guardian, the Mighty One, the All-powerful, the Most High! Exalted be He above their idols! He is Allah, the Creator, the Originator, the Modeller. His are the gracious names. All that is in heaven and earth gives glory to Him. He is the Mighty, the Wise One.'

The Qur'an, sura 59:23–4 tr, N. J. Dawood

The Merciful;
the Compassionate,
the Forgiver,
the Forgiving;
the Clement,
the Generous,
the Affectionate,
the Kind ...

Some of the Ninety-Nine Names of God

Muslims at prayer in Brunei. Islam is the religion of much of south-east Asia.

A painting showing the four archangels bringing a message to Muhammad. Muhammad's face is blanked out, since the Qur'an forbids the representation of any living creature.

practices implied in the Qur'an. The merchants spoke of the old pagan gods but the Qur'an came to emphasize that there is only one God—that 'there is no deity but God'. As opposition grew, the Qur'anic messages began to speak of former prophets who had met with opposition, and of the way in which God had preserved them and their followers and brought disaster on their opponents. Among the stories were those of Noah and the Flood, Lot and the destruction of Sodom, and Moses escaping from Pharaoh.

To Medina

Muhammad's followers were now persecuted in various ways by his opponents, who were often their own relatives. Eventually it became impossible for him to carry on his religious activity in Mecca, and in 622, preceded by about seventy men and their families, he emigrated to Medina. This emigration, the *Hijra*, became the event which marked the beginning of the Islamic era.

Medina was a fertile oasis, but the inhabitants were divided into two hostile groups. Most of them accepted Muhammad as prophet and agreed that they and the emigrants from Mecca would form a single community or federation. Perhaps they were the more ready to accept Muhammad because they had heard from the local Jewish clans that a messiah was expected. They were also hopeful that he would help them to overcome their divisions.

It was at Medina that the religion of Islam took shape. The main ritual forms, modelled on Muhammad's example, were: worship (or prayer), almsgiving, fasting (for the whole month of Ramadan), and the pilgrimage to Mecca (including ceremonies at neighbouring sites). At Medina the messages revealed to Muhammad included legal regulations for matters where Arab custom was unsatisfactory, such as the inheritance of wealth and the avoidance of incest.

The Jewish clans in Medina were associated with Muhammad's federation as allies of Arab member clans, but nearly all the Jews refused to accept him as prophet. They mocked parts of the Qur'an and sometimes actively opposed the Muslims. Muhammad expelled two Jewish clans from Medina and had the men of a third executed. Until after the conquest of Mecca he had few contacts with Christians.

At first, Muhammad had no special political powers at Medina beyond being head of the emigrants from Mecca. After a year or two, however, all his followers there (now called Muslims) became involved in hostilities with the pagan Meccans. By 630 Muhammad was strong enough to take Mecca. He treated his enemies generously and won most of them over to become Muslims. Many

tribes all over Arabia also joined his federation and became Muslims. Because of his successes his authority as head of state was unquestioned.

The first caliphs

'He who honours Muhammad must know that he is dead. But he who honours the God of Muhammad must know that he is living and immortal.' Muhammad died in 632, and with these words his first successor, Abu Bakr, encouraged the Muslim community and pointed them to the task ahead.

On his death, Muhammad left both a religion and a state. At first the state had the form of a federation of tribes or clans, but as it expanded it became more organized. The head of state was known as the 'caliph' (khalifa)—the 'successor' or 'deputy' of Muhammad. Raiding their neighbours had been a normal occupation of the nomadic Arab tribes, and Muhammad and the first caliphs realized that they could not keep peace within the federation unless they found some outlet for the ener-

gies of the tribesmen. They therefore organized raiding expeditions (razzias) in the direction of Syria and Iraq. The aim of these was to obtain booty, including domestic animals.

The first raids from Medina were very successful. There was in fact a power vacuum in the region, because the two great powers of the day, the Byzantine and Persian Empires, had been almost constantly at war for half a century and were now exhausted. In a few decisive battles the Muslims overcame such opposition as the empires presented. Instead of returning to Medina after each campaign, they established forward base camps so that they could go further afield in the following expedition. Following this strategy, they had occupied Egypt, Syria and Iraq within twelve years of Muhammad's death, and were advancing westwards into Libya and eastwards into what is now Iran.

The Byzantine and Persian governors of the provinces fled, and the Muslims made treaties with the local inhabitants, giving them the status of 'protected minorities'. These groups

The Muslim world

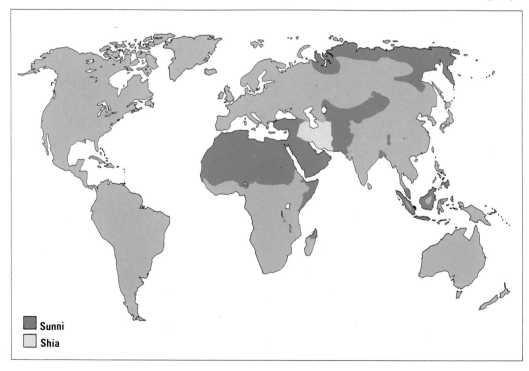

■ Sunni
□ Shia

Muhammad

Lothar Schmalfuss

Muhammad's life is surrounded by legends. They paint a picture of a sort of wonder-working super-human, whose special calling by God was clearly evident to all. The historical facts, however, reveal quite simply a man—a caravan leader who had grown up in bitter poverty, a father who lost most of his children, a moderately successful business man. Above all, a man who perceived in everything that God is in close control, that God is the beginning and end of this world and that he holds in his hands the life of every human being.

Muhammad was born in Mecca, about AD 570. Mecca was a prosperous trading and religious centre of the Arab world. Early in life Muhammad lost his parents. He experienced the misery of being an orphan, but he also learned what it meant to be surrounded by a community wider than immediate family. First he was looked after by his grandfather and then by an uncle. At the age of twenty-five he led the caravans of a business woman, Khadija, so successfully that she offered him her hand in marriage. He was now rich and became a respected and influential citizen of Mecca. He seemed to have reached his goal.

But Muhammad was not satisfied by material security. Early on he had shown a love of solitude. Questions oppressed him. Restlessness drove him round in circles, and before long he came to a severe crisis point in his life. Increasingly he withdrew from business and family and sought the loneliness of the desert. It was there that the event occurred which was to change his life and to affect the history of the world.

The night of destiny

His first biographer, Muhammad Ibn Ishaq, recorded the events of that night. Muhammad was spending time alone on the Hira mountain.

'I was lying asleep,' he reports in his own words, 'when an angel came to me with a piece of material and said: "Read this!" I replied: "I cannot read!" Then he pressed the material against me so hard that I thought I would die. Then he let me go and said again: "Read!" The angel repeated his command once more. Nervously, I replied: "What am I to read?" The angel said:

"Read in the name of your Lord.
He who created and made man from an embryo.
Read, for your Lord is merciful like no one on earth.
He who instructed man by the pen,
He taught him what he did not know."

'I awoke from my sleep,' Muhammad went on, 'and it was as if these words were written in my heart. I came out of the cave and stood on the mountain-side. Then I heard a voice calling to me from heaven: "Muhammad, you are God's messenger and I am Gabriel." I lifted my eyes up and saw him on the skyline. I did not move. When I tried to look away I could still see him.'

The prophet of God

From then on, Muhammad was sure that he had been called to be the prophet of the one God. He returned to Mecca and on the street corners preached about the resurrection of the dead and God's judgement.

'God will judge you according to your works,' he called to the town traders, and he challenged them to submit their lives to God and to practise love towards the poor and imprisoned, to slaves and foreigners. His language had something gripping about it. But many of the citizens of Mecca thought he was possessed, or a dangerous revolutionary. They recognized at once that he was directing his preaching against the polytheism of the town. But this was the focus of the pilgrimages which were their most important source of income. Feeling threatened, the traders' opposition grew. They became increasingly aggressive, forcing Muhammad and his small group of followers to live in a ghetto. When his wife died and, soon afterwards, the uncle who had protected him, Muhammad left Mecca.

Just as Abraham left his ancestral land to form the Jewish nation, so Muhammad left the town of his father and family behind him and went to Medina. AD 622, the year of this journey, or *Hijra*, is the year which marks the start of the Islamic calendar. From then on Islam was no longer just a religion but also a distinct political power. In Medina the community of believers became a state, with Muhammad as its religious and political head, and the social and religious practices of Islam were developed.

Muhammad expected that the Jewish inhabitants of the town would recognize him as God's prophet, but he was disappointed. So he drove out and destroyed the Jewish clans. Enlisting the help of nomadic Arab tribes, Muhammad began armed raids on Mecca, and in 630 he took the town with ease. Surrounded by jubilant followers he rode on a camel straight to the centre of pilgrimage, the Ka'ba. Mecca was quickly cleared of all images and symbols of pagan belief. Then Muhammad raised himself on the saddle and formally announced the end of idolatry and the start of the new age of the one God. There was no resistance, and the victors pronounced no judgement on their former opponents. Mecca remained the focal point and the place of pilgrimage of the new state of God.

Two years later, Muhammad again led the train of pilgrims to the Ka'ba. In front of all the people he declared the last message of God:

'Today I have completed my religion for you and I have fulfilled the extent of my favour towards you. It is my will that Islam be your religion. I have completed my mission. I have left you the Book of Allah and clear commandments. If you keep them you will never go wrong.'

The same year, Muhammad died.

ordered their own internal affairs, but paid tribute or tax to the Muslim governor. The status of protected minority was open only to 'people of the book'—communities who believed in one God and possessed a written scripture, i.e. Jews, Christians and Zoroastrians.

The explosion of Islam

Apart from some periods of civil strife among Muslims, the expansion continued for a century. Westwards the Muslims occupied North Africa to the Atlantic, crossed into Spain, and for a few years held the region round Narbonne in southern France. In the famous battle of Tours in 732 a Muslim raiding expedition was defeated by a French army, but this did not loosen the Muslim hold on Spain. Northwards they raided as far as Constantinople (modern Istanbul), but failed to occupy any of Asia Minor (Turkey). Eastwards, after occupying the whole of Persia and Afghanistan, they penetrated into central Asia and crossed the line of the River Indus in modern Pakistan.

The entrance to a mosque in Damascus. Before prayer, Muslims take off their shoes and wash their feet.

Until 750 this vast area remained a single state ruled by the caliphs of the Umayyad dynasty.

Most of the inhabitants of these regions were not immediately converted to Islam but became protected minorities. The military expeditions, though dignified with the title of 'holy war' (*jihad*), were raids for booty and not to make converts. The idea that opponents were given the choice of 'Islam or the sword' is false, except in the case of pagan Arab tribes. The protected minorities were on the whole well treated, since Muslim rulers felt it to be a point of honour that their 'protection' should be effective. Members of these minorities, however, saw themselves as second-class citizens, and there was a steady trickle of converts to Islam over the centuries. It is in this way that Islam has become the dominant religion in lands which were the original home of Christianity. In the seventh century though, Zoroastrianism—the official religion of the Persian Empire—was in decline, and conversion from it to Islam was quite rapid and extensive.

Consolidation

In 750 the Umayyad dynasty of caliphs, based in Damascus, ended. For the next 500 years, the 'Abbasid dynasty ruled from Baghdad. They never took over control of Islamic Spain, however. They also gradually lost control of other outlying provinces. A local governor with a powerful army would insist on being succeeded by a person of *his* choice, maintaining only weak links with the caliph. In 945 the 'Abbasid caliph was even forced to delegate supreme political and military authority over Baghdad and the central provinces. But there continued to be 'Abbasid caliphs in Baghdad, though without political power, until the destructive Mongol invasion in 1258.

Whereas the Umayyad period was one of growth and adaptation for Islam and the Arabs, the first century or two of 'Abbasid rule was marked by consolidation. All the cultural forms needed for the life of a great empire flourished. A central place was given to the development and

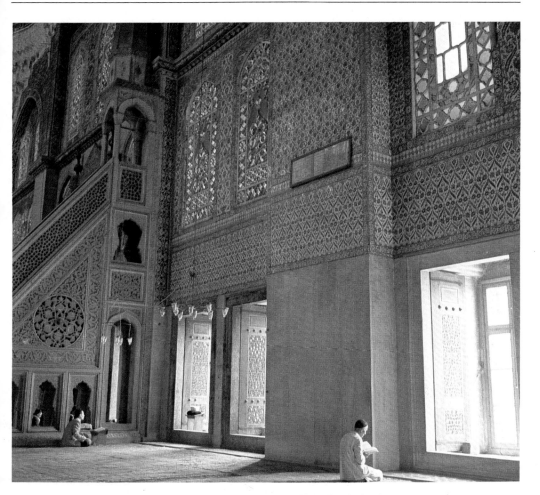

elaboration of Islamic law, the Shari'a, which formed the basis of social structure. The Shari'a was derived in part from rules in the Qur'an, but to a greater extent from the example of Muhammad. His example was known from the collections of *Hadith* (sometimes translated 'traditions')—stories about his deeds and sayings. This study of law or jurisprudence became the core of Islamic higher education.

Subordinate scholarly disciplines were concerned with the text of the Qur'an, the interpretation of the Qur'an, grammar, lexicology and theological doctrine. There were also the 'foreign sciences'—Greek philosophy, medicine, mathematics and natural science. Many Greek books were translated into Arabic and considerable advances were made in the sciences, in literature, in the arts and in the skills of government and administration.

To the east

After 750, military expansion slowed down, and almost the only advance was that into India. Here the climax of Islamic power was under the Mogul emperors from 1556 until 1707, when most of the subcontinent was subject to them. Hindus were treated as 'people of the book' because their philosophers (though not most ordinary Hindus) were monotheists. Though there were group

A Muslim reading the Qur'an inside the beautifully-decorated Blue Mosque in Istanbul.

conversions to Islam, most of the population remained Hindu.

Islamic rule also spread by peaceful methods. Muslim traders with camel caravans took it into the West African steppe, and sea traders carried it to the East African coast. From India it spread, mainly through trade, to Malaysia, Indonesia and the Philippines; and from central Asia it moved into eastern China.

Local people were impressed by the confidence and high culture of the Muslim traders, allowed them to marry local women, and often after a time decided themselves to become Muslims. Converts often kept many of their old customs, and did not immediately observe the Shari'a fully. But over the centuries they moved closer to standard Islam, and at the same time the number of Muslims kept increasing.

The one area where Islam contracted was Spain. Christian military pressure gradually whittled away the area under Muslim control, and in 1492 the last sultan of Granada had to surrender. Muslims continued in Spain for a time, but were executed or driven out by the Inquisition.

The impact of Europe

A new era in the history of Islam began about 1500. The Portuguese sailor Vasco da Gama, having rounded the Cape of Good Hope and disrupted the Muslim trade on the East African coast, reached India in 1498. This was the beginning of the impact of Europe on the eastern part of the Islamic world. In the west the Ottomans had restored the caliphate which had lapsed in 1258, conquered much of south-eastern Europe and the southern coast of the Mediterranean during the fifteenth and sixteenth centuries, and were then in military and diplomatic contact with European states, as well as having commercial dealings. The full force of the European impact, however, was not felt until after the Industrial

Revolution. Napoleon's invasion of Egypt in 1798 is a significant date.

The impact of Europe on the Islamic world (as on Asia and Africa generally) was many-sided: economic, political, intellectual and religious. It began with ocean-borne trade but went on to political interference and finally colonization. As European technology developed in the nineteenth century, the richer Muslims wanted to share in the comforts and conveniences, and independent rulers wanted their countries to have railways and other forms of communication, plumbing, electricity for lighting, telephones, and so forth. Military hardware was high on the list, and then it became necessary to train men to use it. Colonial powers also introduced Western-type education to train men for minor administrative posts. After 1800 the Christian churches sent missionaries to most parts of the world, but in Islamic lands they made few converts and their chief contribution was to the development of education and medical care.

By the early twentieth century, intelligent Muslims were aware of their situation. Movements for political independence grew and were eventually successful. Some industry was developed, based on Western technology. Most Muslim countries adopted an essentially Western educational system, because the religious leaders were not prepared to adapt the traditional Islamic education they controlled. The discovery of vast quantities of oil in the Middle East was at first exploited by Westerners, but later, when taken over by Muslim governments, became a weapon in world politics. Until the end of the Second World War, Muslim countries were united in their struggle to be free of colonialism. Since then, however, splits between 'progressive' and 'conservative' groups have become increasingly apparent.

The Qur'an

Christy Wilson

The Qur'an is the sacred book of the Muslims. It is seen as a perfect revelation from God, a faithful reproduction of an original engraved on a tablet in heaven which has existed from all eternity. Copies of the Qur'an are therefore venerated very highly and are only touched and read by Muslims after ceremonial cleansing. Volumes are usually carefully wrapped in silk or an ornate cloth and placed in an elevated position, such as above a door in a home. Many Muslims memorize in Arabic the whole book—which is almost as long as the Christian New Testament. Those who have done this earn the title of *Hafiz*. And Muslims all over the world quote the short first chapter of the Qur'an in Arabic over and over again in the five daily prayers.

A collection of writings

The word Qur'an comes from the Arabic verb 'to recite', *qara'a*. This bears out the fact that most of the book is in the form of the words of Allah which Muhammad was commanded to proclaim. After the first chapter, the Qur'an consists of 114 chapters (*suras*). These are arranged according to length, the longest near the beginning, the shortest at the end. They are not organized chronologically or even by subject. Rather they are a composite collection of verses written at various periods of Muhammad's life.

All the *suras* start with the words, 'In the name of God, the Merciful, the Compassionate' (except number nine which may originally have been joined to eight). Each of the 114 chapters has a name derived from a prominent or recurring word in the particular chapter: *The Opening* (1), *The Cow* (2), *Jonah* (10), *Joseph* (12), *Abraham* (14), *Mary* (19), *Angels* (35), *Muhammad* (47), *Divorce* (65), *Noah* (71), *Earthquake* (99), *Swift Horses* (100), *Elephant* (105), *Infidels* (109) and *Men* (114).

The *suras* are divided into verses (*ayat*). The word *ayat* also carries the meaning of 'a miracle'. When Muhammad was asked for an authenticating wonder to prove his prophetic role, he simply referred to the Qur'an and its verses: they were his miracle. With its rhymed Arabic prose, the Muslims' holy book certainly has great literary beauty and a special attraction in the original.

The Qur'an does not follow a chronological arrangement, but from internal evidence many of its sections can be placed either in Muhammad's time at Mecca before the emigration of AD 622, or in his time at Medina afterwards. The Medina passages reflect the change in role from being a prophet or preacher to becoming a military leader.

The Qur'an contains several different sorts of writing. Muhammad records experiences of earlier prophets, mostly from the Old Testament, who were often models of his own experiences. There are also frequent proclamations of imminent judgement and of sensuous enticements in heaven and vivid descriptions of the sufferings of the damned in hell. A strict monotheism is taught throughout. Legislative sections for the Muslim community as well as laws governing family relations and inheritances are also included. There are a few historical references: in the thirtieth *sura* the war between the Greeks and the Persians (which probably took place around AD 614) is mentioned.

Proclaimed piecemeal

In the earlier parts of the Qur'an, Muhammad expressed friendship towards Jews and especially Christians as 'people of the book'. Furthermore, the Qur'an acknowledges much Jewish and Christian writing—the Pentateuch (*taurat*), the Psalms of David (*zabur*) and the Gospel (*injil*) of Jesus—as being revelations from God. But later, when the Jewish and Christian people would not accept him as a prophet, the attitude of the Qur'an towards them changes. In order to account for differences between the Jewish faith and the Qur'an, Muhammad charged the Jews with corrupting their scriptures: 'They have perverted the words.' The same charge was made against the Christians.

The angel Gabriel is the one who is credited with revealing the Qur'an to Muhammad. Parts were proclaimed by him piecemeal even though Muhammad claimed that the whole Qur'an existed complete in heaven. *Sura* 25:32 states: 'The unbelievers say, why was the Qur'an not sent down to him as a whole? We wished to strengthen thy heart thereby and we arranged it thus.'

According to Islamic tradition, the Qur'an was originally written on palm leaves, on shoulder-blade bones of camels and on stones. Following Muhammad's death in AD 632, tradition states that the first caliph, Abu Bakr, ordered Muhammad's former secretary, Zaid, to collect and arrange the writings. This was done in co-operation with others and finally an authorized revision of the text was established by Caliph 'Uthman. Other versions in existence were ordered to be destroyed. Thus, although Islam has many sects, all Muslims do use the same Qur'an going back to this original version. (Many groups claim to have other authentic sayings of Muhammad left out of the Qur'an which are called the traditions or *hadith*.)

There are alterations and abrogations within the Qur'an itself. For example, Muhammad originally ordered his followers to pray towards Jerusalem (*sura* 2:150), but when the Jewish people refused to follow him, he changed the direction of prayer to Mecca (*sura* 2:125). Such alterations are explained by *sura* 2:106, 'If we abrogate a verse or consign it to oblivion, we offer something better than it or something of equal value.'

Even though none of the Bible was translated into Arabic until after Muhammad's time, he did have access to Jewish and Christian oral traditions (though this is

A thirteenth-century manuscript of the Qur'an.

disputed by Muslims). For example, one of his wives was a Jewess and another was a nominal Christian from Ethiopia. Having to depend on oral traditions and being acquainted with heterodox forms of Christianity accounts for the fact that Muhammad in the Qur'an misunderstood the Christian teaching concerning the Trinity. In *sura* 5:77 he writes 'They misbelieve who say, "Verily God is the third of three."' He goes on to say 'Oh Jesus, son of Mary, hast thou said unto mankind: "Take me and my mother as two gods beside God"?'. Muhammad thought that Christians worshipped a trinity of a holy family which included God the

Father, Mary the Mother and Jesus the Son. For this reason the Qur'an attacks the sonship of Christ stating that 'God neither begets nor is begotten'.

Another misunderstanding which seems to have come from the influence of Jewish or heterodox Christian teaching was a denial of the crucifixion of Christ. The Qur'an in *sura* 4:156 states 'They slew him not and they crucified him not, that they had only his likeness . . . They really did not slay him.' The Qur'an, however, also teaches that Jesus was born of a virgin, worked miracles, was the Messiah, lived a sinless life, went up alive into heaven and is coming again before the end of the world.

'Praise be to God, the Lord of the worlds! The compassionate, the merciful! King of the day of judgement! Thee only do we worship, and to Thee do we cry for help. Guide Thou us on the straight path, The path of those to whom Thou hast been gracious— With whom Thou art not angry, and who go not astray.'

The most common prayer among Muslims; the words of *sura* 1 of *The Qur'an*

'By the star when it setteth, Your compatriot erreth not, nor is he led astray, Neither speaketh he from mere impulse. The Qur'an is no other than a revelation revealed to him: One terrible in power taught it him. Endued with wisdom.'

The words of Muhammad, *The Qur'an, sura* 53

The Worship of Islam

David Kerr

The Qur'an sees men and women as religious beings. 'I created ... humankind only that they might worship me,' the Muslim hears God say in the Qur'an. Each individual is an *'abd* of God, a term which conveys the twin meanings of 'worshipper' and 'servant' in a single word. And this description applies to all aspects of human life, all of which is lived under the command of God. There is no distinction between worship and the wholeness of human life.

Submission to God

Islam understands itself fundamentally as being 'natural religion', in that *every* created thing exists in dependence upon God, in obedience to his creative and sustaining power and with the purpose of expressing adoration to God. For the human, this should lead to a conscious commitment to a life of thankful and praise-giving obedience to God. The word *muslim* means one who lives his life according to God's will. *Islam* means 'submission to God'.

Worship (*'ibada*) and the activities of the work-a-day world (*mu'amallat*) are joint expressions of the character of *'abd*. The mosque cannot be separated from the market-place, nor politics from praise.

As far as worship is concerned, the Qur'an sees body and spirit as inseparably combined in the wholeness of human worship. Islam has no term for 'spirituality'; for its religious devotion secks to preserve an equilibrium between the 'outward' and the 'inward' in worship. The believer's external acts of worship depend on his internal intention, and the Qur'an is concerned that both should be 'for the pleasure of God'. So while the holy law provides a code of practice as a framework for Muslim worship, the worship depends on the inner dynamic of thankful and praise-giving obedience, the discipline of the soul to 'remember God always'.

The confession of faith

The Islamic code of conduct is founded upon the bedrock of the testimony of faith, the *shahada*. This is the first pillar of Islam. When spoken in Arabic and with sincere intention, it is a commitment to obey God and follow the prophet.

'I bear witness that there is no god but God; I bear witness that Muhammad is the Apostle of God.'

These are the first words breathed into a child's ear at birth and the last which a Muslim would utter with his dying breath—the lantern for life and the hope for the mercy of God in the life hereafter. They point to the one God who has spoken finally through the Qur'an; and they point to Muhammad, 'the Seal of the Prophets', sent to all mankind to transmit and interpret the Qur'an. The words of the *shahada* summon Muslims to worship throughout the world, and their meaning is the heart of prayer and meditation.

Praying together

The Qur'an identifies a human being as 'worshipper'. It also places the individual worshipper, male or female, in the context of a worshipping community.

'Hold fast, all of you, to the rope of God, and do not separate ... and may there spring from you a community who invite to goodness, enjoin right conduct and forbid indecency; such are they who are successful.'

The Shari'a codifies and coordinates the practice of a worshipping community. Worship is a communal act as well as one of individual commitment. To affirm the unity of God (*tawhid*) is necessarily to affirm the unity of the created order and of mankind in right worship.

This community orientation of Islamic worship is symbolized and demonstrated in the ritual of *salat*, the liturgical form of prayer, which it is the duty of all Muslims to observe at fixed hours. Prayer is the second pillar of Islam. There are five prayer times, each preceded by obligatory ritual washing—dawn, midday, mid-afternoon, sunset and night—and they serve to remind Muslims in a regular and disciplined manner of their status before God as 'worshipful servants'. From the moment of the muezzin's call and the preliminary washings *salat* is a communal act.

An expression of this is the common direction (towards the Ka'ba in Mecca) in which all Muslims turn in prayer. Around the globe all are united in direction and in intention within a human circle of worshippers. At a signal from the prayer leader, the *imam*, men and women assemble separately in rows, at the mosque or in the home or place of work, taking care that each person is close to the next. Carefully following the lead of the *imam*, they pray as a single body, quietly reciting words of prayer from the Qur'an. At the same time they bow their bodies in a

Every adult Muslim is encouraged to make the pilgrimage to Mecca once in his lifetime, preferably in the great month of pilgrimage.

series of ritual movements until, from an initial standing position, all are upon their knees with foreheads touching the floor—the whole congregation enacting as a single body its submission before the majesty of God and asking for his guidance and mercy. Each of the five sets of prayers includes the repetition of *Allahu akbar* ('God is greatest') and of the first *sura* of the Qur'an, itself a prayer. At the end of the prayer each person passes the Arabic words of peace to neighbours on right and left: *as-salamu alaikum*, 'peace be upon you'. Private prayers often follow the public service.

The twofold fruit of giving

'O you who believe, perform the *salat* and give the *zakat*.' Prayer is linked closely with almsgiving, the third pillar of Islam, often described by modern Muslims as the pillar of social action. Externally *zakat* is the duty of sharing one's wealth with the poor, the needy, the debtor, the prisoner, the wayfarer—all who are less fortunate than oneself but equally part of the worshipping community and equally precious to God. The Qur'an is less concerned with the quantity, and more with the quality of giving. When it is offered 'in search of God's pleasure and for the

strengthening of their own souls, it is as the likeness of a garden on a hill; the rainstorm smites it and it brings forth its fruit twofold'. The inward attitude is all-important; discretion is preferred to ostentation, and reproach on the part of the giver makes the action worthless.

The Shari'a is meticulous in determining the amounts of alms which should be given on different categories of possessions, but contemporary practice simplifies the matter to an annual rate of 2½ per cent of one's cash balance. But Muslim devotional literature reflects equally the inwardness of *zakat* as 'purification' of the soul. It is a mercy to the giver as much as to the recipient. It is a means to atone for sins which are motivated by human self-centredness, or by irresponsible stewardship of possessions.

The most-loved duty of worship

Special alms are given on the two main religious festivals of the Islamic calendar, the first of which, *'Id al-Fitr* or *Bairam*, marks the end of Ramadan, the holy month of fasting. Fasting (*sawm*) is the fourth pillar of Muslim worship, and involves a total abstinence from food and drink through the daylight hours of the entire month, from early dawn to sunset.

In some ways this is the most obviously communal of the duties of Islamic worship. The physical discipline means that social behaviour of the whole community has to change for the duration of the month; the pace of life slows down and there is time for reflection. It is a period when social relationships are reaffirmed, reconciliations encouraged, and the solidarity of the community is expressed. Mosque attendance swells, particularly on the Night of Power (*laylat al-qadr*) towards the end of the month, when Muslims commemorate the descent of the

Preparation for prayer outside the
mosque at Qum in Iran. The
Muslims of Iran are Shi'ites, the
smaller division of Islam.

Qur'an from heaven and the
beginning of Muhammad's
ministry.

The fundamental intention of
fasting is thanksgiving. Inwardly
the fast is thought of as a dis-
ciplining of the soul to wait
patiently upon God who guides
and provides. This inward aspect
is of great importance. Muhammad is reported to have said that
of all the duties of worship, *sawm*
is the most loved by God since it
is seen only by him.

To Mecca

The fifth of the fundamental
duties of Islamic worship, to be
fulfilled once in a lifetime if at all
possible, is the *Hajj*, the pilgrimage to Mecca and its vicinity.
Here are the most holy of holy
places for Muslims, full of
'memorials' of God's guidance in
times past. There are associations
with Muhammad who began his
life and ministry in the city, and
also with his prophetic precursor
Abraham who, according to the
Qur'an, built the Ka'ba, helped
by his son Ishmael, as a sign of
their submission to God, with the
prayer that God would show
them 'our ways of worship'.

A visit to Mecca has religious
significance for Muslims at any
time of the year. But with the
twelfth month of the calendar,
dhu alhijja, the season of the *Hajj*
or Great Pilgrimage arrives. (At
any other time it is a Little Pilgrimage.) Pilgrims flock to
Mecca, each wearing the simple
pilgrimage garb of white cloth
denoting the state of ritual purification. They congregate in the
Great Mosque and the first rite of
pilgrimage is performed—the
circumambulation around the
Ka'ba. This is followed by running seven times between two
small hills, recalling the plight of
Hagar and her son Ishmael who,
in Islamic, Jewish and Christian

The Festivals of Islam

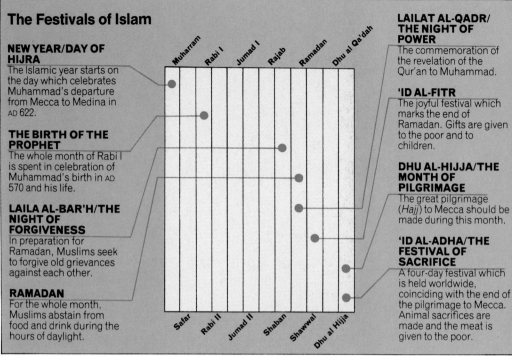

NEW YEAR/DAY OF HIJRA
The Islamic year starts on the day which celebrates Muhammad's departure from Mecca to Medina in AD 622.

THE BIRTH OF THE PROPHET
The whole month of Rabi I is spent in celebration of Muhammad's birth in AD 570 and his life.

LAILA AL-BAR'H/THE NIGHT OF FORGIVENESS
In preparation for Ramadan, Muslims seek to forgive old grievances against each other.

RAMADAN
For the whole month, Muslims abstain from food and drink during the hours of daylight.

LAILAT AL-QADR/ THE NIGHT OF POWER
The commemoration of the revelation of the Qur'an to Muhammad.

'ID AL-FITR
The joyful festival which marks the end of Ramadan. Gifts are given to the poor and to children.

DHU AL-HIJJA/THE MONTH OF PILGRIMAGE
The great pilgrimage (*Hajj*) to Mecca should be made during this month.

'ID AL-ADHA/THE FESTIVAL OF SACRIFICE
A four-day festival which is held worldwide, coinciding with the end of the pilgrimage to Mecca. Animal sacrifices are made and the meat is given to the poor.

tradition, were saved from certain death by a spring of water which God caused to break through the desert sands. This well is named in the Islamic tradition as *zamzam*, and from it the pilgrims may draw holy water before journeying a few miles out of Mecca to Mount Arafat where the *Hajj* comes to its climax. Here the pilgrims observe the rite of 'standing' from midday to sunset in meditation before God. Then they begin the return

Mecca was the birthplace of the prophet Muhammad. It is the centre of Muslim pilgrimage, towards which Muslims turn to pray. The focal point of the city is the cube-like shrine, the Ka'ba, which contains the sacred Black Stone.

journey to Mecca, stopping overnight at Mazdalifa where each pilgrim gathers pebbles. The following day these are thrown ritually against three stone pillars in the neighbouring village of Mina, recalling the moments in Abraham's life when he resisted Satan's temptations to disobey God. God had commanded him to prepare his son (Ishmael) for sacrifice as a test of his obedience (*islam*). The Qur'an tells how the child was ransomed 'with a tremendous victim', and in joyful recollection of this act of divine mercy the pilgrims offer the ritual sacrifice of sheep or camels, the meaning of which is clearly stated in the Qur'an: 'their flesh and blood reach not to God, but your devotion reaches him'.

With the intention of magnifying God and remembering him 'with a more lively remembrance', Muslims throughout the world join with the pilgrims in Mina for the Feast of the Slaughter, which brings the *Hajj* to an end. Muslims remember their corporate identity and responsibility as a worshipping community created by Muhammad. Muhammad believed that this festival was the fulfilment of the Muslim community for which Abraham is said to have prayed before the Ka'ba: 'Our Lord make us submissive to thee, and of our seed a community submissive to thee, and show us our ways of worship, and turn towards us. Lo! thou, only thou, art the Relenting, the Merciful' (Qur'an 2:128).

The Law of Islam

Norman Anderson

Down the centuries the traditional education of a Muslim has rested on twin pillars. Theology taught him what he should believe, and the sacred law prescribed how he should behave. And in practice the law has been the senior partner, for Islam has always been far more explicit about the quality of life God has ordained for his creatures than about the nature of the Creator himself. Although the role of Islamic law has changed considerably in recent years, it can still be described as 'the epitome of Islamic thought, the most typical manifestation of the Islamic way of life, the core and kernel of Islam itself'.

The Path of God's commandments

The sacred law of Islam is called the Shari'a—a word which originally meant 'the way to a watering-place', but came to be used of the path of God's commandments. It is regarded by Muslims as firmly based on divine revelation, derived from four main sources:
● the Qur'an—which, they believe, has existed eternally in Arabic in heaven, and was revealed piecemeal to Muhammad by the angel Gabriel as occasion demanded.
● the *sunna*—or practice of the

Prophet, as enshrined in countless traditions of what he said, did or permitted.
● the *ijma*—or consensus of the Muslim community or of its leading scholars.
● *qiyas*—analogical deductions from the first three sources.

Orientalists have, however, shown that the raw material of the Shari'a was actually provided by pre-Islamic customary law and the administrative practices of early Islam—systematized and Islamicized by scholar-jurists in the light of those Islamic norms which had come to be accepted. They also insist that, for a number of decades, the law was wide open to foreign influences current in the conquered territories or ingrained in the minds of converts to Islam.

The Shari'a has often been classified under five categories:
● what God has commanded
● what God has recommended but not made strictly obligatory
● what God has left legally indifferent
● what God has deprecated but not actually prohibited
● what God has expressly forbidden.

As such its scope is much wider than any Western concept of law, for it covers every aspect of life. Obviously a great deal of it could never be enforced by any

human court, and must be left to the bar of eternity. But in theory, the Shari'a was a divinely revealed blueprint to which every Muslim, from caliph to slave, must attempt to approximate.

In theory, man-made regulations were only appropriate in those matters which God had left 'legally indifferent'. In practice, though, from a very early date, even the official courts allowed a number of 'devices' which eased the inconvenience of some of the Shari'a's precepts.

Muslim rulers, moreover, found its standards of proof too exacting for the maintenance of public order. Muslim merchants found its prohibitions too restrictive for the life of the markets. And local communities of Muslims found its rigid prescripts too alien to their age-old customs. So less rigid courts soon appeared beside the official *qadis'* courts. But the fact remains that, until little more than a century ago, the Shari'a remained the basic (and residual) law—to which lip-service, at least, was almost always paid—through the length and breadth of the Muslim world.

Interpreting the law

But the Shari'a was not a system of law which was either codified or uniform. For although it is regarded as firmly based on divine revelation, it has been developed and elaborated by generations of legal scholars.

The scholars interpreted the relevant verses in the Qur'an and those traditions which they accepted as authentic. They also drew from these sources a plethora of analogical deductions. At first, moreover, any adequately qualified jurist had the right of *ijtihad*—going back to the original sources to derive a rule of law to cover any problem that arose.

At a very early date, however, the Muslim community became divided between the Sunni, or 'orthodox', majority and the Shi'a and Khariji minorities. These two minorities proceeded to split into further exclusive sub-sects, and the Sunni majority divided into a number of different schools or 'rites'. As these schools and sects crystallized, the right of independent deduction was progressively replaced by the duty to accept the authority of the great jurists of the past (*taqlid*). Today even the most learned Sunni jurists are normally considered to be under this authority. The Ithna 'Ashari subsect of the Shi'a (which is still the dominant sect in Iran, for example) still recognizes *mujtahids* who may exercise *ijtihad* in certain circumstances. It is only among the Isma'ili Shi'is that their *imam*—or, in some cases, his representative, the Da'i Mutlaq—can give a wholly authoritative ruling.

Civil law

Since about the middle of the nineteenth century, the position of Islamic law has changed radically throughout the greater part of the Muslim world. First in the Ottoman Empire, next in what was then 'British India', and subsequently elsewhere, the impact of modern life has loosened the sway of the Shari'a in two major ways.

The first change is plain for all to see. In many spheres of life the Shari'a has been displaced by new codes of law, largely derived from the Western world. In the Ottoman Empire, in the 1850s and 1860s, for example, the Commercial Code, the Penal Code, the Code of Commercial Procedure and the Code of Maritime Commerce were all based on French models. But when the Ottoman reformers came to the law of obligations (contract, tort, etc.), they debated whether again to turn to European law or to compile a comparable code derived from Islamic sources.

Eventually the latter view prevailed. So the resultant code (commonly known as the Majalla, completed in 1876) was compiled from the rulings of a selection of Sunni jurists—although all these opinions had received some form of recognition from the Hanafi school. The Majalla was thus of immense jurisprudential significance. For the first time in history, a code of law based firmly on principles derived from the Shari'a was enacted by the authority of the state. And for the first time, again, a compilation was made of provisions of heterogeneous origin selected on the broad principle of their suitability to modern life, rather than their established precedent in one particular school. Moreover, all these new codes were administered in secular courts by personnel trained in modern law schools. It was only the family law which continued to be applied in the age-old way in the Shari'a courts, uncodified and unreformed.

The second change was less obvious but equally important. In 1915 the intolerable lot of Muslim wives under the dominant Hanafi rules virtually compelled the sultan to intervene even in matters of family law. So he issued two imperial decrees permitting wives to request a judicial dissolution of marriage in certain circumstances sanctified by one or other of the Sunnic schools. Once this dyke had been opened the tide came in very fast indeed. In 1917 the Ottoman Law of Family Rights was promulgated based on an extended application of these principles.

In one Muslim country after another, much the same happened. In 'British India' the new secular codes were, of course, based on the Common Law of England rather than the Civil Law of France. Here both secular

Islamic law, the Shari'a, deals with family life and religious requirements as well as matters of civil concern.

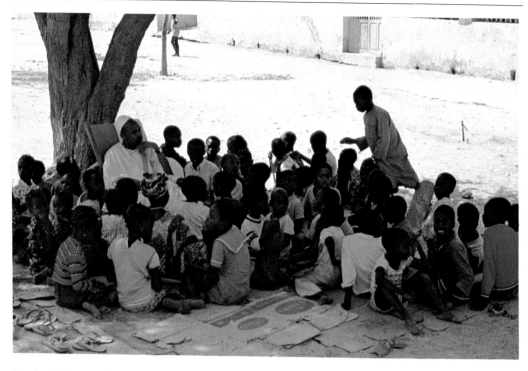

Muslim children are taught the Qur'an in daily lessons. This class is taking place in Senegal.

law and the uncodified family law of different religious communities were administered by the same courts. In Turkey, by contrast, the Shari'a was abolished and European codes (only slightly adapted) were adopted in its place.

In Saudi Arabia, on the other hand, the Shari'a remains dominant—though even there statutory regulations have begun to proliferate. Most Muslim countries, however, now have largely secular codes in all except family law—which must, they insist, remain distinctively Islamic. And even this has been codified—in whole or in part—in a way which makes it more suitable for modern life. In countries such as Somalia and the People's Democratic Republic of Yemen the presence of Marxist influence in such codes is sometimes plain to see.

Thus the present picture is very different from that of the past. Whereas the once-dominant Shari'a is now, for the most part, confined to family law, the current tendency is to produce civil codes which incorporate principles derived from Islamic law alongside those of an alien origin. A few countries have, even more recently, begun to reintroduce some of the Islamic criminal sanctions—a clear evidence of a resurgence of Islamic fundamentalism. In most Muslim countries, moreover, the law—whatever its origin—has been codified by legislative enactments. Thus the authority of the law, once implicit and transcendent, is now, in most countries, constitutional, resting on the will of the people as expressed by their executive or legislature.

A Day in the Life of a Muslim Family

Anthony Harrop

A slight wind sweeps across the flat countryside. There is still no sign of dawn on the eastern horizon. Her family still asleep, Latifa Begum crosses to the tube-well in the yard. She pumps the handle until the clear cold water rises. Neighbours are stirring now. She calls to her eldest child, daughter Safina, 'Tell the boys to get up immediately. Their teacher will soon be here.'

The pale line on the horizon is now a band of mauve shading into yellow. Suddenly, from the newly-installed loudspeaker on the minaret of the mosque 100 yards away, the call to the morning prayer (*fazur*) resounds: 'Wake up, wake up, prayer is better than sleep.'

Prayer

Latifa's husband, Abdul Khaliq, comes out of the house, donning his prayer-cap as he heads for the mosque. As he reaches the gate, his distant relative Abdur Rahman arrives. Rahman is a student, half-way through his ten-year training to become a Muslim religious teacher, a *maulvi*. In order to help him financially during his studies, the family have appointed him to give religious instruction to the children. He leads their prayers each morning.

As they hear his voice the boys run out and together the three of them perform the ceremonial ablutions. Then, with their prayer-mats laid out on the verandah, in careful alignment towards Mecca, they recite the prayer following the example of their teacher. Latifa Begum and Safina, after their own ablutions, also recite the prayer, but separately inside the house, away from the gaze of any outsider, as befits women in Islam.

The prayer finished, Safina joins her brothers for the instruction. Seated on a rush mat on the cement verandah, they recite in unison as Abdur Rahman leads them in a section of the holy Qur'an. The boys are still sleepy and they make many mistakes. But Safina has a good memory and Rahman only has to correct her pronunciation of the classical Arabic. Again and again the section is repeated. After almost an hour, all three children can recite it word-perfect.

Meanwhile, their mother has been preparing breakfast—some rice left over from the previous evening's meal, chapatis, biscuits, a cup of tea for the adults and cow's milk for the children. The teacher stays for the meal, and husband Khaliq comes in.

Part of the community

Khaliq has been delayed at the mosque after the morning prayer. He and the leading religious teacher were talking about payment of the *zakat*, the annual religious tax. The month of fasting (Ramadan) commences in a few weeks' time, and Khaliq's household has been assessed for 200kg of rice, half to be paid

The Muslim community is called to prayer by the muezzin, *who then leads them in prayer.*

during the fast to the mosque authorities for distribution to the poorer members of the village community. As one of the wealthier men of the village, Khaliq's payment of the tax will be a significant contribution to community well-being.

Across the compound from Khaliq's family lives his widowed mother. That afternoon, when the midday sun has lost some of its heat, Khaliq, his mother and Latifa Begum discuss the arrangements for the fast and the payment of the tax:

'Everyone will need a new set of clothes for the festival at the end of the fast. That means fitting out the whole family. And we should also give something to Abdur Rahman,' they decide.

Khaliq's mother wants to invite her two married daughters for *'Id-al-Fitr* ('the Little Festival'). Their husbands will come, too, but will probably only stay a few days. Still, that will almost double the number who must be fed, and the relatives should also receive presents.

'Can we think of any other relative we should give to?'

'Yes, there's my dead cousin's second wife's children,' says Khaliq. 'The boy has a place in a *madrassa* as a charity student, but the family is too poor even to buy him a new suit of clothes.'

'That too is our responsibility,' insists the older lady. 'In addition to our responsibility to our own family, we must pay half the tax during the fast, to help the poorer people in the village to have a better festival'.

'But can we afford it at this time, with so many relatives coming to stay? And in three months' time we shall need a good animal for the sacrifice at the Great Festival.'

'No, we must pay our share of the tax during the fast, even if that means we only have a goat, not a calf to sacrifice.'

The afternoon glides into evening. Dusk breezes dissolve the day's heat to a freshening coolness. Two hours after sunset the day ends as it began, with the late evening prayer *(isha)* echoing around the groves of bamboo and palm, over the thatched houses and out into the still countryside.

Science, Art and Culture in Islam

Lothar Schmalfuss

Islam has produced not only successful army leaders and statesmen but also equally talented poets and musicians, architects and builders. But above all there were the Muslim philosophers and naturalists, whose achievements between the ninth and fourteenth centuries laid the foundations of modern science on which our civilization was built.

For Muslims to start to study the world, they needed a 'supernatural' incentive. Allah was looked on as the Unapproachable, the Impenetrable, so Islam had taught that his creation was similarly unapproachable. It was Mahmun, caliph of Baghdad from 813–833, who supplied that incentive. In a dream, Mahmun saw the ghost of Aristotle, who convinced him that there is no contradiction between religion and reason. Thus freed from all his scruples, Mahmun ordered a 'house of wisdom' to be built. In the library all available books in the world were to be collected.

The works of Greek, Persian and Indian writers were brought together and translated into Arabic, and the knowledge obtained was examined, remodelled and developed. So the starting-point and basis of Islamic knowledge was the Greek conviction that behind the visible chaos of the world there is a fundamental order, ruled by general laws and accessible to human reason. Thus scientific effort pursued primarily philosophical goals, the discovery of the 'basic laws' of the world.

Muslim doctors built on the experience and knowledge of ancient Persia. They discovered the principle of the circulation of the blood, evolved treatment methods for smallpox and practised painless operations under anaesthetics. Their learning, known as the *Avicenna* (after Ibn Sina, the great philosopher and physician) was used as an important textbook in the universities of Europe until the seventeenth century.

In mathematics, Islamic academics learnt from India. From there they adopted the decimal system and also the use of the zero. They called this *sifr*, the empty one. Leonardo de Pisa, who had studied with the Arabs, translated this foreign concept as 'cephirum' and it then developed via 'zefiro' to 'zero'. It was the Arabs also who developed the subject of algebra, using symbols to represent unknown quantities.

Early on, the Arabs had used the stars as guides in the desert. When they became familiar with the work of Ptolemy in the eighth century, they also began to investigate the sky scientifically. Star names and astronomical terms such as zenith, nadir and azimuth are an enduring witness to this work. Scholars also collected their geographical knowledge in atlases and travel guides which recorded the main roads of all known countries, as well as the names and positions of the large towns and their distances one from another. They also calculated the circumference and diameter of the earth.

A worldwide influence

At the height of their culture the knowledge of the Muslims extended to all areas. The fascination they inspired in Europe was enormous. Wherever the West met the East, the West started to learn. In Sicily the court of Friedrich II became a centre of Arabian philosophy and science. In the Levant the Crusader knights became familiar with the Eastern way of life. Above all, this contact took place in Islamic Spain. As early as the tenth century towns were thriving. Cordoba had over 500,000 inhabitants with 700 mosques, 300 public baths and seventy libraries. Its streets and squares were paved and brightly lit at night. Everything which made life pleasant was offered for sale: marzipan, soap and perfume, coffee, damsons and sugar, mattresses, caps and jackets, oranges, asparagus. Their influence spread right through Europe. Travelling singers from Andalusia brought their songs and also Arabic instruments—lute and guitar, trumpet horn and flute. Through Muslim philosophers such as Averroes (Ibn Rushd) and Avicenna (Ibn Sina), Aristotle was rediscovered in the West.

A mosque in Java. Islam is the religion of much of south-east Asia.

In the fine arts, calligraphy, ceramics and architecture, Islam absorbed influences into itself. It took the cultural inheritance of the peoples it conquered and transformed them, creating an all-embracing culture of a unique type. Islamic architecture can be seen in Cordoba, Granada, Marrakesh and Cairo, in Istanbul and Damascus, Agra and Delhi. All reflect the form and style of the country they are in, as well as the Islamic influence which unites them. The 'Islamic' style has a

particular sensitivity for the decorative, and strives to turn the natural appearance of things into the abstract.

The Qur'an teaches that an object and its image are magically united. This was probably the reason why representational art was prohibited.

With the sack of Baghdad by the Mongol invaders in 1258 and the general decline of the Islamic world, the development of art, culture and science in Islam was halted.

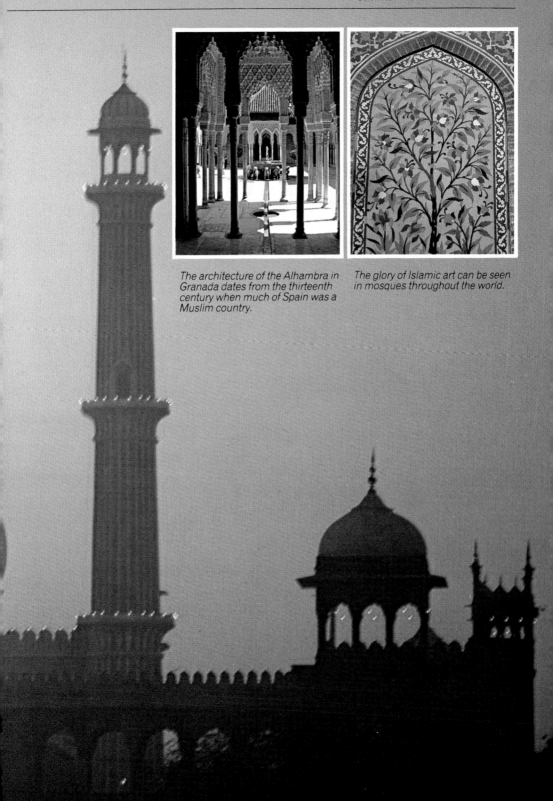

The architecture of the Alhambra in Granada dates from the thirteenth century when much of Spain was a Muslim country.

The glory of Islamic art can be seen in mosques throughout the world.

The Unity and Variety in Islam

David Kerr

Islam has two basic groups—the Sunni and Shi'a. Their origins can be traced back to a question which faced the first generation of Muslims: how was Muhammad, 'the Seal of the Prophets', to be succeeded as leader of the Muslim community? For Muslims, this question was always a religious as well as a political one.

Sunnis—the community consensus

The answer of the Sunnis, who constitute the Muslim majority of approximately 90 per cent, can be summarized as follows. No one could succeed Muhammad in his nature and quality as prophet, for the Qur'an finalized and perfected the revelation of divine guidance and declared Muhammad to be 'the Seal of the Prophets'. Muhammad's successor could therefore be no more than the guardian of the prophetic legacy. He would be a caliph (*khalifa*) with subordinate authority as leader of the believers, having responsibility for the administration of community affairs in obedience to the Qur'an and prophetic precedent. By the process of consensus (*ijma*) the community would select its caliph from amongst the male membership of the Quraish tribe to which Muhammad belonged.

Following Muhammad's death in AD 632, caliphal succession passed from Abu Bakr (632–634) to 'Umar (634–644) to 'Uthman (644–656) and to 'Ali (656–661). These, 'the four rightly-guided caliphs' are deemed to have lived so close to the Prophet that their example, together with Muhammad's, is taken to comprise the authoritative *sunna*, or custom, for all later generations of Muslims to follow.

The Sunnis gradually developed a comprehensive system of community law, the Shari'a. This provided cohesion within the community while allowing for variance between four orthodox law schools, the Malikis, Hanafis Shafi'is and Hanbalis. The principle of *ijma* remained central. Notionally *ijma* is the consensus of the whole community, though in practice it is that of the legal scholars.

After the 'rightly-guided caliphs' the caliphate became a dynastic institution, regarded as the guardian of the Shari'a. But in 1924 it was abolished. The

The vigorously missionary Ahmaddiya sect, founded in India in the early part of this century, is considered heretical by other Muslims. Ahmad announced himself as the awaited saviour of Islam, Christianity and Hinduism.

ijma of contemporary Sunni Islam seems to be that if the Shari'a is observed by the national governments of Muslim states, there is no need for the transnational office of caliph to be restored.

Shi'a—authority and leadership

For Shi'a Muslims the principle figure of religious authority is the *imam*. Muhammad, 'the Seal of the Prophets', completed 'the cycle of prophethood' and with it the possibility of further divine revelation. But Shi'a Muslims believe that he instituted 'the cycle of initiation' for the continuing guidance of the community, by appointing as his successor an *imam*. The *imam* was invested with the qualities of inspired and infallible interpretation of the Qur'an. Accordingly, the Shi'a speak of themselves as

'people of appointment and identification'.

The first *imam* was 'Ali. As cousin, adopted son and later son-in-law of Muhammad (by marriage to Fatima), he was not just a member of Muhammad's tribe but also of 'the people of his house'. This intimate family relationship is significant: the Shi'a believe that 'Ali inherited Muhammad's 'spiritual abilities', his *wilaya*. He was infallible in his interpretation of the Qur'an and leadership of the community. And he passed these qualities on to the sons of his marriage with Fatima, Hasan and Husayn, and they to their descendants in the line of *imams*. The Shi'a believe that 'the cycle of *wilaya*' will continue until the end of human history when, on the Last Day, mankind will be resurrected and judged for the afterlife.

The majority of Shi'a, known as Imamis (most of whom live in Iran), believe that the cycle will

be completed with the messianic return to the twelfth *imam*, often referred to as the *'imam* of the period'. He is said to have been withdrawn into 'occulation' since the third century of Islam. His guidance is still accessible through 'agents' or 'doctors of the law' (*mujtahidun*) of whom the most senior in Iran are the *ayatollahs*. It is they who have the right to interpret the Shari'a and to make religious rulings.

The history of the Imamis has seen two important offshoots. The Saidis, mostly found in Yemen today, do not limit the number of *imams* to twelve and interpret their function in a manner similar to the Sunni caliph. The Isma'ilis, meanwhile, have developed highly esoteric doctrines surrounding the *imam*. They have two major groups, the Nizaris, who look to the Aga Khan as their *imam*, and the Musta'lis (more commonly known as the Bohora Muslims) who believe in a hidden *imam*

The Main Streams of Islam

SUNNI
90% majority
Government by community consensus
led (until 1924) by caliph

Wahhabi

MUHAMMAD   'ALI

Saidis

SHI'A
10% minority
Led by imam,
a successor of 'Ali

Twelvers/Imamis

Seveners/Isma'ilis

Ahmadiyya

who is not descended from Hasan and Husayn.

The two dimensions

Sunni and Shi'a Islam reflect the diversity of the Muslim response to divine revelation. Sunni Islam tends to be more concerned to create and preserve structures of society within which the community may fulfil its God-given responsibilities.

Shi'a Islam began in the martyrdoms of 'Ali and his son Husayn, and has always been conscious of suffering and alienation in the human condition. It searches for answers in a more esoteric interpretation of the Qur'an and Shari'a. But there is obviously no hard and fast distinction. Sunni Islam is also con-

In Shi'ite Islam, religious leaders, mullahs, mujtahids and ayatollahs, define the social and religious law of the community.

cerned with the inner life and Shi'a with the outer. Moreover, the important mystical tradition of Sufism has seen a confluence of Shi'a and Sunni consciousness.

The Future of Islam

Norman Anderson

The initial expansion of Islam in the Middle East, North Africa and Western Europe was achieved by military conquest. Much the same was also true, at a later date, in central Asia, the Indian peninsula and Eastern Europe. In Africa south of the Sahara, Malaysia and Indonesia, on the other hand, Islam spread chiefly by peaceful means—trade, settlement and penetration. But what pattern of expansion or contraction is likely to be seen in the future?

Further expansion by force of arms seems only a remote possibility, except in a few limited areas. But there can be no doubt whatever that a new spirit of self-confidence vis-a-vis the Western world is clearly apparent in the Middle East today—largely based, politically, on the vast reserves of oil in the Gulf area, and the wealth, influence and power which these represent. Throughout Europe and North America, moreover, there are growing numbers of Muslims who are increasingly concerned to preserve their identity and protect their traditions, and Islam is actively competing with Christianity and Marxism for the soul of Africa. But the claim that Islam is attracting significant numbers of converts all over the world has been much exagger-ated. To surmise what may happen in the future, however, we can only look at the trends which are apparent already in the Muslim world. There are a number of pointers.

Increasing secularization?

In many countries where Muslims represent a minority of the population, the current tendency is for governments to put forward uniform national laws which replace the religious laws of the Muslim community. In Kenya, Tanzania, Uganda and Ghana—and even Indonesia, where Muslims not only constitute the majority, but the largest Muslim population in the world—tentative steps in this direction have been taken. In India, however, the large Muslim minority has so far resisted the tendency. Among basically Muslim countries, Turkey officially secularized its law many years ago, and more recently Tunisia, Somalia, the People's Democratic Republic of Yemen (and, until their revolutions, Iran and Pakistan) have introduced certain radical innovations.

So the attitude of some Muslims today represents a distinct retreat from the traditional Islamic position. Ultimately this would reduce Islam to a purely personal matter between an individual and his God, rather than a religion which moulds, and is partially enforced by, society. Yet to erase the social influence of Islam would take many years, very severe repression (as experienced already by many previously solidly Muslim areas of the USSR), or the expulsive influence of a new religion or ideology. On the secular level, probably only communism could achieve this: since a Muslim disillusioned with his religion would find it comparatively easy to switch from one monolithic ideology to another, which may appear to him as more effective.

Radical revolution?

Diametrically opposite, there is the possibility of a fanatical resurgence of Islamic fundamentalism—as seen recently in Iran, Libya and Pakistan. It seems distinctly doubtful, however, whether any future movements of this sort will be able, in the long term, to resist the insidious pressures of modernity and materialism which would assail them from outside.

The middle way?

On the whole, it seems most likely that Islam will neither

In Iran, Muslim self-awareness has been expressed in revolution.

wither away nor return to its primitive past. Rather, it will continue to evolve, adapting itself to its contemporary environment.

If it is to develop in this way, there are certain hurdles to be cleared. The doctrine of holy war (*jihad*), for example, calls Muslims to wage war in all suitable circumstances in order to bring the non-Muslim world under the dominance of Islam. But to join the United Nations Organization with any integrity, Muslim countries must, of necessity, repudiate this classical doctrine—at least tacitly.

Islamic law prescribes the death penalty for a Muslim who 'apostasizes' from Islam. It prescribes stoning for illicit sex relations for any Muslim who has ever enjoyed a valid marriage, amputation of the hand for theft and flogging for certain other offences. For several reasons—including international relations, the Universal Declaration of Human Rights and other international conventions—some of these practices would come under severe criticism today. Similarly, though the Qur'an prohibits 'usury', most Muslim countries now take the view that this does not preclude the receipt of fixed rates of interest on bank deposits or from stocks and shares—although much thought is currently being given to this subject.

From a purely human point of view, it seems probable that Islam will continue to follow the somewhat chequered pattern which at present prevents the many and various countries of the Muslim world from achieving any stable unity. They realize that it is only on such a basis that they can ever exercise a really effective influence; and they can, and do, unite to meet particular threats or needs. But the factors which separate them—economic, political, sectarian, tribal and personal—are so acute that fissures soon appear in any united front.

So it seems likely that the three tendencies—growing secularization, sporadic revivals and evolving adaptations—will continue to co-exist or alternate in the Muslim world.

Christianity and Islam

Contacts and relations between Islam and Christianity have been almost uniformly unhappy. Muhammad himself seems to have been acquainted with only a very distorted presentation of Christian faith and teaching. The initial (and spectacular) Muslim conquests were, moreover, greatly facilitated by sad divisions and bitter disputes between rival Christian churches; and in the succeeding years, large numbers of nominal Christians came to adopt the religion of their new rulers—doing nothing to help mutual understanding. The antagonism was certainly not helped by the long centuries of virtual isolation which followed, broken only by the tragic episode of the Crusades.

During the last two centuries, Christian outreach to Muslims has been renewed. But the impact on the Muslim world has been small in most areas. In part this is because Muslim misconceptions of the Christian faith have proved remarkably resistant. In part it is because the work of Christian missions has all too often been associated with the political and economic imperialism of the West and with the love-hate reaction of most Muslims to European patterns of life and thought. It has also been hindered at times by cultural insensitivity, by an unnecessarily negative attitude to indigenous family and community customs, and by a positive proclamation of the Christian Gospel which has failed to convince because of its lack of theological content, sympathetic presentation or experimental authentication.

Part Six

Religion: or the Fulfilment of Religion?

Jesus

Richard France

Christianity is founded on the worship of Jesus Christ ('Jesus the Messiah') as Son of God, the unique self-revelation of God to man. At the same time it remembers this same Jesus as a real historical figure, a man of insignificant social standing who during his life was unknown outside the obscure corner of the Roman Empire where he lived and died.

Looking for liberation

Born just before the death of Herod the Great, king of Judea, in 4 BC, Jesus lived for a little over thirty years, scarcely travelling outside Palestine throughout his life.

The Jews were a subject people, living either under local princes appointed by the Roman emperor, or under the direct rule of Rome itself. A priestly party, the Sadducees, accepted Roman rule, to which they owed their influence. The Pharisees, who later became the dominant party, were mostly less concerned with politics, and concentrated on the study and application of the Old Testament Law. Some stricter Jews, Essenes, opted out of Jewish society and set up isolated communities—such as *Qumran*—where they could devote themselves to preserving their religious purity. But there were many Jews who resented Roman rule, and from time to time revolts broke out, leading eventually to the disastrous 'Jewish War' of AD 66–73.

The Jews had long hoped for 'the day of the Lord', when God would act to save his people. There were several different hopes of a 'Messiah', a saviour, whom God would send, and such hopes ran high at the time of Jesus. Some saw the Messiah in more spiritual terms, as a priestly or prophetic figure, but in popular expectation he was to be a political liberator, and there were occasional 'messianic' movements centred on popular leaders. Galilee was known as fertile ground for such movements.

Jesus was born at Bethlehem in Judea, but was brought up in Galilee, and most of his public activity was in that region. Judean Jews regarded Galilee as an uncultured, half-pagan area: Jesus' distinct 'northern accent' would have been conspicuous in Jerusalem.

His family was respectable, if not affluent: he was a 'carpenter', or general builder, an important figure in village life. But Nazareth was an obscure village, and Jesus' background was remote from urban culture.

The birth and early life of Jesus

Despite its provincial obscurity, Jesus' family had an honourable pedigree. So his birth took place in King David's town of Bethlehem. Owing to the overcrowding of the town for the Roman census, however, the circumstances were not very regal; his birth in a stable, visited by

The Christian faith depends from beginning to end on Jesus Christ, who was born in Israel around the year 4 BC.

shepherds from the neighbourhood, has become one of the best-known stories in the world.

But, along with the very down-to-earth circumstances of his birth, the Christian Gospels record the fact that it was far from ordinary. Angels proclaimed him the promised saviour, and his parents maintained that he was not conceived by human intercourse, but by the power of God. This bringing together of earthly poverty and obscurity with a miraculous birth is typical of the Gospels' portrait of Jesus, as truly human but also uniquely the Son of God.

Virtually nothing is known of Jesus' life from his infancy until about the age of thirty. He clearly received a sound education in the Old Testament scriptures, presumably in the local synagogue school. However, his upbringing was not in academic studies, but in the practical work of the carpenter.

The event which launched Jesus on his public ministry was the mission of his relative, John 'the Baptist', down in Judea. John called Israel to return to God, and baptized those who responded in the River Jordan. He attracted a large following, and Jesus joined him, was baptized, and himself began preaching. When John was put in prison, Jesus moved back to Galilee, and continued to preach in public.

Healing and preaching

The Gospels summarize Jesus' activity as 'preaching, teaching and healing', and that is how he would have appeared to his contemporaries during the three years or so of his public ministry.

He and his closest followers deliberately adopted a wandering and dependent style of life. They had no permanent home, but moved around as a group, accepting gifts and hospitality when offered. Jesus spoke frequently of the danger of becoming preoccupied with possessions, and called his followers instead to an almost reckless generosity.

As a preacher he drew large crowds, who followed him constantly. He taught with a vivid simplicity and an authority which contrasted sharply with other Jewish religious teachers. We shall consider the content of his preaching later.

Jesus was clearly well-known as a healer from the beginning of his public activity. The Gospels record his curing of many different types of illness and deformity, usually by a simple word and a touch, sometimes by a word alone. There is no elaborate ritual, nor any search for patients; rather a power which responded to physical need as he met it. He is also recorded as an exorcist, driving out demons by a word of command. It was apparently as much for his healing power as for his teaching that he was sought out by the Galilean crowds.

Most of Jesus' recorded miracles are healings, but a number of incidents are recorded where he displayed a supernatural control over nature. Again these were in response to actual needs, not mere arbitrary displays of power, as when he multiplied a little food to feed a hungry crowd, or calmed a dangerous storm on the lake by a command. The

The heart of the Christian message is that Jesus rose from the dead, having conquered sin and death. The picture shows a first-century rock-cut tomb, like the one in which Jesus was buried.

Gospels present him as one who did not go out of his way to gain a reputation as a miracle-worker, but whose personal authority extended beyond his words to a practical control over nature which inevitably made a deep impression on those around him.

Like many other Jewish teachers, Jesus quickly gathered a group of committed followers, known as his 'disciples'. He demanded of them an absolute commitment to the ideals he preached, and to himself personally, and a total dependence on God to supply all their needs. They acted as his spokesmen, going out on preaching and healing missions of their own. An inner group of twelve disciples were his constant companions.

An increasing amount of time was spent in teaching his disciples privately, preparing them to continue his mission. He told them that he would soon be killed, and expected them to be the focus of the new community created by his work. He taught them to see themselves as distinct from other men, and to make it their aim to win others to be his disciples.

Opposition

While Jesus was, at least at first, popular with the ordinary people of Galilee, he very quickly aroused the opposition of the leaders. His attitude was in many respects unconventional, and he posed a threat to the Jewish religious establishment.

He refused to recognize the barriers which divided men from one another in society. His habit of mixing with the ostracized classes, and even of eating with them, earned him the name of 'friend of tax-collectors and sinners'. Women held an unconventionally high place in his following, and not all of them were very respectable. He seemed to delight in reversing accepted standards, with his slogan: 'The first shall be last, and the last first.'

He did not share the general Jewish disdain for Samaritans—a despised minority of mixed blood. He even made a Samaritan the hero of one of his most famous stories, at the expense of respectable Jewish clerics. Although he seldom travelled outside Jewish territory, he welcomed the faith of a non-Jewish soldier and a Syrian woman, and declared that non-Jews, the Gentiles, would even displace Jews in the kingdom of God. As for economic barriers, Jesus deliberately gave up a secure livelihood, and made no secret of his contempt for affluence. It is no wonder that the establishment found him uncomfortable.

On religious questions he was equally radical. He clashed with the religious authorities because of his free attitude to the observance of the Sabbath, the day of rest, and his declaration that ritual purification mattered less than purity of heart. His bold reinterpretation of the Old Testament Law moved consistently away from an external keeping of rules to a deeper and more demanding ethic. He declared the will of God with a sovereign assurance which cut through centuries of evolving tradition, and set him on a collision course with the scribes and Pharisees whose heartless legalism he denounced.

Nor could he please the Sadducees, the priestly rulers. He taught that the Jewish nation was ripe for God's judgement, and predicted even the destruction of the temple on which their national religion was centred. In a symbolic gesture he 'purified' the temple by violently expelling the traders whose presence the priests encouraged. Moreover his enthusiastic popular following threatened to upset the delicate balance of their co-operation with Rome.

All this, we may be sure, did not diminish Jesus' popularity with the ordinary people, who soon came to see him as the expected deliverer, and even on one occasion tried to force him to be their king in rebellion against Rome. But Jesus made it clear that his idea of salvation was not a political one. So gradually his popular following dwindled, as those who wanted a military Messiah became disillusioned. Even one of his twelve closest disciples betrayed him in the end, and none of them under-

'"I'm ready to accept Jesus as a great moral teacher, but I don't accept his claim to be God." That is the one thing we must not say. A man who was merely a man and said the sort of things Jesus said would not be a great moral teacher. He would either be a lunatic—on a level with the man who says he is a poached egg—or else he would be the Devil of Hell. You must make your choice. Either this man was, and is, the Son of God; or else a madman or something worse. You can shut him up for a fool, you can spit at him and kill him as a demon, or you can fall at his feet and call him Lord and God. But let us not come with any patronizing nonsense about his being a great human teacher. He has not left that open to us. He did not intend to.'

C. S. Lewis, *Mere Christianity*

'For God loved the world so much that he gave his only Son, so that everyone who believes in him may not die but have eternal life.'

The New Testament
Gospel of John, 3:16

'The Father and I are one.'

John 10:30

stood his real purpose until after his death.

Death and resurrection

The opposition to Jesus came to its climax at the Passover festival in Jerusalem. Jesus rode into the city in a deliberately 'messianic' gesture—though on a peaceable donkey, not a war-horse—and was enthusiastically welcomed by the crowds, who probably expected him now to declare himself their national leader. Instead, he carried out his demonstration against the temple regime, and engaged in a series of increasingly bitter exchanges with the religious authorities; but he showed no sign of acting against Rome.

Eventually he was arrested by the Jewish leaders with the help of Judas, his disillusioned disciple, and was tried according to Jewish law on a charge of blasphemy, because he claimed to be the Messiah and the Son of God. A death sentence was passed, but a Roman conviction was required to make it effective. This was secured by a charge of sedition, pressed upon the Roman governor by the religious leaders with a show of popular support. So, ironically, the Jesus who had forfeited his popular following by his refusal to take up arms against Rome was executed by Rome as a political rebel, 'the king of the Jews'.

He was executed by crucifixion, the barbaric method reserved by Rome for slaves and rebels. Some highly-placed followers obtained his body and buried it in a nearby tomb.

The cross has rightly become the symbol of Christianity. In that death, with all its cruelty and injustice, is the focus of salvation, and Jesus had already taught his disciples to see it that way, little as they had yet understood him. But the cross alone could have no such significance. It was the sequel that gave it meaning.

Two days later his disciples found the tomb was empty. Their failure to understand this is not surprising—there was much about Jesus they had not understood. But the meaning of it was brought home to them by a series of encounters with Jesus himself, alive and real, though no longer bound by the limitations of time and space (he could appear and disappear suddenly, even inside a closed room).

For a few weeks they met him in a variety of situations, sometimes one or two alone, more often in a larger group. He explained to them again the meaning of his life and death, and the mission he had entrusted to them. Then he left them, and they began to preach to the world that Jesus, triumphant even over death, was Lord and Saviour. It was the resurrection of Jesus which formed the focus of the earliest Christian preaching; it was the risen Lord whom they worshipped.

What Jesus taught

The Gospels sum up Jesus' preaching in Galilee in the challenge: 'The time has come; the kingdom of God is near. Repent and believe the good news!' This summary is a convenient framework for setting out some of the main points of his message.

● **'The time has come'** The Old Testament pointed forward to God's great work of judgement and salvation, when all Israel's hopes and the promises of God would be fulfilled. Jesus saw his mission as this time of fulfilment. In other words, however little he shared popular ideas of a political deliverer, he saw himself as the Messiah, come to save God's people. He called himself the Son of man, echoing a figure in the Old Testament book of Daniel who represented the ultimate deliverance and triumph of the true people of God.

● **'The kingdom of God is near'** The kingdom of God (more accurately, the 'reign of God'; it is an activity, not a place or a community) is central in Jesus' teaching. It means that God is in control, that his will is done. So he called men to enter God's kingdom, to accept his sovereignty and to live as his subjects. He taught them to look forward to the day when this kingship of God, already inaugurated by Jesus ('Yours is the kingdom'), would find its fulfilment when all men acknowledged God as king ('Your kingdom come'), when Jesus himself would return in glory, and share the universal and everlasting dominion of his Father.

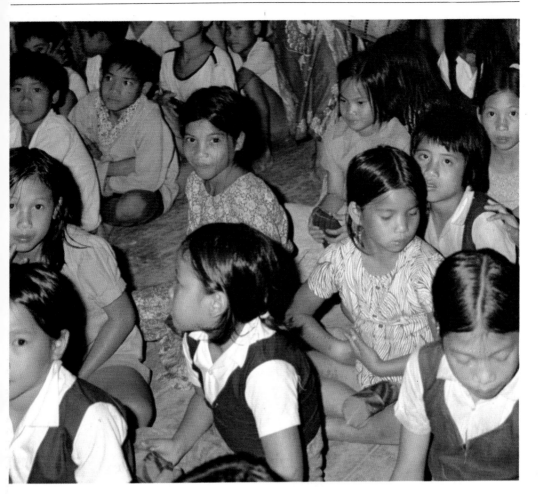

● **'Repent'** Jesus' call was issued primarily to his own people, Israel. He called them to return to their true loyalty to God. He warned them of God's judgement if they refused. There was an urgency in his appeal, and as it was increasingly rejected he spoke of God calling others to be his people instead. Finally, after his resurrection, he sent his disciples to call all nations into the kingdom of God. God's demands are absolute, and disobedience or disloyalty would not be overlooked.

● **'Believe the good news'** Now was the time for deliverance. Jesus preached this not in a political sense, but in terms of the restoration of a true relationship with God. Those who repented would find forgiveness and a new life. And as Jesus predicted his own suffering and death, he saw this as the means of restoration; he was the servant of God whom Isaiah had foretold, 'by whose wounds we are healed'. So he came 'to give his life as a ransom for many', to institute 'the new covenant in my blood', a new people of God redeemed from sin as Israel had been redeemed from slavery in Egypt to be God's special people.

This was the focus of Jesus' teaching, the call to repentance, to membership of a new people of God, forgiven and restored through his atoning death. His famous ethical teaching takes second place, for it is

'I am the bread of life. He who comes to me will never be hungry.

'I am the light of the world. Whoever follows me will have the light of life and will never walk in darkness.

'I am the gate for the sheep ... Whoever comes in by me will be saved.

'I am the good shepherd, who is willing to die for the sheep.

'I am the resurrection and the life. Whoever believes in me will live, even though he dies; and whoever lives and believes in me will never die.

'I am the way, the truth and the life; no one goes to the Father except by me.

'I am the vine, and you are the branches. Whoever remains in me, and I in him, will bear much fruit; for you can do nothing without me.'

Jesus' great statements about himself, from John's Gospel

primarily an ethic for disciples, for those who have thus entered the kingdom of God.

For them life is new. It is focussed on God, their king, but also their Father, for Jesus taught his disciples to depend on God with a childlike trust. Their relations with one another were to be those of members of the same family, inspired by an unselfish, uncalculating love. In this new community many of the world's standards would be reversed, and a concern for material security and advancement would be swallowed up in an overriding longing to see God's kingdom established. It is an other-worldly ethic which has profound this-worldly implications. Jesus expected his disciples to be clearly different, the 'light of the world', showing the world what life was meant to be like. They were to be like God their Father.

Who was Jesus?

He was hailed as a prophet, a man sent by God. In his preaching, teaching and healing he matched up to that role, and as such he is one of a long and noble sequence of men of God before and since. But Christians believe, and his own life and teaching suggest, that he was much more than that.

In his appeal to Israel there was a clear note of finality. This was not just another prophetic warning, but God's last call. Its rejection would spell the end of Israel as God's special people; its acceptance would create a new people of God in whom all God's purposes would reach their climax.

The criterion was not only the response to Jesus' message, but the response to Jesus himself. He called for faith in and loyalty to himself, and presented himself as the final arbiter of men's destiny. He not only proclaimed forgiveness and salvation: by his own life and suffering and death he achieved it. He is the messenger, but he is also the heart of the message. He calls men to God, but he is also himself the way to God.

During Jesus' earthly life his disciples only dimly understood all this, though they understood enough to make them tenaciously loyal to him. But after his resurrection they quickly came to speak of him as more than just a man, and to worship him as they worshipped his Father. And even during his earthly teaching Jesus had prepared the way for this by speaking of himself as the Son of God in a unique sense, and of God as his Father in an exclusive relationship quite different from the sense in which his disciples could use the term. 'All things have been committed to me by my Father. No one knows the Son except the Father, and no one knows the Father except the Son and those to whom the Son chooses to reveal him.'

The worship of Jesus the man as the Son of God did not have its origin in some fanciful piety long after his death, but in the impression he made on his disciples during the three years of his ministry. His resurrection deepened that impression and confirmed it. Without in the least doubting his real humanity, they realized that they had been walking with God.

Community of a Common Life

Chua Wee Hian

For many, the church is a building where Christians gather for worship. Others think of it as an institution where rites such as baptisms, weddings and funerals are conducted. The constant appeals in Western Europe for funds to preserve ancient cathedrals and churches give the impression of the church as a crumbling structure.

But basically the church is *people*. In the New Testament, the Greek word translated 'church' meant 'a called-out gathering'. The church is the people of God called out to know, love and serve the living God. The New Testament uses different pictures to describe it. Portrayed as 'the body of Christ', it is a growing organism with Christ as its head. Pictured as 'the bride of Christ', its members are vitally related to him. To them, Christ entrusts the sacred deposit of biblical revelation—hence the church is 'the pillar and bulwark of truth'.

Although the church has been summoned into existence by God himself, it is made up of ordinary human beings. As such they have their imperfections and limitations. Their perspectives and actions are coloured by the spirit of their generation.

Roots

The church traces its origins to the life, ministry and mission of its founder, Jesus Christ. Through his apostles, he was going to build an indestructible community. Those who confessed their faith in him as the promised Messiah, the 'Son of the living God', were to be the first 'living stones' of God's house. They, and successive generations of Christ's followers, were to be his witnesses. Central to their testimony was the death of Jesus for man's sins. His resurrection confirmed his uniqueness as the world's true Saviour. Men and women were summoned to repent of their sins, to trust him and serve him in the fellowship of his new community—the church.

After an initial period of preaching to Jews only, the early church took the commands of Jesus to witness 'to the ends of the earth' and 'to make disciples of all nations' very seriously. In spite of opposition, the early messengers of the faith, notably the apostle Paul, spread the gospel or good news of Jesus to a spiritually and socially needy world. Those who believed were baptized and incorporated into local churches. By the end of the third century the Christian faith had taken root throughout the Roman Empire.

The majority of believers were drawn initially from the lower classes. The good news of God's love to all people through Jesus Christ appealed to them. Churches as communities that transcended barriers of sex, race and social status welcomed converts in thousands. The political and intellectual elite treated

'Offer yourselves as a living sacrifice to God, dedicated to his service and pleasing to him. This is the true worship that you should offer. Do not conform yourselves to the standards of this world, but let God transform you inwardly by a complete change of your mind. Then you will be able to know the will of God—what is good and is pleasing to him and is perfect.'

Paul's words in his letter to the Romans, 12:1–2

'Whoever comes to me cannot be my disciple unless he loves me more than he loves his father and his mother, his wife and his children, his brothers and his sisters, and himself as well. Whoever does not carry his own cross and come after me cannot be my disciple.'

Jesus' words to those who wanted to follow him; Luke 14:26–27

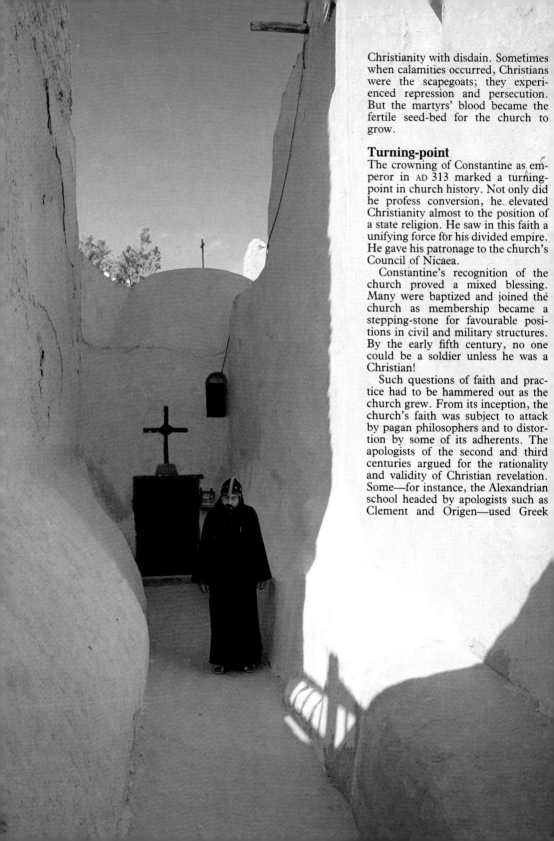

Christianity with disdain. Sometimes when calamities occurred, Christians were the scapegoats; they experienced repression and persecution. But the martyrs' blood became the fertile seed-bed for the church to grow.

Turning-point

The crowning of Constantine as emperor in AD 313 marked a turning-point in church history. Not only did he profess conversion, he elevated Christianity almost to the position of a state religion. He saw in this faith a unifying force for his divided empire. He gave his patronage to the church's Council of Nicaea.

Constantine's recognition of the church proved a mixed blessing. Many were baptized and joined the church as membership became a stepping-stone for favourable positions in civil and military structures. By the early fifth century, no one could be a soldier unless he was a Christian!

Such questions of faith and practice had to be hammered out as the church grew. From its inception, the church's faith was subject to attack by pagan philosophers and to distortion by some of its adherents. The apologists of the second and third centuries argued for the rationality and validity of Christian revelation. Some—for instance, the Alexandrian school headed by apologists such as Clement and Origen—used Greek philosophical language to refute their critics. This led to unwarranted theological speculation. By contrast, Tertullian in the second century declared that there was no common ground between 'Athens and Jerusalem'. The biblical revelation was unique.

It was during periods of relative political calm that the church was forced to define its beliefs in precise theological terms. The nature of Christ as truly God and truly man was publicly debated. Prestigious councils such as those of Nicaea (325), Constantinople (381), Ephesus (431) and Chalcedon (451) formulated and affirmed the great creeds. In the Nicene Creed, Christians confess their belief in 'one, holy, catholic and apostolic church'. These four adjectives reflect the theological identity of the church. They also serve as criteria to evaluate the faithfulness and effectiveness of churches in fulfilling their role and status as God's people.

Unity

'The church is one, because it is the body of Christ—of that there can only be one.' But in what way is the church, with all its diversity of denominations and church traditions, one?

Some churchmen maintain that there should be no separate organizations, and that Christians should strive for visible unity. In the ecumenical climate of this century, the World Council of Churches was established in 1948 to foster dialogue amongst different churches and to advocate union either locally or nationally—and some progress has been made, especially in India and Pakistan.

Other Christians assert that the unity of the church envisaged by Jesus Christ and the apostles is a spiritual union. The unity of believers matches the union between the Father and the Son. Unity is produced by the Holy Spirit and is there amongst those who truly belong to Christ's body. Hence they are exhorted 'to maintain the unity of the Spirit in the bond of peace'.

As the church grew after the time of Constantine, unity was interpreted mainly in terms of adhering to a church tradition under one pope or patriarch. In the fourth and fifth centuries, theological battles were fought amongst the bishops of Rome, Constantinople and, to a lesser extent, Alexandria for primacy. Western Christianity as defined by the Church of Rome sought to impose its structure, liturgy and government on other traditions. Unity was basically maintained through the hierarchy of bishops and the clergy.

The Protestant reformers in the fifteenth and sixteenth centuries, with their rediscovery of personal faith and so the 'priesthood of all believers', opened the door for a greater freedom of liturgy and government. Following the theology of Augustine (354–430), they distinguished between the true church, to which believers of all times belong, and visible churches which have in their membership true and false followers of Christ. But in stressing spiritual unity, Protestant congregations opened the way for divisions based on minor doctrinal interpretations and personalities. Today Protestant Christianity is fragmented organizationally into many different churches, groups and movements, even though the divisions are transcended by the spiritual unity of a common life in Christ.

Holiness

The church is said to be 'holy' in the creed because holiness is the hallmark of God's people. No fewer than 100 passages in eighteen different New Testament writings describe Christians as 'saints': not stained-glass window figures, but those who are separated from sin and set apart for God. The Holy Spirit resides within them, and therefore their lifestyles and behaviour express likeness to a holy God.

Some Christians, particularly those from the second to the fifth centuries, equated sanctity with escape from the contamination of the world. Hundreds of Christians lived alone or in small groups, spending their time in meditation and solitude.

'Love is patient and kind; it is not jealous or conceited or proud; love is not ill-mannered or selfish or irritable; love does not keep a record of wrongs; love is not happy with evil, but is happy with the truth. Love never gives up; and its faith, hope, and patience never fail ... It is love, then, that you should strive for.'

Paul's first letter to the Corinthians, 13:4–7; 14:1

'You have made us for yourself, and our hearts are restless till they find their rest in you.'

Augustine

A monk from the ancient Ethiopian Orthodox Church.

Asceticism became a virtue. Even the celebrated Bible translator Jerome (345–420) denigrated marriage, exalted celibacy and lived as a recluse in Bethlehem.

Not all monks were recluses, however. Monastic communities combined service in their neighbourhood with the disciplined life of their particular orders. In medieval times, monks and priests from the orders were instrumental in establishing educational and medical centres.

Most Christians, however, have seen their concern for holiness as something to be lived out in the world, acting as 'salt' and 'light' within it, as Jesus himself expressed it. Personal piety motivated some to committed social action. A concern for holiness led social reformers such as William Wilberforce (1759–1833) and Anthony Ashley Cooper, seventh earl of Shaftesbury (1801–1885) to fight to abolish the slave-trade and overcome the appalling living conditions brought about by the Industrial Revolution.

A monk from Mt Athos in Greece upholds the centuries-old traditions of the Orthodox church.

A worldwide church

When Christians profess belief in the 'catholic' church, they subscribe to the universality or worldwide nature of the church. Membership in the church transcends racial, social and cultural backgrounds. Members are Christ's witnesses and ambassadors, urging men and women to be reconciled to God through Christ.

When churches faithfully discharge their evangelistic responsibilities in their neighbourhoods and beyond, they multiply and grow. The early churches, starting with the church at Antioch in Syria, were missionary congregations. Whether they sent small apostolic bands of messengers or encouraged their members to share their faith through their natural network of relationships, missionary activity was their constant concern.

The Celtic monastic communities established churches in the British Isles long before Augustine reached Canterbury in 597. In the seventh century, Boniface, the great English missionary-pioneer, won vast areas of Germany to the Christian faith. Christian merchants from Syria and Persia brought the Nestorian form of Christianity to China in the same century.

There is inevitably a creative tension when spiritually-minded church members embark on any missionary venture. These normally attract to their cause dedicated workers and generous lay supporters. Their vitality can create tension with church leaders who are preoccupied with the housekeeping problems of their ecclesiastical structures.

The missionary forces of the Roman Catholic Church were spearheaded by the monastic orders: the Franciscans (founded 1209), Dominicans (1216) and the Jesuits (1540). Hundreds of missionaries accompanied Portuguese and Spanish merchants and soldiers on their expeditions to colonize new lands for the Iberian kingdoms and the pope. Others went as far as India, Japan and China.

Towards the end of the eighteenth century, there was an upsurge of missionary activity on the part of

Protestant churches. The Church Missionary Society, an important missionary arm of the Church of England, was founded in 1799, but its first pioneer workers were Germans. The Moravian Church in Germany had already sent out its own missionaries to Asia and Latin America. William Carey (1761–1834) and Henry Martyn (1781–1812) stirred the imagination of many when they translated the Bible into the main Indian languages. Their sacrificial labours challenged many to serve as missionaries.

The nineteenth century saw thousands of Protestant missionaries from Europe and North America proclaiming the gospel, establishing churches, schools and hospitals in Asia, Africa and Latin America.

Apostolicity

The Roman Catholic Church defines 'apostolicity' in terms of a continuing line of descent from the apostles to the modern-day church through the consecration of its bishops. In contrast, the Protestant reformers interpreted apostolicity in terms of *doctrinal* succession. Christ had entrusted certain revealed truths, embodied in the New Testament scriptures, to his apostles. The church is apostolic in nature in so far as its members continue in the apostles' doctrine and teaching.

The attempts to place ecclesiastical traditions or human reason on a par with or even above biblical revelation have caused deep divisions amongst Christians. The battle for the church to be apostolic in its doctrine is a constant one.

Resilience

At various periods of its history, the church has been threatened with extinction. The early church survived the onslaught of persecution in the first centuries. The Muslim invaders in the seventh and eighth centuries overthrew a vast church structure in North Africa and Turkey. Corruption and decay crept into the leadership of churches. Churches sometimes projected the image of an establishment that protected the interests of the rich and powerful.

But even in times of spiritual decline there has been revival and renewal. Eighteenth-century Britain experienced great spiritual awakenings through the preaching of the Wesleys and George Whitefield. New life flowed into the churches, but the Church of England was unprepared to cope with the masses of new converts. The Methodist Church emerged in order to incorporate many of them.

The church had to contend with the sharp attacks of humanistic philosophies in the nineteenth century; theological liberalism undermined biblical authority. From 1917 onwards vast areas of the world were

A packed church in Zaire.

'When men cease to believe in God, they will not believe in nothing, they will believe in anything.'

G. K. Chesterton

overrun by communism. Its atheistic bias and all-demanding ideology forced Christians either to make a firm stand or to compromise. But the Christian communities in the Soviet Union, Eastern Europe and China continued to flourish in spite of restrictions and opposition.

Today, although there is decline in the West, there is church growth in many lands. In Africa in 1900 the Christian population was estimated at 9 million; today there are around 150 million Christians. African independent churches flourish, with distinctive forms of worship and witness.

In many parts of Latin America, the Christian church is growing more rapidly than the population. Some Pentecostal churches in Chile and Brazil have a membership of several thousand active members per congregation. In the USA, church membership remains at 70 per cent of the population and American missionaries constitute around 60 per cent of today's Protestant missionary task force.

In some parts of Asia, home of the world's great faiths, the church is also growing rapidly. The late '60s provided the stage for a remarkable popular movement in Indonesia. Just after the failure of the communist coup in 1965 and the subsequent vengeance of Muslims, there was a deep vacuum in the lives of many Indonesians. Then, as local Christians and missionaries shared their faith with Muslim community leaders, whole towns and villages embraced the Christian faith.

Membership of the church in South Korea is increasing at the rate of 10 per cent per year. Korean Christians give sacrificially to support missionaries working in other lands. Amongst the 30 million Chinese outside mainland China, there has also been a widespread turning to God. Students around the world have been exceptionally responsive to the gospel.

Traditionally, missionaries are classified as those who are from the West. Today there is a steady growth of a new missionary task force. Between 6,000 and 7,000 missionaries from Asia, Brazil and Africa are engaged in spreading the Christian faith and establishing or strengthening churches in lands other than their own. A new era of partnership is demonstrating the reality of people *from* all nations proclaiming the good news of Jesus Christ *to* all nations.

Christian Beliefs

Howard Marshall

The Christian faith is directly descended from the religion of the Jews. At the time of Jesus this had the following characteristics, as taught in the sacred book of the Jews, the Old Testament:

● Belief in the existence of one God, the Creator and Lord of the universe who is sovereign over all.

● Belief in the fact that man is made in the image of God, but has rebelled against his Creator and stands in danger of judgement.

● Belief that God, who is the righteous judge, is also gracious and merciful. He has provided a way for man to be set free from judgement by the penitent offering of sacrifices.

● Belief that God revealed himself to the nation of Israel and called them to be his people.

● Belief that God would some day establish his rule in a sinful world, setting his people free from their enemies, and appointing his chosen agent, the Messiah, to rule over them for ever.

● The practice of a moral life under the guidance of the Law given in the Old Testament; the maintenance of a religious ritual based on the temple and involving the offering of sacrifice.

The significance of Jesus

These beliefs were decisively affected by the coming of Jesus, his resurrection from the dead, and the gift of the Spirit of God received by his followers. There remained a basic similarity with the Jewish religion but there were some fundamental changes.

The most important of these changes was due to the Christian understanding of Jesus. From a very early date, the Christians began to realize that the Jewish hope of God's chosen agent coming to set up his rule had been fulfilled in Jesus. He was the Messiah whom the Jews awaited. It is the rejection of this by Jews that constitutes the decisive difference between them and Christians. For Christians the coming of Jesus means that God's future plan, announced in the Old Testament, has already begun to happen. God's rule is being established in a new way.

But the way in which it has happened is different from what the Jews had come to expect. They thought that God's rule would be achieved by the military overthrow of their enemies and would lead to their own establishment as the dominant nation. But Jesus attacked not the external enemies of the Jews but the sinfulness of their hearts. The rule of God advances by the conversion of individuals to a new way of life, and the way of violent revolution is firmly rejected.

The death of Jesus

God's action in Jesus was also seen as including sacrifice. The death of Jesus was understood as a means

An African Christian is baptized in the sea, in public declaration of his faith in Christ.

Baptism pictures a person's identification with Christ's death and resurrection. Some churches baptize only adult believers, others baptize children born into Christian families.

of cancelling sin, provided by God himself and displaying his love for sinners. Man's sinfulness must inevitably bring separation from God, or death. But Jesus died this death himself. A variety of pictures—drawn from the slave market, the law court, the temple, and personal relationships—are used to express the fundamental belief that the death of Jesus is the means of reconciling God and man and freeing man from the fear of judgement.

The effect of this understanding was to bring to an end the system of animal sacrifices. They were understood as pictures pointing forward to the spiritual sacrifice of Jesus and now made obsolete by the offering of the perfect sacrifice. Christian worship was no longer a matter of offerings in a temple. Rather it was the expression of gratitude to God for *his* provision of a sacrifice.

At the same time the coming of Jesus was seen as bringing to an end the ritual Law of the Jews which regulated the temple worship and a host of other matters. The ethical principles which lay behind the Law, seen especially in the Ten Commandments, were not abolished, but the detailed ritual and other observances were no longer needed.

In practice, the Jews had come to regard the observance of the Law in minute detail as the means of gaining and maintaining a good relationship with God and obtaining his favour. It was Paul who insisted that God's favour could not be gained by keeping the Law: all have sinned and come short of God's glory. So man's

proper relationship with God can only be that of faith, the grateful and obedient trust which comes to God on the basis of what *he* has done, in contrast to the approach of works which insists that *man* must do something to merit God's favour.

Though Christian worship abandoned the temple, it was deeply influenced by the synagogue, the Jewish meeting-house in which the teaching of the Law was central. But the rejection of the Law as the means of salvation led to a shift in the understanding of the Old Testament. Interest turned more to its prophetic character as a book which looked forward to the coming of Jesus, and it was studied more and more for what it taught about him. At the same time, other writings were increasingly placed alongside it as equally inspired and authoritative scriptures. The writings of the infant church, the letters written by its leaders and the accounts of the ministry of Jesus that we know as the Gospels, were seen as a corpus of scriptures alongside the Old Testament. The whole collection became the Bible of the Christian church.

The recognition that observance of the Jewish Law was no longer binding on Christians together with the simple fact that almost from the beginning non-Jews, the Gentiles, were attracted by the message, led quickly to the development of a community composed of both Jews and non-Jews. Despite initial uncertainties it was recognized that non-Jews did not need to adopt the practices of the Jewish Law, especially circumcision and the observance of Jewish holy days, in order to become Christians. Christianity, which might have remained a Jewish sect, was thus poised to become a world faith, open to all mankind on the basis of belief in Jesus.

The characteristic rites of the new faith, which roughly parallel the Jewish rite of circumcision and the festival of the Passover (which celebrated the deliverance of the people of Israel from slavery in Egypt), were baptism and the Lord's Supper. Baptism was a ritual washing with water which signified cleansing from sin, the reception of God's Spirit, and the dedication of the candidate to God and his entry into the new people of God. The Lord's Supper, or Eucharist ('thanksgiving'), was a token meal of bread and wine—elements used by Jesus at his Last Supper before his death to point to his self-sacrifice and the shedding of his blood to open up a new covenant or agreement between God and his people.

The resurrection of Jesus

Alongside the death of Jesus, his resurrection was the crucial event for the beliefs of Christianity. Christians saw it as God's vindication of Jesus after he had been rejected by the Jewish leaders and put to death. It was the confirmation of his claims to be God's agent, and above all it demonstrated that he was triumphant over the power of sin and death. The resurrection was seen as the decisive stage in the ascent of Jesus to share the throne of God in heaven (to use the picture-language of the New Testament). This belief had several important consequences.

● First, it confirmed the Christian belief that God would act again in history through the return of Jesus at the end of the world. The exaltation of Jesus meant that he was the agent appointed by God to carry out final judgement and to bring in God's eternal reign in peace and justice.

● Second, it led to the conviction that Jesus was to be seen as divine. Already in his lifetime he had displayed a unique consciousness that he was God's Son and that God was his Father. After the resurrection, Christians recognized increasingly that all the functions of God were exercised through Jesus and that he shared in the rule of God. He was to be regarded as the Son of God, who had 'come down' into the world in human form and then 'ascended' to be with God. The consequences of this belief were shattering. Jews and others who believed that there was one God could not accept the Christian claim. Christians for their part had to revise their ideas about God and recognize that, though God is one, alongside the Father there was also the Son; they were each divine in nature, yet in such a way that the Son could be regarded as dependent on the Father. The earthly Jesus was the Son of God made flesh, 'incarnate', become a human being.

● Third, now that Jesus has been exalted to heaven he remains active and living in the same way as the Father is the living God. Sharing the status of the Father, Jesus is now the Lord, so that the relation of the Christian to him is not simply one of belief and trust but also of obedience and commitment. To be a Christian is to make the confession 'Jesus Christ is Lord', a confession that he is both my Lord whom I obey and also the one to whom the whole universe

Radical Christian groups in Russia meet together in homes or out of doors.

will one day bow the knee.

Such faith and obedience is part of a spiritual relationship between the Christian and Jesus. The Christian can be said to be united with Jesus, a whole variety of metaphors from the language of personal relationships being used to express the reality of this link. The new life which the Christian begins when he believes in Jesus is the reproduction of the life of Jesus in him. He dies to his old way of life and rises again to a new God-centred and divinely-inspired life, in the same way as Jesus died and rose again by the power of God. The Christian community is a vast organism or body through which the spiritual life of Christ flows.

The gift of the Holy Spirit and the birth of the church

After the resurrection came the third decisive event which determined the character of Christianity. The Jews already believed in the communication of God's power and guidance to particular individuals, especially the prophets, by the activity of the divine Spirit. The birthday of the church is reckoned from the day of Pentecost when all the believers in Jesus became conscious of the gift of the Spirit given to each one personally. So universal is the gift that a Christian can be defined as a person who has received the gift of the Spirit. The initial experience can be spoken of as a second, spiritual birth, bringing the new life of Jesus to the believer. The Spirit works in the Christian community by giving different abilities to different individuals to enable them to lead and help the church as a whole. He also acts in the life of each Christian to foster the qualities of love and freedom from sin which were seen in Jesus himself.

Thus the Spirit can be seen as the personal agent of God in the lives of individuals and the Christian community. This meant a further development in the understanding of God. The Spirit was recognized as being divine in the same way as the Father and the Son, so that the Christian concept of God had to recognize a fundamental 'three-ness'

or 'Trinity' in the nature of God as one being who exists in three persons. Thus the understanding of God as Trinity, which in this form is peculiar to Christianity and sharply differentiates it from other religions in the same Judaic tradition (Judaism and Islam), sums up the distinctive and vital elements in Christian faith.

Christian belief takes the holiness and judgement of a righteous God seriously. This is seen in the character of the Christian message which includes the warning that all people are sinners who have rebelled against God and therefore face judgement. It is only against this background that the Christian message makes sense as 'gospel', as good news that the same God is merciful and longs for the salvation of all mankind; he has provided the way of forgiveness and life in Jesus. Thus the gospel faces mankind with the alternatives of judgement or life.

Variety and error

The Christian message has naturally been subject to fresh thinking and reformulation down the ages as theologians have tried to express the biblical teaching in ways that are philosophically acceptable and logically coherent. It is not surprising that there have been differences in understanding in different times and places, and that some expressions of Christianity have veered away from the biblical witness.

Thus the doctrines of the Trinity and the incarnation have caused particular difficulty. Since the nature of God, who is infinite, lies beyond the scope of our finite understanding, attempts to explain his nature can lead to dangerous misunderstandings and one-sided statements. This has led to a variety of attempts to simplify the doctrine of God, by restricting full divinity to the Father or by regarding the three persons simply as three different aspects of one God. Theologians have found it hard to believe that Jesus is the eternal Son of God, and some have regarded him as a separate, subordinate being. The tendency in modern times has been to deny that God could truly be united with man in one person, and to say that Jesus was a good man who possessed the divine Spirit to an unusual degree, or that true humanity is the same thing as divinity. Another tendency has been to regard the Spirit as less than a full person.

The Christian understanding of the work of Jesus has also been the cause of difficulty. Some Christians have denied that any sort of action is necessary to enable God to forgive sins and have seen in the death of Jesus nothing more than a demonstration of supreme love. Others have carried the idea of sacrifice over into Christian worship and seen the Lord's Supper as some kind of repetition of Christ's sacrifice on the cross.

At times there have been tendencies to legalism; the need for doing good works in order to merit salvation has been taught. The church has on occasions claimed an authority almost equal to that of God, and developed a hierarchy or set of graded authorities surrounded by pomp and prestige. At other times the doctrine of God as judge has been watered down and replaced by a belief that God will ultimately save all men, no matter how they behaved in this life.

While, therefore, the main thrust of Christian teaching, especially as expressed in the New Testament, is clear, the existence of the various denominations, and of different groups within them, demonstrates that there has been considerable variety and even error in the expression of the faith. Christians need to be prepared continually to go back to the Bible and to test their beliefs and their practice by its teaching. Jesus himself—the Christ of the Bible and of experience—is after all far greater than any human formulation of dogma or teaching about him.

By sharing bread and wine, Christians commemorate and celebrate the death and resurrection of Jesus.

Branches of the Church

Michael Sadgrove

Two historic movements were the primary cause of the various branches of Christianity which exist today. The first was the so-called 'Great Schism' between East and West, usually dated at 1054, although the debate between Greek and Latin Christianity had begun centuries before this. The second was the sixteenth-century disruption generally known as the Reformation whose legacy was Protestantism.

The Eastern Orthodox churches The separation of the Eastern churches from Western Christendom was largely a rejection of the claim of the bishop of Rome to supreme authority. There was also disagreement over the clause added to the Nicene Creed by the Western church in which the Spirit is said to proceed from the Son as well as from the Father, a doctrine rejected by the Orthodox to this day. The best-known members of the Orthodox communion are the Greek and Russian churches, but there are several others, belonging mainly to Eastern Europe and the eastern Mediterranean (reflecting to some extent the Byzantine Empire in which the cultural roots of Orthodoxy belong). Authority in the church belongs not to any individual, but to the Ecumenical Council, whose function is to interpret the 'holy tradition', and administer discipline. Each national church has its own Patriarch; the Patriarch of Constantinople is 'first among equals'.

The Roman Catholic Church The largest single Christian grouping, Roman Catholics, are those who acknowledge the primacy and authority of the pope, the bishop of Rome. As Christ's representative on earth (the 'Vicar of Christ'), the pope stands at the head of a hierarchy of bishops and priests, amongst whom the cardinals have the responsibility of electing the pope. When said to be speaking with full authority (*ex cathedra*) and defining matters of faith or morals, the pope's utterances are regarded as infallible and binding upon all Catholics, although the Second Vatican Council of 1962–65 resulted in greater attention being paid to the authority of the bishops corporately, as an episcopal college. At the centre of Roman Catholicism is the Mass (the communion service), along with six other sacraments: baptism, confirmation, penance (or reconciliation), ordination, marriage and the anointing of the sick ('extreme unction').

The Anglican Church The Anglican 'communion' is a worldwide family of churches in fellowship with the Archbishop of Canterbury, whose status amongst the heads of other Anglican churches is 'first among equals'. The parent Church of England itself is seen by many Anglicans as having roots in Celtic Christianity which flourished in Britain long before Augustine of Canterbury brought Christianity from Rome. Despite the break with Rome at the Reformation, Anglicanism retained a Catholic type of ministry and a liturgy heavily indebted to her Catholic past, but rejecting the doctrines of the papacy and the Mass as sacrifice, together with the concept of priesthood which this implied.

The Lutheran Church, embodying the teaching of the German reformer Martin Luther, represents the chief Protestant presence in Germany and Scandinavia, whence it has found adherents across the world. Only in some countries did the Lutherans retain bishops. The normal form of government is by an assembly (synod) presided over by a general superintendent. Like Anglicanism, Lutheranism adopted a largely conservative attitude towards liturgy, although the preaching of the sermon has always been central.

The Presbyterian churches, in contrast to Lutheranism, followed the principles of John Calvin as exemplified in Geneva at the time of the Reformation, but like the Lutherans stressed the authority of the Bible as greater than that of the church. Church government is in the hands of presbyteries and synods, or courts of ministers and lay elders belonging to a particular region. Like other Reformed churches, Presbyterians have a simple approach to worship, in which the reading and preaching of Scripture, extempore prayers and the singing of psalms and hymns are basic.

Congregationalism stresses the independence of the local church. Independency was largely the result of separatists within English Puritanism making their stand against any involvement with the national church. In common with other 'free churches' such as Baptists and Brethren, they stress the fact that membership is made up of believers, not society at large. The United Reformed Church is a merger of Congregationalists and Presbyterians.

The Baptist churches, now to be found across the world, reject the baptism of infants,

The Main Streams of Christianity

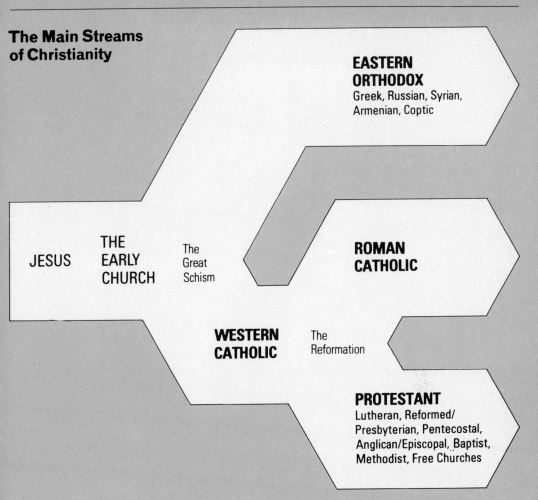

EASTERN ORTHODOX
Greek, Russian, Syrian, Armenian, Coptic

JESUS THE EARLY CHURCH The Great Schism

ROMAN CATHOLIC

WESTERN CATHOLIC The Reformation

PROTESTANT
Lutheran, Reformed/ Presbyterian, Pentecostal, Anglican/Episcopal, Baptist, Methodist, Free Churches

claiming that baptism was given as a sign of an adult's declaration of faith. Baptist churches are essentially independent. Like the other Reformed churches they stress the importance of Scripture.

The Methodist churches owe their origin to the revitalizing movements ('evangelical revivals') of the eighteenth century, and to the evangelistic activity of John Wesley. Although Wesley himself remained an Anglican, Methodist converts were not absorbed into the established church. Churches (or 'societies') are organized into circuits and districts. Government is by a conference of ministers and representatives of church members. The styles of worship include both the highly sacramental and less formal.

Pentecostal churches emphasize the role of the Holy Spirit. The churches are fast-growing, particularly in South America. Services are often characterized by speaking in tongues and prophecy.

The Salvation Army was started in the nineteenth century to bring the gospel and social action to the poor, especially in inner-city areas. Members reject the sacraments.

The Quakers, or Society of Friends, meet for mainly silent worship and inner guidance, and also stress social action. They reject the sacraments and definitions of the faith.

Christian Brethren are independent groups without hierarchy stressing the different ministries of every member, especially in the distinctive communion service; they also stress the primacy of the Bible, and are active in missionary work.

The World Council of Churches was constituted in 1948 as a fellowship of churches united in their loyalty to Jesus Christ 'as God and Saviour'. All the major denominations described above are member churches, with the exception of the Roman Catholic Church, the Christian Brethren and most Pentecostals. The Council exists not so much to sponsor unity schemes as to enable the churches to debate matters of common concern, and where possible, to speak and act as one. It has been particularly active in the fields of social involvement and education, and in taking up the cause of oppressed peoples in Third World countries. Assemblies of the Council meet every seven years.

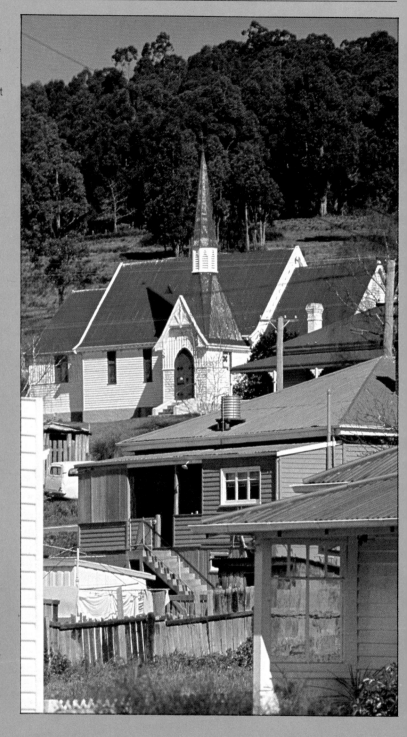

In remote Australian communities the local church serves the needs of the people, as in this country town in Tasmania.

The 'church' is strictly not a building but a gathering of people. But the word is also used of the places where Christians gather for worship, prayer and learning.

The Claim to be Unique

Christopher Lamb

The Christian claim is that Christ is unique: Christianity is not. Christianity can be classified under all the normal headings of a study of human society and religion. It has a long and complex history, leading exponents, a massive literature, distinctive rituals and characteristic social forms. All these can be paralleled by the communities of other world faiths, especially Judaism and Islam, and scholars have compared the 'truth-claims'—for example, the finality of the Qur'an—which are made in the different religious traditions.

This study of comparative religion has alarmed some Christians because in it the features of different religions have been placed side by side and their essential similarity examined. When this process moves from the externals to the inner core of religious faith, Christians often feel their faith is being 'relativized', reduced to the common level of human experience.

Christianity and religion

I believe Christians need fear this kind of study as little as a loving married couple fear the sociologist who tells them they belong to the same sub-group of society and have been culturally conditioned in the same way, and that is why they are happy. They know there is more to it than that! And Christians know that they belong to the human race and that God's creative power has made

them one with all other human beings in the way that their minds and bodies and their social natures work. Therefore it is foolish to resist the idea that, as historians and sociologists look at it, Christianity is one more of the religions of the world. But history and sociology is not the whole story, though it may be told as if it is.

For many who live in the North Atlantic region, however, Christianity is still identified with the culture which has dominated world history in recent centuries by its technological and industrial skills. As this region enters a period of relative decline, Christianity, associated with the past, is thought to be in decline too. So the general impression left by comparative religion seems to be confirmed by observation of present trends. Christianity is relative to other religions, and relative to the success and prosperity of the culture which has adopted it.

Strictly speaking this is undeniable, but it states only part of the truth. The fact is that Christians began as a socially deprived and frequently persecuted group, and for much of their history European Christians belonged to a culture which was backward in comparison with the Muslim community. Moreover, Christianity may be in institutional decline in Europe, but it is certainly not so in Africa, Latin America or east Asia. The resilience

'Give glory to your Son, so that the Son may give glory to you. For you gave him authority over all mankind, so that he might give eternal life to all those you gave him. And eternal life means knowing you, the only true God, and knowing Jesus Christ, whom you sent. I have shown your glory on earth; I have finished the work you gave me to do. Father, give me glory in your presence now, the same glory I had with you before the world was made.'

Jesus' prayer, John 17: 1–5

of Christianity under the harsh conditions of the Soviet Union and Maoist China is also highly significant.

When the student of religion searches for explanations of the past and present vitality of the Christian faith he cannot find the secret in any one culture or any particular stage of economic and cultural development, for that vitality has existed in every kind of human situation. What has always sustained Christians has been the conviction that they have a personal relationship with a unique Saviour who is both God and man.

Christianity and culture

Today Christians in the West have to come to terms with more than the *studies* of religion which have gone on for more than a century in European and American universities. They must adjust to the living presence of people of other faiths as fellow-citizens. Islam is now the second most numerous faith-community in Western Europe, far outstripping Judaism. Western countries have substantial populations of all the principal world faiths, as well as adherents of the cults and new religious movements. Since many of these new citizens are from Asian backgrounds, they encounter prejudice and discrimination because of their skin-colour and way of life. Christians and others have attempted to fight these evils by affirming the value of Asian cultures, and resisting the view that the Western way of life is intrinsically better than any other. Many now accept that only a minimum of adjustment should be required from the newcomers to Western society, and that justice and common sense both point to the basic equality of all cultures.

It is clear that religion and culture are inextricably entwined, and many will go on to assert that the basic equality of all cultures means the radical equality of all religions. Even some who are serious about their own Christian identity will say, 'We have our way to God and they have theirs. Ours is true/works for us, and theirs is true/works for them.' Such attitudes strike most of our Western contemporaries as tolerant, balanced and true to the complex social situations of our time. Often one senses an underlying feeling of guilt about the imperialist exploitation of the past, and the devaluation of Asian cultures which went with it. A new tolerance of faiths is often reckoned to be part of the reparation due to the East from the West.

It is important to notice that Christians with much longer experience of life in multi-faith societies do not often share these attitudes. Christians in the Middle East have maintained their discipleship for centuries without admitting any such fundamental identity between Islam and Christianity. If they had adopted such an idea they would have had no reason to reject Islam for themselves, but they preferred to accept an inferior position in society and occasional persecution rather than put the two faiths on the same level.

A bishop from Sri Lanka noted in 1979 that British Christians were unwilling 'to make critical evaluation of the experience and truth-claims' of other religions, and warned them that this stemmed in part from 'the general loss of self-confidence among many people in the Western world in a post-imperial era. Bishop Wickremesinghe went on to describe how people of different faiths—Buddhist, Hindu, Muslim and Christian—lived and worked together in the same national culture of Sri Lanka, trying to establish justice, peace and prosperity, yet never losing sight of the fact that their respective understandings of the truth were in the end irreconcilable. He talked of what will surely be the experience of many Western nations in the future, how other religions 'are always present before us as alternative explanations of the mysteries of life and death, and especially of suffering. In our region comparative religion is not confined to university faculties or small groups with an interest in this subject. It is a facet of our normal experience and within which we have to make concrete options in the traumatic situations we face as we go through life.'

Christianity and other faiths

Western Christians do not have the same opportunities as Sri Lankans. Nevertheless there are many opportunities to meet people of other faiths, and to study their beliefs at firsthand. It is vital that Christians do not come to easy conclusions about other faiths without some such study of them. Because the claims of the different religions conflict, it is extremely tempting to compare the best of your own faith with the worst of another. Sometimes those who insist that there are positive features in other faiths are thought to be disloyal to their own. There is no doubt that Christian history is full of 'religious tribalism'. Because people were unwilling to believe anything good about other faiths all sorts of inaccuracies and distortions became accepted as fact. Europeans still suffer from the caricature of Islam popularized in the Middle Ages, and Jews have been grossly and consistently libelled by Christians, even by respected church leaders and theologians. This has been one of the principal causes of the centuries-old persecution of the Jews.

Of course Christians have not been alone in misrepresenting other faiths. Muslims have made their own misrepresentations of Christianity, but with the growth of modern communications this 'bearing of false witness' is both unnecessary and dangerous. It mattered less what a Hindu believed about a Christian or a Buddhist about a Jew if they were never likely to meet. But today they will and do. God is not honoured by lies, and the Christian faith is not defended by defaming other faiths. Such defamation is in any case likely to be self-defeating, since uncommitted people who take the trouble to investigate what lies behind the propaganda will feel that it is Christianity which is exposed as false.

But a Christian may happily set aside self-serving descriptions of other faiths and still feel that his study of other faiths must come to a stop somewhere. Even the specialist in his technical vocation of study

In many parts of the world, Christians have seen the need to be involved in education as part of their total contribution to the community.

cannot adequately examine all the possible alternatives to the Christian faith. No religion can be properly understood without a real knowledge of its scriptures in their original language. Is he then to attempt the mastery of Hebrew, Arabic, Sanskrit and Pali, as well as New Testament Greek? It is a lifetime's work to plumb the depths of even one other faith. It is true that there are many scholars to help us, and Christians have actually made much deeper studies of other faiths than, for the most part, scholars of other faiths have made of Christianity. But can a Christian say nothing about his faith and other faiths with confidence unless he can make a claim to be some kind of expert?

To put the same question more sharply: can we be sure that in making Christ central to our lives rather than one of his rivals we are not making a great mistake? Or is that very form of the question evidence of our theological vulgarity, and the Christian faith is really only *our* path to God, neither better nor

worse than many others?

This second position is very widely held, but it is well to be clear what is involved in it. If the Christian path is only one of many, and perhaps not even the best, then it is arrogant to suppose that others may benefit from my religious experience, when that experience is so limited and partial. Evangelism then becomes impossible, and mission must be limited to service, for proclamation would be 'theological imperialism'. The church then is to be limited to biological growth alone. Moreover, *all* the missionary activity of the past must be called in question, including the missionary activity which created the churches of Europe and the ancient churches of the Middle East. In short, the very basis of the church is destroyed, for our existence as Christians is little more than a historical accident and rests on an illusion—the illusion that there was a message to take to the ends of the earth.

If this is the consequence of the conventional view, how can we be

The Christian world (approximate present-day distribution)

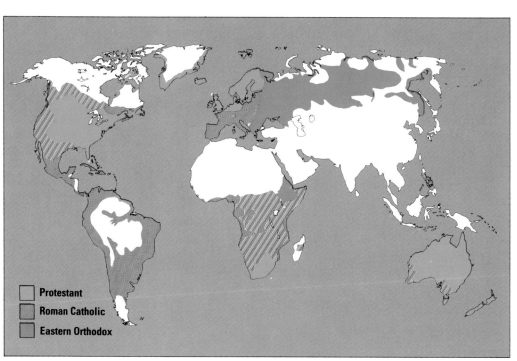

Protestant

Roman Catholic

Eastern Orthodox

sure it is mistaken? The whole question hinges of course on the person of Jesus Christ. For the Christians of the New Testament Jesus Christ is uniquely definitive of the authority and love of God. Jesus himself claimed to be 'the way, and the truth, and the life; no one comes to the Father, but by me'. And shortly after his death and rising again, the first disciples were saying to the Jewish leadership about Jesus: 'There is salvation in no one else, for there is no other name under heaven given among men by which we must be saved.' And the missionary Paul was later to write to a church in Asia Minor that 'He is the image of the invisible God ... he exists before everything, and all things are held together in him.' Jesus is the true centre of human history and the person in whom God has revealed himself with complete authority.

Such is the consistent witness of the New Testament, but how can such a claim be proved? The evidence of the life and death and resurrection of Jesus, and the testimony of his followers over centuries can be set out for inquirers, and evangelists and writers are constantly doing it. But if it were possible to *prove* that Jesus was finally authoritative for men, appointed by God, it could only be done by citing another authority more final than Jesus himself, and the proof would collapse. The most

Young Christians from East Malaysia lead the singing in their open-air church.

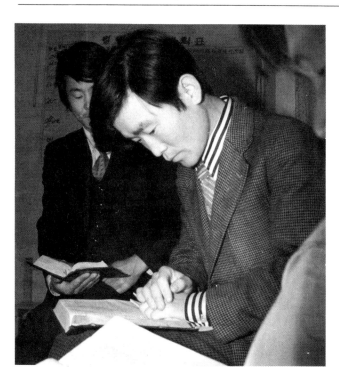

Christian doctors in Korea pray together for God's help before an operation.

'**Before the world was created, the Word already existed; he was with God, and he was the same as God. From the very beginning the Word was with God. Through him God made all things; not one thing in all creation was made without him. The Word was the source of life, and this life brought life to mankind. The light shines in the darkness, and the darkness has never put it out.'**

The opening words of John's Gospel, speaking of Jesus

elegant logic and compelling arguments in favour of Jesus are no more than requests to listen to him and look at him. His life and teaching are self-authenticating—they are their own authority, because only in this way can they be ultimately binding on us.

The uniqueness of Christ

This means that when a Christian sets out to consider the nature of other religious traditions, he does so on the basis of God's self-revelation in Jesus Christ. Jesus is the perfect expression of God's nature in human terms, and in Jesus God has reversed his previous judgement of condemnation on the human race. The Christian finds both his identity and his total security in belonging to God through Jesus, and the community of Jesus. His personal shortcomings and inadequacies, though still a source of pain and grief to him, are not allowed to rob him of his sense of being favoured by God, and he knows the privilege of being used by

God in his plan for the whole of mankind. He prays continually for the special quality of joyous affection which marked the life of Jesus and hopes to pass after this life into his presence.

He looks for echoes and reflections of the Spirit of Jesus everywhere, including the communities of other faiths, and is delighted when he finds them, not trying to belittle them but being glad that 'God has not left himself without witnesses', as the apostle Paul put it when speaking to a pagan audience. For acknowledging the supreme authority of Jesus means a committed mind but not a closed mind. Commitment to Jesus is commitment to a total availability to every human being. Jesus' openness to every kind of person was notorious to his religious critics, who were frequently scandalized by the company he kept. His parables reflected the basic human goodness to be found in the Samaritan, theologically at odds with Judaism. He said about a pagan soldier who took him at his word, 'I tell you this: nowhere, even in Israel, have I found such faith.' Christians need not fear that commitment to Jesus means that they will not be open to others, for his own example precludes that.

At the same time a Christian cannot be loyal to Jesus and also consider the possibility of other fundamental loyalties for himself. He cannot remain a Christian and have an open mind about the final authority of Jesus. If he does it means that he really takes his own judgement as the final authority, usually on some philosophical principle. Of course I have to be responsible in the end for all my judgements, but that is not the same as saying that I am capable of pronouncing my judgement on Jesus. Once I have found where the final word of God is expressed, I can only submit to it. I cannot sit in religious or philosophical judgement on it. I can only respond with my whole being, which is why love, the expression of the whole person, is at the root of Christianity. And human beings are only able to respond in love to God because of the love he has shown them in Christ.

Religion under judgement

Jesus continually sought this whole-hearted response to God, for which another word is 'faith'. 'When the Son of Man comes, will he find faith on earth?' he asked. His complaint against the religion of his day was that it was not whole-hearted but hypocritical. At times it was even manipulative and cynical. Here Jesus passes judgement not just on the religion of his own day but on all established religion, including Christianity in its historic and contemporary forms. Jesus' harshest words are reserved for the Pharisees and the scribes, the religious and theological leaders of Judaism—not because he wanted to destroy the Jewish faith (other rabbis made similar attacks) but because the very best of human religion is inwardly corrupt. Human frustration and evil are not brought about by external things, and cannot be dealt with just by external means: for it is 'out of the heart', said Jesus, that come 'evil thoughts, murder, adultery, fornication, theft, false witness, slander. These are what defile a man; but to eat with unwashed hands does not defile a man.' Religious prescriptions do not reach the heart of the matter, so at the heart of Christianity lies the knowledge that religion is not free from the desperate wickedness of man, for Jesus was condemned and crucified by the *religious* authorities, acting in concert with pagan politicians.

Beyond religion

Christianity in all its historic forms is not unique. It shares in the sinful character of all human activity, and is most at risk when it tries to deny that character. But it carries the message of the uniqueness of Jesus Christ, of his final authority for men and women, and his final solution to the helplessness of a world fit only for the scrap-heap. For Jesus came, not with a new 'religion', a new code or a new philosophy, but to meet human bankruptcy and rottenness with its pain and separation from God and to absorb it into himself by his total obedience to God—to the point of an agonizing and humiliating death. He came also to initiate a new order, a completely new start for the human race, a new creation which began with his own resurrection from death. Men and women are invited to abandon their own futile attempts to reach and please God and simply to put their trust in Jesus, who alone truly knows him. They are invited to become part of the community of those who live by that faith and share the life of Jesus while they wait for the new age in which all will acknowledge him.

So Christians say 'yes' to Christianity as the vehicle of Jesus, but 'no' to it when it betrays that message, as it often has. Christians say both 'yes' and 'no' to other faiths too. Yes, when insights from them fill out and underline and tell in a new vocabulary the glory of God as Jesus has shown him to be. But no, when as so often in human thought and action, the image of God in man is defaced because man has turned his face away from God to bow down to ideas and idols of his own invention, or when the glory of God in Jesus is set aside and controverted. If Christianity is unique, it is only because Christ is. If it ceases to witness to him, it ceases to have any value for the human race.

'Whoever believes in the Son of God has this testimony in his own heart; but whoever does not believe God, has made him out to be a liar, because he has not believed what God has said about his Son. The Testimony is this: God has given us eternal life, and this life has its source in his Son. Whoever has the Son has this life; whoever does not have the Son of God does not have life.'

John's first letter, 5:10–12

'Come to me, all of you who are tired from carrying heavy loads, and I will give you rest. Take my yoke and put it on you, and learn from me, because I am gentle and humble in spirit; and you will find rest.'

Matthew 11:28–29

The Bible

Richard France

The word 'Bible' comes from the Greek *Biblia* meaning simply 'The Books'. The plural is significant: the Bible is a collection of books written over a period of more than 1,000 years, in widely-differing cultural and historical situations, and in a rich variety of styles and language.

Yet this collection has come to be regarded by Christians as a single unit, 'The Bible', as its books have been recognized as standing apart from other books.

The Old Testament

There are two unequal parts to the Bible. The first and by far the larger, called by Christians 'the Old Testament', is simply the Hebrew (and Aramaic) scriptures of Judaism. They present the history and religious thought of the people of God up to the time when Jesus came as the Jews' Messiah.

Christians have always regarded themselves as the legitimate heirs to the religion of ancient Israel, and so accept the books of the Hebrew Bible as fully 'canonical', or part of Scripture. Without them, the specifically Christian scriptures could hardly be understood.

A number of later Jewish works (in Greek) are included in Roman Catholic editions of the Old Testament, sometimes distinguished as 'deutero-canonical', of lesser importance than the Hebrew scriptures. Protestant Bibles do not include these works, which Judaism did not accept as canonical, in the Old Testament; but they are sometimes printed after the Old Testament as a separate section, known as 'The Apocrypha'. Protestant Christians may read them for their interest and profit but do not accept them as Scripture.

The New Testament

The specifically Christian books of the Bible, known as 'the New Testament', comprise twenty-seven writings by Christians of the first century AD, mostly quite short. While most of the writers were of Jewish origin, the books are in Greek which was the common language of the Roman Empire.

They consist firstly of four 'Gospels' setting out from different points of view the life and teaching of Jesus, together with the 'Acts of the Apostles' which is a continuation of the Gospel of Luke to tell the story of the first thirty years of the Christian church. There are then thirteen letters by Paul, the great missionary leader, to churches and individuals; eight other letters by early Christian leaders; and the 'Revelation of John', a visionary work cast in the mould of Jewish apocalyptic literature.

The New Testament writings, while produced within a relatively short period compared with the many centuries of the writing of the Old Testament, are mixed in style and content; even the literary quality of

Beautiful stained glass has been used as a 'visual aid', teaching the stories of the Bible to those who cannot read.

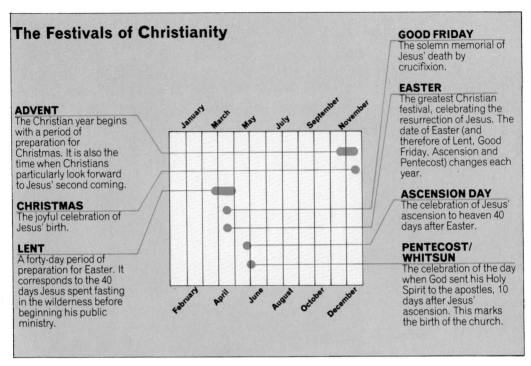

The Festivals of Christianity

ADVENT
The Christian year begins with a period of preparation for Christmas. It is also the time when Christians particularly look forward to Jesus' second coming.

CHRISTMAS
The joyful celebration of Jesus' birth.

LENT
A forty-day period of preparation for Easter. It corresponds to the 40 days Jesus spent fasting in the wilderness before beginning his public ministry.

GOOD FRIDAY
The solemn memorial of Jesus' death by crucifixion.

EASTER
The greatest Christian festival, celebrating the resurrection of Jesus. The date of Easter (and therefore of Lent, Good Friday, Ascension and Pentecost) changes each year.

ASCENSION DAY
The celebration of Jesus' ascension to heaven 40 days after Easter.

PENTECOST/ WHITSUN
The celebration of the day when God sent his Holy Spirit to the apostles, 10 days after Jesus' ascension. This marks the birth of the church.

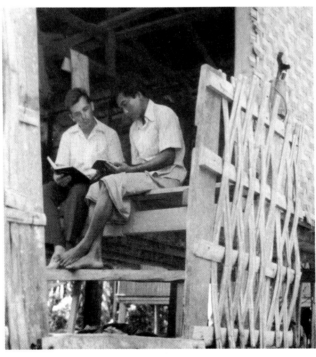

the Greek varies widely. The different interests and personalities of the writers are clear on even a quite superficial reading.

The inspiration of the Bible

Yet Christians have regarded these varied writings of both the Old and New Testaments as a unity, often called the 'Word of God'.

They have spoken of the Bible as 'inspired', meaning by this not merely that it is great literature or that it brings spiritual enlightenment, but that it comes from God.

It is not that its authors were merely passive channels for a divine revelation independent of their own thoughts; the stamp of the writers' personalities on their books is clear. But the classic Christian belief is that what they wrote in their own language, and in their own historical setting, was directed by God so that

Christians read in the Bible of the life and teaching of Jesus, and the principles by which people should live.

the result was no less his word than theirs.

So while the biblical books must be interpreted with proper attention to their background and literary form, what they declare is, Christians believe, God's word to men.

This is why the Bible, for all its variety, is treated by Christians as a unity, progressively revealing not only God's acts, but his mind and will.

The authority of the Bible

In theory, therefore, all Christians accept the Bible as authoritative, both in guiding their actions and in forming their beliefs.

In practice, however, Christians have differed on this. The Protestant Reformation aimed to restore the Bible to a place of authority above the pronouncements of the leaders of the church and the traditions which had grown up. Within Protestant Christianity, the Enlightenment of the eighteenth century led to a new confidence in human reason as the ultimate guide to truth, and the Bible was treated only as a record of human religious development, not as a divine revelation.

Today, while evangelical Christianity accepts the Bible as its supreme authority, more liberal Protestantism increasingly questions its importance. In Roman Catholicism since the Second Vatican Council there has been a remarkable resurgence of interest in the Bible.

Any recognizably Christian faith must be based on the Bible. That is why Bible translation is a major concern of the Christian churches. Teams of translators are at work all over the world, making the Bible available in the mother tongues of even quite small ethnic groups. Today the whole Bible is available in some 250 languages, and the New Testament in 450 more, while translation is in progress in a further 850.

These Peruvian Indians are leaders of their local churches. They are also involved in translating the Bible into their own language.

Christian Worship

Colin Buchanan

All institutions live by their rituals, and religious institutions are no exception. The Old Testament is, from one standpoint, the history of the religious life—including the 'cultic', or worshipping, life—of the people of God. Its pages record the beginnings of Christian worship.

It is recorded in the book of Acts that the infant church began a rhythm of church life which in outline is what would be called 'worship' today. (Indeed, a modern pattern for a Communion service might well have the same elements.) The believers gathered for the apostles' teaching, for prayer, fellowship and the 'breaking of bread'.

The Lord's Supper, Communion or Eucharist, was the distinctive event of Christian worship. Jesus himself commanded it and there is reason to think that the church observed it as a weekly (sometimes a daily) event from the outset. Originally, the commemoration of Jesus, especially his death and resurrection which the 'sacramental' bread and wine signified, was held within the context of a larger meal, called an *agape* or love-feast. But for various reasons this context fell away in the first 150 years after the resurrection, and a ritual meal of solely bread and wine remained.

The New Testament also describes what has been called the Christian 'initiation rite', baptism. This was certainly a means for the new convert to enter the life of the church. But in sharp distinction to contemporary mystery religions, it was open and simple. Baptism was a public 'washing', identifying the believer and his household with the death and rising again of Jesus. Today the churches which are 'Baptist' in conviction hold that this should take place on confession of personal faith. Others baptize children who are 'confirmed' in their faith later, when they themselves come to have a personal belief.

There is other evidence in the New Testament of early church practice. Psalms and hymns were sung. To express corporate solidarity with missionaries, elders or deacons serving the church, there was 'laying on of hands' at their commissioning. The sick were anointed and prayer made for their recovery. Money was collected for other, poorer churches. The 'ministry' of the church was divided amongst those who had the 'gifts of God's Spirit' for both practical and spiritual leadership.

There seems to have been no such concept as 'having a service'. The 'business' part of church life, such as organizing for the care of widows or the relief of famine, was all bound up with the 'worship' part of praying and singing and teaching.

Established patterns

In the post-apostolic years, patterns gradually settled down, and a clear structure of leadership emerged, in which the bishop would normally preside over the worship of the local church. Bishops wrote down for themselves the great thanksgiving prayer they uttered over the bread and wine of communion, and these 'eucharistic prayers' began to be used regularly and over wide areas, as others copied them.

As congregations grew, they sometimes overflowed from the homes in which they originally met. Groups started (even in times of persecution) to put up special buildings for worship. They produced an ever more detailed pattern of the church's year—not only keeping the 'week' of creation (though making the first day of the week

The Orthodox Churches, such as the Armenian Church, emphasize the importance of ritual in their worship of God.

One of the leaders of the protestant Reformation in the sixteenth century was Martin Luther. He preached the message of 'salvation by faith alone' in language which the ordinary people could understand.

holy in place of the seventh), but also keeping annual commemorations: first of all the Passover (when Jesus had died and risen), then Pentecost (when the Spirit had come), and finally Christmas (celebrating Christ's birth) and the 'death day' of the various martyrs.

The Peace of Constantine in AD 313 gave a new boost to church building, and the assimilation of church and state which followed not only encouraged the use of pagan festivals for Christian commemorations (as happened with Christmas), but also started to shape church organization on the lines of the official civic structures. Whole communities were baptized, and the Western concept of 'Christendom' was born. Later, the natural conservatism of the followers of any institution which has rituals ensured that Latin remained in use rather than the language of everyday speech, that fourth-century garments remained in use by those who led the worship (even though fashions changed for other uses) and that church building attracted the energies of architects and builders whilst other civic buildings were neglected.

In many ways the Eastern Orthodox churches have remained closer than any other to the spirit of the fourth and fifth centuries. Generations of a minority position have built in a great regard for the tradition and its conservation. The East has never had a Reformation or even a Vatican II!

In the Middle Ages in the Western church the role of the clergy became much more dominant. Celibacy added to the mystique of the clergy. They alone took an active part in worship. The concept of their special—indeed miraculous—power to transform the bread and wine into the body and blood of Christ gave them the functions of priesthood. The part of ordinary believers was to attend Mass and to adore the presence of Christ. The people could not understand the Latin used for the Bible readings and prayers. Neither did they receive communion, except at Easter, and then (from the late thirteenth century onwards) only the bread.

Reform

The Reformation, which took a stand against these abuses, was essentially a movement of 'the Word'. It involved the return to God's Word written in the Bible, and also a swing in ritual away from drama, colour and movement to a word-centredness, emphasizing intelligibility and an understanding of doctrine. The reformers themselves often tried hard to bring the celebration of communion into the centre of church life, but the longstanding habits of their congregations defeated them. Weekly worship in most Protestant churches focussed on the sermon. In the Lutheran churches there was a growth of hymn-singing to accompany services of the word and of prayers. The Church of England adopted a sober Prayer Book routine, in which the daily round of Bible readings, psalms and prayers took on more importance than preaching.

The Reformation also gave birth to more distinctive traditions. The Anabaptists, for example, included those who not only rejected infant baptism but also gave voice to their emotions in worship, expressing personal piety in prayer in gatherings 'led by the Spirit'. And in the seventeenth century the Quakers originally quite literally 'quaked' before God in worship.

A big change started to affect the whole of English-speaking Protestantism in the eighteenth century. The Evangelical Revival which gave birth to Methodism was characterized by enthusiastic hymn-singing. The hymns were objective in their rich doctrinal content but also expressed emotions towards God. In this revival old metrical psalters were swept aside, and the hymns of Watts and the Wesleys, Cowper and Toplady, started to take their place. Also the Lord's Supper was more frequently celebrated.

Hymns apart, Protestantism has tended to be like Roman Catholicism in that its worship is usually dominated by the man 'up front', and in its solemnity: for the man-in-the-pew religion is not only passive, but also serious. But in the twentieth century, a 'liturgical movement' among both Catholics and Protestants has striven for just those ends which seem so often to have been missed—active participation by the whole congregation, understandable services, and a genuine building up of the fellowship of the body of Christ.

In the Church of Rome this led in time to the Second Vatican Council's reforms of the liturgy, including the admission of local languages into worship, after 1,600 years of Latin. The spillover from this movement into Protestantism along with other shifts of conviction has led to a new emphasis on the corporateness of the sacrament, and on lay participation. Many denominations have gained a new sense that worship might be more than a sermon with some formal preliminaries.

Twentieth century

However, there have always been more radical movements. This century, for instance, has seen the rise of the Pentecostal denominations. These are 'Spirit-directed' rather than 'word-directed', and the characteristic expression in worship has involved a full release of feelings, a free use of body movement and an openness to contributions (not always, but quite often, 'tongues', 'interpretation of tongues' and 'prophecies') from all the worshippers. A parallel movement in the last two decades has been the 'charismatic' movement, which has found a strong home in the 'mainline' Protestant denominations and the Church of Rome.

Today Christianity is once again in a 'missionary' situation in the West, as Christendom fades into secularism. But the various Western forms of Christian worship are not now confined to the West. Young churches flourish in Asia and Africa and

Over the past few years many Christians throughout the world have discovered a new joy and spontaneity in their worship and response to God.

elsewhere. They often tend in worship to be as traditionalist as the Western churches from which they sprang, but the freedom does not exist for them to be culturally relevant to their own contexts. The worship of a truly missionary church loses its respectability, takes on a new edge of realism and, above all, strengthens, unites and equips believers for their daily life and witness in an alien world. Where worship does not build up the body of Christ, the church perishes. The churches of the Western world are slowly awaking to this challenge.

The Christian Life

Michael Sadgrove

The Christian life is the whole life lived before God as he has revealed himself in Jesus Christ. What makes it distinctively Christian is that it is a response to the 'good news', the gospel: that in Christ, men and women enjoy a new quality of life, open to a new dimension of existence and new possibilities of action. As the apostle Paul expressed it in the New Testament: 'I appeal to you, therefore, brethren, by the mercies of God, to present your bodies as a living sacrifice, holy and acceptable to God, which is your spiritual worship.' The word 'therefore' was the link between the gospel he had been describing and the Christian life. It is to be a life of grateful response to what God has done in Jesus Christ.

Christian living

What is it that shapes Christian character and life? Three themes arising out of the New Testament are of particular importance.

● **The kingdom** The 'kingdom' in the first three Gospels means the coming reign of God, and Jesus' preaching of the kingdom is the announcement that this new age has broken in upon our world. With the kingdom comes the summons to accept the rule of God: 'Repent and believe the gospel.' So the Christian life is what marks out the person who belongs to the kingdom, whose values have become the values of a subject claimed by a monarch. In all his praying, behaving and living, the Christian is a kingdom-man, living on the frontier between the old world and the new.

● **Justification** At the heart of the gospel expounded by Paul in the New Testament letters lies the doctrine of justification by faith—being made right with God through trusting in him. In Christ, men and women are freely accepted by God. Their sin is forgiven. They are offered new life in the Spirit as sons and heirs. Reconciliation with God is the unearned and unearnable gift of God. It is offered on the basis of the fact that Jesus Christ died our death, and rose again from death. It is received by faith. The Christian life is therefore a life of freedom, lived in the joyful awareness of an unafraid relationship with God. And it is therefore also a life of glad self-surrender in love to the God who first loved us.

● **The incarnation** 'The Word became a human being and . . . lived among us' is the starting-point of John's Gospel. God has joined himself in Christ to the stuff of the created world and of our own humanity. The Christian life is deeply concerned with what is material, what is human, for it is here that God has met us in his Son. So, on the one hand, Christian life is world-affirming, unashamedly enjoying the goodness of created things. But, on the other, it takes seriously the sufferings and struggles of a world gone wrong, of human beings yearning for wholeness. For to this human condition of suffering and alienation God came in Jesus Christ.

Christian religion

If the word 'religion' means the response of human beings to God, then Christianity is profoundly religious. But because the gospel calls for a total response from man, Christian religion can never be a hermetically-sealed 'spiritual' affair untouched by the demands of human life in the world God has made. Those 'belonging to the Way', as the first Christians were known, were identified by a radically new life-style that included both a Godward dimension of prayer and worship, and a manward dimension of a common life and care for the poor.

So Christian prayer on the one hand and Christian character and conduct on the other are the inseparable parts of Christian religion. For the 'whole duty of man' is to deepen our relationship with God through the spiritual life, and so to grow into mature Christian attitudes and conduct. In the words of the Shorter Catechism, man's chief end is 'to glorify God and to enjoy him for ever'.

Christian prayer

Prayer is possible because God is accessible through Christ. In him, Christians believe, God may be known, loved and adored. And if this is where Christian prayer begins, it must continue with thanksgiving, penitence (asking forgiveness for sin) and supplication (requests to God):

● **thanksgiving**, because in Christ God has revealed his goodwill to man;

● **penitence**, because in Christ God has forgiven and forgives;

● **supplication**, because in Christ God has declared a purpose for history and for humanity.

Prayer in the New Testament

The cry 'Abba!', the familiar Aramaic word for 'Father', is eloquent testimony to the way in which early Christians prayed. Jesus taught his disciples to pray to God as Father. The Lord's Prayer, given twice in the New Testament as the pattern, beginning with the words 'Our Father', has been used as a prayer throughout the centuries by Christians of all traditions. It is basically about the kingdom. The seven petitions that follow all ask in various ways that the blessings of the new age may come upon those who have become members of the kingdom of God. The prayer is nothing if not concrete. It lifts up before God the raw material of human life: material need, failure in relationships with both God and man, the experience of suffering and trial. It is the new age that puts

In the Eastern Church, icons—beautiful paintings of the holy family and the saints—are used as an aid to contemplation and worship.

human experience in its proper perspective.

The spiritual life

How has spirituality developed since New Testament days? There is, of course, a rich heritage of devotion and spiritual life expressed in an infinite variety of ways. But three distinctive approaches can be identified, associated with a Catholic, Orthodox and Protestant outlook.

> '**Jesus said:
> "When you pray, say this:
> 'Father: May your holy name be honoured;
> may your Kingdom come.
> Give us day by day the food we need.
> Forgive us our sins,
> for we forgive everyone who does us wrong.
> And do not bring us to hard testing.'"'**
>
> The Lord's Prayer, Luke 11:2–4

Catholic spirituality

Catholic spirituality is fundamentally 'sacramental'. Because God became man in Christ, the material world is seen as a vehicle for the spiritual. Grace does not destroy nature, but perfects it. And so the 'journey' of the Christian life begins at baptism, with the Eucharist as nourishment, and sacramental confession the means by which the soul is kept on the way that leads to the vision of God. And because the church, with its rites and institutions, is a divine society, the journey is a splendid one, transfigured by the glory of Christ at every stage.

Orthodox spirituality

The Orthodox churches of the East are also deeply rooted in a sacramental understanding of grace. But their distinctiveness lies in their use of icons. An icon is a representation of Christ, the Virgin Mary or one of the saints. But it is more than a mere picture. It is a kind of 'open window' between earth and heaven. The worshipper sees the icon as a proclamation of God's salvation, the material of the object conveying God's grace just as the flesh and blood of Christ had done. But if it 'images' the incarnation, then the icon is also a primary focus for the worshipper's prayers, offered not *to* it but *through* it to the God who is beyond, and yet within it.

Protestant spirituality

What sacraments and icons are to Catholic and Orthodox spirituality, the Bible is to Protestantism. The reading of the scriptures, in the conviction that in them the word of God is to be found, was basic to the prayer of the Protestant reformers. With this went an assurance that the believer had free access to God through Christ, uninhibited by the structures of sacraments and priests erected (as the reformers saw it) by the medieval church. A distinctive mark of early Protestantism was the new value placed on the individual—a consequence of the claim that the individual, justified by faith, mattered to God. The word-orientated 'feel' of traditional Protestantism contrasts sharply with the numinous ethos of symbol and rite that belongs to Catholic spirituality.

Prayer today

Christians today are concerned with relating prayer to life at a number of points. The impact of secularism has led radical theologians to look for more meaningful ways of talking about God and praying in the 'secular city'. Prayer is seen not as withdrawal from the world but as involvement in it. 'Liberation theologians' would go further: the search for political and social goals provides a spirituality of liberation in which prayer is 'made flesh' in the struggle against oppressive economic systems and political regimes.

A parallel development has been to react against the secular and to seek inspiration (often

Following Jesus' example, Christians have always been involved in helping the poor and needy. In 1980, Mother Teresa was awarded the Nobel Peace Prize for her self-sacrificial work in the slums of Calcutta.

'Happy are those who know they are spiritually poor; the Kingdom of heaven belongs to them! Happy are those who mourn; God will comfort them! Happy are those who are humble; they will receive what God has promised! Happy are those whose greatest desire is to do what God requires; God will satisfy them fully! Happy are those who are merciful to others; God will be merciful to them! Happy are the pure in heart; they will see God! Happy are those who work for peace; God will call them his children! Happy are those who are persecuted because they do what God requires; the Kingdom of heaven belongs to them! Happy are you when people insult you and persecute you and tell all kinds of evil lies against you because you are my followers. Be happy and glad, for a great reward is kept for you in heaven. This is how the prophets who lived before you were persecuted.'

The Beatitudes from Jesus' *Sermon on the Mount*

mystical) in other faiths. At the same time within mainstream Christianity, both Catholic and Protestant, the contribution of the 'charismatic' movement has been to encourage the renewal of a spontaneous life of prayer, joyfully liberated from the shackles of formality and convention.

Christian life-style

God's will for human beings is that they should be 'whole': complete in every aspect, whether as individuals, in the intimate relationships of family and community, or in the wider social, national and international context. In Christ, people can become, and indeed are already becoming, what God intended them to be.

Words such as behaviour, conduct, morals, ethics, suggest sticking to rules. A great deal of Christian thinking on morals has looked suspiciously like moralism: the 'oughts' and the 'musts' of duty goading wilful humans into joyless and reluctant obedience. But the Christian life is not something imposed from outside, but something that arises freely and spontaneously from within as the gospel takes root. So Christian behaviour means not only what a Christian does or does not do; it also means how a Christian thinks, and what kinds of values and attitudes he holds as his response to Jesus Christ.

Ethics in the New Testament

How did the early church understand the challenge of the gospel to live 'Christianly'?
● **The Jewish background** Christianity inherited from its Jewish roots the Law of Moses. The Law (with its summary in the Ten Commandments) stood at the centre of Jewish life. God's laws were to be the pattern of a Jew's responsibility towards God and his neighbour. The Law of the Old Testament was not given as a strait-jacket. It was given to guide man's response to a God who had already loved him, and invited him into a relationship of love called the covenant. And so, when Jesus says that all the Law and the prophets hang on the great commandments to love God with all your being, and your neighbour as yourself, he is spelling out what was already there. As the apostle Paul puts it: 'love is the fulfilling of the law.' For Jew and Christian alike, love is the basis of all true response to God.
● **The Sermon on the Mount** Jesus' teaching known as the 'Sermon on the Mount' is the manifesto of the kingdom breaking in with Jesus. The blessings of this new age are for those whom men naturally despise: the poor, the meek, the oppressed. The values of the kingdom, with the seemingly impossible summons to perfection, deal a death-blow to the easier standards of conventional morality. The ethics of the new age call men to live in the light of tomorrow and the coming of God.
● **Paul** If justification by faith is the charter of a Christian's freedom, is he not free to do exactly as he likes? 'Shall we sin, that grace may abound?' No, there is a difference between liberty and licence. Christian liberty is God's gift in an accepting relationship of love. Like all accepting relationships, God's acceptance of a person changes him. It enables him to respond by loving God back—something of which he was not capable before. And so, in a marvellous paradox, God's service is 'perfect freedom'. We can love God *and* do as we want (as Augustine recommended) be-cause what we want as Christians has become precisely what God wants of us: trust, obedience and unconditional love.

Making moral choices

Human life demands that we make moral choices all the time. What is it that determines what is 'right' or 'wrong' in a particular situation? Some may say that a certain course of action is 'natural', or that it leads to the outcome of the greatest good, or that it does not go against the dictates of conscience. All these options have been canvassed by Christians at various times (for example, the concept of natural law invoked by medieval theologians).

But the Christian life is a response to God in Christ, so the overriding criterion for Christian thinking and conduct will be bound up with the gospel and its claims upon us. What was the way of Jesus?

As we have seen, Jesus reasserted the moral values of the Old Testament scriptures. In discussing marriage, he went back to the basic principles of creation, God's intention for man and woman to become 'one flesh'. The principles of creation and law—how God intended man to live—are basic to moral choices. For they are also the most loving way: and in the New Testament they are interpreted in a spirit of Christian love, a spirit of total self-giving. This is not a matter of feeling: what feels loving may not always be in another person's best interests.

In an increasingly pagan society, Christians are having to reaffirm basic moral attitudes on personal and social issues. They can not only point to the right way, they can also point to Jesus as the one who makes it possible to live the right way.

Competing Ideologies Today

It could be said that in the twentieth century popular religion is not religion at all, but the new faiths of existentialism and communism, which together have adherents in so much of the world.

So this book would not be complete without mention, at least, of these ideologies which, though not religions in the strict sense, often have the same place in people's lives as major religions had in the past.

EXISTENTIALISM
Anthony Thiselton

The term 'existentialism' is often used to denote a general attitude towards life and thought. But strictly speaking, there is no single philosophy of existentialism; only a group of highly individual thinkers whom others have labelled 'existentialist'. Some of the features which recur in these thinkers are as follows:
● The priority of the practical over the theoretical.
● The priority of the concrete and personal over the general and abstract.
● The importance of involvement, as against detachment, in the quest for understanding.

Those who attack existentialism would also want to add the following:
● Its pessimism about the possibility of reaching any comprehensive and coherent view of reality.
● Its tendency towards an individualism in which each is free to do his own thing. Truth, it is argued, has been reduced to a matter of what is true 'for me'.

The father-figure of existentialism was **Søren Kierkegaard** (1813–55), whose writings, however, did not become widely known until the early part of this century. After a personal crisis in his life, Kierkegaard came to feel that he had been living on the basis of values derived from his father at second hand, and that he must seek his own more authentic values through firsthand experience and personal decision. In the course of long personal struggles, he came to believe that God was calling him to show in his life and personal commitment what true Christianity meant, in contrast both to armchair philosophy and to nominal Christianity. Christian faith, he believed, was a matter of practical obedience, not theoretical thought. On the positive side, Kierkegaard saw that Christianity was not an 'ism', but a personal commitment. But on the negative side, his devaluing of the Christian community led to an individualistic account of faith which no doubt contributed to his own experiences of deep doubt and anguish.

Martin Heidegger (1889–1976) argued that even the seemingly 'general' questions of philosophy can be asked only concretely from the standpoint of where the thinker already is. He can philosophize only from within his own horizons. To this extent, he can never completely escape the problems imposed by his own finitude and relativity. The Western tradition of philosophy, Heidegger argued, has tended to depersonalize man by ignoring the way in which he is part of his own personal 'world', in which what matters is what matters to him.

Without Kierkegaard's anchorage in Christian faith, this outlook can lead to an increasingly one-sided surrender to relativism and individualism. We find this already anticipated before Heidegger in **Friedrich Nietzsche** (1844–1900) and subsequently developed in **Jean-Paul Sartre** (1905–80) and **Albert Camus** (1913–60). In atheistic versions of existentialism, life is seen as having no rational or universal meaning other than what seems to be authentic for a given individual. The individual must reject society's attempt to impose on him second-hand 'roles' of someone else's making.

In spite of these points of tension between existentialism and Christianity, there are also affinities. These include the priority of the personal over the impersonal (emphasized especially by **Gabriel Marcel**); the recognition of the full implications of human finitude as meaning that I am 'placed' already within 'my' horizons; the importance of personal experiences such as anxiety and guilt in leading to appropriation of truth; and the limitations of mere theorizing over against active decision and practical commitment.

COMMUNISM
Robert Banks

Karl Marx (1818–83) combined and transcended three major streams of thought:
● German philosophical views, especially as filtered through Feuerbach's materialist critique, emphasized the need for human autonomy, a rational society and scientific progress. Marx's debt to them extended as well to his dynamic understanding of history and ideas about human alienation.
● French political theory

was concerned for the politically and economically disadvantaged proletariat who had been bypassed in the bourgeois French Revolution. Marx's debt here embraced its rejection of private property and the emphasis on exploitation by one class of another.

● English economic analysis provided Marx with a description of the mechanics of social change, especially its explanation of the growth of capitalist society. Marx's debt in this area included his concepts of division of labour, surplus value and the like.

All these were fused by Marx into a world-view that was genuinely new. Everything stems from matter, though matter itself is a dynamic phenomenon, giving birth to consciousness, thought, creativity, etc. Man is essentially a social creature who is capable of creating his own destiny. The emergence of primitive technology, however, and its formation of different classes, divided men from each other and locked them into particular social frameworks. All of these gave rise to specific legal, political, moral, religious and cultural systems which were ultimately reflections of the socio-economic base. Each type of society contained contradictions which sowed the seeds of its own destruction. So, from a state of primitive communism there followed classical slave society (or in the East its more despotic Oriental counterpart), feudal society and now capitalist

Jesus described the people of his day as 'sheep without a shepherd'.

society. Out of the inevitable demise of the latter, revolutionary proletarian activity would usher in socialist society. This would be marked by the dismantling of the state and the voluntary rejection of religion, for it would involve the full and free co-operation and contentment of all men.

Revolutionary Marxism?

Since Marx, the world-view he elaborated has undergone a number of modifications at the hands of later Marxist thinkers. His English compatriot **Engels** pushed it in a more scientifically mechanistic and less historically dynamic direction. So too did the Germans **Bernstein** and **Kautsky**, who also tempered Marx's political analysis in a more social-democratic direction. **Lenin**, on the other hand, replaced its view of inevitable capitalist collapse and mass proletarian ascendancy with one justifying a premature seizure of power by a vanguard party representing proletarian interests. His exiled former colleague— **Trotsky**—advocated a continuous revolution rather than simply the unfolding of a critical revolutionary situation.

In China, **Mao Tse-Tung** bypassed the small proletarian class in favour of the larger peasant class to initiate the revolution, thereby omitting what Marx saw as the necessary capitalist preparation for socialist society. Meanwhile, the failure of structural changes behind the Iron Curtain to solve fundamental human problems encouraged some Marxist philosophers to integrate existentialist or

more humanistic elements into their outlook; others developed a more complex understanding of the relation between economic and other structures in the dynamics of social change.

Influential modifications of Marx were undertaken by the leaders of the Frankfurt School of Social Research. These sought to introduce a genuine psychological dimension into his social and political thought and argued that the transition from industrial to technological society rendered much of Marx's outlook irrelevant. The New Left in the '60s, on the other hand, ignored the more rigorous aspects of Marx's social and economic analysis in favour of expressions of moral outrage and belief in a purely political situation. This involved a highly romantic and utopian notion of the preconditions and consequences of revolution.

Russia and the Eastern bloc

Among European countries, Russia seemed least suited to Marx as a prospect for socialism. This was due to its absorption of elements of despotic Oriental society and its rudimentary development of a capitalist base. Modifying Marx's analysis, Lenin first sought to explain the increasingly dynamic success of capitalism in the West by arguing that the success was simply a postponement of its decay arising from exploitation of the colonies of the great powers. He also worked out the organizational theory, principles and

tactics of a revolutionary (though from Marx's point of view premature) seizure of power.

The evolution of Russian communism under Stalin moved even further away from Marxist foundations in a totalitarian direction, though all the basic foundations had been laid by Lenin himself. The dominance of the single leader, the entrenchment of the party, the strengthening of government, the creation of a secret police force, the direct oppression of religious and racial minorities, all showed how powerful were pre-revolutionary Czarist/Oriental attitudes as well as post-revolutionary totalitarian tendencies. The less tyrannical mood under Khrushchev's, and later Brezhnev's, more low-profile, less overtly oppressive, regimes have partially but not radically modified this.

None of the East European communist governments came to power in the same manner as the Bolsheviks in 1917. All owed their existence to Russian interference in their post-war domestic affairs. Even the Yugoslav communist victory pre-eminently sprang out of a war of liberation against the Nazis, not a purely political seizure of power. In differing degrees, particular national institutions, religion and culture in these countries have prevented them from fully imitating the Russian model. (The role of Catholicism in Poland is a case in point.) Yugoslavia represents a more moderate approach with its greater freedom of religion, involvement of workers in industrial decision-making and political independence from Moscow. The

tension between national aspirations and Russian domination has occasionally, though never successfully, disrupted the internal stability of these countries, as in Hungary in 1956 and Czechoslovakia in 1968.

China: Maoism

According to Marx, Oriental societies exhibited a different social and political structure from their Western counterparts. They were by nature essentially static societies rather than dynamic and self-transforming. No disaffected class strong enough to bring about the disintegration of this closed, despotic system existed. And their partial colonization by the West, certainly in the case of China, was insufficient to stimulate them even in a bourgeois-democratic, let alone proletarian-socialist, direction.

For all the Marxist rhetoric, generally quite unsophisticated and at times decidedly vulgar in character, the changes indicated by the communist victory in 1949 were of an essentially different kind. A return to the despotism that pre-dated the 1911 bourgeois Nationalist Revolution under Sun Yat Sen has taken place, though one pushed in a more totalitarian direction. This was centred on Mao Tse-Tung and his ever-changing circle of colleagues. Given the less inherently democratic character of Chinese, as distinct from Russian, society, the extension of ideological as well as bureaucratic control over the population has been more complete. The Cultural Revolution that began in 1966 was an extreme demonstration of the ideological dimension in this process at work. The present leadership seems likely to modify the development of Chinese communism in certain, probably major, respects.

The Third World
The strategy for the establishment of communism in Third World countries has been more the Yugoslav or Chinese than the Russian one. That is, it has generally come about as the result of a war of liberation. In some cases this has occurred in the aftermath of a nationalist war against an occupying power, such as in North Korea against the Japanese. In others, for

example Cuba, it followed a civil war. In Vietnam, a combination of the two was involved. Sometimes, as in Ethiopia, direct Russian assistance was involved in the creation of a communist government. Alternatively, the move in a communist direction has only gradually emerged after liberation occurred: as in the People's Republic of Zaire, and increasingly Angola, though Cuba was the first instance of this. The one example of a popularly-elected Communist government was Allende's in Chile, which was soon sabotaged by internal and external interference.

The strong patriotic aspirations involved in most of these revolutions make it difficult to separate out the specifically communist from the indigenous nationalist elements. Most are developing strong centralized governments engaged in fairly extensive political scrutiny of their subjects. But the basic reason is probably the need to control the means of production as fully as possible so that modernization can take place as quickly as possible. This suggests paradoxically that, more than its anti-capitalist political content, Marxism provides the most

attractive ideological framework by which underdeveloped nations, particularly those antagonistic to former Western masters, can effectively industrialize themselves. Certainly their relations with the communist superpowers have been extremely pragmatic.

A Fusion of Religion: Syncretism

John Allan

'Syncretism' is the name given to any attempt to combine many diverse religious elements into a new system of faith and belief. As this has been a fairly common human impulse down the centuries, the history of syncretism is long and confusing.

In the West, it goes back at least as far as the pre-Christian mystery cults of ancient Rome. The Romans were quite willing to tolerate the existence of private *superstitiones* alongside the official *religio* ordained by the state, and these cults drew from an international background of theological ideas—the cult of Isis from Egypt, Mithras from Persia, Cybele from Asia Minor, to name but three. These

mysteries eventually died out, thanks to a policy of brutal suppression, after the adoption of Christianity as the state religion in AD 392. But the earlier religious cosmopolitanism of Rome (in which, for instance, Augustus highly commended his grandson for visiting the temple in Jerusalem while staying in Palestine) had provided a seed-bed for all sorts of syncretistic schemes—Neo-Platonism, Gnosticism, Hermeticism (incorporating the alchemical and astrological systems of Egypt)—which survived in many guises in different movements, and often penetrated the church itself. For example, Synesius (370–413), who was bishop of Ptolemais

in North Africa, not only wrote Gnostic hymns, but also compiled a commentary on an alchemical treatise and dedicated it to the high priest of the cult of Serapis in Alexandria.

Resistance groups
Throughout the Middle Ages, syncretism flourished mainly amongst popular resistance groups who opposed the theological supremacy of Rome. In the thirteenth century, for instance, the Cathars or Albigensians emerged in the Languedoc area of France, teaching a form of Gnosticism, while at the same time the heresy of the 'Free Spirit' revived Neo-Platonist ideas in the north of Europe. The key to both movements may have been contact with the Arabs; the ideas which Christendom had condemned had passed from the Roman Empire into the keeping of the Arab races, who were now reintroducing them into European life.

At the Renaissance,

Europe experienced an explosion of interest in new ideas, and this often included the old lore of the previously banned movements. The human mind had been liberated from the boundaries set by the censor of the medieval Catholic church, and scholars such as John Dee and Simon Forman saw absolutely no conflict between magical pursuits and Christian orthodoxy. A further source of ideas was added to the syncretistic mix: scholars began to investigate the Jewish Kabbalah, itself a weird mixture of Judaism and magical ideas from many sources. Some daring thinkers went too far (Giordano Bruno's Hermetic ideas led to his death at the stake) but a tradition of speculative thought was established which later led to the foundation of the secret societies and occult groups we know today.

Secret societies
This process began in the eighteenth century, when

the Freemasons (a survival of the medieval craft guilds) were joined and transformed by a number of amateur occultists who suspected that Masonry might be 'the remains of the mysteries of the ancients'. The idea that a secret society of magical wisdom might exist somewhere had been common since 1614, when the 'Rosicrucian Brotherhood' had announced its existence in a manifesto published at Cassel. The likelihood is that the manifesto was a hoax and that no such group had ever formed, but nonetheless the possibility was raised in European minds. Masonry was one of many secret societies in eighteenth-century Europe. Druidism was another variety which grew in popularity in England, and again the fascination was syncretistic—Pythagoras, the Kabbalah, and the Chaldean Magi were claimed to have taught similarly.

Eastern thought

In the late nineteenth century, a growing fascination with Eastern thought in the West led to the flourishing of the Vedantist groups from India and the establishing of religious cults of Western origin with Eastern world-views. In Christian Science, for instance, Mary Baker Eddy taught that pain is an imaginary experience, that God is a 'Principle' rather than a person, that sin, death and evil are unreal. These teachings are markedly Hindu rather than Christian. In Theosophy, Mme Helena Blavatsky claimed to be rediscovering the ancient wisdom (*theosophia*) which lay at the heart of every religion: 'except the

initiates, no one has understood the mystic writing'. But the importance to her thinking of the doctrines of *karma* and reincarnation, together with her claim to be guided by a shadowy brotherhood of 'Masters' usually located in Tibet, shows clearly where the roots of her theology lay.

At the same time, an occult revival centred on Paris led to the foundation of magical and Rosicrucian groups, and the odd claims of a young Persian nobleman named Baha'u'llah brought Islamic syncretism into the West. Baha'u'llah believed himself to be the legendary Twelfth Imam of Islam, due to appear to guide the faithful to a new experience of God, as well as the 'other Comforter' whose coming was promised by Jesus. Thus his teachings—now known as the Baha'i faith—could unite world religions in one, and bring about an era of world peace. Baha'u'llah himself died a young man in 1893, but his impressive and persuasive son 'Abd ul-Baha had remarkable success in spreading the faith in Western high society circles.

This century, the West has seen a remarkable explosion of syncretist groups since the 1960s. The reason for this is probably the search for some kind of spirituality to replace the drug experiences of the psychedelic era. LSD and mescaline had been touted by Timothy Leary and other high priests of the chemical revolution as 'the religion of the twentieth century . . . turn on, tune in, drop out'. But the obvious dangers of drug-taking eventually led to disaffection, which by

1968 allowed a whole variety of Eastern groups to exploit the spiritual gap ex-addicts were experiencing.

'Drugs can't give you eternal peace, but I can,' proclaimed the Divine Light Mission's Guru Maharaj Ji. It is not without significance that both the 'Divine Light' experience and the 'Hare Krishna' experience had already been described (with no religious trappings) in a popular book of the time entitled *Thirty Ways to Get High Without Taking Drugs*.

Doctrinal mix

Most of the Eastern groups were vaguely syncretist: Jesus Christ featured alongside a variety of Hindu figures in the Divine Light Mission's Exhibition of Forty-Two World Saviours. But a Korean-based group, most prominent in the seventies, was the most outspoken in its syncretism. The Unification Church founded by Sun Myung Moon combined Christian ideas and terminology with Taoist notions of God and the complementarity of creation. As its name suggests, the Church sees as its aim the unification of all world religions under a coming messiah, who may well be Sun Myung Moon in person. Some limited attention is paid to Buddhist and Islamic ideas in the group's sacred work, *Divine Principle*, but these traditions add little to the Unification doctrinal mix.

The Unification attempt to combine a foreign religion—Christianity—with more familiar ancestral concepts probably arose out of a desire to forge a new, patriotic faith with Korea as its centre. This has

frequently been a factor in the rise of new syncretist groups. The Rastafarians, for example, with their strange mixture of Christianity and African nationalism, and the Black Muslims, a cross between revivalist Christianity and Islamic theology, have provided an outlet for oppressed people which has allowed them a sense of purpose and of self-respect.

Two more recent trends deserve note. There has been a rise in the popularity of personal therapy or counselling treatments, with names such as Scientology, est, esalen and Exegesis, which rarely admit to being religious, but which all involve the adoption of syncretistic views about the nature of life and the universe. Scientology, for instance (which *does* admit to being a religion, but more often describes itself as 'the modern science of mental health'), combines a course of therapy using a crude lie-detector with a series of ultimately Buddhist teachings: that we are not our bodies but are actually an immortal being called a 'Thetan'; that the Thetan was involved in the creation of the universe and is possessed of theoretically unlimited powers; that we progress through a series of incarnations; that salvation involves personal enlightenment which must be achieved by individual effort unaided by any deity.

Age of Aquarius

Second, the astrological belief that we are now entering the 'Age of Aquarius'—an age in human history when man's consciousness will be expanded and new spiritual powers will be discovered—has led to the proliferation of a whole variety of self-styled 'New Age' groups, with interest in yoga, pyramid power, holistic health, UFO contacts, ley lines and geodetic forces, traditional magic and paraphysical research. These groups will often work together and see themselves as complementary rather than competing. Their basic theology tends to be Eastern but eclectic. Bhagwan Rajneesh, for instance, founder of the Kalptaru Meditation Centres, claims to have built his popularity upon the fact that he follows no one teacher or method, but draws from all. Beshara, another New Age group, claim that 'the man of wisdom, whatever may happen, will never allow himself to be caught up in any one definite form or belief because he is wise unto himself'.

It has been claimed that we are living in the age of the sub-cult, in which people are more likely to look for truth in the small group rather than in the large organized religious system. If this is a correct analysis, the prospects for new syncretisms must be fairer at this moment in history than they have been for a very long time.

Australia, like many secularized countries, has seen a decline in institutional Christianity, though there is a new interest in less formal expressions of faith. But world-wide, Christianity in general is stronger today than ever before.

The Future of Christianity

Robert Linder

*Christians are concerned
to show love for people,
whether their needs are
physical or spiritual.
Medical work has been a
key feature of Christian
activity in the needy parts
of the world.*

Futurology is a tricky business, especially when it deals with religion. Even so, theologians, sociologists, economists, political scientists and occasionally historians attempt to divine the future. Some insight into it can be derived by looking at Christian history, the present world situation and current issues which will affect the future of the faith. From this, perhaps some indication of what Christianity will be like fifty years from now can be gained.

What was the position of Christianity fifty years ago, in say 1930? It was at about that time that the cliché was first invoked that the Western world had entered a 'post-Christian' era. During the next two decades, it appeared to many that this was only too true. Christianity in the USA was in the last stages of the debilitating fundamentalist-modernist controversy. Theological liberalism and religious apathy seemed to have permanently taken over in Europe. Christianity in the non-Western world appeared discredited by its former ties with colonialism. Secular humanism seemed to be the dominant intellectual force in the West, and education was accepted as the panacea for contemporary ills.

Thus, when the Great Depression struck in 1929, most people turned to government and science rather than religion for aid and comfort. At the same time, totalitarian fascism and communism were on the march in Europe and Asia. Many intellectuals in all parts of the world—Marxist and non-Marxist—predicted that it would be only a matter of time before Christianity disappeared altogether.

However, this was not the case. Now, fifty years later, professing Christians are more numerous than ever before in history and their presence seems to be increasingly important with each passing year, even in communist nations. In the 1980s, Christianity has nearly 1,000 million adherents on every continent—clearly out-distancing its nearest rival, Islam, which claims some 585 million followers.

The doom boom

However, though Christianity was growing numerically in the period 1930–80, it was also losing ground in terms of its percentage of total world population and of the population of most developed countries. For example, it decreased from 23.9 per cent of the world population in 1978 to 23.0 per cent in 1979, while the percentage of people affiliated to none of the five major religious systems increased from 40.9 to 42.7 per cent.

Also, the socio-political context of the world has deteriorated significantly since 1930. Incredible as it seems, in the short space of fifty years the world has gone from a major economic depression through a global war to a series of intense localized conflicts, to a period of unbelievable Western affluence, to the precipice of Western collapse and another world war. Not since the Reformation era has an apocalyptic mood been so evident and pervasive in the Western world as it is today. This 'boom in doom' is apparent almost everywhere, in the West as well as in other parts of the world— from the pulpits to the news-stands to the halls of higher learning.

Can or will Christianity help the world meet the threat of economic upheaval and its companion, world hunger? For instance, will Christians play a leading role in the reallocation of wealth necessary in order to feed the world and distribute resources equitably?

The massive problems of politics and economics are compounded by the fact that freedom is in retreat around the globe. Even in the Western democracies, government has become dangerously centralized; in the totalitarian countries it is lord and master. Personal freedom and individual responsibility have been replaced in many lands by personal welfare and corporate responsibility. Technological surveillance and espionage to control people is all too common, even in democratic countries.

How will Christianity respond to these totalitarian trends? In particular, how will the Christians of America respond to increasing fascist tendencies in their country? Can and will Christians in the USA do anything to head off a home-grown brand of American fascism or will they go the way of many believers in Nazi Germany in the 1930s? If America does go fascist in the near future, what will this mean for the cause of human freedom everywhere and for the worldwide missionary enterprise?

Facing issues

Another complicating factor related to economic chaos and the drift toward political totalitarianism has been the great surge of racial movement and unrest. People are leaving

There are flourishing churches in China today, despite the years of official repression.

and will continue to leave their native lands in increasing numbers as modern technology makes it both possible and desirable to do so in the wake of continuing social turmoil. As the different races and cultures rub against each other in great numbers in more and more parts of the world, tension will continue to mount. The movement of large numbers of refugees will be a major factor in world political unrest for years to come. Christianity too will have to cope with the increasingly difficult and interrelated issues of national boundaries, nationalism and population pressures. Christianity could provide a shared world-view which would serve as the 'glue' of multi-ethnic, multi-cultural, multi-linguistic nations.

Some of the recent literature on the subject of civilization's disintegration frankly acknowledges some of these momentous problems but embraces long-range optimism in which computer technology saves the day. Yet in America the polls show that not only have the masses lost faith in traditional political leadership, but people have grown sceptical about the ability of science and technology to solve their problems. In fact, scientific and technological advances have in some cases gone beyond mere problem-solving and begun to dabble with the essence of life itself. Christians will have to speak out on the human manipulation of birth, for example, (especially the growing practice of abortion), the manipulation of behaviour and the manipulation of death.

Can Christianity in fact contribute to the emergence of a new consensus of commonly-held values that will make a difference in terms of the future survival of humanity? For many have wondered, not just if there is a future for religion, but a future of any kind for the human race. Perhaps the bitterest irony is that amidst the general malaise of modern society and the fading confidence of people in their governments, the only major point at which most governments exercise any kind of leadership is in the area of national defence—or what others call the arms

race. While millions of people starve in one part of the world, billions of dollars are spent on nuclear weapons and conventional arms in another. Most alarming, the military build-up and the possibility of a nuclear holocaust have become so familiar to many people that they now seem to dismiss them as threats to human existence. Can Christians act as peacemakers today? Or will Christians subordinate their faith to other considerations such as their country or economic ideology—and join in the killing?

The intellectual foundation for this worldwide political, economic and social drift is a generation cut off from its roots, isolated from its past and from its future, pathologically preoccupied with self. The threat of atomic disaster, ecological problems and the shrinking of resources all tend to concentrate the attention on the present. There is little serious historical and theological thinking being done about the future.

The world also faces the threat of spreading totalitarianism. The most dangerous challenge may come in embattled America where right-wing political forces have experienced a dramatic growth in the 1970s and where fear of the communist menace is still widespread. Elsewhere, totalitarian communist governments have fastened themselves on country after country following the Second World War—China, Cuba, North Korea, Vietnam, Angola and others—and authoritarian regimes of various stripes mark the political landscape of the newly-emerging nations of Africa, Asia and the Middle East. Christians, already suffering under the Marxist regimes of Eastern Europe, have the potential to reverse or head off such developments in many parts of the world if they take a vigorous stand for human rights. Otherwise, Christianity will become once again largely an underground religion throughout much of the world.

Religious revival

The final element which must be considered amongst the 'signs of the times' is the current religious awak-

Christians demonstrate their love of God in loving service to their fellow-men. Pictured right is a recent expedition attempting to bring medical aid by new means to Nepal.

Jesus' last instruction to his disciples was to spread the 'good news' to all the world. Christians today take up this challenge in many ways, such as by using radio.

ening around the world. Although this religious revival extends beyond the Christian religion, it is most intense and significant in terms of the spread of the gospel of Christ. In America, there has been a resurgence of evangelical (conservative biblical) Christianity similar to that which occurred during the nineteenth-century revival known as the second Great Awakening. There have been reports of significant Christian growth in Eastern Europe, Africa south of the Sahara, India, Indonesia and Korea as well as widespread charismatic renewal in Latin America. Historically-speaking, large-scale religious renewal portends the collapse of a civilization (e.g. Rome, the

Middle Ages) or the dawning of a new day of national vigour (e.g. the Wesleyan revival in Britain).

Ironically, while the West experiences economic and political difficulties and Christianity in Western countries struggles to define its social responsibilities, the Christian religion is also experiencing unprecedented growth in many areas where previously it has not been strong. Based on past experiences and present circumstances, it appears that those nations which hold the most promise in the future in terms of Christian growth are Australia (long overdue and currently ripe for great revival), Brazil (where both Catholics and Protestants are enjoying a new spiritual vigour), the Indian subcontinent (where evangelicals appear poised for a new religious offensive), Indonesia (where the Pentecostal movement shows much promise) and Nigeria (the pearl of Africa in terms of both spiritual and economic potential). There are many others. Moreover, the faith will continue to be outgoing and relatively healthy in such places as Poland, Romania, South Korea and the USSR. All of this points to a shift in the centre of spiritual gravity in Christendom away from the USA and Western Europe to the emerging nations during the next fifty years. Thus, the year 2030 could well see countries such as Brazil and Nigeria supplying large numbers of Christian missionaries for work in the USA, Europe and the Muslim world.

The three Christian groups which should continue to expand most dramatically in the coming fifty years are the Roman Catholics, the Baptists and the Pentecostals—mostly because they are most certain about what they are declaring and have the greatest ideological cohesiveness in their proclamation of the gospel. Catholics have begun to experience a period of renewed vigour under the leadership of Pope John Paul II. Baptist work is now present in nearly every nation, and reports of significant gains continue to come not only from the USA but also from the Soviet Union, Romania, India, Burma, Brazil, Nigeria and Zaire.

Many observers feel that the Pentecostal-charismatic movement is the wave of the future, especially in the Third World. Certainly, it has become a potent force in many Latin American countries as well as in some parts of North America, Europe and Asia. In all three groups a decided evangelical thrust can be detected in their current resurgence. A common biblical base, a common commitment to Christ and common external foes could lead them into a much closer relationship by the year 2030.

In the context of these likely developments which will affect the course of Christianity in the next half-century, and in contrast to the destructive forces emerging among the peoples of the world, the Christian religion will continue to have a global impact in at least three ways.

● The faith is being planted more widely today than it (or any other religion) has ever been. This is true of nearly every part of the world with perhaps the exception of the Muslim countries; though here too new opportunities to replant the Christian faith in Islamic lands may occur in the next fifty years, thanks to the increased contact between the West and the predominantly Muslim areas.

● Christianity is more deeply rooted among more peoples than it or any religion has ever been. This does not mean that nominalism or theological liberalism are dead. However, it does mean that today there is in most of the world more serious commitment to Christ on the part of Christians than at any other time in history. This is true in both North America and Europe where the faith has been present for hundreds of years, and it is true for the former colonial areas where fresh, dynamic, indigenous leadership has emerged to replace that previously provided by Western missionaries. Nearly every nation of the world has now formulated statements of the faith in its own language and setting, thus proving once again the universality of the Christian message.

● Christianity in both the Western

There is an explosion in the number of Christians in South America, particularly among the huge student population.

and the non-Western worlds has developed fresh movements and techniques to meet the challenges of the day. An example of this is the 'electronic church' which has emerged to capture a portion of the TV airwaves for the Christian gospel. Evangelical academies, worker-priests and 'liberation theology' are also examples of the remarkable ability of the Christian religion to formulate new strategies to meet the challenge of an ever-needy world.

A new dynamic force

What will Christianity be like in 2030? It will continue to be the most vital spiritual force in the world. It will be the chief custodian of civilization as nations come and go. Moreover, just as the monasticism of the Middle Ages created communities which preserved a commitment to the full Christian life in the midst of a decadent world, so a new monasticism—this time more truly communal by its inclusion of the family—once again will preserve a commitment to the full Christian life in the midst of a decadent world.

Further, Christianity will provide the world with a link to its past, just as it has done since the collapse of Roman civilization. It will survive whatever difficulties engulf the world in the next fifty years and, if history is a faithful guide, will emerge stronger than ever in any new order. It will give larger numbers of people a wholesome connection with their past and a hopeful outlook for the future.

Finally, the Christian faith will continue to give millions of people a sense of balance, stability and purpose in the midst of an increasingly difficult and dangerous world. In addition to the innovations which will be introduced in order to meet new challenges, Christianity will continue to preserve those timeless values so necessary to civilization and life itself: love, peace, faith, sacrifice, discipline, responsibility and recognition of the dignity of all human beings. Long after the demise of the latest gimmicks and fads, Christian believers all over the world will be found listening to the simple preaching of the gospel and enjoying fellowship together and with God.

Part Seven

Rapid Fact-finder

Angela Tilby
John-David Yule

'ABBASID DYNASTY (AD 750–1055) The second great Islamic dynasty which ruled from Baghdad. Under the 'Abbasids the empire enjoyed a period of increased prosperity and trade. Libraries and centres of learning were established throughout the Islamic world. Baghdad fell to the Seljuk Turks in 1055.

'ABDUH, Muhammad (AD 1849–1905) Leader of an Egyptian Islamic reform movement who taught at the orthodox academy of Al-Azhar. He tried to balance the authority of the 'ULAMA' with modern knowledge, believing that faith and reason were complementary.

ABHIDHAMMA PITAKA THERAVADA Buddhist scripture on techniques of mind-training. The aim is to eliminate the idea of the self. It is the key work of Buddhist psychology.

ABRAHAM, ISAAC AND JACOB The three PATRIARCHS who are continually remembered in the Jewish liturgy as the original recipients of God's promise and blessing. According to tradition they are buried in the tomb of the patriarchs in the cave of Mach-pelah in the modern town of Hebron.

ABSOLUTE, THE Term for GOD or the divine often preferred by those who conceive of God predominantly in abstract or impersonal terms.

ABU BAKR MUHAMMAD'S father-in-law and traditionally his earliest convert. He was elected CALIPH after the Prophet's death and ruled for two years, fighting tribes who were trying to break away from the Islamic community. He began the compilation of the QUR'AN.

ADAE Ancestral customs held among the Ashanti and other peoples of Ghana. It refers particularly to the special rites which are held twice every forty-three days and require abstinence from work.

ADI GRANTH Sacred book of Sikhism. It is regarded as the eternal GURU for the SIKH community. It is the central focus of the Sikh home and of the GURDWARA

ADONAI See YHWH

ADONIS Greek god of vegetation whose rites included women mourning at his death and rejoicing at his resurrection. His MYTH describes him as a beautiful youth from Cyprus who was loved by APHRODITE but killed by a boar while hunting. His name is the Semitic *adon* ('lord') and he has features in common with TAMMUZ.

ADVAITA ('Non-twoness') The monist (see MONISM) doctrine of

SHANKARA that all reality is fundamentally one and divine.

AESIR The race of the gods in Norse mythology. It may derive from a root meaning 'wind'.

AFRICAN INDEPENDENT CHURCHES African churches which have arisen in the past 100 years and offer a synthesis of CHRISTIANITY with traditional PRIMAL RELIGIONS. Many have prophetic or charismatic founders and emphasize spiritual healing and communication with ancestors. Some have been a focus of nationalistic aspirations.

AFTERLIFE Any form of conscious existence after the death of the body.

AGAPE Greek word for 'love' which has come to express the Christian understanding of God's love which does not depend on any worthiness or attractiveness of the object of his love. Christians are taught to demonstrate this love to each other in the Christian FELLOWSHIP, and to others. Also, a EUCHARIST meal.

AGE OF AQUARIUS The approaching period of some 2000 years when, because of the precession of the equinoxes, the intersection of the ecliptic with the celestial equator will lie in the constellation Aquarius. This will mark the end of the present Age of Pisces. According to some NEW AGE RELIGIONS, the Aquarian Age will be marked by the decline of institutional and authoritative religion and an increase of self-awareness and spiritual knowledge.

AGNI Indian fire god of Vedic times (see VEDAS). As sacrificial fire, Agni mediates between gods and men and is especially concerned with order and ritual.

AGONES Greek public festivals of sport or drama held in honour of the gods. Most famous were the Olympic Games, dedicated to Olympian god ZEUS.

AHIMSA Indian virtue of non-violence. It usually applies to abstention from harming any living creature and hence to vegetarianism. The doctrine was developed in JAINISM, BUDDHISM and some HINDU sects. In Jain belief violence carries severe penalties of KARMA. MAHATAMA GANDHI applied the idea to the political struggles of the oppressed in his practice of non-violent non-cooperation.

AHKIN High priest of the MAYA who was one of a college of eight or twelve. They were guardians of the arts of writing; they kept the complex Mayan calendar and were experts on cures, SACRIFICE and prescribed methods of DIVINATION.

AHMADIYYA SECT Offshoot of ISLAM founded in India by Mirza Ghulam Ahmad (died 1908) who is believed to be the MESSIAH MAHDI. The sect denies the authority of the 'ULAMA', IJMA' and JIHAD. It is a missionary sect and has gained converts in Asia and Africa.

AHMAD KAHN, Sayyid (born AD 1817) Indian MUSLIM modernist. He believed that scientific advance was compatible with ISLAM and that CHRISTIANITY and Islam had much in common. He taught for some years in England before founding the Anglo-Oriental College at Aligarh.

AH PUCH God of death of the MAYA. Under the title 'lord of seven hells' he is portrayed as a human skeleton. He is accompanied by a dog and a groaning bird.

AHRIMAN See ANGRA MAINYU.

AHURA MAZDA/OHRMAZD ('Wise Lord') ZOROASTER's name for God. His attributes are comparable to those of VARUNA, the Vedic sky god. He demands ethical and ritual purity and he judges the souls of men after death. His symbol is sacred fire.

AKHENATEN Name adopted by Amenophis IV, king of Egypt 1353–1335 BC, in honour of Aten ('the sun disc') whose cult he promoted to the exclusion of all others in a short-lived reform of Egyptian religion. He built a magnificent new capital at el-Amarna.

AKIBA, Rabbi (AD 50–135) Jewish teacher who developed the MISHNAH method of repetitive transmission of teachings. He began the work of systematizing the available interpretations of TORAH, laying the foundations for the work of JUDAH HA NASI. He was also famous for his use of MIDRASH, investing every detail of the Hebrew texts with significance.

ALA/ALE/ANA The earth goddess worshipped by the Ibo people of Ghana. She preserves the fertility of the land and the family. The dead are said to rest in her womb. She is also the guardian of morality: laws and oaths are made in her name.

AL-ASH'ARI (died AD 935) MUSLIM theologian and philosopher who laid the foundations of orthodoxy. He argued that the QUR'AN was eternal, in opposition to a school that claimed eternity belonged only to God. At the same time he claimed that the actual words, recited and written by man, were not eternal.

ALBIGENSIANS The CATHARS of southern France who flourished in the late twelfth and early thirteenth centuries. Their theology was a DUALISM that has been compared with that of the MANICHAEANS although they were probably unconnected. They saw CHRIST as an ANGEL whose teachings had been corrupted by the Catholic clergy. Their most rigorous adherents, the 'perfects', abstained from marriage and avoided animal products.

ALCHEMY Mystical science of chemical manipulation which seeks to change base metals into gold, find the universal cure for illness and discover the secret of immortality. Its study passed from Hellenistic Egypt through the Arabs to medieval Europe. It is also important in TAOISM.

AL-DIN AFGHANI, Jamal (AD 1839–97) Indian MUSLIM philosopher who tried to strengthen the influence of ISLAM as a social and moral movement. He believed that the best practical expression of Islam was democratic government. He worked also for unity in the Muslim world.

AL-GHAZALI (AD 1058–1111) Orthodox MUSLIM legal expert who renounced his post and became a Sufi (see SUFISM). He attacked the incursions of Greek thought into ISLAM and defended the teaching of the QUR'AN. He also defended the Sufi experience of God but denied the possibility of human deification.

AL-HALLAJ (died AD 922) Sufi MYSTIC who was crucified because of his confession 'I am the real' which was taken as a claim to divinity. He considered JESUS OF NAZARETH as the supreme example of human deification and at this death forgave his enemies in imitation of the passion of Jesus.

'ALI Cousin and son-in-law of MUHAMMAD who was elected fourth CALIPH in AD 656. War broke out between 'Ali and the governor of Syria who claimed that 'Ali had plotted 'UTHMAN's death. In AD 661 'Ali was murdered and his son Hasan renounced any claim to the caliphate.

ALLAH The supreme God proclaimed by MUHAMMAD. Allah is one; there are no gods beside him. He is undivided pure spirit, the creator and sustainer of all that is, known to man in the revelation of his holy will in the QUR'AN.

ALLFATHER In early Norse mythology, the oldest of all the gods and the creator god, probably at first a sky god. His attributes were taken over first by TYR and then by ODIN who retained the title Allfather.

ALMSGIVING The giving of free gifts, usually of money, to the poor. In ISLAM it is obligatory (see ZAKAT). In THERAVADA Buddhism the lay community is linked to the SANGHA by their provision of food for the MONKS which is collected on a daily almsround.

AL-RAHMAN AND AL-RAHMIN
('The merciful' and 'the mercy-giver') See BEAUTIFUL NAMES OF GOD.

AMATERASU Japanese sun goddess, the principal deity in SHINTO. She represents the power of light, growth and fertility and her symbol is a mirror. The EMPERORS of Japan claimed descent from her.

AMESHA SPENTAS/ AMAHRASPANDS 'Bounteous immortals' in ZOROASTRIANISM who surround AHURA MAZDA and are also his characteristic attributes. In later Zoroastrianism they are created spirits like ANGELS who help him in his fight with evil.

AMIDA Japanese form of AMITABHA.

AMIDAH ('Standing') The principal Jewish daily prayer, also known as the Eighteen Benedictions, recited standing. Today it actually comprises nineteen benedictions, including prayers for the restoration of ISRAEL and for peace.

AMITABHA ('Infinite light') Celestial BUDDHA worshipped in China and Japan (where his name is Amida). He is believed to live in a 'pure land' in the far west where those faithful to him go after death (see JODO SHINSHU; NEMBUTSA; PURE LAND BUDDHISM).

AMMA Supreme HIGH GOD among the Dogon people of Upper Volta in West Africa. He made the sun and moon out of clay and then united with the earth, producing people. Unusually for a high god, he is worshipped in temples and has his own priesthood.

AMON-RE State god of the Egyptian New Kingdom (sixteenth to eleventh centuries BC). He is a fusion of the sun god, Re, and a Theban god, Amun.

ANA See ALA.

ANALECTS One of the four books of the so-called Confucian canon. It contains the essence of CONFUCIOUS' teaching and was probably compiled about seventy years after his death.

ANANDA One of the most prominent members of the BUDDHA's SANGHA. Traditionally he was the Buddha's cousin and many of the sayings are addressed to him, including the words of comfort shortly before the Buddha's death. He helped to fix the canon of Buddhist SCRIPTURE.

ANATTA Buddhist term indicating that there is ultimately no 'soul' (see SOUL (1)). All beings are merely a series of mental and physical states. Anatta is one of the three MARKS OF EXISTENCE.

ANCESTOR SPIRITS Spirits of the dead in PRIMAL RELIGIONS. They are sometimes thought of as living in a shadowy UNDERWORLD, sometimes in a place of happiness such as the Happy Hunting Ground of North American Indians. They are revered by the living who believe they can appear to them in DREAMS and warn them of danger.

ANCESTOR VENERATION The practice in PRIMAL RELIGIONS of making offerings to the spirits of the dead and expecting to communicate with them through DREAMS.

ANDRIAMANITRA ('The fragrant lord') The HIGH GOD worshipped in the PRIMAL RELIGION of Madagascar.

ANGELS Spiritual beings who in JUDAISM and CHRISTIANITY act as the messengers of GOD. They have two primary functions: to worship God and to support and encourage human beings. In ISLAM the Archangel GABRIEL is associated with the giving of the QUR'AN.

ANGLICAN CHURCHES
Worldwide grouping of churches which recognize the primacy among equals of the Archbishop of Canterbury. They include both catholic and reformed elements and retain BISHOPS.

ANGRA MAINYU/AHRIMAN The chief spirit who is opposed to AHURA MAZDA in Zoroastrian belief. He works continually for evil in the service of the *druj* ('lie'). Later he came to be considered the leader of a vast hierarchy of evil spirits.

ANICCA Buddhist term for the impermanence and changeability which marks all existence.

ANIMISM A term formerly used to describe pre-literary religions. It was dropped because its meaning 'spirit-ism' was felt to be misleading. (See PRIMAL RELIGIONS; TYLOR, EDWARD BURNETT.)

ANTHROPOSOPHY Spiritual system invented by Rudolf STEINER. It stresses the threefold nature of man as physical, etheric and astral body and proposes a programme for spiritual education which includes techniques of MEDITATION.

ANU The sky god of ancient Sumerian religion and HIGH GOD of the Sumerian pantheon. He had little to do with human affairs and delegated his authority to ENLIL. From about 2000 BC he was called King of Gods and Father. His consort was ISHTAR.

ANU/DANU Celtic goddess of the earth and of plenty, and mother of all the Irish gods. The Christian St Anne has attracted some of her legends.

ANUBIS Jackal-headed god of ancient Egypt who conducted souls to judgement and weighed them in the great balance. Known as 'the embalmer', he watched over mummification and was the guardian of tombs and cemeteries.

ANUTU HIGH GOD of the universe worshipped by the Jabem and Bakava people of Papua New Guinea. He was believed to sit on the horizon where the sky meets the sea and hold the sky in his hands. LUTHERAN CHURCH Christians of the area use the name Anutu for God.

APHRODITE Greek goddess of love and patroness of beauty and sexual attractiveness. Her cult was imported from the Near East. The Greeks thought of her as vain and cruel but the Romans identified her with VENUS and honoured her as the mother of Aeneas, ancestor of the Romans. In Cyprus she was worshipped as the MOTHER GODDESS.

API Scythian name for the earth goddess.

APOCALYPTIC Genre of writing in CHRISTIANITY and JUDAISM, concerned with hidden truths, pointing to the ultimate triumph of faith and the judgement of nations. Daniel and Revelation are examples in the BIBLE.

APOCRYPHA Historical and wisdom writings found in the Greek version of the Hebrew scriptures but excluded from the canon of the HEBREW BIBLE fixed at the Synod of Jamnia around AD 100. The Roman Catholic Church accepts its authority, though Eastern Orthodox and Protestant Churches distinguish it from inspired SCRIPTURE.

APOCRYPHAL NEW TESTAMENT Early CHRISTIAN writings in the form of gospels, acts or epistles not included in the Christian canon of SCRIPTURE. Some express heretical teachings.

APOLLO A major god of both Greeks and Romans, though Greek in origin. He is sometimes seen as the sun and is the patron of the arts (especially music), of prophecy, of divination and of medicine. He was the inspiration of the DELPHIC ORACLE.

APOSTLE (1) 'One who is sent', name for the twelve original followers of JESUS OF NAZARETH, also PAUL. The 'apostolic age' is a time of great authority for the Christian CHURCH. (2) Title of MUHAMMAD.

AQUINAS, Thomas (AD 1225–74) Dominican theologian and philosopher whose teachings form the basis of official Roman Catholic theology. He taught a fundamental distinction between faith and reason, asserting that God's existence can be proved, but that the doctrines of the TRINITY and the INCARNATION are revealed and must be accepted on faith.

ARABIC Semitic language related to HEBREW. The language of the QUR'AN and hence of most MUSLIM legislation, theology and prayer. As ISLAM spread to non-Arab peoples, the Arabic language affected the development of their languages and there are African languages, such as Swahili and Hausa, which are a mixture of Arabic and a local dialect.

ARAHAT ('One who is worthy') THERAVADA Buddhist term for one who gains ENLIGHTENMENT by following the discipline of the SANGHA.

ARCHETYPES Term invented by C.G. JUNG to describe the concepts held in common by different people at different items and in different places. He believed that the concept of GOD was the archetype of the self and that it was the object of each individual to discover it.

ARES The Greek god of war, possibly imported from Thrace.

ARIANISM Fourth-century Christian CHERESY of Arius who denied the divinity of CHRIST, claiming that the Son of God was created and not eternal. It was condemned at the Council of Nicaea in AD 325 but flourished until the Council of Constantinople in AD 381.

ARISTOTLE (384–322 BC) Greek philosopher and scientist who taught on every branch of knowledge valued in his time. His work is characterized by acute observation, close reasoning and orderly exposition. His work was rediscovered in the Middle Ages and laid the basis for the theology of THOMAS AQUINAS and for the HUMANISM of the Renaissance.

ARK (1) Israelite religious artefact, probably in the form of a portable miniature temple, which was carried into battle as evidence of the presence of God (see YHWH). In Solomon's TEMPLE the ark lived in the Holy of Holies. (2) A cupboard in the wall of a SYNAGOGUE that faces JERUSALEM, where the handwritten parchment scrolls of TORAH are kept.

ARTEMIS Greek goddess and patroness of virginity, hunting, archery and wild animals. She was also the protector of the newly-born and the bringer of death to women. At Ephesus in Asia Minor, she was worshipped as the MOTHER GODDESS. (See also DIANA.)

ARTHUR Legendary hero of Celtic Britain who may have originated as a Romano-British chieftain. His legends were gradually worked into a coherent Christian framework in which he became the medieval ideal of a Christian king.

ARYAN Word describing the Caucasian people who invaded India around 2000 BC and who gradually imposed their language and culture upon the earlier inhabitants. Related

peoples settled in Iran and Mesopotamia.

ASCETICISM Austere practices designed to lead to the control of the body and the senses. These may include FASTING and MEDITATION, the renunciation of possessions and the pursuit of solitude.

ASGARD The home of the gods in Norse religion. It is a mountainous region rising out of MIDGARD and separated from it by a rainbow bridge.

ASHKENAZIM One of the two main cultural groups in JUDAISM which emerged in the Middle Ages. Their tradition is from Palestinian Jewry and they live in central, northern and eastern Europe. They developed Yiddish as their language, which is a mixture of Hebrew, Slav and German.

ASHRAM In Indian religion, a hermitage or monastery. It has come to denote a communal house for devotees of a GURU. It functions as a centre for building up the commitment of believers and for transmitting the guru's message.

ASHUR Chief god of ancient Assyria. He was a war god and his consort was ISHTAR.

ASHVAGHOSHA Buddhist writer and poet of the first century AD who traditionally lived in north-west India at a royal court. He wrote a verse poem telling the life of the BUDDHA up to the time of his ENLIGHTENMENT.

ASCLEPIOS Greek god of healing whose cult was located at Epidauros. He was struck dead by ZEUS for bringing the dead to life. Snakes were sacred to him and he was thought to be incarnate in their shape (see SACRED SNAKES). His cult was introduced to Rome in the third century BC.

ASOKA (270–232 BC) Indian king who inherited an empire in northern India. He renounced Brahminical statecraft which required him to pursue a policy of imperialist expansion and became a Buddhist lay follower. He had edicts of Buddhist statecraft inscribed on rocks and pillars throughout the country. His example and influence spread BUDDHISM throughout India and beyond.

ASSASSINS Members of a Muslim ISMA'ILI sect which flourished from the eleventh to the thirteenth centuries AD. They were thought to intoxicate themselves with hashish (hence their name) and then go out and murder their enemies.

ASTRAL PLANE The intermediate world, according to THEOSOPHY and SPIRITUALISM, to which the human consciousness passes at death. Some psychics and visionaries are able to project themselves there at will.

ASTROLOGY The study of the influence of the stars on the character and destiny of human beings. The locations of the planets in the field of the zodiac at the time of the subject's birth are the key data considered in the astrologer's analysis.

ATARGATIS Syrian name for the MOTHER GODDESS. She was particularly revered by the Roman Emperor Nero.

ATATURK, Kemal (AD 1881–1938) Founder and first president of the secular Turkish state. He abolished the Islamic law and the caliphate (see CALIPH) and introduced a programme of westernization, including Roman script.

ATHANASIUS (AD 296–373) Bishop of Alexandria who strongly resisted the teachings of ARIANISM and developed the Christian doctrines of the INCARNATION and the TRINITY.

ATHENA One of the great Greek goddesses of Mount OLYMPUS who sprang fully armed from the head of her father, ZEUS. She is the patroness of war, of the city of Athens and of many crafts and skills. She is usually portrayed in full armour, with an owl on her shoulder and the Gorgon's head painted on her shield.

ATMAN SANSKRIT word meaning 'soul' or 'self'. The UPANISHADS teach that atman is identical to BRAHMAN, i.e. the soul is one with the divine.

ATONEMENT (1) Ritual act which restores harmony between man and the divine, when it has been broken by sin or impurity. (2) In CHRISTIANITY, reconciliation between God and man required because of the absolute holiness of God and the

sinfulness of man. As man is incapable of achieving atonement, it is a work of God's GRACE, through the death of Jesus Christ for man's sin.

ATONEMENT, DAY OF See YOM KIPPUR.

ATTIS Vegetation god with a spring festival of death and resurrection which originated in Phrygia. He was worshipped as the consort of CYBELE. In one version of the myth he castrates himself, thus becoming the first of Cybele's eunuch priests.

ATUA Any god or spiritual power in Maori religion.

AUGUR In Roman religion, a member of the college of augurs, whose task was to give prophetic advice through the interpretation of omens. Taking the *auspices*, their principal method, involved observing the flight of birds.

AUGUSTINE (AD 354–430) BISHOP of Hippo in North Africa who was converted to CHRISTIANITY from the teaching of the MANICHAEANS. He stressed the absolute GRACE of God in man's SALVATION and the depravity of man through ORIGINAL SIN.

AUGUSTUS Title of the first Roman emperor, formerly known as Octavian, who ruled 31 BC–AD 14. He pacified and unified the empire, thus facilitating the later spread of CHRISTIANITY. After his death he was declared a god and worshipped throughout the empire.

AVALOKITESHVARA ('Regarder of the cries of the earth') Celestial BUDDHA worshipped by Tibetans and in Korea, Japan and China. The DALAI LAMA is believed to be a reincarnation of him. This Buddha is known under male and female forms and is depicted with a thousand arms, symbolizing endless labour for the welfare of mankind. (See also CHENRESI.)

AVALON Celtic island of immortality replete with miraculous apple trees. Here the hero ARTHUR was taken to recover from his mortal wounds.

AVATAR ('One who descends') In popular Hinduism, Lord VISHNU appears on earth at intervals to assert

ancient values and destroy illusion. The main tradition refers to ten descents, nine of which have already happened. The mythical KRISHNA is the most famous avatar. Some modern cults claim to worship a living avatar.

AVERROES See IBN RUSHD.

AVESTA The SCRIPTURES of ZOROASTRIANISM. It includes the *Gathas*, a series of poems reminiscent of the hymns of the VEDAS which may go back to ZOROASTER himself. They may have been used as a liturgy to ward off ANGRA MAINYU and his evil spirits.

AYATOLLAH ('Sign of God') Iranian term for a great MUJTAHID who has authority in the SHI'A Muslim community.

AZTEC NEW FIRE CEREMONY Ritual which took place at the end of every Aztec cycle of fifty-two years. It was performed at night on a volcanic hill visible from many parts of the valley of Mexico. When the constellation *Pleiades* reached the middle of the sky, the priests signalled that the world would continue for another cycle of fifty-two years. A human victim was sacrificed and a new fire was kindled in his chest cavity.

AZTECS American Indians whose empire in central Mexico flourished from the late twelfth century AD until the coming of the conquistador Herman Cortes in 1519. Their religion centred around a sacred calendar (see TONALPOHUALLI) and featured human SACRIFICE in which the heart torn from a living victim was offered to the gods. (See also CHICOMECOATL; HUITZILOPOCHTLI; NEZAHUALCOYOTL; QUETZALCOATL; TEZCATLIPOCA; TLALOC; TLOQUE NAHUAQUE; XIPE TOTEC; XIUHTECUHTLI.)

B

BA The breath or life-giving force in ancient Egyptian belief. In a ritual ceremony the ba was breathed back into the mouth of a mummified corpse to guarantee the survival of the dead person.

BAAL Divinity of ancient Canaanite or Phoenician fertility religion. The name means 'lord'.

BAAL SHEM TOV (about AD 1700–60) Jewish MYSTIC who founded the movement of HASIDISM. His name means 'Good Master of the Name (of God)' and it is often shortened to BEShT. His original name was Israel ben Eliezer. At the age of thirty-six he developed powers of healing and prophecy. He taught a kind of mystical PANTHEISM. He was greatly loved and became the source of many Yiddish legends and miracle stories.

BABISM See BAHA'I.

BABYLONIAN EPIC OF CREATION/ENUMA ELISH The story of the god MARDUK's fight with the primordial ocean, Tiamat, who is presented as a sea monster. Marduk slit Tiamat in two and made heaven and earth out of the pieces. This MYTH was probably re-enacted every spring at an ENTHRONEMENT FESTIVAL.

BABYLONIAN FLOOD STORY A parallel to the story of the flood in the BIBLE going back to a Sumerian original but best known from the EPIC OF GILGAMESH. It tells the story of a wise king, Utnapishtim, who survived the flood caused by the god ENLIL by taking refuge in a huge boat with his wife and various animals. He was rewarded by Enlil by being transported to a land of immortality.

BAHA'I Offshoot of the Persian Babism movement. The Bab ('gate'; died AD 1850) taught that he had superseded MUHAMMAD and heralded a new faith. One of his disciples, known as Baha'u'llah (1817–1892) developed his teachings into a universalistic religion based on a new scripture, the *Kitab Akdas*. The largest Baha'i communities are in India, Africa and South America; that in the USA is also quite large.

BAIAME HIGH GOD and creator of the world in the belief of the Aboriginals of south-eastern Australia.

BALDER The son of ODIN and FRIGGA, the wisest and most beautiful of the Norse gods. He was killed by the wiles of LOKI but could not be restored to ASGARD because Loki refused to weep for him. His name means 'lord' and he may be connected with the Middle-Eastern dying and rising gods, ADONIS and TAMMUZ.

BAPTISM The SACRAMENT of entry into the Christian CHURCH. By washing in water in the name of the TRINITY, it symbolizes the person's identification with CHRIST's death and resurrection, in dying to sin and being raised to new life. In the case of infants, promises are made on behalf of the child for later CONFIRMATION.

BAPTIST CHURCHES Protestant churches emphasizing the BAPTISM of adult believers by total immersion.

BARK PAINTINGS Paintings scratched on tree bark by Australian Aboriginals, depicting mythical scenes and supernatural figures.

BAR MITZVAH ('Son of the commandment') Ceremony by which Jewish boys, at the age of thirteen, accept the positive commandments of JUDAISM and are counted as adult members of the community.

BARTH, Karl (AD 1886–1968) Swiss Calvinist theologian who reacted against liberalism in theology and declared theology's central theme to be the Word of God.

BAVIDYE In the Kiluba and related Bantu languages, a word meaning 'superior being'. It refers to spirits associated with the community. It also refers to the creator god, often with the addition of *mulubu*: 'old' or 'great'.

BEAUTIFUL NAMES OF GOD Ninety-nine names which characterize the will of ALLAH in ISLAM. Seventy are found in the QUR'AN; the rest are traditional. The most important are *Al-Rahman* and *Al-Rahmin*, 'the merciful' and 'the mercy-giver'.

BEING OF LIGHT A figure occasionally reported to have been seen by those resuscitated from a state of near death. The figure is sometimes identified as CHRIST or an ANGEL.

BELENOS ('Bright') Celtic deity of spring and healing who may have been associated with the sun. The festival BELTANE may reflect his name. He became identified with APOLLO.

BELTANE Celtic spring festival and origin of May Day. The name means 'shining fire' and it is likely that sacred fires were lit for the people to dance round, encouraging the growth of the summer sun.

BENARES/VARANASI/KASHI The most holy city of HINDUISM, situated on the banks of the GANGES. It is a centre for the worship of SHIVA and attracts one million pilgrims every year. The BUDDHA preached his first sermon here, traditionally in the deer park on the outskirts of the city.

BENEDICT (about AD 480–550) Monk and reformer who wrote a Rule of monastic life which has been followed by MONKS and NUNS of the Western church ever since.

BHAGAVAD GITA ('Song of the lord') A section of the MAHABHARATA in the form of a battlefield dialogue between the warrior prince Arjuna and KRISHNA, disguised as his charioteer. Arjuna is unwilling to fight his kinsmen but Krishna encourages him, teaching him that wisdom requires him to fulfil his proper role while at the same time renouncing the consequences of his actions.

BHAGAVAN Indian title meaning 'lord' or 'worshipful'. It is frequently used of VISHNU. It is also a title of honour used by devotees of holy men.

BHAGAVAN SHRI RAJNEESH Indian spiritual teacher and philosopher who founded his own ASHRAM at Pune (Poona) in India. His daily talks and reflections are transcribed and widely published in the West.

BHAJANA An Indian song or HYMN in praise of God usually sung communally at devotional gatherings and accompanied by musical instruments.

BHAKTI Love of, or devotion to God. It is one of the Hindu paths to union with God (see YOGA). It is expressed in popular religion in which the worshipper develops a sense of personal relationship to God, responding to him as though to a father, mother, friend, lover or child, and looking to him for grace.

BHIKSHU ('One who shares') A Buddhist MONK who teaches the DHAMMA and receives his daily food from the community in return.

BIBLE The book of CHRISTIANITY, comprising the Hebrew OLD TESTAMENT and the NEW TESTAMENT which, Christians believe, together form a unified message of God's SALVATION.

BISHOP The most senior order of ministry in the Christian CHURCH, with authority to ordain PRIESTS. Many REFORMED CHURCHES do not have bishops.

BLACK MUSLIMS American Negro movement founded in 1930. Its founder was declared a PROPHET of ALLAH, a claim rejected by orthodox MUSLIMS. The Black Muslims exclude white people from their temples and practise strict morality.

BLACK STONE Sacred object set in the wall of the Muslim KA'BA sanctuary in MECCA. Tradition asserts that it was received by the biblical Ishmael from the archangel GABRIEL. During the rites of pilgrimage (see HAJJ) the faithful try to kiss or touch the stone.

BLACK THEOLOGY A movement developed in the USA which uses the experience of being black in a white-dominated society as a source for theological reflection and Christian action.

BLAVATSKY, Helena Petrovna (AD 1831–91) Founder in 1875 of the Theosophical Society (see THEOSOPHY), who claimed to have received the 'ancient wisdom' after seven years in Tibet being taught by various MAHATMAS. She wrote books defending SPIRITUALISM and various OCCULT teachings.

BODH GAYA Place of the ENLIGHTENMENT of the BUDDHA. Traditionally, he sat for seven days under a peepal tree and then realized the truth of all existence. The tree that witnessed the enlightenment was called the Bodhi-tree. There are many versions of the story.

BODHI In various schools of BUDDHISM, 'awakening', or 'perfect wisdom', or 'supreme ENLIGHTENMENT'.

BODHIDHARMA Traditionally the first teacher of CH'AN Buddhism who moved from southern India to China in AD 520. He introduced the methods of sharp questioning and paradox found today in Japanese ZEN.

BODHISATTVA In MAHAYANA Buddhism a saint or semi-divine being who has voluntarily renounced NIRVANA in order to help others to salvation. In popular devotion bodhisattvas are worshipped as symbols of compassion.

BOG Slavic name for GOD.

BÖN Religion of Tibet before the coming of BUDDHISM. It was a form of nature worship presided over by a chief SHAMAN who communicated with the earth and sky. Though the adherents of Bön violently opposed the introduction of Buddhism, many of their practices were absorbed into the Buddhist system.

BONA DEA Roman fertility goddess whose worship was open only to women. Her rites were celebrated annually in an all-night ceremony presided over by the wife of the chief magistrate.

BOOK OF MORMON Sacred SCRIPTURE of MORMONISM which was revealed to Joseph SMITH. It describes a conflict between two branches of a family which had emigrated under divine guidance from JERUSALEM to America in 600 BC. The Mormons regard it as the completion of the Biblical revelation.

BOOK OF THE DEAD Name given to various collections of SPELLS, often illustrated, buried with the dead of ancient Egypt to assist their souls through the judgement. Commonly the soul is depicted as

weighed in a balance against *ma'at*, a conception of 'right order' (depicted as an ostrich feather), by the god ANUBIS while the scribe THOTH records the result and OSIRIS presides. (See also TIBETAN BOOK OF THE DEAD.)

BOOTHS/TABERNACLES/ SUKKOT Week-long Autumn Jewish festival marking the end of the harvest. Branch- or straw-covered booths remind JEWS of God's protection during their forty-year journey through the wilderness.

BRAHMA The creator god in the Brahmanical period of Indian religion (see BRAHMANISM) whose authority was mocked by the BUDDHA.

BRAHMAN In HINDUISM, the divine, absolute reality. The word is the neuter form of BRAHMA, the creator god of early Hinduism, and originally referred to the holy power evoked through sacrifice.

BRAHMANISM The religion of India at the time of the UPANISHADS and during the early Buddhist period. It was a religion of RITUAL and SACRIFICE with emphasis on the supremacy of the Brahmin class (see CASTE SYSTEM) who held priestly authority over all aspects of life. The use of SANSKRIT was emphasized and there was marked hostility to non-Brahmanical teachings.

BRAHMA SAMAJ Monotheistic HINDU movement founded by RAMMOHUN ROY. It held services influenced by Christian church worship with hymns and theistic readings but failed to make an impact on the Hindu community.

BRAHMINS See CASTE SYSTEM.

BREVIARY Liturgical book containing instructions for the recitation of daily services as followed by the Christian clergy, MONKS and NUNS of the Western church, with the proper hymns, psalms and lessons for each service.

BRIGHID Celtic goddess of poetry, prophecy, learning and healing. The Romans associated her Gaulish equivalent with Minerva. She was absorbed into Irish Christianity as St

Brighid whose feast day coincides with a Celtic spring festival.

BUBER, Martin (AD 1878–1965) Austrian Jewish theologian whose religious roots were in HASIDISM. Although a Zionist, he was critical of the politics of ZIONISM and of Talmudic tradition (see TALMUD). He believed that the central task of JEWS was to build up God's kingdom on the basis of the Jewish belief in an essential dialogue between God and man. He has influenced Christian spirituality and social teaching.

BUDDHA ('The enlightened one') (1) Siddharta GAUTAMA a sage of the SHAKYA tribe who lived in India in the sixth century BC, the founder of BUDDHISM. There is little doubt that there was a historical figure at the source of Buddhism though some branches of MAHAYANA regard this as unimportant. (2) Any human being or celestial figure who has reached ENLIGHTENMENT.

BUDDHAGHOSA Buddhist writer of the fifth century AD who wrote many commentaries on the scriptures and one original work, *The Path of Purity*. The Burmese believe he was a native of Burma but other traditions hold that he was an Indian who worked in Ceylon (Sri Lanka).

BUDDHA IMAGE Representation of the BUDDHA used in all forms of BUDDHISM. The Buddha is most commonly portrayed in the LOTUS POSTURE, but there are also versions of him standing or lying on one side. The various postures and position of the hands symbolize the defeat of evil, the achieving of ENLIGHTENMENT, the preaching of the DHAMMA and the final NIRVANA. The images are psychological aids rather than objects of worship, though in MAHAYANA Buddhism they act as a focus for devotion.

BUDDHISM The great missionary religion which developed from the teaching of the BUDDHA and which spread from India into south-east Asia, later expanding into northern Asia, China and Japan. The two principal divisions are the THERAVADA (HINAYANA) and the MAHAYANA. Special features are found in TIBETAN BUDDHISM, also known as VAJRAYANA or Lamaism.

BUTSU-DAN A Japanese domestic altar to the BUDDHA which contains images or objects of worship and memorial tablets to ancestors. There may be lights, flowers and incense and it is the focus of daily prayer, chanting and the offering of food and drink.

BWANGA 'Medicine' or 'effective cure' in the Bantu languages. It refers particularly to the dynamism or potency for healing or destruction in magical rites and SPELLS.

C

CALIPH ('Deputy' or 'representative') Title of the leaders of the MUSLIM community after the death of MUHAMMAD. The first three caliphs ruled from MEDINA; the UMAYYADS from Damascus, and the 'ABBASIDS from Baghdad. From AD 1517 the caliph was based at Istanbul. Kemal ATATURK abolished the caliphate in 1923.

CALVIN, John (AD 1509–64) French theologian who organized the REFORMATION from Geneva. He emphasized justification by faith and the sole authority of the BIBLE and in particular that each person's eternal destiny was decided irrevocably by God and only those destined for salvation would come to faith.

CAO DAI Religious and political movement which started in southern Vietnam around 1920. It is sometimes called the 'Third Amnesty'. Firmly nationalist, its teachings are a mixture of BUDDHISM and TAOISM.

CARDINAL Member of a college of ordained high officials in the ROMAN CATHOLIC Church who, since 1179, have elected the POPE. Cardinals are appointed by the pope.

CARGO CULTS Term used for new religious movements of Melanesia and New Guinea which imitate European ritual in the hope of thereby receiving European-type material wealth—'cargo'. They look

for the arrival of a MESSIAH who will banish illness and distribute the cargo among the people.

CASTE SYSTEM The division of a society into groups reflecting and defining the division of labour. In India, caste is traditionally seen as the creation of BRAHMA, each caste emerging symbolically from different parts of his body. There are four chief groups: Brahmins, priests, come from Brahma's mouth; Kshatriyas, warriors, come from Brahma's arms; Vaishyas, peasants, come from Brahma's thighs; Shudras, unskilled labourers come from Brahma's feet. Groups of no definite caste were regarded as UNTOUCHABLES and were banished from society.

CATECHISM (1) Instruction on Christian faith; for example, instruction in question and answer form given to those preparing for BAPTISM or CONFIRMATION. (2) A popular manual of Christian doctrine.

CATECHUMEN Candidate in training for Christian BAPTISM.

CATHARS Members of a medieval heretical Christian sect which flourished in Germany, France and Italy before their suppression in the thirteenth century. (See also ALBIGENSIANS.)

CATHOLICISM CHRISTIANITY as practiced by those who emphasize a continuous historical tradition of faith and practice from the time of the APOSTLES to the present day.

CELTS Population group occupying much of central and western Europe during the first millennium BC. They included the ancient Gauls and Britons. They worshipped the MOTHER GODDESS and various local and tribal deities. Evidence from skulls excavated in Celtic sacred places suggests that they practised human sacrifice. Their priests were the DRUIDS.

CERES Roman grain goddess who became identified with the Greek DEMETER.

CERNUNNOS ('The horned one') Celtic horned god associated with the earth and fertility, and protector of the animal kingdom. Usually portrayed sitting cross-legged, he is often accompanied by a stag, or a horned serpent or a bull.

CHAC Rain god of the MAYA. He is portrayed as an old man with a long nose and weeping eyes. He is in quadruple form and faces in all directions. Benevolent and a friend to man, his name was invoked at planting ceremonies.

CHAKRAS According to Tibetan and Indian thought, the six nerve centres of the body from which psychic energy flows. They are: between the eyebrows; at the throat; at the heart; at the navel; at the genitals, and at the base of the spine where KUNDALINI, the serpent-energy, lies coiled. The chakras are sometimes called 'lotus centres'.

CH'AN School of Chinese BUDDHISM formed in perhaps the seventh century AD from a blend of TAOISM and MAHAYANA teachings. The school stressed experience rather than learning and distrusted a too intellectual approach.

CHANG TAO LING (born AD 34) Chinese Taoist priest who established a religious order on Dragon Mountain in Kiangsi. He claimed to have had a vision of LAO-TZU and to have discovered the elixir of life. He ordained his followers who inherited his secret formula and practised various kinds of ALCHEMY.

CHANT Type of singing in which many syllables are sung on a single note or a repeated short musical phrase. Many religions use chanting in worship. Jews and Christians chant the PSALMS; Buddhists and others their own sacred SCRIPTURES. The repetitive nature of chanting can aid MEDITATION.

CHARISMATIC MOVEMENT Renewal movement in Catholic and Protestant Churches stressing the work and manifestation of the HOLY SPIRIT in the life of the church and of the individual believer.

CHASTITY Sexual continence, sometimes undertaken temporarily or permanently as a religious discipline. It is especially valued in CHRISTIANITY where sexual relations are only permissible within marriage.

CHELA In Indian religion, a disciple, student or follower of a GURU.

CHENRESI Form of the Tibetan name for AVALOKITESHVARA, the great BODHISATTVA who is patron of Tibet and is reincarnated in the DALAI LAMA.

CHI/CHINEKE ('Creator') Name for the supreme HIGH GOD among the Ibo people of Nigeria.

CHICOMECOATL AZTEC goddess of maize. Numerous images of her have been found, indicating her popularity. She wears a four-sided head-dress.

CHILAN Soothsayer or godman in the religion of the MAYA, instructed in his arts by the AHKINS. He was usually carried about on a litter and when called on to prophesy, he retired to a darkened room for several days before emerging to give his prophecy in an ecstatic state.

CHINGIS/GENGHIS KHAN (around AD 1167–1227) Mongol 'universal ruler' who succeeded in uniting the various tribes and embarked on a programme of conquest into China, Korea, Russia, the Ukraine and much of the rest of Eastern Europe. On his death he was elevated to divine status.

CHINVAT BRIDGE The bridge of judgement in the teaching of ZOROASTER. Good souls found it broad and easy to cross but wicked souls slipped off as it narrowed, and fell into a chasm of torment.

CHORTEN Tibetan Buddhist shrine, found by roadsides, in fields and at gateways. It is shaped as a pointed dome, often with a spire, crescent and disc at the top, and built on a square base. The construction represents the five elements and may contain RELICS or images or texts of sacred scripture.

CHRIST Greek word for MESSIAH. First applied to JESUS OF NAZARETH by his followers who believed him to fulfil the hopes of ISRAEL, it later became more a proper name of Jesus than a title.

CHRISTADELPHIANS Christian sect founded by John Thomas (AD 1805–71) in the USA, which claims to have returned to the beliefs and practices of the original DISCIPLES. They accept the BIBLE as infallible and are particularly interested in the fulfilment of prophecy. They reject the doctrines of the TRINITY and INCARNATION and have no ordained ministry.

CHRISTIAN Follower of JESUS OF NAZARETH, the CHRIST; a member of the Christian CHURCH.

CHRISTIANITY Missionary religion based on the teachings of JESUS OF NAZARETH, the CHRIST, and the significance of his life, death and RESURRECTION.

CHRISTIAN SCIENCE Unorthodox Christian sect founded in the USA by Mary Baker EDDY in 1866. It began with a small group gathered 'to re-instate primitive Christianity and its lost element of healing'. There are 3,000 Christian Science churches in fifty-seven countries.

CHRISTMAS The festival of the birth of CHRIST celebrated in Western Christendom on 25 December (which is not necessarily the date believed to be the actual date of his birth). The date suggests that it was intended to replace the Roman festival of the birth of SOL INVICTUS in the fourth century AD.

CHUANG TZU Chinese Taoist teacher who lived in the fourth and third centuries BC. He commended a way of life according to nature which disregarded the conventions of CONFUCIANISM. His writings stress spiritual discipline which should lead to MEDITATION on the formless TAO.

CHU HSI (AD 1130–1200) Chinese philosopher who expounded a system rather similar to that of PLATO. He believed that by quiet daily MEDITATION one could see through diversity to the supreme reality behind all phenomena.

CHURCH (1) The community of all CHRISTIANS, seen in the NEW TESTAMENT as the 'body of Christ', of which he is the head. (2) Building used for Christian WORSHIP. (3) A local group, organized section or 'denomination' of the church(1).

CIRCUMCISION The cutting off of the prepuce in males or the internal labia in females as a religious rite. It is widely practised in traditional African religion, either shortly after birth or at puberty. In JUDAISM boys are circumcised at eight days of age in commemoration of ABRAHAM'S covenant with God. Male converts to Judaism undergo this rite. Circumcision is also practised in ISLAM.

CONFIRMATION Christian rite involving the laying on of hands on those who have been baptized, with prayer for the gift of, or strengthening by, the HOLY SPIRIT. It is often the sign of becoming a communicant member of the CHURCH. In Orthodox Churches it is performed at BAPTISM. Roman Catholics are confirmed at about seven years of age. Other Churches which accept confirmation offer it at puberty or later.

CONFUCIANISM The system of social ethics taught by CONFUCIOUS and given imperial recognition in China in the second century AD. Opinion is divided on whether or not Confucianism should be regarded as a religion. (See FIVE RELATIONSHIPS; LI.)

CONFUCIUS/K'UNG FU'TZU (551–479 BC) Chinese civil servant and administrator who became known as a teacher, opening his classes to everyone regardless of wealth or class. His teachings, especially the idea of LI, became the basis of a system of social ethics which greatly influenced Chinese society after his death.

CONGREGATIONALISTS See INDEPENDENTS.

'CONSCIOUSNESS ONLY' SCHOOL Group of Buddhist metaphysicians who argued, after NAGARJUNA, that the world is made up of perceptions emanating from an absolute store of consciousness.

CONSERVATIVE JUDAISM Movement which tries to stand midway between Orthodox and Progressive JUDAISM. It claims to accept the Talmudic tradition (see TALMUD) but to interpret the TORAH in the light of modern needs.

CONVERSION A moral or spiritual change of direction, or the adoption of religious beliefs not previously held.

COPTIC CHURCH The Church of Egypt, a more or less tolerated minority in Egypt since the coming of ISLAM in AD 642. The Church is 'monophysite', i.e. it rejects the teaching about the INCARNATION of CHRIST agreed at the ECUMENICAL COUNCIL of Chalcedon.

CORROBOREE Ceremony of the Australian Aboriginals comprising festive and warlike folk dances.

COUNCILS OF THE CHURCH See ECUMENICAL COUNCILS.

COUNTER-REFORMATION The revival and reform of the Roman Catholic Church as a reaction to the REFORMATION. Its reforms included those of the Council of Trent (AD 1562–63).

COVENANT A bargain or agreement. In JUDAISM the chief reference is to that made with MOSES at SINAI: GOD, having liberated his people from Egypt, promises them the land of ISRAEL and his blessing and protection as long as they keep the TORAH. This confirms the earlier covenants with ABRAHAM and with Noah. The term is also used of God's special relationship with the house of DAVID. With the defeat of the Kingdom of Judah in 586 BC, Jeremiah's prophecy of a new covenant written on the people's hearts came into its own. In the Christian NEW TESTAMENT the sacrificial death of JESUS OF NAZARETH marks the sealing of a new covenant between God and the new Israel, the Christian CHURCH, which completes and fulfills the old covenant.

CRANMER, Thomas (AD 1489–1556) Archbishop of Canterbury under Henry VIII who helped overthrow papal authority in England and created a new order of English worship in his Prayer Books of 1549 and 1552.

CREATION The act of GOD by which the universe came into being. Hence also refers to the universe itself. In JUDAISM, CHRISTIANITY and ISLAM creation is usually thought of as being *ex nihilo*, from out of nothing

that existed before. In HINDUISM it is believed that the universe has been outpoured from God and will contract into him at the end of the age.

CREATION MYTH A story which explains the divine origins of a particular people, a place or the whole world. In some PRIMAL RELIGIONS and ancient religions (see ENTHRONEMENT FESTIVAL) it is ritually re-enacted at the beginning of each year.

CREED Formal statement of religious belief. In CHRISTIANITY, the two creeds used most commonly today are the Apostles' Creed and the Nicene Creed.

CRUSADES The military expeditions undertaken by Christian armies from Europe from the eleventh to the fourteenth centuries intended to liberate the Holy Land from ISLAM.

CUZCO Capital of the INCA empire and site of the great temple of the SUN GOD. In tradition, Cuzco was founded by MANCO CAPAC, the first Inca, on the instructions of the sun god.

CYBELE Phrygian MOTHER GODDESS whose ecstatic rites included a bath in the blood of a sacrificial bull (see TAUROBOLIUM). Her consort was the youthful ATTIS. Her cult spread to Greece in the fifth century BC and to Rome in 204 BC, though here it was virtually banned until the late first century AD because of the scandal caused by her oriental eunuch priests.

CYNIC Follower of the eccentric Greek philosopher Diogenes (about 400–325 BC) who taught that man should seek the most natural and easy way of life, ignoring conventions. He was nicknamed *Kyon* ('dog') and the name stuck to the beggar philosophers who followed him.

D

DAGDA ('Good God') King of the Tuatha De Danann ('People of DANU'), a legendary Irish tribe. The god of wisdom and knowledge, he is patron of the DRUIDS and identified by his magic club and cauldron.

DAGOBA Name for a PAGODA, used in Sri Lanka (Ceylon). Dagobas are bell-shaped buildings and usually enclose a Buddhist RELIC.

DALAI LAMA Former religious and secular leader of Tibet, widely held to be the reincarnation of AVALOKITESHVARA. Since the Chinese takeover of Tibet the Dalai Lama has lived in India. He is still regarded as the spiritual leader of Tibetan Buddhists. (See also LAMA.)

DANU See ANU.

DARUMA Japanese name for BODHIDHARMA. It is also the name of a doll used by Japanese children which resembles Daruma.

DASTUR Parsi priest who is responsible for the rituals of the FIRE TEMPLES and wears a white turban. The priesthood is hereditary. (See PARSIS.)

DAVID King of the Israelite tribes around 1000–962 BC who united them and extended their territory. He stormed the city of the Jebusites and made it his capital, JERUSALEM. He was a musician and poet, to whom a number of psalms in the BIBLE are ascribed. The belief is common to JUDAISM and CHRISTIANITY that the MESSIAH would be a descendant of David.

DEACON Junior minister in the Christian CHURCH. The word means 'servant' and the deacon's functions originally included the distribution of alms to the poor.

DEAD SEA SCROLLS Sacred writings of a breakaway Jewish sect which were discovered in 1947 at Qumran on the western shore of the Dead Sea. The several scrolls and fragments include much of the HEBREW BIBLE as well as hymns, treatises and rules for the life of the

sect. Many scholars identify the sect with the ESSENES.

DEISTS Followers of a movement for natural religion which flourished in seventeenth-century England. They rejected the idea of revelation and held that the Creator did not interfere in the workings of the universe.

DELPHI Greek shrine held to be at the centre or navel of the earth. It was dedicated to APOLLO who slew there a great dragon or python which protected the earlier shrine of the MOTHER GODDESS. There also Apollo established the DELPHIC ORACLE.

DELPHIC ORACLE Most authoritative source of prophecy and political advice in Ancient Greece. Run by the priests of APOLLO, its prophet was a woman, the *Pythia* ('pythoness'), who uttered her oracles in a state of induced frenzy. The message was then interpreted by the priests and delivered in a cryptic, often ambiguous, form.

DEMETER Greek goddess of fertility and growth. Worshipped throughout the Greek world, she was identified with the Egyptian ISIS, the Phrygian CYBELE, and the Roman CERES as the MOTHER GODDESS. Her MYTH concerns the abduction of her daughter Persephone by HADES; yearly, in autumn, the earth becomes barren while she searches for her child. She initiated her own MYSTERY RELIGION—the ELEUSINIAN MYSTERIES—at Eleusis near Athens.

DEMIURGE Term used in GNOSTICISM to describe the creator god, seen as willful, passionate and ignorant. His creation is a cosmic disaster which traps in material existence the divine sparks that emanate from the true God.

DERVISH Islamic MYSTIC belonging to one of the orders which induced ecstasy by movement, dance and the recitation of the names of God.

DEVADATTA Cousin of the BUDDHA and one of his earliest disciples. In some texts he is in conflict with the Buddha and leads a schismatic movement. He was condemned to a period in hell for his misdeeds.

DEVIL Term generally used to describe an evil spirit. In CHRISTIANITY the devil (Satan) is the personification of evil who is permitted to tempt and accuse human beings within the overall providence of God.

DHAMMA/DHARMA The teaching of the BUDDHA—his analysis of existence expressed in the FOUR NOBLE TRUTHS and outlined in the NOBLE EIGHTFOLD PATH. Dhamma is sometimes represented as an eight-spoked wheel. (See also DHARMA.)

DHAMMAPADA One of the best-known texts of the PALI CANON expounding the essence of THERAVADA Buddhist teachings. It encourages the Buddhist disciple to achieve his own salvation, relying on no external saviour or authority.

DHARMA In HINDUISM, cosmic order, the law of existence, right conduct. Also, in BUDDHISM, the teaching of the BUDDHA (see DHAMMA).

DIANA Italian goddess who was associated with wooded places, women, childbirth and the moon. She became identified with the Greek ARTEMIS. The centre of her cult was a grove on the shore of the volcanic Lake Nemi.

DIASPORA The Jewish people who lived scattered among the nations and were therefore in EXILE (2) from the land of ISRAEL. The dispersion of the JEWS came about partly as a result of war and exile, partly as a result of travel and trade.

DIETARY LAWS Rules about food and drink that are characteristic of a particular religion. Thus JUDAISM prohibits the simultaneous preparation or eating of milk and meat products, bans totally the eating of pork and shellfish and regulates the ritual slaughter of other animals for meat. ISLAM proscribes pork and alcohol. JAINISM bans all meat products.

DIEVS Sky god of the Latvian people. He is related to ZEUS and VARUNA.

DIGAMBARAS ('Sky-clad') Members of a major sect of JAINS who followed MAHAVIRA in believing in the virtue of total nudity. Numerous in the warm south of India, they tend to wear robes in public.

DIONYSUS Greek god of wine and of liberation, a dying and rising god identified with OSIRIS. His cult probably came from Thrace or Phrygia. He is associated with vegetation and fertility and appears surrounded by satyrs, nature spirits promoting fertility. He is followed by a host of maenads, frenzied women leading orgiastic rites. Dionysus punishes unbelief with terrible vengeance. In the late Hellenistic world (see HELLENISM) the cult of Dionysus became an important MYSTERY RELIGION.

DIS Roman name for the god of the underworld, the Greek HADES. The name derives from *dives* ('rich'), which translates Hades' euphemistic name, Pluto.

DISCIPLE Follower of a religious leader or teaching. In CHRISTIANITY it refers to the original followers of Jesus in the NEW TESTAMENT and is widened to include all Christian 'followers' throughout history.

DIVALI Festival of light celebrated by HINDUS and SIKHS. For Hindus it marks the return of RAMA from exile and his reunion with SITA as told in the MAHABHARATA. For Sikhs it is a commemoration of the release from prison of the sixth GURU and his return to the city of Amritsar.

DIVINATION The art of the DIVINER.

DIVINE KINGSHIP The belief that kings and queens are descended from the gods and rule with their authority. The ritual purity of the divine king guarantees the community's welfare. Notions of divine kingship are found in some PRIMAL RELIGIONS. (See also PHARAOH; INCA; ENTHRONEMENT FESTIVAL.)

DIVINE LIGHT MISSION Devotional cult of the Indian teacher Guru Maharaj Ji (born 1957) whose devotees in India, Europe and America regard him as a *Satguru*, a perfect teacher in succession to KRISHNA, BUDDHA, CHRIST, MUHAMMAD and others. Initiates receive 'the Knowledge' in a

ceremony which is an introduction to secret MEDITATION techniques.

DIVINER One who tells the future either by reading the signs of nature in the weather, stars or the flight of birds, or by the manipulation of objects such as sticks, stones, bones or playing cards (see AUGUR; HAURUSPEX; I CHING TAROT CARDS). He may also share the powers of a MEDIUM or SHAMAN.

DIVINITIES Name given to minor gods or spirits in PRIMAL RELIGIONS who rule over an area of the world or some human activity—e.g. storms, war, farming, marriage. Divinities are usually worshipped formally with special RITUALS and festivals.

DOCTRINE A religious teaching or belief which is taught and upheld within a particular religious community.

DONN ('The dark one') The Irish god of the dead who lives on Tech Duinn, a rocky island off the south-west coast of Ireland. A god of storms and shipwrecks, he is also the protector of cattle and flocks.

DRAVIDIAN Word describing the pre-ARYAN civilization based in the Indus valley. It was overturned by Aryan invaders around 2000 BC. Today Dravidian peoples inhabit southern India.

DREAMS One of the chief sources of revelation to the individual in PRIMAL RELIGIONS. Dreams may contain warnings or commands or promises of blessing.

DREAMTIME In Australian PRIMAL RELIGION, the mythical period in which, according to Aboriginal tradition, ancestral beings moved across the face of the earth forming its physical features. The dreamtime is recreated in art, painting, chanting, dancing and cult ceremonies.

DRUIDS The priestly caste of Celtic society. It is likely that they presided at sacrifices, made and enforced legal decisions and passed on the traditions of learning, magic, healing and ritual.

DUALISM The belief that reality has a fundamentally twofold nature. Opposed to MONISM it describes the belief that there is a radical

distinction between God and the created world. Alternatively it describes the belief that there are two fundamentally opposed principles, one of good, the other of evil. This moral dualism is the basis of ZOROASTRIANISM. Again it can describe the belief that the mind and the body are fundamentally different yet act in parallel.

DUKKHA Buddhist term for unsatisfactoriness or suffering. Birth, illness, decay, death and REBIRTH are symptoms of a restless and continuous 'coming-to-be' which marks all existence as dukkha.

DURGA ('The inaccessible') In HINDU tradition, the consort of SHIVA in one of her terrifying forms.

E

EASTER The festival of the RESURRECTION OF CHRIST, the greatest and oldest festival of the Christian CHURCH. Its date is fixed according to the paschal full moon and varies from year to year.

EASTERN ORTHODOX CHURCHES Family of self-governing churches looking to the Ecumenical PATRIARCH, the Patriarch of Constantinople as a symbol of leadership. (See also GREAT SCHISM.)

ECUMENICAL COUNCILS Assemblies of Christian BISHOPS whose decisions were considered binding throughout the Christian church. These ended with the GREAT SCHISM though the Roman Catholic Church has continued to assemble councils into the twentieth century. The most important of the Ecumenical Councils were held at Nicaea (AD 325, condemning ARIANISM); Constantinople (AD 381); Ephesus (AD 431, condemning NESTORIANISM) and Chalcedon (AD 451, concerning the INCARNATION of CHRIST).

ECUMENICAL MOVEMENT Movement for the recovery of unity among the Christian Churches. It dates from the Edinburgh 'World Missionary Conference' of 1910 and today focusses in the WORLD COUNCIL OF CHURCHES.

EDDY, Mary Baker (AD 1821–1910) American spiritual teacher and founder of CHRISTIAN SCIENCE. She believed that orthodox CHRISTIANITY had repressed CHRIST'S teaching and practice of spiritual healing and that healing was not miraculous but a natural expression of the divine will. She founded the First Church of Christ Scientist in Boston in 1879; it remains the mother church of Christian Science. She wrote the authoritative work of the movement: *Science and Health (with Key to the Scriptures)* and founded the newspaper the *Christian Science Monitor*.

EL Great god and 'creator of creation' among the Canaanite and Phoenician peoples.

ELDER An officer of the Church in the PRESBYTERIAN and INDEPENDENT CHURCHES. Teaching elders also deal with pastoral care; ruling elders help in church government and administration.

ELECTION God's choice of ISRAEL to be his people as expressed in the COVENANT at Mount SINAI and manifested in the gift of the land of Israel. In JUDAISM the election of the JEWS carries responsibility. They are to bear witness to the reality of God in the world by keeping the TORAH. In Christian theology, the concept is widened to include GENTILE converts to CHRISTIANITY who spiritually inherit the promises made to the PATRIARCHS and to MOSES.

ELEUSINIAN MYSTERIES MYSTERY RELIGION of DEMETER centred at Eleusis near Athens. The Greater Mysteries were held at the time of the autumn sowing and went on for nine days. The myth of Demeter was probably re-enacted and the climax may have been a revelation of a reaped ear of corn. But only initiates were admitted and the exact nature of the mysteries was kept a secret.

ELIEZER, Israel ben See BAAL SHEM TOV.

ELOHIM Plural form of the Canaanite word for a divinity (see DIVINITIES), usually translated 'God' and used as a name of God by the HEBREWS (see also EL). It is sometimes treated as a common-noun plural, 'gods' or 'angels'. (See also ANGELS.)

ELYSIUM Paradise of Greek religion. It was held to be either far away across the sea, or a section of the underworld ruled not by HADES, but by Kronos, one of the ancient Titan race.

EMPEROR, Japanese Since the reign of the legendary JIMMU TENNO, the emperors of Japan claimed divine descent from AMATERASU O MIKAMI. SHINTO thus became an expression of imperial power and nationalism. The divinity of the emperor was formally repudiated in 1945.

ENKI The water god of ancient Sumerian religion.

ENLIGHTENMENT In BUDDHISM, the realization of the truth of all existence which was achieved by the BUDDHA in his meditation at BODH GAYA. Enlightenment or final enlightenment also refers to the passing into NIRVANA of anyone who follows the Buddha's way and attains release from the cycle of birth and REBIRTH. (See also BODHI.)

ENLIL The wind god in ancient Sumerian belief. He persuaded the other gods to plan the destruction of mankind in a great flood. He rewarded the flood's only survivor with the gift of immortality.

EN SOF Name for God used in Jewish MYSTICISM, in particular in the KABBALAH, meaning 'the endless', the absolute infinite whose essence is unrevealed and unknowable.

ENTHRONEMENT FESTIVAL Ancient Near Eastern ritual which re-enacted the creation of the world and the elevation of the creator-deity above the other gods. The part of the god was played by the king who had a sacred status. The festival guaranteed the continuing order of nature and the welfare of the nation. (See also DIVINE KINGSHIP.)

EPIC OF GILGAMESH Babylonian poem dating from the

seventh century BC which includes much earlier material. It tells the story of Gilgamesh's vain quest for the secret of immortality and includes the BABYLONIAN FLOOD STORY.

EPICUREANISM Philosophical school founded by Epicurus (341–270 BC) and holding an atomic theory of the universe. It teaches that the gods are irrelevant to human life, the chief end of which is happiness. Fulfilment comes from the prudent and restrained cultivation of pleasure.

EPISTLE (1) Letter in the NEW TESTAMENT to a Christian community or individual usually from one of the APOSTLES. (2) Letter on doctrine or practice addressed to a Christian community in post-apostolic times.

EROS Greek god of love, Cupid to the Romans, the son of APHRODITE. In Greek literature his cruelty to his victims is emphasized, also his omnipotence. In the Christian era, 'cupids' became angelic beings symbolizing divine benevolence and compassion.

ESOTERIC Word meaning 'inner', suggesting something, (e.g. a knowledge or a teaching) that is available only for the specially initiated and secret from outsiders, and perhaps even from ordinary believers.

ESSENES Jewish group which withdrew to live a monastic life in the Dead Sea area during the Roman period. They were celibates and stressed the importance of ASCETICISM. They also performed exorcisms and rites of spiritual healing and adopted OCCULT practices.

EUCHARIST ('Thanksgiving') The central act of Christian worship, instituted by CHRIST on the night before his death. It involves sharing bread and wine which are sacramentally associated with the body and blood of Christ. (See SACRAMENT.)

EVANGELICALS CHRISTIANS of all denominations who emphasize the centrality of the BIBLE, justification by faith and the need for personal conversion. In Germany and Switzerland, the term refers to members of the Lutheran as opposed to the Calvinist churches.

EVANGELISM The preaching of the Christian GOSPEL to the unconverted.

EXILE (1) The period between 597 BC and around 538 BC when leading JEWS from the former Jewish kingdoms were held in captivity in Babylon. (2) The condition of Jewish life in the DIASPORA, away from the land of ISRAEL.

EXODUS The flight of the people of ISRAEL from Egypt under the leadership of MOSES.

EXORCISM Removal of sin or evil, particularly an evil spirit in possession of someone, by prayer or ritual action.

EZRA Scribe of the Babylonian EXILE who was sent with a royal warrant from the Persian king to reform religion in JERUSALEM. Traditionally he arrived in 458 BC and embarked on a programme to purify the Jewish faith and install TORAH as the central authority in Jewish life.

F

FADY Something which must not be done, something forbidden or TABOO in the religion of Madagascar.

FAITH Attitude of belief in, trust and commitment to a divine being or a religious teaching. It can also refer to the beliefs of a religion, 'the faith', which is passed on from teachers to believers.

FALL OF JERUSALEM The capture of JERUSALEM and the final destruction of the TEMPLE OF JERUSALEM by the Roman general Titus in AD 70 at the end of a revolt which broke out in AD 66.

FAMADIHANA Term for ANCESTOR VENERATION in the religion of Madagascar.

FASTING Total or partial abstinence from food, undertaken as a religious discipline. In PRIMAL RELIGIONS it is often a preparation for a ceremony of INITIATION. In JUDAISM and CHRISTIANITY it is a sign of mourning or repentance for SIN. It is also more generally used as a means of gaining clarity of vision and mystical insight.

FATI-DRA Madagascan ceremony for making blood-brothers.

FELLOWSHIP The common life of Christians marked by unity and mutual love, a creation of the HOLY SPIRIT.

FIELDS OF AARU Paradise of Egyptian mythology, the abode of souls who have passed safely through the judgement before OSIRIS. It is pictured as a place similar to Egypt with a great river and cultivated land.

FIRE SERMON One of the BUDDHA's most famous sermons, traditionally preached at Gaya to 1000 fire-worshipping ascetics, in which he explained that all that exists is burning with lust, anger and ignorance.

FIRE TEMPLES Parsi temples where the sacred fire of AHURA MAZDA is kept continually burning. The fire is kept in a censer on a stone slab hanging under the central dome of the temple. There are no images: the fire symbolizes the purity and goodness of Ahura Mazda. (See DASTUR; PARSIS.)

FIVE PILLARS OF ISLAM Five duties enjoined on every MUSLIM as his response to God. They are: recitation of the creed 'LA ILAHA ILLA ALLAH'; SALAT (ritual prayer); ZAKAT (almsgiving); Saum (fasting in the month of RAMADAN); HAJJ (pilgrimage to MECCA).

FIVE PRECEPTS Ethical restraints for Buddhists, who are to refrain from: taking life; stealing; wrong sexual relations; wrong use of speech; drugs and intoxicants.

FIVE RELATIONSHIPS The codification and application of CONFUCIUS' teaching to the five basic relationships of human life. These are father and son; older brother and younger brother; husband and wife;

elder and younger; ruler and subject. The inferior should show proper deference, the superior proper benevolence. The stress is on reciprocity and Confucius believed that such correct behaviour would weld society in 'the way of heaven'.

FOUR NOBLE TRUTHS The BUDDHA's analysis of the problem of existence—a four-stage summary of his teaching: (1) all that exists is unsatisfactory; (2) the cause of unsatisfactoriness (DUKKHA) is desire (TANHA); (3) unsatisfactoriness ends when desire ends; (4) desire can be ended by practising the NOBLE EIGHTFOLD PATH.

FOUR RIGHTLY-GUIDED CALIPHS Orthodox ISLAM accepts ABU BAKR, 'UMAR, 'UTHMAN and 'ALI as legitimate successors to MUHAMMAD.

FOUR STAGES OF LIFE HINDU outline of man's ideal spiritual life. There are four stages: Student; the Hindu boy learns the scriptures in the house of his GURU and lives a life of chastity; Householder; he marries, has children and earns his living; Forest dweller; when his family are grown up he gradually begins to withdraw from everyday life; Sannyasi (SANSKRIT: 'one who renounces'); he cuts all earthly ties and seeks liberation, often as a wandering beggar.

FRANCIS OF ASSISI (AD 1182– 1226) Founder of the Franciscan order who lived by a simple rule of life rejecting possessions, ministering to the sick and having a special concern for nature.

FREEMASONRY Originally a religious brotherhood of English masons founded in the twelfth century. In the sixteenth century it spread to the European mainland where in Roman Catholic countries it became associated with Deism (see DEISTS). In the UK and USA today it is a semi-secret society which retains certain mystical symbols and ceremonies. Members are committed to a belief in GOD as 'the great architect of the universe', symbolized by an eye.

FREY Norse god of beauty with power over rain and sunshine and the fertility of the earth. His name means 'lord'.

FREYJA Norse goddess and sister of FREY; her name means 'lady'. She is patroness of love and sorcery and drives a chariot pulled by cats. She possesses half the corpses of those who are slain in battle, the other half going to ODIN.

FRIENDS, RELIGIOUS SOCIETY OF See QUAKERS.

FRIGG Chief of the Norse goddesses and wife of ODIN; the goddess of love and fertility. She knows the fates of men but cannot avert destiny.

FUNDAMENTALISM The doctrine that the BIBLE is verbally inspired and therefore inerrant and infallible on all matters of doctrine and history; from *The Fundamentals*, published in 1909.

FURIES Female spirits of retributive justice in Greek mythology. They came from TARTARUS, the Greek HELL, and pursued their victims until these went mad. They upheld the moral order by ensuring that crime was punished. The Greeks called them by euphemistic names, the most common being 'the kindly ones'.

G

GABRIEL One of the archangels of Jewish tradition. In ISLAM Gabriel is associated with the 'faithful spirit' by whom the QUR'AN was revealed to MUHAMMAD. Gabriel also transported Muhammad from MECCA to JERUSALEM and from there to the throne of God in the NIGHT JOURNEY.

GANESHA Elephant-headed god much loved in popular HINDUISM, especially in western India. He is the god of good beginnings and is a symbol for luck and wealth in business and daily life.

GANGES The holy river of India whose waters are sacred for all HINDUS. It is thought to flow from the toe of VISHNU. Pilgrims wash away evil in its waters and the ashes of the dead are thrown into it.

GAUTAMA/GOTAMA Family name of the BUDDHA. Legend depicts him as a great prince born into a royal household. Modern scholars think that his father was probably the head of an aristocratic family living in the town of Kapilavastu.

GENGHIS KHAN See CHINGIS KHAN.

GENIUS (1) In occult religion, a guardian spirit or familiar. (2) In Roman religion, the spirit of a man, giving rise to his maleness. A LIBATION was poured to the genius of the reigning emperor at every banquet.

GENTILE Person who is not a JEW.

GHAT ('Holy place') In HINDU use, a word which can refer to a range of hills, a ritual bathing place or a cremation ground.

GHOST DANCE A dance which sprang out of a religious movement of the 1870s among the North American Indians. It was believed that the dance would lead to the resurrection of all dead Indians on an earth free of disease and death. The movement was destroyed at the Battle of Wounded Knee in 1890. (See also WOVOKA.)

GINNUNGAGAP In Norse mythology the yawning gulf out of which creation sprang. A region of chaos, half of it was freezing fog, the other half flaming heat. In the centre was a roaring cauldron which became the source of all waters.

GINZA The chief scripture of the MANDAEANS, relating the creation of the world and describing the fate of the soul after death.

GLOSSOLALIA Expression in unknown tongues by people in a heightened spiritual or emotional state. In the Christian church it is used to express worship to God and prophetic messages, in other religions to express a state of religious ecstasy.

GNOSTICISM Movement of ESOTERIC teachings rivalling, borrowing from and contradicting early CHRISTIANITY. Gnostic sects were based on MYTHS which described the creation of the world by a deluded DEMIURGE and taught a way of

salvation through *gnosis*, 'knowledge' of one's true divine self. Gnostics contrasted their 'knowledge' with faith, which they considered inferior.

GOBINDH SINGH, GURU (AD 1666–1708) The tenth GURU of the SIKH community. He militarized the Sikhs, requiring them to adopt a distinctive name and dress. He also shifted the focus of authority from the gurus to the sacred scripture, the ADI GRANTH.

GOD (Common noun) A being with divine power and attributes; a deity, a major DIVINITY.

GOD (Proper noun) The creator and sustainer of the universe; the absolute being on whom all that is depends.

GOOD FRIDAY The Friday before EASTER; in CHRISTIANITY, kept by the CHURCH as a holy day, sometimes including FASTING, penance and witness, in memory of the crucifixion of Jesus CHRIST.

GOSPEL (1) One of the four accounts of the 'good news' about JESUS in the NEW TESTAMENT. (2) The Christian message, proclamation, 'good news', referring especially to Jesus' teaching about the KINGDOM OF GOD and to the preaching of the CHURCH about Jesus. (3) The ritual reading of a set portion from the gospels (1) in the context of the EUCHARIST.

GOTAMA See GAUTAMA.

GRACE (1) Unmerited favour, especially in the divine salvation of the unworthy. An essential concept in CHRISTIANITY, where it is contrasted with merit; Christians believe that nobody receives SALVATION because they deserve it, but only by God's grace. (2) A prayer or blessing before a meal.

GRANDFATHER, THE Common name for the supreme GOD among North American Indians. The word is sometimes pluralized and identified with a sevenfold being as in certain other PRIMAL RELIGIONS.

GREAT HOUSE Cult among North American Indians, paticularly those from Delaware and the north-west coast. It centres on a rectangular hall built in alignment with the four points of the compass and which represents the universe. In the centre there is often a pillar with two faces which represents the creator. Ceremonial autumn dances and prayers in the hut mark the beginning of a new year and the start of a new world.

GREAT SCHISM The SCHISM declared in AD 1054 between the Eastern and Western churches resulting from disagreements over the POPE's claim to supremacy, and the doctrine of the HOLY SPIRIT.

GREGORY OF NYSSA (around AD 330–395) Christian theologian who helped develop the doctrine of the TRINITY and expounded the BIBLE as a spiritual path leading to the perfect contemplation of God.

GROUND OF BEING Phrase used by German–US theologian Paul Tillich (AD 1886–1965) to describe GOD. It stresses the immanence of God as depth or ground rather than his transcendence as creator.

GURDJIEFF, George Ivanovich (AD 1873–1949) Spiritual teacher whose book *Meetings with Remarkable Men* relates his search for wisdom. He invented a system of non-identification with the ego which he believed led to the realization of man's true essence. He was influenced by SUFISM. In 1922 he founded an Institute for the Harmonious Development of Man which attracted a number of western intellectuals.

GURDWARA Sikh temple and meeting place, consisting of a worship area which houses the ADI GRANTH, and a cooking and eating area for the symbolic meal which ends Sikh worship.

GURU ('Teacher') A spiritual teacher or guide who, in Indian religion, awakens a disciple to a realization of his own divine nature. In SIKH religion it refers to the ten teachers, from Guru NANAK to Guru GOBINDH SINGH, who ruled the community.

H

HADAD Storm god of Assyria and Babylonia. In the BIBLE he appears as Rimmon, 'the thunderer'. His symbol was lightning and his sacred animal was the bull.

HADES (1) Greek god of the dead and ruler of the UNDERWORLD. He was connected with growth and vegetation and the production of wealth. Because it was considered unlucky to speak his name, he is often referred to as Pluto (the 'rich'). (2) Greek name for the underworld, the abode of the dead. In the Septuagint version of the HEBREW BIBLE it translates *sheol*. In Christian usage it sometimes is used for the interim abode of the departed as distinguished from HELL, the abode of the damned.

HADITH Traditions of MUHAMMAD's words and actions which are not found in the QUR'AN but are a source of authority in Islamic lawmaking. There are many spurious Hadith; one of the major tasks of MUSLIM lawyers has been to categorize Hadith into likely degrees of authenticity.

HAGGADAH A moral or devotional teaching derived from the midrashic exposition of a HEBREW text (see MIDRASH). There are many of them in the TALMUD where they take the form of narrative tales, poems and metaphysical speculations.

HAJJ Pilgrimage to MECCA which is one of the FIVE PILLARS OF ISLAM and which MUSLIMS are obliged to make at least once in a lifetime. It is more meritorious if it takes place in the pilgrim month. On arrival at Mecca, pilgrims make seven circuits of the KA'BA and touch the BLACK STONE. The pilgrims continue to Mina and 'Arafat where sacrifices take place.

HALACH UINIC Ruler of the MAYA. His authority was absolute and he was regarded as a demigod.

HALAKHAH (From HEBREW verb 'to walk') A legal teaching based on the midrashic exposition of a Hebrew text (see MIDRASH).

HAMMURABI (Eighteenth century BC) Mesopotamian ruler who produced a law code laying down punishments for various transgressions and enunciating principles for the conduct of business and social life. The breaking of his code incurred the enmity of the Babylonian gods.

HANUKKAH ('Dedication') Eight-day Jewish festival marked by the lighting of ritual candles which celebrates the rededication of the TEMPLE OF JERUSALEM by JUDAS MACCABEUS in 164 BC.

HANUMAN Monkey-god of popular HINDUISM. In the RAMAYANA he led a monkey army against a host of demons. He can fly and cover huge distances at great speed.

HARA KIRI Vulgar Japanese expression meaning 'belly cutting' which is used for the Japanese traditional practice of ritual suicide among the warrior classes.

HASIDIM ('The pious') (1) The group of Jewish quietist ascetics who were the forerunners of the PHARISEES. (2) A group of medieval MYSTIVS who were particularly important for the development of JUDAISM in Germany. (3) Followers of BAAL SHEM TOV who taught a new kind of HASIDISM in the eighteenth century AD.

HASIDISM Jewish mystical movement with roots in the KABBALAH which arose in the eighteenth century in response to the teachings of BAAL SHEM TOV after a period of persecution by the Cossacks. It stressed the presence of God in everyday life and the value of prayer. Chanting and dancing were used as aids to ecstatic communion with God. The movement was popular and had a wide appeal among ordinary JEWS.

HASINA Madagascan term for spiritual power which is inherent in all living things and is focussed in particular objects and ceremonies. (See MANA.)

HAURUSPEX In Roman religion, a soothsayer who divined from observing the entrails of sacrificed animals. The original *hauruspices* were Etruscans.

HEAVEN The realm of God or of the gods; in CHRISTIANITY the dwelling place of God and the ultimate home of the saved, regarded both as a place and a state.

HEBREW (1) A member of the Semitic tribes which emerged as the people of ISRAEL. (2) The (Semitic) language of the ancient people of Israel, of the HEBREW BIBLE and of the modern state of Israel.

HEBREW BIBLE The Jewish SCRIPTURES which comprise the Books of the Law (see TORAH), the PROPHETS and the WRITINGS. According to tradition the canon was fixed at the Synod of Jabneh about AD 100.

HEIMDALL White god of Norse religion, the watchman of the gods and guardian of the rainbow bridge between ASGARD and MIDGARD. He is a fire god, born of the ice-cold sea and the founder of the different classes of men. He will summon the other gods to fight at RAGNARÖK.

HECATE An earth goddess who probably originated in Asia Minor. Connected with magic and death, she was sometimes known as the ARTEMIS of the cross-roads. She is shown with three faces, carrying torches and followed by baying hounds.

HEL In Norse myth, the queen of the dead. Also her kingdom, the UNDERWORLD, a region of cold, fog and murky gloom, inhabited by the ghosts of the dead. At the battle of RAGNARÖK, Hel will be opened and its hosts will fight on the side of LOKI. The entrance to Hel is guarded by a bloody-breasted dog.

HELL Realm where the wicked go after death. Religious teachings differ over whether this punishment is reformatory or eternal. In CHRISTIANITY, it is total separation from God.

HELLENISM The adoption of the Greek language, culture, philosophy and ideas, particularly around the Mediterranean, from the time of Alexander the Great (356–323 BC). It was the dominant cultural influence during the rise of CHRISTIANITY.

HERA Greek goddess, the wife of ZEUS and Queen of heaven. She was the protectress of women and

marriage and is presented as a model of chastity. She was worshipped throughout the Greek world. Her special bird was a peacock, a symbol of pride.

HERESY The denial of a defined doctrine of the Christian faith. The word means 'chosen thing' and refers to the heretic's preference for his own opinion over the consensus of the CHURCH.

HERM Roadside monument erected in honour of HERMES. Originally they were simply piles of stones; later they were decorated with a phallus and a carved head. There were many *hermae* in Athens.

HERMES Greek messenger god and son of Zeus, protector of travellers, bringer of luck and god of thieves and merchants. He is usually portrayed as a young man in winged hat and sandals, carrying a staff twined with snakes.

HERMETICISM Mystical movement based on a collection of Egyptian scriptures from the first to third centuries AD. The writings drew on Greek and Eastern ideas, and were ascribed to Hermes Trismegistus ('thrice-great HERMES'), who is identified with the god THOTH.

HERZL, Theodore (AD 1860–1904) Leader of the Zionist movement (see ZIONISM). He argued that a national homeland for the JEWS was a necessity. He travelled widely raising support from Christian governments for the Zionist cause. He convened the first World Zionist Congress in 1897 which formulated a political programme for the return to Palestine.

HESIOD Greek poet, probably of the eighth century BC, whose *Theogony* sought to draw together the ancestries of the Greek gods, understanding creation in terms of procreation.

HIGH GOD A god who is acknowledged as the supreme being in PRIMAL RELIGIONS. He is regarded as a creator, sometimes of the universe. He is good and requires moral obedience from men. He is frequently regarded as remote from normal life and is associated with the sky, mountains or other high places.

He is not often worshipped but may be called upon in times of necessity or danger.

HIGH PRIEST Traditional head of the Jewish priesthood and organizer of TEMPLE worship. His function was to enter the Holy of Holies and offer sacrifice on the DAY OF ATONEMENT. It was a key political appointment under the Seleucids and Romans. Talmudic tradition criticizes the corruption of some who held the office, which ceased at the destruction of the Temple in AD 70.

HIJRA ('Going forth') The migration of MUHAMMAD, preceded by some of his followers, from MECCA to MEDINA in AD 622). This was the decisive event for the development of ISLAM for it was in Medina that Muhammad established himself as a religious and political leader and organized his followers as an Islamic community. The MUSLIM calendar counts years 'after Hijra'.

HILLEL Pharisaic Jewish teacher of the first century AD. He was known for his humane and lenient interpretations of TORAH, in contrast to his chief opponent, the stern and rigorous Shammai.

HINAYANA ('Small vehicle') Buddhist term used to indicate the doctrine of salvation for oneself alone in contrast to MAHAYANA. Most Buddhists of south-east Asia prefer the term THERAVADA to describe this school of BUDDHISM.

HINDU Word used by Arabs to describe people living beyond the Indus valley. Today it refers generally to people practising Indian religion who are neither Muslim, Sikh, Parsi nor Jain, and also to their religion, 'Hinduism'.

HINDUISM The religion of India. (See also BHAGAVAD GITA; BRAHMANISM; VEDANTA; VEDAS; UPANISHADS.)

HINENUIOTEPO Guardian of the UNDERWORLD (see RAROHENGA) in Maori religion.

HOA HAO Offshoot of the Vietnamese CAO DAI movement. It is Buddhist-based and has been strongly nationalistic.

HOLI HINDU spring festival which celebrates the love of KRISHNA and RADHA. It is marked by boisterous games which are reminders of Krishna's amorous pranks with the cow-girls as told in the MAHABHARATA.

HOLINESS The sacred power, strangeness and otherness of the divine. In the BIBLE and the QUR'AN the term has moral implications and refers to God's purity and righteousness as well as to that which invokes awe. In CHRISTIANITY, believers are called to reproduce God's holiness in their own lives with the help of the HOLY SPIRIT.

HOLOCAUST (From the Latin BIBLE's word for 'whole burnt offering') The name given to Hitler's extermination of 6 million JEWS in the Nazi death camps in Europe 1941–45. Mass destruction was envisaged as the 'final solution' to the 'problem' of the Jews. The memory of the Holocaust is the key to modern Jewish theology and made the founding of the state of Israel an event of profound significance.

HOLY COMMUNION Name widely used by Anglicans and some Protestants for the Christian EUCHARIST.

HOLY SPIRIT The third person of the Christian TRINITY. In the BIBLE the Holy Spirit is the instrument of divine action and is portrayed as fire or wind. In this sense the Spirit is acknowledged in JUDAISM and ISLAM. The divinity of the Holy Spirit was agreed at the Council of Constantinople in AD 381. He is the source of faith and new life in the believer and the church, giving 'spiritual gifts', guidance, holiness.

HOLY TEMPLE/HOLY PLACE/ HOLY OF HOLIES See TEMPLE OF JERUSALEM.

HOMER Author of the Greek epics the *Iliad* and the *Odyssey* which date from between the eight and tenth centuries BC. According to the historian Herodotus, Homer was the first to detail the characters and functions of the gods of Mount OLYMPUS.

HONEN (AD 1133–1212) Japanese teacher of PURE LAND BUDDHISM. He

taught that repetition of the word NEMBUTSU is all that is necessary for salvation. He is said to have recited it 60,000 times a day.

HORUS Egyptian hawk-headed sky god, associated with the king. The son of ISIS, conceived on the dead OSIRIS, he defeated the evil SETH and assumed the earthly rule Seth had usurped from Osiris.

HSUN-TZU Chinese Confucian scholar of the third century BC who blended the philosophies of CONFUCIANISM and TAOISM. He believed in the correct observance of ceremonial which helped to improve man's evil nature. He was critical of superstition and reinterpreted popular religious practices in rationalistic terms.

HUACA Any of the multitude of DIVINITIES recognized by the INCAS; also, an Inca holy place, shrine or temple.

HUBBARD, Lafayette Ron (Born AD 1911) American science-fiction writer who founded SCIENTOLOGY. This is based on his theories of the mind as outlined in his book *Dianetics: the Modern Science of Mental Health* (1950).

HUBRIS ('Unbridled arrogance') In Greek drama the hubris of man in setting himself up against the gods was a continuous theme. Hubris attracted the anger of the gods and so led to tragedy.

HUIRACOCHA See VIRACOCHA.

HUITZILOPOCHTLI AZTEC god of war and the sun. His name means 'hummingbird wizard' and he was perpetually at war with darkness and night.

HUI YUAN See PURE LAND BUDDHISM.

HUMANISM Way of life based on the belief that what is good for human beings is the highest good.

HUS, Jan (AD 1374–1415) Bohemian reformer who, under the influence of WYCLIFFE's writings denounced the worldliness of the clergy. When he was burnt at the stake he was declared a MARTYR and national hero in Prague. His thought influenced the REFORMATION.

HYMN A sacred song sung in the context of communal worship; a PSALM of communal praise. Hymns are particularly important in Christian and Sikh worship and in the gatherings of the Hindu BHAKTI cults (see BHAJANA).

I

IBN AL-'ARABI (AD 1165–1240) Spanish Sufi teacher and poet (see SUFISM). He taught that the world manifested God and that human beings were created because God desired to be known. MUHAMMAD was 'the seal of the prophets' and Ibn al-'Arabi regarded himself as 'the seal of the saints'. Dante was influenced by his speculations.

IBN RUSHD (AD 1126–98) MUSLIM philosopher, known in the west as Averroes, who was greatly influenced by PLATO and ARISTOTLE. He believed that the Greek heritage was compatible with ISLAM. His synthesis, however, seemed suspicious to the orthodox and he was banished and his books burnt.

I CHING/BOOK OF CHANGES One of the five classics of Chinese literature which was originally attributed to CONFUCIUS but is now thought to be much earlier. It gives instructions and interpretations for a form of DIVINATION using six sticks which can fall in sixty-four significant configurations.

ICON A likeness of a divine figure or SAINT painted on wood or inlaid in mosaic and used in public or private devotion.

'ID AL-ADHA The great festival of the MUSLIM year. It coincides with the offering of the pilgrim sacrifice at Mina near MECCA.

'ID AL-FITR The MUSLIM feast which ends the fasting month of RAMADAN. Greetings cards are exchanged, presents are given and sugary sweets are eaten.

IJMA The consensus of opinion of the MUSLIM community. It is an important principle of Islamic lawmaking.

IJTIHAD ('Enterprise') A way for the Islamic community to develop its law to deal with new situations. It is a ruling given by one MUSLIM teacher, rather than by general consensus (see IJMA). It is controversial whether Ijtihad is always valid or whether the completion of SHARI‘A will render it unnecessary.

IMAM (1) Religious leader and teacher of a SUNNI Muslim community. He leads the ritual prayer of the congregation and is expected to be an interpreter of the QUR'AN. (2) The agent of divine illumination among Shi‘ite Muslims (see SHI‘A) who believe that every age will produce an Imam whose function is to make the truth of MUHAMMAD contemporary. Among the Shi‘a belief in the Imams is an additional article to the usual FIVE PILLARS OF ISLAM.

IMMORTALS Various beings who live in the Realm of Great Purity, according to the teachings of TAOISM. Best known are the 'eight immortals' who are portrayed with a variety of individual characteristics and symbols and feature in Chinese art and drama.

INANNA The MOTHER GODDESS as worshipped in ancient Sumer.

INCA The divine king who ruled over the INCAS.

INCARNATION (1) The Christian doctrine that GOD became man in Jesus CHRIST, so possessing both human and divine natures. (2) A term sometimes used for the HINDU doctrine of the AVATAR.

INCAS Empire centred on CUZCO in modern Peru from around AD 1100 until the Spanish conquest (1532). From the late fourteenth century the empire expanded to include parts of modern Ecuador, Bolivia, Chile and Argentina. The first INCA, MANCO CAPAC, was created by and given absolute authority by the SUN GOD. (See also HUACA; INCAS; PACHACAMAC; PACHACUTEC; TIUHUANACO; VIRACOCHA; VIRGINS OF THE SUN.)

INCENSE Sweet-smelling smoke used in worship, made by burning certain aromatic substances.

INCREASE RITES RITUALS performed by Australian Aboriginals to ensure the continual supply of the particular food associated with the rite.

INDEPENDENCE, DAY OF Jewish festival of thanksgiving on the anniversary of the birth of the state of ISRAEL (4). The liturgy includes prayers for the victims of the HOLOCAUST.

INDEPENDENTS/ CONGREGATIONALISTS CHRISTIANS who uphold the authority and independence of each local church, claiming this system to be the earliest form of church order.

INDEX OF PROHIBITED BOOKS The official list of books which members of the Roman Catholic Church are forbidden to possess or read, first issued in 1557. The *Index* was abolished in 1966.

INDRA ARYAN god of war and storm. There are 200 HYMNS to him in the *Rig Veda* (see VEDAS). He faded from significance in later HINDUISM.

INDULGENCE The remission by the Church of a period of correction in PURGATORY. The sale of indulgences by unscrupulous 'pardoners' was one of the abuses which led to the REFORMATION.

INITIATION Ceremony marking coming of age, or entry into adult membership of a community. It is also used of the secret ceremonies surrounding membership of the MYSTERY RELIGIONS. (See also CONFIRMATION; NAUJOTE; SACRED THREAD CEREMONY.)

INQUISITION Papal office for identifying heretics, founded by POPE Gregory IX and staffed by Franciscans and Dominicans. Torture became an approved aid to interrogation in 1252.

INTERCESSION Prayer offered on behalf of others by a believer on earth or by a SAINT in HEAVEN. In CHRISTIANITY, supremely the work of CHRIST who intercedes for men before GOD.

INTERNATIONAL SOCIETY FOR KRISHNA CONSCIOUSNESS Modern Hindu BHAKTI cult which has been successful in Europe and America. Shaven, yellow-robed devotees chant the MANTRA '*Hare Krishna*' as a way of reaching ecstatic union with God.

INTI The SUN GOD of the INCAS.

IO Supreme being in Maori religion. However, as he has only been referred to since around 1850, he may be derived from Christian teaching.

IQBAL, Muhammad (AD 1876– 1938) Poet, philosopher and president of the MUSLIM LEAGUE. He believed that MUSLIMS needed to study European thought and then construct an authentic Islamic state based on a reformed faith. He is regarded as the spiritual founder of Pakistan.

ISAAC One of the three principal Jewish patriarchs (see ABRAHAM, ISAAC AND JACOB).

ISHTAR Babylonian goddess, mother and wife of TAMMUZ and associated with the fertility rites of death and resurrection. She is also the consort of the Sumerian high god ANU (1). In mythology she is responsible for the great flood which almost destroyed the earth (see BABYLONIAN FLOOD STORY). Worshipped in various forms all over the ancient near East, she was known as Astarte to the Phoenicians and as Ashtoreth to the Hebrews.

ISIS Great Egyptian goddess of motherhood and fertility. The sister and wife of OSIRIS, she restored him to life after he was murdered by SETH. Sometimes represented as cow-headed, she had a great temple at Philae.

ISIS CULT MYSTERY RELIGION based on the MYTH of ISIS and OSIRIS which became particularly popular in the Roman world from the first century AD. Its sacred drama and liturgy express the experience of salvation from sensuality which is open to initiates through the grace of the goddess.

ISLAM (Infinitive of the ARABIC verb 'to submit') Teachings derived from the QUR'AN which is the revelation to MUHAMMAD, a religion of submission to the will of God. (See also ALLAH; MECCA; MUSLIM.)

ISLAMIC SOCIALISM A broad movement which advocates the unity of Qur'anic teachings and socialism.

ISMA'ILIS A group of SHI'A Muslims who believe that the seventh IMAM (2) was the final Imam who has disappeared and will return on the last day (see also ASSASSINS; MAHDI; TWELVERS).

ISMAIL SAFAVI First Shah of Persia who raised an army against the SUNNI Muslim Ottomans, capturing Tabriz in AD 1500. His armies later conquered Iraq. He founded the Safavid dynasty which did not make peace with the OTTOMAN EMPIRE until 1639.

ISRAEL (1) Name given by GOD to JACOB the patriarch and hence to his descendents, the 'people of Israel'. (2) The land promised by God to Abram (ABRAHAM) in the early traditions of JUDAISM. (3) The Northern Kingdom of Israel which seceded from Solomon's kingdom in 922 BC and was destroyed by the Assyrians in 722 BC. (4) The modern state of Israel, founded in Palestine as a Jewish state in AD 1948.

ITZAMNA Chief of the gods of the MAYA. A sky god whose name means 'lizard', he is portrayed as an old man with a long nose. Patron of learning and medicine, he was the inventor of writing.

IXCHEL Moon goddess of the MAYA and consort of ITZAMNA, patroness of childbirth and weaving.

IZANAGI The sky god in SHINTO and the father of AMATERASU. With his consort Izanami he created the islands of Japan.

J

JACOB One of the three principal Jewish patriarchs (see ABRAHAM, ISAAC AND JACOB; ISRAEL (1)).

JADE EMPEROR The supreme divinity in TAOISM, who came into prominence about the tenth century AD. He presided over life and death and kept account of human actions.

JAHANNAM Muslim name for HELL which is frequently mentioned in the QUR'AN as a place of scorching fire and black smoke. Sometimes it is personified as a great monster appearing at the Day of Judgement.

JAIN ('One who has conquered') A follower of the religion known as JAINISM.

JAINISM Religion which emerged in India as a protest against BRAHMANISM. There are 2 million Jains in India today. In Jainism salvation is seen in terms of acquiring god-like omniscience. The asceticism of the Jains has continually influenced mainstream HINDUISM. (See also DIGAMBARAS; JIVA; MAHAVIRA; PARSVA; SVETAMBARAS; TIRTHANKARAS.)

JAMES, William (AD 1842–1910) American psychologist of religion who attempted an analysis and assessment of individual religious experience in his Gifford Lectures, *The Varieties of Religious Experience* (1902).

JANUS Roman god of beginnings whose name derives from *janua*, 'entrance' or 'gate'. He is portrayed with a two-faced head, facing both ways. In Julius Caesar's reform of the calendar, his month became the first of the year.

JAROVIT Slavic war god.

JEHOVAH See YHWH.

JEHOVAH'S WITNESSES Unorthodox Christian sect founded in 1884 by C.T. RUSSELL. It propagates its own version of the BIBLE which it regards as infallible, and stresses the imminent return of CHRIST. Members are pacifists and are forbidden to have blood

transfusions. There may be as many as 3 million Witnesses in 200 countries worldwide.

JEROME (about AD 342–420) Translator of the BIBLE into Latin (the 'Vulgate' version). He wrote many commentaries on the text.

JERUSALEM Fortified city captured by DAVID in the tenth century BC which became the capital and principal sanctuary for the people of ISRAEL. It has remained the focus of Jewish religious aspirations and ideals (see TEMPLE OF JERUSALEM). It is a holy city for CHRISTIANS because of its association with the passion, death and RESURRECTION of JESUS OF NAZARETH. For MUSLIMS it is the holiest city after MECCA. The MOSQUE of the Dome of the Rock stands over the site of Muhammad's NIGHT JOURNEY.

JESUS OF NAZARETH Teacher, prophet and worker of miracles in first century Palestine and founder of Christianity. He taught the coming of the KINGDOM OF GOD with forgiveness and new life for all who believed. His claims to be the promised MESSIAH (or CHRIST) roused opposition from the religious authorities and he was put to death by crucifixion. But after his death his followers claimed that he was risen from the dead and he was seen alive by many. CHRISTIANS, members of his CHURCH, await his promised SECOND COMING which will bring the fulfilment of the Kingdom of God.

JEW (1) A person who is regarded as a member of the Jewish race. According to Jewish religious law Jewishness is inherited through the female line. (2) A person who identifies with JUDAISM, the religion of the Jews.

JIHAD ('Striving') The means of promoting the message of ISLAM by force of arms. MUHAMMAD introduced the idea of a sacred struggle in his war with the Meccans. The QUR'AN understands Jihad as a natural outcome of the FIVE PILLARS OF ISLAM Jihad justified the expansion of Islam under the first four CALIPHS and has been invoked against enemies throughout Islamic history.

JIMMU TENNO Traditionally the first Japanese EMPEROR who began his reign in 660 BC. He was thought to be a great grandson of the sun goddess AMATERASU and was credited with the unification of Japan and the establishment of its government under the guidance of the gods (see KAMI).

JINJA The SHINTO sanctuary. They vary in size from roadside shrines to beautifully located halls surrounded by trees and entered through traditional arched gateways (see TORII). They include halls for ceremonial dances, offerings and prayer rooms.

JINN Spiritual creatures in Islamic belief who are made of smokeless flame. They are capable of belief and unbelief: the good ones are regarded as MUSLIMS.

JIVA A soul or 'life monad' according to JAIN belief. Jivas are infinite and omniscient but in this world KARMA weighs them down into a material existence. Jivas are liberated by acquiring omniscience and this makes them float up to the summit of the universe.

JOCHANAN BEN ZAKKAI Creator of the academic SANHEDRIN in Jamnia after the FALL OF JERUSALEM in AD 70. He led the work of Jewish reconstruction within the limits of Roman law and ensured, through the Sanhedrin, that the Jewish community were represented before the Roman authorities.

JODO Japanese name for PURE LAND BUDDHISM.

JODO SHINSHU ('True Pure Land Sect') A refinement of PURE LAND BUDDHISM founded by SHINRAN. It was characterized by the doctrine of salvation through faith alone and the abolition of the SANGHA.

JOK 'Spirit', 'divinity' or 'god' in several East African languages.

JUDAH HA NASI ('The Prince'; AD 135–217) Leader of the academic Jewish SANHEDRIN in Galilee. He was responsible for compiling the MISHNAH which helped the Jewish community in developing a source of ritual authority in religious teaching. At his death 'Glory departed from Israel'.

JUDAISM The religion that developed from the religion of ancient ISRAEL and has been practised ever since by the JEWS. It is an ethical MONOTHEISM based on the revelation of GOD to MOSES on Mt SINAI and his giving of the Law (see TORAH). (See also ASHKENAZIM; CONSERVATIVE JUDAISM; ORTHODOX JUDAISM; PROGRESSIVE JUDAISM; SEPHARDIM.)

JUDAS MACCABEUS (died 160 BC) Jewish revolutionary who opposed the Hellenizing Seleucid emperor Antiochus Epiphanes who had set up an image of Olympian ZEUS in the TEMPLE OF JERUSALEM. Under Judas sporadic guerrilla revolt became full-scale war. In 165 BC Antiochus was defeated and in the following year the temple was rededicated (see HANUKKAH). Though he achieved religious freedom, he failed to establish a free Jewish state.

JUDGEMENT The divine assessment of individuals and the settling of their destiny, a notion found in many religions. Christianity teaches that judgement is based on the individual's response to Christ.

JUMIS Latvian harvest god.

JUNG, Carl Gustav (AD 1875–1961) Swiss psychiatrist who invented the theory of ARCHETYPES. He investigated the significance of MYTHS, symbols and DREAMS, and found in them evidence for a 'collective unconscious' which was at the root of religion.

JUNO Roman goddess, counterpart of the Greek HERA and wife of JUPITER. She was the patroness of women, marriage, childbirth and family life.

JUPITER/JOVE Principal god of the Romans, identified with the Greek ZEUS. He controlled the weather, particularly lightning and rain and was worshipped throughout Italy as almost a national god.

K

KA The guardian spirit of each individual which, according to Egyptian belief, survived death and lived on in the next world, where it was re-united with BA.

KA'BA ('Cube') The sanctuary in MECCA to which all MUSLIMS turn in prayer. Set in its eastern corner is the BLACK STONE. A pre-Islamic holy place, all its religious images were removed in AD 630 by MUHAMMAD when he purified it to be the central sanctuary of ISLAM. The QUR'AN associates Abraham and Ishmael with the building of the Ka'ba.

KABBALAH Jewish mystical tradition which flourished in the teaching of two schools: the practical school based in Germany which concentrated on prayer and MEDITATION; the speculative school in Provence and Spain in the thirteenth and fourteenth centuries. The tradition originates in Talmudic speculation on the themes of the work of creation and the divine chariot mentioned in the biblical book of Ezekiel. The most famous Kabbalistic book is *Zohar* ('splendour'), a MIDRASH on the PENTATEUCH. (See MYSTICISM; TALMUD.)

KABIR (probably 1440–1518) Indian poet and hymn writer who influenced the development of early Sikhism. He attempted a synthesis of ISLAM and HINDUISM, rejecting the CASTE SYSTEM and CIRCUMCISION, but teaching the love of God, rebirth and liberation.

KAITIAKI Maori word for a guardian spirit.

KALI Consort of the HINDU god SHIVA, a black goddess who is portrayed with a necklace of human skulls and fangs dripping blood. She is both the goddess of destruction and the Great Mother, giver of life.

KALKI In HINDU tradition, the last AVATAR of VISHNU who will descend on a white horse, with a sword, to kill the wicked and bring the world to an end.

KALUNGA Bantu word for the realm of the dead, the sea, the UNDERWORLD. It is also the name of an earth deity.

KAMI Powers of nature which are venerated in SHINTO. They are beneficent spirits who help in the processes of fertility and growth. They were generated by the gods and the Japanese people are descended from them according to Shinto mythology.

KAMMA PALI word for Buddhist concept of KARMA.

KARAITES ('Readers of Scripture') Heretical Jewish school of the eighth century AD which denied the validity of the TALMUD and the oral tradition. They held to a literalist view of TORAH. By the tenth century they had spread throughout the Middle East and Spain. They refused to mix with other JEWS. Under attack by SAADYA BEN JOSEPH the movement gradually disintegrated.

KARAKIA Maori term for any sacred ritual. To be effective and to avoid misfortune it must be recited without error, addition or omission.

KARMA SANSKRIT word for work or action. In Indian belief every action has inevitable consequences which attach themselves to the doer, requiring reward or punishment. Karma is thus the moral law of cause and effect. It explains the inequalities of life as the consequences of actions in previous lives. The notion of karma probably developed among the DRAVIDIAN people of India. In MAHAYANA Buddhism the concept is transformed by the idea of the BODHISATTVA. Merit can be transferred by grace or faith, thus changing the person's karma.

KARO, Joseph (AD 1488–1575) Jewish legal teacher and MYSTIC. He produced the *Shulchan Aruch* (1565) which is one of the most important and cohesive authorities in JUDAISM and is considered to be in accord with the purest Talmudic tradition (see TALMUD). His work is characterized by a devotional tone unusual in legal works.

KASHRUT The code in JUDAISM according to which food is ritually clean or unclean. It refers particularly to meat, which must be slaughtered so as to ensure the minimum of pain and the draining off of blood.

KASHI See BENARES.

KEHUA Maori word for a ghostly being.

KHALSA Originally the militant community of SIKHS organized by Guru GOBINDH SINGH in AD 1699. Now it is the society of fully-committed adult members of the Sikh community. Traditional marks of membership are uncut hair, a comb worn in the hair, knee-length breeches, a sword and a steel bracelet.

KHANDHA See SKANDHA.

KHARIJITES MUSLIM party of seceders from 'ALI, the fourth CALIPH. They opposed the UMAYYAD DYNASTY, believing that the succession should be based on a democratic vote. They were puritans, strongly critical of the moral laxity which developed as Umayyad power increased. Their stance inspired later reforming movements. They still exist as a separate sect in North Africa.

KILIBOB See MANUP AND KILIBOB.

KINGDOM OF GOD The rule of God on earth. In JUDAISM God is king of the universe, the sole creator and ruler. The JEWS are his witnesses and their task is to work and pray for the fulfilment of his rule among all people. The kingdom will be brought by the MESSIAH and will include the restoration of ISRAEL. JESUS OF NAZARETH proclaimed the arrival of the kingdom in himself. Christians share in the kingdom now, and it will be completed and fulfilled at his SECOND COMING.

KITAB AKDAS Scripture of BAHA'I.

KOAN Technique used in RINZAI ZEN to bring about SATORI. It is a mind-bending question given by a teacher to a pupil to help him break through the prison of mental concepts and achieve direct awareness of reality.

KOJIKI SHINTO scripture which is the oldest book in the Japanese language, though it is written using Chinese characters. It contains MYTHS and legends about the creation, the founding of Japan and the ceremonies and customs of the Japanese people.

KOKO Spirits of dead ancestors in the popular cults of the Zuñi people of northern Mexico. The spirits are represented in ceremonial dances in which all participating males wear god-like masks.

KOL NIDRE See YOM KIPPUR.

KONKO-KYO ('The religion of Golden Light') One of the most successful of the Japanese NEW RELIGIONS. It is based on SHINTO but claims to be universal and monotheistic (see MONOTHEISM) and may have 500,000 followers.

KOOK, Abraham Isaac RABBI (AD 1868–1935) First Chief Rabbi of the Holy Land. He believed the Zionist movement to be essentially religious and that the restoration of ISRAEL was necessary for the redemption of the world. He influenced orthodox JEWS in favour of ZIONISM though he was also tolerant of secular Jews.

KORAN See QUR'AN.

KOTEL See WESTERN WALL.

KRISHNA The eighth incarnation of VISHNU according to HINDU tradition. His name means 'black'. Though of noble birth, he was brought up as a cowherd. Eventually he obtained his inheritance and ruled in justice. He was also a great lover: the MAHABHARATA describes his romances with the cow-girls which are seen as a type of God's love for the soul. He is also the main character in the BHAGAVAD GITA where he appears disguised as the charioteer of Prince Arjuna.

KRISHNA CONSCIOUSNESS See INTERNATIONAL SOCIETY FOR KRISHNA CONSCIOUSNESS.

KRISHNAMURTI, Jiddhu (born 1895) Indian spiritual teacher who was brought up by a leading Theosophist Mrs Annie Besant, who proclaimed him as a World Teacher. He renounced this role in 1929 and became a solitary traveller, teaching liberation from dogma and organized religion by the rejection of belief in the individual ego. (See also THEOSOPHY.)

KSHATRIYA See CASTE SYSTEM.

KUAN-YIN Chinese name for the great BODHISATTVA AVALOKITESH VARA, especially when thought of in female form.

KUKAI (AD 774–835) Japanese Buddhist teacher who tried to reconcile BUDDHISM with SHINTO (see RYOBU SHINTO). He is sometimes regarded as a manifestation of the Buddha VAIROCANA. Some believe he exists in a deep trance from which he is able to perform miracles and that he will return one day as a saviour.

KUNDALINI Energy that is coiled like a serpent at the base of the spine, according to TANTRISM. When awakened by YOGA it leaps up the spine to the brain giving an experience of union and liberation, re-enacting the sexual union of SHIVA and SHAKTI.

KWOTH Word for god or spirit among the Nuer people of East Africa.

L

LA ILAHA ILLA ALLAH The first four words of the MUSLIM confession of faith: 'There is no god but God', which continues 'and MUHAMMAD is his prophet'. To accept this creed is to be a Muslim. It is the first of the FIVE PILLARS OF ISLAM. Its words form part of the Call to Prayer which is broadcast from the MOSQUE five times a day in Muslim communities.

LAIMA Latvian goddess of fate.

LAITY (From Greek: *laos*, 'people') The non-ordained members of a religious community (see ORDINATION), or those with no specialist religious function.

LAKSHMI Lord VISHNU's consort. She appears in the *Rig Veda* (see VEDAS) as good fortune. In the RAMAYANA she rises out of the sea

holding a lotus. She is involved in Vishnu's descents to earth as an AVATAR. Some associate her with SITA and RADHA, the consorts of RAMA and KRISHNA.

LAMA Tibetan religious leader, a title formerly applied only to abbots, but later used of any monk. Lamas have been credited with magical powers which are said to be attained through years of arduous training. Their most common feat is telepathy, but they are also reported to be able to leave their bodies at will, cover huge distances at great speed and know the time and place of their own death. (See also BÖN; SHAMAN.)

LAMAISM See TIBETAN BUDDHISM.

LAO TSE/LAO-TZU Traditionally the author of the TAO TE CHING and a contemporary of CONFUCIUS. His name means 'old master' which could have applied to any wandering teacher.

LARES Roman agricultural spirits who were worshipped at cross-roads and in the home as household gods.

LATTER-DAY SAINTS, CHURCH OF JESUS CHRIST OF See MORMONISM; SMITH, JOSEPH.

LECTISTERNIUM A Roman feast in which food was offered to images of the gods which were placed on couches (*lecti*) like human guests.

LENT In CHRISTIANITY a forty-day period of FASTING and penitence before EASTER, originally a period of training and examination for those who were baptized at Easter.

LEY LINES Straight geological lines of spiritual force which some adherents of NEW AGE RELIGIONS believe were discovered and used in the NEOLITHIC PERIOD. Their existence is said to be demonstrated by the many alignments between religious sites, MEGALITHS and unusual topographical features. There is no archaeological or statistical support for this view.

LEZA A name for God as supreme being, found in many parts of East, Central and Southern Africa.

LI CONFUCIUS' concept of propriety or reverence which he believed

should direct all relationships between members of society. Correct application of li was a guarantee of social welfare and harmony.

LIBATION The RITUAL outpouring of drink as an offering to DIVINITIES or ANCESTOR SPIRITS.

LIBERATION THEOLOGY Originating in Latin America, associates SALVATION with the political liberation of oppressed peoples. It is marked by a stress on the challenges to social action contained in the BIBLE, especially the prophetic books and the NEW TESTAMENT, and the reality of the KINGDOM OF GOD as a coming event.

LIMBO According to Roman Catholic doctrine, the dwelling place of souls (e.g. of unbaptized children) excluded from HEAVEN but not subjected to HELL or PURGATORY.

LITURGY ('Public service') (1) Any regular prescribed service of the Christian Church. (2) The EUCHARIST, especially in ORTHODOXY.

LOA Gods or DIVINITIES who are the objects of worship in VOODOO religion.

LOKI The opponent of the AESIR in Norse mythology who is bent on their downfall and the overthrow of the world order. His name may mean 'light' and he is associated with destructive fire. For his part in the death of BALDER he is fettered to underground rocks and poisoned by serpents until the day of RAGNARÖK. His agonies cause earthquakes and volcanoes.

LOKI'S BROOD The children of LOKI who, in Norse mythology, are fathered on the giantess Angrboda. They are the great wolf, Fenriswulf; the world serpent, Jörmungandr, and the goddess HEL. The serpent was cast into the sea where it ringed the world holding its tail in its mouth. Hel was thrown into the UNDERWORLD where she rules over the dead. The wolf was fettered by the AESIR until the battle of RAGNARÖK when he was to swallow ODIN.

LORD'S SUPPER Name for the Christian EUCHARIST favoured by the Protestant reformers who saw the Eucharist primarily as a memorial of CHRIST's death.

LOTUS Type of water lily, a Buddhist symbol of ENLIGHTENMENT. The roots of the lotus are buried in the earth while the flower opens out above the water.

LOTUS POSTURE Style of sitting upright and cross-legged, used as a position for MEDITATION in Hindu and Buddhist practice.

LOTUS SUTRA MAHAYANA Buddhist scripture in the form of a sermon preached by the BUDDHA to a vast throng of gods, demons, rulers and cosmic powers. It contains the essence of Mahayana teachings on the eternity of the Buddha, the universal capacity for Buddhahood and the compassion and power of the BODHISATTVAS. It is especially revered in Japan and is the basic scripture of the NICHIREN Buddhist NEW RELIGIONS.

LUCRETIUS (about 100–55 BC) Roman poet and philosopher who expounded the materialist and rationalist doctrines of EPICUREANISM in his poem *De rerum natura* ('On the nature of things'). He accepted the existence of the traditional gods but located them far away from our world and believed that they had no interest in or influence over events on earth.

LUGH (Irish: 'the Shining One'; Welsh: Lleu) Most honoured of the Celtic gods, a war god, the patron of commerce and moneymaking and prototype of human beings. Skilful in all arts and crafts he is often portrayed as a youthful traveller. His Gaulish name is unknown but Julius Caesar compared him to the Roman MERCURY.

LUPERCALIA Roman festival, possibly in honour of Faunus, an Italian pastoral deity, held on 15 February. Goats or dogs were sacrificed and youths dressed in their skins ran round a course beating people. Originally this may have propitiated a wolf god.

LURIA, Isaac (1514–72) Jewish teacher from Spain who developed the Kabbalistic teachings of the *Zohar* (see KABBALAH). He believed in reincarnation and taught that the dispersion of the JEWS was providential and would lead to universal salvation. His teachings inspired devotional poetry and hymns.

LUTHER, Martin (1483–1546) Founder of the German REFORMATION. He held that only by faith in Jesus CHRIST could man be justified before God, not by any 'works' of religion. So the priesthood and the 'mediating' role of the church are unnecessary.

LUTHERAN CHURCHES Important churches in Scandinavia, other parts of Western Europe and the USA. They value theological study and emphasize the weekly sermon.

M

MACCABEES The family and supporters of JUDAS MACCABEUS. They were the forerunners of the ZEALOTS in fighting a holy war against alien rulers.

MADHVA (AD 1197–1280) Indian philosopher who founded a dualist school (see DUALISM) in opposition to the MONISM of SHANKARA. He was a devotee of VISHNU and believed that God was eternally distinct from the natural world. He may have been influenced by Christian teachings.

MAGI Priestly class of ancient Persia who at first opposed the spread of ZOROASTER'S teachings. By the fourth century BC they had been drawn into the service of the new religion and stressed the ritual and magic elements of it.

MAGIC The manipulation of natural or supernatural forces by SPELLS and RITUALS for good or harmful ends.

MAHABHARATA One of the two great epics of the HINDU scriptures, compiled in the third or second century BC. Ascribed to the sage Vyasa, it tells of the war between two families, the Kauravas and the Pandus. The divine hero of the epic is the AVATAR KRISHNA.

MAHARAJ JI, GURU See DIVINE LIGHT MISSION.

MAHARISHI MAHESH YOGI See TRANSCENDENTAL MEDITATION.

MAHA SABA Semi-religious, semi-political Indian organization founded in 1920. On the right wing of HINDU politics it opposed partition after Indian independence. Members are aggressively nationalistic and resist attempts to modify the CASTE SYSTEM.

MAHATMA SANSKRIT title of great respect or veneration meaning 'great soul'.

MAHATMA GANDHI (AD 1869–1948) Leader of the Indian independence movement and the greatest spiritual and political figure of modern India. Disowning violence, he advocated political change through non-violent resistance. After independence he tried to reconcile the Hindu and Muslim communities. He also campaigned against the social exclusion of UNTOUCHABLES. He was assassinated by a Hindu fanatic.

MAHAVIRA Great JAIN teacher who traditionally lived 599–527 BC, though this is disputed. He abolished the distinctions of the CASTE SYSTEM and tried to spread his teaching among the Brahmins. He starved himself to death at the age of seventy-two, having spent his last years totally naked.

MAHAYANA ('Large vehicle') The form of BUDDHISM practised in Nepal, China, Tibet, Korea and Japan. Mahayana accepts more scriptures than THERAVADA and has developed various forms of popular devotion based on the doctrine of the BODHISATTVAS.

MAHDI 'The guided one' who according to SHI'A teaching will come at the end of the world. The Mahdi is identified with Muhammad al-Mahdi who disappeared in AD 880 and is believed to be hidden until his reappearance. There have been a number of false Mahdis in the Shi'a community.

MAHOMET See MUHAMMAD.

MAIMONIDES, Moses (AD 1135–1204) Jewish philosopher who lived in Spain and later Egypt and attempted a synthesis of Aristotelian and biblical teaching. He listed the THIRTEEN PRINCIPLES of belief which have been treated in Judaism as a creed and are found in the Jewish *Daily Prayer Book*.

MAITREYA The Buddha-to-be, or the next BUDDHA to appear on earth according to MAHAYANA teachings. He is at present a BODHISATTVA awaiting his last rebirth.

MANA Polynesian word for the invisible spiritual power which permeates all things. It has been adopted as a general term in the study of PRIMAL RELIGIONS. It is not necessarily a personal power, though it can be focussed in particular individuals, places and objects.

MANABUSCH ('Big rabbit') Hero of the Algonquin and other North American Indian tribes. He is thought to have restored the earth after a great flood and to have introduced handicrafts and medicine.

MANANNAN Irish sea god, equivalent to the Welsh Manwyddan. He rode on the waves, gave immortality to other gods and possessed magic armour and a magic sword. His symbol is three joined revolving legs, which remains the emblem of the Isle of Man.

MANAQAN TENGRI Mongol name for the god of wild game.

MANCO CAPAC The first INCA who traditionally was created by the SUN GOD on an island in Lake Titicaca. He was instructed to bring civilization to all Indian peoples. He was guided to found the city of CUZCO as his capital.

MANDAEANS Members of a Gnostic sect teaching redemption through a divine saviour who has lived on earth and defeated the powers of darkness. The sole surviving practitioners of GNOSTICISM, about 15,000 still live in Iraq and Iran.

MANDALA A visual aid in the form of a series of coloured concentric circles used in TIBETAN BUDDHISM. Segments of the circles portray different aspects of the BUDDHA'S compassion. Concentration on the mandala enables the disciple to see himself in relation to the Buddha's compassion and thus to achieve ENLIGHTENMENT.

MANES Spirits of the dead in Roman religion.

MANICHAEANS Followers of Mani (around AD 216–276), a Persian teacher whose strict ascetic system was designed to release the divine spark trapped in every person by the wiles of SATAN. Their teaching influenced AUGUSTINE.

MANITO Name used by the Algonquin Indians of North America to refer to spiritual powers. It can apply to all kinds of NATURE SPIRITS or DIVINITIES, friendly or unfriendly.

MANTRA A symbolic sound causing an internal vibration which helps to concentrate the mind and aids self-realization, e.g. the repeated syllable 'om', and in Tibetan Buddhism the phrase OM MANI PADME HUM. In HINDUISM the term originally referred to a few sacred verses from the VEDAS. It came to be thought that they possessed spiritual power, and that repetition of them was a help to liberation. A mantra is sometimes given by a spiritual teacher to a disciple as an INITIATION.

MANUP AND KILIBOB Two semi-divine brothers whose story of separation and reconciliation has played an important part in the PRIMAL RELIGIONS and new religious movements of the Madang area of Papua New Guinea.

MAPONOS Celtic divine youth, worshipped in Gaul and North Britain. The Gauls connected him with healing springs, the British with music. In Wales he is Mabon, son of the Divine Mother. Irish myth speaks of Mac ind Og, the son of DAGDA.

MARA In BUDDHISM, the evil one, temptation.

MARA Latvian goddess of fate.

MARDUK Babylonian deity who superseded the Sumerian god ENLIL. He was associated with the sun and with vegetation. He was addressed as Bel, the Supreme Lord.

MARKS OF EXISTENCE In the BUDDHA's teaching all existence is marked by the three characteristics: DUKKHA; ANICCA; ANATTA.

MARRIAGE, SACRED A religious rite involving real or simulated sexual intercourse which represents the marriage of earth and sky in the fertilization of the soil and the growth of the crops.

MARS Roman war god, regarded second only to JUPITER. Soldiers sacrificed to him before and after battle. Originally he was probably a god of agriculture.

MARTYR ('Witness') Title originally applied to Christians who died rather than renounce their faith during times of persecution. Now a term applied to anyone who dies for a religious belief.

MARY, THE MOTHER OF JESUS Because of her role in the divine plan of salvation, Mary is honoured by all Christians and venerated by Roman Catholic and Eastern Orthodox Christians. The GOSPELS describe her as divinely chosen to be the mother of the Saviour. Roman Catholic churches have attributed an intercessory role to Mary, and developed other doctrines concerning her nature.

MASBUTA Baptismal rite of MANDAEANS.

MASIQTA MANDAEAN ceremony consisting of a sacramental meal held at death to assist the soul to salvation.

MASORETES A group of Jewish scholars from the Babylonian and Palestinian schools who in the ninth century AD supplied the text of the HEBREW BIBLE with vowel points and divided it up into sentences and paragraphs. They also tried to exclude copyists' errors and noted all the variant readings they found.

MASS Name for the Christian EUCHARIST derived from the words of dismissal. The standard ROMAN CATHOLIC term, it emphasizes the sacrificial aspect of the rite.

MATRONAE MOTHER GODDESSES worshipped in Celtic religion. They are often portrayed in groups of three, carrying babies or bushels of fruit or sheaves—clear evidence of their association with earthly and human fertility.

MATSURI Japanese name for a solemn celebration intended to invoke worship of the SHINTO gods and obedience to their moral will. They take place at stated intervals in Shinto sanctuaries.

MAWU Supreme HIGH GOD among a number of West African peoples. He is the creator of gods and the sender of souls into men.

MAX MÜLLER, Friedrich (AD 1823–1900) German philosopher of religion and philologist who taught that religion originated in the personification of the forces of nature. He edited the fifty-one-volume series of translations, *Sacred Books of the East*. He worked in England from 1846.

MAYA Illusion or deception in HINDU thought. Maya is concerned with the diverse phenomenal world perceived by the senses. It is the trick of maya to convince people that this is all that exists and thus blind them to the reality of BRAHMAN and the oneness of existence. (2) Legendary mother of the BUDDHA (1).

MAYA People of an ancient Middle American empire which spread from Yucatan to El Salvador. Mayan civilization was at its height around AD 300–900 and was finally broken up by the Spaniards in the sixteenth century. The Maya developed a complex calendar and a form of writing. Their gods were linked with nature symbols, the most important of which was a double-headed snake. (See also AHKIN; AH PUCH; CHAC; CHILAN; HALACH UINIC; ITZAMNA; IXCHEL; POPOL VUH; YUM KAAX.)

MECCA Holy city of ISLAM, in Saudi Arabia, the birthplace of MUHAMMAD and later the base for his MUSLIM state after its conquest in AD 630. Pilgrimage to Mecca, HAJJ, is one of the FIVE PILLARS OF ISLAM and all Muslims face Mecca to perform ritual prayer five times a day.

MEDICINE MAN See WITCHDOCTOR.

MEDINA Formerly Yathrib, city 169km north of MECCA, the political base for MUHAMMAD from AD 622 until his conquest of Mecca. Pilgrims from Medina were among the first to accept and spread Muhammad's message. The city contains the site of Muhammad's tomb.

MEDITATION Deep and continuous reflection, practised in many religions with a variety of aims, e.g. to attain self-realization or, in theistic religions, to attain union with the divine will. Many religions teach a correct posture, method of

breathing and ordering of thoughts for meditation.

MEDIUM One who is possessed by the spirit of a dead person or a DIVINITY and, losing his individual identity, becomes the mouthpiece for the other's utterance.

MEGALITHS Large stone monuments dating from the late NEOLITHIC PERIOD. Their original function is uncertain but they mark burial mounds and temples and they may have served as a calendar of times and seasons.

MEHER BABA (AD 1894–1969) Indian spiritual leader, regarded by his followers as an AVATAR. From 1925 until his death he did not speak once.

MENCIUS (born 371 BC) Confucian teacher who expanded and developed CONFUCIUS' teachings. He believed that the universe followed a moral order and that knowledge of this order could be attained by MEDITATION.

MENDELSSOHN, Moses (1729–86) German Jewish rationalist philosopher who taught that the three central propositions of JUDAISM are: the existence of God; providence; the immortality of the soul. He believed these to be founded on pure reason and to be the basis of all religion. The revelation to the JEWS preserves the Jews as an ethnic entity. He translated the PENTATEUCH into German and encouraged Jews to become more involved in European culture.

MERCURY Roman god, identified with the Greek HERMES. He presided over trade.

MERIT In BUDDHISM the fruit of good actions which can be devoted to the welfare of other beings. The idea develops in MAHAYANA where it is believed that the BODHISATTVAS have acquired almost infinite supplies of merit which they can transfer to believers.

MERLIN Bard and magician in the romances of the CELTS, later the mentor of ARTHUR.

MESSIAH ('Anointed one') A HEBREW word referring to the person chosen by God to be king. After the

end of the Israelite monarchy it came to refer to a figure who would restore ISRAEL, gathering the tribes together and ushering in the KINGDOM OF GOD. JUDAISM has known several false Messiahs (see ZEVI, SHABBETAI). Modern JEWS are divided as to whether the Messiah is a symbolic or a representative figure and whether the founding of the Jewish state is in any way a prelude to his coming. In the Christian NEW TESTAMENT, JESUS OF NAZARETH is described by Messianic titles, e.g. Messiah, CHRIST, 'the King', 'the One who Comes'. The account of Jesus' entry into JERUSALEM is deliberately phrased in Messianic terms. Jesus himself was cautious about claiming to be Messiah, probably because of its political overtones.

METHODIST CHURCHES Churches deriving from those which joined the Methodist Conference, first established in 1784 by John WESLEY. They are now spread world-wide promoting EVANGELISM and social concern.

MEZUZAH ('Doorpost') Sign placed at the door of a Jewish house, comprising part of the SHEMA.

MIDDLE WAY The BUDDHA's description of his teaching as a mean between the extremes of sensuality and asceticism. It is designed to lead to NIRVANA.

MIDEWIWIN A society of scholars and holy men of the Ojibwa Indians of North America who are charged with the preservation of the traditions of their people.

MIDGARD The home of human beings according to Norse cosmology. Made from the body of the primeval giant, Ymir, it was defended by THOR from attack by giants. Midgard is the middle of the nine worlds; it is in the centre of GINNUNGAGAP and surrounded by sea.

MIDRASH A method of exposition of HEBREW texts designed to reveal the inner meaning of the TORAH. Great attention to detail was paid because the texts were believed to be of divine origin. The method was originally oral; the most important midrashim were recorded and written down.

MIHRAB Semi-circular recess in the wall of a MOSQUE which indicates the direction of the holy city MECCA, which is the direction for MUSLIM prayer.

MIKI NAKAYAMA (AD 1798–1887) Founder of the Japanese religion TENRIKYO. In 1838 she was possessed by a divine being who announced he was the Creator and true God and gave her a series of revelations. Miki Nakayama gave away all her money and practised spiritual healing. Her teachings attracted a wide following. Adherents believe she is still alive, in non-physical form, in the shrine built on the site of her home at the city of Tenri.

MIMI Shy and harmless NATURE SPIRITS of the mythology of northern Australia.

MIMIR In Norse mythology, the fount of wisdom who guards the well of knowledge at the root of YGGDRASIL. He is ODIN'S mentor. In one version of his MYTH, Odin comes to drink from the well and has to sacrifice an eye to do so; in another Mimir's head is cut off and brought to Odin who preserves it as a talking head which gives him advice.

MINARET ('Place of light and fire') A tower attached to a MOSQUE from which the Call to Prayer is broadcast to the MUSLIM community.

MINDFULNESS Buddhist method of contemplative analysis. It has two uses: in MEDITATION, where it refers to the practice of observing the arising and passing away of different mental states until one arrives at detachment; in daily life, where it refers to a quality of carefulness in thought, speech and action which prevents the accumulation of bad KARMA.

MING Chinese emperor (first century AD) of the Han dynasty who, according to tradition, introduced Buddhist scriptures from north-west India. According to tradition he had a dream of a golden man, which he took to be a revelation of the BUDDHA.

MINISTER (1) A lay or ordained Christian who has been authorized to perform spiritual functions (ministries, literally 'service') in the CHURCH. (2) General title for any clergyman, especially those of Protestant denominations.

MINOAN RELIGION Religion of the Bronze Age civilization of Crete. The Minoans probably worshipped the MOTHER GODDESS and reverenced SACRED SNAKES and SACRED BULLS.

MIRACLE An event which appears to defy rational explanation and is attributed to divine intervention.

MISHNAH A compilation of Jewish oral teachings undertaken by Rabbi JUDAH HA NASI in around AD 200. It quickly became second in authority only to the HEBREW BIBLE and formed the basis of the TALMUD. The Mishnah helped Jewish teaching to survive in a period of persecution when the future of the SANHEDRIN was in doubt.

MISSAL Liturgical book containing all that is said or sung throughout the year at the celebration of the MASS. It also includes appropriate directions.

MISSION The outgoing of the Christian CHURCH to the unconverted with its GOSPEL message. It is held that all mankind needs to hear the news of SALVATION.

MISSIONARIES Those who propagate a religious faith among people of a different faith. BUDDHISM and CHRISTIANITY have been the most notable missionary religions.

MITHRA Originally a god of the Indo-Iranians, he was worshipped in the Hindu VEDAS as Mitra and was an important figure in ZOROASTRIANISM, where he was particularly associated with ideas on judgement and the priesthood. To this day, the term for Zoroastrian FIRE TEMPLES is *dar-i Mihr*, 'courts of Mithra'. (See also MITHRAISM; SOL INVICTUS.)

MITHRAEUM Cave-like sanctuary housing a statue of MITHRA slaying the bull.

MITHRAISM Religion of Mithra which flourished throughout the Roman Empire in the second to fourth centuries AD. It was found in almost all parts of the empire, but concentrated in Rome, the Rhine Valley and what is now Hungary and Rumania. Popular among soldiers, it stressed the ethical values of courage and endurance. It was not open to women.

MODERATOR MINISTER of the PRESBYTERIAN CHURCH appointed to constitute and preside over one of the courts that govern the life of the church.

MODIMO/MOLIMO/MORIMO Word for spirit or god in many Bantu languages.

MOHAMMED See MUHAMMAD.

MOIRAI ('Fates') Three goddesses of Greek mythology, described by HESIOD as children of ZEUS and by PLATO as daughters of Necessity. They were Lachesis, who predestines each human life; Clotho, who spins the thread of life, and Atropos, who cuts the thread at death.

MOKSHA SANSKRIT word meaning liberation from the cycle of birth, death and rebirth. Moksha is achieved when virtue, knowledge and love of God cancel out the weight of KARMA which require the self to be reborn.

MONISM the belief that there is only one basic reality in spite of the appearance and experience of diversity. It applies particularly to the beliefs of the HINDU philosopher SHANKARA (see also ADVAITA.)

MONK A member of a male religious community living under vows which usually include poverty, chastity and the wearing of a distinctive form of dress. Monastic orders are found in Christianity and Buddhism. The Buddhist monk is a member of a SANGHA and, additionally to the FIVE PRECEPTS, vows to eat only at set times, not to handle money, use a high bed, use scent or go to stage performances. (See also BENEDICT; BHIKSHU.)

MONOTHEISM The belief that there is one supreme GOD who contains all the attributes and characteristics of divinity.

MOON, Sun Myung (born 1920) Korean engineer, businessman and founder of the UNIFICATION CHURCH. He claims to have authoritative visions of Jesus. Members of the Unification Church accord him a high, if publicly ill-defined, status.

MOONIES Disciples of Sun Myung MOON and members of his UNIFICATION CHURCH.

MORAVIANS Protestant Christians continuing the simple ideals of an earlier group 'The Bohemian Brethren'. They distrust CREEDS and oppose political involvement. They have been active MISSIONARIES since they were founded in AD 1722.

MORMONISM Unorthodox Christian sect founded in AD 1830 in the USA on the basis of the visionary experiences of Joseph SMITH. Under its second leader Brigham Young (AD 1801–77), the Mormons journeyed to found Salt Lake City (1847) where they developed into a strong missionary community. Mormons accept the BIBLE and the BOOK OF MORMON and some other revealed writings. The Mormon Church, officially the 'Church of Jesus Christ of Latter-Day Saints', has over 3 million members, two-thirds of them in the USA.

MORONI See SMITH, JOSEPH.

MORRIGHAN Battle goddess, the nightmare, phantom queen of Celtic mythology. She appears in a trio with Badb, the Crow, and Nemain, frenzy. Together they haunt battlefields, changing shape but often in the form of crows, and foretell war and doom.

MOSES The father of JUDAISM who received the TORAH from God on Mt SINAI having led the people of ISRAEL out of captivity in Egypt. The first five books of the BIBLE are traditionally ascribed to him.

MOSLEM See MUSLIM.

MOSQUE MUSLIM place of public worship, consisting usually of an outer courtyard for ablutions and a large unfurnished inner area where Muslims kneel, sit or prostrate themselves in worship. There is usually one main congregational service in the mosque between noon and 3 p.m. on Fridays.

MOTHER GODDESS/GREAT MOTHER The personification of nature and the natural processes of fertility and growth connected with the earth. Worship of a mother goddess was universal in the Ancient Near East, Asia and Europe (see CYBELE, DEMETER, INANNA, ISHTAR, ISIS). Her worship continues in HINDUISM where the consorts of SHIVA

(DURGA, KALI, PARVATI) have some of her characteristics. There is some revival of interest in her worship among modern feminist groups and practitioners of WITCHCRAFT.

MO-TZU Chinese philosopher and critic of CONFUCIANISM who lived in the fifth century BC. He taught universal love which he believed was the will of heaven. He defended popular religious practices and denounced war and extravagance.

MUEZZIN Person who calls the MUSLIM faithful to prayer.

MUFTI A canon lawyer in ISLAM who gives formal legal advice on questions brought to him in accordance with the QUR'AN, the SUNNA and the law schools.

MUGHAL EMPIRE Indian MUSLIM empire founded by Babur in AD 1526. The third emperor was the liberal Akbar who established good relations with HINDUS. Later rulers succumbed to Islamic puritanism, and after the reign of Aurangzeb the empire declined.

MUHAMMAD (about AD 570–632) Prophet and apostle of ISLAM, the final messenger of God whose message, the QUR'AN sums up and completes the previous revelations to the Jews and Christians. Muhammad saw the expansion of ISLAM in terms of military conquest and political organization and he was outstandingly successful as a commander and ruler in MEDINA and later MECCA.

MUHARRAM Festival kept by Shi'ite MUSLIMS (see SHI'A) commemorating the murder of Al-Huseyn on the tenth day of the month Muharram. A passion play is performed depicting the martyrdom.

MUJTAHID MUSLIM teacher who gives a ruling, legal decision or deduction on the basis of his own learning or authority (see IJTIHAD). In SHI'A Islam, the Mujtahid have great authority.

MUKANDA Male initiation rite among the Kiluba and other Bantu peoples.

MUKISHI Spirit associted with the dead, a spirit of natural phenomena

(see DIVINITIES) or a guardian spirit among the Kiluba and other Bantu peoples.

MULLAH A Persian form of an ARABIC word which means a 'teacher' or 'scholar'—an exponent of the sacred law of ISLAM.

MULUNGU/MUNGU/ MURUNGU In a number of East African languages a name for God as the supreme being.

MUNGU See MULUNGU.

MURUNGU See MULUNGU.

MUSLIM 'One who submits' to the will of God, a follower of ISLAM.

MUSLIM BROTHERHOOD Egyptian puritanical organization founded in AD 1928 by Hasan al-Banna. The brotherhood was influential after World War II and worked against ZIONISM and westernization. It fell into disrepute because of terrorist activities and was dissolved in 1954.

MUSLIM LEAGUE Organization founded in AD 1906 to promote the interests and political aspirations of Indian Muslims. One of its presidents was Muhammad IQBAL.

MWARI The name for God among the Shona people of Zimbabwe and in other Bantu languages.

MYSTERY RELIGIONS Cults based on ancient MYTHS which flourished in Greece, in Rome and throughout the Roman Empire. Initiates went through a dramatic and secret ceremony in which they identified with the divinity at the centre of the myth and experienced salvation and the assurance of immortality.

MYSTIC One who seeks direct personal experience of the divine. He may use PRAYER, MEDITATION or various ascetic practices to concentrate his attention.

MYSTICISM The search for direct personal experience of the divine. There is a distinction between seeing mysticism as leading to identification with GOD (as is common in HINDUISM) and as leading to a union with God's love and will (as in ISLAM, JUDAISM and CHRISTIANITY).

MYTH A sacred story which originates and circulates within a particular community. Some, aetiological myths, explain puzzling physical phenomena or customs, institutions and practices whose origin in the community would otherwise be mysterious. (See also CREATION MYTH.)

N

NAGARJUNA (around AD 100–165) MAHAYANA Buddhist philosopher who taught that the truth of reality was void or emptiness.

NAMANDI Malignant NATURE SPIRITS of the mythology of northern Australia who are thought to attack lonely travellers and to be in constant conflict with the MIMI.

NAMU MYOHO RENGE KYO Formula coined by NICHIREN as the essential truth of the LOTUS SUTRA. It means 'Reverence to the wonderful truth of the *Lotus Sutra*' and it is used by a variety of sects based on Nichiren's Buddhist teachings.

NANAK, GURU (AD 1469–1539) Indian religious teacher and founder of the SIKH religion. He intended to reconcile HINDUS and MUSLIMS and travelled widely preaching a monotheistic faith (see MONOTHEISM) which was influenced by BHAKTI and SUFISM. He appointed a successor to continue his teachings.

NATIVE AMERICAN CHURCH Religious organization of North American Indians founded in 1870. It teaches a synthesis of native religion and Christianity. Its rituals include the ceremonial use of peyote, a spineless cactus containing the hallucinogenic substance mescaline.

NATURE SPIRITS Spirits of trees, hills, rivers, plants and animals which are acknowledged with prayers and offerings in most PRIMAL RELIGIONS.

NAUJOTE INITIATION ceremony of the PARSIS at which a child is invested

with a sacred shirt and thread, symbolic of 'new birth' to adulthood.

NEBO Babylonian god of writing who was the son of MARDUK. His symbol was the pen and his gift of writing gave him the power to prolong life and revive the dead. He resembled the Egyptian THOTH.

NEMBUTSU ('Hail to the BUDDHA AMIDA') The formula of faith taught by the Japanese Buddhist teacher HONEN.

NEMESIS Greek goddess who personified the retribution due to evil deeds. Her vengeance was regarded to be inevitable and exact.

NEMETON 'Sacred place' in Celtic religion, usually an enclosed woodland grove.

NEOLITHIC PERIOD The New Stone Age, from about 10,000 BC until the Early Bronze Age.

NEO-PLATONISM Religious and philosophical movement from the third to the sixth centuries AD. It used the teachings of PLATO as a basis for ascetic practices and mystical experience. Its principal architect was PLOTINUS.

NEPTUNE Italian water god who became associated with POSEIDON and acquired his mythology.

NESTORIANISM CHRISTIAN HERESY that claimed that two separate persons, human and divine, existed in the incarnate CHRIST (as opposed to the orthodox view that God and man are one person in Christ). Although condemned in AD 431 it continued to flourish in Persia. A few groups of Nestorians survive in the present day.

NEW AGE RELIGIONS Term for the various movements which emerged or revived in the mid-1960s, particularly on the West Coast of the USA. These movements were characterized by a sense that man was entering a new phase of religious awareness. Their teachings were often a blend of Eastern and Western MYSTICISM designed to expand individual awareness.

NEW RELIGIONS New sects which have arisen in Japan in the

twentieth century. Many are Buddhist in origin (see NICHIREN), others have SHINTO roots, others are a synthesis, sometimes with Christian elements. (See also KONKO-KYO; P.L. KYODAN; SOKA GAKKAI.)

NEW TESTAMENT The second division of the Christian BIBLE, comprising the GOSPELS, the Acts of the Apostles, the Revelation of John and various EPISTLES.

NEW YEAR, JEWISH See ROSH HASHANAH.

NEZAHUALCOYOTL (AD 1418–72) AZTEC ruler who worshipped TLOQUE NAHUAQUE as the single god from whom all other gods derived their power and being. He built a great temple to him and tried, unsuccessfully, to curb the practice of human SACRIFICE.

NGAI Name for God in several East African languages.

NGANGA Medicine man or healer among the Kiluba and other Bantu peoples; one who practises BWANGA.

NGEWO The supreme HIGH GOD of the Mende people of Sierra Leone. He has neither temples nor priesthood because he has distanced himself from the everyday world since people were becoming too familiar with him.

NIBBANA PALI word for NIRVANA.

NICHIREN (AD 1222–82) Japanese Buddhist reformer who taught that the LOTUS SUTRA contained the ultimate truth and that it could be compressed into a sacred formula: NAMU MYOHO RENGE KYO. He denounced all other forms of Buddhism. When the Mongols threatened Japan he preached a fiery nationalism, urging the nation to convert to true Buddhism. His teachings have provided the inspiration for some modern Buddhist sects (see NEW RELIGIONS).

NIGHT JOURNEY The journey of MUHAMMAD from the temple in MECCA to the TEMPLE OF JERUSALEM which is described in the QUR'AN. Tradition asserts that he travelled on a winged horse accompanied by GABRIEL. By the sacred rock of Abraham, Muhammad met

Abraham, Moses and Jesus. Then he ascended up a ladder of light into the presence of ALLAH. He returned bringing instructions for the faithful.

NIHONGI SHINTO scripture which contains the Japanese CREATION MYTH and legends of the gods. It was originally written in Chinese.

NINIGI The son of AMATERASU in SHINTO belief. At a time of chaos in heaven Amaterasu sent him down to rule the islands of Japan, making him the first Japanese EMPEROR.

NIRVANA/NIBBANA ('Going out', 'becoming cool') In BUDDHISM the state when DUKKHA ceases because the flames of desire are no longer fuelled. It is a state of unconditioned-ness and uncompounded-ness beyond any form of known or imagined existence.

NKULUKULU ('The old, old one') Zulu name for God.

NOBLE EIGHTFOLD PATH In BUDDHISM the way to extinguish desire by adopting: right views; right motives; right speech; right conduct; right means of livelihood; right effort; right mindfulness; right contemplation.

NORNS The Fates of Norse religion. Of giant origin, they are immensely powerful, controlling the destiny of men. They tend and water the trunk of YGGDRASIL. The names of the three norns mean Past, Present and Future. Their association with time makes them more powerful than the immortal gods of ASGARD, since even they are bound to predestined fate. (See also MOIRAI.)

NUADHA Celtic deity who may have originated as an Irish king who relinquished his sacred office yet was saved by LUGH. In Wales he is known as Nudd and he is probably also to be identified with Nodens who had a Romano-British temple in south-west England.

NUMEN In Roman religion, the divine power suffusing nature. From this concept Rudolf OTTO developed the idea that the root of religion was a sense of holy power. This he termed the 'numinous'.

NUN A member of a female religious community as found in CHRISTIANITY and BUDDHISM. Nuns live under vows usually including poverty, CHASTITY and the wearing of a distinctive form of dress. (See also BENEDICT.)

NUT The sky goddess of Egyptian mythology whose body is lined with stars. Every evening she swallows the sun and gives birth to it again each morning.

NYAMBE/ZAMBE/NZAMBI Name for the supreme god in a large area of tropical Africa. It may be linked to a Sudanese word meaning 'power'.

NYAME ('The shining one') Name for the supreme HIGH GOD among the peoples of Ghana in West Africa.

O

OBEAH Religious and magical practices of the West Indies which are usually of West African origin. (See also VOODOO.)

OBO Pile of rocks representing the spirits of the departed in the religions of central Asia.

OCCULT Teachings, arts and practices that are concerned with what is hidden and mysterious, as with WITCHCRAFT, ALCHEMY and DIVINITION.

ODIN Chief of the Norse gods, the ALLFATHER. Originally he was a wild wind god who led the spirits of the dead through the air. The Romans associated him with MERCURY. In later mythology, he visits the earth as The Wanderer. There are two myths of his search for wisdom: the first that he sacrificed an eye as the price for his drinking from the well of MIMIR; the second that he hanged himself upon YGGDRASIL. He is associated with the gallows and there is evidence that victims were hanged on trees in sacrifice to him. As Allfather, Odin watched over the nine worlds and was brought daily reports by two ravens.

Variants of his name include Woden (Anglo-Saxon) and Wotan (German).

OGUN God of iron and metalwork among the Yoruba people of Nigeria. Cyclists, lorry-drivers, soldiers and blacksmiths carry protective charms of Ogun.

OHRMAZD See AHURA MAZDA.

OLD CATHOLIC CHURCHES A group of national churches which have separated from Rome. Since 1932 they have been in communion with the Church of England.

OLD TESTAMENT The HEBREW BIBLE as the first division of the Christian BIBLE.

OLUDUMARE/OLURUN Name for the supreme HIGH GOD among the Yoruba people of Nigeria.

OLURUN See OLUDUMARE.

OLYMPUS, Mount The highest mountain in Greece (2,917m), held to be the home of the twelve greatest Greek gods under the leadership of ZEUS.

OM MANI PADME HUM ('The jewel in the LOTUS') Tibetan MANTRA, whose six syllables are held to correspond to the six worlds of Tibetan Buddhist teaching: *om*, 'gods'; *ma*, 'anti-gods'; *ni*, 'humans'; *pad*, 'animals'; *mi*, 'hungry ghosts'; *hum*, 'hell'. Each world is present as a state of the human mind. The mantra sums up the whole of human existence and is an indispensable aid to self-realization.

ORDINATION Rite in the Christian CHURCH by which men (and in some churches women) are authorized as MINISTERS of the Word of God and the SACRAMENTS. In BUDDHISM the term denotes entry into the SANGHA.

ORIGEN (around AD 184–254) Theologian who tried to present Biblical CHRISTIANITY using the ideas of HELLENISM. He believed that all creatures would eventually be saved, a view condemned as heretical in AD 553.

ORIGINAL SIN The sin of Adam, the first man, in eating from the forbidden tree in the Garden of Eden, expressing independence from God. In Christian teaching the inevitable consequence is seen as separation from God: man is 'fallen', a state inherited by all men and women and resulting in the need for SALVATION.

ORPHISM Religious movement which began in Thrace and flourished in the sixth century BC. It was based on MYTHS of DIONYSUS and Orpheus, who was the supreme minstrel of Greek mythology. It taught a way of liberation through ASCETICISM and held also a doctrine of REINCARNATION.

ORTHODOX JUDAISM Traditional JUDAISM which is Talmudic (see TALMUD) in belief and practice. It is the largest of the modern groupings and it is the form of religion accepted as authentic in Israel.

ORTHODOXY CHRISTIANITY as practised by the Eastern Churches after the GREAT SCHISM. Orthodox Christians are found mostly in Eastern Europe, the Balkan States and Russia.

OSIRIS Egyptian vegetation god, the force behind the cycle of growth and decay. Mythology tells how he had originally lived on earth as a king. He was murdered and later dismembered by his jealous brother SETH. His wife ISIS searched for the pieces of his body and restored him to life. As a symbol of death and resurrection, Osiris became associated with life after death and the judgement of individual souls.

OTTO, Rudolf (AD 1869–1937) German philosopher of religion and author of *The Idea of the Holy* (1917) in which he argued that religious experience sprang from the intuitive and non-rational faculties in man and was characterized by a sense of the 'numinous' (see NUMEN), by awe and dread and amazement.

OTTOMAN EMPIRE (AD 1453–1918) The empire of the Ottoman Turks who were converted to ISLAM. It stretched from the Middle East to the Balkans and at its height to the frontiers of Austria. The Ottomans supported SUNNI orthodoxy against heterodox DERVISH movements. The empire went into slow decline in the eighteenth century and its religious life stagnated.

P

PACHACAMAC Leader of the gods in the religion of the INCAS. A great shrine was built for him near the modern city of Lima, Peru.

PACHACUTEC The ninth INCA (ruled AD 1438–71). A great king, he enlarged the empire and rebuilt the capital CUZCO. He exalted VIRACOCHA as the supreme god of the Incas.

PAGAN Originally a word used by Christians to describe a person who had not adopted the Christian faith. Today it tends to refer to a person who is neither Christian, Jew nor Muslim, or to a person who is irreligious or who adheres to some modern revival of an ancient religion.

PAGANISM The religion and worship of those who are neither CHRISTIANS, JEWS nor MUSLIMS.

PAGODA A Buddhist building in south-east Asia built over Buddhist RELICS and often characterized by a series of superimposed spires. (See also DAGOBA.)

PALAEOLITHIC PERIOD The Old Stone Age, before 10,000 BC in Europe and the Middle East.

PALI Vernacular language of northern India in the BUDDHA'S time and hence the language of early BUDDHISM and the THERAVADA SCRIPTURES. It is related to SANSKRIT.

PALI CANON The basic Buddhist SCRIPTURES—the only scriptures valid among THERAVADA Buddhists. Traditionally the collection began soon after the BUDDHA'S death when his followers met to recite the TRIPITAKA, or 'three baskets' of his teaching. The precise wording of the canon was fixed at a council in the time of king ASOKA.

PAN Arcadian fertility god, patron of shepherds and herdsmen, usually portrayed with goat's horns and legs.

PANCHEN LAMA Title given to one of the leading abbots of TIBETAN BUDDHISM, whose authority paralleled that of the DALAI LAMA, though its emphasis was more on spiritual matters. The Panchen Lama

was believed to be a reincarnation of AMITABHA.

PANTHEISM The belief that all reality is in essence divine.

PAPA Sky god of the Scythians.

PAPATUANUKU See RANGINUI AND PAPATUANUKU.

PAROUSIA See SECOND COMING.

PARSIS/PARSEES Descendants of the ancient Zoroastrian Persians (see ZOROASTRIANISM) living in India, mostly near Bombay. They practise an ethical MONOTHEISM with a RITUAL life that expresses the purity of AHURA MAZDA. The 125,000 Parsis in the world today are divided into three groups, differing over the religious calendar.

PARSVA Legendary founder of JAINISM. Born a prince around 850 BC, he renounced his throne and became an ascetic, finally gaining omniscience. He is considered to be the twenty-second TIRTHANKARA.

PARVATI ('Mountaineer') Consort of SHIVA in HINDU mythology, like Shiva both beautiful and terrifying.

PASSOVER Seven-day Jewish spring festival marking the deliverance from Egypt (see EXODUS). Since Talmudic times (see TALMUD) the festival has begun with a service in the home where unleavened bread, wine and bitter herbs symbolize the joys and sorrows of the exodus. There is a meal and the evening concludes with psalms and hymns which look to God's final redemption of ISRAEL.

PATAGALIWABE HIGH GOD of the Huli people in southern Papua New Guinea. He is a guardian of social ethics who punishes wrong doers with sickness, war, injury or death.

PATRIARCH (1) 'Father-figure'; especially in family and community; in JUDAISM and CHRISTIANITY, refers to the founders of the faith such as ABRAHAM, ISAAC and JACOB. (2) Head of one of the EASTERN ORTHODOX CHURCHES. The Patriarch of Constantinople is a figurehead for Orthodox Christians.

PAUL Apostle of Christianity who established new churches throughout Asia Minor and Macedonia. Originally a Pharisee, he was converted by a vision of Christ on the road to Damascus. He wrote several New Testament epistles. Tradition asserts that he was beheaded at Rome under Nero.

PEKWIN Chief religious leader among the Zuñi people of northern Mexico. His power comes from the Sun Father and his task is the observation of solstices. He directs the people in times of prayer and ritual to ensure the fertility of the land.

PENATES Spirits or gods who protected the Roman household and family and were guardians over the household stores.

PENTATEUCH See Torah (1).

PENTECOST (1) Jewish harvest festival, fifty-two days after Passover. (2) Christian festival marking the coming of the Holy Spirit upon the apostles fifty days after Easter. The second most important Christian festival, it commemorates the beginning of the church.

PENTECOSTAL CHURCHES Churches which have formed from a renewal movement which started in the USA in AD 1906. They teach the experience of 'baptism in the Holy Spirit' which shows itself in speaking in tongues (see glossolalia) and other 'spiritual gifts'.

PERKONS/PERKUNAS Supreme god of ancient Russia, particularly associated with thunder and lightning.

PERKUNAS See Perkons.

PETER Apostle and close follower of Jesus of Nazareth, from whom he received the name Peter: 'Rock'. He held a position of leadership among the early apostles. Tradition asserts that he was martyred in Rome.

PHARAOH In the Bible the title of the king of Egypt. The reigning king was identified with the god Horus and was held to be responsible for the fertility of the land. On death the king became Osiris, his body being mummified and buried in a tomb

which from the Third Dynasty to the end of the Middle Period might be a pyramid.

PHARISEES Jewish anti-nationalistic party that emerged in the time of the Maccabees. They believed that God was universal and taught the individuality of the soul and the resurrection. They prepared the way for the survival of Judaism after the Fall of Jerusalem in AD 70.

PHILO OF ALEXANDRIA (about 25 BC–AD 40) Jewish philosopher who tried to reconcile Greek philosophy with the Hebrew scriptures. His commentaries used allegorical devices to penetrate the meaning of scripture. He developed the Greek doctrine of the *Logos* or Word of God into the status of 'a second God'. His speculations were widely studied by the early Christian fathers.

PHILOSOPHY OF RELIGION The branch of philosophy which investigates religious experience, considering its origin, context and value.

PHYLACTERIES See tephillin.

PILGRIMAGE A journey to a holy place, undertaken as a commemoration of a past event, as a celebration or as an act of penance (see also hajj). The goal might be a natural feature such as a sacred river or mountain, or the location of a miracle, revelation or theophany, or the tomb of a hero or saint.

PILGRIM FATHERS Puritan Christian group who left England for America in the *Mayflower* in AD 1620 and founded the colony of Plymouth, Massachusetts.

PLATO (around 427–347 BC) Greek philosopher and pupil of Socrates. He taught the theory of Forms or Ideas, which are eternal prototypes of the phenomena encountered in ordinary experience. Above all is the Form of the Good, which gives unity and value to all the forms. Plato also taught the immortality of the soul.

P.L. KYODAN ('Perfect Liberty Association') One of the new religions of Japan, founded in 1926. It is based on Shinto but accepts karma from Buddhism and teaches that the ancestors have an influence

on the lives of believers. Its motto is 'life is art' and it sponsors games centres and golf clubs as well as shrines and temples.

PLOTINUS (around AD 205–269) Egyptian philosopher and author of Neo-Platonism whose speculations influenced early Christianity. He dealt with the relationship between the world and the soul and blended Platonic teaching with oriental mysticism. His teachings influenced Augustine.

POLITICAL THEOLOGY Christian movement since the 1960s which stresses the solidarity of theology with the political struggles of oppressed peoples. Its origins are in Latin America but it has many European exponents and has been adopted by the World Council of Churches.

POLYTHEISM The belief in and worship of a variety of gods, who rule over various aspects of the world and life.

PONTIFEX High priest of Roman religion and member of a guild of priests whose president was the *pontifex maximus*. From the fifth century AD the title was applied to Christian bishops, usually the pope.

PONTIUS PILATE Roman procurator of the province of Judea AD 26–36 under whose authority Jesus of Nazareth was crucified. Tradition asserts that he killed himself but the Coptic Church reveres him as a Christian martyr.

POPE Bishop of Rome, Vicar of Christ and head of the Roman Catholic Church, regarded as the successor of Peter. Since the First Vatican Council his pronounce-ments on matters of faith and doctrine have been regarded as infallible.

POPOL VUH The sacred book of a large group of Mayan people. It contains mythology and traditions and dates of the kings of the Maya down to approximately AD 1550.

PORSEVIT Five-headed Slavic god from the island of Rügen.

POSEIDON Greek god of the seas and waters, usually presented as a tall bearded figure carrying a trident. He is responsible for sea storms and earthquakes and is also 'Lord of Horses'.

PRAYER The offering of worship, requests, confessions, or other communication to God or gods, publicly or privately, with or without words; often a religious obligation.

PRAYER WHEELS Wheels and cylinders used by Buddhists in Tibet and northern India. They are inscribed with the MANTRA: 'OM MANI PADME HUM', the powerful effect of which is multiplied as the wheels turn.

PREHISTORIC RELIGION RELIGIONS dating from the period before the development of writing. In the Middle East this is the period approximately up to 3000 BC.

PRESBYTER ('Elder') Term for a Christian minister used in the NEW TESTAMENT interchangeably with BISHOP. Later it was held that the authority of the presbyter (from which comes 'PRIEST') derived from the bishop.

PRESBYTERIAN CHURCHES REFORMED CHURCHES whose teachings and order of worship reflect Calvinism. They are governed by a pyramid of elected, representative courts.

PRIEST (1) One authorized to perform priestly functions including mediation between God or gods and man, the offering of SACRIFICE and the performance of RITUAL in many religions. (2) A Christian minister, the term deriving from PRESBYTER.

PRIMAL RELIGIONS Religious systems of tribal groups having no literary tradition. They are characterized by a belief in various spiritual forces behind natural phenomena, a reverence for ancestors and a tight-knit social system which is sanctioned and held in being by the power of common MYTHS.

PROGRESSIVE JUDAISM Term covering the Liberal and Reform movements which emerged in JUDAISM in nineteenth-century Europe. Both movements are critical of the Talmudic fundamentalism of ORTHODOX JUDAISM and welcome

scientific research on the Bible. They also tend to use the vernacular in worship and interpret the dietary laws more liberally than do the Orthodox.

PROPAGANDA, SACRED CONGREGATION OF Roman Catholic body concerned with MISSION in non-Christian countries. It dates from the COUNTER-REFORMATION.

PROPHET One who speaks for or as a mouthpiece of God or a god. (1) The Old Testament prophets were social and religious reformers of ISRAEL (3) and Judah and of the people of God in exile. It dates God's prospective judgement of Israel; they recalled the people to obedience to God, some offering a hope of a future vindication. (2) In ISLAM 'the Prophet' is MUHAMMAD who brings the word and judgement of God to a final utterance. The authority of the Prophet is an article of the MUSLIM confession of faith.

PROPHETS, THE The second division of the HEBREW BIBLE, including the histories and the prophetic books.

PROTESTANTISM Christian faith and order as based on the principles of the REFORMATION. It emphasizes the sole authority of the BIBLE; justification by faith; the priesthood of all believers. Since the nineteenth century it has embraced liberal trends which have stressed the subjective side of religion.

PSALM A sacred song or poem. The Book of Psalms in the BIBLE provides the basis for much Jewish and Christian worship.

PTAH The chief god of Memphis in ancient Egypt, usually depicted bearded, in mummified shape and carrying three sceptres. He was a creator god, the patron of craftsmen. Merged with Sokar and OSIRIS, he came to have a role in the rituals ensuring the survival of the dead.

PUJA ('Reverence') Refers particularly to temple worship in HINDUISM and to the keeping of rites and ceremonies prescribed by the Brahmins (see CASTE SYSTEM).

PUNCHAU The SUN GOD of the INCAS.

PURANAS Devotional texts used in Indian BHAKTI cults of VISHNU.

PURE LAND BUDDHISM Buddhist sect founded by a Chinese monk, Hui Yuan (AD 334–416). It was characterized by faith in the BODHISATTVA AMITABHA who was the creator of a 'pure land' in the west. Through faith his devotees hoped to be transported there after death.

PURGATORY In ROMAN CATHOLIC teaching, the temporary state of punishment and purification for the dead before their admission to heaven. Its existence was denied by the Protestant reformers.

PURIM ('Lots') Joyful Jewish festival celebrating the story of Esther, wife of the Persian king Xerxes, who defeated the anti-Jewish plot of the king's steward, Haman.

PYRAMID Type of Egyptian royal tomb, usually tapering to the top from a square base, constructed between about 2630 and 1640 BC.

PYTHAGORAS (about 570–500 BC) Greek philosopher, musician and mathematician who taught that number was the basis of reality and that mathematics offered insight into the invisible world. He was influenced by ORPHISM and taught REINCARNATION and a strict vegetarianism.

Q

QIYAS ('Analogy') Principle of Islamic lawmaking by which the answer to a problem may be inferred from the answer to an analogous problem in the QUR'AN or the SUNNA.

QUAKERS Members of the Religious Society of Friends which derives from a puritan group which formed around George Fox in the 1650s. They have no SACRAMENTS and no ordained ministry. Instead authority derives from the 'inner light of the living Christ' in each believer.

QUESTIONS OF KING MILINDA A Buddhist scripture in the form of a discussion between the Greek king Menander and a BHIKSHU called Nagasena.

QUETZALCOATL Mythological figure in MAYA and AZTEC religion. He may have been a king of a pre-Aztec civilization. He is associated with the rediscovery of the complex Mayan calendar. His name derives from the sacred Quetzal bird. In mythology he is a god of the air who descended to earth and taught men the arts of civilization. He opposed the practice of human SACRIFICE. His activities aroused the wrath of another deity and he fled in a boat made of serpent skin and he is often symbolized by a feathered serpent. The name Quetzalcoatl was given to the high priests of Aztec religion.

QUR'AN In ISLAM, the Word of God—the book of God's revelation to MUHAMMAD which was received as a faithful copy of the eternal Qur'an inscribed in heaven. The first three CALIPHS collected the material which was given final form under 'UTHMAN. The Qur'an has a significance for MUSLIMS which can be compared to that of CHRIST for CHRISTIANS.

QURAYSH The tribe of MUHAMMAD, who opposed his attack on idolatry because they were the traditional custodians of the KA'BA. They were defeated in Muhammad's attack on MECCA in AD 630.

R

RABBI ('My master') Jewish religious teacher and interpreter of the TORAH. In modern JUDAISM he or she is a minister to the community, a preacher and a leader of SYNAGOGUE worship.

RABBINIC JUDAISM The religion of the medieval RABBIS who expanded the interpretation of the TALMUD and produced authoritative codes of laws, responses, views and judgements, mostly in the form of correspondence with particular communities.

RADHA Wife of a cowherd in the MAHABHARATA who left her husband to become KRISHNA's mistress. The love of Krishna and Radha is a frequent theme of BHAKTI devotion where it is seen as a type of the love between God and man. The frank eroticism of the stories of Radha is not welcomed by all Hindus.

RADHAKRISHNAN, Sarvepalli (AD 1888–1975) Indian philosopher who became vice-president and then president of India. He taught that there is a basic unity of all religions and that HINDUISM is a useful meeting ground because of its breadth and tolerance.

RADICAL THEOLOGY (1) American movement of the 1960s seeking to reconstruct CHRISTIANITY on the basis of atheism. Its two tenets were that God had 'died' in human experience but that it was still possible to be a follower of JESUS OF NAZARETH. (2) Term sometimes used for theology committed to left-wing politics (see POLITICAL THEOLOGY).

RAGNARÖK The doom of the Norse gods, the end of the world order. ODIN and the gods ride out with the dead heroes of VALHALLA against LOKI and the hosts of HEL. The great wolf (see LOKI'S BROOD) swallows Odin and the whole creation is dissolved in fire. Out of the chaos emerges a new heaven and a new earth. There are Christian influences in some accounts of Ragnarök.

RAROHENGA The place of departed spirits, the UNDERWORLD, in Maori religion. (See HINENUIOTEPO.)

RAHULA Son of GAUTAMA the BUDDHA, by his wife Yashodara.

RAJNEESH, Bhagavan Shri See BHAGAVAN SHRI RAJNEESH.

RAMA The seventh incarnation of VISHNU according to HINDU tradition. His exploits in love and war are described in the RAMAYANA. He is the epitome of righteousness and moral virtue.

RAMADAN Islamic lunar month in which MUSLIMS are obliged to fast from food and water between sunrise and sunset. The old and sick, pregnant women and nursing mothers are exempt, though they are

expected, if possible, to make it up later.

RAMAKRISHNA (AD 1834–86) Hindu Brahmin (see CASTE SYSTEM) who taught that all religions are paths to the same goal. He laid the foundation of Hindu universalism. He was a devotee of KALI, though philosophically he adhered to the teaching of SHANKARA.

RAMAKRISHNA MISSION Indian religious order founded in 1897 by VIVEKANANDA. Its aims are to teach VEDANTA and to care for the sick and needy. It has dispensaries, libraries and welfare centres throughout India and has teaching branches in Europe and the USA.

RAMANUJA (died AD 1137) Indian philosopher who opposed SHANKARA's stress on the oneness of being and denied that the divine lord belonged to a lower order of reality. He believed God and the world were related like body and soul, inseparable but distinct. He was a devotee of VISHNU and believed in the validity of personal devotion to God.

RAMAYANA One of the two great epics of the HINDU scriptures, compiled in the second or first century BC. Ascribed to the sage Valmiki, it tells of the life of the AVATAR RAMA.

RAMMOHUN ROY (AD 1772–1833) HINDU reformer and founder of the BRAHMA SAMAJ in opposition to the idolatry of popular devotion. He believed the VEDAS taught MONOTHEISM, though he also used Christian and Muslim ideas.

RANGINUI and PAPATUANUKU The primeval parents in Maori religion. Ranginui was the sky and Papatuanuku the earth. Their seventy children led by TANE forced them apart and propped the sky up with poles.

RASTAFARIANISM Religious and political movement centred in the Caribbean. It is a cult of Ras Tafari, better known as Haile Selassie (AD 1892–1975), emperor of Ethiopia (1930–74). Rastafarians believe that all West Indians came from Ethiopia and will return there to liberation. They are distinguished by keeping their hair in 'dreadlocks' and by their use of cannabis in worship. They helped develop the *reggae* style of soul music, which they use to express their political and religious aspirations.

REBIRTH Buddhist modification of REINCARNATION in the light of the ANATTA teaching. As there is no SOUL (2), there is no reincarnation as such, but the karmic (see KARMA) residue of one's life and actions are reclothed in the attributes and qualities acquired in the previous life. After a while this karmic 'bundle' is reborn.

'RECITE . . .' The beginning of the passage in the QUR'AN which recounts the revelation of God to MUHAMMAD. The word means making vocal what has already been written.

REDEMPTION God's saving work of buying back or recovering what is his. In JUDAISM it refers to the restoration of ISRAEL; in CHRISTIANITY to the ransoming of sinners from the power of sin and death.

RED HATS Unreformed branch of TIBETAN BUDDHISM whose practices owe much to the former Tibetan religion of BÖN.

REFORMATION The movement within Western CHRISTIANITY between the fourteenth and the seventeenth centuries which led to the separation of the Protestant Churches from Rome. The main issue was the authority of the POPE but doctrinal issues such as the precise meaning of the EUCHARIST and the authority and accessibility of Scripture were also important.

REFORMED CHURCHES Churches which inherit the Calvinist tradition, including Presbyterians, Independents, Calvinistic Methodists and Congregationalists.

REINCARNATION The belief that individual souls survive death and are reborn to live again in a different body, thus passing through a series of lives. Held in pre-ARYAN India, the belief is associated with the doctrine of KARMA. Some traditions believe rebirth is possible only in human bodies; others envisage hellish or heavenly states, while others suggest a transmigration in which human souls are tied to animal or vegetable forms. Some Hindu apologists

explain the doctrine as a mythical way of speaking about the continuity of the human race.

REIYUKAI A NICHIREN Buddhist sect and one of the NEW RELIGIONS of Japan. Founded in 1925, it claims 3 million members.

RELICS Bones or remains of SAINTS, venerated and accredited with miraculous powers in many religions.

RELIGION (From Latin: *religare*, 'to bind, restrain') A system of belief and worship, held by a community who may express their religion through shared MYTHS, DOCTRINES, ethical teachings, RITUALS or the remembrance of special experiences.

RESURRECTION (1) The Christian belief that JESUS OF NAZARETH was raised from death by God the Father who thus vindicated him as MESSIAH and revealed his defeat of death and SIN. (2) The raising of all the dead for JUDGEMENT as taught in JUDAISM, CHRISTIANITY and ISLAM.

RIDA, Rashid (AD 1865–1935) Syrian author and editor of the SALAFIYA periodical *Al-Manat*. He led the Salafiya movement in Egypt and was critical of the secularism of Kemal ATATURK'S Turkish republic.

RINZAI ZEN School of ZEN which employs startling and sometimes violent techniques (e.g. KOAN) to induce SATORI.

RISHIS Great saints or holy men in Indian tradition, many of whom lived as recluses in the forest. The teaching written down in the VEDAS and UPANISHADS is attributed to them. Some are credited with supernatural powers.

RISSHOKO-SEIKAI An offshoot of the REIYUKAI movement which is spreading the teachings of NICHIREN Buddhism beyond the boundaries of Japan. The sect claims 1 million members.

RITES OF PASSAGE Religious ceremonies which mark the transition from one state of life to another. In many religions these transitional periods are felt to be dangerous and to require spiritual protection. Examples include birth rites,

INITIATION rites, marriage rites and funeral rites.

RITUAL Religious ceremonial performed according to a set pattern of words, movements and symbolic actions. Rituals may involve the dramatic re-enactment of ancient MYTHS featuring gods and heroes, performed to ensure the welfare of the community.

ROMA The personification of the city of Rome, worshipped by the Romans as a goddess.

ROMAN CATHOLIC Catholic CHRISTIAN who recognizes the authority of the POPE, the bishop of Rome.

RONGO Maori god of agriculture and peace.

ROSENSWEIG, Franz (AD 1886–1929) Jewish interpreter of the relationship between JUDAISM and CHRISTIANITY. He believed that both faiths manifested one truth. JEWS were witnesses to the holiness of God and were called to live as a distinct community. Christians were to be missionaries, spreading the call of God to all people.

ROSH HASHANAH The Jewish New Year, celebrated as the anniversary of creation. The liturgy is penitential in tone and looks forward to the KINGDOM OF GOD and the MESSIAH. The blowing of the ram's horn proclaims God as king of the universe.

ROSICRUCIANISM Mystical system founded in seventeenth-century Germany and based on an account of a secret brotherhood founded 'to improve mankind by the discovery of the true philosophy'. Several societies came into being based on this originally fictitious 'Meritorious Order of the Rosy Cross' with its private language and magical alphabet. They applied themselves to studies such as ALCHEMY.

RSS/RAHTRIYA SWAYAMSEVAK SANGH ('National self-rule community') Right-wing Hindu political party founded in 1925. It has consistently opposed any separation of the Indian state from Hindu religion.

RTA The cosmic order as understood in the Hindu VEDAS. It is the principle of ethical and physical organization throughout the universe and is the work of the sky god VARUNA.

RUDRA ('The red one') Indian god of destruction in Vedic times (see VEDAS) who was thought to live in the mountains and work with healing herbs. He may be an early version of SHIVA.

RUGIEVIT Slavic god with seven faces from the island of Rügen.

RUMI, Jalal al-Din (Died AD 1273) Sufi MYSTIC and poet, author of the *Mathnavi* and founder of a DERVISH order. He was a nature mystic and often used love and wine as allegories of the experience of the divine.

RUSSELL, Charles Taze (AD 1852–1916) US Bible scholar who started a periodical called *Zion's Watchtower* after being influenced by speculation about the return of CHRIST. This grew into the JEHOVAH'S WITNESSES movement.

RUSSIAN ORTHODOX CHURCH The principal church of Russia since AD 988.

RYOBU SHINTO A Japanese synthesis of BUDDHISM and SHINTO which was evolved in the Heian period (AD 794–1185). The Shinto gods were identified with BODHISATTVAS and AMATERASU with the BUDDHA VAIROCANA. A Buddhist sanctuary was attached to Shinto shrines.

S

SAADYA BEN JOSEPH (AD 892–940) Head of the Jewish academy at Susa in Babylon. He defended the cause of Talmudic JUDAISM (see TALMUD) against the KARAITES and the doctrine of the oneness of God against the Christian TRINITY. He was the first Jewish systematic theologian and he believed in the unity and divine origin of both revelation and reason.

SABBATH Jewish day of worship and rest lasting from Friday sunset to Saturday sunset. The Sabbath is holy because it commemorates God's rest on the seventh day of creation and reminds JEWS of the deliverance from Egypt.

SACRAMENT 'An outward and visible sign of an inward and spiritual grace' (*Book of Common Prayer*). REFORMED CHURCHES count only BAPTISM and the EUCHARIST as sacraments, both being instituted by CHRIST. Roman Catholic and Orthodox Churches add CONFIRMATION, marriage, ORDINATION, penance and extreme unction (the anointing of the sick).

SACRED BEARS In PREHISTORIC RELIGION ritual veneration of the slain bear. It remains common, especially in Arctic and sub-Arctic regions. The Japanese Ainu tribe have bear rituals, as do the Lapps, Finns, Eskimos and North American Indians. Eskimo SHAMANS receive the Great Spirit disguised as a Polar bear. Bear worship is frequently associated with the recognition of the constellation *Ursa Major*; MYTHS concerning the constellation are found among the Greeks and other European and Asian peoples.

SACRED BIRDS Often a symbol of transformation. In Greek mythology ZEUS disguises himself as a swan in pursuit of amorous adventures. The CELTS revere the swan as a symbol of divine transformation and also recognize ravens as appearances of war goddesses (see MORRIGHAN). South and Central American Indians venerate the plumed quetzal (see also QUETZALCOATL). The mythical phoenix of Arabia symbolized the cycle of death and rebirth, the ancient

Egyptians finding in the similar benu a manifestation of the god Re-Atum worshipped at Heliopolis. A bird often symbolizes the departing SOUL freed from the shackles of earthly life. In the BIBLE, the HOLY SPIRIT is described as being like a dove.

SACRED BULLS Symbols of power and strength. They were connected with the worship of the MOTHER GODDESS, especially in the MINOAN RELIGION of ancient Crete where they gave rise to the MYTH of the Minotaur, a bull-like monster who had to be placated with human sacrifices. The slaughter of a bull (see TAUROBOLIUM) was important in some forms of Roman religion.

SACRED SNAKES Frequently associated with the MOTHER GODDESS, especially in MINOAN RELIGION. Because they shed their skin they are symbols of immortality. They are also associated with wisdom and healing (see ASCLEPIOS). In Chinese religion dragons replace snakes as sacred animals. In Norse mythology a Great Serpent, son of the evil LOKI, surrounds the earth. In CHRISTIANITY the snake is a symbol of evil and deceit, especially connected with the biblical MYTH of the Garden of Eden.

SACRED THREAD CEREMONY INITIATION ceremony performed on upper-caste HINDU boys. A sacred thread is placed around the neck indicating that the boy is one of the twice-born and has entered the first-stage of life. (See also NAUJOTE.)

SACRED TREES Objects of religious significance since they connect the earth to the sky. In Celtic religion tree species were sacred to particular tribes: Irish literature speaks of a sacred ash, a yew and an oak, among others. The connection of DRUIDS with the oak is likely but unproved. (See also YGGDRASIL.)

SACRED WELLS Springs, rivers and natural wells often have religious significance, particularly in Celtic religion. Regarded as passages to the UNDERWORLD, votive offerings such as brooches, bracelets and even severed human heads were deposited there. The custom of throwing coins into water may reflect these ancient practices.

SACRIFICE The ritual offering of animal or vegetable life to establish communion between humans and a god or gods.

SADDUCEES Aristocratic Jewish party which emerged in the times of the MACCABEES. They rejected the oral law and late doctrines like the RESURRECTION. They were nationalists and collaborated with the Romans to ensure the survival of the Jewish state. The party collapsed after AD 70.

SAFAVID DYNASTY See ISMAIL SAFAVI.

SAI BABA (Born AD 1926) Spiritual teacher from Brindavan in south India who is regarded by his followers as an AVATAR. Probably the most popular and influential GURU in present-day India, he specializes in curing illness and materializing gifts for his disciples.

SAINT (1) Holy person or dead hero of faith who is venerated by believers on earth and held to be a channel of divine blessing. The Protestant reformers rejected the practice of devotion to saints. (2) In the NEW TESTAMENT and some Protestant Churches, a term for any believer.

SALAFIYA Puritan Islamic party which emerged in nineteenth-century Egypt. It accepted the authority only of the QUR'AN and the SUNNA and rejected the 'ULAMA'. In time it grew closer to the WAHHABI MOVEMENT. It published a journal *Al-Manat* which circulated in the Middle East. (See also RIDA, RASHID.)

SALAT Islamic ritual prayer which is carried out five times a day, facing MECCA and using ritual movements to accompany the words. Salat is one of the FIVE PILLARS OF ISLAM.

SALVATION (1) In the BIBLE, deliverance of God's people from their enemies, and especially from SIN and its consequences, death and HELL; hence also the whole process of forgiveness, new life and final glorification for the believer. (2) In eastern religions, release from the changing material world to identification with the ABSOLUTE.

SAMHAIN Celtic festival marking the beginning of winter, celebrated on 1 November with feasting and carousals. Regarded as a period outside the normal flow of time when the dead could freely return to communicate with the living, it was the subject of many MYTHS and legends, mainly concerning death.

SAMPY Madagascan term for a sacred cult object in which the power and particularity of the people is thought to reside (see TOTEMISM).

SAMSARA ('Stream of existence') Sanskrit word which refers to the cycle of birth and death followed by rebirth as applied both to individuals and to the universe itself.

SANCTUARY A place consecrated to a god, a holy place, a place of divine refuge and protection. Also, the holiest part of a sacred place or building. Historically, in some cultures, a holy place where pursued criminals or victims were guaranteed safety.

SANGHA Community of Buddhist MONKS which started with the BUDDHA's first disciples. The functions of the sangha are to promote through its own lifestyle the best conditions for attaining individual salvation and to teach the DHAMMA to mankind.

SANHEDRIN Jewish supreme council of seventy which organized religious life during the period of independence following the revolt of the MACCABEES. Under Herod the Great the Sanhedrin was divided: the SADDUCEES dealt with political matters; the PHARISEES concentrated on the interpretation of the TORAH. After the FALL OF JERUSALEM (AD 70) an academic Sanhedrin was organized in Jabneh to reorganize Jewish life.

SANNYASI ('One who renounces') The last of the Hindu FOUR STAGES OF LIFE.

SANSKRIT The language of the ARYAN peoples and of the HINDU scriptures. It is an Indo-European language related to Latin, Greek and Persian.

SARIPUTTA One of the BUDDHA's principal disciples, described as the 'Captain of the DHAMMA'.

SATAN In the BIBLE, the personification of evil and identified with the DEVIL.

SATANISM Worship of SATAN or experimentation with evil spirits, which may include the perversion of religious RITUALS, as in a black mass, WITCHCRAFT, or a variety of pseudo-religious and ecstatic practices.

SATGURU See DIVINE LIGHT MISSION.

SATORI ENLIGHTENMENT in ZEN Buddhism.

SATURNALIA Roman festival of Saturn, a mythical king of Rome and father of the god JUPITER, which began on 17 December. A time of banquets and present-giving, some of its characteristics were transferred to the festival of CHRISTMAS.

SAULE Latvian sun goddess.

SAUM See FIVE PILLARS OF ISLAM.

SCHISM A deliberate division or split between Christians which disrupts the unity of the CHURCH.

SCIENTOLOGY Religious philosophy based on the teaching of L. Ron HUBBARD. It teaches development through personality counselling and mind-training, the aim of which is the 'clearing' of the individual and the recognition of his immortal nature.

SCRIBES Officials who organized the religious life of the Jewish community after the EXILE of 586 BC. They regulated the observance of the SABBATH, communal prayer and fasting and were the interpreters of the Law. One of their tasks was to develop 'fences' around the TORAH to prevent its infringement.

SCRIPTURE Writings which are believed to be divinely inspired or especially authoritative within a particular religious community.

SECOND COMING/PAROUSIA The personal second coming of CHRIST which, Christians believe, will be a time of judgement and the inauguration of the KINGDOM OF GOD in its fulness.

SECT SHINTO Term applied to new religious movements and associations in Japan, especially before 1945 when, to be legal, NEW RELIGIONS had to conform to SHINTO patterns.

SEFIROT According to the teachings of Jewish Kabbalistic MYSTICISM (see KABBALAH), the potencies and attributes by which God acts and makes himself known.

SEPHARDIM One of the two main cultural groups in JUDAISM which emerged during the Middle Ages. Sephardic JEWS lived in Spain and Portugal and their traditions go back to Babylonian Jewry. They developed Ladino as their language.

SERAPIS State god of Ptolemaic Egypt whose worship spread throughout the Mediterranean. He took over many characteristics from the ancient Egyptian OSIRIS, but was also associated with the bull god Apis, in turn associated with PTAH. He was both a healing god and a ruler of the UNDERWORLD.

SETH The evil brother of OSIRIS in Egyptian mythology. He murdered his brother and seized his earthly rule until in turn defeated by HORUS. He became the god of war, storms, deserts and disorder.

SEVEN PRECEPTS OF THE SONS OF NOAH The obligations placed on all men and women, regardless of race or faith, according to Jewish teaching. They comprise abstinence from idolatry, blasphemy, incest, murder, theft and the eating of living flesh, and the implementation of justice.

SEVENTH DAY ADVENTISTS Christian sect which emerged from a number of nineteenth-century groups stressing the imminent return of CHRIST. They observe the Jewish SABBATH instead of Sunday. They accept the BIBLE as infallible and require a lifestyle of strict temperance.

SEVERED HEADS A recurring motif in Celtic art and legend. Carvings of human heads are common and niches containing skulls have been found in many Celtic sanctuaries and at the bottom of ancient wells. These probably reflect a tradition of human sacrifice. In legend, severed heads can often talk and distil wisdom.

SHAH WALI ALLAH (AD 1702–62) Indian Sufi writer and teacher (see SUFISM), who led a reform movement aimed at broadening ISLAM into a kind of universal HUMANISM.

SHAIVISM Worship of the Hindu god SHIVA. It is particularly strong in southern India and appeals to extreme ascetics. From Shaivite texts have come the strongest affirmations of MONOTHEISM within HINDUISM.

SHAKTI ('Energy', 'power') A feminine word, particularly associated with SHIVA and his consorts (see KALI; PARVATI; DURGA). In TANTRISM shakti is universal creativity and exists in man as a latent energy which is located at the base of his spine (see KUNDALINI). In tantric YOGA this energy is awakened to travel up the spine and unite with Shiva who is present as mind.

SHAKYAMUNI ('The wise man of the SHAKYAS') One of the names of the BUDDHA.

SHAKYAS Tribe to which the BUDDHA's family belonged. They occupied territory in the Himalayan foothills.

SHAMAN (1) An ecstatic priest-magician among the Tungu people of Siberia. (2) By extension, a similar figure in other PRIMAL RELIGIONS and ancient religions (see also CHILAN). The shaman induces a trance experience in which he is believed to leave his body and visit other worlds. This enables him to convey sacrifices to the gods, to escort the dead to their destination and to return with divine prophecies.

SHAMASH Babylonian sun god and lord of justice who rewards honesty and loyalty and brings retribution on the wicked. He is depicted as giving a ring and sceptre to the lawgiver HAMMURABI.

SHAMMAI See HILLEL.

SHANGO Storm god of the Yoruba people of Nigeria. His symbol is an axe and his sacred animal a ram. Reverence for Shango has travelled to the Caribbean, Haiti and South America where he has a place in VOODOO cults.

SHANKARA (AD 788–820) The best known exponent of classical HINDU philosophy. Developing the thought of the UPANISHADS he declared that only the eternal being is real; the diverse, phenomenal world is an illusion of MAYA. Even the notion of a personal God is part of maya. Liberation comes from realizing oneness with the ABSOLUTE, which is defined as Being, Consciousness and Bliss. (See also VEDANTA (2).)

SHARI'A ('The path') Body of law for the MUSLIM community which derives from the QUR'AN, the SUNNA and other sources, the legitimacy of which is debated in the different schools of law. Shari'a is regarded as divinely authoritative.

SHAVUOT See WEEKS.

SHAYK Sufi spritual teacher (see SUFISM), somewhat analogous to the Hindu GURU.

SHEKINAH The presence or manifestation of God as described in the TARGUMS and later Jewish writings. It came to refer to the indwelling of God in creation. In KABBALAH the Shekinah is exiled from the eternity of God, EN SOF, because of the SIN of man and will only be restored at the final REDEMPTION.

SHEMA The Jewish confession of faith, recited in the morning and evening service. 'Shema' is the opening word in HEBREW of the confession: 'Hear, O Israel, the Lord our God, the Lord is One . . .' Three passages from the TORAH confirm that there is one God and that Israel is chosen to witness to him.

SHI'A/SHI'ITES The minority group in ISLAM, comprising ten per cent of MUSLIMS. They reject the first three CALIPHS, believing 'ALI to be MUHAMMAD's true successor. They also hold that authority resides in the IMAMS(2) who are the infallible messengers of God in every age. The Shi'a live mostly in Iraq, Iran, Lebanon, Pakistan and India. The two main Shi'a divisions are the ISMA'ILIS and the TWELVERS.

SHINGON 'True Word' sect of Japanese Buddhism founded in the ninth century AD and characterized by a complex sacramental and magical ritual which may have been influenced by TANTRISM and by indigenous SHINTO practices.

SHINRAN (AD 1173–1263) Disciple of HONEN and founder of the Japanese Buddhist sect JODO SHINSHU.

SHINTO The indigenous nature religion of Japan which has provided a focus for nationalistic aspirations. (See also AMATERASU; EMPEROR, JAPANESE; IZANAGI; JIMMU TENNO; JINJA; KAMI; KOJIKI; MATSURI; NIHONGI; NINIGI.)

SHIRK ('Associating') In ISLAM the greatest SIN, that of ascribing equals to God. (See also TAUHID.)

SHIVA One of the great gods of HINDU devotion. He is a god of contrasts, presiding over creation and destruction, fertility and asceticism, good and evil. He is the original Lord of the Dance who dances out the creation of the universe. As god of ascetics he is portrayed as a great YOGI, smeared with ashes, holding the world in being through meditation. His symbol is a phallus-shaped pillar denoting procreation.

SHOTOKU, PRINCE Japanese ruler who introduced BUDDHISM as the state religion. During his reign (AD 593–621) he built a Buddhist academy and temple near the state capital at Nara.

SHUDRAS See CASTE SYSTEM.

SHULCHAN ARUCH See KARO, JOSEPH.

SIDDHARTA Personal name of GAUTAMA the BUDDHA.

SIKH ('Disciple') Follower of the Sikh religion which developed in the fifteenth century AD in North India as a synthesis of ISLAM and HINDUISM. (See also ADI GRANTH; GOBINDH SINGH; GURDWARA; KABIR; KHALSA; NANAK; SINGH.)

SIN (1) An action which breaks a divine law. (2) The state of rebellion against God which, in Christian teaching, has been man's state since the Fall of Adam and his expulsion from the Garden of Eden.

SIN Babylonian moon-god and guardian of the city of Ur. He usually appears riding on a winged bull. He is the father of the sun, SHAMASH, and god of vegetation.

SINAI, MOUNT Mountain in the south of the Sinai peninsula where, according to tradition, God revealed himself to MOSES and gave him the Ten Commandments.

SINGH Surname used by SIKHS. It means 'lion' and expresses the militant stance which Guru GOBINDH SINGH impressed upon the Sikh community.

SITA Consort of RAMA in Hindu tradition.

SKANDHA/KHANDHA Term referring to the five factors which compound human personality according to Buddhist teaching. They are form, sense perception, consciousness, intellectual power and discrimination. The relation between them is continuously changing in accordance with the action of KARMA.

SKILFUL MEANS Buddhist practice of compassion in sharing the DHAMMA with the unenlightened. Tradition describes the BUDDHA explaining the Dhamma at different levels to different people. In the LOTUS SUTRA tricks and deceptions are among the skilful means employed to lead the lost to salvation.

SMITH, Joseph (AD 1805–44) Founder of MORMONISM who claimed to be the recipient of a divine revelation to the former inhabitants of America in the form of golden plates inscribed in ancient languages. With the help of the ANGEL Moroni, he translated these and they became the basis of the BOOK OF MORMON. Ordained priest by the heavenly messenger, he founded the Church of Jesus Christ of Latter-Day Saints in 1830. He died at the hands of a mob.

SMITH, William Robertson (AD 1846–94) Scottish theologian and philosopher of religion who

developed the study of comparative religion with his own researches into the religion of Semitic peoples.

SOCRATES (469–399 BC) Greek philosopher and teacher and mentor of PLATO. He taught by a method of question and answer which sought to elicit a consistent and rational response and hence to arrive at a universally agreed truth. He was executed in Athens for corrupting the youth and introducing strange gods.

SÖDERBLOM, Nathan (AD 1866–1931) Swedish theologian and philosopher of religion who developed the study of comparative religion with his own researches into ZOROASTRIANISM.

SOKA GAKKAI 'Value-creating society' of lay members of the Japanese Buddhist sect NICHIREN. It was founded in 1930 in a wave of new cults. It is evangelistic, exclusive and highly organized. It runs its own political party and has schools and a university.

SOL INVICTUS ('Unconquered sun') A name for MITHRA. From the time of the emperor Aurelian (AD 270–275) until displaced by CHRISTIANITY, his was the official imperial cult of Rome.

SOMA The juice of the Indian *soma* plant which may have been fermented or had hallucinogenic properties. It was drunk by gods and men in the VEDAS and was regarded as a mediating god with power over all plants and as a conveyer of immortality.

SORCERER A practitioner of harmful MAGIC. In PRIMAL RELIGIONS sorcerers are sometimes believed to be able to kill others through magic.

SOTO ZEN School of ZEN Buddhism which teaches a gradual and gentle way to SATORI.

SOUL (1) The immortal element of an individual man or woman which survives the death of the body in most religious teachings. (2) A human being when regarded as a spiritual being.

SPELL A formula of words with or without accompanying RITUAL actions which is believed to have the power to manipulate natural or supernatural forces for good or evil ends. The exact form of the spell is often the secret possession of the SORCERER or tribal leader.

SPIRITUALISM Any religious system or practice which has the object of establishing communication with the dead. Most modern spiritualist churches derive from a movement which grew up in mid-nineteenth-century America. Spiritualists seek to communicate with the dead through such means as table-turning and automatic writing. All mainstream Christian churches denounce the practices of spiritualism.

SHRI AUROBINDO (AD 1872–1950) HINDU intellectual and nationalist who attempted a synthesis of Indian and Western thought based on the theory of evolution. He also developed Integral Yoga as a system of YOGA teachings acceptable to East and West.

STEINER, Rudolf (AD1861–1925) Founder of ANTHROPOSOPHY. He originally followed THEOSOPHY and ROSICRUCIANISM but he broke with these groups and developed his mystical ideas into an educational, ecological and medical programme for spiritual progress. He founded a number of highly successful schools which today cater for some 40,000 pupils.

STOICISM Philosophical school founded by Zeno of Citium (approximately 335–263 BC) and named after the porch or *stoa* where he taught in Athens. Stoics believed that the world order reflected the divine intelligence. Men could attain virtue—harmony with the universe—by learning self-sufficiency and behaving with courage and self-control.

STONEHENGE Megalithic monument (see MEGALITHS) on Salisbury Plain, England. It may have been a sanctuary for sun worship or regulated an agricultural and astrological calendar.

STUPA A mound built up to mark a Buddhist holy place or collection of relics. Many stupas in India date from the reign of king ASOKA.

SUBUD Spiritual teaching of the Javanese Muslim teacher Pak Subuh (born AD 1901). It emphasizes submission to the Life Force through a course of spiritual training designed to open up the individual to the reality of GOD and to mastery over the lower nature. The Subud training is open to members of all faiths.

SUFISM Islamic mystical movement originating in the eighth century AD as a reaction to the worldliness of the UMAYYAD DYNASTY. Sufis claimed direct experience of ALLAH through ascetic practices. The orthodox rejected them at first but today Sufi orders are accepted among SUNNIS and SHI'A. (See also ISLAM.)

SUKKOT See BOOTHS.

SUN DANCE Four-day ceremony which grew up among North American Plains Indians in the 1870s as a reaction against white attempts to break up the traditions and beliefs of the people. It was held in the summer inside an immense circular area. The ceremony was crushed by the US army and regulations were imposed against such PAGAN rituals.

SUN-GOD In the INCA religion, the creator of MANCO CAPAC, the first Inca and father to all the Inca rulers. His names include Inti and Punchau.

SUNNA ('Trodden path') The source of authority in Islamic lawmaking which is second only to the QUR'AN. It refers to the words and actions of MUHAMMAD and, in a lesser degree, to the words and actions of the first four CALIPHS.

SUNNI The majority group in ISLAM, comprising ninety per cent of MUSLIMS. They accept the authority of the FOUR RIGHTLY GUIDED CALIPHS and the developed process of law-making guided by the community's legal experts. Sunni Muslims live in the Arab states, in North, West and East Africa and in India and Indonesia.

SUTTA PITAKA The most important collection of THERAVADA Buddhist SCRIPTURES. It consists of sermons of the BUDDHA including the DHAMMAPADA.

SUZUKI, Daisetz T. (AD 1870–1966) Japanese ZEN scholar who

played a major part in introducing Zen Buddhism to the western world. He was a member of the RINZAI sect and was sympathetic to CHRISTIANITY.

SVANTEVIT Slavic god with four heads, from the island of Rügen.

SVETAMBARAS ('White-clad') Members of a major JAIN sect who rejected the DIGAMBARAS' stress on the virtues of nudity. They are numerous in the north of India.

SWAMI General term for a HINDU holy man or member of a religious order.

SWEDENBORG, Emanuel (AD 1688–1772) Swedish scientist who became a MYSTIC and visionary. He taught a kind of pantheistic THEOSOPHY (see PANTHEISM) centred on Jesus Christ in whom he found a Trinity of Love, Wisdom and Energy. He founded the New Church.

SYNAGOGUE Jewish meeting place for worship and study. Synagogues grew out of the TORAH schools of the SCRIBES during the EXILE. After the destruction of the TEMPLE OF JERUSALEM (AD 70), synagogues became the centres of Jewish life. They are built to face JERUSALEM and contain an ARK(2) in which the scrolls of the law are displayed before a perpetual lamp. Worship in synagogues includes readings from the *Torah*, psalms, sermons and communal prayers.

SYNCRETISM The growing together of two or more religions making a new development in religion which contains some of the beliefs and practices of both.

T

TABERNACLES, FESTIVAL OF
See BOOTHS.

TABOO Polynesian word applied to
an object, place or person which is
prohibited because of its holy or
dangerous character. It may include
the sense of being 'marked off' and
therefore separate from everyday
usage.

T'AI CHI The 'absolutely
transcendent' in Chinese philosophy.
The working of T'ai chi in the
production of the YIN AND YANG is
represented by a circle divided into
complementary pear-shaped light
and dark halves.

TALLIT Jewish prayer shawl,
fringed at the four corners and used
during morning prayer and on YOM
KIPPUR.

TALMUD The written
interpretation and development of
the HEBREW scriptures. It is based on
the MISHNAH of JUDAH HA NASI with
the addition of some excluded
teachings and commentary recorded
from the debates and controversies of
the Schools of Babylon on Palestine.
There are two versions: the
Palestinian, compiled while the Jews
were under duress from the Christian
Church, and the Babylonian which is
more detailed and complete.

TAMMUZ Babylonian/Syrian
fertility deity. A young god who, in
mythology, died and was resurrected
after the pattern of the Egyptian
OSIRIS.

TANE/TANENUIARANGI The
creator of vegetation and vanquisher
of darkness in Maori religion.

TANGAROA Maori god of fishes
and the sea.

TANGENY Madagascan ceremony
of giving poison to one accused of a
crime to establish his guilt or
innocence.

TANGIHANGA Maori word for a
funeral gathering.

TANHA ('Craving') The main cause
of suffering as analysed by the
BUDDHA in the FOUR NOBLE TRUTHS.

TANTRISM Tibetan Buddhist
practices which aim at direct
experience of the enlightened self
through symbols, visual images,
repetition of sounds, prescribed
movements, breath control and
ritualized sexual intercourse.

TAO ('Way') In TAOISM, the
underlying principle of reality.

TAOISM Chinese philosophy
outlined in the TAO TE CHING. Its aim is
to achieve harmony with all that is by
pursuing inaction and effortlessness.
Taoism gradually evolved an
elaborate mythological system and
incorporated notions of spirit
possession, ALCHEMY and DIVINATION.
(See also CHANG TAO LING; JADE
EMPEROR; LAO-TZU.)

TAOISM Chinese philosophy
outlined in the TAO TE CHING.

TAO TE CHING Chinese religious
work compiled in the fourth century
BC and ascribed to LAO-TZU, though it
is probably the work of several
writers. It describes the TAO as the
underlying principle of reality which
can only be attained to by passivity.

TARGUM An Aramaic translation
of a HEBREW scripture reading. The
translator was expected to make a free
interpretation. Some of these have
become famous in their own right
and are used by pious JEWS alongside
the appointed text.

TAROT CARDS Set of seventy-
eight cards marked with various
symbolic figures which are shuffled
and dealt as a form of DIVINATION.

TARTARUS Probably an early
name for the Greek god of the
UNDERWORLD, replaced later by
HADES. Tartarus came to signify a
place below the realm of Hades where
particularly wicked men and gods
were sent to be punished. (Compare
HELL.)

TATHAGATA ('One who has
succeeded') Title of the BUDDHA
found particularly in popular
MAHAYANA texts.

TAT TVAM ASI ('Thou that art')
Phrase from the UPANISHADS which
expresses the claim that BRAHMAN, the
divine power sustaining the universe,
and ATMAN, the soul, are one.

TAUHID ('Asserting oneness') The
essential MUSLIM doctrine of the unity
of God. He is oneness in himself
without parts or partners.

TAUROBOLIUM Rite in Roman
religion where initiates entered a pit
over which a bull was slaughtered;
they washed themselves in and drank
the blood. This gave them
participation in the life and strength
of the bull (see also SACRED BULLS).
This ritual slaughter is often wrongly
attributed to Mithraists. It featured in
initiation into the cult of CYBELE and
gave a guarantee of rebirth for twenty
years.

TAWHIRIMATEA Maori god of
winds and hurricanes.

TE AOMARAMA The world of
light and reality in the Maori
CREATION MYTH.

TEPHILLIN ('Phylacteries') Small
boxes containing scriptural texts
written on parchment. They are worn
by JEWS on the head and arm during
daily prayer.

TEMPLE Building designed for
WORSHIP of God or gods, usually
containing a SANCTUARY or holy place
where SACRIFICE may be offered.

TEMPLE OF HEAVEN Great
Chinese temple in Peking where the
Chinese emperors received the
mandate of heaven (see T'IEN) to rule
over the Chinese people. It is still
used for great state occasions.

**TEMPLE OF JERUSALEM/
HOLY TEMPLE** TEMPLE first built
by Solomon on a site bequeathed by
DAVID. It was divided into the Holy
Place and the Holy of Holies where
dwelt the presence of YHWH. This
temple was destroyed in 586 BC. The
second temple was dedicated in 515
BC. It was desecrated by the
Hellenistic Seleucid king Antiochus
Epiphanes but rededicated by JUDAS
MACCABEUS. Rebuilding was begun
under Herod the Great in 20 BC. The
temple was virtually completed in AD
62 but destroyed by Titus in AD 70.

TENDAI Japanese Buddhist sect
based on a former Chinese sect,
T'ien-t'ai, and founded in the ninth
century AD. Tendai was an attempt at
a synthesis between MAHAYANA

teachings which stressed MEDITATION and those that stressed devotion.

TENGRI The supreme god of the Mongols. It was also used as a collective name for gods.

TENRIKYO 'Religion of Heavenly Wisdom' founded in Japan by MIKI NAKAYAMA, and based at the city of Tenri near Nara at the site of the founder's home. This is believed to be the centre of the world and it is the place of divine homecoming for the sect's 2 million adherents.

TE PO Primeval chaos and darkness according to the Maori CREATION MYTH.

TETRAGRAMMATON See YHWH.

TEUTATES, ESUS and TARANIS Gaulish gods mentioned by the Roman writer Lucan (AD 39–65). They required to be appeased by bloody sacrifices. Teutates in particular may have been a god of war, healing and fertility and the guardian of his people.

TEZCATLIPOCA ('That which causes the Black Mirror to shine') Aztec god of night and the north, a magician, symbolized by a jaguar. He was one of the most important of the Aztec gods.

THEISM The belief in one supreme GOD who is both TRANSCENDENT and involved in the workings of the universe.

THEOCRACY ('Divine government') Term describing a state which is constituted on the basis of divine law. It is an important concept in ISLAM where it is sometimes believed that the law of the land should be identical with the SHARI'A. The regime of CALVIN in Geneva was also theocratic.

THEOLOGY (1) A systematic formulation of belief made by or on behalf of a particular individual or CHURCH or other body of believers. (2) The critical study of RELIGION, particularly CHRISTIANITY, with regard to its origins, SCRIPTURES and other texts, DOCTRINES, ethics, history and practices.

THEOPHANY A divine appearance, revelation or manifestation, usually inducing awe and terror in those who witness it. Examples are the appearance of God to MOSES on Mt SINAI amidst thunder, lightning, smoke and trumpet blasts; the appearance of KRISHNA in his divine form 'like a thousand suns' as described in the BHAGAVAD GITA.

THEOSOPHY ('Divine wisdom') A term applied to various mystical movements but which refers particularly to the principles of the Theosophical Society founded by Madame BLAVATSKY in 1875. These comprise a blend of Hindu, Buddhist and Christian ideas, together with particular stress on REINCARNATION, immortality and the presence of GOD in all things. Theosophists also believe in a series of World Teachers who are incarnated to express the divine wisdom.

THERAVADA ('The doctrine of the elders') The form of BUDDHISM practised in Sri Lanka, Burma, Thailand, Kampuchea/Cambodia and Laos, which sticks firmly to the teachings of the VINAYA PITAKA and rejects the doctrine of BODHISATTVAS.

THIRTEEN PRINCIPLES Articles of Jewish faith which were formulated by Moses MAIMONIDES in the twelfth century AD. They assert faith in God as creator, as formless unity, First and Last and only hearer of prayer. They also affirm the words of the PROPHETS, MOSES as the chief of the prophets, the unchanging nature of TORAH, the Creator's knowledge of men, the judgement, the coming of the MESSIAH and the RESURRECTION of the dead. The Thirteen Principles are found in the Jewish Prayer Book.

THOMAS, John See CHRISTADELPHIANS.

THOR Norse god of thunder and lightning. He is portrayed as wild and red-haired, wielding a great hammer. The son of Mother Earth, his wife Sif is a corn goddess. He is associated with agriculture and is the protector of MIDGARD against the giants.

THOTH Ibis-headed Egyptian god, patron of writing and counting, who recorded the weighing of souls in the judgement after death.

THREE BODY DOCTRINE MAHAYANA Buddhist teaching that the BUDDHA exists in three aspects. His human existence was his 'transformation body'. In his celestial existence he appears in his 'enjoyment body'. But the ultimate basis of his Buddhahood is his 'truth body' which unites all three bodies. This is identified with ultimate reality.

THREE REFUGES Brief dedication used by Buddhists and traditionally given by the BUDDHA himself: 'I take refuge in the Buddha; I take refuge in the DHAMMA; I take refuge in the SANGHA.'

THUNDERBIRD A totem (see TOTEMISM) found widely among North American Indians. It represents the eagle, the great bird of the eastern doorway of the world. It also represents thunder spirits who bring rain; the clap of his wings sounds the thunder and the flash of his eyes symbolizes lightning. The Thunderbird is frequently found at the top of Indian TOTEM POLES.

TIBETAN BOOK OF THE DEAD Book of instructions and preparations for death and the rites to be performed for the dying. In TIBETAN BUDDHISM the dying must train in advance, helped by a spiritual teacher, to face the clear light of the Void, reality itself, in such a way as to avoid REBIRTH or at least to ensure a human rebirth.

TIBETAN BUDDHISM/ VAJRAYANA/LAMAISM A mixture of BUDDHISM, TANTRISM and the ancient BÖN religion of Tibet. The two main groups are the RED HATS and the YELLOW HATS. (See also CHAKRAS; CHORTEN; DALAI LAMA; LAMA; MANDALA; PANCHEN LAMA; PRAYER WHEELS; TIBETAN BOOK OF THE DEAD.)

T'IEN ('Heaven') Chinese term sometimes used for the supreme GOD. From around 1000 BC the Chinese emperors were believed to rule by the mandate of heaven.

TILAK, B.G. (AD 1856–1920) Militant Hindu nationalist who wanted to turn India into a great HINDU nation. He provoked non-Hindus to violence, interpreting the BHAGAVAD GITA as a call to arms in the name of Hindu religion.

TIPITAKA The 'three baskets' of the BUDDHA'S teaching, the canon of SCRIPTURE for THERAVADA Buddhists, comprising the VINAYA PITAKA, the SUTTA PITAKA and the ABIDHAMMA PITAKA.

TIPUNA Maori word for ancestors.

TIRTHANKARAS ('Ford-makers') The twenty-four great heros of JAIN belief who help others to cross the stream of existence to liberation. Huge statues of the Tirthankaras, who include PARSVA and MAHAVIRA, are to be found in southern India.

TIUHUANACO ('City of the dead') Centre of a South American civilization which flourished approximately AD 1000–1300. Its god was a weeping god. When the city was taken over by the INCAS, this god became associated with SUN GOD and the city came to be thought of as the holy city of VIRACOCHA.

TIXE Name for God in several Bantu languages of southern Africa.

TLALOC AZTEC god of rain and vegetation. His name means 'he who makes things sprout'. He is portrayed with long fangs and rings round his eyes.

TLOQUE NAHUAQUE Supreme god of the AZTECS. He was an abstract deity, remote from the everyday world. NEZAHUALCOYOTL worshipped him as the supreme god and tried to build a religious philosophy around him as 'the cause of all causes, the unknown god'.

TOHUNGA AHUREWA Maori specialist in the highest sacred knowledge.

TOHUNGA MATAKITE Maori term for a DIVINER.

TOHUNGA TAURA Maori word for a SORCERER, a specialist in the black arts.

TONGUES See GLOSSOLALIA.

TONALPOHUALLI AZTEC sacred almanac which was part of the calendar. It covered a period of 260 days; each day was distinguished by a name and a number, and the days were grouped into numbered weeks. Particular divinities presided over each group of days.

TORAH (1) The five books of the Law (the *Pentateuch*) revealed to MOSES; the first division of the HEBREW BIBLE. (2) 'The teaching', the correct response of ISRAEL to God, outlined in the rules for purity and social justice. It is God's gift to Israel and the way for Israel to fulfil God's call for holiness. (3) The cosmological principle of order which embraces moral and religious instruction as well as the physical ordering of the universe by God.

TORII Gateway to a SHINTO shrine which consists of two vertical posts supporting two horizontal bars, the higher of which is often curved at each end towards the sky.

TOTEMISM (From a North American Indian word meaning 'relative') The belief in some PRIMAL RELIGIONS that particular animals or sometimes plants or other objects have a special relationship with the tribal group and act as its guardians.

TOTEM POLES Tall decorated posts, found especially among North American Indians, which display tribal relationships with ancestors and guardian spirits.

TOWERS OF SILENCE Parsi mounds used for the disposal of corpses. In the belief of the PARSIS, sacred fire must not be polluted by contact with the dead. Corpses are exposed on the mounds where the flesh is eaten by vultures. The bleached bones are finally thrown down a well.

TRANSCENDENT That which is above or beyond common human experience or knowlege.

TRANSCENDENTAL MEDITATION/TM MEDITATION technique taught by Maharishi Mahesh Yogi which has flourished in the West since the 1960s. Practitioners need no religious beliefs. They are taught to meditate for fifteen to twenty minutes twice a day; this reduces stress and aids relaxation. In some states in the USA it has been ruled that Transcendental Meditation is a religion, of Hindu origin.

TRANSFIGURATION The occasion of CHRIST'S appearance in glory to three of his disciples during his earthly ministry. It is celebrated as a feast in the Eastern Churches and by many in the West.

TRANSMIGRATION OF SOULS The belief held by some Hindus that souls are detached from their bodies at death and are attached to other human, animal or vegetable bodies. What the new body will be depends on the individual's KARMA.

TRIGLAV Slavic god with three heads.

TRINITY Christian doctrine of GOD as three Persons, equally God: the Father, the Son and the HOLY SPIRIT, constituting the divine unity.

TRIPITAKA (1) Sanskrit spelling of the (Pali) word TIPITAKA. (2) The SCRIPTURES of Chinese BUDDHISM which include translations of THERAVADA texts, SANSKRIT MAHAYANA texts and some Chinese additions and commentaries. Also called the *San Tsang*.

TRIPLE GEM The BUDDHA as teacher, the DHAMMA as his teaching and the SANGHA as the community who live by his teaching. The 'triple gem' is the core of the Buddhist faith.

TROMBA Madagascan term for possession by spirits.

TUAT The other world in Egyptian mythology, a land of gloom and darkness which is divided into twelve areas, one for each hour of the night. The souls of the dead have to cross this region to enter the judgement hall of OSIRIS.

TWELVERS The majority group among SHI'A Muslims who hold that the twelfth IMAN(2), Muhammad al-Mahdi, will reappear as the MAHDI on the last day. (See also ISMA'ILIS.)

TYLOR, Edward Burnett (AD 1832–1917) British anthropologist who believed that religion originated as 'the belief in spiritual beings'. He called this belief ANIMISM and summarized his arguments in *Primitive Culture* (1871).

TYR The oldest of the Norse gods. Originally a sky god like ZEUS or VARUNA, his attributes were taken over by ODIN. The Romans compared him with MARS because he became a war god, an inspirer of warriors. He is portrayed as having great strength and courage.

U

UFO ('Unidentified Flying Objects') The subject matter for many speculative cults and groups since the 1950s. Members consider the spiritual and practical significances of UFO sightings.

UGUNS MATE Latvian fire goddess.

'ULAMA' The doctors of the law in ISLAM. They are the interpreters of the SHARI'A and the upholders of Islamic orthodoxy. They exist in SUNNI and SHI'A communities.

'UMAR CALIPH after the death of ABU BAKR, from AD 634–644. His rule was a period of dramatic expansion for ISLAM, into Mesopotamia, Persia and Lower Egypt. He was murdered by a Christian slave in the MOSQUE of MEDINA.

UMAYYAD DYNASTY (AD 661–750) The Islamic dynasty based on the Meccan family Umayya. The caliphate was based in Damascus. Under the Umayyads ISLAM spread through North Africa to Spain and as far east as the Indus. There were eleven CALIPHS until the Umayyad period ended in military defeat and the succession of Abu'l 'Abbas as first caliph of the 'ABBASID DYNASTY.

UMMA The MUSLIM community, those who have received God's revelation through MUHAMMAD and live in submission to it.

UNDERWORLD The abode of spirits after the death of the body. In many religions the underworld is a shadowy half-real place presided over by a god of death. (See also DONN; HADES; HEL; HELL; KALUNGA; TUAT.)

UNIFICATION CHURCH Unorthodox sect founded in Korea in 1954 by Sun Myung MOON. Its teachings are ESOTERIC but certainly anti-communist. Its spiritual techniques and practices are controversial.

UNITARIANISM Dissenting movement which spread in England, Poland and Hungary from the sixteenth century. Unitarians reject the Christian doctrines of the TRINITY

and INCARNATION and defend a reason-based ethical THEISM.

UNTOUCHABLES Indians who belong to no caste (see CASTE SYSTEM) and are therefore banished from normal social life. MAHATMA GANDHI called them 'children of God' and worked for their acceptance in Indian society.

UPANISHADS The last books of the Indian VEDAS which were written in SANSKRIT between 800 and 400 BC. They develop the concept of BRAHMAN as the holy power released in sacrifice to the point where it becomes the underlying reality of the universe. The soul, ATMAN, is identified with the holy power, Brahman. They include speculation on how the soul can realize its oneness with Brahman through contemplative techniques.

USINSH Latvian god of spring and patron of horses.

'UTHMAN Son-in-law of MUHAMMAD who succeeded 'UMAR as CALIPH in AD 644. He was regarded as weak and worldly and was murdered in 656 after a period of rebellion. Under his caliphate the final authoritative version of the QUR'AN was produced.

V

VAIROCANA A title for the sun in ancient HINDU mythology. In MAHAYANA Buddhism it became a title for one of the great BUDDHAS. He is regarded as supreme BUDDHA in Java and in the Japanese SHINGON sect. He was said to be identical with the SHINTO sun deity AMATERASU, an identification which helped the development of RYOBU SHINTO.

VAISHNAVISM Worship of, or devotion to, the Hindu god VISHNU. Devotees regard him as the sole deity of whom other gods are mere aspects.

VAISHYAS See CASTE SYSTEM.

VAJRAYANA ('Diamond vehicle') An expression sometimes used for

Tibetan Buddhism, a form of MAHAYANA Buddhism which has distinctive doctrines and practices.

VALHALLA ('Hall of the slain') The part of ASGARD in Norse mythology reserved for dead heroes waiting for the final battle of RAGNARÖK. It had 540 doors and 800 men could march, shoulder to shoulder, out of each door. The dead heroes spent their time drinking, playing games and fighting.

VALKYRIES ('Choosers of the slain') Female servants of ODIN in Norse mythology who choose which side is to have victory and battle and which warriors are to die. They conduct the dead to VALHALLA and wait on them with food and drink. Some MYTHS portray them as witchlike beings, exulting in blood and death.

VAMPYR Spirit of a dead person in Slavic folklore who lives by sucking the blood of the living.

VANIR ('Shining ones') Divine beings of Norse mythology who at first fought with the AESIR and later allied with them and came to live in ASGARD.

VARANASI See BENARES.

VARUNA Indian sky god of the Vedic period (see VEDAS). He produced the cosmic order and was seen as a heavenly ruler and lawgiver as well as a moral guardian of the earth.

VATICAN COUNCILS The first was convened by POPE PIUS IX in AD 1869–70. It resulted in the dogma of Papal Infallibility and attacks on 'modern' thought. The second (1962–65) was called by John XXIII. It led to a drastic modernization of Roman Catholic worship and improved relations with other churches.

VEDANTA (1) 'The end of the VEDAS'. A name for the UPANISHADS, which close the period of HINDU revelation. (2) Indian philosophy based on the teachings of SHANKARA. Its basic tenet is that only BRAHMAN, the Absolute, is fully real. The world of sense experience is contradictory and dreamlike because it is spun from the illusions of MAYA. Release from illusion comes from recognizing the sole reality of Brahman.

VEDAS Scriptures which express the religion of the ARYAN people of India. They comprise HYMNS, instructions for RITUAL and cosmological speculations. There are four divisions: *Rig Veda*, hymns to the Aryan gods who are personifications of natural forces; *Sama Veda*, verses selected for chanting (see CHANT); *Yajur Veda*, prose instructions on matters of ritual; *Atharva Veda*, rites and SPELLS in verse, especially concerned with curing illness.

VENUS Roman goddess of love, identified with APHRODITE and thus honoured as the mother of the Roman people.

VESTA Roman goddess of the hearth and protectress of domestic life. She was regarded as the guardian of the Roman nation. Her cult was under the supervision of six Vestal Virgins who tended the undying flame (traditionally from Troy) which burned in her temple.

VESTMENTS Special garments worn by the Christian clergy during liturgical services (see LITURGY).

VIHARA A dwelling place for members of the Buddhist SANGHA. The term is also used today for any retreat house, temple or Buddhist monastery.

VINAYA PITAKA One of the oldest Buddhist scriptures consisting of the rules of discipline for the SANGHA, and related commentaries.

VIRACOCHA/HUIRACOCHA The uncreated creator god in the religion of the INCAS. He was god of the ancient city of TIUHUANACO and the giver of civilization. PACHACHUTEC, the ninth Inca, exalted him as supreme deity over even the SUN GOD.

VIRGINS OF THE SUN The *Aclla Cuna*, or 'chosen women' of the INCAS. They were selected at the age of ten to serve in the sun temples. Some became sacrificial victims, others wives of the Inca. They were ruled by a chief priestess, the Coya Pacsa, held to be the earthly consort of the SUN GOD.

VISHNU In HINDUISM, god as preserver and life-giver, the creator of the cosmos. He and SHIVA are the two great gods of Hindu devotion. As lawgiver and moral guardian, Vishnu appears on earth from time to time as an AVATAR to reawaken men to knowledge of truth.

VIVEKANANDA (about 1863–1902) Follower of RAMAKRISHNA, and founder of the RAMAKRISHNA MISSION in 1897. An apologist for VEDANTA, he criticized the dogmatism of CHRISTIANITY. Attending the World Parliament of Religions in Chicago in 1893, he commended Vedanta as the highest form of religion.

VOODOO Religion of ninety per cent of the people of Haiti (in spite of the official domination of Roman Catholicism) as well as others in the West Indies and parts of South America. The name derives from a West African word for GOD. In practice Voodoo is highly syncretistic: West African DIVINITIES are worshipped (see SHANGO), often as Christian SAINTS and their sanctuaries are closed during the Christian season of LENT.

W

WAHHABI MOVEMENT Puritanical Islamic movement founded by Al-Wahhab of Arabia (AD 1703–92). Wahhabi accept the authority only of the QUR'AN and the SUNNA. The movement has revived in the twentieth century and is the dominant religious influence in Saudi Arabia.

WAILING WALL See WESTERN WALL.

WANDERING ON In Buddhist thought the continual cycle by which the KARMA of past actions causes the coming-to-be of new mental and physical states which in turn produce more karma and further phases of existence.

WANDJINA Spirit beings of the Australian DREAMTIME who are

believed to have left their shadows on rock and cave walls in paintings and engravings. They are regarded as kindly beings who care for the people, ensure fertility and bring rain.

WEEKS/SHAVUOT Jewish feast celebrated seven weeks after PASSOVER. It has become associated with the giving of the Ten Commandments on Mt Sinai. Also known as PENTECOST (1).

WEREWOLF Human being who has been transformed into a wolf in Slavic folk tradition.

WESLEY, John (AD 1703–91) Founder of the METHODIST movement. He travelled through England on horseback preaching the 'new birth'. Although loyal to the Church of England, he was eventually forced to ordain his own ministers.

WESTERN WALL/WAILING WALL/KOTEL Site in JERUSALEM used by JEWS to lament the FALL OF JERUSALEM and the continuing suffering of the Jews and to pray for restoration. It is believed to be part of the original temple of Solomon, the only part of the temple left standing after the destruction of AD 70. (See TEMPLE OF JERUSALEM.)

WITCHCRAFT The practice of casting harmful SPELLS or charms. Witches are also widely believed to have the power of flying by night and to devour human souls.

WITCHDOCTOR/MEDICINE MAN A healer in PRIMAL RELIGIONS. The terms are rarely used today as they are felt to have misleading connotations.

WORLD COUNCIL OF CHURCHES Body including many Protestant and Orthodox Churches first constituted at Amsterdam in 1948 (see ECUMENICAL MOVEMENT).

WORLD FELLOWSHIP OF BUDDHISTS Society founded in 1950 in Ceylon (Sri Lanka) by G.P. Malaleskera to bring together Buddhists of all traditions and nations with the common intention of spreading Buddhist teaching throughout the world.

WORSHIP Reverence or homage to God or a god which may involve PRAYER, SACRIFICE, RITUALS, singing, dancing or chanting.

WOVOKA (AD 1856–1932) Paiute North American Indian PROPHET and MYSTIC who, reacting against white domination, urged his followers to live in peace, fighting the whites through the power of the GHOST DANCE. His hope of imminent regeneration spread among the Plains Indians. The movement was destroyed at the Battle of Wounded Knee in 1890.

WRATH The righteous anger of God against SIN.

WRITINGS The third and final division of the HEBREW BIBLE, comprising the Wisdom literature (such as Job and Proverbs), the Psalms and the later histories and other material.

WYCLIFFE, John (about 1329–84) English religious reformer who condemned the POPE as Antichrist and began the translation of the BIBLE into English.

X

XIPE TOTEC ('The flayed one') In Mexican mythology, the god of the west and of agriculture, who was skinned alive like the maize. He was represented by the mask of a skinned human face.

XIUHTECUHTLI ('Turquoise lord') The ancient Mexican fire god. His fire burned in every home and temple and he was regarded as a form of the supreme god.

Y

YAHWEH See YHWH.

YAMA In the VEDAS the primordial man who crosses through death and becomes immortal. He is therefore god of death who judges men and consigns them to heaven or hell. His significance as judge faded as the pre-ARYAN doctrine of SAMSARA became established.

YASNA The form of public worship in ancient ZOROASTRIANISM, elements of which are retained by the PARSIS. Part of the AVESTA, it teaches the presence of the divine in all things and refers to many lesser divine beings alongside AHURA MAZDA.

YELLOW HATS Reformed branch of TIBETAN BUDDHISM whose leader is the DALAI LAMA. (See BUDDHISM.)

YGGDRASIL The great ash tree which unifies the creation according to Norse mythology. Its three roots reach ASGARD, MIDGARD and Niflheim, the UNDERWORLD. The tree holds together the nine worlds of giants, dwarfs, men, light elves, dark elves, AESIR, VANIR, the dead and the home of the world-destroyers. The tree of knowledge, it is simultaneously being nourished and destroyed. It is also a symbol of the generation of life: the first man in Norse myth is named Ash.

YHWH The 'tetragrammaton', the sacred name of the God of ISRAEL which was revealed to MOSES. The name means 'I am'. It could not be spoken and the HEBREW 'Adonai' ('the Lord') was substituted when the scriptures were read aloud. The MASORETES put the vowel points for Adonai into the name YHWH which gave rise to the malformation 'Jehovah'. YHWH was possibly pronounced 'Yahweh'.

YIN AND YANG The polarity of energies in Chinese philosophy. Yang is masculine, dynamic, bright and good; yin is feminine, passive, dark and bad. Their production and interplay is represented in a circular diagram (see T'AI CHI). Yin and Yang produce the elements and the cycle of the seasons. They also provided the theoretical basis for the Taoist practice of ALCHEMY (see TAOISM).

YOGA A way to union with GOD in HINDU philosophy. It also forms one of the six classical systems of Indian thought. Traditionally there are eight stages of yoga: restraint; discipline; posture; breathing; detachment; concentration; meditation, and trance. The four main styles of yoga correspond to different personality types: *Karma yoga*, the path of action; *Jnana yoga*, the path of knowledge; *Bhakti yoga*, the path of devotion; *Raja yoga*, the path of insight.

YOGI Indian holy man who has reached ENLIGHTENMENT through yogic practices (see YOGA). (See also TRANSCENDENTAL MEDITATION.)

YOM KIPPUR/DAY OF ATONEMENT Jewish day of FASTING and repentance, the most solemn day of the Jewish year. The liturgy includes a solemn chant, the *Kol Nidre*, which challenges Jews who have strayed from religion to return to faith.

YOUNG, Brigham See MORMONISM.

YUM KAAX Corn god of the MAYA. He is portrayed as a young god holding up a flowering plant.

Z

ZADDIK Jewish teacher in the later Hasidist movement. The Zaddik was seen as the perfectly righteous man who was in mystical communion with God. The Zaddik's house became the meeting place for the HASIDIM(3).

ZAKAT Obligatory almsgiving, one of the FIVE PILLARS OF ISLAM. Originally it was for poor relief and for financing JIHAD. The proportion of the individual's income to be given has varied; at times it has come under state supervision and been levied as a tax, but modern MUSLIM states insist that zakat is quite separate from social welfare.

ZAMBE See NYAMBE.

ZANAHARY The creator god in Madagascan religion.

ZA-ZEN Japanese term for the form of MEDITATION practised in ZEN monasteries. It involves a sitting posture designed to accompany reflection on a KOAN.

ZEALOTS Jewish nationalistic party in Roman times who believed that the Roman presence was a defilement of the land and a flouting of TORAH. In AD 66 they revolted. The war which followed led to the destruction of JERUSALEM and her temple in AD 70. The last stand of the Zealots was at Masada, where 960 of them died in AD 73.

ZEMES DIEVS Latvian god of the farmstead. He is sometimes identified with PERKONS.

ZEMES MATE Latvian earth goddess.

ZEN Japanese Buddhist movement which developed from the Chinese CH'AN school in the thirteenth century AD. It is characterized by the teaching that ENLIGHTENMENT is a spontaneous event, totally independent of concepts, techniques or rituals. Zen aims at harmony in living and uses secular arts such as tea-making and calligraphy to develop effortless skills.

ZEUS Supreme ruler of the Greek gods. Described by HOMER as 'Father of gods and men', he may have originated as a storm god and continued to be regarded as controller of the weather. Although there were many MYTHS about him he did not appear in drama, which suggests that he was held in special awe. Sometimes the name Zeus stood simply for God, as supreme deity.

ZEUS KRETAGENES ('Cretan-born' Zeus) A dying and rising god whose cult flourished during and after the period of the Minoan civilization in Crete. He was associated with the bull and was the original son and consort of the MOTHER GODDESS.

ZEVI, Shabbetai (AD 1626–1716) Kabbalistic RABBI from Smyrna who became the centre of a Messianic movement which spread throughout the Jewish world (see KABBALAH). In 1665 he proclaimed himself MESSIAH. He was later imprisoned and, to the horror of his followers, converted to ISLAM. There were attempts to argue that the sin of the Messiah was a necessary part of redemption, but the movement disintegrated.

ZIGGURAT Ancient Babylonian TEMPLE in the form of a tower rising from a broad base to a narrow top.

ZIONISM The movement to establish a national and permanent homeland for JEWS. In 1897 the first Zionist Congress was organized in Basle by Theodore HERZL in the wake of a wave of European anti-Semitism. Gradually the movement became determined that Palestine was the only realistic place to establish the Jewish state and Jews were encouraged to emigrate and acquire property there. The majority of Jews today support Zionism to the extent that it is manifested in the modern state of ISRAEL.

ZOHAR Most important writing of the Jewish KABBALAH.

ZOMBIE Term used in Haiti and South America for the 'living dead' — those whose souls have been eaten by witches (see WITCHCRAFT).

ZOROASTER/ZARATHUSTRA Prophet and founder of ZOROASTRIANISM. He lived in Persia, either in the tenth and ninth centuries BC, or, more likely, in the seventh and sixth. At the age of thirty he had a revelation of AHURA MAZDA which drove him to preach against polytheism. According to tradition he died performing the fire sacrifice which was the central ceremony of the new faith.

ZOROASTRIANISM The religion of ancient Persia, founded by ZOROASTER, possibly related to the Vedic religion of India (see VEDAS). It was strongly ethical: Zoroaster taught that AHURA MAZDA would judge each individual soul after death. Later there developed a complex doctrinal system speculating about the inner nature of the universe. The expansion of ISLAM drove Zoroastrianism out of Persia (see also AVESTA; PARSIS; ZURVANISM).

ZURVANISM Zoroastrian heresy according to which an absolute being called Zurvan ('time') was the origin of good and evil and the source of the two spirits AHURA MAZDA and ANGRA MAINYU.

Index

Acknowledgements

Maps and charts
Roy Lawrance

Photographs
The photographs in this book are reproduced by permission of the following photographers and organizations.

Australian Information Service 149, 150 (both), back cover (right: aborigines)
Barnaby's Picture Library 87, 105, 139, 170–71, 175, 182, 186, 188 (below), 189, 191, 198, 203, 218, 230, 232, 235, 236, 250, 253 (below), 256, 259, 265, 273, 286, 295, 297, 299, 312, 318, 330, 347, front cover (left: Hindu Divali festival), cover spine
BBC Hulton Picture Library 16
Axel-Ivar Berglund 163
Barbara M. Boal 129, 134 (both), 135, 137
British Museum 123, 132, 140 (right), 316
Michael Cole 385 (all)
Douglas Davies 188 (above), 200(2)
Douglas Dickins 12, 21 (below), 53, 72 (above), 143, 181, 192 (above, both), 193, 194, 211, 214, 227, 229(3), 241, 260, 269, 308, 346, 374, front cover (right: funeral procession, Bali)
W. H. Edwards 21 (above)
Evangelical Union of South America 367, 387
Fritz Fankhauser 70, 76, 248, 254, 276–77, 305, 341, 361, 362, 366, 368–69, 382, 386 (both), front and back cover (main picture: Buddhist monks)
Werner Forman Archive 125
French Government Tourist Office 25

Sonia Halliday 298, 309, 313, 338, 344, 365, back cover (centre: stained glass)
John Hinnells 86
Hirmer Archive 92, 93
Michael Holford 45, 116
Alan Hutchison Library title page, 43, 140 (left), 141, 144, 145 (left), 155, 156, 161, 167, 168, 321, 323, 350
Jewish Education Board 293
Lion Publishing, David Alexander 65, 91, 200(6), 279, 285, 288, 337, 356, 381; from the British Museum: 24, 60, 63, 68, 72 (below), 78 **Jon Willcocks** 29, 152, 153, 348, 353, 377
William Macquitty 10, 17, 19, 36, 51, 57, 73, 77(1,2,3), 82, 172, 185, 188 (centre), 196, 200(3,4), 202, 224, 229(2), 233, 240, 245, 247, 249, 257, 261, 263, 319, 328–29 (all), 332, 373, endpapers, front cover (centre: Japanese girl priest)
The Mansell Collection 89, 102 (both), 103 (both), 106, 107, 108, 290, 370
Wulf Metz 33, 77(5,6,7), 97, 130, 145 (right), 160, 180, 192 (below), 225, 229(1,4), 253 (above), 324, 326, 359
Middle East Photographic Archive 334
Open Doors 351, 383
Ann and Bury Peerless 176, 200(1,5), 205, 207, 209, 220 (both), back cover (left: Jain home shrine)
John Ruffle 62, 77(4), 81, 100
Len Scott 115, 119, 120
Silkeborg Museum, Denmark 114
Derek Swallow 371
Harold Turner 157

The article by the Rev. Robert Brow is reproduced from his book *Religion: Origins and Ideas* by kind permission of the publishers, Tyndale Press.

Exploring
Clinical
Methods
For
Social
Research

The editors and authors gratefully acknowledge the permission granted to reprint the following: The excerpts in Chapter 2, by Clayton P. Alderfer, are reprinted by permission of the University Press of Kansas from *The Life of a Psychologist: An Autobiography* by Fritz Heider, © 1983; and by permission of Random House, Inc., from *Methods of Research in Social Psychology* by J. M. Carlsmith, P. C. Ellsworth, and E. Aronson, © 1976. The excerpt in Chapter 11, by Philip H. Mirvis and Meryl Reis Louis, is from "Little Gidding" in *Four Quartets* by T. S. Eliot, copyright 1943 by T. S. Eliot; renewed 1971 by Esme Valerie Eliot. Reprinted by permission of Harcourt Brace Jovanovich, Inc.

For information address:

SAGE Publications, Inc.
275 South Beverly Drive
Beverly Hills, California 90212

SAGE Publications India Pvt. Ltd.
M-32 Market
Greater Kailash I
New Delhi 110 048 India

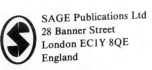

SAGE Publications Ltd
28 Banner Street
London EC1Y 8QE
England

Printed in the United States of America

Library of Congress Cataloging in Publication Data

Main entry under title:

Exploring clinical methods for social research.

Bibliography: p.
1. Social sciences—Methodology—Addresses, essays, lectures. 2. Social sciences—Research—Addresses, essays, lectures. 3. Social sciences—Field work—Addresses, essays, lectures. 4. Participant observation—Addresses, essays, lectures. I. Berg, David N., 1949— II. Smith, Kenwyn K.
H61.E97   1985   300′.72   84-27618
ISBN 0-8039-2432-1

FIRST PRINTING

Exploring Clinical Methods For Social Research

H
61
.E97

Edited by
David N. Berg
Kenwyn K. Smith

 SAGE PUBLICATIONS Beverly Hills London New Delhi

Bull. Paris, December 5, 1945-January 17, 1946
Eleven progressive states of same lithograph, c. 11⅜ × 16⅛″ 28.9 × 41 cm)
Mourlot 17, States I-XI. Collection Bernard Picasso, Paris

I. December 5, 1945

IV. December 22, 1945

III. December 18, 1945

V. December 24, 1945

VI. December 26, 1945

IX. January 5, 1946

VII. December 28, 1945

XI. January 17, 1946

CONTRIBUTORS

Clayton P. Alderfer, *Yale School of Organization and Management*
David N. Berg, *Yale School of Organization and Management*
Cortlandt Cammann, *Institute for Social Research, University of Michigan*
Marshall Edelson, *Department of Psychiatry, Yale School of Medicine*
Jonathon H. Gillette, *Yale University*
J. Richard Hackman, *Yale University*
A. Michael Huberman, *University of Geneva*
Kathy E. Kram, *Boston University School of Management*
Meryl Reis Louis, *Boston University*
Rodney L. Lowman, *North Texas State University*
Matthew B. Miles, *Center for Policy Research, New York*
Philip H. Mirvis, *Boston University School of Management*
Helen Swick Perry, *Cambridge, Massachusetts*
Stewart E. Perry, *Cambridge, Massachusetts*
Alan Peshkin, *College of Education, University of Illinois*
Shulamit Reinharz, *Brandeis University*
Susan J. Schurman, *University of Michigan*
Valerie M. Simmons, *University of California at Santa Cruz*
Kenwyn K. Smith, *The Wharton School, University of Pennsylvania*
Robert I. Sutton, *Stanford University*

PREFACE

Traveling from Christchurch to Queenstown, the view of snowcapped Alps made it hard to keep our attention on the road ahead. Even though on vacation, we had resolved to continue our work on a book about group processes, but we found ourselves distracted by more than just the beauty of the mountains. Our discussions inevitably led to the realization that it would be difficult for the social science community to interpret our concepts without an understanding of the clinical methodology upon which our theories were based. We decided to devote our energies to defining and describing these research methods. Three days later the idea for this book was born.

There are many compatible voices struggling to articulate the contemporary interpretations of a clinical methodology, so we chose to craft an edited volume. A chorus seemed to offer a richness that would be lacking in our duet. In creating this volume, we asked individuals from a variety of fields to write about aspects of their research that they would not normally scrutinize in a public forum. This was a difficult task for both authors and editors. The many iterations were painful, but the quality of the book and the relationships established were worth the effort.

As students learning research methods, we were grateful to an earlier generation of writers who discussed the emotional as well as the intellectual struggles inherent in social research (e.g., Filstead, 1970). We also appreciated those teachers who brought a clinical orientation to our research training. With this volume we seek to continue this tradition.

A tradition is sustained through the efforts of many people. Only some of the names appear in a table of contents or on the cover of a book. In addition to the authors, we want to thank the individuals and organizations who participated in the research described in the following pages. We also want to thank Cheri Coates and Karen Eisenman for typing portions of the manuscript, and Robin Golden for her faith and support when both were needed.

We now recognize that the detour that began on our trip to New Zealand was necessary. In the future we may again need to travel to places foreign to us both, places where we are encouraged to explore our distractions.

> The question is whether the validity of science depends on the achievement of a completely objective, noninvolved, nonprejudicial point of view, or whether the acknowledgment of the necessary relativity, subjectivity, and prejudice involved in any act of perception is, in fact, a truer and more scientific approach to knowledge.
>
> (Susan A. Handelman, *The Slayers of Moses*)

—David N. Berg
Kenwyn K. Smith
New Haven, Connecticut

CONTENTS

INTRODUCTION

Kenwyn K. Smith and David N. Berg

It is one of the contentions of this volume that when we use ourselves as instruments for studying human systems we take on a special responsibility. It is a responsibility to science and to the people with whom we work. We are obligated to struggle to understand the complex emotional and intellectual forces that influence the conduct of our inquiry. These forces are at once the source of our insight and our folly. We must apply the same systematic attention to our analysis of these forces as we do to our analysis of the topics we study. Especially as we move into the field and concentrate our research on the social problems that confront the cultures in which we live, it becomes increasingly important that we examine, describe, and scrutinize who we are, why we do research, how we create knowledge, and how the research process changes us.

This book is an attempt to focus attention on these issues. It is a book about the emotional and intellectual struggles that attend researchers as they formulate ideas, collect and interpret data, and build theory. The chapters in this volume describe struggles with concepts, with methods, with relationships, and with each individual researcher's quest to define his or her place in the social sciences. Not least of all, this book is the product of many individual struggles to *write* about these issues in the belief that both the writer and the reader will learn from such an undertaking.

WHY CREATE THIS BOOK?

All research activity, including fieldwork, laboratory experiments, published articles and books, seminars, and presentations, serves a variety of interests. In its simplest and perhaps most naive conception, the research endeavor serves our interest to know more about the world around us. It also serves the personal interests of the individual researcher and, in some cases, the interests of the individuals and organizations participating in the research. But research, like other

human undertakings, is embedded in a society and enmeshed in the interests of that society. The concerns of a funding agency or supporting institution, the current directions of the profession or discipline, the pressures of career advancement, the subtle influences of class and culture all combine with the desire to know, to form a web of interests served by any research activity. These interests are not easily recognized by the researchers themselves. Some may not be able to see the ways in which their work serves interests other than their own. Others may choose not to see what interests are served because of the difficult questions raised by such an awareness.

Often the methods we choose to conduct research are, wittingly or unwittingly, an expression of the conflicting interests that are being served by the study. Whether in the lab or in the field, these conflicting interests affect our work. In the lab, conflicting interests between researchers and "subject" sometimes lead researchers to use their power to transform the subject's interests into their own interests. Required participation in psychology experiments in universities is an example of this transformation. In other circumstances this conflict has led researchers to lie about their objectives. In the case of field research, the conflict between the interests of science and the interests of the people participating in the study may lead some researchers to return to the controlled environment of the lab. It can also lead to the development of field methods that provide guidelines for accommodating the two sets of interests.

Especially since this volume is devoted to an examination of research methods, we think it is important to be as explicit as we can about the multiple and sometimes conflicting interests served by the creation of this book. In most cases we, like other researchers, do not openly discuss the interests being served by our research nor do we articulate them for others to consider as they think about our work. But since this volume is about research, we believe it is important that we try to convey our thoughts about the interests being served herein. The discussion of the historical, conceptual and personal interests being served by the book is intended also to function as an introduction to the ideas contained in the following pages.

Historical interests. There are many historical themes in the social sciences that the chapters in this volume might address. Over hundreds of years the development of the scientific method has brought with it an increasing separation between knowledge and methods of knowing. In the physical sciences this split served knowledge because scientists were too often and too easily influenced by the needs of their patrons, the

dogma of the Church, or the power of their own beliefs. The standard-ization of a scientific method took a number of important decisions out of the domain of the individual and made them subject to the demands of specific rules of evidence, inference, and generalization. The development of the scientific method meant that a community of researchers could all work toward expanding the existing knowledge about the physical world by using a common language that, on the surface, did not require a common belief other than a belief in the utility of the language itself.

The growth of the social and behavioral sciences, as well as the increasing attention paid to social science by philosophers, has raised a number of important questions about the utility of a research method that is separated from the knowledge it creates. As we learn more about human behavior, as our behavioral science begins to yield fruit, it becomes increasingly clear that we must examine the implications of this knowledge for the research endeavor. In the social sciences, to maintain the split between what we know and how we know it is to handicap ourselves in the service of a belief that social and physical sciences should share the same research methods.

During the past century in particular, social scientists have struggled to integrate their knowledge of human beings with the human practice of research on social systems. Rather than act as if it were possible or advisable for us to step out of our humanity when we do research, these social scientists sought to develop methods that either took account of the researcher's humanity or used it to generate insight into the phenomenon at hand. To be sure, there were also many social scientists who continued to develop methods that took the researcher out of the process as much as possible, convinced then as now that the benefits of such a "removal" far outweigh the costs. It is our view that this separation places severe limitations on what we can learn about social systems precisely because the method itself denies what we already know: that human beings studying human beings are inevitably influenced in complex ways by a variety of social and psychological forces.

This volume attempts to continue the search for ways to integrate our knowledge about human beings with the methods we use to study human systems. We are taking what is usually treated as peripheral and making it central. The book is addressed to both those who have worked to remove the researcher from the research process and those who have attempted to reintegrate the two. The following chapters offer the former an explanation of the necessity of developing clinical methodologies and some examples of their usefulness, and the latter a statement

about the need to bring what we know about the researcher out of the closet.

Conceptual interests. At this point it would probably be confusing to use the term *clinical* to describe those aspects of behavioral science research that acknowledge and utilize the special characteristics of human beings studying human systems. Part of this confusion originates in the current uses of the term, especially in medicine and psychology where *clinical* often refers to a therapeutic activity. Given its current usage in other fields one might ask why we have chosen to redefine this term for the behavioral sciences. There are at least four reasons.

First, especially in psychology, the clinical setting is an arena of professional practice or research in which understanding is sought in the systematic examination of the researcher and the research relationship as well as in an analysis of the human phenomenon being studied. Clinical psychologists in both practice and academe pay close attention to all three aspects in order to inform both their actions and their theories. Psychologists in other subdisciplines often scrutinize the researcher and the research relationship only to the extent that these variables affect what can be known about the psychological issue at hand and then seek to minimize, control, or eliminate their influence whenever possible.

Second, activities that take place in a clinical setting also involve a responsibility to others. Practitioners and researchers alike must struggle to balance the multiple responsibilities they carry. These responsibilities influence the choices they make and the work they do. As a result, much of current practice and theory represents the ways in which professionals have managed these responsibilities. It could be argued that all research in the behavioral sciences has this clinical aspect to it since all research involving human beings also brings with it responsibility whether or not the researcher chooses to attend to it.

A third reason for choosing the term *clinical* is that clinical research or practice necessarily involves the participation of other human beings. In clinical medicine, for example, the physician must learn to work with patients in both the diagnosis and treatment of illness. In the clinical setting it is not enough to know the physiology and chemistry of the human organism; the doctor must also know how to involve the patient. The less the doctor knows, the more he or she must rely on the patient's experience and ability (or willingness) to report that experience. Thus, new knowledge is directly connected to the quality of the doctor-patient relationship and, by implication, the various factors—personal, inter-

personal, organizational, and cultural—that affect that relationship. As behavioral scientists move into the field to do their research or begin to conceptualize the laboratory as an organization, these clinical aspects of research become even more important than they already were. Freud's work is perhaps the best-known example of knowledge that can be created when systematic attention is paid to the information available in a clinical setting—information found not only in the research participant but in the researcher and the research relationship as well.

Finally, our frustration with the current polarization between quantitative and qualitative methods pushed us to seek a concept that would not carry with it the historical baggage born of this controversy. As will become evident, both quantitative and qualitative research can be either clinical or nonclinical, depending upon the stance taken by the researcher and his or her definition of relevant research data.

Our conceptual goal in the chapters that follow is to develop a definition of *clinical* and to explore its relevance for social science research. This will involve further discussions of the distinction between clinical and nonclinical research and an examination of the nature of validity in clinical research. In clinical research, for example, how does one know the difference between knowledge and idiosyncratic whim? How does one learn to trust one's own understanding and how does one evaluate the utility-validity of this understanding? Since we argue that almost all social science research has a clinical element to it, we believe these are important questions for all social scientists.

Personal interests. There are a number of personal interests served by the creation of this volume. Through this work we give further definition to our identities as social scientists. We differentiate ourselves from some in our field and identify with others. In putting forth the ideas in this book we are simultaneously seeking and affirming the worth of these ideas. In working on this jointly, we affirm the importance of our relationship to each other. This activity adds meaning to both our professional and personal lives, and represents one of the tangible products that remain after the work is completed.

We are also aware that this volume is an attempt to increase the legitimacy of a method and the kinds of knowledge it produces. Many of our traditionally trained colleagues come to us for guidance and help when confronted with difficult interpersonal, group, or organizational problems in both research and practice. We suspect that this is more than just colleagial goodwill and that these people find what we know

about human behavior useful. In spite of the fact that *clinical* is often placed in opposition to *academic*, it is clear that clinical knowledge adds to our colleagues' understanding of a human system (and their role in it) and, in some cases, helps them act. In part we write this book to open up a professional conversation about what clinical understanding is and how it contributes to our knowledge about human systems. Whereas this now requires traditional social scientists to converse with colleagues who are often on the fringe of academic respectability, this volume seeks to make that conversation an important and more central part of research in the field.

ORGANIZATION OF THE BOOK

There are four sections to this volume. Each section opens with an introduction and concludes with a brief editorial commentary. The introduction describes the chapters included in the section and the commentary discusses some of the issues and themes raised by them.

Clinical Issues. The three chapters that make up the first section set the stage for the rest of the volume. These initial chapters both pose and seek to answer a number of questions about a clinical method in the behavioral sciences: What is it? What might we learn from such a method? What does it require of researchers who use it? How do we go about it? In this section issues are raised that are then addressed in the chapters that follow.

Clinical Understanding. The five chapters in the second section explore what can be learned from a clinical method and how this knowledge adds to our understanding of human behavior. The chapters range from an epistemological analysis of clinical methods to an examination of the cultural and political influences on what we know about human behavior to a discussion of the ways an action orientation changes how we understand the social world.

Clinical Involvement. The third section includes chapters that focus on the relationships that are part of a clinical method. Some of these chapters examine relationships among researchers and between researchers and the people they work with. Others explore the researcher's relationship with himself or herself during the research process, and still others look at the influence of intergroup relations in the surrounding

culture on the relationship between the researcher and the social system being studied. This section takes a particularly hard look at the personal and emotional demands of clinical research.

Clinical Methods. The final chapters present the clinical side of various research methods including interviewing, participant observation, historical analysis, and qualitative data analysis. Through the description of specific cases, these chapters illustrate some of the dilemmas, challenges, and rewards of a clinical method taken into the field.

In summary, we have sought not only to identify some of the emotional and intellectual struggles in social research but to shed some light on them as well. We hope this volume will provide its readers with some thoughtful companionship as they struggle, inevitably, with some of the issues raised in this book. One's mind, thoughts and feelings, conscious and unconscious, with its links to family and culture, is nurtured by the company it keeps.

Clinical Issues

What is a clinical method? What does it require of the researcher? What is its role in social science? The three chapters in this first section address these questions and identify conceptual themes that are explored in subsequent chapters. Together they initiate a provocative dialogue on the meaning, importance, and challenge of clinical methods.

The first chapter proposes a definition of *clinical* for the behavioral sciences. The authors describe the potential contribution of a clinical method and point out the intellectual and emotional demands on the researcher who wants to use such a method. The coauthors of this chapter emphasize the importance of research relationships—between researchers and research participants, between researchers and their colleagues, and between the various internal "parts" of any individual researcher.

The second chapter struggles with the implications of the fact that researchers are themselves human beings. Using the vehicle of an ongoing conversation between the researcher as scientist and the researcher as self, Alderfer explores how aspects of the researcher as human being influence method development and theory building. Along the way he scrutinizes not only Sigmund Freud and Fritz Heider but himself as well. A clinical method, argues Alderfer, brings the often denied human aspects of the researcher into social research, thereby enhancing its validity and vitality.

The issue of validity is central to Edelson's chapter. He contends that a clinical method must adhere to scientific canons if we are to believe one explanation or hypothesis over another. He addresses the arguments sometimes put forth to exempt a clinical method from scientific standards of inference and concludes that such an exemption is both unwarranted and unwise. Edelson, a psychoanalyst, concludes that psychological phenomena (inside an individual, between researcher and patient, in the scientific community) can be the legitimate domain of a scientifically rigorous clinical method and suggests steps toward this end.

As you read these three chapters, you might reflect on the issues that are alive in your own research work. How do you fit yourself and your work into the social sciences? When do you think about the role of research relationships in the

research process—at the beginning, whenever things go wrong, or as you explain unanticipated findings? What demands for rigor do you experience? How satisfied are you with what you are able to see with your current methodological approach? What forces do you struggle to control inside your self and inside your world, and what influence does this struggle have on your work and your life?

THE CLINICAL DEMANDS OF
RESEARCH METHODS

David N. Berg and Kenwyn K. Smith

The arguments of this chapter are made upon the foundation of three firmly held beliefs. First, the nature and quality of social research findings are powerfully influenced by the relationship between the researcher and the researched. Second, this relationship should receive the same intense scrutiny as other methodological issues in the research process (such as the tools of statistical inference). Third, any system of investigating social reality must address the whole research process, including the research relationship as well as the formal procedures represented in our methodological canons.

The perspective that social science knowledge is developed in the context of a relationship has been acknowledged and discussed by people in many disciplines across many generations (Mannheim, 1936; Sullivan, 1953b; Devereux, 1967; Heron, 1981). Until recently (Morgan, 1983; Reason & Rowan, 1981) there has been little call for the inclusion of a systematic examination of these relationships in the research write-up. Except for a brief explanation of the power of the experimental manipulation or of the rapport developed with informants, it is entirely possible to read an article in psychology, sociology, or even anthropology without knowing much about the research relationships and their impact on the researcher. Important contextual information is therefore not available and we often are forced to supply our own.

Within an academic discipline, research relationships are often assumed to have similar characteristics across studies. In elementary chemistry, for example, standard temperature and pressure are often assumed when findings are reported, but one can easily imagine the confusion if this relationship were altered and not reported. In the social

sciences, however, it is very difficult to assume a standard relationship between the researcher and the researched, given the complexity of this relationship. Even when we seek to standardize our research relationships, we are often unaware of the key characteristics of these relationships until we attempt to apply our findings to other settings. It is usually only then—when they do not fit—that we recognize the special features of our research relationships. To pursue the analogy, we discover that water does not always boil at 212°F when we try to cook an egg in Denver. To say that water boils at 212°F is to say "at sea level" simultaneously if implicitly. As we move to studying complex human phenomena, especially in field settings, we need to be more diligent in our attempts to describe, analyze, and understand the relationships in which we seek our knowledge of social systems.

What makes research relationships in the social sciences complex is the fact that both the researcher and the social system being studied contribute to creating the research relationship. In turn, the relationship has both emotional and intellectual consequences for both parties.

THE CENTRALITY OF RESEARCH RELATIONSHIPS

Research relationships are an important part of social research for several reasons. First, it can be maintained that virtually no information about a person, group, or social system exists without a relationship with that person or social system. Irrespective of whether social phenomena exist independent of our relationship to them, our knowledge of the social world is a consequence of our relationship with this world (in the laboratory, in the field, or in our own lives) or our exposure to the relationships of others (social science research, literature, history).

Sullivan (1953b) discusses this issue in the field of psychiatry, arguing that psychiatric understanding is rooted in the relationship between the psychiatrist and the patient rather than in "objective" data that exist somewhere independent of the psychiatric relationship. This does not preclude the discovery of psychiatric regularities across different relationships. These similarities may indicate a critical pattern in the individual disorders being examined. However, it may also be that these patterns reflect the reality that the doctor-patient relationships are consciously or unconsciously following contours prescribed by a culture or a particular setting.

There are real, not merely philosophical, ways in which our research relationships create what we see. When we examine the creations of a

collection or generation of social researchers we can see regularities in both their research relationships and research findings. These patterns help us to develop our theories. But it is important to remember that different relationships will create different data in social research. Hence we may need to move away from an idealization of standardized relationships, replacing this with a commitment to report and describe the relationships we develop.

Second, research relationships are the vehicle through which the researcher comes to understand a social system. Whether one assumes that each research participant provides a glimpse of an objective social reality or one piece of a mosaic of subjective social realities, the researcher's relationship with the participants and their social systems is an extremely powerful determinant of the quality of the data. Mutual and respectful relationships are more likely to give birth to sensitive thoughts and feelings (in both the researcher and the research participant) than are mistrusting ones.

Third, a description of the research relationship provides the context necessary for interpreting what has been discovered. The mere process of separating the data from their context of origin diminishes the meaning of the data. Preserving as much of the context as possible is an investment in maintaining the meaning of the data.

Critical to the context are the circumstances under which the research was begun. Were participants coerced by authority figures, or by extra points in a college exam, or were mutual benefits established for all parties involved in the research? The reasons why research relationships get established and the interests served by such relationships can be deceptively complex. In its simplest form the relationship grows out of the researcher's desire to understand human behavior and the participants' desire to help or to learn about themselves. However, this simple form is rarely found. There are usually many additional factors that influence the creation of a research relationship and these issues emerge as the relationship develops, constantly shaping its character. Researchers, for example, may differ in their orientation to research, their preferred relationship with a participating individual or social system, their personal or cultural characteristics, and the intellectual or career interests being served by the research. Organizations too may be interested in the research because of its potential value to their primary task, because of their desire to be affiliated with a university, or because they expect the research to provide a rationale for change. As the two parties learn about each other through their interaction on the research, the relationship often changes as the people involved adjust their needs and expectations.

Perhaps the most complex situation is in field research, where many research relationships may exist simultaneously. The number of relationships is not limited by the number of participants since a social system also includes authority structures, work or social groups, and a variety of identity groups (e.g., race, gender, ethnicity, age). Each of these units in a social system (individual, group, organizational) will develop its own relationship with the researcher or research team depending upon the initial characteristics and interests of all people involved and the information collected along the way. As many researchers will attest, the complexity of managing research relationships is magnified by the fact that what happens in one relationship affects others and that skill and awareness in one relationship domain (e.g., individual relationships) do not necessarily carry over to other domains.

WHAT WE MEAN BY CLINICAL

The word *clinical* is an adjective formed from the word *clinic*, a setting where knowledge about a field of endeavor is pursued, accumulated, and applied to problems arising in that field (Morgan, 1984). The Greek word *clinicos* means bed or couch (from the verb *clino*—to cause to lean). In modern usage, an important element of the historical root of the word clinical has been maintained—namely, the delivery of therapeutic service to someone who is "bent over" or in bed. Clinical medicine, clinical psychology, psychiatry, social work, nursing, and most recently clinical sociology are all considered clinical fields because of the professional therapeutic activities involved. But the research aspect of the clinical setting—the role of the clinic in producing professional knowledge that can then be used for therapeutic purposes—has not only faded from view, but given way to a popular view that the clinical and research aspects of a profession are distinct and often conflicting endeavors. In fact, *Webster's New Collegiate Dictionary* (1975) defines *clinician* as "one qualified in the clinical practice of medicine, psychiatry or psychology as distinguished from one specializing in laboratory or research techniques."

In spite of the development of a definition that characterizes clinical as almost exclusively therapeutic and distinct from research, most of the social sciences use the term to refer to specific kinds of research methods. Glassner and Moreno (1982) quote Alfred M. Lee, a former president of the American Sociological Association, as describing participant observation as "a clinical study of social interaction." Like other social scientists, Lee seems to be using the term clinical to describe an

approach to research rather than an application of research to a therapeutic situation. In our experience as well, the term *clinical* is regularly used to refer to an approach to the study of social systems, a method with its own characteristics and its own demands.

We argue that all social research has its clinical aspects. However, these are ignored more often than not and hence the application of the term *clinical* seems inappropriate. In this book, we have chosen to use the term *clinical* for those aspects of research that have the following characteristics:

(1) direct involvement with and/or observation of human beings or social systems;
(2) commitment to a process of self-scrutiny by the researcher as he or she conducts the research;
(3) willingness to change theory or method in response to the research experience *during* the research itself;
(4) description of social systems that is dense or thick and favors depth over breadth in any single undertaking; and
(5) participation of the social system being studied, under the assumption that much of the information of interest is only accessible to or reportable by its members.

(1) The characteristic of direct involvement requires that the researcher have firsthand experience with the social system being studied. Clearly this excludes activities such as secondary analysis of questionnaire data. But what about observation through a one-way mirror, or structured field interviews for a national sample survey, or laboratory experiments with rigid experimenter protocols? With each of these situations there is some direct contact with other human beings; but is this direct involvement? Usually not, since each of these activities prescribes a role for the researcher that is intended to remove him or her from the emotional and unwanted intellectual aspects of the situation. When this psychological removal occurs, then the relationship can be viewed as being without direct involvement. To the extent that this removal does not occur—either because the role itself requires the researcher to examine his or her emotional and intellectual reactions while inside the role (e.g., psychoanalysis, participant observation, group relations training) or because the person in the role is unable (or unwilling) to practice this removal—there is a clinical aspect to the research at hand.

The type and extent of our involvement in social research varies with the project and the researcher, but all researchers have a stake in their research. This stake influences their involvement and brings a clinical

dimension to most research. The involvement may be intense for any number of reasons: career imperatives, belief in the social utility of research findings, or the desire to leave a legacy to the society and culture. For virtually all of us research is seen as a process that informs a professional practice that is itself born of a set of values about progress, justice, fairness, health, happiness, or quality of life.

Direct involvement also implies responsibility. Since, at a minimum, involvement can be understood as the pursuit of the researcher's interests with either the acquiescence or active participation of a social system, the researcher takes on certain responsibilities: responsibilities toward the people participating in the research; and responsibility to behave in accordance with professional standards of ethics, in particular to consider the consequences of one's work for the people involved. For some researchers these responsibilities lead to the development of a contract with participants in which these issues are discussed and specific boundaries or guidelines are laid out including provisions for renegotiating the contract. For others, these issues are left implicit.

In sum, the characteristic of direct involvement includes (1) first-hand experience with the social system being studied; (2) the engagement of the researcher's interests above and beyond his or her interest in science and knowledge for its own sake; and (3) responsibility toward the people participating in the research. Almost all field research in the social sciences, and especially research that has action or policy implications or is part of an intervention designed to help the system involved, has this clinical aspect to it.

(2) The commitment to self-scrutiny on the part of the researcher follows as a direct consequence from the characteristic of direct involvement. As researchers live with other human beings or social systems in the process of doing research, they are inevitably influenced by the relationships. This influence may actually change the researchers, their understanding of the world, values, beliefs, feelings about individuals, groups, or cultures, or it may evoke reactions specific to the research relationship, such as sympathy, anger, pity, condescension, prejudice, love, or hate. In both cases the influence process may go unnoticed by researchers since the process may be slow and the researcher's reactions may be attributed to sources other than the research involvement, especially if involvement is viewed as something to be avoided.

When the influence of the researcher's involvement goes unnoticed, a wealth of information about the social system is lost because the researcher is not attending to the characteristics of the social system that are influencing his or her feelings or reactions and may also be ignoring

the hypothesis that the social system is responding, in part, to the researcher's thoughts and actions. A researcher, for example, may find that he or she avoids certain members of the organization because they make the researcher uncomfortable or ask difficult questions about the researcher's role. This avoidance, in turn, may influence key research decisions.

Self-scrutiny is essential because of the researcher's many and often conflicting interests engaged by the research endeavor. Especially when social science trains its fledgling practitioners to believe that good science is interest free, neutral, and dispassionate, it is all too likely that the influence of the researcher's values, prejudices, gender, group affiliations, career interests, and so on will go purposefully unnoticed or unexamined. Too many of us are taught that our personal involvement in our research renders our work unscientific or illegitimate, as if there is a social scientist somewhere who has no personal involvement or whose involvement has no influence on his or her work. A clinical view of social research contends that this is a myth and that only through a commitment to periodic scrutiny of the researcher's involvement in the research process can the inevitable consequences of doing social research be described, examined, and understood.

Responsibility also brings with it a demand for self-scrutiny. Since what the researcher does not know about his or her own involvement in the research endeavor may affect other people, there is an implicit injunction that the researcher engage in systematic self-scrutiny. While few would argue with this premise, the proof is commitment to a process with this as its goal. Such a process must contend with the natural human tendency to avoid self-scrutiny for fear of learning something unpleasant or unsavory, or something that requires hard, painful decisions. The second characteristic of clinical research is precisely this commitment.

There are many other aspects of the self-scrutiny process, but we will hold our discussion of them until later in this chapter.

(3) The third characteristic of clinical research is *the willingness to change or adapt theory while involved in the research experience.* This does not mean that theory *must* change while the research is in progress, but rather that the researcher is *willing* to change a theory. This, in turn, might change action, data collection, or the type of involvement. This flies in the face of the traditional view that throughout the research process the relationship between data, method, and theory should remain strictly defined and unchanging.

The importance of this characteristic is underscored when viewed in light of the first two characteristics. Direct involvement coupled with a commitment to self-scrutiny by the researcher can result in the

development of new hypotheses about both method and theory at unexpected times in the research process. It would be self-defeating for the researcher to ignore this information, rigidly adhering to the stipulated procedures in order to preserve uniformity at the price of diminished meaning. It is, in fact, easy to see that if one sought to remove oneself from the research experience by minimizing one's involvement or acting as if involvement were unimportant and, in turn, placing little value on self-scrutiny, then it would be logical to separate theory and experience, stipulating precisely the points at which data and experience influence theory development.

(4) Clinical research is predicated on *the preference for dense or "thick" description* (Geertz, 1973) and a choice in favor of *depth over breadth* in any single research undertaking. It is generally accepted that the process of standardization and aggregation sacrifices richness in the service of generalizability. The clinical perspective emphasizes that meaningful generalizations about human behavior in social systems cannot be generated without density of social phenomena. It can be argued, however, that many of the theories about human behavior that meet the standards of science are ultimately rather thin (not very useful or insightful) when confronted with the complexity of social behavior as it occurs in the world.

In clinical research the work of generalization comes after the difficult and time consuming work of description, fraught as it is with the perils of involvement and self-scrutiny. In some instances the process of abstraction may have to be done by people other than those who generate the data. In other instances, the task of theory building on a grand scale may come only in the middle or near the end of a long career in research.

(5) Clinical research emphasizes *the participation of the social system being studied.* As in clinical medicine, clinical research starts with the assumption that all cannot be known merely by an observation of the living system. Some things can be known only when the experience of the system can be conveyed to the clinician in enough detail and depth. Often this communication of detail and depth requires mutual participation in the process of uncovering and understanding the many facets of the system's experience. The system and the researcher must work together to define what is relevant (Torbert, 1983). This takes time, effort, and commitment since the individuals in the social system may not have a language for describing their collective experience and the researcher may not be able to understand the system without a significant depth of mutual involvement and participation.

Real participation occurs only when there has been a mutual exploration that satisfies all parties involved as to the goals, competence,

purposes, and capacities of the people involved. In the case of medicine, for example, the doctor literally depends on the patient's participation for both diagnosis and treatment. The more complicated and rare the disease, the more the patient's participation is important. If the patient does not trust the doctor or the institution in which the doctor works, he or she may not be willing to participate actively in the diagnostic work. A wonderful example of this was Norman Cousins's (1979) participation in his own decisions about how to cure himself. He insisted on treatment that flew in the face of medical wisdom because, as he said, the "doctor latent within him" (lifting a phrase from Albert Schweitzer) told him what was needed for healing in his particular case. Cousins was also fortunate enough to have a doctor who took the research approach that maybe the information accessible to the patient via internal processes, but not confirmable from any external vantage point, might lead to wiser treatment choices.

Participation is particularly important in social research since the perceptions, thoughts, emotions, and beliefs of people constitute the primary subject matter for our investigations.

THE KEY QUESTION

Thus far in this chapter we have highlighted that all social research occurs in the context of a relationship and that there are certain critical characteristics that distinguish what we are labeling as clinical research. The key question that we are moving toward and with which we will conclude this chapter is the following: If clinical research is distinguished by these five characteristics, what kinds of understanding about social systems are likely to emerge from a process with these characteristics? To set the stage for our discussion of this issue, however, it is necessary to elaborate at greater length the role of self-scrutiny in clinical research.

THE ROLE OF SELF-SCRUTINY
IN CLINICAL RESEARCH

When a human system seeks out the assistance (or responds favorably to the overtures) of an applied researcher, it usually does so because it recognizes its need for help in self-reflecting—either on the relationship of its internal parts or on its external relationships with other entities in its ecosystem. Hence, the key work of the researcher involves establishing a way to assist the entity in developing additional insight into its behavior providing, as it were, a system's analog to the self-observing ego in

individual psychology (Smith, 1983b). Given that all systems have difficulty in developing self-reflecting perspectives that are not riddled with misattributions and faulty interpretations, the task of the researcher is both complex and rather tenuous. One of the great difficulties is to avoid having, as it were, the doctor suffering from the same disease that plagues the patient. That is, if the system has major difficulties in self-reflection, then if the researcher (or research team) has the same difficulty, we have the classic situation of the blind leading the blind. For this reason it is absolutely imperative that the skills of self-scrutiny in the researcher be highly developed.

When the research is being conducted by a group, there is a need for self-scrutiny to occur at the individual, interpersonal, and group levels. At each of these levels, the mechanisms for self-scrutiny may differ, but the basic processes are the same: a careful and systematic examination of the conscious and, when possible, unconscious activities of the research system. At the individual level this requires an ability to reflect on one's own experience with a willingness to embrace interpretations that might run counter to one's instincts. For example, if the researcher sees one group in the system as the "bad guys" it may be important to explore the possibility that they might be the "good guys" and then to ask the more difficult question—what is it about my relationship with them or the system as a whole that leads me to use these categories? If the research is being conducted by a group, self-scrutiny must involve attention to group-as-a-whole phenomena such as the dynamics around leadership, influence, authority, intimacy, race, gender, sexuality, power, and intergroup relations.

The value of self-scrutiny is twofold. First, it can help develop both an intellectual and emotional understanding of the dynamics inherent in a human system's struggle to learn about itself, especially those involved in confronting weaknesses, imperfections, failures and problems. Second, self-scrutiny can help uncover valuable information. The scrutiny may be directed at the researchers themselves or at their relationship with the social system. Since all research is approached with some intellectual presuppositions and a variety of emotional predispositions (sometimes called *biases*) it is absurd to act as if this were not the case. Addressing these inevitable influences in a systematic way provides the reader with some of the context in which the research was conducted, allowing others to make independent judgments concerning the role of these factors in the research.

Parallel processes. There is an even more important reason for a research system to have both the commitment to self-scrutiny and the skills to undertake this complex task. Under normal circumstances, the

probability is very high that the processes operative within the researcher (individual or team) will be a playing through, in parallel form, of the key dynamics that are driving the system being researched. We refer to these alignments as parallel processes, defined as the tendency for two or more social systems that have significant contact with each other to show similar affects, behaviors, and cognitions (Alderfer, Brown, Kaplan, & Smith, in press).

An understanding of parallel processes has been part of the therapeutic world for a long time. In this field these processes are referred to as transference and countertransference—concepts that indicate the unconscious tendencies of both the client and the therapist to relate to each other in terms of a prior relationship, transferring to the other attributes of a previous significant individual with whom he or she has been identified (Lidz, 1968). There is a firmly established tradition in psychotherapy to keep a keen focus on countertransference reactions. If they go unnoticed or unexamined, the therapist's understanding of the patient's situation will become distorted, potentially jeopardizing the treatment. On the other hand, if the countertransference can be recognized and scrutinized, it can provide a special kind of insight into the patient's life. It has also been observed that in the supervision of psychotherapy, what transpires in the relationship of the supervisor and the therapist can be a parallel playing out of the therapist-client relationship and vice versa (Searles, 1955; Ekstein & Wallerstein, 1958; Sachs & Shapiro, 1976).

Parallel processes occur not only in interpersonal relationships. They can be found operating in interactions among groups or even at the organizational level. Understanding parallel processes and their impact requires a willingness to deal with emotional reactions that can be disturbing—both in others and in oneself. However, they are only accessible to our understanding if we are willing to do the hard work of self-scrutiny. Turning a blind eye to them does not make them go away; it merely drives them into those areas marked "error" or "the researcher's blind spots" (Berg, 1980; Smith & Crandell, 1984; Alderfer et al., in press).

In summary, the process of self-scrutiny is central to our definition of clinical research because it can yield information about the intellectual and emotional factors that inevitably influence the researchers' involvement and activity, and at the same time provide information about the dynamics of the individual or social system being studied. The self-scrutiny process is difficult and complex precisely because *both* the researcher and the "researched" are simultaneously influencing each other. Since this is occurring in ways that initially are out of the awareness of the parties involved, scrutiny is an absolutely necessary part of social science research.

WHAT UNDERSTANDINGS COME
FROM CLINICAL ACTIVITY?

The purpose of developing the clinical side of social research methods is not to replace what is knowable using traditional approaches but rather to augment it. Through clinical methods we see different aspects of social reality and we look with differently calibrated eyes. Our clinical engagement confronts us with thoughts, feelings, and information that are not accessible under tightly controlled circumstances, and forces us to expand our conceptual horizons beyond the boundaries of our predefined theories.

As part of appreciating the special contribution of the clinical side of research methods, one question we must understand is, What is it that is usually not seen? Then we must move to the question of how new aspects can be seen via clinical methods.

In all of our experience there exists simultaneously what we see and what we do not see, what is known and what is not known. We cannot be everywhere at once and we are incapable of seeing certain things while looking at others. We know, however, that the unseen exists even if we cannot see it because the Gestalt suggests such a side exists (as, for example, in the case of an unfamiliar coin that rests on a table with one side up). We have experience flipping things over, which also contributes to our belief that the underside exists even when we cannot see it. Likewise, in social relationships certain issues, ideas, or emotions are inaccessible. This may be because of implicit, shared agreements to keep certain topics unspeakable. For example, each of us knows things about ourselves, our family, the organization we work in, and the like that we find hard to reveal except under special circumstances. Or it may be that we have no way of really knowing.

We have a sense of the "other side" of physical objects because of our existence as three-dimensional creatures in three-dimensional space. Analogously, our perspective of what's on the other side of social phenomena depends on our view of the structure of the social world and how we interact with it. For example, those who are willing to descend into the depths of Dante's inferno are likely to understand both the manifest and the hidden sides of the human psyche differently than those who have never chosen or been forced to take such a journey.

Perhaps one of the best ways to capture this issue is to illustrate a similar choice point in the evolution of art.[1] When one thinks of a traditional painting, such as a still life of a table, most of what is captured is the top and whatever is placed on the surface. We do not see what is underneath and, if there's a tablecloth, we may not even see the legs. We are left to surmise about the underside, the hidden, extrapolat-

ing from that which is presented. In a way the artist is saying that only what meets the eye is of importance. Then along came cubism, a tradition suggesting everything is important and should be attended to, including the undersides. Even more important, each aspect should be given space within the painting to exist in a way that preserves its essentiality, not subordinating the core of any one element to any other element. In this way the cubists expanded the methods of the traditionalists, representing in two dimensions multiple sides with the goal of preserving a sense of the whole that did not depend on surface structure as the only system of integration. Some critics argued that in the process the artists violated the integrity of the scenes they sought to represent. To this the counterargument was offered that the cubists brought to life different relationships with the objects of their art, thereby expanding the world capable of being represented on canvas. Cubism did not replace anything; it added something.

Although this analogy to art may seem rather pretentious, given the incredible skill and sophistication of that craft, we consider the crossroads we face as social science researchers similar to that confronting artists when cubism had its birth. Are we going to move from being a science that seeks only to represent "reality," or will we become a discipline that makes explicit our interpretive sides and that attempts to represent data, method, and theory in a holistic way?

In this chapter we want to offer a glimpse of what we sense might become our heritage if we can develop adequate clinical sophistication. Again, we turn to art to make our point, and to Picasso. We illustrate with his lithographic work of the *Bull*.[2] If you look at the last photograph of this sequence you may well find yourself asking how a person took a pen, drew five lines, essential and universal, and produced a seemingly effortless distillation of a creature called a bull. In fact it did not happen this way, as the series reproduced here indicates. This bull is a lithograph created via the medium of a stone, and the final representation is the result of eleven iterations on the same stone.

Picasso began with a thick description of a bull, a straightforward image that captured a particular animal. A week later he returned to his lithographic stone and transformed the particular into an animal of brute mass and power. Then, after another week, he scraped the stone again, reducing the size of the bull and in the process leaving clear traces of the artist's personal interaction with his medium. At this stage the focus shifted from mass to surface as white lines were scratched across the body like divisions indicating cuts of meat, as one might find on a butcher's shop poster.

By the midpoint of his series, Picasso had given surface divisions increasing strength over the image. The lines were lengthened and

connected across broader areas of the bull, forcing the body into simpler shapes, as parts were distended. Eventually the bull became centralized again. In portraying the bull, tension between mass, structure, texture, and the animal's individual characteristics was created as Picasso moved to simplify. All remaining hints of representational texture were let go as lines of structure became dominant. By the end the question seems to be how few lines can be used to represent the animal fully in the simplest geometric terms. The simplification to a tiny and empty head surmounted by enormous horns evokes the sense of the bull's unique characteristic—both the universal and the particular represented in the one form.

Picasso's work was the product of a long and complex relationship with both his subject matter and his medium. He was constantly experimenting with his medium and every experiment led to different forms of representation. For our purposes, we can almost imagine him asking a host of methodological questions such as, Where do I start? How do I know when I'm finished? What are the criteria by which I judge the product? How do I know if I have captured the essence of the phenomenon? Need I satisfy only myself? What exactly is the process? How do I conduct this conversation between subject and medium and translate what I learn into further action?

These are questions the clinical side of research evokes: What are the clinical aspects of social research? How do the actions of the researcher make clinical research occur? What are the hazards? What are the demands? What actually is added to our understanding when clinical methods are included in our research? What does it feel like and what are the emotional as well as intellectual signposts along the path of the clinical research process?

We are sure some of our critics will dismiss what we have to say here with the off-handed retort "Are you talking about art or science!" That is exactly our point. When we no longer can distinguish between art and science as separate processes but experience their holism we will have tapped the real meaning of the term *clinical*—knowledge through encounter, valid because it fits with experience, real because it touches the core, the universal and particular simultaneously.

NOTES

1. Our definition of cubism draws heavily upon French (1977).
2. The commentary on Picasso's *Bull* was provided by the National Gallery of Art.

CHAPTER

2

TAKING OUR SELVES SERIOUSLY
AS RESEARCHERS

Clayton P. Alderfer

What becomes acceptable psychology accrues only when all observations, including those which a psychologist makes upon himself, are treated as though made upon "the other one." Thus, we make explicit the distinction between the experimenter and the thing observed. This distinction is obvious in physics, in psychology it is equally valid . . . .

Although a particular experimenter may himself become the object of study by another experimenter, and he in turn by still another, at some stage of such a regress an independent experimenter *must be* [emphasis in original] (i.e., is always) assumed. (S. S. Stevens, 1939, pp. 221-263)

I was attempting to describe some of the dangers of psychological analysis. It can lead to a certain presumption and arrogance when others are seen as mere puppets without freedom and human dignity. The psychologists who stand outside to observe and explain *their* [emphasis mine] mechanisms may feel himself the only exception, the only real person . . . . When I spoke to them [different people in the big city] I had the feeling that I lived; when I talked with psychologists, it was to speak about life but not to live it in the same way. (Fritz Heider, 1983, pp. 28, 47)

The serious problems in life, however, are never fully solved. If ever they should appear to be so it is a sure sign that something has been lost. The meaning and purpose of a problem seem to lie not in its solution but in our working at it incessantly. This alone preserves us from stultification and petrification. (Carl Jung, 1931, pp. 11-12)

Since becoming a social scientist nearly twenty years ago, I regularly have been impressed with what goes on at professional meetings—both inside and outside official sessions. Below are three episodes from the most recent professional meeting I attended. They illustrate the operation of "self effects" among social scientists and suggest that such phenomena readily appear wherever members of the profession gather and individuals decide to be attentive.

(1) Within the first hour of my arrival I was invited to dinner by two colleagues—one I know well enough to call a friend and the other was a new acquaintance. The two people knew each other reasonably well. One was male, the other female. We discussed three topics over dinner: the achievements and adventures of our children; the career movements of common friends coupled with the job openings at our respective universities; and finally, in the taxi on the way back to the meetings, which prominent female and male psychologists were sleeping together and whether they had gotten married yet.[1]

(2) During the conference itself, I gave a talk with the same title as this chapter. The audience was primarily composed of younger members of the profession who reacted positively when I suggested that the self-awareness of the profession—especially of the senior members—was not excessive, and perhaps we might have a more intellectually exciting and practically useful field if we paid more attention to our own consciousness and behavior. Riding in the elevator after the session ended, I was confronted by one of the senior members from the audience, a man senior to me, who said, "Aw, come on, Clay, you're part of the establishment now. You've got to cut this stuff out!"

(3) The final significant event of the conference was a panel of distinguished members who discussed career options for social scientists. Among the group were three men and a woman, whose organizational affiliations included a major university, a consulting firm, a financially successful corporation, and a research laboratory. Listening to these people describe the trials and rewards of their careers, I was suddenly taken with the thought that their organizations, however diverse they were, also had at least one major commonality: They represented the predominantly white male and economically secure sector of our society. I then asked the panel how they thought their organizational location affected their research work. The first person responded, "Just because we are in a wealthy corporation does not mean it is easy to get research money!" Another was unclear about my question. I rephrased it, "I was wondering what difference you think it would make if you had worked for the New Haven, Connecticut,

Welfare Department." Another panelist responded, "Oh, I know what stereotype you are coming from. Well, I served for years on the school board of [a wealthy suburb of a major New England City]. Working for major corporations does not mean you do not serve your communities."

The words "Our Selves" in the title of this chapter are printed correctly; the separate words were selected to indicate several meanings of the term *self*, which we might take more seriously in order to enhance the significance and the quality of social research. I believe these various "selves" are repressed and suppressed by the positivist approach to methodology that most of us are taught and accept. Although avoided and denied, the various aspects of our selves do not go away; instead they operate indirectly and covertly. Professional meetings, manifestly devoted to the sharing of scientific information, are settings where the full range of our personal and professional selves can be seen, if we choose to notice. The three episodes selected were described to illustrate the presence of those frequently unacknowledged and yet most important selves.

In this chapter I shall explore three senses of the term *self*, each taken from a well-developed theoretical position. The various meanings of the concept also have a significant similarity; each accepts and incorporates conscious and unconscious elements. The three theoretical positions are the following: (1) ego psychology (Erikson, 1956); (2) analytical psychology (Jung, 1963); and (3) intergroup theory (Alderfer, 1982).[2]

Ego psychology attends to the conscious and personal unconscious intermingling of the individual's sense of "Who am I?" The theory is concerned with changes in this sense of self induced internally by biological developments such as sexual maturation and aging, including their effects on significant interpersonal relationships, and, externally, by major historical events such as wars and economic transformations.

Analytical psychology focuses on universal symbols of the collective unconscious on their own terms and as a means to examine and illuminate the personal unconscious. *Self* in the language of analytical psychology refers to a favorable coming together of the ego (including the personal unconscious) and the collective unconscious. The collective unconscious includes symbols and myths that may be found across diverse cultures and historical periods.

Intergroup theory concerns the relations among groups taken as entities and the effects for individuals of memberships in interdependent groups. For individuals, selves are shaped by people serving as representatives of groups in relations with other groups. For groups, their internal dynamics and external relations are shaped by the diversity of group affiliations carried by members.

The idea of unconscious processes carries a number of related assumptions, regardless of the theory in which the construct arises. The key idea is that important material is out of awareness and can be brought into awareness. Unconscious material takes the form of symbols, metaphors, and myths. People become expert in understanding unconscious processes by examining their own experience, usually with the aid of a professional therapist or consultant who has developed a disciplined expertise in these matters. Legitimate expertise includes subjecting oneself to analysis before practicing on others. All of the theories include the concept of projection, whereby individuals initially "see" the unconscious material in other individuals or groups before they see it in themselves. All recognize the resistance of people to accepting unconscious dynamics, and all purport to value positively the process of a person taking ownership of her or his unconscious material. The Jungian term for this process is *withdrawing projections.*

I began this chapter with the three examples because they are rich with unconscious material. They would be even richer if I named the individuals involved, and the readers knew about their personal and professional lives. Without doing this, I can make only comparatively general connections between the three concepts of self and the examples.

Example 1. We all were working on our family identities, our fantasies about what men and women do at professional meetings, and our professional identities as receivers and givers of jobs at prestigious universities.

Example 2. As I challenged the old king (a mythological theme) by my words about changing the reigning paradigm of research methodology, I was reminded that I was already a member of the court, from which I could presumably be expelled if I did not "cut it out."

Example 3. A question whose aim was to explore the effects of membership in the white, middle to upper socioeconomic group evoked denial (because we are rich, it is not easy to get research money), avoidance (misunderstanding the question after someone had already answered it), and projection (attributing a "stereotype" to me while giving information that further affirmed the speaker's membership in the group whose membership I asked him to explore).

Professional meetings, of course, are not where research ususally gets done. (My sample of people who have agreed to fill out the JDI after engaging in sexual gossip is not large.) One might argue that profes-

sional meetings serve as a kind of outlet for material that is successfully suppressed while the main work of research is going on. Or, one might view professional meetings as a sort of microcosm of professional behavior in general. What occurs in the official sessions then parallels what shows up in research reports and journal articles, and what occurs in question-and-answer sessions inside and outside official sessions is similar to the unreported material associated with most research projects—no matter how rigorous or carefully controlled.

The remainder of this chapter explores the events around the actual conduct of research rather than professional meetings. The chief question is to what degree the various senses of self importantly influence research processes and products. Efforts to answer follow in four sections.

The first presents two dialogues: (1) Are researchers people when we do research? and (2) How, if at all, do professional organizations in social science affect the behavior and attitudes of their members? Patterned after the Socratic method, these discussions take readers through an example of self exploration by the writer. Readers also may be prodded to engage in similar conversations with themselves or with others.

The second gives biographical and autobiographical material from well-recognized psychologists to illustrate how the operation of "self" dynamics shapes highly regarded research products. Data illustrate all three meanings of the term *self*. In general, the phenomenon of well-known social scientists being subject to biographical or autobiographical study suggests growing awareness of self effects in research.

The third examines the social psychology laboratory as an organization. This major invention of social scientists has had some scrutiny for self effects with attention focused mainly on experimenter-subject relations. I propose to view the laboratory as an organization to identify systemic influences that shape research results without the awareness of the investigators.

Each of these sections provides data pertaining to one or more theories of self. Generally, a section emphasizes one kind of material about the self and includes information relevant to other meanings as well. From this point forward, the text treats readers as if they carried an "intellectual receiver" of three bands—one for each self theory—that is analogous to a radio capable of receiving three stations singly or in combination. The two dialogues focus primarily on the ego-identity of investigators. Secondarily, they attend to group-level issues within social science and between the profession and its publics. Next, the chapter turns to events from the lives of particular individuals. In the first case,

self data emerge from the collective unconscious of the person. In the second instance, the data pertain to ego-identity struggles. Group-level influences are also observable in both accounts. Analysis of the social psychology laboratory leads with group-level effects and also includes information deriving from the ego-identity of investigators.

The fourth portion offers conclusions pertaining to the underlying philosophical issues in self analysis. It also presents the implications of untoward effects of inadvertent and covert self processes on social research and the creative possibilities of effectively harnessing self dynamics to produce more intellectually exciting and socially useful inquiry.

TWO DIALOGUES

The dialogues occur between two persons who may be alive in many of us. Scientist is the individual trained in rigorous methodology undergirded by logical positivist philosophy. He seeks objectivity and is concerned with avoiding bias and preventing loss of control. Self is the whole person speaking. She is sympathetic to critical philosophy and is attentive to avoiding illusion and deception, whether of oneself or of others.

Scientist and Self agree, "We meet to explore these questions: Are social scientists people when they do research? Do the laws and empirical generalizations that social researchers work so hard to develop pertain to themselves? When professional investigators do their work, are they subject to the same lawfulness of behavior and experience as those individuals they study? If not, why not? If so, what difference does it make? These questions may strike readers in a variety of ways."

SELF: Yes, the answers are obvious! Of course social scientists are people!

SCIENTIST: Maybe, but I think the answer should be more tentative. I suppose the "laws" of human behavior apply to social scientists, but we have to be careful about the limits of our findings. There have been comparatively few carefully controlled studies of social scientists.

SELF: True, social scientists are a bit difficult to control—especially after they cease being students and most especially after they have tenure.

SCIENTIST: I meant statistical control and laboratory control, not political or administrative control. You do know the difference, don't you?

SELF: I believe I can recite the ideology of the scientific establishment, if that's what you mean.

SCIENTIST: Would you stop this political innuendo? I am talking about the agreements social scientists make with each other in order to get on

with the business of doing research. These agreements are only political in the largest sense. They serve the aims of social science. Ideology is really an inflammatory word.

SELF: OK. It certainly upsets you a bit, doesn't it?

SCIENTIST: Well, ideology implies lack of objectivity. It suggests that emotional and group forces shape what individual investigators perceive and think.

SELF: That it does.

SCIENTIST: Well, I have difficulty with that. The scientific process is more complicated.

SELF: In what ways?

SCIENTIST: Competent, well-trained social scientists use sophisticated methodological and statistical controls to prevent their own feelings and behavior from influencing their findings in unknown or uncontrolled ways. Social scientists do not inadvertently influence what they study because they have a professional discipline that either prevents such artifacts from arising or permits an assessment of their effects.

SELF: Do you mean the feelings and behaviors of social scientists and their effects are artifacts?

SCIENTIST: Well, not quite. But you know the saying, "One person's artifact is another person's finding."

SELF: Perhaps you mean that the feelings and behavior of social scientists are artifactual when they do research.

SCIENTIST: I guess that's what I mean. But I must say, I experience you as leading me somewhere I am not at all sure I want to go.

SELF: I can understand that. The inevitable conclusion from what you say seems to be that social scientists basically are not people when they do research, except when there are artifactual effects that are unintended and should be corrected.

SCIENTIST: Right, right!! That's what I mean. You've got the idea.

SELF: Do you think the people who are subject to social scientists doing research experience them as people?

SCIENTIST: You mean, "Do our 'subjects' experience us as people?"

SELF: Right, that's what I mean.

SCIENTIST: Well, that is a good question. Perhaps we should study it.

SELF: You mean we should ask the people we study whether they experience us as people studying them?

SCIENTIST: That seems almost nonsensical, doesn't it? What do you think they'd say?

SELF: Of course they experience us as people. I'll bet they even experience us as certain kinds of people or at least as people with certain kinds of characteristics.

SCIENTIST: Well, that's another story. If we asked them what kinds of characteristics social researchers have, do you think we'd have to listen to their answers?

SELF: Why would we ask them if we didn't want to listen to their answers?

SCIENTIST: That's my point. I am not at all sure I want to listen to their answers.

SELF: Then you probaby shouldn't ask them.

SCIENTIST: Right, I think it would be a mistake. Suppose they said things that made us uncomfortable or implied we ought to change.

SELF: It could happen.

SCIENTIST: That settles it. Now I am sure we shouldn't ask. If people gave disturbing answers, I'd probably have an emotional reaction.

SELF: And then your objectivity for future work might be compromised?

SCIENTIST: Absolutely!! For, even after, I might approach the task of data collection with an eye toward how people perceive me; I might never be the same again.

SELF: Well, maybe, but I believe you are over-reacting a bit. Some people do learn to receive feedback about their own behavior with an open-minded attitude. Some even change their behavior in constructive ways.

SCIENTIST: Well, maybe, but then again, maybe not. You know how easy it is to lose one's objectivity if one becomes emotional!

SELF and SCIENTIST now shift their attention to the second question, "In what ways, if any, do professional organizations of social scientists affect the behavior and attitudes of their members?"

SELF: Will you give your answer to this question?

SCIENTIST: Of course, I am a scientist who is sympathetic to other scientists. I avoid no important scientific questions, none, do you hear me? I avoid no important scientific questions!

SELF: Oh, good, would you please answer the question?

SCIENTIST: What question was that?

SELF: In what ways, if any, do professional organizations of social scientists affect the behavior and attitudes of their members?

SCIENTIST: Right, I had forgotten the question. Now that you remind me, I am not sure why you ask.

SELF: I asked because I want to know your answer.

SCIENTIST: What are you, some kind of research person?

SELF: Will that affect your answer?

SCIENTIST: GOOD HEAVENS!! Can't you just answer my question? Answering a question makes me think you are either a research person or some kind of clinical shrink. Which is it?

SELF: Wait a minute! I asked you the question because I wanted to know your answer. PERIOD. That's all. We're colleagues, right?

SCIENTIST: OK! OK! What was the question again?

SELF The question was, "In what ways, if any, do professional organizations of social scientists affect the behavior and attitudes of their members?"

SCIENTIST: Yeah, yeah. Now I remember. Well, I guess I am not sure.

SELF: Isn't the social psychology of organizations built on the assumption that organizations affect the behavior and attitudes of their members? There are many journals, educational programs, research laboratories, divisions of professional organizations, certifications to practice professionally, etc.

SCIENTIST: It is an empirical science. Why don't you go out and collect some data?

SELF: Hold it! We're doing it again. I just want the opinion of a colleague on whether our professional organizations affect the behavior and attitudes of our members. Could you please tell me what you think?

SCIENTIST: All right! You've worn me down. I guess I think the organizations should affect the behavior and attitudes of our members.

SELF: Please wait a minute. I did not ask you what should happen; that's a normative question. I asked your opinion about what does happen; that's an empirical matter.

SCIENTIST: That settles it. I won't answer your question. I am a researcher. I study other people's organizations. That's it!

SELF: Well, what if our professional organizations affect our behavior when we study other people's organizations?

SCIENTIST: Well, what if they do?!? I already said I thought they should.

SELF: But doesn't that suggest we might improve the study of other people's organizations if we understood our own better?

SCIENTIST: Look, cut out this clinical stuff! We're scientists not clinicians. And that's the name of that tune. Because we are in charge, we decide what to study and how. Period. Do you know any real scientists who study their own organizations?

SELF: Thank you very much for not avoiding the question.

The dialogues end here. A reader may relate to them in several ways. First, they are personal material from this writer. They emerged from my self. They represent my internal dialogue with myself. I am both Self and Scientist. Their struggle is my struggle. Second, the dialogues also represent my relationship to the reigning paradigm in social research. With this orientation, I am Self, and Scientist is a representative of the reigning social consensus among well-established, highly respected

social scientists. The point of view of Self is my own, and the responses of Scientist are my perceptions of how the dominant consensus consciously and unconsciously deals with questions of self-reflection. Third, the reader might take these dialogues as a stimulus for constructing her or his own. I do not believe I am alone with the conflict between Self and Scientist. The existence of this book testifies to that assertion. Later sections of this chapter provide additional material pertaining to others' relations with the conflict. A reader who at this time writes her or his own version of the dialogues might experience subsequent sections of this chapter more fully, but, then again, he might not. She probably would, unless she has identified with him excessively. Fourth, a person might relate to the dialogues by enacting them with a colleague. The most interesting results might occur if both people tried both parts for each question.

TWO INDIVIDUAL SELVES
AND THEIR CONCEPTUAL PRODUCTS

Social research as we think of it today is a comparatively recent addition to civilization. The social form was suggested in the early part of the nineteenth century by such writers as August Compte and actually achieved the roots of its present condition in the later 1800s through the publications of scholars such as Wundt, Le Bon, and Freud. From this perspective, the field is close to the end of its first century. During this period, there has been an increasing number of people whose careers have been "being social scientists." We are in a period now when the lives and careers of people born near the start of the twentieth century are drawing to a close. For a variety of reasons—both personal and collective—we see an increasing interest in the personal lives of distinguished social scientists. Some individuals prepare "intellectual autobiographies" as a way of ending their careers. Others, perhaps the more prominent, become the subjects of biographies. Whether stated explicitly or left unacknowledged, the fundamental question of these works is how the personal lives of the social scientists related to their intellectual work.[3]

In this section, I focus on two examples of relationships between selves and conceptual products. The particular people were selected for a variety of reasons. First, I wanted individuals whose contributions I genuinely respect. I did not want to be in the position of disparaging the scholarly work of a person by seeming to reduce it to "nothing more" than acting out of personal conflicts. Second, I wanted the people to be notably different in their preferred styles of working. As one friend put

it, "Everyone knows personality theorists are a little bit nuts, but social psychologists, how could their personal lives affect their science?" Third, of course, there had to be material that either set the stage for relating person and concept or actually made the connection. Fourth, I wanted to examine people through the vehicle of both biographical and autobiographical reports. Sources of error are different in the two forms, and relying on both has the advantage of showing the sorts of associations that are possible from own and from others' data. Finally, I wanted people who represented different generations of behavioral scientists—one from the founding fathers of the 1890s and another from the second generation.

Fritz Heider, with his masterwork of *The Psychology of Interpersonal Relations* (1958), is the first example. The second is Sigmund Freud, with attention to factors that shaped his theoretical conflict about his own seduction theory (Balmary, 1979; Masson, 1984). Heider was a social psychologist not known for embracing depth psychology in his theoretical work. Freud was the founder of a professional movement based on understanding and utilizing unconscious processes.

HEIDER

My attention to Heider's autobiography was stimulated by Harold Kelley's (1984) review, entitled "The Impractical Theorist." Kelley's title was intended to contrast Heider's life and work with that of Kurt Lewin, who was a friend and mentor. Alfred Marrow wrote a biography of Lewin, which he entitled *The Practical Theorist*. Lewin died at a comparatively young age, wrote copiously, and is famous for saying, "Nothing is so practical as a good theory." Heider has lived into his eighties, wrote comparatively few published pieces, and focused his attention on mainly theoretical questions. Lewin is viewed by many as one of the most influential figures in the founding of modern laboratory social psychology and in the start up of action research. Kelley (1984, p. 455) assesses the influence of Heider's (1958) book, *The Psychology of Interpersonal Relations,* as having "enormous influence on modern social psychology, especially in the areas of 'balance' and 'attribution'— perhaps more influence than any other single person."

Kelley begins his review with a quotation from the final paragraph of Heider's autobiography. The full paragraph reads as follows:

> Another happy event was being asked by Roger Barker whether I would consider coming to Kansas, just at the time when I most needed to make a change. That question brought us to this haven where we have made our home for thirty-some years and where our three sons grew up so comfor-

tably. There were many more such turning points in this story that came at exactly the right moment to produce the end effect that seems so happy when I put it all together. As a matter of fact, If I were inclined to be superstitious, I could believe that a friendly spirit arranged the whole sequence of events in which the powers of fortune were so kind to me. (Heider, 1983, p. 190)

Among his numerous transitions, Heider clearly views the move to Kansas as of special significance. As things turned out, it was this change of location that brought the conditions that permitted him to finish his influential book. Kelley recognizes the importance of this transition by calling it "the most dramatic point in Heider's story." Yet Kelley's explanation of the event differs from the one I would give. He reported that Heider felt "cornered" and suffered anxiety attacks. He commented that Heider managed "cognitive restructuring," and it brought him relief. Heider's chief frustration in Kelley's mind was Heider's inability to obtain grant support for his "conceptual research."

Now listen to Heider's (1983, pp. 152-155) own words describing his experience at the time.

I was also frustrated with what I could do during the summer vacations to deal with the ideas about interpersonal relations that I was gradually developing. Somehow my brain does not seem to be very efficient organ. It generates some acceptable products, but only after periods of leisurely dreaming and inactive somnolence. I am not a person of great energy, and the thinking that goes on in my head often seems to be without my personal participation. Nietzsche's words—that one should say, "It thinks," not, "I think"—seems very much to fit my case, and the life I was leading did not seem to give "it" much opportunity.

Gradually, during this period, I developed the idea of writing a book on interpersonal relations, but if I was to do that, I needed more unbroken stretches of free time. I went to New York and to Washington to try to get support from foundations, but everywhere came the same answer: there was nothing available for "conceptual research." A few of the people I talked with said that they, personally, would favor it; the time would come when help would be available—perhaps in five years—but at present it would not be possible to persuade a committee to accept the kind of proposal that I was talking about.

The result of all this was that I felt cornered and became the victim of attacks of anxiety. It is true that they gave me some new insights and were perhaps worthwhile in a way, but on the whole it was a rather unpleasant way of learning about myself. These attacks always came on when I was

lying down for an afternoon nap or for a night's sleep; therefore, even sleep was no longer an escape from what was troubling me. I often formulated my situation or my fate in a kind of picture, partly to realize more clearly what was happening, partly to exaggerate and make fun of it—a way of handling what is unpleasant in life perhaps. The picture accompaniment to the attacks of anxiety was taken from the old story of Prometheus, chained to a rock, with an eagle coming every day to feed on his liver. Though I did not really compare myself to this hero, there was always a ferocious bird that, when I lay down to sleep, came and hacked away at my heart and liver with great gusto. I am sure that this annoying image stemmed from the old Greek saga. I tried to fight the bird off in different ways, but it was very persistent and merciless. It even seemed to me that the more I struggled to repel it, the fierce its attacks became.

My lack of success in getting rid of the bird made me question my approach; so I went back to the philosophy of my earlier years. I asked: "Why do I defend myself so strenuously? After all, I am not so important. Other people are much more important, and there are many more of them!" so I tried to be friendly to the fierce bird. I said to him: "Come on. I am at your service." This cordial invitation had a dramatic effect. It seemed that the one thing against which it was helpless, the one thing it could not stand, was being treated in a familiar way and without respect. The ferocious bird became disgusted and suddenly flew away. When I tried to fill my thinking with the idea "I am not so important" and when I told myself that it did not matter whether or not all those unripe thoughts that I felt growing ever came to fruition, I would feel a sudden relaxation in the region of my heart. My attacks of anxiety stopped. These experiences made me believe very much in a relation between egocentricity, tension, and anxiety, something that is doubtless familiar to people who deal with such problems, recently to people who work with biofeedback.

This was the first time that I had become aware of changes in tension. Since then I have learned more about how to recognize them and how to influence them. I know the pleasant feeling when the blood is flowing out into my limbs and when relaxation is spreading over my body. I try to get this feeling every day as I am going to sleep. The motif "I am not important" still has a place in my mental equipment. I would guess that it has saved me some heartache and frustration, and it is also a balance to counteract the opposed force of my own importance that I have in common with most people.

I should like to add to these remarks about the anxiety attacks that there was the possibility of a mere physiological contributing factor, and that was my smoking. I was never what one would call a heavy smoker. At the time about which I am writing I usually smoked half a pack of cigarettes a day and one or two small cigars with my afternoon tea. However, it was difficult to ventilate my large third-floor study thoroughly. The windows were small and not easy to open, and the air in the room was rather heavy

with smoke and with the dust that inevitably comes from accumulations of books. Eventually, I cut down on my smoking and aired the room more often. These measures may also have contributed to the abatement of my troubles.

To a person familiar with the concepts of Jungian analytical psychology, Heider's dream about his Promethean situation would be taken as an event from the collective—as opposed to the personal—unconscious. According to ancient Greek mythology, Prometheus, himself a god, had angered Zeus, the chief of gods, by giving fire to men and thereby elevating humans to a position too close to the gods. Zeus punished Prometheus by chaining him to a rock and prohibiting either sleep or rest. Zeus also threatened even greater torture if Prometheus did not reveal a great secret. Fate had informed Zeus that one of his sons would dethrone him but had not told him who the mother of this son would be. Prometheus, however, knew who this was and refused to tell. Hermes warned Prometheus that if he did not tell, "An eagle red with blood . . . will tear to rags your body, feasting in fury on the blackened liver" (Hamilton, 1940, p. 72).

Eventually, Heider responds to his dream by talking to the ferocious bird "in a familiar way." From the perspective of analytical psychology, Heider's decision to deal with the bird means that he addresses his unconscious (Jung, 1963, p. 173 ff.). The Promethean drama is archetypal. To reach this point he had to put aside his own ego: "Why do I defend myself . . . I am not so important." Kelley's reflection on Heider's dramatic moment gives a different interpretation. He wrote, "There is a *morality tale* [emphasis mine] for all of us who are inclined to place far great importance on ourselves and our work (Kelley, 1984, p. 456)." Kelley makes no mention of the archetypal contents of Heider's dream. He seems to see putting aside of the egoism as the desirable end state, the "morality tale." My own view, influenced by Jungian psychology, is that the deemphasis on ego was a necessary but not sufficient condition for Heider's development. The remaining step was for him to address the bird—that is, to deal with collective contents from his own unconscious. One could suggest that Heider himself might have been of a similar view; otherwise, why would he have described the dream contents and made the connection to the mythological pattern?

Heider's acceptance of the archetypal material as an explanation for his reduced anxiety, however, remained uncertain. In the subsequent paragraph, he raises the possibility that his change came about from a "mere physiological factor . . . [the reduction of] my smoking." Thus both Kelley as reviewer and Heider as reporter show their struggles

between Scientist and Self. Kelley shows his alertness to the importance of this moment as a crucial turning point in Heider's personal and professional development. Yet he seems to ignore the archetypal material and to prefer an externally based explanation. Heider reports his confrontation with the unconscious and adds a contributing factor in the form of reduced smoking as if he cannot fully state that his own psychic change was as important as it seemed to be.

Ultimately, Kelley sees Heider's change as cognitive restructuring, getting a research grant, and moving to Kansas. He omits the intrapsychic activity that Heider describes and I emphasize, and he draws a different moral injunction than I would. I would argue that Heider makes his self more complete by attending to both ego and unconscious functions. The grant, the move, and the book that were to follow after this dramatic period *reflect* the change in Heider's intrapsychic condition at least as much as they caused it. I suggest that the "friendly spirit" to which Heider refers in the final sentence of his book and to which Kelley attends in the opening sentence of his review is not superstitious at all (at least as the term is usually used) but rather a symbol for the extent to which Heider's self consisted of a favorable integration of unconscious and ego.

FREUD

Discussion of Freud's work pertains to a specific empirical-conceptual element in psychoanalytic theory. Careful scholars of psychoanalytic history know that the issue has been a subject of energetic attention since Freud developed his theory and method. For the most part, debate has been confined to the inner circles of psychoanalytic journals and associations. However, in August 1981, the topic qualified for two major articles in the *New York Times,* and, in 1984, Jeffrey Masson's book *The Assault on Truth: Freud's Suppression of the Seduction Theory* was published by Farrar, Straus & Giroux.

The crucial question pertains to whether reports of early childhood incest from patients who are in psychoanalytic treatment should be viewed as empirically reliable or mainly fantasy. Freud himself stated opinions on both sides of the question. His strongest statement supporting the veracity of patient reports about incestuous experiences came in a paper entitled, "The Aetiology of Hysteria," read before the Vienna Society for Psychiatry and Neurology in April 1896 (Masson, 1984, p. 251). Freud then repudiated his earlier opinion in the well-known book, *Three Essays on the Theory of Sexuality,* first published in 1905.

Masson (1984, 119 ff.) found evidence of correspondence between Freud and Leopold Lowenfeld that suggests that the founder of psychoanalysis gave public evidence of changing his opinion between 1900 and 1902. In personal letters to Wilhelm Fleiss, Freud claimed to abandon the seduction theory in September 1897. Yet Masson (1984, p. 114 ff.) reports a letter to Fleiss from December 1897 in which Freud appears to retain his faith in the original theory. The published version of this later letter to Fleiss, however, was edited by Ernst Kris and Anna Freud to remove evidence of Freud's internal questioning about which theoretical position was preferable.

A reader unfamiliar with the inner realms of psychoanalysis may wonder about the significance—practical and theoretical—of whether Freud and successive analysts held or abandoned the original seduction theory. The crucial issue is the proportion of times when patients' fantasies of seduction are associated with facts of seduction. Few would argue that Freud thought such reports were *always* fantasy. Masson (1984), for example, shows that Freud was familiar with the medical legal literature on child abuse of the 1880s and 1890s. But there is a matter of degree. Freud's later views, which have become a central tenet of orthodox psychoanalysis, take the position that the fantasy of seduction is far more frequent than the fact and that the fantasies are more important for treatment than the (apparently) relatively few instances of actual seduction.

The implications of the later view are wide ranging. Analysts taught to believe that reports of seduction are more likely to be fantasy than reality are less likely to be empathic toward patient reports to the contrary. Existing statistics about incest indicate that the phenomenon is far more likely to occur to women than to men (Herman, 1981; Gelinas, 1983). Thus Freud's later views function not only to dissuade analysts from keeping an open mind to their patients' experiences but also to do so in a manner that is more likely, on average, to be damaging to women than to men.

The effects of gender on the verification of incestuous behavior were in evidence during Freud's period of discovery. Masson (1984, p. 114) provides evidence that Freud's original seduction theory was independently confirmed by Emma Eckstein, a former patient and subsequent supervisee of Freud. Prior to Masson's (1984) work based upon his access to the Freud archives, Marie Balmary (1979) developed a carefully reasoned argument in favor of the original seduction theory by using only published material. Masson (1984, p. 189) identified a number of "recent authors, Florence Rush, Alice Miller, Judith Herman, and Louise Armstrong," who believe that the incidence of sexual violence among children is much higher than is generally acknowledged.

Patients are not the only persons likely to be affected by strictly held beliefs about incest that may be inaccurate. The entire psychoanalytic system of organization and training is also potentially subject to the theory's consequences. Reflecting on the consequences of her reanalysis of Freud's material, Marie Balmary (1979, p. 155 ff.) wrote,

> We have stated that a number of analysts, whose purpose is above all to help their patients . . . have put the theory back in the place from which it should never have left: that of a formulation that can always be revised. . . . The analysts' clinical practice is perhaps more closely allied to Freud's first discovery. . . . It nonetheless remains difficult for an analyst to share with his colleagues those things in this experience that disagree with the reigning theory. . . . It seems to us that their attitude oscillates between two poles: either they accept the theory, reject what they experience, and become embittered workers who haunt psychoanalytic societies seeking from a master or a group something that they would be certain not to understand; or they accept what they experience, reject the theory, grow distant from professional groups, and bear in difficult solitude the burden of their calling.

More recently, Janet Malcolm (1981) has provided a detailed case study of the difficulties and dilemmas of classical psychoanalysis, practiced orthodoxly. Her account, derived from a thorough reading of Freud's work and extensive interviewing of a practicing analyst, portrays a character deeply caught up in the New York Psychoanalytic Society. Her picture of "The Impossible Profession" provides a concrete account of Balmary's first alternative. An example of the second mode of adaptation can be found in Heinz Kohut's writings (e.g., Kohut, 1977, 1984)—especially in his efforts to persuade members of the psychoanalytic establishment to open their minds to his innovations.

> I am fully aware of the strength of the hold that the classical psychoanalytic conception of man has come to exert on our imagination; I know how powerful a tool it has become. . . . And I know, therefore that the suggestion that it is inadequate, or even that in certain respects it leads to an erroneous outlook on man, is bound to arouse opposition. . . . And is it not, to anticipate an argument on the moral side, an escapist move, a cowardly attempt to clean up analysis, to deny man's drive-nature, to deny that man is a badly and incompletely civilized animal? (Kohut, 1977, p. xviii)

Kohut speaks as a respected and accepted member of the psychoanalytic establishment; he was president of the American Psychoanalytic Association, Vice President of the International Psychoanalytic Association,

and Vice President of the Sigmund Freud archives. When he anticipates broad-scale resistance to his efforts at innovation, he knows well the group about which he speaks. The questions are why the conceptual system is so closed, and why it has so successfully resisted change. Answers to these questions turn both on the personality of Freud and on the psychoanalytic organization that was a part of his legacy.

Freud's struggle with formulating the theory brought him to difficult questions about his own family—especially his father. Balmary (1979) reports documentation showing that Freud's father married three times in contrast to the two times of public record. One of Freud's letters to Fleiss during the crucial period when he was changing his mind about the original seduction theory includes the passage, "Then the surprise that in all cases the *father* [emphasis in original] *not excluding my own* [emphasis mine] had to be accused of being perverse—the realization of the unexpected frequency of hysteria, with precisely the same conditions prevailing in each, whereas surely such widespread perversions against children are not very probable" (Masson, 1984, p. 108). At the time he was considering the theoretical revisions, Freud was confronting his own grief about his father's death (Balmary, 1979) and was troubled by incestuous desires about his own daughter (Herman, 1981). Freud himself was not analyzed through a relationship with another person; thus the discoverer of the transference did not take the optimal opportunity to continue his own self-analysis. The inevitable result, if Freud was correct in his own theory, was that he continued throughout life with certain blindspots that might otherwise have been diminished (Neumann, 1979).

Moreover, the Oedipus myth became a key element in psychoanalytic theory, based in part on the invalidity of the seduction theory. As employed by Freud, the myth omits the crime of Laius, who was Oedipus' father. Prior to the birth of Oedipus, Laius had had a homosexual relationship with the son of a friend. This boy subsequently committed suicide due to remorse about his relationship with Laius. In turn Laius was cursed by the gods, and the stage was set for Oedipus to kill his father and marry his mother. Freud's use of the myth in his theory omits the role of Oedipus' father, and the psychoanalytic theory thereby also protects Freud's memory of his own father (Balmary, 1979; Alderfer, Charleen J., 1982). Freud's theory of ego development was tied to a partially misunderstood version of an archetypal myth.

To report these facts about the founder of psychoanalysis and to trace out their implications is also to enhance my respect for Freud's courage and genius. For some people, saying aloud that an acknowledged great

person had limitations, retained certain blind spots, and demonstrated natural human frailties is an anathema. I believe otherwise. Freud's deepest commitment was to the relentless pursuit of truth about human psychology. He made many of his major discoveries through self-analysis. It seems only natural, and quite in keeping with both the spirit and the content of his work, that succeeding workers would employ the essential tenets of his own method to improve upon his contribution.

Masson's (1984) efforts to explain Freud's change of mind about seduction theory suggest additional forces that may have influenced the founder of psychoanalysis. When Freud presented the original seduction theory he was met by stony silence from the psychiatric community of his era. Initially Freud stood firm in the face of this resistance, but eventually, if Masson's report is sound, he did change his mind in response to peer pressure. Beyond the generic social forces, Freud may also have been subject to a much more personal kind of influence. Masson (1984) strongly suggests that Wilhelm Fleiss, Freud's trusted confidant of this era, was himself abusing his son, Robert Fleiss. Masson's (1984) evidence is based on very careful reading of several books by Robert Fleiss, who turned out to become a prominent analyst himself. Robert Fleiss wrote, "I have clarified the picture of my father in the two expert and thorough analyses, the last in middle age with Ruth Mack Brunswick," who was a member of Freud's innermost circle (Dyer, 1983). Again, it appears that a woman plays an important part in the clarification of conditions surrounding the development of the seduction theory.

Finally, there is the role of Freud's daughter Anna in managing the historical data surrounding the theory. From her father's death until her own demise, Anna Freud's role as symbolic leader of the psychoanalytic movement and inheritor of her father's authority was widely recognized. In her adult years, Anna Freud's relationship to her father was close. Dyer's (1983, p. 44) biography states, "In later years the psychoanalytic Zeus had no intention and no reason for relinquishing his daughter to lesser mortals." Anna Freud received her training analysis from her father (Dyer, 1983, p. 26) and throughout Sigmund Freud's mature adulthood and declining years, Anna served "as colleague, companion, secretary, nurse, and business and personal courier" for her father (Dyer, 1983, p. 56). In preparation of his study about the seduction theory, Masson (1984, pp. 112-114) uncovered several instances where Anna, sometimes working with prominent male colleagues in the psychoanalytic establishment, had omitted key elements of Sigmund Freud's correspondence that bore directly on the older Freud's internal

debate about the soundness of the revised theory. Anna's special place as keeper of her father's historical legacy and as key figure in the careers of many prominent male psychoanalysts may have further served to keep data relevant to the seduction hypothesis from being adequately examined.

The drama surrounding Freud's seduction theory shows signs of both ego-identity and intergroup forces shaping the theorist's product. Within his own psychology, Freud showed evidence of being deterred from greater accuracy by unresolved feelings about his father, a close friend, and his colleagues of the day. Eventually he took a theoretical position that not only was probably in error but also in such a manner that it was more detrimental to women than to men. Furthermore, it is possible that this theoretical problem was preserved from scrutiny by Freud's own daughter acting in cooperation with some of her most distinguished male colleagues in psychoanalysis.

With the cases of Heider and Freud we have different ways in which the selves of the psychologists apparently influenced their work. For Heider, the focus of attention was the effect of his self analysis on releasing his own productivity, which led ultimately to the production of his masterwork. The actual content of Heider's self awareness was not of major concern, although Heider himself throughout his autobiography made numerous connections between his own life experiences and his theoretical formulations. The chief theory for explaining Heider's change was Jung's analytical psychology. For Freud, on the other hand, the main issue pertained to the content of a major element in his theoretical concepts. There is evidence of both ego-identity forces and intergroup dynamics shaping Freud's thinking. Beyond Sigmund Freud's individual decision about his theoretical position, there were also the enormous forces of the psychoanalytic movement, which served to reduce the likelihood of detecting Freud's apparent error and correcting it.

The Heider and Freud cases were similar in that both men themselves seemed to avoid full confrontation with the self forces influencing their work. Both were also assisted by colleagues in their denial. Heider spoke to diminish the importance of his dream work directly after reporting it, and Harold Kelley, an ardent admirer of Heider, wrote as if the archetypal material played no part in Heider's change. Freud's struggle with the seduction theory was covered over by his own hand, by his favored daughter's management of his literary estate, and by orthodox analysts who followed after the father and his daughter. The dialogue between Self and Scientist was alive and well for Heider and Freud and for their respectful followers.

THE ORGANIZATIONAL PSYCHOLOGY
OF THE SOCIAL PSYCHOLOGY LABORATORY

Beginning with papers by Martin Orne (1962) and Henry Reicken (1962) and continuing to the present, social psychologists have been concerned with the social complexities of their laboratories. By now there is an extensive empirical literature on the "social psychology" of the social psychology laboratory (Rosenthal, 1966; Rosenthal & Rosnow, 1969, Wuebben, Straits, & Shulman, 1974). The effect of this research has been to stimulate a notable degree of self criticism and reflection on the part of social psychologists (Festinger, 1980). Three conceptual positions have emerged for dealing with the empirical findings about the social psychology laboratory. These approaches differ in the degree to which they attempt to achieve a holistic sense of the laboratory as a social system. Labels for the respective orientations reflect varying degrees of conceptual integration between laws applicable to the laboratory and to its "subjects."

(1) *Laboratory as technology.* The contemporary emphasis in this orientation is on the laboratory design as derived from the assumptions of analysis of variance. Writers of this school emphasize the rational justification for laboratory procedures. Usually there are three:

(1) random assignment of respondents to conditions;
(2) independent observation of each respondent's data; and
(3) control over extraneous sources of variation through experimental procedures.

If all three assumptions are satisfied, investigators believe that they can draw valid causal inferences about the relationship between independent and dependent variables. From the perspective of laboratory as technology the subtle forms of communication and behavior that have been identified in empirical studies are error. The aim is either to control their appearance through tightly and precisely executed procedures or to cancel out their effects through strictly randomized assignments of people to experimental conditions. In the laboratory as technology, there is minimal conscious incorporation of what is known about human behavior into the conduct of laboratory activities, except in the form of independent variables.

(2) *Laboratory as carefully managed interpersonal relationships.* The focus in this orientation to laboratory behavior is on the experimenter-respondent relationship. There is acceptance of the subtle authority

dynamics in this relationship, and efforts are made to take account of these dynamics in a manner that presumably more adequately permits investigators to make valid inferences about the relationships between independent and dependent variables. Included in these efforts are controls that vary experimenter expectancies about research outcomes and that replace live experimenters with video- or audiotape recordings. These approaches accept as valid that complex social processes occur in social psychology laboratories. They tend to respond to these phenomena either by making key authority figures in the laboratory (i.e., the experimenter) more psychologically distant from respondents or by increasing the degree of deception utilized during experimental procedures. Rosenthal (1966), for example, suggests doing more than double-blind procedures according to which two levels of experimenters do not know what is expected from the experimental treatments. He suggests actively misleading experimenters so they believe the opposite of the expected results. If such experiments also involve deceiving respondents, which they often do, this mode of coping with the authority dynamics of the laboratory results in deception now in two directions— among those in authority (namely, the experimenters) and between those in authority and those in submission (namely, the experimenters and the respondents). Thoughtful researchers (e.g., Rosenthal, 1966, p. 288 ff.; Carlsmith, Ellsworth, & Aronson, 1976, p. 93 ff.) now discuss the "ethics" of being dishonest with respondents and usually conclude that they find no evidence of harm being done or that the advances in knowledge outweigh any potential harm. Committed experimenters generally do not question what happens in the social system of the laboratory as a whole when there is widespread and officially supported deception going on among several key groups. In order to do this, it would be necessary to have a theory about the laboratory as a social system.

(3) Laboratory as social organization. This orientation views the laboratory as a human organization.

A *human organization* is a set of interdependent human groups who consciously accept a collective mission and therefore subordinate group interests when necessary and who publicly receive support from the larger social order for the legitimate pursuit of their collective mission.

A *human group* is a collection of individuals who have interdependent relations with each other; who perceive themselves as a group by reliably distinguishing members from nonmembers; whose group identity is recognized by nonmembers; who acting alone or in concert have interdependent relations with other groups; and whose roles for the

group are a function of expectations from themselves as individuals, from other group members, and from nongroup members (Alderfer, 1984).

Figure 2.1 provides a schematic diagram that portrays the significant groups that shape the human system of the social psychology laboratory. Like any other organization, the laboratory can be analyzed in terms of organization groups that are determined by the organizational position of members and by identity groups based upon the biological origin of people. Both classes of groups and their interaction importantly influence what happens in organizations (Alderfer, 1977, 1984).

In terms of organization groups, there are bodies both outside and inside the system. Within the system there are at least three and as many as five hierarchical levels. Each lower level is somewhat dependent on the immediately higher level; the middle levels (confederates and experimenters) also often have aspirations to move upward in the laboratory hierarchy. This view of the internal dynamics of the laboratory includes a place for all of the findings about demand characteristics, experimenter bias, and the like, and it puts these phenomena into a larger context of the intergroup dynamics inside the system. It raises questions about whether the primarily interpersonal orientation of researchers such as Rosenthal (1966), Orne (1962), and others is adequate to explain or to manage laboratory events. It suggests that intergroup dynamics of hierarchy, for example, are likely to affect how subjects relate to confederates, how confederates relate to experimenters, and how experimenters relate to senior investigators (Smith, 1982a).

Outside the laboratory organizations there are at least three organization groups that potentially influence what happens inside the system. The ultimate aim of research is publication, which is controlled by journal editorial boards. These groups are carefully selected to include individuals who have demonstrated their capacity to meet existing standards of social research—either as senior statespersons or as very promising younger members. Human subjects committees represent the public interest, ideally, and their objective is to be sure that respondents are appropriately warned and protected from potentially harmful behavior by investigators. These committees are frequently populated by the same kinds of people who belong to editorial boards. Informally, members of the field acknowledge that investigators tell review committees only as much as is necessary to gain their approval, and the committees do only what they must in order to maintain credibility with the governmental bodies that require their operation in order to provide funding. Finally there are the funding bodies, private and public. Laboratories receive support within universities by means of space,

equipment, and supplies. They receive external support through funding. Members of these review bodies are characteristically senior established members of the field whose own investigations have laid the groundwork for contemporary directions. In sum, the laboratory is a complex social organization of groups, the natural dynamics of which one would expect to produce carefully controlled, systematically biased information (like any other human organization) unless conscious efforts where taken to reverse such normal tendencies.

There has been some conceptual analysis identifying properties of the internal hierarchy of the laboratory (Argyris, 1968). The fact that laboratories as organizations produce different empirical results while replicating the same experiment was shown by Vidmar and Hackman (1971). Wuebben, Straits, and Shulman (1974) have summarized a variety of studies showing that subjects, who are treated statistically as independent observations because they are asked to remain silent about experimental procedures, in fact show a marked propensity to tell others (potentially in their group) about laboratory events. These sorts of findings do not fit with the concept of laboratory as impersonal technology or with the idea that effective control can be maintained by dealing only with experimenter-respondent relationships. The findings are consistent with the model of laboratory as social organization.

Identity group effects of laboratory organizations have also been shown empirically. Among experimenters, people have long accepted as an element of laboratory lore that certain studies were more likely to show results if female subjects were employed. When carefully reviewed, a vast array of social influence experiments were shown to have results dependent in part on gender differences between investigators and respondents (Eagly & Carli, 1981). Roberts (1981) has also brought together a series of papers describing gender effects in the groups external to the laboratory organization, while Boykin, Anderson, and Yates (1979) have done similar work with regard to race.

An example of the interaction of identity group and organization group dynamics follows.

Sixty-three college women were recruited as volunteers to participate in a series of group discussions on the psychology of sex. This format was a ruse, created in order to provide a setting in which subjects could be made to go through mild or severe initiations in order to gain membership in a group.

Each subject was tested individually. When a subject arrived at the laboratory, ostensibly to meet with her group, the experimenter explained to her that he was interested in studying the "dynamics of the group

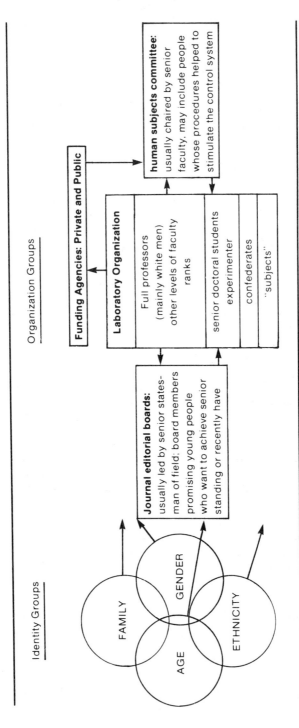

Identity Groups

Organization Groups

Funding Agencies: Private and Public

Laboratory Organization

Full professors
(mainly white men)
other levels of faculty
ranks

senior doctoral students
experimenter
confederates
"subjects"

human subjects committee:
usually chaired by senior
faculty, may include people
whose procedures helped to
stimulate the control system

Journal editorial boards:
usually led by senior states-
man of field; board members
promising young people
who want to achieve senior
standing or recently have

FAMILY

GENDER

AGE

ETHNICITY

Figure 2.1 The Social Psychology Laboratory as Human Organization

discussion process" and that, accordingly, he arranged these discussion groups for the purpose of investigating these dynamics, which included such phenomena as the flow of communications, who speaks to whom, and so forth. He explained that he had chosen as a topic "The Psychology of Sex" in order to attract a large number of volunteers and that this had proved to be a successful device, since many college students were interested in this topic. He then went on to say that this topic presented one major drawback, namely, many of the volunteers were embarrassed and found it more difficult to participate in such a discussion than they might have if the topic had been a more neutral one. He explained that this study would be impaired if any member failed to participate freely. He then asked the subject if she felt she could discuss this topic without difficulty. The subjects invariably replied in the affirmative.

The instructions were used to set the stage for the initiation. The subjects were randomly assigned to one of three experimental conditions: a severe-initiation condition, a mild-initiation condition, or a no-initiation condition. The no-initiation and mild-initiation conditions constituted the control groups. . . . The experimenter told these subjects [in the mild and severe conditions] that he had to be absolutely certain that they could discuss sex frankly before he could admit them to a group. Accordingly, he said that he had recently developed a special test which he was now using as a "screening device" to eliminate those girls who would be unable to engage in such a discussion without undue embarrassment. In the severe-initiation condition, this embarrassment test consisted of having each subject read aloud (to the male experimenter) a list of twelve obscene words and two vivid descriptions of sexual activity from contemporary novels. In the mild-initiation condition, the girls were merely required to read aloud a list of relatively inoffensive words related to sex. This elaborate procedure constituted the empirical realization of the independent variable.[4]

Suppose the material presented above was reframed into the language of intergroup theory to make the self dynamics of the laboratory more explicit; what would the account look like? Here is one possibility.

Two male Stanford University advanced graduate students in their late twenties[5] invited female undergraduate women to participate in a study about the psychology of sex. After attracting the women to the laboratory on the ruse that the study was about sex, the men explained that their interest was really about the dynamics of the group discussion process.

To establish three levels of severity of initiation the senior older men told the junior younger women that they would have to take a test to determine whether they would become too embarrassed to participate freely in the experiment and thereby impair the results. Women in the no-initiation

condition simply were asked to say that they had no qualms about discussing sex. Women in the mild-initiation condition were required to read aloud a list of relatively inoffensive words related to sex. Women in the severe-initiation condition were required to read aloud to a senior older male experimenter a list of twelve obscene words and two vivid descriptions of sexual activity from contemporary novels.

When the initiation activities were finished the women were asked to "sit in" on a group discussion by means of listening through earphones. In fact, there was no live discussion, and the women were told not to speak, lest they discover that no one would respond. To be sure the junior younger women would not inadvertently uncover this deception, the senior older male publicly disconnected the microphone that the women might otherwise have used to speak to the fictitious group.

Carlsmith, Ellsworth, and Aronson (1976) explicitly discuss the use of deception in this and in other experiments at several points in their text. They devote an entire chapter to ethical issues, including a section on deception, and they provide another chapter on methodological concerns about deception. Thus, they show an awareness of ethical problems with deception, and they report data that questions empirically whether deception has the intended effects. They also discuss problems as well as advantages of the Aronson and Mills (1959) study. In a 1984 interview with *Psychology Today*, Aronson stated, "I've found it increasingly difficult to do the kinds of experiments we were doing 15 or 20 years ago. For one thing, we've gotten much more concerned ethically about lying to people while conducting an experiment. This limits the kinds of questions we can ask and the realness of the experience we can create in the laboratory" (Aronson, 1984, p. 45).

As I understand their analysis, however, a split occurs between experimenter behavior that serves laboratory realism and experimenter actions that satisfy truthfulness. The quotation in the preceding paragraph, for example, takes the position that a reduction in lying limits investigations of certain questions. Another place where the split occurs is in debriefing after the experiment. Here again, the writers raise a variety of important questions about the debriefing process and caution against experimenters being callous, cavalier, arrogant, or insensitive. They recognize the unequal status of experimenter and subject, and they acknowledge that the authority difference may influence how the subject responds to debriefing. My sense is that they want experimenters to behave as sensitive and caring authority figures, and they want subjects to act cooperatively. A more difficult question, which they do not address, is how benevolent authority figures act when their scientific interests conflict with their subjects' human interests. Several statements from the book do bear on the question:

No amount of post experimental gentleness is as effective in relieving a subject's discomfort as an honest account of the experimenter's *own* [emphasis in original] discomfort. Although no one enjoys being deceived, much of the displeasure may stem from a feeling that one's deceiver is feeling smug about it. (p. 102)

It is important to allow the *subject* [emphasis in original] to decide whether or not it was valuable. . . . The experimenter has no right to assume that this commitment to science is shared by the subject. (p. 103)

It is conceivable that some subjects might feel that they must act like "good sports" or help the experimenter save face and so may pretend to be in good spirits while remaining in inner turmoil. . . . A good way of getting a subject to reveal any lingering disturbances or uncertainty about the experiment is to solicit suggestions for improving the experiment. (p. 104)

In addition, this procedure [of encouraging criticims of the experiment] often allows the subjects to admit that they were (or still are) upset . . . by the deception; if this should occur, further efforts must be made to bring the subjects to a full understanding of the reasons for the procedure and an acceptance of their own response to it. (p. 306)

Viewed in interpersonal terms, these assertions could be conceptualized as advising experimenters to be warm, supportive, self-revealing, and empathic to subjects in the debriefing so that the people leave the experiment feeling good about themselves and about the experimenter. The experimenter has a further interest in the subjects' feeling good and closely identified with the experimenter, as Carlsmith et al. recognize when they write, "The experimenter who has been open and honest in dealing with the subject during the post-experimental debriefing period can be reasonably confident that few subjects will break faith" (1976, p. 307). Viewed through the concepts of intergroup theory, the experimenters are using their authority and interpersonal skills to bring the deceived subjects into their own group after the experiment is over. Instead of the subjects feeling angered at social scientists who have deceived them, they will feel like cherished members of the higher status group and "keep faith" as an act of loyalty to their new group. Intergroup analysis would focus more on creating conditions through which subjects can express their anger at the people who deceived them, assuming that the aims of debriefing are to deal with the consequences of the deception and to assist subjects with unburdening themselves of the anger that usually arises in people who learn that they have been consciously and willfully deceived. Intergroup theory applied to the problem of respecting the dignity of individuals brought into the laboratory for scientific purposes argues for strengthening the boundaries of

the subject group so they can stand autonomously in relation to the experimenters, not weakening those boundaries by drawing the subjects closer and more subordinate to their deceivers.

A related question that Carlsmith et al. (1976) do not address is whether an "open and honest" postexperimental debriefing is realistically possible after an experiment that has actively and consistently misled subjects. In the Aronson and Mills (1959) study, the senior men lied twice to the junior women about the purpose of the experiment. First they said it was about the psychology of sex, and then they said it was about the process of group discussion. They also lied twice about what the women were doing. First they said the women had to take a test, and then they said they were to sit in on a group discussion. Thus, there were at least four substantial lies in that study. The textbook authors come close to seeing the problem when they acknowledge that some experimenters use the debriefing period for additional deception. They state, "If experimenters continue to violate this aspect of the contract, subjects will have no way of knowing for sure when the experimenter is telling the truth and when expressed sincerity might be a further ploy" (p. 109). I accept that Carlsmith et al. (1976) want consciously to keep deception out of the debriefing period. But behavioral reality may exceed their wishes. How does one tell the truth about the experiment—which means uncovering all the lies—and then convince the people who were subjects that "now" one is telling the truth? This is especially difficult when the experimenters—for a variety of reasons— act in a manner that keeps subjects' anger and resentment largely suppressed. Carlsmith, Ellsworth, and Aronson (1976) represent the more self-reflective end of the scale among dissonance researchers. Although I believe they miss important aspects of how organizational groups within the laboratory create a self-maintaining culture of deception, they do not deny that serious problems exist in the realm of interpersonal relationships. Leon Festinger (1980, pp. 249-250), the founder and original leader of the dissonance tradition, however, concludes a book devoted to examining fifty years of social psychology research with statements such as the following:

No one would want to minimize the importance of ethical considerations.

I don't want to dwell too long on such difficult [ethical] problems.

These ethical issues never seemed extraordinarily difficult to me.

In none of these issues do questions of harm to the subject arise in any real form. . . . There is also no real issue of invasion of privacy or maintaining confidentiality that cannot be adequately dealt with.

Scientist speaks loudly and clearly through Festinger's words.

In the concepts of intergroup theory, the understanding, the use, and the explanation of deception in the laboratory is a function of group relations inside the laboratory and outside. Inside are usually at least three hierarchical levels—principal investigator, experimenter, and subject. Outside is often a national network. In the case of dissonance work, Leon Festinger is still at the top even though he "left the field" nearly twenty years ago (Festinger, 1980). The Carlsmith et al. (1976) textbook is a product of a national network. Aronson's (1984, p. 43) *Psychology Today* interview shows that Festinger remains an important authority figure for him, and Festinger's 1980 book on *Restrospectives on Social Psychology* indicates that Festinger and the national network remain important for each other.

The Aronson and Mills (1959) experiment also provides important illustrative data about the effects of gender groups in the laboratory organization. Unlike the phenomena of deception, the dynamics of gender in the laboratory do not receive significant self-reflective attention by the textbook authors because their implicit theory of interpersonal dynamics in the laboratory does not recognize gender differences. The kinds of questions intergroup theory would raise about the Aronson and Mills (1959) study include these:

(1) What does it mean when an all male research team uses their university based authority to persuade an all female group of respondents to engage in sexually explicit talk in one-to-one encounters with higher status men?

(2) What does it mean when the study is selected seventeen years later by a two-male/one-female team of textbook authors to illustrate "the advantages of laboratory experimentation"?

(3) What does it mean when a mixed gender team does not examine the effects of gender dynamics when they review the Aronson and Mills (1959) experiment?

These are among the kinds of answers that intergroup theory provides:

Question 1. The strong tendency for only men to occupy senior positions in organizations and for women to have access only to junior roles was characteristic of many organizations during the era when the study was done (Alderfer, 1977). When Aronson and Mills (1959) designed their study, probably they were simply participating in the cultural norms of those times. As male graduate students aspiring to advance in the then male-dominated field of social psychology, they would be unlikely to perceive the problematic features of the gender relations in their study, or, if vaguely uneasy, they would be unlikely to raise such a question among themselves or with their supervisors.

Question 2. At the time of the textbook writing, the authors show some awareness of gender dynamics. In a footnote at the conclusion of the experiment's description, they write, "It is important to remember that this experiment was carried out in 1959, a time when female undergraduates were unaccustomed to seeing (much less verbalizing) explicit obscene words and descriptions of sexual activity. As in most social psychological research, the independent variable must be understood in the cultural context of time and place" (1976, p. 30). The point of this footnote is to caution readers in 1976 that the 1959 experimental treatment might not work in contemporary times because of the changed societal relations between men and women. I believe the authors are unaware that they give an unconscious message about gender dynamics by selecting this study as the first illustration in a section of their book entitled "The Advantages of Experimentation." If their way of working included reflecting on how their own identity group memberships affected their work as some versions of intergroup theory propose, then they would have been much more likely to question themselves thoroughly about how gender dynamics were portrayed in the book (Alderfer, 1984). A situation of two more senior men (Carlsmith and Aronson) working with a less senior woman (Ellsworth) would be accepted as a legitimate subject for inquiry whenever gender dynamics were relevant to the work.

Question 3. The Aronson and Mills (1959) experimental procedure employs one of several possible relationships between men and women in the experimental treatments. The full set of possibilities is (a) male experimenters and female subjects; (b) male experimenters and male subjects; (c) female experimenters and male subjects; and (d) female experimenters and female subjects. The study used only case a. On the surface, I do not see anything in dissonance theory that explains why this particular option was appropriate for testing the theory and the others were not. If that is correct, then the experiment would be stronger if more than one of the conditions were employed; it would be strongest if all four were used. My hypothesis is that neither b, c, nor d would have produced results similar to a. However, if only one of the additional conditions had failed to reproduce the original findings, then the study would have an important source of invalidity—termed a subjects X treatment interaction by Campbell and Stanley (1963). In this regard, it is interesting to note that the textbook authors (1976, p. 221) consider a study by Gerard and Matthewson (1966), which used electric shocks instead of sexually explicit talk and kept condition a the same, as a valid replication of Aronson and Mills (1959). In several senses this study

does replicate the earlier one. Men are in the dominant position in the laboratory again. Women are subject to stressful experimental treatments by men again. The results are consistent with dissonance theory predictions again. And, once more, the textbook authors do not question whether there was a possibility of a subjects X treatment source of invalidity. Intergroup theory suggests that on this issue, if the writers had been able to discuss their own gender dynamics, they would have been more likely to identify a subjects X treatment as a potential source of invalidity in both experiments.

As stated at the outset of this chapter, the aim of the section on the social psychology laboratory was mainly to illustrate the operation of group-level self effects. Individuals are nevertheless involved, and, as a matter of custom, we do mention names such as Aronson, Mills, Festinger, Carlsmith, Ellsworth, and others. But the main point of the analysis was to view these individual people as group representatives. Chief organization groups were dissonance researchers as a functional group and roles in the laboratory as hierarchical groups. The primary identity groups were men and women. I recognize that readers unfamiliar with intergroup theory may have difficulty focusing on the people as group representatives. That nevertheless is what examining the laboratory with the concepts of intergroup theory leads one to do.[6]

CONCLUSIONS AND IMPLICATIONS

In the preceding sections I have presented a variety of data to illustrate the operation of self effects in the conduct of professional meetings, in the construction and modification of theories, in the execution of laboratory experiments, and in the teaching of research methods. The data for these illustrations typically did not come from published research reports. Rather they usually came from more personal reports by the authors themselves or their biographers. As the standards for social research stand today, much of what I have written would not be considered scientific. Needless to say, I wish to question those standards. An essential quality of the scientific method is a process of continuing correction. Concretely, this means a persistent quest for better methods, improved theories, and less misleading data. Should we put investigators and their organizations consciously into the theory-method-data dialogue rather than mislead ourselves by acting as if investigators are not people when they do research and professional organizations have no effects on the behavior and attitudes of their members except those intended by research hypotheses?

The three quotations that began this chapter represent a continuum of acceptance for self dynamics in social research. Stevens, the committed positivist, argues that the independent observer *must be* assumed. Heider, the self-reflective theorist, notices the self-inflation of psychologists who place themselves outside the phenomena they observe, and Jung, the depth psychologist, observes that our really serious problems in living are never fully solved and warns us about the potential loss of vitality if they should appear to be. The person familiar with the dynamics of projection may notice that the conditions desired by Stevens are closest to the circumstances that are most likely to induce observers to dissociate and deny their own experience and to project it upon "the others" they study. Heider appears to be at least subliminally aware of this tendency toward splitting, which pursuit of a distantly objective social science seems to promote. Jung, on the other hand, argues that we escape our psychological problems only with the achievement of stultification—an assertion that seems remarkably in accord with Heider's sense that when he spoke to psychologists, he had a sense of not living in quite the same manner as he did when relating to others.

I believe the quest for objectivity in the sense demanded by Stevens and enacted by Scientist in our dialogues is founded on a complex of fears, which are extraordinarily difficult for individual social scientists to acknowledge to themselves—let alone to critical colleagues. The cornerstone of this complex is that allowing for greater consciousness of their own experience would unleash powerful emotions—in others, to be sure, but also in themselves. The next step is the belief that these emotions will get out of control and disrupt any realistic possibility of rational understanding. As a result there is a decided—one could almost say compulsive—desire to control. The acceptable language is experimental control or statistical control, but the focal tension beneath the language of rationality is a fear of disorder or chaos. In order to cope with these fears, the regime in authority adopts repressive measures and resists mightily efforts to examine the fundamental bases of their assumptions.

The choice, however, is not between chaos and repressive control. One need not decide between the apparently cool, detached, robotlike investigator dressed in a white coat, perhaps shown on a video tape, and the unrestrained, enmeshed, overpersonal "human being" who "goes native" and loses all sense of a professional role and behavior. The alternative orientation—and it is a way of being, not a commitment to a particular methodology—is a theory-based and disciplined approach to self examination. Difficult and emotionally problematic features of methods are brought forward and examined; they are not denied, sup-

pressed, or in other ways covered over. Problems of different self-perspectives are "controlled in" rather than "controlled out" so that conscious dialogue and dialectic is possible. In fact, the idea that these phenomena can be controlled out simply does not stand up under scrutiny from self analysis. Philosophically, the basic orientation partially is present in the idea of a crucial experiment which consciously pits alternative theories against one another in order to choose the better. It is also partially present in the clinical concept of "working on" (and sometimes "working through") key conflicts. Effective dialogue and dialectic, however, does not assume that one or more contending viewpoints must be eliminated. New syntheses that incorporate valid elements of several apparently conflicting perspectives may emerge.[7]

The conscious incorporation of self dynamics into research procedures of all kinds—field and laboratory, individual and collective—is not a straightforward, easily achieved change. It is not, for example, simply adding another independent variable to the design of laboratory studies, as is the habitual response of investigators steeped in this tradition. It involves fundamental reconceptualization of what investigators do when they do research, and it implies significant behavioral change by researchers.

Few may think this sort of change is desirable. None may find it is possible. In light of the broad-scale resistance that is already well documented, I shall not suggest that such changes *should* occur. Instead, I outline the kinds of changes that would permit a serious engagement of self dynamics in social research only to show the concrete meaning of acting in accord with the analyses presented above. As Scientist might say, "I shall attempt to change no one's behavior, no one do you hear me, NO ONE! And furthermore, I shall make no recommendations about organizations, NONE, do you understand that?" To which Self might respond, "I shall not insist that you do anything that is contrary to your basic nature." The implications of this follow:

(1) Accept the autobiographical self expressive nature of social and psychological research.
   (a) Select individuals for the profession based on their interest in and capacity for self-reflection. Include both issues of individual development (needs, values, modes of coping) and group membership (gender, ethnicity, hierarchical position).
   (b) Provide education and training (and reeducation and retraining) to encourage a continuing sense of self-reflection and self development for researchers throughout their careers.
   (c) Ask people to file autobiographical statements every 7-10 years, in accord with adult development theory, to encourage self-reflection

and to provide data for literature reviewers who wish to include information about investigators in their analyses.

(2) Increase consciousness of the problematic features of social science organizations as both investigatory and professional bodies. Decide to address actively the features of the system that are likely to shape research results covertly if they are not explicitly examined.

(a) Enlarge the methods sections of research reports to include much more detailed and thorough accounts of the relations among investigators in their different roles and between investigators and respondents.

(b) Provide education and training (and reeducation and retraining) on the diagnosis and design of social organizations for investigators (Alderfer, 1980a).

(c) Establish a shared understanding that progressive social science organizations have periodic "audits" by visiting professionals who examine and report on how the human system is understanding and managing the problematic features of its own social organization. Make these studies available to members of the system so they can learn from them and to other scholars who wish to investigate how properties of the human system may influence research findings produced or interpreted by its members.

Each proposal provides for a long-term view of how the individuals and the institutions of social research might change to incorporate self dynamics creatively in social research. Individual changes lead to a greater sense of personal vitality with self reflection among particular people. Institutional changes create conditions that permit utilization of self dynamics in particular studies. To the degree that we can examine in our various selves the phenomena we investigate in others, we shall move toward a more conscious understanding of social science, withdraw many of our unconscious projections, reduce repressions that have long supported an illusory concept of objectivity, and move toward a profession that engages its members and its public in self enhancing inquiry.

NOTES

1. This chapter is a sequel to an invited speech I gave at the American Psychological Association convention in September, 1979 entitled, "Why Organizational Psychologists Act Like Fruitcakes." It has not been easy to get that speech published. People who wish to receive the first paper may write to me, and I will respond gratefully. Portions of this chapter were presented as a colloquium for the Social Psychology Program at Yale University on February 20, 1984, and as a keynote address at the Fifth Annual I/O and OB Graduate Student Convention at Old Dominion University on April 28, 1984.

I, of course, did not participate in this talk about sexual behavior. When it was over, I pulled out two copies of the Job Description Index that I carry for such moments and

asked my friends to complete them. Both refused and asserted that the questionnaire items were not relevant to their recent experience. I add this footnote to indicate that, unlike others, I retain scholarly attitudes and inappropriate objectivity even during the most trying moments at professional meetings.

2. I choose to undertake this exploration by leading with theory rather than with the vast array of confusing and inconsistent empirical findings on the self as they have been accumulated by a variety of authors such as Wylie (1961, 1968) and Gergen (1971). This choice reflects both an intellectual prejudice and an enactment of the major theme of this chapter. The intellectual bias is nicely stated by Northrup (1947, p. 22):

> Galilei would have thrown and shot off all kinds of projectiles, carefully observing and describing what happened, gathering more and more detailed empirical information until this information added up to a generalization which was the answer. It is likely that had Galilei done this, he or his successors would still be observing, with the problem unsolved.

This is to place one's energy on the side of theoretical development when a choice is necessary between conceptual statements and empirical findings. Philosophically this chapter belongs to the critical as opposed to scientific orientation to theory (Geuss, 1981). Critical theories aim at emancipation rather than domination of the external world; reflect upon themselves rather than "objectify" the phenomena they attend to; and are accepted or rejected both by normal positivist empirical standards and by judgments from those the theory aims to serve. The aim of this chapter is to free social research from a variety of dysfunctional limiting conditions that arise because methods of self-reflection are largely avoided by the vast majority of U.S. social scientists. The approach here will provide linear statements that describe and explain self-reflective processes; report data from several empirical traditions that illustrate failure and success at self-reflection; and offer material to evoke self-reflective behavior by readers. I am indebted to David Morgan for calling my attention to critical philosophy.

3. Samples of biographical works include Jones (1953) on Freud, Hannah (1976) on Jung, Marianne Weber on Max Weber (1926), Marrow on Lewin (1969), and Perry (1982) on Sullivan. Autobiographical examples include those of Jung (1963), Roethlisberger (1977), Heider (1983) and the edited series by Krawiec (1972) on contemporary psychologists.

4. This excerpt was taken from *Methods of Research in Social Psychology,* a textbook on the conduct of laboratory experiments by J. Merrill Carlsmith, Phoebe C. Ellsworth, and Elliott Aronson (1976, pp. 29-30). The experiment described by the authors was published by Aronson and Mills (1959). The description of the experiment was given in a section entitled "The Advantages of Experimentation" in Carlsmith et al.'s book.

5. The material on the ages and university location of Elliot Aronson and Judson Mills at the time of the study was taken from the Biographical Directory of the American Psychological Association (1975).

6. On a personal note, I do want to acknowledge the valuable assistance I received from Elliot Aronson on an earlier version of this paper. This in no way implies that he agrees with what I say—only that he gave me extensive comments that I found very helpful.

7. A good example of a dialectic made of incorporating self dynamics into research may be found in Rober Tucker's (1984) recent paper, "Towards a Philosophy of Social Science for Black-White Studies."

THE HERMENEUTIC TURN AND THE SINGLE CASE STUDY IN PSYCHOANALYSIS

Marshall Edelson

FACING THE CHALLENGE
OF THE "CLINICAL" DEMANDS
OF SOCIAL SCIENCE RESEARCH

Science, above all, teaches us to doubt—to question our conceptions of the world. It is an institutional embodiment of Freud's reality principle. It requires us to justify our beliefs about the world on empirical grounds. To provide such grounds, we pit our own hypothesis against a rival hypothesis and, when the data we obtain favor our own hypothesis over its rival, we consider what alternative explanations would account for our having obtained these data even if our own hypothesis were false.

Two kinds of deviation from the values and norms of science must especially concern social scientists. The scientistic deviation refuses to accept the demands of a thoroughgoing skepticism. Although this rebellion is disguised by an apparently zealous conformity to "science," it is revealed when an investigator neglects the "clinical" or human demands of social science research. He ignores, in other words, personal and social forces operating in such research, which influence what data are and can be obtained.[1]

The hermeneutic deviation also refuses to accept the demands of a thoroughgoing skepticism, but rebellion here is expressed by "dropping out"—abandoning the quest for scientific knowledge altogether. Under some circumstances, perhaps, this deviation has its beginnings when meeting the clinical demands of social science research becomes an end in itself.

The scientistic deviation expresses itself in the overinfatuation of some scientists with the form of conventional research designs. A research design, however, is merely a means to enable an investigator to argue that provisional acceptance of a test hypothesis over rival and alternative hypotheses is justified; the argument is the substance. A particular research design is rationally valued only if it does its job in the study of persons or social systems, no matter how successful it has been in other kinds of studies. In the social sciences, the intrapersonal processes of the investigator, his values and biases, his conscious and unconscious wishes, fears, anxieties, and defenses against impulses and dysphoric affects, influence what information he is able to obtain from the human subjects with whom he interacts and how he interprets the information he does obtain. Unavoidably, he affects his subjects and they affect him. The intrusion of the personal and the social in social science research is a major source of alternative hypotheses, which would account for his having obtained the data favoring his own hypothesis, even if this hypothesis of his were false. The possible influence of such factors casts doubt on the conclusion that his data necessarily support his hypothesis. Ignorance or willful neglect of the clinical aspects of social science research will lead the investigator to overestimate his own hypotheses and to interpret the data he obtains uncritically.

Many papers in this volume are concerned with the scientistic deviation in social science research; this chapter shall have very little more to say about it. The concern here is rather with the second deviation, which strongly asserts itself currently in the psychoanalytic community. Some psychoanalysts at least, and their allies in the humanities and social sciences, regard the emphasis in science on testing hypotheses not as an expression of the reality principle but rather as some eccentric offshoot of an aberrant logico-philosophical movement (*logical positivism* is the usual epithet) that is out of touch with what most scientists do. This attitude leads quickly to the conclusion that testing hypotheses is not what "we" are up to—because psychoanalysis is a special science, with its own rules of inference and evidence (whatever these might be) and its own mode of understanding ("Verstehen"), or because it is not science at all but a hermeneutic endeavor, which in its objectives more resembles "reading" (i.e., interpreting) a text than explaining a state of affairs. In the context of a discussion of responses, evasive or otherwise, to the clinical demands of social science research, it should be noted that likening the psychoanalyst's activity in making clinical interpretations to the humanist's activity in interpreting a text quite plays down the reciprocal interactions of psychoanalyst and analysand as well as the crucial contribution to clinical interpretation made by the analysand's own activity.

The recoil from the discipline of hypothesis testing may take a less extreme form, apparent, for example, in a tendency to deprecate work in the context of justification and to emphasize disproportionately discovery and the invention of explanations as quintessential scientific activities. Those who are enthusiastic about the psychoanalytic case study join its detractors in relegating such case studies to the context of discovery, since both groups believe that, however richly suggestive the ideas generated and however satisfyingly complex the explanations proposed, case studies lack design controls, and cannot, therefore, provide scientific support for the credibility of psychoanalytic hypotheses.

In this chapter, questions are raised about all these versions of the hermeneutic turn in psychoanalysis—and by extension in any of the social sciences.

SOME PERNICIOUS EPISTEMOLOGICAL JUSTIFICATIONS OF THE CASE STUDY

Recently, in *Hypothesis and Evidence in Psychoanalysis* (1984), I took the position that psychoanalysts can and should conform to the canons of procedure and reasoning that characterize science and distinguish it from other human endeavors, especially so when they use clinical data from the psychoanalytic situation to provide support for psychoanalytic hypotheses. It will certainly be held by some colleagues that, as a psychoanalyst, I have given away too much when I accept the view of science held by those who question the scientific status of psychoanalysis, and especially those (e.g., Grunbaum, 1984) who believe that data obtained in the psychoanalytic situation cannot be used to *test* psychoanalytic propositions.

In my experience, this kind of response from colleagues comes eventually to rest on an appeal to epistemological justifications for the proposal that psychoanalysis is and should be exempt from scientific canons. The methods of study and manner of reasoning in psychoanalysis are—and must be—different, so the argument goes, because the way in which psychoanalysts acquire knowledge, as well as the kind of knowledge they acquire, differ qualitatively from the way in which natural scientists acquire knowledge and the kind of knowledge they acquire. First, the phenomena, and our ways of knowing them, are subjective rather than objective. Second, our interest is in knowing or understanding the meaning or meanings of phenomena and not in determining their status as cause or effect. Third, we seek to understand (rather than explain or predict) phenomena—and in all their complexi-

ty, wholeness, and uniqueness, not merely as exemplars or instances of generalizations about relations between or among a set of relatively few variables that are themselves the colorless result of a process of conceptual analysis or abstraction from multifaceted phenomena.

These differences, the argument concludes, justify a preference for the case study and all its relatives over the experiment and all its relatives. Just contrast the former's richness, narrative complexity, presentation of a unique individual who is to be understood as a whole, and emphasis on the subjective and the qualitative, with the latter's preoccupation with deductive and inductive schemata, reliance on quantification and prediction in testing hypotheses, concern with empirical generalizations involving simple relations among a few variables, and efforts to control (e.g., hold constant or eliminate) the influence of many factors in order to demonstrate the influence of an isolated few.

In this chapter, I shall examine what is meant by references to subjectivity, meaning, and complexity and uniqueness (which are contrasted with objectivity, causality, and abstraction and generalization), and I shall reject these epistemological justifications of the case study, and the view based on them of psychoanalysis as a hermeneutic enterprise, a special "science," exempt from ordinary canons of scientific method and reasoning. I shall conclude, perhaps unexpectedly in light of what has gone before, that the case study is indeed a valuable method in psychoanalysis and, specifically, is capable of providing data that will test psychoanalytic hypotheses—just as clinical methods, in general, are valuable in the same way in social science. The use of such a method, however, not only does not imply rejection of, but can and indeed should conform to, the canons of method and reasoning that are characteristic of science no matter what its subject matter is. The psychoanalytic case study in particular, and case studies in general, should not only *not* be relegated to the context of discovery but can and should be used to make various kinds of arguments that justify on empirical grounds provisional acceptance of some hypotheses as more credible than others.

SCIENCE

Certain presuppositions, stated below in italic, underlie ordinary canons of scientific method and reasoning. It is difficult to conceive that those who want exemption from the canons are indeed prepared to discard the presuppositions.

(1) *The actual world is as it is independent of our descriptions or knowledge of it; our values, preferences, and emotional responses to it; and our attempts to understand or explain it.* To deny that there are

brute facts indifferent to our wishes and feelings, to talk as if there is no actual world, only symbolic forms constructed by symbol-making organisms, is to show oneself somewhat deficient in a sense of reality. Of course, our values, wishes, and emotions influence what questions we ask, what problems we address, and how we interpret states of affairs— specifically, how we classify them and what significance we attribute to them; but that this is so does not constitute an insurmountable obstacle to testing and revising our beliefs about the actual world. Here, for one, we are able to depend on our senses, our instruments for obtaining information, which accommodate to brute reality and do not merely assimilate what is observed to already existing schemata, as well as on canons of scientific method and reasoning.

(2) *The scientist, therefore, adheres to a correspondence theory of truth.* A scientist asserts that a certain state of affairs obtains in the actual world. If the state of affairs does obtain, the assertion corresponds to reality: It is true. If it is not true, then it is false. The truth-status of a sentence expressing such an assertion is independent of our state of knowledge or our capacities for acquiring knowledge. If a sentence is true, it is true whether or not we know it is true or are able to construct an argument concluding that, given the empirical data and the way these data were obtained, this sentence is more credible than its rivals and, therefore, should be provisionally accepted as true.

(3) *All hypotheses are underdetermined by data, facts, or evidence. There is no criterion for deciding that some hypothesis is the best (the one, the certainly true) hypothesis. There are only criteria for deciding that some hypothesis, which is a member of a set of hypotheses, is a better (more credible) hypothesis, given the available evidence, than the other members of that set of hypotheses. In general, a hypothesis will not be accepted provisionally as credible just because positive instances of it are observed; it will be so accepted only if evidence favors it over rival hypotheses.*

Any data obtained are entailed by, and therefore in that sense explained by, any one of an indefinite number of rival hypotheses about the actual world. It is always the case that any one or any combination of a number of causally relevant factors may have been responsible in the research situation for generating particular data. A scientist is always faced with the problem, then, of obtaining data that favor his hypothesis over another, and of eliminating from consideration possible plausible alternative explanations other than the truth of his hypothesis of how he came to obtain these data.

It follows that scientific knowledge is never certain. Scientific belief in the truth of a hypothesis is always provisional, relative to the rival hypotheses that have been challenged by the hypothesis; the available

data that have been brought to bear to support the hypothesis over its rivals; and the alternative hypotheses also capable of accounting for these data that have been eliminated. Scientific belief is inevitably relative, therefore, to the conceptual tools and methods for acquiring knowledge we have and the background knowledge we presume to be true when a hypothesis is tested.

Data do not support a test hypothesis unless those data can be argued to favor a test hypothesis over some rival hypothesis about a domain. Further, these data must have been obtained in a way and under circumstances justifying the conclusion that the truth of the test hypothesis is a more credible explanation for the fact that these data have been obtained than plausible alternative hypotheses. Contrary to what is assumed by many clinicians, observations, no matter how great their number, cannot be said to support a hypothesis just because they are consistent with or entailed by it.

(4) *The canons of scientific method and reasoning are independent of subject matter. These canons do not depend in any way upon and are not altered by what domain an investigator chooses for study; they are not affected, in other words, by what kinds of observable or hypothetical entities, and what kinds of properties attributed to these entities, constitute the subject matter of any particular science.*

Scientific activity may be said to occur in either the context of discovery or context of justification, depending on what objectives, and therefore what skills and attitudes, are given priority.

Scientific activity occurs in two analytically distinguishable phases, discovery and justification. These are embedded in the work undertaken, for example, when a scientist devises a model, evaluates it, revises it, evaluates it again, revises it again, always with the objective of coming closer to what is true of the actual world. Science cannot do without either discovery or justification.

In the context of discovery, establishing a frame of reference for investigation (selecting a domain, identifying the kind of entities constituting the domain, deciding what kind of properties are of interest that may be attributed to such entities), and inventing powerful iconic and/or discursive causal explanations of facts of interest, have priority. Decisions in the context of discovery are not constrained in any simple way by what is true of the world. These decisions are matters of conceptual invention. While there are many circumstances and heuristics that appear to facilitate acquisition of insights leading to the formulation of new hypotheses, it is quite difficult to state precisely what these are. A hypothesis may come to a scientist as the result of a dream, or following immersion in—or painstaking examination of—a body of data. Neither

route automatically decides that the hypothesis will survive, or fail to survive, tests of its scientific credibility.

In the context of justification, taking a skeptical or critical attitude toward causal explanations and subjecting them to rigorous empirical tests have priority. Here, the question is not how powerful or otherwise satisfying an explanation is, but how accurate it is. Accuracy is evaluated by addressing two questions: How warranted is the conclusion that a causal explanation is better (i.e., more credible) than some rival? How warranted is the conclusion that the truth of this causal explanation accounts better for the fact that certain favorable data have been obtained by an investigator than do alternative explanations?

SUBJECTIVITY

In criticizing subjectivity, meaning, and complexity and uniqueness as epistemological justifications for exempting the case study from canons of scientific reasoning and method, I do not of course intend to deny that, for example, insight into one's own motives as well as special interpersonal skills may be required to obtain data in case studies (whether of persons, groups, or organizations). Nor do I intend to devalue the use of case studies to achieve objectives other than acquiring and evaluating scientific knowledge. (See Edelson, 1984, pp. 70-73, for a discussion of various objectives a case study may have.)

What I am arguing is rather that such epistemological justifications as these do not work to exempt the case study that purports to make a contribution to scientific knowledge from canons of scientific reasoning and method. These canons apply in acquiring and evaluating scientific knowledge of any kind and therefore apply also in case studies in psychoanalysis in particular—and clinical studies in social science in general—if these are to be used as a means of justifying claims about the actual world.

What is meant by references to subjectivity when warrant for exemption from scientific canons is sought? Here are some possibilities.

(1) *There is no actual world that is as it is independent of any particular observer's descriptions or experience of it. What we have are sets of unique symbolic representations of "reality" and these constitute the only reality we shall ever know.*

Currently, in psychoanalysis, this assertion takes the form of emphasizing an analysand's language and his rules for using it in different ways in thought and communication (a hermeneutics) rather than to what in the actual world the analysand refers or what in the actual world is responsible for his capacity to use language at all or his various uses of

language on particular occasions. If any "explanation" occurs here, in answering, for example, such questions as "Why does the patient say that?", it consists of references to syntactic (form-determining and form-transforming) and semantic (content-determining and content-transforming) rules, which are then applied to decode or translate one verbal production (what is to be explained) into another verbal production (the explanation). When there is no concern, as here apparently there is not, with what constraints or conditions actually determine what syntactic and semantic rules have been in fact used on a particular occasion by an analysand, then an infinite number of translations are possible and there is no way to assess the truth of a claim that such and such *is* (not just *may be*) in this instance the translation of such and such. If this description captures at all what is meant in some references to subjectivity, then out of considerations of consistency it makes little sense to talk of science or scientific knowledge at all. This is not to say that the attitudes, beliefs, and activities just described might not have considerable value of another kind.

It is possible that what is at issue behind this kind of reference to subjectivity are simply an investigator's preferences

(a) for a particular kind of data—the verbal reports of a subject over classifications or ratings of the subject's behavior by others;

(b) for assessing and attributing causal status to how objects or states of affairs in reality are represented by, look to, or are interpreted by, different subjects (or the same subject at different times), over assessing and attributing causal status primarily or solely to intrinsic features of a subject's situation.

These preferences do not constitute grounds for abandoning canons of scientific method and reasoning, or make it impossible on logical grounds ("in principle") to conform to such canons.

(2) *In psychoanalysis and the social sciences the investigator's stance must be subjective rather than objective if he is to acquire knowledge of his subject rather than about his subject.*

(a) *The investigator must be involved with, rather than a detached observer of, the subject. He acquires knowledge of, rather than about, the subject through empathic identifications with him, or by noticing the various internal states stirred in himself, as a participant who interacts with, is influenced by, and reciprocally responds to the subject he studies.*

(b) *The investigator inevitably brings to bear all his own biases, preferences, and values, and he responds with his own largely unconscious anxieties and his largely unconscious defenses against the*

impulses and anxieties aroused in him, as he interacts with the subject.
These aspects of his own mental life determine how he influences the
subject and, therefore, what the subject says to him and shows him; what
he selects or is able to receive of what the subject says to him and shows
him; and how he interprets what is said or shown, when it is ambiguous
(as it usually is).

My response, when the above statements capture what is meant by
subjectivity, is as follows.

(a) We may suppose that the investigator who uses empathic identifications or reciprocal responses as a means of knowing is in the context
of discovery. What he concludes from observation of his own internal
states, what hypothesis about the subject he forms as he makes such
observations, remains to be tested against plausible rival and alternative
hypotheses.

However, we may also regard the investigator's reports of his internal
states as the same kind of data as the subject's reports of his internal
states. For example, if a kind of investigator-state, or report of such a
state, is associated or correlated with a kind of subject-state, or report of
such a state, that itself becomes a fact to be explained or a fact that might
provide support for one hypothesis over another.

(b) The way in which aspects of the mental life and propensities of the
investigator determine what data are accessible to him, what data he
selects or notices, and how he interprets such data, is a strong argument
for the implementation of the canons of scientific method and reasoning. For here we describe, in fact, a plausible alternative account of how
the investigator might come to obtain observations that seem to support
his conjectures about the subject, even if these conjectures are false.

To be a skilled observer requires the ability to acquire the kind of
insight into one's own mental life and propensities that will expand one's
observing capacities. The canons encourage the investigator to become
aware of his characteristics as an instrument for making observations,
and to discover what systematic and random influences upon his observations arise from his own nature.

In addition, these canons check the investigator's overinvestment in
his own conjectures, counter his credulity where these are concerned,
and provide him with the means to give primacy to the reality principle
rather than to the pleasure principle. Such canons, above all, impose a
conceptual discipline upon the investigator to seek out, to imagine, and
explicitly to formulate rivals to the belief he seeks data to support, and
alternatives to the explanation he favors in accounting for the data he
obtains; he must wrestle with these. The value of a case study, with
respect to its contribution to scientific knowledge, is diminished when it

makes no mention of rival or alternative hypotheses and how these are assessed in relation to the hypothesis the data of the case study supposedly support. It is clear, for example, that Freud's extended consideration of rival and alternative hypotheses in *The Interpretation of Dreams* enhances the value of that work.

Is it really true that, because of biases, values, and unconscious meanings, there can be no agreement about what the facts are? Judges can be used to classify or rank order the contents of protocols of psychoanalytic sessions (Luborsky, 1967, 1973; Luborsky & Mintz, 1974), judges who are blind to the purposes of the investigator and who do not necessarily share his biases. Such judges, no matter the differences in their intrapsychic processes, can be shown to be capable of agreement among themselves in carrying out such tasks.

If an investigator is smuggling in evaluative assessments, preferences, or proposals as matters of fact, then it is possible to make use of conceptual analysis to expose this deception.

(3) *We work within a subjective frame of reference, not in the objective frame of reference of the natural scientist. What we study is "inside" the subjective life of the subject. There is nothing objective "out there" to measure; and objective methods, in general, are unavailing applied to subjective phenomena.*

(a) *We do not study the subject as a physical object, as a natural scientist would. We study wishes and beliefs, the whole range of kinds of psychological entities or intentional states. These are individuated by subject; by content (object, state of affairs); and by psychological mode (a subject's psychological state, or attitude or relation to the content)— and not, for example, by spatiotemporal location. These psychological entities or intentional states are not physical objects.*

(b) *We do not study the intrinsic properties of states of affairs, events, or objects as the natural scientist does, but rather how they seem to, how they are interpreted by, and what they signify or mean to the subject. Inevitably, therefore, we study irrational as well as rational phenomena, and the rationality and logical arguments of the natural scientist have no relevance in any effort to understand such subject matter.*

If this is what is meant by subjectivity, my response is as follows.

(a) Neither the canons of scientific method and reasoning nor the character of scientific explanation are dependent on the subject matter of science, the choice of a domain for study, what kind of entities are selected for study, or what kinds of properties are attributed to such entities. Edelson (1984, especially pp. 86-101) and Searle (1983), for example, have shown, in somewhat different formulations, how psychological entities or intentional states can be individuated, and that the

choice of a domain of such entities for study, or of the kinds of properties to be attributed to them, does not need to affect in and of itself the
scientific status of that study. There is no reason to suppose a priori that
there are no regular relations between and among kinds of wishes and
beliefs (or other such entities). There is no a priori logical basis for
concluding that the causes of the properties of, or the causal relations
between and among wishes and beliefs (or other such entities), or the
causal efficacy of such properties or relations with respect to other
phenomena, cannot be studied according to the canons of scientific
method and reasoning, however difficult such study might prove to be.

Measurement in this subjective realm is possible. If an investigator is
able to classify kinds of psychological entities or intentional states, for
example, according to the kinds of contents characteristic of each, or is
able to order them, for example, according to their relative strength or
intensity, as in everyday life we certainly in a rough and ready way
already do, and as every psychoanalyst certainly does, he is making use
of a kind of measurement. Such nominal and ordinal measurements are
not to be despised. Even if in this realm we never achieve the level of
equal-interval measurement (i.e., each entity has so-and-so many equal
units of some property), nominal and ordinal measurements are sufficient to carry out much scientific work.

(b) Suppose that the relations of interest, those that lead to fruitful
explanation, are just those that depend on the way in which the subject
himself classifies the states of affairs, events, or objects that are the
contents of his psychological or intentional states; or that assignment of
a particular psychological entity or intentional state of a subject to a
class depends critically on whether or not the investigator believes that
that entity or state is for that subject a member of that class. This sort of
subjectivity does not constitute an intrinsic obstacle to work according
to scientific canons. What is important here is that the investigator be
able to specify in what way his hypothesis that the subject classifies a
particular entity or state in a particular way is supported by evidence.

To do this, the investigator must keep very clear the difference
between his data and his inferences or hypotheses about the subject.
That such and such is a content of a psychological or intentional state of
the subject, according to the subject's own statement, may be accepted
as data. If an investigator wishes to be very cautious, he may accept as
data only that the subject reports that such and such is a content of a
psychological or intentional state of the subject's own.

The psychoanalyst's assignment of the content of an analysand's
verbalizations to a class of contents characterized by a state of affairs in
which one object *takes in or merges* with another object, or a state of

affairs in which one object *hides away or keeps in* another object, or a state of affairs in which one object *penetrates* another object with a third object—or the psychoanalyst's inference that for the analysand the content is so classified—may be based upon such evidence as the particular choice of words used by the analysand in describing his psychological or intentional states. The evidential status of the analysand's choice of words constitutes one reason for the psychoanalyst's careful attention to the nuances associated with the exact words used by the analysand; he would and should not be satisfied by some rough approximation to or translation of these words by someone other than the analysand.

These considerations about classification apply also to assigning relative strengths or intensities to psychological or intentional states.

What also seems to be at issue behind both these kinds of references to subjectivity (3a and b above), besides the two preferences previously mentioned, is an investigator's unproblematic (with respect to scientific canons) preference for regarding performances or behaviors as effects of internal states, or as manifestations or realizations of dispositions or propensities, over regarding performances or behaviors in and of themselves as both the causes and effects of interest.

(4) *Objectivity as a characteristic of scientific method depends on the possibility of intersubjective agreement, at least in principle, among observers. In psychoanalysis, however, such intersubjective agreement is impossible. The psychoanalyst can read anything he wants into what the analysand says. One psychoanalyst will hear as "anal efforts to control" what another psychoanalyst hears as "compensatory strivings to overcome a sense of inferiority." So, Freudian, Adlerian, and Jungian psychoanalysts all claim that the data support their hypotheses. Surely, what we have here are different stories, each with its own value, and no way to choose between them on grounds of veridicality.*

Meehl (1983) gives this particular problem of subjectivity extended consideration in one of his characteristically brilliant papers. He argues convincingly that there are ways to achieve intersubjective agreement about the inferences made from the analysand's reports.

The general problem is just what degree of intersubjective agreement can be achieved about what the data are. When Meehl refers to the subjectivity of inference in psychoanalysis, however, he means in part by "inference" how data are classified; the problem becomes the possibility of intersubjective agreement about such classifications. In his example, he argues there is a way of achieving intersubjective agreement about how a set of utterances by an analysand in a particular psychoanalytic session should be classified according to type of theme. However, the classification of themes Meehl presents (i.e., the kind of facts he picks

out to be explained) seems to me to be dependent on psychoanalytic theory in just the way I argue in what follows that it must not be.

My own response to the problem of achieving intersubjective agreement is as follows.

(a) The difficulty in achieving intersubjective agreement in psychoanalysis follows from the preoccupation with seeking confirming instances, without regard to the problem of excluding plausible alternative explanations of the occurrence of such instances.

(b) More attention must be paid to keeping clear the difference between data and inferences based on data. Data include, for example, that such and such is the content of an analysand's psychological or intentional state, according to his own statement; or that such and such a content is assigned to one or another class or rank—where the classifications or bases for ranking involve reference to nontheoretical properties of such contents; or even that one kind of content, so classified, co-occurs regularly with another kind of content, or that the strength of one kind of psychological or intentional state covaries with the strength of another kind. Inferences from data include interpretations or hypotheses about the analysand entailed by a conjunction of particular psychoanalytic hypotheses (making use of theoretical concepts) and particular data. The interpretations of psychoanalysts clearly are not first-order facts, and should not be, as they often are, presented as such.

If incompatible inferences about an analysand, based on different theories, are made by different psychoanalysts, then the same kinds of scientific arguments about the relation between rival or alternative hypotheses and evidence I shall describe in the penultimate section of this chapter must be used to decide which inference or hypothesis is to be provisionally accepted over another.

In connection with the need to keep clear the difference between data and inferences or interpretations, note that the classification "taking in or merging," "hiding away or keeping in," and "penetrating" is not the same as the classification "oral," "anal," and "phallic." The former classification is based on rather commonsense notions—knowledge, for example, of metaphors and figures of speech; it is not knowledge of the psychoanalytic theory of psychosexual development. Therefore, this classification may be considered nontheoretical, not because no theory is required to use it, but because carrying out a classification of psychological or intentional states according to these notions does not require knowledge of psychoanalytic theory, which the investigator wants to use these data to test. (Here, we have some way of understanding the emphasis on metaphors and figures of speech in Freud's writing and in psychoanalytic practice.)

That this classification is nontheoretical, in the sense described, is so, even if considerations based on psychoanalytic theory have led to a decision to use such a classification. In the same way, the usefulness of characterizing physical objects in terms of location in space and time is certainly suggested by Newtonian theory, but knowledge of that theory is not required, although knowledge of some theory is required, to assign a physical object to a particular spatiotemporal location.

It is quite otherwise with a classification such as "oral," "anal," and "phallic." In my opinion it is a mistake to consider a statement such as "the analysand's utterance or state is anal" as a typical data statement in psychoanalysis. For, if the distinction nontheoretical-theoretical is not kept in mind, an investigator is in peril of guaranteeing acceptance of a theory by assuming it to be true prior to any empirical justification for accepting it as true, and smuggling it into the very constitution of the facts that are held to test it. Including as a premise in an argument the very conclusion that is supposed to follow from a set of premises results in tautology.

Clearly none of this denies that all data are both theory laden and corrigible. What is asserted here is that data must not be laden with the very theory one is using them to support, and that what are regarded as facts at any time are those nontheoretical assertions about the actual world about which it is easiest, at that time, to achieve intersubjective agreement.

MEANING

Psychoanalysis is not natural science. It is a hermeneutics, an explication of the meaning of what the analysand reports, which is regarded as a text to be interpreted (in the sense "decoded" or "translated"). The relations to be explored are between signifiers and what they signify, symbols and what they represent, signs and what they refer to, allude to, or stand for—not between causes and effects.

Psychoanalysis is the study of a signifying or symbolizing function. If that study involves explanation at all, it is closer to the kind of "explanation" exemplified by answers to questions about the meaning of words, phrases, concepts, or proverbs than it is to causal or functional explanations exemplified by answers to questions about the origin or source of some state or condition, how some change or difference in state or condition has come about, or how something works. What is at issue are logical connections (in a broad sense), denoted by such terms as "means," "symbolizes," "is a paraphrase of," "implies," or "is by analogy like"—primarily conceptual connections between linguistic entities

(including descriptions of nonlinguistic entities), or their counterparts, rather than intrinsic connections obtaining in the actual world between or among nonlinguistic entities themselves. (See Sherwood, 1969, for a discussion of explanation in terms of significance, as distinct from explanation in terms of origin, genesis, or function.)

The case study is not a scientific argument. It is not an account of causal connections. It is a story, which reveals the complex, coherent network of signifiers and signifieds that makes sense of the analysand's symptoms, dreams and parapraxes. It translates and decodes, rather than causally explains, these.

My response to this characterization of psychoanalysis and the case study follows.

A careful reading of Freud's work reveals that he persistently sought causal and functional explanations of mental phenomena. See Shope (1973), in his excellent paper on Freud's uses of the term "meaning," and my comparison of Freud's theory of dreams and Chomsky's theory of language (Edelson, 1972, 1975) for citation of relevant passages. Certain passages of Freud's (occasional rather than preponderant) do allude, often metaphorically, to symbolizing activities in human life. I think these could be argued to indicate an effort on Freud's part to clarify by analogy aspects of the subject matter he is studying, including in some instances aspects of the clinical activity of the psychoanalyst—while at the same time perhaps he paid too little attention to disanalogies—rather than to indicate any abandonment on his part of the explanatory objectives he so clearly pursues. There is no more reason to suppose that just because Freud refers to language, symbols, representations, and symbolic activity (part of his subject matter), he has rejected, or should have rejected, canons of scientific method and reasoning than to suppose that just because Chomsky studies language (his subject matter) his theory of linguistics cannot be a theory belonging to natural science and that he cannot be seeking causal explanations in formulating it.

Of course, that Freud sought causal and functional explanations is no reason to suppose psychoanalysis continues to do so, but I would argue that clinical psychoanalytic theory as we know it, which is what is applied as far as I know in most current instances of psychoanalytic treatment, exemplifies causal and functional explanation; any other characterization of the clinical theory of psychoanalysis involves a rather bizarre misreading of it or is in the service of a radical revision of it. In the latter case, there is no particularly good reason to call the revision a version of psychoanalytic theory.

For psychoanalysis, the *meaning* of a mental phenomenon is a set of unconscious psychological or intentional states (specific wishes or impulses, specific fears aroused by these wishes, and thoughts or images

that might remind the subject of these wishes and fears). The mental phenomenon substitutes for this set of states. That is, these states would have been present in consciousness instead of the mental phenomenon requiring interpretation had they not encountered, at the time of origin of the mental phenomenon or repeatedly since then, obstacles to their access to consciousness. If the mental phenomenon has been a relatively enduring structure and these obstacles to consciousness are removed, the mental phenomenon disappears as these previously unconscious states achieve access to consciousness.

That the mental phenomenon substitutes for these states is a manifestation of a causal sequence. An example of one such causal sequence: A wish leads to an image of a dreaded state of affairs, which the subject believes will follow upon the gratification of the wish. Therefore, imagining the gratification of the wish, and believing that gratification to be possible and imminent, produces anxiety. Anxiety may lead to changes in states of consciousness and to various operations (e.g., the dreamwork, primary process, defense mechanisms) upon these psychological or intentional states, which determine the form and content of the mental phenomenon that comes to substitute for them. The psychological or intentional states, in conjunction with or by means of the various operations upon them, cause the mental phenomenon to come into being (i.e., make it happen).

For psychoanalysis, the *meaning* of a mental phenomenon is also the purpose (e.g., the wish fulfillment) the mental phenomenon serves, and here we may have reference to the functions it serves both in keeping rejected contents out of consciousness in order to avoid dysphoric affects such as anxiety, and in providing unconscious motives, drives, or impulses a means of expression (i.e., a path to satisfaction).

Meaning, in the first sense, requires causal explanation of a mental phenomenon (i.e., an answer to the question, What makes it happen?). Meaning, in the second sense, requires functional explanation of a mental phenomenon (i.e., an answer to the question, To what end does it serve as a means?). With reference to meaning (in the first sense, especially) Freud writes of that which fills a gap, repairs a discontinuity, or finds its place in psychic continuity (i.e., fits in with other psychological or intentional states in conscious mental life or belongs to a sequence of such states that has been interrupted). With reference to meaning in either sense, Freud writes of that which, by virtue of psychoanalytic explanation, gives intelligibility or significance to a mental phenomenon that does not make sense. (For a similar account of meaning in psychoanalysis, see Shope, 1973.)

The following points are especially important.

(a) Semantic explanation, which refers to meaning or significance (see, e.g., Sherwood, 1969), is not, in psychoanalysis at least, a noncausal kind of explanation. Suppose the question is, Why does the analysand fear the snake so? Suppose the answer to that question is, A snake stands for or symbolizes a penis. It is easy to see that by itself this is no answer at all; for one thing, it leads immediately to the question, Why does the analysand fear a penis so? The question is about an inexplicable mental phenomenon (i.e., "fearing the snake so") and its answer depends on an entire causal explanation of the kind described above. "A snake stands for or symbolizes a penis" makes sense as an answer only if it is understood as shorthand for a causal explanation of that kind. Similarly, to say that the child stands for or symbolizes the boss is not a satisfactory answer (it does not even sound right) to the question, Why does this father beat his child?

(b) Causal and functional explanations are, given the above account, two different perspectives on, or two different ways of talking about, the same relations between or among events or states of affairs. Explanation in terms of purpose or function (reference is to a means-end schema) should not be contrasted as teleological (i.e., determination by ends) to causal explanation (i.e., determination by antecedents). No *future* state of affairs is required by functional explanation to explain what obtains or occurs in the present. Causal efficacy resides in the representation in the present of possible future states of affairs; in a present image of, orientation to, or anticipation of a possible future state of affairs; in a present desire or wish that an imagined state of affairs obtain in the actual world; in a present intention to make that imagined state of affairs happen; in a present plan for bringing that imagined state of affairs into being, a plan that is based on beliefs about means-ends relations.

An unconscious image of an end state of affairs modeled on past memories of the gratification associated with that kind of state of affairs can dominate psychological life, even in the absence of conscious intentions to make such a state of affairs happen. The subject repeatedly imagines that kind of state of affairs, acts to bring it about, interprets whatever he perceives as that kind of state of affairs, and then acts and responds in terms of this interpretation. The image is endowed with the power to compel the subject to repeat over and over again his attempt to resurrect that kind of state of affairs.

(c) Empirical generalizations describing statistical associations or correlations entail and therefore may be used to "explain" or predict singular facts. They are also themselves facts the scientist wishes to

explain. To do so, he has recourse to causal mechanisms. In the absence of an explanation that spells out a causal mechanism, an empirical generalization remains a description of an accidental relation, rather than, for example, a scientific law.

Causal explanation (e.g., as explicated by Harre, 1970) traces how one event or state of affairs leads to, produces, or generates another. To elaborate such explanations, a scientist may call on a regress of causes and effects—for example, may identify an antecedent event or state of affairs as an even more remote cause, or interpolate between any cause and effect of interest other cause-and-effect links that constitute steps from the one to the other.

Causal explanation may also make use of a move from whole to part or from part to whole. How the parts or constituents of a kind of enduring structure are organized or relate to each other, and what properties such constituents have (usually different from properties the structure itself has), may be shown to produce or generate facts about such structures. Conversely, facts about a structure may be shown to result from, or involve, responses by the structure to causally relevant events or states of affairs in its situation; situation and structure, then, form the larger whole of which the structure itself is a part.

So, physicists explain macro-characteristics of physical objects (e.g., temperature, the change from water to ice) in terms of the properties of and relations among micro-constituents of such objects. Freud explains psychological phenomena as the result of both the properties of and relations among intrapsychic constituents (e.g., wishes and beliefs) of a psychological system and the impact of that system's relations with situational objects (including its own body). Talcott Parsons explains sociological phenomena as the result of the interaction between internal relations (inputs and outputs) among the subsystems of a social system and that system's external relations to conditions, resources, and obstacles, in its situation.

Freud wishes to account for the properties of mental phenomena, including why they should have such and such contents, by causes that are also mental. The mental phenomenon that does not make sense is both caused by and is the realization of a set of relations among hypothetical (i.e., unconscious) psychological entities or intentional states, which do make sense, somewhat as the properties of water or ice both are caused by and are the realization of the movement of molecules under different conditions of volume and pressure—molecules that have properties unlike those of water or ice.

A major contribution of psychoanalytic theory is not to rest content with empirically observable properties or regularities (co-occurrence or covariation) but to spell out the mechanisms by which the properties of

and relations among a set of psychological entities or intentional states cause (make happen, produce, generate) and are realized by a phenomenon with somewhat different properties than they have. A single case study is often used to spell out causal mechanisms; this is a particularly important feature of Freud's case studies. What is called a psychoanalytic narrative by some is in part at least an effort to explicate causal mechanisms, to show how one kind of state of affairs or event can lead to, produce, or generate another, or how relations among constituent entities can cause or be realized by the properties of a certain kind of structure.

COMPLEXITY AND UNIQUENESS

The case study captures the subject completely, presents the subject vividly, matches with fidelity the complexity of the subject, and preserves what is unique about the subject—in a way that no objective-quantitative study can.

But scientists do not presume to capture "all the phenomena." They seek to study a specified domain or domains, constituted by certain kinds of elements, which are characterized in certain ways. An interest in vivid presentations more often than not disguises a reliance on rhetorical persuasion as a strategy for compelling belief in place of logical argument about the relation of hypothesis and evidence. An emphasis on complexity more often than not disguises a shrinking from the necessary work of abstracting out aspects of reality—properties of interest (ultimately variables)—in order to investigate just the relations between or among these. Discouraging talk of countless variables (and the different kinds of relations, and the possibly very complicated network of relations, between or among them) is no substitute for beginning to specify what these variables are and to map their interrelations.

Those who emphasize the *complexity of psychological phenomena* perhaps appreciate too little the complexities of physical phenomena. We may say, for example, that such an event as striking a match causes such an event as fire. A moment's reflection reveals the complexities here. Such necessary conditions as the presence of oxygen, and the dryness of the match and of the surface against which it is struck, must be distinguished from causes. A cause makes the difference; it makes something happen. The necessary conditions contribute to the production or generation of the effect, but they cannot by themselves cause it.

The concept *cause* implies a capacity or power to produce, bring about, make happen, or generate, and also implies a causal mechanism,

which explicates the nature of this capacity or power. But a great many things are, if not causes, *causally relevant*. Anything is causally relevant if it makes a difference. A kind of event or state of affairs is causally relevant—even if it cannot be shown to or does not determine an effect (i.e., bring it about without exception)—if it increases the probability of that effect from what the probability of it would be in the absence of that kind of event or state of affairs. (A kind of event or state of affairs can also be causally relevant, but in a negative sense, if it decreases its probability.) Causally relevant events or states or affairs may not have the power or capacity to produce or generate an effect, even if they are necessary conditions without which the effect will not occur. These necessary conditions are often part of, or used by, a postulated causal mechanism; without them, therefore, a cause cannot produce its otherwise expectable effect.

In psychoanalysis, Freud distinguishes not only between dispositions or propensities (e.g., fixations), favoring circumstances (e.g., fatigue or debility), instigating causes (frustration and regression), and essential causes (unconscious conflict), but also between the mental cause of a mental phenomenon such as a dream (e.g., its motive force) and the sources of the manifest contents of that dream (recent indifferent impressions, somatic stimuli, symbols), those materials that are made use of in generating the dream but that themselves do not have the power to cause it.

Concentration and abstraction, and in this sense a simplification of the phenomenal world, are essential to science. No scientific theory ever seeks to explain everything there is to be explained. That would be impossible. No set of hypotheses can encompass all properties, for some of these belong to different kinds of elements and are at different levels of analysis. Unfocused indiscriminate impressionability, passive promiscuous immersion in phenomena, in and by themselves cannot bring forth scientific thought. No one can advance scientific knowledge who bemoans that dissecting out certain features of a person (or a cell, for that matter) is destructive to its complexity, or that no person (or cell), event, state of affairs, or structure is exactly like any other (which, of course, is always true). Striving to get it all, to get more and more of it, not to miss anything, as if the more phenomena, the more truth, to capture the look as well as the physics of the rainbow, are not so much anti-scientific as in many ways just beside the point for scientific work.

Discussions of the *uniqueness of the individual* more often than not miss the point that scientists are interested in relations—ultimately, relations between or among variables. Every statement about relations between or among kinds of states of affairs, properties, or amounts of

properties is a generalization over a set of instances in each one of which values of different variables coincide. The set of instances may be generated by a group of persons, each instance by a different person. In the case study of a person, the set of instances are generated by that one person; each instance, for example, is a different exemplar of a kind of mental phenomenon or performance produced by that person, or is a different time-slice of that person. The phrase "individualizing or idiographic versus generalizing or nomothetic science" marks a pseudo-issue, as Holt (1962) has decisively and devastatingly argued. I add only the following to his discussion.

The same kind of reasoning about hypothesis and evidence may be used in studying a domain whose elements are collectives (societies, organizations, groups, or families); a domain whose elements are persons; a domain whose elements are cultural objects (books, movies, games or athletic contests); or a domain whose elements are physical objects. A single person, a single cultural object, or a single society, organization, group, or family, each with its distinctive elements and their properties, may each constitute a domain that is the subject of a single case study. We may study the interpersonal transactions or interactions bounded by a particular single collective; or the intrapersonal events or entities bounded by a particular single person—the perceptions, beliefs, memories, feelings, wishes, dreams, symptoms, dysfunctional performances, or achievements of, or objects produced or occasions occupied by that person.

In each kind of domain, a limited set of properties of the elements of the domain and the relations between or among these properties is what is of interest. Each element, generated by the single case regarded as a domain of such elements, together with the property or properties the element exemplifies, is the focus of a potential act of observation. The methods of making and recording observations, and the mode of reasoning about the relation between hypotheses and the evidence provided by such observations, are not fundamentally different in the study of an intrapersonal domain from those used in the study of a population of persons. In both, for example, groups of elements allocated to different conditions, or samples of different kinds of elements, may be compared. In both, each element observed instantiates a particular value of every variable of interest.

A hypothesis is always a hypothesis about a particular domain. The question raised when a hypothesis is tested is whether it, rather than some rival hypothesis, can be provisionally accepted as true about that domain. One may also raise a question about the scope of a hypothesis. Different arguments about the relation of hypothesis and evidence are

required, depending on whether the question is about the truth of a hypothesis about a particular case (e.g., Does a postulated relation hold for a particular subject?) or the question is about generalizability (e.g., Under how many conditions to which the subject is exposed or for how many such subjects does the postulated relation hold?).

Statements asserting that certain relations between particular concepts or variables hold for a single case, that in a single case one kind of state of affairs is causally relevant in bringing about another kind of state of affairs, or merely that a single case has a certain kind of property, are just as much hypotheses as statements making similar claims about populations of such cases. Indeed, contrary to an attitude sometimes apparent in critics of case studies, it is not necessarily a trivial achievement to provide evidence making a causal hypothesis about a single case scientifically credible, even if it is not also possible to provide evidence from a study of the case that would justify generalizing the same hypothesis to other cases. (A series of cases, however, might provide evidence justifying such generalization.)

THE CASE STUDY AS A SCIENTIFIC ARGUMENT

It is pernicious to relegate case studies to the context of discovery, for it discourages rigorous argument about the relation of hypothesis and evidence in such studies. My impression is that, in fact, in most case studies that have had an impact on the scientific community, there is a challenge, even if it is latent, to at least one rival set of concepts and hypotheses—a challenge that indeed motivates the case study. There is also an argument, however informal, that the data of the case study give greater support to the challenging than to the challenged set of hypotheses. The scientific value of such a case study ultimately depends upon the adequacy of that argument.

Such an argument usually presupposes that the author of a case study is able convincingly to provide warrant for the following assertions.

(a) He can reliably identify instances of nontheoretical states of affairs. Consider Luborsky's painstaking explication of criteria (1967) for deciding whether what is reported is to count as an instance of momentary forgetting, or Freud's discussion (1900) of what shall count as a dream.

(b) He can make such an identification without using—or depending upon procedures, instruments, or tests which presuppose the truth of—the test hypothesis he is proposing, or any other hypothesis that entails or follows from that test hypothesis. Consider the background

theoretical knowledge, which is not being tested, that is presupposed by the use of a thermometer, a microscope, or free association in obtaining the facts that are to serve as evidence for hypotheses that themselves do not depend in any way on this background theoretical knowledge. (For a discussion of what is presupposed by the method of free association, see Edelson, 1984.)

The contribution of the case study to scientific work is increasingly held to be both limited and minimal (e.g., Kazdin, 1980, especially pp. 9-32). The prevalence of two arguments especially about the relation of hypothesis and evidence in such studies has done much to discredit them. These two arguments should not be used. One argument is that an empirical instance of a hypothesis, which follows logically from it, confirms the hypothesis, and that is sufficient to enhance its scientific credibility. Indeed, the argument, implicit if not explicit, is that the greater the number of positive instances of a hypothesis obtained, the more credible the hypothesis. Another equally dubitable argument concludes from the mere concomitancy of two states of affairs, events, or processes reported in a case study that one is the cause of, or causally relevant in the production of, the other.

What arguments, then, can and should an author of a case study use? In general, a case study shall be considered to provide some support for a test hypothesis—to make it to some extent scientifically credible— only if the author of the case study argues and is justified in arguing that all three of these assertions about it are true.

(1) The test hypothesis has the power to explain the kind of observations made and reported in this case study, and some rival hypothesis does not. The observations are predictable or expectable if the test hypothesis is true, but are not predictable or expectable if the rival hypothesis be true instead.

(2) In this case study, the test hypothesis ran a real risk of being rejected in favor of that rival hypothesis.

(3) The test hypothesis accounts better than some alternative hypotheses for the fact that the observations apparently favoring it were obtained by the author of the case study.

It is my thesis that arguments such as the following about the relation between hypothesis and evidence can and should be used when the data are obtained by case study (or, generally, by clinical methods in social science) just as much as when they are obtained by experimental or objective-quantitative methods. (For a discussion of the contributions of Platt, Hacking, Popper, Campbell and Stanley, and Glymour to the formulation of one or another of these arguments, see Edelson, 1984.)

Indeed, if it were not possible to make these arguments when the data are obtained by case study, much of my objection to what I have called pernicious epistemological justifications of the case study would lose its cogency.

EXPLANATORY POWER AND
THE VANQUISHED-RIVAL ARGUMENT

Authors of case studies should not, as they often do, confuse explanatory power and scientific credibility. Explanatory power is necessary, but it is not sufficient, to establish credibility. Von Eckhardt (1982) makes the distinction clear and claims (incorrectly, I believe) that Freud in his case studies ignored it to the detriment of the scientific value of these studies. The argument "because data statements confirm a hypothesis (i.e., follow logically from it), the hypothesis is scientifically credible" is, as has been previously pointed out, an unacceptable argument.

Even if an author of a case study should succeed in arguing conclusively that his hypothesis "explains" (i.e., entails) his data, it does not, if he wishes also to argue for its scientific credibility, absolve him from the responsibility to test it in his case study. He tests it both by exposing it to at least some risk of rejection and by pitting it against rival and alternative hypotheses. Any attempt of this kind on his part, limited though it may be, will do much more than mere submission of a record of confirming instances of the hypothesis to convince a reader that the hypothesis is to some degree worthy of provisional belief and to inspire a reader to want, and perhaps even to carry out, additional tests.

What is especially important is presentation of some version of the vanquished-rival argument. The author of the case study shows that given the evidence, his hypothesis is more credible than one or more of its rivals. The rival hypothesis, which is held or entertained prior to the attempt to obtain evidence to support the test hypothesis, expresses a belief about the domain of interest different from that expressed by the test hypothesis. The author of a case study may argue that

   (a) the rival hypothesis entails that a particular event or outcome, the occurrence of which is consistent with or deducible from the test hypothesis, will not occur, and so that it did occur favors the test hypothesis over the rival hypothesis;

   (b) the rival hypothesis entails that a particular event or outcome, the occurrence of which is either likely, probable, or expectable given the truth of the hypothesis, is rare, improbable, or unexpected given the the truth of the rival hypothesis, and so its occurrence favors the test hypothesis over the rival hypothesis; or

(c) the rival hypothesis does not entail that a particular event or outcome will occur or will not occur (it has nothing to say about such an event or outcome), while the test hypothesis entails that the event or outcome will occur and so that it did occur favors the test hypothesis over the rival hypothesis.

An important subspecies of the vanquished-rival argument is the Bayesian probabilistic impact-of-new-information argument. The author of a case study may argue that the way in which new information, obtained in a study, changes both the prior probability attached to the proposition that a test hypothesis is true, and the prior probability attached to the proposition that a rival hypothesis is true, favors the test over the rival hypothesis. (Prior probabilities are based on information available before the study.) In other words, given new information, posterior probabilities are now attached to the two propositions and these posterior probabilities favor the test over the rival hypothesis. This argument is implicit in much clinical reasoning, including that which goes into working out a differential diagnosis, or deciding upon, or changing, a patient's diagnosis, given new information about the patient. (Note that this argument does not involve simply the different probabilities some event or outcome has under different hypotheses, as in the vanquished-rival argument [b above] but rather the probabilities attached to hypotheses themselves.)

THE RISKY-PREDICTION ARGUMENT

Suppose that the failure of a particular event or outcome to occur under conditions of investigation would be held to favor a rival hypothesis over a test hypothesis. Suppose that, given prior background knowledge, the probability that the particular event or outcome under conditions of investigation will indeed fail to occur is very high. To predict, then, nevertheless, that under conditions of investigation the particular event or outcome will in fact occur because the test hypothesis is true is to subject the test hypothesis to a correspondingly very great risk of rejection. If, therefore, the particular event or outcome subsequently under conditions of investigation does indeed occur, its occurrence provides correspondingly very strong support for the test hypothesis.

It is important, if an author of a case study is to be able to make this argument, for him to anticipate and identify with the critical skepticism his hypothesis will inevitably encounter by subjecting it to a real risk of rejection. If the cards are not to be stacked in favor of his hypothesis, he must choose a particular case or obtain observations in studying that

case in a way that makes rejection of the hypothesis not only possible but indeed more probable than acceptance of it.

Any wish to accept a hypothesis must be checked by making it difficult to accept it, by setting it up to be rejected. The author of a case study will, therefore, specify which observations, if he had obtained them, would have led him to reject his hypothesis—and how he proceeded in such a way that just these observations not only might have occurred but (though they did not occur) were very likely to have occurred. He will show that he avoided particular steps that might have prevented their occurrence and in fact took particular steps to increase the likelihood that, if they could be obtained, they would be obtained.

Any one of the following arguments may be used to justify a claim that the hypothesis in a particular case study survived a real risk of rejection: (1) the least likely case argument; (2) the rare cause argument; (3) the improbable outcome argument; (4) the convergence argument; and (5) the bootstrap argument.

The least likely case argument. If a hypothesis is a generalization of the kind "all dreams are wish fulfillments," then a counterexample falsifying the hypothesis is "this dream is not a wish fulfillment." A case that might be chosen for study, then, is one involving a dream which appears not to be a wish fulfillment, given existing knowledge (which does not include the test hypothesis).

For example, the dream in the case study is made up of images of misery and pain. On the commonsense background assumption, which at the time of testing the hypothesis is widely accepted, that human beings do not wish for misery and pain, the expectation is that evidence obtained in a study of such a dream will show that the dream is not a wish fulfillment. The choice of this kind of dream for study increases the probability that the test hypothesis will be rejected. If, even so, the evidence obtained does show that the dream is a wish fulfillment, that improbable outcome counts more toward establishing the credibility of the test hypothesis than such an outcome would have counted if the dream chosen for study had been made up of images of joy and pleasure.

Similarly, in testing a hypothesis that all societies are rule governed, a society whose members are apparently all wild and lawless, or a primitive society whose members as children of nature are thought to behave spontaneously, might be chosen for study. Or, in testing a hypothesis that an unconscious conflict involving homosexual impulses is causally necessary to produce a certain kind of psychopathology (e.g., paranoia), a patient who is apparently unconflicted about his homosexual behavior but who is also paranoid might be chosen for study.

The rare cause argument. In testing a causal hypothesis, if the supposed cause of an effect is known to occur relatively rarely in a population, a case study in which these two events co-occur is a more convincing instance of the hypothesis than a case study in which the supposed cause is known to occur relatively frequently in the population.

A hypothesis describes a relationship, for example, between a childhood event, such as the one postulated by Freud in the Rat Man Case (a child is punished by his father for masturbating) and a mental phenomenon in adulthood (e.g., a neurotic symptom). In what follows, assume the frequency of the mental phenomenon in the population remains constant. If the childhood event occurs relatively frequently in the population, then a case that manifests the mental phenomenon is, quite probably, a case in which the childhood event also occurred, even if there is no causal relation between the two. In other words, the probability of obtaining a confirming instance of the hypothesis is relatively high, even if no causal relation between the childhood event and mental phenomenon actually exists.

However, if the childhood event occurs relatively rarely in the population, then a case that manifests the mental phenomenon is, quite probably, a case in which the supposed childhood event did not occur unless the two are causally related. Here the probability of obtaining a negative instance of the hypothesis is relatively high, if the two are not related. When an author of a case study postulates a cause that he knows occurs relatively rarely in a population, he can argue with some justification that he has thereby increased the probability of rejecting his hypothesis and that, therefore, obtaining a positive instance of his hypothesis in his case study counts more toward establishing the credibility of that hypothesis than if he had postulated a relatively frequently occurring cause.

In passing, note here that the report of a rare case of something is to be distinguished from a report in which a rare cause is postulated to explain something. A rare case is one that is known to occur—or that a review of the literature shows to have occurred—very infrequently. Since there is so little opportunity to observe such a case, it may be thought worthwhile just to describe "the facts" in detail, even if the state of knowledge is such that no hypothesis presents itself to account for these facts and no hypothesis's credibility seems undercut by them. Facts, however, are always relative to a choice of elements and ways of characterizing elements and, therefore, presuppose some sort of assumptions about what in the phenomena is worth noting. The scientific value of such a report tends to be overrated, therefore, since it is unlikely that

the author will include just those facts that will turn out to be relevant to a consideration of hypotheses that are at some later time of interest.

The improbable outcome argument. The improbable outcome argument may take the form of (a) the unexpected prediction argument; or (b) the precise deduction argument.

The unexpected prediction argument. When an author of a case study makes a prediction, he asserts that a state of affairs has obtained, does obtain, or will obtain, or that an event has occurred, is occurring, or will occur, when in fact he cannot know that the assertion is true. It is not based on direct experience. It does not follow logically from any background knowledge available to him. It does follow logically from the hypothesis he tests by making the prediction. If this hypothesis is true, then his prediction must be or is likely to be successful; if the prediction should turn out to be unsuccessful, then the hypothesis must be or is likely to be false.

The probability that his prediction will turn out to be successful is, given his background knowledge, low indeed. Essentially, then, the author of the case study tests his hypothesis by deducing from it what is, based on established knowledge and excluding the hypothesis in question, an improbable state of affairs or event.

The predicted state of affairs or event will probably not occur. Its failure to occur, which is expected, would suggest rejection of the test hypothesis. Therefore, if this improbable state of affairs or event does occur, the hypothesis has survived a real risk of rejection. This unexpected occurrence, then, counts more toward establishing its credibility than the occurrence of a state of affairs or event observed in the course of studying a case, which also follows from and is therefore explained by the hypothesis but which was not predicted.

That a state of affairs obtains or an event occurs when the author of a case study knows it obtains or occurs is completely probable. He cannot claim that the hypothesis has run any risk of rejection unless he has predicted the state of affairs or event before knowledge of it. What has already been observed in a case study may be regarded, if no existing knowledge accounts for it, as in that sense "unexpected," but it is certainly not improbable in the sense of unlikely to occur. (It has in fact already occurred.) The author of the case study, in referring to such an "unexpected" observation and its relation to his hypothesis, has only demonstrated that this hypothesis has more explanatory power than other hypotheses in the body of knowledge previously available to him. He has not, however, exposed that hypothesis to any risk of rejection.

To do that, he, not knowing an event has occurred or will occur, must predict that given his hypothesis it will occur or has occurred, when existing knowledge leads to the prediction that it is impossible for it to occur (or that it should occur only very, very infrequently).

An "unexpected" observation may simply be one that a case study documents has not been reported before. A case study may be written to record such an unusual observation and to announce what hypothesis the observation has instigated the author to formulate in order to explain it or what hypothesis is called into question by it. The unexpectedness (in the sense just described) of this kind of observation contributes nothing at all to making the intended-to-be-explanatory hypothesis credible, although it may cast real doubt on the credibility of a hypothesis with which such an observation is incompatible.

There is no way to guarantee that an author of a case study will take a critical attitude toward his own hypothesis and will do everything he can to subject it to some risk of rejection. That is one reason that both the possibility of replication and the fact of replication are so important in scientific work. Even when an observation in a case study is described as unexpected because its occurrence when predicted was improbable, a reader cannot be certain that it was actually predicted. An author of such a study may write his story as if he predicted first and observed later, although in fact he observed first and "predicted" later.

Similarly—when multiple independent predictions are made from a hypothesis or a set of hypotheses and no existing knowledge entails that they should be jointly successful, or when a predicted outcome is measured in a variety of ways—an author of a case study may not reveal, or may report but ignore, how many of his predictions in fact did fail; he may report only positive findings. Indeed, any researcher may not calculate, or may calculate but ignore, what proportion of his positive findings would in fact have been expected to have occurred by chance even if his hypothesis were false. Achieving some successful predictions among many unsuccessful ones does not justify rejecting a plausible alternative hypothesis—that the proportion of successful predictions was itself a matter of chance.

Taking a pessimistic view of the capacity of people to be skeptical of their own ideas, one may say that how determined an author of a case study or any research is to be critical of his own hypothesis can be decided ultimately only from the fate of tests of his hypotheses carried out by others. However, since whether an assertion is actually a prediction (in the sense given to that term here) determines in part at least whether a hypothesis has run a risk of rejection, it is important for an author of a case study at a minimum to document that he has in fact

made a prediction when that is how he justifies his claim that his hypothesis has run such a risk. He should specify, for example, what he knew and didn't know when he made the prediction, what procedures he followed in making the prediction, and just exactly what prediction he made. Did he predict from one *part* of a session, interview, or psychological test to another; from one *entire* session, interview, or psychological test to another; or from one kind of information to another kind of information? How precise was his prediction? His documentation should show, if true, that he took particular steps to elicit, discover, or search out observations damaging to his hopes, and that the observation he did make was not one that just anyone, without the aid of his hypothesis, could easily have stumbled over.

The precise deduction argument. A hypothesis does not, of course, run much risk of rejection if a prediction from a hypothesis or an observation deducible from and therefore explained by a hypothesis is one of a set of a few grossly discriminated states of affairs or events. Not much of what is possible can be excluded by a prediction or deduction when the possible outcomes an author of a case study specifies are few in number or vaguely discriminated, or both, or if—as frequently happens— he does not even specify the states of affairs or events excluded by his hypothesis, while emphasizing what state of affairs or event follows from it. The freedom from risk of rejection is even more enhanced when the occurrence of any one of a relatively large subset of possible states of affairs or events is considered to be compatible with the truth of the hypothesis.

The degree of risk of rejection a hypothesis runs increases as the degree of precision of a prediction or deduction from that hypothesis increases. The degree of precision of a prediction or deduction increases as the degree of fineness of discrimination of possible outcomes increases. The degree of fineness of discrimination is measured by how many possibilities are discriminated and how free the discrimination is from vagueness. Precision in a case study may depend, for example, upon how detailed the description of conditions is that must be satisfied for a state of affairs or event to be counted—or to fail to be counted—as a positive instance of a hypothesis. Degree of precision also increases with every increase in the size of the subset of possible outcomes that are negative instances of a hypothesis (those inconsistent with it) relative to the size of the subset of possible outcomes that are positive instances of the hypothesis.

The degree of precision of a prediction or deduction from a hypothesis may be used to argue that the hypothesis has indeed run a risk of rejection. The more precision, the greater the risk. The greater the risk,

the more severe the test. A hypothesis surviving a more severe test than a comparable rival hypothesis has, other things being equal, more credibility than its rival.

Mathematicization and quantification acquire their value in scientific work both from the lack of vagueness or ambiguity in what is deduced or predicted from a hypothesis and from the enormous range of possible outcomes excluded by a prediction or deduction, both of which ensure that the tested hypothesis runs a high risk of rejection. There is no reason not to try to approximate in a case study achievement of such desiderata: (a) specifying an exhaustive set of mutually exclusive possible outcomes (states of affairs or events), which are discriminated from each other as sharply, with as little vagueness and ambiguity, as possible; (b) making this set of well-discriminated possible outcomes as large as possible; (c) specifying which of these outcomes follow from a hypothesis and which at the least cast doubt upon it; and (d) attempting always as much as possible to make the size of the subset of negative possible outcomes much greater than the size of the subset of positive possible outcomes.

The convergence argument. An author of a case study shows that he can make multiple independent deductions from the same hypothesis. The deductions are independent if and only if (a) the different observations, which are used to arrive at the same conclusion, are obtained from different sources, by different methods, or in different settings or life epochs, or involve different kinds of subject-performances, and when possible are obtained by different unrelated observers; and (b) no available knowledge entails that these different kinds of observations are actually of the same sort (have the same cause) and should coexist. The author may then argue that since each deduction independently has exposed his hypothesis to the possibility of being rejected, he has, by making multiple independent deductions, increased the opportunities for such rejection and therefore the risk the hypothesis has run in the case study.

The improbability of the assumption that the hypothesis is false, given a set of such observations, makes the argument more than merely an argument for the explanatory power of the hypothesis. In arguing about explanatory power, that a vast number of observations follow deductively from a hypothesis is what is emphasized. Here, the emphasis is on different kinds of observations obtained by different and independent routes. In each study or with each different method, different alternative hypotheses, which might have accounted for the data, will be regarded as plausible and may be eliminated. If so, it is more probable

that the test hypothesis is true than that (1) the test hypothesis is false, and (2) in each study some different alternative hypothesis, which was not eliminated from consideration, accounts for the occurrence of the event or outcome.

The bootstrap argument. A subset of independent but interrelated hypotheses are jointly supported if they converge upon the same outcome. For example, one hypothesis in conjunction with some data entails the occurrence of an event or outcome (that a variable has a particular value) and another hypothesis in conjunction with some other data entails the occurrence of the same event or outcome (that the variable has that value), and the event or outcome occurs (the variable is observed to have that value). Or, if a variable is theoretical, one hypothesis in conjunction with some data entails that it has a particular value, and another hypothesis in conjunction with this computed value entails the occurrence of an event or outcome (that another variable has a particular value), and the event or outcome occurs (this other variable is observed to have that value). In each instance, it is possible that the expected event or outcome may not occur; then, one hypothesis at least among the subset of hypotheses must be false. The subset of hypotheses runs this risk repeatedly, as each prediction is checked. Glymour (1980) has shown how the author of a case study (Freud, in the Rat Man Case) can carry out such a test of a subset of his hypotheses.

ALTERNATIVE EXPLANATIONS OF THE EVIDENCE

An alternative hypothesis expresses some belief about which factors operating during the process of obtaining data, or operating in the situation in which data are obtained, might have led to the occurrence of an event or outcome held to support a test hypothesis (i.e., what factors might account for the data obtained) even if the test hypothesis were false. Similarly, an alternative hypothesis could express some belief about what factors of this kind might have been responsible for the failure of an event or outcome to occur (when its occurrence would have been held to support a test hypothesis) even if the test hypothesis were true.

If different observations favoring a test hypothesis are obtained in very different ways, in the same case study, in different case studies, or in different kinds of studies, it can be argued that it is improbable that these independent observations should all, or in so vast a proportion of instances, be obtained if the test hypothesis were in fact false. Since the favorable observations were reached by such different routes, in each one of which different alternative explanations were relatively implau-

sible or eliminated, it is not parsimonious to assume that different alternative hypotheses each time—rather than the test hypothesis all through—account for obtaining the observations.

This line of thought leads to the suggestion that the same hypothesis should be tested by carrying out different kinds of studies, including the case study, in each one of which a different alternative explanation for the data cannot be considered to be really plausible or, if plausible, is controlled or eliminated. Replication of a case study with similar subjects—preferably, for example, by different investigators, working in different settings, and perhaps following somewhat different methods, but testing the same hypothesis—can also be convincing on much the same kind of reasoning. The case series for this reason continues to influence clinical practice, despite the disrepute in which the case study is held.

The use of various designs in single case study, which make use, for example, of carefully documented comparisons of phenomena of interest under different conditions over time (including a baseline period of observation), or which enable the investigator to show that the level of some symptom or performance of a subject's is over time consistently higher under one condition than under another, and which eliminate various alternative hypotheses as less plausible than a test hypothesis, are well described in such works about developments in the methodology of single subject research as Barlow, Hayes, and Nelson, 1984; Campbell and Stanley, 1963; Chassan, 1979; Edelson, 1984, especially Chapters 4 and 11; Kazdin, 1982; and Shapiro, 1963. (For additional citations, see Edelson, 1984.) As these works also make clear, it is possible to perform statistical tests in some single case studies in an attempt to reject a particular kind of alternative hypothesis—the null hypothesis that the apparently favorable outcome probably came about as the result of chance or extraneous factors.

Finally, the appropriate, effective use of "historical controls" (e.g., previous clinical experience) or "external controls" (in general, the use of data from other sources to make relevant comparisons in a case study) in order to eliminate alternative hypotheses from consideration are described by Bailar, Louis, Lavori, and Polansky, 1984; Campbell and Stanley, 1963; and Lasagna, 1982.

CONCLUSION

The case study does not necessarily imply deviation from canons of scientific method and reasoning. It should not be relegated to the context of discovery. The case study can be an argument about the

relation between hypothesis and evidence. The probative value of a case study (i.e., its ability to test a hypothesis) depends on the validity of the author's use of it to claim that his hypothesis or set of hypotheses has explanatory power, has run some risk of rejection, and is more credible than rival or alternative hypotheses.

The author of a case study should carefully separate facts from hypotheses (inferences, interpretations). He should specify his hypothesis and which outcomes of his study he would consider to be warrant for rejecting that hypothesis. He should present not only evidence supporting a hypothetical causal link, but evidence for the hypothetical mechanism by virtue of which the cause has the power to produce or generate the effect. He should describe one or more rival hypotheses about his subject matter and present an argument for favoring his hypothesis over its rival or rivals. He should describe one or more alternative hypotheses, which would account for his having obtained the evidence he regards as supporting his hypothesis even if his hypothesis were false, and present an argument (even if it is a nondesign argument) for favoring his hypothesis over such alternative hypotheses. He should indicate specifically the way in which the scope of his hypothesis is limited by counterinstances, if he is not prepared to reject his hypothesis because of these counterinstances.

Such a case study would not have to be justified by the claim that considerations of subjectivity, meaning, and complexity and uniqueness required the author to abandon ordinary canons of scientific method and reasoning.

NOTE

1. Throughout this chapter *he* and *his* are used in their generic form unless otherwise specified.

Commentary

A common thread binding the three chapters in this first section is the theme of doubt. The authors encourage us to keep a healthy skepticism in the forefront of our research lives: When we think we have *the* explanation we should entertain the possibility that the conclusions we find compelling may be a consequence of our reactions to the nature of the research topic or the research relationship and might lead us to believe flawed or myopic explanations of the world.

The exhortation to preserve doubt is not an invitation to negativism; it is not a claim that nothing can be known, that reality does not exist, that nihilism is the only logical conclusion to our endeavors. Rather it is a statement of the contention that doubt forms the foundation of good research. Doubt is the precondition to the questioning nature of our work. At the intellectual level it keeps us open to the possibility of alternative explanations. At the emotional level it makes us open to learning about that which runs counter to our instincts or biases. Doubt in research is an affirmation that scrutinizing our selves, the process by which we draw our inferences, and the unconscious dynamics operative beneath our manifest actions are the hallmarks of a complete research method.

In all three chapters there is a recognition that research is a process that is deeply involving. It cannot be undertaken in any mechanistic way. It puts methodological and personal demands on the researcher. The theme of involvement is the cornerstone of Section III of this book but it is evident that even as the introductory ground is covered, involvement surfaces as a powerful issue.

We are all aware that the research process is demanding. Our methods courses teach us a great deal about these demands. None of us, however, is really prepared for the overwhelming demands that result from the unconscious material Alderfer's chapter addresses. It is easy to think of the unconscious as a source of bias, a contaminating force that interferes with the purity of our rational processes. Most research perspectives take the view that unconscious dynamics are error to be minimized. Alderfer argues that unconscious dynamics are always present and play a powerful role in the creation of data and theory. The quality of this creative force will depend on how we are able to treat the unconscious material. Nurture it, explore it, give it legitimacy, and it may become one of the researcher's greatest allies. Invalidate it, ignore it, or legislate it out of our work and it may well become a serious detractor.

Alderfer suggests that the unconscious material with which we all must struggle may derive from a variety of sources. Our upbringing, the roles we played (or are playing) in our families, the historical context in which we live, our professional training, our locations in social hierarchies, the culture (or cultures) to which we belong, and the symbols out of which our realities are

constructed all mix to give us unconscious lives that contain individual, institutional, and collective dimensions. By granting legitimacy to these "invisible" sides, the split between the self and scientist lessens and we are able to draw on a much broader array of data to inform our understanding. The manifest becomes understood in relation to the latent just as the lines of tension beneath the surface are understood in relation to the deep structure of Picasso's *Bull*.

Edelson's chapter begins where the Alderfer argument leaves off. Once this additional information is made clearer, he asks, What do we do with it? Edelson argues that it should be treated like all other evidence. Simply that it is unconscious, emotional, or relational information does not excuse if from rigorous rules of inference. He does not subscribe to the often held view that traditional science is irrelevant to data not represented in physical forms. He affirms that the investigator who would draw lines of any kind, even in single case research, must be able to specify the rules of operation by which the categories are created and the links made. These must be contrasted with other categories and links created by similar rules or with explanations that might result from alternative rules of operation. Edelson is strong in his claim that what we view as knowledge should be built upon hypotheses and evidence that have been subjected to the canons of science.

The clinical side of research methods is often labeled "soft" in contrast to the tight experimental and statistical procedures regularly characterized as "hard." In the opening section of this book the authors make clear that the clinical side requires hard and disciplined work. The nature of the work cannot be routinized quite like experimental methods, making it difficult, not soft. This section puts the issue of rigor in clinical research squarely in front of us. In some ways it is a "call to arms." For those who lay claim to the term "clinical" but ignore the hard work, this is a reminder that there are standards in clinical work and that clinical research skills bring with them obligations that should not be compromised. For those who would grossly misrepresent the clinical as idiosyncratic whim, this section seeks to educate and to warn: This level of dismissal is destructive and runs the risk of creating divisions that endanger our science and our profession. For those dedicated to serious clinical scrutiny, this section is a statement of what guides the clinical dimensions of our work.

Clinical ~~~~

The question in this section is not primarily *what* we know but *how* we know about the social world. Each of the five chapters that follow examines some of the factors that influence how we understand human behavior. These factors are always present, always shaping what we notice, what we choose to ignore, our criteria, and our concepts. A clinical method seeks to understand these influences in pursuit of an epistemology, a theory of knowing, that describes the many different ways by which the social world is known.

Using the concept of "action usable knowledge," Cammann explores the implications for research of adopting "usefulness" as a criterion for social science knowledge. He makes clear that the way we learn about social systems and, consequently, what we are likely to understand about them are very dependent on why we want to know. Smith's chapter complements Cammann's with its analysis of the influence of context on meaning. Smith urges us to consider the contextual issues we often overlook as we attribute meaning to events and he offers suggestions on how to broaden our field of vision to include both figure and ground. Together these two chapters send us off into a sea of alternative ways of understanding social reality.

The third and fourth chapters, by Perry and Reinharz, respectively, examine the cultural, political, and sexual influences on how we think about human behavior and social institutions. Perry's chapter views ideas as cultural products and shows, for example, how the meaning and complexity of a concept such as color are powerfully influenced by cultural socialization. He takes the issue further by illustrating how all knowledge carries with it the cultural and political values of the society that spawns it. Reinharz, in a feminist critique of sociological theory, painstakingly examines the ways in which sexist and racist nonconscious ideologies are manifest in the sociological literature. In her analysis of a number of prominent sociological texts, Reinharz points out that the sociological establishment's unwillingness to systematically mistrust *how* it came to know the social world created serious and destructive distortions. Her chapter urges social scientists to scrutinize cultural and political influences on their methods of knowing.

Finally, Lowman's chapter offers some thoughts on a clinical way of knowing, differentiating it from nonclinical approaches. His chapter includes a description of the skills, knowledge, and attributes of the clinical researcher—

the prerequisites for clinical understanding. Lowman examines the person and the training behind clinical knowledge.

How do we understand the core issues in people's lives? There appear to be many ways, just as there are many ways to know a sunset. Any epistemology must come to understand the many ways of knowing and the many influences on knowing if it hopes to aid researchers in learning about the social world. Each of the chapters in this section takes us a step toward developing such an epistemology.

ACTION USABLE KNOWLEDGE

Cortlandt Cammann

For more than ten years now, I have been working as an agent of change in organizations. During that period, I have done a lot of learning, often painfully, about what it takes to be successful in helping organizations to change. There is still much that I do not know, but one conclusion that I have drawn is that there are a number of forms of knowledge that are helpful to people who are trying to create organizational change that are not of central focus in many graduate programs in organizational behavior or organizational development. My purpose in writing this chapter is to describe the areas of knowledge that I believe can help people who want to conduct change, in hopes that these areas will become legitimate domains for teaching and research in the future. I do not intend to argue against traditional theory and research. These are very useful for people who want to understand organizations. They are not, however, complete. Conducting change work requires knowledge that has less academic acceptance, and approaches to using knowledge that vary somewhat from the orientations that are often taught in graduate schools. Collecting information that is scientifically acceptable, for example, requires following a variety of procedures that are often not feasible within organizational settings. Change agents have no less requirement for valid information about organizations they are working in than do scientists, but they need to be able to collect the

AUTHOR'S NOTE: I cannot acknowledge all of the people whose ideas have influenced the ideas presented in this chapter. A broad range of literature has influenced my thought, although the works of Clay Alderfer, Chris Argyris, and Ed Lawler have been particularly important. Colleagues like David Berg, Lee Ozley, Stanley Seashore, and Debbie Tracey have done much to shape my thinking, and clients have continually been a source of ideas. The editors of this volume provided much valued help in sorting through my ideas. While the ideas here are my responsibility alone, I appreciate the many ideas and critiques that have shaped my thoughts.

information whether they can use scientific data collection procedures or not. Consequently, change agents need to develop less scientific—but still valid—ways of understanding the way an organization works.

In the sections that follow, I will describe some of the key elements of knowledge that are useful to people who are trying to act in actual time settings to create change.

KNOWLEDGE OF NORMATIVE MODELS AND VISIONS

Throughout my student career, I learned that the scientific approach is based on impartiality. As a scientist, one is supposed to look at problems dispassionately, consider all options, and design empirical ways to test one option for explaining a phenomenon against another. Of course, there was always the reality of science, which did not match this ideal too closely, but the logical, empirical approach was clearly the ideal. As I began to work with organizations in creating change, I came to realize that this value helps little in the world of change.

The scientific problem of accurately describing a phenomenon and the way it works can be idealized as a rational process. Organizational change, however, is not a rational process and rational models do not seem to be the most useful ones for guiding its creation. It is rare to find people in organizational settings who are willing to "rationally" experiment with options to find out which one is "best" so that a change can be made in the "most favorable" direction. Power, politics, personal viewpoints, distrust of rational arguments, and individual interests all make such approaches untenable. Imagine, for example, the likelihood that the scientists in a university community would do an experiment to test the true value of the tenure system by randomly assigning a group of full professors at a selected set of universities to the tenured and nontenured conditions to test the results.

I also found that I could not comfortably take the role of disinterested scientist in doing change work. I could not easily help an organization do something that I personally did not believe would be successful or that would hurt the quality of work life of the people who worked in the organization. While not a dispassionate view, I hoped that my work would make a difference in the way people would experience their organizational lives. I knew that I would make mistakes and that all change runs the risk of leaving some people feeling worse off, but I could only work comfortably if I felt that the directions were, as best I could tell, positive ones according to the belief system that I hold.

Consequently, I concluded that I could not view my work as an agent of change as being purely experimental. I was engaged in a process of

trying to create worlds that I felt were valuable both in order to learn how to do it and to see if they were viable improvements as I believed. As I came to these conclusions, I discovered two interesting things. The first, ironically, was that "scientific" findings did in fact facilitate organizational change. There were times when I or people that I was working with would present a theory in some area such as job design, and the people in the organization would say, "Let's do it." They were not doing it for rational reasons, however. They rarely inquired about the nature of the evidence for the theory, and never asked what competing theories there were. They wanted to act because they saw the theory as a clear direction that had been proven by science and proposed by experts. In many cases changes made in this way were viewed as successful since the people who were involved became convinced that the change represented a better way to do their work. When they made the change they found that their prophecy was right. Whether an independent evaluator would agree was often a mute point.

The second thing I learned was that the clearer I was about my own values and the type of world I wanted to create, the more effective I could be as an agent of change. It made it easier for me to figure out how I wanted to act as I moved from situation to situation and dealt with the inevitable, unexpected problems that develop when a change is underway. It made it easier to communicate effectively my own vision of a better future so that organizations could decide whether they wanted to work with me. And it made it easier for me to help organization members develop their own vision of the future so that they could figure out how to design changes that would help them get there.

Together these learnings led me to the conclusion that normative models are an essential ingredient in the process of change. Organizational change is an uncertain activity in which neither the change agent nor the people in the organization can control all the forces that will influence the change that occurs. A downturn in the organization's marketplace, a change in key leadership positions, a new technology developed by a competitor, a tornado, and other unforeseen events can disturb efforts at planned change. Further, organizations are maintained by a complex set of interdependent forces, and any set of changes will create secondary reactions that will disturb the change process and alter the intended results. Consequently, change is unlikely to be created successfully by any planned sequence of activities. Rather, it requires an image of the result that is desired, and people who can invent activities as necessary to bring the result about. Normative models of organizational functioning play an essential role in helping people develop and share the image of the organization that they wish to create.

INFLUENCE

A second problem that I rapidly discovered was that theories of organizational dynamics described what I would see in organizations, but did not help me figure out what I should do to change them. To create change it was not enough to know what had to change; I also needed to know how to influence people to make the change.

INFLUENCING INDIVIDUALS

One of the first areas I needed to understand was how to influence individuals. All stages in a change process, from the creation of a vision to the alteration of specific behaviors and systems, require people to change, and one of the essential jobs of a change agent is to help them change in constructive ways.

In many cases, influencing the people I worked with was not too difficult. They often shared my basic values and beliefs: Individual development is good; people should have as positive a work experience as possible; things can be accomplished more effectively by having people cooperate together; and doing things well is preferable to doing them poorly. In these cases, exercising influence inolved helping people see that there were ways to accomplish these objectives that were more effective than the ones that they were using. Generally speaking, if it were possible to create the conditions where these individuals were not being punished for changing, the process of influence involved getting them to focus on the values they held and to find ways of realizing their goals. At this point, I think our field is developing better and better theories for explaining and guiding this type of influence process. This type of knowledge is very important for people who are trying to help others change.

There were other situations that I found much more difficult. There were people who resisted changes because they did not understand them, because they felt it would be harmful rather than helpful to the organization, because they expected to be disadvantaged by it, or because they preferred stability to uncertainty. Often these individuals could be left alone and allowed to watch the change to see if they could become more comfortable with it. Equally often, however, resistant individuals occupied critical positions; if they did not support the change, it would have been hampered.

Over time, I have helped organizations use a variety of strategies to influence individuals in these situations. These have included the use of organizational rewards and punishments ("you will be fired if you don't

change"), the use of authority ("changing is one of your key job objectives"), personnel movement (put the person in a job that isn't critical so that they won't block the change), education (send them to a T-group), exposure to other situations where the change has worked (send key managers to other similar organizations to talk to people who made the changes successfully), and so forth. Each time the decision of what to do has involved struggling with the dilemma of trying to influence the people without using an influence process that is contrary to the values and directions of the change being made. Sometimes the attempts have been successful, other times they have failed. I know of change situations where people who were not able to manage in participative ways were moved out of key positions autocratically, which then undermined the credibility of the change effort. In other cases, the same actions have been seen as an indication that the management of the organization was serious about participation.

Understanding how to influence people who resist change is one of the most difficult tasks facing someone trying to help organizations develop. It is not an area that our current theory explores in much detail, and represents a domain where we need to understand better both the knowledge and the skill that is involved if we are going to help people learn to act more effectively as agents of change.

INFLUENCING PROCESSES

In addition to learning how to influence individuals, I found that acting as an agent of change involved being able to influence the process by which things got done in the organizations I was working with. I often found myself in situations where I knew what should be done, but the flow of action and interaction made it impossible for me to get it done. I found myself in meetings where people would not listen to each other and critical information was not being shared. I watched groups fighting without ever identifying the problems they were fighting about. I watched individuals carefully manipulate the flow of conversation so that decisions they opposed would never be made. I watched people make decisions without considering what appeared to be obvious and better alternatives, and groups founder in ways that led them to conclude that working together was inefficient and impossible. In all of these situations I found that the flow of events was overwhelming my ability to create change, and that I needed to learn how to influence the process if I were going to produce a useful result.

For example, in dealing with Union-Management Quality of Worklife projects, the leaders on both sides often have opinions, feelings, and

assumptions about the other side that need to be expressed or they will continue to influence the perception of events and the nature of reactions. Yet, if this does not happen at an appropriate time and in an appropriate context, the sharing of information can create anger and reinforce the adversarial nature of the relationship. I needed to find ways of identifying the right time for this type of sharing, and to learn ways to help the people involved do it successfully.

Similarly, reward, budget, and management systems often put managers in a position that makes it difficult for them to allow change. Unless these issues are addressed relatively early, it can be fruitless to attempt too much floor-level change. I needed to understand the appropriate sequencing of change attempts to enable people to make the necessary changes. Then, I needed to learn how to develop contracts and planning mechanisms so that appropriate sequences could be developed.

Finally, managers in organizations develop their own style of exercising influence. Once they develop an image of a change they would like to create, they are likely to use their previously developed skills of influencing others to make the change happen. This can create a problem if their previous style is autocratic and manipulative and the change objective is to create increased participation and openness. I found that I was often frustrated because key managers who were working to create a change would frustrate themselves by the way they tried to influence others to make the changes come about. Ordering subordinates to be participative was generally not the most effective way to get participation implemented, particularly when the subordinates had no more idea about what being participative was than did the manager. I needed to learn how to help other people exercise influence in a different way than they had in the past. This involved helping them find different mechanisms (e.g., groups), different approaches (e.g., problem solving), and different personal styles (e.g., listening) so that they could exercise influence in a manner that was congruent with the type of organization that they were trying to develop.

The ability to influence the processes by which things are done in an organization is an important skill for people who work as agents of change. People in our field know a great deal about the different types of processes that exist and the effects of using them, but this knowledge needs to be better integrated into our teaching programs and needs to be taught as skills to be learned, not just as knowledge to be acquired.

INFLUENCING SYMBOLS AND PRINCIPLES

Finally, I learned that I needed to understand how to influence the symbols and principles that guide the activities of organizations if I

wanted to have a significant effect. I found that creating change in a large organization could be a lot like trying to shape a balloon. I could help a group learn to solve problems effectively, only to have the membership change. I could help set up a cooperative union-management group, only to have union-management tensions from other areas erode the cooperation in the group. I could help one group of managers learn to work in a participative manner, only to find that none of the people they worked with were changing and that eventually they went back to their old approaches because it was easier. The basic problem was that each change activity had the potential of becoming an isolated event that was disconnected from the mainstream of the organization. Unless there was a way to integrate different change activities and give them a coherent thrust, they ran the risk of becoming isolated ineffectual activities.

In part the solution to this problem was to influence key individuals and key organizational processes so that the change activities were central to the functioning of the organization. I have found, however, that this is not enough. The changes need to be reinforced by symbols and principles that are communicated and meaningful for all of the people in the organization. These symbols and principles become a map that people in the organization can use to make sense out of change activities and to see their centrality for the organization. They are the vehicle for helping people to realize that isolated change activities are part of a pattern of change that will not go away; they give shape to the balloon.

While I am convinced that influencing symbols and principles is a critical task for people conducting organizational change, I do not think we know enough about how this can be done. Symbols can be powerful, but we need to learn a lot more about their use and effects so that they can be used more effectively as tools in creating change.

KNOWLEDGE THAT LINKS THEORY AND ACTION

Another discovery that I made early in my consulting work was that having a theory that helped me to understand was not necessarily the same as having knowledge that could guide my action. I can vividly remember sitting in meetings where I was trying to understand the group dynamics so that I could help the group develop. There was a period of time where I would have to sit down after the meeting to figure out what was going on and what I could do about it. Then there was a period of time when I could figure out what was going on while I was watching the group, but still needed to sit down and think about it before I could

figure out what to do. The most frustrating period came next. I could see what was going on, and I could figure out what I should do to influence it, but the lag time was a few minutes and by the time I figured it out it was too late. Finally, I reached the point where I could understand what was happening and be able to act appropriately almost without thought.

From the perspective of an agent of change, knowledge is not helpful unless it can be turned into action. This action can take many forms, but for people who are trying to develop organizations, it means that the knowledge must help them move from the perception of events to a plan of action to the execution of the plan within very short time frames (often minutes or seconds), and under circumstances that are not conducive to reflection. It is one thing to be able to plan a change strategy in the quiet of your office, and another to try to figure out how to move it forward in the middle of a meeting where representatives from sales and manufacturing are yelling angrily at each other about who is at fault for the fact that there will not be enough business in the next six months for the plant to survive.

There are two characteristics of knowledge that seem to make it useful as a basis for action. First, knowledge is more useful when it encompasses a whole action sequence. Frequently, knowledge is passed on in a symbolic form through writing or discussion. Consequently, it results in understanding that fits a pattern, but is not linked closely to reality or action. For example, we read an article that says participation in planning changes can be helpful in creating effective implementation and includes research to justify the claim. This article is convincing, so the next time we are involved in creating change we try to do it in a participative way. As a result, we learn that there are a few things that the article did not cover. It did not provide enough description of the context so that you could recognize the organizational conditions under which participation will work; it didn't give guidelines for figuring out who should participate when dealing with anything more complex than a few work groups; it didn't help identify the characteristics of people who will resist the participation or for whom a participative approach might not be appropriate; it did not provide guidelines on how to hold a successful participative meeting (or even suggest that this might be an issue); it didn't describe how you would feel when a meeting you were leading began to deteriorate, or how to react constructively; and it did not indicate that acting participatively requires certain skills on the part of the change agent.

Useful knowledge helps the change agent predict how events are likely to unfold following specific actions; what roles and activities are going to be required; how being in the flow of action will feel; what

emotional, political, developmental, and rational dynamics are likely to be triggered and how they can be managed; and how each sequence of intervention activities will fit into the broader pattern of organizational transformation that is under way. Personally, I find theories and models to be the most useful when they are linked to cases that illustrate their application, when they include descriptions from the view of people trying to use them to create change, and when I can use my own direct experience to test them and find out how they can help me in my work. Abstract ideas that are minimally specified and illustrated are interesting for stimulating my thoughts but are not directly helpful in guiding my actions.

Second, knowledge will be more useful in guiding change if it is composed of complementary simple models that together create a holistic view. This particular form of organizing knowledge has a number of advantages for the change agent. First, models can help a change agent develop an understanding of the situation that can serve as a basis for action. A change situation is usually full of information, and the change agent's problem is to organize the information into a picture that can be used to guide change activity. Models, analogies, metaphors, and other forms of symbolic representation are crucial in helping change agents get the most out of the information available to them. They provide schema that can help the change agent notice information that is available, and they provide a tool for generating hypotheses and predictions. By helping the change agents focus on critical information and by helping them predict the consequences of events, the models can help change agents work more effectively.

For example, I find that a systems model can be a useful way to organize my understanding of an organization. It highlights the fact that an organization and each subunit within it represent entities that need to be understood. It gets me to focus on the relationship between the system and its environment, on the way it is organized to transform its inputs into outputs, and on the nature of the boundaries that exist within and outside of the organization. It makes it easy for me to ask what the ideal state of the organization would be like, and to contrast it with the way the organization is at the moment. The form of the systems model is very simple and I can carry it around in my head as a picture, yet it allows me to organize a great deal of information and keep my understanding of the organization integrated. I can easily use the systems model to generate analogies to other organizational systems with similar characteristics to the organization I am working with, which helps me develop a richer understanding of the organization and link what I am doing to elements of my past experience.

To be helpful in change situations, the models need to be quite simple. Complex models are fine for trying in retrospect to sort out what happened, but they are of little help when you are in the middle of a situation that demands action. A model that says behavior is an interactive function of complex personality variables, situational factors, and interaction dynamics is not very helpful when the problem is to decide what to say next to the vice-president of manufacturing to get permission for an experimental project. A model that gives action guidelines (e.g., present all the available information in a way that gives the vice-president valid information, free informed choice, and will create internal commitment to the results) is much more helpful when there is little time to plan. Of course, simple models must be consistent with reality and with the objectives of the intervention in order to be helpful.

Just as simplicity makes models easier to use under real time circumstances, concreteness makes them easier to link to the situation in which one is acting. In spite of my training, which has taught me the value of abstract theory, I find that much of my change work relies on using metaphors and examples to understand what is happening and to explain ideas to others. If a picture is worth a thousand words, a metaphor is worth a dozen correlations. The most helpful theories are those that are able to combine simple, abstract theory with metaphors and examples in a way that makes them usable in concrete situations.

Finally, the models will be more useful if they easily fit together to create a holistic picture of what is happening in the organization. Our models tend to describe organizational patterns at different levels of analysis. We use these constructions to help us understand the complexity of organizational events, but the stream of activities is always a totality that we break apart conceptually. The activity of a change agent becomes a part of that stream; so even though our action may be based on a theory that exists at one level of analysis for purposes of simplicity, the consequences of the action occur at all levels simultaneously. For example, many Quality of Worklife interventions use the tool of a joint Union-Management Steering Committee to coordinate and oversee project activities. Often, the membership is developed to give the committee good representation of the different groups in the organization that need to be included in the intervention. Such designs are based on organizational and intergroup theories, and generally will produce the expected consequences if they are appropriately developed. The consequences of these committees at the individual level can be quite severe. As the members of the Quality of Worklife committee begin to learn more about the members of other groups, they begin to change their views and become different from the people they are on the committee to

represent. This can cause personal stress, alienate them from their support group, and make it more difficult for the committee members to maintain their places in the organization. This is a necessary part of the change process, and if the individuals are able to maintain their credibility they can begin to change the groups that they represent. If the individual consequences of the intervention design are not recognized and dealt with, the organizational consequences that are expected may not develop.

To summarize, my experience as a change agent has led me to believe that action usable knowledge has some important characteristics. The conceptual elements of knowledge need to be connected with appropriate behavioral skills so that understanding can be linked to action in an effective way. The knowledge needs to include simple, concrete models that can be used to interpret events and guide actions in real time settings, and the models need to be congruent enough to be used simultaneously. Finally, the models need to be framed in very concrete terms so that conclusions from the models can easily be translated into sequences of actions.

CREATING CHANGE REQUIRES KNOWING YOURSELF

The final type of knowledge that is critical for people who are creating change is self-knowledge. In helping people to develop visions, or influencing people to help make visions a reality, the change agent is the primary tool in creating change. Consequently, it becomes very important for change agents to understand themselves and the consequences of their behavior. The extent to which change agents understand themselves will determine their effectiveness in a variety of ways.

First, much of a consultant's effectiveness depends on the adequacy of the consultant's organizational diagnosis. It is easy for the diagnosis to be distorted by individual preferences and biases, but this can be easily counteracted if the consultants know their biases and systematically look for alternative explanations for events. Similarly, the diagnosis will be influenced by the information that the consultant collects. If the consultant tends to collect information in some areas and not others or to interact with some people and not others, he or she can get a distorted picture of what is happening. This can be prevented by actively balancing the information sources used. My personal experience is that it is bothersome to keep checking my understanding of the organizations that I am working with and I do not like systematically talking with

people that I don't find pleasant, but I also find that when I do these things, I develop a much better and more complete understanding of the organization I am working with.

Second, one of the best, most direct sources of information for change agents is their own direct experience. When consultants feel that the organizations they are working with are discounting their needs, manipulating them to do things that they do not want to do, or channeling their efforts so that they cannot work on problems in a holistic way, they are getting direct information about the way in which the organization affects people who deal with it. The problem in using this type of information is that the change agents must know themselves well enough to be able to distinguish between their reactions and the organizational causes that may affect others in different ways. My experience has been that when I can do this task well, it gives me a quality of understanding of the organization that I cannot get in any other way because it is the only time when I am learning about the organization directly instead of by inference or report.

Third, change agents are more effective if they are able to identify and accept the consequences of their actions as well as the limits on what they can do. It can be difficult to accept that helping a manager figure out how to ethically and humanely remove a subordinate from a key job may be increasing the pain for the subordinate because it delays the decision, or that strategies for influencing key managers are not being successful in helping them to change. Recognition of failure is an important ingredient in changing approaches when necessary, and looking carefully at the consequences of actions is critical for reducing the chances of failure in creating change.

Fourth, change agents are more effective if they can use their intuition to design action. Many situations are complex enough and emotional enough that rational planning and designing will not work. The change agent cannot consciously integrate all of the necessary information, and the appropriate actions may not be anything that the change agent has done before. In such circumstances, all the effective change agents that I know work from their intuition and frequently are able to invent effective interventions. Working intuitively in this way requires a lot of self-confidence: It requires acting in ways that feel right but are not easily rationally defensible. I do not believe that this self-confidence can be built without both understanding oneself and experimenting with using intuition and evaluating the results.

Finally, change agents need to be able to deal with interpersonally stressful situations. Creating organizational change involves the creation of pain. People feel pain as they change and as they see change in the

organizational world that they are used to living in, and often the change agent is seen as the cause of the pain. Change agents need to understand why they are disliked, sabotaged, and resisted so that they keep up their activity when the activity is appropriate and stop when it is not. In this context, it is also important that change agents be able to keep a clear vision of the objectives of the change project and a clear understanding of progress that is being made. There are times when everyone involved in a change project will doubt whether it can succeed (including the change agent), and it is only by keeping grounded in the vision and the progress that it is possible to keep moving forward.

CONCLUSION

In this chapter I have described types of knowledge that can help people conduct organizational change and that are not typically provided in our current graduate programs. I have argued that change agents need knowledge that is useful in facilitating action and that action usable knowledge has a number of characteristics:

(1) It includes normative theories that change agents and their clients can use to develop pictures of the futures that they want to create.
(2) It includes knowledge about the use of influence, the consequences of its use, and the ethics of being influential.
(3) It includes models, metaphors, and maps that can be used to create an understanding of organizational events and patterns in real time frames and normal conditions. These models must be simple and holistic but, more important, the change agent must be able to use the models that work best at the time and switch or create new models when the old ones lose their predictive power.
(4) The knowledge and skill must facilitate intervention activity. It must help a change agent produce the right action at the right time to produce intended consequences.
(5) It must include knowledge of oneself. In the end, it is the change agent who is the tool for change; and the better change agents understand themselves, the more effective they are going to be in accomplishing their objectives.

Taken together, these knowledge requirements suggest that to train change agents effectively we may need new theories and different approaches to training than current graduate programs generally provide. It suggests that there is a positive value to normative theories of organizations that has often been overlooked, that theories that are concrete, simple, and not broadly generalizable may have as much value

as more abstract and general ones, and that theories and practices that help develop the skills of change agents may be as valuable as theories and practices that allow us to describe and evaluate what they do. We need to examine the types of knowledge we are building in our field, and change our theories and methods so that we can effectively prepare people to fill the role of agents of change.

EPISTEMOLOGICAL PROBLEMS IN
RESEARCHING HUMAN RELATIONSHIPS

Kenwyn K. Smith

One special epistemological bind plagues our attempts to research human relationships. The dilemma? That the research process is itself a relationship. Hence, whatever we observe about the relationships of the groups and people we research may be just as relevant to our relationship with them. There is probably no endeavor for which the truism *what one knows depends upon how one knows* is more applicable.

Consider the topic of ethnocentrism (Sumner, 1906; Levine & Campbell, 1972)—the tendency for groups in conflict to see their own actions in a positive light while viewing the behavior of others negatively. Typically, when we are embroiled in the dynamics of ethnocentrism we posture our social distance from others so that we can see in their actions whatever we wish. If we stay far enough away we can overlook the differences among their members and make the attribution that their actions are an expression of their character as a whole. Meanwhile we can maintain that our actions are a consequence of the forces to which we are being subjected. Only as each group transcends the boundaries separating them is it possible to recognize that others appear as they do less because of what they're like than as a result of the filters through which they're being examined.

AUTHOR'S NOTE: The ideas in this chapter were formulated in my collaborative work with Valerie M. Simmons. We are grateful to H. Peter Dachler for his exhaustive and exhausting commentaries on our earlier writings, which led to the recognition it was not possible to elaborate our arguments in a single paper. This stimulated the decision to abandon the original paper in favor of working on this book. The price was that the passage of time, distance and our respective personal developments made the ongoing coevolution of our thoughts on this topic no longer possible.

Could it be that decades of research on human interactions have been, in part, a consequence of the ethnocentrism of social science? Certainly, many methodological standard-bearers have exhorted us to remain distant and detached from the object of our research, to eliminate any subjective encounter that might contaminate our findings. And certainly for a long time our field pursued questions posed by white male researchers in forms such as "Do black students perform more poorly than whites because of lower intelligence?" or "Will women be able to handle the emotional strains of managerial responsibility?" or "What personality characteristics cause bizarre behavior in developing children?" It took a Herculean civil rights effort to have these issues reframed in interactive terms—so that school performance of all children could be seen as a consequence of a wide range of social processes; so that demonstrative releases of emotion, which women seem to be more capable of, could be viewed as adaptation superior to the ulcers and coronary attacks so often experienced by men in powerful positions; so that the "acting out" behavior of a child in a family could be seen as giving expression to feelings on behalf of the family as a whole.

With the benefit of hindsight it is possible for us, as white males, to admit that racial and gender-based ethnocentrism was at play in our research endeavors. But the more troubling question is whether our current social theory is still being driven by a subtler but just as powerful form of the same process. If so, how might we recognize it? And if it is unavoidable, how can we at least learn from it?

In this chapter, I want to raise some of the dilemmas involved in researching relationships in organizations. I wish it were possible to formulate a methodology that might lead to the development of a general theory of relationships, but that task is clearly beyond my reach. There are, however, some interim steps that I feel we can take. Some of these are central to this chapter. These concerns are formulated both as minefields to be sidestepped and as a crossroads that requires the researcher to make critical epistemological decisions.

An example of a theoretical choice point faced by psychological researchers in the past was the tendency to look at the characteristics of the actors in interaction as opposed to the characteristics of the *interaction patterns* themselves (Goffman, 1959). This has led to enormous energy being poured into measuring, in microscopic detail, the characteristics, dimensions, properties, and so on of the entities engaged in the interaction while transforming the interaction itself into exclusively statistical terms. This mind-set has encouraged researchers to take what might be described as characteristics of the relationship, objectifying them (calling them "things"), and then putting them into one of the

entities enacting the relationship. This, I believe, is a misattribution; it is analogous to noticing a figure emerging from a ground in gestalt psychology and treating the boundary that distinguishes figure from ground as a characteristic of either the figure or the ground (Sherif & Sherif, 1969). As Wilden (1980) points out, the boundary is neither an attribute of figure nor of ground. It is best understood as a statement about the relationship between figure and ground.

As a precursor to the development of a general theory of relationships, we need to formulate ways to translate into a relational form that which appears on the surface to be an attribute of an entity. When we hear complaints about poor leadership, can we recast this as a statement about the relationship of a group with its idealizations (goals)? When a group member is being discussed in derogatory terms, can we think of this as being an expression of within-group dynamics rather than a statement of reality about the individual's character? When we hear of workers being described as uncooperative, or management as uncaring, can we pose this in terms of intergroup relations between management and labor?

I am not proposing that a relational frame is the *only* right one for understanding organizational phenomena. It does seem important, however, for us to develop an adequate theory of social *relations* so that we can meaningfully debate the relative merits of relational perspectives with the more traditional views. Otherwise we live with the danger of being driven by our shared epistemological blindspots.

SETTING THE FRAME

The terrain still to be mapped in this field is enormous. Hence, in this chapter I want to take on a modest task that consists of two phases. First I want to discuss four of the key minefields that I think researchers of human relationships must deal with. These are (1) the problems of dialectical thinking in organizational action; (2) the trade-offs between stability and resilience; (3) the existence of invisible texts—the role of rules and the difficulty of gaining access to latent content; and (4) the close link between process and structure in organizations. In the second part of this chapter I wish to point out three types of clinical research skills I consider necessary for a theory of relationships to have a reasonable chance of evolving. These are the art of double description, the art of contextualization, and the art of reframing.

CRITICAL MINEFIELDS

THE PROBLEM OF DIALECTICAL THINKING

A great deal of organizational research is done as a response to pleas for external help from organizations that are having problems. Invariably, implicit in an organization's thinking about the nature, cause, and solution to its problem may be found faulty logic such as "Since A is the problem, not-A must be the solution" (Watzlawick, Weakland, & Fisch, 1974). Hence the request for assistance often comes in the form of "please help us implement not-A." It is commonplace to be presented with requests such as "We're having problems with our present workers, so we want you to help us design a new selection system," or "The workers are complaining about pay, so we'd like you to build a new incentive system," or "We're obviously not going in the right direction, so we want your help in selecting a new chief executive officer." Such thinking is fraught with A/not-A dilemmas.

For the action researcher who needs to understand what's going on before any attempts to produce change are made, it is necessary to confront this type of thinking head on. While problems may become manifest in the form of A, it is rare that not-A provides any type of solution.

Bateson (1972), in one of his delightful metalogues with his daughter, makes clear the A/not-A problem as he addresses her question "Why do things get in a muddle?" He points out that while there may be just one way for things to be properly organized there are a large number of ways in which they can become disorganized. Certainly, by negating organization, you get disorganization. However, negating disorganization in no way leads to organization. Organization and disorganization are two conditions of a logically different kind (Russell, 1960) and the pathways from one to the other are not mirror images of each other.

As researchers, all of us need to be very careful not to buy the logic that the solution to a problem consists of doing the opposite of what created the problem in the first place. While in mathematics a negative multiplied by a negative produces a positive, this is not the case in the day-to-day human condition. This is most evident if I'm unhappy (a condition defined in negative terms). Negate nonhappiness and it does not automatically follow that I will be happy. I'm just as likely to become depressed, or something worse than the original unhappiness. This means that every organizational problem formulation must be undergirded by a good diagnosis before actions designed to create solutions are taken.

Another type of faulty logic that comes from dialectical thinking can be found among those organizational actors that view themselves as problem-solvers. While their solutions may be effective after a problem has surfaced, the solution mentality tells us *nothing* about what to do to avoid the problem in the first place. This key dilemma can be seen in the following analogy. If your house is burning down, the solution is to have firefighters douse it with water. Who of us, however, to avoid having our house burn down would argue that daily we should spray it with water! Understanding an organizational problem requires a different logic when our goal is to avoid the problem in the first place as opposed to solving it after it has occurred.

One way in which the action-researcher is regularly confronted with a dialectical dilemma is when he or she is called in and asked for help—a typical beginning point for a great deal of our organizational research. It is usual that an organization seeks the assistance of outsiders when it can no longer work out what to do to help itself. Hence it approaches the outsider as the expert and in the process puts itself into the functional equivalent of the dependent, inept child at the feet of the all wise parent. Now, as every parent knows, the best help is often to support the child in the stumbling process. Telling him or her how to walk is often less useful than encouraging the faltering steps. When an outsider enters into a helping role, taking on the mantel of the expert, it is just as likely that he or she will become trapped in a relationship in which the actions seen as helpful are the opposite of what is needed. Anyone invited in as an expert would be well advised to treat the invitation for help as diagnostic data about the patterns of dialectical thinking operative in the organization's self-reflections. To accept the request for help without appropriate diagnosis is to rob the research process of many options that may prove valuable.

STABILITY VERSUS RESILIENCE

One set of cybernetics concepts that is helpful in thinking about relationships is the contrast between stability and resilience. Traditional systems theory has argued that living systems operate on the principle of homeostasis. This means that if there is a disturbance, either internally or externally produced, that leads to some type of disequilibrium, energy from the system will be poured into restoring equilibrium as quickly as possible because instability threatens the system's basic order.

Recent theory (Jantsch & Waddington, 1976; Jantsch, 1980) has proposed a rival thesis that operates on the principle of order through fluctuation. Instead of viewing fluctuation as equilibrium disturbing, it

is seen as a major vehicle for creating order. The converse of homeostasis is argued. The key point is that around equilibrium order is threatened. However, far from equilibrium, order is maintained. Within this frame of thinking, the viability of relationships depends more on resilience than upon stability.

Drawing the distinction between stability and resilience is important for our attempts to understand relationships in organizations. Holling (1976) defines *stability* as the capacity of a system to "return to an equilibrium state after a temporary disturbance; the more rapidly it returns and the less it fluctuates, the more stable it is." On the other hand, *resilience* may be viewed as a measure of the persistence of a system and its ability to absorb change and disturbance while still maintaining the same relationships with other entities in its ecosystem. These two concepts, when taken together, make it possible to think of an entity becoming more unstable as a result of large fluctuations; but learning how to survive with these fluctuations makes for greater resilience in that a lot of changes can be absorbed.

The contrast between stability and resilience may be seen in comparing *fail-safe* with *safe-fail* strategies. Since the stability view emphasizes equilibrium, this makes the maintenance of a predictable world all-important. On the other hand, a resilience view focuses on persistence, with the emphasis being upon keeping options open and examining events from a regional rather than a local perspective. Here the assumption is that the future will be unexpected rather than predictable; thus whatever stability there is will be less a result of general stasis and more an equilibrium created out of a dynamic network of the complex intersection of internal and external forces (Smith, 1984a).

There is a marked difference between the stability and resilience approaches as to the focus of interest in the generation and maintenance of order. Within the stability frame, the focus is on keeping the relationships among the inner parts ordered so that the whole remains basically the same. Within the resilience frame, the order is "located" more external to the entity. The key patterns are the relationship between the entity and others in its ecosystem. So long as these external patterns can be survived, with the various fluctuations generated by many entities banging into each other as part of the dynamic of the ecosystem, then the long-term order of the entity will be preserved. This may be, however, at the price of significant internal disorder. That is, the trade-offs may often be resilience at the cost of instability and stability at the cost of loss of resilience.

With the interpersonal, intragroup, and intergroup interactions that constitute a large proportion of the key relationships in organizations,

conflict often emerges. Then choices have to be made as to how they are to be handled (Simmel, 1955). There are several potential paths.

(1) Conflict may be viewed as relationship disturbing and therefore to be eliminated or minimized. This translates into either barring the troublesome themes from surfacing or trivializing them when they do, producing an overall cordiality that, at best, is superficial. The relationship appears stable so long as it remains contextually bound, but it could not be described as resilient.

(2) Conflict may be viewed as relationship disturbing but legitimate since turbulence is an integral part of closeness. This perspective places resilience above stability, with the turbulence being viewed as a part of growth and creativity—painful, but in the nature of things.

(3) Conflict may be denied, displaced, and then enacted elsewhere in the system. When conflict is avoided, often it simply gets moved to some other part of the system, creating disorder elsewhere while allowing stability to be maintained in the location from whence the conflict originated.

The particular implications of stability versus resilience approaches in research relations are rather profound. These concepts can help us map some of the delicate territory around one critical minefield. It has always been my experience that as I approach a new organization I want the entry process to go smoothly—for there to be a clear and logical way to negotiate a research contract. This rarely happens. However, when entry has gone easily for me the project has turned out to be more difficult than when entry was hard. Without a doubt my best research relationships have evolved when entry was so turbulent and difficult that I thought it would be almost impossible. When in the midst of such turbulence, the expectation of a favorable outcome has given me little comfort. But from a distance I can see that easy entry seems to set the relationship in stability terms; then, when subsequent conflict between them and me surfaces, the potential disequilibrium stresses our relationship, making the brittleness painfully visible. A difficult, turbulent entry, on the other hand, means that from the outset both researcher and the researched have to confront differences, learn how to manage their conflicts, and decide to proceed in the light of the knowledge that the relationship may be rather disturbing. Such struggles seem to create resilience. And the exasperating thing I've learned is that when entry takes a long time, when it seems protracted and involves moving gradually into the complexity of the system, the overall project is richer.

The stability-resilience trade-off becomes most visible on occasions when feedback is being given. Since valuable feedback involves learning to discuss that which normally is not talked about, many sensitivities

must be approached. As internal members struggle with these difficult themes, there is always the likelihood that rather than confront the message they will turn and kill off the messenger. A resilient relationship between researcher and the system, built out of turbulent struggles earlier, makes this phase both more survivable and more rich than a relationship built on the principles of stability.

INVISIBLE TEXTS, LATENT CONTENT, AND RULES

Whenever we observe interactions among people or between groups, our task as researchers is to look for some kind of order. We may do this by trying to identify the patterns latent in what we see, or by mapping onto our observations category systems already established in our awareness from other social situations. In the former case we are struggling with an *emergent* order, whereas in the latter case we're involved with *imposed* order. In our field we already know a lot about the epistemologies relevant to imposed order. The standard scientific approach of deriving hypotheses from established theory and then seeking empirical evidence to confirm or disconfirm our propositions is predominantly driven by an ordering principle of an imposed kind.

The task of mapping the emergent order is a very different type of process. It requires that we look, as it were, to an invisible text latent within what is seen and derive the unwritten text that ties the surface behavior into a coherent whole. This type of ordering requires a derivative approach and is full of speculation.

Perhaps the most simple, though very powerful, concept of invisible text is that of rules. At some level, all behavior is driven or rather contoured by rules, usually known to those who enact them but mysterious to outside observers.

An example of what is meant by latent rules may be seen in the following event. In Australia there is a football game unlike anything know to Americans. It is played with a ball about 1½ times the size, but the same shape, as an American football, on an oval field approximately 200 yards by 120 yards at the longest and widest points, respectively. Each team has 18 players with opponents guarding each other across the whole field, as in basketball. The game involves kicking, jumping, catching, punching, bouncing, and running with the ball. At the end, the score may be Team A 15-18-108 defeated Team B 14-22-106. For me, a fun thing to do is to sit a group of American sports buffs in front of a video, without sound or commentary, and ask them to derive, merely from their observations, the rules by which the two teams play. The processes they go through and the conclusions they draw are fascinating. Of course, in the sports example above there are such things as explicit rules

known by the players, whereas in regular social discourse the rules are implicit. For the observer not knowing the rules, the sports game is but a jumble of what appears to be pointless acts. However, once the rules are understood there is a template that binds together, into a coherent whole, behaviors that would otherwise appear unlinked.

In the case of the game, there is an easy path to knowing the rules. We can ask the players. However let's imagine we were watching some young children playing a pick-up game of Australian football in the parking lot. Chances are they would have been playing according to the rules they had absorbed through normal socialization but which they could not actually describe. To ask them why they do X or Y would probably bring the unenlightening explanation "because that's what you do!" Their behavior is governed by rules they know implicitly but which are not part of their awareness they can comment upon. Their awareness or knowledge of the rules is encoded within their behavior and not in any system of self-commentary upon their behavior.

The key issue is to comprehend the idea that latent within all social discourse may be found invisible texts that are only visible beneath or between the lines of the observable text. If the explicit text is difficult to comprehend, by unraveling the latent text it may be possible to notice links between parts that otherwise may appear uncoupled.

A key element of latent texts and ground rules is that they provide a powerful contouring of subsequent experiences. They give us a template, a type of master mold from which all subsequent experience is approached and upon which our perceptions are mapped. These templates, these latent scripts, serve as guides to action as powerful in their regulatory force as the rules of grammar are for the formulation of a verbal communication.

To provide an example of learning to look for the latent text beneath a set of surface exchanges I want to discuss something that happened to me during a lengthy study of a public school system in the New England town of Ashgrove (Smith, 1982a). For months I had been working as a participant observer in the system, tracing the relations among various groups such as the town politicians and the elected board of education, the superintendent's office, the principals in the high school, and the like. I had reached the point of having access to a tremendous amount of information, having sat for hours in clandestine caucuses in dark political crevices, read scores of files, and observed hundreds of hours of meetings, and so on. My presence had appeared to be accpeted and I no longer felt vulnerable to being excluded.

Then in quick succession I had two experiences with the board of education that raised the question as to the appropriateness of the open access I had been given. One was at a clandestine caucus of the Demo-

cratic board members being held in the early hours of the morning in one of their homes. The atmosphere was highly charged. They were hatching a scheme of enormous complexity. Suddenly someone became concerned that I was present. "Shred his notes," suggested one person. "That won't work. It's all in his head by now anyway," returned another. Suddenly, two of the board members, grown men, highly esteemed in the community, jumped up, put their fingers close to my scalp and chanted in high pitched voices, "scramble your brain, scramble your brain" as though they were ritualistically subjecting me to some exorcism or symbolic electric shock treatment that would eliminate my memory.

A few days later I was sitting as a lone outsider observing a closed meeting of the whole board of education, a practice that had been ritualized. My observing presence was as much part of the landscape as the old furniture that made up the board room—at least, so I thought. Suddenly someone suggested I should be asked to leave. A heavy debate continued around me as they examined the pros and cons of my being permitted to remain. I was rescued. "You've got to be crazy throwing him out of here. He's got the goods on every one of us," offered one of the Democrats. "Do you want to alienate him now? Lest there be any doubt, I've told him everything I think about every one of you in this room, things I wouldn't tell you to your face and my bet is he knows all of your reactions to me too!" This burst killed the discussion. They proceeded with their business, letting me continue my observation.

The two experiences puzzled me and caused me to look beneath the surface in what for me were new ways. What was happening to me was data about the board of education, but what was this data telling me? My surprise was not so much that I was nearly thrown out—I expected that and in fact was somewhat amazed I was not often asked to leave. But in each of these instances was the issue of timing. Why now? This was what was central. The experience and my subsequent struggles to deal with it taught me a new way to look at Ashgrove, and the board of education in particular, for the pattern I observed was intriguing. Once I had seen it clearly, it was easy to recognize from then on. The latent script was that whenever two internal factions within the board were about to engage in some horrendous fight, they as a whole first attacked some other group or person. If it was not someone else it was me. Living through this experience and allowing myself to generate new hypotheses directly from the experience made it possible to gather data of a quite different kind to check out my emerging suspicions about the covert rules of interaction that dominated the Ashgrove system.

THE CLOSE RELATIONSHIP
OF PROCESS AND STRUCTURE

At first blush organizations appear to have some structures and some processes. The structures seem fixed and given. The processes seem changeable and volitional. I would like to argue, however, that this is true primarily at the level of appearances. Dig underneath or go behind what we label as process and structure and we will see in large part that they are fundamentally the same. I want to be careful not to overstate the case. Hence let me concede that some structures, virtually by definition, are fixed. For example, water is always H_2O, made up of a very precise combination of hydrogen and oxygen. Alter the structure and you no longer have water. However, most of the structures we are dealing with in human organizations are not like water. Rather, they are processes that have been repeated so often that they have the appearance of being fixed.

To illustrate this point let's consider an example. In the earliest formation stages of a stream there is no structure. All we have are drops of water following a path of least resistance. However, if these drops always travel along the same route, in time the aggregation of the individual meanderings of the water drops creates what is experienced as a structure—a stream. Then other living organisms in the environs (plants, animals) come to count on the predictability of the water's behavior, and begin to act as though the stream were a firm structure. The act of treating the stream as a structure causes a secondary set of processes to emerge. Vegetation springs up around the water path, animals make tracks to the best drinking spots, and so on. In the process, another set of augmentary structures are created. That is, the process of the stream becoming experienced as a structure generates other processes, which in time also are repeated so often that they too seem fixed. In some cases the emergence of these secondary structures helps to reinforce the primary structure even more. For example, the development of vegetation around the stream heightens the regularity of the water cycle, thereby reinforcing the viability of the stream. In no time we have an interlocking network of structures that together make up what we may describe as a system.

It is very important for us, however, to recognize that these structures are actually processes repeated over and over again. Hence it does not really make sense to talk of the structures separate from the processes that constitute them. In fact, processes and structures are really one and the same thing. They merely become manifest in different ways depending on whether we are looking at their static or their dynamic character-

istics. Bacharach and Lawler (1980) capture this reality for us nicely by defining structure as the crystalization of processes that have become repeated so often that their patterning appears fixed.

In human interactions it is not at all uncommon to have an event occur that does not appear to fit the prevailing structures. We usually label it as aberrant and see it as a process that is threatening the established structures. It would, of course, be more accurate to describe it as a process that is a little different from the other processes that have become repeated so often in homogenized form that they are experienced as structures.

When the "aberrant" occurs we can ask, "What is it about the nature of this event that makes it not fit the established order?" We may equally ask what is it about the established order (structure, crystallized processes) that makes it impossible to expand in order to incorporate the "aberrant," thereby treating it as a normal event? The point is that the "aberrant" is only aberrant because of the tightness of the definition of the structure (crystallized processes). If the structure were less homogeneous, the "aberrant" would be merely a part of the heterogeneity of a much looser structure.

Because structure tends to be viewed as given and because other processes have become linked to it, creating a "system of structures," and since individual acts appear as volitional, pressure is experienced by the individual actor (person, group, or whatever) to make its actions fit the structure rather than the other way around. This is especially so because it is so much more convenient. To have the new act destabilize the whole edifice of structured processes would require much more work. To deal with the nonfitting acts as deviance or error makes life more simple.

The particular relevance of this set of thoughts to our research endeavors is the following. As we draw maps of our observations of organizational actions, there are some events (interactions) that appear not to fit. At this point we confront a choice. Is there something about these particular events (acts, people, circumstances, and so on) that makes them unusual? Or is there something about the restrictions of the maps, contours, or structures that make these events appear as unusual? We can look (1) to the character of the aberrant, (2) to the tightness of the structure, and (3) to their relationship with each other as possible places for explanation.

All too often, however, we fall into the trap of looking only at the "aberrant." As a result we overlook the fact that the "aberrant" may fulfill a very critical function for the prevailing structures (crystallized processes). This has been elaborated for us in group theory (the func-

tions of the social deviant—Dentler & Erikson, 1959), in intergroup theory (the role of the "out" group—Simmel, 1955), and in the family literature (the role of the "acting out" family member—Minuchin, 1974). What we need are much more general theories that provide automatic ways of examining the relationship of the "normal" with the "aberrant." And we also need to recognize that this will be the exact opposite of how the organization (its members, its dominant coalitions) thinks because to give credence to the aberrant would threaten the prevailing system of structures. And the very nature of organization involves the maintaining and elaboration of those structures.

SUMMARY

Thus far I have discussed four epistemological dilemmas that plague our understanding of human relationships. (1) The problem with typical organizational thinking is that it falls into dialectical binds. If A is defined as the problem, not-A is seen as the solution. This is faulty logic. (2) Relationships are easier to manage when they are stable. However, those that are built on the principles of stability may not be very resilient when conflict and turbulence arise. (3) While relationships may appear to be of a particular form when examined at the surface level, their texture is made up, in large part, of dynamics that are invisible. Seeking out the latent content and the hidden rules that drive relationships is an important element of organizational work. (4) Process and structure are two terms that evoke different images for the organizational researcher. However, they are tightly related to each other and in most ways are basically the same thing. Hence, when we are working on structures we are also working on processes, and vice versa. To treat them as separate or separable is a false dichotomy. These four dilemmas are merely a sample from the large array of concerns that need to be rethought as we push toward methodologies that will facilitate the development of an adequate theory of relationships.

NECESSARY SKILLS •

The question we are now confronted with is whether there are ways out of these methodological woods so heavily mined with epistemological dilemmas. To this I have no clear answer—at least not yet. But there are some starting points. I want to suggest the importance of three craft skills that I believe, if developed more fully and drawn together, may provide us with critical new possibilities. These are the following: the art

of double description as reported by Bateson (1979); the art of contextualization (Jakobson & Halle, 1956; Christians & Carey, 1981); and the art of reframing (Watzlawick, 1978).

THE ART OF DOUBLE DESCRIPTION

The essence of the double description process may be seen in an examination of vision. If we had only one eye, the world would appear as two dimensional. Since we have a second eye it is possible to gain information about depth. If we look at the world with one eye *what* we see is the same as if we're looking with two eyes, except that as a consequence of the second eye we can see differently. The information added creates a different kind of picture than that generated by monocular vision. There is nothing more right about one picture or the other. It's just that the mere existence of two types of pictures (descriptions) of the one scene enables extra perspective, extra insight to be incorporated that would not be possible without the capacity to make contrasts.

Bateson (1979) provides a superb example of the increment of insight produced by a second language of description, without the addition of any extra so-called objective information, in his comparison of algebra and geometry.

In algebra we can say $(a + b)^2 = a^2 + b^2 + 2ab$. In geometry we can represent this same statement as follows:

	a	b
a	a^2	ab
b	ab	b^2

In one sense absolutely nothing extra was added by the geometric description; the second language added no new information. However, it did lead to an increment in understanding the relation of $(a + b)^2$ to its product.

Bateson (1979) further illustrates this issue by asking the question "what is the sum of the first ten odd numbers?" An individual could write out the series $1 + 3 + 5 \ldots + 19$ and add them. Or they could note that

The sum of the first odd number is 1
The sum of the first two odd numbers is 4
The sum of the first three odd numbers is 9
The sum of the first four odd numbers is 16
The sum of the first five odd numbers is 25, etc.

Soon the trick can be learned that "the sum of the first ten odd numbers must be the square of the ordinal name, which in this case is 10, hence the answer is 100." What has been learned here is the difference between the *ordinal* name of a given odd number and its *cardinal* value. The ordinal name of the number 5 in the above series is 3. Hence the sum of the first 3 odd numbers will be 9, and so on.

The addition of the second system of description that led to the pattern dealing with the ordinal names has enabled us to move from talking arithmetic to talking about arithmetic. The switch has been from numbers to attributes of numbers.

Double description, or better still, multiple description, enables us to create multiple maps of single observations. And these multiple maps facilitate contrasts that otherwise would not be possible. Since all science, in the final analysis, depends upon the information generated by differences and similarities, we as investigators must generate multiple observations. One way to do this is to observe the same phenomenon in multiple cases—the traditional view of the variable n in research. Another is to generate multiple perspectives on the same phenomenon, an alternate way of thinking about n, made possible by multiple description.

For our task of studying relationships the key issue is whether we can create at least one description (or a number) that casts our concerns in interactive terms. Again, Bateson (1979) provides a useful illustration of this basic process. He suggests we examine a dog and a rabbit involved in a game of chase. If we view them as separate entities, we end up asking questions such as, When does the dog chase the rabbit? and, What level of self/other knowledge does the dog have? However, if we view the whole dog-rabbit as a single system, the pertinent questions change, for now the only critical information is *relational.* We are no longer in the bind of whether the rabbit ran because the dog chased it, or whether the rabbit, by running, *told* the dog to chase it. Instead we have a system of A and B combined and our focus can be the patterns that characterize the A-B entity as a whole.

In this example we can see that by shifting the level of analysis from the entities A and B to the entity of the A-B interaction, we are forced to draw new boundaries that generate different patterns of similarity and difference, demanding in turn different types of descriptions. These new patterns are no more or less right than those noted when observations were made from a noninteractional frame. However, the extra description does force upon us a tension without which we could easily become locked into a single, reified interpretation.

THE ART OF CONTEXTUALIZATION

The importance of context in social discourse cannot be overemphasized. Since social entities (individuals, groups, organizations) all strive to give meaning to experience, their sense-making processes are very important.

The work of Jakobson and Halle on metaphor (1956) highlights the centrality of context in the creation of meaning. For example, the metaphor "blanket" as discussed by Jaynes (1976) evokes a very different meaning in the following two sentences: "The thick snow blankets the ground" and "The thick smog blankets the city" (Smith, 1982b). In the former context, the metaphor "blanket" conjures images such as protection and warmth until some period of awakening whereas in the latter case the images are of suffocation from which escape is desirable (Smith & Simmons, 1983).

There are many different levels of context that can be important. For example, an interpersonal exchange between two individuals may mean radically different things depending on the group, the intergroup, and the organizational context in which it is occurring (Alderfer & Smith, 1982; Berg, 1984). Two white males holding a conversation about what it means to be white in a group of workers where everyone else is black would be quite a different exchange than if all the other members were white. The meaning of the conversation would again be equally influenced by the larger organizational context if the setting in which this group of workers belonged were managed by only whites while all but these two workers were black.

Each level of analysis that we use as a context within which to set a relational event can create a different set of meanings. Set the event in five contexts and we may get as many as five sets of meaning validly attached to that which is observed.

An example of the relevance of the issue of contextualization can be seen in the following. At one time when I was observing an organization adjusting to a strike I listened intently to a lengthy conversation of corporate executives who were discussing structure. Their concern was that during normal times they had a formal structure for the organization's operations that really did not operate very effectively. In fact, they all agreed the organization remained viable because of the powerful informal structure that existed. Few obeyed the formal rules. There were a large number of informal networks that enabled managers and workers to get things done despite the system rather than because of the system. One perspective taken in this exchange was that the strike offered the opportunity "to clean up our act," expressed as follows:

"Let's take this chance to make formal many of those informal procedures we've agreed work so effectively; at least that way we won't have to be always sneaking around behind the back of the formal procedures." A counterperspective was offered. "No. That's a big error. You don't seem to understand that the informal structure only works *because* it is juxtaposed beside the formal structure. I wouldn't tamper with the informal at all. In fact, if we formalize it we'll probably kill it off."

They debated at length. It was very sophisticated. The issue was whether the informal processes that were so effective would be viable if it were not for how they tied to the formal structure that in fact contextualized them. This latter thought prevailed in this situation with very creative consequences. The executives agreed that surviving the strike would probably depend on whether some new informal networks and procedures emerged. They concluded that to tamper directly with the informal networks would be an error. Rather, they saw their best option to be to change certain elements of the formal structure, the domain over which they had legitimate power, with the hope that their changes would prompt the necessary readjustment in the informal system they believed would be beneficial. They could not accurately predict what the new informal system would look like, but they were able to press certain structural levers that stirred a very creative period of informal realignments.

THE ART OF REFRAMING:
BOTH A CONCLUSION AND A BEGINNING

In the above section, I pointed out the importance of context on the meaning of an event. How the context is used as a frame for an exchange influences the nature of the event. The context may exist ready-made for the experience. No interpretation is required, for the context is self-evident. More often than not, however, there is no immediately "right" context available, or else there are numerous possible contexts, each with validity, but also each generating its own meaning out of the event. In this setting, the researcher has to choose the frame or frames to be used and the choice will shape the meanings that will be infused into the event or events being examined.

A great deal has been written on framing, especially in the family therapy literature (see Watzlawick, 1978; Haley, 1973; Selvini Palazzoli, Boscolo, Cecchin, & Prata, 1978). Hence, for the discussion here I will limit myself to simply pointing out that the process of double/ multiple descriptions and thus our theorizing about relationships are primarily based on multiple framing. Slot an event into a singular frame and all we

have is one description. Frame it multiply and then we have multiple descriptions, thereby creating the possibility of numerous meanings. This art of creating multiple meanings is as central to the clinical side of the research process as the concept of sample size is to the procedures of the logical positivist.

Some aspects of framing are self-evident. Other aspects are very complex. For example, it is not all that difficult to understand the multiple frames that can be created by mapping events into a variety of explicit external contexts, as I've discussed. However, events may also be framed by internal contexts—by what might be called the "inscape" (in contrast to the "landscape") for events that can be meaningfully framed by the dynamics latent within them.

Perhaps the best way to capture what I mean by this is to draw upon an analogy we can take from music—the concept of *voicing*. Hofstadter (1979) provides a wonderful description of the basic principles of voicing. A simple melody such as Three Blind Mice has a single theme, the line any of us would sing if invited to join in this song. This we think of as the main voice. This single theme, however, can be played against itself by having "copies" of the theme join in after a fixed time-dealy. The first voice enters with the theme, then a copy joins in a few bars later with exactly the same theme. Then after an equal delay a third voice enters, and so forth. In order for a simple round like this to work each of its notes must be able to serve in a dual or triple role. That is, it must be able to be simultaneously part of the melody and part of the harmonization of the same melody. In this sense, it is both a voice in its own right *and* a frame for another voice. In the triple round the same note must fulfill the melody (voice) and dual harmonization (two frames). This is the simple concept of voicing—that is, the delayed repetition of copies of the same theme.

There are numerous complex versions of voicing. For example, a second type of complexity may be introduced by staggering not only in time but in pitch. Thus the first voice might commence the theme in one key, the second voice joins in after an appropriate delay, not on the same note but five notes higher, while a third joins in later yet another five notes higher, overlapping the first two. A third type of complexity may be created by having the second voice singing twice as quickly or twice as slowly as the first, and so on. This is formally referred to as dimunition and augmentation, respectively, since the change in pace either shrinks or expands the theme. A fourth complexity involves the *inversion* of the theme. This means making the melody jump down whenever the original theme jumps up, and by exactly the same amount. A fifth complexity—one that represents a great deal of sophistication—is playing the

theme backward in time. The complexities go on and on, with the elaboration of concepts like the "countersubject," and so forth. The details, for our purpose here, do not matter.

What is of value is to recognize that each event that we social researchers make into data for our theories has both context (settings in which it is embedded) and latent texts (scripts), which are the behavioral equivalent of musical voices. Hence the richness of the meanings of the data we are working with depends almost entirely on our capacity to see/hear/sense/intuit that which is beyond the manifest and then to make these into frames that will give us multiple descriptions to make into the fibre from which the fabric of our theories is constructed.

This, I would argue, is at the core of the clinical skills we must develop if we are to give ourselves a fighting chance of creating a theory of relationships. It is only when we have learned how to formulate anew the substance out of which we build our theories that we will be ready to generate epistemologies adequate to the tasks of understanding organizational relationships. I do not know what the journey will involve. But I'm convinced the foundation skills for setting off on the journey into this terrain are the skills of multiple description, contextualization, and reframing.

6

LOOKING AT RESEARCH IDEAS AS BEHAVIORAL DATA

Stewart E. Perry

The first clinical demand of social science requires researchers to recognize their own humanity as it inheres in their basic research concepts. In this chapter, I want to suggest an intellectually respectable perspective for responding to that demand. I will do so by presenting the view that research ideas (like all ideas) are pieces of human behavior and therefore are themselves susceptible to scientific analysis and understanding in the same way as any other behavioral data.[1]

All too often in the course of research we as social scientists work with our scientific research ideas as if they had an existence and a meaning quite apart from the human beings who use them. We too often consider that our careful use of scientific techniques and methods somehow provides us with a means to transcend the common ground of frail humanity that we otherwise share with everyone. We are, in fact, apt to approach research as a way of shedding our humanity. It cannot be done.

Harry Stack Sullivan reminded his trainees that physicists (in the Einsteinian revolution) discovered themselves moving about among their own data (Perry, H., this volume). Thus psychiatrists (and, by extension, all social scientists) should not be surprised to find themselves as participants in all their observations of human behavior. Here I will suggest further that all of us engaged in research will discover ourselves embedded also in the midst of our working concepts. Although social scientists, like other scientists, have long since recognized that all our data are shaped by the concepts that we choose to use, we have not yet accepted the notion that in our ineluctable humanity we have not only chosen the concepts but have also shaped them to fit our human condition. In that manner we fashion both our ideas and any resultant information.

Let me jump in with a case illustration from the research in a major psychiatric hospital where I worked for five years in the mid-1950s as a

participant observer studying the relationship between the social setting of the hospital and the theories, methods, and research problems of the researchers (Perry, S., 1966). I have recently learned that something odd has been happening in the intervening years at that hospital.

When I was there in the mid-1950s, the most significant mental health problems that the staff studied were defined mainly in the research frameworks of "psychotherapy," "social structure," "social epidemiology," and "cultural milieu." It is true that at that time the hospital also sponsored research in the biology and chemistry of both the normal and the disordered brain. For example, there was a lot of work on brain analogs to lysergic acid diethylamide (long before the hippies discovered LSD). However, the then preferred research frameworks 'had'[2] to be included in the brain chemistry projects. That is, concurrently with brain chemistry questions the researcher was strongly encouraged to consider social and psychological questions. Even if one was rather single-mindedly a brain chemist and not at all a Leonardo in the whole range of psychiatry, one was expected to link one's work somehow to the preferred framework.

During the intervening years in that same hospital, the situation has completely reversed itself. Now, as I have learned from current staff members, what is really valuable to research is generally cast in biological and chemical frameworks. Little goes on as of now that relates to the previously honored rubrics of "social," "cultural," and "psychotherapeutic." How has this come about?

Thomas Kuhn's (1962) work on the paradigmatic shifts in science might make this change recognizable. He has argued that new findings can pile up to such a persuasive degree that previous ways of thinking about scientific puzzles are jettisoned in favor of other ways that had been around for a good while but not accepted. But that is not true in this case. Nothing over the last twenty years in the results of psychiatric research either at that hospital or elsewhere provides the disinterested observer with a 'scientific' rationale for that shift. Indeed, at many other respected settings the social-psychological-cultural rubrics still hold sway.

TOOLS FROM DEVELOPMENTAL PSYCHOLOGY

To understand what has happened to the research ideas in this one case (and, by implication, in similar cases), I would want to seek tools for studying the behavior of the persons using the research ideas, rather than tools for studying the ideas themselves. I would want to begin at the beginning—the very beginning: How do children grow up to use ideas? That is, by looking at events in child growth and development one might

find general processes that ultimately produce the researcher and his or her research ideas (Piaget, 1970). For the case of the research hospital, developmental psychology does not offer immediate explanatory assistance but it does provide the best overall entry into the perspective of the behavioral analysis of ideas and provides the bridge for moving on to sociological and political science tools that will aid in looking at the hospital puzzle. Along the way I believe it will become evident that anthropology, economics, and all the other social sciences can also be relevant to the study of ideational behavior in science and elsewhere.

So, to begin with, an idea is, after all, embodied in a word or phrase, and that would immediately suggest examining the process by which the child comes to learn and deal with words, shuffling and reshuffling them until they satisfy her or him as somehow referring to what she or he wants them to refer to. No matter how one might try to escape the constraints of relying on words—by using numbers, for example, as if these too were not simply a special type of word—we cannot elude all that learning to use words implies in human behavior. It is true that at least some physical scientists report that they tend to formulate their concepts in 'mental pictures' of 'physical structures.' Having done so, however, the physicist then faces the task of translating the internal images into socially communicable mathematical formulae and verbal expression.

Surely, the most limiting and at the same time most releasing of all the child's early learning experiences for developing ideas, including scientific ideas, is the language the child is brought up to use—and will manipulate for purposes of research reports. Consider only the simplest situation, in which the language of one's childhood is the language of one's scientific field. If this is one of the major European tongues, it is a magnificently flexible tool indeed. In one sense, a contemporary European language is inexhaustible, for probably any language can express anything if its users can coin new expressions, new terms.

By contrast, traditional literary Arabic does not permit language development. Partly this has to do with certain religious strictures about the number of words in the Koran; and thus there is a sacred speech and a secular one, the vernacular Arabic. For those of the Arabic cultures, the traditional literary language is the only language to be used for truly valuable ideas. That means that the advancement of science must take place outside the realm of "valuable ideas." Consider how this might constrain diplomatic communication among devout Moslems about the ethics of scientific technologies in nuclear energy and nuclear arms.

But even if a language is growing or, more to the point, because it can grow, the variety of ideas that *might* be expressed in it will never be mastered even in the largest dictionary. At the same time, each people

and each person is constrained, as Whorf (1950) has made us well aware, from thinking certain thoughts and from expressing certain ideas because the language in current use lacks certain words and expressions. When we learn another language, we can begin to see that our previous world of ideas is only a limited sector of an unknown range or spectrum of possible ideas.

Schachtel (1947), the clinical psychologist, told us that the rich experience of children in their 'naive' interactions with the physical and interpersonal world is whittled down by the lack of appropriate words (or schemata) available to them, their parents, and their other associates for latching on to the experience. Without the linguistic schemata as vessels in which to catch the heavy rain of experience, all memory of the broad range of sensation, for instance, that is open to the child is restricted or distorted into a distribution that will fill the available words with the meanings that significant others assign to them. Children thus come to recognize and remember only those parts of the world that people in their culture group have recognized before. And if by chance a child has vividly sensed or felt something that does not fit the choice of words that is available, so that he or she creates new words or combinations of words, the child may be disciplined or subtly controlled to forget it. Gaps in memory, then, have a systemic source, Schachtel argued, far beyond the reasons for repression that Freud described. And experience in the present is subject to the same constraints as experience recalled.

One of the ways that later researchers have discovered that this is so is by the comparison of reactions of people, from different language backgrounds, to what the researchers call the same stimulation. A rather dramatic array of evidence occurs with respect to color. Color, in terms of twentieth-century Western science, is a combination of hue (that is, places on a spectrum measured within the range of 100 to 700 millimicrons); chroma (that is, saturation or purity); and brightness or brilliance (called *value* in technical colorimetry). True, those three dimensions constitute a very specialized language for technical purposes, but, after all, most readers of this book will recognize the concept of color and will be albe to discriminate red from orange, and so on.[3]

Color, however, is not a universal concept; and quite apart from so-called color blindness, not all people recognize what you and I might call the same colors. For example, the Haununóo, a central Philippines culture group, have no such concept, and it requires a special investigative technique in anthropology to discover exactly what elements they do respond to in the discrimination of something comparable to what Americans would call different colors (Conklin, 1955; Frake, 1969). It turns out that the Haununóo discriminate colors according to a four-

way system of darkness or lightness and redness or greenness. The latter terms of distinction apparently arise from a rural perspective and imply dryness versus succulence, what one might discriminate by the state of the stem of a plant during different seasons of the year.

Thus the child in this Philippine culture can and must do different things in the recognition of coloration compared to the child in the United States. Similarly, U.S. children of different backgrounds will latch on to variant color distinctions. The child of artist parents may see something different in the tomato reds than the child of a farm family discriminates. But even Americans of homogeneous background can give corollary evidence of the influence of the conceptual categories of language upon perception. In American English there are some colors that can be identified with a one-word name; others need a phrase. It is harder for American college students presented with color chips to recognize colors that need a phrase; and they do not agree with each other as much on those colors as they do on the colors identifiable by one word. The same color chip study done with the Zuñi Indians, using the Zuñi language, gives similar results for responses to one-word colors versus those requiring Zuñi phrases (Brown & Lennenberg, 1954).

Such studies provide good evidence that language really constricts or opens powers of perception. That is, the world, as each person is able to formulate it, really is different depending upon the schemata that the person is trained to use to describe it. What is true for color discrimination is true for other sorts of experience. In growing up, one is taught to make only a limited number of conceptual discriminations.

TOOLS FROM OTHER SOCIAL SCIENCES

Because discrimination, perception, and conceptualization can vary so with early developmental experiences, including language, some specialists argue that the reason that people throughout the world can communicate at all is because some concepts are physiologically built into the body's equipment (Chomsky, 1971). Thus, in addition to tools in developmental psychology, physiology is another set of behavioral science tools to examine ideas as behavioral data. The special case of toxic hallucinations is only the simplest matter to be considered in that perspective. Much more intriguing and fundamental is the issue of the 'fit' between our body equipment and the physical world around us such that we *can* apprehend that world (Campbell, 1977). However, there are still other tools to consider before returning to the case of the research hospital.

Given the variations deriving from each person's own history, the research ideas in use or created by the person must somehow reach a shared core of meaning, however refined and simultaneously impoverished by the requirements of sharing. Only thus is the user accepted and heard in her or his social groupings, including academic departments and research laboratories. Ultimately, the user has to seek a minimum of consensus with others by which her or his ideas can be validated. At that point new social rules as well as interpersonal sensitivities come into play, and one would seek tools from social psychology, sociology, and political science.

Of course, philosophers and kings of many times and places have wondered how it might be possible to engineer a consensus (establish a set of shared rules) that would be dependable over the years and require acceptance on its own terms. That is another way of asking, as scientists do, how can we reach the truth about a certain experience? But truth itself is an idea; and as an idea it too has its own ties with the particular times and places in which it occupies attention. For example, Merton (1957: chap. 16) has suggested some reasons to suppose that science and its version of truth requires or at least flourishes best in a democratic setting. However, even in science, nondemocratic forms of behavior play a necessary role, as I will note later on.

Yet even a dictator may ask, How can I establish a criterion of true knowledge that is free of the ties of time and place and person, including my own time, place, and person? The person in authority may recognize his or her own mortality, so how will the truth live on after the ruler? One solution is to institutionalize a means of succession—the king is dead, long live the queen. Thus authority might survive human mortality, but of course the new monarch may turn out to have very different ideas. Then those who have lived under both regimes must ask themselves, Which one represents the truth?

In so-called Western society, it is very important to make the distinction between what is 'true' and what is 'untrue.' While other societies may have other priorities, in Western civilization a good deal of effort has gone into working out justifications for the label *true*. A whole set of different criteria have come to be recognized, and one may choose among them: Does it fit with other ideas held to be true (the criterion of consistency)? Is it a guide for successful action (the criterion of usefulness)? Does it produce dependable predictions beyond itself (the criterion of new knowledge or new truth)? Is it what some very trustworthy and expert person says (the criterion of authority)? Does it seem simpler and yet do the same thing as another more complicated formulation (the criterion of aesthetic economy)? And so on.

What makes us as researchers feel sure that the way we decide on the truth or falsity of an idea is itself the true way to do that? How did we learn to decide by that particular means? It may seem at first blush that science, dependent on so-called self-correcting research, is different from other ways of determining truth. Yet science as a system of ideas is, in fact, a very successful social institutionalization of authority about truth.

Very much like the temporal succession of other interpreters of truth, scientists provide for a succession that manages thereby in part to transcend place, time, and person. Some of the authority of science lives on in the succession of the particular scientist's students, some in acceptance of her or his students and ideas in other kingdoms and duchies— other laboratories. But it must be recognized that science is a human transmission of authority, even if one is thereby merely recognizing that no individual scientist can manage to retest all that has gone before, even in his or her own narrowly defined field. Thus all must take on authority that some other criterion besides authority was at one time applied.

The very humanity of science as revealed in its dependence upon its own system of authority makes it accessible to the rest of society. Science is vulnerable to competing views through its always-present loopholes, vulnerable to entry by the surrounding nonscientific environment that supports and defines its boundaries. This is so, even though the authority of 'science' may be accepted not only by scientists but also, to some extent, by most of the nonscientists in their environment. Acceptance occurs, however, only if it will not fundamentally interfere with the authority of the nonscientists. For example, South African political elites accept the truth of scientific statements except when those statements conflict with the implications of their racial views. So, generally speaking, science as a way of life and as a set of ideas is relatively acceptable to European-oriented people today so long as it does not interfere with their other ways of life and other views. And thus science remains enmeshed in the tangles of those other ways of life and other views.

Scientists, nevertheless, often claim stoutly that their activity is independent of the realms of political, religious, and other such competing institutions, ideas, and ways of life. After all, science as a way of life and as a way of determining the truth of statements has grown up on the denial of the relevance of social and cultural ties that might bind it to a particular moment in history. Thereby the authority of science—not linked to political or other authority, but only to its own standards— seeks to determine truth in a way that will live forever.

However, if we scientists and researchers are to give ourselves this special superhuman eternal status, we must have some superhuman means at our disposal, and that, so far, we have not been able to demonstrate. In fact, it is only religious or spiritual realms—so much in opposition to science—that have so far been able to 'demonstrate' superhumanity. So we, as scientists, recognizing the way human beings behave, will have to come to the conclusion that scientific ideas can no more escape their political environment, for example, than the political environment can escape the onslaught of scientific ideas. There will always be some sort of interchange between each pattern of social activity and any others within the tangent environment—a cross-cultural exchange, so to speak.

WORKING IN A RESEARCH SETTING

In our personal lives as researchers, then, we will encounter, wittingly or unwittingly, such exchanges. Sometimes the exchanges are very visible, and sometimes they seem to come upon us without our having recognized it until it has happened. In biology, one visible exchange was Stalin's decree on Lysenkoism in which Stalin underwrote the Russian agronomist Lysenko's scientific hypothesis that environment-induced changes in plants are inheritable. Somewhat less visible has been the exchange that became the reversal of what is more valuable science and less valuable science at my old research hospital, which, as it happens, is a mostly federally supported hospital.

I do not have sufficient careful information by which to explain that shift in valued research questions, but I believe the following is a reasonable hypothesis. Most observers will agree that federal policy, beginning in the Nixon administration, came to downgrade social science in general as not being a part of 'real science' and as therefore not deserving the same support. Under Reagan, the broad social forces expressed in his even more stringent policies are also expressed in the yardstick being used at the research hospital. Because of the hospital's virtually full dependence upon federal funds, it is especially vulnerable to the definitions of federal policymakers at the highest levels, and so the reversal occurred.

Eventually, of course, such pressures can generate their own resistance. Social scientists systematically entered the political arena as lobbyists in 1981 to protect their access to federal funds—and, ultimately, their status as a part of science. A lobbying organization now operates under the name of the Consortium of Social Science Associations.

Be that as it may, suppose you were a research scientist at that hospital in the early period and were a brain physiologist; or suppose you were a research scientist in this later era and were a social psychologist. In either instance, you could, of course, pack up your files and go to an intellectually more congenial research institution; and indeed researchers in all sorts of settings are doing this all the time.

The opportunity for that sort of mobility varies. On the one hand, for example, the choices tend to narrow as the scientist becomes older, unless she or he is of sufficient stature to create her or his own institutional setting. On the other hand, generally the older one is, the more likely it is that one has already found or created a congenial setting. Nevertheless, whatever the choice, to stay or to go, the research is shaped.

Do the ideas themselves get shaped in this situation or is this just a matter of more resources for selected research topics? Also, does the overall course of development of the ideas in the entire affected field get shaped? Such questions require their own systematic study, but they should sensitize the researcher to his or her own intellectual accommodations to the research work setting. Probably, the more uncongenial the environment, the more cautiously and carefully you will progress to protect your work against potentially well-founded criticism. So, what effect will that have upon the leaps of thought that mean so much in scientific development? What sort of person would you have to be to make those leaps when others in the setting do not share your perspective, when you are isolated by your choice of research topics? That suggests the matching of the researcher's personality predilections to particular social settings—still more sophisticated questions to be explored in the field of scientific ideation (Kohn & Schooler, 1983).

By contrast, the more uncritical and supportive the research environment, perhaps the more apt you will be to trade ideas swiftly and lightheartedly, and the more apt you are to be less self-critical in your own research and the conceptual definitions you formulate and use. Is the more congenial environment apt to perpetuate what in the long term will be viewed as a dead end, when the support group runs out of energy, resources, and, ultimately, members?

As soon as one no longer concedes a scientific idea as *essentially* having its own life apart from the human context in which it is grown, these and a whole host of other ideational behavior questions can be raised. And these questions can themselves be pursued according to the rules of scientific research.

I do not think it is too much to jump from the accessibility of such questions to the further issue of instituting new criteria for scientific

truth. By that I do not mean to suggest that newer criteria would turn out to be better; but I do suggest that if our human environment is a part of scientific truth and knowledge, then somehow or another we as social scientists need to take that into account in our efforts to calibrate our research ideas and their results. Is it enough to say, "Well, the results have been replicated elsewhere, so everything must be okay"? The "elsewhere" may share some very crucial social and other behavioral characteristics that help to produce identical results. To counter this, one might wish to rely most upon an "elsewhere" that is quite different. But, what are the factors that should be varied for truth's sake? That is not at all clear; and that makes the relatively unexplored field of scientific ideational behavior that much more important to the social sciences researcher.

Explorations in the field can begin with examining the influential environment of one's own behavior in the research setting (Friedman, 1967). On the one hand, this examination can be considered merely, say, the sociology of knowledge, or perhaps merely as a radical empirical critique of one's methodology—simply taking one step further what the scientist has always insisted on: a careful and thorough description of research technique, now including hitherto overlooked behavioral parameters. On the other hand, if "methodology" or "sociology of knowledge" is the conceptual category for the study of ideational behavior in research, we may be using familiar categories of thought to isolate us subtly from an experience that requires other forms of formulation. We miss the point to which Schachtel alerted us and which we encounter mechanically in any computer today. Without a proper program, we can not accept data, no matter how valuable. The first step is surely for us to adopt the wonder with which the child encounters the world and engages ever anew in the struggle of discovery and formulation.

NOTES

1. This presentation attempts to provide in a readable format a sort of summary of a book of some ten chapters, now in process. I have indicated only a few exemplary references that might be consulted. The most rewarding and comprehensive approach to the problem presented here is Donald T. Campbell's challenging William James Lectures at Harvard University, 1977, still in manuscript form but available from Campbell at Lehigh University.

2. I will use single quotation marks as flags that the word is a troublesome gloss for something more complex—as a translator might signal that a word that has been selected does not adequately translate what is in the original.

3. The general point I want to make about variations in color discrimination does not depend upon choosing between Land's retinex theory of color perception or the more standard view (Ingle, 1985).

FEMINIST DISTRUST:
Problems of Context and Content in Sociological Work

Shulamit Reinharz

We do not know exactly what is on the Other Side until we arrive there—and the journey *is rough.* (Daly, 1978)

CONVENTIONAL AND ACADEMIC DISTRUST

One of the hallmarks of both the modern attitude and the scientific method is distrust. We moderns do not trust one another because we see that self-interest takes precedence over other considerations. Skepticism also pervades our relation to scholarship. Science requires that we do not simply accept assertions, but rather that we seek evidence according to standardized criteria. We must question if the author employed the correct methods; if the interpretations of data reflect bias; if the instrumentation was appropriate, and so on. In addition, we have recently discovered that certain methodological, epistemological, and social psychological dilemmas are constraints in the production of social science knowledge.[1] Thus, a social scientist learns to compound conventional distrust with academic distrust.

We are also taught that distrust can be suspended when someone's work has been found acceptable according to certain criteria. True, at

AUTHOR'S NOTE: The following people provided helpful reviews of this chapter: Loraine Obler, Gordon Fellman, Barbara Gruber, Anne Mulvey, Margaret Fearey, Oliva Espin, Brinton Lykes, Hortensia Amaro, Tracy Paget, Maurice Stein, Irving K. Zola, Barrie Thorne and Liz Stanley. Evan Harriman typed the manuscript and helped prepare the references.

some later point we might uncover new criteria or evidence that force us to reexamine previous assertions. But this possibility should not lead us to a relativist position, wherein one says, "Since I can never know anything with certainty, nothing can be judged."

Conventional criteria for determining the worth of scholarship do not include the extent to which findings match one's personal experience (see, e.g., Toby, 1955). In fact, it is believed that there would be no unique purpose for scholarship if it coincided with personal experience. Experience, it is believed, is the foundation of idiosyncratic claims on limited instances. In sum, the attitudes of the modern scholar/scientist include distrust of others' work, belief in the value of particular criteria for judging work, and disdain for personal experience.

FEMINIST DISTRUST

Feminism adds another dimension to this modern attitude. It suggests that conventional and academic distrust are limited because, as Kuhn has discussed, they function within a dominant paradigm erroneously equated with reality (Brandwein, 1984, p. 5). Feminism proposes that this paradigm is not sufficiently recognized as a paradigm. Therefore, feminist distrust applies to work *within* the conventional paradigm compounded by distrust *of* the paradigm itself. Feminists have alluded to this problem when referring to "personal tension" (Westkott, 1979) or "ontological anguish and exile" (Vickers, 1982). Only rarely has the attitude been labelled *distrust* (Lugones & Spelman, 1983).

The anguish mentioned by Vickers refers to a related problem—the lack of a solution to the problem of distrust (see, however, Register, 1979, p. 8). Feminist theory and research should, of course, be the solution, but these are still relatively new and somewhat problematic. For instance, the degree and nature of feminist anguish vary among the disciplines (Stacey & Thorne, 1984). And even in a single field there is more divergence than consensus. Moreover, feminism includes a heterogenous set of beliefs ranging from radical and separatist to liberal, reformist, and even conservative (Firestone, 1970), resulting in minimal consensus about guideposts for research (Reinharz, 1981). Furthermore, it is somewhat dangerous even to discuss the topic of feminist anguish without jeopardizing the fragile hold feminist scholars have on their jobs as researchers and teachers (Westkott, 1979, p. 430; Bernard, 1981, p. 17). Feminists do not as yet have sufficient resources to own or control settings for research. Finally, because feminism provokes among those who think in its terms a reevaluation of all aspects of one's life,

acceptance of a feminist perspective introduces self-doubt. Thus, feminist consciousness places added demands on the researcher.

FOREMOTHERS OF FEMINIST DISTRUST

Feminist sociologists' distrust originated in the awareness that sexism was pervasive in the discipline, making it wrong, conservative and embarassing (Friedan, 1963, chap. 6). Kate Millett, writing from outside the field, was one of the first to make this point: "Modern research . . . takes patriarchy to be both the status quo and the state of nature" (1969, p. 78). For the sociologists who wrote during the early phase of this second wave of the American women's movement (see Gornick & Moran, 1971), the capacity to articulate a feminist critique was rather remarkable. After all, these women had been socialized within the dominant paradigm (Bernard, 1981, p. 14).

Nevertheless, as they discovered that the scholarship in which they had been trained was embedded in a patriarchal paradigm, they began to claim that there was strain and even incompatibility (Wittig, 1982) between "their" academic discipline and their feminist consciousness. For example, Daly (1978) argued that reform of patriarchal scholarship is impossible unless new language is used. Stanley and Wise (1983) argued that patriarchy is so intertwined with heterosexuality that to eliminate the former would mean little without eliminating the latter, the prospects of which were nil. This argument has been applied to other components of the dominant paradigm—such as classism, racism, capitalism, ageism—all of which render conventional scholarship partial and leave attempts at generalization limited (see, e.g., Reinharz, Bombyk & Wright, 1983; Ladner, 1973; and Schwendinger & Schwendinger, 1974).

Furthermore, feminist scholars' thinking about method became influenced by the effectiveness of consciousness raising in generating a social movement and in forming the groundwork for the articulation of feminist theory (see Reinharz, 1983). Because of the central role of consciousness-raising in the history of contemporary feminism, some feminist scholars give it a central role in all forms of feminist scholarship (see, e.g., Lugones & Spelman, 1983). MacKinnon, a well-known feminist theoretician, has expressed this view:

> Consciousness-raising is the major technique of analysis, structure of organization, and theory of social change of the women's movement. In consciousness-raising, often in groups, the impact of male dominance is

concretely uncovered and analyzed through collective speaking of women's experience, from the perspective of that experience. . . . Its claim to women's perspective is its claim to truth. (1982, pp. 519, 536)

The adoption of this position, however, encourages a methodological and epistemological shift that seems to take us out of the tradition of sociology—and conventional science—altogether (see Smith, D. E., 1974).

A few years after the Millett insight, Daniels wrote that when a feminist perspective is applied to the work of sociologists, "we are forced to rethink the structure and organization of sociological inquiry" (1975, p. 340) in all its aspects. In other words, she implied that sexism in the *content* of conventional sociological research was part and parcel of the sexist *context* in which sociological research was done, in particular, the university and other "normal" institutions.

In both arenas—content and context—some feminist sociologists have come to feel that we have to begin again. We have made some strides with regard to content—textbooks that have a feminist, sociological orientation have begun to appear (Bernard, 1981; Andersen, 1983) as have guides to the elimination of sexism in teaching (Thorne, 1982) and in theory and research (Millman & Kanter, 1975; ASA, 1980; Bowles & Duelli-Klein, 1983; Roberts, 1981; Stanley & Wise, 1983). Feminist criticism of all the disciplines, not just sociology, has even broken into the public arena (Fiske, 1981; Howe, 1982) and projects have been funded to mainstream some feminist materials. But this is only a beginning.

CONTEXT: THE MALE-CENTERED INSTITUTION

Research is a socially organized activity done in the context of socially structured institutions such as universities, hospitals, and research institutes. From a feminist perspective, the university is male-dominated rather than woman-centered (Bart, 1971; Bernard, 1973; Rich, 1979). It is a place in which men dominate, in part because they predominate (only approximately 17 percent of university faculties are female; U.S. Department of Labor Statistics, 1979) and because they earn more than the women do (in 1981 women college teachers earned 80 percent of what their male colleagues earned; Kendrigan, 1984, p. 36; see also Ehrenreich & Stallard, 1982). And even though male faculty earn more than women on average, at all ranks, with the same length of service, and at the same age, courts have ruled that this does not constitute discrimination against female faculty members (see *On Campus with Women*, 1982, p. 5).

It is a place in which men who want to succeed marry, whereas women who want to succeed don't.[2] The same pattern holds for having children.[3] These patterns combine, so that "married women are substantially less likely to earn tenure than unmarried women who are still less likely to earn tenure than married men with children" (Hu-DeHart, 1982, pp. 8-9). Thus, it is less likely that research will be conducted by married women with children than by other groups. It is probably even less likely that research will be defined and conducted by gays or lesbians, or by people from racial and ethnic minorities.

The university, from the perspective of feminists, is a place where sexual harassment is common (Somers, 1982; Verba, 1983); a place where the names of persons found guilty of sexual harassment are not always divulged, thus allowing the practices to continue;[4] a place which is increasingly dangerous to women in terms of rape (*On Campus with Women*, 1982, p. 1); a place where there was so little attention to women's existence, that women's studies had to be created. It is a place where recruitment procedures have been demonstrated to be inequitable (Szafran, 1984); a place where as one goes up the academic ladder—from student to lecturer and through the professional ranks to the ranks of highest administration—there are fewer and fewer women (Committee to Study the Status of Women in Graduate Education and Later Careers, 1974); a place where there are more demands made on women than on men (e.g., affirmative action activities, sexual harassment committees, women's role conferences) and there are also fewer role models for women to emulate. It is a place where feminists, minorities, and women in general must compete with each other since there is little room to move up (for a discussion of this issue, particularly with regard to tenure, see Freeman, 1979). It is a place where textbooks and classics abound with sexist language. And finally, it is a place where most of these factors are not considered very important or where they are no longer considered important.

Although we may want it to be otherwise, this context is reinforced by the *content* of the work done within the university, including much of its research. This is because research is conducted within disciplinary methodological and theoretical *traditions* that act as constraints. Although the origins of the disciplines were developed at a time when society differed in major ways from the present, certain structures such as sexism were pervasive then as now, and through their influence on the tradition continue to influence the content of current research.

Generally, the methodological and theoretical traditions are learned during the socialization process; internalized, and then used and trans-

mitted (Reinharz, 1979, 1983). Feminist consciousness raises doubts about these disciplinary conventions, particularly epistemology. Within sociology, this questioning of tradition calls into question the dominant positivist paradigm. It is to this that I now turn.

CONTENT: THE POSITIVIST PARADIGM

Modern social science is conducted in the framework of positivist philosophy (Alexander, 1982; Coser, 1975; Giddens, 1974; Polkinghorne, 1983).

> Positivism stands for a certain philosophical attitude concerning human knowledge . . . it is a collection of rules and evaluative criteria referring to human cognition: it tells us what kind of contents in our statements about the world deserves the name of knowledge and supplies us with norms that make it possible to distinguish between that which may and that which may not reasonably be asked. (Kolawowski, 1969, p. 2)

One of the key components of the positivist view is that knowledge must be concerned with *observable* phenomena whose explanations must be limited to forces that are not metaphysical or religious in nature. The explanations, however, need not consist of observable phenomena but can be ideas. In my view, the invocation of these explanatory ideas constitutes a defection from the very innovation that positivism was supposed to introduce. I will explain this problem in the context of feminist distrust.

There are three assumptions in the positivist paradigm. First is the assumption that there is a clear-cut distinction between observable phenomena on the one hand and metaphysical entities or religious phenomena on the other (Alexander, 1982). It is assumed that this distinction is obvious and not a result of human interpretation rooted in particular interests.

This assumption leads to the second underlying view: that there is a dichotomy between the object of study and the person who is conducting the study. This distinction is referred to as the subject/object dichotomy. It allows those who work in the positivist framework to believe that "the investigator's commitments have no influence on his or her data . . . [and that] generalizations are based solely on objective evidence" (Alexander, 1982, p. 6). The insistence on subject/object differentiation has been linked by feminist theories to the male child's need for individuation in relation to his mother (Keller, 1982). Feminists see in this insistence a defensive, even dangerous, need for differentiation, distance, and separation, which characterizes patriarchal culture.

In addition, positivist philosophy assumes that procedures can be applied to observable phenomena in a way that produces certain knowledge with which everyone is compelled to agree by virtue of rules of logic and mathematics. These three assumptions lead those working in the positivist perspective to disregard the context in which phenomena are embedded (Mishler, 1979; Cicourel, 1982), to believe that "facts" are unproblematic (Thomas & Edmondson, in press), to be disinterested in the unique human experience (Polkinghorne, 1983, p. 21), and to be intolerant of ambiguity.

Positivism is contrasted with speculative, introspective subjectivism, defined as prescientific, arbitrary, and incapable of producing lawlike generalizations from specific instances. Positivism posits that the rules that apply to the study of the physical environment can be applied to all phenomena, because human behavior, like nature, is law-like. Finally, positivism implies that because empirical observation is definitive, the certainty of science yields legitimate *power*. In their rejection of theology, positivists took the power from God and put it in the hands of scientists. The subject/object dichotomy inherent in positivist philosophy complemented the androcentrism of the culture in which it was formulated and the personal views of the people who worked within it. Together they formed a deep male-centeredness[5] which erased women's experience and set the stage for feminist distrust. I shall attempt to document this statement in the following section.

POSITIVIST ORIGINS AND SEXISM

A French male aristocrat, Claude Henri de Rouvroy de Saint-Simon (1760-1825), should be credited with having developed the framework of positivist philosophy. He also linked this philosophy with social goals. He believed that empirical social science could be harnessed for "organizing and rationalizing human relations" (Schwendinger & Schwendinger, 1974, p. 68). In other words, when speculation and philosophy were replaced by the scientific method, a positive society could be created.

Saint-Simon did not rid himself of religion, but instead attempted a synthesis of science and religion. Yet he called this positivism. Having been profoundly influenced by the French Revolution, his description of the ideal society which could be brought about through the application of positivist principles reflects a mix of protecting vested interests and supporting democracy:

> I believe that all classes of society would benefit from an organization on these lines: the spiritual power in the hands of the scientists, the temporal

power in the hands of the property-owners, the power to nominate those who should perform the functions of the leaders of humanity, in the hands of all; the reward of the rulers, esteem. (Saint-Simon, 1964, p. 11)

A student of Saint-Simon's, August Comte (1790-1857), is generally thought of as having defined positivism and having dedicated his life to its widespread adoption. He believed that the power of positivism was such that using its principles, social scientists could construct the ideal society free of social problems. Ironically, the ideal society envisioned by this French Catholic man was infused with religious symbols and rituals. For example, in the ideal society built on positivist principles, Comte believed women would play the role of "guardian angel" and would be worshipped. As for the reproduction of society, a Virgin Mother would give birth to children by means of artificial insemination (Kolawowski, 1969, pp. 62-63).

Historians of social science "explain" Comte's development of religious idealism from the foundations of scientific positivism by reference to his long periods of mental illness. This explanation avoids acknowledgment of the fact that positivism cannot escape being interwoven with values and pragmatics. However, studying the development of Comte's philosophy raises doubt about the ability of positivism to withstand the influence not only of individual psychopathology but also political ideologies, religious beliefs, and values of other kinds. Particularly apparent is the inability of positivism in general, and positivist sociology in particular, to withstand the influence of patriarchal ideology.

Emile Durkheim, an anticlerical French Jew, considered by most sociologists as a founding figure because he defined social phenomena and showed how they should be studied, stipulated rules that should be followed in order to discover empirically based knowledge. His book, *The Rules of Sociological Method* (1895/1938), states that all preconditions must be eradicated, thus assuming that they *can* be. Durkheim earns his place as a founder of sociology because he produced both a model and the standards for empirical research in his classic study, *Suicide* (1951). This study contains much material on the differential rate of suicide among men and women. As is well known, Durkheim used suicide statistics to develop his theories. But it is generally not discussed that he *inferred* or *speculated* about the motivations of the people who had committed these suicides. The inferences drew on ideas held subjectively by Durkheim, which may be referred to as *the ideology that underpinned a surface positivism*. For example, Durkheim's explanation of the greater rate of suicide among married women than among married men includes the following:

Women's sexual needs have less of a mental character because, generally speaking, her mental life is less developed. These needs are more closely related to the needs of the organism, following rather than leading them, and consequently finding in them an efficient restraint. Being a more instinctive creature than man, woman has only to follow her instincts to find calmness and peace. She thus does not require so strict a social regulation as marriage, and particularly as monogamic marriage. (1951, p. 272)[6]

This passage is one of many that illustrate how positivist philosophy and research procedures were unable to eliminate the influence of patriarchal social ideology.[7] What this means is that thought, which had been believed to be governed by the rules of objectivity, was not objective at all, but rather a reflection of the social relations in which it was produced. This link converted the liberating potential of positivism to a new form of tyranny (Myrdal, 1969).

THE SOCIOLOGY OF KNOWLEDGE AND SEXISM

The thesis that science, thought, and culture are mental superstructures that reflect the social substructure (Stark, 1958) is the central tenet of the sociology of knowledge, defined first by Karl Marx and elaborated later by Karl Mannheim, C. Wright Mills, Robert K. Merton, and others. This idea, sometimes referred to as "historical realism" (Suppe, 1977; Gergen, 1973), claims that "science is a human activity which takes place in various *historical* contexts and is not a process of formal logic attaining timeless truths" (Polkinghorne, 1983). Because the sociology of knowledge position represents a radical critique of science, it is a framework that feminists have found useful (see, e.g., Sherman & Beck, 1979; Bernard, 1981). Feminists have shown that it is not only the class structure of the historical period that influences the production of knowledge, but also the sex of the writer, because social conditions differentially affect men and women, making the perspectives of each a reflection of their sex-based ideology.

Mannheim, the man identified as the definer of the field, stated that the sociology of knowledge endeavors "to comprehend the theories and their mutations in close relation to the collective groups and typical total situations out of which they arose and whose exponents they are" (cited in Stark, 1958, p. 12). The whole point of this endeavor is to unveil the connection between social relationships and the knowledge accepted in a particular period. Essentially, the connection between the two rests on

the values that underpin both. Unfortunately, however, these values are not easily recognized at the moment, but become more apparent with the occurrence of social change and social conflict (Merton, 1957; Shaskolsky, 1970).

Despite the sociology of knowledge, the relation between knowledge and the fact that it was produced by men in a patriarchal society was rarely, if ever, considered by scholars in this field, leading to extraordinary contradictions. For example, Stark devoted an entire book to showing that thought was rooted in social conditions, and that different people's perceptions of the "same phenomenon" depend on their interests. Yet, here is an example he offered in support of his thesis:

> When a man and a woman see a lady passing in the street, they will (unless the man happens to be a fashion designer!) receive different impressions and images of her. The man's mind is likely to register her features and bodily form rather than her frock, the woman's her frock rather than her features and bodily form because their order of values is in all typical cases different from that of the majority of males . . . men on the one hand, women on the other—are constituted by nature, not by social forces, and the eye-opening interest or value is rooted in the instinctual rather than the social life (though it certainly is not purely instinctual, as our reference to the dress-designer is sufficient to demonstrate). (Stark, 1958, p. 133)

Despite the author's commitment to the basic premise of the sociology of knowledge, he claimed that *sex differences* in the production of thought are *not* rooted in social circumstances, but are instinctual. Patriarchal ideology stood firm despite the sociology of knowledge insight because it was an integral part of the thinking of social scientists, characteristic not only of positivists but of their sociology of knowledge critics as well.[8] It was so taken for granted that it could not be seen.

This confounding of seemingly "scientific" assertions with ideological beliefs is a central concern of feminists. To explore instances of its occurrence is to engage in a kind of consciousness-raising about the discipline (Lopata, 1976, p. 176). Recognition of this interpenetration of social science and social ideology brings in its wake distrust of sociological theory, concern about the value of accumulated social science knowledge, and questions about the distinction between science and ideology. As Eisenstein argued, "to the degree that sociology is rooted in a male world-view, it is as much ideology as it is science. The dichotomization between science and ideology does not hold" (1982, p. 36). In other words, feminist uncovering of patriarchy suggests that both what was thought to be positivist and the supposedly scientific critique of positivism were ideologically infused.

A pure form of positivism could function only in a society that has no divisions or interests, including the interests of the social scientists (Berg, 1984). The feminist critique of social science supports the view that since interest-free knowledge is logically impossible, we should feel free to substitute explicit interests for implicit ones. Feminism challenges us to articulate our values and, on the basis of these, to develop new theories and formulate new research practices.

SEXISM IN OUR "TRUSTED" CONTEMPORARY CLASSICS

Cultural attitudes toward women at the time in which American sociology was being defined were also sexist (Schwendinger & Schwendinger, 1974, pp. 290-334). These attitudes became part of American sociology in terms of its body of knowledge and its professional associations (Deegan, 1981). As a result, the contributions of female sociologists were not acknowledged and had little influence in shaping the discipline. This pattern continues (Welch & Lewis, 1980).

Hand in hand with this discriminatory context was the pejorative writing about women among both positivist sociologists and their sociology of knowledge critics. I will clarify this statement by presenting examples from the writing itself. I located this material by looking at esteemed sociology books, not in terms of their major arguments, but rather in terms of their asides, illustrations, and examples. I looked not at what the authors thought needed explaining, but at what they thought did not—that is, their taken-for-granted assumptions. To me this is a first strategy for working away from feminist distrust—facing the preconceptions squarely. Examples writers use reveal the images with which they think and build their arguments. The examples writers offer can be likened to Thematic Apperception Test pictures used by psychologists to trigger their subjects' way of looking at the world.

For example, a much praised book still widely adopted in sociology courses, Peter Berger's *Invitation to Sociology* (1963), does not look very inviting to me when the images are examined. Upon reexamination, the fact that many sociologists accepted this book as a self-definiton is rather alarming.[9] Berger's use of analogies and images is extensive throughout the book. Here are a few examples at the start of the book:

> Perhaps some little boys consumed with curiosity to watch their maiden aunts in the bathroom later became inveterate sociologists. (p. 19)

> The geologist looks at rocks only at appropriate times, and the linguist speaks English with his wife. Anthropologists use the term "culture shock" to describe the impact of a totally new culture upon a newcomer.

In an extreme instance such shock will be experienced by the Western explorer who is told, half-way through dinner, that he is eating the nice old lady he had been chatting with the previous day—a shock with predictable physiological, if not moral consequences. (p. 23)

On page 44 we learn the "sociological principle" that men are happy when their families are not around so that they can conveniently "use marginal people for their pleasure." On page 45 we learn that Veblen was an inveterate seducer of other people's women. (People *are* men, they *have* women.) On page 55 we learn that youth ends when a man decides to join the church and remain faithful to his wife. Here is Berger's definition of middle-age:

The middle-aged Joe Blow, having accepted the fact that his wife will not get to be any prettier and that his job as assistant advertising manager will not become any more interesting, looks back on his past and decides that his earlier aspirations to possess many beautiful women or to write the definitive novel of the half-century were immature. (p. 59)

According to Berger, social mobility has occurred

when the girl of one's teenage daydreams is transmuted into an ignorant though pretty peasant, [when] even Mama, who used to be the orb around which the universe revolved, has become a silly old Italian woman one must pacify. (p. 60)

Whereas sociologists usually asserted that wives acquire their socioeconomic status through their husbands, Berger seems inadvertently to suggest otherwise:

Most individuals to whom an executive career is open marry the "right" kind of wife (the one that David Reisman has called the "station-wagon" type) almost by instinct. (p. 85)

Perhaps, as Berger suggested earlier, sociology is inviting to those boys who are titillated by watching others. In the following definition of sociology's power, the little boy who used to peep through the keyhole to watch his maiden aunt in the bathroom, now is seen observing couples in their bedrooms:

A sociologist can predict whether a man of a certain class has sexual relations with his wife with the lights turned on or off. (p. 81)

Sociologists may self-consciously claim that marriage and the family are the foundations of a stable society, but actually find them miserable institutions:

> The idea that a man should fixate his sexual drive permanently and exclusively on one single woman with whom he is to share bed, bathroom and the boredom of a thousand bleary-eyed breakfasts was produced by misanthropic theologians. (p. 85)

Berger concludes his "inviting" book by explaining that sociology is humanistic, even though it is so difficult to be a humanist in our culture:

> It is not easy to introduce a humanistic dimension into research designed to determine the optimum crew composition of a bomber aircraft, or to discover the factors that will induce somnambulent housewives in a supermarket to reach for one brand of baking powder as against the other. (pp. 169-170)

In my view, the problem with these excerpts is not eliminated by calling them a "writing style." Rather there seems to me to be a sociological vision that underlies the images. My point is that the writing of sociologists reveals their view of society, a view that sees women primarily as stupid, sexually unexciting wives *or* objects of sexual desire and violence.

Another "trusted classic" of contemporary sociology that defined the field and is in its seventeenth printing (at least) rarely used images that referred to women, but if so only as wives whose significance was as possessions that helped define the character of men:

> We ... want to know how much each is influenced by his contemporaries, and in which realms of life this influence is more important—in the choice of one's car, the books one reads, the wife one takes, the profession one pursues? (Inkeles, 1964, p. 53)

With Luckmann, Berger coauthored *The Social Construction of Reality* (1967), a work that represents a cornerstone of contemporary sociological theory in the sociology of knowledge tradition. In this book women appear only once in the index, referring to the ill effects on boys if their father is "absent" and their mother's and sisters' presence influences them to be effeminate. Women make their appearance here only as vehicles of potential harm. It is almost ironic that Berger and Luckmann end their book with this revealing conclusion:

Sociology takes its place in the company of the sciences that deal with man as man . . . [the] object is society as part of a human world, made by men, inhabited by men, and, in turn, making men, in an ongoing historical process. It is not the least fruit of a humanistic sociology that it reawakens our wonder at this astonishing phenomenon. (p. 211)

Criticism of the limited view of women that is an integral part of structural-functionalism, one of the most widely accepted among contemporary sociological theories, is well known (Millett, 1969, pp. 310-329). Yet even critics of structural-functionalist theory, advocates of conflict models, may unwittingly integrate sexist imagery into their theory. Sexist imagery is present in the works of humanistic critics of mainstream sociology, just as sexist practices were prevalent in humanistic social movement organizations that attempted to alter American society before the resurgence of the women's movement. For example, here are some images used in Derek Phillips's *Abandoning Method*:

Imagine a situation where Mrs. Jones' husband has behaved toward her in an abusive and violent manner over a period of several years. Finally after he has pushed her down a flight of stairs, Mrs. Jones obtains a knife and kills her husband. We might want to say that this situation fits a typical formula of causal ascription: no B without A. Had he not been so violent and abusive, had he not pushed her down the stairs, she would not have killed him. However, to support such a causal assertion it is also necessary to show that, if A is not present, B will not occur, or that whenever A occurs B will follow. But B could conceivably occur without A; Mrs. Jones could have killed her husband for a great variety of reasons; he beat the children, or insulted her mother, or snored too loudly. And there are too many abusive and violent husbands for us to say with any degree of certainty that their behavior will always be followed by their wives' killing them. So concepts such as motive, reason, and purpose have doubtful and indeterminate application. (1973, p. 174)

The misogyny in this excerpt is apparent in the implicit ridicule of a woman whose murder of her husband could have occurred for four apparently equivalent reasons: her husband's violence toward her, his beating of their children, his insulting her mother, or his snoring. She becomes absurd if she is considered willing to murder for snoring. By casting doubt on her reasonableness, she is demeaned and he is almost excused. To me, this conjecture about her motive speaks louder than Phillips's explicit disdain for violent husbands.

In a previous discussion of the concept of probability, Phillips uses the following telling example:

A man who "flirts" with a woman at a party by ripping off her clothes and throwing her to the floor will almost certainly be seen as exceeding the rules of flirting. (1973, p. 159)

These examples reflect the workings of a misogynist imagination in a patriarchal culture. Yet it is this same imagination that these writers think of as sociology and that has been legitimated as such. Violence toward women and the view of women as ridiculous, particularly in their evaluation of men, is embedded in the writing of people thought of as reliable interpreters of society. Recognizing that sociology written by men has been "male sociology," not "sociology," can be a way of sidestepping the problem of distrust (see also Patai, 1983).

SEXISM IN CONTEMPORARY TEXTBOOKS

Even contemporary textbooks contain pejorative references to females despite recent public recognition of the need to expunge sexist writing from publications (Miller & Swift, 1980). In my view, these textbooks reinforce prejudice against women and other groups even when they disparage negative beliefs about them. When illustrations are ostensibly directed at undermining associations between certain groups and negative traits, people are reminded of these associations. Again, this problem arises in the examples and analogies, not in the explicit argument of the books. For example, one of the most highly regarded textbooks in sociology contains the following:

> Suppose you were once cheated by a shopkeeper you thought to be Jewish. You might conclude from that one event that Jewish shopkeepers are dishonest in general. Subsequently you'd probably take special note of dishonest actions by other Jewish shopkeepers, while ignoring honest Jews and dishonest non-Jews. Some people take special note of all lazy blacks they come across and ignore energetic blacks and lazy whites. Others notice irrational and emotional women while overlooking stable women as well as unstable men. (Babbie, 1983, p. 12)

Babbie returns to a discussion of Jews, blacks, and women when explaining the principle of deduction:

> Suppose, for example, you had decided that all Jewish shopkeepers were dishonest, and then *one of them* walked four miles to return the wallet that you left on the store counter. What would you do? In *our* casual, day-to-day handling of such matters, we often make up information that

would resolve the contradiction. Maybe the shopkeeper isn't really Jewish after all. Or maybe the shopkeeper was just casing your house with a later burglary in mind. (emphasis added)

Perhaps that hard-working and energetic black at work is just trying to get promoted to a soft executive post. Perversely, people often doubt the general femininity of the woman who is tough-minded, logical and unemotional in getting the job done. Concluding that she's not really a woman protects the general conclusion that women are irrational and flighty. (Babbie, 1983, p. 12)

In this methods textbook, necessary and sufficient causes are explained by scenarios about anti-Semitism:

Let's postulate, for example, that being an anti-Semite is a necessary cause for murdering Jews in the streets. Non-anti-Semites don't do it. This causal relationship is not at all diminished by the fact that the vast majority of anti-Semites do not murder Jews in the streets. (Babbie, 1983, p. 58)

The racism and sexism that I believe pervade such examples begin with seeing certain groups as "them" rather than "us." Since pronoun use reveals the author's identifications, one strategy for dealing with distrust is to look specifically at the way an author uses pronouns. To do this means to treat scientific writing not only as a source of information as defined by the author, but also as a text revealing something about the author. Although the passive voice of much scientific writing hides the author's voice to a large extent, clues can sometimes be found in introductions, conclusions, and asides. The pronouns with which the author writes reflect the perspective through which the author sees.

Another window on the author's implicit sociology is the use of adjectives. In the passages quoted above, some groups are given adjectives and others are not. People who are black are called black because they are a kind of person, whereas people who are white are not called white. Blacks are shown to be a variation of people, whereas whites are the people of which other groups are variations. The objects of derision or violence are specified as blacks, Jews, or women, but the agents of prejudice are labelled vaguely as people, not as groups with characteristics of their own such as Christians, men, or whites. This language use conforms to what psychologists have shown—namely, that men are seen as the norm, women as the deviation. The strategy out of distrust that flows from this idea is to not label blacks as blacks or women as women unless everyone is labelled in terms of race and gender. In addition, one

could eliminate adjectives altogether and write about women or blacks as if they represented the universally human (see Patai, 1983). Reading social science with these ideas in mind reveals the extent to which contemporary prejudice can be reinforced by contemporary social science.

Examples keep women pregnant, homosexuals feared (Rosnow & Rosenthal, 1984, pp. 137-138), and the elderly stupid. The metaphor of the witch/woman/bad as a contrast with science/male/good is common. For example, Rosnow and Rosenthal (1984) contrast an old woman with the implicitly normative young man and middle-aged male magistrate, casting her as a weird, benevolent witch. Abrahamson (1983, p. 12) does likewise in his reference to the Sphinx, who was part monster and part woman, slain by Oedipus (here a symbol of science) after he acquired knowledge. The scientist as Oedipus and woman as "other" is perhaps the most succinct clue to the paradigm from which positivism has not yet been freed.

The problem is not resolved by looking at qualitative research texts written by men. For example, when using metaphors to discuss the researcher's attitudes, Douglas draws on sexual/military imagery:

> A research assault on a social institution is often analogous to a military assault on a nation. (1976, p. 31)

> The researcher, like the wise lover, *never presses his* case to the point where an explicit "no" is possible—*unless his* situation is desperate or unless there is no tomorrow. (emphasis added; 1976, p. 32)

The feminist researcher is likely to feel alienated from methodological instruction such as this (see also Gurney, in press). In Douglas's world, researchers are men who ensnare other men into acknowledging their deviance vis-à-vis women. For example, he explains that his clever dinner party tactics enabled him to trick a businessman into revealing that his company kept a list of callgirls for special customers (1976, pp. 66-67). He explains the idea of self-deception by reference to a man who tries to convince a "friend" to give up a girlfriend because he "wants the girl." Women appear frequently in this text, but only as the duped party, the whore, or the girlfriend manipulated by others.

FINAL THOUGHTS ON REREADING SOCIOLOGY

A male sociologist in a patriarchal milieu sees the world not only as a sociologist but also as a male, oftentimes in aggressive, manipulative, sexualized ways (unless he has gone out of his way to change his

consciousness and behaviors through specific feminist commitments). In addition, he writes for a male audience who sees the world in the same terms. If this is so, then the challenge for the female and/or feminist sociologist is to figure out how to use selectively the sociological tradition—that is, to determine what she can trust.

In the classic sociological texts women were perceived only as objects, if they were perceived at all. Yet women made up half the society the sociologists were writing about. Rereading sociology leads to the conclusion that male sociologists have been unable to transcend their society's commonplace ideas.[10] In addition, despite the claims of objectivity (a supposed product of positivist methodology), the attitudes apparent in the work of male sociologists are not unlike those of their class and gender. What Simone de Beauvoir said of society in general was also true of sociologists. Women were defined by male sociologists as "the other" or were not there at all. Hatred and fear of women has been given the label *misogyny*. Perhaps a new word—*gynopia*—is needed to point out the inability to perceive the very existence of women as fully human actors.

Feminist distrust of sociology stems from the insulting, inaccurate, and entirely "other" nature of much theory, methodological instruction, and even humanistic criticism. But then the question remains, What theory and method would be a useful alternative? If it were only a question of defining new topics relative to women's lives and correcting specific sexist biases in research (see ASA, 1980) or teaching (Gappa & Pearce, 1982) things would be *relatively* simple. But the problem seems deeper than that.

Perhaps the answer is that sociology can never be free of sexism in a world characterized by misogyny and gynopia. Positivist science did not free thought of prejudice. Rather, social movements, political power, and consciousness raising seem to have made the most significant impacts in this regard. In my view, there is a continued need for consciousness-raising among social scientists, focused on the questions, To what extent does our research incorporate the prejudices of the day, and to what extent does it transcend them?

Although I have focused on distrust, I have also mentioned some means of working with distrust. First is to reexamine classic and contemporary sociological texts written by men in terms of their gendered authorship in a patriarchal society. This reexamination should seek the implicit sociology revealed in asides, examples, and metaphors. The use of pronouns and the phrase "of course" are other clues. Second is to seek missing historical and neglected contemporary works written by women and use them to build a modern sociology. These two consciousness-rais-

ing strategies redefine "sociology" as "male sociology" and "female sociology" as "sociology" (Patai, 1983). Third is to search for a postpositivist paradigm based on feminist and other critical assumptions (for an example, see Thomas & Edmondson, in press). These assumptions include recognition of one's values and the extent to which one is embedded in one's research (see Reinharz, 1979, 1983). Fourth is the construction of new contexts in which we can do our postpositivist feminist sociological work. These new contexts include institutions that have been transformed from competitive and bureaucratic to cooperative and egalitarian. In these new institutions, knowledge producers would be demographically representative of the population at large. It goes without saying that these new institutions would be physically and psychologically safe. In the meantime, a sociology grounded in values other than those that define our society may have to be carried out in alternative settings alongside the university (see Nebraska Feminist Collective, 1983; Reinharz, 1983). Since the context in which knowledge is created affects the knowledge that is created, our attempts to develop an unalienating social science will always be linked to our ability to develop a fully humane society.

NOTES

1. See Rosnow and Rosenthal (1984) for a discussion of the methodological and epistemological problems of artifacts and values, and see Peters and Ceci (1982) for a discussion of the social psychologically based inconsistency in the evaluation of scientific work.

2. "Fewer than half of women academics are married, compared to almost 90% of the men" (Hu-DeHart, 1982, p. 8).

3. "About one-third of the women in academe have children, compared to more than two-thirds of the men, and these women tend to have fewer children than men with families" (Hu-DeHart, 1982, p. 8).

4. Names of sexual harassers are sometimes written in women's bathroom stalls as a way of alerting potential victims.

5. I am indebted to Barrie Thorne, who suggested this phrase (personal communication, 1984).

6. Part of this quote is discussed in Nebraska Feminist Collective (1983). To Durkheim's credit, it must be said that he did not lump all women in one category but rather recognized the differences among types of women, depending, in this case, on whether or not they were married. Similarly, Durkheim recognized that marriage has differential consequences for the male and female partner. He thereby implicitly accepted a conflict-of-interests model of marriage—a model that feminists are also developing in contrast with the structural-functionalist model.

7. See also, Durkheim, *The Division of Labor in Society* (1933/1964, pp. 55-63).

8. Anti-positivists, phenomenologists, critical theorists, and Marxist sociologists seem to have been similarly encumbered by and not cognizant of their patriarchal

assumptions. For this reason, although the feminist sociological critique has benefitted from these preceding critical perspectives, it has not been satisfied by them.

9. When I was preparing to teach an introductory social psychology course in 1982, I asked colleagues at various universities which books they thought were best and Berger's was hailed as a twenty-year-old classic worth using nowadays. I continously see praise for the book. For example, Westhues (1982), a humanistic sociologist, annotates a reference to it as "a little book that brims over with clarity and cordiality" (p. 32).

10. The extent to which this is true is continuously being discovered. For example, Charlotte Schwartz and Merton Kahne have shown that in the theorizing of medical sociologists there has been an unwitting and implicit assumption that the physician is a white male and the patient is a woman, child, or person compromised economically or socially (1983, p. 335). They show that these assumptions have almost undermined the theory built on them.

WHAT *IS* CLINICAL METHOD?

Rodney L. Lowman

This chapter and this book should not have had to be written in 1985. It is astounding and in many ways preposterous to imagine that those who study and attempt to change social systems should be oblivious and often downright hostile to the idea of "clinical" methods. That a collection such as this one will likely be at the fringe of social science studies is a sad statement about the narrow-mindedness of a field that potentially could do much to improve the lives of persons who live, work, and play in social systems.

But just as good clinical change agents must begin with clients as they now are and not as they would like for them to be, so too this chapter makes the assumption that its readers are persons for whom clinical method is a fairly recent, and in many ways still novel, concept. The chapter therefore asks and attempts to address such questions as the following. How does one think "clinically"? How does the epistemology of clinical method differ from that of more traditional approaches used to understand social systems? How can quality standards be applied to such methods to assure that they are rigorous? These questions, and others, will constitute the central themes of this chapter. True to its subject, the presentation incorporates my own experiences and perceptions to illustrate how social scientists function when they use clinical methods.

The term *clinical* originated with the medical profession. In medicine, *clinical* refers to those aspects of study that are based on actual treatment and observation of patients as distinguised from experimental or laboratory study (*Webster's New Twentieth Century Dictionary*, 1971). Clinical methods of teaching or research therefore refer to those that are closely tied to the real-life manifestations of that which is studied or treated, as opposed to paradigms, models, or analogues from other species. *Experience-based* is an appropriate descriptor.

Although clinical methods are well established in the health care professions, the same cannot be said of those who study or attempt to change social systems. The animosity that has characterized the debates between traditional researchers and those more clinically oriented goes beyond the natural rivalry that might arise between proponents of different methodologies used to study the same phenomenon. Exemplary of the depth of feelings on both sides is the following anecdote. A fews years ago, a group of researchers were invited by the Industrial/Organizational (I/O) Psychology Division of the American Psychological Association to present a symposium for its annual convention on the topic of "parallel processes in organizational research." The theme of similarities between the behaviors studied and those of the researchers was an old one for clinical psychologists but apparently a radical one for the I/O group, which, after soliciting the symposium, insisted that a critic be sent along to challenge the views to be presented (K. Smith, personal communication, 1984). At the sparsely attended symposium the critic proceeded to lambast the presentations, primarily on the basis that "parallel processes" had nothing to do with research. The critic went so far as to inquire of one member of the audience who had asked a sympathetic question of the presenters whether he was wearing beads. This experience suggests more than a difference of scientific paradigms: It implies a threat of some significance. One does not fight that which has no importance.

If animosity extends both to clinical methodology and to its substantive findings, it is useful to ask why. Part of the answer lies in a difference of abilities and of world views of the type of persons who are attracted to the two methodologies (which will here be called *traditional* and *clinical*). Traditional researchers bring a "scientific" orientation to their subject matter. They look at the world through representational eyes: The accurate symbolization of reality is more important than empathic understanding or learning through introspection or observation. This type of personality is probably best described by Holland's (1973) "Investigative" type: analytical, distant, asocial, more interested in working with ideas or things than with people (e.g., Osipow, 1973; Roe, 1961).

The person who studies from what might be called the *phenomenological,* or *clinical*, perspective, in contrast, is more likely to be at least as oriented to other people as to ideas or things. Intuition and the understanding of phenomena on the basis of experience form an important research tool for this type of investigator's approach. In Holland's terms, the typical "clinical" researcher probably has both "Social" and "Investigative" components. It is possible, particularly for those who

study organizations and social systems, that those attracted to the clinical methodologies are persons for whom research methods are relatively sterile or "juiceless" unless they involve meaningful interaction with people. Clinical methods, in this view, may be one possible way of adjusting to a misfit between themselves and the general field of which they are part.

It is appropriate to speculate on the personal dynamics that cause one to be attracted to a field like organizational psychology. In my experience, graduate students in the area of organizational and social systems studies who have been attracted to clinical research and change methodologies have been those who have had some interest in working with people and who felt themselves alien to mainstream organizational research methods, yet who for one reason or another had seriously considered—and rejected—the more unambiguously "clinical" areas of study. Thus, individuals may choose such a field as a relatively safe way of handling personal conflicts. While something about psychology attracted and kept them (rather than choosing a field like business management), they chose a psychological specialty that is both applied and emotionally "safe." The ones who actively struggle with the "clinical" issues are probably those for whom the desire to help, to understand themselves, and/or to work with other people have not yet been fully suffused with intellect or power drives.

These divided loyalties, unassisted by a sympathetic audience of either faculty or peers, can make for considerable personal conflict. In my own case, for example, I trained in both clinical and organizational psychology and have struggled for years to find or create a setting compatible with what seem to me, if not the profession, to be complementary perspectives. I have learned to expect almost no understanding, much less appreciation, from the vast majority of my traditionally trained colleagues. The professional life of the clinically oriented social systems researcher or interventionist is, in 1985, a lonely one.

It would of course be bad psychology to pretend that career choice decisions are made solely on the basis of personal psychological dynamics, or that personality is the exclusive determinant of one's approach to research. One's abilities constitute another critical determinant. An intriguing work by Gardner (1983) presents a theory of "multiple intelligences." Gardner's work reminds us of the narrowness of our present concepts of what qualifies as intelligent behavior by identifying seven kinds of intelligence: linguistic, spatial, kinesthetic, musical, logical-mathematical, and two kinds of interpersonal intelligence. How abilities relate to personality and vocational interests is still an unsettled question in the professional literature (e.g., Osipow, 1973), but it is plausible

that persons who are attracted to clinical methods in the social sciences are those whose abilities tend toward the verbal-linguistic and interpersonal, while those who are specialists in the traditional, quantitative methods are more skilled in the spatial and mathematical abilities. Such differences, if empirically confirmed, would likely result in very different approaches to both research and life, and could explain some of the hostility directed at clinical methodologists by traditional researchers.

Clinical method is of interest and importance, however, only if it illuminates and clarifies what cannot be accomplished by other, better-established methodologies. It is no good to develop clinical approaches if all they do is keep intellectual misfits less discontent. Clinical methodologies worth developing are those that uniquely add to understanding and that have widespread applicability. They are perhaps most useful as exploratory devices for those aspects of a field of inquiry that are uncharted; for studying complex social systems as a whole that cannot be examined easily, if at all, by the traditionalist's scientific scrutiny; and as the methodology of choice for interpersonally based change strategies.

WHY CLINICAL METHODS ARE NEEDED

The study of social systems needs clinical methodologies if only because so little has been learned from traditional approaches. As one example, Miner (1984) illustrates the limitations of many of the theories that have predominated in the literature in one area relevant to this discussion—industrial/organizational psychology. A similar concern was raised by Gordon, Kleiman, and Hanie (1978), who empirically demonstrated that few of the research findings of organizational psychology differed significantly from common sense.

Traditional I/O psychology, particularly personnel psychology, has most successfully created technically sophisticated studies of rather small subsystems of life in organizations, especially personnel selection and evaluation. In the day-to-day experiences of most organizations, these are important, but clearly delimited, concerns. Moreover, quantitative sophistication is no substitute for veridicality to experience. Studies in social systems of personality, emotions, and complex interactions of personal and structural aspects have been rare. Even case studies that accurately reproduce the real-life experience of members of an organization are few. It is as if Freud were to have attempted to understand neurosis solely by reference to intellect, ignoring emotions.

Since traditional methodologies have had over fifty years to apply their methodologies to the problems of social systems and have had such

little impact on the day-to-day behavior of these systems, then perhaps it is time for other research methods to be given a real chance to explore the same territory. Such opportunity would require primarily the legitimization of clinical methods as proper research tools. Were clinical methods to be seriously integrated into the curricula of relevant graduate training programs, perhaps a new, more clinically sensitive, generation of scholars and practitioners with astute observational and change agent skills would become attracted to the field.

DIFFERENTIATING CLINICAL AND TRADITIONAL METHODS

"Clinical" methodologies differ from traditional ones in their perceptual and inferential processes, in what is acceptable as "data," and in the researcher's relationship to the phenomenon being studied. Clinical researchers include cultural anthropologists, scientifically oriented interventionists, and even some artists and novelists. A clinical researcher considers as a primary requirement that he or she have a basic, personalized, and ultimately well-integrated understanding of the phenomenon being studied. Whether the product be a therapeutic statement, a canvas, or a journal article, the effective clinical methodologist clearly conveys depth and complexity of understanding.

APPLIED SCIENCE

The distinction between the clinical and the traditional approaches is something regarded as the "subjective" versus the "scientific." This is misleading. As Herma puts it: "The real opposition is not between more or less scientific disciplines, but between a theoretical and an applied science. All practical applications of scientific knowledge introduce personal factors such as experience, skill, intuition, and invention" (1968, p. 122).

It is in these "personal factors" that organizational behaviorists are so inadequately trained. In contrast, psychotherapy provides an example of a field that is unabashedly "clinical" in orientation. Attention is directed both in training and in practice to the development of expertise in observation, interpersonal competence, and in the juxtaposition of theory with experience (e.g., Greenson, 1967; Paul, 1973). Observational skills, timing, intuition, and a comparison of the observed and the theoretical are obviously needed for success as a psychotherapist.

Clinical methods may be more suited for some undertakings than for others. Microsurgery and plumbing do not obviously lend themselves to clinical methods. It is likely that important criteria for determining whether clinical methods will be able to make a substantive contribution include that they be applied to phenomena that cannot adequately be represented by traditional scientific method alone (at least at that stage of the science's development), that the phenomena be directly observable by those with appropriate skills and training, and that there be sufficient complexity that traditional methods of experimental control are not applicable.

It is illustrative that one of the most important contributions to understanding psychopathology even today is the work of Freud. Those researchers who have tried to apply traditional methodologies to such constructs as unconscious processes (e.g., Silverman, 1976) have added rather little understanding when compared to Freud's. While not abandoning scientific principles, Freud used his investigative and observational genius to create methods appropriate to his subject matter. The technique of free association provided a relatively standardized method for observing and working with a great diversity of client problems. These methods were decidedly toward the "clinical" end of the "traditional-clinical" spectrum of research methods. Controlled studies with high interrater reliabilities were no substitute for the insightful observations by one man of his patients' behaviors.

By analogy, in the social systems area the researcher or interventionist might learn a great deal by the feel of an organization, its physical plant, bulletin boards, responses to an unstructured interview with a few representative employees, or through observation of the posture and voice tones of a supervisor and subordinate as they interact. Such a methodology might study the memoranda, advertisements, the financial history of the organization, and the nonverbal behaviors manifested by key organizational members in a meeting. For the clinical investigator *all* behavior is potentially important. The ability to observe, classify, and interpret behavior accurately rests critically on the skills and personality of the clinician.

SYSTEMIC PERSPECTIVE

The clinical methodologist is perhaps best able to view a complex social structure as a system. While heavily acknowledged as a desirable theoretical foundation for studying organizations (e.g., Katz & Kahn, 1978), systems theory has been adequately incorporated into relatively few empirical studies of organizations or social systems. The best examples of the application of systems theory to date are case studies such as

those by Newhouse of the airplane manufacturing industry (1982) and Levinson's detailed case studies of organizations (1972), though the latter are tainted by a rather mechanistic fixation on psychoanalytic theory.

The clinical investigator is better able to examine behavior systematically because of not being bound to one research paradigm, which by its nature limits the number of hypotheses that can be measured or considered at any one time. The clinician is free to introduce hypothesized explanatory constructs without the necessity of having to measure such variables "scientifically." This does not mean that anything goes, but rather that the clinician may consider as explanations alternatives not empirically measured by the investigator, such as the relative influence on an organization of such events as the death of its founder, its recently having successfully marketed a new product, or a protracted strike that occurred three years prior to the study.

The clinical researcher is also free to examine many different types of data, even though some data sources may be less rigorously measured. For example, a psychotherapist may inquire in some detail about events that historically have been important to a client and may accept a subjective interpretation of the meaning of these events independent of their "objective" truth or falsity. The clinician can also observe multiple data sources simultaneously—the tone of voice with which a client speaks about her or his mother, the discrepancy between gestures and words, or the difference in the amount of time devoted to one subject rather than another.

THE PRODUCT

Traditional researchers seek to reduce information about social systems to quantitative data that can be analyzed statistically. Clinicians recognize that numbers are only one way to express knowledge and make liberal use of alternative ways of reporting findings. The case study and the qualitative description of clinical experience are regarded as acceptable forms in which to present results, particularly those of complex systems. Works such as those of Jaques (1952), Sofer (1961), Whyte (1948), and Watzlawick, Weakland, and Fisch (1974) are illustrative of good clinical writings (especially concerning social systems) and of both the values and the limitations of this approach.

DEVELOPMENTAL PERSPECTIVE

The clinician thinks in developmental terms in two primary ways. First, the age of a person or a social system provides a good indicator of the types of issues that are generally important at that particular life or

developmental stage (e.g., Levinson, Darrow, Klein, Levinson, & McKee, 1978; Kimberly & Miles, 1980). The developmental perspective helps the researcher or interventionist tailor the inquiry or change project to methodologies that are likely to be relevant and important to the client.

Second, a developmental approach suggests the need for theories and observations that are dynamic rather than static, since change is recognized as being the natural state of a person or system. The clinical method pays special attention to events, not just to variables, in attempting to understand change in a social system, recognizing the importance of both historical happenings and of variables that can be expressed and analyzed mathematically. The clinical method values these views while also recognizing the inadequacies of existing theories of the developmental phases of organizations. Unlike the study of individuals, in which multiple theories of predictable life stages have been developed and tested in literally thousands of studies, we do not yet have comparable developmental theories for social systems and have virtually no empirical studies in this area. The clinical investigator must therefore be sensitive to patterns of growth and development without reliably knowing the stages through which the social system will predictably pass. It is precisely for a problem like this that clinical methodologies are best suited.

INFERENTIAL AND EPISTEMOLOGICAL PROCESSES

Any method of inquiry must articulate methods for moving from the data collected to generalizations about the data. The traditional researcher characteristically moves from theory to data to statistical tests of theory. The clinical researcher moves from observation of behavior to interpretation to hypothesis generation. The traditional researcher relies on logico-deductive models of inference; the clinician, on intuitive models and on the interaction between the researcher and the object being studied. While in traditional research "truth" is established through the quantitative analysis of data, in clinical research other methods must be used. In psychotherapy, for example, the therapist's perception is a hypothesis whose accuracy or inaccuracy will be judged, among other things, by the response of the patient. Criteria have been developed by psychotherapists to determine whether or not an interpretation is accurate. For example, Malan (1979) asserts that accurate interpretation will be followed by an increase in the client's rapport with the therapist. What is important in this context is not the validity of

this particular approach to establishing "truth" but rather the illustration of a method in which investigative approaches are carefully integrated with their subject matter.

Similarly, in working with an organization, a clinically oriented interventionist might conclude that an apparent problem of low productivity really stems from father-son rivalry and the owner-father's ambivalence toward giving up control of the organization (e.g., Levinson, 1983). Again, the interventionist translates client-presented data to theories or understandings that would explain the behavior and about which the client may be unaware. The veracity of the theory is confirmed, if at all, by the reception it receives from the client in an interactive process, as previously discussed. The clinical inferential process is therefore personalistic and highly related to the skill, intuition, and competence of the therapist or researcher.

WORKING ON MULTIPLE LEVELS

The clinical approach, at least to individuals, addresses its subject matter from multiple levels. It is not content to deal only with the surface manifestations of a behavior. Recognizing that behavior is determined by both conscious and unconscious factors, and that it is typically overdetermined by multiple sources of causality, the clinician seeks an understanding of both the rational and the irrational.

It is the unconscious processes that have largely been ignored by traditional researchers of organizations and social systems. Most of the theories of behavior in organizations are comfortable only with the most overt and "rational" causes of behavior, despite the fact that unconscious factors may, at least at the individual level, be highly deterministic of such behaviors as procrastination, goal setting, and work accomplishment. In the clinical approach, special sensitivity to the less easily measured aspects of behavior is stressed. Interactions among cognitive, affective, and value-related determinants of behavior are all taken into account by the clinical investigator.

ACTIVISM

The clinical researcher is a more active participant in the process of learning. Rather than rigidly controlling the type of data that is elicited or trying to minimize personal observations that might lead to alternative hypotheses to those originally considered, in the clinical approach the investigator is actively a part of the process of learning. The clinical investigator tries different types of interpretations and observes the client's responses. The clinical investigator also recognizes that his or

her own behavior is always influential in determining what will be observed (e.g., Lowman, 1982b). It was one of Freud's important contributions to recognize that a separate psychology was not needed to explain the therapist and the patient: Similar concepts and principles apply to both. Researchers cannot act in isolation from what they research without seriously jeopardizing their understanding. Clinical researchers or interventionists recognize that they are necessarily part of the system they seek to change or to understand, and therefore make an active effort to integrate that reality into research methods.

EMOTIONAL DEMANDS
OF CLINICAL METHODS

Because the person of the clinical investigator is so prominent in the interaction, clinical methods are affectively demanding of the researcher. If, as was speculated earlier in this chapter, traditional investigators typically enter the field of research as a way of assuring predictability and order in their lives, clinical methods are a radical, and presumably unappealing, departure. The clinical researcher involves him- or herself in all phases of an investigation. Moreover, clinicians are sensitive to unconscious and well-defended explanatory causes, which may put considerable strain on their own defense mechanisms. The extreme ambiguity associated with experience-driven, as opposed to data- and theory-driven, approaches also requires expertise in coping with considerable uncertainty.

WHO CAN AND WHO CANNOT CONDUCT
CLINICAL STUDIES

Clinical methods demand far more of the researcher than do traditional methods. Clinical researchers place themselves in the thick of the data-gathering process and place their person on the line in the process of collecting data or making interventions. Because of these working conditions, clinical researchers or interventionists are far more likely to experience anxiety, intrusion into their personal dynamics and defenses, and, since depth rather than superficial understanding is sought, the arousal of anxiety in the persons being studied.

Curiously, the personal qualities, skills, and abilities required for the successful clinical researcher have been poorly researched. Berg (1980) and Sofer (1961) come closest, among existing literature. Table 8.1 presents a hypothesized and admittedly speculative listing of the job skills, knowledge, and desired attributes of the clinical researcher or

TABLE 8.1   Job Skills, Knowledge, and Attributes of the Clinical Researcher

(1) *Job Skills*
    A. Ability to establish relationships of trust, acceptance, warmth and concern
    B. Ability to diagnose a client's condition, to gather and interpret evidence from a variety of sources, to use oneself as a diagnostic instrument
    C. Ability to communicate at the level of the recipient, to give and receive feedback in minimally threatening ways, to communicate with a minimum of contradictory messages, to help others acknowledge ownership of their own ideas and feelings
    D. Ability to execute a well-developed sense of timing, especially when working under stress
    E. Ability to be pragmatic, emphasizing the applied and practical aspects of behavior
    F. Ability to work under conditions of high stress, high uncertainty and ambiguity, high frustration, loneliness and professional isolation

(2) *Job Knowledge*
    A. Organizational and interpersonal dynamics
    B. Principles of change and changing
    C. Individual personality dynamics
    D. Ethics
    E. Standards of professional practice

(3) *Personal Attributes*
    A. Cognitive complexity and high intelligence
    B. Interpersonal competence, including:
       B1. Openness and honesty
       B2. Awareness of and control over one's own personal psychological defenses
       B3. Cognitive flexibility
       B4. Self awareness and self acceptance
    C. Moderate needs for affiliation, achievement, and power
    D. "Helping" orientation
    E. High need for personal competence
    F. Comfort with intuitive methods
    G. Imagination and cognitive flexibility

interventionist. In this table there are numerous presumed personal characteristics that either should be made the focus of clinical methodological training or criteria of selection for those entering the field.

The skills outlined in Table 8.1 are primarily interpersonal. It is likely that the characteristics that make for a successful clinical investigator will rarely be found in traditional researchers. Miles (1979) makes the point that as qualitative methods increase in popularity, they may become an "attractive nuisance" to those unprepared by training or temperament for their complexities. Such individuals may do more

harm than good by using these methods. The task for traditional researchers is not to abandon or even necessarily to supplement the methodologies with which they personally are familiar and skilled, but rather to encourage and support nontraditional researchers to develop outstanding examples of studies using their particular methods. Even more important, the traditionalist should attempt to learn from the findings of clinical studies—which is hard to do if personal aversion perverts interest or attention.

THE URGENT NEED FOR QUALITY CONTROL IN CLINICAL APPROACHES

When they are bad, clinical methods can be very bad indeed. They are more subject to abuse than traditional approaches. They may invite weak researchers or those who are simply in the wrong field. Because the role of the clinical researcher or interventionist is so much more personalized, there is far more need for checks on the quality of the work.

The controls and checks that a clinical methodology requires are different from those appropriate to traditional research. In training psychotherapists, for example, clinical supervision models make extensive use of one-to-one supervision with audio- and videotapes of actual trainee-client interactions. Supervision is regarded as a long-term process and an ongoing need beyond one's formal years of training. It is recognized that the opportunities for distortion of data based on personal needs or the therapist's own psychopathology are many; an external party to the client-therapist relationship provides a needed outside perspective to minimize possible negative consequences to the client.

In general, bad clinical methods are probably much worse than bad traditional methods. Because there is more agreement on the methodologies and rules of evidence for the traditional than for the clinical approach, inferior work of a traditional nature can more easily be discovered. Bad clinical research may be ignored or never presented so that there is no external jury or, worse, only sympathetic admirers to evaluate its merit. Since clinical research methods are still in their infancy, it is up to those persons who perform clinical studies, whether as researchers or as interventionists, to impose their own requirements for quality control. For those still in graduate school, the task will often be to seek out interested faculty and fellow students, perhaps those in other areas of study such as psychiatry or clinical psychology, to develop the supervisory and support relationships needed.

TRAINING CLINICAL SKILLS

Curiously, there has been rather little attention directed toward how to train clinical skills in the few applied behavioral science training programs that give any attention at all to clinical methods. Such programs would benefit first by providing comprehensive rather than piecemeal programs for training these skills (e.g., Lowman, 1982a). Second, such programs could make the assessment and development of the requisite interpersonal skills or aptitudes major criteria for the selection of students and faculty, and for the measurement of acquired competencies. There appears to be little awareness by students, faculty, or program administrators of more traditional programs of what would be required to train persons competent in clinical methods. A course or two tossed into what is essentially a research curriculum may be worse than no training in clinical methodology. Alderfer and Berg (1977), Lippitt, Watson, and Westley (1958), and Sofer (1961) are among the few authors who have demonstrated much understanding of what would be needed to train clinical skills. My own perspectives on training clinical skills in applied behavioral science settings are similar to those just cited. I would add the following additional recommendations:

(1) Responsibility. Medical training models impose, appropriately, a rigid system of control to assure the protection of the client. The concept of personal responsibility for the client is so strongly part of the culture that no one would expect to challenge it with impunity, and breaches are dealt with rather severely. There is no comparable ethic among those who would attempt to change or to study social systems. Such an ethos would require far more rigorous standards of selection than now exist, but also the creation of training paradigms embodying such standards from the very beginning of training.

(2) Personal self-awareness. To take responsibility for another implies the need to subordinate one's own needs, defenses, and conflicts to the needs of the client. To experience the client role firsthand is an appropriate adjunct to the training in clinical research methods. In my experience, personal therapy is especially needed by those attracted to the clinical study of social systems to address conflicts in the areas of counterdependency and in the experience and exercise of power. In addition, personal therapy can provide a better foundation for the ongoing examination of roles suggested by Berg (1980).

Self-awareness proceeds both by intensive self-exploratory methods and by examining one's cognitive and personal strengths and weak-

nesses. Clinicians have no monopoly on self-awareness, only models of training that give members of the profession explicit opportunity to discuss, and, if need be, to challenge one another's self-perceptions. Participation in intensive, personally intrusive laboratory experiences and completion of psychological testing can enhance self-awareness.

(3) Peer support. If my hypotheses of professional isolation, loneliness, and a basic desire for strong interpersonal relations by clinical researchers are valid, strong peer support may provide one mechanism for countering professional isolation. Group solidarity may be fostered by a number of well-established means that need not be elaborated here. Mentoring (Levinson et al., 1978), while important, should not be overemphasized since its contribution may be slight compared to the heady innervation that is precipitated by the discovery of psychological congruity with a relevant group of peers. Moreover, the peer relationship may be less prone to the apparently natural demise of the mentoring relationship. (For similar reasons, I have always favored sending teams rather than individual students into organizations to learn change methodologies. While intensive supervision by an experienced instructor is also provided and considered important, the team tends to be where the more long-lasting learning occurs.)

(4) Diagnostic and conceptual skills. Students of social systems are perhaps among the worst trained diagnosticians of any major helping profession. The scarcity of diagnostic theory severely limits the ability to acquire skills in social system diagnostic practice. Moreover, the weak understanding of individuals by those oriented to study or change of social systems does not facilitate the ability to think complexly in terms of individual-group-system interactions.

In the absence of adequate diagnostic taxonomies, the clinician may best proceed in developing an understanding of diagnostic principles by experience-based tutorage from those with relevant clinical experience. Matching learning to appropriate interventions by those so inclined would best, at this stage of learning, proceed similarly.

(5) Ethics. Existing codes of ethics of medicine and psychology provide reasonable bases from which to formulate guidelines for practice. Elaborating such codes to the practice of research and intervention in social systems (as opposed to work with individuals) is needed. Integration of ethical concerns with the training of social science inquiry is also important.

CONCLUSION

Clinical methodologies are not for everyone. They are far more demanding than traditional methods in terms of emotionality, activity levels, and in the need for observational acuity and technical integration. Clinical researchers will probably always, and perhaps even appropriately, constitute a minority of social systems researchers. Most persons with skills amenable to clinical methods will probably find more compatible settings with more and better role models in fields such as cultural anthropology, clinical psychology, or psychiatry. It is hoped that someday soon there will be a Freud of organizations, of communities, and of other branches of social sciences to exemplify fully the potential of clinical methodologies. In the meantime, such clinical researchers face a lonely undertaking.

While the need will always be there for the rational scientist, advances in clinical methods of social science inquiry and intervention must await challengers, people able to look at the field with new visions and new understandings, to say that what we know and how we know it is both personally and professionally insufficient. The task of the social sciences is to legitimize such methodologies of inquiry, to encourage those clinically inclined to approach their work with rigor and discipline, and to sanction the belief that there are multiple ways to study the same phenomenon. Like the unrecognized gifted artist, clinical researchers in social systems need also to be protected from the existential despair that may be an inevitable part of the legacy of the innovator and that may lead, prematurely, to abandonment of inquiry.

In the future, clinical and traditional research methodologies might best be combined, each making a distinct and complementary contribution. It is time to make respectable the work of clinical researchers and to realize the limitations of our traditional approaches. The field of applied social science studies is rather urgently in need of intellectual rehabilitation. As Robert Pirsig put it in a different context,

> Classic understanding should not be overlaid with romantic prettiness: classic and romantic understanding should be united at a basic level. . . . At present we're snowed under with an irrational expansion of blind data-gathering in the sciences because there's no rational format for any understanding of scientific creativity. . . . We have artists with no scientific knowledge and scientists with no spiritual sense of gravity at all, and the result is not just bad, it is ghastly. (1974, pp. 293-294)

Commentary

The common bond that draws the chapters of this section together is the underlying question of how our ways of knowing shape our understanding of the social world. When we take these chapters as a whole, it is possible to make some clear assertions. There are important differences among us that affect our judgments about what constitutes relevant data or valuable knowledge including our gender, our interest in social action or basic science, and our source of support. The list of factors that makes a difference is long, but the general point is straightforward. The knowledge we create is, in part, a product of the culture or cultures in which we live, the groups to which we belong, the institutions that support us, and the values we hope our knowledge will sustain.

The chapter by Cammann puts before us the central concern. Knowledge is not an island, absolute unto itself. It is a set of relationships that are tied explicitly to criteria we value. The very elaboration of different criteria forces us to "count" knowledge differently. In this case, Cammann is interested in knowledge that he describes as action usable in organizational change projects. He contrasts this type of knowledge with what is knowable via methods that require "detachment and objectivity."

In a way, the pursuit of "pure" knowledge is the pursuit of an illusion made possible by the protection of institutions such as wealthy private universities that do not ask that applicability be a key criterion for funding. This point is wonderfully illustrated by Perry's example of the way changes in what was viewed as acceptable knowledge in a psychiatric hospital mirrored almost perfectly the shifts in the economic and political agendas of the funding agencies on which the hospital depended. Devastating as the thought may be in some academic circles, knowledge appears often to be a pawn in the hands of public policymakers. We may not have evolved as far as we would like to think in separating social knowledge from the desires of those who, at a given moment, dominate our society.

The chapter by Reinharz is a stark reminder that knowledge is a product of intergroup relations. What has passed as knowledge has been a product of ways of knowing that contain within them dynamics that elevate men and preserve their power while devaluing women and denigrating their humanity. Had there been a chapter written in a similar vein by a black American we would see the all-pervasiveness of the problem of social dominance.

These chapters inevitably lead us to the question of what type of ordering process we might use to create alternative hypotheses about the world, or knowledge less truncated by a single way of knowing. In the answer to this question we can observe a similar pattern in each chapter. All the authors struggled with the issue of influence—the influence upon them of social and organizational forces and, in turn, the researchers' influence on how and what they know. All saw knowledge as a product of these influences. None of the authors seemed totally at peace with this realization. It touched something deep

and catalyzed further struggle. Each needed to find some resting place, a touchstone that would provide a foundation for their assessments as well as some emotional comfort.

There were differences in where each author came to rest. Perhaps the place where these differences were most evident was in the writing style each used. Cammann writes, "If it's action usable for me in a particular setting, I'll settle writes about his struggles, the professional angst he feels comes through on the written page. The writing style reflects the source of his understanding. Cammann writes, "If it's action usuable for me in a particular setting, I'll settle for that as knowledge." A personal foundation presented in a personal style. In contrast, Smith went to the level of relationships, Reinharz to her group identification with women, Lowman to the discipline of his profession, and Perry to the domain of politics, culture, and the world of ideas. In each case the writing style seemed consistent with the content presented.

The overall gestalt of this section is that there are many ways of knowing. This recognition comes from looking at clinical issues in a systematic way. We can know by coming up close and seeing what works for us, by entering into relationships, by developing an awareness of our group and intergroup identities, by accepting the discipline of a particular field and by examining the way our knowledge reflects our culture.

The question may well be asked, Is it possible to know anything for sure? This may be one dilemma raised by this section. There is, however, another place to come to rest. Having established that different understandings arise from different ways of knowing, we now have many more hypotheses, ideas, and concepts to use as rival explanations for our research findings. This opens up the possibility of a much broader knowledge base. If our goal is richness and potency of explanation, the more alternatives that are rigorously mapped, the less likely we are to suffer the frustration of "significant" results with trivial importance.

Clinical Involvement

After reading the five chapters in this section, one is struck by the relationship between clinical involvement and self-scrutiny. One could argue that involvement is a powerful stimulus for self-reflection, but it is also apparent that the willingness to engage in self-scrutiny opens up possibilities for involvement and learning. In each of the following chapters the authors describe both their involvement (with themselves, with colleagues, with research participants) and their struggles to gain some self-understanding. Together the chapters support the contention that involvement and self-scrutiny enhance both researcher and research.

In the first chapter Hackman takes us through his struggle, still incomplete, to find his own clinical "voice." It is a deeply personal account of successes and failures, anger and hurt, pain and hope. As he describes this odyssey, Hackman offers us glimpses of the repercussions occurring in his significant relationships with colleagues who are strongly identified with the clinical tradition and with others who are skeptical of it. As Hackman finally completes a chapter he says he did not want to write, it becomes clear that the personal struggle and the professional relationships are closely linked.

The second chapter is concerned with the *researcher's* emotions during research with human systems. Berg's contention is that many of our research methods are designed to protect us from the various sources of anxiety present in social research. The chapter includes an analysis of two short cases that illustrate how important the exploration of the researcher's anxiety is to the conduct of research. Berg calls on us to examine and report the emotional dynamics of research relationships since they are an inevitable consequence of the researcher's involvement.

In the third chapter Louis helps Mirvis explore the transferential dynamics present in a research project and the impact they had on Mirvis's actions, perceptions, and research role. Mirvis takes the risk of showing us some of his family history in an effort to uncover its initially subtle but ultimately powerful effect. The chapter shows a researcher willing to explore how his *whole* self becomes involved in the research relationships that make up social research.

The fourth chapter describes how Kram's research on mentoring forced her to confront the influences of her own group memberships on her study. She takes us through numerous examples of research issues that led her through a process of self-reflection and then back again to decisions about the research. In

some cases Kram had not anticipated that the research would cause her to scrutinize the impact of her age and sex on *her* behavior as well as the behavior of the participants in her study.

In the final chapter, Peshkin recounts two fascinating stories about his ethnographic studies of the educational systems in two midwestern towns. Peshkin spent a year in each town and only *after* writing major research reports on both studies did he begin to realize that his findings were heavily influenced by the "persona" evoked by each setting. One of the central issues in both settings was the nature and function of intolerance in these communities. Peshkin slowly discovered that the *concept* of intolerance takes on very different intellectual forms depending on whether the researcher identifies himself or herself with the tolerant or the intolerant. The narrative itself is a marvelous description of self-discovery.

The five chapters in this section are filled with emotion. Each of the authors struggles to convey what research involvement *feels* like—the pain, the intensity, the dawning awareness, the learning. It is difficult to describe feelings with words, but the emotion, the involvement, and the commitment to self-scrutiny come through.

ON SEEKING ONE'S OWN CLINICAL VOICE:
A Personal Account

J. Richard Hackman

It probably is significant that I do not want to be writing this right now. Since it may help readers make sense of what I am about to say, let me take a few paragraphs to reflect on why I have put this paper off until the last conceivable minute—and still find myself less than eager to proceed with the task.

First, I have no special commitment to the promulgation and use of clinical research methods. Clinical methodology is one of many sets of tools, all of which are flawed in some ways, that are available to researchers interested in making sense of individual, group, and organizational phenomena. The clinical approach is one about which I have tried to do some learning over the last decade or so, and one that has proven helpful to me in my scholarly work. But I do not feel called to espouse or explain clinical methods; that can be done more appropriately (and better) by colleagues who are more experienced and expert in the use of these methods than I am.

Moreover, my dominant motivation right now is to get on with my research, not to write about methodology. I am trying to understand certain group and organizational dynamics, and I want to develop and frame my understanding so that it contributes to others' learning and, I hope, enhances their ability to act competently in pursuing their objectives. In short, I want to spend my time these days *doing* it, not writing about how one does it, and certainly not reflecting on how I happen to have developed my own ways of doing it. This chapter comes at the wrong time in the evolution and execution of my own work and I wish I had not committed to write it.

My continuing ambivalence about clinical methods has been evident to me (and to the editors) in thinking about this chapter—as the paragraphs above surely make clear. One of the ways I respond when I am feeling ambivalent about something is to wallow in it for a while, and

then put my head down and charges ahead in one direction or another. I have wallowed in this project for many months now, and finally agreed with one of the editors that it is time to put my head down and charge—to see if anything worth sharing with others comes out. What follows is the product of that negotiated agreement.

OVERVIEW

If one can characterize my involvement with clinical methodologies as something of a struggle (as I have experienced it, this is not a bad metaphor), then it may be useful to discuss how the struggle began. Although one could reflect back well into childhood in attempting to trace the roots of any scholar's conceptual and methodological orientation, I will begin with my years in graduate school—for it is there that I learned what "research" meant and developed my initial approach to scholarly work. Then I will review a series of events that occurred as I was leaving graduate school and starting my academic career that provided the impetus for my engagement with clinical methods.

What I have to say about the process of seeking my clinical "voice" follows that introductory material. The theme I have chosen to use in organizing my thoughts about that process (and this should not now be a surprise) is ambivalence. As I made choices to engage with the clinical world, I found ambivalence everywhere I turned: on the part of my colleagues in experimental social psychology, on the part of colleagues who identify themselves with the clinical tradition, and (perhaps most of all) within myself. For me, then, to talk about the development of clinical voice *is* to talk about ambivalence—how it is expressed and how it is dealt with, by the learner and by his or her colleagues.

The essay ends with something of a balance sheet expressing my present view of the assets and liabilities of clinical methods for the kind of work I do. This provides me an opportunity to assess whether the time and emotional energy I have expended in beginning to learn clinical methods have been well spent (I conclude that it *has* been worth it). It also gives me a platform to express my present views about the value of clinical approaches for organizational research, teaching, and intervention (I conclude that these methods offer opportunities that are not otherwise available) and about the risks that inhere in the use of clinical approaches (I conclude that the risks are serious, particularly if clinical methods come to be seen as the only legitimate way to learn about and help people and social systems, but that they can be managed).

This essay is, of necessity, highly personal in character. As someone trained that the person and the personal pronoun have no place in

writing intended for one's scholarly colleagues—and being someone who values his personal privacy a great deal—that necessity makes me uncomfortable. My hope is that by opening the curtains a bit on the experiences I have had (and the feelings that have accompanied them) in the course of my development to date as a scholar and teacher, I may be able to serve as a kindred spirit at a distance for others who are travelling the same road—and who may be feeling as alone on that road as I often have felt.

WHEREFROM CAME THIS CLOSET CLINICIAN?

To the best of my recollection, Freud was mentioned in class once during my four years as a doctoral student in psychology at the University of Illinois in the mid-1960s—and that was to identify him as a figure in the history of psychology of little relevance to contemporary psychologists. That was surprising to me. Although I had taken only a couple of psychology courses as an undergraduate (my major was mathematics), I arrived at graduate school with the impression that Freud was at the core of the discipline. But I adapted quickly to the highly quantitative and empirical orientation of my doctoral program, and found that I could "do psychology" pretty well.

I had what I believed to be (and still believe to be) superb training in experimental social psychology at the hands of people like Joe McGrath, Ivan Steiner, Fred Fiedler, and Marty Fishbein. We had to take two minors in those days, and mine were psychological measurement (a special strength of Illinois psychology) and sociology (just enough involvement to convince me that I was not a natural sociologist, and that I had little interest in becoming one). My only exposure to organizational psychology at Illinois was one doctoral seminar that was mainly spent trying to figure out if there was anything about organizations that might be interesting to study (I concluded there probably was not).

Quantitative data were at the core of the Illinois program in those days, and I learned well how to collect and analyze them in accord with state-of-the-art measurement and statistical techniques. "Dustbowl empiricism," a term sometimes applied to the kind of research that was done at Illinois, is an offensive term to me because it demeans the impressive capability those people had to use numbers and statistics to make sense of phenomena whose complexity defied comprehension in other ways. The psychologists with whom I worked were smart, thoughtful, and insightful; I admired them then, and I do today.

My dissertation research was squarely in the Illinois paradigm. Tony Morris and I collaborated to collect data on 108 experimental groups, each of which performed 4 of 108 different tasks we had written, yielding 432 transcripts of group interaction (the focus of Tony's dissertation) and 432 written group products (the focus of mine). The research design was beautifully counterbalanced, the analysis was sophisticated, and for some time thereafter I characterized the dissertation as "the best piece of research I will ever do."

Yet, even as I was preparing to leave Illinois, I experienced a vague and troubling disaffection with the work. I kept trying to figure out how to apply the dissertation findings, to use them to make a constructive difference in something I cared about. I could not come up with much, at least in part because I could not figure out from the data *why* our task manipulations had such large effects on group performance outcomes. Standard arguments about the inherent virtues of basic research provided little solace.

This uneasiness with my research may have contributed (although if it did I was not aware of it at the time) to my decision about which of three academic positions to accept. The options were Wake Forest College (which was appealing because of my interest in undergraduate liberal arts education), Carnegie Institute of Technology (which had a fine group of potential colleagues in experimental social psychology), and Yale (where I would have an appointment in something called "industrial administration" with a token secondary appointment in psychology). I went to the Yale interview mainly because it was Yale— and that seemed quite something for a kid from the Midwest who had never been east of Ohio. On the way, I tried to read a book by Chris Argyris (a senior faculty member at Yale of whom I had never heard) but I could not understand it. On the way back, I wondered why I was so engaged by what was going on in that strange department where people were looking at organizations and behavior within them using methods and concepts that were wholly foreign to me. A few weeks later, when I found myself fudging the numbers on my decision-making balance sheet so that Yale would come out a little higher than it had the first time, I decided to throw caution (and the balance sheet) to the wind and go east.

IMPETUS FOR LEARNING

One cherishes what one knows how to do, and I cherished my skills as an experimental social psychologist. I could barely wait to bring them to bear on the organizational issues that were so much alive at Yale. But it

gradually became clear that I did not have all the skills I needed to do the kind of teaching and research I wanted to do, or to have the constructive influence on organizational practice I wanted to have. The signs that I needed some more learning came from diverse parts of my life at work, and their cumulative impact was powerful.

In laboratory research. Still smarting over my inability to comprehend fully the reasons for the large performance differences among groups in my dissertation research, I decided to do a careful reading of the group interaction transcripts. I reasoned that if one looked at what happened in high-performing groups and compared that to what transpired in groups that performed poorly, then surely one would discover what was *really* responsible for the observed performance differences. So I selected appropriate subsets of transcripts and (with considerable anticipation) carefully read and studied them.

When I finished, the anticipation had turned to dismay: I had no idea what to make of what I had read.[1] Despite the fact that I had available for my use one of the best data sets on group performance ever compiled, I was unable to frame a reasonable answer to the fundamental question in the group effectiveness paradigm: "How come some groups perform so much better than others?" Neither multivariate statistics nor verbatim reading of the interaction transcripts had provided much help. So how, I asked myself, *does* one understand a group, anyway? It was a most troubling question, and one I knew I would have to take on.

In field research. One of my early experiences in field research resulted (I believe) in a manager losing his job—a consequence of my good intentions coupled with inexperience, incompetence, and lack of supervision in managing field relationships.

The project dealt with shop-floor motivational questions, and involved collection of data using questionnaires and interviews. Early on, I experienced the project as enjoyable and relatively easy to manage. The top manager who had initiated the research seemed enthusiastic, it was exciting to learn about the organization and how it conducted its business, and data collection was going smoothly—although some people did seem guarded and uneasy about talking with me. (When I sensed uneasiness, I would let the individual "off the hook," even to the extent of ignoring the interview questions and filling the scheduled time with casual conversation with the interviewee.)

Things were not so smooth and relaxed when the time arrived to present the research findings to the organization. For one thing, the top manager seemed to have lost interest in the project (he claimed that pressing business matters were fully occupying him). And when I arrived

for one feedback session, I found myself scheduled with the executive committee of the union (with whom I had not met as a group before, and who asserted that they were there to see which managers I had identified as incompetent). My protestations that that was not what the project was about fell on deaf ears, and when I refused to name names, they ended the session and left.

I kept trying to make contact with the top manager until, one day, I learned that he had dismissed the manager of the department where the research had been done—and, I was told, had used the research findings as part of his justification.

This shocked me about as profoundly as anything else I can recall in my professional work (even now, many years later, I find it hard to write about the events of the project). The only positive outcome of the research was that it jolted me (finally) into realizing how I and my research had been used, how unaware I had been of what was actually transpiring throughout the life of the project, and how grossly unskilled I was in comprehending and managing research in organizational settings. It was clear that if I was going to do research in the field, I was going to have to learn a lot of things I had not been taught in graduate school.

In teaching. One of my first teaching assignments was a large section of introductory psychology. T-groups were much in vogue at the time, and the staff (I was one of four) decided that everybody in the course should have a three-hour T-group experience. We scheduled hundreds of students into small groups, reserved rooms around campus for the group meetings, and lined up dozens of trainers to facilitate them.

On the evening of the event, one of the trainers failed to appear, and another instructor suggested that I substitute for him. I declined politely but I was aghast. I could not comprehend how a trained clinician could suggest that someone with no group training whatever lead a T-group— even if it was only a three-hour "demonstration." While the dubious worth (and the risks) of the whole enterprise of one-shot T-groups for all introductory psychology students was not something I understood at the time, I at least had enough sense to realize that one needed some training to lead such a group. I did not have it, I had serious reservations about the behavior of some of those who did, and I figured that it might make sense to learn a little about that stuff—considering that I billed myself as someone not only interested in groups, but knowledgeable about them.

In the department. The climate of the Department of Industrial Administration (subsequently Administrative Sciences) at Yale in the

late 1960s provided persistent support for exploring alternative ways of behaving, teaching, and learning—and many of these explorations were rooted in the clinical tradition. It was impossible to be a member of the Yale organizational behavior group in those years and not be affected in some way by clinical thought and practice.

The events that affected me were separately of small consequence but collectively had great impact. For example,

— attempting to line up Fritz Steele's vote for an upcoming faculty appointment, and his using the occasion to inquire about my personal model of organizational politics. By the time the conversation was over, he had gently prodded me toward expanding my thinking about social influence in organizations, and had modeled for me an alternative way of being influential that I found as intriguing as it was unfamiliar;

— participating in a fairly intense debate with my faculty colleagues (at one of our evening discussions at Argyris's house) on whether or not there really is such a thing as "unconscious motivation," and finding myself disturbed at how my own thinking about human behavior was restricted by assumptions I had never thought seriously about, let alone questioned;

— trying to respond to concerns raised by graduate students about how "authority dynamics" might be affecting what was happening in my course, and not even being sure what it was they were talking about.

With all of these events and more, I increasingly realized that I was standing just outside the real inner circle. It was not the best of motives, but I wanted to be in the inner circle—and this, coupled with the experiences enumerated above, led me to decide to test the clinical waters. I had no idea at the time whether I could do even the basics of research and teaching using clinical methods—it all seemed mysterious, special, and (perhaps partly for those reasons) incredibly attractive.

TESTING THE WATER

There was (and is) no programmatic character to my explorations of clinical teaching and research methods. There were, however, some signal learning events and activities that helped me (1) see that I had overblown the mystique of group, clinical, and experiential methods; (2) discover that becoming moderately competent in their use was not out of my personal reach; and (3) learn some skills and develop some attitudes about research and teaching that were new to me. In no particular order, they include the following.

Engagement with Alderfer, Argyris, and Torbert. Clay Alderfer received his doctorate from the Yale organizational behavior program

in 1966 and went off to teach at Cornell just as I was arriving in New Haven. Two years later he returned to Yale, and there was a clear expectation on the part of the senior faculty that he and I had some things to learn from one another. It was true. We jumped into collaborative work, starting with a jointly taught course on research methodology that attempted to meld clinical and experimental research approaches. A couple of years later, we wrote a joint research proposal (which compared work design and team building as points of departure for initiating organizational change) and began a lengthy (and ultimately unsuccessful) series of negotiations to find an organization where we could do the research. These activities provided many opportunities for me to learn about clinical methods—both cognitively and by observing (and, at times, modeling) Clay's behavior.

The intellectual pivot around which organizational behavior at Yale revolved in the late 1960s was Chris Argyris. Indeed, after Don Taylor became chairman of psychology and Wight Bakke passed away, Chris was the only senior faculty member in our group. He kept after me: reading my scholarly work carefully and commenting on it in ways that forced me to think hard about what I was doing, why, and how; and confronting me persistently and constructively about my research and teaching. His obvious commitment to learning and understanding was a model for me, and his high expectations of me helped keep my motivation and standards high. While my involvement with Chris was an important part of my development as a scholar and teacher, it also was highly frustrating: It seemed that every time I thought I was getting it, it turned out that I was not, and I began to sense how difficult clinical skills could be to learn.

Bill Torbert (a doctoral student at the time) seemed to "have it," but I could not understand exactly what it was he had—and I was supposed to be one of his advisors. We taught an experimental (and moderately experiential) undergraduate course together, and in some sense it was a miserable failure: Our attempt to promote self-directed learning turned out instead to promote disengagement from the course for many of our students.[2] Yet the course did help me understand better than I had before that one must behave in order to learn, that failure is a necessary part of the learning process, and that blind or unexamined behavior is grossly insufficient for someone who aspires to understand people and social systems.

A couple of years in a couples' T-group. Four couples (we varied in age, work situation, and experience in group training) decided to meet regularly to explore personal and interpersonal issues in marriage. The

group became a supportive setting in which I could learn about (and practice dealing with) unconscious, emotional, and interpersonal phenomena that previously I had ruled out of consideration on the grounds that they accounted for trivial variance—or that they could not be addressed in a systematic, "scientific" matter. I discovered that some of my preconceptions were little more than defensiveness, and that maybe I even had some skill in dealing with issues that before had seemed either not worth the trouble or beyond my competence.

Half a year of individual "developmental" therapy. During one of my first official Yale leaves, I decided to do some personal emotional learning and signed up for a period of therapy with a highly recommended individual to "look inside." It was a glorious rationalization: In retrospect, I believe I actually wanted to get rid of some problems I was having with myself, and I acted as if coming in for fifty minutes once a week and letting the therapist do his good work on me would take care of it. It did not, of course, but the experience was valuable in helping me shed the view that this clinical stuff was somehow magic. Therapy was a constructive and worthwhile thing for me to have done (and something I have repeated), but for reasons different than those on my mind when I first signed up.

The Oshry power laboratory. Ken Smith (a doctoral student in our program) had attended a "power laboratory" led by Barry Oshry and came back enthusiastic about what he had learned. What he said and wrote about the experience fascinated me, so I decided to try it out. The laboratory helped me comprehend the full power of group and intergroup forces for the first time, and also forced me to acknowledge the ways I had kept myself from having to deal with them—both in my work and in my life. (To find yourself arm wrestling for real with a valued friend and colleague through a jagged window you have just broken to force your way into his residence tends to shake you up a bit.) Yet when I compared my ability to understand and deal with group and intergroup dynamics with that of the staff (and that of other participants, some of whom were repeat attendees), I felt naive and ignorant. This experience, as much as any other, hammered home the fact that I had to *learn* this stuff. I could not go on saying I was a psychologist (of all things!) interested in groups and organizations without opening myself to phenomena that can have tidal (rather than ripple) effects on what transpires within them. I needed to understand these forces, to figure out how to study them, and to discover ways to use them in studying other things. I was, I felt, ready for a major push forward in my learning about unconscious and group dynamics in organizational life.

GOING FOR IT—AND COMING UP SHORT

After deciding to try to expand and deepen my clinical skills (there was no exact date the decision was made, but at some point it became clear that I was going to proceed), I expected my learning to unfold gradually but consistently. I had not anticipated the ambivalence I would find on every side—and on the inside. Since I have come to believe that experiencing and dealing with ambivalence is an integral and necessary feature of such learning, I will describe my encounters with it below.

THE CLINICAL ESTABLISHMENT

I imagined that once I presented myself for learning (I was motivated and reasonably well prepared, surely an attractive student) I would be welcomed into the fold of those interested in clinical and experiential methods of research and teaching. I was wrong. Those in a position to teach me tended instead to reject me, something they had not done before I implicitly "announced" myself as a serious student. (That the announcement was implicit may have been part of the reason for this— and a sign of my own ambivalence about proceeding.) The rebuffs came from a variety of sources, ranging from an organization dedicated to experiential education to students in our program at Yale. For example:

— National Training Laboratories (NTL) rejecting my application to participate in a workshop on experiential approaches to job design (an area in which I had done quite a bit of empirical and conceptual work) on grounds that I was unqualified to attend. (I had not previously taken their basic human interaction laboratory.)

— Offers to participate in teaching our experiential introductory master's course, and to apprentice myself in our group dynamics course, being ignored or rejected by my clinically oriented faculty colleagues.

— As I began to experiment more with experiential and clinical method-ologies in the classroom, students identified with that group doing things to keep me in the "traditional" camp—and, occasionally, to encourage conflict between the two groups. When I did a classroom session on field diagnostic methodologies, for example, one such student wondered aloud to his colleagues (within my earshot) how much of what I covered would "have to be un-taught" the next semester in the experiential course he would be helping with. (Students identified with traditional teaching and research methodologies have engaged in similar behavior, although aimed in the opposite direction. Apparently some students feel it is in their best interest—or, perhaps, they are just more comfortable—if faculty stay in their historically proper places.)

Events such as these keep happening, and they frustrate and anger me. On the one hand, some of my clinically oriented colleagues claim that their approach is where the *real* learning about people, groups, and organizations is to be had. This, they say, is where the action is in our field, and the presence of a clinical stream of teaching and research in our program is one of its most distinctive and attractive features. On the other hand, they behave toward me (and some other interested faculty) in ways that preclude our becoming involved with them in these cutting-edge activities. The message, as I receive it, is that I am not ready (or, perhaps, not able—it has never been clear) to learn what they have to teach.

How is this to be understood? From the point of view of the clinical establishment, Hackman's interest is surely a compliment: He says that what we do is sufficiently interesting and important that he wants to learn more about it. But perhaps it also is a threat: If Hackman learns how to do it, our comparative advantage diminishes—particularly if he should turn out to be a good student. So we find ourselves ambivalent about helping him learn.

That is, of course, raw speculation—I cannot speak for my colleagues. My response to what I have encountered has been to learn as best I can on my own, with lots of trial and error, and to work with students who "straddle" the two groups whenever appropriate and possible. And I believe I have learned some things that are both interesting and different from the core doctrine of the clinical cohort in organizational behavior. That is one of the advantages of doing it on your own—you discover what *you* discover. But it has created even more problems with the clinical establishment: Hackman is not only *doing* it, he's getting it *wrong*. (But maybe he's getting it right. How are we ever to tell if we keep him at arm's length?)

THE SOCIAL PSYCHOLOGY ESTABLISHMENT

Colleagues identified with mainline social psychology seem to harbor a wish that I would continue to be the same guy I was when I left Illinois. The signs of this are subtle, but they also are plentiful and they keep coming. For example:

— A former Yale colleague calling to tell me (with a chuckle) that there is controversy in the social psychology world about what my name is. This individual (who knows me as "Richard") was at a conference heavily attended by experimental social psychologists, including colleagues from my Illinois days (who knew me as "Dick"). When my work was discussed at the conference, he reported, there was explicit and occasionally vigorous disagreement about my name: Is he Richard, or is he Dick?

While my colleague called because he thought it was funny, his interpretation was that my social psychologist colleagues *really* wanted me to be the person they used to know, the one who did things the scientifically correct way, rather than the one who may have been led astray by his more clinically oriented colleagues out east.

— A faculty member on the West Coast who writes me shortly after I have delivered a paper at a university near her own proposing some new approaches to methodology for group and organizational research, telling me that she heard that Hackman has "thrown over all his previous work, and is starting over with some really far-out methods." She wanted to know if it was true. Hackman had, of course, done no such thing; indeed, he was trying to *build* on what we have learned about theory and method to date, to take the next incremental step in improving our scholarly tools. Is it an expression of ambivalence that the presentation was coded as a wholesale switching of sides?

— Social psychologists writing or calling about my work on groups, inviting me to be on review boards, to speak at conferences, to consider applying for grants they know about, saying "these new directions you are taking are just what we need, just the way the field should be evolving." Yet, some of them see in their own work little movement in the directions they applaud in mine. Is it that I am to serve as the point person in edging toward new kinds of methods and theories so that they do not have to?

In all, I sense among my colleagues in social psychology some gentle encouragement for me to come back home. I feel they would welcome me, forgive me for the errors of my recent ways, and even give me back my old room. In fact, I do want to reengage with mainline social psychology. These people are my friends, and in a real sense my professional family of origin. Moreover, I am encouraged by what seems to be a renewed interest in relationships and groups among members of the social psychology establishment. But the guy who is coming back is different from the guy who left—and he is returning with some new tools and with a belief that the old homestead might be more interesting and durable if a few structural modifications were made. I wonder if the welcome mat will be kept out once that is realized.

MYSELF

Part of the ambivalence I receive from my colleagues—whether of the clinical or the social psychological persuasion—has been internalized, and part of my ambivalence is wholly self-generated. While I cannot sort out the sources, here are the signs I see:

— Getting a tiny rejection (e.g., having an offer to co-teach a course declined) and turning that into a major event. This allows me to continue to feel virtuous without having to actually do what I hesitantly suggested

I'd like to do. It is characteristic of me, and one of my unattractive features: Someone puts my nose a little out of joint, I put it the rest of the way out of joint and work to keep it there. I am a great victim.

— I do not know how good I really am at using clinical methods, and I may be behaving in ways that keep me from finding out. When I have worked collaboratively with clinically oriented colleagues, for example, I invariably wind up taking greater responsibility for the conceptual part of the activity, while they manage the experiential part. I have resented that—but I also regularly have colluded with it (and on occasion have even suggested such a division of labor). How worried am I that I will, eventually, discover that I am not very talented in the use of clinical and experiential methods? To what extent does that fear keep me from putting myself squarely on the line?

— There are numerous learning opportunities open to me that I have not accepted, such as finding an appropriate time to participate in a Tavistock conference. Given my interest in groups and in the exercise of authority as a way to create conditions that foster work team effectiveness, I need the learning that a Tavistock experience could provide. Moreover, my clinically oriented colleagues have actively encouraged me to enroll. Yet things keep getting scheduled in a way that makes it impossible. How am I to understand that in the context of my avowed commitment to learning clinical skills?

— I find it far easier to help and nurture others than to be helped and nurtured by them. I spend a great deal of my professional time teaching others, and almost none of it in a student role. Indeed, I get reasonably uneasy when I am being taught or helped, when I am dependent on somebody else for something I want or need. When I learn, I *prefer* to figure things out for myself, even if it takes longer or is more painful. If I am going to become expert in clinical methods, at some point I am going to have to come to terms with this issue—and I am still unsure how willing (or able) I am to do that.

— When I am with "traditional" colleagues I often espouse the clinical view of things, but when I am with clinically oriented colleagues I often raise questions that imply that I favor more traditional methods of research and teaching. This may merely reflect my tendency to behave in a counterdependent fashion on occasion, but it also has a self-protective character that can inhibit learning. That is, if I play the role of skeptic (regardless of the group I am with), how seriously will members of that group take my espoused wish to learn from them? Does my probing, skeptical stance (something I generally value in myself) actually cover resistance to learning new and potentially anxiety-arousing material?

SUMMARY

Happily, despite all the ambivalence listed above, there are some things that are relatively unambiguous—things that have made it possible for me to continue learning, despite the opposing pulls I have experienced and my personal conflicts about moving further toward developing my clinical voice.

For one, a handful of colleagues have consistently supported my attempts to learn new skills. I will not embarrass them by giving their names here, but it pleases me that they include people from both sides of my professional life, people with strikingly different professional values and personal orientations toward research and practice. Their support and encouragement have made it possible for me to stick my neck out on occasion in ways I probably would not otherwise have done.

Moreover, I have finally learned what it is I do well—and that provides a solid base from which I can take some risks to expand my knowledge and skills. What I do best, it turns out, is *neither* (1) designing clever experiments or doing powerful multivariate analyses of massive datasets, nor (2) probing deeply submerged emotional dynamics or reaching out for remote but fascinating possible interpretations of what might *really* be going on within a person, a relationship, a group, or an organization. Instead, my particular specialty is *inductive conceptualization*. I can take massive and confused sets of materials (virtually any materials) and make sense of them. I do this relatively effortlessly, and generally I do it well. The point is that this skill is useful both in making sense of massive tables of data *and* in comprehending seemingly chaotic transpirings in groups and organizations. The movement I have made is not so much away from data tables (I still enjoy studying and trying to make sense of them) but toward using my skills in new ways in researching, teaching about, and intervening with groups and organizations.

Knowing what it is that I can do well has made it easier to keep trying to develop skills and methods that I can use in exercising my specialty. Even if I come up short in learning activity, or if I try a new method that fails, I have something that I and my colleagues value to fall back on. I need that, and I have great admiration for people (such as some graduate students) who are able to engage in personally risky skill-development activities even before they have a good sense of their core professional competence.

CONCLUSION

Let me conclude by reflecting on some of the lessons I have learned thus far from my engagement with clinical methods. First I discuss why I have come to believe that the struggle to develop a clinical voice is ultimately worth the effort it takes, and then address some aspects of clinical methods (and some behaviors occasionally exhibited by clinical researchers) that I would like to avoid in my own work.

WHY THE STRUGGLE IS WORTH IT

Moving away from either/or thinking. Most of us trained in scientific methods have long ago adopted the "hypothesis testing" way of thinking about research: Either you reject the null hypothesis or you do not, and the numbers that emerge from the research design and statistical analysis tell you which is correct. "Don't give me any of this 'significant at the .06 level' nonsense," we admonish students in our research methods classes. Follow the formula, and truth will be revealed as a binary state. It is a neat, clean, either/or way of thinking. There is no messy middle to worry about.

Despite the fact that we regularly violate our own admonitions when we need to understand some particularly complex phenomenon or data set, most of us have either/or thinking well ingrained in how we comprehend and explain our phenomena. "Is this theory or that one correct?" we ask, and then proceed to design a horse-race study to compare them. "Does variable x cause outcome y, or doesn't it?" "Is the leader's style democratic or is it autocratic?" And the list goes on.

If social systems were binary, traditional research methodologies (and the kind of thinking they promote) would be appropriate. But organizations are more complex than that: There are multiple routes to the same outcome, causes often are intercorrelated and have redundant effects, a single event can result in a variety of different outcomes (some of which are not predictable from things we can measure beforehand) and occurrences in organizations often have multiple meanings even for the same observer (let alone for people with different stakes who watch from different perches). Either/or thinking invites us to overlook such complexity and messiness, or to suppress it, in the interest of experimental control. And, unfortunately, what is overlooked or suppressed may be near the heart of the phenomena we are trying to understand.

Clinical methods, when appropriately used, offer a way to avoid getting trapped by our own methods and cognitive styles—not merely by acknowledging that the world is more complex than either/or thinking suggests, but by providing a way of understanding multiple causes, effects, perceptions, and realities. It is hard to imagine how one could develop and test a rich and useful understanding of behavior in organizations without clinical methods.

Learning more from fewer cases. While I would not argue for a fully idiographic approach to group and organizational research, my guess is that we will learn more about our phenomena if we spend more time gathering better data about fewer cases—something for which clinical

methodologies are particularly well suited. Consider, for example, an organizational researcher who is interested in understanding how white males in organizations accommodate increasing numbers of women and blacks in their midst, or one who seeks to identify the conditions required for decision-making groups in organizations to become more effective. If one of these researchers had some time and energy available to use in enriching his or her repertoire of research skills, which of the following would you recommend—(1) learning LISREL and collecting the large quantities of data required for appropriate use of that methodology, or (2) learning clinical methods and using them to study intensively a smaller number of cases? Is there any contest? Then why do so few of us do the latter and so many of us do the former?

Developing better ways of communicating research findings. One of the rarely acknowledged virtues of clinical methods is that the findings they generate often defy being placed in the format normally used for presenting the results of scholarly research. If, for example, one has large amounts of qualitative data (perhaps including data about the researcher's own involvement with and reactions to the organization), how can that material be presented in a method-results-discussion journal format? And what if one's conclusions are based on a large number of small and specific observations, each of which provides frail support for any conclusions, but which collectively provide a sturdy interpretive base? How does one write a results section containing such material in a way that allows readers to see and test for themselves the link between data and conclusions?

Problems such as these require that nontraditional ways of presenting what we learn in our research be explored. And that, of course, raises some fundamental questions about how we come to believe what we think we have found, how we can best teach others (including people whose skills and scholarly orientations differ from our own) what we have discovered, and how we can present our findings in ways that invite constructive use of the lessons learned.

Some might view these questions as illustrating problems with clinical methods; one cannot, after all, apply a standard template to the analytic results and crank out a journal article. I prefer to view them more optimistically, as occasions for addressing matters that *should* be on a scholar's mind much of the time but that usually are not—precisely because we have available to us widely accepted methods for doing and writing up research. To be involved with clinical research methods, then, requires that one worry a lot about how to communicate one's findings to others. That is, in my view, a worthy use of a scholar's time.

Moving toward new kinds of theories. Using clinical methods to study organizational behavior involves much more than simply applying concepts and methods developed in traditional individual and group clinical work to organizational phenomena. Such concepts and methods generally do not sufficiently take account of contextual and structural factors. Indeed, they often center our attention on phenomena that may themselves be derivative (or even epiphenomenal) in organizational settings (e.g., on aspects of group interaction that are far more significant for self-analytic groups than for teams operating in social systems where there are tasks to be performed, clients to be served, bosses to manage, and organizational control systems to contend with).

Using clinical methods in organizational settings, then, invites us to conceptualize group and organizational phenomena in ways that address both (1) the unconscious and emotional dynamics that are prominent in the work of clinical psychologists, and (2) the contextual and structural factors that powerfully shape what happens in purposive social systems. Such conceptualizations surely would be richer than those favored either by orthodox clinical psychologists or by students of organizations who rely on traditional research methodologies—and they just might turn out to be more valid and useful as well. While it is hardly new to notice that the methods one uses affect what one chooses to study (as well as the kinds of interpretations and conclusions that emerge) it is important nonetheless—and it is one of the advantages of clinical methods for organizational research.

TRAPDOORS AND MINEFIELDS

Glibness. A number of people who claim to be clinical researchers have this talent, and it is one that I share. It worries me about them, and it worries me about me. How can we distinguish genuine clinical insight from mere personal impressions glibly presented? How can we protect ourselves, our students, and the participants in our research from findings dressed up in the language of clinical interpretation that are, in fact, little more than unsupportable speculations?

Particularly distressing to me are clinicians who arrive on the research scene (virtually any research scene) with a ready-made interpretive apparatus (for example, involving authority dynamics or "basic assumption" behavior) that they then tailor to fit whatever group or organizational situation they encounter. Worse, such devices can be used by a facile commentator in a way that defies rebuttal (e.g., by characterizing attempts at disconfirmation as evidence of defensive

resistance to accepting what is really going on and, therefore, as additional evidence for the validity of the interpretation).

It is *hard* to generate clinical interpretations of behavior in social systems that can be tested and disconfirmed with data, and too many researchers who don the clinical cloak are unwilling (or unable) to do the intellectual and methodological work required to protect themselves from the temptation to engage in glib, seamless interpretation.

The priesthood. To this outsider, the clinical establishment seems to have the quality of a priesthood: You are either in or out, and if you are in you have to accept the doctrine. While I acknowledge and accept the need to establish high standards of excellence for those who would use clinical methods (or any other research method, for that matter), I disagree with those who insist that using clinical methods requires one to accept a certain system of beliefs and values. I am also too old to be as respectful as perhaps I should be of the gatekeepers of clinical methodologies.

It should be clear from this chapter that I want to be an "associate member" of the priesthood—welcome at services, allowed to do a baptism now and then, encouraged to continue my studies, but free to be heretical and to practice other religions as well. That seems to me an altogether reasonable aspiration. Yet I also must acknowledge the possibility that my feelings about the matter (which, obviously, are strongly held) are simply one more sign of a deep-seated ambivalence about what I am studying—and the fact that in this arena I am a novitiate rather than a priest.

Failure. I am generally against it—particularly when it makes me look stupid, hurts others unintentionally, or results in research reports that are incorrect or misleading. Yet failure is an important component of learning—and learning is obviously something I am for. This dilemma can loom large for the student of clinical methods, because the stakes are high both for the learner and for the organization where the learning activities take place.

How can the essential opportunities for learning from failure be provided without either (1) placing ourselves or the social systems we are studying at greater-than-necessary risk, or (2) cutting the level of risk to the point where we neither fail *nor* learn? Teachers of clinical methods have thought hard about precisely this question and have come up with pedagogical devices that appear to chart a reasonable course between the horns of the dilemma. But it can be troublesome nonetheless when

one is just starting to learn clinical methods, particularly for those of us who have difficulty finding colleagues who are willing to teach us.

Risking the core scholarly values. I have little patience for people who make clinical interpretations of events and, when asked for the data and the logic of inference used to generate those interpretations, respond with a statement such as "If you know how to look you can see it." Such assertions (which I have heard far too often) combine the worst features of glibness and the priesthood, and I find them wholly at variance with the core values of scholarly work.

Whatever clinical methods I wind up using in my future research, I am reasonably certain that they will seek to promote (rather than dismiss) three core values: (1) trustworthy, verifiable data as the basis for interpretations and inferences; (2) means of assessing the meaning of those data that are accessible to other scholars; and (3) sound logic of inference in drawing conclusions from data.

Clinical methodologies greatly expand the kinds of data that are available for scholarly work, and may unearth hypotheses that otherwise would go unnoticed (including hypotheses that centrally involve the person of the data collector and his or her relationship to the data source). That is all to the good—but it is also insufficient. In my view, those of us who use clinical methods are obligated to subject our data and inferences to the same skeptical scrutiny we would apply to a layperson's interpretation of what is going on in a group or organization.

SUMMARY

This chapter has charted my halting and tentative attempts over the years to expand my repertoire of research tools by learning something about clinical methods for organizational research. Having summarized above my present assessment of certain benefits and risks associated with the use of those methods, let me close by posing a question that surely is on the minds of at least some readers: Why in the world would Hackman ever write an essay such as this?

It is a question I have asked myself more than once—particularly when I found myself putting events and feelings on paper that I would prefer to keep private, or when the account of my professional development bored even me. My answer has much less to do with any imagined virtue of self-disclosure than with the loneliness of learning clinical methods. Often, when feeling incompetent, rejected, or unsure

of just what it was I was doing, I also felt professionally alone. There were few people around who could help me make sense of what was happening, or to reflect with me on whether or not my explorations were worth the trouble.   ·

Ironically, the process of writing this chapter has provided such colleagueship in good measure—from the editors of the book especially, but also from others. That fact suggests that I could have obtained more support along the way if I had more actively sought it. Moreover, it highlights an unanticipated function the chapter has served: It has provided an occasion for reengaging with colleagues on both the clinical and social psychological sides of my professional life about what I have been doing and how they have been reacting to it. After writing a rough draft of the chapter and discussing it with the editors, I realized that I also had to show it to Joe McGrath and Clay Alderfer—because they are important actors in the events recounted here, certainly, but also because my attempts to learn clinical skills are entwined with and consequential for my relationships with them. In their reactions, both provided not only helpful substantive suggestions but also (and more important) personal reflections and challenges that reaffirmed their importance to my continuing development as a scholar.

So writing this essay has served more functions than I suspected it would when, a few months ago, I set my ambivalence temporarily aside and began to put words on paper. To the extent that some readers may be dealing with issues and feelings similar to those I have experienced, I hope they find an instant of recognition (and, perhaps, a bit of encouragement) in the words of someone who has been travelling a similar path.

NOTES

1. It never occurred to me at the time, despite my finding that task factors controlled considerable variation in group performance, that I might be looking in the wrong place—that the clues I was seeking might lie outside rather than within groups. Only much later, when I began observing groups operating in their natural organizational habitats, did I come to entertain this possibility.

2. What we did and what we learned are described in Torbert and Hackman, "Taking the Fun out of Outfoxing the System," in Runkel, Harrison, and Runkel, *The Changing College Classroom* (1969).

ANXIETY IN RESEARCH RELATIONSHIPS

David N. Berg

The methodological appendix has a long and illustrious history in social science field research. It is often the section of the report in which we learn the real story about the researcher's discoveries and how he or she felt during the months or years of field research. This appendix, often titled "Method," contains a rich description of the research procedures, the relationships formed with the people who participated in the study, and the dilemmas or problems faced by the researcher along the way. It is the story behind the story and, ironically, it can become the central feature of a research report (e.g., Dalton, 1959; Whyte, 1955) long after the findings have been updated.

The value of the appendix is in the insight it provides about the struggles—emotional and intellectual—that make up field research. The fact that these accounts and insights are often appended to the main text testifies to the belief that the information in the appendix is tangentially germane to the knowledge reported. Other evidence suggests that social scientists are not particularly interested in the role research relationships play in developing our understanding of social systems. A recent volume on organizational assessment, for example, included new articles on a variety of research methods, but adopted a fourteen-year-old article on the effects of research relationships on behavioral science knowledge (Lawler, Nadler, & Cammann, 1980). Yet the frequency with which authors feel compelled to include such appendixes and the interest with which we all read them suggest that the appended information plays an important role in how we understand the body of the text.

This chapter begins with the assumption that the information found in methodological appendixes is too important to be relegated to the

AUTHOR'S NOTE: I would like to thank David Morgan, Jeff McNally, Vicki Van Steenberg, Cortlandt Cammann, Leroy Wells and Richard Hackman for their helpful comments on an earlier draft of this chapter.

very end of a research report. In particular, the emotional as well as the intellectual consequences of research involvement need to be described and examined because of the influence they exert on the development of both theory and method (Devereux, 1967). For the participants, the emotions generated by research involvement include fear, mistrust, anxiety, apprehension, excitement, interest, dependency, and reactivity. Some of these emotions have been studied by social scientists in an effort to learn how to minimize their influence on the research process. Much less attention has been paid to the emotions generated within researchers as they conduct research. It is a startling omission (albeit with some notable exceptions) considering that once one has participated in field research it is impossible to overlook the powerful emotions stirred by the undertaking.

When a description of the emotional dynamics of the research relationship is missing from a research report, the reader is denied access to the researcher's perception of the emotional context in which the study was conducted. This is important information because no matter how hard researchers try to wall off their emotions—whether in the lab or in the field—they are rarely, if ever, successful. The absence of a description and analysis of these emotional dynamics in our research reports does nothing to diminish the effects of these emotions, it merely hides them from systematic scrutiny. A piece of the framework necessary to interpret the findings is lost.

When attention has been paid to the role of emotions in social research, interesting questions and dilemmas have been raised. Anthropologists have struggled with the effects of the researcher's ideology and culture on his or her fieldwork (e.g., Von Laue, 1975; Mead, 1973; Freeman, 1983). Fieldwork in ethnography has sought to define a role for the researcher that provides the ethnographer with a "native's" view of the culture while maintaining a certain reflective distance from that culture. The process of deepening emotional involvement happens gradually as the representatives of two cultures come to know each other. The question of interest to the social scientist is how and in what ways this emotional involvement influences the conduct of research (Devereux, 1967).

Research in the psychotherapeutic professions has also attended to this question—specifically, to the effects of the therapist's emotional relationship with the patient on his or her understanding of the patient's situation. The emotions involved in the therapeutic relationship may derive from unconscious personal, interpersonal, or cultural factors and often exert a powerful influence on the therapist's behavior. The example of countertransference in psychoanalysis (the analyst's reactions to the patient, which originate in the analyst's unconscious

reactions to relationships in early childhood) has not only identified this phenomenon, but also provided other social scientists with a strong rationale for attending to the effects of their own emotional involvement. This work has made the examination of these questions a domain of inquiry in its own right.

George Devereux, an anthropologist and a psychoanalyst, also explored in great detail the emotional consequences for the researcher of conducting behavioral science research. His example of a European anthropologist observing a castration ritual in a tribal setting makes poignantly clear the possible emotional influences on the collection, analysis, and interpretation of behavioral science data (1967). Devereux was particularly interested in the anxiety that was aroused in social research. One of his conclusions was that the development of research methods that specified a distant, uninvolved relationship between researcher and research participant was an unconscious attempt to defend the researcher against the anxiety aroused in behavioral science research.

Whether one agrees with Devereux or not (I confess I do) his work serves as a point of departure for this chapter. In it I will explore the role of anxiety in social research. The first section discusses possible sources of anxiety in the research process. The second examines two short cases to illustrate the influence of anxiety on field research. The final section addresses the implications of the previous two sections for social science research.

The focus of this chapter is anxiety. It is not the only emotion that attends social research and it may not be the most frequently experienced, but it is arguably the most troublesome and therefore the most rewarding for examination. Unlike some emotional reactions to research relationships, anxiety often provides its own veil—a veil that is neither transparent enough to allow easy access nor opaque enough to allow easy dismissal. We know, however vaguely, what is behind the veil. We know what it feels like. But most of us have only a clouded understanding of the role it plays in our research.

ANXIETY

An examination of the sources of anxiety in research relationships begins with a working understanding of the concept of anxiety in general. For an individual, May (1977) defines anxiety as "the apprehension cued off by a threat to some value that the individual holds is essential to his [or her] existence as a personality" (p. 180). In his discussion of anxiety May raises the following points:

(1) the diffuse and often vague sense of apprehension is associated with a threat to "core" patterns of security each individual develops;

(2) when the security base of an individual is threatened, and since it is in terms of this security base that the individual experiences himself or herself in relation to other objects, the distinction between subject and object breaks down;

(3) the reaction to the threat is disproportionate to the objective danger because some internal conflict is involved (i.e., it is the subjective experience of threat that determines the level of anxiety);

(4) repression, or the unconscious removal of the source of threat from conscious awareness is a central feature of subjective or neurotic anxiety;

(5) the capacity for anxiety is not learned, but the quantities and forms of anxiety in a given individual are;

(6) fear, as distinguished from anxiety, is a differentiated emotional reaction to a specific, "objective" danger that is external to the individual (pp. 180-199).

He concludes with a statement about threats to a culture that exacerbate the anxiety experienced by individuals: "The[se] threats . . . are not threats which can be met on the basis of the assumptions of the culture but rather are threats to those underlying assumptions themselves." (p. 212) If we substitute "group" for "culture" May has provided us with a definition of group-level anxiety which is consistent with other work in group dynamics (Bion, 1961). This group-level anxiety adds to the anxiety experienced by individuals.

What then are the sources of anxiety in research relationships and what individual values or group-level assumptions might be threatened by research involvement? The following discussion is based on the view that research relationships have the potential to arouse some degree of anxiety because the relationship is felt to be the source of threat in three areas: personal, professional, and group-level. Personal anxiety is aroused by threats to the individual's psychological identity—that is, by threats to the way he or she responds to the surrounding world. Professional anxiety is aroused when the researcher feels there is a threat to the research itself. Group-level anxiety is aroused in the special case where research is done by a team and threat is experienced as a result of the emotional dynamics of groups. These three areas are not independent since one could argue, at a minimum, that personal anxiety will influence both professional and group-level anxiety, but it is also true that each of the three makes a unique contribution to the anxiety experienced in social research. For that reason we will examine each separately.

Personal anxiety. There are a number of sources of personal anxiety in research relationships. First, unlike research in the physical sciences, the study of human behavior involves researchers in self-study. Whether or not the social scientist is motivated to study human behavior in order to gain some measure of self-awareness (as some have argued), the act of studying human behavior has an element of self-analysis. The social scientist often confronts the difficult task of self-scrutiny without conscious awareness or choice. Anxiety may surface because the research relationship "forces" the researcher to confront personal weaknesses, unconscious conflicts, or current struggles in the development of his or her identity (Balmary, 1979; Devereux, 1967).

This anxiety is like that of the painter who undertakes a self-portrait and finds that it is much more difficult than painting the portrait of someone else. The artist is simultaneously painting an image and his or her relationship to that image. In the case of a self-portrait the work involves "staring into" the artist's relationship to him- or herself. Whatever anxiety is inside the artist is now made a part of the work process. In addition, self-analysis always brings with it the threat that the "patterns of security" developed to protect an individual's identity will themselves be questioned.

Second, as with any relationship, research relationships include transference and countertransference reactions. Since most field research involves complex authority relations (e.g., inside the research team, between the research team and numerous levels of the system being studied) it provides fertile ground for unconscious reenactments of parental and familial conflicts. Since transference reactions are unconscious, the anxiety that attends them is not easily traced to its source and may be misattributed to other events in the research relationship.

A third source of anxiety comes from the group identities the researcher brings to every research relationship. Each of us is not an anonymous scientist in the relationship with research participants. We also carry with us a variety of group memberships that contribute to our identity: race, gender, age, ethnicity, and social class (Alderfer, 1977). These group memberships can be a source of anxiety in two ways: (1) The groups to which the researcher and the research participant belong may have a history of conflict, hostility, or suspicion that may, in turn, affect the level of anxiety for one or both. The uncertainty surrounding these intergroup relations and the unspoken norms that make it difficult to discuss the effects of intergroup history on interpersonal relations heighten this anxiety. (2) The salience of a particular group membership (e.g., ethnicity) in a research relationship may raise unresolved

issues in the researcher's own identity (e.g., whether, or how much, to identify with an ethnic tradition) that may cause anxiety (McGoldrick, Pearce, & Giordano, 1982; Babad, Birnbaum, & Benne, 1983).

It is possible to consider these three areas as representing anxiety that springs from our present, our individual histories, and our collective histories. For each of us, these anxieties are different but are evoked by the relationship with individuals, groups, and organizations who participate in the research.

Professional anxiety. Doing research with human systems also brings with it different kinds of professional anxiety. In the course of a research project researchers may face situations that question their professional abilities or competencies as well as the assumptions underlying the research itself. To the extent that research is an important part of the researcher's identity, this anxiety can be strong. A few sources of professional anxiety are discussed below.

Multiple responsibilities—especially responsibilities to the participating social system—can cause anxiety. No longer do researchers' actions influence only their findings, publications, or careers. Research conducted with the active participation of a social system necessarily involves the needs and objectives of that system and obligates the researcher to consider these in the course of the research. The researcher's actions can and do affect individuals and organizations. When information is fed back or discussed with an organization, for example, the possible consequences carry with them a significant responsibility. This responsibility may overlap with other professional or scientific responsibilities (e.g., measurement standards, confidentiality) but it may also involve decisions not covered in professional manuals (Mirvis & Seashore, 1979). The increased uncertainty and the risk of failure caused by multiple responsibilities can be potent sources of anxiety.

Control is another source of anxiety in field research. Field settings increase the complexity of the scientific tasks. There are more uncertainties, more potentially relevant factors for explaining events, and more activities outside the control of the researcher. In addition, researchers often share what control they have in order to design a project that is useful for the participating social system. The objective in moving from the laboratory to the field is to gain insight into human behavior in nonlaboratory settings. Yet research methods transferred from the lab often work at cross purposes to this objective, urging the researcher to assert quasi-experimental control so that the influence of specific variables can be isolated and cause-and-effect relationships

inferred. The researcher in the field may struggle to retain control in the belief that this is the only way to produce and publish scientific research. As the researcher's control seems to slip away, so it seems does his or her opportunity for theory building that is predicated on control. The attendant anxiety is especially troublesome since it involves the individual researcher's relationship to social science as a profession.

Research with social systems invariably involves a relationship with an existing authority structure. A research "contract" is often drawn up between the researcher and representatives of one or more authority structures (e.g., labor and management; paid and volunteer staff; physicians and patients). In these situations the values, expectations, and desires of the social system's authority structure must be examined, understood, discussed, and reconciled (if possible) with the values of the research project. There always exists the possibility that misunderstanding or differences can lead the authority structure to undermine the research activities. It is also possible that the researcher will need to confront the authority structure with unpleasant or unwanted information. The fact that research projects often originate near the top of the authority structure means that researchers inevitably attract the prevailing attitudes toward those with authority. Since these processes are ongoing over the life of the project as new dilemmas and decisions are faced, managing the relationship with the authority structure can be a source of anxiety.

A researcher's professional investment in a project can also be a source of anxiety when combined with uncertainty, multiple responsibilities, and shared control. Consider a young assistant professor on the verge of producing his or her first major theoretical contribution who is one year away from a tenure review. Under these conditions a great deal more anxiety may attend every unexpected event in an important research project. In fact, the position of the researcher may actually imbue a research relationship with the career anxiety he or she is experiencing. It is misleading to assume that because researchers are scientists they are not human beings. Research is an activity embedded in a profession. Most of us earn our living or part of it doing research. As a result, all of the anxieties associated with earning a living (e.g., advancement, security, recognition) are also part of the research process. Uncertainty in our research relationships can threaten not only our research but our lives as well.

A final source of professional anxiety has been suggested by the work of Jaques (1955) and Becker (1973). Both of these authors argue that social institutions (organizations, rituals, traditions) are the means by which individuals and groups defend themselves against certain forms

of anxiety. In Jaques's (1955) view, social systems play a role in defending the individual from paranoid and depressive anxiety; in Becker's (1973) view, culture in general is a collective way of managing the anxiety associated with death. If it is true that social systems have a role in defending their members against anxiety, then researchers who seek to understand these social systems may be treading on very sensitive ground. The process of looking into a social system (the thoughts and feelings of its members, their frustrations and satisfactions, the meaning of their participation) may increase the anxiety experienced by the participants, which in turn may increase the anxiety experienced by the researchers.

Group-level anxiety. Teams or research groups raise the possibility of a third type of anxiety in social research. Strictly speaking, most of these anxieties stem from the tensions any team encounters as it struggles to become an effective group (Bion, 1961; Bennis & Shepard, 1956; Smith & Berg, 1984) and would occur during any kind of research. These sources of anxiety include (1) *individual differences*—the anxiety that arises from the exploration of individual strengths and weaknesses; (2) *trust*—the anxiety associated with learning to trust others while protecting oneself from exploitation; (3) *conflict*—the anxiety derived from the fear that conflict will destroy the group, no matter how strong the espoused belief that conflict is necessary for group development; and (4) *leadership and authority*—the anxiety born of the emotions surrounding both leading and following, fears of being misled, or fears that whatever authority structure is adopted will become tyrannical.

These are only examples of the anxieties that accompany the development of a group. A research team that works with a living system can develop additional sources of anxiety rooted in its relationship to the social system it studies. As the research team develops its own group identity there is inevitably some degree of ethnocentrism with respect to other groups (e.g., the site organization). This ethnocentrism can cause the research team to project its own internal hostility and anxiety onto the site organization, subsequently experiencing this organization as a source of threat and anxiety. And while it is possible that research teams meet with hostile or mistrustful reactions from research participants, it is also likely that these reactions are exaggerated by the ethnocentric tendencies of the team itself.

The use of a research group also carries with it the possibility of mirroring or parallel processes in its relationships with other groups involved in the research (Alderfer et al., in press; Ekstein & Wallerstein, 1958; Berg, 1980). Parallel process (described in the opening chapter of

this volume) refers to the tendency of living systems in a relationship to develop internal, emotional dynamics that parallel each other. As a result, research teams may experience whatever anxiety exists in the participating system, often mistaking this anxiety for their own. In this case the research team's anxiety can be used to develop hypotheses for understanding the dynamics of the research site.

CASES AND CONSEQUENCES

We have examined anxiety as an example of powerful and complex emotions that can be engendered by a researcher's involvement with a social system. But of what consequence are these emotional effects? Do the emotional dynamics of a research relationship create different data? Would we be justified in interpreting "findings" differently if we knew the emotional characteristics of the relationship that spawned the findings? It is to these questions that I now turn. In the following two cases, anxiety stemmed from specific characteristics of the research relationship and in each case the effects of the anxiety were analyzed as part of a postmortem on the events described.

Case 1. I (white, male researcher) approached a predominantly female public relations firm with a proposal to study the influence of ideology (feminist) on organization. I was interested in learning how an organization committed to an "alternative" structure and value system differed (if at all) from a traditional hierarchical organization in the way it handled a range of issues common to organizational life, (e.g., accountability, decision making, control, evaluation). After some discussion to which I was not privy, the president reported that the study could proceed but that the firm was very busy and could not devote a great deal of time to the project. I planned an entry phase designed to acquaint members of the organization with the purposes and activities of the study. At the conclusion of this phase it was my intention to draft a "contract" between myself and the organization describing the expectations and responsibilities of everyone involved. The study was to be totally voluntary, but a minimum level of participation was necessary for the study to have any validity.

After some initial, short interviews with a cross-section of organization members, I became aware of a number of tensions between various groups in the firm: feminists and nonfeminists; upstairs (clerical) and downstairs (professional); black and white. Initially I succeeded in recruiting representation from each group for a liaison system (Alderfer,

1980a) to help manage the research, but soon a number of people (feminist, upstairs, black) began to withdraw. In spite of this I continued to plan the project, concentrating on those people who remained interested. I solicited reactions to my ideas and drafted the contract. Finally I distributed the draft contract to everyone in the firm and invited them to see me or call me at an office set aside for this purpose. No one called or came by.

This unmistakable expression of a lack of interest and involvement was very disturbing. I called a colleague and asked for help in analyzing the situation. That discussion and subsequent reflections on the evolution of the project led me to some conclusions about my own actions during the entry phase.

(1) Lack of involvement in the project had been characteristic of the firm's reaction to the study from the beginning. I *knew* that this lack of involvement needed to be examined during the entry phase if there was to be a successful project since the richness of the case study would depend upon the firm's willingness to become active partners in the research. But I feared that the lack of involvement might also mean that if the project became at all troublesome, the firm would simply terminate the research. Without realizing it, my anxiety about the project's possible termination led me to avoid any actions that might produce disagreements or conflict in the firm. One of the issues avoided was the apparent lack of interest in the study.

(2) The tensions between internal subgroups in the firm became increasingly important during the entry phase. I *knew* that the project was becoming enmeshed in the existing intergroup conflicts—if one group was in favor of it, the other group was not. The conflicts in the firm about ideology, work delegation, and treatment of minorities began to play themselves out around the question of the study. I felt some responsibility for stirring up this conflict, especially in an organization that took pride in its solidarity and struggled to survive in a business environment that was hostile to the firm's avowed ideological goals. In spite of the fact that these conflicts threatened to engulf the project, my anxiety moved me *away* from discussing these issues with the firm's staff. The anxiety about being responsible for igniting these issues combined with the fear that any disruption would terminate the project caused me actively, albeit unconsciously, to avoid these issues and their potential influences on the study.

(3) When first contacting the organization, I was concerned about the implications for the research of a male researcher doing a study with an almost all-female firm. I realized that the absence of a woman on the research team would seriously affect the data collection and analysis, but hoped that an internal liaison group might address this problem.

When, at an introductory meeting, no mention was made of this issue except in a joke ("Can he type?"), I assumed that the firm had decided that sexual dynamics were not an issue. Upon reflection I began to understand my quick acceptance of this explanation.

It seemed that sexual dynamics were important in two ways. First, my identity had been influential in the firm's decision to go ahead with the study. (I learned about this when papers of mine that had been circulated during the entry phase were returned to me along with a "comments" sheet.) Because I was male, the firm reasoned, my research results (assumed to be laudatory about the firm) would be more acceptable to the larger, male-controlled society. In this way, I was treated as a representative of men who could communicate with his own group in ways that women could not. The decision to allow the study was based partly on the belief that the researcher, *by virtue of his male identity*, could be used to influence men. My anxiety about the intergroup aspects of a male researcher working in a female organization led me to accept the belief that gender would have no effect on the project. From the beginning I had been curious about the apparent lack of attention to gender issues and I suspected there were concerns not being expressed, but I decided not to push it. What would I do if a number of women in the firm resented my presence? What if some of the women did not like me? The anxiety raised by these questions led me away from the topic and from any actions that would have raised the issue of sexual politics.

The second influence of sexual dynamics was more personal. Only upon reflection did I realize the role of sexuality in the project. My attraction to some of the women in the firm and my desire to be liked by them seemed so unprofessional and engendered so much anxiety that I could not admit or examine these feelings. I subsequently discovered that these feelings influenced my choice of whom to interview, which in turn influenced my perception of the firm. Although the influence was subtle, with hindsight it is clear. The topic was so fraught with anxiety that I was totally unaware of most of the sexual aspects of the project until over a year after its conclusion.

The project ended when I decided that the divisiveness in the firm threatened the participation rate in the study. It was almost certain that a significant number of people would refuse to participate and the validity of the diagnostic goals of the study would be seriously undermined. The research relationship was terminated.

Case 2. Two black men and three white women chose to work together on an organizational diagnosis (Alderfer, 1980a) with a nonprofit service organization (NSO). The five-person team was part of

a graduate-level course and the team members were students. The purpose of the course was to learn about the theory and practice of organizational diagnosis and to provide interested organizations with some help in understanding their problems and their potential. NSO was a predominantly black organization that served a predominantly black constituency although, like most organizations of its kind, it was embedded in a white community. The executive director asked the class instructor if a student team could come to explore the possibility of a diagnostic project.

In a class of twenty-two students only three were members of a minority group and two of them chose to be on the NSO team. This was noticed and discussed in class. Both black members of the NSO team said they felt some pressure from the class to join the NSO team since an all-white team could not do a diagnosis in an all-black organization. Each had chosen the NSO project for personal reasons, but both felt this pressure and expressed it to the class. The discussion was a difficult one for the class, and the process whereby the project teams were chosen was not extensively examined.

The team sent one black man and one white woman to the initial meeting with the executive director, a black, female Ph.D. in psychology, to discuss the possibility of a project. The students reported that the meeting was an uncomfortable one. The executive director, not the team members, controlled the meeting and asked a lot of questions. In particular, she had asked the team about how they were handling the topic of race relations in their team. She also asked how the team was handling male-female relations and pointed out that the combination of black men and white women had historical meaning in the black community and might affect the diagnostic team's relations with NSO. The executive director was also clear that she thought it was absolutely crucial for white students to be involved since NSO existed in a white world, depended on that world for support, and had to manage its relationships with that outside world as did any other nonprofit organization. The students came away from the meeting feeling that they had been on the defensive most of the time.

In reviewing the meeting, the entire team became increasingly alarmed at what they perceived to be their loss of control of the entry meeting. The agenda they had prepared had quickly dissolved and the students who had met with the executive director felt they had been unprepared for the discussion that she had initiated. At one point the team members who had *not* been present at the meeting blamed their representatives for losing control. At the end of the review meeting the entire team was wondering if they could handle the power and obvious competence of the executive director.

A few days later the team met with the instructor of the course to discuss a draft of the "contract" between the diagnostic team and NSO. The students had drafted the contract. The instructor was struck by the formal, legalistic style and language of the draft. It began: "The diagnostic team, hereafter designated 'Team' agrees to . . . " and proceeded to outline the rights and obligations of the parties involved. The aims and goals of the diagnosis were obscured by the language and the impression left by the document was one of mutual mistrust. As the instructor read the words back to the team members, they began to discuss the emotional aspects of their relationship with NSO and its effects on them.

(1) The initial meeting with the executive director had shaken the entire team. They had entered the meeting feeling in control and believing that they should control the entire project since the diagnostic expertise rested with them. The loss of control during the meeting caused anxiety about the whole project. One reason for the formal, controlling contract language was to reassert the team's control. The team realized it had been unprepared to share influence with the executive director. When she asserted her willingness to take control, the team feared that the project might be taken away from them.

(2) The initial meeting also created anxiety about race and gender relations. The team had not confronted these issues among its members during its formation meetings—perhaps because it felt a necessity to present a united front to the rest of the class—but the meeting with the executive director made it much harder to avoid the racial and sexual dynamics inside the team. This very difficult and anxiety-producing set of issues, coming as it did in the early stages of the team's development, threatened the group's cohesiveness. Although the team discussed race (individual feelings and experiences), in a way it seemed that the team's survival as a *work* group depended on not probing too deeply into the topic of racism because this might uncover feelings that could not be managed easily. The executive director had identified precisely those issues that had the greatest potential for fragmenting the team (and thereby jeopardizing the project and the course). In part, the team's reaction provided the group with an external "threat" that helped build the team's cohesiveness.

(3) Finally, the experience with the executive director caused the team a great deal of anxiety about its competence. Team members voiced concerns about their skill in managing unpredictable, emotional situations. The "contract" they had drafted attempted to specify the behavior of both parties in a variety of possible circumstances in order to reduce the likelihood that the team would have to struggle with unforeseen issues and the trust, or lack thereof, in their relationships

with each other. It was the instructor's belief that the draft contract would have decreased the chances that the project would proceed, perhaps unconsciously saving the team from an experience that might have forced them to struggle with the issues of competence and race.

Eventually the team rewrote the contract and conducted a diagnosis with NSO that was praised by the executive director for its accuracy and thoughtfulness. Throughout the project the team did struggle with its own process, racism, sexuality, and scapegoating—topics that, according to team members, never seemed to be "worked through" satisfactorily.

Reflections. It would be a mistake to label these two cases "bad" field research or the work of neophyte researchers. It is possible that these examples are oversimplified in the service of illustration, but the theme presented in both cases is an important one. In each case, anxieties arising from the research relationship influenced the researchers' behavior. It is difficult to assess how these experiences influenced the researchers' understanding of human behavior, but there can be no doubt that this was the case. We can be sure that there would be differences in the theories that might have evolved had the researchers' reactions been different or been managed differently. Although it is tempting to try to evaluate which reactions are "right" and which are "wrong," the unavoidable descriptive statement is that our understanding of human behavior is embedded in a particular relationship with the human systems in which the research is conducted.

IMPLICATIONS

The implication of this discussion is that the emotional dynamics in research relationships are an important variable in the social science research process. They are not merely sources of bias or reactivity, but rather the context in which research happens, influencing both the process and the outcome. This suggests that the field needs to pay more attention to this variable.

Specifically, we should begin to *examine* more closely the effects of research relationships on researchers. Just as the examination of countertransference is an integral part of psychoanalytic practice, the examination of the researcher's reactions to the research relationship should be an integral part of field research. We need to struggle to identify the ways in which we choose methods, topics, and activities that help us to defend ourselves against the feelings generated by research in and about human systems. Perhaps most important, we need to

entertain the hypothesis that these feelings are an inevitable part of social science research—especially when we use ourselves as the research instrument. Our understanding of human behavior will be very different if we merely "cope" with our reactions instead of examining them and attempting to learn about ourselves and about human behavior through this examination.

If we are to examine the research relationship we must *train* applied behavioral scientists to be able to face and to struggle with the difficult personal, professional, and group issues that arise in research. This kind of training requires supervised experience in the exploration of unconscious processes at the individual and group levels. As this chapter suggests, the struggle to understand the role of anxiety in one's research involves both self-examination and the examination of relationships in which the researcher is involved. We must learn to design our research based on an awareness of the inevitable presence of anxiety in our work rather than on the wish that it could be eliminated. We must be willing to examine our involvement in our profession, including our satisfactions and frustrations and the role professional achievement plays in our lives at various stages of the life cycle. If we conduct ourselves and our research in flight from the anxiety that is part of our work, we will produce knowledge that is an artifact of this response.

Perhaps even more important, we must strive to develop researchers who are able to use the experience of anxiety to guide and enhance their understanding of social systems. Most often, the emotions generated by research relationships are not merely the expression of an individual researcher's personal history. Instead, they are the product of a specific human being engaged with others in the study of social systems. These emotions can be a window into the researcher's internal dynamics, but they can also broaden his or her understanding of the social world by providing additional kinds of data from which to construct hypotheses and, in some cases, by providing different kinds of hypotheses. Anxiety in particular, because of its roots in the unconscious experience of threat, may alert us to some of the more powerful forces affecting the social system we study and our work with it.

Training also raises the issue of supervision. I do not believe we are currently training researchers to make the examination of difficult emotions part of their research work. If we believe such an examination is important and useful for the development of meaningful theories about human behavior, then our desire to provide training in this area may outstrip our ability to do so. We, the generation responsible for the training of future social scientists, may find it necessary to train ourselves first. We may have to learn to learn from each other in ways

that are neither familiar nor comfortable and we may find it necessary to look outside our particular disciplines for the supervision and guidance we need.

Finally, it is important that we begin to *report and describe* the emotional dynamics in the research relationship when we publish our findings and our theories. Just as scientific standards urge us to publish our F-tables so that readers can check our data or draw their own conclusions from our presentations, it is important that we report the relationship context and not bury it in a footnote or an appendix. Especially because we are usually so close to this particular variable, we should require ourselves to examine it and describe it so that others might observe its possible effects. Only by reporting these relationship variables can we begin to develop theories about the effects of certain kinds of research relationships on the research process.

CONCLUSION

Every theory that emerges from field research has been constructed in the context of a research relationship. Often we do not know as much about this relationship as we do about the "findings" that grow out of it. Sometimes knowledge of the characteristics of this relationship would powerfully influence our understanding and critical evaluation of a theory. Sometimes the influence would be trivial. To know more about these relationships we must make a commitment to examine, describe, and report them in our work. This commitment would further add to the complexity of social science research, making it a personally taxing endeavor far beyond mere hard work and intellect. It could be argued that the relatively minor role given to the study of research relationships is designed to spare us this pain.

SELF-FULL RESEARCH:
Working Through the Self as Instrument
in Organizational Research

Philip H. Mirvis and Meryl Reis Louis

This chapter recounts conversations between the authors to illustrate how the self enters into the research process, where and why, and even when it should; hence the title "Self-Full Research." It considers the study of a corporate acquisition and focuses on Mirvis's work as an "instrument" in the research. For the past eight years, I (Mirvis) have been studying the impact of the acquisition of DC, a 1000-person manufacturing firm, by a conglomerate called GrandCo. Meryl Louis has studied how newcomers bring their needs, values, family histories, and interpretive frameworks to the task of making sense of a culture new to them (Louis, 1980). We talked over this study of DC, and my needs, values, family system, and sense of things, in search of ways that my self, and therefore other selves, can influence organizational research.

Meryl and I first talked about DC and me. The case study concerned a "white knight" acquisition: DC had been the target of an "unfriendly" takeover bid by an unwanted, some said unscrupulous, buyer. GrandCo had saved DC by outbidding this firm and securing majority ownership of DC's stock. It had become DC's new "parent" company. I felt the impact most immediately and fully through my relationship to DC's chief executive. Lester Richardson, DC's head and son of its founder, was called a "wounded leader" following the acquisition. He had fought to keep DC independent but had failed and been forced to turn to GrandCo. He was depressed after the sale. His wife reported that he did not want to face work, that he could not rid himself of his disappoint-

AUTHORS' NOTE: We would like to thank Joan Sieber and the editors for their assistance with this chapter.

ment and pain. My mother had once said this about my dad. My father, a business executive, lost his job in a corporate acquisition in the early 1970s. He, too, became depressed. He died a short time later—unemployed.

So Meryl and I talked about families and growing up. I still see myself as a child of the sixties, then at the fringe of the antiwar movement, at the core today, continuing to question the place of politics, business, war, and injustice in the society and in my own life. GrandCo had come to the rescue of DC. It was also big business and, in DCers' eyes, full of aristocrats who expected people to knuckle under, bureaucrats who expected people to follow their rules, and politicians who knew how to get people to play the game their way. In my story of the acquisition, these characterizations served to focus observations and interpretations. GrandCo became a symbol; and DCers took on personae based upon the way they related to GrandCo, its bigness, its values, its badness.

Our talk came back to concepts. My initial conceptions of myself in the research focused on the inner me, neglecting other facets of my self, as well as the research participants, the family system in DC, indeed the context in which they and I lived and worked. Conversation led to the realization that my self and their selves together shaped the research. "Sounds like transference and countertransference," said my clinically minded self, "or boundary relations." We laughed at this. I added, "In this paper I want to communicate my own selfness as a kind of affirmation of personhood or of universal self-fullness. That sounds trite. But I am fearful that in communications about who I am, what truths I find, how I get screwed up . . . I will only introduce a bunch of concepts." Meryl replied, "I have less concern. Your selves, their selves, make up multiple stories. We'll tether concepts to experience."

SELF AS INSTRUMENT

"Have you seen the movie *Silkwood*?" Meryl recalled an image of the lead actress putting her arms through a glass and into long, thick, rubber gloves while handling radioactive material. The material could be seen, even touched with rubber gloves, but as the hands became an instrument, they were demonstrably and intendedly separate from the material in their grasp. What was the reason for this? Clearly, to protect a self from radiation. Did this not also protect the material from contamination? We then conjured the material, aware of the separations and protections, winking at a handler. Suppose instrument is persona: Would it do to study responses to a thick, rubber glove?

I related a story Charles Perrow had told me of how merchants in the Middle Ages had turned "souls" into "hands." The Christians of that time had many holidays and worked in cottage industries. The merchants, seeking greater output for trade, organized them into factories and gradually eliminated most of the religious holidays. "Hands reach, grasp, mold, form," said I. "I see souls with wings, more ethereal, not really a body part, or else maybe in the form of a heart." Meryl countered that the self lives in many realms. There is the self as the secular, pragmatic actor in life space. Then there is the more spiritual self, maybe—in deference to me—with wings.

After the meeting, Meryl prepared some notes that began:

> Phil . . . Help. What are we arguing? Try this: It has been widely assumed that the researcher should "stay out of the way," bracket his or her self aside with a narrowly circumscribed research/scientist role.

> We are (are we?) arguing, however, that: (1) This *does not* happen and we are going to highlight ways and places that the self sneaks into inquiry, wanted or not; (2) Further, it *should not* happen (this total bracketing of the self) for "good" research occurs when the self is there in more than a narrowly defined role; "good" research comes about from managing the way the self enters in, beyond the research role.

> So we hope to show (don't we?) that it is neither possible nor desirable to screen out the self; but you gotta pay attention to how and when the self shows up.

Neither of us subscribes to notions of value-free science. Many have shown how personal and societal values are deeply embedded in what researchers study, how they study it, what conclusions are drawn, how their work is used. Nor can we accept the idea of self-less research. To do so is to accept mechanization of the research, alienation in research relations, and ultimately the absence of identity for the researcher. This simply does not match our research experience.

The self is, of course, bracketed in research. The case study here involves research in an organization by a university-based researcher. That establishes a context that defines the research. The study was to focus on the impact of the acquisition on DC executives, the workforce, and, more broadly, the DC culture. Its purposes were for scholarly research and to contribute to DC's learning. My self, therefore, would be put into focused and purposeful research and action roles. Such role definitions narrow and channel the ways that the self enters into the research effort. Futhermore, I was an outsider to DC. People were eager to tell their story of the acquisition, but also protective of their privacy and unsure how the information would be used by the organization.

Such defensiveness constrains self-expression in research relations (Argyris, 1952).

Mirvis and Seashore (1979) use concepts of roles and role systems to explicate research relations and call upon researchers to work jointly with research participants in negotiating and implementing research roles. This was accomplished in the initial contracting meeting for the acquisition study. I also sought to work openly with DCers to examine personal values, purposes, thoughts, and feelings as these are expressed in the research effort (Mirvis, 1982). That much is essential for researchers who make use of clinical research methods (Berg, 1980). These prescriptions loosen brackets on the research/scientist role and the role of research participants. They free people to be more effective as "secular, pragmatic actors in life space." Our concern here, however, is with the nonconscious, historic, symbolic, even universalistic brackets that, much as rubber gloves, protect the self but also intrude on the research process, interpretations, and recommendations. Our concern is with developing an awareness of those parts of the self and the need to examine openly, and tighten or loosen, their bracket in the conduct of self-full research.

The canons of clinical methodology can be a bane or boon to self-full research. Through the method itself, the self experiences past, present, and future, the good and bad, the essential and nonessential. Self experiences itself and the experience can be "irradiating." The canons prescribe that researchers objectify themselves, as in the classical bracketing of clinical therapy. This can provide an informative diagnostic data base about behavior in organizations (Alderfer, 1968), but it excludes some significant insights into organizational dynamics by keeping the researcher, figuratively, behind the glass (Mirvis, 1980). The alternative is to subjectify the self, and thus intensify and personalize experience, but that risks contamination (Evered & Louis, 1981). The self as instrument must be both subject and object, clinician and in the clinic, to meet the demands of self-full clinical research. The gloves must be removed; the handler must wink back. This requires introspection, reflection, self-awareness and mutuality, empathy, the capacity to share. The stories of the acquisition, of DC, and of me reflect my efforts, in the course of everyday fieldwork, to put myself clinically into research. Conversations with Meryl took place on holidays. They are our sharing of souls.

RICHARDSON

I first met Richardson when I was a student at an American Management Association seminar for college students. I was searching

for career direction in my life and attended the seminar to learn more about business. This was a difficult time in my life as I was in a stage of rebellion anchored in maturation but focused on the outside world of Vietnam, capitalism, the military-industrial complex. The dreaming, achieving, powerful side of me envisioned and embraced social change. The vehicle, I reasoned, could be the work organization if only more participative, democratic, humane practices could be introduced and sustained. "Not that this would end the war," I told Meryl, "but that it was a place to begin and one where I could assume a place."

That Richardson was a father figure for me was not in my conscious awareness at that seminar. I was in a rough relationship with my father at that time as he had become the embodiment of some of the evils I saw in the world. Still, his ways and values and warmth also led me to want to understand more of the business world to see what it might hold for me. Richardson was an image of possibility. He was an advocate of humanistic business values and linked them with participation, delegation, and group effort in his stewardship of DC. He described his management philosophy and DC's practices in the language of behavioral science. After the seminar he urged me to learn more about behavioral science at Yale and to come and visit him at DC some day.

My father died later that year. Several years later, as a graduate student, I began a study of work life in DC. Richardson was the sponsor of the study and saw it as an extension of his philosophy and the DC way. The study took on added dimension following DC's acquisition. It was agreed that a chronicle of the acquisition, based upon clinical interviews with key executives, analyses of memoranda, and careful listening to tapes of key acquisition-related meetings, could help DC to learn from its experiences. I did some background research and then met with Richardson. There my identification with this father figure hit me.

Richardson was the wounded leader at that time and I had heard from others of his depression and withdrawal following the sale to GrandCo. I asked him first about his current career situation. He clarified that things were status quo—he hoped to become a group vice-president in GrandCo but it looked as though he would have to report to a GrandCo official named Schmidt, a man he neither liked nor respected. I then asked if he had any contingency plans and he stated, "In my view, my career planning is off the subject" and cautioned me against taking any "sidepaths." The interview became contentious. I was accused of asking many "loaded questions." My experience was of playing "gotcha games" with my father as we discussed politics, business, and values in that stormy time of my life.

Out of the blue I told Richardson about my father, his firing after an acquisition, his death, all with my voice cracking, tears in my eyes.

Richardson, arms folded in his lap, head bowed, just nodded. A month earlier, in negotiations about the study, Richardson had warned me that careers could be at risk in this study of the acquisition. I sensed his wounds during the interview and felt that more than a career might be at stake.

In my briefing of top DC executives following the first round of data gathering, I focused on the death-and-dying imagery many had used to describe reactions to the sale. There were the denial and anger they had expressed at a key in-house meeting and the lingering tensions over who was to blame for the failure to prevent the sale. We talked openly about Richardson's culpability and all agreed that his guilt was baseless for it was impossible to stop a "speeding truck." There was a strong consensus that Richardson's wounding had left managers uncertain of his career plans. This uncertainty—never discussed between Richardson and top managers—was proving to be a drain on their energies. It was agreed that in the next months Richardson would have to get on with his career planning and DCers with their own.

THE SELF SYSTEM

I followed Richardson's advice after the management seminar and explored the behavioral sciences at Yale. My first professor was Richard Hackman and he turned me on to McGregor, Likert, finally Argyris. Richardson knew of all their works and had worked with Argyris in crafting the management system at DC. The behavioral science courses I took, including a T-group and a seminar on Freudian psychology, provided an inspiration. Now, I went back to reread the papers I had kept to look at myself from that period.

One of the papers addressed boundary relations.

The logic of my paper followed the lines of object relations theory and addressed libidinous tensions arising from fears of abandonment. My tendency had been to intellectualize relationships with the T-group leader and hold on through attention-gaining comments and insights. In this study of DC, I recognized my intellectual bonds to Richardson, which we had talked about in negotiating the study. Part of my role was to offer a distinct perspective on the impact of the acquisition—one that Richardson did not see or could not grasp. My insight was that Richardson's wounding was a source of anxiety for all DC executives and clouded their relations with him. That insight seemed to match the experience of DCers and stimulated career planning in DC.

The other paper covered identification with my father. Periodic cuts to the finger are sufficient data for this male to accept the ubiquity of

castration anxiety. I had studied internalization of my father's moral values and masculine role. The paper covered what was accepted and what was rejected—from my vantage in college days. My link to my dad had brought me to the management seminar where I met Richardson. Resolution of conflicts with my dad was, sadly, cut short by his death. With Richardson I could grow to full manhood. I hoped to work with him and learn with him in this study of DC.

My identification with Richardson and the transference of love focused on his masculinity, his values, his intellect, his fatherliness. His wounding was akin to the wounding of my father. I did not want to lose him either. My researchings helped to unearth the tensions that his career uncertainties were creating in DC. At the briefing meeting several began to talk about his leaving and how DC would get along without him. Richardson went to the window. I stated, "Don't throw him out," then sheepishly mumbled something about the need to think through executive transitions, to let Richardson make up his own mind.

The coincidence of Richardson's life story and of my own father's makes the intensity of the identification with a research participant in this instance unusual. "But wasn't it Richardson who brought you into DC's world?" It was, and that alone augurs for some mutual identification among the research self and the other selves in the organization. Meryl noted, too, the potential for countertransference. Indeed, Richardson had treated me like a son, a good son at that. It is understandable that a young man would link his soul to a competent, mature male. And Richardson was half-Jewish. I am half-Jewish too—on my father's side. The tapes of our conversations show that I said that Richardson's mother was a Catholic. That is wrong. My mother was the Catholic. From her I learned that souls have wings.

GRANDCO

GrandCo was set up from the first research negotiations. Richardson felt it was "damn near suicidal" to involve them in the study, despite my research inclinations. According to him, GrandCo's "protect your ass" orientation would quash the study. They were not open to data; they were not willing to problem-solve the problems of combining the two firms. Their style was to be "nice and genteel" and "to sweep problems under the rug." I pressed. He said,

> I am reluctant to come to this conclusion because I really place a value on informed choice.... In effect, I'm saying I'm going to deprive GrandCo of a choice [to be in the study].... It's a choice I don't want to bother them with.... We are so deviant already.... We have to use our shots carefully.

It was recognized that this would limit the validity of the study. There would be no data gathered from GrandCo and no chance for GrandCo people to become involved in the study at all. I would be hearing only one side of the story, and likely a side slanted to "fit people's needs." Richardson was afraid of GrandCo and felt that the risks of involving them in this study were too great to take.

Relations between DC and GrandCo had been bad from the start. When Richardson was wounded another DCer set the combination strategy. He saw GrandCo as a "technostructure" that would enslave DC, an octopus that would engulf them, an amoeba that would absorb them. He urged DC executives to "repel all borders" and to "avoid kissing the enemy's ring before the results of the battle were announced." He set the strategic tone for months of conflict that would follow between the two firms.

There were many levels to the conflict between the two firms. One conflict was between Richardson and his boss at GrandCo. Schmidt was described by Richardson and others as a bastard who worked through henchmen and who was thoroughly unprofessional. Another was between the business systems of the two firms. GrandCo was financially oriented, tight on controls, organizationally bureaucratic. DC was product oriented, loose on controls, less policy driven, more open and flexible. The deepest conflict, the most troubling to DCers, concerned the value systems in the two firms. Here DCers made distinctions between the authority of knowledge and the power of aristocrats, the political environment and the family feeling. GrandCo people were Theory X, technocrats, turkeys, whereas DCers saw themselves as Theory Y, people oriented, just good God-fearing folk.

SYMBOLIC SYSTEMS

It was this latter conflict that hooked me. No doubt characterizations of GrandCo as an octopus or amoeba are archetypal images. I used them to convey the depth of DCers' anxieties about joining with GrandCo in my briefing meeting. They were not my images, however, for I never experienced GrandCo in that way. No doubt, too, my absence of contact with GrandCo people, based in Richardson's fears, led me to stereotype GrandCo. Maybe Schmidt was the bad father. Maybe GrandCo was like that bad company that took the job away from my dad. No doubt that my sense of GrandCo's size, DC's account of the "wars," and DCers' descriptions of those technocrats led me to picture GrandCo people as strong, tough, and skilled—the same muscle crowd that wreaks havoc in the world today. But all that did not hook me; what did was values.

Symbols are expressions of the self. To a God-fearing boy like I was, prone to intellectualization, values become a common language to talk

about, think about, often be myself. Values were a common bond between DCers and me. We used value talk to express our purposes and what we were doing with the research. In the contracting meeting Richardson talked about evangelizing GrandCo. That failed. Following the sale to GrandCo, DC executives had prepared a list of twenty-five values to be preserved in the combination. My researchings were to help DC "keep religion"—to learn from its response to the acquisition in service of maintaining its values.

My briefing on the results of the first round of data gathering shows me unhooked from the amoebas, the parents, the wars, even the techno-crats. I focused on the roots of DC's stategy in DCers' anger, reactive-ness, and wounded leadership. All agreed that the strategy of resistance had been self-defeating. I traced conflicts to commonplace emotions and to the natural happenstance of an acquisition. By the time of the briefing DCers recognized all of that as well. Finally, I mirrored for them their perceptions of GrandCo as ethnocentric, polarizing, and evaluative. They knew as much and said so; although some belittling was justified, their views had surely been tainted. DCers left the briefing in collective spirit. Richardson was asserting himself again and vowed to at least work more openly with Schmidt. The strategy of resistance was abandoned and DCers agreed to work more authentically with Grand-Co, to test their perceptions, and to avoid fights for fighting's sake. I felt great about the briefing. Full of myself. But myself was not fully in *what I said.*

"You seem angry at GrandCo, seem to be stereotyping them." What I had left unsaid but was just below the surface was my feeling that GrandCo's values were potent and bad. Meryl drew a distinction between ethnographic and phenomenological ways of knowing. In the former, one learns by taking others' perspectives—those of different insiders or native groups. In the latter, one learns by putting oneself in the live situation and reflecting on one's own experience—something like "going native" and reporting on one native's perspective. Where was I actually and ideally in those terms?

In my briefing, I could take DC's side and see GrandCo in one way, but I could also take GrandCo's side and in that way help DCers better understand GrandCo's point of view. As DCers stepped back from their relationship with GrandCo, they could see the two perspectives too.

"But how did you experience GrandCo?" "I didn't," I stammered, for I never met any of their executives. I had read a book about the firm and talked to a former employee; I did not really like any of what I had heard or read. "So," Meryl said, "whatever GrandCo is for you is really what comes from DCers' experiences of GrandCo and your experience of DCers." "Mmmmm." "Are values a shorthand for whatever GrandCo

means to you?" "Mmmmm." "Why values, Phil?" Maybe I was "externalizing" myself. We had never heard of such a concept and agreed that Freud would likely turn over in his grave. "I really wanted DC to hold onto its values—I was an evangelist, too, and GrandCo people were heathens." Then I called them callous capitalists with no sense of human feeling: "Those fucking bastards were kicking my boys around." Meryl asked who I symbolized in the story. Talk turned to families.

BATES AND DAVIS

Bruce Bates was a role model for me—maybe an ego ideal. He was the Human Resources Officer in DC and chief implementer of the DC philosophy and value system. I first worked with him when the studies of worklife began in DC and he was a strong backer of the acquisition study. Like Richardson, he too voted against GrandCo's involvement in the study. He could find no evidence that GrandCo was interested in learning about the acquisition and DC's reaction; he saw no prospects for GrandCo people mutually addressing problems that might be unearthed by the research. He could not keep his "integrity" if GrandCo was in the study so long as the relationship was that way.

Bates was a great conceptualizer and reader of organizational process. I once told him that a part of me thirsted for the day-to-day impact and family feeling that a business position should provide. He seemed to embody an ideal businessperson cum social scientist. Bates was my guide through the first round of data collection on the acquisition. He had thought of "jumping ship" after the sale but stayed on to protect DC's interest. He had fought against the reactive strategy, but his efforts to promote a more proactive strategy had failed. Bates proposed several concepts that were useful at the briefing. One was the death-and-dying model used to characterize DC's denial of the legitimacy of GrandCo and their anger at losing their independence. His concepts, his guidance, and the change in his own approach to GrandCo helped reshape DC's strategy and set DC and GrandCo on a more cooperative track.

Richardson's career planning speeded up after the briefing meeting and it became clear that DC needed a new executive vice-president. The decision was to be made using DC's participative selection system and, in recognition of GrandCo's interest and in the spirit of cooperative relations, Schmidt of GrandCo was asked to join the selection committee. It was quickly agreed that several internal candidates were qualified for the job. Following months of interviews with the candidates, analysis of ratings of their peers and subordinates, and discussions within the committee, the field narrowed to two. One was Bates. He was distinguished by his intellect, his leadership in participative management, and

his human relations management style. The other was Robert Davis, head of the major operating divisions in DC, and known for his line experience and financial acumen. His was the traditional route to the top in DC.

The committee was divided over the candidates. Then Schmidt announced he was in favor of looking for an external person, maybe someone in GrandCo. Richardson flew to GrandCo headquarters to meet with him. One week later Davis was named DC's new executive vice-president.

The second round of data gathering began shortly after this announcement. Amongst interviewees there were varied opinions as to how the decision had been made. Some saw it as an honest business decision—that the "best man" had won—and pointed with pride that GrandCo could be involved in this participative way. Others said that Bates's conflicts with GrandCo during the first year of combination had hurt him, that GrandCo needed to find a guy who could play the game more in their way. Still others said that "the deck was stacked" and GrandCo's power made the decision in Davis's favor.

Interviewees reported a surge of momentum after the decision. They had moved into the acceptance phase in the death-and-dying sequence and had established parameters of control with GrandCo. Business was improving and many sensed a stronger pace in DC. As I prepared my report, a major business decision was made. Several divisions in DC were combined and Bates, the human resource man, was named the new general manager. Davis had initially been against his appointment. The selection committee saw it as a "natural," however, and Davis and Bates met to "get the bugs out." This decision was hailed throughout DC. The family feeling was back again.

FAMILY SYSTEMS

The vice-presidential selection had been a real battle. As I told Meryl the story, we agreed that it sounded like the description of a family system. Meryl wondered where the researcher was in that family system: Where were the indebtednesses, alliances, conflicts, vendettas, and whatever else? Battles can be embedded in the experience of being in a family. "How do you feel about Davis?" "A fair amount of ambivalence." "You have an older brother, don't you?"

Bates was "pissed off" by the vice-presidential decision. So was I. As I reentered the room I mumbled that my brother was more like Davis than Bates—"In some ways," I added. "And aren't you more like Bates?" Meryl wondered. My brother had been a Junior Achiever, a business

major in college, a Harvard MBA. He had taken a T-group course and hated it. I had never fit into Junior Achievement and had eschewed business training. I was reminded that I had characterized Bates as Richardson's "son" in DC; so who was Davis? We swirled awhile. Meryl recalled that I had forecasted an impending bloody battle between Davis and Bates in a cautionary note attached to the first round briefing report. "Impending; but you already know it's bloody, don't you?" I let out a moan. "What's the struggle with the brothers?" At the oddest times the fire in the wood stove needs tending, so I took out the poker and tended to it.

I still have a hard time talking about myself in relation to my family and my brother. Brotherly rivalries are not uncommon, and I may have carried such a rivalry into my relationship with Davis. I identified with Bates's ways of thinking, his style, and his appreciation of life. In Davis I saw confidence, groundedness, a sense of responsibility—all aspects of my brother that I admire and resist in myself. The rivalry may be linked to family position. Older brothers show Davis's traits, and also tend to value property, to get along with authority figures, and to have a taste for running a business. Second brothers do not. We tend to be more spirited, more quixotic in thinking, and centered upon people; we may talk but never seem ready to run the show.

Now, these traits are not ascribed to Davis or Bates. They do fit with my own family system. In DC, Davis was older than Bates and clearly the more experienced manager as he came from a line position. His was also the traditional route to the vice-presidential post. All of these criteria stick in my brotherly craw. Bates's obstinate manner estranged him from GrandCo and, curiously, his orientation to people was seen as softness, which hurt him as well. Those same curious traits cohabit in many second brothers. We resent them used against us by impersonal authority figures and institutions.

The second report intimated that the struggle between the brothers was not resolved. There was the possibility that Bates would leapfrog Davis and examples were drawn from GrandCo to explicate the likelihood. Younger brothers have such wishes; Meryl sensed that mine were farfetched. What is more, I cited Davis's promotion and the organizational structure decisions as signs that DC was abandoning its value system and that true family feeling was being lost. In the report, I asked managers to consider whether DC risked deculturation. I urged them to rededicate themselves to their old values and to seek to integrate the changes.

The report was read with interest. Richardson and Bates wanted to meet as we had done after round one and discuss the report and its action implications. Davis and other officials in DC, members of his

alliance, felt that a meeting was unnecessary. For them the report slowed progress and my warnings seemed vague and without action implications. Months went by. Then I got a letter from Richardson saying a decision had been made that no briefing would take place.

It's one thing to not put your heart into things. Emptiness and futility are its companions. But I had put my heart and soul into the second round report. And it was not recognized; it did not make a difference to anyone. The symbol system went to work. GrandCo, Schmidt, Davis, a hidden subculture in DC were in cahoots. "With whom?" "Well," I said, "I guess the military-industrial complex doesn't map very well to reality." Then, I added,

> With the contingency crowd, the crowd that questions the "sufficiency" of participative management in a world of rock throwers; I went after them in my dissertation; the crowd that says tough, rationalistic, autocratic management fits well in certain environments. Whose ends are served by that? Makes more sense to be tight, kick ass when the environment says. . . . Says who? That damn competing values crowd. . . .

DISINTEGRATION

Richardson left DC before the third round of data gathering. We talked before his leaving. I asked him whether my story was wrong, whether I had lost all objectivity, whose issues were being worked in the story: DC's, his, or my own. Heady, warm, but inconclusive. I then asked him about DC's future. He was of two minds. He was a strong believer that the culture of a company takes on the values of its leader. With a new man heading DC, the culture could change and change fast. At the same time, Richardson also believed that cultures are ingrained in people, ideas, functions, rituals, traditions. DC people would influence the new president. DC's way of life would resist disintegration and assimilation into GrandCo.

Davis was named the new president of DC. The transition was handled well. Richardson went to all DC locations to say goodbye and was followed by Davis, who met with all DCers and presented himself to them in customary group, family-style meetings. Interviewees made no comments on the reasons surrounding Richardson's departure. My sense was that it was better left unsaid. They did express loss—of their own father figure—and of the family symbol he set for DC. Interviewees also commented on some changing norms amongst top management, less process discussion, less extensive participation in decisions, less joking and horseplay. Many commented as well that GrandCo was having a greater influence over some decisions in DC.

Nonetheless, there was also keen excitement, a sense that DC was moving again. New products were being developed, the market was coming out of the recession, profits would be up again. Bates was doing a "super" job; Davis was full of energy; the company was healthy again.

There was a briefing following the third round of data gathering. No report was requested; I was just asked to give my impressions in the context of reviewing the worklife data. I talked about the disintegration of DC and urged top managers not to resurrect the old culture but rather to reculturate and set a new path. One said we were all "feeling the elephant." So an elephant was drawn depicting cultural options. One option was for the elephant to sit on the people; another was to use its trunk to call attention to new challenges. One option was for the elephant to stand on its hind legs and lead the herd; another was for it to listen to people and to use its head. The elephant had to walk through tall grass to sustain profitability. It also had to carry people—all DCers—on its back. One stated that the group was like blind men each feeling a part of the elephant. They had to share their feelings; give the elephant a heart.

The elephant was presented to all DCers at worklife briefing meetings. So was the task of reculturation. Meetings were held throughout DC to the end of feeling the elephant and giving the elephant a heart. A new statement of beliefs and values has been drafted and is circulating through DC today. Davis is meeting with DCers at all locations in group, family-style meetings to learn their reactions.

MYTHIC SYSTEMS

Acquisitions and mergers beget myths (Hirsch, 1980). There is the "war and western" genre with battles, bombings, shootouts, and ambushes. These have heroic referents in raiders, the big hat boys, gunfighters, and the tombstone makers. There are nautical myths, with pirates and safe harbors, and gamesmanship, with moves, countermoves, and strategy plays. There are the courtship myths with wooing, playing hard to get, marrying, and the afterglow.

Many myths surfaced around the acquisition of DC. The company that sought to take them over was seen as a "rapist." GrandCo, in traditional chivalry, was cast as the white knight that rode to rescue. DC was, of course, the damsel in distress. Following the sale, many in DC referred to it as a marriage.

DCers had their own myth born at the time Richardson assumed leadership of the company some eight years before the sale. The top management went on a retreat, talked over their values, visions, hopes,

and selves, and embarked on a path toward more participative, soulful stewardship of the corporation. They saw their realm as Camelot, with Richardson as Arthur and top managers as Knights of the Round Table. Their rites included poetry, skits at management meetings, a sense of themselves in a holy crusade.

I felt a part of this myth, like another member of the realm. I was the kingdom's scholar, its storyteller. I wrote an epic poem about the acquisition. In the land of Camelot there lived a princess, it began, and traced the preacquisition history to the point of the threatened rape. It celebrated the beneficence of the white knight but warned of the covetous nobles and grasping beast in its castle far away. The financial people and technostructure were symbolized that way. There came to pass months of struggle, with jousts over principle and skirmishes over power, the poem read, tracing the roots of DC's combative strategy and the consequences. Then came the visit to the Land of the Scholars, the new strategy, the new relationship, later the new realities. The final stanzas read:

> Kingdoms come and Kingdoms go, Princesses marry and marriage means change. Beasts do battle and nobles count money, but battles do end and more than gold makes a reign. The days of Camelot are passing, what call ye the next days? Will harvests still flourish? Will the princess still shine? With the old spark gone, will a new one arise?

> Scholars can ponder and knights dream of glory. But the answers to these questions await the princess's story.

I do not know the princess's story today. I have lost touch with the reality of DC. A story *could* be written about a security-driven man, Richardson, who installed a Mickey Mouse system, participative management, who was not man enough to handle an acquisition, who had a namby-pamby human resource director; and now some real men have taken over the business, who are realistic about participation, who know what business is all about, who have gotten the place cleaned up. A story about war or a western, of the forces of light and darkness, could be the tale. "It ain't my story. I do not see that story in DC, I do not experience that myself," I told Meryl.

"What was your experience?" "I am losing touch with myself." My father was gone at DC, my values were being recast, the big villains were wreaking injustice on my boys, and maybe my brother was trying to keep the whole thing together. Bates was writing poetry about his search for the "path with the heart." I was blathering to Meryl.

We then talked, necessarily so, about clinical supervision. Researchers who use themselves as instruments need that in the field. Ken Benne

(1959) has done some thoughtful writing on neurotic anxiety as it expresses itself in organizational research and consultation. Needless to say, I have my neuroses and my normal anxieties as well. Benne makes a distinction between neurotic anxiety and rational fear "based upon the sober fact that both 'change agent' and 'client' change during a process of consultation. And change may involve disintegration of a self and its associations without valid re-integration and rebuilding" (p. 63).

TURNING TO OTHERS

There was another person working with DC, another man I identified with, another man who guided me along the way. Garfinkle, a clinical psychologist, worked with DC to implement its management system alongside Richardson and Bates. He has met Schmidt, knows the people at GrandCo, and does not think my anxieties are neurotic; he is feeling them himself. Garfinkle participated in the executive vice-presidential decision committee. He discussed values and character with Davis and cast his lot with Bates. Garfinkle finds GrandCo to be "benevolent/authoritarian," as he is wont to say, and committed to conventional business wisdom.

Garfinkle believes in octopuses and amoebas as valid psychic images and metaphors for corporate behavior. He finds GrandCo's values to be antithetical to genuine concern for people and, thus, to DC's participative systems. He is not sure whether DC's value system can be preserved. Garfinkle, more deeply than I, feels the loss of Richardson. He, more so than I, feels the loss of value of his work in DC. He told me, sadly, that he would never again find a client like Richardson and an organization like DC used to be.

Our earlier discovery that DCers, their selves, histories, and situations, shaped my self in the research process comes back to me now. As I live the DC myth through Richardson, Bates, even Garfinkle, the story reads one way. By contrast, the new human resources man at DC, after a discussion of my current views, tells me he believes that DC's Camelot is ahead. Richardson's predecessor had his myth, Richardson had his, and the new generation will have their own. He believes that Richardson's legacy will live on in DC through its rituals and its practices, newly defined in a new culture, but at core, at the level of value, the same. A professional colleague to whom I described DC's current efforts at reculturation said it sounded like organization development in the 1980s. He said I had to "let go" of my sixties' images, get with today. So I told Meryl, "I am not sure what is going on in DC; I am not sure of my self."

TURNING TO SELF

We then talked about the therapeutic aspects of doing particular forms of social science—as therapy for the self. Certainly researchers study topics that envelop personal life issues and characters that bring to the fore central life themes. Such encounters can enable the self-minded researcher to gain insights into ways the self influences the research process and, perhaps, work through some of the issues in the successful management of research relations. We then kibitzed about power mongers who study power, the brains who study things like sense-making. It seemed the powerless, isolated, and brainless studied these too. Thus, we concurred that there is always some pathology in the self-selection of a field of study, an area of inquiry, a line of interpretation. "One reason people study particular issues, interpret data in particular ways, even make interventions of a particular sort is to maintain an issue, to keep it fixed, to make it legitimate," said Meryl. We noted that that could normalize experience, even reveal a universal in life drama. It could also be a sign of pathology.

My psychodynamic self found certain psychodynamics in DC. The issues were of authority, manliness, weakness, models of leadership. My symbolic self found symbolism in GrandCo's power and values, in DC's Camelot and conquest, totems of goodness and taboos of badness. My familial self found family feeling, then upset; a place for me, then betrayal. Those selves intertwine an instrument, shape it and are shaped by it. My relations with DCers, the setting, the circumstances, and my self activated all these self systems in my data gathering, interpretations, and interventions. I was intertwined with all the selves in DC too, and in this sought the universal self. "Hadn't my story of DC's acquisition, the myths and all, revealed something about all of us? About people in transition? About the meaning of life—for DCers? for me?"

"So where's the pathology?" I hollered at Meryl. Silence was the reply. I told her of the latest developments in the story. I have been talking to Bates about the research, talking about the ways I portrayed him, confessing that Davis was being cast as something of a bad guy, little more than a caricature. Bates suggested I talk to Davis, let him know my feelings, see if we could get a better fix on each other. At this writing it has been three weeks and I still have not called him. One more thing. Bates, Davis, and I agreed that it was time GrandCo knew about the study. I had some worries that this would create problems in DC, but both assured me that the relationship, at this point, could withstand them. Schmidt now has several draft papers about the history of acquisition. I have not called him to learn of his reaction either.

"What are you afraid of?" "I do not want to change the story at this point!" It will be a fuller, richer, more valid story once I learn more about Davis and learn more about GrandCo; I know that, but I certainly am hesitating. "Would it mean more than giving up the myth, the aesthetic of the story?" "Mmmmm." "Is there another danger?" "I'm afraid of losing my anger," I said. "Suppose these guys are not caricatures, suppose values are relativistic, suppose I do bring their world into me? I would lose my anger." "Then there's the pathology."

Therapy for the self in the research process must be premised upon not only the limits of the self but also of its possibilities. In this study, and in this dialogue, I am seeking my self of being and becoming. It is a developmental task. My brother and I are really connecting of late. We have talked about our dad, what life is like for him as the older brother, and what life is like for me. I find myself more conscious of ways we are similar as well as our differences. I am dealing better with my anger, fear, and tightness around corporate "big boys." Some of this has to do with my own maturity; some comes from growth experienced in preparing this work! I am also letting go. Not of the core; but I am trying out a new identity, less judgmental, narrow, and exclusive, and more accepting, broad, and inclusive. I am planning to let go of the story soon. Oh, I will continue my research in DC. But I will be listening more openly, more aware of my own self, more responsive to what DC really might become.

These selves of being and becoming transcend the other self-systems and gain expression in instrument, too. The systems of self, family, symbol, and myth to live in these selves and, in the experience of being and becoming, can be developed. I am developing in my life and in my research world, too. Progress is slow; but talking about it seems to help.

As we concluded our conversations we thought about constructing one of those strips that turns over on itself and then returns back. "What do you call that damn thing, Meryl?" "A Möbius strip." It might go from the self into the research, the research into the self, the research letting go of the self, the self letting go of the research. "Seems a technocratic image to me." Meryl agreed, offering Eliot instead:

> We shall not cease from exploration
> And the end of all our exploring
> Will be to arrive where we started
> And know the place for the first time.

(T. S. Eliot, *Four Quartets,* 1971)

ON THE RESEARCHER'S
GROUP MEMBERSHIPS

Kathy E. Kram

The primary purpose of this chapter is to draw on my own experiences to illustrate the potent effects that one's personal characteristics have on the formulation and implementation of social science investigations. Through a discussion of two major research projects I will highlight how my age, gender, and professional group identifications shaped both the definition of the problems that I studied and the manner in which each study was carried out, as well as the nature, quality, and validity of the major findings. On the assumption that such self-understanding is a necessary prerequisite for the development of effective clinical field skills (Berg, 1980), I will also identify several strategies for achieving awareness of how one's group memberships influence the research process.

In my attempt to understand how my personal characteristics have shaped my research endeavors, I have found that an intergroup perspective on the research process is extremely useful. This theoretical perspective suggests that individual, interpersonal, group, and organizational relations can be understood by examining the group memberships of the parties involved and the relationship among these groups in the broader social context (Alderfer, 1984; Alderfer & Smith, 1982; Rice, 1969; Smith, 1977; Smith, 1982a). Thus, for example, my interactions with the individuals that I interviewed for both studies were shaped by the group memberships that each of us brought to these interpersonal transactions. In addition, my formulation of the research problem and my interpretation of the data were shaped by my memberships in particular age, gender, and organizational groups. This theoretical orientation provides a framework for exploration of how one's personal identity shapes the research process.

HOW GROUP MEMBERSHIPS AFFECT
THE RESEARCH PROCESS

An intergroup perspective suggests that the behavior of the researcher, the relationships between researcher and client, and the
relationship between the researcher and the data that are collected can
be understood by considering the groups that each of the actors in the
research process represent (Rice, 1969; Alderfer, 1984; Alderfer &
Smith, 1982). The basis of this claim is that all individuals are part of
collective social processes that shape their behavior through the groups
to which they belong.

The effects of these group memberships on the research process are
found in first considering which group membership may be shaping the
behavior of the researcher as well as the transactions between researcher
and client system members. Once these salient group memberships are
identified, intergroup theory suggests that the relationships between
these relevant groups in the larger social context will parallel behavior at
the individual and interpersonal levels (Alderfer, 1984; Alderfer &
Smith, 1982). Thus, for example, the impact of being a young female
researcher in a male-dominated setting can be best understood by
considering the well-documented dynamics of token women in all-male
work groups (Kanter, 1977; Wolman & Frank, 1975), and how these
may be operating in the research setting. Similarly, the impact of being
an academic researcher in a corporate setting can be understood by
considering the nature of ongoing relations between industry and
university groups. In both examples, relevant factors to consider are the
nature of group boundaries, power dynamics, affective patterns,
cognitive formulations, and leadership behavior manifested among the
groups of interest (Alderfer, 1984).

In practice, this conceptualization requires the researcher to ask
several important diagnostic questions during the research process.
First, how are my group memberships shaping my perceptions,
behavior, and affective reactions as I formulate the research questions
and move forward to data collection and analysis? Second, how are my
group memberships shaping research participants' reactions to me and
their willingness to respond authentically to questions and probes
throughout the data collection process? Third, how do the group
memberships of all parties involved in the research process shape the
nature and quality of data that are finally collected? Fourth, how do my
group memberships shape the interpretation of findings at the conclusion of the investigation?

Discussion of two major research projects serves to illustrate the
value of attending to the researcher's group memberships. The first

involved a biographical interview[1] study of pairs of junior and senior managers in one corporate setting; the primary purpose was to investigate the nature of mentor relationships. The second study, which evolved directly out of the findings of the first, involved a biographical interview study of relationships with peers that managers experience at three different career stages; the primary purpose was to investigate alternatives to hierarchical relationships that might provide critical mentoring functions. In both cases, retrospective analysis of how salient group memberships shaped definition of the research problem, design and implementation of data collection, as well as interpretation of findings, has illuminated how my personal characteristics and those of the research participants shaped these endeavors.

STUDY 1: MENTOR RELATIONSHIPS IN MANAGERIAL CAREERS

The study was designed to explore the nature of mentor relationships, those relationships between junior and senior adults in a work context that are perceived as being supportive of individual development. In one corporate setting 18 pairs of managers were interviewed individually about their career histories and about their relationships with each other. Analysis of these interview data resulted in a conceptualization of the range of developmental functions that are provided in these relationships, a dynamic view of how these relationships unfold over time, and a delineation of the psychological and organizational forces that limit the value of these development alliances (Kram, 1983; Kram, 1985).

At the conclusion of this study, much progress had been made toward understanding the nature of mentor relationships and defining a broader conception of developmental relationships. The critical role of relationships in adult and career development was confirmed, the complexities of cross-gender relationships were illuminated, and new questions about the role of peer relationships in career development provided the impetus for the second study. The content and context of this project determined that my age, gender, and graduate student role would significantly influence definition of the problem, collection of the data, and interpretation of the findings.

DEFINING THE PROBLEM

Attendance at a seminar on adult development led by Daniel J. Levinson was a major catalyst for choosing the topic for my dissertation project. This intellectual experience was critical because it introduced

me to a conceptual scheme that would guide my research for years to come (Levinson, Darrow, Klein, Levinson, & McKee, 1978). I now realize how much my own stage of development shaped my decision to do research in this area and to define the focus and scope for the study as I did.

I found the seminar particularly relevant to understanding the course of my own life during my early adult years. At age 27, I had encountered several hurdles in my professional and personal life that I was able to address effectively because, in part, of several important relationships with more senior colleagues. Although unconscious at the time, a primary motivation for pursuing this study was to better understand the role of these relationships in my own life. The adult development perspective not only legitimized the challenges and crises that I had experienced, but provided some insight into a kind of adult relationship that was key to their resolution in the early adulthood period (Levinson et al., 1978; Erikson, 1968; Jung, 1933).

My age also affected how I defined the methodology for studying the nature of mentor relationships. Pairs of managers in a corporate setting were identified by first approaching juniors in the age range of 25-35 about their significant relationships with seniors, and then inviting those significant others to participate in a parallel interview sequence. Intuitively, I felt more inclined to approach the juniors first; this reflected my relative comfort and identification with this group, in contrast to the group of mentors who would later be identified. This early choice had unanticipated consequences for the range of data that were collected and for the analysis of both groups' personal accounts. For example, I learned very little about the multiple protégés that a mentor may have at a given point in time since I contacted the seniors about the relationship identified by the junior. In addition, my tendency to identify with the juniors made it more difficult to develop insight into the seniors' experience of the mentor alliance.

My gender appears to have influenced the definition of the project in two major ways. First, the decision to study relationships and their role in adult and career development, rather than some other feature of the developmental perspective, reflects the strong relationship orientation in my own life. This is consistent with my sex role socialization in earlier years as well as with my contemporary experiences (Gilligan, 1982; Baker-Miller, 1976). Clearly, the study of subjective and personal experiences in relationships attracted my attention far more than the study of more objective organizational processes.

My gender also influenced the definition of the research sample. I was compelled to have women in the sample so that I could examine sex

differences in patterns of individual development and in relationship dynamics. The demographics of the research site made it impossible to find more than one female mentor, but I was able to locate eight cross-gender alliances in which the junior was female. These gender comparisons were a high priority for me in this study, and continue to be a theme in each successive research project that I design. It is interesting to note that race comparisons were not included in the study; had I been other than white, I suspect this oversight would not have occurred.

My organizational role and affiliation affected the design of this project in two ways. First, my graduate school mentors encouraged me to utilize a biographical interviewing methodology; this was clearly most appropriate for the task at hand, but also frequently discounted in traditional academic arenas as not sufficiently rigorous. Most certainly the freedom, guidance, and encouragement that I received as I learned the methodology and implemented it influenced the course of this study. The findings are rich, and they clearly strengthen conclusions drawn from more traditional research methodologies.

Second, the location of the research site was facilitated by my dissertation chair and mentor. His ongoing relationship with a local corporation enabled easy access to this site, and minimized my initial anxieties about entering the field for this study. While I did explore other options, I chose to work at the site where the positive reputation of my mentor preceded me. With my increased knowledge of the dynamics of mentoring, I now understand why at this point in time I chose to follow in his footsteps. While the research relationship was an extremely positive one, I gained insight into the organizational influences on mentoring alliances from a particular setting. Hence the findings are limited by this design choice.

Finally, it is interesting to note that my age, gender, and organizational role significantly shaped my working hypotheses about the nature of mentor relationships. First, I suspected that these developmental alliances were primarily beneficial to the junior in the pair because of my own experiences to date in which I was yet too young to appreciate how my mentors benefited from teaching and coaching me. Second, I suspected that cross-gender alliances would be somehow different from same-gender alliances, based on discussions that I had had with my male peers about their relationships with their mentors; those hypotheses that emerged from the research were far more comprehensive than I could begin to articulate at the outset of the study. Third, I wrongly assumed that mentor relationships would look just like the ones that I had experienced during my academic career; variations due to organizational setting, nature of the profession, and individual differences had

yet to be identified through the research process. These working hypotheses, shaped by my group identifications, could have posed threats to the validity of the data collection and analysis; with the aid of clinical supervision (discussed later), I was able to acknowledge them and continue to generate alternative explanations and interpretations.

COLLECTING THE DATA

In this phase the intergroup perspective suggests that the group memberships of both researcher and interviewees are relevant. Group memberships of both parties shape key elements of the interview, such as rapport building, information sharing, and termination processes.

First, it was easier to build rapport with individuals of similar age to me than it was with the senior managers who were identified as mentors. I found myself far less anxious in approaching a young manager in his or her late twenties than I did in approaching a manager in his fifties. My own historical attitudes toward those older and in positions of authority were idealization; I assumed that they would not be interested in talking with a novice researcher. My anxiety and discomfort delayed the rapport-building process. As I examined familiar feelings from the past and questioned their relevance in the present, I was able to challenge these preliminary assumptions. With this increased self-awareness, I became less anxious about asking those in authority positions to take the time to participate in the interview sequence. I also had a sense that I became more credible and easier to talk with for the senior managers; data collection proceeded more openly once this age barrier was overcome.

Similarly, my age enhanced my ability to understand and empathize with the junior managers' experiences, making it relatively easy for me to ask relevant, probing questions. In contrast, interviews with senior managers were sometimes more stilted; I was unable to identify with their experiences, my empathy was more limited, and hence I was more often surprised. My questions to the seniors were not as finely tuned, and indeed I learned from them which questions needed to be asked in order to obtain adequate understanding of their points of view.

Gender similarities and differences had parallel effects on the interview transactions. Membership in the same-gender group facilitated rapport and identification, while membership in opposite-gender groups frequently created sexual tension and/or the lack of empathy or rapport, particularly early in the interview sequence. In my interviews with female research participants, I found it quite easy to build rapport and to empathize with their personal accounts. The corresponding

threat to valid data collection, however, was the degree to which I identified with many of their experiences. Frequently I found myself pursuing tangents to the predesignated questions because of personal interest in their comments. Or, my strong identification with their accounts caused me to project some of my own reactions and experiences rather than listen openly to theirs.[2] Thus, while similar gender group identifications facilitated rapport, they simultaneously presented a threat to the validity of the data.

In my interviews with male research participants there were both advantages and disadvantages resulting from our gender group differences. On the one hand, sexual tensions and awkwardness frequently hindered the interview process, particularly when I asked male mentors about their relationships with female protégés. On the other hand, if these tensions could be managed over the course of the interview sequence so that sexual attractiveness was enhancing rapport rather than threatening it, here and now data on cross-gender relationship dynamics could be observed. While identification and rapport were more difficult to achieve in cross-gender interview transactions, the potential benefits of these encounters were great.

Age and gender group differences between researcher and participants provided several opportunities to learn from the transferences and countertransferences that evolved during the interview sequences (see Chapter 1 for definitions). I hypothesized that the senior male managers' reactions toward me were, in part, a replication of their feelings toward their junior female colleagues. These transferences were very useful in developing insight into sex role dynamics and intimacy concerns in cross-gender mentor alliances; when I experienced their attempts to keep me in a "one-down" position or their flirtatious behavior as a distraction from the interview task, I suspected that this same behavior might occur in their roles as mentors. Similarly, my reactions to these same male senior managers provided insight into the authority dynamics in mentor relationships. By comparing these countertransferences with the personal accounts of junior managers, I was able to further understand how attitudes toward authority shape the phases of a mentor relationship.

Finally, to a lesser extent, my role as graduate student also influenced this phase of the research process. This organizational group membership, given its low status, low power, and transient nature, contributed to feelings of uncertainty about my own competence and the likelihood that I would complete a project of significant merit and importance. At the same time, I can hypothesize that research participants frequently wondered whether this study would have significance and whether I had

sufficient experience to conduct the interviews and analysis effectively. This particular barrier was surmounted during the interview sequences as I demonstrated competence, answered relevant questions about me and the study, and became aware of how my own performance anxiety was shaping the interview process.

ANALYZING THE DATA

In practice, the analysis of interview data cannot be entirely separated from the collection of the data. In clinical research of this kind, these two phases of the research process are intimately intertwined. As interviews are conducted, initial insights emerge about the phenomenon that is being studied. These new insights influence the kinds of questions that seem important to ask in subsequent interviews. This inductive process is characterized by continuous movement between data and concepts until the time when sufficient categories have been defined to explain what has been observed. This methodology is described by Glaser and Strauss (1967) as the "constant comparative method of analysis."

Clearly, in this kind of inductive and "messy" process, there are many ways to cut the data; and the researcher's perspectives on the world, shaped by his or her group memberships, will determine which course is chosen. In delineating the functions of mentor relationships, I identified two types: career functions and psychosocial functions (Kram, 1985). Whereas other studies of mentoring have tended to emphasize the career functions (Missirian, 1982; Kanter, 1977; Clawson, 1980; Phillips-Jones, 1982), I paid particular attention to how these developmental relationships supported psychosocial growth as well as career advancement. In retrospect, this is a reflection of what I had recently experienced in my own professional life; several relationships with senior colleagues that extended support beyond instrumental advancement concerns to broader personal and professional dilemmas.

Second, in delineating the phases of a mentor relationship (Kram, 1983) I devoted considerable attention to the separation phase of the relationship. This was undoubtedly due to the fact that at the time of the study I was beginning to anticipate leaving graduate school and separating from several people who had provided a variety of mentoring functions. The complexity of feelings that I experienced, including sadness, appreciation, anger, and excitement as I began to say goodbye to a most significant mentor, fueled my desire to understand intellectually this critical relationship phase. Clearly current developmental concerns in my own life (e.g., whether I would continue to flourish apart from my mentor) shaped which categories were emphasized in my

analysis. It was only after I completed my own separation that I could expand my analysis to present a more comprehensive description of all of the relationship phases.

In a similar fashion, my work offered a much more comprehensive picture of the juniors' experiences of the mentor relationship than it did of the seniors' experiences. Even with arduous analysis of transcripts and interview notes, the juniors' personal accounts were more fully brought to life in the written analyses because I was able to empathize and identify with many of their experiences. It was only through extensive discussion with my senior colleagues and further informal interviews with age peers of the seniors in my sample that I developed a full appreciation for the significance of assuming the role of mentor. From this experience I learned that more consistent effort and extra grappling with the data will be required to develop adequate understanding of personal accounts from people with vastly different group memberships than those of the researcher.

As in the interview phase, the use of self in the analysis is a critical resource for the researcher. Organizing themes and categories emerge in the interaction between the researcher and the data that have been collected as one's own reactions to the data and to the interview phase of the project are examined. Thus, whenever I had strong affective responses to the data as I was studying interview transcripts, I referred back to personal reactions that I had noted during the interview phase as well as to my own experiences in mentor relationships for further insight. I then had three sources of data rather than only one to draw upon in formulating new interpretations.

The most vivid example of this use of multiple sources of data from self and research participants is found in my analyses of the dynamics of cross-gender mentor relationships. I noted that my relationships with male mentors and peers had been somewhat guarded as they and I experienced both the excitement and threat of increasing intimacy. I, and I suspect some of them, avoided frequent one-on-one contact. And, in some instances, I felt trapped in stereotypical role relationships where I played the "helpless" student and they "rescued" me, or I played the "cheerleader" while they expressed their knowledge and creativity. These stereotypical roles minimized discomfort with sexual attraction but they were extremely dysfunctional since they reduced my competence, intellectual contributions, and sense of autonomy.

The downside risk of using one's own personal reactions and experiences in efforts to understand the data of research participants is that analysis of their accounts will be distorted by the researcher's own projections and transferences. Indeed, I had to reassess my analyses of

cross-gender dynamics when I noted that only the junior women's points of view were well articulated; this indicated to me that my interpretations of these relationships were significantly biased by my age and gender group identifications.

Finally, as the analysis phase is completed, implications for research and practice are identified. As with the choice of categories and themes for analysis, this "choicepoint" is also shaped by the personal characteristics of the researchers. As one who, at the time, was moving out of the role of graduate student into the role of professor, I was particularly intrigued with how organizational circumstances shape the course of a mentor relationship. Similarly, as one who would be leaving several significant relationships with senior colleagues, I was interested in the findings that suggested that relationships with peers might provide critical alternatives to the hierarchical mentor relationship. Finally, as the solo woman entering an all-male work group, I remained curious about how organizational contexts shape the dynamics of cross-gender alliances. Each of these has become a focus of inquiry for me since Study 1 was completed.

STUDY 2: PEER RELATIONSHIPS
AS MENTORING ALTERNATIVES

This study was designed to explore the nature of relationships with peers in work settings that support individual development. The first study indicated that while mentor relationships provide critical developmental functions in both early and middle career years, they endure only a few years and they are relatively unavailable to most people in organizations (Kram, 1985). I decided to explore relationships with peers in work settings because they were frequently mentioned by participants in the first study as providing a variety of supportive functions, particularly in the absence of mentors.

In order to investigate the role of peer relationships in career development, 15 individuals spanning three age groups (25-35, 36-45, 46-64) were interviewed about their career histories and about relationships along the way that had supported their development. They were asked to describe in depth two such relationships with peers. These significant others were then invited to participate in a parallel interview study about the relationship and the personal and organizational context in which it evolved. The majority of the original 15 research participants identified two peer relationships, 3 identified only one, and 1 identified none. Thus 25 relationship pairs were studied, and they were all located in one large *Fortune 500* manufacturing firm.

This study resulted in the delineation of a continuum of peer relationships that extend across a lifetime, providing unique functions at different career stages (Kram & Isabella, 1985). The results highlighted how relationships with peers can provide critical mentoring functions (Kram & Isabella, 1985).

The similarities between Studies 1 and 2 are readily apparent: a biographical interview methodology was utilized; the unit of analysis was the relationship; personal and organizational factors that shaped the evolution of relationships were examined; and the critical role of each kind of developmental relationship in psychosocial and career development was investigated. Given these similarities, it is not surprising that many of the group membership influences outlined in the discussion of Study 1 also characterized this second study. I discuss Study 2 in order to highlight several striking differences in each major phase of the research process due to variations in age and organizational group memberships. These comparisons reinforce the potent effects of personal characteristics and intergroup forces on social science investigation.

DEFINING THE PROBLEM

A number of interesting questions evolved from the mentoring study that defined several options for future research. Indeed, in seminar discussions of the findings, colleagues frequently pursued those that further explored the potential negative consequences of mentoring alliances or, alternatively, those that would illuminate differences in these developmental relationships across organizations and the practical implications of such variations. While these areas piqued my interest, and have subsequently become subjects of investigation, at the time that Study 2 was defined, relationships with peers presented the most intrigue for me. This choice was clearly shaped by the age- and career-related developmental tasks that I faced at the moment.

Four years had passed since the inception of the first study, and I had experienced many personal and professional changes during that period that influenced the kinds of relationships that I needed and that were available to me in my new work setting. At age 32, I had a strong desire to experience greater mutuality in my relationships with colleagues, and even early images of providing mentoring functions to my junior colleagues. I was aware of missing my graduate school mentors, and yet I also sensed that I was too old to recreate such relationships. This transition period, in moving from student to professor, from my twenties to my thirties, and from single to married provided the impetus to explore the potential of peer relationships in a work context.

Growing older and experiencing these major transitions also compelled me to develop a far more complex view of relationships. Whereas I entered the mentoring study with a working hypothesis that individuals generally have one mentor who guides and supports them, I could now see how relationships change, personal needs change, and, more often than not, individuals have a variety of hierarchical and peer alliances within and outside the work context that support their development. This increasing awareness of the complexities of relationship dynamics was a driving force behind investigation of other types of developmental alliances.

My organizational group membership significantly shaped the design of this project. As a junior professor, I felt a sense of urgency to conduct new research and very little time in which to do so, given the varied responsibilities of the role. In addition, the need for ongoing colleagueship on research endeavors sparked my interest in working with others on the study rather than recreating the solitary dissertation experience. Finally, in the role of teacher and scholar, I wanted the opportunity to guide others in learning about research. These forces contributed to my decision to put together a team of two doctoral students and myself; this team not only shaped the course of data collection and analysis, but it also provided an opportunity for me to experience many of the mentoring and peer dynamics that were the subject of my ongoing investigations.

At this point in time, I was acutely aware of how changes in organizational position and age are catalysts for changes in relationship needs and possibilities. Thus, I was convinced that the study should include individuals at early, middle, and late career stages rather than just a sample of juniors who are launching new careers. The mentoring study provided the opportunity for me to develop greater capacity to relate to and understand those at other stages than my own. Ideally, our research team would have representatives from the three major career stages; however, the graduate students with the interests and skills to participate were about my age with several years of work experience outside of academia. Awareness of the effects of group memberships on each stage of the research process would at least enable us to be aware of the limitations of our age homogeneity.

The research team did provide one dimension of diversity that was absent in Study 1; we were two women and one man. Thus, we had constructive counterpoints on gender-based issues, the capacity to conduct same-gender and cross-gender interviews, and the opportunity to examine—within one research team—how gender affects mentoring and peer alliances in terms of power relations, affective

responses, competition, and intimacy. Because we were age peers but not organizational peers, my relationships with my colleagues had characteristics of both mentoring and peer alliances.

COLLECTING THE DATA

In this study, most of the interviews were conducted by the doctoral students on our research team. My organizational role as professor and teacher prompted me to give up total immersion in the data collection process in order to adopt a clinical supervisor role. I negotiated entry into a research site, conducted several exploratory interviews and then through the remainder of data collection met with the team on a weekly basis to discuss their experiences in the field and to set up data analysis procedures.

It was during this phase of the project that we began to utilize our own experience to learn about peer relationships. First, there was considerable ambiguity about the boundaries and definitions of our interpersonal relationships. While organizationally I was to serve as a mentor in conducting research of this kind, at least one member of the team felt more comfortable with me as a peer rather than as a supervisor. I contributed to the confusion in the situation by feeling some ambivalence and anxiety about assuming the expert and mentor role for the first time. Gradually, as we took the time to process our experiences working together, we learned about the difficult dynamics—competition, resentment, struggles for control—that frequently emerge in peer relationships and in mentor relationships during certain phases. These were also the dynamics that were less likely to surface in our interviews, where we were primarily investigating the supportive nature of peer alliances. In retrospect, this self-study was essential to overcoming significant obstacles to getting our work done well. At the same time, attending to these process issues significantly enhanced our understanding of the relationships that we studied.

As in Study 1, age and gender group memberships of researchers and participants shaped the data collection process. In general, similarities promoted empathy and rapport during the interview sequences as well as threats to valid interpretations due to researchers' projective identifications. Differences, on the other hand, promoted the opportunity to learn firsthand how such differences shape the relationships that were the focus of investigation, as well as threats to valid data collection posed by predictable resistances, transferences, and countertransferences. These group and intergroup forces are significant, and would be even more so if the population studied were also characterized by socioeconomic, racial, or cultural backgrounds that were vastly different

from those of the researchers. It appears that one way these complexities are managed is to choose (albeit unconsciously) to do research in settings where group membership differences between researcher and participants are minimized.

ANALYZING THE DATA

The process of analysis proceeded in a similar fashion to that described in Study 1. The team of researchers proved to be invaluable at this phase to the extent that the range of possible organizing categories and themes was quite extensive and each of us could bring our own perspective (and group memberships) to bear on the interpretation of the data. Most threats to validity were minimized by the active involvement of three researchers, each of whom had unique contributions and questions; tendencies to distort the data as a result of particular group memberships and associated projections or transferences were checked by our colleagues on the team.

My previous work on mentoring unknowingly presented a threat to valid interpretation of the data because I was inclined to use concepts from the first study to organize the data in the peer study. Fortunately, my colleagues pushed me to search for categories and concepts that were truly grounded in the interview data. The "messy" process of reviewing transcripts and trying to make sense of them was even "messier" with three sets of eyes. At times each of us wondered whether the struggles and disagreements over interpretations would result in greater insight and understanding at the completion of the project. In retrospect, it is clear to me that our gender differences enhanced our understanding of same-gender and cross-gender relationships; and our similarities in age, but differences in organizational group memberships, enabled us to define the continuum of peer relationships and to identify unique forms of these developmental relationships at different career stages.

Our own efforts to be an effective team enhanced our understanding of the "underside" of peer relationships. Whereas our interviewees focused almost entirely on the contributions that their relationships with peers made to their development, our conflicts, competitive dynamics, struggles for control, and difficulties in establishing open and trusted communication produced another set of data that provided a balanced view of the benefits as well as the limitations of peer relationships.

The most unanticipated consequence of this phase of the research project was the additional insight that I developed into what it is like to be a mentor. During this project, I began to truly empathize with the

mentors that I had interviewed years before, and to understand more fully the range of challenges and affective experiences that characterizes this generative stance toward junior colleagues. Changes in my age and organizational group memberships were a catalyst for this increased awareness and insight.

IMPLICATIONS

This retrospective analysis from an intergroup perspective offers several guidelines for future research endeavors:

(1) At the outset of a study, the salient group memberships shaping the research process should be identified so that they can be consciously managed. These will depend on the content and the context of the study. It is not difficult to imagine how the questions, methods, and obstacles encountered during the research reported here would differ if I had had other personal characteristics.

(2) It may be necessary to modify a research strategy in order to increase the likelihood that group membership influences will enhance rather than interfere with the research process. Comparisons of the two studies of developmental relationships indicated that the introduction of a team of researchers enhanced the research process by creating diversity in gender and organizational group memberships. Both studies would have been strengthened by the inclusion of researchers who were older and/or of a different racial group.

(3) If the relevant group memberships appear to create insurmountable obstacles to valid data collection and analysis, then the research endeavor should be discontinued or significantly modified. When group memberships are such that little empathy and rapport can be established between researcher and participants, or characteristics of the researcher make valid interpretation of the data very unlikely due to a frame of reference that distorts rather than facilitates insight, professional integrity can only be maintained by a decision to discontinue the project and to pursue questions that can be adequately addressed.

(4) Systematic study of group membership influences is necessary at the outset of each new research endeavor because the complexion of these forces will undoubtedly differ from one project to the next. While certain group memberships of the researcher never change (like gender or race), organizational memberships change as one's career evolves, as illustrated in my transition from student to professor. Each study presents a context with new actors; even if the researcher's group memberships are stable, unique dynamics are created by their interaction with those of a new set of research participants.

*(5) The potent influences of group memberships necessitate the use of
finely tuned clinical skills.* Self-awareness, relationship skills that enable
effective management of field relationships, and the diagnostic skills to
understand and manage these inevitable intergroup forces, are absolutely necessary to complete a project that meets the standards of valid
investigation (Isabella, 1983).

MANAGING GROUP MEMBERSHIPS EFFECTIVELY

I conclude that managing group membership influences is a primary
responsibility of every individual who is engaged in social science
investigation. Three major vehicles exist for supporting efforts to
identify and consciously manage these intergroup forces: systematic
self-study, clinical supervision, and the use of a research team.

SYSTEMATIC SELF-STUDY

Understanding the effects of one's own group memberships on the
research process is not an easy task. It requires inquiry into one's past to
discover how identity group memberships have shaped current values
and perspectives that are brought to one's work. In addition, it requires
observation of one's current experiences and interactions in order to
develop insight into how both identity group and organizational group
memberships are affecting one's relationships and activities. Such self-
awareness is difficult to achieve, and frequently a painful rather than
enjoyable experience.

There are several solo activities that can support productive self-
study. First, keeping a personal journal on a regular basis facilitates
insight into one's reactions to events and the forces that are contributing
to them. In essence, the same skills that are utilized in the research
process can be applied to the study of self. Data is collected in a
systematic way and then analyzed using concepts and themes that aid
organization and insight. Often this is facilitated in personal therapy,
where self-analytic work with a trained professional supports the
ongoing process of inquiry. Second, taking field notes during a research
project enables systematic study of self as one is engaged in the research
setting. More focused than the personal journal, field notes attend to
specific events related to each phase of the research process. Here,
reactions during interviews and during periods of data analysis can be
recorded and then referred back to as one attempts to understand the
projections and transferences that may have shaped the study as it
unfolded.

These solo activities are often difficult to perpetuate, particularly when there are so many external demands taking energy and time that could otherwise be used for systematic self-study. Another avenue is collaborative study with others who have similar aspirations to achieve self-awareness as well as personal and professional effectiveness. Experientially based courses in interpersonal effectiveness, group dynamics, and/or clinical field methods provide a context in which such learning can occur. Not only does this kind of structure facilitate regular self-study, but it provides an opportunity for individuals to get feedback from colleagues that is likely to enhance self-understanding. In addition, these learning contexts provide discussion of relevant conceptual frameworks that can be utilized with colleagues or in solo pursuits to develop further understanding of how one's personal characteristics affect one's experiences as a researcher.

CLINICAL SUPERVISION

A one-on-one relationship with a more experienced teacher, colleague, or mentor, provides the opportunity for an individual to enhance self-awareness, relationship skills, and diagnostic skills that are needed to identify and manage group membership influences effectively, especially since individuals are limited by blind spots, biases, and resistances. Berg (1980) describes this as an apprenticeship in which a young researcher can learn the requisite clinical field skills by working closely with another who is both well-trained and interested in the student's continuing learning and development. In this context, the student has the opportunity to develop his or her identity as a researcher by examining personal values and skills, and to expand self-awareness and a range of clinical field skills through the supervisor's role modeling, coaching, and counseling.

Clinical supervision includes ongoing self-study, study of the here-and-now relationship between student and supervisor, and study of the experiences one has in research sites in ongoing projects. Thus, three opportunities are created for identifying salient group memberships and how they influence one's activities in research endeavors. Through self-disclosure, feedback from one's supervisor, and joint exploration of both parties' experiences in their relationship, psychological processes of projection, transference and resistance are examined, the impacts of particular group memberships are discovered, and personal, relationship management, and diagnostic skills are further developed (Berg, 1980).

Clinical supervision serves different purposes at each stage of the researcher's career. Early it is likely to be a mentoring relationship— later it will be more peerlike.

CREATING A RESEARCH TEAM

This vehicle serves several of the functions provided by clinical supervision: colleagues can act as sounding boards for each other, they can provide feedback on particular methods of data collection and analysis, and, through joint investigation, they can enhance each other's learning as well as the scope and quality of the research project through each colleague's unique contributions to the team. As long as members have the needed skills and a commitment to building effective working relationships among themselves, a research team has great potential to reduce the threats to valid data collection and analysis discussed earlier.

The composition of a research team can be designed to enhance group membership influences. First, by creating diversity in identity group and organizational group memberships, a collective wisdom is generated that prevents narrow thinking, obstacles to rapport in data collection, and distortions in analysis. Second, where homogeneity does exist, representatives of the same groups have an opportunity to learn more about the meaning and impact of these memberships by exploring common experiences and perspectives. Finally, to the extent that representation among team members resembles the population of research participants, it is more likely that parallel processes will evolve. Thus what occurs in the team can be analyzed and related to what goes on in the field, and vice versa. This helps generate appropriate questions, causes data collection to be more open, and allows analysis to reflect more accurately participants' accounts.

One difficulty is that research teams are not readily available; it is frequently difficult to find individuals with the requisite skills and schedules to launch a collaborative effort. In addition, this vehicle requires a range of clinical skills to manage the group process so that the team enhances rather than detracts from the research process.

CONCLUSION

A researcher's group memberships always shape his or her investigations; systematic understanding of these influences is essential so that they can be managed effectively. The discussion of two studies of developmental relationships illustrated how gender, age, and organizational group memberships affected each phase of the research process.

In some instances these personal characteristics enhanced the effort by facilitating rapport and empathy. In other instances, these same factors created limitations and threats to valid data collection and analysis.

The clinical skills necessary to identify and manage effectively group membership influences are not easily attained. Just as training in theory and method generally takes years of intensive study, so do skills in self-awareness, building and managing field relationships, and diagnosing how one's identity in the role of researcher affects the process of inquiry. These skills cannot be developed fully within the context of a graduate program; more likely than not, the foundation is created during this training and socialization period. From then on, however, systematic self-study, clinical supervision, and the use of research teams will be essential to facilitate ongoing understanding and effective management of these potent forces.

NOTES

1. Biographical interviewing is a data collection methodology designed to reconstruct research participants' life or career histories. It is like a traditional interview method in that there is a list of topics to be covered and questions to be asked. However, each interview is different from the others because unique questions and comments are utilized in response to the individual's way of telling his or her own story. This flexibility facilitates joint investigation by enabling the interviewee to manage his or her personal exploration. Comparisons across interviews are based on an integrated understanding of each person and each relationship. For further explanation of this method, see Levinson et al. (1978).

2. Projective identification is an unconscious process by which an individual projects parts of his or her self onto another. This process facilitates empathy and rapport; however, it poses a threat to valid data collection and interpretation because what are noted as attributes of the research participant may really be characteristics of the interviewer that have been projected.

VIRTUOUS SUBJECTIVITY:
In the Participant-Observer's I's

Alan Peshkin

A way of seeing is always a way of not seeing.

(Kenneth Burke)

It is psychologically impossible for scientists' perceptions to be uncontaminated by social conditioning.

(Henrika Kuklick)

Quidquid perciptur, runs the Thomistic adage, *per modum percipientis percipitur:* Whatever is perceived is perceived through the character of the one who perceives.

(Michael Novak)

Subjectivity, so it is thought, compromises a researcher's most faithful rendering of a phenomenon because it leads to emphases and omissions that result in skewed portrayals. Nonetheless, these days researchers report their subjectivity with a straightforwardness bordering on aplomb. In this chapter, I discuss my personal encounter with subjectivity, which Webster defines as "the quality of an investigator that affects the results of observational investigation," and, I would add, other types of investigation as well. This quality I take to be an amalgam of the dispositions stemming from one's class, statuses, gender, and values. To me, the issue is not whether subjectivity is a persisting aspect of social research—it undoubtedly is. The issue is subjectivity's variable nature at the hands of the very same researcher. The question to consider, I now realize, is, Which of the researchers' personal qualities will a research experience elicit? This realization arose in the course of working as a participant observer in two different field settings where I pursued my studies of the school-community relationship.

AUTHOR'S NOTE: I am indebted to Elliot Eisner, Walter Feinberg, David Spain, and Robert Stake for usefully critical comments on this chapter.

ON SUBJECTIVITY

Like good soldiers imbued with their side's truth, social scientists may align themselves in opposing camps, so taken by the orthodoxy of their own perspective that they scorn those with contrary views (see Phillips, 1983, and Eisner, 1983, for example). The contending—and contentious—true believers may identify themselves as realists or empiricists, on the one hand, and idealists, on the other. As generally defined, these two traditions are in conflict (for example, see Riley, 1974), whereas in the actual practice, as opposed to the abstract discussion, of social science, researchers seldom are struck by the ineluctability of either one. They tack, so it seems, between alternating—even simultaneous—understanding and awareness of their own project in terms of the realist's objectivity and the idealist's subjectivity. Even those who unequivocally endorse an idealist orientation would be embarrassed by a critic's claim that prejudice so dominated their work that what they had seen was primarily in their beholding eye. Those oriented toward idealism do not want to exalt prejudice, subjectivity's stepchild; their orientation derives from a recognition of the impossibility of value-free research, the consequent inevitability of researcher-object interaction in social research, and, most important for my purpose in this chapter, the sense that subjectivity is the salt of creativity.

That personal factors penetrate all points of the research process is a matter of record (Peshkin, 1982a). Although it would be farfetched to claim that we could predict what researchers would study if we but knew enough about them, their choice of topics for investigation is far from random. Notwithstanding the opportunism generated by the availability of funds, we are generally attracted to a limited, if not a narrow, band of topics. Choice of topic is a starting point for the interplay of subjectivity in social science inquiry.

In this regard, note the acknowledgments of several sociologists. Shulamit Reinharz, reflecting on her choice of dissertation topic, writes,

> In the subtle matter of selecting a research problem and site, the researcher's conscious and unconscious needs seek fulfillment. . . . I plunged into the study of a mental hospital . . . to grapple with the personal pain of having friends of my own recently hospitalized for psychiatric problems. (1979, p. 141)

Reisman observes that Lazarsfeld

> used to remark that he undertook the Teacher Apprehension Study because it gave him a chance to put to work his passion for newly

discovered contextual analysis. But . . . it was no accident that the subject was academic freedom: he cared about that. (1979, p. 226)

Of course, our personal proclivities do more than incline us to investigate certain problems. They lead us to take sides—Stein chooses that of gypsum workers, not their boss's (1971, p. 143); Metz, whose work focuses on schooling, concludes, "I did have a personal predilection favoring the side in the debate which gave more rights of participation to children" (1981, p. 13). And they lead us to make decisions that we see, usually in retrospect, were not governed by strict concerns for objectivity and dispassion. For example, anthropologist Morris Freilich writes,

> The biases which stem from the personality of the researcher are many and include the selection of a given type of community to study . . . and selection of given types of natives as key informants. (1970: 568)

An Indian anthropologist, Madan, reports that in his study of Kashmiri Brahmins he obtained data on conflict among kinfolk from some families who chanced—again, the personal factor—to take him "into the domain of their privacy" (1975, p. 151).

Although it may be no serious matter that what we choose to investigate derives from personal inclinations, we would take as serious the charge that our conclusions are subjective. But can subjective factors be removed from the social scientist's conclusions? Can we claim to set aside our personal orientations at the end of our studies any more than we did at the beginning and thereafter? I think not. Sociologist Daniels writes, following her procedurally difficult study of the American military, "If women can study male societies from which they are specifically excluded," it may be useful to think of the value of other "alien" persons studying other groups. "It is not argued," she says, "that such observers will learn the same things that less alien persons might. Some perspectives will be lost, others will be gained" (1967, p. 267). When English sociologist Roy Wallis says that other investigators of Scientology could well reach conclusions different from his (1977, p. 164), we must wonder what, indeed, we should make of Wallis's conclusions about Scientology, or, for that matter, of Daniels's about the military. Does anything go? Is social science reduced to mere personalistic wallow? These questions will be answered in the course of this chapter, but first I will discuss my personal experiences that prompted this reflection on subjectivity. These experiences made me realize how abstract my previous understanding of subjectivity was, and they provided the basis for the particular point I intend to make about subjectivity.

TWO STUDIES, TWO VIEWS:
WHOSE OX IS GORED?

Some insights and understandings may be acquired by virtue of the experience of others. As parents, we often hope this will prove true, trusting that our children will profit from what we know and thereby forego the anguish of what we have experienced. As adults, we acquire some insights and understandings vicariously through the graphically portrayed documentation of others. We may continue believing that we have grasped what they have communicated until we come to deeper belief through personal experience—as I did in the case of subjectivity.

I have been investigating the relationship between schools and their host communities in a variety of environmental settings. Among other sources of data (interviews, questionnaires, and documents), I learn about the phenomena that interest me by taking the role of participant observer, thereby becoming a resident in the site of my study for an extended period of time (12 to 18 months) and living the life of the community's residents to the fullest extent possible for an outsider.

Underlying the distinctions different definitions of participation-observation contain is the critical fact that in this data-collecting mode researchers are immersed in the lives of others whose behavior and beliefs are the essence of their data. Notwithstanding this personal immersion, sociologist Gans notes about participant observation that "it requires surrender of any personal interests one might have in the situation being studied in order to be free to observe it" (1968, p. 304). These "personal interests" are the basis for the "*human* participant observer" who, along with the "*research* participant observer," is present as we conduct our studies (for elaboration of this distinction see Freilich, 1970, pp. 535-536). Thus, fieldworkers each bring to their sites at least two selves—the human self that we generally are in everyday situations, and the research self that we fashion for our particular research situation. In reality, much as we may intend to surrender our personal interests, Gans's ideal remains out of reach because participant observation, especially within one's own culture, is emphatically first person singular. The human *I* is there, the I that is present under many of the same political, economic, and social circumstances as when one is being routinely human and not a researcher.

Behind this I are one's multiple personal dispositions—the result of the aforementioned amalgam of one's class, statuses, gender, and value orientations—that may be engaged by the realities of the field situation. Because of the unknown and the unexpected aspects of the research field, we do not know which of our dispositions will be engaged, but they

are likely to be our enduring ones, those invested with the greatest affect. If we knew in advance which personal factors would be engaged and what selectivity would result, our studies might turn out differently.[1] But we do not know, at least not always, and not with certainty, and thus I come to Mansfield and Bethany.

THE STUDY OF MANSFIELD[2]

The midwestern village of Mansfield is on no one's list of quaint, charming villages, of places one must visit. Because of its isolated location, Mansfield is usually reached only by intention. I went there because it was truly a rural community, shaped essentially by the requisites of the corn and soybean fields that make it an island, contiguous with no human settlement of any size. Of course, its adults not employed in agriculture commute to factory jobs in small cities (the nearest approximately 45 minutes away), places where Mansfielders also do their major shopping, take their recreation, and receive their medical services.

Mansfield's school district population of about 2200 people contains a native-born majority who married locally and stayed to raise their children in these quiet confines. In the course of two years in Mansfield—one spent living in the house of an 84-year-old widower, a former coal miner and farmer—I learned many intriguing things about village life. Before coming to Mansfield, I thought of such places as interruptions on the way to somewhere else, places that I could not avoid because no expressway skirted their grain elevators, dying Main Streets, and obtrusive stop signs. Their two-story, white frame houses looked like a movie set for a film I would not want to see, somnolent settings the world had passed by, as would I once I got beyond their reduced speed zone.

As researcher, not motorist, in Mansfield, I asked students, teachers, and parents to tell me about their community. "I'm from Chicago, a city boy," I'd say, "so tell me what it's like to grow up here, to live here," indeed, though I never asked, to die here. And they did. Mansfield was not every resident's favorite place, but it was to the village's mainstream majority about whom I wrote my book (Peshkin, 1978). They told me that privacy was scarce in Mansfield. It was like living in a fishbowl. They explained, however, that it was caring, not nosiness, that motivated them to be informed about their neighbors. When someone dies, neighbors close in with a level of support that moderates the impact of death's loss. Old folks have their caretakers, a nearby family that voluntarily looks after the aged who live alone and have no one to shovel their

snowy sidewalks or haul out their garbage. I heard a great deal about shades being watched—if an oldster's shades are not raised by the usual time, concerned neighbors call to be sure that everything is okay; and also about chimney smoke in winter—neighbors check (just a quick glance out a window) to see if smoke is visible. As long as it is, the furnace is working properly.

When young Mansfielders grow up, they stay at home or close to it, notwithstanding their adolescent impulse as high school seniors to depart for distant shores, fed up with the village's intimacy and nurturance. Yet, when they do leave, it is most often to another small town located within the area they knew while growing up. When they move farther away, they often return for the high school's annual homecoming celebration, because this ritual roundup includes everyone, not just the members celebrating their fifth or fifteenth reunion. And when they retire, those who had moved away often move back to spend the rest of their lives where they feel most at home. This idyllic picture, presented without the blemishes, was basically confirmed by my questionnaire data and by readers of my Mansfield study who said they thought they were reading about their own home towns.

In regard to their school system, Mansfielders usually elect school board members who are both natives and farmers. These gentlemen operate as guardians of their community, hiring teachers and administrators who, in their terms, are "country." The more I learned about Mansfield High School, the educational focus of my study, the more I realized that through local control it had developed into an effective means for reproducing local values and behavior. In short, Mansfield High School fit Mansfield: the level of academic discourse, the many extracurricular activities, the models projected by teachers, and the emphasis on volunteerism and athletic competition—all reflected the lives of those adults who felt they belonged in Mansfield and who comprised their school system's host community.

THE STUDY OF BETHANY

Fundamentalist Christian schools are newsworthy these days, their numbers reputedly increasing in recent years by two, then three, and finally four newly opened schools per day. They open in small towns and large cities; they open in places where public schools are closing due to declining enrollment. Together with their expanding churches and popular television preachers, and their religiously oriented New Right politicians, they form a fundamentalist trinity. I thought it important to understand the fundamentalist's role in contemporary education.

For my study, I gained access to Bethany Baptist Church and its K-12 Bethany Baptist Academy (BBA). As in Mansfield, I focused on the academy's high school, concerned about the relationship between BBA and its host community encompassed by Bethany Baptist Church's 1500 members. I moved to Hartney, the city of approximately 50,000 people in which Bethany's church and school are located, and found an apartment in the home of a Bethany church family. They were stalwart Christians and kind, generous people who accepted me as a family member during my 18 months with them.

Bethany Baptist Church is run by Pastor Muller. He built its membership, its church building, and its school by attracting a large core of dedicated followers; they volunteer when work needs to be done, recruit new members in response to their scriptural imperative to proselytize, and aid their troubled brethren with money, time, or prayer as needed. As I sensed when I conducted interviews, and verified when I administered a questionnaire, a large majority of parents, teachers, and students center their away-from-home life around church and school activities.

Bethany Baptist Academy is physically separated from its church only by a parking lot. Otherwise, church and school are not separate in any way: The same interpretation of scripture underpins both institutions. Church leaders consider the school as integral a part of the church's establishment as its Sunday morning services. This is the basis for their argument that Christian schools, except for health and safety standards, are no more rightfully subject to state control than churches.

In its advertising brochure, BBA presents itself as "a school with a difference"; it means to be distinguished from its public school counterparts in terms of its philosophy, the conduct and appearance of its students and teachers, and the "integration," as they call it, of scripture and all subject matter, whether English, social studies, or mathematics.

Bethanyites claim their academy is a God-centered school, a necessary alternative to the Man-centered public school. They support this claim in several ways. Every person the academy hires in any capacity must already be a born-again Christian and willing to become a member of Bethany Baptist Church. Teachers, students, and their parents pledge themselves to observe church and school regulations. The student pledge is notable for its 24-hour coverage that requires students to obey the rules all the time, wherever they are; the same coverage applies to teacher behavior. The librarian censors what the library acquires in order to keep out doctrinally unsafe materials. Moreover, fully persuaded that scripture is God's word and, accordingly, absolute, eternal, and universal truth, Bethany's church and school strive to indoctrinate their beliefs. Their doctrine is not merely school stuff to be learned for

recitation and tests and then forgotten; it is meant to be the foundation for their entire life, ideally for the life of all people everywhere.

Spirituality pervades the school—in its daily, pre-class devotional session, its prayers said at the outset of each class, its daily Bible study class, its thrice-weekly chapel, and its requirement that students always carry a Bible except during physical education. Informal social groupings tend to bring together students of equivalent degrees of spiritual commitment. When asked about their futures, the vast majority of students affirm they will attend a Bible-believing Christian college, marry a born-again Christian, send their children to Christian schools, and live with the Bible at the center of their lives.

In every respect, Bethany Baptist Academy is fully the agent of its church community, its educators neither allowed nor willing to differ in any way from what fundamentalist doctrine endorses. As in Mansfield, a sense of community prevails in Bethany, and its school provides welcome recruits to its community.

TWO VIEWS

One primary legacy of my study at Mansfield was an enhanced awareness of my own commitment to community. This community-supporting I was, in fact, the primary I who shaped the data collection and developed the interpretations in preparation for the resulting manuscript. In the span of years from 1972 when the project began to 1978 when the manuscript was published, I reinforced my a priori commitment to community. I believe this happened because of continually making manifest in my analysis and writing what previously had been latent. In retrospect I can see that this element of subjectivity that served and directed me at Mansfield was a potential obstacle to seeing in subsequent studies because my community orientation had become accustomed to center stage. It was the veteran I, practiced in directing my efforts as I pursued, across different settings, the common issue of the school-community relationship.

Another legacy from Mansfield was the understanding that local schools do more than help children develop their social skills and economic potential; and they do more than politically socialize them. In stable, basically homogeneous places like Mansfield, schools also contribute to the viability of their communities by providing an often critical set of community maintenance functions (see Peshkin, 1982b).

The title of my book about Mansfield conveys the story I meant to tell: *Growing up American: Schooling and the Survival of Community.* Its conclusions celebrate Mansfield and its high school, both flawed in

several ways, clearly not meant for everyone, but comfortable and comforting places for Mansfield's aforementioned mainstream majority. I liked Mansfield and its people. In a world rife with alienation and insecurity, the Mansfields of America strike me as special places, worthy candidates for survival. When I drew my conclusions, I identified Mansfield's racism, which I muted by calling it "anti-black sentiment"; I identified its limited capacity to socialize adolescents for a world exceedingly more complex than its own little cosmos; and I identified its tendency to exact conformity as the price of belonging. I noted these attributes because they are important concerns to me and to our society. I also wanted to preempt the accusation that I ignored Mansfield's negative side. But, having stated the negative side, I could then send up my linguistic signal—"nevertheless," which indicates a shift in directions—and proceed to assert what I felt most strongly:

> Bearing in mind the dilemmas they raise, cannot a nation's Mansfields be nurtured rather than threatened by modern society? Must one equate goodness with largeness, mindlessly allowing all the dimensions of life to increase without regard to the quality of life that results? (Peshkin, 1978, pp. 209-210)

I entered Bethany's world expecting to find a sense of community— and I did; I expected to find a school that accurately reflected and reinforced the dominant behavior and values of its community—and I did. Mansfield prepared me for Bethany. However, Bethany provided me with more than just another manifestation of the school-community relationship; indeed, Mansfield's school-community relationship is loose compared to Bethany's nearly perfect fit. I was able to see in practice that an institution based on absolute truth of necessity strives to be a total institution (Goffman, 1961). No less a degree of control is congruent with the organizational imperatives of absolute truth.

In addition, my fieldwork there was an unexpected occasion to be defined, labeled, and judged, and, therefore, to learn unexpected things about myself. At Mansfield, I was the child of the city exploring the *terra incognita* of rural life, the white, academic urbanite who was not directly threatened by the village's racism and cognitive insularity. Mansfielders were content with my self-definition. They needed most to know not my antecedents but whether I was trustworthy and would hear their paeans to the rural life. At Bethany, much as I wanted to be the non-Christian scholar interested in learning about the fundamentalist educational phenomena that was sweeping the country, I discovered, so to speak, that being Jewish would be the personal fact that would bear on my

research; it became the unavoidably salient aspect of my subjectivity. Bethanyites were content for me to define my research self, but could never rest easy with my unsaved human self. I became forcibly aware that the threats to my identity as a Jew were not just a matter of history.

For, in the course of inculcating their adolescents with doctrine and the meaning of their Christian identity, Bethany's educators taught us both that I was part of Satan's rejected, humanist world; I epitomized the darkness and unrighteousness that contrasts with their godly light and righteousness. They taught their children never to be close friends, marry, or go into business with someone like me. What they were expected to do with someone like me was proselytize, share their Truth, so I, too, by accepting Jesus as my personal savior, could be born-again and escape an eternity in hell. Although the children did not proselytize me, their mentors frequently did—over a bowl of soup in the lunch room, in the hall after leaving a meeting, but mostly in the course of our interview sessions.

The experience of Bethany's church and school as a total institution, and my perception of their evangelism as arrogance, turned my focus away from the very facts at Bethany that had so impressed me at Mansfield: its nurturant community and efficacious, community-maintaining school. Why? Because Mansfield had not gored me, and Bethany did. Thus, in the first paper I wrote about Bethany, called "Fundamentalist Christian Schooling: Truth and Consequences," I discussed the costs to its participants and others and I concluded as follows:

> I hope the day never comes when our society—feeling threatened by the success of Christian schools—believes that they must be suppressed or curtailed in any way. . . . I trust that my concern, and that of others, about their costs never exceeds the level of concern abolitionist Wendell Phillips expressed in his 1852 speech. . . . Studying Bethany Baptist Academy has rekindled my appreciation of Phillips' wise call for "eternal vigilance" if a nation is to preserve its liberty. (1983, pp. 23-24)

The academy's fundamentalist orthodoxy made me concerned about the resultant insularity of its students; its unrelenting evangelical efforts made me concerned about a future society (like those my persecuted ancestors lived in) that contained no place for me *as I am*. To repeat, Bethany gored me.

Given my differential reactions to community in Mansfield and Bethany, I was compelled to reflect on who I was and was not at Mansfield, whose racism I euphemized and toward whose intimate community I urged respectful consideration, and on who I was and was

not at Bethany, whose evangelism I deplored and toward whose community and educational juggernaut I urged eternal vigilance.

I had indeed discovered my subjectivity at work, caught red-handed with my values at the very end of my pen—where I believe they belong. For example, if I were a black American studying Mansfield, would I, could I, moreover, should I have been able to see beyond its obvious racism in order to exalt its uncommon sense of community? And would I have been free—Is not one subjected to those personal factors composing one's subjectivity?—to learn how schools function to maintain such communities? My commitment to community—helped by being white—directed my attention to the school's nonacademic, community maintenance functions. Without understanding these functions, we do not fully grasp what schools mean to people in many villages, small cities, and stable urban neighborhoods. If I were a black American in Mansfield, I could find other true things to write about, other stories to tell.

Furthermore, if I were a born-again Christian studying Bethany's school, could I, would I, moreover, should I have been able to see beyond the extraordinary contribution it makes to my well-being as a Christian in order to identify how its teachings threaten outsiders? And would I have been able to spot Bethany's paradox, one likely to disturb nonfundamentalists? Bethany's school legally exists because our pluralistic society has laws that secure the private, religious school's right of establishment. Yet nothing in BBA's educational policy and practice supports pluralism. Both school and church are doctrinally monolithic. If I were a born-again Christian studying Bethany, I could find other true things to write about, other stories to tell.

Of course, as a white researcher I still see Mansfield's racism, and as a Jewish researcher I still see Bethany's successful school and community. Seeing, however, is not enough; it leads me merely to point out, not focus on, Mansfield's racism and Bethany's community. I concede that subjectivity need not blind me to perspectives other than those following naturally from my subjectivity. However, since these other perspectives are not reinforced by my personal dispositions, they fail to get the same attention as those that are. They fail, therefore, to be explicated and connected to other aspects of the phenomenon under study, and expanded so that the promise of the perspective is most fully exploited.

I do not dwell, for example, on Mansfield's limited social opportunities that preclude knowing almost anyone unlike themselves. As a result, I do not explore how tolerance and certain types of community are inversely related. There is a story worth telling about this inverse relationship; I did not so much reject telling it as I felt drawn to tell the

one I did. I feel at liberty to spin a particular story—the gift of my subjectivity—but not out of thin air; my story must be borne out by facts that are potentially available to any other researcher. I do not ask, however, if it is the best story, as though there invariably is just one story most worth telling. I do strive to relate the story that best follows from my construction of a setting. This construction results in my particular perception and ordering of facts, and my particular interpretation.

The failure to exploit fully other themes than the one I have chosen may be seen as a shortcoming, but I see it as the reality of social research conducted in complex settings. Such settings support many stories, so to speak, not all of which can be told—or told most effectively—by any one researcher. Thus, my subjectivity is simultaneously enabling and disabling, as it impels me to entertain and develop some research possibilities and restrains and delimits me from developing others.

Subjectivity has assumed a usefully concrete form to me as a consequence of my participant-observer experience in Mansfield and Bethany. So informed, I may more consciously take account of its effects on my research procedure, from its beginning to its end, rather than just writing the after-the-fact, *pro forma* section in one's manuscript that says, "This is who I am. Reader, beware!" Such sections should be written, but their writing should not be the first occasion for considering how subjectivity has encroached upon one's research process. After all, if my subjectivity grants me a license to pursue a certain line of thinking, it does not warrant the self-congratulatory conclusion of, "Eureka! This is it!" The virtue of subjectivity is that it concentrates and focuses attention; and it produces an "it." Since in doing so subjectivity has also narrowed my perception and awareness, I need to know both what has moved me and what has not; I need to discover what interpretations I slight or ignore in the course of exploiting the ones that I favor.

CONCLUSIONS

As noted, my subjectivity narrows what I see and shapes what I make of what I see. By disposing me to choose, I select from the array of N possibilities those that I will make something of. I bring my biases or inclinations to my research. Unlike clothing, they are preexisting states that cannot be shed and thereby prevented from interacting in some way with the objects I study. That they will interact is unavoidable; just how they will do so is uncertain. My subjectivity, furthermore, is one basis for my distinctiveness, although not a unique distinctiveness, peculiar solely to me. Otherwise, my work would be marked by idiosyncracy that

locates what I have seen exclusively in my eyes and in those of no other's. If my work is to become acceptable to the corpus of social science, it should not be the product of hallucination, delusion, or illusion (Polanyi, 1958, p. 302). That is, if what I see cannot be squared with the real or imaginable perceptions of others, I may have had an interesting personal experience but I have missed the boat.

If subjectivity is both unavoidable and virtuous, does this make objectivity avoidable and unvirtuous? I think not. My *Webster's* circularly defines objectivity as the state of being objective, and defines objective, more usefully, as "independent of what is personal or private in our apprehension and feelings; expressing or involving the use of facts without distortion by personal feelings or prejudices."[3] Because objectivity directs attention to the relationship between personal dispositions and distortion, it is a good thing. Distortion is bad; we all agree. Shaping is good, at least better than distortion. Passion and prejudice distort, while values and other personal orientations shape, or so it seems as I think of these terms.[4]

Objectivity, however, does more than alert us to the potential association between distortion and personal dispositions, and most assuredly between distortion and prejudice, a distinction that *Webster's* fails to make; the above definition wrongly presents personal feelings and prejudice as identical. This pertains to my central point: The mistaken notion that "true" science is value-free has compelled even those who know better to feel guilty about the legitimate role of subjectivity in the course of their research. Personal dispositions, what I have defined as subjectivity, are the researcher's allies. If you stand where I do, and think, or understand how I think, as I do, then you may see what I see: a community in Mansfield and a total institution in Bethany. Not thinking as I do, but in ways that I find imaginable, you may see misery in Mansfield and blessings in Bethany. Both sets of outcomes are warrantable. The researcher's prejudices are not allies; nor is the belief that every aspect of a phenomenon is fair game for his subjectivity. Objects do have attributes that are generally singular in nature—that is, about which one true or fitting statement can be made using the linguistic conventions peculiar to the observer's culture. Included in these attributes are traits denotable by number, sex, and color. If I am subjective, if personal states affect how I represent denotable qualities, then I have erred.

One can find good company for the belief that there is no value-free social research, and no less good company for the insistence that there is no virtue in a runaway subjectivity that has become subjectivism, defined as the view that attaches "supreme importance to the subjective

elements in experience" and also as the belief that "individual feeling . . . is the ultimate criterion of the good and the right." By exalting one's singularity, subjectivism gives no scope for verifying one's perceptions and interpretations by the generally accessible experience of other investigators. Subjectivity is not subjectivism. When others agree with my perceptions and interpretations, I believe I have achieved a creditable intersubjectivity, not a discreditable group illusion.

From those who accept their subjectivity but abhor subjectivism, one hears an abundance of injunctions that reflect a concern to keep the former from deteriorating into the latter. Nadel espouses teamwork in anthropological research as "a means of overcoming the limitations of the personality" (1951, p. 50; see also Diesing, 1971, p. 281). Becker urges researchers to avoid that sentimentality which hinders them from investigating "some matter that properly should be regarded as problematic" (1974, p. 119). Barzun and Graff emphatically advise that what one knows as a consequence of one's subjectivity be tested in all ways possible with the evidence available to competent scholars (1957, p. 146). Eisner elaborates an argument opposing the view that subjectivity is tantamount to relativism. Among the six points he would have us ask of theories or interpretations are the following: Do they have "instrumental" utility? Are they consistent with other theories or interpretations? And do they offer economical and elegant accounts of the data? (1983, p. 4). These many injunctions attest to the seriousness of the researcher's concern to preclude the dysfunctional consequences of passion, prejudice, and subjectivism.

My subjectivity is functional and the results it produces are rational. But if they are rational only to me and no one else, not now or ever, then I have spawned illusions and my views are bound to be ignored. When I disclose what I have seen, my results invite other researchers to look where I did and see what I saw. My ideas are candidates for others to entertain, not necessarily as truth, let alone Truth, but as positions about the nature and meaning of a phenomenon that may fit their sensibility and shape their thinking about their own inquiries. If, somehow, all researchers were alike, we would all tell the same story (insofar as its nondenotable aspects are concerned) about the same phenomenon. By virtue of subjectivity, I tell the story I am moved to tell. Remove my subjectivity and I do not become a value-free participant observer, merely an empty-headed one (Diesing, 1971, p. 280).

Since I know now which I's were most tellingly present at Mansfield and Bethany, I am alerted to these, which *might* be present in my next study. But, in fact, I do not know which of the possible configurations of my personal dispositions will be most engaged when I next assume the

role of participant observer and immerse both my human and research selves in someone else's life. When I do know, I will perhaps then be aware of what force has shaped my research procedure from beginning to end. I may also be aware of what I have not seen or seen imperfectly, for these are the costs virtuous subjectivity exacts for its particular perceptual gifts.

NOTES

1. It is inaccurate to compare methods in terms of engagement-nonengagement, since one's data, however collected—by telephone or face-to-face interviews, by observations of naturalistic behavior behind one-way mirrors or of behavior in a staged setting, or by library research—end up as data in hand. They become stimuli to the researcher and, accordingly, can engage some aspects of the researcher's human selves. The participant observers' proximity to their data sharply accentuates this process.

2. This and all other names mentioned in regard to Mansfield and Bethany, the site of the second study described here, are pseudonyms.

3. This definition, and all others quoted in this section without citation, are from the *Webster's Third New International Dictionary*.

4. There is an Orwellian Newspeak here that I must acknowledge—I shape, but you distort.

Commentary

In the introduction to this section we suggested that one theme common to each of these five chapters was the experience of pain. The authors, either explicitly or implicitly, point to how the pain surfaced and how it influenced their lives. There is also some additional pain in acknowledging, retrospectively, how their response to the pain clouded their perceptiveness and led to actions that might have been different "if they knew then what is clear now."

In both the Hackman and Berg chapters the pain emanated from sources inside the researcher. Anxieties that threaten are first defended against and then, as the defenses are noticed, attempts are made to understand the source of these internal reactions. The pain becomes the stimulus for the self-reflection process. In the chapters by Mirvis and Louis and by Kram, the self-reflection is focused primarily at the level of the interaction. The pain triggered an examination of the relationship with other people and with the research topic itself. Peshkin focuses at a different level. He noticed how the two communities of Mansfield and Bethany evoked very different responses in him, creating an imbalance in his sympathies. He saw the positive side of the community dynamics in one setting and the negative side in the other, using benign language in one study and malignant language in the other to describe processes that at their core were similar.

The pain described in each of the five chapters was both a consequence of and a contribution to the deep levels of involvement the researchers experienced in their investigations. Kram expresses this most clearly when she identifies that her interests in researching first mentor and then peer relationships grew out of her own experiences with developmental relationships. The very recognition of her involvement meant that she expected that scrutinizing her personal reactions would yield worthwhile data—not only for the purpose of minimizing bias, but as a valuable source of insight. Thus committed to self-scrutiny, Kram was also committed to struggling with what she uncovered about herself and her research relationships, and this in turn heightened her level of involvement.

The levels of involvement, the commitment to self-scrutiny, and the pain were emotionally costly, but there were also significant gains. In each of the chapters there is a sense of rejuvenation. In Hackman's experience it is clear that his struggles are, in part, a consequence of his desire to push important relationships to greater levels of significance. This may involve pruning relationships he has grown beyond, or it may mean incorporating parts of himself he has not wished to accept. In any case, the tone is one of a desire to live his professional life in a fuller way. Even the choice of his title suggests a voice that has been present but underdeveloped.

Learning how to reframe anxiety as the possibility of new figures emerging from undifferentiated backgrounds is the key to Berg's chapter. Instead of

staying with the posture of defending oneself against the pain of anxiety, the reframing has a vitalizing quality to it. This is also seen in the Mirvis and Louis account of how much Mirvis was reliving the pain of his relationship with his father when dealing with Richardson at DC. It could be argued that the pain was worth it, for through his examination of the transference process Mirvis was aided in understanding better his father's experience and thereby their relationship as father and son. Mirvis was also able to appreciate more fully some of the problems for Richardson and some of the human costs brought about by the merger.

For Kram, the benefits that came from the pain included her ability to take on new roles. Her struggles to understand the mentor-mentee relationship brought her to the inevitable position of taking on the mentor role herself, a position that seemed so foreign to her just a few years earlier when she began her own work. Peshkin's chapter is a rich description of the process of reclaiming parts of ourselves that we leave behind or split off in the service of "objective" research. From reading the chapter we have the sense of a person whose awareness of his own involvement in research deepened as a result of what he learned from the pain of self-scrutiny.

Another theme that cuts across the chapters is the struggle with ambivalence. Hackman makes it the centerpiece of his chapter, but throughout the section there are signs of deep reluctance on the part of each researcher. Despite this reluctance, each moved ahead in some way, somehow making the ambivalence a companion in work. We argue that perhaps the central clinical skill is learning how to see ambivalence diagnostically, without becoming paralyzed by it and without blaming others for its existence. Perhaps the most powerful critique of positivist methodologies is that they funnel experience into either/or frameworks. Contradictions demand resolution. Something is either true or false. The clinical approach suggests that it is possible for seemingly contradictory data to coexist and to express a truth. In fact, the clinical perspective reminds us that data often appear contradictory because of the way we frame them. It is in the nature of the question that one determines the nature of the answer.

Taking an intellectual position that allows and encourages us to frame issues in "both/and" ways triggers deep emotional ambivalence. It is stressful to live with contradiction. If we cannot change this ambivalence internally, our predisposition to reduce it may cause us to prematurely "choose" one side or another. No one is equipped to attend to the clinical side of research until he or she has begun to learn about ambivalence and is willing to scrutinize its role in social research.

The issues addressed in Section III feel to us to be at the heart of the clinical method. In many ways Section II is the head and Section IV is the body. Each part, of course, has no existence or meaning without the others, but the heart feels special.

Clinical Methods

The first four chapters in this section examine the application of a clinical method to a variety of research activities: archival analysis, interviewing, historical analysis, participant observation, and biographical research. The question addressed by these chapters is, How does a clinical approach change our theories about data collection and our methods of doing it? The final chapter presents a model for managing the process of analyzing and presenting qualitative data. All five chapters attempt to come to grips with the implications for research methods of clinical involvement.

In the first chapter, Simmons describes her experience reconstructing an organization's prehistory. Initially the work involved extensive archival analysis and interviewing. In the second phase, however, Simmons struggled to reconcile seemingly contradictory descriptions of events, actions, and chronologies. The "method" she developed for understanding what these contradictions meant grew out of her willingness to treat contradiction as evidence. Gillette, too, is concerned with history. He provides us with a definition of history and a role for historical analysis in social science research. In examining the assumptions underlying the historical and social scientific perspectives on "here and now" behavior, he finds them distinct but complementary and concludes his call for more historical analysis with some cautions about the demands it places on the researcher.

Perry's chapter is a reflection on a twenty-year process of creating a biography. In particular, she examines the way in which she evolved a participant observation method for studying the life of Harry Stack Sullivan. At critical phases of her research Perry found that her ability to open *herself,* emotionally and intellectually, to *his* environment provided valuable insight into Sullivan's life. By examining her own reactions and those of the people around her, she was able to piece together some of the powerful forces that shaped Sullivan's life.

Early in the chapter by Sutton and Schurman we read about an interviewer who calls a respondent to schedule an interview only to receive an angry and abusive reaction to this apparently innocent request. The rest of the chapter describes what these two ISR researchers learned about conducting interviews on "hot" emotional topics. As they learned about respondents' reactions to layoffs and plant closings, they also learned about research relationships. The chapter concludes with an analysis of the ways researchers might handle emotionally "hot" topics and the ways interviewing methods must change to accommodate such research.

The final chapter deals with the inevitable dilemmas facing qualitative researchers who must record, analyze, and present an overwhelming amount of data. Huberman and Miles argue that this process is constantly being shaped by the researcher's latent theories about the social system. They believe we must allow these theories an explicit role in the data reduction process so that both the theories and the reductive analysis can be scrutinized by the researcher and the research participants.

The chapters in this section point to the many clinical choices present in all research activities. Facing these choices, making them, and understanding them fully is an essential part of a clinical method. These choices are often made difficult by the emotional and intellectual risks they present, but to avoid or finesse them can imperil the validity and integrity of the research.

RECONSTRUCTING AN ORGANIZATION'S HISTORY:
Systematic Distortion in
Retrospective Data

Valerie M. Simmons

I expected to be bored. I could already picture myself sitting in a bleak, bureaucrat's office, hunting through file after file of dusty documents, reading the six hundredth memo, stopping to worry the paper cuts in my cuticles, yawning.

I was after information about the history of "Dexter" (a pseudonym), a public service organization we (Kenwyn K. Smith, Terri B. Thames, and Judith Marx) had been studying for nearly two years. Our research team had been trying to understand how a new organization develops (see also Smith & Simmons, 1983), and had started daily participant observation soon after the first staff were hired. Spurred on by Sarason's (1972) admonition that a new organization's early development could be understood *only* in historical context, I had taken on the investigation of Dexter's "prehistory" for my dissertation research.

I had not expected to be drawn back through time some fifteen years, back to when Dexter was only a glimmer in its parents' eyes—nor that Dexter would turn out to have had so many parents. I had not thought that it would be so hard to find the beginning of planning for an organization only two years old; perhaps the metaphor of the human life cycle increasingly applied to organizations (Kimberly & Miles, 1980) had led me to expect a gestation period only nine months long.

Certainly I had not expected to relive those fifteen years of planning history with an intensity and vividness that took over my life. For the six months it took me to reconstruct the history of planning for Dexter, I lived my here-and-now life only as a shadow, drifting off in the middle of dinner conversations to ponder the day's new data, or in the midst of

intimate moments with friends to think about relationships among the people I'd met in search of Dexter's past.

Reconstructing the past brings about a peculiar relationship between the researcher and the *time* she or he relives. I found that historical research demands that we understand how the complex cognitions and emotions experienced *at* an event—already an imperfect representation—become further degraded and reinterpreted over time in the memories of those who were there. But an understanding of cognitive/emotional distortion is not enough. Historical research demands that we acknowledge the central role of empathy—the researcher's empathy—in that reconstruction process.

In historical research, the only data available are the memories of people who participated in the history, tapped through retrospective interviews, and surviving paper records produced by participants at the time. Using empathy as a method is to use these memories and documents as the grounding for building a model of a particular history, reconstructing the gestalt from which those writings and memories emerged. The researcher must conduct a dialogue with the experience (of others) and with social, clinical, and cognitive psychological theory, gradually coming to see the raw data in light of those ideas that make it make sense.

But empathy is a process during which the researcher becomes increasingly involved with the past and must scrutinize the emotions of that involvement as second-order data—a kind of validity test—of the completeness of that empathic understanding. As I came to know the participants in Dexter's creation, through pieces of memories and fragments of interactions recorded on paper, I came to feel what it *must have been like* for those people to be invested in creating Dexter. As I reconstructed the network of relationships among these people and, using general theory about groups, began to see which investments and perceptions were shared, I began to feel for the groups, and then for the intergroup interactions across boundaries, and finally for the system as a whole.

Organizational research, even in the present, involves internalizing the conflicting perceptions of participants. This process can be an emotionally risky undertaking, as an introjection of a system in full-blown conflict feels just as awful as a raging inner conflict. A system researcher must suffer the conflict until a transcendent theoretical/ emotional framework emerges that makes it *all* make sense (Marshall, 1981).

Such a framework must *order* empathic insights correctly in time, so that the development of emotional attachments and the progression of

events feed into one another as the history actually unfolded. I found that the single most valuable method of historical research was to read through the data from the beginning after every datum had been painstakingly located and placed in proper order. It was only then that I could make sense of the inconsistencies, and only then that I could feel the first stirring of an idea, the coincidences of fragments of ideas about Dexter, the churning of political organizing in the community, the grim grinding processes of the bureaucracy, the tragedies of conflicts in the making, the casualties of those caught in the explosions of system conflict, the powerful cathexis of planners to an emergent dream, and the pain of being severed from that dream, leading inevitably to the recent past, when the Dexter *I* had lived during the just past two years finally made sense. When I finished that chronological pass through history, I felt I had myself given birth to Dexter. I was not bored.

In this chapter, I present some ways in which I learned to think about distortion in retrospective data, including the constraints on encoding an event in memory when it happens, the further distortions of memory that may occur with the passage of time, and the difficulties in interpreting self-report data. I then describe the gradual evolution of a model of Dexter that helped me understand *how* each person's data was distorted and which was a tool for using both distortion and "truth." Then I address the ways in which I came to deal with some of my own distortions and how I came to trust the experience of empathy as a final validity check. The chapter concludes with a discussion of how we might meet the overwhelming demands of such methods.

RECONSTRUCTING A HISTORY OF DISTORTIONS

When I began this research, I intended to use both retrospective interviews and archival documents as data but fully expected that the interviews would yield the richest and most reliable data—memos and official planning documents are known to be carefully crafted public presentations that often bear little resemblance to the complex realities out of which they emerge. I found exactly the opposite: The gestation of Dexter was preserved in those dusty files in a form that allowed analysis of the fictional nature of documents and insight into the reality behind them, but human memories of events stretching some fifteen years into the past were so degraded and distorted that only a sophisticated application of clinical rigor could sort out what they actually represented.

DISTORTIONS IN ENCODING

I have always tended to take cognitive psychology seriously, and if there is any single message from recent work in cognition and perception, it is that the simple act of perceiving an event is greatly constrained by our cognitive capacities and that the representation that gets stored in memory is a highly interpreted one. When an interviewer asks, "What happened at that committee meeting in January of 1975?" she or he must keep in mind that several factors intervene between the event and participants' perceptions of that event: the opportunity to observe, selective perception, and interpretation.

Participants' memories of a single event seem to differ systematically with controversy and investment in the *meaning* of events. With the passage of time, initial perceptions of an event are likely to change even more as participants "forget," or get the chronological order of events confused, or reinterpret past events every time a new event intervenes and clouds original interpretations with current dynamics.

DISTORTIONS IN REPORTING

Finally even these highly degraded and distorted memories of an event are available only through the interview process so that both the interviewer's cognitive limitations and the dynamics of the relationship between interviewer and informant intervene further between past "reality" and current understanding. Retrospective interviewing is not just a simple matter of deciding whether the informant is telling the "truth."

THE LIMITS OF "TRUTH"

Although I thought that I understood the dynamics of interviewing and the highly interpretive nature of self-report, an event early in my interviewing process reminded me how easy it is to mistakenly trust memories reported by a key informant. I had accepted an invitation to

Figure 14.1 Factors Intervening in the Encoding of Events

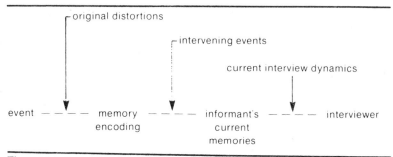

Figure 14.2 Factors Intervening in the Reporting of Events

lunch from a Dexter woman I had grown to know and trust through the two years of participant observation of Dexter's present. When I arrived at her house, the table was laid and a good bottle of Cabernet open to toast our friendship; as the bottle was consumed, we talked as women often do, and my informant revealed intimate, risky details of her private life. I recall reflecting to myself that I really trusted Carol to tell me the truth, and her revelations about her private life were evidence that she trusted me.

We were talking about recent events at Dexter, so I decided to probe to see what she knew about the recent firing of an employee. I knew, through other sources, that the employee had been fired to avoid a scandal of some proportions from the employee's activities outside Dexter. I recorded that event in my journal:

> I probed once about D.L.—she didn't bat an eyelid. She said that she got fired for being ugly and obnoxious. I'd bet money she doesn't know.

I was congratulating myself on the richness of my informant system and feeling pretty smug about knowing "the truth" when my complacency was shattered by the realization of what this analysis implied for historical interviewing. Even if I could assure myself, as I could with Carol, that the informant was doing his or her best to tell me the truth, I might have a seriously misleading version of "truth." *And I would have no way to know.* Carol, like all of us, had filled in the simple "fact" of a firing with an interpretation that made it make sense to her. Had I not held a privileged piece of information, I would have recorded Carol's interpretation as the truth.

This event gave me a paranoia that was to serve me well throughout my restrospective interviewing: a test of rigor that demanded that every "fact" be seen as the informant's interpretation of events to which she or

he may have had severely limited access and about which an interpretation might have been crafted. I trusted very little from then on, and took interview reports as data about the reality out of which interpretations emerged rather than as "objective" facts.

THE VALUE OF DISTORTED INTERVIEW DATA

How then can valuable data be gleaned from the residue of old memories? It requires taking seriously the relatively simple warnings of cognitive and clinical psychology: Memories are highly selective, opportunistic, contextually encoded, and frequently reinterpreted fragments that represent the factual "truth" only slightly. But had I stopped there, I would have thrown out a lot of good data. I recorded in my research journal that I did not trust my interview data and was reluctant to include them:

> It's slowly dawning on me that I just don't have much confidence in people's ability to reconstruct a chronology—they just can't seem to be very accurate about dates, and it seems hard—impossible—for them to go back to prior emotions. The latest ones leave too heavy an imprint.

> I feel confident in getting a general feel for the reality set of their role, but I'm reluctant to pin it into the very specific time frame of my archival chronology. Interviewing people is frustrating -they just don't have good enough memories. This past is more important to me than it is to most of them.

It was only after I turned in desperation to a closer examination of archival data that I was able to construct a framework of people and groups, changing through time, that enabled me to move from rejecting interview data as "distorted" into building a Dexter-specific model of distortion that enabled me to make sense of both distortion and fact.

BUILDING A MODEL OF DISTORTION

Although knowledge of the kinds of distortions that can occur is necessary to retrospective understanding, it is not sufficient. Knowing only that memories about Dexter were distorted was no help; such knowledge is paralyzing (which may be why so many people choose to deny the inevitable subjectivity of data). The only way out of the wilderness for me was to construct slowly a Dexter-specific model of events and people's emotional investments as a guide to sorting out *how* data were distorted—what was "true" in what context at what time for each person.

DISTORTIONS ABOUT INVOLVEMENT

I had begun retrospective interviewing with current Dexter employees who had participated in Dexter's planning. I was using a nomination technique, asking each informant, "Who else was involved in Dexter's planning?" I began with A.L., a current Dexter administrator, who told me of endless committee meetings with representatives from community groups and public agencies who had a stake in Dexter's creation. When I asked A.L. who had represented the local criminal justice system in meetings, he drew a blank. For long minutes, he had a puzzled look on his face, as he searched his memory without success.

I knew, from minutes of meetings, that A.L. had sat through many meetings with representatives of the criminal justice system, people whom he knew well; yet he had "forgotten" them. Triangulating A.L.'s self-report against archival evidence, I was able to form hypotheses about the reasons for this peculiar distortion. Perhaps the criminal justice system had been shut out of the real action; perhaps the real planning took place behind the scenes, so that the committee meetings were only a charade of participation; perhaps A.L. had been involved in conflictual interactions with the representatives of the criminal justice system, so that he wished to "forget" that they were present. These hypotheses, formed out of an analysis of distortion in self-reports, led me to seek evidence about the relationship between A.L. and the criminal justice system and about behind-the-scenes planning activities. Some hypotheses turned out to be supported, others contradicted. None would ever have been formed had I not taken "forgetting" as potential data.

My Dexter-specific model of distortion evolved through this research, gradually refining my research techniques. For example, while I originally set out to use informant "nominations" to tell me who else had been involved in the planning process, I changed my technique to first probe for self-generated (systematically distorted) nomination lists and follow up with questions about who else was peripherally involved but not important, who represented the most deviant perspective, or who might disagree most with the informant's perceptions.

Thus, self-report data were valuable not only for what was there but for what was left out. When I interviewed G.D., a man who had been centrally involved in ten years of Dexter planning, he could not remember many names. Since I knew from committee meeting minutes how many long hours he had spent with these people, I tried the

hypothesis that his "bad memory" was saying something important about his relationship to these others. After this interview, I recorded in my journal my

> overwhelming sense of G.D.'s isolation (self-imposed)—he's just not attuned to others—he forgets names and the contributions of others.

From this observation and an evolving model of distortion, I was able to generate and test the hypotheses that G.D. felt himself to be the real central planner, that he engineered a sham of participation in public meetings, and that he was personally deeply invested in Dexter, so deeply that he was blind to the investments of others.

DISTORTIONS OF TIME

This interview contributed another corollary to my evolving model of distortion. As I listened to G.D. tell the story of Dexter's planning history, I got the impression that for *most* of the years of planning, G.D. had worked in a warm, collaborative partnership with B.K. G.D. spoke of his friend B.K. with great warmth and affection, and described at some length the plans they made together. I recorded in my journal that "from G.D.'s eyes, he and B.K. were the whole show."

Piecing together a chronology of events and actors from archival documents, I was surprised to learn that G.D. and B.K. had worked together for only six short months. Setting this partnership in the context of an accurate time frame, it became apparent that G.D. had distorted his encoding of the passage of time to *expand* the length of a warm partnership and *shrink* the time during which he had been dealing with other relationships of less importance to him personally. Eventually, this piece of "distorted" data led me to understand how terribly conflictual the planning process had been for participants and how they sought relief from the stress of conflict by retreating to behind-the scenes planning and cooperative relationships. Intervening events (i.e., the more recent warm relationship between two actors) had further distorted memories of the stream of time.

DISTORTIONS VISIBLE IN THE INTERVIEW

In the first half-hour of talking with G.D., I thought that he had played a relatively uninvolved part in the Dexter story: He did not remember much about the details of the history, he claimed not to know much about Dexter present, and he did not seem to care that its

administration had been taken away from his agency. Only when I began asking about archival records did I get clues that his detachment might be misleading. G.D.'s files on Dexter were not packed away in storage (as one might have expected from a project over five years dead); they were within arm's reach of G.D.'s chair. At first he had denied me free access to the files, but he offered to go through them to pull out relevant documents. I watched his final expressions as he leafed through files; his brow wrinkled with concentration, a wry smile flashed across his face, he sighed deeply, closed his eyes, shook his head, and suddenly turned to start piling files in my arms. "It's just too depressing—it all comes rushing back," he sighed. "I couldn't stand to go through these papers again."

That brief glimpse of emotion was the first clue I had that G.D. had had a more deeply personal investment in Dexter than he would admit; it was the data from which a hypothesis eventually emerged suggesting that G.D.'s identification with Dexter planning was shared by a small, cohesive group of planners, each of whom came to identify more strongly with Dexter planning than with the agencies that each represented. This was a conceptual breakthrough in understanding how planning proceeded in the midst of constant community chaos.

RECONSTRUCTING NETWORKS

When I began this historical study, I began keeping notecards, one for each person, to note official job titles and agency affiliations; when I had enough information, I began drawing charts of the system, placing each actor in his or her proper position. My "errors" troubled me; I would think that I had placed a person correctly, only later to find contradictory evidence—a different job title, or even worse, a "mistake" in agency. Just about the time I was ready to start all over, despairing at the many such "errors," I realized that in a system as political as the one I was studying, promotions and transfers must have been a consistent phenomenon.

I started over, this time noting *dates* carefully, and was unable to construct a series of system charts, showing not only the configurations of actors and interest groups in each slice of time, but also the movements of each actor through promotions, demotions, transfers, and relocations to a new agency—data that again helped me to "make sense" of some anomalies: A "state" person who seemed to take the perspective of "county" people was no longer puzzling when I learned that he was a former county politician; a psychiatrist's virulent animosity toward the "medical model" suddenly made sense when I

learned that years before he had been forced out of the state psychiatric group which had planned Dexter on a medical model.

In these ways, I gradually moved from a bare bones outline of people and agencies into an understanding of individual and group investments in Dexter planning; I began to understand why their actions were reasonable, given the total reality from which they operated.

EMPATHY AS A VALIDITY TEST

I do not know when it was that I realized how emotionally involved I was becoming in the Dexter history, nor when I became self-conscious about using my own emotions as a test of validity. Despite my training in clinical aspects of qualitative methods, which taught me to pay attention to my own emotions as an interviewer and participant observer in the present, I had not expected to become emotional about the past.

One of the most important intergroup conflicts in Dexter present was a well-developed antagonism between county and state, both of whom funded and held Dexter responsible. I felt myself originally to be relatively neutral in this enthnocentrism, but as I talked to people and read documents, I noticed that I was constantly being drawn into judgments about who was "right" and who was "wrong."

When I realized how long and hard state bureaucrats had worked to get legislative approvals for the plans, I respected the state position, and saw the county as ungrateful for the state's "gift" to them. When I interviewed people in the county who had volunteered their time for grass-roots organizing and lobbying, I began to understand their feeling that the state had "grabbed the control and the credit" for Dexter. I admired county efforts to gain local control, the struggle of the "little people" against the huge state bureaucracy, and despised the state's sham of encouraging "community input." When I interviewed state bureaucrats, however, I shifted position again when I realized how community protests actually endangered the funding and construction of Dexter's buildings. After spending a rainy Saturday in the local newspaper office, leafing through old papers for stories about Dexter, I was

> struck by the prevalence of county protests to *any* project—freeways, housing developments, on and on. It seems the essence of the bored rich-meddling syndrome. I went away feeling what a pain in the ass those county people are—all those whining letters about not being included!

But a few weeks later, following a trail of official letters between the state and the county, promises given and forgotten, I began to see again how "the state really led the county on—I'm beginning to see how the county felt screwed by the state."

Only after riding this emotional roller-coaster several times was I able to integrate my own feelings about county and state into an intergroup framework that allowed me to take account of both perspectives on the struggle: I could understand how county and state people justified their own feelings and how they came to despise the other group, without myself judging one perspective to be "right." I wrote in my journal, "I've gone back and forth so much with emotional identifications so many times that I now feel very sympathetic to just about everyone. I think I've got it."

However, the most biasing emotional attachment I had was still hidden to me: Having become so close to current Dexter employees, and having lived through the intense emotions of their early confusion and fights, I *blamed* the planners, both county and state, for having botched the planning and caused Dexter so many troubles after it opened. Sarason's (1972) proposition that new organizations inherit conflict from the planning history was emotionally convenient for me; it allowed me to give academic respectability to my own emotional agenda of absolving the Dexter I knew and loved from responsibility for its early failures. Only a coincidental event saved me from my own bias.

PHYSICIAN, HEAL THYSELF

About the time I had finished gathering data and placing it in proper time perspective, I had to stop thinking about Dexter's history of unresolved conflicts to prepare a speech for the American Association of University Women. I had been selected "Woman Scholar of the Year" by the local chapter of AAUW and was to accept the award at a banquet.

I was struck by the juxtaposition of "woman" and "scholar" and began thinking about my own life, how I had struggled with the contradiction of being "smart" and a "girl" during the 1950s, when those two images were mutually exclusive. I traced my life history through phases of trying to be a woman (giving up my intellectual promise) and trying to be a scholar (giving up my feminine promise) and saw that I had flipped back and forth several times, each time trying to resolve the conflict between woman and scholar by denying the need for one or the other.

As I worked on my speech, I began to realize that just as the old societal images of women and of scholars had begun to loosen and shift, so had I begun to integrate the previously contradictory images in my personal identity: I was a woman scholar, and although the *external* world still did not welcome women in academics, the *internal* conflict was slowly being resolved. My inability to resolve the woman/scholar conflict had slowly resulted in a new internal image that transcended the split. I decided to title my speech "The Value of Unresolved Conflict" and congratulated myself on being able to tolerate the conflict, unresolved, for so long.

When I returned to work on the Dexter history of conflicts, I realized what I had done. Working through my own emotions in another context had allowed me to see the possibility that unresolved conflict, no matter how painful, might have long-term benefits in creating something new. I could not allow myself to draw a conclusion about myself that I refused to consider for Dexter, so I examined the hypothesis that the planners' inability to resolve conflicts had been good for Dexter too. I had to admit that it was so. Despite the pain of conflicting images of what Dexter should be, Dexter had indeed begun to evolve into a public service agency that transcended previously contradictory images, no matter how awkwardly. I began to forgive the planners, and with that emotional breakthrough, I could begin to craft theory about conflict in the creation of new organizations without making emotional attributions of blame.

HISTORICAL SENSE-MAKING

So, given the logistical problems and emotional demands of reconstructing history, was it worth it? Did my hard-won historical understanding make Dexter's early development make sense, as Sarason (1972) had claimed?

It did, beyond my expectations. I had selected, from Dexter's first year, five key conflicts, issues with which Dexter struggled and by which it was nearly destroyed during those early months:

Which referral agency's needs was Dexter to serve?
What population was Dexter to serve?
What would constitute "success" for Dexter?
Who would pay for Dexter?
Who would Dexter be controlled by—county or state?

My historical search was focused on trying to find whether those conflicts had arisen during the planning and, if so, how planners had dealt with them. When I began searching for Dexter's planning history, I looked first to find its beginning. I began nearly every interview with the questions, "When do you first remember hearing any mention of Dexter?" and "Who first thought of creating Dexter?" They turned out to be very difficult questions.

After months of investigation, I began to think that *any* "origin question," even for an organization as young as Dexter, was doomed to be clouded in myth. It turned out that at least four separate groups thought that *they* had first thought of Dexter, and furthermore, that it was their hard work that brought Dexter to life. Along with feelings of parenting came feelings of ownership, and each group was certain that its needs were most pressing, knew which population was most appropriate for Dexter to serve, and who should pay for Dexter.

The irony of Dexter's beginning was that while conceptions that arose simultaneously in separate parts of the community flowed into a wave of demand sufficiently powerful and persistent to overcome bureaucratic inertia and bring Dexter to life, the divergent perceptions of origin coexisted without resolution throughout the planning, almost guaranteeing that Dexter would later be torn apart by its identity crisis.

A CHRONOLOGICAL PASS THROUGH TIME

After I had finally assembled papers and notes from archives and memories, I began the most painstaking task of my already obsessive venture: Beginning with the first myths of origin, I worked my way slowly through time, picturing events, trying to imagine feeling as the participants did, slowly building an image of the reality out of which each person and group produced documents, took stands, responded to others, and made decisions.

It was only then, with all data available to me simultaneously, that I was able to play memories against each other, make sense of the divergence between private opinions and public documents, and finally gain empathy both for participants and, in a new and startling way, for the actions of the system as a whole.

The emotional impact of making a chronological pass through time was powerful. In the early years, I felt the hope and determination of those many parents of Dexter, and could see how they all were part of a more general wave of belief sweeping the country during the sixties, a

belief that all social problems could indeed be cured, given enough money and ingenuity. I felt them struggle with each other, and watched with feelings much like those of the audience to a Greek tragedy as the separate realities began to clash with one another, at tremendous human cost: public and private arguments, escalating into conflicts that ruined some careers and may have been responsible for a suicide. In the most conflictual periods of history, when people were behaving in the most unkind ways to each other, I hated them all; I was disgusted with the history, and had to force myself to sit down at my desk to continue working. I noticed that the planners of that era were avoiding work, too. My emotions paralleled theirs.

After participating empathically in such ugliness, which I could then see was a nearly inevitable result of so many diverse interests claiming legitimacy to participate in planning Dexter, I began to doubt my own conviction that participation was necessarily a "good" way to run society. Again, my feelings paralleled the planners'. Only by achieving a state of simultaneous empathy with clashing segments of this system could I at last understand *why* the planners had chosen to avoid conflict, to postpone resolution of such vital issues, and to withdraw behind walls of secrecy, creating a sham of public participation. For several years, progress and withdrawal from controversy were directly related. I began to think that this was the only way Dexter could possibly have been brought to life.

From the hard-won perspective of the historian, I could at last "see" the staggering cost of creating Dexter—the thousands of hours of time put into meetings, preparation of memos, telephone calls, lobbying (one single public hearing included the participation of 109 agencies and 37 individuals, with a transcript running several volumes). I had touched the emotions of only a few of the people who lived that history, yet I sat at my desk and wept for their humiliation, their hard work, and their failures. When I finished the history, I felt I had lived through those years of struggle and had myself given birth to Dexter. I was not sure it was fair to bring Dexter into a world so harsh and inevitably disappointing.

And yet with a longer range of vision, I was able to see that Dexter was not doing so badly after all. I could see that those long years of conflictual relationships among those who felt they "owned" Dexter had slowly, painfully, set the patterns for relationships in the present; conflict that had been chaotic in the early years was still present in current relationships, but more regulated, more manageable, and with

some hope of benefit. Dexter present was managing, albeit with struggle, to meet some of the needs of all of its parents, to fulfill some of the dreams of integrating fragmented services into a single setting, to serve (with uncertain success) the populations whose need had stimulated planning fifteen long years earlier.

I finished my work (Simmons, 1983) with a profound respect for the difficulty of creating new life forms in a world set up for old ones and with a sense that change might indeed be inevitable, but only in retrospect. In process, to those participating in change, there are only hard choices and the limits of human perseverance.

THE CLINICAL DEMANDS OF HISTORY

I would advise anyone contemplating historical work to first read Lawrence Durrell's *Alexandria Quartet*, a series of four novels containing so much truth about social realities that it is fiction only in the most trivial sense. In these novels, Durrell leads the reader through a complete explanation of the meaning of a series of events, only to reveal how totally wrong we can be when we understand social reality from only a single perspective.

I struggled with Durrell's lesson during this research and constantly warned myself that no matter how thoroughly I thought I understood Dexter's history, I might get a totally different understanding if I talked to just one more person or searched through just one more set of files. I recorded this constant anxiety in my research journal:

> As I reach the end of the history, I keep getting exhausted—but there's still more data to be gathered! Going to the state offices sucks the life out of me. I just can't deal with any more commissions or task forces. I noticed _____'s office today, but I couldn't bear the thought of learning more, so I just walked away. I feel *bloated* with data, and nauseous because it's squirming around in a confused tangle. It's as if there are zones of data, with infinite confusion at the most distant points gradually giving way to a patterned understanding at the core. But because this network stretches outward (and deeper) endlessly, I *always* feel the anxiety of that outer rawness, and I try to find form in it, and if I get more data, I *do*, but that just moves the circle farther out into the void. I want to stop—I'm overwhelmed.

Although reconstructing the Dexter history was an obsessive act unequalled in my experience, I was constantly plagued with the certainty that it was "wrong." This was not just scientific caution—I

knew that many of the people who had lived this history would eventually read my account, and I worried both that they might be hurt, embarrassed, or angry and that they would make fun of my "erroneous" conclusions.

It is no wonder that people do not use historical methods more with in-context phenomena. I would be willing to bet that I know as much as anyone has ever known about a particular set of events, but I *still* feel acutely ignorant about the full historical context of Dexter's beginnings. In retrospect, my single most valuable scientific safeguard was that continuous paranoid voice in my ear, telling me "You don't *know* that—you might be wrong!"

To make use of that vague anxiety, that epistemological paranoia, is a methodological task of the greatest demands:

- to acknowledge, fully and shockingly, the highly degraded, distorted, and constantly reinterpreted nature of human memory;
- to build, with the aid of theory about how humans construct realities for themselves, setting-specific models of distortion that help us to make use of both the "fact" and the "fiction" of human perception;
- to acknowledge, deconstruct, and make use of the emotional involvement of the historian as yet another participant in the construction of explanations for events; and
- to trust the guidance of those vague feelings of anxiety, using emotional empathy as a final test of validity.

ARE WE UP TO THE DEMANDS?

There seem to be three major sets of demands for doing research with attention to the complexities presented in this chapter: the demand that we be broadly educated in the social sciences and that we personally overcome the fragmentation of disciplinary boundaries in doing methodical research; the demand that we become personally educated about our own psychological processes, both as they affect our interactions with "subjects" and as they affect our own interpretations of the world we study; and the demand that we develop and disseminate methodological knowledge—not just methods, but rather understanding *of* method—far more sophisticated than our current prescriptions for research. A fourth is a meta-demand: that we alter the system of professional expectations to support and allow research which may be less "certain" than we are led to believe should be the case, legitimating the attendant anxieties of both researchers and the scientific community.

In this chapter, I have mentioned only two areas of psychology that I used extensively in this work: clinical psychology and cognitive psychology. It is exceedingly rare for an organizational researcher to receive training in the fundamentals of human cognition and human emotionality, along with organizational theory, yet these are only two areas among many that enrich a researcher's perspective. Since all disciplines in the social sciences and the humanities deal with human behavior, can we afford to pretend that these diverse disciplines do not all tell us something essential about humans? I think not, yet the pressures in higher education for increasingly differentiated, specialized, and narrow training are in sharp conflict with the pragmatics of institutional resources and the limits of human endurance. To "know" in the abstract, too, is not the same as "knowing" for oneself, and the demands of self-understanding suggested by this chapter mean that researchers should seek understanding of their own biases, blind spots, and cognitive limitations with as high a priority as theoretical knowledge. The anti-clinical bias in much of "scientific" psychology, which worships at the altar of detached objectivity, must be confronted directly as a defense against the implications of applying theory to oneself. The stigma of entering into individual psychotherapy must be transformed to a routine and essential part of graduate training, as must "consciousness raising" at the social level; we must come to understand how all of us are encased in the perspective of our ethnic, gender, and class backgrounds, as well as our own psychodynamic histories. The need to transcend all such filters is, sadly, mired in the impossibility of understanding the social world without them.

Our work as researchers must be supported by methodological theory that is informed by social theory, so that our methods do indeed take account of subjectivity as an inevitable, evolving social construction. These paradigmatic conflicts—the need for certainty against the impossibility of certainty—have seemed unresolvable, but after a long period of defensive prescriptions in methodological literature, we are finally beginning to see literature that takes on the challenge of methods for people studying people as they really are (e.g., Putnam & Pacanowsky, 1983; Morgan, 1983; Reason & Rowan, 1981).

The demand that we begin to make use of the ephemeral experience of empathy as a validity check is perhaps risky, as one person's empathy is another person's projection. No one but I will ever come to know the Dexter history as I have known it, nor come to have the same "making sense" of it as I. I must live with the anxiety that my hard-won understanding may be yet another, deeper fantasy to fulfill some

personal agenda. I face that agonizing conflict with every word I write, resolving it only temporarily.

At heart, perhaps the conflict is one between the ideal that our intellect tells us must be found if we are to keep from fooling ourselves about what we know about the social world, and the reality that none of us is quite up to the challenge. There are limits to my capacity to endure internal conflict without fleeing into dissonance-reducing simplifications, but these limits are expanded when the intensity of the struggle is legitimized in the community of organizational scholars, and shared as an integral part of the process of research.

HISTORY IN THE HERE AND NOW:
The Development of a Historical Perspective

Jonathon H. Gillette

Recent organizational behavior literature reflects an emerging concern among social scientists that current scientific methods are failing to capture the dynamic qualities of organizations. A particularly frequent criticism is that researchers ignore past events and assume that they can understand a system by examining only the present (Kimberly & Miles, 1980).

While a review of the literature basically confirms this view, there have been some attempts to take into account the influence of an organization's past. Sarason (1972), for example, focused much of his attention when examining new organizations on their "prehistory." Some have proposed development models that, by definition, attend to the passage of time. (See Levinson et al., 1978, for individuals; Bennis & Shepard, 1956, for groups; and Kimberly & Miles, 1980, for organizations.) Others have done longitudinal studies (Lawrence & Dyer, 1983). Finally, a number of social scientists have examined an organization's past while researching its here-and-now dynamics through examining archival material and reconstructing past events in interviews. All these methods attempt to gain an understanding of the present through a greater sensitivity to the past (e.g., Alderfer & Brown, 1975). Their techniques, however, are often mentioned only in passing and have not been clearly connected to the social science methodology in use.

What is lacking is an explicit formulation of an interdisciplinary approach that brings together the historical and social science paradigms of analysis. Such a formulation would contain a specific set of constructs to guide the historical inquiry and its interpretation. It would mean that the researcher attended to the past as an integral part of any analysis of an ongoing system.

The development of an interdisciplinary perspective is not an easy task. History and organizational behavior have distinctive world views. Each has traditions that emphasize different foci and methods and, in some basic way, deny the validity of the other (Lifton, 1974). Bringing them together is analogous to trying to be simultaneously a member of two separate and distinct groups. Consider the following chart in which each field is presented as an ideal type:

Social Scientist/O.B. Practitioner   Historian

Praises

The scientific tradition   The literary tradition
- theory based   - data led
- replicable   - written in narrative form
- objective   - personal, subjective

Attacks

The non-scientific tradition   The historical tradition
- no explicit theory   - theory driven
- data arranged to suit end goals   - failing to deal with unexplain-
- missing data   ed variance
- no system of replication   - preserving false dichotomy be-
                                                    tween data that can and cannot
                                                    be counted
                                                  - acts as if past has no influence

What the chart makes clear is that the two fields are in many ways polar opposites. It is not hard to imagine a social scientist dismissing a historian's work as "novel," or to imagine a historian dismissing a social scientist as having "good numbers that mean nothing." Any interdisciplinary formulation would need to contend with these polarities. Is the evidence presented in a scientific or literary mode? What are the criteria for selecting evidence in the first place? What are the standards for distinguishing good work from bad? Further, these polarities are not likely to lead to a resolution that eliminates the tension between the two perspectives. Rather, any resolution will have to carry, as its price, some form of internal tension.

The goal of the particular mix of history and social science offered in this chapter is to gain a greater understanding of the present through an increased sensitivity to the past. This mix is new. Others, in particular the psychohistorians, have used an interdisciplinary mix of history and social science. Their process has involved doing traditional historical research through the lenses of new social science theory. They have sought to reinterpret past events through newly developed paradigms (Lifton, 1974). This particular model of uniting history and social

science does not help a researcher studying present events who wishes to become sensitive to influences from the past. Such research requires an opposite resolution: the conduct of social science research through the lenses of a historical perspective.

This chapter attempts to take the first steps in developing such a historical perspective within social science research. Part one of the chapter examines the discipline of history, outlining the main components of its perspective, and describing the modes of historical inquiry. Part two proposes two steps in the development of a historical perspective: acquiring an understanding of historical works and doing actual historical research in an ongoing organization.

WHAT IS HISTORY?

At its simplest, history is the systematic study of the past. Its roots are in a literary tradition, and many of the great historians of the past were also great writers. As writers, they have struggled to recreate the past in a form accessible to readers in the present. As historians, they have a perspective that includes events preceding, during, and after the time of events studied. It is a perspective that seeks understanding across time boundaries.

The historical perspective consists of a number of different elements. These are (1) a basic assumption, (2) a sensitivity to context, (3) a narrative form, (4) the temporal position of the researcher, and (5) levels of analysis.

BASIC ASSUMPTION

Historical perspective has at its core a basic assumption that guides the inquiry. Phillip Rieff (1974), a psychohistorian, articulated it as follows: "The past is not simply dead weight to be cast off by enlightened minds, but active and engaged, threatening to master the present." Such an assumption is woven into the fabric of historical exposition, affecting its interpretation of individual behavior. Consider this passage from Trotsky's (1932) *History of the Russian Revolution*:

> Foremost in our vision will stand the great, moving forces of history, which are super-personal in character. . . . Moreover, we hope to show in what follows, partially at least, just where in a personality the strictly personal ends—often much sooner than we think—and how frequently the "disturbing traits" of a person are merely scratches made by a higher law of development.

Individual behavior and personality are influenced by the past: What is often interpreted as personality may instead be a reflection of the forces of the past. The historical perspective is based on the assumption that individuals are affected by events over time. Historical research, then, provides not just a tour of the past, but a method for understanding the past's relationship to and influence on the present.

This basic assumption requires a researcher to look beyond the experiences of any single individual. Just as social scientists have explored collective behavior as something distinct from any individual's behavior, so the historian seeks a perspective that interprets interconnections across individual time periods. Thus the historian is able to understand events and behaviors in a way that is unavailable to the individual participants.

A SENSITIVITY TO CONTEXT

A historical perspective is built on a belief in the importance of context. The emphasis is on building interpretation from the contextual ground up; there is an accompanying skepticism concerning theory. Both of these components have important methodological consequences, as noted in Lipset and Hofstadter's (1968) comparison of history and sociology:

> History must be concerned with the analysis of the particular sets of events or processes. Where the sociologist looks for concepts which subsume a variety of particular descriptive categories, the historian must remain close to the actual happenings and avoid statements which, though linking behavior at one time or place to that elsewhere, lead to a distortion in the description of what occurred in the set of circumstances being analysed.

This skepticism of theory exists despite many historical works that present large theoretical statements. Historians would argue that the process used to develop their broad interpretations was qualitatively different from the social science process of generalization in that theories simply follow the data and any large conclusions are solidly based on specific contextual data.

In the final analysis, historians contend that there are elements of understanding that will always evade any theoretical application.

> Most important, historians must always appreciate the limitations of using a single interpretive point of view.... Every model, by scaling down reality into a series of more easily comprehended components, inevitably reduces the complexities of history. Even when our models have accounted for goals, strategies, SOPs[Standard Operating Procedures], political influence, and outcomes, there remain those pieces of the picture

which are still irreducible. . . . Some elements of history will always remain stubbornly intractable, beyond the reach of the model builders. (Davidson & Lytle, 1983)

THE NARRATIVE FORM

Key to a historical perspective is the creation of the narrative. A critical element is that the narrative flow from the events themselves rather than from a theoretical model. Tuchman (1981) notes,

> As to treatment, I believe that the material must precede the thesis, that chronological narrative is the spine and the bloodstream that bring history close to "how it really was" and to a proper understanding of cause and effect; that, whatever the subject, it must be written in terms of what was known and believed at the time, not from the perspective of hindsight, for otherwise the result will be invalid.

The narrative is richly descriptive, and presents conclusions only after building the contextual fabric of the era for the reader. It is a collection of data, arranged through a literary medium and tolerating the use of imagination as long as the presentation remains rooted in the data.

The validity of a narrative lies in its ability to incorporate both previously known and newly discovered data. Historians have nightmares about discovering a relevant piece of research that has been left out of their analysis. From the data, the narrative must develop a perspective that makes sense of individuals and their behavior in the context of their time. The reader can, with this perspective, understand events in a way that no individual participant could. Validity is literary rather than scientific. It is the compelling nature of the narrative that distinguishes good work from bad: how tightly argued it is, whether it takes into account all the relevant information, and whether it evokes an instinctively believable image of the past.

THE TEMPORAL POSITION OF THE RESEARCHER

The above criteria for validity must themselves be understood as a product of their temporal position in the discipline of history. That is, judgments concerning validity shift as time passes. Historians fifty years ago interpreted the American Revolution as a radical break from the past, while more recent reinterpretations see it as a means of conserving that past. Every historian's interpretive lens, its selection and interpretation of data, is influenced by the time in which the historian lives.

Thus, historical perspective not only requires that we attempt to understand others in the context of their times, but that we begin to understand ourselves, including the influences of our present on our

theories and interpretations. Threats to validity can arise either from a failure to account for the specific historical context of the events being described, or from failure to recognize assumptions of our own research framework that are based on our historical rootedness. In fact, historians also study themselves; the field of historiography attempts to examine how historians have been influenced by their circumstances.

LEVELS OF ANALYSIS

One of the difficulties in discussing history is that the same word is used whether you look at individuals, organizations, or society as a whole. Each has its own history. In order to clarify what is being analyzed, history can be conceived of as having a number of different levels. The word *level* comes from social science and is used to differentiate work done on individuals, groups, and organizations. Having a clear sense of these different levels can greatly aid in understanding how past events combine and interact. It makes it possible to differentiate between, for example, whether people find themselves unemployed during the Great Depression at the beginning or the end of their working lives.

Hareven (1977, 1982) was the first to begin looking at historical levels. She attempted to examine these differences by organizing history into three levels of time. One is *individual time*. This is essentially an understanding of the developmental stage of any single individual, including both chronological age and relationships to others (e.g., marriage, adolescence). Another is *organizational time*. This refers to an organization's developmental stage—for instance, whether it is expanding or bureaucratizing. A third is what Hareven calls *historical time*. This represents the overall social, economic, institutional, and cultural context of the larger society.

Despite the confusion of having the third level called "historical," this framework begins to bring together a number of theories to enrich and deepen each other. The various developmental theories noted in this chapter's introduction can all plot their particular dynamics on a single chart, each line of which represents a different level of analysis. Individual, group, system, and societal dynamics may cross over, pull at, intensify, or smother each other. This structure allows us to frame an analysis that keeps track of changes that have taken place at a particular level simultaneously with changes that have taken place in the context surrounding that level. It provides the opportunity to see a connection between changes within an organization and changes within the larger society.

In summary, history has a simple definition: It is the study of the past. It has a basic assumption that the past is actively engaged in the present. It is context sensitive and has a skepticism of theory. It relies on a

narrative as its main form. In addition, it operates at a number of levels simultaneously, challenging us to understand both the past and ourselves.

DEVELOPING A HISTORICAL PERSPECTIVE

Given an accurate and thorough understanding of history, the task still remains of training the researcher to be sensitive to historical influences while examining ongoing systems. The goal is for the researcher to develop a historical perspective as an additional way of understanding the here-and-now.

This chapter suggests two actions through which an increasing historical perspective may develop: studying current historical works and conducting historical research within the organization under consideration. These actions incorporate all the elements of history that were outlined in the previous section, as well as having implications for how research is carried out.

STUDYING HISTORY

Studying current historical works helps in understanding the historical forces that are influencing one's working theories and one's role as a researcher/interventionist in a system. Social scientists have not been particularly interested in such an examination (Gergen, 1973; Schlenker, 1974). It is one thing to acknowledge history as something that needs to be controlled for internal validity (Campbell & Stanley, 1963). It is quite another to accept a relationship between history and the development of particular general theories.

The purpose, then, is to try to understand our historical position as researchers. This is clearly an ongoing task, one that seeks *understanding* of historical forces rather than elimination of their influence. The first step is to examine what assumptions in one's own set of theories remain unexplored and unchallenged. A great deal of recent work, especially by labor historians, is relevant to studies in organizational behavior. These writings discuss work structures (Friedlander, 1975; Hareven & Langenback, 1978), workers' control (Montgomery, 1979), bureaucracy and complex organizations (Clawson, 1980), scientific management and work designs (Noble, 1977), and corporate welfare programs (Meyer, 1981).

These works challenge social science researchers' assumptions about the nature of a research relationship, raising important questions about the system theories most investigators learn early in their training. Historical attitudes toward three major topics stand out as important challenges to conventional social science assumptions: views on the

nature of bureaucracy, the nature of a research relationship, and the scope of a study.

Bureaucracy. It is a commonly held assumption that bureaucracy is an inevitable form that results when organizations grow in size and complexity. Katz (1971), however, finds compelling evidence in school systems organized in the early 1900s that "bureaucracies are bourgeois institutions designed to repress working people." His evidence on school systems is extended by David Tyack (1974), who states,

> Bureaucratization was *partially* a response to the complexities of urbanization and population growth *but* not the result of a preordained imperative. Rather the drive to bureaucratize urban schools, which flowered after 1890 in cities across the nation, was part of an effort by elites and educational professionals to turn political questions into administrative issues by removing decision making from the public arena to the hallways and offices of bureaucratic organizations where educational experts could operate free from the pressures of public opinion.

Dan Clawson (1980), comes to similar conclusions by examining the metal working industry. He analyzes a little-known form of production known as "inside contracting," a form he claims is craft centered:

> A distinction can be made between craft and bureaucratic forms of production; in craft production most or all of the basic decisions about how to produce a product are made by persons who are themselves directly involved in physically producing it; in bureaucratic production these decisions are made by people not in the work crew.

Eventually, inside contracting was abolished and replaced with a bureaucratic form. Clawson finds no evidence to support the traditional justification for bureaucratic forms:

> Why was inside contracting abolished? The two most important reasons were, first, the attempt to shift income from contractors to the company and second, the wish to establish and maintain an "acceptable" social hierarchy. Neither considerations of efficiency nor dissatisfaction with inside contracting's technical capacity to perform the work were significant issues at the time.

Research relationship. The second major challenge historians pose to social scientists concerns the forces shaping a researcher's relationship with an organization. A number of historians have pointed out the ways in which the relationship between corporations and academia has shaped the nature and scope of research questions, and that this relationship changes over time (Perrow, 1973). Consider the work of

Noble (1977), which focuses on technology and the rise of engineers and engineering schools.

As Christopher Lash writes in the preface to Noble (1977),

> The notion of technological determinism has dominated popular understanding of the industrial revolution. Changes in technology are assumed to have been the principal cause of industrialization, and the whole process is seen purely as a technological revolution.

Noble challenges that assumption by examining the rise of industrial engineering. He argues that engineers, and their choice of technology to develop, were dominated by the imperatives of economic and social control:

> In short, they ventured to design a new (yet old) social order, one dominated by the private corporation and grounded upon the regulated progress of scientific technology. Forces of production and social relations, industry and business, engineering and the price system—the two poles in the dialectic of social production—collapsed together in the consciousness of corporate engineering under the name of management.

Social scientists, especially in organizational behavior, have origins that parallel engineers and can, in some way, be seen as social engineers of organizations. Their ties to management and management science are reflected in their research topics and their location in management schools. This creates a "form of consciousness," to use Noble's phrase, that prevents a close examination of the ways intervention may be colluding with the forces for social and economic control.

It is important to note that the image that emerges is not one of social scientists harking to the beck and call of corporate greed. It is, instead, more an image of researchers who do not engage in a process of self-reflection. Concepts such as the "free flow of information" become valued because they are thought to be neutral or value free. The consequences are not always so neutral. Consider the consequences of the children's television show, *Sesame Street*. It was originally designed to provide key skills to those who were entering school with the lowest levels of competence. The results were intended to bring the top and the bottom closer together, by starting them in school with the same basis of skills. However, just the opposite happened. Since those at the top had a built in higher learning rate, exposure to *Sesame Street* put them even farther ahead. While all children's skills increased, parity decreased even further.

Scope of the study. Another prevalent assumption about organizational research is that the dynamics inside the system drive the behavior of its members. In essence, the belief is that one can understand behavior

in organizations by restricting the scope of the study to the inside of the organization. Recent historical work by Gutman (1976) and Montgomery (1979) points to the importance of understanding working class culture inside *and outside* the factories. They refute the traditional historical interpretation that it is the factories and the bosses who are responsible for primary socialization into the workplace. Workers socialize other workers, both inside and outside the factory walls. My own work on New Haven Italian workers in a metal working industry confirms this interpretation. The metal workers sought to bring their larger community values into the factory (Gillette, 1983). An understanding of this interpretation might enable researchers to see how "resistant" behavior in the workplace may be a statement of community values, rather than just a battle with the boss.

DOING HISTORICAL RESEARCH

The second step in developing a historical perspective is to do actual historical research. This step influences both the processes of diagnosis and of intervention.

Diagnosis. A historical perspective can be developed while analyzing an ongoing system. The work involves examining past documents and interviewing members of that system about the past. The goal is to be able to put together time lines, sequences of events over time, for each of the levels outlined earlier in this chapter. The analysis seeks to understand events by looking at behavior among levels, connected across time.

It must be pointed out from the start that each source of historical data has some strengths and weaknesses. Documents are often easy to obtain but notoriously inadequate in describing the emotions and, in many cases, the exact actions taken by members of a system. Oral accounts are fallible because of memory loss and personal reinterpretations of past events. However, these two sources, taken together, can begin to help the researcher understand events of the past and how the current dynamics are connected to them.

As each level of time—individual, group, organizational, and societal—is charted, the power of this form of analysis lies in the new diagnostic insight the interaction of different levels of time lines provides. Consider the following case as an example of how various levels of time can be brought together:

> In the late 1960s, a large manufacturing company decided to set up an independent subsidiary—one that would be structured differently—to attract what they thought would be a different kind of worker and a

different kind of customer. The plant was small, run by the workers (who rotated the managerial duties) and emphasized increased contact between workers and customers. Despite a general shift in the larger society away from alternative structures, the subsidiary was successful and popular through the 70s and into the early 80s.

In 1982, the plant's environment changed, in that two similar subsidies were established in the same area. No longer a monopoly, the plant had to define more clearly just what made it special. The organizational structure had already moved toward a more traditional management structure. The physical plant had been redesigned to make the space occupied by workers and managers more differentiated. The process of manufacturing had originally been run by teams of four, but now most workers worked alone.

There was a variety of data available to them as they faced their re-examination. They were still turning a good profit and attracting highly skilled, highly motivated workers. Yet some of the new workers were experienced in more traditional forms of manufacturing. Among the old workers, some had strong feelings about the team method while others were worn out by it.

The plant decided to become more traditional. The question, then, is how to understand that decision. Certainly, the changes in the plant's environment are a factor, along with a trend that had been developing over time toward a more traditional structure. Theories put forth by scholars such as Dimaggio and Powell (1983) analyze similar trends by pointing out the tendency in organizations to conform to a standard structure over time. But is this analysis sufficient to explain the phenomenon? What is taking place at the other levels of the system?

At the individual level, all of the workers were between 35 and 42 years old, with the vast majority having worked at the plant since its opening and, in fact, never having worked elsewhere. Thus, for many of these individuals, issues of mid-life transition were powerful and disturbing. Many talked about leaving, but few had clear ideas as to what else they would do. For many, the financial stress of educating their children was increasing while their pay continued to be near the statewide low.

At the group level, two major factions had existed within the plant for most of its history: one that had always sought a more traditional approach, and one that had always pushed for alternatives. Since the plant was small, conflict between the two groups had often been seen as a clash of personalities. As long as the two groups remained in some state of parity, the system was able to satisfy both groups with small adjustments. However, in the last three years the traditionalists had gained dominance by securing the leadership position for one of their members and by the departure of a major leader of the other group. Developmentally, the traditional group had gained greater cohesion, while the alternative group unraveled more and more.

Finally, fiscal pressures that had been building up inside the parent company for a number of years began to influence the plant. Its original justification, as a choice based on its production structure, was replaced by a justification based on money. The plant, since it had fewer managers, had a lower per unit cost. In other words, what had made it legitimate to members of the system hierarchy changed.

Thus, the plant's movement toward a more traditional program was not just a function of events on any one of these levels; rather, each made an important contribution the rest. The decision can be seen as a synergistic response to a number of historically based patterns that reinforced each other.

The above case illustrates how one might interpret the historical data available in a system, as well as giving a sense of the kind of information one might need to seek. An additional factor must be kept in mind. The historical mind holds to the notion that the narrative or story follows wherever the data leads. To implement this aspect of historical research, a social scientist must be willing to expand, alter, or even contract the original parameters of a study. It is quite possible that the organization can be understood without seeking data outside the system. But it may also be true that some understanding of the larger system, such as the neighborhood from which the members originate, may be essential. The experience of historians is that the scope of the study is determined through the process of the research itself.

Intervention. The inclusion of historical research may also influence interventions in a system and may alert practitioners to the insufficiency of a here-and-now analysis as a guide for change. Consider the following example:

> A group of inner city high school teachers was meeting regularly with an outside consultant to learn how to integrate theories of group dynamics into daily classroom management. In one particular session, the consultant's agenda was to demonstrate that the teachers were consistently acting as if they had no power or influence. He used, as an example, the issue of how dirty the building was, and refused to accept the teachers' refrain that they could not change that aspect of the school. In the process of resisting the consultant, the teachers became more aware of their denial of their own authority and power. The consultant left the session feeling that he had made an important contribution to their learning and had made an appropriate intervention.
>
> The consultant had correctly analyzed their "acting as if" mode and was able to show it to them in a way that they accepted and which elicited a commitment to change. But he did not understnd the historical aspect of their resistance to taking power, particularly in relation to the upkeep of the building. His failure to do this meant that he had no sense of the utility of the particular resistance that emerged. In fact, that resistance was an important defense for those teachers and enabled them to work effectively

in their classrooms. Time and time again, the system as a whole had threatened to drown them with its needs. Within a year after this particular program, two significant teachers left, suffering from burnout.

These teachers had, over time, created a boundary between themselves and the rest of the system, in order to prevent the system from overwhelming them. Historically, this boundary had served them well. They had done a number of projects that had accomplished some reform, while managing to continue teaching. The consultant had no sense of their previous interaction with the system, nor did he have a sense of how the myth of total powerlessness had emerged within the group. An alternative intervention might have been to build a boundary that was based on a more accurate sense of reality. This might have enabled the myth to be examined, lessening its deleterious effects on their performance, while preventing the removal of the myth from opening up the floodgates. This type of understanding would only have been possible if the history of that system and group had been examined.

IMPLICATIONS

The development of a historical perspective has a number of implications. First, the researcher is more likely to enter an organization with an expanded set of alternative hypotheses. This is especially beneficial if the research goal is to understand the multiple perspective in an organization. Here, knowing the history of the various groups may allow for their viewpoints to be recognized, then understood. Since most researchers are not from the same group or class as many members of the organizations they study, understanding other group history is a way to have some empathy even before entering an organization.

Second, new ways of interpreting data collected from an organization may open up. It is one thing to come up with information, for example, that workers in a garment factory are taking home unused pieces of fabric. However, it is another thing to interpret or even label it. The management might call it "stealing" and, to most outsiders, this makes sense, since it is assumed that the material bought by management belongs to management. But there is also an alternative interpretation: The workers have, by tradition, been granted ownership of any bolt of cloth they worked on, so that any charge of stealing would be a change in the way the cloth has been accounted for in the past.

A third implication concerns the process of generating and interpreting theory. To some extent, all theories seek to portray root processes that would take place no matter what the historical setting. In order for this to be true, the theorist must be able to distinguish historical content from theoretical process. Lifton (1967) raises this issue in his examination of the work of Freud:

The central dilemma here for depth psychology is its extreme suscep-
tibility to specific historical imagery and conflict. That imagery, moreover,
directly reflects the prevailing sense among the people of a particular
culture and epoch of their own nature. . . .

The fact that Freud's model of libido and repression of the instinctual
sexual impulses was put forth during the late Victorian era, at a time when
society was struggling with these issues, does not invalidate the generalizability of his ideas; their power lies precisely in that generalizability. But
it does raise the important point—not only for Freud but for our own
work now— of the influence of historical forces on the psychological
theories we choose to develop.

Lifton goes on to argue that, today, the fear of death is the content
that has replaced the position held by sexual repression in Freud's day.
The root psychological dynamics remain, while the content shifts
according to culture and time.

Finally, all of this is not without some cost to the researcher; the
demands of this type of work are heavy. Interdisciplinary work has been
said to be "the process by which the unknowns of one's own subject are
multiplied by the uncertainties of some other science." Venturing into a
new field where there are no set guidelines creates internal tension,
especially when that area is bounded by two competing perspectives. In
this particular mix, it is hard not to lose one's sensitivity to unexplained
data while doing social science research. Maintaining a tension between
the two is essential.

Additional difficulties arise. The method requires the researcher to
start off with, and to retain longer, more alternative hypotheses of
behavior. This is not the traditional scientific method of narrowing
possibilities toward the most likely answer; rather, it consciously seeks
to widen the field of possible answers. This increases both the
uncertainty any researcher has concerning the ability to understand a
complex system and the volume of data that needs to be examined. Few
have the resources or, more especially, the time to carry out a full
historical examination.

The process of challenging one's own assumptions requires naviga-
tion between the two extremes of self-doubt and self-righteousness.
Basic philosophical issues that challenge the ability of researchers to
know themselves, much less an organization, remain. And, certainly,
nothing is more infuriating than being told, "I am self-conscious of my
history: you are not." However, between these two poles lies an
opportunity to gain a richer perspective on oneself and the forces that
influence one's theories. In turn, the investigator can develop a greater
sensitivity to the system's memory as well as its here-and-now dynamics.

USING PARTICIPANT OBSERVATION TO CONSTRUCT A LIFE HISTORY

Helen Swick Perry

"Imagine the embarrassment of the physicist to have found that he was among his own data," Harry Stack Sullivan observed in a 1943 lecture to students in the Washington School of Psychiatry. He was reminding his audience, most of whom were psychiatrists in training, that they were engaged in participant observation in their work with patients and that they, too, were among their own data. Twentieth-century physicists had been forced to this realization by the discovery of relativity; they could no longer deal with absolute "truth." The student of human behavior had been struggling much longer with this blurring between the observer and the observed. Even the biographer, as I was to discover in constructing the life history of Harry Stack Sullivan, is forced into the role of participant observer.

When I began in the 1960s to gather data on Sullivan's early life in Chenango County, New York State, with the idea of writing his biography (Perry, H., 1982), I thought of my task in formal terms; I was in search of facts, correspondence, pictures, and interviews with relatives and friends. Yet almost immediately I dimly perceived that I had begun a new look at my own early life in ways that would extend far beyond my formal encounter with psychoanalysis some two decades earlier. As a female biographer of a male subject, I had to begin at a new level to cross the gender gap in much the same way that a therapist of one sex undertakes work with a patient of the other sex. Although my beginnings were superficially different from Sullivan's in important ways, I shortly discovered that "we are all much more simply human than otherwise," as Sullivan (1953a, p. 16) noted. In unexpected ways, I

AUTHOR'S NOTE: An earlier version of this paper, entitled "A Methodological Approach to Interpersonal Biography," was presented on January 26, 1980, in New York City at a symposium on "Psychoanalysis 1980: Converging Views," sponsored by the William Alanson White Institute of Psychiatry, Psychoanalysis and Psychology.

kept finding strange islands of similarities in our encounters with family, friends, and community, although Sullivan was born almost twenty years before me. And I learned to understand that differences in ethnicity, religious identification, and gender paled before the similarities of our human existence.

As I measured my own life and the lives of people in Sullivan's early background against the development of his life and his "durable achievements as a contributor to culture history" (Sullivan, 1947), I found myself, during the period that I worked on the biography, becoming much more sophisticated about the use of participant observation. Yet I had already used that tool for over a decade before in studying patients in three mental hospitals and in making a community mental health study of the Haight-Ashbury district in San Francisco (Perry, H., 1970). It is one thing to ferret out the current life and meaning of an ongoing social setting; it is another to reconstruct the life of a child growing up in a rural community at the turn of the century, over fifty years before my study began. Participant observation was a crucial tool for both kinds of endeavors.

The formula for writing an interpersonal biography, which is another term for the use of participant observation in gathering data for a life history, came from Sullivan himself. During his brief but productive life, Sullivan got around to commenting on many facets of society, including the writing of biography. Only a small portion of his writings are in book form and indexed, so I had forgotten that he had ever mentioned biography.[1] Only after I had already completed a good part of my research and an appreciable amount of the writing did I happen on his formula for writing biography, and I was astonished to see how I had operationally been forced into the avenues that he had so succinctly defined. The passage—which I used as an epigraph for the biography—comes from Sullivan's review (1947) of Ruth Benedict's book on Japanese society, *The Chrysanthemum and the Sword:*

> Biography usually fails to integrate its subject person with the significant others who facilitated and handicapped his durable achievements as a contributor to culture history, and rarely indicates whence came his skills and limitations in the interpersonal relations which made his contribution effective. A survey of at least the near past and present of the culture-complex which he influenced is required to validate this sort of biographical data, to give it dependable psychiatric or social psychological meaning. The phenomenon of Freud without its setting in the contemporary society of Vienna has been followed by the phenomena of Freud's evangelists and Freud's detractors, also without sensitivity to the nuances of cultural differences within the major context of the Western world.

It is difficult to picture in diagrammatic fashion the intricacy and range of this process, representing as it does an important amalgam of the methods of social anthropology and the particular insights of dynamic psychiatry. When one begins to apply this approach in a systematic way, new insights and exciting connections appear as if by magic. The task becomes increasingly complex as one proceeds. Thus I had to inform myself in detail on the lives of more than a dozen people in Sullivan's early environment in order to have some idea of how their lives intertwined with his and helped to define him. Eventually I had to reconstruct his interaction with several friends and colleagues in his adult life and examine both the overlapping similarities that initiated the interaction and the differences that enlarged the scope of Sullivan's thinking.

In beginning with his early life, I first had to look at the geography and history of the area in which he grew up; his limited access to mass communication, which was mainly the daily newspaper published in the county seat; and the economic conditions, the mental health, the religious tensions, and the educational facilities of that time and place. All these factors affected the personalities that most intimately impinged on his early life. I also had to be alert to the anxieties implicit in those people I talked to, emergent from their own particular life histories, as measured against the impact of the general culture. There is no way to do a complete examination of all these factors, but after one has immersed one's self in reconstructing this kind of intimate data on the people and the culture-complex that surrounds any child in the process of growing up, certain obvious insights appear that can be verified, mainly by the way the assets and limitations of these early encounters are played out in the later life.

On my first field trip to Chenango County, I did not immediately recognize that I had any particular interest in studying the community intensively or my own interaction with it, although I was familiar with William Foote Whyte's classic study (1955) of an Italian-American urban community. Whyte set out to study the values of that community with the specific goal of understanding and defining the life-style of that group; from the outset this necessitated an evaluation of his own values and social class. Unlike me, he began his task by looking at the neighborhood as a whole, but eventually he had to concentrate on how these values were reflected and played out in the lives of particular people on whom he focused. I was originally intent on establishing one important fact about Sullivan's early life that I needed for an introduction to the collection of Sullivan papers on which I was then working— documentation for his hospitalization with a schizophrenic break,

which he once mentioned to me (Perry, H., 1982, pp. 3-4). Although I was never able to find documentation for this—in hospital records, for instance—I began almost immediately to sense the input of the community into the mental life of its inhabitants. Thus I was confronted with cogent information on the life of the community over a period of many years. I was faced with vital information on what it was like to grow up as an outsider (the grandson of Irish immigrants) in this tightly structured and still remote part of the Eastern United States. Even though I arrived on the scene over a half-century after Sullivan had moved away, I began to relive the world in which he found himself, through interviews, through information that I found in the daily county newspaper for that period, and through the entire life of the county as reflected in the newspaper. Preeminently that included clear clues to patterns of mental disorder in the county. Shortly I was to discover through U.S. Census Bureau reports that Chenango County had the highest suicide rate for all rural counties in the United States in 1908, the year Sullivan graduated from high school. Out of such data I was forced to move from the particular career line of one person into a wide look at the total picture and then back again.

Either a study of a person living in a culture-complex or a study of a culture-complex as it is filtered through a variety of people is defined quite precisely by Sullivan (1947) in his review of Benedict's book:

> Any *person* is to a great degree a function of his past interpersonal history, the immediate present, and the well- or ill-foreseen neighboring future. Any *people* is an interlocking dynamic network of a great many contemporary persons, each with past, present, and neighboring future with considerable identities and similarities—roughly equaling the culture—and some significant differences [emphasis added].

Sullivan is here using the word *people* to represent what the anthropologists usually call *society*. He is making a contrast between the word *person* and the word *people*. This interplay of the two approaches to human behavior reached its highest point in a series of articles written by Sullivan near the end of his life, one of which was called significantly "Towards a Psychiatry of Peoples" (Sullivan, 1948).

Benedict, by a so-called coincidence, grew up in the same county as Sullivan, although the religious, social-class, and ethnic identification of their families set them apart, and they never knew each other in those years. During World War II, Benedict used this dual approach of person and people in her book on the Japanese. In making a wise recommendation to the United States government on the necessary retention of the

Japanese Emperor in the postwar period, she began by analyzing the complex meaning of the relationship of the people to their emperor through the use of literature, historical studies, and interviews with Japanese-Americans living in this country at the time of World War II. She herself had never been in Japan, and because of the war, she had no access to people living in Japan during the course of her study. Her role as a participant was therefore extremely difficult as she had to acquire a sympathetic feel for values so different from her own, with no firsthand contact with the then current situation in Japan and no firsthand knowledge of the country itself. Yet the Japanese people themselves feel that her study is one of the best ever done on their life and values.

As I went along in my task of trying to figure out what early experience had informed Sullivan's theory, I became more and more aware of my own experience in growing up and to what extent I had assets and liabilities for my participant observation of Chenango County in general and of Sullivan in particular. Partly I underwent a kind of personal sociological analysis, which became an important expansion of my earlier psychoanalytic experience. For the first time I had to face the fact that I had the bias and the blind spots of a WASP. I had never considered that I could be defined as belonging to an elite class. Indeed, partly in keeping with the ideas of the Society of Friends, in which my maternal grandfather had been raised, I was well acquainted with the belief that all men are equal in the sight of God and felt that I accepted this formulation in my daily life. For a variety of familial and personal reasons I was identified with the underdog on most political issues. Yet this was essentially an elitist attitude in which I felt that I must be generous with those who had less.

My own father and mother had been raised on farms in Niagara County, not too distant in social values from the WASPs in Chenango County, including Ruth Benedict. As a child I had spent vacations on relatives' farms in Niagara County, although I myself was raised in a small, largely working-class town just outside of Washington, D.C., where my scientist father had a government job. So, many of the people in Chenango County were much like my relatives; I felt comfortable talking to them.

I also slowly made friends with some of Sullivan's cousins and other Irish-Americans in the county, most of whom were Catholic. Only slowly and painfully did I begin to realize that my unconscious feeling of superiority to Catholics in particular and, more generally, to people who were closer to immigrant status than I was represented a considerable handicap in my explorations.

I had made several brief visits to the county early in the 1960s, but in 1963 I decided that I must make a more formal study of Sullivan's early life and that I would spend a month in the county. Through an Irish-Catholic friend, Miss Loretta Macksey—someone who had known Sullivan as a child—I found a rooming house near where Miss Macksey lived. On my first Sunday there, my (Protestant) landlady asked me which church I went to, and I immediately surmised that it was inconceivable to people in that area that as an adult I had given up attending church. I told her that as a child I had gone to the Congregational church, but that my mother was Quaker on her father's side and Methodist on her mother's side, and that my father was raised as a Baptist. She smiled knowingly—this pattern of different Protestant sects was well known to her, and she was sympathetic. She thought that I would be comfortable in her church, which as I remember was Methodist, and I dutifully accompanied her to church each Sunday. Miss Macksey, the Irish-Catholic neighbor, queried me about my religion after the first Sunday. She told me that I was so sympathetic to the Irish people that she had assumed that I must be part Irish. I told her that I had a great grandmother on my father's side who was Irish, but I had never known her at all; she asked me whether she was Catholic, and I told her that I really did not know.

Subsequently Miss Macksey, who was related to some of the Stack cousins, made arrangements for me to spend an evening with these cousins who happened to be on a visit from Brooklyn, N.Y., to this village where they had grown up. The visit supplied me with new understanding of Sullivan's general background, but I was also questioned by them. One of their main questions centered around whether Sullivan had really been buried by the Roman Catholic Church. When I said that he had and that I knew because I had attended the funeral, they challenged me sharply: How could I know if I were not a Catholic? At some point, Miss Macksey intervened for me; she told them that I was very understanding of the situation of Irish Catholics in Chenango County—"we were treated like skunks at a Sunday School picnic"—and she said that my own grandmother (exaggerating the immediacy of the relationship) was born in Ireland—but in the "northern part," she noted. This was news to me, but I was too startled to protest; so I simply accepted this interpretation, which, I understood, was given in good faith.

I finally recognized that Miss Macksey had explained my not being Catholic, though partly Irish in background, in such a way that my acceptance in the Irish-Catholic part of the community would be expedited: That is, I had the understanding of the Irish through my

"grandmother" and the only reason I was not Catholic was because that part of my family had come from the "northern part" of Ireland where Protestants had dwelt for many centuries. That is, my ancestors in Ireland had not turned coat during one of the famines in Ireland, which would have been the worst possible explanation. During the great potato famine in particular, the inhabitants in the south and west of Ireland, far from the cities, were in most danger of starvation, and the English charitable organizations fed thin soup to the Catholic farmers only if they would renounce the Catholic church; the people who succumbed to this temptation were termed "soupies" by their neighbors. In Chenango County, by contrast, some of the Irish Catholics had become Protestant with much less of an excuse; no one had to starve in America, staunch Catholics noted, and therefore the tendency to become Protestant here as a way of making it faster up the ladder was a sign of an even greater weakness. So it was that Miss Macksey had carefully defined me in such a way that I would not be subject to such criticisms (even about my great grandmother) and that I would be accepted in the Irish-Catholic community in Chenango County.

This encounter also provided me with some insight into why Sullivan had specified that he wanted a Catholic funeral—a fact that caused a good deal of questioning among his psychiatric colleagues, most of whom had abandoned the religion of their own childhoods. They felt that Sullivan saw formal religion as often antithetical to good mental health and as a potential problem, particularly during adolescence. How could he specify a Catholic funeral? I understood his decision completely only after I had spent considerable time in Chenango County. They were keeping score there. The community's questioning continued indefinitely: Was a convert, in either direction, punished by God? And did someone, no matter how far he wandered from the teachings of the Catholic church, finally come back to the fold at the end? Regardless of all else, some church had to provide burial services; it was inconceivable that it would be omitted. In the end, Sullivan remained true to the expectation of those Stacks and Sullivans who were still Catholic. From these two experiences, I had a clear view of the importance of religion in the life of the county.

I would like to mention two other happenstances that were critical in my work. On one of my first visits, I discovered in the county newspaper for 1908 an item on Harry Sullivan's taking a state scholarship examination for Cornell University. He won a scholarship and attended there for less than a year. My father, a farm boy, had also won a state scholarship to Cornell five years earlier and had graduated from there. In my family, there was a story told by my paternal grandmother of how

homesick my father had been in the metropolis of Ithaca so far away from home, and of how he had packed his trunk and returned home at Thanksgiving time in his freshman year, determined not to return to Cornell. His paternal grandfather had talked him into going back. A Sullivan cousin remembers that Harry as a freshman had not wanted to go back to Cornell after his first trip home at Thanksgiving. There was clear evidence here of the culture shock of a farm boy encountering a more sophisticated and complex community and of the significance of travelling even fifty miles in that period. But over time and after making some blunders, I found out that there was a difference between the homesickness of my father and that of Harry Sullivan.

To begin with, my father's family belonged to the farming community in which they lived—they were Protestant, lived on a fruit farm in the most lush section of Niagara County and had a substantial house and farm buildings. The family did not consider it essential at all that my father go to college, nor were they particularly impressed with the fact that my father had won a scholarship. Thus his return from college, not wanting to go back, was treated matter-of-factly by his parents; indeed, it was only his grandfather who encouraged him to return and lectured my father's parents on the fact that they should make more of an effort to go down to Ithaca on the train and visit their son. By contrast, Harry's reluctance to return to Cornell was completely unacceptable to his mother. She felt that Harry's only hope was education; even though he was not yet 17 years old when he went to Cornell, she would not accept the possibility that he could not make it at college. It was in that first year at Cornell that Harry's marks begin to fail and he was finally placed on probation for almost a year; he never went back to Cornell. However limited my father's encounter with larger centers of population before he went to Cornell, he had gone to market in Buffalo many times as a boy to sell farm produce and had looked with awe and wonder on the houses along Delaware Avenue. Moreover, he was almost three years older than Harry was upon entrance. My father, having been kept out of school each fall to help with harvesting, did not finish the required work in high school until he was 19 years old. The very similarities of their backgrounds underscored the differences.

Another area for participant observation emerged as I began to hunt for Sullivan's preadolescent chum—a formulation peculiarly evocative for me, as for many of Sullivan's students. In 1947, I first heard him lecture about the importance of the chum in the years just before adolescence. A person might suffer considerably, he said, from losing the companionship of a chum, through death or through the family's moving away. Although I had had considerable analytic experience by

then, I had never explored the impact of a chum in my own growing-up years. That night at home, I wrote, almost automatically and entirely autobiographically, a short story entitled "The Lost Chum." For the first time I recognized why I had lost my best friend; she had moved not too far away but into a better neighborhood than ours, and her mother wished to terminate all contacts with the old neighborhood. Thus I had a strong personal interest in locating Sullivan's chum, even many years later.

As I talked to teachers, neighbors, and relatives who knew Sullivan as a child, I began to ask, "Did he have a particular friend in school or near home?" From all of them there was a consistent answer—it was Clarence Bellinger, the boy who lived on the next farm. He was Sullivan's *only* friend. They were both living on farms and attending the village school, and they were not totally accepted in that society made up of village children; so they clung together and dreamed together. They had handicaps for the true friendship of peers, for Clarence was five years older than Harry. Yet this relationship was a good deal better than nothing. They were both only children, with mothers who insisted on their becoming famous. The first one to become a psychiatrist was Clarence, and eventually Harry followed suit. Both of them had their first mental hospital experience at St. Elizabeths Hospital under William Alanson White, who himself was more than familiar with Chenango County, as I shall comment on shortly.

Finding Sullivan's chum opened up new avenues that I could explore participantly. For Clarence and Harry were both outsiders in the village school, partly because they were both living on farms. But Harry was the only Irish-Catholic boy in the village school, and Clarence's family did not go to any church—an even more unusual deviation from the norm. Thus Clarence's position was even worse than Harry's. In another dimension I too was an outsider in the school that I attended as a child; my parents arranged for their children to attend the city schools because they were better than the local schools, so that we were rejected by the children in the local schools as being high hat and yet were outsiders in the city schools. Such stories are often a significant part of growing up in the diverse society that is America, so that we peculiarly need the comfort of a chum in whom we can confide with impunity in the delicate years of transition to adulthood.

I shortly began to be aware of many other apparent coincidences as I proceeded with my task. In every significant relationship that Sullivan had, whether in childhood or adulthood, and that I explored, there were strange bands of commonality that one might term, in a mystical sense, auspicious coincidence, as if Sullivan were fated to find this or that

person in his journey through life. I would like to redefine these so-called coincidences. I would posit that in a diverse society in which there is still relatively a good deal of chance for upward mobility, all of us have areas of experience that one can think of as almost isolated strands of life. Many of these experiences are kept well hidden in order to protect self-esteem. All of us who manage to survive become adept at locating the person whose experience at some critical point produces a situation in which we can confide within that delimited area; or, equally true, we withdraw because we become acutely sensitive to the anxiety in the other person that triggers our anxiety in the same area of experience, either because we have had the same experience and are trying to forget it or because the other person's experience is too different and unsettling. Because Sullivan's early life was peopled with an unusually small number of significant people, he seems to have had an uncanny sense for finding these bands of commonality and these areas that aroused anxiety in him.

I would like to begin by examining one simple basis for common experience—time and place (or geography). At the turn of the century, geography in rural United States was a much more important variable than it is now, selecting a limited range of people and experiences. When one adds to that variable another dimension—that of the mental health problems that exist in a particular community— then one has a strong common basis for understanding in general the problems of mental health there. One can talk with another about a similar population, with the same general problems of ethnicity, economics, religion, and so on. Having established some consensus, then one can pool one's knowledge with another's to extrapolate from this a common statement about mental health and disorder. The overlap of time and place in the lives of William Alanson White and Sullivan offers an example of this phenomenon.

In the same year that Sullivan was born, White came as a young physician to Binghamton State Hospital in Broome County, adjacent to Chenango County. This hospital was the usual resource for mentally disturbed patients in Chenango County. A few years after White left Binghamton in 1903, Ross McClure Chapman became a staff physician there and then later became superintendent at Sheppard and Enoch Pratt Hospital outside Baltimore. Sullivan's first hospital work was as a liaison person to St. Elizabeths in Washington, D.C., under White; his first important post as a psychiatrist was under Chapman at Sheppard. In other words, all of these people—Bellinger, White, and Chapman, who were each in his own way notable influences on Sullivan's life—had been exposed to the mental health problems of the same geographic area

at about the same time. The difference was in the nature of the exposure: White and Chapman were exposed as young adults and professionals; Bellinger and Sullivan were 16 and 11, respectively, when White left Binghamton for St. Elizabeths, where he began a brilliant career as superintendent. For White, Binghamton was his only intensive work with patients on the wards; he reports that after he left there, he never again had the same opportunity to spend time with patients on the wards. But his view of patients had the same experiential flavor as Sullivan's, partly because they both had knowledge of the same kind of mental health problems in all kinds of people as they existed in that period in the environs of Binghamton State Hospital. Thus both White and Sullivan articulated the same feeling about patients. White (1938, p. 58) wrote of his Binghamton experience as illustrating that "these patients are very much more *like* the rest of us than they are *different* from us [emphasis in original]." Sullivan was more poetic in stating the same observation: "We are all much more simply human than otherwise, be we happy and successful, contented and detached, miserable and mentally disordered, or whatever." White's experience of that area of the country was not limited to the hospital. He writes of riding through the same countryside during the period that Sullivan was growing up:

> As I read over the pages of this book I am reminded of my experiences in Binghamton as a consultant. These experiences took me in many instances to near-by small towns and to the outlying districts, and I became acquainted with the country doctors, men who studied medicine and started their practice many years before and who, as a result, were schooled by experiences of the most varied kind. The country doctor then spent most of his time in his buggy making his calls, sometimes miles apart. . . .

> As I traveled with the country doctor along the roads on the way to and from his patients he talked to me confidentially about his work, and as we passed houses and people he would often note that here was where so-and-so lived and there was such-and-such a person. He knew about them and he knew about their families because he had lived with them or as their neighbor for years, had been their principal adviser. . . . He knew that if one of the members of such-and-such a family sustained a fracture that there would probably be delayed union. He knew that in another family a moderate temperature usually resulted in delirium. And in this family that we were passing he knew the husband and the father to be a shiftless, irresponsible and unreliable person and the oldest son to take after him very much in these respects, whereas the daughters were very much more like their mother, who was a substantial and stable woman, because it was the mother in this family who had the ability to hold the little group together and hold them to constructive ends. (pp. 270-271)

Thus geography and an overlapping time frame tended to create a commonality for White, Chapman, and Sullivan—and to a certain extent for Bellinger. But a similar commonality at another level existed for the Swiss psychiatrist Adolf Meyer and Sullivan; the ingredients of their common experience were more complex than what I have just described. That is, Meyer, born in Switzerland, came to the United States as a young man and had his first experience as a neuropathologist in a state hospital in Kankakee, Illinois. As a young immigrant who had suffered in transition to the new society, Meyer found himself losing interest in the examination of the brains of dead patients and turned to searching out the stories of these patients before they died. Many of the patients had been immigrants like himself, and they had lost their way in a new country. Under the influence of the founders of Hull-House in Chicago, Meyer began to develop a knowledge of the whole person and of the social stress of transition.

Thus the bond between Meyer and Sullivan did not come from geographic commonality but from the experience of being an outsider as it related to schizophrenic problems. They both recognized the need for a preventive psychiatry in order to minimize the impact of transition in this diverse society. Moreover, both of them had some firsthand experience with mental illness in the family: Meyer's mother suffered a serious mental illness after her oldest son left for America; she was then alone, a widow with all her children gone from home. Her illness had a profound effect on Meyer, since he had always considered her one of the sanest people he had ever known. And Sullivan's own personal bout with mental illness had its beginnings in part in the lonely and disturbed life of his mother, as both of them tried to cope with being outsiders in a WASP community.

Finally, White, Sullivan, and Meyer began their careers in psychiatry in mental hospitals that cared for a wide spectrum of patients of many different social classes and ethnic origins. White, Meyer, and Sullivan were all skeptical of psychoanalysis as *the* answer to mental health problems in a democratic and diverse society; it was an important tool, but the real answer would depend on developing data on the recurring problems in the general society that could be tackled scientifically—that is, by developing *life histories* on a wide spectrum of people. It seems significant that in 1938, Meyer cited Sullivan as being the person who had been active for years "in bringing anthropology and the study of personality together under a lead of psychiatry" (Meyer, 1952, p. 452).

To delineate adequately the use of differences in order to enrich the total experience of both persons is a much more complicated task. In brief, to the extent that one makes skillful use of areas of commonality

with a stranger, one can proceed to learn about a wide gamut of experiences from the other person that are different from one's own. That too is exemplified over and over again in Sullivan's life. Thus his early and close collaboration with Edward Sapir brought together two people who varied in their ethnic, religious, and social class identities. Sapir, at five, came to this country with his mother, a Lithuanian Jew, and his father, an itinerant cantor; his father shortly disappeared, and Edward, as the only surviving child, was raised after the age of ten in New York City where his mother devoted herself to expediting his career as a student. He won scholarships to the Horace Mann School, followed by a four-year scholarship to Columbia University, where he did graduate work under Franz Boas in linguistics and cultural anthropology. Sullivan's education, by comparison, was spotty and casual, and largely obtained from long hours in libraries while he earned his way through a second-rate medical school in Chicago. It was the situation of their first meeting in 1926 that provided an immediate commonality. Sapir had sought out Sullivan in order to gain some understanding of the tragic illness and death of his first wife; she had suffered a mental disorder—emergent, again, from too many cultural transitions: from the role of outsider in her move as a teenager from Lithuania to the United States where she attended Radcliffe College, and finally, after marriage, travelling to Ottawa in Canada, where she found herself often alone with her young children while her husband was away engaged in his fieldwork. In this early encounter with Sullivan, Sapir gained a new understanding of the tragedy that had almost overwhelmed him. And Sullivan found a gifted thinker who understood in a participant way the importance of Sullivan's clinical insights. They could then go on from there, exploring for the next decade, until Sapir's untimely death in 1939, the richness of their differences, so that the differences in themselves became the source of new intellectual adventures.

So it is that beyond the theme of commonality, which appears over and over again in Sullivan's life and work, there is the stronger theme of using participant observation to overcome one's own anxieties in meeting a stranger, so that one can move from some slight area of commonality to the larger realm of differences in experience and life pattern that make each stranger an opportunity for growth.

In 1946, Sullivan summarized his approach to the field of psychiatry and psychiatric research; he might have used the same words in alerting anyone engaged in research into human behavior:

> Individual differences, especially those which are principally matters of language and customs in people from widely separate parts of the world,

may be extremely impressive and may present great handicap to discovering the significant differences in relative adequacy and appropriateness of action in interpersonal relations, which constitute extraordinary success, average living, or mental disorder.

The therapist or the research psychiatrist, however, participates intelligently in interpersonal relations with his confrere only to the extent that these handicaps are successfully overcome or evaded and finds opportunity to gain skill in this particular in his dealings with any stranger. (Sullivan, 1953a, pp. xii-xiii)

NOTE

1. At the time that the review was written and published (1947), I was working for Sullivan and was responsible for preparing the manuscript for publication; while I remembered some thirty years later the general content of the review, I was astounded to discover the reference to biography while I was sorting out Sullivan's professional relationship to Benedict.

ON STUDYING EMOTIONALLY HOT TOPICS:
Lessons From An Investigation Of
Organizational Death

Robert I. Sutton and Susan J. Schurman

We anticipated that a study of organizational death would require us to face strong emotion. This research entailed interviews with decision makers who had been in the thick of organizational death. Their reports were needed to help generate a theory of this organizational transition. We felt ready for this challenging fieldwork because of lessons gained from prior research with relatively benign topics. But we were unpleasantly surprised by the level and diversity of emotion encountered during initial efforts to interview managers, administrators, and union leaders. These expeditions into the real world at first strained our research skills, as well as our self-esteem. Later, they enlightened us about the unique demands of studying topics that evoke red-hot emotion.

Consider two of our early adventures. Schurman tried to call an informant at her home; the informant's husband answered. Schurman's field notes reveal,

> His response caught me completely off-guard. First he started yelling (literally) at me about graduate students, worthless social science research, voyeurism, etc., and assured me that his wife would have no interest in talking to me. Gradually, as he discovered a receptive audience, he turned from his tirade on grad students to the topic of the closing, which he termed 'the greatest screw job in the history of the state.' During the conversation the informant's son was standing in the background stirring his father on to further grievances about the closing. We were on the phone about 50 minutes.

Schurman was shocked by the conversation. She and Sutton spent an hour talking about the episode in an effort to make sense of it, and its implications for subsequent data gathering. Schurman also complained that working on this study was turning out to be far more effort than she bargained for, primarily because of the amount of emotion evoked by organizational death.

Anger was expressed by other gatekeepers, as well as by many informants with whom we spoke. One informant whom Sutton telephoned, for example, was a well-educated professional. Sutton expected at least the pretense of courtesy. He explained the nature of the research and asked if the informant wished to participate The professional told Sutton that he was a "mother-fucker." The informant got over his anger, however, and eventually participated in a series of enlightening interviews. Sutton worried about this conversation. He worried that, because of the level of emotion associated with organizational death, the research would cost more money, take more time, and cause more stress among members of the research team than first anticipated. He also worried that collecting quality data about this topic would be hampered by this red-hot emotion.

These two examples illustrate angry responses, and their influence on two researchers. Other profound emotional responses were also encountered throughout the research. One informant, for example, placed extreme and unwarranted faith in our ability to help him understand what he had just endured in the management of a dying organization. Another informant was very calm, but persistently lied to us, as well as to others, about his intentions and past behavior. Still other informants were so depressed that they reported feeling "numb."

The profound threat associated with this topic is illustrated by questionnaire responses of 23 informants who had been members of the eight defunct organizations. These managers, administrators, and union leaders were asked to compare the closing experience with five increasingly threatening life events: (1) receiving a parking ticket; (2) an argument with a friend or relative; (3) a serious illness; (4) a divorce; (5) the death of a spouse. On the average, the 23 former members reported that involvement in the closing was somewhat worse (3.39 on a five point scale) than having a serious illness. That organizational death can entail a profound strain is accentuated by the responses of 9 of the 23 (39%) former members. These 9 people revealed that the closing was comparable to divorce or the death of a spouse.

Working with these distraught informants taught us some important lessons. Perhaps the primary methodological lesson is that studying hot topics requires a more complex exchange relationship between research-

er and informant. In return for providing data, informants expected us to listen, give them feedback, or give them advice—in short, to provide them with social support (House, 1981). Our experience with emotionally cold topics (e.g., a study of personnel practices) and warm topics (e.g., quality of work life) had not sufficiently prepared us for the strength and range of this need.

The remainder of the chapter explores this and other lessons gained from our research on organizational death and extends them to additional topics that arouse strong emotion among informants. We first consider conditions that give rise to hot topics. Then we describe the altered exchange relationship that arises when working with distressed informants, the influence of this relationship on the researcher, and coping techniques for the researcher. Next, the third section explores methods for enhancing the quality of data collected from distraught informants. Finally, the fourth section introduces some sticky ethical dilemmas that arise in high temperature research.

CONDITIONS THAT GIVE RISE TO
EMOTIONALLY HOT TOPICS

Predicting which topics give rise to red-hot emotion is important: They place unique demands on the relationship between researcher and informant, and a special combination of methods is required for gathering high-quality data on such topics. Conditions likely to give rise to emotionally hot topics are proposed in Figure 17.1. The figure builds on the Institute for Social Research's model of social-environmental determinants of stress and health (Katz & Kahn, 1978). Starting from the left of the figure, distraught informants may be encountered when studying profound transitions at four levels of analysis: community, organizational, work group, and individual.

The purpose of this model is *not* to offer a formal theory of stress, strain, or disruptions, although it does have some elements of such a theory. Rather, its purpose is to provide researchers with indicators or "tip-offs" that the topic is emotionally hot. Thus, the presence of these disruptions does not assure that one will be working with distraught informants; nor does their absence make certain that one will not be working with such informants. In addition, these transitions are interdependent rather than independent. In our study of organizational death, for example, an economic depression in Michigan led to more frequent organizational deaths, which in turn led to the demise of more work

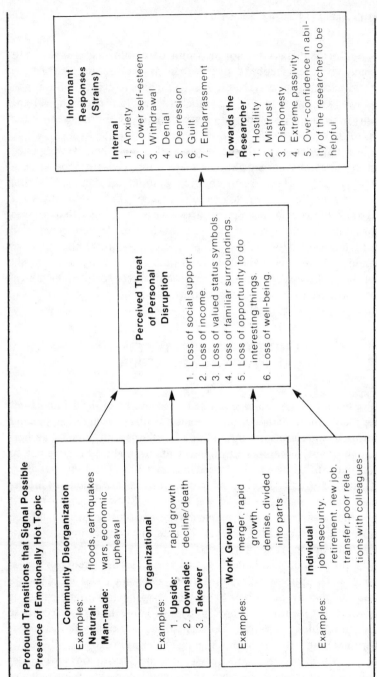

Figure 17.1 Conditions that May Give Rise to Emotionally Hot Topics in Organizational Research

groups. These social system transitions increased the occurrence of individual job loss, transfers, and early retirement.

These transitions, separately or in combination, may cause the informant to perceive (and objectively experience) personal disruption. The researcher is studying a hot topic to the extent that a high proportion of informants will experience or have experienced the threat of personal disruption. Disruption of organized response appears to be stressful for all organisms (Mandler & Watson, 1966).

These profound disruptions have two varieties of effects on informant responses that are relevant to our discussion. These informant responses (see Figure 17.1) include internal reactions to stress, such as anxiety, lower self-esteem, withdrawal, denial, depression, guilt, and embarrassment. These are typical reactions (usually labelled strain) to occupational stress (see, for example, Cobb & Kasl, 1977; Katz & Kahn, 1978).

Yet informant responses are not exclusively internal. These strains spill over to the informant's relationships with other people, including the researcher. Hostility, mistrust, dishonesty, passivity, and overconfidence in the researcher's ability to help the informant are thought to be common responses to this disruption. These and similar responses place unique demands on the study of hot topics.

This model for predicting the presence of a hot topic may prove helpful, but it must be used along with practical research skills. It is important, for example, to ask colleagues for advice about the topic that one is studying. Moreover, preliminary expeditions into the real world are essential if a high temperature topic is suspected. Such expeditions enhanced our research. Sutton interviewed several informants, and most were distraught. He did not fully appreciate the distinct demands of emotionally hot topics immediately, but these expeditions did improve the research design. These early warnings were also helpful because they encouraged him to seek people for the research team who had strong field skills.

Finally, the research worker must also consider the content of the data collected and the research methods employed. Strong emotions should be expected to the extent that informants are directly queried about threats of personal disruption. Thus, in our study of organizational death, questions about organizational size rarely evoked strong emotion. In contrast, questions about the fate of employees or decision makers were often followed by strong emotion. In addition, the strength of emotional responses is linked to the data-gathering methods used. Qualitative methods that entail working closely with informants create arenas in which strong emotional responses toward the investigator are possible.

THE RELATIONSHIP BETWEEN RESEARCHER
AND INFORMANT

This chapter has a persistent theme: Working with distraught informants requires special skills. The investigator studying a hot topic is compelled for ethical reasons, and forced for practical reasons, to enter into a different kind of relationship with informants than is customary for research on cold topics. Investigators conducting cold research have generally not had to give much in exchange for what they get. The price of data is usually the intrinsic satisfaction the informant gains for contributing to the lofty, but intangible, goal of scientific knowledge.

Upset informants expect more in exchange. They often expect the researcher to abandon the traditional, emotionally neutral posture and adopt a more clinical posture. This section describes the altered exchange relationship, its influence on the researcher, and coping strategies for the researcher.

THE ALTERED EXCHANGE RELATIONSHIP

A variety of authors have prescribed a reciprocal relationship between researcher and informant (e.g., May, 1980; D'Aunno & Price, 1983; Cassell, 1980). These recommendations are usually based on moral and epistemological considerations. In contrast, we found that a reciprocal relationship was unavoidable for studying hot topics. Many informants simply would not tolerate an asymmetrical relationship. They usually expected, and sometimes demanded, greater than ordinary inducements in exchange for participating in the research.

The additional inducement expected most often by the upset informants we worked with is best described as social support (Cobb, 1976; House, 1981). House's four dimensions of social support are useful for illustrating the range of help that distraught informants can be provided:

(1) *emotional support:* providing empathy, trust, and simply listening to the informant;
(2) *appraisal support:* providing data that allow the informant to compare him- or herself to similar others;
(3) *informational support:* providing information that allows the informant to cope with problems, usually information that helps people help themselves; and
(4) *instrumental support:* instrumental actions that directly help an informant in need.

The exchange relationships in our research extended to the first three forms of support only.

All informants expected us to provide them with some emotional support. In exchange for providing us with data about the closing, they expected us to listen attentively when they discussed personal problems. We had to be careful to strike a balance between how much we should gently prod informants back to the content of our questions and how much we should simply listen. Although this is always a challenge for interviewers, the magnitude is far greater when working with distressed informants. It was not uncommon for our gentle prods to be answered with hostile comments such as, "So I thought you wanted to hear my story." And many other informants simply ignored our efforts to structure the conversation and continued to talk about whatever they wished.

Some informants sought appraisal support. This is consistent with research suggesting that human beings in distress have a strong need to compare themselves to similar others (Singer, 1980). Singer proposes that social comparison allows humans in distress to evaluate and adjust their responses. Informants often asked us, "What did managers in other closings do in this situation?" Although we often sidestepped such questions, we sometimes felt it was appropriate to respond; it would help informants who had done much to help us. The ex-president of a defunct hospital (who had been extremely helpful) questioned us persistently about efforts other dying organizations had made to help displaced employees. His organization provided assistance for the unemployed that was superior to the other organizational deaths we had studied. We felt compelled to tell him this fact.

In contrast to emotional and appraisal support, we gave little informational support to informants. We did not give specific advice about managing closings, for example. Nonetheless, the feedback that we gave in exchange for participation included not only a complete journal article on "Managing Organizational Death" (Sutton, 1983); it also included a complete copy of the special issue of the journal in which the article appeared, which was on "The Management of Organizational Decline." This was provided because so many informants insisted that they had better get plenty of feedback about our findings. Finally, in looking back, we should have arrived at interviews with a list of therapists or at least referral agencies. Such information might have been needed by those who were suffering profound psychological distress.

Social support is a resource that those who study emotionally hot topics may exchange for data. We found that listening and understanding, rather than making judgments (which are so rampant in organiza-

tional death), was what informants wanted most often. The pressure of managing these responsibilities can be difficult for the researcher. This problem is addressed next.

THE INFLUENCE ON THE RESEARCHER OF WORKING WITH DISTRAUGHT INFORMANTS

The members of our research team responded in a variety of ways to working with informants who were angry, depressed, confused, distrustful, or otherwise difficult. Anger and guilt were perhaps our most common reactions. Our anger tended to arise in response to informant anger. At times, we would have to work very hard not to lose our tempers at informants who attacked us personally. Sutton, for example, was tempted to holler at the foul-mouthed professional described in the introduction to this chapter.

Perhaps the greatest anger, however, was evoked in response to the head of a dying organization who lied about us behind our backs. This administrator never directly refused to be interviewed. Instead, he always claimed "I'm too busy, call me back later." His superior was one of the informants in our research. The superior contacted the administrator and asked if he had any knowledge of our research. The administrator claimed he had not heard of our study and expressed anger at us for studying the organization without his permission. Yet, he had heard of the study *and* given us permission. Sutton and two other members of the research team were very angry at this dishonest informant who made them look bad. Moreover, we were extremely frustrated because we perceived that it was not possible to tell the superior the "true" story because of research ethics. This incident took much time—we held many meetings to decide how to handle this fellow. Our anger toward him was so strong, however, that most of the meeting time was spent complaining about this "liar," which hindered the progress of the research.

Guilt was also a common response among those of us on the research team. We worried that the fellow who accused social scientists of voyeurism was correct. Moreover, we often worried that participation in our research increased the work load of informants who were already overwhelmed with hundreds of tasks. Sutton worried about his impact on an informant who had a heart attack shortly after participating in the research. Sutton had put much pressure on this distressed fellow to produce archival data about the closing, and the informant had complained a great deal about the extra work.

The distress evoked within us by these emotional episodes sometimes interfered with our performance on subsequent research tasks. Some

members of the research team responded to their own guilt and anger with psychological detachment from informants and with procrastination. The psychological detachment made it more difficult for us to feel and act concerned in response to the troubles of other informants. Such responses may have interfered with our performance, particularly because social support (which requires the expression of concern) was the primary resource expected by informants.

A second response to this stress was procrastinating about telephoning potential informants. Sutton, for example, put off planned phone calls to other informants for several weeks after he was verbally assaulted by the professional.

Clearly, not performing research tasks interferes with the quality of the research. But psychological and behavioral detachment are not without virtue. These "time outs" helped us to continue our long-term efforts. Despite the widely advertised evils of procrastination, putting off phone calls for a few weeks helped us regain our ability to be supportive and reduced the probability that we would abandon the research. Other coping strategies for researchers who study hot topics are explored next.

COPING STRATEGIES FOR THE RESEARCHER

Our experience suggests some steps that can be taken to manage the negative influence of distraught informants on researcher well-being and performance.

Anticipate the emotional temperature of the topic. As suggested above, forecasting that the research topic is hot helps eliminate a poor study design. The model presented earlier can help researchers anticipate emotionally hot topics. When an initial assessment suggests that the topic is hot, a research strategy may be needed that is appropriate for the special demands of gathering data from distraught informants.

We learned a variety of ways to plan for strong emotion. Sutton enlisted the help of a clinical psychologist after his first encounters with distraught informants. Following from the psychologist's suggestions, Sutton designed an "initial observation form." The form included open- and closed-ended questions about the potential informant's emotional responses—including anger, depression, and denial. This form prepared us for the crucial first few minutes with informants. It made salient the importance of initial contacts (usually telephone calls) and it prepared us to expect profound affect.

As implied above in the discussion of procrastination, we also learned not to contact people when we were distracted or distressed. We noted a positive correlation between our psychological preparedness and our success in obtaining informant participation. Similarly, we found conducting interviews when tired or upset to be an error.

Develop necessary clinical skills. The implications of our experience are clear: Greater skill at providing support increased the chances of informant cooperation and satisfaction, and reduced researcher stress. This suggests the research team studying a hot topic should be composed of people who can provide support. This means not only selecting people with such skills, but also using techniques such as role plays to help interviewers learn how to cope with upset informants. In our research, the degree of a researcher's clinical skill often determined failure or success at gaining entry to a research setting.

Build in a social support for the researchers. Studying hot topics increases the researcher's own need for social support. After our initial encounters with informants revealed the emotional intensity we would be facing, we found ourselves relying on each other for emotional support. Later, as additional researchers were added, we adopted regular meetings in which part of the time was devoted to discussing difficult encounters with informants. While this kind of research can certainly be conducted by solitary researchers, we recommend collaboration as a means of obtaining social support.

METHODS FOR ENHANCING THE QUALITY OF DATA COLLECTED FROM DISTRAUGHT INFORMANTS

Studying hot topics may require abandoning the "standard rules" of the research game derived from the traditional scientific method. This notion was suggested above and will be explored further in this section. Specifically, we consider (1) retrospective data; (2) nonparticipants; and (3) deviations from common field research practices.

RETROSPECTIVE DATA

The use of retrospective data is usually discouraged by methodologists. The negative effect of "history" (Cook & Campbell, 1979) on efforts to specify causal relationships is widely known. Similarly, research on shortcomings in human inference (Nisbett & Ross, 1980; Fischhoff, 1982) suggests that human judgments about the occurrence and causes of past events confirm the definition of *recollect* from *The*

Devil's Dictionary (Bierce, 1911): "to recall with additions something not previously known."

Our research concerned organizations that had recently closed and thus used much retrospective data. And our concern about the hazards of relying on human recollections influenced the research design. Effort was put forth to interview multiple informants with diverse perspectives in each closing. Moreover, much time was spent gathering pertinent organizational records, which provided prospective data. Finally, we attempted to study two closings prospectively: One attempt was moderately successful, but the other was terminated by management before much data could be gathered.

A primary lesson for studying emotionally hot topics is that, in contrast to cold topics, retrospective research has distinct strengths. When people are trapped in the turmoil of an organization closing or other profound transition, they often do not have either the time or the inclination to speak with a curious behavioral scientist. In the aborted effort to study the large department store, for example, the research was terminated partly because the management was so busy orchestrating the complex transition that they did not have time to speak with us. Management also worried that we would leak information to the press about the closing that could damage the reputation of the parent organization. In this closing, and other ongoing closings, we were told to call back after the crisis had passed because people would have time to participate only after it was over. Moreover, fears about leaks to the press would be less salient to management after the closing was complete.

Several potential informants also asserted that it was rude to study them during the throes of distress. One woman (a gatekeeper) told Schurman that it "was outrageous that you people would call at a time like this. Don't you have any idea what an upsetting thing this is?" Similarly Wortman and her colleagues (1980) report that it is impossible (and insensitive) to study rape victims immediately after an assault or to interview victims of spinal cord injuries while they are suffering acute pain. Data collection must be retrospective in such cases.

This discussion also implies that, in emotionally hot research, response rates among individuals and organizations are likely to be higher with a retrospective design. Thus, even using the logic of the traditional scientific method, the quality of the sample obtained when using retrospective data may help compensate for the hazards of human recollections. This is not a design consideration in studies of most cold topics. And perhaps more important, it can be unethical or simply rude to invade the privacy of people while they are suffering severe distress.

NONPARTICIPANTS

Our research also revealed that people who *decline* to participate in hot research may provide more useful evidence than can be gathered from nonparticipants in cold research. This lesson is an important by-product of the "initial observation form" we used to summarize initial conversations with potential informants. When potential informants were unable or unwilling to participate in an extended interview, they were often willing to have a short telephone conversation about the closing. These responses were recorded on the observation form. The profound emotion generated by this transition caused many "nonpartici-pants" to give us detailed information, which taught us additional lessons about organizational death.

Refusals to participate often came from gatekeepers rather than directly from the chosen informant. The comments made by gatekeepers (such as the one described above who told Schurman that her call was an "outrageous" act) also gave us valuable information. As a result, the initial observation form had provisions for recording gatekeeper responses.

DEVIATIONS FROM COMMON FIELD
RESEARCH PRACTICES

Standard practices for collecting questionnaire and structured inter-view data emphasize that the research should *not* be described to the subject in detail. This form of "error from the investigator" (Webb, Campbell, Schwartz, Sechrest, & Grove, 1981) is thought to bias re-sponses during the remainder of the interview. Similarly, consider the instructions given to professional interviewers at the University of Michi-gan's Institute for Social Research:

> Remember not to be too specific about the interview in introducing yourself and the survey to the respondent. It is important that you avoid introducing a bias into the interview which might predispose the respon-dent to answer in a particular way. Very general statements such as: "We are interested in how people are getting along these days" or "We're talking to people all over the country to see how they feel things are going in the world today" are usually quite successful. (Interviewer's Manual, Survey Research Center, 1976, pp. 7-8)

We tried to follow these instructions during our pretesting efforts. We soon learned, however, that potential informants would rarely tolerate such vague statements. Because of the attributes of organizational

death, many had recently learned to mistrust fellow human beings greatly. They responded to vague descriptions of the study with pointed questions such as "Exactly what are you going to do with this information?" and "Exactly what is in this project for you?" Thus, we found it was necessary to give them a relatively detailed summary of our research design. While such information probably biased the interviews, it was better than conducting no interviews at all.

The stress and paranoia generated by hot topics requires researchers to make the nature of the exchange relationship more explicit. D'Aunno and Price (1983) suggest that explicit negotiation of all research relationships is desirable because "when this exchange is negotiated openly in a context of mutual respect, the product should be both more scientifically sound and more useful to the community." While explicit negotiation of the exchange relationship may be desirable in emotionally cold or warm research (despite its biasing effects), it is essential when studying topics that evoke profound hostility, depression, guilt, and confusion among informants. Participants in hot research often have more to lose than those in cold research, and demands for information about what they are getting involved with are justified.

Along similar lines, we found that this exchange relationship forced us to reveal more about ourselves than is customary, or deemed desirable, in emotionally cold research. One very nervous informant spent a full hour responding to Sutton's interview questions with his own questions about Sutton's personal life. Sutton gently told him, "I'd rather not answer such personal questions." The informant became angry and said, "You are asking me all these personal questions, why the hell can't I ask you a few?" While such profound pressure for self-disclosure by the interviewer was unusual, our research suggests that there is greater pressure for self-disclosure in red-hot research. This appears necessary because informants need to trust the interviewer more than in cold or warm research, and moderate levels of self-disclosure can encourage such trust.

Hot topics may also force the investigator to abandon widely accepted practices about the use of interview protocols. Common instructions to interviewers include "Ask the questions exactly as they are worded in the questionnaire," "Ask the questions in the order in which they are presented in the questionnaire," and "Ask every question specified in the questionnaire" (Survey Research Center, 1976; Babbie, 1973).

The qualities of the exchange relationship likely to emerge when studying emotionally hot topics conflict with this demand for control over the subjects' behavior. Informants we interviewed would often insist on telling their own story in their own way. In addition, we

sometimes did not ask questions from our interview just exactly as they were worded because an informant, we judged, would be offended. We also frequently deviated from the order in which questions were presented in the interview. If an informant talked about the aftermath of the closing before speaking about how the decision was made (especially if he or she was upset about it) we would let him or her talk.

Thus, strong expectations held by informants who participate in emotionally hot research may interfere with or make impossible the use of a highly structured protocol. While deviations from the interview protocol are common in studies that seek to discover hypotheses, such pressures are even stronger when working with distraught informants. Our research calls into question the ethics of using only closed-ended response options (such as Likert scales) when studying hot topics. While we did leave informants with a questionnaire at the end of the interview, this was done after the exchange relationship had been negotiated.

ETHICAL DILEMMAS

Some sticky ethical dilemmas arise in high temperature research. These dilemmas can be separated into two categories, corresponding to a pair of major ethical requirements governing research conducted with human subjects: informed consent and voluntary participation.

INFORMED CONSENT

We have argued that discovering hypotheses requires a flexible research design that can be altered as the study proceeds. We have further argued that informants in our study demand greater knowledge of the research design than is typically encountered in emotionally cold research. The conventional standard of informed consent is difficult to apply in this case because it creates an ethical dilemma. To what exactly is the participant consenting? How much information is necessary for consent to be informed? One practical solution to this problem is to portray the research design to prospective participants with more certainty and specificity than actually exists. The researcher is then faced with the possibility that the research plan will change and the participant will have an inaccurate impression of the study. Sutton, for example, told a number of participants that he planned to use closed-ended survey questions extensively. As the study evolved, these data proved less useful and played a much smaller role than anticipated. Did these participants have informed consent?

A related ethical difficulty concerns whether or not distraught participants can be considered informed and consenting. Consider one interview that Sutton had with an informant who was very angry and upset. Sutton judged that much of what the informant said was confused and distorted, possibly as a result of extreme anxiety. Sutton recalls wondering "Should I end this interview? This guy is really upset." Sutton also wondered how to terminate the interview gracefully. It was difficult to decide which was worse: to continue the interview or try to end it. How does the investigator judge when an informant is too upset? Can prematurely terminating an interview compound the informant's distress?

Sutton's response to the distraught informant in the above example illustrates yet another ethical problem in hot research. After weighing the pros and cons of continuing or ending the interview, Sutton elected to continue. One explanation for this decision is that, despite Sutton's reservations about the impact of the interview on the informant, his role as researcher caused Sutton to make the wrong choice. Conflicting role demands such as this can lead to ethical dilemmas for any research conducted in organizational settings (Mirvis & Seashore, 1979) and are especially likely in emotionally hot research.

VOLUNTARY PARTICIPATION

True voluntary participation may be a rare event in organizational research (Mirvis & Seashore, 1979; Schurman, 1982). Role expectations for organization members reduce or eliminate their freedom to refuse participation. Mirvis and Seashore observe that "researchers are dealing with a social system composed of people who have positions in a hierarchy . . . researchers cannot approach participants in the study as individuals because they behave within an interdependent framework of rights and responsibilities" (p. 79).

The reality of social organization is that, depending on their position in the hierarchy, people can be subtly coerced into "volunteering." Although the effects of such coerced participation are generally acknowledged to be benign, even by many who are critical on ethical grounds (e.g., Wax, 1980), it is not clear that the results of involuntary participation in hot research are benign. Such participation may exacerbate an already distraught person's emotional discomfort. The problem of potential coercion compounds the difficult ethical issue in emotionally hot research previously discussed.

None of the ethical problems described are unique to emotionally hot research, although we have tried to show that they are both more likely and more salient in such research. They are endemic to social research,

especially research that relies on qualitative methods. The traditional ethical safeguards are both difficult to apply and relatively meaningless in such research. Some researchers have proposed alterations to the traditional ethical framework governing social research. Wax (1980) has suggested that consent be viewed as a *process* in which the informant and researcher develop a certain relationship within which consent is a progressive development based on shared understanding rather than an *event*. Similarly, Mirvis and Seashore (1979) have argued that the task of the "action-researcher" is to "create ethical relationships" with organization members.

The notion that doing ethical social science stems not from a priori contracts between researchers and subjects, but from the development of ethical relationships between researchers and informants, has a firm basis in both philosophy and practice. Implementation of such a concept in organizational settings on hot research topics is not without serious problems. Few clear guidelines exist about how to form such relationships with multiple organizational actors or how to maintain such relationships with conflicting actors.

We recommend that researchers studying hot topics in organizations turn to the applied organizational change literature for models of developing ethical relationships with informants.

CONCLUSION

The study of hot topics that evoke red-hot emotion creates an arena for the researcher in which both costs and benefits are greater than for cold topics. The advantages are potentially great: Hot topics often concern more pressing social problems, problems of more import to informants, and topics of greater interest to both scholars and the general public. The difficulties associated with hot topics are also greater, however. These include requirements for more resources for the amount of data gathered, more threats to the validity of findings because "tried and true" approaches are less likely to be effective, and greater risk of ethical dilemmas.

This chapter has introduced some guidelines for researchers who choose to face these hazards and opportunities. We proposed a model to help researchers identify conditions that give rise to emotionally hot topics. We specified some attributes of the exchange relationship that emerge when distraught informants expect social support from the researcher in return for the data they provide. Next, it was suggested that hot topics call into question some widely accepted research

practices. Finally, we introduced some ethical dilemmas that are exacerbated by the unique demands of hot topics.

We end this article with a suggestion and a comment. First the suggestion. We urge our colleagues to take special care to document the natural history of research on emotionally hot topics. Little is known about conducting it in nontherapeutic settings, and documentation of both successful and unsuccessful approaches is needed to improve the quality of future research. We are especially concerned that those who conduct hypothesis testing research on hot topics will hesitate to be open about natural history since, as Van Maanen observes, "coming clean" is less common in this variety of research (Van Maanen, Dabbs, & Faulkner, 1982).

And now the comment. In exploring the peculiarities of emotionally hot research we have questioned the unqualified value of the traditional scientific method as a guiding force for all organizational research. We do not, however, believe that assumptions and methods that stem from the traditional approach are flawed. On the contrary, they are valuable and appropriate for many (but not all) research problems.

Along these lines, we contend that a wide range of methods must be used in parallel to best discover the qualities of organizations and of life within them. This call may sound trite, as it is repeated often in the literature. We are concerned, however, by how widely it is ignored by those who study organizations. We worry about some harsh battles we have recently witnessed between colleagues of different perspectives. Nasty exchanges have been observed about the relative virtues, for example, of applied versus basic, quantitative versus qualitative, and macro versus micro views of organizations.

Disagreement is valuable when it enhances knowledge. Yet, much of what we have observed can only be described as poorly disguised warfare over the value of one's "turf" rather than sincere efforts to enhance knowledge. In the spirit of seeking enhanced knowledge about organizations, it is our hope that research on emotionally hot topics continues and grows because it is an important *addition* to the organizational studies literature.

ASSESSING LOCAL CAUSALITY IN QUALITATIVE RESEARCH

A. Michael Huberman and Matthew B. Miles

"Causality" has a bad name these days among social scientific researchers. Mention the term and you can expect most of your colleagues, to borrow the surrealists' dictum, to reach for their epistemological pistols. Logically enough, the quickest draws are those of action theorists, phenomenologists, ethnomethodologists, and interpretive sociologists, for whom exercises in causal deduction or causal inference represent the worst sort of neopositivism.

Our own work during the past few years has been to reinstate the legitimacy and power of causal analysis in empirical research, and to reinstate it, in particular, in the type of clinical or qualitative research described in this volume. We argue that the determination of causal influence is both appropriate and feasible in social research, and that it need not be done solely with the algorithms of structural equations, covariance matrices, or confirmatory factor analysis.

For us to claim that the determination of causal relationships is both legitimate and feasible in qualitative research has a tantalizing shock value in such a volume as this. It is a strong claim, smacking of hubris; how can it be justified, both conceptually and operationally? That is the agenda for this chapter. First, we shall examine some of the epistemological issues rumbling away beneath the issue of causality. Then we identify the types of causal determination one is called upon to make in social research, and describe the kinds of clinical knowledge enabling a researcher to do this. We draw from past work in analytic induction, social judgment, and qualitative studies to define the requirements of a good methodology for causal analysis.

Having grounded these procedures conceptually, we then ground them operationally, by illustrating at the nuts-and-bolts level just how one can work with qualitative data, incrementally and analytically, to build causal "maps" of local settings and events.

Finally, in covering this terrain, we shall be attentive to the stream of meaning-communicating and meaning-negotiating transactions between the researcher and informants in the field, and how those transactions affect the determination of causality.

We have approached this chapter—and our work—in a systematic, cognitive way, believing that drawing valid conclusions about causality is the product of thoughtful or sense-making activity, both on our part and the part of the people whose lives we are studying. We state our views crisply for clarity, and hope they will not be mistaken for smugness or dogma.

CAUSAL REALISM AND CAUSAL IDEALISM: FINDING THE MIDDLE GROUND

Arguing about the epistemological bases of causal deduction and inference has become so elaborate, passionate, and discipline-specific that it is more straightforward to state a stance and flesh it out, than to erect the ritual conceptual scaffold that will justify one's preferences and elegantly cut opponents' throats. The epistemological litmus test here is how one responds to Hume's classic dilemma: How can one postulate unobservable *connections* among events? The events themselves can be observed, as can the recurring associations between those events, but the *relationships* between these events require our adding more than we can observe.

For a causal idealist, whatever we choose to add—latent variables, constructs, propositions, laws, theories—involves an *arbitrary decision* as to how, conceptually, we prefer to carve up the social universe. Some regularities may be there to be observed, at least temporarily, and the links we postulate between them may be plausible. So, too, are the theories we generate to coordinate those plausible links into a meaningful set—but it is *we* who put the meaning there. The world, as Hanson (1958, p. 14) has put it, is not held together by cosmic glue. Or, more brutally, as Wittgenstein wrote in the *Tractatus,* "causes are superstitions."

For a causal realist, on the other hand, the belief is that the constants or regularities observable in the social world can be expressed in the form of *lawful statements* whose validity is independent of individual cognition. There are lawful patterns out there to be discovered, whether

or not we are aware of them or can articulate them. By specifying the conditions under which these processes obtain, by accurately predicting their presence or absence, and by progressively correcting the extant bodies of explanation, we can get a progressively better fix on the laws undergirding events in the world.

It is important to say that causal idealism and causal realism represent a *continuum* more than a dichotomy. There are few people operating at the conceptual extremes, apart from the epistemologists still trying to sharpen distinctions. Scratch those epistemologists, however, and you will find many of them taking a personal stance nearer the middle than at the poles. Virtually no one contends that social processes are wholly solipsistic, nor will anyone claim that such processes correspond to Kantian categories. More important, there are virtually *no* working researchers at the extremes. For example, the social phenomenological research derived from Husserl and Schutz has invariably contained some systematic, inferential procedures for determining such lawful constructs as indexality, et cetera rules, typification, or reflexivity. Conversely, most major neopositivist (i.e., realist) methodologists (see Snow, 1974; Cronbach, 1975; Cook & Campbell, 1979) have shifted toward more perceptual, context-embedded, and interpretive inquiry.

As with all continua, there are middle points—the ones that disappear when militant conceptual partitioning tries to force us into one camp or the other. In the middle lie several, conceptually coherent epistemologies, of which perhaps the best known is "transcendental realism" (Bhaskar, 1975, 1982; Harré, 1972; Manicas & Secord, 1982). Since our own stance is largely reflected here, let us briefly review the basic tenets.

As causal realists, these authors postulate a social patterning that exists independently of cognizing experience. This patterning is not a description of classes of events, but rather an expression of the *causal properties* of structures operating in the world. In that sense, theoretical entities are not hypothetical, but real. This is the operative passage in Manicas and Secord:

> Scientific explanation is not subsumption. Rather, it is causal explanation, and it demands that we show how in each particular case a particular causal configuration occurred that had just the achieved result. . . . Explanation thus requires knowledge of the causal properties of the configured structures *and* a historical grasp of the particular and changing configuration. (p. 403)

Such terms as "historical grasp" and "changing configuration" reflect the middle-groundedness of this theory. Transcendental realists assume that social patterns will change—and that social theory, as a social and historical product, has to chase after those changes. They also assume that while we can *explain* social phenomena, we cannot really *predict* them. There will always be an enormous range of co-determining variables, forming complex, shifting configurations.

The consistencies we seek are, in effect, idiosyncratically organized. There is neither full determination nor complete closure, but there are recurrent contingencies and causal tendencies that can be identified and mapped, so as to render some explanations more powerful, more fully saturated, than others. Finally, social behaviors and structures arise in part from motivated human acts—understandings, meanings, intentions—so that the phenomenological dimension is a necessary, although not sufficient, component of those lawful processes we seek to explain.

A positivist epistemology that makes short shrift of correspondence theory, empirical probabilism, and predictive validity, while still making coherent claims to verifiable explanation, is an interesting one. It is especially interesting because it incorporates some of the core components of the idealist position as well—socially generated meanings, intentionality and reflexivity, historicism. In doing this, transcendental realism, like other middle-ground epistemologies (e.g., Campbell, 1975), enables us to draw methods from both the psychometric and phenomenological traditions—to wed clinical/qualitative approaches to actuarial/quantitative techniques.

But its more immediate interest is reflected in the excerpt just cited. The stress is on *causal*, rather than on purely *functional*, explanations. One is not talking about "interdependencies" or "functional relations" among variables—the customary way of sidestepping the issue of causal inference—but about *directional* influences exerted among patterned interactions.

At the same time, transcendental realists are demanding that the governing patterns be continuously connected to the empirical relationships from which they are derived. That is, causal analysis must be *contextualized*, case by case. Thus we cannot translate events and processes into equations "representing" them, as one would routinely in mathematical modeling. We have to stay with the "real" world, and build up to a smaller number of more-inclusive properties that actually function as causal agents in that world. We can identify, perhaps even determine, "local" causality, and can overlay two or more local cause maps, but cannot determine "general" causality—because there is none.

Just *how* we should go about this is not yet clear, but some of the contours are there. We shall need to stay close to the settings themselves. We must define the "variables" we observe there in contextually meaningful ways, listening closely to how actors in the setting define them. We must avoid context-stripping data transformations (e.g., converting descriptors to numbers). And we must ground the inferred causal patterns in the specific events and processes constituting them, not plaster existing theoretical constructs onto them. From this initial list, it is already clear that the methodologies we shall need derive more from a qualitative research paradigm than from a correlational or experimental one.

CLINICAL KNOWLEDGE AND CAUSAL INFERENCE

First things first: What is local causality knowledge *of*? It is knowledge, we have said, of recurring, patterned social phenomena whose recurrence and pattern we infer from concrete empirical instances. We infer it post hoc: We can explain it (the past is determined), but cannot really predict it (the future is not). Such knowledge is often awesomely complex and multilayered. It is unstable, as are any sociohistorical phenomena, so that we must periodically unbundle and reassemble our explanations, unless we work at the most superordinate or general level of theory—which is typically too general to pack much explanatory power for the relatively specific and contingent nature of local determinisms. If we choose to work descriptively, as an ethnographer would, we might agree easily on *what* constitutes an account of local events and processes. But we are shooting higher here, for the *why* and *how* of the what, and there will be several plausible—and contending—explanations in play at that level. The higher the level of inference, the more uncertain and multiple become the truth estimates.

So how will we know when our causal explanations are correct? No metaphysical buzzer is going to go off. Credible analysts will always find legitimate points of disagreement. We are solving neither puzzles nor crimes, which have straightforward algorithms for finding unequivocal solutions. On the other hand—and this is important—some explanations *are* likely to be more compelling than others: They will get more agreement from credible judges; they provide a closer fit with the complete (albeit imperfect, forcibly ambiguous) set of data. It may be that no single explanation is unequivocally correct; but some are better than others, and not anything goes.

Cognitive psychologists and artificial intelligence analysts would say that in the issue of local causality we have an "ill-structured" (Simon, 1977) or "wicked" (Churchman, 1971) problem on our hands, and that this has important consequences for the ways in which the problem can be solved. We are in a propositional "problem space" that is closer to resolving real-world issues like alcoholism or pollution than to determining chemical reactions and physical laws. That is, we *can* resolve the chemistry of alcoholism and the physics of pollution, but we will not have solved the problem of how to deal with either. Worse, if we try to force the situation into one in which the problem *can* be solved by the rules, algorithms, and classical analytic techniques that we use for "well-structured" problems, we will, at best, have resolved only the well-structured part of the ill-structured problem—without knowing exactly which part that was.

In other words, problem spaces for which there exists a single, correct solution usually have either the solution contained in the formulation of the problem (as, for example, in logical deductions) or have preestablished rules—axioms, symbol strings, symbolic transformations—that, when correctly applied, produce the correct solution. Those well-structured problems are amenable to solution by these sets of rules and procedures, but this is not the case for ill-structured problems—like those of determining local causality. That tells us, for instance, that path analysis is not the appropriate solution to the problem of determining local causality. Nor would the formal procedures of logical and inductive inference be useful: They have not traditionally contended with real-world problems in a real-world problem space. We may be able to use some statistics and some procedures of inductive inference—indeed, we shall want to—but we cannot use them *conventionally* if our aim is to generate or to verify causal explanations of naturally-occurring social phenomena.

In short, the resolution of ill-structured problems is not well worked out. Churchman (1971) and others (e.g., Mitroff & Sagasti, 1973; Wood, 1983) have outlined appropriate "inquiry systems" for wicked problems—a "Kantian" approach to partly wicked problems and a "Hegelian" approach to very wicked ones. Unfortunately, the procedures are not well operationalized, and the guarantor of validity is the classic one: the degree of fit between, on the one hand, extant theory and theoretical predictions and, on the other, the data collected under the presumptions of the theory. There are real problems with this line of thought, especially if one subscribes to the middle-ground epistemologies. The "theory" is usually too broad-gauged to be "fitted" to local determinisms; local phenomena easily lend themselves to competing theoretical

explanations; more contingent or condition-specific theories often trail far behind the sociohistorical shifts that best account for the data; and "prediction" is, as we said before, a dicey business. So while we are conceptually grateful to the wicked problem/inquiry system approach for indicating what kind of methodology is appropriate to the study of local causal determinism, we are still, technically speaking, naked.

Where does one look? There are a multitude of technologies contending for our minds, but few that claim to take on (1) multifaceted, context-specific social phenomena, *without* the use of (2) preestablished algorithmic or standardized transformations of those phenomena, and *still* come up with (3) causal or deterministic explanations.

Overall, we have borrowed from three methodological traditions. First, we have looked to standard procedures of analytic induction. Next, we have borrowed from the literature on clinical and social judgment. Finally, we have adapted various qualitative methodologies, both in the ethnographic and interpretive traditions. Let us briefly list what we have taken from each.

COMPONENTS OF AN ECLECTIC METHODOLOGY

Analytic induction. The general procedures of analytic induction (e.g., Swinburne, 1974; Hesse, 1974) are iterative; they follow a succession of question-and-answer cycles that entail examining a given set of cases, then modifying and refining that examination on the basis of subsequent cases. Progressively, the analyst scans the data for clusters of similar appearing or similarly functioning variables, and for the relationships among these phenomena. From these, working typologies and hypotheses are drawn, then tested during the next cycle of scanning, clustering and patterning. This requires an "investigative" approach (Douglas, 1976) to the conduct of fieldwork, if one adapts this model to social research.

Inductively derived conclusions are valid in the relaxed sense that they are probable, reasonable, or likely to be true. The premises and the evidence make the conclusions more compelling than any equally detailed rival. "Compelling" can be defined in a number of ways: as best-fitting to the rest of one's current knowledge of an issue; as functionally efficient when applied the next time; as internally complete and cohesive; as more consonant with the regnant constructs or pieces of theory. These alternatives are not mutually exclusive, and taken cumulatively they make for increasingly stronger claims. One can also add to this list. For example, we have looked for "phenomenological

compellingness" in our conclusions—that is, conclusions with which several informants at a given field site concur independently. Such conclusions correspond to, although they are *not* necessarily formulated identically with, respondents' own explanations. While this list is a hybrid, there are a few inductivists who have systematized such criteria when the analyst is working with real-life, wicked data gathered from imperfect sources (see Rescher, 1976, 1980, on inductive plausibility).

So analytic induction can provide a general investigative approach for conducting qualitative research, along with some workable criteria for assessing the trustworthiness of conclusions. It can also offer some criteria for determining causal influence: the standard canons of temporal succession, constant conjunction, and directional influence. We shall be illustrating them shortly. Note for now, however, that these three are obviously weak criteria, necessary but nowhere near sufficient for the kinds of multilayered, interactive processes we are trying to pin down in the field. But when one combines them with some of the other criteria we have listed—conceptual consonance, fittingness, functional efficiency, and corroboration from local informants—they can make causal claims much weightier.

Clinical and social judgment. Theoretically, analysts using analytic induction procedures and criteria with complex, real-life data sets would generate more "valid" conclusions. The closest empirical analogue we have found is that of the "exceptional clinician" (Dunn, 1982), "connoisseur," or "expert." Overall, the analytic induction literature has described *general* procedures for essentially nonclinical or noninteractive investigations, while the clinical and connoisseurship literature has been more domain specific and much of it has focused on whether and how an individual can outperform standardized instruments and machine-generated diagnoses. Furthermore, much of it focuses more on how people *learn* to do things than on how much they *know* about what they are doing. But there may be useful insights here. Let's see.

If we start with the notion of the researcher as a qualitative judge (much like a clinician) applying techniques of analytic induction to complex, real-life data sets in order to explain the underlying patterns, the prognosis is a poor one. There is a long stream of research (e.g., Meehl, 1954, 1965; Goldberg, 1970; Dawes, 1971; Faust, 1982) showing that clinical judgments,[1] whether in medical or lay settings, are consistently less accurate than statistical/actuarial ones.

Some of the related studies are hair-raising. For example, Taft (1955) demonstrated that "expert" judges can be wrong more often than untrained ones. Oskamp (1965) showed how clinicians came to feel

increasingly confident of their initially *erroneous* judgments as they got more and more *accurate* information. Tversky and Kahneman (1971) were easily able to catch mathematical psychologists in the act of making biased inferences from samples to populations. Mahoney and De Monbreun (1977) found conservative ministers outperforming psychologists, physicists, and engineers on hypothesis-testing skills. Closer to our specific topic, Sherman and Titus (1982) showed how causal inferences are made in the very process of taking in information. Cognitively, comprehension brings into play the causal explanations needed to bind together meaningfully the bits of information being encoded. Finally, Read (1982) has shown how, in complex stimulus situations, one often engages in causal reasoning based on no more than a single instance.

The cognitive processes underlying the biases in clinical reasoning have been well studied (see Nisbett & Ross, 1980). Essentially, they turn around faulty heuristics for *selecting information* from a complex stimulus field (over-reliance on vivid data), for *judging the frequency and probability* of an event (overdependence on cognitively "available" information), for *classifying* persons and objects (ignoring base-rate information), and for *revising initial judgments* (succumbing to an "anchoring" effect). Typically, the clinical or qualitative judge scans the environment more readily for confirmatory rather than for disconfirmatory information—the so-called "cognitive confirmation effect." Alternatively, human judges will generate correct strategies but then fail to use them consistently. Oftentimes, the more complex the stimulus situation, the more primitive the cognitive processing.

Where does this leave us? It suggests, for starters, that the shift from predesigned instrumentation to human judgments combining scientific and experiential knowledge is fraught with danger if one is making claims to validity. Any "clinical" researcher operating in a natural setting had best be well armed with the safeguards against bias described in the social judgment literature.

Qualitative methodology. Let's consider the situation from a causal realist's perspective. Most qualitative researchers work alone in the field. Each is a one-person research machine: defining the problem, drawing the sample of informants and subsettings, designing the instruments, collecting the information, then reducing, analyzing, interpreting, and writing up that information. A vertical monopoly, overseen by a Promethean entrepreneur.

How do we know whether the resulting account is surreal or real? By "real" let us simply mean for now that another researcher, working

independently at the same site, would not come up with wholly contradictory findings. Since the published report usually contains few methodological details, we cannot look there. Nor can we blindly accept the robustness of the field researcher's customary tools of the trade for avoiding biases—for example, "bracketing," extensive time on site, thorough description of the setting. These are all desirable procedures, but there seems to be no empirical confirmation that (1) these procedures do, in fact, yield bias-free data and (2) a given field researcher was actually using them rigorously. What we need are specific indications of how the researcher got to the principal conclusions and verified them in such a way as to address the main biases in making social judgments that we have just reviewed.

Still, the qualitative research tradition, as exemplified by ethnographic and phenomenological studies, is a promising one for a causal realist working in ill-structured problem spaces. For one thing, qualitative researchers contend with complex, contextualized social facts, whereas the clinical and problem-solving literature has dealt largely with impersonal, contrived, simplified, or decontextualized settings. Checkmating strategies and simulated clinical folders are pallid proxies for real-life problem resolutions and explanations.

For another thing, careful documentation of naturally occurring events is the basis for making case study inferences. Still another appealing trait is that informants' accounts provide the basis for making sense, at least initially, of the analyst's observations. The notion that informants are *local connoisseurs*—that they have potentially a far more differentiated and complex representation of their surroundings than the analysts is likely to acquire in the time available on site—is a compelling one, provided one can sort out the more from the less plausible versions offered by local informants.

Finally, the social anthropological tradition has a potentially powerful blend of analytic detachment (usually through theory testing) and extensive local acquaintance (usually through vicarious or real social participation)[2] that approximates some of the "confirmatory" procedures of analytic induction, clinical diagnosis, and complex problem-solving found in the empirical research literature. In short, if an analyst of local causality can pluck selectively from the storehouse of methods used in qualitative field studies, he or she will find tools allowing for (1) the study of intact social settings, (2) flexible access to people best able to reflect on the determinants of these local environments, and (3) direct observation coupled with continuous testing of the emerging data against diverse explanations drawn from comparable settings. Such

selective plucking, we have argued, is conceptually coherent and legitimate from a causal realist's stance. And if it is combined with some standard procedures for making analytic and causal inferences, together with safeguards against the prevalent biases in clinical and social reasoning, we may have a basic repertoire for doing qualitatively derived causal analyses.

OPERATIONAL APPROACHES TO ASSESSING LOCAL CAUSALITY

Like others, we have wrestled with these epistemological and methodological issues for several years. About ten years ago, each of us moved independently from small-scale, exploratory work into a multi-year venture with qualitative research, and did some subsequent reflection on our learnings and frustrations (Huberman, 1981; Miles, 1979). We then collaborated on a three-year, multiple-setting field study keyed to a national survey (Huberman & Miles, 1983b, 1984). In the course of that project, we undertook a separate study of the procedures actually used in the analysis of qualitative data (Miles & Huberman, 1981).

The task was to document in detail the successive analytical steps taken during single-case and across-case analyses, all the way from the initial coding of field notes to the more explanatory cross-site analyses. Each of the analyses fed into a detailed self-documentation form on which we recorded the successive steps in data-reduction and analysis, the decision rules used, the bases for drawing conclusions, the confidence held in the conclusions, and the strengths and weaknesses of the analysis. These inquiry episodes were then de-bugged, refined, and extended into a sourcebook (Miles & Huberman, 1984) which also incorporated recent work of other qualitative researchers. The examples shown below come from the sourcebook (for a rapid overview, see Huberman & Miles, 1983a). Through training sessions, dissertations, additional studies, and peer critiques, the methodology has been refined further.

Let us now draw selectively from the sourcebook to illustrate how a field researcher can assess local causality through the use of analytic induction, including inferential procedures for determining causal influence, in combination with field ethnographic and phenomenological techniques, and with some simple verification devices to control for the most common clinical biases listed above.

QUALITATIVE DATA ANALYSIS

First, however, a map of the general terrain. We consider that qualitative analysis consists of three concurrent flows of activity: data reduction, data display, and conclusion-drawing/verification. *Data reduction* is the process of selecting, focusing, simplifying, abstracting, and transforming the raw information appearing in field notes. The process occurs continuously throughout the life of the study, *not* only at the end. In fact, even before the data are collected, the researcher is deciding, often without full awareness, which conceptual framework, which settings, which research issues, which data collection approaches will be pursued, and which not. As data collection proceeds, there are further episodes of reduction—for example, writing interim summaries, coding, teasing out leitmotifs, making clusters and partitions, writing memos. In short, data reduction is not separate from analysis; it *is* analysis, which entails a progressive sharpening, sorting, and organizing of the data as the study unfolds.

A second component is *data display*. Most qualitative data are displayed as narrative text, a format we find cumbersome, dispersed, sequential rather than simultaneous, poorly structured, and prone to selective, hasty, oftentimes poorly justified conclusion-drawing. We have come to understand that such displays as matrices, graphs, networks, charts, and figures are more economical and rigorous devices. They force further analysis and ordering; they oblige the analyst to look at *all* the data, not just an alluring segment. They open up avenues of further analysis otherwise masked in the welter of raw field notes, and they force the analyst to peel away the decorative from the jugular.

The third stream of analysis activity is *conclusion-drawing and verification*. This is the basic inductive cycle, whereby the researcher notes relationships, regularities, covariations, and configurations and begins to piece them together into larger, more data-encompassing units. These Gestalts become working typologies and hypotheses that are progressively modified and refined as they get used in the next pass at the setting.

It is the verification part of the cycle that modifies the emerging conclusions. It may be as brief as a fleeting second thought crossing the analyst's mind during coding, followed by a short excursion back to the original field notes. Or it may be thoroughgoing and elaborate, with an analytic "audit" being performed by a critical analyst or with an attempt to replicate the finding in another setting or subsetting.

In this view the three types of analysis activity form an interactive, iterative cycle. The researcher moves steadily among these nodes during

and after the data collection, generating, then verifying the main findings. Progressively, the core explanatory issues emerge, are sharpened, checked out, and amended, and then checked out again until they resist the combined assault of several verification devices.

We shall see shortly that the mechanics of generating a local causal analysis follow the same sequence, except that it is the *last* such exercise, building hierarchically from the previous, more fragmentary cycles of collecting, reducing, displaying, and verifying information from the field. For now, however, one should note that the general analytic strategy is consonant with other inductive approaches on the market, be they "constructive," "generative," or "grounded" (Goetz & LeCompte, 1981; Becker, 1958; Zelditch, 1962; Glaser, 1978). What all have in common is the notion of continuous analysis during data collection, in a gradual funneling, focusing sequence. What is distinctive about our version, perhaps, is that it is thoroughly *operationalized*. While other qualitative researchers may well have used similar methods, they have, as a rule, given few indications of how they were actually derived and how they are used.

THE RESEARCHER AND THE RESEARCHED

One more preliminary note. All such analytic approaches, operationalized or not, share a common characteristic of creating cognitive distance between the researcher and the setting. To conduct interim analyses, the field researcher steps back or out, sifts the data, then steps back in. The "stepping back" is consequential. Actually getting the data, of course, can imply any point on the *verstehen* continuum from intersubjective resonance to nonparticipant observation, and the field notes from most points on the continuum will reflect the world view of informants as that view is habitually expressed and made coherent. But during the stepping-back analysis cycle, those notes are *translated*—analytically metabolized into investigative hunches, constructs, propositions, questions, presumed relationships. Analytic induction as a research act inexorably pushes the "emic" toward the "etic" and, thereby, tilts in the direction of the neopositivism exemplified in transcendental realism and other middle-ground epistemologies. No matter how "grounded" or phenomenologically sensitive the fieldwork, the resulting analytic transpositions will redefine and abstract the context into other units, imperfectly isomorphic with those used by local actors to define and explain their setting.

Similarly, when one speaks of "verification," as we have just done, one infers that informants' accounts can be misleading, contradictory,

or self-deceptive, and will need to be "checked out." Of the dozen tactics for testing or confirming findings that we have elaborated (see below), about a third entail double-checking accounts furnished by local informants. Here again, the researcher is in an ambivalent stance vis-à-vis the informant, vacillating between a trusting/mistrusting and a partner/suspect relationship. Once again, the investigative or forensic metaphor comes to mind: the qualitative researcher as intellectual detective in a social sphere in which informants are unlikely to volunteer the conflictual or affectively loaded information that the researcher needs in order to piece together the setting. There is, of course, a continuum of investigative stances within the inductive mode, the most extreme being that of Douglas (1976), for whom the informant is invariably a source of mistrust, deceit, or self-delusion, presenting various "fronts" that the researcher then seeks to penetrate. But even the gentler, more phenomenological stances put distance between research-er and researched; the difference is one of degree, not of nature.

That distance is not necessarily to be deplored, and it may even make the validity of causal inference stronger. As we will note later, treating respondents as colleagues, and inviting confirmation/disconfirmation of a researcher-generated causal map can lend much confidence— exactly because of the researcher-researched difference in perspectives.

BUILDING A CAUSAL MAP OF THE LOCAL SETTING

While transcendental realists can legitimate nonstatistical causal analysis on epistemological grounds, they do not show how it is done. We have taken a cut at operationalizing the procedures through the elaboration of what we have called *causal networks*. A causal network is a visual rendering of the most important independent and dependent variables in a field study and of the relationships among them. The plot of these relationships is *deterministic* rather than solely correlational. It is assumed that some factors exert a directional influence on others (X brings Y into being or makes Y larger or smaller) and that the web of these relationships can be mapped. In addition, a causal network has associated text (the causal narrative), describing the meaning of the connections among factors.

Getting started.[3] In the approach we generally favor, the first building blocks of causal analysis are the—deliberately general—conceptual framework and research questions, when these are available, along with the codes that the researcher uses to label various chunks of the field notes. Next come the reflective remarks and added marginal remarks

made during the transcription of field notes. These are typically modest, data-shaping exercises. They alert the analyst to variables that go together and that contrast with other variables, and they invite a closer look at something that might be an underlying theme or pattern. All this means that *discrete* variables are getting clumped into *tentative families*. If they can stay in that family through successive data-gathering, -analyzing, and -verification cycles, they are good candidates for a "box" in the causal network.

Finding patterns. Marginal and reflective remarks often translate into what we have called *pattern codes*. These are in effect meta-codes, still bigger bites of data; they often turn into candidates for inclusion in a causal network. In essence, they signal a theme or pattern that makes a local difference. For example, in one study we came up with a pattern code, "TEAMS," which described a conflict between two administrative factions in a school district. The code stuck; it recurred and eventually got amalgamated into a stream of variables on the causal network ("career advancement motivation" and "climate in district office") that, in turn, determined the key outcomes.

Moving up a notch, pattern codes are extended into memos—written comments on emerging descriptive or explanatory concepts that cluster events and processes in the field, keeping them anchored to the context in which they appear (see Glaser, 1978). Memos, in turn, are combined with reflective remarks and pattern codes to generate *interim summaries* and *site analysis meetings* between researchers. These are intended to force out the emerging thematic and explanatory pieces—to move carefully from description to inference.

How, specifically, one moves up the inferential chain is something we have tried to document and then operationalize in the form of "tactics" for generating meaning. The tactics progress from elementary clustering and partitioning exercises (counting, noting patterns, making plausible associations, clustering, making metaphors, splitting variables, subsuming particulars into the general) to more inductively ambitious exercises (factoring, noting relations between variables, finding intervening variables, building a logical chain of evidence, making conceptual/ theoretical coherence). The latter devices, with results checked against the properties of the setting, then modified and refined, combine discrete pieces of data into the evidential chain that has a beginning causal logic.

One notes, approximately at first, which variables are present or absent together in the setting and which appear unconnected to those. Then, more systematically, the analyst begins to plot the variables that

are coming regularly into play *before* others, are varying concomitantly *with* others, or are having a directional *influence* on others, with that influence changing when *other* variables are taken into account. In conducting these analyses, the researcher is simply applying the standard canons of inductive inference: temporal precedence, concomitant variation, and directional influence. He or she is also constructing the rudiments of a causal map that contains assumptions about the *directions* of influence among *sets* of variables. These assumptions, of course, will need to be made explicit and checked out during the next time on site—or, if one is off the site, checked out within the available data set. More on this verification process shortly.

Generating causal fragments. It is at this point that the analyst assembles the fragments of the emerging causal map. Here is a specimen list of decision rules for doing this:

- Translate the pattern codes into variables—that is, something that can be scaled (high to low, big to little, more to less).
- Rate the variable (e.g., high, moderate, low). How much of it is there in the site?
- Draw a line between pairs of variables that covary—that appear together consistently at the site or have some kind of relationship (e.g., more of one variable goes with less of another).
- Draw a directional arrow between each variable that comes first (temporally) and those later ones it appears to influence. *Influence* here means that more or less of one variable determines to some extent the rating on another. The rating of the second variable might have been different had the first one not been there.
- If two variables covary and are related but seem only to have a tepid or oblique influence on one another, there is probably another, latent variable that needs to be invented to join the two. Review the full list of codes to see if one fits here. (The analytic tactic here, listed earlier, is *finding intervening variables.*)

Figure 18.1 is an example of a causal fragment. The figure puts together themes having to do with the mastery of a new educational practice. The story can be told quickly. A demanding project with high implementation requirements (1) began with inadequate preparation (2) and was bailed out by high levels of assistance (3), which increased local efforts (4) and facilitated practice mastery (5). The (–) sign indicates reverse causal influence: Low preparation leads to high assistance.

The intent here is to stimulate thinking, not to get closure. The analyst should try to assemble a few such fragments without necessarily connecting one to another—should play around, do some causal

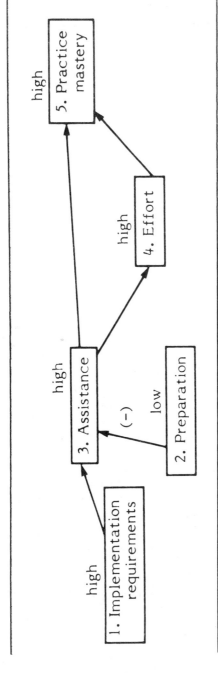

Figure 18.1 Causal Fragment: Mastery of a New Educational Practice

noodling—yet be careful not to connect variables that do not go together *empirically*, even if on logical grounds they should.

A useful next step is to take these fragments out to the field during later data collection to see how, and whether, they work. This can include some *member checks* (Guba & Lincoln, 1981)—that is, submitting the diagram to an informant to get confirmation and qualification (e.g., *some* preparation was decent, some assistance did not have an effect on levels of effort, some users were competent and experienced enough to do without preparation or assistance and still get high practice mastery). That might suggest that the next iteration of the network should have an arrow from a new box labeled "user competence" to the "effort" variable (4) and to the "practice mastery" variable (5).

Testing or confirming findings. Trying out the causal fragments on those being researched is, we suggest, good and necessary medicine. Good medicine, because it buffers each progressive inductive cycle as one moves from particulars to generals and from description to inference. Necessary medicine because, as we noted earlier in reviewing the literature on clinical and social judgment, the qualitative researcher is vulnerable to a pack of biases of which he or she is often, at best, remotely aware. In most cases, these biases break down into a series of "faulty heuristics," which operate, perversely enough, at the crucial moments in a field study: when the researcher is making inductive inferences or generalizing. Since the causal analysis is the hierarchical queen of these lower-level conclusions, its validity and reliability live or die by the trustworthiness of the more elementary and fragmented exercises in generating meaning.

The obvious remedy is to catalogue the most frequently appearing biases, and work out some operationally defined procedures for correcting each of them. Social anthropologists have done some of this work already (e.g., by addressing the "holistic fallacy," the "elite bias," and the "cooptation" or "going native" problem), but many of the solutions are not well operationalized, and most assume that one has several months on site.

In our research and in the sourcebook, we have chipped away at this issue and have reframed it by working out a dozen operationalized techniques for verifying conclusions in qualitative research. A simple list gives the flavor of these tactics:

- Checking for representativeness
- Checking for researcher effects

- Triangulating (by sources, methods, levels, and researchers)
- Weighting the evidence
- Making contrasts/comparisons
- Checking the meaning of outliers
- Using extreme cases
- Ruling out spurious relations
- Replicating a finding
- Checking out rival explanations
- Looking for negative evidence
- Getting feedback from informants
- Documenting and auditing conclusions.

For example, the representativeness problem addresses the faulty heuristics of generalizing abusively from instances to sets of instances. In this case, as in the others, we advise that the qualitative researcher *assume* that he or she is selectively sampling and drawing inferences from a weak or nonrepresentative sample of cases—be they people, events, or processes. In other words, you are guilty until you prove yourself innocent. You can prove your innocence in at least one of four ways: (1) simply increase the number of cases, (2) look *purposively* for contrasting (negative, extreme, countervailing) cases, (3) sort the cases systematically and fill out weakly sampled case types, and (4) sample randomly within the universe or people and phenomena under study.

The last two procedures, not coincidentally, correspond to the stratification and randomization conventions used by experimentalists to enhance internal validity. But, whereas the experimental researcher uses these procedures *early*, as anticipatory controls against sampling and measurement error, the qualitative researcher uses them *later*, as verification devices. That allows one to let all the candidate people and data in, so that the most influential ones will have an equal chance of emerging. But you *still* have to carry the burden of proof that the patterns you ultimately discover are, in fact, representative.

Generating a causal network variable list. About three-quarters of the way through data collection, the researcher should be ready to assemble the remaining pieces of the causal network. A useful first step is to generate the full set of network variables. This, too, is an exercise in playful brainstorming. The idea is to list all the events, factors, outcomes, processes, and so forth that seem to be important, then to turn them into variables. For instance, several fights between employees will become "organizational conflict." The first pass should be exhaus-

TABLE 18.1   List of Antecedent, Mediating, and Outcome Variables

Antecedent or Start Variables	Mediating Variables	Outcomes
Internal funds	External funds	Stabilization of use
Career advancement motivation	Program adoption (NDN)	Percentage of use
	Program concept initiative (IV-C)	Student impact
Assessed adequacy of local performance	Program development (IV-C)	User capacity change
Environmental turbulence	District endorsement	Institutionalization
	Building endorsement	Job mobility
	Influence of innovation advocate	
	Implementation requirements	
	Adequacy of initial user preparation	
	Program-district fit	
	Program-building fit	
	Program-user fit	
	Assistance	
	User commitment	
	User skill	
	Program transformation	
	Teacher-administrator harmony	
	Validation effort (IV-C)	
	Stability of program leadership	
	Stability of program staff	
	Organizational transformation	

tive, the next one more selective. That is, once a full set of variables is down, the list should be combed for redundancies and overdifferentiation (e.g., three types of fighting between employees). As a rough rule of thumb, fifteen variables are probably too few and forty too many. As an illustration, Table 18.1 is a list of core variables generated in a school improvement study we conducted (Huberman & Miles, 1984).

In a single-site study, the variable list is a straightforward procedure. In a multiple-site study, by contrast, we are at a decisive moment. For cross-site comparisons, the same variables are going to be used to analyze five, ten, or twenty sites. For this to happen, theoretically *each* of the variables has to be empirically meaningful at *all* the sites. Of course one should leave slack for the probability that there will be a handful of *site-specific* variables in addition. They are of two types: those that are influential at only one site and those that are influential at most but not all sites. In the former case, the final causal network will contain a site-specific variable, labeled as such. In the latter case, some

network variables will be dropped (with an explanation) from the sites at which they contribute little to the analysis.

Drawing the causal network. In principle, most of the items on the variable list will have been prefigured, explicitly or implicitly, in the pattern codes, interim summaries, and memos we reviewed earlier. They will also have emerged during the progressively multivariate displays we have alluded to. Analyzing *conceptual clusters* in the setting, for example, allows the analyst to tease out the relationships within one of the variable families. *Effects matrices* are exercises that identify incipient cause-effect relations. Then, *both* clustering and cause-effect inferencing are combined in *site dynamics matrices.* In other words, the causal analysis is being done incrementally; one is testing individual paths more rigorously and, at the same time, building an integrated map.

Finally, the *event-state* network get us almost there; let us illustrate how. Figure 18.2 is an excerpt from an event-state network for one of the field sites in a twelve-site study we conducted. As the figure indicates, *events* are key, observable, or verifiable actions whose influence is judged to be decisive, and *states* are the consequences of those (and sometimes of other) events. The double-numbering (for number 4 and number 7) indicates that these items are thematically or functionally similar. This sets up the final causal network. Figure 18.3 is an excerpt, with the variable numbers keyed to the corresponding "variables" in the event-state network.

Let us now take a look at a fully drawn causal network (Figure 18.4). It will look initially overwhelming to the reader because it condenses mountains of inferential data into one, integrated display. But stay with us for some simplifying explication.

Drawing the network is probably done best the same way one should analyze it: stream by stream. Some streams—unbroken chains of variables—are long: Look at the one that runs directly from box 1 through boxes 8, 9, 10, to 30, even to 32. Others are, conveniently, shorter; the bottom stream from 5 to 35 and 33 is a short one. Within an unbroken stream, there are usually eddies leading in different directions or ending up at the same place via a different route. They should also be drawn in.

Streams can be most easily drawn—especially if the event-state net-work is used as the semi-final cut—from antecedents forward in time. It is also possible to take a dependent variable and work backward, but then it is important to run it forward again to be sure the links are coherent and empirically justified. One will usually find that there are cross-stream connections, and they can be drawn in as the network evolves.

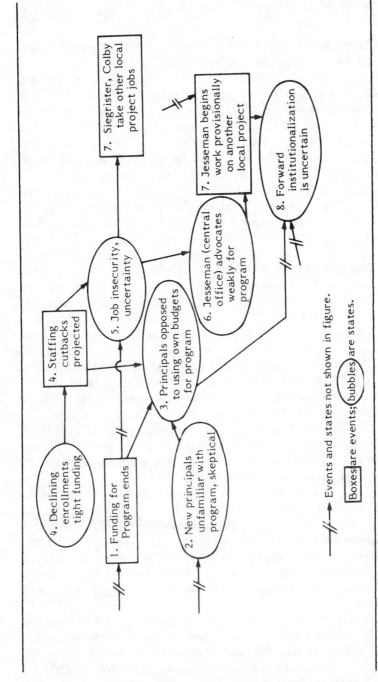

Figure 18.2 Excerpt from an Event-State Network

1. Funding for Program ends
2. New principals unfamiliar with program, skeptical
3. Principals opposed to using own budgets for program
4. Declining enrollments tight funding
4. Staffing cutbacks projected
5. Job insecurity, uncertainty
6. Jesseman (central office) advocates weakly for program
7. Siegrister, Colby take other local project jobs
7. Jesseman begins work provisionally on another local project
8. Forward institutionalization is uncertain

⎯⎯→ Events and states not shown in figure.

Boxes are events; bubbles are states.

372

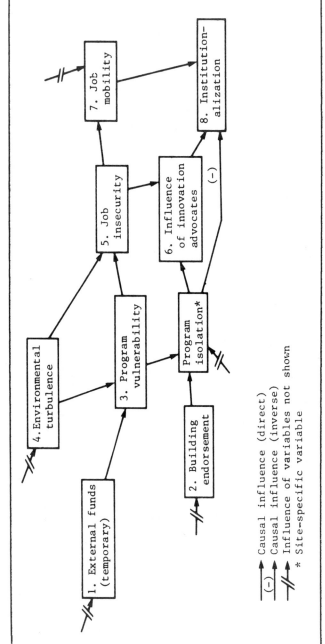

Figure 18.3 Excerpt from a Causal Network

373

Figure 18.4 Causal Network for Perry-Parkdale CARED Program

Causal influence (direct) →
Causal influence (inverse) (−)

1 mod/low Assessed adequacy of local performance

2 high State mandate

3 high Search for programs*

4 low Internal funds

5 high Career advancement motivation

6 high Search for add-on funds*

7 high Program–district fit

8 high District endorsement

9 Program adoption

10 high Implementation requirements

11 Program demand characteristics

12 low Program–building fit

13 high Program vulnerability*

14 high External funds (temporary)

15 high Competition for funds & students*

16 high Environmental turbulence

17 high Dissemination effort*

18 mod/high Assistance

19 high Adequacy of user preparation

20 high User commitment

21 high User quality (competence)

22 low Building endorsement

23 high Program isolation*

24 mod/low Influence of innovation advocates

25 high Job insecurity

26 high User skill

27 mod Stabilization of use

28 mod/low Program transformation

29 low Organizational transformation

30 mod/high Student impact

31 mod/low Percentage of use

32 low Institutionalization

33 high Job mobility

34 high User capacity change

35 high External network development*

ANTECEDENT VARIABLES ——— INTERVENING VARIABLES ——— OUTCOME VARIABLES

*Variable specific to this site

374

Often, these streams and eddies have a name—a scenario or theme—and this makes them easier both to analyze and to render. For example, along the bottom stream variables 5, 17, 35, and 34 have a "cosmopolizing" theme: People go outside their environments in connection with a new project and the experience both stretches them and sets up possible career shifts. Or, again, staying along the bottom of the network, boxes 4, 16, 25 and 33 add up to a "casualty" stream: low money, high turbulence (usually in the form of budget cuts), staff instability, and ultimate staff reassignments.

Alternatively, the streams can be labeled according to the level of dependent variables (e.g., high student impact scenarios, low institution-alization scenarios, high job mobility scenarios). These similarly named scenarios can be very different. For instance, as we just saw, one high job mobility scenario involves a promotion or desirable transfer, whereas another involves an unwanted reassignment or even a layoff.

Causal network narratives. Drawing conclusions from the network should wait until the analyst has a more coherent sense of what is on it. Like all time-related representations, this one tells a story—really, several stories. One should write out a chronological narrative for each of the major streams. In this case, one starts at the beginning. Here is an excerpt from the narrative for the causal network shown in Figure 18.4:

> The first three antecedent variables (1, 2, and 4) worked out this way: The state mandate (2) for well-planned career education programs, together with assessment of local performance as less than adequate (1), led to a search for new programs (3), which proved to be a good fit (7) with district characteristics, and hence to district endorsement (8), and to adoption of the program (9).
>
> But these were not sufficent causes of adoption. Inadequate local funds (4) to cover existing programs led to a ceaseless search for add-on funds (6) as almost a "way of life" for the district. That search led to getting temporary external funds (14) for a three-year period; they were the other basic cause of adoption (9).
>
> The program, when adopted, proved to have substantial implementation requirements (10), which dictated the need for assistance (18), and also exerted a good deal of pressure for careful selection of high-quality staff (21), and for careful preparation (19) of them to carry out the program. The heavy implementation requirements (10), and to some degree the assistance provided (18), induced a good deal of user commitment (20), and in turn user skill (26), which was also high because of staff quality (21). High user skill, in conjunction with the fact that the program was quite well stabilized (27) by late 1980, brought about a reasonable degree of student impact (30).

That stream of causality refers essentially to internal program dynamics. What was happening at the *district and building* level?

Moving back to program demand characteristics (11), we note that certain aspects of the program (such as its removing students from high school control, and from high school courses and activities) caused poor fit between the program and the sending buildings (12). That poor fit led to lack of endorsement (22) from building principals, counselors and teachers. Poor endorsement was further weakened by the presence of competition for funds and for students (15), induced by the fact that the external funds (14) were temporary in nature.

Writing the narrative usually does several things. It forces the analyst to be less mechanistic and more coherent: Turning a network into clear text requires one to be fully explicit about what is causing what. Corrections and revisions are likely. Second, it provides an opportunity for expansion: The analyst can explain why variables are related, why they are rated differently, why some precede others, which ones matter more, and so on.

In the same vein, the narrative brings back the *context*, pinning down the conditions and contingencies under which the abstracted variables actually play out. As transcendental realists emphasize, our task is to show how *in each particular case* the causal configurations occurred, then to provide a theoretical redescription of the case that is isomorphic to its components.

Auditing and verification. Finally, both the network and the narrative constitute materials that can be handed to a colleague, to a critic, and to site informants for auditing and verification.

By *auditing*, we mean that a second reader goes carefully over the conclusions to check their robustness.[4] The auditor's task is *not* to generate another network or narrative, but to go through the original one with the kind of fine-grained, nitpicky review that secondary analysts visit on their peers in statistical studies. One of the important assumptions here, which we derive directly from the work on ill-structured problems and appropriate inquiry systems, is that *more than one* causal network may be valid, that there is no single solution to the exclusion of the others but that some solutions are more compelling and robust than others. It is the auditing process that keeps the orginal analyst inferentially honest and, at the same time, informs the reader of the credibility of the analysis.

There is no simple answer to the question of what to do when you and your auditor disagree sharply about some aspect of the analysis

procedures or conclusions. Here are some responses we have found ourselves making:

(1) Arguing, "explaining," clarifying one's point of view until both agree that the original cut was right, or that some revision is needed.

(2) Going back to the original data to see if they really support the conclusions drawn; more often than not, an auditor can usually suggest some *new* data that could be used to verify or disprove the conclusions. The familiar technique of *triangulation*—using other data sources, methods, or analysts—is relevant here.

(3) Jointly recasting the particular procedure used (for example, drawing a new network with revised paths and some new variables, together).

(4) Turning the tables and inviting the auditor to become the analyst, with the analyst taking a look at the product. This is, naturally, most labor intensive, and useful only when heavy disagreements exist. (We have found, by the way, that heavy disagreements are in fact rare—and that when they do exist, there is often a social-psychological underpinning involved: The auditor and analyst belong to different subgroups, are uneasy with each other, etc. It pays to work on the real relationship issue, and not to camouflage it as a "data" issue.)

Finally, here are some reponses we do NOT ever recall having made:

(1) Giving the problem to the local authority figure (research director, principal investigator, etc.).

(2) Finding a third, fourth or fifth party, and going by majority rule.

(3) Saying to the original analyst, "Ok, it's your baby. Do it any way you like."

What these responses have in common is a sort of mechanical, disengaged quality, along with the assumption that important substantive issues can be managed by nose-counting or pulling rank.

Feeding the network *and* narrative back to the site is very useful; it serves as a verification device and as an opportunity for the analyst to learn more. Both the graphics of the network and the details of the narrative have in our experience turned out to be helpful decoding and sense-making tools for site informants. The causal networks provide information at macro-analytic levels of inference that most informants initially either discount or swallow whole for their esoteric, "scientific" appearance. But the narratives bring the local actors back into their own surround—and then deepen their understanding and critique of the network. As the symbolic interactionists have shown well, people do not

act towards social structures or roles or constructs; they act toward *situations* and *events*, and are likely to understand meta-situational language only to the extent that it is directly plugged into the events and situations described in the narratives.

We have worked up feedback forms for verifying causal networks and narratives through local informants' reactions. Generally speaking, we have tried to pick people from a particular site who (1) are reasonably knowledgeable about the phenomena we are studying, non-defensive, and articulate; (2) come from several different roles and perspectives; (3) are themselves of an inquiring, curious turn of mind. (Naturally, all these criteria cannot usually be met—and probably should not be, lest we merely recreate an ideal image of ourselves in the guise of site informants.)

The forms we have used are described in a previous work (Miles & Huberman, 1984, pp. 142-143). In brief, they present the network and the narrative, then ask the respondent for comments on its accuracy, and to cross out or add boxes, cross out or add arrows, change box weights—and to explain the rationale for doing this. Since we consider this professional work, we offered site people a modest reader's fee ($25-50).

People seem to enjoy doing this work. It lets them see rapidly how the researcher has put the pieces together, and they then run that view against their own perspective. When that perspective is different, informants can quite easily re-draw parts of the network or re-draft parts of the narrative.

Our experience has been that site informants do not differ sharply from our analyses, suggesting only marginal changes—which are, however, often illuminating. Sharp differences would suggest a great deal either about the quality of our field work or some real or perceived danger to the informant.

To illustrate the latter, we should cite an experience where one of us, in an earlier project, fed back *complete case studies* to site personnel. Almost everyone found things in the detail of the cases that either upset them, or could genuinely damage their careers; we were threatened with suit in four of five sites. Such concerns were in fact valid, we judged, and the relevant material was deleted or disguised.

Causal networks, however, are far less likely to tread such dangerous ground. They are abstracted analyses, general maps of what happened and why, and they do not identify specific actors who are blameworthy, misguided, incompetent, or the like.

FROM LOCAL TO MULTIPLE-SETTING CAUSALITY:
A BRIEF NOTE

A case is more than a case. It has components found in other cases; it is, after all, an aggregate of instances that we could simply not comprehend if we did not have, in our own experience, corresponding instances taken from elsewhere. The problem, of course, is that these instances are idiosyncratically organized within each case, and being so organized, they may *mean* different things from one context to another. The Bible probably has it right: Each case is like *no* other, like *some* other, and like *all* others.

Given the current growth in multisite qualitative studies (see Smith & Louis, 1982), we badly need approaches to drawing coherent, valid meaning from more than one case. However, even middle-range epistemologists have made a strong argument for determining local causality, case by case, and an equally strong argument against any such thing as "general" causality. Others, too, have been wary of moving from the idiographic to the nomothetic—or, as Lewin had it, from the Galilean laws obtaining in single cases to the Aristotelian laws affecting *classes* of objects. But there may well be a middle ground here: finding causal determinisms in more than one context, with similar events and processes coming into play. Is there a way of plotting them without recourse to multivariate statistics and without erasing the setting-specific configurations and thereby rendering each case, literally, meaning-less?[5] We think there may be, and have enjoyed tinkering with the mechanics of bringing it off. Given space constraints, we will provide only a brief summary here; the interested reader should consult Miles and Huberman (1984, pp. 197-209).

Essentially, the analyst looks at each of n causal networks (and their associated narratives when needed). For each network, one extracts the *sub*network of boxes and arrows that lead directly to the dependent variable being analyzed. Variables that have no path from them to the outcomes—even through other variables—are ignored. Within each subnetwork, there is a careful effort to isolate and name the streams involved (for example, the "casualty" and "cosmopolizing" streams already mentioned).

The next step is that of matching the variable streams to those in other cases that have similar outcomes. There are two approaches to this: (1) general "pattern matching" at a global level; and (2) in a more detailed analytic mode, putting the variables in an "antecedents matrix" (Miles & Huberman, 1984, pp. 203-205) showing, for the full set of sites, the immediate and remotely causal variables.

Either of these approaches helps the analyst to cluster the streams and to develop scenarios that are more general for sites as wholes. The work then moves up a notch, by clustering *sites* into families (for example, in twelve sites, we found one family of two sites we called "win-lose" because they included both successful and unsuccessful job mobility streams).

The final step involves verifying the scenarios within families: Are the variables the same? Do they have the same value? Are the outcomes at the same level? Do the narratives support the "familyness"? And do families with *different* levels of outcome show different, or differently loaded, variables?

Such a description is rather abstract. We have found, however, that using these procedures does permit one to produce *generalized* causal networks reflecting the shared and the idiosyncratic elements of sites within the same family. We typically found from two to four sites in a family within our set of twelve sites.

CONCLUDING COMMENT

In this chapter, we have tried to spell out a coherent and manageable approach to nonstatistical research that allows for the analysis of local causal influence without disfiguring the configuration of context-specific phenomena. In developing that approach, we have also tried to include some components that many analysts tend to obscure or omit, in particular the epistemic bases for the methodologies proposed *and* the nuts and bolts of the methodologies themselves. Until we can get some agreement on those issues, taken *together*, we will continue to talk past one another in a dialogue of the deaf about clinical qualitative research, like the more comic characters in a Chekhov play or the more tragic characters in a Pinter play. And this, in turn, will put us researchers in the incongruous position of being unsure of what we mean when we pretend to "explain" why our informants behave as they do—they who have worked out consensual and functional ways of going about *their* business and of making perfectly good sense of it.

NOTES

1. These studies use a considerably narrower, simpler, definition of *clinical* than that used elsewhere in this book. But there is no guarantee that clinical judgment more broadly or complexly defined will necessarily produce valid knowledge—which is what we are after.

2. Scriven (1979, p. 69) puts it well in remarking that cause-hunting, like lion-hunting, "is only likely to be successful if we have a considerable amount of relevant background knowledge."

3. This account, with its step-by-step detail, is only possible because we repeatedly carried out self-documentation of our analytic moves, as described above. Reviewing our documentation forms both taught us something about our own fallability as analysts and showed us the usefulness of the procedures as they gradually emerged in an iterative fashion. For more detail see Miles and Huberman (1984, pp. 243-248).

4. This auditing will be much deeper and better if the analyst also has kept some form of documentation of the procedures followed and has recorded the ideas and feelings that surfaced during the process. Even if that has not been done, it is useful to have an auditor do some retrospective interviewing: "What led you to decide on *that* variable as an antecedent?" "Where were your doubts at that point?" "Why do you feel so sure about that stream's name?"

5. In *The End of the Road*, John Barth captures the dilemma nicely when he has his protagonist observe that the authors of (medical) textbooks, like everyone else, can read generality only by ignoring enough particularity.

Commentary

As Helen Swick Perry delved into the biographical details of Harry Stack Sullivan's life she found herself thinking about her father. There were many similarities in the early lives of these two men and, as Perry reported, on occasion she found it hard to keep separate her reflections on each of them. Her relationship with Sullivan's history made salient her relationship with her father, stirring contemporary emotions. The past and the present, other and self all came together in a caldron of fused thoughts and feelings. It would have been understandable if Perry had put aside this overwhelming experience, but her work as investigator turned to the task of drawing new distinctions, separating father from Sullivan, present from past, self from other. At the conclusion she writes, "the very similarities underscored their differences."

This concept, the relationship of similarities and differences, is the essence of the scientific method. It is not possible to have "information" without distinctions. It is difference that creates data. The task of science is to distinguish and to link together that which has been distinguished. It must be noted that the concept of difference is likewise dependent on the concept of similarity. If not for similarity there would be no difference. Without darkness we could not know light. Darkness allows us to have the concept of light. The concepts of darkness and light give meaning to each other because they have a critical similarity.

In many ways the description of science in the preceding paragraph is like the process of identity development in a child or an adolescent. Only as distinctions are made can relationships develop. Only as the two-year-old learns how to say no does the concept of yes have real psychological meaning. Only as we separate from our parents can we know who we are. Significantly, these differentiations can occur only if there are meaningful connections in the first place. The process of becoming fully integrated, both internally and with the external world, depends on clear distinctions being drawn. This enables new similarities and connections to develop. The analogy between the activities of the scientific method and the process of individual identity development underscores the truly human character of scientific work.

At the collective level, too, distinctions play a role in enabling us to identify similarities. In the same way that individuals cannot be understood apart from the groups and organizations to which they belong, science must be understood in terms of its context. If, as Reinharz points out in Section III, the evolution of a community of scientists has been an attempt to formulate an authority system capable of combating the tyranny of political rulers, the distinction between the authority of science and the authority of the king affirms their *similarity* as systems of authority.

Each of the chapters in this section struggles with issues of similarity, differentiation, and integration. Simmons, as she introjected the discrepancies in the archives, confronted a choice: Should she search for what caused the discrepancies or should she search for what the discrepancies might tell about

the system's prehistory. Taking the debate inside, she fused the past and the present, outside and inside, system and person, and as she lived with these contradictions was able to draw distinctions that informed her about the past and the present. She *created* new perspectives, new insights, and new theories through the process of incorporation, fusion, differentiation, and integration.

Gillette, by describing the distinction between history and social science shows the presence of history in the here-and-now of social research. Sutton and Schurman struggled with the fact that they were unable to carry out interviews on certain topics using the detached method their training demanded. In the process they realized that those highly structured methods needed to be understood and used differently in different contexts. Their attempts to act similarly in very different settings taught them about the ways they needed to act differently.

This same topic undergirds the chapter by Huberman and Miles. They argue that distinctions are always being made and that these choices should be recorded as they are made. At the same time Huberman and Miles suggest that clustering—delineation by similarity—is an important part of the data reduction process. Distinguishing and clustering are the key processes in the analysis of causal chains and they are the foundation of validity in the clinical side of research.

In conclusion, we would like to point out that the purpose of this volume has been to make finer distinctions, to draw lines not previously drawn, and to make links among that which is now distinguished. We do not believe that this is in opposition to science. It is intended to affirm that the application of the activities of science to science itself is what nourishes science, keeping it vital and expanding its capacity to respond to the demands of the social world of which it is a part.

REFERENCES

Abrahamson, M. (1983). *Social research methods*. Englewood Cliffs, NJ: Prentice-Hall.

Alderfer, Charlene Hareven, J. (1982). Freud, a potential family theorist. *Network, 2*, 9-10.

Alderfer, C.P. (1968). Explorations in consulting-client relationships. *Human Organizations, 27*, 260-265.

Alderfer, C.P. (1977). Group and intergroup relations. In J.R. Hackman & J.L. Suttle (Eds.), *Improving life at work*. Santa Monica, CA: Goodyear.

Alderfer, C.P. (1980a). The methodology of organizational diagnosis. *Professional Psychology, 11*, 459-468.

Alderfer, C.P. (1980b). Consulting to underbounded systems. In C.P. Alderfer & C.L. Cooper (Eds.), *Advances in experiential social processes* (Vol. 2). New York: John Wiley.

Alderfer, C.P. (1984). An intergroup perspective on group dynamics. In J. Lorsch (Ed.), *Handbook of organizational behavior*. Englewood Cliffs, NJ: Prentice-Hall.

Alderfer, C.P., & Berg, D.N. (1977). Organization development: The profession and the practitioner. In P.H. Mirvis & D.N. Berg (Eds.), *Failures in organization development and change* (pp. 89-110). New York: John Wiley.

Alderfer, C.P. & Brown, L.D. (1975). *Learning from changing*. Beverly Hills, CA: Sage.

Alderfer, C.P., Brown, L.D., Kaplan, R.E., & Smith, K.K. (in press). *Group relations and organizational diagnosis*. New York: John Wiley.

Alderfer, C.P., Kaplan, R.E., & Smith, K.K. (1974). The effect of variations in relatedness need satisfaction on learning desires. *Administrative Science Quarterly, 19*, 507-532.

Alderfer, C.P., & Smith, K.K. (1982). Studying intergroup relations embedded in organizations. *Administrative Science Quarterly, 27*, 35-65.

Alexander, J. (1982). *Theoretical logic in sociology: Positivism, presuppositions, and current controversies*. Berkeley: University of California Press.

Andersen, M. (1983). *Thinking about women: Sociological and feminist perspectives*. New York: Macmillan.

Argyris, C. (1952). Diagnosing defenses against the outsider. *Journal of Social Issues, 80*, 24-34.

Argyris, C. (1968). Some unintended consequences of rigorous research. *Psychological Bulletin, 70*, 185-197.

Aronson, E. (1980). Persuasion via self-justification: Large commitments for small rewards. In L. Festinger (Ed.), *Retrospections on social psychology* (pp. 3-21). New York: Oxford University Press.

Aronson, E. (1984). A missionary for social psychology. *Psychology Today, 18*, 40-45.

Aronson, E., & Mills, J. (1959). The effect of severity of initiation on liking for a group. *Journal of Abnormal and Social Psychology 59*, 177-181.

ASA (American Sociological Association). (1980). Sexist biases in sociological research: Problems and issues. *Footnotes*. Status of women in sociology.

Babad, E.Y., Birnbaum, M., & Benne, K.D. (1983). *The social self*. Beverly Hills, CA: Sage.

Babbie, E.R. (1973). *Survey research methods*. Belmont, CA: Wadsworth.

Babbie, E.R. (1983). *The practice of social research* (3rd ed.). Belmont, CA: Wadsworth.

Bacharach, S.B., & Lawler, E.J. (1980). *Power and politics in organizations*. San Francisco: Jossey-Bass.

Bailar, J., Louis, T., Lavori, P., & Polansky, M. (1984). Studies without internal controls. *New England Journal of Medicine, 311,* 156-162.

Baker-Miller, J. (1976). *Toward a new psychology of women.* Boston, MA: Beacon Press.

Balmary, M. (1979). *Psychoanalyzing psychoanalysis: Freud and the hidden fault of the father.* Baltimore, MD: Johns Hopkins Press.

Barlow, D.H., Hayes, S.C., & Nelson, R.C. (1984). *The scientist practitioner.* New York: Pergamon Press.

Bart, P. (1971). Sexism in social science: From the iron cage to the gilded cage—the perils of Pauline. *Journal of Marriage and the Family, 33,* 742.

Barzun, A., & Graff, H.F. (1957). *The modern researcher.* New York: Harcourt Brace Jovanovich.

Bateson, G. (1972). *Steps to an ecology of mind.* New York: Ballantine.

Bateson, G. (1979). *Mind and nature.* New York: Bantam.

Becker, E. (1973). *The denial of death.* New York: Free Press.

Becker, H.S. (1958). Problems of inference and proof in participant observation. *American Sociological Review, 23,* 652-660.

Becker, H.S. (1974). Whose side are we on? In G. Riley (Ed.), *Values, objectivity, and the social sciences* (pp. 107-121). Reading, MA: Addison-Wesley.

Benne, K.D. (1959). Some ethical problems in group and organizational consultation. *Journal of Social Issues, 15,* 60-67.

Bennis, W.G., & Shepard, H.A. (1956). A theory of group development. *Human Relations, 9,* 415-457.

Berg, D.N. (1980). Developing clinical field skills: An apprenticeship model. In C.P. Alderfer & C.L. Cooper (Eds.), *Advances in experiential social processes* (Vol. 2). New York: John Wiley.

Berg, D.N. (1984). Objectivity and prejudice. *American Behavioral Scientist 27,* 387-402.

Berger, P. (1963). *Invitation to sociology: A humanistic perspective.* Garden City, NY: Doubleday.

Berger, P., & Luckman, T. (1967). *The social construction of reality: A treatise in the sociology of knowledge.* Garden City, NY: Doubleday.

Bernard, J. (1973). My four revolutions: An autobiographical history of the American Sociological Association. *American Journal of Sociology, 78,* 773-791.

Bernard, J. (1981). *The female world.* New York: Free Press.

Bhaskar, R. (1975). *A realist theory of science.* Leeds, UK: Leeds Books.

Bhaskar, R. (1982). Emergence, explanation and emancipation. In P. Secord (Ed.), *Explaining social behavior: Consciousness, behavior and social structure.* Beverly Hills, CA: Sage.

Bierce, A. (1911). *The devil's dictionary.* New York: Albert and Charles Boni Inc.

Biographical Directory of the American Psychological Association. (1975). Washington, DC: American Psychological Association.

Bion, W.R. (1961). *Experiences in groups.* London: Tavistock.

Bowen, E.S. (Bohanan, L.) (1954). *Return to laughter.* New York: Harper & Row.

Bowles, G., & Duelli-Klein, R. (Eds.) (1983). *Theories of women's studies.* London: Routledge & Kegan Paul.

Boykin, A.W., Anderson, J.F., & Yates, J.F. (Eds.). (1979). *Research directions of black psychologists.* New York: Russell Sage Foundation.

Brandwein, R. (1984). Feminist thought-structure: An alternative paradigm of social change for social justice. Paper presented at a conference, Toward social and economic justice, Brandeis University, Waltham, MA, March 23-25.

Brown, R.W., & Lennenberg, E.H. (1954). A study in language and cognition. *Journal of Abnormal and Social Psychology 49*: 454-462.

Buraway, M. (1979). *Manufacturing consent*. Chicago: University of Chicago Press.

Campbell, D.T. (1975). Degrees of freedom and the case study. *Comparative Political Studies, 8*(2), 178-193.

Campbell, D.T. (1977). Descriptive epistemology: Psychological, sociological and evolutionary. Unpublished paper, William James Lectures, Harvard University, Cambridge, MA.

Campbell, D.T., & Stanley, J.C. (1963). *Experimental and quasi-experimental designs for research*. Chicago: Rand McNally.

Carlsmith, J.M., Ellsworth, P.C., & Aronson, E. (1976). *Methods of research in social psychology*. Reading, MA: Addison-Wesley.

Cassell, J. (1980). Ethical principles for conducting fieldwork. *American Anthropologist, 82*(1), 28-41.

Chassan, J. (1979). *Research design in clinical psychology and psychiatry* (2nd ed.). New York: Irvington.

Chomsky, N. (1971). *Problems of knowledge and freedom*. New York: Pantheon.

Christians, C.G., & Carey, J.W. (1981). The logic and aims of qualitative research. In G.H. Stempel & B.H. Westley (Eds.), *Research methods in mass communication*. Englewood Cliffs, NJ: Prentice-Hall.

Churchman, C.W. (1971). *The design of inquiring systems: Basic concepts of systems and organization*. New York: Basic Books.

Cicourel, A. V. (1982). Interviews, surveys, and the problem of ecological validity. *American Sociologist, 17*(1), 11-20.

Clawson, D. (1980). *Bureaucracy and the labor process*. New York: Monthly Review Press.

Clawson, J. (1980). Mentoring in managerial careers. In C.B. Derr (Ed.), *Work, family and the career*. New York: Praeger.

Cobb, S. (1976). Social support as a moderator of life stress. *Psychosomatic Medicine. 38*(5), 330-344.

Cobb, S., & Kasl, S.V. (1977). *Termination: The consequences of job loss* (HEW Publications No. NIOSH 77-224). Washington, DC: U.S. Department of Health, Education and Welfare.

Committee to Study the Status of Women in Graduate Education and Later Careers (1974, March). *The higher the fewer*. University of Michigan.

Conklin, H. C. (1955). Haununóo color categories. *Southwestern Journal of Anthropology 11*, 339-344.

Cook, T.D., & Campbell, D.T. (1979). *Quasi-experimentation: Design and analysis issues for field settings*. Chicago: Rand McNally.

Coser, L. (1975). Presidential address: Two methods in search of a substance. *American Sociological Review, 40*, 691-700.

Cousins, N. (1979). *Anatomy of an illness as perceived by the patient: Reflections on health and regeneration*. New York: Norton.

Cronbach, L. (1975). Beyond the two disciplines of scientific psychology. *American Psychologist, 30*, 116-127.

Culler, J. (1977). *Ferdinand de Saussure*. New York: Viking.

Dalton, M. (1959). *Men who manage*. New York: John Wiley.

Daly, M. (1978). *Gyn/ecology: The metaethics of radical feminism*. Boston, MA: Beacon Press.

Daniels, A.K. (1967). The low-caste stranger in social research, In G. Sjoberg (Ed.), *Ethics, politics, and social research* (pp. 267-296). Cambridge, MA: Schenkman.

Daniels, A.K. (1975). Feminist perspectives in sociological research. In M. Millman & R.M. Kanter (Eds.), *Another voice: Feminist perspectives on social life and social science* (pp. 340-380). Garden City, NY: Doubleday.

D'Annuo, T., & Price, R. (1983). Methodology in community research I: Context and objectives. In K. Heller, R.H. Price, S. Reinhart, S. Riger, & A. Wandersman (Eds.), *Psychology and community change*. Homewood, IL: Dorsey.

Davidson, J. W., & Lytle, M. H. (1983). *After the fact: The art of historical detection*. New York: Random House.

Dawes, R. (1971). A case study of graduate admissions: applications of three principles of human decision-making. *American Psychologist, 26*(2): 180-188.

Deegan, M. J. (1981). Early women sociologists and the American Sociological Society: The patterns of exclusion and participation. *The American Sociologist, 16*(1),: 14-24.

Dentler, R.A., & Erikson, K.T. (1959). The functions of deviance in groups. *Social Problems, 7*, 98-107.

Devereux, G. (1967). *From anxiety to method in the behavioral sciences*. Paris: Mouton.

Diesing, P. (1971). *Patterns of discovery in the social sciences*. New York: Aldine.

Dimaggio, P., & Powell, W. (1983). The iron cage revisted: Institutional isomorphism and collective rationality in organizational fields. *American Sociology Review, 48*, 147-160.

Douglas, J. (1976). *Investigative social research: Investigative and team research*. Beverly Hills, CA: Sage.

Dunn, W. (1982). *The theory of exceptional clinicians*. Pittsburgh: University of Pittsburgh, Program for the Study of Knowledge Use.

Durkheim, E. (1895/1938). *The rules of sociological method*. Chicago: University of Chicago Press.

Durkheim, E. (1933/1964) *The division of labor in society*. New York: Free Press.

Durkheim, E. (1951). *Suicide*. New York: Free Press.

Dyer, R. (1983). *Her father's daughter: The work of Anna Freud*. New York: Jason Aronson.

Eagly, A.H., & Carli, L.L. (1981). Sex of researchers and sex-typed communications as determinants of sex differences in influenceability: A meta-analysis of social influence studies. *Psychological Bulletin, 90*, 1-20.

Edelson, M. (1972). Language and dreams. In R. Eissler et al. (Eds.), *Psychoanalytic study of the child* Vol. 27. (pp. 203-282). New York: Quadrangle Books.

Edelson, M. (1975). *Language and interpretation in psychoanalysis*. Chicago: University of Chicago Press.

Edelson, M. (1984). *Hypothesis and evidence in psychoanalysis*. Chicago: University of Chicago Press.

Ehrenreich, B., & Stallard, K. (1982, August). The nouveau Pon. *Ms.*, p. 220.

Eisenstein, Z. (1982). Comment. *The American Sociologist, 17*(1), 29-35.

Eisner, E. (1983). Anastasia might still be alive, but the monarchy is dead. *Educational Researcher 5*, 13-14, 23-24.

Ekstein, R., & Wallerstein, R.S. (1958). *The teaching and learning of psychotherapy*. New York: International Universities Press.

Erikson, E.H. (1956). The problem of ego identity. *Journal of American Psychoanalytical Association, 4*, 56-121.

Erikson, E.H. (1968). *Identity, youth and crisis*. New York: W.W. Norton.

Evered, R., & Louis, M.R. (1981). Alternative perspectives in the organizational sciences: Inquiry from the inside and inquiry from the outside. *Academy of Management Review, 6,* 385-395.

Faust, D. (1982). A needed component in prescriptions for science: Empirical knowledge of human cognitive limitations. *Knowledge, 3,* 555-570.

Festinger, L. (Ed.). (1980). *Retrospections on social psychology.* New York: Oxford University Press.

Filstead, W. (1970). *Qualitative methodology.* Chicago: Markham.

Firestone, S. (1970). *The dialectic of sex: The case for feminist revolution.* New York: William Morrow.

Fischhoff, B. (1982). For those condemned to study the past: Heuristics and biases in hindsight. In D. Kahneman, P. Slovic, & A. Tversky (Eds.), *Judgment under uncertainty: Heuristics and biases* (pp. 335-353). Cambridge: Cambridge University Press.

Fiske, E. (1981, November 23). Scholars face a challenge by feminists. *The New York Times,* pp. 1, 12.

Frake, C.D. (1969). The ethnographic study of cognitive systems. In S.A. Tyler (Ed.), *Cognitive Anthropology.* New York: Holt, Rhinehart & Winston,

Freeman, D. (1983). *Margaret Mead and Samoa: The making and unmaking of an anthropological myth.* Cambridge, MA: Harvard University Press.

Freeman, J. (1979). The feminist scholar. *Quest, 5,* 26-36.

Freilich, M. (1970). Toward a formalization of field work. In M. Freilich (Ed.), *Marginal natives* (pp. 485-585). New York: Harper & Row.

French, M. (1977). *The women's room.* New York: Jove.

Freud, S. (1900). The interpretation of dreams. *Standard edition of the complete psychological works of Sigmund Freud.* London: Hogarth Press.

Freud, S. (1933). *New introductory lectures on psychoanalysis.* New York: W.W. Norton.

Friedan, B. (1963). *The feminine mystique.* New York: Dell.

Friedlander, P. (1975). *The emergence of a UAW local, 1936-1939: A study in class and culture.* Pittsburgh: University of Pittsburgh Press.

Friedman, N. (1967). *The social nature of psychological research: The psychological experiment as a social interaction.* New York: Basic Books.

Gans, H.J. (1968). The participant observer as a human being: Observations on the personal aspects of field work. In H. Becker et al. (Eds.), *Institutions and the person* (pp. 300-317). Chicago: Aldine.

Gappa, J.M., & Pearce, J. (1982). *Sex and gender in the social sciences: Reassessing the introductory course.* Washington, DC: American Sociological Association.

Gardner, H. (1983). *Frames of mind: The theory of multiple intelligences.* New York: Basic Books.

Geertz, C. (1973). *The interpretation of cultures.* New York: Basic Books.

Gelinas, D.J. (1983). The persisting negative effects of incest. *Psychiatry, 46,* 312-332.

Gerard, H. B., & Matthewson, G. C. (1966). The effects of severity of initiation on liking for a group: A replication. *Journal of Experimental Social Psychology, 2,* 278-287.

Gergen, K. (1971). *The concept of self.* New York: Holt, Rinehart & Winston.

Gergen, K.J. (1973). Social psychology as history. *Journal of Personality and Social Psychology, 26,* 309-320.

Geuss, R. (1981). *The idea of a critical theory.* Cambridge: Cambridge University Press.

Giddens, A. (Ed.). (1974). *Positivism and sociology.* Portsmouth, NH: Heinemann Educational Books.

Gillette, J. (1983). *Ethnic workers in New Haven.* Unpublished manuscript, Yale University.

Gilligan, C. (1982). *In a different voice.* Cambridge, MA: Harvard University Press.

Glaser, B.G. (1978). *Theoretical sensitivity.* Mill Valley, CA: Sociology Press.

Glaser, B.G., & Strauss, A.L. (1967). *The discovery of grounded theory: Strategies for qualitative research.* Chicago: Aldine.

Glassner, B., & Moreno, J.D. (1982). Clinical sociology and social research. *Sociology and Social Research, 66*(2), 115-126.

Glymour, C. (1980). *Theory and evidence.* Princeton, NJ: Princeton University Press.

Goetz, J.P., & LeCompte, M.D. (1981). Ethnographic research and the problem of data reduction. *Anthropology and Education Quarterly, 12*(1), 51-70.

Goffman, E. (1959). *The presentation of self in everyday life.* Garden City, NY: Doubleday.

Goffman, E. (1961). *Asylums.* Garden City, NY: Doubleday.

Goldberg, L. (1970). Man versus model of man: A rationale, plus some evidence, for a method of improving on clinical inferences. *Psychological Bulletin, 73*(4), 422-432.

Gordon, M.E., Kleiman, L.S., & Hanie, C.A. (1978). Industrial-organizational psychology: Open thy ears o house of Israel. *American Psychologist, 33,* 893-903.

Gornick, V., & Moran, B. K. (1971). *Woman in sexist society: Studies in power and powerlessness.* New York: Ballantine Books.

Greenson, R.R. (1967). *The technique and practice of psychoanalysis* (Vol. 1). New York: International Universities Press.

Grunbaum, A. (1984). *The foundation of psychoanalysis.* Berkeley: University of California Press.

Guba, E.G., & Lincoln, Y.S. (1981). *Effective evaluation.* San Francisco: Jossey-Bass.

Gurney, J. (in press). Not one of the group: The problem of sexism in field work. *Qualitative Sociology.*

Gutman, H., (1976). *Work, culture and society in industrializing America, 1815-1919.* New York: Knopf.

Haley, J. (1973). *Uncommon therapy: The psychiatric techniques of Milton H. Erickson.* New York: Ballantine.

Hamilton, E. (1940). *Mythology.* New York: New American Library.

Hannah, B. (1976). *Jung: His life and work.* New York: G.P. Putnam's Sons.

Hanson, N. (1958). *Patterns of discovery.* Cambridge, U.K.: Cambridge University Press.

Hareven, T.K. (Ed.). (1977). *Family and kin in American urban communities, 1700-1930.* New York: Franklin Watts, New Viewpoints Press.

Hareven, T.K. (1978). *Transitions: The family and the life course in historical perspective.* New York: Academic Press.

Hareven, T.K. (1982). *Family time and industrial time.* Cambridge, U.K.: Cambridge University Press.

Hareven, T.K., & Langenback, R. (1978). *Amoskeag: Life and work in an American factory city.* New York: Pantheon.

Harre, R. (1970). *The principles of scientific thinking.* Chicago: University of Chicago Press.

Harre, R. (1972). *Philosophies of science.* Oxford: Oxford University Press.

Harris, M. (1979). *Cultural materialism.* New York: Random House.

Heider, F. (1958). *The psychology of interpersonal relations.* New York: John Wiley.

Heider, F. (1983). *The life of a psychologist: An autobiography.* Lawrence: University of Kansas Press.

Henry, J. (1963). *Culture against man.* New York: Random House.

Herma, J.L. (1968). The therapeutic act. In E.F. Hammer, (Ed.), *Use of interpretation in treatment technique and art.* New York: Grune & Stratton.

Herman, J.L. (1981). *Father-daughter incest.* Cambridge, MA: Harvard University Press.

Heron, J. (1981). Philosophical basis for a new paradigm. In P. Reason & J. Rowan (Eds.), *Human inquiry: A sourcebook of new paradigm research.* New York: John Wiley.

Hesse, M. (1974). *The structure of scientific inference.* London: Macmillan.

Hirsch, P.M. (1980). Ambushes, shootouts, and Knights of the Roundtable: The language of corporate takeovers. Presentation to the Academy of Management, Detroit.

Hofstadter, D.R. (1979). *Gödel, Escher, Bach: An eternal golden braid.* New York: Vintage.

Holland, J. (1973). *Making vocational choices.* Englewood Cliffs, NJ: Prentice-Hall.

Holling, C.S. (1976). Resilience and stability of ecosystems. In E. Jantsch & C.H. Waddington (Eds.), *Evolution and consciousness.* Reading, MA: Addison-Wesley.

Holt, R. (1962). Individuality and generalization in the psychology of personality. *Journal of Personality, 30,* 377-402.

House, J.S. (1981). *Work stress and social support.* Reading, MA: Addison-Wesley.

Howe, F. (1982). Feminist scholarship: The extent of the revolution. *Change,* April, 12-20.

Huberman, A.M. (1981). Splendeurs, miseres et promesses de la recherche qualitative. *Education et Recherche, 3*(3), 233-249.

Huberman, A.M., & Miles, M.B. (1983a). Drawing valid meaning from qualitative data: Some techniques of data reduction and display. *Quality and Quantity, 17,* 281-339.

Huberman, A.M., & Miles, M.B. (1983b) *Innovation up close: A field study in 12 school settings: Vol. 4. People, policies and practices: Examining the chain of school improvement* (D.P. Crandall and associates). Andover, MA: The Network, Inc.

Huberman, A.M. & Miles, M.B. (1984). *Innovation up close: How school improvement works.* New York: Plenum.

Hu-DeHart, E. (1982). Women and minority academics in the United States: Academic freedom or academic repression in the 1980s? Paper presented at the National Emergency Civil Liberties Committee Foundation Conference on Academic Freedom in the 1980s, New York, May 21-22.

Ingle, D.J. (1985). The goldfish as a retinex animal. *Science, 227* (4687), 651-654.

Inkeles, A. (1964). *What is sociology? An introduction to the discipline and profession.* Englewood Cliffs, NJ: Prentice-Hall.

Isabella, L. (1983). *Evaluating qualitative research: Five criteria.* Paper presented at the Academy of Management Meetings, August.

Jakobson, R., & Halle, M. (1956). *Fundamentals of language.* The Hague: Mouton.

Jantsch, E. (1980). *The self-organizing universe.* New York: Pergamon.

Jantsch, E., & Waddington, C.H. (Eds.). (1976). *Evolution and consciousness.* Reading, MA: Addison-Wesley.

Jaques, E. (1952). *The changing culture of a factory.* New York: The Dryden Press.

Jaques, E. (1955). Social systems as a defense against persecutory and depressive anxiety. In M. Klein, P. Heimann, & R.E. Money-Kyrle (Eds.), *New dimensions in psychoanalysis.* London: Tavistock.

Jaynes, J. (1976). *The origin of consciousness in the breakdown of the bicameral mind.* Boston, MA: Houghton Mifflin.

Jones, E. (1953). *The life and work of Sigmund Freud.* Garden City, NY: Doubleday.

Jung, C. G. (1931). The stages of life. In J. Campbell (Ed.), *The portable Jung* (pp. 3-22). New York: Viking.

Jung, C.G. (1933). *Modern man in search of a soul.* New York: Harcourt Brace Jovanovich.

Jung, C.G. (1963). *Memories, dreams, reflections.* New York: Pantheon Books.

Kanter, R.M. (1977). *Men and women of the corporation.* New York: Basic Books.

Kaplan, A. (1964). *The conduct of inquiry.* Scranton, PA: Chandler.

Katz, D., & Kahn, R.L. (1978). *The social psychology of organizations* (2nd ed.). New York: John Wiley.

Katz, M.B. (1971). *Class, bureaucracy and schools.* New York: Praeger.

Kazdin, A. (1980). *Research design in clinical psychology.* New York: Harper & Row.

Kazdin, A. (1982). *Single-case research designs.* New York: Oxford University Press.

Keller, E. F. (1982). Science and gender. *Signs: Journal of Women in Culture and Society,* 7(3): 589-602.

Kelley, H.H. (1984). The impractical theorist. *Contemporary Psychology, 29,* 455-456.

Kendrigan, M. L. (1984). *Political equality in a democratic society: Women in the United States.* Westport, CT: Greenwood Press.

Kimberly, J.R., & Miles, R.H., & associates (1980). *The organizational life cycle.* San Francisco: Jossey-Bass.

Kohn, M.H., & Schooler, C. (1983). *Work and personality.* Norwood, NJ: Ablex.

Kohut, H. (1977). *The restoration of self.* New York: International Universities Press.

Kohut, H. (1984). *How does analysis cure?* Chicago: University of Chicago Press.

Kolawowski, L. (1969). *The alienation of reason: A history of positivist thought.* Garden City, NY: Doubleday.

Kram, K.E. (1983). Phases of the mentor relationship. *Academy of Management Journal, 26,*(4), 608-625.

Kram, K.E. (1985). *Mentoring at work.* Glenview, IL: Scott, Foresman.

Kram, K.E., & Isabella, L.A. (1985). Mentoring alternatives: The role of peer relationships in career development. *Academy of Management Journal,* forthcoming.

Krawiec, T.S. (Ed.) (1972). *The psychologists* (Vols. 1-2). New York: Oxford University Press.

Kuhn, T.S. (1962). *The structure of scientific revolutions.* Chicago: University of Chicago Press.

Ladner, J. (Ed.). (1973). *The death of white sociology.* New York: Vintage.

Lasagna, L. (1982). Historical controls. *New England Journal of Medicine.* 307, 1339-1340.

Lawler, E.E., Nadler, D.N., & Cammann, C. (1980). *Organizational assessment: Perspectives on the measurement of organizational behavior and quality of work life.* New York: John Wiley.

Lawrence, P., & Dyer, D. (1983). *Renewing American industry.* New York: Free Press.

Levine, R.A., & Campbell, D.T. (1972). *Ethnocentrism.* New York: John Wiley.

Levinson, D.J., Darrow, C.N., Klein, E.B., Levinson, M.H., & McKee, B. (1978). *The seasons of a man's life.* New York: Ballantine.

Levinson, H. (1972). *Organizational diagnosis.* Cambridge, MA: Harvard University Press.

Levinson, H. (1983). Consulting with family businesses. What to look for, what to look out for. *Organizational Dynamics, 12*(1), 71-80.

Lidz, T. (1968). *The person.* New York: Basic Books.

Lifton, R.J. (1967). *Death in life: Survivors of Hiroshima.* New York: Basic Books.

Lifton, R.J. (1974). *Explorations in psychohistory: The Wellfleet papers.* New York: Simon & Schuster.

Lippitt, R., Watson, J., & Westley, B. (1958). *The dynamics of planned change.* New York: Harcourt Brace Jovanovich.

Lipset, S., & Hofstadter, R. (1968). *Sociology and history: Methods.* New York: Basic Books.

Lopata, H. L. (1976). Sociology. *Signs: Journal of Women in Culture and Society, 2*(1), 165-176.

Louis, M.R. (1980). Surprise and sense making: What newcomers experience in entering unfamiliar organizational settings. *Administrative Science Quarterly, 25,* 226-251.

Lowman, R.L. (1982a). Clinical psychology at work. *The Clinical Psychologist, 35*(3), 19-20.

Lowman, R.L. (1982b). Parallel processes in conducting organizational research. Paper presented at the meeting of the American Psychological Association, Washington, DC (ERIC Document Reproduction Service N. ED 223712).

Luborsky, L. (1967). Momentary forgetting during psychotherapy and psychoanalysis. In R. Holt (Ed.), *Motives and thought* (Psychological issues monograph 18/19, pp. 177-217). New York: International Universities Press.

Luborsky, L. (1973). Forgetting and remembering (momentary forgetting) during psychotherapy. In M. Mayman (Ed.), *Psychoanalytic research* (Psychological issues monograph 30, pp. 29-55). New York: International Universities Press.

Luborsky, L., & Mintz, J. (1974). What sets off momentary forgetting during psychoanalysis? *Psychoanalysis and Contemporary Science, 3,* 233-268.

Lugones, M.C., & Spellman, E.V. (1983). Have we got a theory for you: Feminist theory, cultural imperialism and the demand for "the woman's voice." *Women's Studies International Forum, 6,* 573-581.

MacKinnon, C. A. (1982). Feminism, Marxism, method and the state: An agenda for theory. *Journal of Women in Culture and Society, 7*(3), 515-44.

Madan, T.N. (1975). On living intimately with strangers. In A. Beteille & T.N. Madan (Eds.), *Encounter and response* (pp. 131-156). Delhi: Vikas.

Mahoney, M., & De Monbreun, B. (1977). Psychology of the scientist: An analysis of problem-solving bias. *Cognitive Therapy and Research, 1*(3), 229-238.

Malan, D.H. (1979). *Individual psychotherapy and the science of psychodynamics.* London: Butterworth.

Malcolm, J. (1981). *Psychoanalysis: The impossible profession.* New York: Knopf.

Mandler, G., & Watson, D.L. (1966). Anxiety and the interruption of behavior. In C.D. Spielberger (Ed.), *Anxiety and behavior.* New York: Academic Press.

Manicas, P.T., & Secord, P.F. (1982). Implications for psychology of the new philosophy of science. *American Psychologist, 38*(4), 390-413.

Mannheim, K. (1936). *Ideology and utopia.* Translated by L. Wirth and E. Shills. New York: Harcourt Brace Jovanovich.

Manning, P.K. (1979). Metaphors on the field: Varieties of organizational discourse. *Administrative Science Quarterly, 24*(4), 660-671.

Marrow, A.J. (1969). *The practical theorist: The life and work of Kurt Lewin.* New York: Basic Books.

Marshall, J. (1981). Making sense as a personal process. In P. Reason & J. Rowan (Eds.), *Human inquiry: A sourcebook of new paradigm research.* Chichester, England: John Wiley.

Masson, J.M. (1984). *The assault on truth: Freud's suppression of the seduction theory.* New York: Farrar, Straus & Giroux.

May, R. (1975). *The courage to create.* New York: W.W. Norton.

May, R. (1977). *The meaning of anxiety* (rev. ed.). New York: Washington Square Press.

May, W.F. (1980). Doing ethics: The bearing of ethical theories on fieldwork. *Social Problems, 27*(3), 358-370.

McGoldrick, M., Pearce, J.K., & Giordano, J. (1982). *Ethnicity and family therapy.* New York: The Oxford Press.

Mead, M. (1973). *Blackberry winter.* New York: William Morrow.

Meehl, P. (1954). *Clinical versus statistical prediction.* Minneapolis: University of Minnesota Press.

Meehl, P. (1965). Clinical versus statistical prediction. *Journal of Experimental Research in Personality, 63*(1), 81-97.

Meehl, P. (1983). Subjectivity in psychoanalytic inference. In J. Earman (Ed.), *Testing scientific theories.* Minneapolis: University of Minnesota Press, 349-412.

Merton, R.K. (1957). *Social theory and social structure.* New York: Free Press.

Metz, M.H. (1981). The impact of ethnographer's roles on the research process. Paper presented at the annual meeting of the American Educational Research Association, April, Los Angeles.

Meyer, A. (1952). *The collected papers of Adolf Meyer, Vol. 3: Medical teaching* (E.E. Winters, Ed.). Baltimore, MD: Johns Hopkins Press.

Meyer, S. (1981). *The five dollar day: Labor, management and social control in the Ford Motor Company, 1908-1921.* Albany: SUNY Press.

Miles, M.B. (1979). Qualitative data as an attractive nuisance: The problem of analysis. *Administrative Science Quarterly, 24*(4), 590-601.

Miles, M.B., & Huberman, A.M. (1981). *The realities of school improvement: Analysis of qualitative data* (NIE grant G-81-0018). New York: Center for Policy Research.

Miles, M.B., & Huberman, A.M. (1984). *Qualitative data analysis: A sourcebook of new methods.* Beverly Hills, CA: Sage.

Miller, C., & Swift, K. (1980). *The handbook of nonsexist writing.* New York: Lippincott and Crowell.

Millett, K. (1969). *Sexual Politics.* New York: Ballantine.

Millman, M., & Kanter, R.M. (1975). *Another voice: Feminist perspectives on social life and social science.* Garden City, NY: Doubleday.

Miner, J. (1984). The unpaved road over the mountains: From theory to applications. *The Industrial-Organizational Psychologist 21*(2), 9-20.

Minuchin, S. (1974). *Families and family therapy.* Cambridge, MA: Harvard University Press.

Mirvis, P.H. (1980). The art of assessing the quality of life at work. In E.E. Lawler, D. Nadler, & C. Cammann (Eds.), *Organizational assessment.* New York: John Wiley.

Mirvis, P.H. (1982). Know thyself and what thou art doing. *American Behavioral Scientist, 26*, 177-197.

Mirvis, P.H., & Seashore, S.E. (1979). Being ethical in organizational research. *American Psychologist, 34*, 766-780.

Mishler, E. (1979). Meaning in context: Is there any other kind? *Harvard Educational Review, 49*(1), 1-19.

Missirian, A.K. (1982). *The corporate connection: Why executive women need mentors to reach the top.* Englewood Cliffs, NJ: Prentice-Hall.

Mitroff, I., & Sagasti, F. (1973). Epistemology as general systems theory: An approach to the design of complex decision-making experiments. *Philosophy of Social Science, 3*, 117-134.

Montgomery, D. (1979). *Worker's control in America*. Cambridge: Cambridge University Press.

Morgan, D. (1984). Some thoughts on the etiology and meaning of the clinical demands of research methods. Unpublished notes, Yale University.

Morgan, G. (Ed.). (1983). *Beyond method: Strategies for social research*. Beverly Hills, CA: Sage.

Myrdal, G. (1969). Biases in social research. In A. Tiselius & S. Nilsson (Eds.), *The plan of values in a world of facts*. New York: John Wiley.

Nadel, S.F. (1951). *Foundations of social anthropology*. New York: Free Press.

Nebraska Feminist Collective (1983). A feminist ethic for social science research. *Women's Studies International Forum, 6*(5), 535-544.

Neumann, E. (1979). Freud and the father image. In E. Neuman (Ed.), *Creative man* (pp. 232-245). Princeton: Princeton University Press.

Newhouse, J. (1982, June 14). A sporty game: I. betting the Company. *The New Yorker*, 48-105.

Nisbett, R.E., & Ross, L. (1980). *Human inference: Strategies and shortcomings of social judgment*. Englewood Cliffs, NJ: Prentice-Hall.

Noble, D. (1977). *American by design*. New York: Knopf.

Northrup, F.S.C. (1947). *The logic of the sciences and the humanities*. New York: Meridian Books.

On Campus with Women. (1982). Vol. 34, pp. 1-2, 5. Washington, DC: Project on Status and Education of Women.

Orne, M.T. (1962). On the social psychology of the psychological experiment. *American Psychologist, 17*, 776-783.

Osipow, S.H. (1973). *Theories of career development* (2nd ed.) Englewood Cliffs, NJ: Prentice-Hall.

Oskamp, S. (1965). Overconfidence in case-study judgments. *Journal of Counseling Psychology, 29*(3), 261-265.

Patai, D. (1983). Beyond defensiveness: Feminist research strategies. *Women's Studies International Quarterly, 6*(2), 177-189.

Paul, I.H. (1973). *Letters to Simon on the conduct of psychotherapy*. New York: International Universities Press.

Perrow, C. (1973). *Complex organizations*. Glenview, IL: Scott Foresman.

Perry, H.S. (1970). *The human be-in*. New York: Basic Books.

Perry, H.S. (1982). *Psychiatrist of America: The life of Harry Stack Sullivan*. Cambridge, MA: Belknap Press.

Perry, S.E. (1966). *The human nature of science: Research psychiatrists at work*. New York: Free Press.

Peshkin, A. (1978). *Growing up American: Schooling and the survival of community*. Chicago: University of Chicago Press.

Peshkin, A. (1982a). The researcher and subjectivity: Reflections on an ethnography of school and community. In G. Spindler (Ed.), *Doing the ethnography of schooling* (pp. 20-47). New York: Holt, Rinehart & Winston.

Peshkin, A. (1982b). *The imperfect union: School consolidation and community conflict*. Chicago: University of Chicago Press.

Peshkin, A. (1983). *Fundamentalist Christian schooling: Truth and consequences*. Paper presented at the Annual Meeting of the American Educational Research Association, April, Montreal, Canada.

Peters, D.P., & Ceci, S.J. (1982). Peer-review practices of psychological journals: The fate of published articles submitted again. *The Behavioral and Brain Sciences, 5*, 187-255.

Phillips, D.C. (1973). *Abandoning method*. San Francisco: Jossey-Bass.

Phillips, D.C. (1983). After the wake: Postpositivistic educational thought. *Educational Researcher, 5*, 4-12.

Phillips-Jones, L. (1982). *Mentors and proteges*. New York: Arbor House.

Piaget, J. (1970). *Genetic epistemology* (E. Duckworth, Trans.). New York: Columbia University Press.

Pirsig, R.M. (1974). *Zen and the art of motorcycle maintenance*. New York: William Morrow.

Polanyi, M. (1958). *Personal knowledge*. London: Routledge & Kegan Paul.

Polkinghorne, D. (1983). *Methodology for the human sciences*. Albany: SUNY Press.

Project on the Status and Education of Women (1982). *On campus with women, 34*, 1-12.

Putnam, L.L., & Pacanowsky, M.E. (Eds.). (1983). *Communication and organizations: An interpretive approach*. Beverly Hills, CA: Sage.

Read, S. (1982). Once is enough: Causal reasoning from a single instance. *Journal of Personality and Social Psychology, 45*, 2, 323-334.

Reason, P., & Rowan, J. (Eds.). (1981). *Human inquiry: A sourcebook of new paradigm research*. Chichester, England: John Wiley.

Register, C. (1979). Brief, a-mazing movements: Dealing with despair in the women's studies classroom. *Women's Studies Newsletter, 7*(4), 7-10.

Reicken, H.W. (1962). A program for research on experiments in social psychology. In N.F. Washburne (Ed.), *Decisions, values, and groups* (pp. 25-41). Elmsford, NY: Pergamon Press.

Reinharz, S. (1979). *On becoming a social scientist: From survey research and participant observation to experiential analysis*. San Francisco: Jossey-Bass.

Reinharz, S. (1981). *Dimensions of the feminist methodological debate*. Paper presented at the American Psychological Association annual meetings, Los Angeles.

Reinharz, S. (1983). Feminist research methodology groups: Origins, forms, functions. In V. Peraka & L. A. Tilly (Eds.), *Feminist re-visions: What has been and might be* (pp. 197-228). Ann Arbor: University of Michigan Press.

Reinharz, S., Bombyk, M., & Wright, J. (1983). Methodological issues in feminist research: A bibliography of literature in women's studies, sociology and psychology. *Women's studies international forum, 6*(4), 437-454.

Reisman, D. (1979). Ethical and practical dilemmas of fieldwork in academic settings: A personal memoir. In R.K. Merton et al. (Eds.), *Qualitative and quantitative research: Papers in honor of Paul Lazarsfeld* (pp. 210-231). New York: Free Press.

Rescher, N. (1976). *Plausible reasoning*. Amsterdam: Van Gorcum.

Rescher, N. (1980). *Induction*. Pittsburgh: University of Pittsburgh.

Rice, A.K. (1969). Individual, group, and intergroup processes. *Human Relations, 22*, 565-584.

Rich, A. (1979). Toward a woman-centered university. In *On lies, secrets and silences* (pp. 125-155). New York: W.W. Norton.

Rieff, P. (1974). Freud and the authority of the past. In R.J. Lifton (Ed.), *Explorations in psychohistory: The Wellfleet papers*. New York: Simon & Schuster.

Riley, G. (Ed.) (1974). *Values, objectivity, and the social sciences*. Reading, MA: Addison-Wesley.

Roberts, H. (Ed.) (1981). *Doing feminist research*. London: Routledge & Kegan Paul.

Roe, A. (1961). The psychology of the scientist. *Science, 134*, 456-459.

Roethlisberger, F.J. (1977). *The elusive phenomena*. Cambridge, MA: Harvard University Press.

Rosenthal, R. (1966). *Experimenter effects in behavioral research*. New York: Appleton-Century Crofts.

Rosenthal, R., & Rosnow, R.L. (Eds.). (1969). *Artifact in behavioral research*. New York: Academic Press.

Rosnow, R.L., & Rosenthal, R. (1984). *Understanding behavioral science*. New York: McGraw-Hill.

Runkel, P. J., Harrison, R., & Runkel, M. (Eds.). (1969). *The changing college classroom*. San Francisco: Jossey-Bass.

Russell, B. (1960). *Our knowledge of the external world*. New York: Mentor Books.

Sachs, D.M., & Shapiro, S.H. (1976). On parallel processes in therapy and teaching. *Psychoanalytic Quarterly 45*, 394-415.

Saint-Simon, Henri de (1964). *Social organization, the science of man, and other writings*. (F. Markham, Ed. and Trans.). New York: Harper & Row.

Sarason, S.B. (1972). *The creation of settings and the future societies*. San Francisco: Jossey-Bass.

Schachtel, E.G. (1947). On memory and childhood amnesia. *Psychiatry, 10*, 1-26.

Schein, E.H. (1984). *Organizational culture*. Unpublished manuscript, Sloan School of Management, MIT.

Schlenker, B. (1974). Social psychology and science. *Journal of Personality and Social Psychology, 29*, 1-15.

Schurman, S.J. (1982). *Political realities of conducting evaluation research in the public sector*. Paper presented at the American Psychological Association Annual Meeting, Washington, DC.

Schwartz, C. G., & Kahne, M. J. (1983). Medical help as negotiated achievement. *Psychiatry, 46*, 33-350.

Schwendinger, H., & Schwendinger, J. (1974). *The sociologists of the chair*. New York: Basic Books.

Scriven, M. (1979). Maximizing the power of causal investigations: The modus operandi method. In W. Popham (Ed.), *Evaluation in education: Current applications*. Berkeley, CA: McCutchan.

Searle, J. (1983). *Intentionality*. Cambridge: Cambridge University Press.

Searles, H.F. (1955). The informational value of the supervisor's emotional experiences. *Psychiatry, 18*, 135-146.

Selvini Palazzoli, M., Boscolo, L., Cecchin, G., & Prata, G. (1978). *Paradox and counterparadox*. New York: Jason Aronson.

Shapiro, M. (1963). A clinical approach to fundamental research with special reference to the study of the single patient. In P. Sainsbury & N. Kreitman (eds.), *Methods of psychiatric research*. New York: Oxford University Press.

Shaskolsky, L. (1970). The development of sociological theory in America: A sociology of knowledge interpretation. In L.T. Reynolds & J. M. Reynolds (Eds.), *The sociology of sociology*. New York: David McKay.

Sherif, M., & Sherif, C. (1969). *Social psychology*. New York: Harper & Row.

Sherman, J. A., & Beck, E.T. (1979). *The prism of sex: Essays in the sociology of knowledge*. Madison, WI: University of Wisconsin Press.

Sherman, R., & Titus, W. (1982). Covariation information and cognitive processing: Effects of causal implications on memory. *Journal of Personality and Social Psychology, 42*(6), 989-1000.

Sherwood, M. (1969). *The logic of explanation in psychoanalysis*. New York: Academic Press.

Shope, R. (1973). Freud's concept of meaning. In B. Rubinstein (ed.), *Psychoanalysis and contemporary science* (Vol. 2, pp. 276-303). New York: Macmillan.

Silverman, L.H. (1976). Psychoanalytic theory: "The reports of my death are greatly exaggerated." *American Psychologist, 31*(9), 621-637.

Simmel, G. (1955). *Conflict and the web of group-affiliations*. (K.H. Wolff & R. Bendix, Trans.). New York: Free Press.

Simmons, V.M. (1983). Conflict in open systems: Planning for a new organization. Unpublished doctoral dissertation. College Park, MD: University of Maryland.

Simon, H., (1977). *Models of discovery*. Boston, MA: D. Reidel.

Singer, J.E. (1980). Social comparison: The process of self-evaluation. In L. Festinger (Ed.), *Retrospections on social psychology*. New York: Oxford.

Smith, A.G., & Louis, K.S. (1982). Multimethod policy research: Issues and applications. *American Behavioral Scientist, 26*(1).

Smith, D. E. (1974.) Women's perspective as a radical critique of sociology. *Sociological Inquiry, 44*(1), 7-15.

Smith, K.K. (1977). Some notes for O.D. consultants: Learning how to interact with client systems. *Australian Psychologist, 11*(3), 281-289.

Smith, K.K. (1982a). *Groups in conflict: Prisons in disguise*. Dubuque, IA: Kendall-Hunt.

Smith, K.K. (1982b). Philosophical problems in thinking about organizational change. In P.S. Goodman et al (Eds.), *Change in organizations* (pp. 316-374). San Francisco: Jossey-Bass.

Smith, K.K. (1983a). Social comparison processes and dynamic conservatism in intergroup relations. In L.L. Cummings & B. M. Staw (Eds.), *Research in organizational behavior* (Vol. 5, pp. 199-233). Greenwich, CT: JAI Press.

Smith, K.K. (1983b). A role for community psychologists: As participant-conceptualizers. *Austrialian Psychologist, 18*(2).

Smith, K.K. (1984a). Rabbits, lynxes and organizational transitions. In J.R. Kimberly & R.E. Quinn (Eds.), *Managing organizational transitions* (pp. 267-294). Homewood, IL: Irwin.

Smith, K.K. (1984b). Toward a conception of organizational currents. *Group and organization studies, 9*(2), 285-312.

Smith, K.K., & Berg, D.N. (1984). *Paradoxes of group life*. Unpublished manuscript, University of Pennsylvania.

Smith, K.K., & Crandell, S.D. (1984). Exploring collective emotion. *American Behavioral Scientist, 27*(6), 813-828.

Smith, K. K., & Simmons, V. M. (1983). A Rumpelstiltskin organization: Metaphors on metaphors in field research. *Administrative Science Quarterly, 28*(3), 377-392.

Snow, R., (1974). Representative and quasi-representative designs for research in teaching. *Review of Educational Research 44*, 265-292.

Sofer, C. (1961). *The organization from within*. Chicago: Quadrangle.

Somers, A. (1982). Sexual harassment in academe: Legal issues and definitions. *Journal of Social Issues, 38*(4), 23-32.

Stacey, J., & Thorne, B. (1984). *The missing feminist revolution in sociology*. Paper presented at the Annual Meeting of the American Sociological Association, San Antonio, TX, August 27-31.

Stanley, L., & Wise, S. (1983). *Breaking out: Feminist consciousness and feminist research*. London: Routledge & Kegan Paul.

Stark, W. (1958). *The sociology of knowledge: An essay in aid of a deeper understanding of the history of ideas*. London: Routledge & Kegan Paul.

Stein, M.R. (1971). The eclipse of community: Some glances at the education of a sociologist. In A.J. Vidich et al. (Eds.), *Reflections on community studies* (pp. 207-232). New York: Harper & Row.

Stevens, S.S. (1939). Operationalism and logical positivism, *Psychological Bulletin, 36,* 221-263.

Sullivan, H.S. (1943). *Conceptions of modern psychiatry,* Lecture 1 from 1943-1944 series of unpublished lectures, Washington School of Psychiatry.

Sullivan, H.S. (1947). Review of R. Benedict's *The chrysanthemum and the sword. Psychiatry 10,* 214-216.

Sullivan, H.S. (1948). Towards a psychiatry of peoples. *Psychiatry, 11,* 105-116.

Sullivan, H.S. (1953a). *Conceptions of modern psychiatry.* New York: W.W. Norton.

Sullivan, H.S. (1953b). *The interpersonal theory of psychiatry.* New York: W.W. Norton.

Sumner, N.G. (1906). *Folkways.* New York: Ginn.

Suppe, F. (Ed.). (1977). *The structure of scientific theories* (2nd ed.). Urbana, IL: University of Illinois Press.

Survey Research Center. (1976). *Interviewer's manual* (rev. ed.). Ann Arbor, MI: Institute for Social Research.

Sutton, R.I. (1983). Managing organizational death. *Human Resources Management, 22*(4), 391-412.

Swinburne, R. (Ed.). (1974). *The justification of induction.* London: Oxford University Press.

Szafran, R.F. (1984). *Universities and women faculty: Why some organizations discriminate more than others.* New York: Praeger.

Taft, R. (1955). The ability to judge people. *Psychological Bulletin, 52*(1), 1-23.

Thomas, D. L. & Edmondson, J. E. (in press). The rise of family theory and critiques from philosophy of science and hermeneutics. In M.B. Sussman & S. K. Steinmetz (Eds.). *Handbook of marriage and the family.* New York: Plenum Press.

Thompson, J.D. (1967). *Organizations in action.* New York: McGraw-Hill.

Thorne, B. (1982). Guidelines for introductory sociology. In J. M. Gappa & J. Pearce (Eds.), *Sex and gender in the social sciences: Reassessing the introductory course.* Washington, D.C. American Sociological Association.

Toby, J. (1955). Undermining the student's faith in the validity of personal experience. *American Sociological Review, 20,* 717-718.

Torbert, W. (1983). Initiating collaborative inquiry. In G. Morgan (Ed.), *Beyond Method.* Beverly Hills, CA: Sage.

Trotsky, L. (1932). *The history of the Russian revolution.* New York: Simon & Schuster.

Tuchman, B. (1981). *Practicing history.* New York: Ballantine.

Tucker, R.C. (1984). *Towards a philosophy of social science for black-white studies.* New Haven, CT: Yale University.

Tversky, A., & Kahneman, D. (1971). The belief in the law of small numbers. *Psychological Bulletin, 76*(2), 105-110.

Tyack, D. (1974). The one best system. Cambridge, MA: Harvard University Press.

United States Department of Labor Statistics. (1979).

Van Maanen, J., Dabbs, J.M., Jr., & Faulkner, R.R. (1982). *Varieties of qualitative research.* Beverly Hills, CA: Sage.

Verba, S., with DiNunzio, J. & Spaulding, C. (1983, September). *Unwanted attention: Report on a sexual harassment survey.* Report to the Faculty Council of the Faculty of Arts and Sciences, Harvard University. (mimeo)

Vickers, J. M. (1982). Memoirs of an ontological exile: The methodological rebellions of feminist research. In G. Finn & A. Miles (Eds.), *Feminism in Canada*. Montreal: Black Rose Books.

Vidmar, N. & Hackman, J.R. (1971). Interlaboratory generalizability of small group research: An experimental study. *Journal of Social Psychology, 83*, 129-139.

Von Eckhardt, B. (1982). Why Freud's research methodology was unscientific. *Psychoanalysis and contemporary thought, 5*, 549-574.

Von Laue, T.H. (1975). Transubstantiation in the study of African reality. *African Affairs, 4*, (10), 401-419.

Wallis, R. (1977). The moral career of a research project. In C. Bell & H. Newby (Eds.), *Doing sociological research* (pp. 146-169). New York: Free Press.

Watzlawick, P. (1978). *The language of change*. New York: Basic Books.

Watzlawick, P., Weakland, T., & Fisch, R. (1974). *Change*. New York: W.W. Norton.

Wax, M.L. (1980). Paradoxes of "consent" to the practice of fieldwork. *Social Problems, 27*, (3).

Webb, E.S., Campbell, D.T., Schwartz, R.D., Sechrest, L., & Grove, J.B. (1981). *Nonreactive measures in the social sciences* (2nd ed.). Boston: Houghton Mifflin.

Weber, M. (1926). *Max Weber: A biography*. New York: John Wiley.

Weick, K. (1976). Educational organizations as loosely coupled systems. *Administrative Science Quarterly, 21*(1), 1-19.

Welch, M., & Lewis, S. (1980). A mid-decade assessment of sex biases in placement of sociology Ph.D.'s: Evidence for contextual variation. *American Sociologist, 15*(3), 120-127.

Westhues, K. (1982). *First sociology*. New York: McGraw-Hill.

Westkott, M. (1979). Feminist criticism of the social sciences. *Harvard Educational Review, 49*(4), 422-430.

White, W.A. (1938). *William Alanson White: The autobiography of a purpose*. Garden City, NY: Doubleday.

Whorf, B.L. (1950). *Four articles on metalinguistics*. Washington: Foreign Services Institute, Department of State.

Whyte, W.F. (1948). Status in the kitchen. In W.F. Whyte (Ed.). *Human relations in the restaurant industry* (pp. 33-46). New York: McGraw-Hill.

Whyte, W.F. (1955). *Streetcorner society* (2nd ed.). Chicago: University of Chicago Press.

Wilden, A. (1980). *Systems and structure* (2nd ed). London: Tavistock.

Wittig, M. (in press). Metatheoretical dilemmas in the psychology of gender. *American Psychologist*.

Wolman, C., & Frank H. H. (1975). The solo woman in a professional peer group. *American Journal of Orthopsychiatry, 45*(1).

Wood, P., (1983). Inquiring systems and problem structure: Implications for cognitive development. *Human Development, 26*, 249-265.

Wortman, C.B., Abbey, A., Holland, E.A., Silver, R.L., & Janoff- Bulman, R. (1980). Transitions from the laboratory to the field. In L. Bickman (Ed.), *Applied Social Psychology Annual, 1*. Beverly Hills, CA: Sage.

Wuebben, P.L., Straits, B.C., & Shulman, G.I. (1974). *The experiment as a social occasion*. Berkeley, CA: Glendessary Press.

Wylie, R. C. (1961). *The self concept*. Lincoln: University of Nebraska Press.

Wylie, R.C. (1968). The present status of self theory. In E.F. Borgatta & W.W. Lambert (eds.), *Handbook of personality theory and research (pp. 728-787)*. Chicago: Rand-McNally.

Zelditch, M. (1962). Some methodological problems of field studies. *American Journal of Sociology 67*, 566-576.

DATE DUE

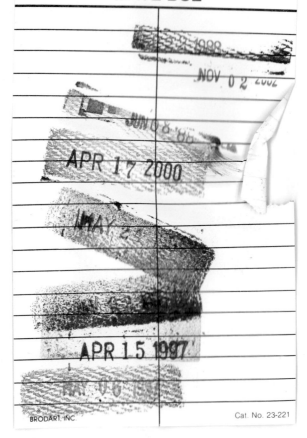

NOV 0 2 2002

APR 1 7 2000

MAY

APR 15 1997

BRODART, INC.   Cat. No. 23-221

her when he caught her eye. She took her seat and he was left to stare at her thick chestnut hair laced with the scent of fresh oranges—*like a Creamsicle,* he thought.

Standing at his podium, Fuller said, "The first business of the day is to read the best paper turned in on Friday." He flipped open a manila folder and Nathan's mouth went dry. Would the piece be his? He had thought it the best creative writing he'd ever done, an essay about the role of music in everyday life.

"Let me begin by saying that most of you did very ordinary writing—a situation I hope to correct as we are immersed in good writing by great masters and thinkers from the past. Only one standout in this first bunch."

Nathan's heart thudded. Fuller leaned over the podium. "The writer is number four-five-four." Nathan's heart sank. "The piece is a free-form poem titled 'Wings to Fly.' " Nathan slumped in his chair and Fuller began to read:

> *I have fashioned wings of wax and feathers and*
> > *carefully formed them as things of beauty.*
> > *And utility.*
> *Snow white.*
> *Pale yellow.*
> *They glow like cat's eyes.*
> *And I have tied the wings to my thin, earthbound*
> > *arms, and found a place*
> *on a high rock from which to hurl*
> > *myself.*

I'll pass just above the sea, being careful not to let
the feathers drench.
I'll pass low away from the sun and suddenly I am
flying, flying.
And I wait for night to fall so that I can fly higher.
Suddenly this space is too safe.
And night will come too dark.
For if I only fly and do not soar, how will I know
the universe
How will I know what lies inside. Of me?
For starlight is pale and far away.
Stars prick darkness but are not warm.
And so I choose to soar. Upward into blue-lit sky
and closer to the sun until I feel the wax
dripping, melting, trickling into the sea of
glass-still water.
And yet, unafraid, I fly straight toward the sun.
Straight toward the Son.
Will I be caught?
Or will I melt into the sea below?

Fuller looked up at the hushed classroom, his expression intense. He walked to the blackboard and
wrote the final few lines for them to see. Nathan was
struck by the different spellings of *sun/Son,* each with
a different meaning, and by the imagery that linked
them.

Fuller continued. "I leave each of you to ponder the
mind-set of this writer and to glean the message there

for all of us." He returned to his podium, tucked the paper into the folder. Nathan yearned to hear this teacher read one of his pieces with such reverence. "And please note, there wasn't a four-letter word in the piece. Ladies and gentlemen, English is an amazing language, full of both plentiful and beautiful words. Several of you peppered your work with four-letter words. Why? Shock value? Do you think I don't know these words? Frankly, I think using them shows weakness of mind and lack of talent. Stretch yourselves, writers. Make me *care* about your pubescent thoughts in poetic language, not gutter-speak."

Students shuffled feet and shifted at their desks. Nathan cut his eyes sideways on the chance that the writer might subtly reveal himself with a look of pride or embarrassment or satisfaction, but all expressions were merely curious.

When the class was over, Nathan scooped up his books, walked quickly to catch up with Lisa in the crowded halls. "How are you doing?" he asked, falling in step beside her. She looked at him, startled. Did no one even dare speak to the Great Lisa?

"Why do you ask?"

Her question caught him off guard. Usually people said, "Fine" or "Life sucks" or anything other than "Why do you ask." He said, "I mean, you weren't in class Friday. I thought maybe something happened."

"Are you my social secretary, Malone?"

At least she remembered his name. "You said you liked

Fuller's class, but you didn't show. I thought maybe something went wrong. It's an inquiry, not an inquisition."

"I had an appointment," she said quickly. "Nothing sinister."

After an awkward moment, he asked, "So, who do you think writer four-five-four is?"

"Was it yours?"

"I wish."

"It was okay," she said with a shrug.

"The reference to classical mythology was a nice touch. And the use of *sun* with two meanings was pretty cool."

She stopped and foot traffic flowed around them. "You read mythology, Malone? Or did you pick it up from Saturday morning cartoons?"

He felt color seep into his neck at her put-down. He didn't understand why she was being so caustic and unfriendly. "I've read a lot of the old Greek and Roman stories. And I thought the poem Fuller read was deep. Didn't you?" He held her gaze like a firebrand, determined not to let her get away with it.

She blinked, turned. "I like mythology too. Not sure if I liked the poem. I've got to go."

He stepped in front of her. "Homeschooling isn't a free ride, you know. I had to work hard and pass regular performance tests. I think public school—this school—is a cakewalk. Kids don't seem like they care much about their classes, and most of them can't carry on a conversation beyond next week's football game or who's dating whom."

She didn't respond right away, but he could tell he'd

gotten her attention. "Don't think that I feel like home-schooling is inferior to this, because I don't." She sounded apologetic. "I think you're lucky to have been able to be homeschooled. It implies somebody cares for you."

"Are you saying nobody cares for you?"

The halls were almost empty now and she took a few steps backward toward the outside door. "Wrong assumption, Malone."

It had been a stupid thing for him to ask. Of course somebody cared about her. She probably had a hundred somebodies who cared about her. He screwed up his courage. "Want to talk about it over coffee some-time? I can call you."

"A date?" she asked.

"Why not? Pick a time and place."

"I don't date."

He watched her step through the doorway into the bright afternoon sunlight. The motorcycle was waiting, and this time Nathan saw the driver more clearly: a lanky man with muscular arms and chest, work boots and dirty jeans. He wore a dark helmet and his long hair stuck out from under it. He handed Lisa a helmet and she slung her leg over the Harley's seat, slipped her book bag onto her back. The man gunned the motor, kicked off from the curb. Nathan watched the cycle speed away.

Nathan told Skeet all that had happened on the ride home. Skeet listened and didn't remind him about his prediction that Nathan would tumble for Lisa. "Takes courage to ask, man."

"I don't believe she doesn't date," Nathan grumbled.

"Hey, here's something to cheer you up. Crestwater's playing Highland Friday night, and Highland's better. Which means that Roddy has a good chance of getting his butt kicked. Want to come watch with me?"

"Why not." Nathan's disdain for the jocks had grown over the past few days. They really did act as if they were a superior breed when he knew they weren't. Rumor was that two had paid underclassmen to write papers for them, and if their teachers knew about it, they let it slide.

"And"—Skeet drummed on the dashboard—"rumor is there's going to be a party after. Location to be revealed."

An illegal party. Nathan knew his parents would never let him go. But then, why should he have to tell them? He was perfectly capable of attending a party without getting into trouble. It was about time that he struck out on his own, blew off steam and had some fun.

5

*L*isa Lindstrom was unable to pinpoint the exact moment Nathan Malone came on her radar; she just knew that she slowly became aware of him, like a buzz one starts to hear in a quiet room. One minute all is silent, then a sound begins to break through a person's subconscious and annoys until the person has to stop what she's doing and go find the source. She tried to ignore him, this noise, but one day he broke through—she looked up and saw the most incredible blue eyes, fringed with thick dark lashes, staring at her. Nathan's eyes.

She determined to steer clear, keep him at arm's length as she did so many others, which would have been easier if she hadn't sensed intelligence and sensitivity behind his eyes. Why couldn't he be self-absorbed like Roddy and his jock friends? Or shy? Or avant garde and far out like the goths? Instead he was lean, dark-haired and blue-eyed—an apparition sent to bedevil her when she had no time for it.

"Is that the guy?" Charlie Terry asked Friday afternoon when Lisa climbed onto the back of the cycle.

"What guy?"

"The one staring at you from the doorway."

Lisa disliked the teasing tone in Charlie's voice. "I should have kept my mouth shut and never mentioned him to you."

"Why? I'm in favor of you finding somebody good enough for you."

"Sorry. It's not on my to-do list." Lisa shoved on a helmet, fastened the chin strap.

"It should be."

"Well, it isn't."

"You're being stubborn, Lisa."

"My life. My choice." Charlie was dirty from the construction site where he worked, but she wrapped her arms around his chest anyway. "We leaving or sitting here all day?"

Charlie gunned the engine and kicked off from the curb.

By the start of the fourth quarter, it was evident that Highland was the better football team. Crestwater's cheerleaders attempted to whip up the crowd, but enthusiasm was low. "Go team!" Skeet shouted.

Only Nathan knew his friend was cheering for the other team. "Your school spirit is awesome."

"Ain't it, though?" Skeet grinned, watching Roddy limp to the sidelines between two coaches. "Oo-o-o. Did the big mean tackle hurt you, Roddy?"

"I don't think he can hear you."

"And I don't want him to either." Skeet grinned again. "I'm going to grab a soda before they close the concession stand. Want anything?"

"I'm good." Nathan watched Skeet pick his way down the bleachers. The crowd was beginning to thin, leaving the dismal game despite the cheerleaders' frenzied shouting. Nathan's gaze stopped cold on Lisa. She was sitting below him and to the far left beside a heavyset short-haired girl. His view of her had been blocked by others. Nathan was almost at the top of the bleachers, and he could see the parking lot. With cars pulling out, it was easier to distinguish the layout, and off to one side, he saw her Harley. It gleamed black and silver when headlights struck it. He didn't see her "driver," so that probably meant she'd ridden it to the game herself.

Nathan's heart beat faster. Should he go down and accidentally bump into her? What would he say? He weighed his options, but before he could act, Skeet was back and Nathan decided to do nothing. He didn't want to drag Skeet with him and risk a rebuff.

"I got a party update," Skeet said. He pulled out a napkin with a crude map drawn on it. "It's near Lake

Lanier. Some kid's grandfather owns land out there and it's very private."

"That's pretty far out. You sure you want to go?" Nathan was having second thoughts. He'd told his parents there was a school dance after the game and they'd extended his curfew until twelve-thirty. He hadn't liked lying to them, especially to his mother, because she was so scared for him when he was out of her sight.

"Come on," Skeet said as Highland made another touchdown. "We have to celebrate Highland's victory some way or another."

By the time they arrived at the designated farmland site, the party was in full swing. Cars were parked haphazardly on wet grass and a large bonfire danced in a fire pit. Kids swarmed around the crackling flames and among coolers full of beer and wine drinks. Music boomed from a portable amp hooked to a generator. Couples had already paired off and were dancing or slipping away into the darkness with blankets.

"Does this guy's grandfather know about this?" Nathan asked.

"I doubt it. But we'll be long gone by the time he hears about it. Smell that sweet air?" Skeet asked. "Weed. Want some? It'll cost a few bucks."

"No, and neither do you." Nathan struggled with his conscience. On the one hand, he felt daring and bold; on the other, guilty. He shouldn't even be here. What so many of the kids took as their regular rites, Nathan had never done. He'd spent a lifetime pinned in place by his parents, and now he was a social retard—even by Skeet's standards, who was hardly a party animal.

Skeet had no chance to argue his case for a joint because the sound of a cycle reverberated in the already noisy night air. Nathan turned and saw Lisa on her Harley. His mouth went dry. Skeet said, "I never expected her to show."

"Wasn't she invited?"

"Dude, no one here was invited. Word went around and whoever wanted to come, did." Skeet looked thoughtful. "It's just that she doesn't party with us high school dweebs."

"Well, she's here."

Skeet's eyes narrowed. "You aren't thinking that you're going to get her to look your way, are you?"

"No," Nathan said hastily, although it was exactly what he was thinking. "I was just making an observation."

Skeet rocked back on his heels. "Listen, I'm going to go get a beer. Want one? Or should I bring you a bottle of spring water?"

Nathan didn't really like beer—he'd tasted it on the sly at certain homeschool parties—but he didn't like the way Skeet was riding him either. "Bring me a beer," he said as Skeet walked away.

He kept an eye on Lisa as she tied her helmet to the cycle. He waved. She saw him, gave a halfhearted wave in return, but it was all he needed to hustle over to her side. He said, "I saw you at the game with some girl."

"Jodie Price. She's a friend."

"She didn't come with you to the party?"

"Jodie didn't want to come. She hates crowds." A damp chill had fallen on the field, and fog hovered just above the grass in the distance. Lisa watched several of the cheerleaders clumped together around the fire. "Not all girls travel in packs," she added.

"Why *did* you come?"

"Haven't you heard? I'm a party girl."

The two images he had of Lisa, one of a party princess and the other of a loner, didn't mesh. He was about to tell her that when a voice shouted, "Fight!"

Kids rushed toward the bonfire. Nathan and Lisa went to see what was happening. In the middle of the semicircle formed around the fire and the beer stash, Skeet was standing between Roddy and two of his fellow players. The three of them held bottles of beer and looked roaring drunk and as big as tanks. Roddy was in Skeet's face, which looked pale but stony in the firelight. Roddy gave Skeet a shove. "Who invited you, faggot?"

Skeet said nothing, and that only seemed to make Roddy madder.

Nathan shouldered his way through the crowd and broke into the open. "Hey, leave him alone."

Roddy looked up, and Nathan saw that the side of his face was swollen and that his eye was turning black—hits from the game, Nathan assumed. "Who're you? A fellow faggot?" For some reason, this made a few in the crowd laugh.

Nathan stood beside Skeet. "I'm his friend." He was scared, but Roddy's rattlesnake meanness made Nathan mad. "He's not doing anything to you."

"He's breathing my air."

Again, laughter.

"Then let me remove him from your illustrious presence."

Nathan's sarcasm wasn't lost on Roddy, who cursed him. He leaned into Nathan's face. "I'm going to kick your ass first."

"How about mine, Roddy? Going to kick mine too?" The voice was Lisa's, and the crowd parted and started buzzing as she stepped into the circle next to Nathan and Skeet.

Roddy swayed and called her a skank.

"Hey!" Nathan said. "You can't talk like that to her."

"Says who? You with her, faggot-boy?"

"Nobody's with me," Lisa said. Firelight flickered over her face, reflecting in her eyes, now dark as the night sky. "But if you touch any of us, it won't look too good on the police report," she said. "You know, the one I'll file and that will go on your permanent record for the Georgia coach to read when he's considering you for scholarship money."

Nathan could hardly believe her bravado. Roddy was hateful when he was sober, downright venomous when he was drunk.

Roddy's expression twisted, but he didn't take a swing at any of them. Nathan held his breath. Rod's two buddies grabbed his arms. "Come on," one said. "They ain't worth it."

Roddy swore some more, tossed what was left of his beer at Skeet and Nathan, and swaggered off. The crowd gave the three football players a wide path, mumbling among themselves, then turned away. Skeet wiped beer from his cheek with his sleeve. "He could have killed us."

Nathan's knees felt wobbly, but he didn't let on. "He's a jerk—" he started.

The night was split by the wail of sirens. Somebody screamed, "Cops!" and the kids scattered like roaches across the field toward their cars.

"No, firetrucks!" another voice amended, but no one was listening.

Skeet pulled Nathan's arm. "Let's boogie."

Nathan was looking at Lisa, sprinting for her cycle. Instantly he knew what he was going to do. He reached into his pocket, grabbed his keys and pressed them into Skeet's hand. "Take my car."

"But—"

"Just park it on the street in front of your house. Put the keys under the floor mat."

"How will you—"

"Do it!" Nathan took off running, catching up to Lisa's cycle just as she was revving the engine. He threw his leg over the seat behind her.

"Get off!"

"No way."

She hesitated. "You'll slow me down. We'll end up in jail."

"I'm riding with you."

"Off, Malone."

"You'd better move it."

"You don't have a helmet."

"Then you'll just have to drive real careful."

The field was almost empty of cars now, and the red cast of the firetruck's lights could be seen swirling in the gloom, hurtling across the field toward the bonfire that glowed and crackled against the dark ground and pale, thickening fog.

"Hang on," Lisa ordered. Leaning forward, she aimed the big Harley in the opposite direction from the fast-approaching truck. In seconds, Nathan was flying through the night, his arms holding her to him.

6

*N*athan hunkered down, hanging tight. Riding the Harley was like riding a wild horse, the ground so bumpy that he thought his teeth would jar loose. The dark night surrounded them, and all Nathan saw were blurs of branches shooting past as Lisa kept close to a tree line parallel to a fence. Eventually she hit a dirt road, pelting them with gravel as she turned onto it. The cycle finally hit the solid asphalt of the highway and the ride smoothed.

Nathan watched the white line of the road streak below his feet. His head filled with the noise of the machine and the aroma of her leather jacket. He was freezing, but also wild with the pleasure of the ride and the nearness of Lisa. He would have ridden to the ends of the earth with her, certain that he'd never experienced a greater high than this moment in time.

Lights began to fly past and he realized that they were back in civilization. The cycle slowed, turned again and stopped under glaring lights in a gas station. They both sat on the machine and breathed hard. Slowly the sound of a country song from a nearby car broke into Nathan's consciousness, bringing him back to earth.

"You can let go now," Lisa said.

Unable to feel his cold-numbed fingers, he did so stiffly. He got off the bike, flexed. "We made it." He grinned.

She dismounted the cycle, brushed past him. "I need gas."

He took the pump handle from her, reached into his pocket and pulled out money. "How much?"

"I can buy my own gas."

"I owe you. I invited myself along."

She took a ten-dollar bill from him and headed for the building. Nathan filled the Harley's tank, staring at the beautifully airbrushed red heart emblazoned with her name in fancy letters on a purple ribbon. He'd never felt more alive. Being close to Lisa had awakened him, and he tried to think of a way to keep the feeling going. He glanced around, caught sight of a huge bookstore directly across the street—the kind that stayed open extra late.

She returned, handed him his change just as the pump clicked off. "Can you call your friend to come get you?"

He felt a moment of panic. "Can't I bum a ride

home? I don't live too far from Crestwater. Don't you have to head that way to get home yourself?"

"Afraid I'll dump you out here, Malone?"

"Terrified," he answered truthfully, but kept his tone unemotional. "How about some coffee? I'm cold, aren't you?" He gestured across the street and watched emotions he couldn't read cross her face.

"I need to be going. . . ."

"Come on. It's warm in there. A cup of coffee. What can it hurt?"

Inside the bookstore, which smelled of newly printed books and fresh lemon oil, he bought them each a mug of mocha coffee, then found two easy chairs among the stacks. He watched Lisa sip from her cup and fumbled for a thread of conversation. "You did a brave thing back at the party, standing up to Roddy."

"You're the one who almost got his head knocked off."

"Thanks for intervening. He would have killed me and Skeet and never thought twice about it."

She smiled over the top of her cup, and it was as if someone had turned on a current through his body. "Rod's a bully. He's big, dumb and drunk. In the morning all he'll be is sober."

Nathan grinned. "But still big and dumb?"

"Count on it." She warmed her hands around the cup. "Why did he go after Skeet?"

Nathan shrugged. "I guess because he can. I heard you stood him up last year for the prom. Why?"

She arched an eyebrow. "Because I could." He laughed and she added, "Football season will be over soon and Rod will fade into the background. He won't have staying power, believe me."

Nathan wanted to take her hands in his, but he hesitated. What if she wouldn't stand for it? He asked, "So what kind of music do you like?" She named a couple of bands. "I'm into country," he said. "Not the twangy kind, but the modern kind."

"You mean those songs about somebody doing somebody wrong?"

"I think of them as songs from the heart about life. Skeet and I play in my garage and work up some juice. He's on keyboard. I play guitar. I—um—I've written a few songs myself. Don't expect them to go platinum or anything." She looked more interested. Of course. She liked to write too.

"Ever get any bookings?"

"Not since Morgan Frey's ninth birthday party. Skeet and I were fourteen and the girls thought we were stars." He grinned at the memory. "Our band lacks depth. We need more members."

"A singer?"

"The *right* singer would be good. You a singer?" He didn't dare to hope.

"I can't sing a note."

"So that's a look at my life. How about you? What do you like to write?"

"Nothing that will ever get published."

"You don't know that."

"Sure I do." She took another sip of coffee. "I'll never send them anyplace. The only person who reads my stuff is Fuller, and that's for a grade."

"I want my songs to get published. It would be a kick to hear them on the radio someday."

She continued to drink the coffee, and silence lengthened between them. He searched for something else to say to her, to make her look at him with interest, to have her think he was cool. He should face it: He was dull and boring with a small, uninteresting life. Why should she talk to him?

"What was it like to be homeschooled?" she asked. "Didn't you get lonely?"

"I was alone, but not too lonely. We did things with other homeschoolers—field trips, joint projects. I made it into the citywide spelling bee in seventh grade, but lost in the third round: *excavate* tripped me up. I'm going to use that word in a song someday, just to prove I can. Plus homeschooling has some real perks—the cafeteria lines are really short and the food's incredible."

That made her smile. "Your mother didn't mind having you home all day?"

"She likes to teach. How about you? Have you always gone to Crestwater?" He knew the answer, but he wanted to hear her voice, have her eyes meet his.

"We moved here last January from Valdosta after construction work dried up for Charlie. He got a job here real easy, and there's a lot of building going on in Atlanta. Mom works as an office coordinator for the same construction firm. As for me, well, one high school is pretty much like any other."

"Who's Charlie?"

"The man who lives with Mom and me."

"Your stepdad?"

"No," she said, leaving him to wonder.

His parents were boringly conventional and had been married forever. "Is he the guy who sometimes rides your cycle and picks you up at school?"

"We share my cycle when his truck's down. But the Harley's mine. Charlie bought it for me."

Nathan had many questions he wanted to ask, but she was finished with her coffee, and he saw that she was getting restless. "Want another cup?"

"No thanks." She asked a salesperson passing by for the time.

It was after midnight and his stomach knotted. He didn't want to be late getting home, but he didn't want the evening with Lisa to end. "You going to miss your curfew?" he asked.

She stood. "I don't have curfews. But I'll bet you do, don't you, Malone?"

He felt embarrassed, hating to confess that he still had rules and limits set by his conventional parents. "Until twelve-thirty, but I don't care if I'm late."

"Come on," she said. "I'll drive fast."

Getting on the cycle, he said, "My car's at Skeet's. He's just down the street from me. It'll be best if I park my car in my driveway tonight."

"Whatever," she said, and the engine roared to life.

There was little traffic and she got him to his car in less than twenty minutes. She cut the engine before hitting the top of his street and coasted. At Skeet's street, he hopped in his car, fished out the key from under the floor mat.

"I'll walk this to the corner before I start up." Lisa began pushing the Harley.

"How about a movie next Saturday night?" he whispered loudly, leaning out the window.

"I told you, Malone, I don't date."

Disappointed, he watched her disappear around the corner.

Nathan drove his car into his driveway, jogged to the front door and turned his key in the lock as the hall clock struck the half hour. He had made it. He took the stairs two at a time, quietly slipped into his bedroom and threw himself across his bed, euphoric. He'd spent part of an evening with Lisa and it had left him soaring, and hungry for more of her. He'd get her to go out with him again. He didn't know how, but he would.

He heard one of the twins begin to cry, and soon after, the other started. They would be hungry, and his mother would come down the hall to their room to nurse them. And knowing his mother, she'd peek into his room to check on him. Nathan quickly struggled under the covers, pulling the sheet up just as he heard his door creak open. *All tucked in, Mom.* He heard the door close, and after a few minutes the twins quieted down. Nathan got out of bed, turned on a flashlight and found a legal pad. His head and heart were full of music and he wanted to write it down. Lisa had done that. She'd filled him with hope and fire.

Lisa sat for a long time at the corner, balancing her cycle and looking back at Nathan's house. She saw a dim light go on in an upstairs room and wondered if it was his room. She fumbled in her jacket pockets, searching for a cigarette. She remembered stashing one, but now she couldn't find it. She didn't smoke much, but once in a while she craved a hit of nicotine.

Her search turned up empty and she swore under her breath. Charlie had most likely confiscated it. "You shouldn't smoke," he told her whenever he caught her with a cigarette.

"Why not? It's not as if I'll die of lung cancer."

"It doesn't look ladylike. It's a stinking habit."

"You should talk. Who do you think I steal them from?"

"Just 'cause I smoke don't mean you should."

"You worry too much, Charlie."

Lisa shivered. The light in the window blinked off. She should never have had coffee, or sat and talked to Nathan, or allowed him to put his arms around her waist and press his body against her back. Stupid of her.

She turned on the cycle's engine and the noise splintered the quiet night. Dogs barked. Lisa roared off, determined to put this night behind her—as well as the guileless, blue-eyed boy who wrote country music and made her feel so totally alive.

7

"*H*ow was the game?" Karen Malone asked the next morning at breakfast.

"We lost." Nathan sat hunched over his cereal bowl, desperately wishing he was upstairs in bed instead of getting ready to go outside for a morning of yard work with his father, who was already waiting for him in the garage.

"I saw that much in today's paper. I'm asking if you had a good time."

"Mom, it was a football game. I sat in the stands with Skeet. We cheered. We lost. We came home."

"Really?" Her eyes narrowed. "Then why do the clothes you stuffed in the laundry hamper smell like stale beer?"

Nathan went hot all over. "You smelled my clothes?"

"And the inside of your car smells like beer too."

"Aw, come on—"

"*You* come on." She stood at the counter looking furious. "Did you drink last night? Tell me the truth."

"No, I didn't drink. And thanks for the vote of confidence."

"Did Skeet?"

Nathan slammed his spoon down on the table. "We weren't drinking. If you have to know, the beer got spilled on us."

"I don't want you hanging around with kids who drink."

Nathan knew she was on a roll and he didn't want to hear it. He stood up, headed for the garage. "I need to get started. Skeet's coming over later. Grill him if you don't believe me."

"Don't walk away from me while we're talking."

"*You're* talking. I'm not supposed to speak, right? I told you we weren't drinking. I made curfew. And I'll wash my own laundry so the smell of beer won't touch anything sacred." He slammed out of the kitchen.

His father looked up from shaking a bag of grass seed into the dispenser for overseeding the lawn, something he did every fall. "Storm over?"

"It's never over with her. She doesn't trust me."

"She's scared, that's all." Craig paused. "*Were* you drinking last night?"

Nathan threw up his hands. "I can't believe you asked me that! No, I wasn't drinking." He saw no reason to confess that he would have if Roddy hadn't shown up.

"All right. Cool down. I believe you."

Nathan shoved his feet into old gardening sneakers. He stomped over to the push aerator, a piece of equipment with a large heavy drum and spikes for making holes in the lawn. It would leave the hard Georgia clay more pliable and ready to accept the new grass seed his father would scatter. The job was long and difficult, but suddenly Nathan felt like taking his frustration out on the earth. "What's she going to do when I move away next fall? Follow me to college?"

"Don't burn your bridges, son. You may have to take a HOPE Scholarship."

"What! And live at home?" The HOPE Scholarship was money from the state lottery given to students with a B average, and it paid for tuition as long as the student maintained good grades. However, it was only available for students to attend state schools, which would mean Nathan couldn't go away to college, but would have to remain in state, and most likely at home.

"Business is down. We may not be able to afford to send you away."

"That's just great. You know college is my only hope of getting away from her."

"Don't talk as if your mother's trying to ruin your life. College is a privilege, not a right."

"She won't let go, Dad. You know that's true. I

thought the twins would mellow her out. I thought going to Crestwater would get her to step back, but no, she's still dogging me." He kept thinking of Lisa and the extraordinary freedom she had to come and go, to not have a curfew.

"Your mother's been through a lot. This whole family's been through a lot."

"Old news," Nathan said stubbornly. "No one can change the past and I shouldn't be the one to pay because Mom's afraid."

"They're my fears too," his father said quietly, but quickly added, "Listen, she *will* get involved with the twins, especially as they get older. She's tapped out right now, tired all the time. Cut her some slack, okay?"

"Why do I have to be the one?"

"Because you're the one who matters most." His father looked resigned. "And because I've given my whole life to make things better for her. To make it up to her somehow."

Nathan felt deflated. No matter how their history got discussed, it always came back to ground zero. He used to think that their family history was a vicious circle, but now that he was older he saw that it was more like a spiral, moving not round and round, but downward, ever downward.

Nathan was in his room picking on his guitar that afternoon when Skeet came by after finishing his shift at the grocery store. "Hey, man. I'm busting to know what happened last night." Skeet tossed his wadded apron onto the bed and plopped on the floor in front of Nathan. "I know you rode off with Lisa. Where'd you go?"

"As far away from the field as we could get." Nathan perked up. Talking about Lisa was a sure way to bring him out of his funk.

"Which would be . . . ?"

Nathan grinned. "We ended up having coffee at some bookstore and talking. Then she brought me home."

"Oh man, you lucky dog!"

"It was a wild ride. I don't think the girl knows the meaning of fear."

"And you got to hold her body? You actually put your arms around her?"

"I got to hang on to her for my *life*. You ever ride across a bumpy field on a Harley?"

"Not lately." Skeet pulled a candy bar from his shirt pocket and offered half to Nathan, who refused it. "So now what?"

"That's what I'm trying to figure out." He put down the guitar. "The girl's got secrets, Skeet."

"How do you know this? Did she say, 'I've got a secret'?"

Nathan shook his head. "She didn't have to. I just know it in my gut."

"And you want to know her secrets."

"I do."

"Gee, most guys just want to get in her pants."

Nathan scowled. "That's crude."

"And that thought's never crossed your mind?"

"Knock it off, Skeet. Don't talk about her like she's some kind of sex prize."

Skeet looked contrite. "Sorry, man. I just can't believe you're immune to that part. She's beautiful, and every guy at school wants her. What makes you think you can score? And I don't mean in a crude way. But score with her in a real way."

"Maybe I can't. But I won't know if I don't try."

"Got a game plan?"

Nathan sat back down, picked up his guitar. "Maybe I'll write a song for her."

"Need my input?" Skeet wiggled his fingers.

"Not yet. I'll let you know." Nathan couldn't concentrate with Skeet staring up at him, so after a few minutes he set down the instrument. "Want to shoot some hoops?"

"Great!"

They passed through the kitchen, where Nathan's mother was busy creating supper. "Hey, Skeet."

"What's cooking, Mrs. M?"

"Meatloaf, mashed potatoes and gravy."

Nathan remained sullen. She knew he loved her special meatloaf, and this was her way of saying she was sorry about their fight that morning.

"There's plenty," Karen said. "Want to stay?"

Skeet's face broke into an eager smile. "You bet! Double my gravy portion."

Nathan led the way out the door to the side of the house where the basketball hoop hung, not yet willing to accept her peace offering.

If Nathan thought he'd be able to have any kind of familiarity with Lisa on Monday, he was wrong. She didn't come to school for two days, and when she did show up, she acted preoccupied and rushed out of Fuller's class like a whirlwind. Nathan hardly had a chance to speak to her.

Fuller pulled a pop quiz on Thursday and passed back the results on Friday. Nathan had scored a ninety on the test, but attached to it was his first creative paper as 705, and it was a spiderweb of red ink. His stomach knotted as he read the teacher's notes. Fuller had found the paper "pedantic, plodding and a rehash of old ideas." He'd urged Nathan to try something "fresh and innovative" for his next effort. The teacher had added, "You write well-constructed sentences, so I know you have a command of grammar rules. But good writing isn't always about rules. It's also about feelings and emotions offered in an original format. Think outside the box."

For some reason, Fuller's criticism stung him like the tentacles of a jellyfish. Instead of impressing the teacher, he'd humiliated himself. He wondered what Fuller had written on Lisa's paper, then remembered that she'd skipped that day. And how about 454? What wonderful praise had Fuller heaped on that person's paper?

"You up for a session?" Skeet's voice broke into Nathan's dark thoughts. "I don't have to work this afternoon, and I don't want to hang around my house."

"Sure." Nathan shoved his papers into his notebook and headed for the parking lot with Skeet.

"Bad news?"

"No. Just a test." By habit, Nathan searched the lot the instant they were outside.

"She already left," Skeet said. "I saw her take off a few minutes ago."

Nathan shrugged. "It doesn't matter."

"You giving up?"

"Do I look like a quitter?"

Skeet grinned. "You're the man."

Later, Nathan raised the garage door, plugged in his electric guitar, and let Skeet cut loose on the keyboard. Nathan preferred his acoustical guitar, but at the moment he felt like making noise, and his mother and the twins were off shopping, so no one was there to shush him. He let the music crank and, pulling fevered, frenzied sounds from the steel strings, closed his eyes and let the music take him to another zone. He was aware of nothing until Skeet's playing fell off and he opened his eyes to complain and then saw why Skeet had stopped.

At the end of his driveway, Lisa sat wrapped in

leather and staring at him from the seat of her Harley. His heart leaped. He laid down the guitar and started for the door. She quickly backed her Harley onto the street, kicked off.

"Lisa!" he yelled. "Wait! Lisa!"

By the time he'd sprinted to the end of his driveway, she was gone.

8

*N*athan squirmed through the remainder of the weekend, arrived early at school on Monday and waited in the parking lot for Lisa, hoping that today wouldn't be one of the days that Charlie's truck was broken. He was rewarded by the sound and sight of her cycle just after the first tardy bell. He didn't care if he was late to first period, he was going to talk to her. She pulled into her space and he stepped from behind the car parked next to it. "Good morning."

She looked startled. "Same to you." She unstrapped her book bag from the seat. He eased in front of her. "Are you stalking me, Malone?"

"Why did you come by my house on Saturday?"

"I was out for a ride. You own the streets?"

"Why my street?"

She tried to shove past him, but she couldn't. "Don't let it go to your head, Malone. You don't mean anything to me."

He jammed his hands into the pockets of his jacket. "Sure I do, Lisa. You just haven't accepted it yet." He had no idea where he'd gotten the nerve to say such a thing. Chalk it up to being angry.

She rolled her eyes. "Guys are so vain. A cup of coffee and a ride home is not the basis for a lasting relationship. Now excuse me."

"If you would like to really hear us play, Skeet and I are holding an audition Saturday afternoon in my garage for a drummer—some guy Skeet met at work who thinks he'd like a stab at it."

"I hope it goes well for you." She'd walked around to the opposite side.

"Three o'clock," he added as the last bell sounded and she hurried toward the building.

Lisa was cool to him in Fuller's class. Nathan didn't push it. He held out hope that his invitation wouldn't be ignored. Whether she admitted it or not, there was an undercurrent flowing between them. Like static electricity that snapped at unexpected moments, he could feel it. And he craved it.

On Friday, Fuller collected more of the class's original papers. When the bell rang Nathan was surprised when Lisa turned in her desk and asked, "Did you submit one of your songs to Fuller?"

"No."

"Why not?"

"They're private."

She looked skeptical. "You want some big country singer to sing your songs, but you don't want someone as good as Fuller to judge them first, is that it? You can't have it both ways, Malone."

"They're not the kind of poetry Fuller would appreciate. Songs need music to make them sound right. You ever read the words to a song, a song you might love when it's played? It can sound pretty dumb because the words depend on the music to drive them."

"Coward," she said, then picked up her books and left.

He cleaned the garage on Saturday, rolled out the piece of carpet he and Skeet used for practice, even vacuumed it, and set up a side table with sodas on ice. Skeet was impressed. "All for an audition with a drummer? He may suck."

"We should at least look like we're serious and sort of professional. Okay—semiprofessional," he amended when Skeet gave him a kooky look.

"What's next? A tour bus?"

The drummer arrived right on time, a kid named Larry who proceeded to set up his gear and tell Nathan and Skeet how his former band had played a few bar mitzvah parties, some birthday celebrations for socially connected Atlanta debutantes, and a country club before breaking up.

"We're not into rock," Nathan explained.

"I can dig it," Larry said.

Except that he couldn't. The rhythm of country seemed to totally defeat Larry, and after half an hour, Nathan was ready to throw his drum set out the door. He was edgy too because he kept hoping Lisa would show, and just as he was giving up on the possibility, she rolled into his driveway. His heart leaped and he couldn't hide a smile.

Lisa wasn't alone. Her rider was the girl Nathan had seen her with at the football game. Lisa boldly walked into the garage, and the girl followed hesitantly. "Are these auditions open?" Lisa asked.

"To you they are, baby," Larry called out.

She gave him a look that would have peeled paint and turned toward Nathan. "This is my friend, Jodie Price. She's a hell of a singer and you should give her a chance."

Skeet walked over. "We don't need a singer."

Jodie pulled on Lisa's arm. "Let's go. I told you this was a bad idea."

Nathan saw the scared look on Jodie's face and realized that Lisa had strong-armed her into coming. He also felt instantly sorry for the girl because he knew what it was to be an outsider. "Did Lisa tell you we're country?"

"My favorite," Jodie said. She was a short girl with a round face, short dark hair and brown eyes. She was heavy, but pretty in her way. She kept fidgeting, and Nathan figured Jodie would rather be anyplace but here.

"We should give her a try," Nathan told Skeet.

Skeet grimaced, but returned to his keyboard.

"How about some classic Patsy Cline?" Nathan picked up his acoustical guitar. It felt funny to be auditioning people for their band, more their hobby than anything else.

"I know 'Crazy' and 'Sweet Dreams,' " Jodie said. "Actually, I know all her songs."

"Let's try 'Crazy.' " Nathan looked straight at Lisa.

She ignored his look, walked over to the table, plucked a soda from the cooler and sat on an old folding chair.

Nathan played a few riffs. Skeet picked up the melody, and even Larry managed to come in softly with his snare drum. Jodie stepped up, opened her mouth and sang the words with a magical timbre that sent goose bumps up Nathan's back. Who knew that such a voice could come out of this shy, plump little girl? *Lisa had known.*

They stopped and started a few times, but eventually got through the song. When the last note had faded, Lisa jumped up, clapping. "Didn't I tell you she was good?"

"You're good," Nathan told Jodie, who turned red and shuffled her feet.

Skeet came over. "Yes. But we never planned on adding a singer."

"It's all right," Jodie said, dropping her gaze to the floor.

"You should practice some more together," Lisa interjected. "See what comes of it. What kind of a band are you if you don't have a singer?"

"Want to try it again next week?" Nathan asked.

Jodie shrugged. "I—I guess so."

"Give Skeet a way to get hold of you."

"What about me?" Larry asked.

"Same thing." He turned to Lisa. "Take a walk with me."

"Where?"

"Around back."

He unlatched the high wooden gate and led her down the path to his mother's eye-popping backyard of winding trails, clusters of trees, shrubs, and flowers, and gurgling koi pond. Many of the leaves were tinged with the colors of autumn. By November, the trees would be dormant and bare.

"Whoa," Lisa said when they rounded the corner of the house. "Some backyard, Malone."

"My mother's hobby." He kept his eyes on Lisa. "Why did you bring Jodie over here?"

"To sing with your band."

"Skeet and I just mess around. We don't have a serious band."

"You should. You sounded pretty good to me."

"Jodie would never have done this if you hadn't dragged her."

"So? She's got a great voice. She just needs confidence. Your band can give that to her, and in the bargain, your band will be better. I'm doing you both a favor."

"Where do you know her from?" He never saw Lisa hang with anyone at school, and Jodie was the type who faded into the woodwork in a school the size of Crestwater.

"She lives in my apartment building. I heard her singing out on the playground one day last summer. She didn't see me. She was sitting on a swing. The place was empty and she was just singing out loud. I told her I thought she sounded great. She was embarrassed, but once we got to know each other, we became friends. She has talent, and your band's a good start for her. Not everyone can be on *Star Search* or *American Idol.*"

"What do you get out of it, Lisa?" He kept digging for Lisa's motives, which he figured were present, but he couldn't grasp what they were. "What exactly do you want?"

She didn't say anything at first. He kept looking at her, at her violet eyes, at her lips, full and shimmering with gloss. It made his knees weak. "No one can give me what I want, Malone." She surprised him by looping her arm through his. "Show me around. Where I live we only get flowers planted at the entrance. The place is mostly asphalt, parked cars and a few scraggly trees, watered daily by dogs. I'm telling you, those trees are toxic. No one can go near them."

Nathan walked with Lisa. He knew the gardens well, since he helped his mother tend them, so he talked about specific plants and apologized for what wasn't blooming. "You should really come in the spring," he said. "I'll bet there are a thousand flowers then."

She seemed totally into the tour and for once he was glad his mother had taken such pains with the yard.

They stopped at the koi pond and Lisa sat on the bench, leaned out over the water and watched the exotic fish come to the surface in a school of fluttering fins.

"They're beggars," Nathan said. "We can hand-feed them."

"Really? Can I?"

"I'll have to go get some bread from the house."

"No, that's okay. Some other day."

Did that mean she might actually come again? He'd been trying to get her attention and spend more time with her, and all it might have taken was an invitation to feed some fish.

She sat back, closed her eyes and breathed in the air. She was so beautiful that he wanted to kiss her. Of course, she'd probably push him into the pond if he tried. Her eyes opened and focused on the magnificent magnolia tree in the center of the yard. "Big tree."

"Mom planted it when I was three."

Lisa studied the beds around the tree, set off by a meandering row of bricks and Spanish tile. "You know, it sort of looks like there was something else there at one time. Before the flower beds and tree."

"There was."

"Tell me."

His heart pounded and his mouth tasted bone-dry. It was the thing his family never spoke about. "We used to have a swimming pool. Mom liked the tiles too much to rip them out."

"And your parents covered it over? We have a pool

at my complex, but it's toxic too." She wrinkled her nose. "Too many little kids peeing in it. So why did you all fill yours in with dirt? Too much trouble to take care of? Your mom wanted gardens and trees instead?"

The pounding in Nathan's ears was almost a roar. He wanted to tell her but wasn't sure if he should. It was their family business, and besides, it might turn her off, one thing he didn't want to do. Nathan took a deep breath and stared out across the sun-splashed lawn. "We covered it over because it's where my sister drowned."

9

"She *drowned?*"

"When she was six. It was a long time ago." Nathan felt hot and knew color was seeping up his neck. He should have kept his mouth shut.

Lisa stared at him, a range of emotions he couldn't decipher playing across her pretty face. He knew she had questions, but he hoped with everything inside of him that she wouldn't ask any. He'd said too much already. "That's very sad," she finally said, and reached over and stroked his hand.

He jerked back, but only because it was so unexpected. "We don't talk about it," he said, regretting pulling away from her.

She didn't seem to be bothered by his rejection. The koi thrashed at the pond's surface, and Nathan watched Lisa's reflection undulate in the water. He saw something on her face that he couldn't describe but that spoke to his heart. *Sadness? Understanding?* More than anything, he wanted to put his arms around her, hold her close. He could have spent forever next to her, imagining her in his arms with this mysterious thread somehow connecting them.

"Forever" ended abruptly when Skeet crashed through the foliage. "There you guys are! Jodie thought you'd run off and left her." His pique turned to apology when he looked at their faces. "Sorry, dude."

Lisa jumped up. "I've got to get home too."

The three of them hurried back to the garage, and Jodie looked relieved when she saw them. Larry was long gone. Dusk had fallen and the driveway was dark. Nathan turned on a light and watched the girls climb onto the Harley. "You sing great, Jodie," he called out. "Next week again, you hear?"

"I'll be here," Jodie said.

"You can come too," he said to Lisa.

"I'll bring Jodie, but I can't stay." Lisa was back to her cool, elusive self.

A wind had kicked up and Nathan watched them drive off, feeling as cold and scattered as the dry leaves tumbling around his feet.

Lisa eased into the dark apartment. "Mom?" No answer. Then she remembered it was bingo night at the Catholic church. Her mother wasn't Catholic, but she loved bingo.

"Lisa? Back here," Charlie called.

She flipped on a lamp, tossed her book bag on the sofa and went down the hall to the apartment's third bedroom, where Charlie had set up the television, DVD, his recliner and an over-the-hill couch. He muted the TV with the remote control and waved her over. He was freshly showered, his long hair pulled back in a ponytail. He smelled of leather and lime soap. "I made some soup for us," he said. "It's on the stove. You hungry?"

"Jodie and I stopped for a burger."

"How'd her audition go?"

"She wowed them."

Charlie grinned. "So you were right about them needing her, weren't you?"

Lisa tugged off her boots, propped her feet on the old scarred coffee table. "They asked her back next week."

"They any good?"

"They've got a ways to go before they can play in public."

"And the young man?"

"What about him?" She kept seeing Nathan's face, almost expressionless, when he told her about his drowned sister. Lisa was intensely curious about it, but knew how it felt to have someone pile on questions you didn't want to answer. Some secrets were best left buried.

"You still like him?"

"I don't like anybody, Charlie. Not in the way you're thinking. You know I can't."

"That's all in your head, little girl. You told me you wanted to try out everything, remember? Well, loving somebody is part of the trying-out business."

"Not for me." She stared at the figures on TV, characters running around wildly in some movie, looking extremely stupid without a sound track. "Why do you stay, Charlie? Mom's never here. I'm—well, you know how I am. Why do you waste your time on us?"

"Your mom's not a strong person, Lisa," Charlie drawled after a minute of reflection. "Not all her fault," he added. "Life's just worn her down. You and me *are* strong. So we pick up the slack, make it easier for those who aren't strong. This young man—"

"Nathan Malone," she said, hating to say his name because a name made a person real. It breathed life into someone who otherwise remained in the shadows.

"This Nathan, is he strong?"

She thought about that, about the way he'd looked at her when she told him to get off her bike that night in the woods, about how he'd cornered her in the parking lot and forced her to listen to him, about the look on his face when he'd told her about his sister. "He doesn't discourage easily. Yes, he's strong."

Charlie leaned back in his recliner. "That's good, Lisa. 'Cause you're going to need a strong one."

The Saturday jam sessions proved to be the highlight of Nathan's weeks. Not only was their band improving, their sound maturing, but it was also when he could see Lisa without the clutter of the classroom surrounding them. She had proven standoffish, and he'd been unable to connect with her as he had that night in the bookstore or the afternoon by the koi pond. Every day she rushed out of Fuller's class, offering Nathan a breezy goodbye, acting as if they'd never shared a moment together. On Saturdays, she brought Jodie to Nathan's garage and either waited for her to finish or left and returned for her later. By November, when the first cold snap hit Atlanta, Nathan was desperate to be alone with her again.

"Keep Jodie and Larry busy," Nathan instructed Skeet one Saturday before the others arrived.

"How?"

"Figure it out. I want to get Lisa off to myself for a little while."

"You've been making cow eyes at her for a month and she hasn't taken the hint," Skeet said. "What makes you think a few minutes alone with her today will make a difference?"

"If I wanted an argument, I'd have asked my mother," Nathan growled. "She's out with the twins. Dad's playing golf. I want a chance to be alone with Lisa. Are you going to help me or not?"

Skeet bowed from the waist. "I'm your servant."

The practice went well, and as soon as it was over, Skeet stepped up to Jodie. "Hey, can you and Larry take a sec to go over some parts of the last number with me?"

"What about Nathan?" Jodie asked.

"Don't need him for this."

Nathan set his guitar aside. "Mom left a plateful of cookies for us in the kitchen."

Larry whooped. "I *love* your mother's cookies!"

"It's cold out here," Lisa said. She'd been sitting in an old lawn chair, flipping through a magazine.

"I'll brew some hot chocolate," Nathan said.

"That would be good," Jodie said eagerly.

Nathan turned to Lisa. "Could you help me carry stuff?"

She hesitated, but Jodie gave her a pleading look. "All right," she said, not sounding happy about it. She followed Nathan indoors.

The kitchen looked spotless, and the smell of chocolate chip cookies spiced the air. Nathan pulled a gallon of milk from the refrigerator and poured some into a pan, rummaged in the pantry for cocoa and sugar, all the while maintaining a stream of conversation. "You were right about Jodie. She's great. Larry's talking about getting us a gig or two for the holidays. He has connections from his old days and we think we might give it a try—"

"Nathan, it's okay. You don't have to talk me to death. I don't mind helping you with the food. I don't mind being alone with you."

He was glad for the dim light. She couldn't see how embarrassed her words made him feel. He put the pan of milk on the stove and turned on the gas burner.

"Okay, you found me out. I do want to be alone with you."

"Why?"

"Because you never even look my way at school."

She crossed her arms. "It's nothing personal."

He forced a laugh. "Well, it feels personal. It feels like you think there's something wrong with me. Like I'm not worth another conversation, or another cup of coffee. Why can't you stand being alone with me?"

"That isn't true."

"Then why can't we be friends?"

"We are. I found your band a singer, didn't I?"

"You did that for Jodie. The fact that she helps our band is bonus points. Not all of us are projects for Lisa to manage, you know. What do you get out of it?"

"I—it's complicated. My life is complicated."

"How so? Have you got a job?" She shook her head. "Then what? You don't have curfews. You cut school at will. You don't hang with anyone. What's complicated?"

"Why do you care?"

"Because *you* care. You stand up for me and Skeet to a guy like Roddy. You become an advocate for a girl like Jodie. Your 'I don't give a damn' routine doesn't hold up with me."

"I'll work on it." She looked shaken, tried to brush past him.

He caught her arm. "Not so fast." And before he could stop himself, he'd pulled her against his chest and kissed her full and hard on the mouth. She fought him at first, but he didn't let go, and as the kiss lengthened, it deepened. His blood sang in his head, tore through his veins like wildfire. He raised his hands and cupped her face, pushed his tongue between her lips. She didn't resist, but put her arms around him and kissed him willingly.

The hiss of milk boiling over on the stove was what finally seeped through Nathan's consciousness and broke them apart. They stood staring at each other while the milk sizzled and a burning smell singed the air. Nathan's hands were shaking and his heart was almost jumping from his chest. Lisa's eyes looked huge and deep. Her breath was ragged and louder than the boiling milk. She stepped backward, turned to the stove and shut off the flame. "It's a mess," she mumbled, and he was certain that she wasn't talking only about the burned milk.

He came up behind her, wanting to touch her, hold her, but she sidestepped him. "Don't," she said.

Nathan walked across the floor to the kitchen island. He rested his palms on the cool granite, licked his lips, and tasted her all over again. "I'm not sorry," he said.

"Nothing's changed," she said, sounding stubborn.

Her words wounded him. He'd put himself on the line with that kiss, opened his heart and invited her inside, and now she was pulling back. Again. "Sure it has." He crossed to the refrigerator. "We have to heat more milk."

* * *

There were only three days of school the following week because of Thanksgiving. Lisa missed the first two and on the third slipped into her seat in Fuller's class just as the bell rang. Nathan ached with frustration. Had she not come to school simply to avoid him? He'd thought about calling her but kept losing his nerve. Plus, there was no listing for her in the phone book. Better to deal with her face to face. But at the moment, he was staring at her back and Fuller was talking about poets Nathan had no interest in. Lisa lifted her hair and gathered it into a barrette, and Nathan was left to stare at the nape of her beautiful neck. He wanted to put his hands around her neck and shout, *Don't you know you're making me crazy!*

". . . poets today have difficulty being heard because poetry has few advocates in today's world," Fuller was saying.

Nathan squinted at the base of Lisa's neck, where a tiny grid of blue dots disappeared into her hairline. Had she started a tattoo and then changed her mind? He'd always wanted one, but never had the courage to get one. His mother would have hit the roof and grounded him for life if he had. But Lisa—well, she apparently could do whatever she wanted.

". . . read a nice piece of work to you today." Fuller's voice broke through Nathan's thoughts. "It's a love poem by one of our own and resonates without being cloying. I thought it quite good. It was written by student seven-oh-five."

Nathan's heart seized.

10

*N*athan heard shoes shuffle, papers rustle. Usually Fuller called out every number except Nathan's, and he read student 454's work more often than any other. Nathan slumped low in his desk chair, cut his eyes sideways, wondered if he was wearing a sign announcing, LOOK HERE! I'M STUDENT 705! He sure hoped not. He'd tried for weeks to write well enough to be picked, but his work always came back swimming in red ink. According to Fuller, it lacked originality. It lacked conviction. He scribbled, "You write well, but it feels forced and dry"—whatever *that* meant. And now today, while Nathan was in total turmoil because of Lisa, Fuller had discovered something worthy to be read aloud. His stomach tightened.

Fuller cleared his throat and began reading Nathan's work.

> *"I stand and watch you from afar.*
> *I wish upon you, like a star.*
> *You see me not.*
> *You come.*
> *You go.*
> *Still, I love you better than you know."*

Fuller lowered the paper and a girl on the side of the room said, "That's just *so* romantic."

"Why?" Fuller asked.

Nathan's ears felt on fire. He slunk lower in his seat. He'd written the poem late one night when he'd been longing for Lisa. The words had come quickly, easily, like water from a faucet. He'd been nuts to turn it in as an assignment.

No one spoke, and Fuller said, "It's short and to the point. And we like it because it came from the writer's heart, not his head. And that, my future Writers of America, is where all good writing comes from—a person's heart. And once you tap into it, your work will come alive. Trust me."

Nathan left the room slowly that day, not wanting to talk to anyone, especially Lisa, because he was certain he was wearing the poem's authorship across his face like a billboard. He was suddenly glad about the long holiday weekend. He and Skeet hadn't scheduled practice either. It meant four days without seeing Lisa. Four days. Ninety-six hours. Five thousand, seven hundred and sixty minutes to distance himself from the confession of his heart, now made public.

On Friday afternoon Skeet came over and asked, "Can I borrow your wheels to go see Jodie?"

Nathan was shooting baskets in the driveway. "Why?"

"I want to see her."

Nathan stopped mid-dribble, tucked the ball under his arm and stared hard at his friend. "You got something going with Jodie?"

Skeet's face turned beet red. "We—um—have been talking on our cells and seeing each other at school."

"Why didn't you tell me you liked her?"

Skeet shrugged. "I didn't know how. You've had your head up your butt for weeks. I thought you would notice eventually."

Nathan shook his head, felt apologetic and stupid at the same time. "I should have noticed. Sorry, man."

"So can I take your car?"

"Jodie lives in the same apartment building as Lisa, doesn't she?" Skeet nodded. "Give me fifteen to clean up and I'll drive you over myself." He tossed the ball into the garage.

"I thought you might," Skeet said, with a wry grin.

Magnolia Gardens, the apartment complex where Lisa and Jodie lived, was a maze of yellow and brown rundown-looking buildings with a faded red tennis court, sans nets, and a pool long past its prime. Small signs pointed the way to the back. Jodie lived near a yard full of little kids climbing on old playground equipment. Cars were parked everywhere, and Nathan ended up blocking in a car that Skeet said belonged to Jodie's divorced mother.

Jodie opened her door, and the smile she beamed at Skeet told the story of how she felt about him. Nathan couldn't believe he'd been so blind and preoccupied not to have seen it before. "Lisa lives in the left front ground-floor apartment through the next stairwell over," Jodie told him.

Nathan thanked her and beat a quick retreat. A wreath made of fall foliage and orange ribbon hung on the scarred front door of Lisa's apartment. Nathan wiped his sweating palms on his jeans and rang the bell.

"Can I help you, son?" A man's voice came from behind Nathan.

Nathan walked back out to the parking lot to where the man was working under the raised hood of an old truck. He wore a ponytail and was dressed in dirty jeans, a sweatshirt and a jacket. "I'm Charlie Terry," he said, wiping his hands on a soiled rag.

"Nathan Malone." They shook hands.

"I'm guessing you're looking for Lisa."

"I was in the area. Brought my friend to visit Jodie." The excuse sounded lame even to Nathan's ears.

"Lisa's out with her mom doing some Christmas shopping."

Of course. His mother had taken off early to do the same thing. His father had twins duty.

"They've been gone awhile, so I expect they'll be back soon. If you want to wait around, you can."

Nathan didn't have anything else to do. He couldn't barge in on Skeet and Jodie, and he couldn't drive off and leave Skeet. "If you don't mind."

Charlie smiled. He was tall and well muscled. His skin was deeply tanned and his hands looked like worn leather. His voice, thick as honey, sounded Southern. "You know anything about engines?"

"Just that cars need them to move."

That made Charlie laugh. "This old heap should be sold for scrap, but I keep hobbling her together. Cheaper than a new one." He ducked back under the hood.

Nathan leaned in to see a maze of wires, and the smell of oil assailed him. "What's wrong?"

"I think it's the alternator." When Nathan said nothing, Charlie added, "It sends electrical current to the battery. If the alternator doesn't work, the car won't start."

"I thought the battery had the electricity."

Charlie cocked his head and grinned. "You really *don't* know much about cars."

"Or girls either," Nathan said before thinking.

Charlie laughed, straightened. "Women are a mystery, all right. Even Shakespeare thought so." Then he proceeded to quote several passages about women from different Shakespearean plays. Nathan recognized only a few, but Charlie's rich voice made each line sound heavy with meaning. Charlie finished with, " 'Who ever loved, that loved not at first sight?' That's from *As You Like It.*"

Was Charlie making fun of him? Had he figured out how much Nathan cared about Lisa? And how little Lisa cared about him? "There's been a few songs written about it too," Nathan said. "I guess no one can figure them out."

Charlie looked amused. "Not that we don't keep trying." He worked with the wires, attaching several to a black gizmo. "Now, hooking up an alternator, this makes sense. Machines are fixable and they're logical too." Finally he said, "Get in and turn the key. Let's see if I've done this right."

Nathan scooted across the torn bench seat and turned the key. The engine sputtered, then came alive. He hopped out. "That's pretty cool."

"What—making a truck start? A monkey could do it if you showed him how."

"They say a monkey could write a novel if you leave him at it long enough. That doesn't mean the novel will be any *good.*"

Charlie slapped Nathan's shoulder. "Right again."

Nathan felt pleased that Charlie seemed to approve of him, because he knew that even though the man wasn't Lisa's father, Lisa thought a great deal of him. Nathan poked his head under the hood of Charlie's truck and was studying the perplexing engine when Lisa's voice asked, "What are you doing here, Malone?"

Nathan jumped and banged his head on the edge of the raised hood. He saw stars.

"Now look what you've done," Charlie said. "He's bleeding."

Nathan reached up. His hair felt sticky, and when he looked at his hand, he saw blood.

"Are you all right?" Lisa looked anxious.

"I—I think so. Do you have a twin sister? I see two of you."

Charlie chuckled. "Take him inside and fix him up, girl."

Once inside the apartment, Lisa sat Nathan on a chair in the small dining area and clamped a folded paper towel onto his head wound. "I'll be right back."

He waited, looking the place over. It was sparsely furnished, with few decorations on the walls. The apartment looked lived in, but not homey. The front door opened and a woman entered carrying several department store sacks. "You okay? Charlie told me what happened. I'm Jill Lindstrom, Lisa's mother." She was an older version of Lisa, except that her hair was bleached blond with dark roots showing.

"I'm all right," he said.

"Let me see." She lifted the paper towel. "Scalp cuts bleed something fierce, but I don't think it's too deep."

Lisa returned with a damp cloth and antiseptic cream. The two women hovered over Nathan, making him feel nervous and embarrassed. A little cut didn't warrant so much attention. After a few minutes they were finished, and Nathan said, "Thanks."

Jill sized him up. "So you go to school with Lisa."

It was more a statement than a question, but Nathan said, "Yes, ma'am. I'm Nathan."

" 'Ma'am?' " She looked amused. "Don't call me ma'am, makes me feel old."

Nathan colored. He'd been raised to say *yes, sir* and *yes, ma'am.* "I—I didn't mean—"

Jill squeezed his arm. "Why, aren't you the cutest thing! You're blushing." She turned to Lisa. "Hang on to him, honey. Gentlemen are hard to come by."

"Mother!"

"Well, he is cute," Jill insisted. "He's adorable. And just look at those eyelashes. Boys shouldn't have eyelashes that long. It's not fair."

Lisa shot her mother a threatening look. "Don't you have something to *do,* Mom?"

Jill smiled brightly. "Reckon I can put away the things we bought." She went over and picked up the sacks. "Now, you come back any time you want, Nathan. Any friend of Lisa's is always welcome here." She breezed down the hall.

Lisa waited until a door shut, then turned to Nathan. "You sure you're all right?"

He saw that she was flustered and he pressed his advantage. "Maybe I should come over tomorrow for a checkup."

"Don't push it, Malone."

He caught her wrist. "Why do you always call me by my last name?"

"First names are too personal."

"I've heard you call others by their first names. Why be personal with them and not me?"

"You ask too many questions."

He eased her onto his lap, felt her tense up. "I'm not going to bite, Lisa."

"Why are you here anyway?"

He explained about Skeet and Jodie. "Did you know they liked each other?"

"Sure. Didn't you?"

"I was clueless." He rested his hand against the small of her back, felt the warmth of her skin through her clothing. "Did you plan for them to hit it off?"

"No one can plan those kinds of things. But I was hoping they'd like each other. And now they do."

"So why them and not us?"

She stiffened and her eyes looked shuttered. "There is no us, Malone."

"There could be." He got an idea, lifted her up and stood. "Tell you what. Come home with me today. My mother's one of those Christmas freaks who has to put up a tree right after Thanksgiving. We'll be decorating it tonight. You can help." She started to shake her head, but he caught her face between his palms and kissed her lightly. "I'm your patient, remember? You need to keep an eye on me, see to it that I don't slip into a coma from this nasty head wound I suffered while trying to help fix Charlie's truck. It's the least you can do, Lisa."

11

"Tell me, Lisa, have you chosen a college yet?"
Nathan's mother asked at dinner that night. His
parents had been surprised when he had shown up
with Lisa and announced that she was staying for dinner and the tree-decorating ritual. He'd never brought
a girl home for dinner before, plus they'd always done
tree trimming only as a family. Karen had eyed Lisa
like an interloper and even flashed Nathan a few questioning looks that he ignored.

"Not yet," Lisa said. "I'm not planning on going to
college."

Nathan glanced at his mother, knowing that Lisa
had uttered heresy. Her answer had surprised him too,
though.

"Nathan's going to college," Karen declared.

"He should," Lisa said. "He's smart."

"Lisa's smart too," Nathan said, feeling a need to defend her.

"So what will you do in lieu of college?" Karen asked. The twins, in matching high chairs beside the table, sucked on matching pacifiers. At four months, neither could sit up on her own, but the chairs had a semi-reclining position, and the two together in matching reindeer outfits looked adorable.

"I stopped making plans years ago."

Nathan wondered what she meant by that.

Just then Abby dropped her pacifier and let out a wail. Lisa bent and retrieved the thing. "I'll go rinse it off."

"I'll do it." Karen took the pacifier.

The moment she left the dining room, Nathan's father said, "It's okay if you don't want to go to college. It's not a capital offense."

"My mother already has the twins enrolled," Nathan added, irritated by his mother's third degree.

Karen swept back into the room. "What about your parents? What do they want you to do?"

"They pretty much let me do what I want."

Karen looked shocked. "Really?"

"It's a long story."

Nathan watched Lisa withdraw. She wasn't going to say anything that revealed more than she wanted. Lisa had walls around her that no one breached. He willed his mother to change the subject.

Karen apparently got his mental message because she said to his father, "Did you get the tree set up?"

He and Nathan had wrestled the overly large fir into its tree stand earlier. "It's standing. But I still need to put the lights on it."

"And I need to get the girls in bed."

Lisa slid her chair away from the table. "How about if Nathan and I clean up?"

"Thank you." Karen's voice was crisp.

Alone in the kitchen with Lisa, Nathan said, "I'd like to hear your long story someday."

Lisa looked over at the refrigerator at Molly's drawing hanging dead center. "And I'd like to hear yours."

Nathan glanced at the artwork. It had hung there for so long, he sometimes failed to see it. "Not much to tell. I was three when it happened. Molly was six. She sneaked out of the house during naptime and drowned in the pool. I don't really remember much about it at all."

"Do you remember Molly?"

He shrugged. "Sometimes I think I do. But I get the images all mixed up with the photos Mom keeps of her in our photo albums. So I can't really say for sure that I remember her. But that's okay, because Mom never lets any of us forget her."

Lisa reached over and removed a glass that Nathan was holding. "You were squeezing it so tight, I thought you might break it," she explained quietly.

"I guess you've seen enough of my blood for one day, huh?"

"After we finish here, can I see your room?" she asked, changing the subject.

Nathan took her all over the house, room by room. She asked questions, and he wondered what she thought of his lifestyle, different from hers. He wondered too what *did* matter to her. She seemed more relaxed than ever, smitten with the twins, and not intimidated by his parents. The girl was a puzzle and a surprise, all in one package.

They ended up in the basement, right outside the door of what had been his classroom for so many years. She asked, "Do you miss being homeschooled?"

"No."

"But you're not crazy about Crestwater either."

"I don't feel like I fit either place. This is too isolated. The other, too fragmented. I'm not sure my mom did me any favors."

"My mother couldn't have done it for me. Charlie could have, but he had to work to pay the bills. Besides, he never graduated from high school."

"You're kidding. He was quoting Shakespeare to me."

Lisa smiled. "I never said he wasn't educated. He reads all the time. He's the smartest man I know. Maybe even smarter than Fuller. He took courses at a college but he says he screwed some things up. I don't know the story, but he likes working with his hands outdoors, and he's been good to us. He understands life can give you a bad hand."

"How long has he—" Nathan faltered. This wasn't any of his business.

"Lived with us?" Lisa didn't appear offended. "He

moved in when I was nine, and he's been with us ever since."

He wanted to ask about her real father but didn't have the guts. Besides, what did it matter? Charlie was the dad in her life, and that was what counted.

"We're ready to trim the tree," Nathan's father called from the top of the basement stairs.

Upstairs, Nathan's mother had set out a tray of hot chocolate and warm cookies and a large bowl of popcorn. A fire crackled in the fireplace, and boxes of beautiful decorations flanked the tree, now aglow with ribbons of tiny white lights. Christmas carols played on the audio system.

Karen stayed busy decorating the mantel with pine branches, silk magnolias, candles and a platoon of glass and china angels. Craig sat on the floor, gobbling cookies and untangling light strings for the stair banister.

"Your house looks like a still-life painting," Lisa whispered to Nathan. They stood together trimming the tree. "You do this *every* year?"

"For as long as I can remember. Don't you put up a tree every year?"

"Sure. Just not like this."

She didn't elaborate, and he was left to wonder what her Christmases had been like.

From one of the boxes, Lisa picked out an obviously homemade ornament—a Styrofoam ball thick with flaking gold glitter. "Your craft project?"

Before Nathan could say a word, his mother yelled,

"Don't drop that!" She rushed across the room, seizing the ball from Lisa's hands and cradling it tenderly in her own.

"I—I'm sorry," Lisa stammered.

Karen looked flustered. "I didn't mean to yell. It's just that this one has special meaning for me. I-it was made by someone special." She hung it reverently on the highest branch she could reach.

Lisa sidled Nathan a look of understanding, then offered, "If you really want to preserve it, maybe you should buy one of those special cases used for showing off baseballs. They can be sealed airtight, and that will really keep the ornament from falling apart. And I noticed a drawing on your refrigerator. It can be laminated, and that will keep it from falling apart too."

Nathan saw by his mother's expression that she had never thought of these things. She was stuck in a time warp about Molly and couldn't see the obvious. "Good ideas," he said. "Don't you think so, Mom?"

"Yes," Karen said stiffly. "I'll look into your suggestions."

When the tree was fully decorated, they stood around it, admired it, and sipped hot chocolate. Nathan had hoped to have Lisa stay and watch a movie with him, but once the tree was complete, she asked him to drive her home. "It was nice to meet you," Karen told Lisa, but her voice held none of the warmth Lisa's mother's had held when she first met Nathan.

He drove her home, nervous about saying good

night because he wanted to kiss her in the worst way. He pulled in next to Charlie's truck, but before he could turn off his engine, she jumped out of the car. "I had a good time."

"Hey, wait up. I'll go with you."

"No. I think Charlie and Mom are asleep," she said, leaning into the passenger window. "I'll see you in school on Monday."

Confused, and burning with desire, Nathan watched her hurry up the walk. He just couldn't figure her out. They'd had a good time together. She wasn't one bit put off by his mother. Lisa's own family seemed nice enough, if unconventional, so he didn't think they were the problem. So what was it? What made Lisa run?

I stand and watch you from afar. I wish upon you, like a star. . . . The words of his own poem returned, and with it, all the confused longing he'd felt the night he'd first written it. "Still, I love you better than you know," he said aloud, and swore to himself he would get inside her heart. Somehow.

"Did you have a good time?" Lisa's mother asked when Lisa let herself into the apartment. She was sitting on the worn sofa, scratching off silver finishes from a stack of lottery tickets.

"Mom, why do you waste your money this way?"

"Simple—if I don't play, I can't win. When I strike it rich, you and Charlie both will be eating your words. Now tell me about your dinner at Nathan's."

"I had a great time."

"Well, he's cute as can be and he sure seems nice."

"He is nice."

"And his family?"

"They're nice too, although I don't think his mother likes me."

Jill sank against the sofa. "That's crazy. Why wouldn't she like you?"

"Just a feeling."

"Have you—" Jill faltered. "You know . . . said anything to him yet?"

"I'm not going to do that."

"I don't get why you're so secretive. It's nothing to be ashamed of."

"Mom, please don't lecture me. You all agreed to let me play by my own rules."

"Yes, but—"

Just then Charlie came into the room. "Let her be, Jill. She knows what she wants."

Jill's expression turned sour, and she scraped furiously at another ticket.

Charlie handed Lisa a piece of paper. "Your call came Wednesday. I didn't tell you until now because I wanted you to have a good holiday. You're set up for two-thirty, five days a week."

"Two-thirty! But that means I'll have to leave school at one-thirty, and for weeks I'll miss half of the only class I really like."

"Your teacher will understand. If you have a problem, I'll speak to him."

"Fuller knows already." Lisa struggled against the lump in her throat. "I—I just thought I'd have more time to be normal."

Charlie squeezed her shoulder. "I'm sorry, baby girl."

Lisa fought back tears, pushed past him, and went to her room. She didn't want to cry. Not over something no amount of tears could ever change.

*F*uller never looked up from his lecture notes the first day that Lisa walked out of his class a half hour early. All eyes in the room watched her, including Nathan's, and although Lisa had been polite to him in the halls, she acted as if Friday night had never happened. Every time he looked at the Christmas tree, he saw her carefully hanging ornaments and smiling at him. She'd had a good time, he was sure of it; but now she had returned to her cool, elusive self. She was still a dream he chased.

On Friday, he caught up with Jodie and Skeet holding hands in the hallway and asked Jodie if she knew what was going on with Lisa.

"She doesn't confide in me," Jodie told him, her expression sympathetic.

"I thought you were friends."

"We are, up to a point. She's nice to me, but she keeps to herself. Sorry, Nathan."

"Will she bring you to practice tomorrow?"

"My mom's dropping me. She doesn't have to work this Saturday, and she wants to hear me sing. She won't stay long. That's all right, isn't it?"

"Sure. Yeah. Whatever." Nathan's pent-up frustration almost got the best of him. "Sooner or later I'm going to figure it out," he said stubbornly.

"I hope you do," Jodie said. "And when you do, will you tell us? I can't figure Lisa out either."

The Saturday practice went well, although Nathan's heart wasn't in it. He missed Lisa's presence and kept wondering where she was and what she was doing. And who she might be doing it with. That line of thinking had come about because of his mother's questioning. The minute Nathan had appeared in the kitchen to grab breakfast, Karen had asked, "So, is Lisa coming by today?"

"I don't know." He stubbornly held out hope that she might stop by, since she knew they would be rehearsing.

"If she comes, will she be riding that motorcycle?"

"It's how she gets around, Mom." Of course, his mother had noticed Lisa in the garage on Saturdays, but she'd not connected Nathan's feelings for the girl until he'd brought her home for dinner, so now her motorcycle was an issue.

"I think motorcycles are very dangerous. It's a wonder her parents let her have one."

"Does this mean Abby and Audrey won't be getting matching cycles when they're sixteen?"

"Don't be impertinent."

"Well, don't rag on Lisa." He hunkered over his cereal bowl, willing his mother to let him eat in peace.

"Do you *like* this girl, Nathan?"

"I like her."

"As a girlfriend?"

"A guy can dream."

His mother looked exasperated. "I can't believe she's your type. There are so many nice girls out there."

He dropped his spoon with a clank into his now empty bowl. "What's my type, Mom? Have you already picked out the perfect girl for me?"

"Well, no . . . it's just that Lisa seems so . . ." She searched for words, and Nathan felt his blood pressure going up. "Well, so much more mature than other high school girls I've met."

"I'm seventeen! I know what I like, and it's not some Barbie type."

"It's not about your ages," Karen added hastily. "It's an attitude. A disposition. I don't know how to describe it."

"Well, then please don't." He stood, then dumped his bowl and utensils in the dishwasher.

"Nathan, I'm not your enemy."

He grimaced.

"I care about you. The wrong girl at this time in your life could be disastrous. Lisa's pretty and she's so-phisticated. Just because you two may be the same age, and in the same grade in high school, doesn't mean she's on the same wavelength as you. Why, she's proba-bly dating much older boys. I—I just don't want to see you get hurt."

He exited the kitchen with his mother's words run-ning around in his brain, and now, hours later, the words were still wedged there. Hadn't Skeet told him months ago that Lisa went out with college guys? Hadn't he known her reputation all along? Why would she even give a second look at a dork like Nathan? Yet the kiss he'd taken from her hounded him. She'd re-turned his kiss. Their mouths had fairly sizzled with it. And she'd treated him with a kind of tenderness that defied her hard-boiled image.

"Hey, Nate! You listening?" Skeet's voice jarred him out of his mind game.

Startled, Nathan looked up, somewhat surprised that he still was standing in his garage. "Sorry," he mumbled. "Tell me again."

"Larry has gotten us an audition at the VFW in Doraville, for a Christmas party. You think we're ready to tackle a whole evening of music for a live audience?"

Nathan looked from face to face of his band. Each looked excited, expectant, waiting for him to decide. A dance party for old codgers wasn't exactly the Grand Ole Opry.

"It pays," Larry said. "Not a fortune, but money's money."

"It's a place to start," Jodie offered.

"And the crowd may be hard of hearing, which couldn't hurt," Skeet joked.

Nathan shrugged. "Why not? Set it up."

Skeet, Larry and Jodie passed around high fives. "I've already given them an audition tape," Larry said. "That's why they asked us. They'll be printing up letters for the membership and want to know what we call ourselves. Any suggestions? We've got to have a name."

After a few minutes of reflection, Nathan said, "How about The Heartbreakers?"

The others tested it aloud. "Works for me," Skeet said, throwing his arm around Jodie. "We can always change it later if we want."

Nathan agreed.

Nathan was never certain when the idea to follow Lisa came to him. It just did. He rejected it at first. *Juvenile. Stupid. Boneheaded.* But another week of watching Lisa pick up and leave class early set him on the path to see what was going on with her for himself. He chose Friday as the day to do it, skipping Fuller's class altogether and waiting in the parking lot for her to emerge from the school building and climb onto her cycle. He'd never ditched a day of school in his life—mostly because homeschooling gave him plenty of freedom and he'd never needed to—but things were different now.

He sat hunched behind the wheel of his car and only straightened a little when Lisa appeared half a parking lot away. She snapped on her helmet, took off with a roar. He eased his car out of the lot and onto the street, careful to stay well behind her and keeping traffic in between. "You're pathetic, Malone," he said out loud, annoyed that he'd been reduced to a common sneak, but he didn't turn back.

He watched her pink helmet bob as she wove in and out of moving cars. She turned into a large parking garage and he crept inside once she was well out of sight. He'd been concentrating so hard on keeping up with her that he didn't know exactly where he was—just near some large buildings. To be safe, he drove up to the uppermost level and found a space. He looked around. The place was totally generic, with no signs to indicate anything except floor level and section. Cautiously he emerged from his car, crossed to a bank of elevators. He rode down with a group of strangers, stepped out when they did and was surprised to see himself inside a hospital lobby.

Lisa went to a *hospital* every day? That didn't make sense. The place looked mammoth. The atrium soared above him, and sunlight pouring through skylights turned the area yellow gold. A giant decorated Christmas tree filled up one corner of the lobby near a gift boutique.

"May I help you, young man? You look lost."

He turned to see an information desk and an elderly woman dressed in a pink uniform. "I—I'm not sure," he said, walking over.

"Are you here to see a particular doctor? Perhaps have testing done?"

"I—um—was supposed to meet a friend here, but I can't remember where she said to meet her." The lies were falling easily off his tongue, so Nathan forged ahead.

"Well, if the person's come for day surgery—"

"No. I don't think so. She comes every day, though."

The woman looked thoughtful. "Perhaps chemotherapy. Or maybe dialysis. But that's usually every other day. Radiation is a possibility. How long has she been coming?"

Every word fell like hammer blows on Nathan's heart. He backpedaled. "You know, I passed her car in the parking garage. I'll just wait for her there."

The woman smiled, gave her attention to another man who had stepped up to her desk.

Nathan retreated to the garage, his heart pounding. Was Lisa sick? He thought about it. She didn't look sick. She never acted sick. Why would she come here every day? A job? He could handle that. He'd known a girl who was a teen volunteer at a hospital. She had wanted to be a doctor. But why would Lisa be so secretive about a volunteer job?

There *had* to be an explanation. Maybe she was seeing a psychiatrist. That would be ironic, because he was the one acting nuts! And people didn't see shrinks every day, if he remembered correctly. All at once, he was out of conjectures. He would have to find her cycle in the huge garage, wait for her, and confront her. Humiliating as it would be, asking her was the only way to *really* know.

A big black cycle with a painted red heart was easier to spot than a specific car, and Nathan found her Harley two floors below where he had parked. He wished he'd worn his watch, but he hadn't, so he wasn't sure how long he waited, but eventually, he heard the click of boot heels on concrete coming closer.

He was leaning against the concrete wall in front of her cycle when she saw him. She blinked, confused over seeing him out of context.

He stepped forward. "Hi, Lisa."

"How did you—"

His cheeks flamed red. Suddenly, revelation seemed to wash over her. "Did you *follow* me?"

"Yes," he said softly. "I have to know why you leave school early and come here every day."

Impulsively, she swore at him, adding hotly, "Who do you think you are? What gives you the *right* to follow me?"

"I took the right." Nathan stepped closer until he was almost nose to nose with her. "I took it because . . . because, you see . . . I love you."

13

*H*is confession sounded so anguished, his expression looked so vulnerable, that Lisa was reminded of the glass angels on his fireplace mantel. With the right well-chosen words, she could break him, and now was the time to do it if she was ever going to be free of him. *Except* . . . Emotion clogged her throat, moisture filmed her vision, blurring his face, turning his features shimmery. She whispered, "That makes no sense. You hardly know me."

Nathan watched Lisa's eyes fill with tears. He touched her cheek, fully expecting her to shove him backward. He wasn't sorry for what he'd said. He *did* love her. "It's not about *knowing*, Lisa. It's about *feeling*. Believe me, I wish I didn't feel the way I do about you. I think about you all the time—first thing in the morning. Last thing at night."

She seemed to crumble from the inside out. Her shoulders heaved and he took her slowly into his arms, pressed his cheek against her thick dark hair, let her cry hard and long. If he could have stretched the minutes into eternity, he would have; he wished they could be someplace else, anywhere other than a cold, lonely hospital parking garage. Cars circled past them, but no one seemed to notice them. Nathan was glad for that.

When her sobs lessened, Nathan stroked her hair, lifted her chin. She was beginning to shiver from the cold, and her whole body trembled.

"Don't look at me," she said. "Crying makes me look awful."

"Not to me." He had no tissue to offer her. "My car's up a couple of floors. Let me take you someplace warmer. Want some coffee?"

"My ride . . . ," she said, looking at her cycle.

"I'll bring you back for it."

He was amazed when she didn't argue. He took her to his car, got her tucked inside, turned on the heater full blast and slowly wound his way down to the street level. There he got his bearings, drove to the closest coffee shop and walked her inside. The shop had an empty sofa in a corner, so he settled her there, bought them both steaming cups of fresh coffee and sat next to her so that he was touching her. "Talk to me," he said.

Her hands were icy cold, and she warmed them around the cup. He wanted explanations, and she was loathe to give them. Her opportunity to cut and run had passed and she knew it. "I'll tell you everything."

Her voice held the raspy sound of weeping. "Just not right now. I—I need some time to pull it all together in my head."

He was disappointed, but he sensed a change in her, a difference that he hoped wouldn't disappear. He told himself to be patient. "Tell me when and where," he said.

"Come to my apartment later. Mom's playing bingo tonight and Charlie will be out with some of his friends."

"What time?"

"After seven."

"And you promise to be there?"

"I'll be there."

"And you'll let me in?"

A tiny smile crept into her heart over his distrust. She knew he was already *in*. "I'll let you in."

Nathan was cheerful at dinner that night, making conversation without his parents' having to pry things out of him. He offered snippets from his day, omitting his ditching adventure without even a qualm of conscience. All he could focus on was getting out of the house and going to be with Lisa. He cleared the table and loaded the dishwasher quickly, and as soon as his mother reappeared from bathing the twins, he announced that he and Skeet were headed to the mall and a movie.

He had been on rocky ground with his mother for a week, their discussion about Lisa standing like a wall between them. Nathan was glad she didn't give him her usual third degree when he went out—he could recite her line of questions from memory—and he was grateful for the break. He was also grateful that his father had been working long hours at his office and hadn't been sucked into the mother-son conflict.

Nathan drove to Lisa's, parked in front of her building, went to her door and knocked. He felt great relief when she opened the door.

"I made us popcorn," she said. "You want a cola?"

He did. The place was lit by two lamps, and from the back hall he heard the television. "Um—how are you feeling?"

She gave him a funny look. "I feel fine, Malone."

For a minute he thought she might have reverted to her old ways. "Me too," he said.

That made her smile. "Want to see my room?"

"Seems fair. I showed you mine."

Lisa's room was especially large, with a bathroom on one end and a wall of closet doors on the other. He realized it was really the apartment's master bedroom, which made him wonder why she'd gotten it instead of her mother and Charlie. "Nice," he said, panning the room, taking in everything at once.

His gaze rested on the room's focal point, a photographic mural of treetops filled with fiery red blossoms. It ran the length of the room's longest wall, across from a quilt-covered queen-size bed, which was under a window and heaped with decorative pillows. There was a desk, no computer, floor pillows, and a short bookcase stuffed with books and CDs. He walked to the mural, touched the paper and its crimson flowers. "Looks real."

"It's the tops of royal poincianas—flame trees," Lisa said from behind him. "When we lived in Miami, there was one in our backyard, and every spring it put out these incredible red-orange flowers. I loved it. I used to have tea parties under it. The tree's leaves are very tiny, so when I stood under it and there was any kind of breeze, the shadow patterns looked like lace on my skin, and I felt like a princess. The branches grow up really high and form a canopy, like an umbrella. When I was a kid, I thought it would one day touch the sky, and then I planned to climb up it and touch the sky too." Lisa ran her palm along the mural, caressing the paper flowers as she talked.

"It's a pretty tree," he said, more fascinated by Lisa's descriptions and revelations than by the mural. "I've never seen one before."

"They don't grow this far north. I wish they did." She cast a longing look at the photograph.

Nathan didn't get her attachment, but then he didn't understand his mother's obsessive interest in their backyard either. "I've got to admit, it's kind of a different look for a bedroom."

"What did you expect to see? Posters of rock stars?"

"I've learned not to have expectations when it comes to you, Lisa."

She arched an eyebrow, thrust the bowl of popcorn at him. He took a handful, went to her bed and began to sort through pillows. "Quite a collection." They were in all sizes and shapes. Some looked like animals, others were richly decorated with tassels, braids and beads. One was shaped and decorated like a motorcycle.

"My mother gives them to me. She likes to shop and add to my stash. I don't know what I'm going to do with all of them when I—"

She stopped so abruptly, Nathan was caught off guard. Her face looked flushed. "When you what?"

"Leave. You know, move on."

He wasn't sure that was what she'd meant to say.

"Give them away, I suppose," she said.

"Talk to me, Lisa." Nathan was growing impatient for her to move into the real reason he'd come over.

She tossed him a floor pillow and settled cross-legged onto another, then put the popcorn bowl between them. She looked nervous, not at all like her usual in-control self. "What do you want to know?"

"Duh. The hospital."

"It's a boring story."

"I've got all night."

"What, no curfew?"

"You're procrastinating."

"Yes, I am. On purpose. It's something I hate to talk about."

He sat perfectly still, watching the light play on her hair and cheekbones. He wanted to lay her down and kiss her.

"When I was eleven, almost twelve, I started having

bad headaches. I began seeing double, staggering and falling down for no reason. We lived in Miami then. Me and Mom and Charlie." She stared over Nathan's head as she spoke.

"Your real dad?"

"Not part of the picture. He was long gone."

"Go on."

"We had a little house in North Miami. There was a yard and my tree. I had school and friends."

"And headaches," Nathan said, reminding her of the original tack.

"I was put in a hospital. I had all kinds of tests— lots of needles and big scary-looking machines aimed at me. God, I hated it so much." She shuddered. "In the end, they told us I had a brain stem glioma." She paused. "*Glioma.* It's a pretty word, don't you think?"

His heart pounded with increasing dread. "If you say so."

"But it's not a pretty thing, Malone. No, glioma isn't pretty at all." She looked at the mural of the trees. "It's a kind of brain tumor. Most are malignant, and so was mine. It was growing in my upper cerebellum." She clamped a hand to the base of her neck. "You remember what the cerebellum does from biology class, don't you?"

He tried to nod.

"Refresher course." She held up a finger. "It coordinates body movements and lies next to the brain stem, which controls breathing and heartbeats and swallowing.

My little glioma cells were slow growing—a good thing, but also very stubborn . . . as in hard to kill." She plucked at the fringe on her floor pillow while she talked. "They couldn't do surgery: the tumor was too close to the brain stem. Chemo doesn't affect the type of cancer I had. That left radiation. So, they mapped out a field on my neck, marked it with small permanent blue dots."

She lifted her hair, turned so that he could see the dots. He'd seen them before and recalled thinking they might have been part of a tattoo she'd decided against. Now he saw that they were laid out in a grid pattern, and more marks had been added. Her hair had been cut too, shaved up the back of her neck and into the base of her skull. The outer layer of hair had been left alone, and it covered the marks and the shaved area when it hung loose. He wanted to touch her neck, trace his fingers along the path. "I see them."

She let go and her hair fell like a curtain over the telltale grid. "I went for treatments five days a week, for many weeks. Radiation doesn't hurt; it makes you tired, though. I was pretty scared. I had to lie really still with this monster machine aimed at my neck and the grid. The room had a large glass window and I could see my radiologist, Dr. Glickman, and Charlie from the table. Charlie called the machine a zapper because it was going to zap and destroy the bad cells. He said it was like a video game, and I understood that because he and I would play Nintendo for hours and every time either of us made a kill, Charlie said that was just like the radiation treatments killing my cancer cells."

"It must have worked," Nathan said. "You're here."

"It worked. To a degree. They never said I would be cured. Just that the best we could hope for was halting the growth for a time. Most people with brain cancer live two to five years after treatments, if they're lucky. I've made it six."

Nathan's heart was pounding so hard, he thought it would pop from his chest. He tasted bile. "Meaning?"

"It's growing again."

14

athan was reeling. Lisa had a brain tumor. The look on her face was open and guileless, her violet eyes, clear and pure. How could such a terrible thing be happening to someone so young and beautiful? "What are the doctors doing for you now?"

"Radiation again. I go five days a week."

That explained her leaving school early and the hospital visits. "Haven't they figured out some other way to treat this thing by now?"

"Not yet."

Her answer upset him. What had medical science been doing for all this time? What about all the cancer research he'd heard about, even read about? Why couldn't any of it help Lisa? "What about in other cities? Other countries?"

"Atlanta has a renowned cancer treatment center. Some of the best doctors in the world are here."

"And they still only use *radiation*?"

"I won't do experimental treatments."

"But why not? If it will help?"

"I don't know if they will help. Most don't, according to research. Gliomas are . . . well, just a bitch to deal with. And . . . and it's not the way I want to spend what's left of my life, hopping from one experiment to another. In and out of hospitals. Feeling like crap." She smiled ruefully. "I'd rather live like I was dying, not die without ever living."

"And your mom and Charlie are letting you *do* this?" Nathan couldn't believe what he was hearing. His mother would have tied him down and made him try every medical hope out there if the same thing were happening to him.

"I'm eighteen, Malone. I can do what I want. And they let me have control. I don't *have* to finish high school, you know. It's kind of silly in a way. But I want to graduate. For some dumb reason, I really do."

Subdued, he asked, "Is the radiation working? Is the tumor shrinking like last time?"

"Too soon to tell."

"But it probably will. I mean, the radiation worked before."

She tossed a kernel of popcorn at him. "Hey, Malone, don't freak out on me. It is what it is."

He jumped up, started pacing. "Well, it sucks! Big-time."

Lisa stood up too. "Now listen to me. There are

some rules for you that go along with this information I just dumped on you."

"What rules?"

"You can't tell anyone about this. Not Skeet, not anyone. You hear me?"

"Why?"

"Because I won't have that whole school staring at me and whispering about me every time I walk down the hall."

"But—"

"Would *you* want Roddy and his little friends making fun of *you*?"

"They wouldn't—"

"Oh please! Grow up. I went through it before. At my other school, kids acted like I had the plague. Half the middle school wouldn't come near me. Some even did gimp imitations . . . you know, dragging their leg and scrunching up their faces like a Frankenstein monster."

"They made *fun* of you? That's sick."

"The shrink I saw at the time said—and now I'm quoting: 'It's how they cope with their own fears about getting cancer themselves.' So what? It didn't make it hurt any less."

"But this is high school. Don't you think people might have matured by now?"

She crossed her arms. "Do you? Some of the 'mature ones' make oinking sounds whenever Jodie walks past. You saw for yourself how they go after Skeet for no known reason. I don't want them to know one thing about me. You got that?"

Of course, he understood, but he still couldn't get over it. Apparently homeschooling had shielded him from a lot of things. "So no one but me knows about you?"

"Fuller knows."

Nathan said, "And Charlie and your mother."

"They've lived with it for a long time. I'm almost glad the waiting is over. It was like waiting for the other shoe to fall because—" Her voice caught and she looked away. His heart squeezed, but he waited for her to finish. "Because we always knew it would come back. And now it has."

It explained a lot to Nathan. Her recklessness and in-your-face attitude. Her disdain of school cliques and rules she didn't like. Her refusal to let anyone get close to her. Lisa had chosen *not* to care because it protected her from hurtful things she thought were far worse than cancer. Nathan got something else too. By allowing Lisa to handle what was happening to her, and by giving her the freedom to come and go as she pleased, her mother and Charlie kept her with them. "I'll keep your secret," he said.

"I mean it. If this gets out, I'll leave this place so fast . . ." She let the implications sink in.

Nathan moved closer, so close he could feel the heat from her body. "What I said earlier, about loving you . . . this doesn't change anything."

She looked incredulous. "I have cancer, Malone. Go find a normal girl."

"I don't care. I love you, Lisa. And I'm not splitting. Get used to it."

Nathan watched Lisa leave Fuller's class every day, and his heart ached because he knew where she was going. He gritted his teeth when he heard others in their class call her "Diva" or speculate on what she might be doing with Fuller on the side for the privilege of walking out each day. Nathan wanted to hurt them. They were stupid. Mean and stupid. He couldn't wait for the Christmas holidays to come, because he swore to himself that he would spend every free minute with her.

"Where's your head, man?" Skeet asked at practices. "This gig is next Saturday and you're off in la-la land. We need you here, with us."

"Sorry," Nathan mumbled, and forced himself to concentrate on the music.

Lisa rarely came to rehearsals, which they had increased to include three afternoons a week. When she did visit, she sat in the shadows. He was careful not to look her way if Skeet went off on him, because he knew she'd think it was her fault.

"Do you *get* that these guys are paying us *money* to be good?" Skeet said. "And that if they like us, it can lead to other gigs?"

"I said I was sorry. Let's start again."

The worst was his mother's prying. "What's *wrong* with you?" she demanded one night at the dinner table.

"Nothing."

"Don't tell me that. It's like you've crawled into some dark cave. If school is too much for you—"

"What's too much for me is the way you hound me."

"Don't talk to your mother like that," his father ordered.

Their loud voices started Abby crying in her high chair. Seconds later Audrey joined in. "Now look what you've done," his mother snapped. She offered each girl a teething ring.

His father, the peacemaker, said, "Nate, I've talked to my boss and they're making a place for you in the mailroom for the time you're out of school over the holidays."

"Thanks, but no thanks. I don't want to work over the holidays."

"What! I went to bat for you, son. They're doing this as a favor for me."

"Dad, I'm sorry, but not this year."

"You said you needed the money."

"I'm making a little cash with the band for two parties."

"Money you'll have to split four ways. What's the matter with you? Why are you acting this way?"

Nathan didn't answer. He stood, wadded his paper napkin. "I'm finished with supper. I've got a big paper to do."

"Don't walk away from this table," his mother shouted.

Abby wailed and threw down her teething ring, and Audrey followed suit. Nathan kept moving.

* * *

"If this place was any dorkier, we could register it." The comment came from Larry as the band was setting up on the stage of the VFW in Doraville.

The room was old, tired-looking, with cheap paneled walls, long tables and metal chairs, and an open area around a dusty stage for dancing. Tinsel had been taped on the walls, along with Happy Holidays signs, and gaudy decorations hung on an artificial tree that had seen better days. The American flag, along with banners and photos of VFW members, covered another wall.

"You'll feel better when they pay us," Skeet said, flexing his fingers and running chords on his keyboard.

"Did you see the guy who let us in? He's older than God. I just hope nobody keels over dead tonight," Larry said.

"I'm like, *so* nervous," Jodie said. She was wearing jeans and a red shirt with some sequins sewn on the collar and cuffs.

"You'll be great, babe," Skeet said.

Nathan said nothing. He tuned his guitar and watched the door. Lisa had promised she would come. The event was scheduled to start in forty-five minutes and she hadn't shown up, but there was plenty of time.

An elderly man came up to the stage and introduced himself as the president of the group. "You *can* play the old ones, can't you? The *good* country songs?"

"Jodie here sounds just like Patsy Cline," Nathan said, his gaze on the door.

"Yes, we like Patsy. And Loretta and Reba too. Real country, you know."

"We won't let you down," Skeet said.

The room began to fill with elderly couples, and the tables grew crowded. The smell of barbecue drifted from the kitchen. At some point the band was introduced, and Nathan and his friends began to play. They were tight and nervous at first, but once Jodie got over her butterflies, they hit a groove and their sound mellowed out. Couples actually began to dance to the music. Everything would have been perfect except that Lisa never arrived. Nathan gave up watching the door and got into the music, torn between loving her and loathing her for jerking him around.

By ten o'clock the guests were gone, and The Heartbreakers were packing up their gear. Skeet said, "This didn't last long. Maybe we can play to a younger crowd next time."

"The next one's a birthday party with a Western theme," Larry said. "The guy's turning forty."

"Not much better."

Jodie took a swig from a soda. "It's all right with me. I got to sing."

"Like an angel," Skeet said. "You all want to grab some burgers? I'm starved."

Larry and Jodie agreed enthusiastically.

Nathan was in no mood for socializing. He pushed outside, carrying two guitar cases and a box with a special mike for his acoustical guitar, and headed for his car.

"How'd it go, cowboy?" The question came from Lisa. She was wrapped in a long suede coat and leaning against her bike.

Nathan's heart leaped with pleasure at the sight of her. He brushed past her, determined not to let her know. How could she stand there so nonchalant, as if she hadn't known how important their very first paid engagement was to them? "You're a little late for the party."

"I'm here to make it up to you. Hop on. I have another party for us to catch."

He wanted to say, *Forget it.* He wanted to blow her off the way she'd done to him.

"Hey, Lisa." Jodie came up and hugged her friend. "We were great! Sorry you missed it."

"I'll bet you were."

Not a word of apology, Nathan thought, but even as he thought it, he locked his gear in his trunk and handed Skeet the keys. "Go on without me."

"You sure?"

"Park at your house. Like last time." Nathan got onto Lisa's bike; she handed him a helmet and started the engine. He settled into the hard leather seat, angry at himself for not being stronger and walking away. Furious. But it didn't matter. Nothing mattered except being with Lisa. Nothing.

15

"Where are we going?" Nathan shouted above the road noise and the sound of the Harley's engine.

"Fraternity row at Tech."

Nathan wasn't sure he liked the idea of hitting a party at Georgia Tech, but he didn't want to argue with her. She could have gone without him, but she hadn't.

By the time she parked her cycle on the lawn of a fraternity house, Nathan was cold and not in a great mood. Light poured from every window of the old house, music blared out to the sidewalk, and people spilled onto the lawn in drunken groups. Lisa headed inside and Nathan followed. The smell of booze was strong, and Lisa wasted no time in grabbing them both bottles of beer. "Drink up," she said, tipping her bottle upward.

Nathan took a sip from his.

"Hey, Lisa, baby! Long time no see." A guy came up from behind them and swooped Lisa up in his arms. "Where have you been, sweet thing?"

"Around. There are other places to party, you know." She pulled away, nodded toward Nathan. "Meet a friend of mine."

The guy glanced toward Nathan. "Any friend of Lisa's . . ."

"I got it."

"You looking over the Greeks?"

"Not yet," Nathan said.

"Well, this is party central. If you're into partying, that is." He put his arm around Lisa's waist. "And if you're with Lisa, you *got* to be into partying." He kissed her cheek, and she shooed him away.

"What?" Lisa said to Nathan, looking irritated.

"Why are you doing this? To show me how cool you are?" He was angry at her and jealous of every guy she had a past with.

"Life's short." She turned on her heel and melded into the crowd.

Her words stung. Nathan elbowed his way behind her, caught up with her just as she was heading to dance with some other guy who was nuzzling her neck. Nathan watched and seethed. If she was trying to hurt him, she was succeeding. He didn't think the song would ever end, and when it did, he shoved through and caught her up under his arm. "Wondered where you got off to." He told the guy, "I use the head and next thing you know, I'm dateless. But now I'm here to take her off your hands."

The guy, who looked glassy-eyed, gave a drunken shrug and staggered off. Lisa said, "Don't go possessive on me, Malone."

The music screamed around them. All he wanted to do was get her out of there.

"I need another beer," she said.

"Take mine."

She held it against her temple and Nathan saw perspiration prickling her upper lip. Her skin looked pale and clammy, and she was trembling.

"Come with me." Shielding her, he wove them both through the room to the front door and outside into the chilly night air. She stumbled. He led her across the lawn and away from others. "What's wrong?" He didn't figure she'd had enough beer to be drunk, but something was definitely going on with her.

"Go away," she said. She dropped the bottle, staggered behind a hedge of bushes, and fell to her knees. He heard her vomiting. He plowed through the brush and knelt beside her. "What can I do?"

"Nothing." Her face was contorted with pain.

"Let me help you."

She pressed the heels of her hands into her eyes. "Bad headache."

Nathan's gut seized. "Just lie down." She needed no urging. He ripped off his jacket and made a pillow for her head. He remembered that she'd stuffed her long coat into a saddlebag on her cycle. "I'll be right back." He raced to where they'd left the Harley, quickly pushed it to where she was lying. He could hear her moaning. He fumbled in the saddlebag, grabbed her coat and covered her. "Tell me what to do."

"Nothing . . . to . . . do . . . ," she managed.

He couldn't watch her suffer. He rummaged through the bags, pulling out lipstick, a hairbrush and then her cell phone. He found Charlie's preprogrammed number, punched it. When Charlie answered, Nathan said, "Lisa's sick. We need help."

Nathan held Lisa, smoothing her hair and rocking her until Charlie's pickup arrived at the curb. "Over here!" Nathan shouted. Charlie ran over, scooped up Lisa as if she were a small child, walked her to the truck and laid her on the front seat. "Help me with the cycle," he said to Nathan.

Together, they lifted the machine into the bed of the pickup and Charlie swiftly secured it. "It happened so fast," Nathan said. "One minute we were dancing. The next she was in horrible pain."

"Sit up front and hold her while I drive," Charlie said.

Nathan did as he was told, all the while his heart hammering with fear. Lisa moaned. "She'll be all right, won't she?"

"She needs to go to the ER. Morphine's the only thing that helps when the headaches are this bad."

Charlie made record time on the freeway, pulled into the semicircle parking in front of the emergency room at Grady Hospital reserved for ambulances, and lifted Lisa from Nathan's arms. "Park the truck. Meet me inside."

By the time Nathan found a space and went inside, Charlie was filling out paperwork in an area crammed with waiting patients. He said, "They took her into triage. They called her doctor. Nothing to do now except wait."

Charlie turned in the paperwork, returned to the chair Nathan held open for him. They sat side by side, Charlie looking at the floor, Nathan pushed back against the wall. After a few minutes, Nathan said, "How often does this happen to her?"

"The headaches come and go. No pattern. No warning."

"Does it mean the radiation isn't helping?"

Charlie glanced over at Nathan. "She's told you about that?"

"Yes."

"That's good. I told her she should."

"It stinks. Her being sick and all."

"It does," Charlie said. "Things went pretty good for a long time. We almost forgot the tumor would grow again." Charlie's use of *we* made Nathan aware that Lisa's mother hadn't shown up. He wondered about it, but didn't know how to ask. "If you need to leave—"

"Not until I know she's okay," Nathan told him, aware that he was way past his curfew, and not caring.

"It could take a while."

"I'll wait."

At some point, a doctor appeared and talked to Charlie. When he left, Charlie said, "They're going to keep her for observation."

"When can she leave?"

"Probably tomorrow. We can go back and see her, though."

A nurse in green scrubs led them to a curtained-off area. Lisa was on a bed, eyes closed. An IV line was taped to her arm, and the tubing ran to a bag of clear liquid hooked to a pole. To Nathan, she looked child-like, as pale as paste, as fragile as bone china. All he wanted to do was hold her.

Charlie bent and kissed her forehead. "Hey, princess."

Her eyelids fluttered open. "It was a bad one, Charlie." She looked drugged and her speech slurred. She focused on Nathan, her expression confused. "Why are you here?"

"Don't you remember the party?"

"Sort of. I got sick."

"From the pain," he clarified, forgiving her every-thing.

"You should have gone home. You'll get in trouble."

"And miss this adventure? No way."

Her eyelids drooped. "Keep . . . my . . . secret, Malone."

Once she was asleep, Charlie said, "I'll take you home, Nathan." Everyone seemed to call him by his first name but Lisa. "I'll talk to your parents if you want me to."

"I'll handle it," Nathan said.

They left the ER.

Nathan made no pretense of sneaking into his house. He went into the kitchen and to the refrigerator. From a chair at the table, his mother raised up like an apparition. "You are so grounded, mister."

"Okay," Nathan said. He extracted a cola, shut the door, popped the tab.

"Is that all you have to say for yourself?" She snapped on the overhead light. "Where *were* you? Do you know what time it is?"

He glanced at the clock, saw that it was after four in the morning, thought better of telling her the obvious, and took a long drink from his cola. "I went to a party with Lisa."

"Without permission?"

"Call me wild and crazy."

Karen came closer. "Don't be flip. Why didn't you call? I've left a dozen messages on your cell phone. I've been worried sick!"

In truth, he'd forgotten about his cell phone. "I turned it off while our band played tonight and forgot to turn it back on. Sorry."

"Oh, please!" She stomped to the counter. "Did you ride on that girl's cycle?"

"We did." He knew she wouldn't have asked if she didn't already know the answer.

"Skeet said you had."

"You called Skeet?"

"What was I supposed to do? You weren't home and I could see your car in his driveway."

"Hope you don't get him in trouble. You know how his old man is."

"That's your fault too." She banged her fist on the cold granite top.

"I'd like to go to bed now."

She glared at him. "Sleep fast because there are some new rules. You *will* be going to work today and every day of your school break with your father. You *will* come home with him and go nowhere else. You hear me?"

He wanted to protest, but knew that it would be useless at the moment. She was mad and needed time to cool off. He also knew that there was no way he was going to remain under house arrest for two weeks. One way or another, he was going to see Lisa over the holidays.

"You want to talk about it?" Nathan's father asked as they drove into work the next morning.

"No." Nathan's eyes were closed, and he had tipped the passenger's seat as far back as it would go. Three hours of sleep had done him more harm than good.

"Why do you go out of your way to provoke her, son?"

"I don't mean to."

"But you know her hot buttons and lately it seems

like you make up new ways to push them." They rode in silence before his father said, "Is this girl *this* important to you?"

Nathan raised his head. "Yes. She is."

His father's jaw tightened. "You be careful, all right?"

Nathan knew what his father was thinking, and he didn't need a lecture about safe sex at the moment. Nathan knew how to protect his body. He had no idea how to protect his heart. "I'll be careful," he said.

Nathan's father cut his eyes sideways. "Your mother loves you. You need to understand where she's coming from." In the parking garage, Craig turned off the engine but didn't move to get out of the car.

Now what? Nathan wondered.

"Do you remember anything about that day?"

Nathan didn't have to be a rocket scientist to know which day he was talking about—the day that had changed their lives forever. "You mean the day Molly died," he said.

16

"Why are you bringing this up now?" Nathan asked. He really didn't want to talk about it.

"I think it will help you see things from her—*our* perspective," his father said.

"Right now?" All Nathan wanted to do was go inside, get to work and call about Lisa.

Ignoring his question, his father continued. "We bought our house in late July, about three years after we were married. It was a big house and much more than we could afford, but your mother's grandfather had died and left her a small inheritance. That's what we used for the down payment. We figured we'd make the payments over the life of the mortgage somehow."

Nathan looked straight ahead as his father talked, at the cold cement wall of the parking garage, and wondered why earthshaking information seemed to be delivered to him in parking garages.

"One of the reasons your mom loved the house was because it had a pool. Did you know she was on her high school swim team?" His dad didn't wait for Nathan to reply. He plunged ahead. "Molly was especially excited about it, but neither of you could swim and we didn't want to be foolish, so we fenced in the pool and I installed a special latch up high where little fingers couldn't reach. Your mom wanted the two of you to learn from the best, so she hired a certified teacher for you and Molly."

"I don't remember."

"No reason you should. You were barely three. In September, Molly started first grade. You both had taken two lessons, but Molly was certain that she could swim. She threw tantrums when your mother made her wear water wings. She kept saying she was a 'big girl.' She didn't need them, only babies like Nathan needed them."

His father pinched the bridge of his nose wearily. Nathan wished he'd stop the story, yet knew he wouldn't, and worse, Nathan knew he should hear it. "You got sick," his dad explained. "Kids' stuff, ear infection, congestion. You were miserable and awake for about three nights in a row and your mom was awake with you. By Saturday, you were on an antibiotic and getting well. Best of all, you were sleeping again too. Molly was too old for naps, but we insisted on her having a quiet time in her room. I was out playing golf that day. Your mom was so tired that she lay down and fell sound asleep when you did."

Nathan's heart was racing now because he knew where the story was going, and it was making him sick to his stomach.

"Molly was a precocious child, such a smart, clever little girl. Once you and Mom were asleep, she sneaked out of her room, down the stairs. She even dragged a dining room chair to the gate and stood on it so she could reach the latch." He took a breath, and his voice took on a raspy quality. "And she got it open. Your room was overlooking the backyard at that time, and you must have seen her in the pool from your window because when Mom came into your room and asked if you knew where Molly was, you said, 'Molly go swim.' "

From the deepest recesses of his memory, Nathan heard a wailing sound. He wasn't sure if it was the sound of his mother's anguish or a siren. He shook his head to clear out the noise. In his mind, he saw a bird's-eye view of the backyard, a blue-water pool and someone floating facedown. *A memory?* Again, Nathan wasn't sure. Emotion clogged his throat and he couldn't speak.

"The paramedics came but couldn't do anything for her. Molly was dead. After the funeral, we hired a contractor to take out the pool. We put in gardens to remind ourselves that life goes on. I believe that everything your mother plants is a tribute to Molly's memory."

Nathan knew it was true.

"At any rate, your mother never forgave herself for falling asleep, and *you* became the focus of her life." His father squeezed Nathan's shoulder. "I know you want to grow up, son. I know you feel smothered sometimes. All I want you to realize is *why* she's this way and—and to be kind to her."

Nathan cleared his throat. "She shouldn't blame herself, Dad. It was an accident."

"We know that in our heads, but in our hearts—" He paused. "Well, in your heart you tell yourself you should have prevented it from happening. If she had lived, Molly would have graduated from high school by now, gone to college or gotten a job, maybe even gotten married. No way of ever knowing, of course. When a child dies, dreams die."

Nathan's insides turned cold. Lisa's face materialized on the concrete wall outside the car's windshield as his father's words went through him like a sword.

Going back to work at his dad's office in downtown Atlanta wasn't difficult for Nathan. Not only was he warmly greeted by his dad's colleagues, he had use of the company van for errands and deliveries, plus free time. The first opportunity, he called Lisa's cell and was relieved when she answered. She was home.

"Charlie told me how much you helped. Thanks for that. Did you get in much trouble?"

"Not too much."

"How did your gig go? I never asked you, and I

should have. I wanted to come, but the headache came on. I took some stuff and thought I'd knocked it out. I was wrong."

"We got paid, so they must have liked us." He paused. "Do you get headaches like that very often?"

"Please don't ask me questions about my health. I really don't like talking about it."

Didn't she understand how worried he was about her? Didn't she know that he couldn't simply forget what was happening to her? He didn't want to scare her off though, or have her retreat into her isolation mode, so he asked, "When can I see you?"

"Aside from radiation treatments, I'll be hanging around until school starts back up."

He told her about work and said he'd be sticking close to home evenings. "But we can meet for lunch when I have a delivery out your way."

She read between the lines. "I thought you said you weren't in trouble."

"Maybe just a little bit of trouble."

"I'll meet you wherever you want."

Nathan felt elated. "I'll let you know."

On Saturday, The Heartbreakers played at a man's fortieth birthday party. After dropping off Skeet and Jodie, Nathan fought the urge to go to Lisa's and instead went home like a good boy, arriving before the eleven-o'clock news. On Sunday afternoon, Nathan wheedled time out of his mother to go Christmas shopping at the mall. He bought toys for the twins, a sweater for his mother, a dress shirt for his dad and a video game for Skeet. He spent the bulk of his money on a heart-shaped necklace for Lisa. Two days before Christmas, he met her in one of the city's public parks and gave it to her. The day had turned blustery, the sky gray, but sitting on the park bench watching her unwrap his gift made him forget everything except being near her.

"It's beautiful," she said, holding it up to catch the light.

Like you, he wanted to say, but knew it would sound too corny. "Let me put it on you."

She stroked the gold heart once he snapped the catch. "I have something for you too." She reached into the oversize handbag she was carrying and pulled out two wrapped items. One was a CD of a hot country band. "You have it?"

He didn't. He unwrapped the other gift and discovered a book on how to market songs—how to sell music, and names and addresses of agents, houses and music industry labels.

"I haven't thought about selling my songs in a while."

"Why not? You can't forget your dreams."

"Pipe dreams."

"Has Fuller read any of your work out loud yet?"

"A couple." Nathan squirmed, not wanting her to know he'd written the one poem for her. Which didn't make sense because he'd all but laid his heart at her feet. "How about you? He read any of your stuff?"

"Some."

"Some is more than a couple."

"A figure of speech." She looked up at the low gray clouds blanketing the sky. "I wish it were spring."

"It's not too far away."

"Far enough," she said.

Right after Christmas, Nathan got the idea of inviting Lisa to his house. How could his mother object to that? They'd be right there under her watchful eye. Karen agreed, but Nathan saw by his mother's expression that she wasn't thrilled with the idea. What surprised him was that Lisa agreed to come. And she came often, making a guarded peace with his mother by talking about flowers and Lisa's beloved flame trees.

"I've never seen one," Karen confessed.

"Experts consider royal poincianas one of the most beautiful species of tree in the world," Lisa told her.

"I'll look it up on the Internet," Karen promised.

Lisa adored the twins, and they always smiled when they saw her face. Nathan told her, "I think Audrey really likes you. She's the shy one, and doesn't take to many people."

"They're really cute. You're lucky to have siblings."

"Huge age gap though. They'll give Mom something to do when I'm gone."

"She'll miss you."

"Don't think she hasn't mentioned it several hundred times. If she had her way, I'd live in this basement until I was an old man." Ever since his father's talk, Nathan anticipated his mother's protectiveness, but it hadn't made him like it any better. "How about your mom? She doesn't smother you."

Lisa looked thoughtful for a moment. "She's over the smothering stage. We have an understanding, remember? I appreciate her and everything, it's just that this isn't what she signed on for. You know, having a sick kid."

"That's not your fault."

"It doesn't matter. It's still a handicap. Mom wanted to travel, see the country, maybe even the world. She had plans for her and Charlie to get married and travel all over in an RV once I moved away."

"Why don't they get married?"

"We'd lose our insurance. Right now my treatments are covered, but if anything changes . . ." Lisa shrugged. "She likes to buy lottery tickets. She thinks that if she could hit a jackpot, our lives would change for the better."

That didn't make any sense to Nathan. "Would it?"

"She wants to take me places and show me things. Sometimes she acts like I'm not sick at all." Lisa smiled tightly. "At least Charlie's a realist."

"But the tumor *could* shrink again. It could go away for another long long time, couldn't it?"

"That's what gambling is all about, isn't it? Playing the odds."

Nathan screwed up his courage and asked, "What are the odds?"

She didn't answer, only patted his cheek. "You want to play another video game? I can't let you think you're better than me with a joystick."

Nathan didn't like the way she changed the subject, but the discussion was over and she wouldn't return to it.

17

Classes resumed with the new year. Nathan dropped the job and concentrated on getting homework completed in order to spend more time with Lisa. Besides, his crisis with his mother was over. She lightened up when he brought home straight As for first semester, and he'd been more respectful of her concerns about him.

Lisa left Fuller's classroom each afternoon for only the first couple of weeks in the month. When she began to stay for the full class period, Nathan asked, "Is radiation over?"

"Over. Except for feeling tired. I think I could sleep for a week."

"How—" She shot him a cautionary look and he remembered her warning not to ask about it. "I have a right to know," he groused.

She arched a perfect eyebrow, spun on her heel and walked away. He stood in the hall feeling left out and angry. He loved her. She should tell him something. He considered going to Charlie but discarded the idea because he knew Lisa wouldn't like it if he did.

At the end of January, Fuller called Nathan up after class once the room had emptied. The teacher said, "The school system is doing a joint effort with all senior English and art departments. They want to compile and publish the best student work in the metropolitan area. To this end, they're asking teachers in these disciplines to submit the best of their best student efforts." He steepled his fingers together. "I would very much like to submit the poem you wrote last semester. Is that all right?"

Nathan's jaw dropped. "*My* poem?"

Fuller riffled through a folder. "This one."

Nathan glanced at the paper, but naturally, he knew the words by heart. "I—I guess it's okay. Is it really good?"

"I wouldn't submit it if I didn't think so. Do you mind if I put your name on the work instead of your number?"

"I—I guess so." He stood as if rooted.

"Something else, Mr. Malone?"

"Did you pick others from our class?"

"Three others."

"How about the poem about Icarus? I never forgot that one."

"Why is that your concern, son?"

Nathan felt his face redden. "It isn't. I—I've just always wondered about the writer."

"It doesn't matter," Fuller said, straightening the folder. "The student won't give permission for the work to be submitted."

"You should come to the Valentine's dance with me." Nathan said the words lightly, right after he and Lisa had completed a game of Ping-Pong in his garage.

"Why should I do that?"

"Because I asked you to."

Lisa tossed the paddle on the table, slipped on her jacket. "That's sweet of you, but I hate school dances." She started for her cycle, parked in the driveway.

He caught her arm. "Skeet wants to take Jodie. They need wheels. I thought we could double."

"Can't you loan him your car?"

"Not without you and me in it."

She struggled not to grin. "So going to the dance would be a rescue mission? For Skeet and Jodie?"

"Pretty much." Nathan's heart hammered. He wanted to hold her and kiss her beautiful mouth.

"Well, since you put it like that." She threw her leg over her Harley.

"It's a date?" His heart was doing cartwheels.

"It's a date."

The Valentine's dance was held at one of Atlanta's posh country clubs. Nathan had looked forward to it for days and had rented a tux, bought Lisa a corsage,

142

washed and waxed his car. When he and Skeet arrived at the apartment complex, Skeet hurried off to get Jodie, and Nathan went to Lisa's. She opened the door herself and Nathan gave a low whistle. She wore a long gown of midnight blue that shimmered when she moved. Her hair hung loose, not piled in fancy curls and sprayed stiff. "You're staring. This look all right?" she asked.

"I have no words."

Her features softened. "I'll report that to the saleslady."

"Where're Charlie and your mother?" Nathan realized Lisa was alone. *His* mother had taken a ton of photos before he could step out the door, plus given him a disposable camera with instructions to get shots of himself and his friends at the dance.

"They took a few days off and went to the casinos at Cherokee. A little vacation. Because it's Valentine's Day, Mom said she felt lucky."

He could tell that Lisa wasn't happy about the trip. "I feel lucky too. I'm with you," he said.

When they stepped into the main ballroom, heads swiveled and people whispered at the sight of them.

Jodie clung to Skeet. "Why is it that I can sing to a hundred strangers, but I can hardly walk into this room with kids I've gone to school with for years without breaking into a cold sweat?"

"If you did start singing, they'd fall at your feet," Skeet said.

"I miss our band," Jodie said with a sigh.

Larry had dropped them in favor of drumming for a rock group.

"We'll reorganize," Skeet told her.

But Nathan knew they wouldn't. Every free minute he had, he wanted to spend with Lisa. The band was a distant third behind Lisa and keeping his grades up. He had been applying to colleges, and in March he'd sit for the SATs again. He'd done fine on the test in October, but now he might do better. And better could mean a scholarship and going away to college.

The four of them found an empty table. "Punch?" Skeet asked. He left and returned minutes later balancing four cups. He set them on the table, looked about covertly, reached into his pocket and pulled out a half pint of whiskey. "Want some? I took it from the old man's stash."

Nathan sidled Lisa a glance. He didn't want to drink, but he would if she did.

Lisa shook her head. "Not tonight."

Relieved, Nathan turned down Skeet's offer too. Skeet looked disappointed. "You two aren't much fun."

"We're a lot of fun," Lisa said, patting his hand. "Jodie, get this guy dancing before he gets too loaded." Once they were alone, she asked Nathan, "Are you going to ask me to dance?"

"I can only dance to the slow ones," he confessed, remembering how she had danced at the frat party. "The other kind of dancing wasn't on my home-schooling schedule."

As soon as the music slowed, they went out onto the crowded floor. From the moment he took her in his arms, Nathan was certain he wouldn't be able to let go when the music stopped. Her perfume, a mixture of some spring flower and fresh rain, intoxicated him. The curve of her waist under his hand made him lightheaded. Her cheek rested on his shoulder, sending shivers straight through him, turning him clumsy and oafish.

Without warning, he felt a bump and turned to see the faces of Roddy and his date, a cheerleader named Crissy. "Whoops," Roddy said, without a hint of regret. Then he did a double-take as he looked from Nathan to Lisa.

Quickly Nathan ducked Lisa between two other couples, putting distance between them and the scowling Roddy. Nathan felt on top of the world. "Did you see the look on Rod's face? Now I know how Neanderthals felt when one brought home the biggest mastodon," he crowed in Lisa's ear.

She stopped dancing. "Are you comparing me to an extinct furry elephant?"

"No, no. I—I just meant—"

She burst out laughing. "I wish you could see *your* face, Malone."

He pulled her closer. "What I meant to say, he can't figure out how a babe like you would be seen with a doofus like me."

"Good recovery. But you're not a doofus," she said. "A dork, maybe, but no doofus."

"Thank you for raising my social status. I was really worried."

She laughed and it sounded like music.

By the time the dance was over and they'd stopped for coffee and arrived back at the apartment complex, Nathan was high on his own adrenaline, hating for the evening to be over, ever mindful of the curfew his mother had imposed. The notion of it brought him down. Skeet was feeling no pain, and once Nathan had parked and Skeet had exited the car with Jodie, Skeet said, "I'm going to crash on Jodie's sofa. Her mom will let me. I can't go home like this because the old man will kill me."

"He won't care if you're gone all night?"

"Get real. He keeps wishing I'd disappear."

Jodie steadied him, and Nathan watched them walk away.

"Come on," Lisa said, taking Nathan into her place. She kicked off her strappy high heels as she walked in the door. "Want a soda?"

"Sure." Suddenly, he didn't care about his stupid curfew. He was with Lisa, and that's where he wanted to be.

She poured them both a soda, gathered up the hem of her dress and retreated to her room. Nathan followed hesitantly. She flopped onto her bed, resting on her elbows, the long dress clinging to her every curve. He stood awkwardly at the door. She patted the bed. "I won't bite."

He sat next to her. "Well, fair warning: I *might*."

She studied him thoughtfully. "Thank you for tonight."

"That's my line."

"It gave me something I've always wanted."

"What's that?"

"Normal." Her expression had gone soft and serious. "Tonight I was a normal high school girl, going to a normal high school dance with three normal high school friends. I really had a good time."

He set down his drink, scooted closer to her. "I've never done it before either. I'm glad we got to do it with each other." He tucked her hair over her shoulder. "Lisa, I—"

She moved away from him, toward the headboard. "Are you going to get sentimental on me, Malone?"

He moved next to her. "Yes." He took her in his arms, kissed her mouth. She tasted of cold cola and cherry lip gloss and it made his head swim. When the kiss broke, he saw that her cheeks were damp. "Are you crying?" It wasn't the result he had hoped for.

She swiped her cheek, laughed self-consciously. "It's the sweetness of it all. You have no idea how wonderfully and terribly sweet this is to me. Sweet and normal."

He was confused because her emotions seemed all over the place—one minute joking, the next crying. Girls were baffling. "What can I say? I want to make you happy."

"Really?"

"I wouldn't have said it if I didn't mean it."

Tears pooled in her eyes. "I don't want you to leave," she said softly. "I don't want to be left alone."

His heart hammered as he realized how alone they were. The idea of staying made him lightheaded. He cupped her face, stared deeply into her violet eyes, and there he saw something else he'd never seen before. Her bravado was stripped away. He saw fear and loneliness. He saw pain and raw need. Her walls were down, and he knew he couldn't leave her. "Let me make a call," he told her.

He went into the hall and with shaking fingers punched in his home number. His mother answered on the second ring. "Mom?"

"Are you all right?"

"Mom, I'm fine."

"What's wrong?"

"Nothing's wrong. I'm going to be late, that's all."

"How late will you be?"

He took a deep breath. "I'll be home in the morning, first thing."

"You'll *what*? You have no permission—"

"Mom, don't."

"You don't call me and announce that you're staying out all night! Where are you anyway?"

"I'm safe. I—I'm with Lisa."

"Where are her parents?"

His mother was too insightful, for he'd hoped he wouldn't have to tell her everything until the next day. Still, he wasn't going to lie to her either. "They're not here."

Dead silence, then, "Have you been drinking?"

"Not a drop. Let me talk to Dad."

When his father came on the line, Nathan said, "I'm calling because I don't want Mom calling the police. I'm safe, sober, and sane. I know what I'm doing. Trust me. Please."

His mother came back on the phone. "This is ridiculous, Nathan. You can't—"

"But I am. I'll be home in a few hours."

"That girl is poison!"

"Mom . . . I love you." He cut off the call, turned off his cell phone and flipped it closed. He went back into the room to be with Lisa.

18

The next morning Lisa surprised him by coming to his house with him. "You don't have to," he said. "Yes, I do."

They rode in silence and walked into the kitchen hand in hand. His parents were at the table, his father flipping through the newspaper, his mother feeding the twins. Karen looked up, and her angry expression gave way to one of surprise. The twins squealed when they saw Nathan and Lisa. Karen returned to feeding them cereal and bananas. "Sit down until I finish with the girls," she said.

Nathan first poured himself and Lisa cups of coffee. He nodded at his father, who raised his eyebrows and returned to his paper. The tension in the room was like summer air before a rainstorm, thick and oppressive, and except for the burbling of Audrey and Abby, no one spoke. When the girls were finished eating, Karen washed them up and carried them to their playpen in the other room, where they could be seen from the doorway. The moment she stepped back into the kitchen, Lisa said, "It was my fault Nathan didn't come home last night. He did it as a favor to me because I asked him to."

Karen was in no mood for either excuses or apologies. "I know you both think my rules are old-fashioned and provincial. I know you both believe that enlightened parents let their kids make the rules. I know you have freedoms that Nathan doesn't have, Lisa. But common sense dictates that rules and safeguards are for a person's protection, not simply an annoyance to be circumvented any way possible."

Nathan knew she was just getting warmed up.

"What are you two *thinking*? Spending the night together? Do you believe I'm so stupid as to not remember teenage hormones? For god's sake, what if you got pregnant? You'd ruin both your lives!"

Nathan felt heated embarrassment and anger over his mother's tirade. He wanted to yell back at her, but Lisa spoke first, her voice calm, quiet. "That won't happen, Mrs. Malone. I won't get pregnant because, you see, I won't live long enough to ever have a baby."

She went on to tell Nathan's parents everything about her tumor, much as she'd told Nathan. Her voice was soft, her eyes dry, as if the fear and pain she'd felt last night in her room had vanished with the rising of the sun. At some point, his mother sat down at the table, her face a mask of disbelief. "And now the second round of radiation is over," Lisa said. "Unfortunately it hasn't helped much. The tumor hasn't shrunk, but at least it's dormant. We don't know for how long."

This was news to Nathan, and he felt as if he'd been punched.

"They want to try a new kind of Gamma Knife radiation, but it's a long shot too. The tumor's just too close to some vital brain tissue."

"Are you going to do it anyway?" Nathan's question turned Lisa's attention his way.

"I want to graduate. A person needs goals and that's mine. So if I do it, it won't be until after school's over." She looked again at Karen and Craig. "I swore Nathan to secrecy, made him promise to tell no one what was happening to me. He kept that promise and I hope you won't hold it against him. It's my story. My life. Please . . . don't . . . punish him."

From the other room, Audrey wailed because Abby had bopped her on the head with a plastic block. Karen pushed herself up from the table with both hands, wavered for a moment as if she were shouldering a heavy weight. "I—I have to think about this, Lisa."

"I understand."

She paused at the doorway, her back to them. "I— I'm sorry that you're sick."

"So am I," Lisa said.

Nathan's father cleared his throat. "Thank you for telling us."

"You needed to know."

Karen said, "I had a daughter once and lost her."

"Nathan told me."

"I miss her every day."

Nathan caught sight of Molly's old drawing still stuck to the refrigerator across the room. The drawing had been laminated. A lump formed in his throat that he could not swallow.

Oddly, Nathan's family did not talk about Lisa's illness at his house, and the incident of his staying out all night melted away. He ran into Lisa's mother and Charlie whenever he went over to get Lisa, and they were friendly to him. "You're such a nice young man," Jill would tell him if she was home. "I told Lisa she should find a nice guy and leave those losers behind."

Nathan was hesitant to hear more about "those losers." There were some things he didn't want to know.

Charlie always greeted him with a smile and a handshake. "You've settled our girl down . . . something I've been trying to do for years," he told Nathan one time.

"I'm thinking of pulling the plugs from her cycle and then she'll depend on me one hundred percent."

That made Charlie laugh. "It's a plan."

In the following weeks, Lisa came over more often, and by mid-March on a sunny Saturday morning she actually helped Nathan and his mother replant pansies in the flower beds. Karen pulled up the limp and wasted plants, hit hard by winter, and Nathan dug small holes for Lisa, who plucked fresh plants from a flat of multicolored flowers and poked them into the prepared ground. "You sure you want to do this?" he asked during a break. His mother had gone inside to make a pitcher of lemonade because the spring day had turned hot.

"I like doing it. It makes me feel good to know that something beautiful will grow because I planted it."

"They're just pansies. We'll rip them out in May and June and plant hot-weather flowers."

"So? They're pretty now." She examined one closely, puffed a breath onto fragile lavender flower petals. "I think these are my favorites. The color's perfect." She glanced over at him. "Why are you smiling?"

"Just remembering that girl on the motorcycle who used to blow me off. You're not so tough."

"And you're not so nerdy."

"Is that what you thought of me?"

She gave him a look of pure innocence. "That's my secret."

He grinned, decided to ask her what had been on his mind for weeks. "How come you won't let Fuller submit your pieces in that countywide student works book?"

"I wasn't asked." They were sitting on the ground, and she grabbed her knees and pulled them against her chest.

"Sure you were. You're number four-five-four."

"Who told you that?"

"No one told me. I just know that you are. The poem about flying into the sun—I liked it a lot. You wrote it, didn't you?"

"I've always wanted to fly. Yes, I wrote it."

He was elated because he had figured out her identity. "I *knew* it was you."

He also knew that her poem was a metaphor for death. He got it, but just as he had learned not to ask questions about her health, he didn't bring it up. "Submissions don't close until next week. You should let Fuller submit it."

"Did you tell him he could use yours? You know, the one about loving someone from afar?"

He grinned sheepishly—no use denying it now. "How long have you known?"

"Since the day he first read it. You really do wear your heart in your eyes, Malone."

"A turnoff?"

In answer, she leaned forward and kissed his mouth.

"Hey, Nate, Lisa, wait up."

Nathan and Lisa turned at the sound of their names in the hallway as they were leaving school. Skeet and Jodie were heading straight at them. "What's up?"

"Have you heard about Roddy?"

"Don't think so. What's happened?"

"He's flunking and won't walk for graduation." Skeet sounded downright gleeful.

"He has to go to summer school, and a lot of college coaches have backed off from scholarship offers," Jodie added. "I guess the term *dumb jock* really applies, huh?"

"He could have studied," Lisa said. "He thought he could coast because he could play ball."

"Couldn't happen to a nicer guy," Skeet said.

"You're getting far too much pleasure out of this, my man," Nathan said, grinning.

"It's been a long time coming." Skeet chuckled. "Hey, prom's next month, and I think we should all go together."

Nathan hadn't broached the subject with Lisa yet, although he assumed that they would be going. He still wasn't a hundred percent sure of her. She was moody and could retreat into her own world without warning. "I agree. What do you say?"

"You drinking again?" Lisa asked Skeet.

Skeet made a face. "No way. I was hungover for two days."

"Prom *is* a rite of passage," Nathan reminded Lisa.

"A new adventure," Jodie said, looking hopeful. "And it wouldn't be the same without the two of you."

"Plus," Skeet said with a covert glance around, "it'll be a sort of celebration. Come April, I'll be eighteen and I'm moving into my own place."

"What are you talking about?" This was the first Nathan had heard of this.

"Larry and two other guys rent an apartment together and one of the guys is moving out. Larry asked me if I wanted to move in and I jumped at the chance."

"It makes sense," Jodie said. "You know how his stepfather treats him."

"How're you going to pay for it?" Nathan asked, taken aback by Skeet's announcement. There was a time when Skeet told him everything first.

"I've got money saved. And as soon as school's out, I'll get a car. My mom said she'd get me one if I graduated. Then I'm starting into the management training program at the grocery store. My supervisor asked me if I wanted to. He said I had 'potential.' Think of it! Winston George Andrews has potential."

"What about college?"

"You're college material, Nate, not me." Skeet slapped him on the shoulder. "This is a cool move, man. I'll be living on my own *and* collecting a full-time paycheck."

"I'm glad for you," Lisa said.

"So that's why prom is even more of an event. We'll be celebrating the start of my new life."

"A worthy cause," Lisa said, her eyes bright with an inner light only Nathan saw.

In late March, Lisa told Nathan that she would be out of classes for a week. "For some tests," she said vaguely. "I'll call you when I surface."

Grateful that she'd told him that much, he hunkered down and missed her like crazy. By the following Saturday, he hadn't heard from her. He called her cell number, only to have some voice announce that the number was no longer in service. She hadn't told him she was planning on getting a new cell number either.

He grabbed his car keys and told his mother, "I'm heading over to Lisa's."

At the complex, Nathan wove around to the back, parked in an available space, and jogged toward her apartment. The door was open, and when he stepped inside, he was greeted by two handymen in coveralls. A carpet steaming machine stood near freshly painted drywall. Otherwise, the place was empty.

"Can I help you?" one of the painters asked.

"The people who live here . . . where are they?" His heart hammered and he felt cold all over. *Where is she?*

"I guess they've moved, buddy. We get called in to repaint and clean the carpets after a tenant goes. According to the front office manager, there's been nobody here for almost a week now."

*N*athan skirted the painters and went straight to Lisa's room, where only blank walls and hollow echoes greeted him. The mural of the flame trees had been partially ripped from the wall and lay in shreds on the carpet like shed skin. He bent and retrieved a swatch, turned it over to see the bright blossoms, and remembered how Lisa's hands had caressed the paper the night of the dance. A million dreams ago.

He wadded the paper, threw it at the wall and left. He jogged across the parking lot to the front office, where he burst inside, startling the woman behind the front desk. "The people in 5193, Charlie Terry and his family . . . where are they?"

The woman sized him up. "Calm down, young man." She picked up a clipboard, turned several sheets of paper, ran her finger down a column, looked up. "They've moved."

He gritted his teeth. "Where?"

"Even if I had that information—which I don't—laws prohibit me from revealing it."

"They didn't tell you *anything*?"

She sighed. "Mr. Terry simply came in last week and said they were leaving."

"There must be a forwarding address! A phone number!"

"No, there isn't. Mr. Terry said that he'd notify us as to where to mail his deposits. Which he may not get back since he failed to give our customary two weeks' notice."

"But—but . . ."

"I'm sorry," the woman said. "I have no other information for you. You'd best run along now."

"If—if Charlie calls, will you ask him to *please* contact Nathan?"

"I'm not a message service."

"Please!"

She agreed, but Nathan saw by her expression that as soon as he was out the door, she'd forget his name.

Nathan went to Jodie's apartment and pounded on the door. Jodie opened it, took one look at Nathan and asked, "What's wrong?"

"Where's Lisa gone?"

Skeet padded up behind Jodie in bare feet. "Hey, man."

"Lisa's gone? I—I didn't know," Jodie said, peeking

out the door and toward Lisa's apartment. "Lisa's gone," she said over her shoulder to Skeet.

"But you live just down the parking lot from her! All her furniture is out. They're repainting. She's moved. How can you not know?"

"Hey, Jodie says she doesn't know. Don't be in her face," Skeet said.

Jodie tugged at Skeet's arm. "He didn't mean anything by it." She turned back to Nathan. "I swear, I don't know. I'm in school all day and Mom works. I didn't see a trailer or moving van when I *was* home."

"But you're her friend!"

"She often doesn't call me, especially now that Skeet and me are together. You know how she is, she keeps to herself a lot."

Nathan slumped against the doorjamb. "Why would she do this? Why would she leave without telling me?"

"Oh, Nathan, I'm so sorry!" The words came from his mother. "And you had no idea they'd just pick up and go?"

"Lisa told me she had to go through some tests."

"Maybe the test results showed something that needed immediate attention."

Nathan didn't find comfort in that thought. "But why wouldn't she say something to me? Why would she and her family sneak out of town? All their cell phone numbers don't work, and they left no way to reach them."

Karen lifted Abby from a changing table and handed her to Nathan. She picked up Audrey and laid her on the table, fetching a paper diaper from a shelf below. "She's a very independent girl, Nathan. She doesn't think or act like you do."

"What's that supposed to mean?" Abby tried to grab his lower lip.

"Don't get defensive. I've actually come to like the girl. But she *is* different. You must admit that."

"Different isn't a bad thing." His mother's analysis annoyed him.

"No, but different is, well, *different.* She plays by different rules, guards her privacy like a junkyard dog, and has never made you any promises that you've talked about. Which leads me to think she understands her dilemma and purposefully doesn't form attachments."

The truths were too much for Nathan. Lisa had made him no promises. *He* was the one who had made them. *He* was the one who had pledged his undying love and tried with all his heart to keep and protect her. And now she had vanished. "She shouldn't have left this way," he said, more hurt than angry.

"I agree," his mother said. "But remember, people have reasons for making the choices they do, and although we don't understand them, we must accept them."

"But how will I know how she's doing? How will I know when she gets really sick?"

His mother relieved him of Abby and, balancing each baby on a hip, said, "That is the worst part, Nate . . . the not knowing. I've wondered thousands of times if Molly cried for me to rescue her from the water. I don't know. I'll never know."

He saw emotional pain etched in her face just before she turned and carried the twins downstairs. He felt for her, and for himself, both now united by grief.

Nathan couldn't concentrate at school, and after a week he considered asking his mother to supervise him for the final two months of high school. The twins were older and maybe she could handle his schooling like before. Maybe he could even test out and receive his diploma in the mail. Crestwater was just a big, indifferent institution as far as Nathan was concerned, and he wanted out. Certainly except for himself, Skeet and Jodie, no one seemed to notice that Lisa wasn't there. "She came and went a lot," Jodie told him. "People got used to it."

"And she didn't exactly go out of her way to make friends," Skeet said.

Those things didn't matter to Nathan. Lisa was gone and there was a hole in his life large enough to walk through. Even his guitars brought him no comfort. His music had dried up. He felt empty of song.

Fuller called Nathan up to his desk before Easter break. The final bell had sounded, the room had cleared, and in his raspy voice he said, "I wanted to tell you that your poem has been selected for the countywide book that will be published in the fall. Congratulations."

There was a time when the news would have elated Nathan. Now it was just information.

"The competition was stiff," Fuller went on to say. "Thousands of entries, but only two hundred chosen, plus sixty-five student art projects. Nice job, Mr. Malone."

"Were any others picked from Crestwater?"

"One more. At the last minute, student four-five-four allowed me to also submit their work, which surprised me. I'd thought persuading this student was a lost cause."

"The Icarus poem."

"That was the one. How did you know?"

"I asked the author about it, and she told me she had written it, and I told her she should let you submit it."

"So then you know everything?"

"Yes." Nathan's gaze held Fuller's. "I don't suppose you know what happened to the author, do you?"

"Sadly, no. The only message a teacher gets from the administration is that a student will no longer be in class and has left our area." He shook his head. "Pity. She was quite gifted."

Nathan's brief flare of hope that Fuller might know something about Lisa's whereabouts dimmed. "Thanks," he said dully.

"Mr. Malone, *you* too are talented. Also, you're a good student, and if you ever need faculty recommendations on college applications, I'll be glad to write one for you."

"Thanks again." Nathan scooped up his books and went to the door.

"You aren't alone in missing student four-five-four, Mr. Malone."

Skeet and Jodie hung with Nathan over the break and worked hard to raise his spirits. They were playing a video game in his basement one morning when Jodie asked, "Do you know why Lisa was so secretive about her personal life? I've always wondered."

"She never told you anything?" This surprised Nathan because he figured girls shared every morsel of information they possessed.

"Do you know something?"

Now that Lisa had fled, there was no reason to keep her secret. It might also help his two friends realize that his sense of loss wasn't just the pinings of a lovesick puppy. He set down his game controller and without any buildup told them all he'd known for the past many months. Jodie's expression turned to shock, then she cried. "Cancer? Lisa has brain cancer?"

Skeet went slack-jawed. "Get out."

"It's true. All those months she skipped out of last period, she was going for radiation treatments."

"I—I remember she'd sometimes get headaches," Jodie said, blowing her nose. "She told me they were migraines."

"Much worse," Nathan said.

"So I guess she got worse?" Skeet ventured.

"The first question I'll ask, if I can track her down before . . ." He couldn't finish the sentence.

Jodie said, "Tell me again how you've tried to find her."

Nathan went down his list. "All dead ends."

"Did you go to the construction company where Charlie and her mom worked?"

Nathan sat upright. "No. I didn't."

"People get final paychecks. If they left quickly, the place may have a way to reach them."

"You're a genius!" Nathan jumped up, renewed hope surging through him, followed swiftly by disappointment. "I don't know where they worked."

"I do," Jodie said.

"Let's go."

"Wait a minute," Jodie said. "I have an idea, so let me handle this. Besides, I think a curious friendly girlfriend trumps a desperate hysterical boyfriend in this instance."

Eventually they drove to the site where Jodie knew Lisa's mother had last worked, and parked across the street. Before Nathan and Skeet could get out of the car, Jodie stopped them. "Sit. It's best I go alone."

"But—" Nathan started.

"Tie him up if you have to," she told Skeet. Taking her purse and a shopping bag, she crossed the street and entered the construction trailer.

Time dragged and Nathan thought he'd jump out of his skin from the suspense. "What's taking so long?"

"It's only been fifteen minutes, dude. She'll come through," Skeet said. "This girl's outstanding."

It seemed as if an eternity had passed before Jodie emerged from the trailer and came back across the street. She scooted into the backseat.

"Well?" Nathan demanded. "Don't make me go postal."

Jodie grinned and handed him a folded slip of paper. "Charlie Terry's new cell phone number."

Nathan snatched it. "You did it, Jodie! Man, you're terrific!"

"I told you so!" Skeet reached around and hugged her. "How did you do it?"

"I went to the only woman in there. She's taken over Lisa's mother's job, and I said that I was Lisa's best friend and that she'd left before the yearbooks came out and that I *had* to make sure she got hers because it *is* her senior year . . . blah-blah-blah." She pulled a book from her bag and grinned. "I cried too. Real tears."

"Brilliant," Skeet stated. "Especially since new year-books aren't even out yet."

"Last year's edition was a convincing prop. I just waved it around and she never got too close a look at it."

"Did she say where they've moved?" Nathan asked, staring at the cell number and committing it to memory.

"Someplace in Miami," Jodie said. "You'll have to get Charlie to tell you where."

20

Nathan waited until he was alone to make the call on his cell phone. Charlie answered on the second ring.

"It's me, Charlie. It's Nathan Malone. Please don't hang up."

After a pause, Charlie's soft drawl came through. "I knew you were resourceful, son. How did you find us?"

"From where you used to work," Nathan told him.

Charlie chuckled. "I told Lisa that it was a mistake for her not to tell you we were leaving. I said you'd figure out something."

"H-how is she?"

"Bad."

Nathan felt his stomach heave. "I want to see her."

"She doesn't want you to see her like this—the way

she is now. You know how she gets when she digs in her heels."

"I know, and I don't care. Please tell me where you are. I'm coming."

"We're in Miami. That's a good ten-hour drive from Atlanta."

"So?"

"Your parents might not like it."

"I'm coming," Nathan repeated, knowing he had one monster of a fight in front of him.

That evening after the twins were in bed, Nathan packed a duffel bag. He went down to the kitchen, stood in the doorway, watched his mother roll out pastry dough and gathered his courage. At the table, his father sat fiddling with his laptop. Nathan wondered why he hadn't noticed this about the two of them before—they liked being in the same room with each other, even if they were doing different things. *Togetherness.* He had wanted that with Lisa.

Nathan stepped into the lighted room. "Mom, Dad . . . I've found Lisa. I just talked to Charlie and he told me where they are in Miami."

Both his parents turned his way. Karen said, "That's a relief. How is she doing?"

"Not so good."

His father shook his head. "That's too bad. I'm sorry."

"I want to go and see her."

169

"When?" Craig asked.

"As soon as possible. I could leave in the morning."

"Tomorrow's a school day."

"I don't care."

"You've just come off spring break," Karen said. "You still have six weeks of school left. You can't just pick up and leave."

"I haven't taken a single sick day this year. My grades are perfect. I can afford to take the time."

"Well, I can't," Karen said. "I can't just drop everything and go with you. And neither can your father. Have you thought about trying to drive all that way with the girls?"

"I'm not asking you to go."

It took a second for his statement to sink in, and when it did, his mother declared, "Well, you can't go by yourself."

"Why not?"

"Oh, Nathan, let's not have an argument. You can't go to Miami alone. You don't know a soul there and you have no place to stay. It's unrealistic to expect Lisa's family to take you in."

"I wouldn't even ask them. They're living in a motel while Lisa's in this special facility."

His mother returned to her pastry project. "No, son. You aren't going."

He walked over to the counter where she stood, removed the rolling pin, guided his mother to a chair, sat her down and crouched in front of her. Holding both her hands in his, he said, "She's dying, Mom."

"I—I understand that, but—"

"Let me ask you something," he interrupted. "What would you give if you could spend one more day with Molly? Just one?"

Tears welled in Karen's eyes. "That's not fair."

"I have a chance to see Lisa one more time. Please don't try to take it away from me."

"Karen." They both glanced at Nathan's father, who had spoken. "Let him go."

Tears spilled onto Karen's cheeks. "But—"

Craig held up his hand. "I'll call my old boss, Bernie Steadman. He and his family live near Miami now and I know they'll let Nathan stay with them. Our son will be all right. And he should have the opportunity to do this."

Nathan hadn't expected his dad's support, but he was grateful.

Karen pulled away, wiped her cheeks. Her shoulders slumped, but Nathan knew she had capitulated. "You'll call every few hours?"

Nathan rose. "Twice a day. I promise."

"What if—?"

"I'll be fine, Mom. Really."

"How long will you stay?"

"For as long as she'll let me be with her."

The Sisters of Mercy, a Respite and Haven for the Terminally Ill, was an amazingly beautiful facility set on several acres in Coral Gables, Florida, a suburb of Miami. Nathan drove slowly along the driveway, which was sheltered by banyan trees, palms, and palmettos and bordered by brilliantly hued flowering hibiscus bushes and bougainvillea vines of hot fuchsia pink. It seemed that he was off in a tropical wilderness instead of near a city. The main building where he was scheduled to meet Charlie looked like a Spanish hacienda crowned with red barrel roof tiles. With its cream-colored stucco walls, decorative wrought iron, large wooden beams overhead and red-clay Spanish tile underfoot, the place looked more like a resort than a hospital. Yet it *was* a hospital— one that specialized in caring for the dying.

The lobby was peppered with groupings of sofas and comfy chairs. A nun, in a crisp short white dress, a pale blue apron, and a starched white head covering, sat behind a carved desk of darkest wood. A simple wooden cross hung around her neck. "May I help you?"

Before he could answer, he heard his name called from across the lobby. He looked up to see Charlie and Jill, heading toward him. Charlie shook his hand, then showed him to a side porch, where people sat visiting patients around bamboo tables. Ceiling fans moved the perfumed tropical air.

"Aren't you a sight for sore eyes," Jill said, with a big smile. "Are you settled in?"

"Yes, with a friend of my dad's over on Key Biscayne." Now that he was actually here, Nathan felt nervous and anxious. It had been weeks since he'd seen Lisa, and he didn't know what to expect. "This is a nice place," he said, glancing around.

Jill beamed a smile. "We want my baby to have the best. We don't do the Catholic thing, but the sisters here know that. They're real kind to everybody. There's a waiting list, but Lisa's doctor at Emory made the arrangements and we're real grateful. I just couldn't stand to think about my little girl stuck in that apartment in Atlanta, or some pathetic nursing home. She always liked Miami, you know. So this is where we brought her."

"Does Lisa know I'm here?" Nathan asked.

"She didn't want you to come at first," Charlie said.

"If you changed her mind, thank you."

Charlie chuckled. "I didn't exactly, but I did tell her I thought it was the *nice* thing to do."

Jill said, "It's not that Lisa doesn't care about you. It's just . . . just that things are so bad for her. She wanted you to remember her the way she was."

"When can I see her?"

"She's outside in the courtyard, under that big tree."

Nathan saw her then through the screen. She sat in a wheelchair, a throw across her lap, shadows and sunlight sprinkling through lacy leaves of a single great tree that spread umbrella-like over the entire stone courtyard. The tree blazed with red blossoms, like a living fire. *A flame tree.*

He walked to the screen door and Charlie walked with him. "A few things you need to know before you go out there," Charlie said. "They shaved her head for the Gamma Knife procedure that didn't work."

"Hair doesn't matter to me," Nathan said.

"And one more thing," Charlie said. "She's blind."

At the sound of his approach, Lisa turned toward him. She only had sounds to guide her now, but she was getting good at distinguishing between approaching nuns and others. "Hello, Malone."

Nathan halted in front of her chair, a knot in his throat so big that he couldn't speak right away. She looked small and thin, fragile in the chair, her shorn head covered by a silk scarf. All the frustration and resentment he'd been nursing since she'd left without a word to him evaporated.

"So, do you like my new look?" she asked. "I've heard that bald is in."

He stooped, took her hands. "You're beautiful."

"Liar."

"I love you."

She stiffened. "Why did you come?"

"To tell you that."

She sighed, turned her face aside. "I wanted to crawl off and die alone. I thought it was the best thing."

"Not for me. I want to be with you."

"Don't make this any harder, Malone."

He sat on the cool gray stones at the foot of her chair. "Jodie and Skeet say hello. Mom and Dad say that they miss you. Fuller says both our poems made the cut for the best of Atlanta student works book. The twins are standing up on their own now. We missed the prom."

"The twins are standing?" Lisa ignored the other announcements.

"They walk around holding on to furniture. They fall a lot, but they keep getting up and doing it again. They're pretty cute. For girls."

Lisa smiled, imagining the babies in her mind's eye. "How are Charlie and my mom doing?"

"They're sad, but they're okay."

"Good. I wish . . ." She didn't finish, but reached out. He leaned into her touch, and her fingers followed the contours of his face and then his hair. "Your hair's longer."

"No time to get it cut." His voice almost broke.

"I miss riding my cycle," she said wistfully. "I loved the sense of freedom it gave me."

"Remember that party when I climbed on the back and wouldn't get off?"

"We talked for an hour at that bookstore."

"I thought you were bored."

"I thought you just wanted bragging rights—you know, locker-room talk about how you bagged Lisa Lindstrom for a night."

"If I could have lived in your back pocket, I would have."

"I'm sorry about that frat party."

He shrugged, realized she couldn't see his movement. "I was crazy jealous. I couldn't stand it. I hated every guy you'd ever been with."

"That night you stayed with me, after the Valentine's dance—"

"A highlight of my life." He smoothed her lap blanket. "You regret it?"

"Not at all."

His heart skipped a beat. "I loved you more, if that's possible." He saw moisture fill her sightless eyes. "Lisa, I'm glad you got to come here . . . to this place."

She smiled. "When I first came, I could still see, and when I saw this tree, I knew it was where I wanted to be. Isn't it beautiful?"

"Beautiful," he said, without taking his eyes off her.

She took a deep breath and he heard her weariness in it. "I should go back to my room. I don't want to embarrass myself by falling out of my chair out here. Tell Charlie when you go inside."

"I'll send him out." Nathan wasn't ready to leave. He never wanted to leave her, yet he got up slowly. She was shutting down and he understood that he must respect her privacy. "Thank you for letting me come."

"Did I have a choice? You're a very persistent guy, Malone." Her smile lingered.

"A favor?"

"What?"

"Say my first name. You never call me by my first name."

"Nathan."

From her lips, it sounded like a prayer. He rocked back on his heels, struggling not to cry.

She said, "We had a great ride, didn't we?"

He bent and kissed her lips quickly before she could pull away. "We had a great ride."

He cautiously stepped backward, keeping her in his sight as long as possible. A breeze stirred the air and the towering flame tree above her. A shower of tiny red petals fluttered down, twirling and falling to bathe her in a thousand flashes of pure crimson.

She felt them fall, lifted her face toward the sky and caught them on her cheeks, eyelids, soft lips.

Sunlight and shadow flicked over her, reminding Nathan of Spanish lace entwined with tears of brightest red.

She raised her arms, caught drifting petals in her lap and upturned palms; she was Icarus ready to touch the sun.

Nine days later, on a warm Thursday morning when he rolled out of bed to face another day of his waning hours of high school, Nathan picked up his cell phone to stuff it in his backpack. He flipped it open to check on battery life and saw that he had a text message. His heart thudded and his fingers went cold and numb. Still, he punched in the code to access the message. In abbreviated form, it read:

"Lisa took flight 3:09 this morning. Charlie"

21

Nathan pushed the wheelbarrow across the backyard while balancing the tree it carried. The twins squealed as he passed them. They were contained inside their baby corral, a sturdy plastic fence that encircled most of the surface of the patio. The corral was heaped with toys, but Abby wanted out and let him know it.

"I'm busy, Ab," he told her, even though she couldn't understand. Audrey pulled herself up beside her sister and joined the clamor.

"They want you to play with them," his mother said. "They adore their big brother." She'd been weeding the flower beds next to the patio. She wiped her hands on a towel tied around her waist, and came toward him. "What kind of tree did you buy?"

Nathan set down the barrow. "A weeping willow."

"That's fitting," she said, with a sympathetic smile. "A good choice, son." His mother fingered the bright green foliage budding on the branches. "It will need full sun. And lots of space; they grow quite large."

"It's a dwarf variety."

"Smart thinking."

"So, where should I start digging?"

His mother scanned the yard. "I've really packed it in, haven't I? How about in the middle, maybe ten yards or so from the magnolia."

"Molly's magnolia?" He was surprised. That tree was practically sacred.

"Your tree for Lisa should have a place of honor," Karen said quietly.

He pushed the wheelbarrow to the middle of the yard, then counted off ten long paces from the great magnolia. It was dotted with cream-colored flowers, their heavy perfume filling the air. He took out a shovel and sank it into the hard red Georgia clay. Within minutes sweat was running off his body and blisters were forming on his palms. Every drop of sweat, every throb of his hands was for Lisa's sake, and he welcomed the pain.

School was out; graduation a memory. In another month, he'd be leaving for college—and leaving his boyhood behind forever. He'd accepted an academic scholarship to a small college in Kentucky that had offered him full tuition for his freshman year. It had come buoyed by his high SAT scores, good grades, and several letters of recommendation—the best one from Max Fuller. Kentucky was a good choice, he thought. Not too far away, but far enough. He needed a change of scenery.

"I'll help you dig," his mother said, coming up beside him.

"That's okay. You were right—it's something a person needs to do alone."

She nodded, looked toward the patio when Audrey let out a wail. Abby had thrown her own sippy cup over the side of the corral and had taken her sister's in consolation. His mom sighed. "I'd better go referee."

Nathan watched her cross the lawn and pick up Abby's cup. He chuckled, imagining how busy his mother was going to be with them over the years. He loved his little sisters, the only sisters he would ever know in the cycle of life. A cycle neither Molly nor Lisa had gotten to fulfill. He had thought a lot about Molly lately. Although he hadn't known her well, hardly remembered her, in fact, she had left a gaping wound in his family when she'd left. Just as Lisa had left a wound in his heart when she died.

Lisa had been one of a kind—secretive, hardheaded, independent, wild and daring, but also smart, witty, well read, a gifted writer, loyal to her friends, and kind to the underdogs of life. And she would always be his standard of measure for loving someone again.

The hole had grown deep and Nathan tossed down

the shovel. He loosened the dirt in the container holding the tree, and with both hands lifted it free of the bucket. He set it in the hole, picked up the shovel and began to fill in around the root-ball. Next he would water it thoroughly so that it could begin its own life cycle in his mother's gardens.

As he worked, from inside his head, and quite unexpectedly, music began to form, beautiful notes that needed his guitar for purest expression. The music drifted in and out, and he savored it. Then words formed, fragments of a song. What had Fuller said about good writing? *It comes from the heart, not the head.* And so he hummed while he waited for the new music to make the journey from his mind to his heart and into his soul.

Lurlene McDaniel began writing inspirational novels about teenagers facing life-altering situations when her son was diagnosed with juvenile diabetes. "I want kids to know that while people don't get to choose what life gives to them, they do get to choose how they respond."

Her many novels, which have received acclaim from readers, teachers, parents, and reviewers, are hard-hitting and realistic but also leave readers with inspiration and hope.

Lurlene McDaniel lives in Chattanooga, Tennessee.

Lurlene McDaniel began writing inspirational novels about teenagers facing life-altering situations when her son was diagnosed with juvenile diabetes. "I want kids to know that while people don't get to choose what life gives to them, they do get to choose how they respond."

Her many novels, which have received acclaim from readers, teachers, parents, and reviewers, are hard-hitting and realistic but also leave readers with inspiration and hope.

Lurlene McDaniel lives in Chattanooga, Tennessee.